PROBLEMS AND MATERIALS
ON COMMERCIAL LAW

PROBLEMS AND MATERIALS ON COMMERCIAL LAW

SEVENTH EDITION

DOUGLAS J. WHALEY
JAMES W. SCHOCKNESSY PROFESSOR OF LAW
THE OHIO STATE UNIVERSITY

1185 Avenue of the Americas, New York, NY 10036
www.aspenpublishers.com

Permissions
Aspen Publishers
1185 Avenue of the Americas
New York, NY 10036

Printed in the United States of America

1 2 3 4 5 6 7 8 9 0

ISBN 0-7355-3481-0

Library of Congress Cataloging-in-Publication Data

Whaley, Douglas J.
    Problems and materials on commercial law / Douglas J. Whaley.—7th ed.
        p. cm.
    Includes index.
    ISBN 0-7355-3481-0
    1. Commercial law—United States—Cases. I. Title.

KF888 .W48 2002
346.7307—dc21

2002035618

About Aspen Publishers

Aspen Publishers, headquartered in New York City, is a leading information provider for attorneys, business professionals, and law students. Written by preeminent authorities, our products consist of analytical and practical information covering both U.S. and international topics. We publish in the full range of formats, including updated manuals, books, periodicals, CDs, and online products.

Our proprietary content is complemented by 2,500 legal databases, containing over 11 million documents, available through our Loislaw division. Aspen Publishers also offers a wide range of topical legal and business databases linked to Loislaw's primary material. Our mission is to provide accurate, timely, and authoritative content in easily accessible formats, supported by unmatched customer care.

To order any Aspen Publishers title, go to *www.aspenpublishers.com* or call 1-800-638-8437.

To reinstate your manual update service, call 1-800-638-8437.

For more information on Loislaw products, go to *www.loislaw.com* or call 1-800-364-2512.

For Customer Care issues, e-mail CustomerCare@aspenpublishers.com; call 1-800-234-1660; or fax 1-800-901-9075.

Aspen Publishers
A Wolters Kluwer Company

To my students, who, through the years,
have taught me as much about
Commercial Law as I taught them.

SUMMARY OF CONTENTS

CHAPTER 8.   NEGOTIATION   353

CHAPTER 9.   HOLDERS IN DUE COURSE   361

CHAPTER 10.   THE NATURE OF LIABILITY   435

CHAPTER 11.   BANKS AND THEIR CUSTOMERS   503

CHAPTER 12.   WRONGDOING AND ERROR   581

CHAPTER 23.   BANKRUPTCY AND ARTICLE 9   1035

This book explores commercial law by focusing on a series of Problems designed to encourage the student to concentrate on the exact statutory language in the Uniform Commercial Code and related statutes. Representative cases and textual notes are also included.

Unfortunately, students reared on the case method sometimes have trouble concentrating on Problem after Problem. Such an attitude here can be academically fatal. As a guide to the degree of concentration required, I have used a hierarchy of signals. When the Problem states "Read §3-302," I mean "Put down this book, pick up the Uniform Commercial Code, and study §3-302 carefully." When the instruction is "See §3-302," the reader need look at the cited section only if unsure of the answer. "Cf. §3-302," or simply "§3-302," are lesser references, included as a guide for the curious.

I have edited the footnotes out of most cases; the ones that remain have been stripped of their original numbering and have been consecutively numbered with my other textual footnotes. Unless clearly indicated otherwise, all footnotes in the cases are the court's own.

Douglas J. Whaley

Columbus, Ohio
November 2002

PROBLEMS AND MATERIALS ON COMMERCIAL LAW

PART 1

SALE AND LEASE OF GOODS

Chapter 1
BASIC CONCEPTS

I. INTRODUCTION

The law of Sales is contained in Article 2 of the Uniform Commercial Code, but you should be aware that a major rewrite of that Article is in the works, though its completion keeps being postponed. At the time of publication of this book it was unclear when the revised version would be finished and available for enactment, and the author has learned the folly of trying to teach an unfinished draft of a statute. What to do? The answer is that the materials that follow cite to the original version of Article 2, but the issues raised are equally relevant to the revised version when and if it is promulgated. If by the time you read this the revised Article 2 is available, use it to answer the Problems posed. At the beginning of the revised Article there should be a table translating the old citations to their newer counterparts, so use this table to home in on the relevant sections of the revised Article.

Article 1 of the Uniform Commercial Code is a general Article whose rules are applicable to all the Articles that follow (unless they state otherwise). It contains general principles such as a section explaining how the Code is to be construed (§1-102), a section preserving the common law unless obviously changed by the Code (§1-103), a command that *good faith* be imposed in all UCC transactions (§1-203), and, most importantly, a huge definition section (§1-201) explaining the meaning of terms used throughout the rest of the statute. Article 1 itself has recently been rewritten, and the 2001 version has been sent to the states for adoption. It should be widely adopted, though it has one controversial provision: new §1-301, which allows the parties to a UCC transaction to adopt the law of *any* jurisdiction and have it apply to their disputes, even if that jurisdiction has no obvious connection to the parties or the matter at issue. Citations in this book are to the original numbering of Article 1, but the new Article also has a table at its front translating the old numbers to the new ones, should that become relevant in your studies. For an extended discussion concerning the new Article 1, see the Symposium thereon in 54 S.M.U. L. Rev. 469-1048 (2001).

Finally, a word about the Official Comments to the various sections of the Uniform Commercial Code. These Comments were not enacted into law, but since they were written by the drafters of the UCC, and appended thereto, and since they explain what the drafters intended the sections to mean, they obviously are very persuasive in convincing the courts to follow them when litigation arises. On the other hand, if you, future attorney, have a case in which a Comment *hurts* your argument, you might point out that in many jurisdictions the Official Comments were not available to the legislature at the time it adopted the Article concerned (so they are often not part of the legislative history), and many of these Comments have the look of "Oops, we meant to say . . ." or "We knew we could never get this through the legislature, so we are trying to change the law by Official Comment," and thus can be safely ignored. In any event, the Official Comments are a tool that will be useful to you in your exploration of the Uniform Commercial Code, and you should not hesitate to use them.

II.   SCOPE OF ARTICLE 2

A.   *"Transactions in Goods"*

Article 2 of the Uniform Commercial Code applies to *transactions in goods*. Read §2-102. The word *transactions* is not defined in the Code.

Look at §2-106(1); does that help? Much is encompassed within these parameters. Both the delivery of a multi-billion dollar space shuttle to the U.S. Government and the purchase of a package of chewing gum at a local store trigger the application of Article 2 of the Code. *Goods* is defined in §2-105. Read it, and work through the following materials.

PROBLEM 1

Does Article 2 of the Code apply to the following matters?

(a) The sale of an insurance policy? — *no*

(b) The sale of real property? What about the sale of a house apart from the realty? See §2-107. *no*

(c) The sale of building materials as part of a construction project? See the case following this Problem.

(d) The sale of standing timber? Crops? See §2-107. *yes*

(e) A defective spinal plate given a patient in a hospital operating room? See McCombs v. Southern Regional Medical Center, Inc., 233 Ga. App. 676, 504 S.E.2d 747, 37 U.C.C. Rep. Serv. 2d 36 (1998). The preparation of false teeth by a dentist? See Carroll v. Grabavoy, 77 Ill. App. 3d 895, 396 N.E.2d 836, 27 U.C.C. Rep. Serv. 940 (1977). The injection of a drug (for which the patient was separately billed) into a patient's eye as part of an operation? See Providence Hospital v. Truly, 611 S.W.2d 127, 30 U.C.C. Rep. Serv. 785 (Tex. Civ. App. 1980).

(f) The sale of membership in a health spa?

(g) The sale of the entire assets of a clothing store? See Article 6, particularly §6-103.

(h) The sale of electricity? Compare In re Pacific Gas and Electric Co., 271 B.R. 626, 47 U.C.C. Rep. Serv. 2d 598 (Bankr. N.D. Cal. 2002), with New Balance Athletic Shoe, Inc. v. Boston Edison Co., 29 U.C.C. Rep. Serv. 2d 397 (Mass. Super. Ct. 1996).

Milau Associates, Inc. v. North Avenue Development Corp.

Court of Appeals of New York, 1977
42 N.Y.2d 482, 368 N.E.2d 1247, 398 N.Y.S.2d 882,
22 U.C.C. Rep. Serv. 561

WACHTLER, J. A massive burst in an underground section of pipe, connecting a sprinkler system to the city water line, caused substantial water damage to bolts of textiles stored in a warehouse. The plaintiffs who were commercial tenants of the building sought recovery against

both Milau Associates, the general contractor which built the warehouse, and Higgins Fire Protection Inc., the subcontractor which
designed and installed the sprinkler system. The suit was brought on
the alternative theories of negligence and breach of implied warranty
of fitness for a particular purpose.

Evidence adduced at the trial indicated that the break followed
the occurrence of a phenomenon known as a "water hammer"—a
sudden and unpredictable interruption in the flow from the city water
main, followed by a back-surge and build-up of extreme internal
pressure when the flow was again released. According to the plaintiffs'
experts, this "hoop tension" caused a crack to develop at the root of a
V-shaped notch discovered toward the end of the conduit; the fracture
traveled along the length of the vulnerable section of pipe with a
tearing action and the torrential result.

The "stress-raising" notch was alleged to have been produced by a
dull tooth on the hydraulic squeeze cutter used by Higgins to cut sections of the commercially marketed pipe furnished by the subcontractor as specified in the work contract with Milau. Although the
400-foot-long connection had been carefully tested and had functioned
properly in conjunction with the remainder of the system inside the
building, only a few months in operation had caused enough rusting at
the base of the notch, plaintiffs contended, to affect the integrity of the
entire system. The defendants produced offsetting expert opinion that
the pipe itself was neither defective as manufactured nor improperly
installed.

The trial judge, having denied plaintiffs' request to charge that
the contractors had impliedly warranted the fractured pipe to be fit for
its intended purpose, submitted the case to the jury on the sole
question of negligent installation. The jury returned a verdict in favor
of the defendants, finding neither want of due care by Higgins nor
negligent supervision by Milau.

The textile companies contest the trial court's restrictive rulings
on the law of warranty. They assert that the V-shaped notch found in
the ruptured section of pipe is adequate proof that this crucial
component of the sprinkler system supplied by Higgins was defective.
It is their contention that the jury would have been justified in finding
a defect in the "goods" furnished under the hybrid sales-services
contract without necessarily finding negligence on the part of either
defendant. The plaintiffs argue that this defect made the pipe unfit for
its intended purpose and that they were entitled to have the jury
decide whether there was a breach of an implied warranty under

§2-315 of the Uniform Commercial Code or by application of common law warranty principles.

The majority at the Appellate Division found the record to be "devoid of any evidence that the pipe installed by Higgins was unfit for its intended purpose" (56 A.D.2d 587, 588), and concluded that neither the Code nor the case law could be invoked to grant the extension of warranty protection sought by the plaintiffs. While we agree with this result, we have some difficulty with that court's caveat that, "in a proper case, the implied warranty provisions of the Uniform Commercial Code might apply to the 'sale of goods' aspect of a hybrid sales-services contract (see Schenectady Steel Co. v. Trimpoli Gen. Constr. Co., 43 A.D.2d 234 [concurring opn. by Greenblott, J.], aff'd, 34 N.Y.2d 939)." (56 A.D.2d, p.588.)

The sales-services dichotomy has been recognized and developed from the days of the law merchant.[1] In a more contemporary formulation, this court in Perlmutter v. Beth David Hospital (308 N.Y. 100, 104) held that, "when service predominates, and the transfer of personal property is but an incidental feature of the transaction," the exacting warranty standards for imposing liability without proof of fault will not be imported from the law of sales to cast purveyors of medical services in damages. In that case we held that this prohibition could not be circumvented by conceptually severing the sale of goods aspects of the transaction from the overriding service component so that a hospital's act of supplying and even separately charging for impure blood plasma could not in logic or common sense be separated from a physician's contribution in administering the plasma during the course of treatment. Viewed in its entirety, we held in *Perlmutter* that the transaction could not be characterized in part or in its underlying nature as one for the sale of goods, for Mrs. Perlmutter had checked into the hospital to restore her health, not to purchase blood.

The fact that in *Perlmutter* our "service predominates" analysis led to a conclusion of law which was also supported by policy considerations peculiar to the impure blood cases does not strip its analytic

---

1. From its inception, the "English rule" served as a basis for applying the commercial law of sales whenever a transaction resulted in a transfer of chattels. Applying this formulation in Lee v. Griffin (112 Eng. Rep. 716 [K.B. 1861]), Justice Blackburn held that a contract to manufacture and fit a set of false teeth was subject to sales remedies. Courts in this country, however, generally followed the "labor rule," under which the law of sales would not be applied if the contract required a workman "to put materials together and construct an article for the employer" (Mixer v. Howarth, 21 Mass. [4 Pick.] 205, 207 [1838]).

approach of vitality. The court made no attempt to mask the fact that reallocating the risk of loss by imposing warranty liability on no greater proof than the adverse result itself would place untoward economic and health-care burdens on hospitals and patients alike. However, the court's sensitivity to these policy considerations, rather than restrict the scope of its holding, should suggest the need to assess all hybrid transactions along the sales-services continuum both legally and pragmatically.

As suggested in *Perlmutter,* those who hire experts for the predominant purpose of rendering services, relying on their special skills, cannot expect infallibility. Reasonable expectations, not perfect results in the face of any and all contingencies, will be ensured under a traditional negligence standard of conduct. In other words, unless the parties have contractually bound themselves to a higher standard of performance, reasonable care and competence owed generally by practitioners in the particular trade or profession defines the limits of an injured party's justifiable demands (e.g., Aegis Productions, Inc. v. Arriflex Corp., 25 A.D.2d 639 [recognizing that in cases where "the service is performed negligently, the cause of action accruing is for the negligence," and "if it constitutes a breach of contract, the action is for that breach"]).

The parties to the contract underlying this action were perfectly free at the outset, although not after the fact, to adopt a higher standard of care to govern the contractors' performance. Indeed, under a subcontract in which Higgins undertook to design and put together a sprinkler system tailored to the needs of the commercial tenants, the subcontractor was obligated to "furnish and install a wet pipe sprinkler system all in accordance with the requirements of the New York Fire Insurance Rating Organization, including . . . one 8¢ City water connection from pit at property line to inside of factory building. . . ." Additionally, by affixing its corporate signature to the standard form construction subcontract, the fire protection specialist "expressly warranted" that "all materials and equipment [which it] furnished and incorporated would be new" and that "all *work* under this subcontract shall be of good quality, free from faults and defects and in conformance with the contract documents. All work not conforming to these standards may be considered defective" (emphasis added).

Section 2-313 of the Uniform Commercial Code requires that a "seller's" affirmation of fact to a "buyer" be made as part of the basis of the bargain, that is, the contract for the sale of goods. The express warranty section would therefore be no more applicable to a service contract than the Code's implied warranty provisions. Of course, where the party rendering services can be shown to have expressly bound itself to the accomplishment of a particular result, the courts will enforce that promise (e.g., Robbins v. Finestone, 308 N.Y. 543; Frankel v. Wolper, 181 App. Div. 485, *aff'd*, 223 N.Y. 582).

Here the textile company plaintiffs had the opportunity to plead and test the construction of the written warranty provided in the work subcontract at the trial level. They opted instead to prove fault, and if that failed, to seek enforcement of a warranty imposed by law for the sale of goods unfit for their intended purpose. They were unable to convince a jury that Higgins had performed negligently. And they failed as well to demonstrate that the work subcontract was anything other than precisely what the parties had understood it to be; an agreement outlining the materials to be employed and the performance obligations to be assumed by a construction specialist hired to install a sprinkler system. Both the subcontract and the agreement between Milau and the owner were on their face and at heart no more than a series of performance undertakings, plans, schedules and specifications for the incorporation of the specialized system during the erection of a building—a predominantly labor-intensive endeavor. In the final analysis, the parties contemplated the workmanlike performance of a construction service. The fact that something went wrong less than six months after that service was performed does not change the underlying nature of the agreement governing its performance.

Given the predominantly service-oriented character of the transaction, neither the Code nor the common law of this State can be read to imply an undertaking to guard against economic loss stemming from the non-negligent performance by a construction firm which has not contractually bound itself to provide perfect results (see Schenectady Steel Co. v. Trimpoli Gen. Constr. Co., 43 A.D.2d 234, 238-239; id. pp.239-240 [Cooke, J., concurring in part]; Ben Constr. Corp. v. Ventre, 23 A.D.2d 44; see also North American Leisure Corp. v. A&B Distributors, Ltd., 468 F.2d 695; 1 Anderson, Uniform Commercial Code [2d ed.] §§2-102:5, 2-105:10; 1955 Report of the N.Y. Law Rev. Commn., p.361). In fact, where courts in other jurisdictions have purported to apply an implied warranty of fitness to transactions which in essence contemplated the rendition of services, what was actually imposed was no more than a "warranty that the performer would not act negligently" (e.g., Bloomsburg Mills, Inc. v. Sordoni Constr. Co., 401 Pa. 358), or a "warranty of workmanlike performance" imposing only the degree of care and skill that a reasonably prudent,

skilled and qualified person would have exercised under the circum-
stances (e.g., Union Marine & Gen. Ins. Co. v. American Export Lines,
Inc., 274 F. Supp. 123; Pepsi Cola Bottling Co. v. Superior Burner Serv.
Co., 427 P.2d 833), or an "implied warranty of competence and ability
ordinarily possessed by those in the profession" (Wolfe v. Virusky, 306
F. Supp. 519). (See generally Greenfield, Consumer Protection in
Service Transactions Implied Warranties and Strict Liability in Tort,
1974 Utah L. Rev. 661, 668-673.) The performance of Higgins and
Milau was tested under precisely this standard and found free from any
actionable departure.

To be sure, particularly in cases involving personal injury, the
absence of an enforceable contractual relationship for the technical
sale of goods will not necessarily result in the foreclosure of all
remedies, at least where the policies favoring the imposition of strict
tort liability for the marketing of defective products are present (see,
e.g., Victorson v. Boch Laundry, 37 N.Y.2d 394; Velez v. Craine & Clark
Lumber Corp., 33 N.Y.2d 117) or where manufacturing misjudgments
create an unreasonably dangerous condition (see Micallef v. Miehle,
Co., 39 N.Y.2d 276). However, in the products liability cases, "[r]ather
than arising out of the 'will or intention of the parties,' the liability imposed on the manufacturer . . . is predicated largely on considerations
of sound social policy" (Victorson v. Boch Laundry, supra, p.401,
quoting Codling v. Paglia, 32 N.Y.2d 330, 340-341), including consumer
reliance, marketing responsibility and the reasonableness of imposing
loss redistribution. Yet the language and policies of the tort-based cases
"should not be understood as in any way referring to the liability of a
manufacturer [or tradesman] under familiar but different doctrines of
the law of contracts for injuries sustained by a customer or other
person with whom or for whose benefit the manufacturer previously
has made a warranty or other agreement, express or implied" (Victorson v. Boch Laundry, supra, p.400).

The appellants here, however, had at no time in the course of
litigation sought to invoke these doctrines to redress their no less real
but somehow less impelling economic loss. Additionally, to a much
greater extent than professionals and tradesmen in the services arena
where standards are usually set contractually, sellers of goods typically
encourage mass public reliance on their products' fitness and safety
through advertising, packaging and other promotional devices. This
phenomenon is reflected in the fact that the Code's warranties
attaching to sales of goods are underpinned by an assumption of some
form of reasonable reliance by the unleveraged buyer.

No such situation presents itself here and we can find no reasonable basis in policy or in law for reading what would amount to a warranty of perfect results into the contractual relationships defined by the parties to this action.

Accordingly, the order of the Appellate Division should be affirmed.

The hot issue currently vexing the courts is whether Article 2 applies to transactions involving the sale of software, and this very issue is one of the major stumbling blocks to the promulgation of the proposed new version of Article 2.

The Uniform Computer Information Transactions Act (UCITA) is a controversial statute proposed by the National Conference of Commissioners on State Laws (but rejected by the American Law Institute, the other body approving changes to the Uniform Commercial Code) that deals with the sale or licensing of software. If widely enacted, it will cover the computer program field and remove this issue from Article 2. At this writing there is so much opposition to the statute, which is thought to be very anti-consumer, and at this writing (late 2002) it has only been enacted (with some changes) in Maryland and Virginia. Indeed four states have enacted so-called bombshelter statutes, forbidding the application of UCITA to its contracts, even if the parties were to choose UCITA as the relevant law.

In the meantime the courts have taken all sorts of stands on the issue of the applicability of Article 2 to software sales. Some courts say that this is not primarily a transaction in *goods*, and therefore use the common law instead of the Code; see Honeywell, Inc. v. Minolta Camera Co., Ltd., 41 U.C.C. Rep. Serv. 2d 403 (D.N.J. 1991). Others apply the Code either by analogy, see I.Lan Systems, Inc. v. Netscout Service Level Corp., 183 F. Supp. 2d 328, 46 U.C.C. Rep. Serv. 2d 287 (D. Mass. 2002), or because the parties seemed to assume that Article 2 governed the transaction. However, the vast majority of courts have routinely applied Article 2, finding that the sale of software *is* the sale of goods. The leading case is Advent System Ltd. v. Unisys Corp., 925 F.2d 670, 13 U.C.C. Rep. Serv. 2d 669 (3d Cir. 1991); see also Dahlmann v. Sulcus Hospitality Technologies, Corp., 63 F. Supp. 2d 772, 39 U.C.C. Rep. Serv. 2d 299 (E.D. Mich. 1999), Softman Products

Co., LLC v. Adobe Systems, Inc., 171 F. Supp. 2d 1075, 45 U.C.C. Rep. Serv. 2d 945 (C.D. Cal. 2001).

Analysts Intern. Corp. v. Recycled Paper Products, Inc.

United States District Court, Northern District of Illinois, 1987
1987 WL 12917, 45 U.C.C. Rep. Serv. 2d 746

GRADY, Chief Judge.

This diversity case is before us on the motions of plaintiff/counterdefendant Analysts International Corporation ("AIC") to dismiss the counterclaim of defendant/counterplaintiff Recycled Paper Products, Inc. ("RPP") pursuant to Federal Rule of Civil Procedure 12(b)(6) and for partial summary judgment under Federal Rule of Civil Procedure 56. For the reasons below, we deny the motion for summary judgment and grant the motion to dismiss in part.

FACTS

The facts of this case, although many, are not complex. RPP is an Illinois corporation which publishes and supplies greeting cards and other gift products to retail stores nationwide. RPP's Statement of Facts at 1 ("RPP Facts"). AIC is a Minnesota corporation, with an office in suburban Chicago, which develops, designs, markets, and implements computer software systems. AIC's Statement of Facts at 2 ("AIC Facts"). RPP sought to computerize its system of reordering merchandise; it conceived of a computer-assisted merchandising program ("CAMP") which would automatically process computer-scannable order tickets sent to RPP by its customers. RPP Facts at 2. From the ticket, CAMP would identify the customer, store location and desired product; the computer would analyze the customer's credit, and the product's sales and inventory history, and determine whether to ship the desired product, substitute a different product, or reject the order altogether. Id. at 3. CAMP would also send out invoices and credit the sales force with their commissions. Id.

In late January 1983, RPP drafted the CAMP proposal, which was later refined in August 1983. AIC Facts at 3. RPP decided to hire an outside computer programming firm to develop and implement CAMP. RPP Facts at 3. In the fall of 1983, RPP solicited bids from several software houses, including AIC. AIC supplied RPP with promotional literature. Id. at 4-5. RPP contracted with AIC to send a consultant to conduct a "feasibility study." Id. at 6. After three months of studying RPP's business operations, AIC concluded that it could design, develop and implement the CAMP system. Id. at 7. RPP paid AIC $16,000, calculated at an hourly rate, for the study. Id.

AIC and RPP then entered into a contract. The parties dispute almost every material term of the contract, which was partly in writing and partly oral. On January 17, 1984, AIC sent RPP a letter stating the project would take 36 weeks and would be completed in October 1984, at a price of $278,000. RPP Facts at 8. AIC contends that the price was only a rough estimate and that RPP had agreed to pay AIC on an hourly basis. AIC Facts at 5. RPP claims AIC gave it constant assurances that the price was fixed and that the project would not run past October 1984. RPP Facts at 8-9. The contract was later mutually modified to expand the capacities of CAMP—at an additional cost of $124,210, but the October completion date remained. RPP Counterclaim at ¶24 ("CC"). AIC began to work on the project and submitted biweekly invoices which indicated they were computed on an hourly rate basis; RPP approved and paid the invoices. AIC Facts at 5.

In October 1984, AIC announced the work would not be completed on time; the CAMP system was implemented during the latter part of December 1984. RPP Facts at 13. The system was not tested and personnel were not trained on the system before implementation. Id. RPP states that AIC knew of problems in CAMP all along and did not tell RPP. Id. at 10-12. The program did not perform any of its intended functions. Id. at 13. Between January and June 1985, RPP suffered severe business disruptions. Id. Among other problems, the system would credit customers with undeserved discounts, orders were erroneously filled, and sales commissions were not properly credited. Id. at 14-17. Throughout this period, AIC tried to fix the program. RPP continued to pay AIC's invoices, totaling $928,689. AIC Facts at 6. RPP hired outside auditors to assess the state of CAMP in May 1985. RPP Facts at 18. The auditors concluded that the system would have to be redone in its entirety. Id. AIC claims that its system was substantially fixed by May 1985. AIC Facts at 6. Nonetheless, AIC worked on CAMP until October 1985, when it left RPP's premises because of RPP's refusal to pay an outstanding bill of $330,386. Id. AIC instituted this lawsuit to recover the unpaid account balance under breach of contract and fraud theories. RPP countersued in a nine-count complaint also alleging breach of contract and warranty, and fraud, among other things. AIC has moved for summary judgment on RPP's breach of contract and warranty counts. It also has moved to dismiss RPP's counts charging common law and statutory fraud, negligent misrepresentation, malpractice, and RICO. We begin with the motion for summary judgment.

MOTION FOR SUMMARY JUDGMENT

AIC moves for summary judgment on RPP's counterclaim for breach of contract and for breach of an express warranty, implied warranty of merchantability and warranty of fitness for a particular purpose. (Counts I-IV respectively.) We begin with Counts III and IV for breach of the implied warranties found in Sections 2-314 and 2-315 of the Uniform Commercial Code, Ill. Rev. Stat. ch. 26, ¶¶2-314, 2-315 (1985) ("UCC"). AIC argues that its agreement with RPP was to provide services, not goods, and that the implied warranties of merchantibility and fitness for a particular purpose apply only to sales of goods. AIC Memorandum in Support of Summary Judgment at 13 ("AIC S/J Mem."). RPP argues that software transactions are governed by the UCC and in any event, the nature of the contract is a disputed question of material fact for the jury. RPP Memorandum in Opposition to Summary Judgment at 13 ("RPP S/J Mem.").

On a motion for summary judgment, the moving party has the burden of establishing that there is no genuine issue of material fact and that it is entitled to judgment as a matter of law. Chrysler v. Gallagher, No. 85 C 5930, Memorandum Op. at 6 (N.D. Ill. Jan. 29, 1987) (Grady, J.), citing Cedillo v. International Ass'n of Bridge and Structural Iron Workers, 603 F.2d 7 (7th Cir. 1979). AIC has provided uncontroverted evidence that it did not sell computer hardware, or any "off the shelf" software to RPP. AIC S/J Reply at 2. In further support of its motion, AIC proffers RPP's concession that their agreement entailed substantial design and programming services to be rendered by AIC. AIC S/J Reply at 2; RPP S/J Mem. at 14. This evidence, however, does not establish that AIC is entitled to judgment as a matter of law. The legal issue presented is whether the UCC applies to the purchase of CAMP—a computerized automatic merchandise re-ordering system. This, in turn, depends on whether the agreement involved is one for a "transaction in goods." Ill. Rev. Stat. ch. 26, ¶2-102. AIC argues that agreements to write custom developed computer programs are not transactions in goods. AIC S/J Mem. at 14-15. As support, AIC cites cases holding that the subject of computer program contracts is the skill of the programmers, and not the tangible discs and tapes on which the programs would be stored, so that the transactions were not within Article 2 of the UCC. Data Processing Services, Inc. v. L.H. Smith Oil Corp., 492 N.E.2d 314 (Ind. Ct. App.

1986); Liberty Financial Management Corp. v. Beneficial Data Processing Corp., 670 S.W.2d 40 (Mo. Ct. App. 1984). We are not persuaded by the reasoning found in these cases. Data Processing, for example, found the transaction to be "clear cut" because no "hardware" was sold. 492 N.E.2d at 314. The plaintiff instead retained the computer programmers to develop an "electronic data processing system" to meet its needs. Id. And although the end result would be stored on discs and tapes, it was the programmers "knowledge, skill, and ability" which was the subject of the contract. Id. at 319. The court mentioned a few paragraphs earlier that plaintiffs contracted for a data processing system. The court's analysis of such a system in terms of discs, on the one hand, and skill on the other, obscures the synthetic nature of software. Software has both tangible and intangible elements. Note, Software and the UCC, 65 Boston U.L. Rev. 129, 131 (1985). Focusing on one aspect of software to the exclusion of the other loses sight of the whole of the contract, which was for a computer system. Obviously the knowledge of the programmer is important, but only insofar as it enables him to produce the software according to the contract. See RRX Industries, Inc. v. LabCon Inc., 772 F.2d 543, 546 (9th Cir. 1985) (programmers' services incidental to contract for software); Triangle Underwriters, Inc. v. Honeywell, Inc., 604 F.2d 737, 742-743 (2d Cir. 1979) (notwithstanding extensive designing services, transaction for computer software was a sale of goods).

AIC next argues that where a transaction primarily involves creative efforts resulting in a unique work product, the contract is one for services. AIC S/J Mem. at 14. AIC cites two Illinois authorities, neither of which we find persuasive. See Nitrin, Inc. v. Bethlehem Steel Corp., 35 Ill. App. 3d 377, 342 N.E.2d 65 (1st Dist. 1976); Boddie v. Litton Unit Handling Systems, 118 Ill. App. 3d 520, 455 N.E.2d 142 (2d Dist. 1983). In *Nitrin,* plaintiffs sued a general contractor for damages sustained when a specially manufactured piece of equipment broke down. The court noted that the 41-page contract between plaintiff and general contractor, drafted by the plaintiff, clearly indicated that the general contractor was responsible only for design and engineering work. Id. at 77. The court held that because the contract did not concern the sale of goods it was not within the purview of the UCC. Id. The situation before us contrasts markedly with *Nitrin,* for the contract between the parties here is hardly explicit; the only written embodiment of their agreement is a letter, drafted by AIC, which refers not to AIC's responsibility for services but for "system delivery" at the end of October. RPP S/J Mem. at Exhibit 8 (Letter of January 19, 1984).

In *Boddie*, plaintiff was a postal worker who was injured by machinery specifically manufactured for the Postal Service. The *Boddie* court explicitly held that the UCC governed the contract under which the machine was sold to the Postal Service's general contractor. 455 N.E.2d at 150, 151. The plaintiff, however, was not in the class of protected people who could seek recovery under the UCC. We do not see how this case supports AIC's position. Furthermore, we can find no Illinois support for AIC's position that specially commissioned goods involving creative efforts are outside of the UCC.

Where an agreement involves both goods and services, Illinois uses the "dominant purpose" test to determine whether an agreement is one for goods rather than for services and is therefore governed by Article 2 of the UCC. Snellman v. A.B.Dick, No. 81 C 3048, Memorandum Op. at 20 (N.D. Ill. Mar. 20, 1987) (Grady, J.). The court must inquire whether the "essence or dominant factor" in the formation of the contract was the provision of goods. *Snellman* at 21 (citing Sally Beauty Co. v. Nexxus Products Co., Inc., 801 F.2d 1001, 1007 (7th Cir. 1986)). RPP has provided much evidence by way of deposition to support its position that the essence of the contract was for a computer program and that the service aspect, though substantial, was an incident to the product. RPP S/J Mem. at Freidmann Dep. 51-52, 81, 109-10, 121-122; Keiser Dep. at 53, 72-73, 105, 171, 182-186, 220-221, 268; Lohmeyer Dep. at 643, 644. AIC has produced no contrary evidence.

We conclude that except for the provision of a good—a computerized reordering system—the agreement in this case would have no purpose. Had RPP gone to a computer store and bought this software off the shelf, there would be no doubt that the software was a good. Because no "off the shelf" software was adequate, AIC was expected to do a great deal of work, to be sure, but that work was to result in the production of a computer program. To call that work "service," implying that it was service rendered to RPP, is to beg the question. Any supplier of a specially designed item must necessarily perform whatever work is required to create or produce the item. But this does not make the undertaking a "service" to the purchaser of the item. AIC itself has admitted that "the end product of [our] services has almost always been an operating computer program or software system designed to conform to the requirements of each specific client." RPP S/J Mem. at Exhibit 18.

We therefore hold that RPP's agreement with AIC was a transaction in goods and was within the purview of the UCC. RPP is entitled to put on proof at trial of breaches of the implied warranties of merchantability and of fitness for a particular purpose. AIC's motion for summary judgment on Counts III and IV is denied. . . .

Anthony Pools v. Sheehan

Maryland Court of Appeals, 1983
295 Md. 285, 455 A.2d 434, 35 U.C.C. Rep. Serv. 408

RODOWSKY, J. This products liability case presents questions of implied warranty and of defense to strict liability in tort involving an inground, gunite swimming pool and its diving board. Analysis of whether there is any implied warranty and, if so, whether it can be excluded takes us into the problem of hybrid transactions and into Md. Code (1975), §2-316.1(1) and (2) of the Commercial Law Article (C.L.).[2]

Plaintiffs, John B. Sheehan (Sheehan) and his wife, Pilar E. Sheehan, of Potomac Woods, Maryland, sued Anthony Pools, a division of Anthony Industries, Inc. (Anthony) in the Circuit Court for Montgomery County. Sheehan sustained bodily injuries when he fell from the side of the diving board of the plaintiffs' new, backyard swimming pool. The swimming pool had been designed and built by Anthony. Anthony also designed and manufactured the diving board which it installed as part of the swimming pool transaction.

The swimming pool is 16 feet by 40 feet, with a depth from 3 feet to 8 feet. Its style is "Grecian," which means that there is a curved alcove in the center of each of the 16 foot sides. The 6-foot-long diving board in question was installed over an imaginary centerline bisecting the alcove at the deep end of the pool. Anthony had completed its work by mid-June of 1976. On August 21, 1976 the plaintiffs entertained at a pool party. Sheehan testified that he had not previously used the diving board. He said that on that evening he emerged from swimming in the pool, stepped up onto the diving board, and, while

---

2. C.L. §2-316.1 in relevant part provides:

"(1) The provisions of §2-316 do not apply to sales of consumer goods, as defined by §9-109, services, or both.

"(2) Any oral or written language used by a seller of consumer goods and services, which attempts to exclude or modify any implied warranties of merchantability and fitness for a particular purpose or to exclude or modify the consumer's remedies for breach of those warranties, is unenforceable. However, the seller may recover from the manufacturer any damages resulting from breach of the implied warranty of merchantability or fitness for a particular purpose."

walking toward the pool end of the diving board, slipped and fell from the right side of the diving board and struck the coping of the pool.

Plaintiffs advanced two theories of liability. First, skid resistant material built into the surface of the top of the diving board did not extend to the very edge of the board on each side. It stopped approximately one inch short of each edge. This condition, it was claimed, breached an implied warranty of merchantability. Plaintiffs also presented testimony directed toward proving that use of the "defective" diving board, particularly as positioned in the alcove, was unreasonably dangerous.

At the end of the plaintiffs' case, the trial court directed a verdict for Anthony as to liability founded on warranty, because the written contract between the parties conspicuously provided that the express warranties which it contained were in lieu of any other warranties, express or implied. The case went to the jury on a strict liability in tort theory. Verdict was in favor of the defendant, and judgment was so entered.

Plaintiffs appealed to the Court of Special Appeals which reversed and remanded for a new trial. That court said that "the swimming pool package purchased by the Sheehans constitute[d] 'consumer goods'" so that C.L. §2-316.1 rendered ineffective Anthony's attempt to limit the implied warranty of merchantability. Sheehan v. Anthony Pools, 50 Md. App. 614, 619, 440 A.2d 1085, 1088 (1982). The granting of the directed verdict based on the contractual limitation was held to be error. Judgment based on the jury verdict was reversed because of error in the instructions. As to that issue, Judge Moore, writing for the court, concluded:

> In the instant case, it is our view that while the trial court was eminently correct in rejecting the defendant's request for a contributory negligence instruction, the matter should not have ended there. On the basis of the facts involved and of the Sheehans' specific request, an instruction should have been granted that Mr. Sheehan's inadvertent or careless use of the diving board and the pool would not bar his recovery. On the other hand, giving such an instruction would also have required an appropriate instruction on assumption of risk, i.e., that the defendant was entitled to prevail if Mr. Sheehan had discovered the defect, was aware of the danger, and then proceeded unreasonably to use the diving board and pool. [Id. at 625-626, 440 A.2d at 1092.]

We granted Anthony's petition for certiorari which raised three questions. In essence, the petition asks us to review (1) the implied warranty issue; (2) the inadvertent use instruction issue; and (3) whether the Court of Special Appeals erred "in holding, as dictum that contributory negligence is not a defense in a strict liability case."

1

The warranty issue, as presented here, involves only the implied warranty of merchantability under C.L. §2-314. Plaintiffs do not argue that their warranty claim is based upon any express warranty or that the diving board was to be used for other than its ordinary purpose. Anthony contends that the Sheehans' swimming pool is not "goods," that exclusion of implied warranties is allowed, and that a directed verdict on the plaintiffs' warranty count was proper. We agree with the Court of Special Appeals that the directed verdict was improper in this case, but we reach that conclusion by a somewhat different route.

Title 2 of the Commercial Law Article is the Maryland Uniform Commercial Code Sales. C.L. §2-101. Unless the context otherwise requires, that title "applies to transactions in goods. . . ." C.L. §2-102. For purposes of title 2, and with certain exclusions not here relevant, "goods" means "all things (including specially manufactured goods) which are movable at the time of identification to the contract for sale. . . ." C.L. §2-105(1). C.L. §2-314(1) in part provides that "[u]nless excluded or modified (§2-316), a warranty that the goods shall be merchantable is implied in a contract for their sale if the seller is a merchant with respect to goods of that kind." C.L. §2-316(2) permits the exclusion or modification of the implied warranty of merchantability by language which mentions merchantability and which, in the case of a writing, is conspicuous. The Maryland UCC, in §2-316.1, then states that the "provisions of §2-316 do not apply to sales of consumer goods, as defined by §9-109, services, or both," and that any "language used by a seller of consumer goods and services, which attempts to exclude or modify any implied warranties . . . is unenforceable." C.L. §9-109(1) provides that goods are " '[c]onsumer goods' if they are used or bought for use primarily for personal, family or household purposes."

The May 25, 1976 contract between Anthony and the plaintiffs is a printed form designed for use in Anthony's Washington, D.C. region. It is a single sheet of paper, approximately 15" by 20", with printing on both sides. The face of the document is three columns wide. The lefthand column on the face is headed "Retail Installment Contract." Under that column are set forth Anthony's contractor license numbers in Virginia, Maryland and the District of Columbia, a statement of the buyer's right to cancel a home solicitation contract, federal truth-in-lending disclosures and a detachable notice of cancellation. The next two columns on the face are entitled "Swimming Pool Construction Agreement." Anthony "agrees to construct for and sell to" the plaintiffs, called "'Buyer,'" the "swimming pool and related equipment described below (herein collectively called the 'work') to be installed at" the plaintiffs' home for a fixed cash price. Below this covenant, under the heading "Plans and Specifications," are two columns listing 47 items, some of which are automatically included and some of which are optional. These items appear under the headings, "General Construction Specifications," "Hydraulic and Filtering Specifications," "Color-Coordinated Exclusive Deck Equip.," "Automatic Pool Equipment" and "Other Anthony Features." In the subject contract Anthony's obligations included pool layout, structural engineering, obtaining construction permits, excavation, use of engineered steel reinforcing throughout the pool structure, guniting the pool structure, finishing the pool interior with hand troweled, waterproof plaster, installation both of a six-inch band of water-line tile and of coping and installation of a filter, a pump, a skimmer and a specified model of six foot diving board. The reverse side of the contract contains two columns of terms and conditions, including the implied warranty exclusion.

The subject contract presents a mixed or hybrid transaction. It is in part a contract for the rendering of services and in part a contract for the sale of goods.

Burton v. Artery Company, 279 Md. 94, 367 A.2d 935 (1977) addressed the applicability vel non of the Maryland UCC Sales to hybrid contracts. The issue presented was whether the four-year statute of limitations under §2-725(1), or the general three-year statute, applied to a contract to landscape around a construction project of 13 buildings. The contract called for the furnishing and planting of hundreds of trees, of hundreds of shrubs, and of sod. We there adopted the test enunciated in Bonebrake v. Cox, 499 F.2d 951 (8th Cir. 1974), a case holding that the sale and installation of bowling lanes, with associated equipment, is a contract of sale and not of services. That test is whether "the predominant factor . . . , the thrust, the purpose, reasonably stated, is a transaction of sale with labor incidentally involved," or vice versa. 279 Md. at 114-115, 367 A.2d at 946. Applying that test, the court held the contract in *Burton* to be predominantly a transaction in goods. See also Snyder v. Herbert Greenbaum & Associates, 38 Md. App. 144, 380 A.2d 618 (1977) (contract to furnish and install over 17,000 yards of carpet in 228 apartments was predominantly a sale of goods).

G. Wallach, The Law of Sales Under the Uniform Commercial Code (1981), §11.05[3] at 11-28 describes the current state of the law concerning implied warranties in hybrid transactions to be as follows:

> The general pre-Code approach to this issue was to examine the transaction to see whether the goods aspect or the service aspect of the transaction predominated. If the service aspect predominated, no warranties of quality were imposed in the transaction, not even if the defect or complaint related to the goods that were involved rather than to the services. This mechanical approach remains the most popular method of resolving the issue.[3]

The few reported holdings concerning whether Article 2 of the UCC applies to swimming pool installations have involved a variety of types of pools and are not uniform. A Connecticut trial court decision dealt with the alleged breach of the implied warranty of merchantability in the installation of an aboveground swimming pool. Its sides were plywood panels, braced by a 29 × 4" support. A vinyl liner was laid within the sides. That court applied the predominant purpose test. It held that the owners did not offer any adequate evidence on the apportionment between labor and material and equipment, and so they failed to meet the burden of establishing the existence of a warranty under the UCC. Gulash v. Stylarama, Inc., 33 Conn. Supp. 108, 364 A.2d 1221 (1975). A vinyl liner pool was also involved in Riffe v. Black, 548 S.W.2d 175 (Ky. App. 1977). The walls of that pool consisted of prefabricated steel which was set into an excavated site. Sand was troweled for the bottom of the pool. Leaking had resulted from the contractor's failure both to reseal the liner after a wrinkle had developed during installation and to repair the hole which developed later. The Kentucky court applied a predominant purpose test and necessarily classified the contract as one for the sale of goods. It was held that the warranty provisions of that state's UCC "apply to

---

3. Among recent decisions applying the predominant purpose test are: White v. Peabody Construction Co., Inc., 386 Mass. 121, 434 N.E.2d 1015 (1982) (contract for the construction of a housing project was one for services so that there was no warranty implied under the UCC on the windows or frames, which leaked); Milau Associates v. North Avenue Development Corp., 42 N.Y.2d 482, 368 N.E.2d 1247, 398 N.Y.S.2d 882 (1977) (there is no warranty of merchantability on a section of pipe which ruptured and which had been installed as part of a sprinkler system in the course of construction of a new building); Northwestern Equipment, Inc. v. Cudmore, 312 N.W.2d 347 (N.D. 1981) (contract for the repair of the transmission in a used bulldozer is a contract for services and carries no implied warranty of fitness for a particular purpose, even though the charges for parts exceeded the charges for labor).

services when the sale is primarily one of goods and the services are necessary to insure that those goods are merchantable and fit for the ordinary purpose." Id. at 177. Judgment for the pool owners was affirmed. Ben Construction Corp. v. Ventre, 23 A.D.2d 44, 257 N.Y.S.2d 988 (1965) is not a UCC case, but it is analogous. It presented the claim of the pool owners for return of moneys paid, based on a section of the New York Personal Property Law. The pool is described in the opinion only as "installed." Judgment for the defendant contractor was affirmed, 3-2. In the majority's view, the contract was for work, labor and services and was not a sale, while the dissent viewed the transaction as primarily a sale of a swimming pool with an incidental agreement to install.

The Court of Special Appeals has recently held that C.L. §2-601's "perfect tender" provisions do not apply to a contract for the installation of an inground, concrete swimming pool. There was no transaction in goods because the pool was not movable. Chlan v. KDI Sylvan Pools, Inc., 53 Md. App. 123, 452 A.2d 1279 (1982) [No. 192, September Term, 1982, decided December 7, 1982].

Here, Anthony undertook the construction of an inground, steel reinforced, gunite swimming pool with hand finished plaster surfacing, tile trim and coping. The Sheehans were not buying steel rods, or gunite, or plaster or tiles. The predominant factor, the thrust, the purpose of the contract was the furnishing of labor and service by Anthony, while the sale of the diving board was incidental to the construction of the pool itself. The question thus resolves itself into whether the predominant purpose test, which we applied in *Burton* for the purpose of determining whether the UCC statute of limitations governed that transaction, should be applied to determine whether the sale of the diving board, included in the Anthony-Sheehans transaction, carries an implied warranty of merchantability under §2-314.

Were the predominant purpose test mechanically to be applied to the facts of this case, there would be no quality warranty implied as to the diving board. But here the contract expressly states that Anthony agrees not only to construct the swimming pool, but also to sell the related equipment selected by the Sheehans. The Sheehans are described as " 'Buyer.' " The diving board itself is not structurally integrated into the swimming pool. Anthony offered the board as an optional accessory, just as Anthony offered the options of purchasing a pool ladder or a sliding board. When identified to the contract, the diving board was movable. See C.L. §2-105. The board itself remains detachable from its support, as reflected by a photograph in evidence. The diving board, considered alone, is goods. Had it been purchased by the Sheehans in a transaction distinct from the pool construction agreement with Anthony, there would have been an implied warranty of merchantability.

A number of commentators have advocated a more policy-oriented approach to determining whether warranties of quality and fitness are implied with respect to goods sold as part of a hybrid transaction in which service predominates. See Farnsworth, Implied Warranties of Quality in Non-Sales Cases, 57 Colum. L. Rev. 653 (1957); Comment, Sale of Goods in Service-Predominated Transactions, 37 Fordham L. Rev. 115 (1968); Note, Products and the Professional: Strict Liability in the Sale-Service Hybrid Transaction, 24 Hastings L.J. 111 (1972); Note, Contracts for Goods and Services and Article 2 of the Uniform Commercial Code, 9 Rut.-Cam. L.J. 303 (1978); Comment, Sales-Service Hybrid Transactions: A Policy Approach, 28 Sw. L.J. 575 (1974). To support their position, these commentators in general emphasize loss shifting, risk distribution, consumer reliance and difficulties in the proof of negligence. These concepts underlie strict liability in tort. See Phipps v. General Motors Corp., 278 Md. 337, 363 A.2d 955 (1976).

A leading case applying a policy approach in this problem area is Newmark v. Gimbel's Incorporated, 54 N.J. 585, 258 A.2d 697 (1969). There the patron of a beauty parlor sued for injury to her hair and scalp allegedly resulting from a lotion used in giving her a permanent wave. Because the transaction was viewed as the rendering of a service, the trial court had ruled that there could be no warranty liability. The intermediate appellate court's reversal was affirmed by the Supreme Court of New Jersey which reasoned in part as follows (id., at 593, 258 A.2d at 701):

> The transaction, in our judgment, is a hybrid partaking of incidents of a sale and a service. It is really partly the rendering of service, and partly the supplying of goods for a consideration. Accordingly, we agree with the Appellate Division that an implied warranty of fitness of the products used in giving the permanent wave exists with no less force than it would have in the case of a simple sale. Obviously in permanent wave operations the product is taken into consideration in fixing the price of the service. The no-separate-charge argument puts excessive emphasis on form and downgrades the overall substance of the transaction. If the beauty parlor operator bought and applied the permanent wave solution to her own hair and suffered injury thereby, her action in warranty or strict liability in tort against the manufacturer-seller of the product clearly would be maintainable because the basic transaction would have arisen from a conventional type of sale. It does

not accord with logic to deny a similar right to a patron against the beauty parlor operator or the manufacturer when the purchase and sale were made in anticipation of and for the purpose of use of the product on the patron who would be charged for its use. Common sense demands that such patron be deemed a customer as to both manufacturer and beauty parlor operator. [Citations omitted.]

The court was careful to limit its holding to commercial transactions, as opposed to those predominantly involving professional services. Id. at 596-597, 258 A.2d at 702-703.

1 R. Anderson, Uniform Commercial Code (1970), §2-102:5 at 209 refers to *Newmark* as illustrative of a possible trend in the law and states:

It is probable that a goods-services transaction will come to be subjected to Article 2 of the Code insofar as the contractor's obligations with respect to the goods themselves are involved, at least where the goods involved could have been purchased in the general market and used by the plaintiff-customer.

A warranty of fitness for particular purpose under §2-315 of the UCC was implied in Worrell v. Barnes, 87 Nev. 204, 484 P.2d 573 (1971). In that case a contractor was engaged to do some carpentry work and to connect various appliances in the plaintiff's home to an existing liquified petroleum gas system. The appliances were not supplied by the contractor. Suit was for damage to the plaintiff's home resulting from a fire. The plaintiff produced evidence that the fire was caused by a defective fitting installed by the contractor which had allowed propane to escape. Dismissal of the plaintiff's claims, based on the Nevada version of strict liability in tort and based on implied warranty, was reversed. The court reasoned that, because it had held that the contractor had sold a product so as to bring into operation the doctrine of strict liability, "so also must we deem this case to involve 'goods' within the purview of the Uniform Commercial Code." Id. at 208, 484 P.2d at 576.

1 W. Hawkland, Uniform Commercial Code Series (1982), §2-102:04, at Art. 2, p.12 has suggested what might be called a "gravamen" test in light of the decision in *Worrell*. He writes:

Unless uniformity would be impaired thereby, it might be more sensible and facilitate administration, at least in this grey area, to abandon the "predominant factor" test and focus instead on whether the gravamen of the action involves goods or services. For example, in Worrell v. Barnes, if the gas escaped because of a defective fitting or connector, the case might be characterized as one involving the sale of goods. On the other hand, if the gas escaped because of poor work by Barnes the case might be characterized as one involving services, outside the scope of the UCC.

In this state, the provisions of C.L. §2-316.1(1) and (2) reflect an implicit policy judgment by the General Assembly which prevents the mechanical application of the predominant purpose test to cases like the one under consideration. Subsection (1) states that §2-316, dealing in part with the manner in which an implied warranty of merchantability may be excluded or modified, does not apply to "consumer goods . . . services, or both." Under subsection (2) language "used by a seller of consumer goods and services" to exclude or modify implied warranties is unenforceable. The hybrid transaction is covered by, or at least embraced within, those terms.

Under the predominant purpose test, as applied by a majority of the courts, a hybrid transaction must first be classified as a sale of goods in order for there to be UCC-based, implied warranties on the goods included in the transaction. If goods predominate and they are consumer goods, §2-316.1 would render contractual disclaimers of implied warranties ineffective because that section applies to a seller of consumer goods. In such cases the result of applying the predominant purpose test is consistent with §2-316.1. If, however, the predominant purpose test results in classifying the transaction as a contract for services there would, under the majority approach, be no UCC-based, implied warranties on goods included in the transaction. But, §2-316.1 declares that a seller of consumer services may not contractually disclaim implied warranties. In the hybrid transaction, at least one effect of §2-316.1 is to render ineffective contractual disclaimers of implied warranties on consumer goods included in a consumer service transaction. Section 2-316.1 is at least partially predicated on a legislative understanding that warranties under the UCC are implied as to the goods included in such transactions. An all or nothing classification of the instant transaction under the predominant purpose test would mean there could be no UCC-based, implied warranties on the diving board and would be contrary to the legislative policy implicit in §2-316.1. Consequently, we cannot use that test in order to determine whether UCC-based warranties are implied as to consumer goods in a transaction that is predominantly for the rendering of consumer services.

The gravamen test of Dean Hawkland suggests the vehicle for satisfying the legislative policy. Accordingly, we hold that where, as part of a commercial transaction, consumer goods are sold which retain

their character as consumer goods after completion of the performance promised to the consumer, and where monetary loss or personal injury is claimed to have resulted from a defect in the consumer
goods, the provisions of the Maryland UCC dealing with implied
warranties apply to the consumer goods, even if the transaction is
predominantly one for the rendering of consumer services. The facts
of the instant case, however, make it unnecessary for us presently to
decide whether §2-316.1 would require that UCC-based, implied
warranties also extend to consumer goods which are used up in the
course of rendering the consumer service to the consumer.

Thus the diving board which Anthony sold to the Sheehans as part
of the swimming pool construction contract carried an implied
warranty of merchantability under C.L. §2-314. Anthony's contractual
disclaimer of that warranty was ineffective under C.L. §2-316.1. As a
result, the trial court erred in relying on the disclaimer as a basis for
directing a verdict in favor of Anthony on the warranty count. . . .

Judgment of the court of special appeals affirmed. Costs to be paid
by Anthony Industries, Inc.

B. Merchants

PROBLEM 2

Portia Moot, a third-year law student, sold her car to a fellow
student. Does Article 2 of the UCC apply to this transaction? Would
§2-314 apply to the sale?

Siemen v. Alden

Illinois Appellate Court, 1975
34 Ill. App. 3d 961, 341 N.E.2d 713, 18 U.C.C. Rep. Serv. 884

MORAN, J. Plaintiff sued defendants to recover for injuries he
sustained while operating an automated multi-rip saw. The three-count
complaint sought recovery on theories of strict tort liability for sale of a
defective product, breach of warranties, and negligence. Plaintiff
proceeds on this appeal against defendant Korleski only. He appeals
the order of the trial court granting defendant's motion for summary
judgment on count one, alleging strict tort liability, and count two,
alleging breach of warranties.

Plaintiff had owned and operated a sawmill since 1961. In 1968, he decided to purchase a multi-rip saw to increase his production of decking pallets. Upon the suggestion of a customer, plaintiff contacted Lloyd G. Alden, manufacturer of the saw in question. Alden informed plaintiff that a new saw could not be delivered in less than six months and suggested that plaintiff contact defendant Korleski who owned two of the Alden saws. Plaintiff contacted defendant who advised him that he indeed had two saws: the one he was currently using, and an older one purchased in 1962 which had not been used since 1965. Thereafter the parties met on two occasions at defendant's sawmill to discuss plaintiff's possible purchase of the older saw. At the first meeting, defendant demonstrated the newer saw which operated in the same manner as the one plaintiff was considering purchasing. Plaintiff's son accompanied him to the second meeting at which time plaintiff was first shown the saw in question. It was sitting, partially dismantled, in a corner and was covered with boards and sawdust. Defendant informed plaintiff that it was [not] in operating condition and that plaintiff would have to supply and install saw blades, motor, shiv, belts, pulleys, and a sawdust removal apparatus in order to use it. Thereafter, the parties agreed on a purchase price of $2900.

Plaintiff's injury, which precipitated the instant suit, occurred in 1970 when a cant of wood exploded while being fed through the saw in question.

On appeal, plaintiff contends that summary judgment in favor of defendant should be reversed because (1) defendant had a sufficient relationship to the saw which injured plaintiff to subject him to strict liability for sale of the defective product, and (2) under the Uniform Commercial Code, ch. 26, §2-314 and §2-315, (Ill. Rev. Stat. 1971, ch. 26, §§2-314, 2-315), the defendant is liable for implied warranties.

In Suvada v. White Motor Co., 32 Ill. 2d 612 [2 U.C.C. Rep. Serv. 762] (1965), the Illinois Supreme Court adopted the provisions of Section 402A of the Restatement of the Law of Torts, 2d (1965), which states:

> *Special Liability of Seller of Product For Physical Harm to*
> *User or Consumer*
>
> (1) One who sells any product in a defective condition unreasonably dangerous to the user or consumer or to his property is subject to liability for physical harm thereby caused to the ultimate user or consumer, or to his property, if
>
> > (a) the seller is engaged in the business of selling such a product, and

(b) it is expected to and does reach the user or consumer without substantial change in the condition in which it is sold.

(2) The rule stated in Subsection (1) applies although

(a) the seller has exercised all possible care in the preparation and sale of his product, and

(b) the user or consumer has not bought the product from or entered into any contractual relation with the seller. [Restatement of the Law of Torts, Second, ch. 14, §402A.]

The plain language of the rule limits the application to a seller engaged in the business of selling the product which proved defective. This limitation is buttressed by the comment accompanying the rule in that the occasional seller is explicitly excluded. (Restatement of Torts, 2d, Comment, page 350. See 55 I.B.J. 906 (1967).) Plaintiff contends that because the sale of the saw occurred within the scope and conduct of defendant's business, and because defendant modified the machine to suit his own purposes thereby creating the condition which led to plaintiff's injury, defendant had a relationship to the saw sufficient to subject him to strict liability. Plaintiff's argument fails to overcome the clear requirement of the rule that the seller be engaged in the business of selling the particular product. In the instant case, defendant asserted and plaintiff has not denied that defendant's only sale of a saw or sawmill equipment was to plaintiff. It is therefore apparent that the sale is an isolated transaction and does not come within the provisions of 402A. Balido v. Improved Machinery Inc., 105 Cal. Rptr. 890, 895 (1973).

Plaintiff claims that under §§2-314 and 2-315 of the Uniform Commercial Code (Ill. Rev. Stat. 1971, ch. 26, §§2-314, 2-315) a genuine issue of material fact exists as to defendant's liability arising from his saw-related knowledge and skill, and plaintiff's ultimate reliance upon this knowledge in purchasing the saw. Section 2-314 states in pertinent part:

Unless excluded or modified . . . a warranty that the goods shall be merchantable is implied in a contract for their sale if the seller is a merchant with respect to goods of that kind. . . .

Section 2-104(1) of the Uniform Commercial Code (Ill. Rev. Stat. 1971, ch. 26, §2-104(1)) defines a merchant as:

[A] person who deals in goods of the kind or otherwise by his occupation holds himself out as having knowledge or skill peculiar to the practices or goods involved in the transaction or to whom such knowledge or skill may be attributed by his employment of an agent or broker or other intermediary who by his occupation holds himself out as having such knowledge or skill.

Defendant [*sic*—Plaintiff?] argues in his reply brief that plaintiff [*sic*—defendant?] falls within the terms of §2-104(1) and is therefore a merchant for purposes of §2-314 by virtue of his "holding himself out as having knowledge or skill." This test, however, is not the standard for determining who is a merchant within the meaning of §2-314. The Committee Notes to §2-104 (S.H.A. 1971, ch. 26, §2-104, Committee Notes ¶2, page 97) and to §2-314 (S.H.A. 1971, ch. 26, §2-314, Committee Comments, ¶3, page 232) make it clear that the definition of merchant within §2-314 is a narrow one and that the warranty of merchantability is applicable only to a person who, in a professional status, sells the particular kind of goods giving rise to the warranty.

A person making an isolated sale of goods is not a "merchant" within the meaning of the scope of this section [2-314] and, thus, no warranty of merchantability would apply. [S.H.A. 1971, ch. 26, §2-314, Committee Comments, ¶3, page 232.]

The record is clear that defendant is engaged in the sawmill business. The sale in the instant case was an isolated transaction and therefore did not come within the terms of §2-314. Balido v. Improved Machinery, supra.

Plaintiff also claims that §2-315 of the Uniform Commercial Code (Ill. Rev. Stat. 1971, ch. 26, §2-315) is applicable to the transaction in the instant case. The provision reads:

Where the seller at the time of contracting has reason to know any particular purpose for which the goods are required and that the buyer is relying on the seller's skill or judgment to select or furnish suitable goods, there is unless excluded or modified under the next section an implied warranty that the goods shall be fit for such purpose.

This section imposes two requirements: first, that the seller know of the particular purpose for which the goods are required, and second, that the buyer rely on seller's skill or judgment in selecting the product. Here, the first requirement is met in that it is undisputed that defendant knew plaintiff's purpose for buying the saw: the making of pallets. As to the second requirement, plaintiff asserts that the following facts create a genuine issue of material fact as to plaintiff's reliance on seller's expertise: plaintiff neither owned nor had experience with a multi-rip saw whereas defendant had been operating one for about six years; Alden referred other customers to defendant for demonstrations of the saw; and defendant explained safety requirements for operating the saw and made recommendations on operating procedures. Impliedly, according to plaintiff, defendant had expertise due to his experience with the saw, and Alden considered defendant to have that expertise by its referral of other customers to defendant for demonstrations.

Defendant, on the other hand, asserts that there was no genuine issue of material fact indicating that plaintiff relied on defendant's skill or judgment in purchasing the saw, and supports this assertion with the following facts: plaintiff made his original inquiry to purchase an Alden-brand saw upon the advice and suggestion of a customer; after learning of the six-month delivery delay, plaintiff contacted defendant regarding the used Alden saw rather than investigating the purchase of a different brand; plaintiff's statement in his deposition, "in my search for a gang-rip saw I was directed to Ed Korleski," indicates that he had decided to purchase such a saw prior to any contact with defendant; and plaintiff brought his son to view the saw to see "whether he thought [the saw] was what [they] needed," suggesting that plaintiff relied on his son's judgment, not the defendant's.

It is not the facts that are in dispute, but the conclusion or inference to be drawn from them, i.e., do plaintiff's facts raise a question of his reliance on defendant's judgment in selecting the saw sufficient to submit the issue to the jury for determination. We find plaintiff's facts insufficient to raise a question of material fact as to his reliance upon defendant's skill and knowledge; no facts indicated that plaintiff relied on defendant's expertise in making his decision to purchase the saw. Rather, the uncontroverted facts establish that plaintiff had decided to purchase an Alden saw prior to his initial contact with defendant. We hold therefore that the trial court properly granted defendant's motion for summary judgment.

Judgment affirmed.

Notice that the definition of *merchant* in §2-104(1) refers not only to those who deal in the goods involved, but also those merchants who deal in the *practices* of the kind involved in the transaction. Official Comment 2 explains:

The special provisions as to merchants appear only in this Article and they are of three kinds. Sections 2-201(2), 2-205, 2-207 and 2-209 dealing with the statute of frauds, firm offers, confirmatory memoranda and modification rest on normal business practices which are or ought to be typical of and familiar to any person in business. For purposes of these sections almost every person in business would, therefore, be deemed to be a "merchant" under the language "who . . . by his occupation holds himself out as having knowledge or skill peculiar to the practices . . . involved in the transaction . . ." since the practices involved in the transaction are non-specialized business practices such as answering mail. In this type of provision, banks or even universities, for example, well may be "merchants." But even these sections only apply to a merchant in his mercantile capacity; a lawyer or bank president buying fishing tackle for his own use is not a merchant.

On the other hand, in Section 2-314 on the warranty of merchantability, such warranty is implied only "if the seller is a merchant with respect to goods of that kind." Obviously this qualification restricts the implied warranty to a much smaller group than everyone who is engaged in business and requires a professional status as to particular kinds of goods. The exception in Section 2-402(2) for retention of possession by a merchant-seller falls in the same class; as does Section 2-403(2) on entrusting of possession to a merchant "who deals in goods of that kind."

A third group of sections includes 2-103(1)(b), which provides that in the case of a merchant "good faith" includes observance of reasonable commercial standards of fair dealing in trade; 2-327(1)(c), 2-603, and 2-605 dealing with responsibilities of merchant buyers to follow seller's instructions, etc.; 2-509 on risk of loss; and 2-609 on adequate assurance of performance. This group of sections applies to persons who are merchants under either the "practices" or the "goods" aspect of the definition of merchant.

PROBLEM 3

Are the following persons merchants?

(a) Amanda, who quit her teaching job on Friday and on Monday opened a hat store?

(b) Tom Tiller, a farmer selling his produce to a wholesaler? Compare Loeb & Co. v. Schreiner, 294 Ala. 722, 321 So. 2d 199, 17 U.C.C. Rep. Serv. 897 (1975) ("Although a farmer might sell his cotton every year, we do not think that this should take him out of the category of a 'casual seller' and place him in the category with 'professionals.'"), with Continental Grain Co. v. Brown, 19 U.C.C. Rep. Serv. 52 (W.D. Wis. 1976) ("A sale of 75,000 bushels of corn for a total price in excess of $212,000 is not a 'casual' sale."). See also Vince v.

Broome, 443 So. 2d 23, 37 U.C.C. Rep. Serv. 1498 (Miss. 1983) ("Some farming operations are worth millions of dollars. . . . It would stretch the imagination to conclude that all these operations were exempt from coverage under the Commercial Code."); Ohio Grain Co. v. Swisshelm, 40 Ohio App. 2d 203, 318 N.E.2d 428, 15 U.C.C. Rep. Serv. 897 (1973) (the modern farmer is more than "a simple tiller of the soil, unaccustomed to the affairs of business and the market-place. . . . Only an agribusinessman may hope to survive."); Harvest States Cooperatives v. Anderson, 217 Wis. 2d 154, 577 N.W.2d 381, 36 U.C.C. Rep. Serv. 2d 662 (1998) (man who had some cows and made occasional sales of corn not a merchant).

III.   SCOPE OF ARTICLE 2A

In recent years equipment leasing has become big business. It now accounts for well over $200 billion in outstanding contracts worldwide and is predicted to far exceed that amount by the end of the first decade of the new millennium. Leasing goods (as opposed to pur-chasing them) has certain advantages. It may be desirable for accounting reasons because the lease obligation is not reflected as an asset/liability, thus improving the balance sheet ratios. At various times there have been tax advantages to leasing goods, though the tax laws have fluctuated on this through the years.[4]

A major problem with all this is that the law of personal property leasing has not been clearly defined. It originally developed from the law of bailments and, by analogy, from the law governing the lease of real property, though it fit comfortably into neither. Where the law was unfavorable or nonexistent, model equipment leases were promul-gated by various bodies. See, e.g., Antin, An Equipment Lease Form, 8 A.L.I.-A.B.A. Course Materials J. 117 (1983). Since the adoption of the Uniform Commercial Code, many courts have applied Article 2 to leases, either stating that this was the intention of the drafters—see §2-102, stating that Article 2 applies to "transactions" in goods—or using Article 2 by analogy. Since many of Article 2's sections apply only if a

---

4. It has always been malpractice for the author to say the word "tax" out loud, and this book therefore expresses no opinion on the current position of the Internal Revenue Code on this or any other subject.

"sale" occurs—defined in §2-106(1) to require the passing of title from the seller to the buyer—the Code's rules have to be stretched a great deal to encompass a true lease of goods.

Added to this difficulty was the fact that many so-called leases were not true leases at all, but instead were sales of the goods involved disguised as leases. This was done for various reasons: the bookkeeping and tax considerations mentioned above, plus the desire to escape from the necessity of complying with either Article 2 or the secured transactions rules of Article 9. The original wording of §1-201(37) contained a skeletal test for telling a true lease from a disguised sale: if the lessee had the option to become the owner of the leased goods at the end of the lease period for nominal or no consideration, a sale was effected. To this, courts deciding cases under both Article 2 and Article 9 added elaborate tests for telling a true lease from a disguised sale.

In 1987 the last of the various bodies involved approved for adoption a new version of the Uniform Commercial Code containing Article 2A, entitled "Leases." It is modeled in large part (some say too much)[5] on Article 2. Throughout the rest of this book, reference will be made to sections of Article 2A, particularly where those sections deviate from the similar rules in Article 2.[6]

First, however, it is important to appreciate the kind of leases to which Article 2A applies. Reference must now be had to the 1987 version of §1-201(37).[7] If a so-called "lease" does not pass the tests described therein, Article 2A is not triggered. Instead, the "lease" will be governed by Articles 2 and 9 because the lease will typically then be a disguised sale on credit, with the "lessor's" interest in reality being nothing more than the reservation of a security interest.[8]

---

5. "The Article 2A draftsmen's desire to follow the Article 2 model on occasion resulted in virtual unintelligibility to all but the most experienced and knowledgeable." Report of the Uniform Commercial Code Committee of the Business Law Section of the State Bar of California on Proposed California Commercial Code Division 10 (Article 2A) (1987), reprinted in 39 Ala. L. Rev. at 979, 984 (1988). California has adopted Article 2A with major overhauls to some of its sections. See also Kripke, Some Dissonant Notes About Article 2A, 39 Ala. L. Rev. 791 (1988).

6. The original version of Article 2A contained so many flaws that it was redrafted in 1990. The 1990 version is the one referred to in this book.

7. In the new version of Article of he Uniform Commercial Code, the correct section number for the definition of a "security interest" is §1-203.

8. Professors James White and Robert Summers deal with Article 2A in their splendid treatise on the Uniform Commercial Code: see Chapters 13 to 15 in Volume 2 (4th ed. Practitioner Treatise Series 1995). This work is published in two editions: a multi-volume work for practitioners and a one-volume student edition. All further citations, unless noted, are to the student edition: J. White & R. Summers, Uniform Commercial Code (5th ed. 2002) [hereinafter White & Summers].

Read the very complicated definition of "security interest" in
§1-201(37), concentrating on the major part of it that attempts to distinguish between a true lease and a security interest (that is, a sale on
credit disguised as a lease). What are we to make of this definition?
The happiest thing about it (despite its formidable size) is that it does
draw some bright lines to help attorneys tell leases from secured
transactions:

1.   As under the original definition, if at the end of the lease
      period the lessee becomes the owner of the property for little
      or no consideration, a secured transaction and not a lease
      has been created.
2.   If the contract contains a clause that permits the lessee to
      terminate the lease at any time and return the leased goods
      (the so-called walk away test), a true lease has resulted. Such
      a right of termination is not an attribute of a sale of goods.
3.   If the lease is for the entire economic life of the leased goods,
      with or without renewal, a disguised sale has occurred.

Other than that, each lease must be evaluated on its own. It does
not necessarily answer the central question if the lessee pays
consideration equal to or even greater than the fair market value of
the leased goods as long as the lease does not cover the total economic
life of the goods. Nor does the lessee's assumption of major duties
(taxes, risk of loss, etc.) necessarily indicate a lease or a sale of goods.
      Use the definition and the above tests to answer the following
Problem.

PROBLEM 4

B.I.G. Machines, Inc., leased a computer to Helen's Flower
Shoppe for a five-year period. The machine was new and had cost
B.I.G. Machines $10,000. Helen's Flower Shoppe promised to pay
$225 a month as rent. Is this a lease or a disguised sale? Is your answer
affected by the following considerations?
      (a) The lease provided that the lessee could terminate the lease at
any time and return the computer to the lessor.
      (b) Assume there was no such option as described in (a), but the
goods had no value at the end of the five-year period.
      (c) Assume instead that the rental amount is only $150 a month
and the computer will be worth $3500 at the end of the five-year

period. The lease has a clause giving Helen's Flower Shoppe the option to purchase the computer for that amount at that time. Is this a true lease? What if the lease *requires* the lessee to renew this lease at the end of the five-year period for another five years? s/✓

IV. INTERNATIONAL SALES

Effective January 1, 1988, the United States became bound by a treaty: the United Nations Convention on Contracts for the International Sale of Goods [hereinafter CISG].[9] The Convention covers only issues of contract formation and the rights and duties of the parties thereto. It excludes coverage of products liability issues; it does not address matters touching on contract validity, such as fraud, illegality, etc. The leading text on the CISG to date is J. Honnold, Uniform Law for International Sales Under the 1980 United Nations Convention (3d ed. 1991).

PROBLEM 5

Hegemony Enterprises, headquartered in New York, is about to sign a contract for the sale of men's clothing to Cosas Americana, a retailer in Mexico City. You are the lawyer for Hegemony Enterprises, and a company official calls you with the following questions:

(a) Will the CISG apply to this transaction? See CISG Articles 1 and 2.

---

9. The countries that have ratified the Convention as of this writing are Argentina, Australia, Austria, Belorussia (Belarus), Bosnia and Herzegovina, Bulgaria, Canada, Chile, China, Cuba, Czech Republic, Denmark, Ecuador, Egypt, Estonia, Finland, France, Georgia, Germany, Ghana, Guinea, Hungary, Iraq, Italy, Lesotho, Lithuania, Mexico, Moldavia, Netherlands, New Zealand, Norway, Poland, Romania, Russian Federation, Singapore, Slovak Republic, Slovenia, Spain, Sweden, Switzerland, Syria, Uganda, Ukraine, United States, Venezuela, Yugoslavia, and Zambia. Note how much international trade is *not* currently subject to the treaty; major players such as Great Britain, Japan, Korea, and Taiwan are not signatories. The United Nations has provided a telephone number that can be called to obtain an up-to-date list of the countries adopting the Convention: (212) 963-7958 or 963-5048.

(b) If Hegemony Enterprises wants the law of New York to apply, can the parties so stipulate in the contract and avoid the CISG? See Article 6.

(c) If Hegemony Enterprises were selling toys to Cosas Americana, would the CISG apply? See Article 2(a).

Chapter 2
CONTRACT FORMATION

The basics of contract formation should be reassuringly familiar to you from Contracts class. Perhaps the UCC approach to the Statute of Frauds, the Parol Evidence Rule, and offer and acceptance were covered there. If not, as you learn these rules rather than review them, contrast the UCC approach with the common law approach.

I. THE STATUTE OF FRAUDS

Read §2-201, which is quite a change from the common law Statute of Frauds. At common law, when a contract fell within the Statute, *all* its terms and conditions had to be in writing or the contract was not enforceable. Under §2-201, a contract can be enforced even if a main term is omitted or misstated. The only term necessary for a sufficient memorandum under §2-201(1) is *quantity*. Not only are the standards lessened by the Code, but also four exceptions are provided: merchant confirmation letters, special manufacture, part performance, and admission in legal proceedings.

PROBLEM 6

On December 10, James Ross, president of Ross Ice Cream Shoppes, Inc., phoned Robert Scott, president of Amundsen Ice Company, and negotiated the purchase of two tons of ice from Amundsen at $256/ton. As they talked on the phone, Scott picked up a memo pad enscribed "Amundsen Ice Company From the Desk of the President," wrote on it "2 tons Ross Co.," and then scribbled his initials on it. When the parties hung up the phones, Scott placed the memo on a spindle marked "Orders." Ross wrote Scott a letter beginning "Dear Bob: This is to confirm our ice purchase deal . . . ," which described their transaction completely. Scott received the letter on December 14. On January 17, Scott phoned Ross and denied the existence of the contract detailed in the Ross letter. Answer these questions:

(a) Does the memo pad note satisfy §2-201(1)? See §1-201(39) and Official Comment 39.

(b) What legal effect did the December 14 letter have? Same result if Ross's letter failed to mention the quantity? Even if the letter satisfies the Statute of Frauds, is it conclusive as to the existence and terms of the contract? See Hinson-Barr, Inc. v. Pinckard, 292 S.C. 267, 356 S.E.2d 115, 4 U.C.C. Rep. Serv. 2d 36 (1987).

(c) Did Scott's denial of the terms contained in Ross's letter avoid the operation of §2-201(2)? Suppose Scott had immediately written Ross a letter stating, "You haven't stated the terms correctly. We only agreed to sell you 1½ tons." Would that letter be a sufficient notice of objection? See Simmons Oil Corp. v. Bulk Sales Corp., 498 F. Supp. 457, 31 U.C.C. Rep. Serv. 1236 (D.N.J. 1980); Annot., 82 A.L.R.4th 709.

(d) If there had been no confirmation letter, suppose Ross files suit and Amundsen responds with a demurrer—may the trial court judge dismiss on the pleadings? Compare Franklin County Coop v. MFC Serv., 441 So. 2d 1376, 37 U.C.C. Rep. Serv. 1465 (Miss. 1983), with Triangle Marketing, Inc. v. Action Indus., Inc., 630 F. Supp. 1578, 1 U.C.C. Rep. Serv. 2d 36 (N.D. Ill. 1986). If Scott admits the contract formation in a deposition, would §2-201(3)(b) be satisfied? See Reiss-

man Intl. Corp. v. J.S.O. Wood Prod., Inc., 10 U.C.C. Rep. Serv. 1165
(N.Y. Civ. Ct. 1972). Does §2-201(3)(b) always require the judge to
permit the matter to go to trial? See M & W Farm Serv. Co. v. Callison,
285 N.W.2d 271, 27 U.C.C. Rep. Serv. 1239 (Iowa 1979); compare the
majority and dissenting opinions in DF Activities Corp. v. Brown, 851
F.2d 920, 7 U.C.C. Rep. Serv. 2d 1396 (7th Cir. 1988).

St. Ansgar Mills, Inc. v. Streit

Supreme Court of Iowa, 2000
613 N.W.2d 289, 42 U.C.C. Rep. Serv. 2d 58

CADY, Justice.

A grain dealer appeals from an order by the district court granting
summary judgment in an action to enforce an oral contract for the sale
of corn based on a written confirmation. The district court held the
oral contract was unenforceable because the written confirmation was
not delivered within a reasonable time after the oral contract as a
matter of law. We reverse the decision of the district court and remand
for further proceedings.

I.   BACKGROUND FACTS AND PROCEEDINGS.

St. Ansgar Mills, Inc. is a family-owned agricultural business
located in Mitchell County. As a part of its business, St. Ansgar Mills
buys corn from local grain farmers and sells corn to livestock farmers
for feed. The price of the corn sold to farmers is established by trades
made on the Chicago Board of Trade for delivery with reference to five
contract months. The sale of corn for future delivery is hedged by St.
Ansgar Mills through an offsetting futures position on the Chicago
Board of Trade.

A sale is typically made when a farmer calls St. Ansgar Mills and
requests a quote for a cash price of grain for future delivery based on
the Chicago Board of Trade price for the delivery. The farmer then
accepts or rejects the price. If the price is accepted, St. Ansgar Mills
protects the price through a licensed brokerage house by acquiring a
hedge position on the Chicago Board of Trade. This hedge position,
however, obligates St. Ansgar Mills to purchase the corn at the stated
price at the time of delivery. Thus, St. Ansgar Mills relies on the farmer
who purchased the grain to accept delivery at the agreed price.

Duane Streit formerly resided in Mitchell County and currently
practices veterinarian medicine in Carroll County. He also raises hogs.

He owns a large hog farrowing operation in Carroll County and a hog finishing operation in Mitchell County near Osage. Streit purchased the Osage farm from his father in 1993. Duane's father, John Streit, resides in Mitchell County and helps Duane operate the Osage finishing facility.

Duane and his father have been long-time customers of St. Ansgar Mills. Since 1989, Duane entered into numerous contracts with St. Ansgar Mills for the purchase of large quantities of corn and other grain products. Duane would generally initiate the purchase agreement by calling St. Ansgar Mills on the telephone to obtain a price quote. If an oral contract was made, an employee of St. Ansgar Mills would prepare a written confirmation of the sale and either mail it to Duane to sign and return, or wait for Duane or John to sign the confirmation when they would stop into the business.

John would regularly stop by St. Ansgar Mills sometime during the first ten days of each month and pay the amount of the open account Duane maintained at St. Ansgar Mills for the purchase of supplies and other materials. On those occasions when St. Ansgar Mills sent the written confirmation to Duane, it was not unusual for Duane to fail to sign the confirmation for a long period of time. He also failed to return contracts sent to him. Nevertheless, Duane had never refused delivery of grain he purchased by telephone prior to the incident which gave rise to this case.

On July 1, 1996, John telephoned St. Ansgar Mills to place two orders for the purchase of 60,000 bushels of corn for delivery in December 1996 and May 1997. This order followed an earlier conversation between Duane and St. Ansgar Mills. After the order was placed, St. Ansgar Mills completed the written confirmation but set it aside for John to sign when he was expected to stop by the business to pay the open account. The agreed price of the December corn was $3.53 per bushel. The price of the May corn was $3.73 per bushel.

John failed to follow his monthly routine of stopping by the business during the month of July. St. Ansgar Mills then asked a local banker who was expected to see John to have John stop into the business.

John did not stop by St. Ansgar Mills until August 10, 1996. On that date, St. Ansgar Mills delivered the written confirmation to him.

Duane later refused delivery of the corn orally purchased on July 1, 1996. The price of corn had started to decline shortly after July 1, and eventually plummeted well below the quoted price on July 1. After Duane refused delivery of the corn, he purchased corn for his hog operations on the open market at prices well below the contract prices of July 1. St. Ansgar Mills later told Duane it should have followed up earlier with the written confirmation and had no excuse for not doing so.

St. Ansgar Mills then brought this action for breach of contract. It sought damages of $152,100, which was the difference between the contract price of the corn and the market price at the time Duane refused delivery.

Duane filed a motion for summary judgment. He claimed the oral contract alleged by St. Ansgar Mills was governed by the provisions of the Uniform Commercial Code, and was unenforceable as a matter of law under the statute of frauds. He claimed the written confirmation delivered to John on August 10, 1996 did not satisfy the statute of frauds for two reasons. First, he was not a merchant. Second, the confirmation was not received within a reasonable time after the alleged oral agreement.

The district court determined a jury question was presented on whether Duane was a merchant under the Uniform Commercial Code. However, the district court found the written confirmation did not satisfy the writing requirements of the statute of frauds because the delivery of the confirmation to John, as Duane's agent, did not occur within a reasonable time after the oral contract as a matter of law. The district court found the size of the order, the volatility of the grain market, and the lack of an explanation by St. Ansgar Mills for failing to send the confirmation to Duane after John failed to stop by the business as expected made the delay between July 1 and August 10 unreasonable as a matter of law.

St. Ansgar Mills appeals. It claims a jury question was presented on the issue of whether a written confirmation was received within a reasonable time. . . .

III. STATUTE OF FRAUDS.

The statute of frauds is one of the most well-known and venerable rules applicable to contract law. Generally, it establishes an exception to the proposition that oral contracts are enforceable in a lawsuit if sufficiently proven by requiring certain types of contracts to be in writing and signed by the party against whom enforcement is sought. See Iowa Code §554.2201(1).

The statute of frauds originated in 17th century England to combat the use of fraud and perjury by litigants in court proceedings to establish oral contracts. See 2 E. Allan Farnsworth, Contracts §6.1, at 82-83 (2d ed. 1990). At the time, court rules prohibited parties to a lawsuit from testifying as witnesses in their case, and, consequently, an oral contract could only be established with testimony of third parties. See Azevedo v. Minister, 86 Nev. 576, 471 P.2d 661, 663 (1970). This prohibition allowed witnesses to be persuaded to give false testimony on behalf of a party in an effort to establish an oral contract, leaving the other party at a distinct disadvantage. See James J. O'Connell, Jr., Boats Against a Current: The Courts and the Statute of Frauds, 47 Emory L.J. 253, 257 (1998) [hereinafter O'Connell].

In 1677, in response to this unsavory practice of using perjury to establish oral contracts, Parliament enacted the statute of frauds to require certain contracts to be supported by written evidence to be enforceable. 29 Car. 2, ch. 3 (1677) (Eng.); see Hugh E. Willis, Statute of Frauds—A Legal Anachronism, 3 Ind. L.J. 427, 427 (1928). The statute included contracts which were not only particularly susceptible to fraud, but those which posed serious consequences of fraud, including contracts for the sale of goods or property. See O'Connell, 47 Emory L.J. at 258.

Despite a difference in the court rules which gave rise to this statute of frauds, our American legal culture quickly adopted the principle. James J. White & Robert S. Summers, Uniform Commercial Code §2-1, at 50 (2d ed. 1980) [hereinafter White & Summers]. Iowa adopted the statute of frauds in 1851. See Iowa Code §§2409-2410 (1851). The statute of frauds also became a part of the Uniform Sales Act in 1906, which Iowa subsequently adopted in 1924. See 1919 Iowa Acts ch. 396 (initially codified at Iowa Code §§9930-10007 (1924)). This statute required all contracts for the sale of goods to be in writing. Over time, the Uniform Sales Act was replaced by the Uniform Commercial Code.[1] The Uniform Commercial Code continued to adhere to the statute of frauds, but was limited in its provisions to the sale of goods in excess of $500. Iowa enacted its version of the Uniform Commercial Code in 1966 including the statute of frauds. See 1965

---

1. After six years of deliberating, the National Conference of Commissioners on Uniform State Laws produced the 1952 Official Text of the Uniform Commercial Code. See William A. Schnader, A Short History of the Preparation and Enactment of the Uniform Commercial Code, 22 U. Miami L. Rev. 1, 1-2 (1967). In 1954, Pennsylvania was the first state to formally adopt the text. See 13 Pa. Const. Stat. §§1101 to 9507 (1953). By 1968, the Uniform Commercial Code was effective in 49 states, the District of Columbia, and the Virgin Islands. See Uniform Commercial Code Table, 1 U.L.A. 1-2 (Master ed. 1989). There have been three official revisions, the 1972, the 1978, and the 1987 Official Texts, offered by the Permanent Editorial Board, a board established in 1961 to keep the Code up to date. See William A. Schnader, The Permanent Editorial Board for the Uniform Commercial Code: Can it Accomplish its Object?, 3 Am. Bus. L.J. 137, 138 (1965).

Iowa Acts ch. 413. Iowa's statute of frauds for the sale of goods now provides:

> Except as otherwise provided in this section, a contract for the sale of goods for the price of $500 or more is not enforced by way of action or defense unless there is some writing sufficient to indicate that a contract for sale has been made between the parties and signed by the party against whom enforcement is sought or by that party's authorized agent or broker.

Iowa Code §554.2201(1) (1995).

Although the statute of frauds has been deeply engrained into our law, many of the forces which originally gave rise to the rule are no longer prevalent. White & Summers §2-1, at 51. This, in turn, has caused some of the rigid requirements of the rule to be modified.

One statutory exception or modification to the statute of frauds which has surfaced applies to merchants. Id. §554.2201(2). Under section 554.2201(2), the writing requirements of section 554.2201(1) are considered to be satisfied if, within a reasonable time, a writing in confirmation of the contract which is sufficient against the sender is received and the merchant receiving it has reason to know of its contents, unless written notice of objection of its contents is given within ten days after receipt. Id. Thus, a writing is still required, but it does not need to be signed by the party against whom the contract is sought to be enforced. The purpose of this exception was to put professional buyers and sellers on equal footing by changing the former law under which a party who received a written confirmation of an oral agreement of sale, but who had not signed anything, could hold the other party to a contract without being bound. See White & Summers §2-3, at 55; Kimball County Grain Coop. v. Yung, 200 Neb. 233, 263 N.W.2d 818, 820 (1978). It also encourages the common, prudent business practice of sending memoranda to confirm oral agreements. White & Summers §2-3, at 55.

While the written confirmation exception imposes a specific ten-day requirement for a merchant to object to a written confirmation, it employs a flexible standard of reasonableness to establish the time in which the confirmation must be received. Iowa Code §554.2201(2). The Uniform Commercial Code specifically defines a reasonable time for taking action in relationship to "the nature, purpose and circumstances" of the action. Id. §554.1204(2) [UCC §1-204]. Additionally, the declared purpose of the Uniform Commercial Code is to permit the expansion of commercial practices through the custom and practice of the parties. See Iowa Code Ann. §554.1102 cmt. 2 (course of dealings, usage of trade or course of performance are material in determining a reasonable time). Furthermore, the Uniform Commercial Code relies upon course of dealings between the parties to help interpret their conduct. Iowa Code §554.1205(1). Thus, all relevant circumstances, including custom and practice of the parties, must be considered in determining what constitutes a reasonable time under section 554.2201(2).

Generally, the determination of the reasonableness of particular conduct is a jury question. See Pirelli-Armstrong Tire Co. v. Reynolds, 562 N.W.2d 433, 436 (Iowa 1997); see also Harvey v. Great Atl. & Pac. Tea Co., 388 F.2d 123, 125 (5th Cir. 1968) (passing judgment on the reasonableness of conduct of the parties must be accomplished in light of all the circumstances of the case and should rarely be disposed of by summary judgment). Thus, the reasonableness of time between an oral contract and a subsequent written confirmation is ordinarily a question of fact for the jury. Mortgageamerica Corp. v. American Nat'l Bank, 651 S.W.2d 851, 856 (Tex. Ct. App. 1983); Schiavi Mobile Homes, Inc. v. Gagne, 510 A.2d 236, 238 (Me. 1986) (reasonableness of parties' time for action is a question of fact). It is only in rare cases that a determination of the reasonableness of conduct should be decided by summary adjudication. *Harvey*, 388 F.2d at 125. Summary judgment is appropriate only when the evidence is so one-sided that a party must prevail at trial as a matter of law. Ridgeway v. Union County Comm'rs, 775 F. Supp. 1105, 1109 (S.D. Ohio 1991).

There are a host of cases from other jurisdictions which have considered the question of what constitutes a reasonable time under the written confirmation exception of the Uniform Commercial Code. See Gestetner Corp. v. Case Equip. Co., 815 F.2d 806, 810 (1st Cir. 1987) (roughly five-month delay reasonable in light of merchants' relationship and parties' immediate action under contract following oral agreement); Serna, Inc. v. Harman, 742 F.2d 186, 189 (5th Cir. 1984) (three and one-half month delay reasonable in light of the parties' interaction in the interim, and non-fluctuating prices, thus no prejudice); Cargill, Inc. v. Stafford, 553 F.2d 1222, 1224 (10th Cir. 1977) (less than one-month delay unreasonable despite misdirection of confirmation due to mistaken addressing); Starry Constr. Co. v. Murphy Oil USA, Inc., 785 F. Supp. 1356, 1362-63 (D. Minn. 1992) (six-month delay for confirmation of modification order for additional oil unreasonable as a matter of law in light of Persian Gulf War, thus increased prices and demand); Rockland Indus., Inc. v. Frank Kasmir Assoc., 470 F. Supp. 1176, 1179 (N.D. Tex. 1979) (letter sent eight months after alleged oral agreement for two-year continuity agreement unreasonable in light of lack of evidence supporting reasonableness of delay); *Yung,* 263 N.W.2d at 820 (six-month delay in confirming oral agreement delivered one day prior to last possible day of delivery unreasonable); *Azevedo,* 471 P.2d at 666 (ten-week delay reasonable in light of immediate performance by both parties following oral agreement); Lish v. Compton, 547 P.2d 223, 226-27 (Utah 1976) (twelve-day delay "outside the ambit which fair-minded persons could conclude to be reasonable" in light of volatile price market and lack of excuse for delay other than casual delay). Most of these cases, however, were decided after a trial on the merits and cannot be used to establish a standard or time period as a matter of law. Only a few courts have decided the question as a matter of law under the facts of the case. Compare *Starry,* 785 F. Supp. at 1362-63 (granting summary judgment), and *Lish,* 547 P.2d at 226-27 (removing claim from jury's consideration), with Barron v. Edwards, 45 Mich. App. 210, 206 N.W.2d 508, 511 (1973) (remanding for further development of facts, summary judgment improper). However, these cases do not establish a strict principle to apply in this case. The resolution of each case depends upon the particular facts and circumstances. *T. o. C.*

In this case, the district court relied upon the large amount of the sale, volatile market conditions, and lack of an explanation by St. Ansgar Mills for failing to send the written confirmation to Duane in determining St. Ansgar Mills acted unreasonably as a matter of law in delaying delivery of the written confirmation until August 10, 1996. Volatile market conditions, combined with a large sale price, would normally narrow the window of reasonable time under section 554.2201(2). However, they are not the only factors to consider. Other relevant factors which must also be considered in this case reveal the parties had developed a custom or practice to delay delivery of the confirmation. The parties also maintained a long-time amicable business relationship and had engaged in many other similar business transactions without incident. There is also evidence to infer St. Ansgar Mills did not suspect John's failure to follow his customary practice in July of stopping by the business was a concern at the time. These factors reveal a genuine dispute over the reasonableness of the delay in delivering the written confirmation, and make the resolution of the issue appropriate for the jury. Moreover, conduct is not rendered unreasonable solely because the acting party had no particular explanation for not pursuing different conduct, or regretted not pursuing different conduct in retrospect. The reasonableness of conduct is determined by the facts and circumstances existing at the time.

Considering our principles governing summary adjudication and the need to resolve the legal issue by considering the particular facts and circumstances of each case, we conclude the trial court erred by granting summary judgment. We reverse and remand the case for further proceedings.

Article 2A has a Statute of Frauds similar to §2-201, though the amount of the lease must be at least $1,000 before a writing is required, and the writing must describe the leased goods and the lease term in order to satisfy the Statute. See §2A-201. There is no "merchant's confirmation" subsection in this section because (according to the Official Comment) that situation does not often arise in lease transactions.

There is no Statute of Frauds for international sales under the CISG unless the country adopting the Convention stipulates that its own Statute of Frauds will apply. See Articles 11 and 96.

PROBLEM 7

The city manager of Thebes, Utah, which is world-famous for its beautiful desert golf course, orally ordered a huge water tank to be made in the shape of a golf ball on a tee from Tanks of America, Inc. The price was agreed to be $30,000, and the city sent Tanks a down payment check for $3,000, signed by the city comptroller and marked "Tank" on the memo line. Tanks of America built the tank and was in the process of painting "City of Thebes" on the side when a representative of a newly elected city administration called and said that the new administration considered the contract unenforceable. Answer these questions:

(a) Does the check satisfy §2-201(1)? Where is the *quantity*?

(b) What legal argument can Tanks of America make based on §§2-201(3)(a) and 2-201(3)(c)? See Harvest States Cooperatives v. Anderson, 217 Wis. 2d 154, 577 N.W.2d 381, 36 U.C.C. Rep. Serv. 2d 662 (1998) (good discussion of specially manufactured goods exception). Does the City of Thebes have a good response to the §2-201(3)(c) argument? See W.I. Snyder Corp. v. Caracciolo, 373 Pa. Super. 486, 541 A.2d 775, 7 U.C.C. Rep. Serv. 2d 993 (1988).

(c) If the city had promised to sign a written contract but had never gotten around to doing so, can promissory estoppel or equitable estoppel be used to circumvent §2-201? Reread §1-103, and see Allen M. Campbell Co. v. Virginia Metal Indus., Inc., 708 F.2d 930, 36 U.C.C. Rep. Serv. 384 (4th Cir. 1983); Billings & Henderson, Promissory Estoppel, Equitable Estoppel and Farmer as a Merchant: 1973 Grain Cases and the UCC Statute of Frauds, 60 Utah L. Rev. 59 (1977); Annot., 29 A.L.R.4th 1006.

PROBLEM 8

Tomorrow, Inc. (a computer software company), and Systems Unlimited (a company specializing in advising other companies how to maximize their computer operations) entered into a written joint venture contract by which Tomorrow, Inc., promised to design and sell to Systems Unlimited software that would enable the latter's customers to receive engineering drawings by phone. The parties agreed that their arrangement was "non-exclusive" (meaning either was allowed to deal with other buyers and sellers of the same product). The contract described the obligations of the parties in some detail and stated that the contract would terminate after two years unless renewed. In fact, after working with Tomorrow, Inc., for only six months, Systems Un-limited decided it could develop its own software cheaper than buying it from Tomorrow, Inc., so it faxed a letter to the latter stating that their contract was at an end. Systems Unlimited declined to purchase any further software. Tomorrow, Inc., which had incurred substantial start-up costs in developing the software for this contract, was astounded and promptly filed suit. Systems Unlimited sought refuge in the Statute of Frauds, arguing that the contract signed by the parties stated no quantity. Does §2-201(1) always require a specific quantity? Look at the statutory language very carefully. Compare §2-306. See also Advent Sys. Ltd. v. Unisys Corp., 925 F.2d 670, 13 U.C.C. Rep. Serv. 2d 669 (3d Cir. 1991); White & Summers §2-4 n.9.

At both the federal and state level statutes have been enacted to facilitate electronic commerce as civilization moves from the world of paper into cyberspace. The states acted first, with many of them adopting the Uniform Electronic Transactions Act (UETA), and the federal government followed with the similar Electronic Signatures in Global and National Commerce Act, 15 U.S.C. §7001, commonly known as "E-Sign." The latter statute applies only in jurisdictions not adopting UETA. Both statutes should be in your statute book.

The basic thrust of these statutes is to allow electronic records in most commercial transactions even if other statutes, such as the Statute of Frauds, require a written signature. However, with certain exceptions (utility cut-off notices, notices of default, repossession, foreclosure, and eviction, insurance cancellations, etc.), almost all legal notices can now be accomplished electronically. This would include the various disclosures required by the consumer laws studied in this book. There are a number of unsettled issues.

Both of the statutes mentioned above require that where a consumer is involved, he/she must have *agreed* to electronic disclosures, but it is unclear exactly what this means. The federal statute is broader, requiring that there be *electronic agreement or confirmation of agreement,* and this agreement must be "affirmative"; 15 U.S.C. §7001(c)(1)(C)(ii). This means that the consumer must have agreed electronically to receive electronic records or have confirmed this consent electronically. UETA is less clear about this, though the Comment 4 to §5 indicates that the consumer's agreement to receive electronic communications must be actual and not imposed unconscionably as part of the fine print in a written contract.

There is also no consensus on what electronic communication means. Is it sufficient for the required information to be posted on a website (the so-called Come and Get It notice) that the consumer must periodically access (which, of course, most won't do) to keep informed? In the 1990s AOL posted rate changes only on its website, making customers agree that this was sufficient notice of any hike in the rate, only to back down when nineteen Attorneys General objected that the practice was unfair and deceptive. What about email notification? Must it be highlighted in such a way that the consumer will recognize its importance and not delete it as "spam"? If the consumer has switched email addresses, then what? Must the sender do something with bounced-back messages? These issues and others will have to await case resolution. For a summary of the consumer issues and suggested resolutions, see Jean Braucher, Rent-Seeking and Risk-Fixing in the New Statutory Law of Electronic Commerce: Difficulties in Moving Consumer Protection Online, 2001 Wis. L. Rev. 527.

II. THE PAROL EVIDENCE RULE

Read §2-202 and its Official Comment.

PROBLEM 9

Lawyers for Swinging Singles Magazine negotiated for an entire year with Space Age Aircraft Co. to obtain a contract for the construction of a special Swinging Singles airplane. (The plane was to be black and silver, with the Swinging Singles emblem painted on the tail; it was to contain a living room, a bed chamber, a swimming pool and hot tubs, and a dance floor.) The resulting 30-page contract also contained a *merger* clause, stating that all prior negotiations were merged into the written contract that contained all the terms of the agreement. The contract was signed by both parties. Does §2-202 bar the introduction of evidence of the following?

(a) An alleged precontract agreement that Space Age would provide free flying lessons to Hi Handsome, president of Swinging Singles, Inc.? The contract says nothing about this. See the test found in Official Comment 3 to §2-202.

(b) An alleged precontract agreement that Swinging Singles could use the plane for two months, and if they did not like it, they could return it for a full refund?

To aid in the construction of agreements, the Code looks to the customs within the industry (called *usage of trade*), the parties' past contacts with one another (called *course of dealing*), and the parties' behavior during the existence of the contract in question (called *course of performance*) and presumes that these matters are relevant in fleshing out the express terms of the contract. See Nanakuli Paving & Rock Co. v. Shell Oil Co., 664 F.2d 772, 32 U.C.C. Rep. Serv. 1025 (9th Cir. 1981) (good discussion of these terms). Read §§1-205 and 2-208[2] carefully. Their relationship to §2-202 is explored in the case below.

Columbia Nitrogen Corp. v. Royster Co.

United States Court of Appeals, Fourth Circuit, 1971
451 F.2d 3, 9 U.C.C. Rep. Serv. 977

BUTZNER, J. . . .

I

Royster manufactures and markets mixed fertilizers, the principal components of which are nitrogen, phosphate and potash. Columbia is

---

2. In the new Article 1 of the Uniform Commercial Code, "course of performance" has been taken out of Article 2 and placed in §1-303(a).

primarily a producer of nitrogen, although it manufactures some mixed fertilizer. For several years Royster had been a major purchaser of Columbia's products, but Columbia had never been a significant customer of Royster. In the fall of 1966, Royster constructed a facility which enabled it to produce more phosphate than it needed in its own operations. After extensive negotiations, the companies executed a contract for Royster's sale of a minimum of 31,000 tons of phosphate each year for three years to Columbia, with an option to extend the term. The contract stated the price per ton, subject to an escalation clause dependent on production costs.

Phosphate prices soon plunged precipitously. Unable to resell the phosphate at a competitive price, Columbia ordered only part of the scheduled tonnage. At Columbia's request, Royster lowered its price for diammonium phosphate on shipments for three months in 1967, but specified that subsequent shipments would be at the original contract price. Even with this concession, Royster's price was still substantially above the market. As a result, Columbia ordered less than a tenth of the phosphate Royster was to ship in the first contract year. When pressed by Royster, Columbia offered to take the phosphate at the current market price and resell it without brokerage fee. Royster, however, insisted on the contract price. When Columbia refused delivery, Royster sold the unaccepted phosphate for Columbia's account at a price substantially below the contract price.

II

Columbia assigns error to the pretrial ruling of the district court excluding all evidence on usage of the trade and course of dealing between the parties. It offered the testimony of witnesses with long experience in the trade that because of uncertain crop and weather conditions, farming practices, and government agricultural programs, express price and quantity terms in contracts for materials in the mixed fertilizer industry are mere projections to be adjusted according to market forces.[3]

---

3. Typical of the proffered testimony are the following excerpts:

"The contracts generally entered into between buyer and seller of materials has always been, in my opinion, construed to be the buyer's best estimate of his anticipated requirements for a given period of time. It is well known in our industry that weather conditions, farming practices, government farm control programs, change requirements from time to time. And therefore allowances were always made to meet these circumstances as they arose."

"Tonnage requirements fluctuate greatly, and that is one reason that the contracts are not considered as binding as most contracts are, because the buyer normally

Columbia also offered proof of its business dealings with Royster over the six-year period preceding the phosphate contract. Since Columbia had not been a significant purchaser of Royster's products, these dealings were almost exclusively nitrogen sales to Royster or exchanges of stock carried in inventory. The pattern which emerges, Columbia claimed, is one of repeated and substantial deviation from the stated amount or price, including four instances where Royster took none of the goods for which it had contracted. Columbia offered proof that the total variance amounted to more than $500,000 in reduced sales. This experience, a Columbia officer offered to testify, formed the basis of an understanding on which he depended in conducting negotiations with Royster.

The district court held that the evidence should be excluded. It ruled that "custom and usage or course of dealing are not admissible to contradict the express, plain, unambiguous language of a valid written contract, which by virtue of its detail negates the proposition that the contract is open to variances in its terms. . . ."

A number of Virginia cases have held that extrinsic evidence may not be received to explain or supplement a written contract unless the court finds the writing is ambiguous. E.g., Mathieson Alkali Works v. Virginia Banner Coal Corp., 147 Va. 125, 136 S.E. 673 (1927). This rule, however, has been changed by the Uniform Commercial Code which Virginia has adopted. The Code expressly states that it "shall be liberally construed and applied to promote its underlying purposes and policies," which include "the expansion of commercial practices

---

would buy on historical basis, but his normal average use would be per annum of any given material. Now that can be affected very decidedly by adverse weather conditions such as a drought, or a flood, or maybe governmental programs which we have been faced with for many, many years, seed grain programs. They pay the farmer not to plant. If he doesn't plant, he doesn't use the fertilizer. When the contracts are made, we do not know of all these contingencies and what they are going to be. So the contract is made for what is considered a fair estimate of his requirements. And, the contract is considered binding to the extent, on him morally, that if he uses the tonnage that he will execute the contract in good faith as the buyer. . . ."

"I have never heard of a contract of this type being enforced legally. . . ."

Well, it undoubtedly sounds ridiculous to people from other industries, but there is a very definite, several very definite reasons why the fertilizer business is always operated under what we call gentlemen's agreements. . . .

"The custom in the fertilizer industry is that the seller either meets the competitive situation or releases the buyer from it upon proof that he can buy it at that price. . . . [T]hey will either have the option of meeting it or releasing him from taking additional tonnage or holding him to that price. . . ."

And this custom exists "regardless of the contractual provisions."

"[T]he custom was that [these contracts] were not worth the cost of the paper they were printed on."

through custom, usage and agreement of the parties. . . ." §1-102. The importance of usage of trade and course of dealing between the parties is shown by §2-202, which authorizes their use to explain or supplement a contract. The official comment states this section rejects the old rule that evidence of course of dealing or usage of trade can be introduced only when the contract is ambiguous. And the Virginia commentators, noting that "[t]his section reflects a more liberal approach to the introduction of parol evidence . . . than has been followed in Virginia," express the opinion that *Mathieson,* supra, and similar Virginia cases no longer should be followed. §2-202, Va. Comment. See also Portsmouth Gas Co. v. Shebar, 209 Va. 250, 253 n.1, 163 S.E.2d 205, 208 n.1 (1968) (dictum). We hold, therefore, that a finding of ambiguity is not necessary for the admission of extrinsic evidence about the usage of the trade and the parties' course of dealing.

We turn next to Royster's claim that Columbia's evidence was properly excluded because it was inconsistent with the express terms of their agreement. There can be no doubt that the Uniform Commercial Code restates the well established rule that evidence of usage of trade and course of dealing should be excluded whenever it cannot be reasonably construed as consistent with the terms of the contract. Division of Triple T Service, Inc. v. Mobil Oil Corp., 60 Misc. 2d 720, 304 N.Y.S.2d 191, 203 (1969), *aff'd mem.,* 311 N.Y.S.2d 961 (1970). Royster argues that the evidence should be excluded as inconsistent because the contract contains detailed provisions regarding the base price, escalation, minimum tonnage, and delivery schedules. The argument is based on the premise that because a contract appears on its face to be complete, evidence of course of dealing and usage of trade should be excluded. We believe, however, that neither the language nor the policy of the Code supports such a broad exclusionary rule. Section 2-202 expressly allows evidence of course of dealing or usage of trade to explain or supplement terms intended by the parties as a final expression of their agreement. When this section is read in light of §1-205(4), it is clear that the test of admissibility is not whether the contract appears on its face to be complete in every detail, but whether the proffered evidence of course of dealing and trade usage reasonably can be construed as consistent with the express terms of the agreement.

The proffered testimony sought to establish that because of changing weather conditions, farming practices, and government agricultural programs, dealers adjusted prices, quantities, and delivery schedules to reflect declining market conditions. For the following reasons it is reasonable to construe this evidence as consistent with the express terms of the contract:

The contract does not expressly state that course of dealing and usage of trade cannot be used to explain or supplement the written contract.

The contract is silent about adjusting prices and quantities to reflect a declining market. It neither permits nor prohibits adjustment, and this neutrality provides a fitting occasion for recourse to usage of trade and prior dealing to supplement the contract and explain its terms.

Minimum tonnages and additional quantities are expressed in terms of "Products Supplied Under Contract." Significantly, they are not expressed as just "Products" or as "Products Purchased Under Contract." The description used by the parties is consistent with the proffered testimony.

Finally, the default clause of the contract refers only to the failure of the buyer to pay for delivered phosphate. During the contract negotiations, Columbia rejected a Royster proposal for liquidated damages of $10 for each ton Columbia declined to accept. On the other hand, Royster rejected a Columbia proposal for a clause that tied the price to the market by obligating Royster to conform its price to offers Columbia received from other phosphate producers. The parties, having rejected both proposals, failed to state any consequences of Columbia's refusal to take delivery—the kind of default Royster alleges in this case. Royster insists that we span this hiatus by applying the general law of contracts permitting recovery of damages upon the buyer's refusal to take delivery according to the written provisions of the contract. This solution is not what the Uniform Commercial Code prescribes. Before allowing damages, a court must first determine whether the buyer has in fact defaulted. It must do this by supplementing and explaining the agreement with evidence of trade usage and course of dealing that is consistent with the contract's express terms; §§1-205(4), 2-202. Faithful adherence to this mandate reflects the reality of the marketplace and avoids the overly legalistic interpretations which the Code seeks to abolish.

Royster also contends that Columbia's proffered testimony was properly rejected because it dealt with mutual willingness of buyer and seller to adjust contract terms to the market. Columbia, Royster protests, seeks unilateral adjustment. This argument misses the point. What Columbia seeks to show is a practice of mutual adjustments so prevalent in the industry and in prior dealings between the parties that it formed a part of the agreement governing this transaction. It is not insisting on a unilateral right to modify the contract.

Nor can we accept Royster's contention that the testimony should be excluded under the contract clause:

> No verbal understanding will be recognized by either party hereto; this contract expresses all the terms and conditions of the agreement, shall be signed in duplicate, and shall not become operative until approved in writing by the Seller.

Course of dealing and trade usage are not synonymous with verbal understandings, terms and conditions. Section 2-202 draws a distinction between supplementing a written contract by consistent additional terms and supplementing it by course of dealing or usage of trade. Evidence of additional terms must be excluded when "the court finds the writing to have been intended also as a complete and exclusive statement of the terms of the agreement." Significantly, no similar limitation is placed on the introduction of evidence of course of dealing or usage of trade. Indeed the official comment notes that course of dealing and usage of trade, unless carefully negated, are admissible to supplement the terms of any writing, and that contracts are to be read on the assumption that these elements were taken for granted when the document was phrased. Since the Code assigns course of dealing and trade usage unique and important roles, they should not be conclusively rejected by reading them into stereotyped language that makes no specific reference to them. Cf. Provident Tradesmen's Bank & Trust Co. v. Pemberton, 196 Pa. Super. 180, 173 A.2d 780 (1961). Indeed, the Code's official commentators urge that overly simplistic and overly legalistic interpretation of a contract should be shunned.[4]

We conclude therefore that Columbia's evidence about course of dealing and usage of trade should have been admitted. Its exclusion requires that the judgment against Columbia must be set aside and the case retried. . . .

---

4. Referring to the general provisions about course of dealing and trade usage, §1-205, Comment 1 states:

"This Act rejects both the 'lay dictionary' and the 'conveyancer's' reading of a commercial agreement. Instead the meaning of the agreement of the parties is to be determined by the language used by them and by their action, read and interpreted in the light of commercial practices and other surrounding circumstances. The measure and background for interpretation are set by the commercial context, which may explain and supplement even the language of a formal or final writing."

QUESTION

If the merger clause in the contract between Columbia and Royster had stated that it barred all evidence of usage of trade and course of dealing, would the decision have been different? See Southern Concrete Servs., Inc. v. Mableton Contractors, Inc., 407 F. Supp. 581, 19 U.C.C. Rep. Serv. 79 (N.D. Ga. 1975).

III. OFFER AND ACCEPTANCE

A. General Rules

Common law rules of contract formation had too many technicalities and formalities to suit the drafters of the UCC. If, as often happens, persons in business form contracts on a very informal basis, the Code does all it can to give legal meaning to the resulting deal. Read §§2-204, 2-205, and 2-206 before doing the next Problems.

PROBLEM 10

Mastervoice TV ordered 20,000 fuses from the Generous Electric Company, the order stating "Reply by return mail." Instead of a formal reply, Generous immediately shipped the fuses. When the fuses arrived, they were found to be defective. Mastervoice, which had to procure substitute goods elsewhere to meet its production schedule, sued Generous Electric for breach of warranty. Answer these questions:

(a) At what moment was the contract formed? — want suit = Acceptance

(b) Can Generous make this defense: "There was never any contract since our alleged act of acceptance (the shipment of *defective* goods) did not comply with requirements of Mastervoice's offer (which contemplated only shipment of *good* fuses)"?

(c) Instead of the above, assume that when Generous received the order it discovered that it no longer manufactured the type of fuses Mastervoice wanted, but that it did carry a very similar type of fuse that it believed would suit Mastervoice's needs. The shipping manager for Generous was unable to get through to the relevant people at Mastervoice, so in the end Generous shipped the slightly different fuses along with a cover note saying, "These are similar to the fuses you ordered, but may not be right for you. If they are not suitable, we will gladly take them back without charge." Is Generous now in breach because it shipped nonconforming goods? See §2-206(1)(b).

PROBLEM 11

For years P. Dreamer had wanted a Rolls Royce Silver Shadow with burgundy-colored trim (he had seen one in an ad and salivated). He saw one on the lot of Posh Motors. After Dreamer had dickered loud and long over the terms with Paula Posh, president of Posh Motors, they finally agreed on a price. Dreamer said he wanted to clear the deal with his wife before signing anything, so Posh promised she would hold the car for the Dreamers until the next day at noon. When Mr. and Mrs. Dreamer arrived at the dealership the next morning, the car was gone. Posh had made a better deal with another buyer. Do the Dreamers have a good cause of action? See §2-205. Does §1-103 help?

B. The Battle of the Forms

> As long as there are merchant buyers and sellers of goods, there will be forms with self-serving boilerplate. And as long as the transactions proceed without incident—which may be after a long while and many sales—their forms will pass like ships on a foggy sea. But when at last one of their transactions sinks, each retreats to the shelter of its favorable terms to claim victory.

Dependable Component Supply, Inc. v. Pace Electronics Inc., 772 So. 2d 582, 43 U.C.C. Rep. Serv. 2d 521 (Fla. App. 2000).

The "battle of the forms" is a much litigated problem that arises from two sources: (1) the business practices of either negotiating deals orally and then exchanging printed forms that no one reads until a dispute arises, or dealing at arms length with non-matching purchase orders and acknowledgments, and (2) the complexities of §2-207 and its Official Comment.

Subsection (1) to §2-207 is meant to reverse the common law rule that an *acceptance* that was not the *mirror image* of the offer was (impliedly) both a rejection and a counteroffer. Under §2-207(1), an acceptance adding new terms creates a contract based on the original offer, unless the *acceptance* very clearly states otherwise. As to what happens to the additional terms, see §2-207(2).

If, in spite of all logic and business judgment, the parties exchange documents that cannot be reconciled so as to produce a contract, no contract results, and either party may, on discovering this mishap, back out of the deal *if* that party acts prior to the beginning of performance. If performance has begun (with the parties wrongly believing a contract exists), subsection (3) of §2-207 regulates the ensuing mess.

PROBLEM 12

The Magic Carpet Co. had a long and profitable business relationship with Alibaba Carpet Manufacturers of Bagdad, Illinois. Fifty-five times Alibaba had sold carpets to Magic Carpet. Each sale was carried out in the following manner. A partner of Magic Carpet telephoned Alibaba's order department and ordered a certain quantity of carpet at the price listed in Alibaba's catalog. After each oral order was placed, the credit department was consulted to determine if Magic Carpet was paid up. Then, if the credit was okay, the order department of Alibaba typed the information from the order on one of its printed acknowledgment forms, each of which had the following paragraph printed conspicuously on its face:

> The acceptance of your order is subject to all of the terms and conditions on the face and reverse side hereof, all of which are accepted by buyer; it supersedes buyer's order form, if any. It shall become a contract either (a) when signed and delivered by buyer to seller and accepted in writing by seller, or (b) at seller's option, when buyer shall have given to seller specification of assortments, delivery dates, shipping instructions, or instructions to bill and hold as to all or any part of the merchandise herein described, or when buyer has received delivery of the whole or any part thereof, or when buyer has otherwise assented to the terms and conditions hereof.

The provisions on the reverse side of the form provided, among other things, that the seller disclaimed all warranties, express or implied. Each acknowledgment form was signed by an employee in Alibaba's order department and mailed to the Magic Carpet Co. Shortly thereafter, the carpet was shipped. Magic Carpet always received the acknowledgment form before the carpet. They placed each form in a file, accepted delivery of the carpet, and paid for it promptly. On the 56th sale, the accepted and paid-for carpet proved to be non-conforming. Magic Carpet sued Alibaba for breach of warranty. Alibaba replied that its form disclaimed all warranties.

Answer these questions:

(a) Was a contract formed between Magic Carpet and Alibaba?
See §2-207(1).

(b) Was the disclaimer of warranties part of that contract? See §2-207(2).

Problem 12 is based on Dorton v. Collins & Aikman Corp., 453
F.2d 1161, 10 U.C.C. Rep. Serv. 585 (6th Cir. 1972), where the court
clearly and competently sorted through the complexities of §2-207.
The most infamous case involving §2-207 is Roto-Lith Ltd. v. F.P.
Bartlett & Co., 297 F.2d 497, 1 U.C.C. Rep. Serv. 73 (1st Cir. 1962). In
Roto-Lith, the court failed to appreciate the change wrought in the
common law by §2-207 and essentially reapplied *the mirror image rule*
and *the last shot doctrine.* The case was widely criticized and was finally
overruled by the First Circuit in Ionics, Inc. v. Elmwood Sensors, Inc.,
110 F.3d 184, 32 U.C.C. Rep. Serv. 2d 1 (1st Cir. 1997). White and
Summers discuss §2-207 exhaustively. See White & Summers §1-3.

PROBLEM 13

Humpty Dumpty Corp. was a company that demolished old
buildings to clear sites for new construction. Humpty Dumpty
proposed to sell a large quantity of used bricks to the Kings Horses
Company on the condition that Kings Horses would pick up the bricks
and haul them away. The seller made a formal written offer, stating the
quantity (2½ tons), the price ($22,000), and a delivery date of June 15.
Kings Horses accepted, enclosed a check for $22,000, and changed
the delivery date to July 20. The president of Humpty Dumpty calls
you and asks if Kings Horses has breached the contract if it does not
pick up the bricks on June 15. What do you advise him? See §2-207(3)
and Official Comment 6. See also §2-309; Richardson v. Union
Carbide Industrial Gases, Inc., 790 A.2d 962, 47 U.C.C. Rep. Serv. 2d
119 (N.J. Super. 2002) (good discussion of the so-called knock-out rule).

Diamond Fruit Growers, Inc. v. Krack Corp.

United States Court of Appeals, Ninth Circuit, 1986
794 F.2d 1440, 1 U.C.C. Rep. Serv. 2d 1073

WIGGINS, J. Metal-Matic, Inc. (Metal-Matic) appeals from judgment entered after a jury verdict in favor of Krack Corporation (Krack)

on Krack's third-party complaint against Metal-Matic. Metal-Matic also appeals from the district court's denial of its motion for judgment n.o.v. We have jurisdiction under 28 U.S.C. §1291 (1982) and affirm.

FACTS AND PROCEEDINGS BELOW

Krack is a manufacturer of cooling units that contain steel tubing it purchases from outside suppliers. Metal-Matic is one of Krack's tubing suppliers. At the time this dispute arose, Metal-Matic had been supplying tubing to Krack for about ten years. The parties followed the same course of dealing during the entire ten years. At the beginning of each year, Krack sent a blanket purchase order to Metal-Matic stating how much tubing Krack would need for the year. Then, throughout the year as Krack needed tubing, it sent release purchase orders to Metal-Matic requesting that tubing be shipped. Metal-Matic responded to Krack's release purchase orders by sending Krack an acknowledgment form and then shipping the tubing.

Metal-Matic's acknowledgment form disclaimed all liability for consequential damages and limited Metal-Matic's liability for defects in the tubing to refund of the purchase price or replacement or repair of the tubing. As one would expect, these terms were not contained in Krack's purchase order. The following statement was printed on Metal-Matic's form: "Metal-Matic, Inc.'s acceptance of purchaser's offer or its offer to purchaser is hereby expressly made conditional to purchaser's acceptance of the terms and provisions of the acknowledgment form." This statement and the disclaimer of liability were on the back of the acknowledgment form. However, printed at the bottom of the front of the form in boldface capitals was the following statement: "SEE REVERSE SIDE FOR TERMS AND CONDITIONS OF SALE."

On at least one occasion during the ten-year relationship between Metal-Matic and Krack, Allen Zver, Krack's purchasing manager, discussed the limitations of warranty and disclaimer of liability terms contained in Metal-Matic's acknowledgment form with Robert Van Krevelen, Executive Vice President of Metal-Matic. Zver told Van Krevelen that Krack objected to the terms and tried to convince him to change them, but Van Krevelen refused to do so. After the discussions, Krack continued to accept and pay for tubing from Metal-Matic.

In February 1981, Krack sold one of its cooling units to Diamond Fruit Growers, Inc. (Diamond) in Oregon, and in September 1981, Diamond installed the unit in a controlled-atmosphere warehouse. In January 1982, the unit began leaking ammonia from a cooling coil made of steel tubing.

After Diamond discovered that ammonia was leaking into the warehouse, Joseph Smith, the engineer who had been responsible for building Diamond's controlled-atmosphere warehouses, was called in to find the source of the leak. Smith testified that he found a pinhole leak in the cooling coil of the Krack cooling unit. Smith inspected the coil while it was still inside the unit. He last inspected the coil on April 23, 1982. The coil then sat in a hall at Diamond's warehouse until May 1984, when John Myers inspected the coil for Metal-Matic.

Myers cut the defective tubing out of the unit and took it to his office. At his office, he did more cutting on the tubing. After Myers inspected the tubing, it was also inspected by Bruce Wong for Diamond and Paul Irish for Krack.

Diamond sued Krack to recover the loss in value of fruit that it was forced to remove from the storage room as a result of the leak. Krack in turn brought a third-party complaint against Metal-Matic and Van Huffel Tube Corporation (Van Huffel), another of its tubing suppliers, seeking contribution or indemnity in the event it was held liable to Diamond. At the close of the evidence, both Metal-Matic and Van Huffel moved for a directed verdict on the third-party complaint. The court granted Van Huffel's motion based on evidence that the failed tubing was not manufactured by Van Huffel. The court denied Metal-Matic's motion.

The jury returned a verdict in favor of Diamond against Krack. It then found that Krack was entitled to contribution from Metal-Matic for thirty percent of Diamond's damages. Metal-Matic moved for judgment n.o.v. The court denied that motion and entered judgment on the jury verdict.

Metal-Matic raises two grounds for reversal. First, Metal-Matic contends that as part of its contract with Krack, it disclaimed all liability for consequential damages and specifically limited its liability for defects in the tubing to refund of the purchase price or replacement or repair of the tubing. Second, Metal-Matic asserts that the evidence does not support a finding that it manufactured the tubing in which the leak developed or that it caused the leak. We address each of these contentions in turn. . . .

DISCUSSION

A. METAL-MATIC'S DISCLAIMER OF LIABILITY FOR
    CONSEQUENTIAL DAMAGES

If the contract between Metal-Matic and Krack contains Metal-Matic's disclaimer of liability, Metal-Matic is not liable to indemnify

Krack for part of Diamond's damages. Therefore, the principal issue before us on this appeal is whether Metal-Matic's disclaimer of liability became part of the contract between these parties.

Relying on Uniform Commercial Code (U.C.C.) §2-207, Or. Rev. Stat. §72.2070 (1985), Krack argues that Metal-Matic's disclaimer did not become part of the contract. Metal-Matic, on the other hand, argues that §2-207 is inapplicable to this case because the parties discussed the disclaimer, and Krack assented to it.

Krack is correct in its assertion that §2-207 applies to this case. One intended application of §2-207 is to commercial transactions in which the parties exchange printed purchase order and acknowledgment forms. See U.C.C. §2-207 comment 1. The drafters of the UCC recognized that "[b]ecause the [purchase order and acknowledgment] forms are oriented to the thinking of the respective drafting parties, the terms contained in them often do not correspond." Id. Section 2-207 is an attempt to provide rules of contract formation in such cases. In this case, Krack and Metal-Matic exchanged purchase order and acknowledgment forms that contained different or additional terms. This, then, is a typical §2-207 situation. The fact that the parties discussed the terms of their contract after they exchanged their forms does not put this case outside §2-207. See 3 R. Duesenburg & L. King, Sales and Bulk Transfers under the Uniform Commercial Code (Bender's U.C.C. Service) §3.05[2] (1986). Section 2-207 provides rules of contract formation in cases such as this one in which the parties exchange forms but do not agree on all the terms of their contract.

A brief summary of §2-207 is necessary to an understanding of its application to this case. Section 2-207 changes the common law's mirror-image rule for transactions that fall within article 2 of the U.C.C. At common law, an acceptance that varies the terms of the offer is a counteroffer and operates as a rejection of the original offer. See Idaho Power Co. v. Westinghouse Electric Corp., 596 F.2d 924, 926 (9th Cir. 1979). If the offeror goes ahead with the contract after receiving the counteroffer, his performance is an acceptance of the terms of the counteroffer. See C. Itoh & Co. v. Jordan International Co., 552 F.2d 1228, 1236 (7th Cir. 1977); J. White & R. Summers, Handbook of the Law Under the Uniform Commercial Code §1-2 at 34 (2d ed. 1980).

Generally §2-207(1) "converts a common law counteroffer into an acceptance even though it states additional or different terms." Idaho Power, 596 F.2d at 926; see U.C.C. §2-207(1). The only requirement under §2-207(1) is that the responding form contain a definite and seasonable expression of acceptance. The terms of the responding form that correspond to the offer constitute the contract. Under §2-207(2), the additional terms of the responding form become proposals for additions to the contract. Between merchants the additional terms become part of the contract unless the offer is specifically limited to its terms, the offeror objects to the additional terms, or the additional terms materially alter the terms of the offer. U.C.C. §2-207(2); see J. White & R. Summers, §1-2 at 32.

However, §2-207(1) is subject to a proviso. If a definite and seasonable expression of acceptance expressly conditions acceptance on the offeror's assent to additional or different terms contained therein, the parties' differing forms do not result in a contract unless the offeror assents to the additional terms. See J. White & R. Summers, §1-2 at 32-33. If the offeror assents, the parties have a contract and the additional terms are a part of that contract. If, however, the offeror does not assent, but the parties proceed with the transaction as if they have a contract, their performance results in formation of a contract. UCC §2-207(3). In that case, the terms of the contract are those on which the parties' forms agree plus any terms supplied by the UCC. Id.; see Boise Cascade Corp. v. Etsco, Ltd., 39 U.C.C. Rep. Serv. (Callaghan) 410, 414 (D. Or. 1984); J. White & R. Summers, §1-2 at 34.

In this case, Metal-Matic expressly conditioned its acceptance on Krack's assent to the additional terms contained in Metal-Matic's acknowledgment form. That form tracks the language of the §2-207(1) proviso, stating that "Metal-Matic, Inc.'s acceptance . . . is hereby *expressly made conditional* to purchaser's acceptance of the terms and provisions of the acknowledgment form" (emphasis added). See *C. Itoh & Co.*, 552 F.2d at 1235. Therefore, we must determine whether Krack assented to Metal-Matic's limitation of liability term.

Metal-Matic argues that Krack did assent to the limitation of liability term. This argument is based on the discussions between Zver for Krack and Van Krevelen for Metal-Matic. Some time during the ten-year relationship between the companies, these two men discussed Krack's objections to the warranty and liability limitation terms in Metal-Matic's acknowledgment form. Krack attempted to persuade Metal-Matic to change its forms, but Metal-Matic refused to do so. After the discussions, the companies continued to do business as in the past. Metal-Matic contends that Krack assented to the limitation of liability term when it continued to accept and pay for tubing after Metal-Matic insisted that the contract contain its terms.

To address Metal-Matic's argument, we must determine what constitutes assent to additional or different terms for purposes of

§2-207(1). The parties have not directed us to any cases that analyze this question and our research has revealed none. We therefore look to the language and structure of §2-207 and to the purposes behind that section to determine the correct standard.

One of the principles underlying §2-207 is neutrality. If possible, the section should be interpreted so as to give neither party to a contract an advantage simply because it happened to send the first or in some cases the last form. See J. White & R. Summers, §1-2 at 26-27. Section 2-207 accomplishes this result in part by doing away with the common law's "last shot" rule. See 3 R. Duesenberg & L. King, §3.05[1][a][iii] at 3-73. At common law, the offeree/counterofferor gets all of its terms simply because it fired the last shot in the exchange of forms. Section 2-207(3) does away with this result by giving neither party the terms it attempted to impose unilaterally on the other. See id. at 3-71. Instead, all of the terms on which the parties' forms do not agree drop out, and the UCC supplies the missing terms.

Generally, this result is fair because both parties are responsible for the ambiguity in their contract. The parties could have negotiated a contract and agreed on its terms, but for whatever reason failed to do so. Therefore, neither party should get its terms. See 3 R. Duesenberg & L. King §3.05[2] at 3-88. However, as White and Summers point out, resort to §2-207(3) will often work to the disadvantage of the seller because he will "wish to undertake less responsibility for the quality of his goods than the Code imposes or else wish to limit his damages liability more narrowly than would the Code." J. White & R. Summers §1-2 at 34. Nevertheless, White and Summers recommend that §2-207(3) be applied in such cases. Id. We agree. Application of §2-207(3) is more equitable than giving one party its terms simply because it sent the last form. Further, the terms imposed by the code are presumably equitable and consistent with public policy because they are statutorily imposed. See 3 R. Duesenberg & L. King, §3.05[2] at 3-88.

With these principles in mind, we turn now to Metal-Matic's argument that Krack assented to the disclaimer when it continued to accept and pay for tubing once Metal-Matic indicated that it was willing to sell tubing only if its warranty and liability terms were part of the contract. Metal-Matic's argument is appealing. Sound policy supports permitting a seller to control the terms on which it will sell its products, especially in a case in which the seller has indicated both in writing and orally that those terms are the only terms on which it is willing to sell the product. Nevertheless, we reject Metal-Matic's argument because we find that these considerations are outweighed by the public policy reflected by Oregon's enactment of the UCC.

If we were to accept Metal-Matic's argument, we would reinstate to some extent the common law's last shot rule. To illustrate, assume that the parties in this case had sent the same forms but in the reverse order and that Krack's form contained terms stating that Metal-Matic is liable for all consequential damages and conditioning acceptance on Metal-Matic's assent to Krack's terms. Assume also that Metal-Matic objected to Krack's terms but Krack refused to change them and that the parties continued with their transaction anyway. If we applied Metal-Matic's argument in that case, we would find that Krack's term was part of the contract because Metal-Matic continued to ship tubing to Krack after Krack reaffirmed that it would purchase tubing only if Metal-Matic were liable for consequential damages. Thus, the result would turn on which party sent the last form, and would therefore be inconsistent with §2-207's purpose of doing away with the last shot rule.

That result is avoided by requiring a specific and unequivocal expression of assent on the part of the offeror when the offeree conditions its acceptance on assent to additional or different terms. If the offeror does not give specific and unequivocal assent but the parties act as if they have a contract, the provisions of §2-207(3) apply to fill in the terms of the contract. Application of §2-207(3) is appropriate in that situation because by going ahead with the transaction without resolving their dispute, both parties are responsible for introducing ambiguity into the contract. Further, in a case such as this one, requiring the seller to assume more liability than it intends is not altogether inappropriate. The seller is most responsible for the ambiguity because it inserts a term in its form that requires assent to additional terms and then does not enforce that requirement. If the seller truly does not want to be bound unless the buyer assents to its terms, it can protect itself by not shipping until it obtains that assent. See *C. Itoh & Co.*, 552 F.2d at 1238.

We hold that because Krack's conduct did not indicate unequivocally that Krack intended to assent to Metal-Matic's terms, that conduct did not amount to the assent contemplated by §2-207(1). See 3 R. Duesenberg & L. King, §3.05[1][a][iii] at 3-74. . . .

The jury verdict is supported by the evidence and consistent with the UCC. Therefore, the district court did not err in denying Metal-Matic's motion for a judgment n.o.v.

PROBLEM 14

Would the following clause in the seller's acknowledgment to the buyer's order form be a material alteration under §2-207(2)(b): "Any disputes concerning this contract shall be subject to binding arbitration"? See Aceros Prefabricados, S.A. v. TradeArbed, Inc., 282 F.3d 92, 46 U.C.C. Rep. Serv. 2d 596 (2d Cir. 2002). If this clause were in an acknowledgment of an international sale of goods to which CISG applies, would it be valid? See Article 19; Filanto, S.p.A. v. Chilewich Intl. Corp., 789 F. Supp. 1229 (S.D.N.Y. 1992), *appeal dismissed*, 984 F.2d 58 (2d Cir. 1993); Comment, The U.N. Convention on the International Sale of Goods and the "Battle of the Forms," 13 Fordham Intl. L.J. 649 (1990).

Bayway Refining Co. v. Oxygenated Marketing and Trading A.G.

United States Court of Appeals, Second Circuit, 2000
215 F.3d 219, 41 U.C.C. Rep. Serv. 2d 713

JACOBS, Circuit Judge:

Plaintiff-appellee Bayway Refining Company ("Bayway") paid federal excise tax on a petroleum transaction, as the Internal Revenue Code requires a petroleum dealer to do in a sale to a buyer who has not procured an exemption under the applicable tax provision. In this diversity suit against the buyer, Oxygenated Marketing and Trading A.G. ("OMT"), Bayway seeks to recover the amount of the tax it paid. One question in this "battle of the forms" contract case is whether, under N.Y. U.C.C. §2-207(2)(b) (McKinney 1993) a contract term allocating liability to the buyer for an excise tax is an additional term presumed to have been accepted (as the seller contends) or (as the buyer contends) a material alteration presumed to have been rejected. The United States District Court for the Southern District of New York (McKenna, J.) granted summary judgment in favor of the seller, Bayway.

We conclude that, in the circumstances presented: (i) the party opposing the inclusion of an additional term under §2-207(2)(b) bears the burden of proving that the term amounts to a material alteration; (ii) the district court properly granted summary judgment in favor of the seller, because the additional term here did not materially alter the contract; and (iii) the district court properly admitted evidence of custom and practice in the industry despite the fact that it was first proffered in the moving party's reply papers. Accordingly, we affirm.

BACKGROUND

Bayway and OMT are in the business of buying and selling petroleum products. Bayway contracted to sell to OMT 60,000 barrels of a gasoline blendstock called Methyl Tertiary Butyl Ether ("MTBE"). On February 12, 1998, OMT faxed Bayway a confirmation letter, which operated as the offer, and which stated in pertinent part:

> We are pleased to confirm the details of our purchase from you of MTBE as agreed between Mr. Ben Basil and Roger Ertle on [February 12, 1998.] . . .
>
> This confirmation constitutes the entire contract and represents our understanding of the terms and conditions of our agreement. . . . Any apparent discrepancies or omissions should be brought to our notice within the next two working days.

Bayway faxed its confirmation to OMT the next day. That document, which operated as the acceptance, stated in pertinent part: "We are pleased to confirm the following verbal agreement concluded on February 12, 1998 with your company. This document cancels and supersedes any correspondence in relation to this transaction." Bayway's acceptance then set forth the parties, price, amount and delivery terms, and undertook to incorporate the company's standard terms:

> Notwithstanding any other provision of this agreement, where not in conflict with the foregoing, the terms and conditions as set forth in Bayway Refining Company's General Terms and Conditions dated March 01, 1994 along with Bayway's Marine Provisions are hereby incorporated in full by reference in this contract.

The Bayway General Terms and Conditions were not transmitted with Bayway's fax, but Paragraph 10 of its General Terms and Conditions states:

> Buyer shall pay seller the amount of any federal, state and local excise, gross receipts, import, motor fuel, superfund and spill taxes and all other federal, state and local taxes however designated, other than taxes on income, paid or incurred by seller directly or indirectly with respect to the oil or product sold hereunder and/or on the value thereof.

This term is referenced as the "Tax Clause."

OMT did not object to Bayway's acceptance or to the incorporation of its General Terms and Conditions (which included the Tax Clause). OMT accepted delivery of the MTBE barrels on March 22, 1998.

The Internal Revenue Code imposes an excise tax, payable by the seller, on the sale of gasoline blendstocks such as MTBE "to any person who is not registered under [26 U.S.C. §4101]" for a tax exemption. 26 U.S.C.A. §4081(a)(1)(A)(iv) (West Supp. 1999). After delivery, Bayway learned that OMT was not registered with the Internal Revenue Service for the tax exemption. The transaction therefore created a tax liability of $464,035.12, which Bayway paid.

Invoking the Tax Clause, Bayway demanded payment of the $464,035.12 in taxes in addition to the purchase price of the MTBE. OMT denied that it had agreed to assume the tax liability and refused to pay that invoice item. In response, Bayway filed this diversity suit alleging breach of contract by OMT.

Upon Bayway's motion for summary judgment, the district court held that the Tax Clause was properly incorporated into the contract. See Tosco Corp. v. Oxygenated Mktg. & Trading A.G., No. 98 Civ. 4695, 1999 WL 328342, at *3-*6 (S.D.N.Y. May 24, 1999). The fact that Bayway had failed to attach a copy of the General Terms and Conditions was irrelevant because OMT could have obtained a copy if it had asked for one. See id. at *3. The court then analyzed the contract-forming documents, applied the "battle of the forms" framework set forth in N.Y. U.C.C. §2-207(2), and concluded that OMT failed to carry its burden of proving that the Tax Clause materially altered the contract. See id. at *3-*6. The court therefore granted summary judgment in favor of Bayway.

DISCUSSION

On appeal, OMT argues (i) that it succeeded in raising genuine issues of fact as to whether the Tax Clause materially altered the Bayway/OMT contract and (ii) that the evidence of custom and practice in the industry, upon which the grant of summary judgment turns, was improperly admitted. . . .

We affirm for substantially the reasons stated by the district court. We hold—on an issue of first impression in this Court—that in a "battle of the forms" case governed by N.Y. U.C.C. §2-207(2)(b), the party opposing the inclusion of an additional term bears the burden of proving that the term works a material alteration. Viewing the evidence in the light most favorable to OMT, we conclude that OMT failed to shoulder that burden. Finally, we hold that the district court properly admitted the evidence concerning industry custom and practice.

A.   BATTLE OF THE FORMS

Bayway argued its motion for summary judgment on the basis of New York law, presumably because one of the additional terms incorporated by its acceptance is a New York choice-of-law provision. OMT has accepted New York law as controlling for purposes of Bayway's summary judgment motion. [The court quoted §2-207(1) and (2).]

It was undisputed in the district court that Bayway's confirmation fax is effective to form a contract as an acceptance—even though it stated or referenced additional terms (including the Tax Clause)—because it was not made expressly conditional on OMT's assent to the additional terms. See id. §2-207(1). Therefore, under §2-207(2), the Tax Clause is a proposal for an addition to the contract. See id. §2-207(2). The parties are both merchants within the meaning of the U.C.C. See id. §2-104(1), (3). The Tax Clause therefore is presumed to become part of the contract unless one of the three enumerated exceptions applies. See id. §2-207(2). In its defense, OMT invokes the "material alteration" exception of §2-207(2)(b).

1. Burden of Proof

The allocation of the burden of proof under this exception to §2-207(2) is a question of New York law, see United States v. McCombs, 30 F.3d 310, 323-24 (2d Cir. 1994) (holding that, under the Erie doctrine, federal courts sitting in diversity apply the forum state's law concerning burdens of proof), and is answered in the text of New York's U.C.C. §2-207(2). Section 2-207(2)(b) is an exception to the general rule of §2-207(2) that additional terms become part of a contract between merchants. That general rule is in the nature of a presumption concerning the intent of the contracting parties. Thus if neither party introduced any evidence, the Tax Clause would, by the plain language of §2-207(2), become part of the contract. To implement that presumption, the burden of proving the materiality of the alteration must fall on the party that opposes inclusion. Accordingly, we hold that under §2-207(2)(b) the party opposing the inclusion of additional terms shoulders the burden of proof. In so doing, we join almost every court to have considered this issue. [Citations omitted.]

2. Materiality and Per Se Materiality

A material alteration is one that would "result in *surprise* or *hardship* if incorporated without express awareness by the other party." N.Y. U.C.C. §2-207 cmt. 4 (emphasis added).

Certain additional terms are deemed material as a matter of law. For example, an arbitration clause is per se a material alteration in New York because New York law requires an express agreement to commit disputes to arbitration. See Marlene Indus. v. Carnac Textiles,

Inc., 45 N.Y.2d 327, 408 N.Y.S.2d 410, 413, 380 N.E.2d 239 (1978); see also N.Y. U.C.C. §2-207 cmt. 4 (listing as examples of per se material alterations, inter alia, waivers of warranties of merchantability or fitness for a particular purpose and clauses granting the seller the power to cancel upon the buyer's failure to meet any invoice). OMT characterizes the Tax Clause as a broad-ranging indemnity clause, and analogizes it to these per se material alterations. We reject the analogy. The Tax Clause allocates responsibility for the tax payable on a specific sale of goods. See Union Carbide Corp. v. Oscar Mayer Foods Corp., 947 F.2d 1333, 1335, 1337 (7th Cir. 1991) (distinguishing between "open-ended" tax liability, which is a material alteration, from "responsibility for taxes shown on an individual invoice," which is not). And unlike an arbitration clause, which waives a range of rights that are solicitously protected, the Tax Clause is limited, discrete and the subject of no special protection. Unable to show that the Tax Clause is a material alteration per se, OMT must prove that in this case the Tax Clause resulted in surprise or hardship.[5]

3. Surprise

Surprise, within the meaning of the material alteration exception of §2-207(2)(b), has both the subjective element of what a party actually knew and the objective element of what a party should have known. See American Ins. Co. v. El Paso Pipe & Supply Co., 978 F.2d 1185, 1191 (10th Cir. 1992); In re Chateaugay, 162 B.R. at 956-57. A profession of surprise and raised eyebrows are not enough: "[C]onclusory statements, conjecture, or speculation by the party resisting the motion will not defeat summary judgment." Kulak v. City of New York, 88 F.3d 63, 71 (2d Cir. 1996). To carry the burden of showing surprise, a party must establish that, under the circumstances, it cannot be presumed that a reasonable merchant would have consented to the additional term. See Union Carbide, 947 F.2d at 1336.

OMT has adduced evidence that the Tax Clause came as an amazement to OMT's executives, who described the term's incorporation as "contract by ambush" and a "sl[e]ight-of-hand proposal."

---

5. Even if an additional term that places the tax liability on the opposing party was a material alteration per se, New York law allows a party to rebut this conclusion in some limited circumstances with a sufficient showing that the additional term reflects the custom and practice in the particular industry. See Avedon Eng'g, 126 F.3d at 1285 & n.15 (discussing New York law); Schubtex, Inc. v. Allen Snyder, Inc., 49 N.Y.2d 1, 424 N.Y.S.2d 133, 135, 399 N.E.2d 1154 (1979). As discussed below, Bayway's evidence that the Tax Clause reflects the custom and practice in the petroleum industry is compelling and unrebutted.

Thus OMT has sufficiently exhibited its subjective surprise. As to objective surprise, however, OMT has alleged no facts and introduced no evidence to show that a reasonable petroleum merchant would be surprised by the Tax Clause. See In re Chateaugay, 162 B.R. at 957 (including as types of evidence proving objective surprise "the parties' prior course of dealing and the number of written confirmations that they exchanged, industry custom and the conspicuousness of the term"). OMT had no prior contrary course of dealing with Bayway, and offered nothing concerning trade custom or practice.

Ordinarily, our inquiry into surprise would end here. However, in response to OMT's claim of surprise, Bayway introduced evidence that the Tax Clause reflects custom and practice in the petroleum industry, and on appeal OMT argues that Bayway's own evidence raises a genuine issue of material fact as to whether such a trade practice exists. Although the evidence was introduced by Bayway, we are "obligated to search the record and independently determine whether or not a genuine issue of fact exists." Jiminez v. Dreis & Krump Mfg. Co., 736 F.2d 51, 53 (2d Cir. 1984) (quoting Higgins v. Baker, 309 F. Supp. 635, 639 (S.D.N.Y. 1970)) (internal quotation marks omitted).

Upon our review of the evidence, we conclude that Bayway has adduced compelling proof that shifting tax liability to a buyer is the custom and practice in the petroleum industry. Two industry experts offered unchallenged testimony that it is customary for the buyer to pay all the taxes resulting from a petroleum transaction. One expert stated that "[t]his practice is so universally understood among traders in the industry, that I cannot recall an instance, in all my years of trading and overseeing trades, when the buyer refused to pay the seller for excise or sales taxes."

OMT cites the standard contracts of five major petroleum companies that Bayway introduced to illustrate contract terms similar to the Tax Clause. OMT argues that only three of the five place the tax liability on the buyer, and that there is therefore an issue of fact as to whether the Tax Clause would objectively surprise a merchant in this industry.

OMT misconstrues the evidence. Three of the contracts—those of CITGO Petroleum, Conoco, and Enron—mirror the Tax Clause. A fourth, Chevron's, differs from the others only in that the cost of the taxes is added into the contract price rather than separately itemized. Thus Chevron's standard contract affords OMT no support.

The fifth example, the Texaco contract, is silent as to the tax allocation issue in this case. But on this unrebutted record of universal trade custom and practice, silence supports no contrary inference.

Moreover, common sense supports Bayway's evidence of custom and practice. The federal excise tax is imposed when taxable fuels are sold "to any person who is not registered under [26 U.S.C. §4101]." 26 U.S.C. §4081(a)(1)(A)(iv). The buyer thereby controls whether any tax liability is incurred in a transaction. A trade practice that reflects a rational allocation of incentives (as trade practices usually do) would place the burden of the tax on the party that is in the position to obviate it—here, on OMT as the buyer.

Viewing Bayway's evidence in the light most favorable to OMT, we conclude that allocating the tax liability to the buyer is the custom and practice in the petroleum industry. OMT could not be objectively surprised by the incorporation of an additional term in the contract that reflects such a practice.

4. Hardship

To recapitulate: A material alteration is one that would "result in surprise *or* hardship if incorporated without express awareness by the other party." N.Y. U.C.C. §2-207 cmt. 4 (emphasis added). Although this Official Comment to the U.C.C. seemingly treats hardship as an independent ground for finding that an alteration is material, courts have expressed doubt: "You cannot walk away from a contract that you can fairly be deemed to have agreed to, merely because performance turns out to be a hardship for you, unless you can squeeze yourself into the impossibility defense or some related doctrine of excuse." Union Carbide, 947 F.2d at 1336 ("Hardship is a consequence [of material alteration], not a criterion. (Surprise can be either.)"); see also, e.g., Suzy Phillips Originals, Inc. v. Coville, Inc., 939 F. Supp. 1012, 1017-18 (E.D.N.Y. 1996) (citing *Union Carbide* with approval and limiting the test for material alteration to surprise); In re Chateaugay, 162 B.R. at 957 (same).

We need not decide whether hardship is an independent ground of material alteration, because even if it were, OMT failed to raise a genuine issue of material fact as to hardship. OMT's only evidence of hardship is (generally) that it is a small business dependent on precarious profit margins, and it would suffer a loss it cannot afford. That does not amount to hardship in the present circumstances.

Typically, courts that have relied on hardship to find that an additional term materially alters a contract have done so when the term is one that creates or allocates an open-ended and prolonged liability. See, e.g., St. Charles Cable TV, Inc. v. Eagle Comtronics, Inc., 687 F. Supp. 820, 827 (S.D.N.Y. 1988) (finding a hardship in "shift[ing] all risks for any dispute to the buyers"), *aff'd*, 895 F.2d 1410 (2d Cir.

1989) (unpublished table disposition); Charles J. King, Inc. v. Barge LM-10, 518 F. Supp. 1117, 1120 (S.D.N.Y. 1981).

The Tax Clause places on a buyer a contractual responsibility that bears on a specific sale of goods, that is (at least) not uncommon in the industry, and that the buyer could avoid by registration. The cry of hardship rings hollow, because any loss that the Tax Clause imposed on OMT is limited, routine and self-inflicted.

OMT failed to raise a factual issue as to hardship or surprise. Summary judgment was therefore appropriately granted in favor of Bayway. . . .

For the foregoing reasons, we affirm the judgment of the district court.

Courts call the clause that ends subsection (1) of §2-207 ("unless acceptance is expressly made conditional on assent to the additional or different terms") the *proviso* clause. The proviso clause acts just like a railroad switch. If it is *not* used as part of the accepting form, then the purported acceptance *does create* a contract, and the parties are directed to subsection (2) to determine its terms. If the proviso is put into the accepting document, the exchange of forms does not create a contract, and the parties are directed to subsection (3) to see what results from their dealings. My point is this: the presence or absence of the proviso shunts the parties into either subsection (2) or subsection (3), *but never both*.

PROBLEM 15

On April 25, Plastic Furniture Mart sent a purchase order for 100 tables to the Ersatz Manufacturing Company. In addition to the usual boilerplate language, the purchase order also stated: "BUYER OBJECTS IN ADVANCE TO ANY TERMS PROPOSED BY SELLER THAT DIFFER IN ANY WAY FROM THE TERMS OF THIS PURCHASE ORDER." Ersatz received the order, and on May 3 it sent back its own acknowledgment form, which disclaimed all warranties and contained this clause: "THIS IS NOT AN ACCEPTANCE UNLESS BUYER ASSENTS TO ALL CHANGES MADE BY THIS ACKNOWLEDGMENT FORM." Neither party read the details of the other's form. On May 6, Ersatz shipped the tables. Is there a contract? See §2-207(3). Did Ersatz make a warranty as to the condition of the tables? See §2-314. On May 3 was there a contract?

Leonard Pevar Co. v. Evans Products Co.

United States District Court, District of Delaware, 1981
524 F. Supp. 546, 32 U.C.C. Rep. Serv. 720

LATCHUM, J. This is a diversity action by the Leonard Pevar Company ("Pevar") against the Evans Products Company ("Evans") for an alleged breach of express and implied warranties in Evans' sale to Pevar of medium density overlay plywood. Defendant denies liability, claiming that it expressly disclaimed warranties and limited its liability in its contract with Pevar. The parties agree that their respective rights and liabilities in this action are governed by the Uniform Commercial Code. The parties have filed cross motions for summary judgment pursuant to Rule 56, F.R. Civ. P. This court will deny both motions because it finds material facts that are in genuine dispute.

I. FACTS

In the fall of 1977, Pevar began obtaining price quotations for the purchase of medium density overlay plywood to be used in the construction of certain buildings for the State of Pennsylvania. As part of this process, Pevar's contract administrator, Marc Pevar, contacted various manufacturers of this product. Evans was one of the manufacturers contacted and was the supplier that quoted the lowest price for this material.

On October 12, 1977, Marc Pevar had a telephone conversation with Kenneth Kruger of Evans to obtain this price quotation. It is at this juncture that a material fact appears in dispute that precludes this court from granting summary judgment. Pevar claims that on October 14 it again called Evans, ordered plywood, and entered into an oral contract of sale. Evans admits that Pevar called Evans, but denies that Evans accepted that order.

After the October 14th telephone conversation, Pevar sent a written purchase order to Evans for the plywood. In the purchase order, Pevar did not make any reference to warranties or remedies, but simply ordered the lumber specifying the price, quantity and shipping instructions. On October 19, 1979, Evans sent an acknowledgment to Pevar stating, on the reverse side of the acknowledgment and in boilerplate fashion, that the contract of sale would be expressly contingent upon Pevar's acceptance of all terms contained in the document. One of these terms disclaimed most warranties and another limited the "buyer's remedy" by restricting liability if the plywood proved to be defective.[6]

II.   STATUTE OF FRAUDS

Evans contends that if Pevar and Evans entered into an oral contract, it would be unenforceable because it would be in violation of the statute of frauds. Section 2-201 generally provides that an oral contract for the sale of goods in excess of $500 is unenforceable. Section 2-201(2), however, provides an exception. If a written confirmation is sent to the receiving party, and the receiving party does not object to the confirmation within ten days, then the oral agreement may be enforceable. The court finds that Pevar's written purchase order constituted a confirmatory memorandum and Evans' acknowledgment failed to provide sufficient notice of objection to Pevar's confirmation. The acknowledgment did not deny expressly the existence of the purported contract; rather, it merely asserted additional terms. Thus, the statute of frauds will not bar Pevar from proving the existence and terms of the contract for the reasons given in Marlene Industries Corp. v. Carnac Textiles, Inc., 45 N.Y.2d 327, 380 N.E.2d 239, 240 (1978) where the court stated:

6. Both of these terms were in boldface type:

"9. Unless seller delivers to buyer a separate written warranty with respect to goods, to the extent legally permissible the sale of all goods is 'as is' and there is hereby excluded and seller hereby disclaims any express or implied warranty, including, without limiting the generality of the foregoing, any implied warranty of merchantability or any implied warranty of fitness for any particular use or purpose; provided, however, there is not hereby excluded or disclaimed any implied warranty that seller owns goods or any implied warranty that goods are free from any security interest or other lien or encumbrance of which buyer has no knowledge at the time of contracting to buy such goods."

"12. Buyer shall afford Seller prompt and reasonable opportunity to inspect Goods as to which any claim is made by Buyer. Seller reserves the right, in its sole discretion, within the 90 calendar day period following receipt of any claim made by buyer, to repair any claimed defect in goods or to substitute other goods therefor and, by making such repair or replacement, seller shall have no further liability or obligation to buyer with respect to such goods, if any defective goods are not so repaired or replaced by seller, seller's liability and obligation shall be limited to the stated purchase price of such goods, and buyer shall be obligated at its expense to return the goods to seller, seller shall in no event be liable or obligated for buyer's manufacturing costs, lost profits, good will or other indirect, special, incidental or consequential damages."

This case presents a classic example of the "battle of the forms," and its solution is to be derived by reference to section 2-207 of the Uniform Commercial Code which is specifically designed to resolve such disputes. . . . [S]ubsection (2) of section 2-201 [is not applicable], for that statute deals solely with the question whether a contract exists which is enforceable in the face of a Statute of Frauds defense; it has no application to a situation such as this, in which it is conceded that a contract does exist and the dispute goes only to the terms of that contract. In light of the disparate purposes of the two sections, application of the wrong provision will often result in an erroneous conclusion. As has been noted by a recognized authority on the code, "[t]he easiest way to avoid the miscarriage this confusion perpetrates is simply to fix in mind that the two sections have nothing to do with each other. Though each has a special rule for merchants sounding very much like the other, their respective functions are unrelated. Section 2-201(2) has its role in the context of a challenge to the use of the statute of frauds to prevent proof of an alleged agreement, whereas the merchant rule of section 2-207(2) is for use in determining what are the terms of an admitted agreement." [Duesenberg, General Provisions, Sales, Bulk Transfers and Documents of Title, 30 Business Law, 847, 853].

See also C. Itoh & Co. (America) Inc. v. Jordan International Co., 552 F.2d 1228, 1233 (C.A. 7, 1977). Section 2-201, therefore, has no application to this case; this action involves the application of §2-207.

III. BATTLE OF THE FORMS

Turning now to §2-207, it provides: [the court quoted §2-207].

Section 2-207 was intended to eliminate the "ribbon matching" or "mirror" rule of common law, under which the terms of an acceptance or confirmation were required to be identical to the terms of the offer or oral agreement, respectively. Dorton v. Collins & Aikman Corp., 453 F.2d 1161 (C.A. 6, 1972). The drafters of the Code intended to preserve an agreement, as it was originally conceived by the parties, in the face of additional material terms included in standard forms exchanged by merchants in the normal course of dealings. Alan Wood Steel Co. v. Capital Equipment Enterprises Inc., 39 Ill. App. 3d 48, 349 N.E.2d 627 (1976). Section 2-207 recognizes that a buyer and seller can enter into a contract by one of three methods. First, the parties may agree orally and thereafter send confirmatory memoranda. §2-207(1). Second, the parties, without oral agreement, may exchange writings which do not contain identical terms, but nevertheless constitute a seasonable acceptance. §2-207(1). Third, the conduct of the parties may recognize the existence of a contract, despite the previous failure to agree orally or in writing. §2-207(3).

A.   ORAL AGREEMENT FOLLOWED BY CONFIRMATION

Section 2-207(1) applies to those situations where an "oral agreement has been reached . . . followed by one or both of the parties sending formal memoranda embodying the terms so far as agreed upon and adding terms not discussed." Uniform Commercial Code, Comment 1 to §2-207. These additional terms are treated as proposals under §2-207(2) and will become part of the agreement unless they materially alter it. *Dorton,* supra, 453 F.2d at 1169-70.[7]

In the present case, paragraphs 9 and 12 of Evans' acknowledgment, which disclaimed warranties and limited liability, may include terms not in the original agreement. Generally, these types of clauses "materially alter" the agreement. Uniform Commercial Code, Comment 4 to §2-207. Nevertheless, the question of a material alteration rests upon the facts of each case. See *Dorton,* supra, 453 F.2d at 1169 n.8; Medical Development Corp. v. Industrial Molding Corp., 479 F.2d 345, 348 (C.A. 10, 1973); Ebasco Services Inc. v. Pennsylvania Power & Light Co., 402 F. Supp. 421, 442 (E.D. Pa. 1975). If the trier of fact determines that the acknowledgment includes additional terms which do not materially alter the oral agreement, then the terms will be incorporated into the agreement. If they materially alter it, however, the terms will not be included in the agreement, and the standardized "gap filler" provisions of Article Two will provide the terms of the contract. If the facts reveal that no oral agreement was created, then §2-207(1) may still apply, but in a different manner.

7. The "unless" proviso in §2-207(1) does not apply to confirmatory memoranda because the parties have already entered into an agreement and one party does not have the power pursuant to §2-207 to terminate it unilaterally.

"Confirmation connotes that the parties reached an agreement before exchange of the forms in question. The purpose of the Code drafters here must have been to make clear that confirmations need not mirror each other in order to find contract. Simply stated, then, under this first clause of section 2-207(1) it is reasonable to assume that the parties have a deal, that there is a contract even though terms of the writing exchanged do not match. All of the language following the comma in subsection (1) simply preserves for the offeree his right to make a counter-offer if he does so expressly. This phrase cannot possibly effect the deal between parties that have reached an agreement and then exchanged confirmations. In that situation it is too late for a counter-offer and subsection (2) must be applied to determine what becomes of the non-matching terms of the confirmations."

Air Products & Chemicals, Inc. v. Fairbanks Morse, Inc., 58 Wis. 2d 193, 206 N.W.2d 414, 422-23 (1973), quoting Section 2-207 of the Uniform Commercial Code—New Rules for the "Battle of the Forms," 32 U. Pitt. L. Rev. 209, 210 (1971).

B.   WRITTEN DOCUMENTS NOT CONTAINING IDENTICAL TERMS

The second situation in which §2-207(1) may apply is where the parties have not entered into an oral agreement but have exchanged writings which do not contain identical terms. If the court determines that Pevar and Evans did not orally agree prior to the exchange of documents, then this second situation may apply. In such a case, both Pevar and Evans agree that Pevar's purchase order constituted an offer to purchase. The parties, however, disagree with the characterization of Evans' acknowledgment and Pevar's acceptance of and payment for the shipped goods. Evans contends that the terms disclaiming warranties and limiting liability in the acknowledgment should control because the acknowledgment constituted a counteroffer which Pevar accepted by receiving and paying for the goods. Evans argues that by inserting the "unless" proviso[8] in the terms and conditions of acceptance of the acknowledgment, it effectively rejected and terminated Pevar's offer, and initiated a counteroffer; and when Pevar received and paid for the goods, it accepted the terms of the counteroffer.

Evans relies upon Roto-Lith, Ltd. v. F.P. Bartlett & Co., 297 F.2d 497 (C.A. 1, 1962) for the proposition that a buyer accepts the terms of the seller's counteroffer merely by receiving and paying for shipped goods. In *Roto-Lith*, the buyer of goods sent a written purchase order to the seller. The seller thereafter sent an acknowledgment, accepting the purchase order in part, but also added terms which disclaimed warranties and limited liabilities. The buyer received the goods but did not object to the seller's terms. The court found that the seller's acceptance (acknowledgment) was expressly conditional on assent to the additional terms, and therefore, a counteroffer. It held that the buyer accepted the terms of the counteroffer when it received and paid for the goods.

Roto-Lith has been widely criticized because it does not reflect the underlying principles of the Code. Rather, it reflects the orthodox common law reasoning—that the terms of the counteroffer control if the goods are accepted unless the counterofferee specifically objects to those terms. The drafters of the Code, however, intended to change the common law in an attempt to conform contract law to modern day business transactions. They believed that businessmen rarely read the terms on the back of standardized forms and that the common law, therefore, unduly rewarded the party who sent the last form prior to

---

8. Section 2-207(1) "unless" proviso provides: "unless acceptance is expressly made conditional on assent to the additional or different terms." Evans traced this language in its acknowledgment.

the shipping of the goods. The Code disfavors any attempt by one party to unilaterally impose conditions that would create hardship on another party. Thus, before a counteroffer is accepted, the counter-offeree must expressly assent to the new terms.

This court joins those courts that have rejected the *Roto-Lith* analysis. *Itoh,* supra, 552 F.2d at 1235; *Dorton,* supra, 453 F.2d at 1166; Uniroyal, Inc. v. Chambers Gasket & Manufacturer Co., 380 N.E.2d 571, 577-78 (C.A. Ind. 1978); Falcon Tankers Inc. v. Litton Systems, Inc., 355 A.2d 898, 906 (Del. Super. 1976). See also Construction Aggregates Corp. v. Hewitt-Robbins Corp., 404 F.2d 505 (C.A. 7), *cert. denied,* 395 U.S. 921 (1969). "It finds that [t]he consequence of a clause conditioning acceptance on assent to the additional or different terms is that *as of the exchanged writings there is no contract.* Either party may at this point in their dealing walk away from the transaction" or reach an express assent. *Itoh,* at 1236, quoting Duesenberg & King, Sales & Bulk Transfer (Bender) §3.06(3) at 73. Without the express assent by the parties no contract is created pursuant to §2-207(1). Nevertheless, the parties' conduct may create a contract pursuant to §2-207(3).

C.   CONDUCT ESTABLISHING THE EXISTENCE OF A CONTRACT

Section 2-207(3) is the third method by which parties may enter into a contract. This section applies when the parties have not entered into an oral or written contract. Section 2-207(3) provides that "[c]on-duct by both parties which recognizes the existence of a contract is sufficient to establish a contract for sale although the writing of the parties do not otherwise establish a contract." As *Dorton,* supra, 453 F.2d at 1166 noted:

> When no contract is recognized under Subsection 2-207(1) . . . the entire transaction aborts at this point. If, however, the subsequent conduct of the parties—particularly, performance by both parties under what they apparently believe to be a contract—recognizes the existence of a contract, under Subsection 2-207(3), such conduct by both parties is sufficient to establish a contract, notwithstanding the fact that no contract would have been recognized on the basis of their writings alone.

Section 2-207(3) also provides that where a contract has been consummated by the conduct of the parties, "the terms of the particular contract consist of those terms in which the writings of the parties agree, together with any supplementary terms incorporated under any other provisions of this Act."

In this case, the parties' conduct indicates that they recognized the existence of a contract. If this court finds after trial that Pevar and

Evans did not enter into an oral agreement, §2-207(3) will apply. The terms of the contract will include those terms in which Pevar's purchase order and Evans' acknowledgment agree. For those terms where the writings do not agree, the standardized "gap filler" provisions of Article Two will provide the terms of the contract. *Itoh*, supra, 552 F.2d at 1237.

An Order will be entered in accordance with this Memorandum Opinion.

QUESTION

Assume that you are an attorney representing a seller who frequently receives purchase orders triggering §2-207's rules. Your client wants to disclaim warranties. What do you advise?

— Get Rid of the P.O. - and make the other side signs the K and B aware of all of the provision.

Klocek v. Gateway, Inc.

United States District Court, Kansas, 2000
104 F. Supp. 2d 1332, 41 U.C.C. Rep. Serv. 2d 1059

VRATIL, District Judge.

William S. Klocek brings suit against Gateway, Inc. and Hewlett-Packard, Inc. on claims arising from purchases of a Gateway computer and a Hewlett-Packard scanner. . . . For reasons stated below, the Court overrules Gateway's motion to dismiss, sustains Hewlett-Packard's motion to dismiss, and overrules the motions filed by plaintiff.

A. GATEWAY'S MOTION TO DISMISS

Plaintiff brings individual and class action claims against Gateway, alleging that it induced him and other consumers to purchase computers and special support packages by making false promises of technical support. *Complaint,* ¶¶3 and 4. Individually, plaintiff also claims breach of contract and breach of warranty, in that Gateway breached certain warranties that its computer would be compatible with standard peripherals and standard internet services. *Complaint,* ¶¶2, 5, and 6.

Gateway asserts that plaintiff must arbitrate his claims under Gateway's Standard Terms and Conditions Agreement ("Standard Terms"). Whenever it sells a computer, Gateway includes a copy of the Standard Terms in the box which contains the computer battery power cables and instruction manuals. At the top of the first page, the Standard Terms include the following notice:

> *Note to the Customer:*
> This document contains Gateway 2000's Standard Terms and Conditions. By keeping your Gateway 2000 computer system beyond five (5) days after the date of delivery, you accept these Terms and Conditions.

The notice is in emphasized type and is located inside a printed box which sets it apart from other provisions of the document. The Standard Terms are four pages long and contain 16 numbered paragraphs. Paragraph 10 provides the following arbitration clause:

> DISPUTE RESOLUTION. Any dispute or controversy arising out of or relating to this Agreement or its interpretation shall be settled exclusively and finally by arbitration. The arbitration shall be conducted in accordance with the Rules of Conciliation and Arbitration of the International Chamber of Commerce. The arbitration shall be conducted in Chicago, Illinois, U.S.A. before a sole arbitrator. Any award rendered in any such arbitration proceeding shall be final and binding on each of the parties, and judgment may be entered thereon in a court of competent jurisdiction.[9]

Gateway urges the Court to dismiss plaintiff's claims under the Federal Arbitration Act ("FAA"), 9 U.S.C. §1 et seq. The FAA ensures that written arbitration agreements in maritime transactions and transactions involving interstate commerce are "valid, irrevocable, and enforceable." 9 U.S.C. §2. Federal policy favors arbitration agreements and requires that we "rigorously enforce" them. Shearson/American Exp., Inc. v. McMahon, 482 U.S. 220, 226, 107 S. Ct. 2332, 96 L. Ed. 2d 185 (1987) (quoting Dean Witter Reynolds, Inc. v. Byrd, 470 U.S. 213, 105 S. Ct. 1238, 84 L. Ed. 2d 158, (1985)); *Moses*, 460 U.S. at 24, 103 S. Ct. 927. "[A]ny doubts concerning the scope of arbitrable issues should

---

9. Gateway states that after it sold plaintiff's computer, it mailed all existing customers in the United States a copy of its quarterly magazine, which contained notice of a change in the arbitration policy set forth in the Standard Terms. The new arbitration policy afforded customers the option of arbitrating before the International Chamber of Commerce ("ICC"), the American Arbitration Association ("AAA"), or the National Arbitration Forum ("NAF") in Chicago, Illinois, or any other location agreed upon by the parties. Plaintiff denies receiving notice of the amended arbitration policy. Neither party explains why—if the arbitration agreement was an enforceable contract—Gateway was entitled to unilaterally amend it by sending a magazine to computer customers.

be resolved in favor of arbitration." *Moses,* 460 U.S. at 24-25, 103 S. Ct. 927.

FAA Section 3 states:

> If any suit or proceeding be brought in any of the courts of the United States upon any issue referable to arbitration under an agreement in writing for such arbitration, the court in which such suit is pending, upon being satisfied that the issue involved in such suit or proceeding is referable to arbitration under such agreement, shall on application of one of the parties stay the trial of the action until such arbitration has been had in accordance with the terms of the agreement, providing the applicant for the stay is not in default in proceeding with such arbitration.

9 U.S.C. §3. . . . [T]he Court concludes that dismissal is appropriate if plaintiff's claims are arbitrable.

Gateway bears an initial summary-judgment-like burden of establishing that it is entitled to arbitration. [Citations omitted.] Thus, Gateway must present evidence sufficient to demonstrate the existence of an enforceable agreement to arbitrate. See, e.g., Oppenheimer & Co. v. Neidhardt, 56 F.3d 352, 358 (2d Cir. 1995). If Gateway makes such a showing, the burden shifts to plaintiff to submit evidence demonstrating a genuine issue for trial. Id.; see also Naddy v. Piper Jaffray, Inc., 88 Wash. App. 1033, 1997 WL 749261, *2, Case Nos. 15431-9-III, 15681-8-III (Wash. App. Dec. 4, 1997). In this case, Gateway fails to present evidence establishing the most basic facts regarding the transaction. The gaping holes in the evidentiary record preclude the Court from determining what state law controls the formation of the contract in this case and, consequently, prevent the Court from agreeing that Gateway's motion is well taken.

Before granting a stay or dismissing a case pending arbitration, the Court must determine that the parties have a written agreement to arbitrate. See 9 U.S.C. §§3 and 4; Avedon Engineering, Inc. v. Seatex, 126 F.3d 1279, 1283 (10th Cir. 1997). When deciding whether the parties have agreed to arbitrate, the Court applies ordinary state law principles that govern the formation of contracts. First Options of Chicago, Inc. v. Kaplan, 514 U.S. 938, 944, 115 S. Ct. 1920, 131 L. Ed. 2d 985 (1995). The existence of an arbitration agreement "is simply a matter of contract between the parties; [arbitration] is a way to resolve those disputes—but only those disputes—that the parties have agreed to submit to arbitration." *Avedon,* 126 F.3d at 1283 (quoting *Kaplan,* 514 U.S. at 943-945, 115 S. Ct. 1920). If the parties dispute making an arbitration agreement, a jury trial on the existence of an agreement is warranted if the record reveals genuine issues of material fact regarding the parties' agreement. See *Avedon*, 126 F.3d at 1283. . . .

The Uniform Commercial Code ("UCC") governs the parties' transaction under both Kansas and Missouri law. See K.S.A. §84-2-102; V.A.M.S. §400.2-102 (UCC applies to "transactions in goods."); Kansas Comment 1 (main thrust of Article 2 is limited to sales); K.S.A. §84-2-105(1); V.A.M.S. §400.2-105(1) (" 'Goods' means all things . . . which are movable at the time of identification to the contract for sale. . . ."). Regardless whether plaintiff purchased the computer in person or placed an order and received shipment of the computer, the parties agree that plaintiff paid for and received a computer from Gateway. This conduct clearly demonstrates a contract for the sale of a computer. See, e.g., Step-Saver Data Sys., Inc. v. Wyse Techn., 939 F.2d 91, 98 (3d Cir. 1991). Thus the issue is whether the contract of sale includes the Standard Terms as part of the agreement.

State courts in Kansas and Missouri apparently have not decided whether terms received with a product become part of the parties' agreement. Authority from other courts is split. Compare Step-Saver, 939 F.2d 91 (printed terms on computer software package not part of agreement); Arizona Retail Sys., Inc. v. Software Link, Inc., 831 F. Supp. 759 (D. Ariz. 1993) (license agreement shipped with computer software not part of agreement); and U.S. Surgical Corp. v. Orris, Inc., 5 F. Supp. 2d 1201 (D. Kan. 1998) (single use restriction on product package not binding agreement); with Hill v. Gateway 2000, Inc., 105 F.3d 1147 (7th Cir.), *cert. denied*, 522 U.S. 808, 118 S. Ct. 47, 139 L. Ed. 2d 13 (1997) (arbitration provision shipped with computer binding on buyer); ProCD, Inc. v. Zeidenberg, 86 F.3d 1447 (7th Cir. 1996) (shrinkwrap license binding on buyer);[10] and M.A. Mortenson Co., Inc. v. Timberline Software Corp., 140 Wash. 2d 568, 998 P.2d 305 (2000) (following *Hill* and *ProCD* on license agreement supplied with software).[11] It appears that at least in part, the cases turn on whether the

---

10. The term "shrinkwrap license" gets its name from retail software packages that are covered in plastic or cellophane "shrinkwrap" and contain licenses that purport to become effective as soon as the customer tears the wrapping from the package. See *ProCD*, 86 F.3d at 1449.

11. The *Mortenson* court also found support for its holding in the proposed Uniform Computer Information Transactions Act ("UCITA") (formerly known as proposed UCC Article 2B) (text located at www.law.upenn.edu/library/ulc/ucita/UCITA _99.htm), which the National Conference of Commissioners on Uniform State Laws approved and recommended for enactment by the states in July 1999. See *Mortenson*, 998 P.2d at 310 n.6, 313 n.10. The proposed UCITA, however, would not apply to the Court's analysis in this case. The UCITA applies to computer information transactions, which are defined as agreements "to create, modify, transfer, or license computer information or informational rights in computer information." UCITA, §§102(11) and

court finds that the parties formed their contract *before* or *after* the vendor communicated its terms to the purchaser. Compare *Step-Saver*, 939 F.2d at 98 (parties' conduct in shipping, receiving and paying for product demonstrates existence of contract; box top license constitutes proposal for additional terms under §2-207 which requires express agreement by purchaser); *Arizona Retail*, 831 F. Supp. at 765 (vendor entered into contract by agreeing to ship goods, or at latest by shipping goods to buyer; license agreement constitutes proposal to modify agreement under §2-209 which requires express assent by buyer); and *Orris*, 5 F. Supp. 2d at 1206 (sales contract concluded when vendor received consumer orders; single-use language on product's label was proposed modification under §2-209 which requires express assent by purchaser); with *ProCD*, 86 F.3d at 1452 (under §2-204 vendor, as master of offer, may propose limitations on kind of conduct that constitutes acceptance; §2-207 does not apply in case with only one form); *Hill*,105 F.3d at 1148-49 (same); and *Mortenson*, 998 P.2d at 311-314 (where vendor and purchaser utilized license agreement in prior course of dealing, shrinkwrap license agreement constituted issue of contract formation under §2-204, not contract alteration under §2-207).

Gateway urges the Court to follow the Seventh Circuit decision in *Hill*. That case involved the shipment of a Gateway computer with terms similar to the Standard Terms in this case, except that Gateway gave the customer 30 days—instead of 5 days—to return the computer. In enforcing the arbitration clause, the Seventh Circuit relied on its decision in *ProCD*, where it enforced a software license which was contained inside a product box. See *Hill*, 105 F.3d at 1148-50. In *ProCD*, the Seventh Circuit noted that the exchange of money frequently precedes the communication of detailed terms in a commercial transaction. See *ProCD*, 86 F.3d at 1451. Citing UCC §2-204, the court reasoned that by including the license with the software, the vendor proposed a contract that the buyer could accept by using the software after having an opportunity to read the license.[12] *ProCD*, 86 F.3d at 1452. Specifically, the court stated:

---

103. In transactions involving the sale of computers, such as our case, the UCITA applies only to the computer programs and copies, not to the sale of the computer itself. *See* UCITA §103(c)(2).

12. Section 2-204 provides: "A contract for sale of goods may be made in any manner sufficient to show agreement, including conduct by both parties which recognizes the existence of such contract." K.S.A. §84-2-204; V.A.M.S. §400.2-204.

> A vendor, as master of the offer, may invite acceptance by conduct, and
> may propose limitations on the kind of conduct that constitutes accep-
> tance. A buyer may accept by performing the acts the vendor proposes
> to treat as acceptance.

ProCD, 86 F.3d at 1452. The *Hill* court followed the *ProCD* analysis,
noting that "[p]ractical considerations support allowing vendors to enclose the full legal terms with their products." *Hill*, 105 F.3d at 1149.[13]

The Court is not persuaded that Kansas or Missouri courts would
follow the Seventh Circuit reasoning in *Hill* and *ProCD*. In each case
the Seventh Circuit concluded without support that UCC §2-207 was
irrelevant because the cases involved only one written form. See *ProCD*,
86 F.3d at 1452 (citing no authority); *Hill*, 105 F.3d at 1150 (citing
ProCD). This conclusion is not supported by the statute or by Kansas or
Missouri law. Disputes under §2-207 often arise in the context of a
"battle of forms," see, e.g., Diatom, Inc. v. Pennwalt Corp., 741 F.2d
1569, 1574 (10th Cir. 1984), but nothing in its language precludes application in a case which involves only one form. The statute provides:

> Additional terms in acceptance or confirmation.
>   (1) A definite and seasonable expression of acceptance or a
> written confirmation which is sent within a reasonable time operates

13. Legal commentators have criticized the reasoning of the Seventh Circuit in
this regard. See, e.g., Jean R. Sternlight, Gateway Widens Doorway to Imposing Unfair
Binding Arbitration on Consumers, Fla. Bar J., Nov. 1997, at 8, 10-12 (outcome in
Gateway is questionable on federal statutory, common law and constitutional grounds
and as a matter of contract law and is unwise as a matter of policy because it
unreasonably shifts to consumers search cost of ascertaining existence of arbitration
clause and return cost to avoid such clause); Thomas J. McCarthy et al., Survey:
Uniform Commercial Code, 53 Bus. Law. 1461, 1465-66 (Seventh Circuit finding that
UCC §2-207 did not apply is inconsistent with official comment); Batya Goodman,
Honey, I Shrink-Wrapped the Consumer: the Shrinkwrap Agreement as an Adhesion
Contract, 21 Cardozo L. Rev. 319, 344-352 (Seventh Circuit failed to consider principles of adhesion contracts); Jeremy Senderowicz, Consumer Arbitration and
Freedom of Contract: A Proposal to Facilitate Consumers' Informed Consent to Arbi-
tration Clauses in Form Contracts, 32 Colum. J.L. & Soc. Probs. 275, 296-299 (judiciary
(in multiple decisions, including *Hill*) has ignored issue of consumer consent to an
arbitration clause). Nonetheless, several courts have followed the Seventh Circuit
decisions in *Hill* and *ProCD*. See, e.g., M.A. Mortenson Co., Inc. v. Timberline Software
Corp., 140 Wash. 2d 568, 998 P.2d 305 (license agreement supplied with software);
Rinaldi v. Iomega Corp., 1999 WL 1442014, Case No. 98C-09-064-RRC (Del. Super.
Sept. 3, 1999) (warranty disclaimer included inside computer Zip drive packaging);
Westendorf v. Gateway 2000, Inc., 2000 WL 307369, Case No. 16913 (Del. Ch. March
16, 2000) (arbitration provision shipped with computer); Brower v. Gateway 2000,
Inc., 246 A.D.2d 246, 676 N.Y.S.2d 569 (N.Y. App. Div. 1998) (same); Levy v. Gateway
2000, Inc., 1997 WL 823611, 33 UCC Rep. Serv. 2d 1060 (N.Y. Sup. Oct. 31, 1997)
(same).

as an acceptance even though it states terms additional to or different from those offered or agreed upon, unless acceptance is expressly made conditional on assent to the additional or different terms.

(2) The additional terms are to be construed as proposals for addition to the contract [if the contract is not between merchants] . . . .

K.S.A. §84-2-207; V.A.M.S. §400.2-207. By its terms, §2-207 applies to an acceptance or written confirmation. It states nothing which requires another form before the provision becomes effective. In fact, the official comment to the section specifically provides that §2-207(1) and (2) apply "where an agreement has been reached orally . . . and is followed by one or both of the parties sending formal memoranda embodying the terms so far agreed and adding terms not discussed." Official Comment 1 of UCC §2-207. Kansas and Missouri courts have followed this analysis. See Southwest Engineering Co. v. Martin Tractor Co., 205 Kan. 684, 695, 473 P.2d 18, 26 (1970) (stating in dicta that §2-207 applies where open offer is accepted by expression of acceptance in writing or where oral agreement is later confirmed in writing); Central Bag Co. v. W. Scott & Co., 647 S.W.2d 828, 830 (Mo. App. 1983) (§2-207(1) and (2) govern cases where one or both parties send written confirmation after oral contract). Thus, the Court concludes that Kansas and Missouri courts would apply §2-207 to the facts in this case. Accord *Avedon,* 126 F.3d at 1283 (parties agree that §2-207 controls whether arbitration clause in sales confirmation is part of contract).

In addition, the Seventh Circuit provided no explanation for its conclusion that "the vendor is the master of the offer." See *ProCD,* 86 F.3d at 1452 (citing nothing in support of proposition); *Hill,* 105 F.3d at 1149 (citing *ProCD*). In typical consumer transactions, the purchaser is the offeror, and the vendor is the offeree. See Brown Mach., Div. of John Brown, Inc. v. Hercules, Inc., 770 S.W.2d 416, 419 (Mo. App. 1989) (as general rule orders are considered offers to purchase); Rich Prods. Corp. v. Kemutec Inc., 66 F. Supp. 2d 937, 956 (E.D. Wis. 1999) (generally price quotation is invitation to make offer and purchase order is offer). While it is possible for the vendor to be the offeror, see *Brown Machine,* 770 S.W.2d at 419 (price quote can amount to offer if it reasonably appears from quote that assent to quote is all that is needed to ripen offer into contract), Gateway provides no factual evidence which would support such a finding in this case. The Court therefore assumes for purposes of the motion to dismiss that plaintiff offered to purchase the computer (either in person or through catalog order) and that Gateway accepted plaintiff's offer (either by completing the sales transaction in person or by agreeing to ship and/or shipping the computer to plaintiff).[14] Accord Arizona Retail, 831 F. Supp. at 765 (vendor entered into contract by agreeing to ship goods, or at latest, by shipping goods).

Under §2-207, the Standard Terms constitute either an expression of acceptance or written confirmation. As an expression of acceptance, the Standard Terms would constitute a counter-offer only if Gateway expressly made its acceptance conditional on plaintiff's assent to the additional or different terms. K.S.A. §84-2-207(1); V.A.M.S. §400.2-207(1). "[T]he conditional nature of the acceptance must be clearly expressed in a manner sufficient to notify the offeror that the offeree is unwilling to proceed with the transaction unless the additional or different terms are included in the contract." *Brown Machine,* 770 S.W.2d at 420. Gateway provides no evidence that at the time of the sales transaction, it informed plaintiff that the transaction was conditioned on plaintiff's acceptance of the Standard Terms. Moreover, the mere fact that Gateway shipped the goods with the terms attached did not communicate to plaintiff any unwillingness to proceed without plaintiff's agreement to the Standard Terms. See, e.g., *Arizona Retail,* 831 F. Supp. at 765 (conditional acceptance analysis rarely appropriate where contract formed by performance but goods arrive with conditions attached); Leighton Indus., Inc. v. Callier Steel Pipe & Tube, Inc., 1991 WL 18413, *6, Case No. 89-C-8235 (N.D. Ill. Feb. 6, 1991) (applying Missouri law) (preprinted forms insufficient to notify offeror of conditional nature of acceptance, particularly where form arrives after delivery of goods).

Because plaintiff is not a merchant, additional or different terms contained in the Standard Terms did not become part of the parties' agreement unless plaintiff expressly agreed to them. See K.S.A. §84-2-207, Kansas Comment 2 (if either party is not a merchant, additional terms are proposals for addition to the contract that do not become part of the contract unless the original offeror expressly agrees). Gateway argues that plaintiff demonstrated acceptance of the arbitration provision by keeping the computer more than five days after the date of delivery. Although the Standard Terms purport to work that result, Gateway has not presented evidence that plaintiff expressly

---

14. UCC §2-206(b) provides that "an order or other offer to buy goods for prompt or current shipment shall be construed as inviting acceptance either by a prompt promise to ship or by the prompt or current shipment . . . " The official comment states that "[e]ither shipment or a prompt promise to ship is made a proper means of acceptance of an offer looking to current shipment." UCC §2-206, Official Comment 2.

[handwritten: neither arbitration nor return of product requirement made a condition of original sale.]

agreed to those Standard Terms. Gateway states only that it enclosed the Standard Terms inside the computer box for plaintiff to read afterwards. It provides no evidence that it informed plaintiff of the five-day review-and-return period as a condition of the sales transaction, or that the parties contemplated additional terms to the agreement.[15] See *Step-Saver,* 939 F.2d at 99 (during negotiations leading to purchase, vendor never mentioned box-top license or obtained buyer's express assent thereto). The Court finds that the act of keeping the computer past five days was not sufficient to demonstrate that plaintiff expressly agreed to the Standard Terms. Accord *Brown Machine,* 770 S.W.2d at 421 (express assent cannot be presumed by silence or mere failure to object). Thus, because Gateway has not provided evidence sufficient to support a finding under Kansas or Missouri law that plaintiff agreed to the arbitration provision contained in Gateway's Standard Terms, the Court overrules Gateway's motion to dismiss. . . .

[handwritten: motion to dismiss overruled]

15. The Court is mindful of the practical considerations which are involved in commercial transactions, but it is not unreasonable for a vendor to clearly communicate to a buyer—at the time of sale—either the complete terms of the sale or the fact that the vendor will propose additional terms as a condition of sale, if that be the case.

Chapter 3

WARRANTIES

The law of warranty has borrowed its concepts from the legal coffers of tort, contract, and property. The UCC divides warranties into two basic types: warranties of *title* and warranties of *quality*.

I. THE WARRANTY OF TITLE

Read §2-312.

PROBLEM 16

Fast Eddie stole Mabel Stanley's car from a shopping center in Phoenix. He drove it to Las Vegas, where he sold it for $500 to Sealed Lips Used Cars. This firm somehow obtained a Nevada certificate of title for the car, which showed clean title in Sealed Lips. The car was then sold for $2,000 to a bona fide purchaser, Frederick Duty. Duty drove it for a month until a bad run at the roulette wheel forced him to sell it in order to finance further recreational activity. Another bona fide purchaser, Samuel Pirate, bought the car from Duty for $1,900. He drove it for only one week before the Nevada State Police impounded it and returned it to Mabel in Phoenix. Pirate sued Duty for breach of the warranty of good title.

(a) Duty argues that he *thought* he had good title, and since he was not negligent or in any way at fault in so believing, the warranty was not breached. Does this defense succeed? See Brokke v. Williams, 766 P.2d 1311, 7 U.C.C. Rep. Serv. 2d 1404 (Mont. 1989).

(b) Duty argues that he *did* have good title, and hence the warranty was not breached. Did he? See §2-403(1); Inmi-Etti v. Aluisi, 63 Md. App. 293, 492 A.2d 917, 40 U.C.C. Rep. Serv. 1612 (1985) (*Nemo dat qui non habet*—"He who hath not cannot give").

(c) Would your answer to (b) change if Fast Eddie had bought the car from Mabel with a bad check? See §2-403.

(d) Does the law give any relief to Duty? See §2-607(5)(a) (describing a procedure known as *vouching in*).

PROBLEM 17

Before the Nevada State Police found Mabel's car, discussed in the last Problem, they accidentally impounded a very similar car owned by P. T. Boss. Boss had recently purchased the car from Croupier Motors. In order to convince the police that they had made a mistake and should release the car to him, Boss had to hire an attorney, Arnold Sunglasses. The latter did retrieve the car and then sent Boss a bill for $400. Boss forwarded the bill to Croupier Motors, along with a cover letter to the effect that title problems were the seller's headache per §2-312. Should the car dealership pay Sunglasses's bill? See Official Comment 1 to §2-312; White & Summers §9-12 (Practitioner ed. only); Frank Arnold Contractors, Inc. v. Vilsmeier Auction Co., 806 F.2d 462, 2 U.C.C. Rep. Serv. 2d 845 (3d Cir. 1986). See also §2-607(5).

PROBLEM 18

Sellers can sometimes evade or disclaim the warranty of title. Determine if the warranty is present in the following situations:

See Brophe v. Williams

(a) The sales contract has this clause: "The product is sold 'As Is' and seller makes no warranties, express or implied, as part of this sale." See Official Comment 6 to §2-312. _also see 312(2) & its comt t(2)_

(b) Repossession Motors sold a car on credit to a customer who returned it after failing to make the first payment. It then conducted an _yes_ Article 9-type resale. (See §9-610.) Does the resale buyer get the benefit of a §2-312 warranty? See Official Comment 5.

(c) Ted Traveler walked into the men's room of the bus depot and, to his surprise, was offered an expensive watch at a bargain rate from a _No_ stranger. He bought the watch. Is there a warranty of title in this transaction? See §1-205(2).

Note that the warranty of title also includes:

(1) a warranty that there are no security interests (or other liens) on the goods other than those of which the buyer knows (§2-312(1)(b)), and

(2) a warranty given by merchant sellers against claims based on patent infringement or the like (§2-312(3)).

If the buyer furnishes specifications to the seller (which happens where the goods are to be specially manufactured to the buyer's order), the _buyer_ automatically makes a warranty to the seller that protects the latter from infringement claims. Section 2-312(3). This is the _only_ situation under the UCC where the buyer is the warrantor.

II. WARRANTIES OF QUALITY

Warranties of quality are subdivided into two types: express warranties and implied warranties. For an excellent study of the UCC's warranties of quality, see Special Project, Article Two Warranties in Commercial Transactions, 64 Cornell L. Rev. 30 (1978), and Special Project, Article Two Warranties in Commercial Transactions: An Update, 72 Cornell L. Rev. 1307 (1987).

A. Express Warranties

An express warranty arises when the seller does something affirmative to create buyer expectations about the characteristics or performance of the goods. Typically this means that the seller will make oral or written representations about the product in advertisements, the verbal sales pitch, or the written contract. These representations must have some substance to them (more than mere "puffing") to rise to the dignity of an express warranty. In the Code's words, they must "relate to the goods" (an obvious requirement) and become part of the *basis of the bargain* (a not-so-obvious or explainable requirement). Under the now-replaced Uniform Sales Act (§12), the buyer had to prove *reliance* on the statement alleged to be an express warranty. Does *basis of bargain* mean this? Read Official Comment 3 to §2-313. Most courts have adopted a test suggested by Professor Williston that a statement goes to the basis of the bargain if its natural tendency is to induce the buyer to purchase (even though that is not the sole reason). See White & Summers §9-5; Nordstrom §§66-68. This means that if the statement, however made, has any substance to it so that it *might* have played some part in the buyer's decision to buy, the burden is on the *seller* to prove that the buyer did *not* rely. If the seller cannot meet this burden, the buyer has the benefit of an express warranty. Read §2-313 carefully.

PROBLEM 19

(a) The salesman at the lot of Smiles Pre-Owned Vehicles told the woman buying the car that it was in "A-1 shape." She bought the car, but it broke down the next day, stranding her in the country. Was this oral statement mere puffing? See Wat Henry Pontiac Co. v. Bradley, 202 Okla. 82, 210 P.2d 348 (1949); White & Summers §9-4. Is it an easier case if the seller tells the buyer that the used car is in "mint condition"? See Taylor v. Alfama, 481 A.2d 1059, 39 U.C.C. Rep. Serv. 1235 (Vt. 1984).

(b) When the farmer looked over the young chickens he was contemplating purchasing from the poultry company, he complained that they looked pretty scruffy. The salesman explained that that was because they were on half-feed and that when they were placed on full-feed, they would "bloom out, straighten up, and fly right," and they would "do a good job in your chicken house." The farmer purchased the chickens, and two months later they started dying in droves. The farmer sued, claiming breach of an express warranty. Is he right? Is this a question of law or of fact for the jury? See Woodruff v. Clark County Farm Bureau Coop., 153 Ind. App. 31, 286 N.E.2d 188, 11 U.C.C. Rep. Serv. 498 (1972).

(c) Portia Moot, a third-year law student, had taken the course in sales, so when she went to buy a used car, she listened very carefully to the sales pitch. The smarmy salesman was quite friendly, but he only made two statements about the car she bought: "This is a great car!" and "You're going to love it!" In fact, the car broke down a great deal, and Portia quickly grew to hate it. Does she have a cause of action here?

(d) Assume that the car salesman told Portia that the used car she was contemplating purchasing had been thoroughly inspected by the car dealership's crack repair department and was "mechanically in perfect condition." However, Portia was suspicious about the reliability of the car and before she bought it, she took it to her own favorite mechanic for an inspection. She didn't buy the car until her mechanic cleared it as fine. When the car broke down a few days later, she decided to bring suit on the express warranty. What defense will the car dealership raise?

PROBLEM 20

Upon graduation from law school, Andrew Loner hung out his shingle and waited. Mr. and Mrs. Consumer were his first clients, and they told him the following story. Two weeks earlier they had visited a wallpaper store, Paper & Paste, Inc., and inquired about vinyl wallpaper for their dining room. The salesman told them that the "finest" wallpaper in the store was Expenso-Paper, a vinyl wallpaper selling at $25 a roll. When he learned that the Consumers had never before put up wallpaper, the salesman assured them that Expenso-Paper "goes up easily, can be put on with any paste, and dries immediately." He said that it "would look wonderful" and, moreover, that Expenso-Paper "was used by Mary Magic," the famous movie star, in her dining room. He showed them a sample book and they picked out a pattern they liked and ordered 10 rolls. When the paper arrived the next week, it proved to be very stiff and hard to work with. It tore easily and refused to stay flat on the wall (it either bubbled or, due to its heavy weight, fell down on drying). In addition, it was dyed a darker color than the version of the pattern in the sample book. The final result was that the Consumers' dining room looked terrible. To top it all off, the Consumers discovered that Mary Magic did not own a home (she lived exclusively in hotels).

Upon complaining to Paper & Paste, the Consumers were told by the manager that Expenso-Paper needs a special brand of paste, to wit, Expenso-Paste. They were also told that Expenso-Paper was an inferior brand and that next time they should buy Super Wall, a better product that the store carried.

The Consumers told Loner that they signed the contract without reading it and that the statement about Mary Magic's dining room was made *after* they signed the agreement. Loner (and you) have to answer these questions:

(a) Which of the salesman's representations amount to express warranties?

(1)   finest?
(2)   goes up easily?
(3)   can be put on with any paste?
(4)   dries immediately?
(5)   would look wonderful?
(6)   was used by Mary Magic?

Do you see any other express warranties?

(b) Is the Mary Magic statement part of the *basis of the bargain*, arising as it did after the contract was signed? See §2-209(1); Official Comment 7 to §2-313.

PROBLEM 21

Balding Paul bought a wig from Hair, Inc. He became annoyed when the wig changed colors slightly from season to season. He did not do anything about it until one day, while thumbing through a newspaper, he noticed an ad for Hair, Inc., that claimed that their wigs did not shrink or change color. On checking back, he discovered that Hair, Inc., had run an identical ad during the week prior to his purchase of the wig. He sues. On the witness stand Paul confesses that he never saw the ad until a year after his purchase of the wig. Is this admission fatal to his recovery on a theory of express warranty? See *Winston Indus., Inc. v. Stuyvesant Ins. Co.*, 55 Ala. App. 525, 317 So. 2d 493, 17 U.C.C. Rep. Serv. 924 (1975) (buyer held protected by manufacturer's warranty on mobile home even though he never received a copy).

B.   Implied Warranties

In many ways implied warranties are the legal opposites of express warranties. An express warranty is created only where the seller does something *affirmative* (opens his mouth and says something, takes out a newspaper ad, displays a sample). Implied warranties, on the other hand, are *automatically* part of the contract unless the seller (or the circumstance) does something affirmative to get rid of them. Implied warranties are implied as a matter of law; they are sometimes referred to as "children of the law." Like express warranties, the seller's intention to create any implied warranty is completely irrelevant.

1. Merchantability (2-314)

The implied warranty of merchantability (which is easier to spell and pronounce if you think of it as two words — *merchant* and *ability* — tacked together) is not given a precise definition in the Code. The basic idea is that the item must be saleable and conform to the normal expectations of the parties. Notice that §2-314(2), which you should now read, sets minimum standards for its meaning. Clever lawyers can make much of the laundry list found in that subsection.

Shaffer v. Victoria Station, Inc.

Washington Supreme Court, 1978
91 Wash. 2d 295, 588 P.2d 233, 25 U.C.C. Rep. Serv. 427

DOLLIVER, J. On March 26, 1974, plaintiff Shaffer ordered a glass of wine at the Victoria Station, a restaurant operated by defendant. In the course of taking his first or second sip, the wine glass broke in Mr. Shaffer's hand, resulting in alleged permanent injury.

Plaintiff brought this action based upon three theories: negligence, breach of implied warranty under the Uniform Commercial Code, and strict liability under the theory of Restatement (Second) of Torts §402A (1965). The manufacturer of the glass was named as a defendant, but was never served. Prior to trial, as counsel and the trial judge were discussing proposed instructions, plaintiff's attorney indicated that he could not prove negligence, and wished to submit the case to the jury on the grounds of breach of warranty and strict liability. Plaintiff then took a voluntary nonsuit on the negligence issue. At the same time, the court ruled the case sounded in negligence alone, and granted the defendant's motion for dismissal. The Court of Appeals affirmed. Shaffer v. Victoria Station, Inc., 18 Wash. App. 816, 572 P.2d 737 (1977). We reverse the Court of Appeals.

I

Defendant argues the Uniform Commercial Code does not apply
since the restaurant was not a merchant with respect to wine glasses as
defined in §2-104 and, since the glass itself was not sold, there was no
passing of title as required under §2-106. Plaintiff, however, points to
§2-314 as being decisive. We agree. Section 2-314 reads, inter alia:

> (1) Unless excluded or modified (§2-316), a warranty that the
> goods shall be merchantable is implied in a contract for their sale if the
> seller is a merchant with respect to goods of that kind. Under this
> section the serving for value of food or drink to be consumed either on
> the premises or elsewhere is a sale.
>   (2) Goods to be merchantable must be at least such as . . .
>   (c) are fit for the ordinary purposes for which such goods are
> used; and . . .
>   (e) are adequately contained, packaged, and labeled as the
> agreement may require; . . . .

It is our opinion that, when the Uniform Commercial Code states
"the serving for value of food or drink to be consumed either on the
premises or elsewhere is a sale" and that such food and drink must be
"adequately contained, packaged, and labeled as the agreement may
require," it covers entirely the situation before us. Plaintiff ordered a
drink (a glass of wine) from defendant. Defendant sold and served the
glass of wine to plaintiff to be consumed by plaintiff on the premises.
The wine could not be served as a drink nor could it be consumed
without an adequate container. The drink sold includes the wine and
the container both of which must be fit for the ordinary purpose for
which used. Plaintiff alleges the drink sold—wine in a glass—was unfit
and has, therefore, stated a cause of action.

In addition to the language of §2-314, we believe the language of
§1-103 is applicable. It states:

> Unless displaced by the particular provisions of this Title, the prin-
> ciples of law and equity, including the law merchant and the law relative
> to capacity to contract, principal and agent, estoppel, fraud, misrepre-
> sentation, duress, coercion, mistake, bankruptcy, or other validating or
> invalidating cause shall supplement its provisions.

Plaintiff urges that cases which apply the Uniform Commercial
Code where the goods are leased rather than sold (see, e.g., Baker v.
Seattle, 79 Wash. 2d 198, 484 P.2d 405 (1971)), or are under a bail-
ment for mutual benefit (see, e.g., Fulbright v. Klamath Gas Co., 271

Ore. 449, 533 P.2d 316 (1975)), be extended to the facts before us. We believe this is unnecessary. A more straightforward and less tortuous approach is that adopted in Hadley v. Hillcrest Dairy, Inc., 341 Mass. 624, 171 N.E.2d 293 (1961). In that case, a bottle of milk delivered to the plaintiff's home shattered and cut the plaintiff's hand. The Massachusetts Supreme Judicial Court, relying on the Massachusetts sales act (which was not, as argued by defendant, significantly different in its applicable part from the Uniform Commercial Code), held at 627, "In our view it is immaterial whether or not the property in the jug passed to the plaintiff." The court goes on to cite Geddling v. Marsh, (1920) 1 K.B. 668. In that case, a retailer received bottled mineral water from the manufacturer and was injured by an exploding bottle. The court found the bottles were not sold to the retailer but held the retailer could recover under a breach of an implied warranty of fitness. The court said at 671-672:

> In this case there was only one contract—namely, a contract between the plaintiff and the defendant that the plaintiff should be supplied with mineral waters. Mineral waters could not be supplied except in bottles, and therefore the plaintiff was asking to be supplied with mineral waters in bottles. That undoubtedly is a contract of sale, and I will assume that in that contract there might be a condition that the bottles should not be bought by the plaintiff but should be hired; but the question the county court judge had to consider was whether the bottles were not "supplied under a contract of sale." This was a contract of sale none the less because there was a special provision with regard to the bottles. The section, in my opinion, extends not only to the goods actually bought under the contract but to goods "supplied under the contract of sale." This particular bottle was thus "supplied under a contract of sale," and it follows that it should be reasonably fit for the purpose for which it was supplied. In fact it was not reasonably fit and in consequence of that unfitness the plaintiff was injured.

See also Sartin v. Blackwell, 200 Miss. 579, 28 So. 2d 222 (1946). Plaintiff has a cause of action both on the face of the statute and under the principles of case law elucidated above.

II

Strict liability

We also hold an action lies under the strict liability theory of Restatement (Second) of Torts §402A (1965). The policy questions of strict liability and their application to retailers have been previously determined. See Seattle-First Natl. Bank v. Tabert, 86 Wash. 2d 145,

542 P.2d 774 (1975); Ulmer v. Ford Motor Co., 75 Wash. 2d 522, 452
P.2d 729 (1969). The only question remaining is whether §402A
applies to the transaction here. In addressing this issue, the Court of
Appeals expressed concern over an uncontrollable broadening of the
doctrine of strict liability:

> Were the wine glass in question held to be a mere facet of the sale
> of the "glass of wine" and thus a "product" for the purposes of section
> 402A, the theory of strict liability would be greatly and unnecessarily
> expanded. The reasonably clear standard of engagement "in the
> business of selling . . . a product" would be abandoned in deference to a
> less predictable question—whether the injury-producing aspect of the
> sale was necessary to the sale. If a wine glass renders a restauranteur
> strictly liable because he could not sell wine without it, what of other
> tablewear, the waiters and the bus boys, the furnishings to effect an
> attractive atmosphere, or the building housing the establishment? The
> argument could be made that numerous aspects of a restaurant's
> operation, or that of any other retailer, are integral to each sale. To
> ignore the fact that this allegedly defective glass was never sold would
> create great uncertainty as to the limits of strict liability.

Shaffer, at 820-821.

We do not agree with the gloomy view of the Court of Appeals of
the consequences of allowing the plaintiff to proceed with this action.
We hold the sale of a glass of wine is subject to the strict liability
provisions of §402A. If their predictions as to future lawsuits come to
pass, we will deal with the litigation at that time. Confirmation of the
applicability of §402A to this case is given in comment h, which says:

> The defective condition may arise not only from harmful in-
> gredients, not characteristic of the product itself either as to presence or
> quantity, but also from foreign objects contained in the product, from
> decay or deterioration before sale, or from the way in which the product
> is prepared or packed. No reason is apparent for distinguishing between
> the product itself and the container in which it is supplied; and the two
> are purchased by the user or consumer as an integrated whole. Where
> the container is itself dangerous, the product is sold in a defective
> condition. Thus a carbonated beverage in a bottle which is so weak, or
> cracked, or jagged at the edges, or bottled under such excessive pressure
> that it may explode or otherwise cause harm to the person who handles
> it, is in a defective and dangerous condition. The container cannot
> logically be separated from the contents when the two are sold as a unit,
> and the liability stated in this Section arises not only when the consumer

drinks the beverage and is poisoned by it, but also when he is injured by the bottle while he is handling it preparatory to consumption.

Restatement (Second) of Torts §402A, comment h at 351-352 (1965).

Plaintiff has stated a cause of action under theories of implied warranty of fitness and strict liability. The Court of Appeals is reversed.

QUESTIONS *yes, could be contributory neg.*

1. Would it be a defense to the restaurant that it was not negligent in any way in connection with its handling of the wine glass? See Official Comment 13 to §2-314; La Fountain v. Sears, Roebuck & Co., 680 F. Supp. 251, 6 U.C.C. Rep. Serv. 2d 1091 (E.D. Mich. 1988).

2. If a casino serves its patrons free drinks at the gaming tables and one of the drinks proves to contain chips of glass, would the Washington Supreme Court reach the same result it did in the last case? See Levondosky v. Marina Assocs., 731 F. Supp. 1210, 11 U.C.C. Rep. Serv. 2d 487 (D.N.J. 1990).   *— yes, still implied warranty of fitness*

By far the most important segment of §2-314(2) is found in subsection (2)(c): to be merchantable the goods must be "fit for the ordinary purposes for which such goods are used." (Or, as the South Carolina courts have put it since 1793, "a sound price warrants a sound commodity.") When you think about it, a warranty that the goods are fit for their *ordinary purpose* is a big warranty. It is the warranty that the goods will work, and it is typically the only warranty that the buyer needs. When sellers disclaim the implied warranty of merchantability (and they often do), why do buyers not routinely complain? *— b/c don't have to pay for it.*

PROBLEM 22

Consider the following: *good question*

(a) Are cigarettes that cause lung cancer merchantable if used over a period of years? See Franklin E. Crawford, Fit for Its Ordinary Purpose? Tobacco, Fast Food, and the Implied Warranty of Merchantability, 63 Ohio St. L.J. 1165 (2002); White & Summers §9-8. If the seller's advertisements stated that the cigarettes were "mild," would that create an express warranty?   *— possible*

(b) Officer Krupke, a New York policeman by profession, sold his family car to his next-door neighbor, Maria, telling her it was a "good car." In fact, it was falling apart and blew up the first time she drove it. Has Krupke breached the implied warranty of merchantability? See §2-104(1); Official Comment 3 to §2-314; §1-203. Should §2-314 be extended so that the warranty is made by all sellers? See Hillinger, The Merchant of §2-314: Who Needs Him?, 34 Hastings L.J. 747 (1983).

PROBLEM 23

Natty Bumpo was driving through upstate New York when a deer ran in front of his car. He swerved to avoid it and ran into a tree. His major injuries came from his sudden contact with the inside of the driver's door, where he smashed up against sharp points on the door handle, the window lever, and an ashtray. Natty sued the car manufacturer, the Mohican Motor Company, for breach of the warranty of merchantability. His theory was that the manufacturer should have designed a much safer car. The manufacturer's defense was that the car was fit for its ordinary purpose and that Natty had misused it. How should this come out? See Larsen v. General Motors Corp., 391 F.2d 495 (8th Cir. 1968); Nordstrom §82; Comment, Intended Use and the Unsafe Automobile: Manufacturers' Liability for Negligent Design, 28 Md. L. Rev. 386 (1968); Annot., 76 A.L.R.2d 91.

Daniell v. Ford Motor Co.

United States District Court, New Mexico, 1984
581 F. Supp. 728, 38 U.C.C. Rep. Serv. 464

BALDOCK, J. . . . In 1980, the plaintiff became locked inside the trunk of a 1973 Ford LTD automobile, where she remained for some nine days. Plaintiff now seeks to recover for psychological and physical injuries arising from that occurrence. She contends that the automobile had a design defect in that the trunk lock or latch did not have an internal release or opening mechanism. She also maintains that the manufacturer is liable based on a failure to warn of this condition. Plaintiff advances several theories for recovery: (1) strict products liability under §402A of the Restatement 2d of Torts (1965), (2) negligence, and (3) breach of express warranty and implied warranties of merchantability and fitness for a particular purpose, §§2-313, 2-314, & 2-315 (1978).

Three uncontroverted facts bar recovery under any of these theories. First, the plaintiff ended up in the trunk compartment of the automobile because she felt "overburdened" and was attempting to commit suicide. Deposition of Connie Daniell at 4-5 (May 25, 1983). Second, the purposes of an automobile trunk are to transport, stow and secure the automobile spare tire, luggage and other goods and to protect those items from elements of the weather. Affidavit of Hugh Daley at 3 (January 17, 1983). Third, the plaintiff never considered the possibility of exit from the inside of the trunk when the automobile was purchased. Deposition of Connie Daniell at 16 (May 25, 1983). Plaintiff has not set forth evidence indicating that these facts are controverted. See F.R. Civ. P. 56(e).

The overriding factor barring plaintiff's recovery is that she intentionally sought to end her life by crawling into an automobile trunk from which she could not escape. This is not a case where a person inadvertently became trapped inside an automobile trunk. The plaintiff was aware of the natural and probable consequences of her perilous conduct. Not only that, the plaintiff, at least initially, sought those dreadful consequences. Plaintiff, not the manufacturer of the vehicle, is responsible for this unfortunate occurrence.

Recovery under strict products liability and negligence will be discussed first because the concept of duty owed by the manufacturer to the consumer or user is the same under both theories in this case. As a general principle, a design defect is actionable only where the condition of the product is unreasonably dangerous to the user or consumer. Restatement 2d of Torts, §402A (1965); Skyhook Corp. v. Jasper, 90 N.M. 143, 147, 560 P.2d 934, 938 (1977). Under strict products liability or negligence, a manufacturer has a duty to consider only those risks of injury which are foreseeable. N.M.U.J.I. Civ. 14.2 & 14.3 and U.J.I. Civil Committee Comment under 14.2 & 14.3 (1980 & 1983 Supp.) (strict products liability); Kelly v. Montoya, 81 N.M. 591, 593, 470 P.2d 563, 565 (Ct. App. 1970) (negligence). A risk is not foreseeable by a manufacturer where a product is used in a manner which could not reasonably be anticipated by the manufacturer and that use is the cause of the plaintiff's injury. The plaintiff's injury would not be foreseeable by the manufacturer.

The purposes of an automobile trunk are to transport, stow and secure the automobile spare tire, luggage and other goods and to protect those items from elements of the weather. The design features of an automobile trunk make it well near impossible that an adult intentionally would enter the trunk and close the lid. The dimensions of a trunk, the height of its sill and its load floor and the efforts to first lower the trunk lid and then to engage its latch, are among the design features which encourage closing and latching the trunk lid while standing outside the vehicle. Affidavit of Hugh Daley at 3 (January 17, 1983). The court holds that the plaintiff's use of the trunk compartment as a means to attempt suicide was an unforeseeable use as a matter of law. Therefore, the manufacturer had no duty to design an internal release or opening mechanism that might have prevented this occurrence.

Nor did the manufacturer have a duty to warn the plaintiff of the danger of her conduct, given the plaintiff's unforeseeable use of the product. Another reason why the manufacturer had no duty to warn the plaintiff of the risk inherent in crawling into an automobile trunk and closing the trunk lid is because such a risk is obvious. There is no duty to warn of known dangers in strict products liability or tort. Garrett v. Nissen, 84 N.M. 16, 21, 498 P.2d 1359, 1364 (1972). Moreover, the potential efficacy of any warning, given the plaintiff's use of the automobile trunk compartment for a deliberate suicide attempt, is questionable.

The court notes that the automobile trunk was not defective under these circumstances. See Rudisaile v. Hawk Aviation, Inc., 92 N.M. 575, 577, 592 P.2d 175, 177 (1979). The automobile trunk was not unreasonably dangerous within the contemplation of the ordinary consumer or user of such a trunk when used in the ordinary ways and for the ordinary purposes for which such a trunk is used. Skyhook Corp. v. Jasper, 90 N.M. 143, 147, 560 P.2d 934, 938 (1977); Restatement 2d of Torts §402A, comment i.

Having held that the plaintiff's conception of the manufacturer's duty is in error, the court need not reach the issues of the effect of comparative negligence or other defenses such as assumption of the risk on the products liability claim. See Scott v. Rizzo, 96 N.M. 682 at 688-689, 634 P.2d 1234 at 1240-1241 (1981) (in adopting comparative negligence, the New Mexico Supreme Court indicated that in strict products liability a plaintiff's "misconduct" would be a defense, but not a complete bar to recovery), and also see Bendorf v. Volkswagenwerk Aktiengesellschaft, 88 N.M. 355, 540 P.2d 835 (1975) (precomparative negligence assumption of the risk defense). The court also does not reach the comparative negligence defense on the negligence claim.

Having considered the products liability and negligence claims, plaintiff's contract claims for breach of warranty are now analyzed. Plaintiff has come forward with no evidence of any express warranty regarding exit from the inside of the trunk. N.M. Stat. §2-313 (1978). In accordance with Rule 56(e) of the Federal Rules of Civil Procedure

and Local Rule 9(j) (D.N.M. October 25, 1983, as amended), summary
judgment on the express warranty claim is appropriate.

②Any implied warranty of merchantability in this case requires that
the product must be fit for the ordinary purposes for which such goods
are used. N.M. Stat. Ann. §2-314(2)(c). The implied warranty of merchantability does not require that the buyer must prove reliance on the
skill and judgment of the manufacturer. Vitro Corp. of America v.
Texas Vitrified Supply, 71 N.M. 95, 106, 376 P.2d 41, 48 (1962) (Reese,
Jr., G., D.J.). Still, the usual and ordinary purpose of an automobile
trunk is to transport and store goods, including the automobile's spare
tire. Plaintiff's use of the trunk was highly extraordinary, and there is
no evidence that that trunk was not fit for the ordinary purpose for
which it was intended.

Lastly, plaintiff's claim for a breach of implied warranty of fitness
for a particular purpose, N.M. Stat. Ann. §2-315 (1978), cannot withstand summary judgment because the plaintiff has admitted that, at the
time she purchased the automobile neither she nor her husband gave
any particular thought to the trunk mechanism. Deposition of Connie
Daniell at 15 (May 25, 1983). Plaintiff has admitted that she did not
even think about getting out from inside of the trunk when purchasing
the vehicle. Id. at 16. Plaintiff did not rely on the seller's skill or judgment to select or furnish an automobile suitable for the unfortunate
purpose for which the plaintiff used it.

Wherefore,

It is ordered that defendant's Motion for Summary Judgment is
granted.

QUESTION

Would the court have reached the same result if the plaintiff had
been accidentally trapped in the trunk?[1]   N O

2. Fitness for a Particular Purpose   (2 - 315)

Where the buyer wants to use the goods for something beyond
their *ordinary* purpose, a warranty of merchantability is not enough.

---

1. In 1998, during a three-week period, eleven children died from being locked
inside automobile trunks. As a consequence of these and similar accidents, the
National Highway Traffic Safety Administration has required that all automobiles
manufactured after September 1, 2001, have an interior release mechanism in the
trunk.

But the buyer may be able to sue for breach of the implied warranty of fitness for a particular purpose if the buyer can satisfy all of the elements of §2-315. Read the section and its Official Comment.

PROBLEM 24

When Christopher Wren finished building a recreation room in his basement, he wanted a heater for it. He saw an ad for the A-1 Hotblast Heater, which seemed to be what he needed. A good friend of Wren's named Inigo Jones ran a nearby appliance store. Wren went there and told Jones that he wanted the A-1 Hotblast Heater for the new room. Jones knew the room well; he had helped build it. When the heater arrived, it worked perfectly, but it simply did not have the capacity to heat the room. May Wren sue Jones for breach of either §2-314 or §2-315? See Comment 5 to §2-315. See Englebreacht v. W.D. Brannan & Sons, Inc., 501 S.W.2d 707, 13 U.C.C. Rep. Serv. 1015 (Tex. Civ. App. 1973).

PROBLEM 25

Harold Thumbs went to the Easy Paint Store and bought a can of green paint, which the store mixed on the premises from various pigments. Harold used the paint on his dining room walls, but due to a miscalculation on his part, he ran out when he was half finished. He took the empty paint can back to the store. He told the clerk that he was only half done with the job and needed another can, which the clerk promptly mixed and sold him. Harold finished the painting and then noticed two things: (1) the dried paint gave off an offensive odor, and (2) the paint from the second can did not match the first. What cause(s) of action does he have?

PROBLEM 26

Donald Souse ordered a martini at the Tired Executives Club. When he bit into the olive, he cracked his new $2,000 dentures on a pit. Is there a cause of action under either §2-314 or §2-315? See Hochberg v. O'Donnell's Restaurant, Inc., 272 A.2d 846, 8 U.C.C. Rep. Serv. 674 (D.C. 1971).

Courts faced with this last problem (harmful substances in food) have split into two camps: those that deny liability if the object is a *natural substance*, as opposed to a *foreign object*, and those that permit recovery even where the consumer is injured by a natural substance as long as the biter's "reasonable expectation" is that it would have been removed. The problem reoccurs in the cases as gourmands encounter stones in cherry pies, pits in olives, or, as in the classic case below, bones in fish. See Annot., 7 A.L.R.2d 1027.

Webster v. Blue Ship Tea Room, Inc.

Massachusetts Supreme Judicial Court, 1964
347 Mass. 421, 198 N.E.2d 309, 2 U.C.C. Rep. Serv. 161

REARDON, J. This is a case which by its nature evokes earnest study not only of the law but also of the culinary traditions of the Commonwealth which bear so heavily upon its outcome. It is an action to recover damages for personal injuries sustained by reason of a breach of implied warranty of food served by the defendant in its restaurant. An auditor, whose findings of fact were not to be final, found for the plaintiff. On a retrial in the Superior Court before a judge and jury, in which the plaintiff testified, the jury returned a verdict for her. The defendant is here on exceptions to the refusal of the judge (1) to strike certain portions of the auditor's report, (2) to direct a verdict for the defendant, and (3) to allow the defendant's motion for the entry of a verdict in its favor under leave reserved.

The jury could have found the following facts: On Saturday, April 25, 1959, about 1 P.M., the plaintiff, accompanied by her sister and her aunt, entered the Blue Ship Tea Room operated by the defendant. The group was seated at a table and supplied with menus.

This restaurant, which the plaintiff characterized as "quaint," was located in Boston "on the third floor of an old building in T Wharf which overlooks the ocean."

The plaintiff, who had been born and brought up in New England (a fact of some consequence), ordered clam chowder and crabmeat salad. Within a few minutes she received tidings to the effect that "there was no more clam chowder," whereupon she ordered a cup of fish chowder. Presently, there was set before her "a small bowl of fish chowder." She had previously enjoyed a breakfast about 9 A.M. which had given her no difficulty. "The fish chowder contained haddock, potatoes, milk, water and seasoning. The chowder was milky in color and not clear. The haddock and potatoes were in chunks" (also a fact of consequence). "She agitated it a little with the spoon and observed that it was a fairly full bowl. . . . It was hot when she got it, but she did not tip it with her spoon because it was hot . . . but stirred it in an up and under motion. She denied that she did this because she was looking for something, but it was rather because she wanted an even distribution of fish and potatoes." "She started to eat it, alternating between the chowder and crackers which were on the table with . . . [some] rolls. She ate about 3 or 4 spoonfuls then stopped. She looked at the spoonfuls as she was eating. She saw equal parts of liquid, potato and fish as she spooned it into her mouth. She did not see anything unusual about it. After 3 or 4 spoonfuls she was aware that something had lodged in her throat because she couldn't swallow and couldn't clear her throat by gulping and she could feel it." This misadventure led to two esophagoscopies at the Massachusetts General Hospital, in the second of which, on April 27, 1959, a fish bone was found and removed. The sequence of events produced injury to the plaintiff which was not insubstantial.

We must decide whether a fish bone lurking in a fish chowder, about the ingredients of which there is no other complaint, constitutes a breach of implied warranty under applicable provisions of the Uniform Commercial Code, the annotations to which are not helpful on this point. As the judge put it in his charge, "Was the fish chowder fit to be eaten and wholesome? . . . [N]obody is claiming that the fish itself wasn't wholesome. . . . But the bone of contention here—I don't mean that for a pun—but was this fish bone a foreign substance that made the fish chowder unwholesome or not fit to be eaten?"

The plaintiff has vigorously reminded us of the high standards imposed by this court where the sale of food is involved (see Flynn v. First Natl. Stores Inc., 296 Mass. 521, 523) and has made reference to cases involving stones in beans (Friend v. Childs Dining Hall Co., 231 Mass. 65), trichinae in pork (Holt v. Mann, 294 Mass. 21, 22), and to certain other cases, here and elsewhere, serving to bolster her contention of breach of warranty.

The defendant asserts that here was a native New Englander eating fish chowder in a "quaint" Boston dining place where she had been before; that "[f]ish chowder, as it is served and enjoyed by New Englanders, is a hearty dish, originally designed to satisfy the appetites of our seamen and fishermen"; that "[t]his court knows well that we are not talking of some insipid broth as is customarily served to convalescents." We are asked to rule in such fashion that no chef is forced "to reduce the pieces of fish in the chowder to minuscule size in an effort to ascertain if they contained any pieces of bone." "In so ruling," we are told (in the defendant's brief), "the court will not only uphold its reputation for legal knowledge and acumen, but will, as loyal sons of Massachusetts, save our world-renowned fish chowder from degenerating into an insipid broth containing the mere essence of its former stature as a culinary masterpiece." Notwithstanding these passionate entreaties we are bound to examine with detachment the nature of fish chowder and what might happen to it under varying interpretations of the Uniform Commercial Code.

Chowder is an ancient dish preexisting even "the appetites of our seamen and fishermen." It was perhaps the common ancestor of the "more refined cream soups, purees, and bisques." Berolzheimer, The American Woman's Cook Book (Publisher's Guild Inc., New York, 1941) p.176. The word "chowder" comes from the French "chaudiere," meaning a "cauldron" or "pot." "In the fishing villages of Brittany . . . 'faire la chaudiere' means to supply a cauldron in which is cooked a mess of fish and biscuit with some savoury condiments, a hodgepodge contributed by the fishermen themselves, each of whom in return receives his share of the prepared dish. The Breton fishermen probably carried the custom to Newfoundland, long famous for its chowder, whence it has spread to Nova Scotia, New Brunswick, and New England." A New England Dictionary (MacMillan and Co., 1893) p.386. Our literature over the years abounds in references not only to the delights of chowder but also to its manufacture. A namesake of the plaintiff, Daniel Webster, had a recipe for fish chowder which has survived into a number of modern cookbooks[2] and in which the removal of fish bones is not mentioned at all. One old time recipe recited in the New English Dictionary study defines chowder as "A dish made of fresh fish (esp. cod) or clams, stewed with slices of pork or bacon, onions, and biscuit. Cider and champagne are sometimes

---

2. "Take a cod of ten pounds, well cleaned, leaving on the skin. Cut into pieces one and a half pounds thick, preserving the head whole. Take one and a half pounds of clear, fat salt pork, cut in thin slices. Do the same with twelve potatoes. Take the largest pot you have. Try out the pork first, then take out the pieces of pork, leaving in the drippings. Add to that three parts of water, a layer of fish, so as to cover the bottom of the pot; next a layer of potatoes, then two tablespoons of salt, 1 teaspoon of pepper, then the pork, another layer of fish, and the remainder of the potatoes. Fill the pot with water to cover the ingredients. Put over a good fire. Let the chowder boil twenty-five minutes. When this is done have a quart of boiling milk ready, and ten hard crackers split and dipped in cold water. Add milk and crackers. Let the whole boil five minutes. The chowder is then ready to be first-rate if you have followed the directions. An onion may be added if you like the flavor." "This chowder," he adds, "is suitable for a large fishing party." Wolcott, The Yankee Cook Book (Coward-McCann, Inc., New York City, 1939) p.9.

added." Hawthorne, in The House of the Seven Gables (Allyn and Bacon, Boston, 1957) p.8, speaks of "[a] codfish of sixty pounds, caught in the bay [which] had been dissolved into the rich liquid of a chowder." A chowder variant, cod "Muddle," was made in Plymouth in the 1890s by taking "a three or four pound codfish, head added. Season with salt and pepper and boil in just enough water to keep from burning. When cooked, add milk and a piece of butter." The recitation of these ancient formulae suffices to indicate that in the construction of chowders in these parts in other years, worries about fish bones played no role whatsoever. This broad outlook on chowders has persisted in more modern cookbooks. "The chowder of today is much the same as the old chowder. . . ." The American Women's Cook Book, supra, p.176. The all embracing Fannie Farmer states in a portion of her recipe, fish chowder is made with a "fish skinned, but head and tail left on. Cut fish in 2-inch pieces and set aside. Put head, tail, and backbone broken in pieces, in stewpan; add 2 cups cold water and bring slowly to boiling point. . . ." The liquor thus produced from the bones is added to the balance of the chowder. Farmer, The Boston Cooking School Cook Book (Little Brown Co., 1937) p.166.

Thus, we consider a dish which for many long years, if well made, has been made generally as outlined above. It is not too much to say that a person sitting down in New England to consume a good New England fish chowder embarks on gustatory adventure which may entail the removal of some fish bones from his bowl as he proceeds. We are not inclined to tamper with age old recipes by any amendment reflecting the plaintiff's view of the effect of the Uniform Commercial Code upon them. We are aware of the heavy body of case law involving foreign substances in food, but we sense a strong distinction between them and those relative to unwholesomeness of the food itself, e.g., tainted mackerel (Smith v. Gerrish, 256 Mass. 183), and a fish bone in a fish chowder. Certain Massachusetts cooks might cavil at the ingredients contained in the chowder in this case in that it lacked the heartening lift of salt pork. In any event, we consider that the joys of life in New England include the ready availability of fresh fish chowder. We should be prepared to cope with the hazards of fish bones, the occasional presence of which in chowders is, it seems to us, to be anticipated, and which, in the light of a hallowed tradition, do not impair their fitness or merchantability. While we are buoyed up in this conclusion by Shapiro v. Hotel Statler Corp., 132 F. Supp. 891 (S.D. Cal.), in which the bone which afflicted the plaintiff appeared in "Hot Barquette of Seafood Mornay," we know that the United States District Court of Southern California, situated as are we upon a coast, might be expected to share our views. We are most impressed, however, by Allen v. Grafton, 170 Ohio St. 249, where in Ohio, the Midwest, in a case where the plaintiff was injured by a piece of oyster shell in an order of fried oysters, Mr. Justice Taft (now Chief Justice) in a majority opinion held that "the possible presence of a piece of oyster shell in or attached to an oyster is so well known to anyone who eats oysters that we can say as a matter of law that one who eats oysters can reasonably anticipate and guard against eating such a piece of shell. . . ." (p.259.)

Thus, while we sympathize with the plaintiff who has suffered a peculiarly New England injury, the order must be:

Exceptions sustained.

Judgment for the defendant.

QUESTIONS

1. Is the court saying that a natural substance does not breach the warranty or that the plaintiff's reasonable expectation should have included the bone? See Phillips v. Town of West Springfield, 405 Mass. 411, 540 N.E.2d 1331, 9 U.C.C. Rep. Serv. 2d 535 (1989).

2. Would the plaintiff have recovered if she had been born and reared in South Dakota and was on her first visit to New England?

3. Would the result be the same if the plaintiff had purchased a *can* of fish chowder and encountered the bone?

PROBLEM 27

Carry Nation, on the advice of her beautician, Parker Pillsbury, bought a hair dye named "Intoxicating Fragrance" and proceeded to use it in accordance with the instructions on the package. Unfortunately the product contained alcohol, to which Ms. Nation was allergic, and she suffered considerable burn damage to her scalp and ears. When she sued the manufacturer, Harper's Hair Products, Inc., the basic defense was that only 0.5 percent of the population had this allergic reaction. Is this a good defense? See Jeneric/Pentron, Inc. v. Dillon Company, Inc., Chemichl Inc., Chemichl AG., 171 F. Supp. 2d 754, 45 U.C.C. Rep. Serv. 2d 769 (D. Conn. 2001); M. Dixon & F. Woodside, Drug Product Liability (1988); W. Freedman, Allergy and Products Liability (1965); 3 L. Frumer & M. Friedmen, Products Liability §49.01 (1988); Comment, Strict Liability and Allergic Drug Reactions, 47 Miss. L.J. 526 (1976); Annot., 53 A.L.R.3d 298.

C. Warranty Disclaimers and Limitations

1. Disclaiming Express Warranties

The drafters of the Uniform Commercial Code thought that it was basically unfair for a seller to create an express warranty and then try to disclaim it, so they drafted §2-316(1) in such a way as to make disclaimer of an express warranty virtually impossible. Read it. The proper way to avoid liability for an express warranty is *to not make it in the first place.* Note that express warranties are created by *affirmative* seller conduct. The seller must take out an ad, publish a booklet, say something orally about the product, or point to a sample or model, or the warranty will never arise. Having done one of these things and created buyer expectations that the product will comply with the representations made, the seller must live with the liability assumed. See Official Comment 4 to §2-313; Travis v. Washington Horse Breeders Assn., 111 Wash. 2d 396, 759 P.2d 418, 6 U.C.C. Rep. Serv. 2d 1093 (1988).

Bell Sports, Inc. v. Yarusso

Supreme Court of Delaware, 2000
759 A.2d 582, 42 U.C.C. Rep. Serv. 2d 714

WALSH, Justice:

This is an appeal from a Superior Court denial of judgment as a matter of law, or alternatively, for a new trial following an award of damages in a product liability action. The defendant-appellant claims error on the part of the trial judge in ruling on the qualifications of plaintiff's expert witnesses and in permitting the substance of that testimony to establish a jury question on claims for breach of warranty. The appellant further asserts that the jury verdict was internally inconsistent and that the Superior Court should have declared a mistrial after discharging a juror for cause during trial. Upon careful review of the record, we conclude that the Superior Court did not abuse its discretion in permitting the testimony of plaintiff's experts nor in submitting the issues of breach of warranty to the jury. We further conclude that the jury's verdict did not lack consistency and that the refusal to grant a mistrial was not error.

I

On October 20, 1991, Brian J. Yarusso ("Yarusso"), then 22 years of age, was riding his off-road motorcycle[3] at a dirt motocross track located off Church Road in Newark, Delaware. Yarusso was wearing a full complement of safety equipment in addition to the helmet that is the subject of this dispute. While traveling over a series of dirt moguls, or bumps, Yarusso hit one of the moguls in such a way that he was catapulted over the handlebars of the motorcycle. He landed on his head, flipped over and came to rest face down in the dirt. As a result of his fall, Yarusso sustained a burst fracture of the C5 vertebral body and was rendered a quadriplegic.[4]

Yarusso filed suit in the Superior Court against Bell Sports, Inc. ("Bell"), the manufacturer of the Bell Moto 5 helmet he was wearing at the time of the accident. Yarusso's suit against Bell was predicated on a claim that the enhanced injuries he suffered were the proximate result of a defect in the helmet's design. The Bell Moto-5 is a full-face motocross helmet that was designed for off-road use. It complies with federal Department of Transportation ("DOT") standards and is also certified by the Snell Foundation, a leading worldwide helmet research and testing laboratory. The helmet is constructed of a fiberglass outer shell, an inner crushable liner, and a retention system consisting of a chinstrap and D-ring pull-tab. While all three of these components are designed to interact, the inner liner is considered the most important safety feature of the helmet. The expanded polystyrene material of which this liner is primarily constructed is designed to compress upon contact with a solid object.

Yarusso's complaint contained alternative grounds for recovery. He alleged negligence in the design and construction of the helmet, breach of express warranties and breach of an implied warranty of merchantability. Yarusso's express warranty claim arose from specific

3. "Off-road" motorcycles are equipped with motors, tires, seats and suspension components specifically designed to function effectively under adverse riding conditions typical of motocross tracks, woods, and fields. They are generally much lighter in weight than motorcycles designed for street use, have a higher degree of suspension clearance/compliance, and are usually not equipped with horns, lights, and other features required for legal street operation.

4. Dr. Joseph Cusick, a neurosurgeon, described Yarusso's specific injuries. He testified that Yarusso's C5 vertebral body sustained major damage due to a "severe axiocompression load, usually . . . without much extension or flexion." The magnitude of the load was sufficient to crack the bone, push the spinal disk into the soft bone, and "explode" the disc into the spinal cord and some of the other disks.

textual representations in the helmet's accompanying owner's manual (the "manual"), the relevant portions of which are as follows (emphasis printed in manual also reproduced below):

> Five Year Limited Warranty: Any Bell helmet found by the factory to be defective in materials or workmanship within five years from the date of purchase will be repaired or replaced at the option of the manufacturer, free of charge, when received at the factory, freight prepaid. . . . This warranty is expressly in lieu of all other warranties, and any implied warranties of merchantability or fitness for a particular purpose created hereby, are limited in duration to the same duration as the express warranty herein. Bell shall not be liable for any incidental or consequential damages. . . .
>
> Introduction: Your new Moto-5 helmet is another in the long line of innovative off-road helmets from Bell. . . . [T]he primary function of a helmet is to reduce the harmful effects of a blow to the head. However, it is important to recognize that the wearing of a helmet is not an assurance of absolute protection. NO HELMET CAN PROTECT THE WEARER AGAINST ALL FORESEEABLE IMPACTS.
>
> Helmet Performance: The Moto-5 is designed to absorb the force of a blow first by spreading it over as wide an area of the outer shell as possible, and second by the crushing of the non-resilient inner liner. Damage to the helmet after an impact is not a sign of any defect in the helmet design or construction. It is exactly what the helmet is designed to do.
>
> NOTICE: No helmet can protect the user from all foreseeable impacts. To obtain the maximum protection offered by any helmet, it must fit firmly on the head and the chinstrap must be securely fastened.

Yarusso testified at trial that he purchased this particular helmet based on the specific assertions, quoted above, that "[t]he primary function of a helmet is to reduce the harmful effects of a blow to the head."

Yarusso's implied warranty of merchantability claim arose out of his contention that the helmet was not merchantable because it was sold as an off- road helmet but was designed to function for "on-road" use. Because the helmet met DOT street helmet standards, Yarusso claimed that it was actually designed with a very stiff liner that would effectively function for on-road use but would not protect a rider against foreseeable off-road falls, where the impact surface could conceivably be softer.

A pivotal factual issue at trial was whether the helmet liner properly crushed, as designed, at the time Yarusso's head impacted the ground after his fall. Yarusso claimed that the injuries to his neck were caused by the stiffness or density of the liner material at the helmet crown. At trial, he offered expert testimony by Maurice Fox ("Fox"), a safety consultant who had been employed by a helmet manufacturer during the 1970s. Fox opined that Yarusso's helmet sustained the majority of the fall's impact at its crown where the liner was too dense to crush sufficiently, thereby transmitting excessive force to Yarusso's neck, resulting in his paralysis. Fox's testimony however, was directed primarily at Yarusso's negligence claim against Bell, which the jury subsequently rejected.

Joseph Cusick, M.D. ("Cusick"), a neurological expert, similarly testified that the neck injuries sustained by Yarusso were consistent with impact at the top, or crown, of the helmet. Cusick further testified that a 20-30% reduction of force to Yarusso's body would have been sufficient to avoid injury because his body would have been able to withstand this lower level of force.

Richard Stalnaker, Ph.D. ("Stalnaker"), a biomechanical engineer, also testified on behalf of Yarusso and largely affirmed Fox's opinion. His testimony was crucial in the jury's determination that Bell had breached express and implied warranties. Stalnaker determined that the force of Yarusso's impact with the ground was equivalent to 60 foot pounds, and that adequate crush of the helmet liner would have reduced it significantly to avert injury. Although Stalnaker modified the analytical process used to reconstruct the accident to coincide with that presented by Bell's expert reconstruction witness at trial, Bell's counsel rejected an opportunity to delay the trial and requested only a mistrial. Because the trial judge determined that the factual foundation for Stalnaker's testimony was unchanged despite his use of an alternative analytical, she denied the motion for mistrial leaving the matter for attack through cross-examination.

Bell offered its own expert testimony at trial disputing the helmet's point of impact from the accident and asserting the inability of any helmet to protect its user from severe neck injuries. The principal designer of the helmet, James Sundahl ("Sundahl"), testified that any helmet must be designed to protect its user from a multitude of accident types. He further opined that in circumstances involving a helmet's impact with a soft surface, the surface itself, rather than the helmet, absorbs a greater portion of the energy. When questioned about the representation in the helmet's manual, Sundahl testified that it was "wrong."

James McElhaney, Ph.D. ("McElhaney"), a professor of biomechanics at Duke University, testified for Bell and disputed Yarusso's contention that the helmet was impacted at its crown. McElhaney testified that the front of Yarusso's helmet liner was crushed in a fashion indicating a substantial blow to that area. Both Sundahl and McElhaney presented evidence of industry-wide research to the effect that no helmet can offer "any significant protection of the neck because the mass of the torso is so much more than the energy levels that a helmet can manage." Bell's experts claimed that this helmet and helmets in general are designed to protect users from head and brain injuries and the helmet in this case did precisely that.

Upon the conclusion of Yarusso's case, he abandoned his failure to warn claim. At the close of all the evidence, Bell moved for judgment as a matter of law as to liability. The trial court granted judgment as a matter of law on Yarusso's breach of implied warranty for a particular purpose claim, but denied Bell's motion on the remaining counts. The jury was then charged on the remaining claims of negligence, breach of implied warranty of merchantability and breach of express warranty.

On the second day of jury deliberations, one juror notified the trial court that he had reviewed outside information regarding motorcycle helmets in connection with securing a motorcycle licensing examiner's certificate. The jury also notified the court that they were deadlocked. The trial judge subsequently interrogated the juror who had disclosed his outside knowledge out of the presence of the remaining jurors. The trial judge determined that while the juror had not yet shared this extraneous information with other jurors, he had violated the direct instruction to decide the case solely from the evidence presented. The trial judge dismissed the juror prompting a motion from Bell for a mistrial, which was denied. Because both parties had agreed at the outset of the trial to accept a jury of eleven members, the remaining jurors were permitted to deliberate.

Through specific answers to interrogatories, the jury ultimately found that Bell was not negligent, but had breached an express or implied warranty, which proximately caused Yarusso's enhanced injury. Yarusso was awarded $1,812,000 in damages. Bell objected that the verdict was inconsistent and renewed its motions for judgment as a matter of law or alternatively for a new trial on liability only, all of which were denied by the Superior Court. This appeal followed. . . .

III

By its verdict, the jury specifically determined that Bell had not negligently designed the Moto-5 helmet but that Bell had breached "an express or implied warranty" when it sold the helmet and that "conduct proximately caused Brian Yarusso to suffer enhanced injuries." Bell argues on appeal that Yarusso failed, as a matter of law, to establish an evidentiary basis for recovery under either express or implied warranty and the trial court should have granted judgment in its favor as to those claims.

Preliminarily, we note that the jury was permitted to find liability under alternative forms of breach of warranty, express or implied, without differentiating between the two. Bell did not object to the warranty claims being submitted in that format and, thus, the verdict may be sustained if there is record and legal support for recovery under either theory.

A.

The statutory basis for a claim for damages based on breach of an express warranty arising out of a sale of goods under Delaware law is found in this State's counterpart of the Uniform Commercial Code, Title 6, section 2-313 [which the Court quoted].

The official commentary to that section under the U.C.C. indicates that the drafters intended its warranty provisions to be construed and applied liberally in favor of a buyer of goods. See U.C.C. §2-313 cmt. 1 (1977) ("Express warranties rest on 'dickered' aspects of the individual bargain, and go so clearly to the essence of that bargain that words of a disclaimer in a form are repugnant to the basic dickered terms."); U.C.C. §2-313 cmt. 3 ("In actual practice affirmations of fact made by a seller about the goods during a bargain are regarded as part of the description of those goods; hence no particular reliance on such statements need be shown in order to weave them into the fabric of the agreement."); U.C.C. §2-313 cmt. 4 ("[A] contract is normally a contract for a sale of something describable and described. A clause generally disclaiming 'all warranties, express or implied' cannot reduce the seller's obligation with respect to such description. . . ."). The language of the U.C.C.'s official commentary may be applied by analogy to the sale of goods governed by 6 Del. C. §2-313 in the reconciliation of any ensuing express warranty disputes. Thus, Bell's argument in this case that the express warranty terms in the manual are strictly limited to the "Five Year Limited Warranty" section, which also contained a purportedly effective disclaimer of those terms, is unfounded.

Formal wording is not necessary to create a warranty and a seller does not have to express any specific intention to create one. See Pack & Process, Inc. v. Celotex Corp., Del. Super., 503 A.2d 646, 658-59 (1985). Here the additional terms found in the manual's "Introduction" and "Helmet Performance" sections (stating that "the primary function of a helmet is to reduce the harmful effects of a blow to the head . . ." and ". . . the [helmet] is designed to absorb the force of a blow by spreading it over as wide an area of the outer shell as possible . . .") are textual representations constituting affirmations of fact upon which a buyer is entitled to rely. While this Court does not appear to have specifically addressed the issue, other courts have held that express warranties can arise from similar textual representations found in owners' manuals even where not specifically labeled as such. See e.g., Kinlaw v. Long Mfg. N.C., Inc., 298 N.C. 494, 259 S.E.2d 552, 557 (1979); Hawkins Constr. Co. v. Matthews Co., 190 Neb. 546, 209 N.W.2d 643, 654-55 (1973).

The restrictive provision of 6 Del. C. §2-316(1), renders Bell's effort to disclaim any express warranties in the manual's "Five Year Limited Warranty" ineffective as a matter of law. See U.C.C. §2-316(1) cmt. 1 (stating that "this section . . . seeks to protect a buyer from unexpected and unbargained language of disclaimer by denying effect to such language when inconsistent with language of express warranty. . . ."). While the manual contains disclaimers warning potential users that the helmet cannot prevent all injuries, other representations were made to assure a potential buyer that the helmet's liner was designed to reduce the harmful effects of a blow to the head. Those representations constituted essential elements of a valid express warranty that may not be effectively disclaimed as a matter of law. See Jensen v. Seigel Mobile Homes Group, 105 Idaho 189, 668 P.2d 65, 71-72 (1983) (holding that one principle of the law of warranty is to hold a seller responsible for its representations and assuring that a buyer receives that which he bargained for).

Bell argues that even if an express warranty was created and not effectively disclaimed here, the manual's textual representations promise only to prevent injuries to the head, not to a user's neck. Furthermore, Bell argues, the helmet's liner did crush as designed, thereby precluding a finding that the warranty was breached. Yarusso counters this argument by pointing out that injuries to the neck may logically follow a blow to the head, the helmet's liner did not sufficiently crush to prevent his injury and, as a result, he did not get what he bargained for. Upon review of the evidence, much of which was admittedly supplied by testimony of Yarusso's experts, the jury came to a logical conclusion that an express warranty was made in the helmet's manual. Upon consideration of this representation in relation to the specific facts of this case, they also concluded that the warranty was breached. In view of the evidence presented by the experts for both parties on the relationship between the helmet's design and the risk of neck injury, a factual predicate existed for the jury to determine whether there was a basis for recovery under the express warranty claim. The Superior Court did not err in submitting that issue to the jury.

B.

Our holding sustaining the jury's verdict on the claim of breach of express warranty renders an in-depth consideration of Bell's implied warranty arguments unnecessary, since the jury was permitted to find a breach of warranty on alternative grounds. The Superior Court in rejecting Bell's post-trial motions also declined to rule on the merits of Bell's attack on the implied warranty finding in view of the jury's finding of liability on the express warranty claim. We also are not required to address Bell's contention that Yarusso was obligated, as a matter of law, to present evidence of a safer alternative design. See Mazda Motor Corp. v. Lindahl, Del. Supr., 706 A.2d 526, 530 (1998). We note, however, that Yarusso's experts never claimed that a helmet can reduce the probability of a user's neck injury in all circumstances, and they were not required to present evidence that a helmet could be designed to achieve this. Expert evidence was presented, however, that a helmet could be designed with a softer liner that would, in theory, limit the amount of force placed on the user's neck, thereby reducing the probability of partial-load direct downward neck injuries, particularly upon impact with harder surfaces. There was, thus, a sufficient factual predicate for submission of the implied warranty claim to the jury.

IV

In a related vein, Bell next argues that the jury's finding for Yarusso on breach of express and implied warranties is inconsistent with its finding that Bell was not negligent. Because the jury found no product defect leading to negligent conduct on Bell's part, it could not have properly found, the argument runs, that a defect existed in the helmet upon which any warranty claims relied. See Ruffin v. Shaw Indus., Inc., 4th Cir., 149 F.3d 294, 301 (1998) (holding that the requirements of both actions are nearly alike and that a finding on one claim often "applies equally" to the other); Prentis v. Yale Mfg. Co., 421 Mich. 670, 365 N.W.2d 176, 186 (1984) (both actions "involve identical evidence and require proof of exactly the same elements"). In essence, Bell contends that because its product was not defective, a verdict in favor of Yarusso on warranty and negligence claims was precluded.

A claim for breach of warranty, express or implied, is conceptually distinct from a negligence claim because the latter focuses on the manufacturer's conduct, whereas a breach of warranty claim evaluates the product itself. See Cline v. Prowler Indus. of Md., Inc., Del. Supr., 418 A.2d 968, 978, n.19 (1980) (the focus of a negligence claim is the manufacturer's conduct and the breach of an accepted standard of conduct); Borel v. Fibreboard Paper Prod. Corp., 5th Cir., 493 F.2d 1076, 1094 (1973) (in a products liability case with inconsistent verdicts, it is within the jury's prerogative so long as evidence supports the finding); Community Television Serv. v. Dresser Indus., Inc., D.S.D., 435 F. Supp. 214, 216 (1977) (jury could find defendant neither negligent nor strictly liable while finding as a matter of law that representations in a brochure created an express warranty that defendant breached). Based on the foregoing authorities, we find no fatal inconsistency between the jury's verdict negating negligence but finding breach of warranty. . . .

The judgment of the Superior Court is AFFIRMED.

PROBLEM 28

When Portia Moot went to buy a new car, she asked the salesman how many miles to the gallon it would get. He replied that it would get "between 30 and 35 M.P.G. in the city and 40 to 45 on the highway." Delighted, she bought the car. The very best the car ever did, even in highway driving, was 27 M.P.G., and Portia was upset. When she threatened a lawsuit, the dealership pointed out the following three clauses in the contract she had signed that it relied on to avoid liability. This contract said nothing about miles per gallon of gas. In your opinion is there any way around these clauses?

(1) "This is the entire contract, and there are no other matters agreed to by the parties that are not contained herein."

(2) "There are no other express or implied warranties except those contained herein."

(3) "No salesperson has the authority to give express warranties other than those contained herein." (As to this last clause, see White & Summers §12-4, and the brief reference to the matter in Official Comment 2 to §2-316.)

2. Disclaiming Implied Warranties

In contrast to express warranties, implied warranties are much more easily disclaimed. Since they are created by the legislature of the enacting state and not by seller conduct, there is less unfairness in their destruction as long as the seller or the circumstances alert the buyer to the disclaimer. Read §§2-316(2) and 2-316(3) carefully.

Cate v. Dover Corp.

Texas Supreme Court, 1990
790 S.W.2d 559, 12 U.C.C. Rep. Serv. 2d 47

Doggett, J. We consider the enforceability of a disclaimer of implied warranties. The trial court upheld the disclaimer and granted summary judgment in favor of Dover Corporation. The court of appeals affirmed. 776 S.W.2d 680. We reverse the judgment of the court of appeals and remand this cause to the trial court for further proceedings consistent with this opinion.

In September 1984, Edward Cate, doing business as Cate's Transmission Service, purchased from Beech Tire Mart three lifts manufactured and designed by Dover Corporation to elevate vehicles for maintenance. Despite repairs made by Beech and Dover, the lifts never functioned properly. Dover contends that Cate's subsequent claim against it for breach of the implied warranty of merchantability is barred by a disclaimer contained within a written, express warranty.

This warranty is set forth on a separate page headed in blue half inch block print, with the heading: "YOU CAN TAKE ROTARY'S NEW 5-YEAR WARRANTY AND TEAR IT APART." The statement is followed by bold black type stating, "And, when you are through, it'll be just as solid as the No. 1 lift company in America, Rotary." The text of the warranty itself is in black type, contained within double blue lines, and appears under the blue three-eighths inch block print heading "WARRANTY." The disclaimer of implied warranties, although contained in a separate paragraph within the warranty text, is in the same typeface, size, and color as the remainder of the text.

An implied warranty of merchantability arises in a contract for the sale of goods unless expressly excluded or modified by conspicuous language. Tex. Bus. & Com. Code Ann. §§2.314(a), 2.316(b) (Vernon 1968). Whether a particular disclaimer is conspicuous is a question of law to be determined by the following definition:

A term or clause is conspicuous when it is so written that a reasonable person against whom it is to operate ought to have noticed it. A printed heading in capitals (as: NON-NEGOTIABLE BILL OF LADING) is conspicuous. Language in a body of a form is conspicuous if it is larger

or of other contrasting type or color. But in a telegram, any stated term is conspicuous.

Id. §1.201(10). Further explanation is provided by comment 10 thereto:

> This [section] is intended to indicate some of the methods of making a term attention-calling. But the test is whether attention can reasonably be expected to be called to it.

In interpreting this language, Dover argues that a lesser standard of conspicuousness should apply to a disclaimer made to a merchant, such as Cate. Admittedly, an ambiguity is created by the requirement that disclaimer language be conspicuous to "a reasonable person *against whom it is to operate.*" Comment 10, however, clearly contemplated an objective standard, stating the test as "whether attention can reasonably be expected to be called to it."

We then turn to an application of an objective standard of conspicuousness to Dover's warranty. The top forty percent of the written warranty is devoted to extolling its virtues. The warranty itself, contained within double blue lines, is then set out in five paragraphs in normal black type under the heading "WARRANTY." Nothing distinguishes the third paragraph, which contains the exclusionary language. It is printed in the same typeface, size and color as the rest of the warranty text. Although the warranty in its entirety may be considered conspicuous, the disclaimer is hidden among attention-getting language purporting to grant the best warranty available. . . .

Although this is a case of first impression in Texas, the facts here parallel those reviewed in other states. In Massey-Ferguson, Inc. v. Utley, 439 S.W.2d 57, 59 (Ky. Ct. App. 1969), a disclaimer hidden under the heading "WARRANTY and AGREEMENT" was found not to be conspicuous:

> It is true that the *heading* was in large, bold-face type, but there was nothing to suggest that an exclusion was being made; on the contrary, the words of the headings indicated a *making* of warranties rather than a *disclaimer.*

(Emphasis in original.) Similarly, in Hartman v. Jensen's, Inc., 289 S.E.2d 648 (S.C. 1982), the court found that placing a disclaimer under the bold heading "Terms of Warranty" failed to alert the consumer to the fact that an exclusion was intended. Dover's disclaimer similarly fails to attract the attention of a reasonable person and is not conspicuous. . . .

Dover argues that even an inconspicuous disclaimer should be given effect because Cate had actual knowledge of it at the time of the purchase. Because the object of the conspicuousness requirement is to protect the buyer from surprise and an unknowing waiver of his or her rights, inconspicuous language is immaterial when the buyer has actual knowledge of the disclaimer. This knowledge can result from the buyer's prior dealings with the seller, or by the seller specifically bringing the inconspicuous waiver to the buyer's attention. The Code appears to recognize that actual knowledge of the disclaimer overrides the question of conspicuousness. For example, §2.316(b) does not mandate a written disclaimer of the implied warranty of merchantability but clearly provides that an oral disclaimer may be effective.[5] Similarly, §2.316(c)(3) allows an implied warranty to be excluded or modified by methods other than a conspicuous writing: course of dealing, course of performance, or usage of trade. When the buyer is not surprised by the disclaimer, insisting on compliance with the conspicuousness requirement serves no purpose. See R. Anderson, Uniform Commercial Code §2-316:49-50 (1983). The extent of a buyer's knowledge of a disclaimer of the implied warranty of merchantability is thus clearly relevant to a determination of its enforceability. See Singleton v. LaCoure, 712 S.W.2d 757, 759 (Tex. App. Houston [14th Dist.] 1986, *writ ref'd n.r.e.*) (relying in part on buyer's acknowledgement to enforce disclaimer). The seller has the burden of proving the buyer's actual knowledge of the disclaimer.

As this is a summary judgment case, the issue on appeal is whether Dover met its burden by establishing that there exists no genuine issue of material fact thereby entitling it to judgment as a matter of law. City of Houston v. Clear Creek Basin Authority, 589 S.W.2d 671, 678 (Tex. 1979). All doubts as to the existence of a genuine issue of material fact are resolved against the movant, and we must view the evidence in the light most favorable to the Petitioner. Great American Reserve Ins. Co. v. San Antonio Plumbing Supply Co., 391 S.W.2d 41, 47 (Tex. 1965). In

5. Tex. Bus. & Com. Code §2.136, comment 1 (section seeks to protect buyer from unexpected and unbargained language of disclaimer by permitting exclusion of implied warranties only by conspicuous language or other circumstances which protect buyer from surprise); see also Weintraub, Disclaimer of Warranties and Limitation of Damages for Breach of Warranty Under the UCC, 53 Tex. L. Rev. 60, 66 (1974); J. White & R. Summers, Uniform Commercial Code §12-5, n.76 (2d ed. 1980) (seller may effectively disclaim by orally explaining inconspicuous written disclaimer, provided word "merchantability" used).

support of its claim that Cate had actual knowledge of the disclaimer, Dover relies on Cate's deposition testimony, as follows:

> *Q:* Do you know, or do you remember what kinds of warranties you received when you bought the lifts?
>
> *A:* I may be wrong, but I think it was a five year warranty.
>
> *Q:* What was your understanding of that warranty?
>
> *A:* Any problems would be taken care of within the five year period.
>
> *Q:* Do you know if that warranty was from Beech Equipment, or from Dover?
>
> *A:* I believe it was from Dover.
>
> *Q:* Did you receive any written documentation in regard to that warranty?
>
> *A:* Yes, ma'am.

Although it is clear that Cate understood the warranty to extend for only five years, it is not clear that he understood any other limitations or exclusions. Merely providing a buyer a copy of documents containing an inconspicuous disclaimer does not establish actual knowledge. Dover has failed to establish that as a matter of law Cate had actual knowledge of the disclaimer.

We hold that, to be enforceable, a written disclaimer of the implied warranty of merchantability made in connection with a sale of goods must be conspicuous to a reasonable person. We further hold that such a disclaimer contained in text undistinguished in typeface, size or color within a form purporting to grant a warranty is not conspicuous, and is unenforceable unless the buyer has actual knowledge of the disclaimer. For the reasons stated herein, we reverse the judgment of the court of appeals and remand to the trial court for further proceedings consistent with this opinion.

SPEARS, J. concurs and files a separate opinion (in which MAUZY, J. joins).

RAY, J. files a concurring and dissenting opinion.

SPEARS, J. Although I concur in the court's opinion, I write separately to declare that the time has come for the legislature to consider the realities of the marketplace and prohibit all disclaimers of the implied warranties of merchantability and fitness.

These implied warranties, created by common-law courts long before the adoption of the UCC, developed to protect purchasers from losses suffered because of "the frustration of their expectations about the worth, efficacy, or desirability" of a product. W. Keeton, Prosser and Keeton on the Law of Torts §95A (5th ed. 1984). Implication of these warranties into every goods contract, without regard to the parties' actual assent to their terms, served "to police, to prevent, and to remedy" unfair consumer transactions. Llewellyn, On Warranty of Quality, and Society, 39 Colum. L. Rev. 699, 699 (1936); Humber v. Morton, 426 S.W.2d 554, 557-558 (Tex. 1968). These implied warranties also serve other important purposes: they create incentives to produce and market higher quality products; they discourage shoddy workmanship and unethical trade practices; and they place responsibility on those who profit from the sale of goods, have the greatest control over the products, and are better able to bear the risk of loss. See *Humber*, 426 S.W.2d at 562; Decker & Sons v. Capp, 139 Tex. 609, 610, 164 S.W.2d 828, 829 (1942). Section 2-316 of the U.C.C., however, subverts all of these purposes by giving sellers almost unlimited license to disclaim implied warranties.

We live in an age when sellers of goods "saturate the marketplace and all of our senses" with the most extraordinary claims about the worth of their products. Anderson, The Supreme Court of Texas and the Duty to Read the Contracts You Sign, 15 Tex. Tech L. Rev. 517, 544 (1984); Henningsen v. BloomField Motors, Inc., 161 A.2d 69, 84 (N.J. 1960). Yet, the same sellers under the carte blanche granted them by §2-316 of the U.C.C. refuse to guarantee and indeed expressly disclaim that their products are merchantable or even fit for their intended purposes. Under §2-316, not much is actually required for an effective disclaimer. To disclaim the implied warranty of merchantability the seller need only include the word "merchantability" in a conspicuous fashion. Tex. Bus. & Com. Code Ann. §2-316(b) (Vernon 1968). To disclaim the implied warranty of fitness the seller must use a writing and must make the disclaimer conspicuous. Id. at §2-316(2). No particular form of words is needed to disclaim an implied warranty of fitness, nor does §2-316 require the buyer to be actually aware of the disclaimer before it will be enforced. All implied warranties can be disclaimed by the mere inclusion of expressions like "as is" or "with all faults." Id. at §2-316, comment 1. Finally, as today's majority makes clear, §2-316 does not even require the disclaimer to be conspicuous if the buyer's actual knowledge of the disclaimer can be shown.

By establishing specific "requirements" for disclaimers §2-316 ostensibly "seeks to protect a buyer from unexpected and unbargained language of disclaimer." Tex. Bus. & Com. Code §2-316, comment 1 (Vernon 1968). In reality, however, §2-316 completely undermines implied warranties. Implicitly, §2-316 adopts the position that disclaimers should be enforced because society benefits when parties to a contract are allowed to set *all* the terms of their agreement. The problem with this position, and with §2-316 generally, is two-fold: it ignores the fact that governmental implication of protective terms into private contracts is commonplace (e.g., the *implied* warranties of merchantability and fitness); and, more importantly, it rests on the faulty premise that contractual disclaimers are generally freely bargained for elements of a contract.

Freedom of contract arguments generally, and §2-316 specifically, presuppose and are based on "the image of individuals meeting in the marketplace" on equal ground to negotiate the terms of a contract. Rakoff, Contracts of Adhesion: An Essay in Reconstruction, 96 Harv. L. Rev. 1174, 1216 (1983). At one time, this image may have accurately reflected marketplace realities. However, the last half of the twentieth century has witnessed "the rise of the corporation" and, increasingly, the displacement of physical persons as sellers in consumer and commercial contracts. Phillips, Unconscionability and Article 2 Implied Warranty Disclaimers, 62 Chi.-Kent L. Rev. 199, 239 (1985). This development has led to innumerable situations in which consumers deal from an unequal bargaining position, the most prominent example being the ubiquitous standard form contract which is now used by most sellers of goods and which invariably contains an implied warranty disclaimer. See Melody Home Mfg. Co. v. Barnes, 741 S.W.2d 349, 355 (Tex. 1987); *Henningsen,* 161 A.2d at 86-89; Slawson, Standard Form Contracts and Democratic Control of Lawmaking Power, 84 Harv. L. Rev. 529, 529 (1971) ("standard form contracts probably account for more than ninety-nine percent of all the contracts now made"); L. Vold, Handbook of the Law of Sales 447 (2d ed. 1959) (dramatic rise in corporate power has yielded the standard form contract whose terms are drafted by the seller and usually contain implied warranty disclaimers).

The great majority of buyers never read an implied warranty disclaimer found in a standard form contract.[6] Even when implied

---

6. See Restatement (Second) of Contracts §211, Comment b (1981):

> A party who makes regular use of a standardized form of agreement does not ordinarily expect his customers to understand or even to read the standard terms. One purpose of standardization is to eliminate bargaining over details of individual transactions, and that purpose would not be served if a substantial number of customers retained counsel and reviewed the standard terms. . . . Customers do not in fact ordinarily understand or even read the standard terms.

Id.; see also Rakoff, Contracts of Adhesion: An Essay in Reconstruction, 96 Harv. L. Rev. 1174, 1179 n.21 (1983) (citing numerous commentators who declare that standard terms not read or understood, and some empirical studies asserting same proposition);

warranty disclaimers are read, their legal significance is not generally understood. Such disclaimers include unfamiliar terminology (e.g., "implied warranty of merchantability"), and comprehending their legal effect requires one not only to understand what substantive rights are involved, but also to grasp that these rights have been lost via the disclaimer. Phillips, Unconscionability and Article 2 Implied Warranty Disclaimers, 62 Chi.-Kent L. Rev. 199, 243 (1985); see also Federal Trade Commission, Facts for Consumers (Mar. 23, 1979) (more than 35% of those surveyed mistakenly believed that an "as is" disclaimer meant the dealer would have to pay some, if not all, costs if a car broke down within 25 days of a sale). Finally, even if a buyer reads and understands an implied warranty disclaimer, chances are he will be without power to either strike these terms or "shop around" for better ones. If the buyer attempts the former, he will likely run into an employee who is unauthorized to alter the form contract; if he attempts the latter, he will likely confront a competitor who offers substantially the same form terms. *Henningsen*, 161 A.2d at 87. In short, the "marketplace reality" suggests that freedom of contract in the sale of goods is actually nonexistent; a buyer today can either take the contract with the disclaimer attached or leave it and go without the good. . . .

The realities of the modern marketplace demand that the legislature prohibit implied warranty disclaimers by repealing §2-316 of the U.C.C. Without such action, Texas courts will be forced to rely on "covert tools," such as the unconscionability provision in §2-302 or the "conspicuous" requirement in §2-316, to reach a just and fair result in disclaimer suits. When these tools are used, guidance, predictability and consistency in the law is sacrificed, while limited judicial resources are spent policing unjust bargains that could have been avoided. Were it up to the judicial branch, the courts could declare such disclaimers void as against public policy. If the legislature has the interests of Texas citizens at heart, it will repeal §2-316 because, no matter how conspicuous, such disclaimers are abusive of consumers.

MAUZY, J. joins in this concurring opinion.

RAY, J. I concur in that portion of the court's opinion requiring that a written disclaimer of the implied warranty of merchantability must be conspicuous to a reasonable person. I write separately, however, to take issue with the court's immediate erosion of that

---

Phillips, Unconscionability and Article 2 Implied Warranty Disclaimers, 62 Chi.-Kent L. Rev. 199, 243 (1985) (many sales do not involve a written sales contract that is presented before the goods change hands; usually, the disclaimer is inside the package and is not seen until after the sale is completed).

standard by permitting a showing of actual knowledge of the disclaimer to override a lack of conspicuousness.

The statute, on its face, provides for no actual knowledge exception. There is no room for judicial crafting of those omitted by the legislature. I would hold that the extent of a buyer's knowledge of a disclaimer is irrelevant to a determination of its enforceability under §2-316(b) of the U.C.C.

The effect of actual knowledge is subject to debate among leading commentators on commercial law. The purpose of the objective standard of conspicuousness adopted by the court today reflects the view that "the drafters intended a rigid adherence to the conspicuousness requirement in order to avoid arguments concerning what the parties said about the warranties at the time of the sale." J. White and R. Summers, Uniform Commercial Code §12-5 (2d ed. 1980). An absolute rule that an inconspicuous disclaimer is invalid, despite the buyer's actual knowledge, encourages sellers to make their disclaimers conspicuous, thereby reducing the need for courts to evaluate swearing matches as to actual awareness in particular cases. See W. Powers, Texas Products Liability Law §2.0723 (1989). Today's decision condemns our court to a parade of such cases.

PROBLEM 29

(a) A statement buried in the fine print of a used car purchase agreement states that "There are no express or implied warranties that are part of this sale." See §§2-316(2), 1-201(10).

(1) Are the implied warranties effectively disclaimed?

(2) If the car dealership asks you to redraft this clause so as to comply with the Code, what changes would you make in the language?

(3) What changes would you make in the physical appearance of the clause in the contract? Is it all right to put the disclaimer in a clause labeled WARRANTY? See Hartman v. Jensen's, Inc., 289 S.E.2d 648, 33 U.C.C. Rep. Serv. 889 (S.C. 1982).

(4) Can the car dealer win the legal dispute by arguing that usage of trade (§1-205) permits the burial of warranty disclaimers in the fine print? (For an annotation collecting the automobile warranty disclaimer cases, see Annot., 54 A.L.R.3d 1217.)

(b) The words AS IS are written with soap in large letters across the front windshield of the used car. See §2-316(3)(a). Is this effective to disclaim implied warranties? Express warranties? Annot., 24 A.L.R.3d

465. Must the "as is" language be conspicuous? See §2-316(3)(a); Lumber Mut. Ins. Co. v. Clarklift of Detroit, Inc., 224 Mich. App. 737, 569 N.W.2d 681, 33 U.C.C. Rep. Serv. 2d 1105 (1997); R. J. Robertson, Jr., A Modest Proposal Regarding the Enforceability of "As Is" Disclaimers of Implied Warranties: What the Buyer Doesn't Know Shouldn't Hurt Him, 99 Com. L.J. 1 (1994).

(c) The car salesman asks the buyer, "Would you like to examine the car?" and the buyer, who is in a hurry, says, "No." Effective disclaimer? See §2-316(3)(b); see also Official Comment 8.

(d) Remember Ted Traveler (Problem 18), who walked into the men's room of the bus depot and bought an expensive watch? We decided there was no warranty of title in that transaction. However, a warranty of quality is a separate question. Are there implied warranties in this sale? See §2-316(3)(c).

PROBLEM 30

Joe College bought a new car from Flash Motors, relying on the seller's extravagant claims about the car's superior qualities. He signed a purchase order on August 1, and the car was delivered two weeks later. In the glove compartment he found the warranty booklet and on reading it was dismayed to learn that the actual written warranty was very limited in coverage. Is he bound by the written warranty's terms? What argument can he make? See Comment 7 to §2-313; §2-209; White & Summers §12-5 at 427.

Bowdoin v. Showell Growers, Inc.

United States Court of Appeals, Eleventh Circuit, 1987
817 F.2d 1543, 3 U.C.C. Rep. Serv. 2d 1366

WISDOM, J. This appeal raises a single question: whether the defendants effectively disclaimed the implied warranties of fitness and merchantability with respect to a high pressure spray rig that caused injuries to the plaintiffs. The district court concluded that a disclaimer found in the instruction manual that accompanied the spray rig when it was delivered to the purchaser was conspicuous and therefore effective. We disagree. Even assuming that the disclaimer was otherwise conspicuous, it was delivered to the purchaser *after* the sale. Such a post-sale disclaimer is not effective because it did not form a part of the basis of the bargain between the parties to the sale. The decision of the district court is therefore reversed.

FACTS

At the time this controversy arose, the plaintiffs in this action, Rachel and Billy Bowdoin, raised chickens in Sampson, Alabama, for Showell Growers, Inc., a Maryland corporation. Under their contract with Showell Growers, the Bowdoins were required once a year to give a thorough cleaning to their chicken house and the chicken coop pallets. To aid them in this annual task, Showell Growers lent the Bowdoins a high pressure spray rig. In December 1980, Mrs. Bowdoin was using the spray rig to clean the pallets when an article of her clothing caught in the safety shield covering the spray rig's power take-off shaft. Mrs. Bowdoin was pulled into the shaft and suffered severe injuries.

The spray rig in question was manufactured by FMC Corporation, an Illinois corporation. The safety shield and drive shaft component was manufactured for FMC by NEAPCO, Inc., a Pennsylvania corporation. Showell purchased the spray rig from FMC through an FMC dealer, Brushy Mountain Co-op of Moravian Falls, North Carolina. Two weeks after the sale, the spray rig was shipped to Brushy Mountain and then delivered to Showell Growers. An instruction manual was included with the spray rig when it was delivered to Showell Growers. The last page of the instruction manual included a purported warranty disclaimer, which stated: *"The foregoing warranty is expressly in lieu of any and all other warranties, express, implied, statutory or otherwise (including, but without limitation, the implied warranties of merchantability and fitness for a particular purpose). . . ."*

Usually, FMC required its dealer and the purchaser to complete an "agriculture delivery report" before a sale. The report contains a disclaimer of the implied warranties of fitness and merchantability. The purchaser is required to read the report and sign it acknowledging that he has read the warranty information. The report is then returned to FMC. The record shows that no agriculture delivery report was completed in connection with the purchase by Showell Growers.

In 1982, the Bowdoins filed a diversity action against Showell Growers and FMC in the United States District Court for the Northern District of Florida. The Bowdoins later added NEAPCO as a defendant. The Bowdoins sought to recover on a number of counts including one count alleging breach by FMC and NEAPCO of the implied warranties of fitness and merchantability. FMC and NEAPCO moved for summary judgment on this count. The district court concluded that the law of Alabama applied to the warranty claims and that under Alabama law, FMC and NEAPCO had effectively disclaimed the implied warranties with the disclaimer in the instruction manual. The district court therefore granted summary judgment in favor of FMC and NEAPCO, and dismissed with prejudice the Bowdoins' implied warranties claims.

The Bowdoins now appeal that ruling. The sole issue on appeal is whether the district court correctly determined that FMC and NEAPCO had effectively disclaimed the implied warranties. The Bowdoins contend that the district court's ruling in favor of FMC and NEAPCO is erroneous for several reasons: the disclaimer was not part of the bargain and is therefore ineffective; the disclaimer is not conspicuous as required under Alabama law; the spray rig comes within the classification of "consumer goods" and therefore a manufacturer cannot disclaim implied warranties; the disclaimer is unconscionable; and finally, even if the disclaimer is effective as to FMC, it is ineffective as to NEAPCO, which manufactured the drive shaft and safety shield component. We conclude that the disclaimer is ineffective as to both FMC and NEAPCO because it did not form a part of the basis of the bargain. We therefore do not reach the Bowdoins' other arguments.

DISCUSSION

Under the Uniform Commercial Code as adopted by Alabama and virtually every other state, a manufacturer may disclaim the implied warranties of merchantability and fitness provided that the disclaimer is in writing and conspicuous, and provided that the disclaimer is part of the parties' bargain. If a disclaimer was conspicuous to the purchaser *before the sale,* a court will generally hold the disclaimer effective based on the assumption that the disclaimer formed a part of the basis of the bargain. If, however, the disclaimer was not presented to the purchaser before the sale, the court will hold such a disclaimer ineffective because it did not form a part of the basis of the bargain. This "basis of the bargain" rule protects purchasers from unexpected and coercive disclaimers.

We turn now to determine whether the FMC disclaimer was a part of the basis of the bargain. The parties agree that for purposes of this analysis, the Bowdoins stand in the shoes of Showell Growers. The question therefore is whether the disclaimer is effective as to Showell Growers. We conclude that it is not.

Showell Growers purchased the spray rig at least two weeks before it was delivered. When the rig was delivered, an instruction manual was enclosed, and in that instruction manual is the disclaimer upon which FMC and NEAPCO rely. The disclaimer was never brought to Showell's attention.

Such a post-sale disclaimer is ineffective. "By definition, a disclaimer that appears for the first time after the sale in something supplied by the seller is not a part of the basis of the bargain and therefore is not binding on the buyer. Thus, the buyer is not bound by the disclaimer to which he had never agreed at the time of the sale and which first appears in the manufacturer's manual delivered to the buyer with the goods [or] the manufacturer's printed material brochure, or warranty booklet that accompanies the goods. . . ."[7]

The leading Alabama decision on disclaimers of implied warranties is in harmony with this position. In Tiger Motor Co. v. McMurtry, the Alabama Supreme Court addressed the validity of a disclaimer of implied warranties with respect to an automobile. The evidence showed that the day after the sale took place, the automobile was delivered to the purchaser along with the disclaimer. The evidence also showed that the disclaimer was never called to the purchaser's attention before the sale. The court concluded that the disclaimer was ineffective. Decisions of other courts construing the same provisions of the Uniform Commercial Code have also concluded that a post-sale disclaimer is not effective. [Citations omitted.]

FMC attempts to distinguish these cases on three grounds. First, FMC argues that unlike the purchasers involved in most of the cases, who were, for the most part, individual consumers, Showell Growers is a sophisticated commercial enterprise. But FMC has not offered and we have not found a post-sale disclaimer case in which such a distinction was material. Indeed, several of the cases in other states did involve commercial transactions between sophisticated commercial enterprises or businessmen, and the results reached were not affected: Courts consistently held that post-sale disclaimers were ineffective.

FMC next argues that here the post-sale disclaimer was effective because it was conspicuous. Specifically, FMC asserts that the cases which have held post-sale disclaimers ineffective involved "egregious facts involving the combination of the failure of a disclaimer to be conspicuous and its appearance subsequent to the parties' transaction."

---

7. R. Anderson, 3 Uniform Commercial Code §2-316:32, p.345 (footnotes omitted).

FMC's argument is, however, wrong on both the facts and the law. Several of the cases holding post-sale disclaimers ineffective did not even mention whether the disclaimer was otherwise conspicuous. And the cases to which FMC is apparently referring typically involved not one disclaimer but two: one in the sales contract and the other in a document delivered after the sale, such as an instruction manual or a warranty. In those cases, the courts held both disclaimers ineffective: the disclaimer in the sales contract because it was in small print and therefore not conspicuous, and the post-sale disclaimer because it was not a part of the basis of the bargain. In these cases, as in the cases involving only a post-sale disclaimer, the courts generally did not discuss whether the disclaimer was otherwise conspicuous. The absence of such a discussion is not surprising, because as a general rule the conspicuousness of a post-sale disclaimer is immaterial. By definition, a post-sale disclaimer is not conspicuous in the full sense of that term because the reasonable person against whom it is intended to operate could not have noticed it before the consummation of the transaction. A post-sale disclaimer is therefore not effective merely because it was otherwise conspicuous.

Finally, FMC argues that its post-sale disclaimer is effective because of prior dealings with Showell Growers that put Showell on notice that FMC's practice was to disclaim implied warranties with respect to high pressure spray rigs. Showell Growers had previously purchased an FMC spray rig similar to the one that caused Mrs. Bowdoin's injuries. The instruction manual accompanying the first spray rig contained a disclaimer of implied warranties, and according to one Showell employee, that instruction manual appeared to be identical to the one accompanying the spray rig in question. From this, FMC argues that Showell was on notice that FMC was disclaiming the implied warranties with respect to the second spray rig.

This argument misses the point. Even assuming that the mere similar appearance of two instruction manuals could put a purchaser on notice that a disclaimer in the first would also be found in the second, FMC's argument fails for the same reason its argument that a post-sale disclaimer can be effective if it was otherwise conspicuous failed. A disclaimer must be conspicuous before the sale, for only then will the law presume that the disclaimer was part of the bargain. In this case, Showell Growers did not receive the second instruction manual until after the second sale was consummated. The disclaimer in that instruction manual was therefore without significance. This is not less true merely because earlier Showell had received a similar instruction manual. Until it received the second instruction manual, it could not know what it would look like or what it would contain.

CONCLUSION

We conclude that the post-sale disclaimer of implied warranties found in the instruction manual that accompanied the FMC spray rig is ineffective because it did not form a part of the basis of the bargain. The decision of the district court is therefore reversed, and the district court is instructed to reinstate the Bowdoins' breach of implied warranties of fitness and merchantability claims against FMC and NEAPCO.

Rinaldi v. Iomega Corp.

Delaware Superior Court, 1999
41 U.C.C. Rep. Serv. 2d 1143

COOCH, J.

I. INTRODUCTION: FACTUAL AND PROCEDURAL HISTORY

This proposed class action was commenced in September 1998 on behalf of all persons who have purchased purportedly defective "Zip drives" from January 1, 1995 to the present. The Zip drives are manufactured by defendant Iomega Corporation, a computer storage device maker incorporated in Delaware and based in Utah. A Zip drive is a large capacity personal computer data storage drive. The complaint alleges inter alia that the alleged defect, said by Plaintiffs to be commonly known as the "Click of Death," causes irreparable damage to the removable magnetic media storage disks on which the drives store data. Plaintiffs also allege that the defect renders the data on the disks unreadable and that when another drive attempts to read the data from a disk that has been infected, the defect transfers to the second drive, causing further damage.

Plaintiffs' complaint has four counts. Count I alleges that Defendant breached the implied warranty of merchantability by manufacturing a product that was not fit for the ordinary purpose for which such products are used and that Defendant's disclaimer of the implied warranty of merchantability contained in the packaging of the product was ineffective because it was not sufficiently "conspicuous" as required by 6 Del. C. §2-316(2). Count II alleges that Defendant was negligent in manufacturing and designing the Zip drive without using the reasonable care, skill, and diligence required when placing such a product into the stream of commerce. Count III alleges that Defendant committed consumer fraud in violation of the Delaware Consumer Fraud Act by falsely misrepresenting through advertising to the consuming public that the Zip drives were suitable for their intended purpose. Count IV alleges that Defendant was negligent in failing to warn the consuming public about the risks of its product when it knew or should have known that the product could cause damage when used for its intended purpose. . . .

Defendant's Motion to Dismiss Count I on the grounds that Plaintiffs have failed to state a claim for breach of the implied warranty of merchantability is GRANTED since the Court finds that the disclaimer is "conspicuous." . . .

Defendant contends that Plaintiffs' claim for breach of the implied warranty of merchantability has failed to state a claim because Defendant's disclaimer of the implied warranty of merchantability, contained within the packaging of the Zip drive, effectively disclaimed all liability. The sole issue to be resolved here is whether Count I of the complaint should be dismissed because Defendant's disclaimer of the implied warranty of merchantability was not "conspicuous," as required by 6 Del. C. §2-316, because the disclaimer was contained within the packaging of the Zip drive product itself and therefore not "discovered" by the purchaser prior to the purchaser's purchase of the product.

Defendant's disclaimer inside the Zip drive package provides:

> EXCEPT AS STATED ABOVE IN THIS PARAGRAPH, THE FOREGOING WARRANTIES ARE IN LIEU OF ALL OTHER CONDITIONS OR WARRANTIES, EXPRESS, IMPLIED, OR STATUTORY, INCLUDING, WITHOUT LIMITATION, ANY IMPLIED CONDITION OR WARRANTY OF MERCHANTABILITY OR FITNESS FOR A PARTICULAR PURPOSE AND OF ANY OTHER WARRANTY OBLIGATION ON THE PART OF IOMEGA (capitals in original).

The above disclaimer appears near the bottom of a document labeled "IOMEGA LIMITED WARRANTY" located inside the packaging.

6 Del. C. §2-316(2) provides, in pertinent part, ". . . to exclude or modify the implied warranty of merchantability or any part of it the language must mention merchantability and in the case of a writing must be conspicuous. . . ." 6 Del. C. §2-316(2) is identical to §2-316(2) of the Uniform Commercial Code.

The usual arguments concerning the conspicuousness require-ment of U.C.C. §2-316(2) have been based on issues such as the size of the type set and the location of the disclaimer in the warranty itself. Defendant contends that the conspicuousness requirement has been met regardless of the location of the disclaimer inside the Zip drive package so long as the disclaimer is "noticeable and easily readable." Defendant asserts that "modern commercial realities of how contracts are formed with consumers of prepackaged products necessitates that the terms of [its] warranty disclaimer be given effect."

Plaintiffs do not claim that the disclaimer was improperly worded, that the text of the disclaimer was improperly placed in the rest of the warranty or that the typeface of the disclaimer was too small, but in-stead argue that the disclaimer, located in the packaging of the prod-uct, could not realistically be called to the attention of the consumer until after the sale had been consummated, thus rendering the dis-claimer not "conspicuous" as a matter or law and therefore ineffective.

Although similar issues of additional terms to a contract such as a shrinkwrap license,[8] an arbitration clause[9] and a license agreement,[10] each physically located within the packaging of the product, has been litigated in other jurisdictions, the parties have cited no case directly addressing the effectiveness, under U.C.C. §2-316(2), of a disclaimer of the implied warranty of merchantability by virtue of its location within the packaging of a product itself, nor has the Court found any such case.

The issue of conspicuousness, generally, under §2-316 has been the topic of various law review articles, periodicals and texts,[11] and has been the subject of much litigation. As stated, however, no authorities have been located that squarely addressed the issue in this case. The traditional focus has been on the "mention"[12] of merchantability and the visible characteristics of the disclaimer, such as type set and location within the warranty document itself. In determining if a

8. ProCD, Inc. v. Zeidenberg, 7th Cir., 86 F.3d 1447 (1996).

9. Hill v. Gateway 2000, Inc., 7th Cir., 105 F.3d 1147 (1997), *cert. denied*, 118 S. Ct. 47 (1997).

10. M.A. Mortenson Co. v. Timberline Software Corp., Wash. App., 970 P.2d 803 (1999).

11. See, e.g., Bernard F. Kistler, Jr., U.C.C. Article Two Warranty Disclaimers and the "Conspicuousness" Requirement of Section 2-316, 43 Mercer L. Rev. 943, 945-953 (1992); Jeffrey C. Selman and Christopher S. Chen, Steering the Titanic Clear of the Iceberg: Saving the Sale of Software From the Perils of Warranties, 31 U.S.F. L. Rev. 531, 533-536 (1997); William H. Danne, Jr., Construction and Effect of UCC §2-316(2) Providing That Implied Warranty Disclaimer Must Be "Conspicuous," 73 A.L.R.3d 248, Vol. 73 (1976).

12. 6 Del. C. §2-316(2).

disclaimer of the implied warranty of merchantability is effective as being "conspicuous," the secondary authorities and courts have often looked to the purpose of §2-316.[13] The purpose of that section is to "protect a buyer from unexpected and unbargained for language of disclaimer."[14] That purpose is the real backbone in determining if a disclaimer is conspicuous when looking at factors beyond the mentioning of merchantability and type set.

Analogous support for this Court's conclusion that the physical location of the disclaimer of the implied warranty of merchantability inside the Zip drive packaging does not make the disclaimer inconspicuous can be found in some cases from other jurisdictions. In ProCD, Inc. v. Zeidenberg,[15] the Seventh Circuit held that a shrinkwrap license located inside the packaging of the computer program was enforceable as an additional term of the contract, and stated that the commercial practicalities of modern retail purchasing dictate where terms such as a shrinkwrap license should be located. The ProCD court held that it would be otherwise impractical for these additional terms to be located on the outside of the box in "microscopic" type. The ProCD court stated, "[t]ransactions in which the exchange of money precedes the communication of detailed terms are common." The ProCD court then looked to other sections of the U.C.C. that dealt with the issue in terms of acceptance and rejection of goods: "A buyer accepts goods under §2-606(1)(b) when, after an opportunity to inspect, [the buyer] fails to make an effective rejection under §2-602(1). [The seller] extended an opportunity to reject if a buyer should find the license unsatisfactory." The ProCD court continued its analysis and observed that

> Consumer goods work the same way. Someone who wants to buy a radio set visits a store, pays and walks out with a box. Inside the box is a leaflet containing some terms, the most important of which usually is the warranty, read for the first time in the comfort of home. By [the buyer's] lights, the warranty in the box is irrelevant; every consumer gets the standard warranty implied by the UCC in the event the contract is silent; yet so far as we are aware no state disregards warranties furnished with consumer products.[16]

13. Ronald A. Anderson, Anderson on the Uniform Commercial Code, §2-316:144-153 (3d ed. 1983); Debra L. Goetz, Special Project: Article Two Warranties in Commercial Transactions, An Update, 72 Cornell L. Rev. 1159, 1264-1275 (1978).
14. U.C.C. §2-316 cmt. 1 (1962).
15. 7th Cir., 86 F.3d at 1447.
16. Id. at 1452.

Plaintiffs argue that ProCD is inapposite because it specifically concerned the validity of a shrinkwrap license which is not governed by U.C.C. §2- 316(2). Although that is correct, ProCD stressed that "the U.C.C. . . . . permits parties to structure their relations so that the buyer has a chance to make a final decision after a detailed review" of the contract terms.[17] All of the additional terms, which included the shrink-wrap license, became part of the contract in ProCD.

In Hill v. Gateway 2000, Inc.,[18] the Seventh Circuit relied on ProCD in holding that an arbitration clause located inside the packaging of a computer was enforceable as an additional term to the contract, and stated, "[p]ractical considerations support allowing vendors to enclose the full legal terms with their products . . . [C]us-tomers as a group are better off when vendors skip costly and ineffectual steps such as telephonic recitation, and use instead a simple approve-or-return device."[19] In holding that the arbitration clause was effective, the Hill court concluded that an additional term physically located outside of the contract was nevertheless an enforceable term of the contract.

In M.A. Mortenson Co. v. Timberline Software Corp.,[20] the Washington Court of Appeals relied on *ProCD* and *Hill* and held that a licensing agreement located inside the packaging of a software program was enforceable as an additional term to the contract. In *Mortenson* the court stated, ". . . the terms of the present license agreement are part of the contract as formed between parties. We find that [the purchaser's] installation and use of the software manifested its assent to the terms of the license. . . ."[21] As in *ProCD* and *Hill,* the *Mortenson* court held that a licensing agreement located within the packaging of the product, not in the contract itself, was an enforceable additional term of the contract.

Other courts have also addressed the issue of the physical location of the disclaimer of the implied warranty of merchantability from different perspectives. Thus in Step-Saver Data Systems., Inc. v. Wyse Technology,[22] the United States District Court for the Eastern District of Pennsylvania discussed the location of a disclaimer of the implied warranty of merchantability inside computer software packaging and held the location of an additional term (in *Step-Saver,* a disclaimer) is

17. Id. at 1453.
18. 7th Cir., 105 F.3d at 1147.
19. Id. at 1149.
20. 970 P.2d at 803.
21. Id. at 831.
22. E.D. Pa., C.A. No. 89-7203, 1990 WL 87334, Broderick, J. (June 21, 1990).

to be considered independently of conspicuousness. The *Step-Saver* court held that "[t]here is no question that pursuant to the U.C.C., limitation of warranty and remedies are valid when packaged with the product so long as the limitation is clear, conspicuous and one that a reasonable person would have noticed and understood."[23] The holding in *Step-Saver* that conspicuousness and location are to be considered independently is not directly on point with the issue at bar. However, the *Step-Saver* court relied on the purpose behind §2-316 in finding that so long as a disclaimer of the implied warranty of merchantability is one that could be noticed and understood, the disclaimer is conspicuous.

This Court has addressed the issue of conspicuousness under §2-316(2) in Lecates v. Hertrick Pontiac Buick Co.[24] In *Lecates,* a case on which Plaintiffs rely, the issue was whether the implied warranties were effectively disclaimed by an automobile dealer when the car that was sold malfunctioned, causing physical injuries. The court held that the seller's disclaimer of the implied warranty of merchantability located in a sales invoice satisfied the conspicuous requirement of §2-316(2). In *Lecates,* the specific question was whether or not the disclaimer had been delivered by the seller to the buyer only after the sale had already been consummated. The *Lecates* court addressed this narrow issue in light of the specific facts in that case and observed that disclaimer clauses have been held ineffective "if it appeared that the documents in which such clauses appeared were given to the buyer after the sale had been consummated."[25] *Lecates* addressed the issue of what terms and conditions were a part of the contract at the point of contract consummation, but here, Defendant's disclaimer of the implied warranty of merchantability was an additional term of each contract between each plaintiff and Defendant to purchase the Zip drives. Defendant's sales of the Zip drives to the six plaintiffs were each not "consummated" until after each plaintiff had had an opportunity to inspect and then to reject or to accept the product with the additional terms that were enclosed within the packaging of the Zip drive.

The commercial practicalities of modern retail purchasing make it eminently reasonable for a seller of a product such as a Zip drive to place a disclaimer of the implied warranty of merchantability within the plastic packaging. The buyer can read the disclaimer after payment for the Zip drive and then later have the opportunity to reject the contract terms (i.e., the disclaimer) if the buyer so chooses. This Court

23. Id. at *7.
24. Del. Super., 515 A.2d. 163 (1986).
25. Id. at 170.

concludes that Defendant's disclaimer of the implied warranty of merchantability was effective despite its physical placement inside the packaging of the Zip drive and has satisfied the conspicuousness requirement of 6 Del. C. §2-316(2).

Defendant's Motion to Dismiss Count I on the grounds that Plaintiffs have failed to state a claim for breach of the implied warranty of merchantability is granted. . . .

QUESTION

see pg 131 for context

Do these last two cases conflict? If so, which is right and which wrong? — *Issue when do you have a transaction.*

3. Limitations on the Warranty

Sometimes a seller is willing to give a warranty to the buyer, but wants in some way to limit the scope of the liability that a breach creates. The Code permits such a limitation, but puts various restrictions on its use. Read §§2-316(4) and 2-719.

Wilson Trading Corp. v. David Ferguson, Ltd.

Court of Appeals of New York, 1968
23 N.Y.2d 398, 244 N.E.2d 685, 297 N.Y.S.2d 108,
5 U.C.C. Rep. Serv. 1213

JASEN, J. The plaintiff, the Wilson Trading Corporation, entered into a contract of sale with the defendant, David Ferguson, Ltd., for the sale of a specified quantity of yarn. After the yarn was delivered, cut and knitted into sweaters, the finished product was washed. It was during this washing that it was discovered that the color of the yarn had "shaded"—that is, "there was a variation of color from piece to piece and within the pieces." This defect, the defendant claims, rendered the sweaters "unmarketable."

This action for the contract price of the yarn was commenced after the defendant refused payment. As a defense to the action and as a counterclaim for damages, the defendant alleges that "[p]laintiff has failed to perform all of the conditions of the contract on its part required to be performed, and has delivered . . . defective and unworkmanlike goods."

The sales contract provides in pertinent part:

> 2. No claims relating to excessive moisture content, short weight, count variations, twist, quality or shade shall be allowed *if made after weaving, knitting, or processing,* or more than 10 days after receipt of shipment. . . . The buyer shall within 10 days of the receipt of the merchandise by himself or agent examine the merchandise for any and all defects. [Emphasis supplied.]
>
> 4. This instrument constitutes the entire agreement between the parties, superseding all previous communications, oral or written, and no changes, amendments or additions hereto will be recognized unless in writing signed by both seller and buyer or buyer's agent. It is expressly agreed that no representations or warranties, express or implied, have been or are made by the seller except as stated herein, and the seller makes no warranty, express or implied, as to the fitness for buyer's purposes of yarn purchased hereunder, seller's obligations, except as expressly stated herein, being limited to the *delivery of good merchantable yarn of the description stated herein.* [Emphasis supplied.]

Special Term granted plaintiff summary judgment for the contract price of the yarn sold on the ground that "notice of the alleged breach of warranty for defect in shading was not given within the time expressly limited and is not now available by way of defense or counterclaim." The Appellate Division affirmed, without opinion.

The defendant on this appeal urges that the time limitation provision on claims in the contract was unreasonable since the defect in the color of the yarn was latent and could not be discovered until after the yarn was processed and the finished product washed.

Defendant's affidavits allege that its sweaters were rendered unsaleable because of latent defects in the yarn which caused "variation in color from piece to piece and within the pieces." This allegation is sufficient to create a question of fact concerning the merchantability of the yarn (Uniform Commercial Code, §2-314, subd. [2]). Indeed, the plaintiff does not seriously dispute the fact that its yarn was unmerchantable, but instead, like Special Term, relies upon the failure of defendant to give notice of the breach of warranty within the time limits prescribed by paragraph two of the contract.

Subdivision (3) (par. [a]) of section 2-607 of the Uniform Commercial Code expressly provides that a buyer who accepts goods has a reasonable time after he discovers or should have discovered a breach to notify the seller of such breach. (Cf. 5 Williston, Contracts [3d ed.] §173.) Defendant's affidavits allege that a claim was made immediately upon discovery of the breach of warranty after the yarn was knitted and washed, and that this was the earliest possible moment that the defects could reasonably be discovered in the normal manufacturing process. Defendant's affidavits are, therefore, sufficient to create a question of fact concerning whether notice of the latent defects alleged was given within a reasonable time. (Cf. Ann., 17 A.L.R.3d 1010, 1112-1115 [1968].)

However, the Uniform Commercial Code allows the parties, within limits established by the code, to modify or exclude warranties and to limit remedies for breach of warranty. The courts below have found that the sales contract bars all claims not made before knitting and processing. Concededly, defendant discovered and gave notice of the alleged breach of warranty after knitting and washing.

We are, therefore, confronted with the effect to be given the time limitation provision in paragraph two of the contract. Analytically, paragraph two presents separate and distinct issues concerning its effect as a valid limitation on remedies for breach of warranty (Uniform Commercial Code, §§2-316, subd. [4]; 2-719) and its effect as a modification of the express warranty of merchantability (Uniform Commercial Code, §2-316, subd. [1]) established by paragraph four of the contract.

Parties to a contract are given broad latitude within which to fashion their own remedies for breach of contract (Uniform Commercial Code, §2-316, subd. [4]; §§2-718; 2-719). Nevertheless, it is clear from the official section 2-719 of the Uniform Commercial Code that it is the very essence of a sale contract that at least minimum adequate remedies be available for its breach. "If the parties intend to conclude a contract for sale within this Article they must accept the legal consequence that there be at least a fair quantum of remedy for breach of the obligations or duties outlined in the contract. Thus any clause purporting to modify or limit the remedial provisions of this Article in an *unconscionable manner* is subject to deletion and in that event the remedies made available by this Article are applicable as if the striken clause had never existed." (Uniform Commercial Code, §2-719, official comment 1; emphasis supplied.)

It follows that contractual limitations upon remedies are generally to be enforced unless unconscionable. This analysis is buttressed by the fact that the official comments to section 2-302 of the Uniform Commercial Code, the code provision pertaining to unconscionable contracts or clauses, cites Kansas City Wholesale Grocery Co. v. Weber Packing Corp. (93 Utah 414 [1937]), a case invalidating a time limitation provision as applied to latent defects, as illustrating the underlying basis for section 2-302. . . .

However, it is unnecessary to decide the issue of whether the time limitation is unconscionable on this appeal for section 2-719, subd. (2) of the Uniform Commercial Code provides that the general remedy provisions of the code apply when "circumstances cause an exclusive or limited remedy to fail of its essential purpose." As explained by the official comments to this section: "where an apparently fair and reasonable clause because of circumstances fails in its purpose or operates to deprive either party of the substantial value of the bargain, it must give way to the general remedy provisions of this Article." (Uniform Commercial Code, §2-719, official comment 1.) Here, paragraph 2 of the contract bars all claims for shade and other specified defects made after knitting and processing. Its effect is to eliminate any remedy for shade defects not reasonably discoverable within the time limitation period. It is true that parties may set by agreement any time not manifestly unreasonable whenever the code "requires any action to be taken within a reasonable time" (Uniform Commercial Code, §1-204, subd. [1]), but here the time provision eliminates all remedy for defects not discoverable before knitting and processing and section 2-719, subd. (2) of the Uniform Commercial Code therefore applies.

Defendant's affidavits allege that sweaters manufactured from the yarn were rendered unmarketable because of latent shading defects not reasonably discoverable before knitting and processing of the yarn into sweaters. If these factual allegations are established at trial, the limited remedy established by paragraph two has failed its "essential purpose" and the buyer is, in effect, without remedy. The time limitation clause of the contract must give way to the general code rule that a buyer has a reasonable time to notify the seller of breach of contract after he discovers or should have discovered the defect. (Uniform Commercial Code, §2-207, subd. [3], par. [a].) As indicated above, defendant's affidavits are sufficient to create a question of fact concerning whether notice was given within a reasonable time after the shading defect should have been discovered.

It can be argued that paragraph two of the contract, insofar as it bars all claims for enumerated defects not reasonably discoverable within the time period established, purports to exclude these defects from the coverage of the express warranty of merchantability. By this analysis, the contract not only limits its remedies for its breach, but also purports to modify the warranty of merchantability. An attempt to both warrant and refuse to warrant goods creates an ambiguity which can only be resolved by making one term yield to the other (cf. Hawkland, Limitation of Warranty under the Uniform Commercial Code, 11 How. L.J. 28 [1965]). Section 2-316 (subd. [1]) of the Uniform Commercial

Code provides that warranty language prevails over the disclaimer if the two cannot be reasonably reconciled.

Here, the contract expressly creates an unlimited express warranty of merchantability while in a separate clause purports to indirectly modify the warranty without expressly mentioning the word merchantability. Under these circumstances, the language creating the unlimited express warranty must prevail over the time limitation insofar as the latter modifies the warranty. It follows that the express warranty of merchantability includes latent shading defects and defendant may claim for such defects not reasonably discoverable within the time limits established by the contract if plaintiff was notified of these defects within a reasonable time after they should have been discovered. . . .

In sum, there are factual issues for trial concerning whether the shading defects alleged were discoverable before knitting and processing, and if not, whether notice of the defects was given within a reasonable time after the defects were or should have been discovered. If the shading defects were not reasonably discoverable before knitting and processing and notice was given within a reasonable time after the defects were or should have been discovered, a further factual issue of whether the sweaters were rendered unsaleable because of the defect is presented for trial.

The order of the Appellate Division should be reversed, with costs, and plaintiff's motion for summary judgment should be denied.

Chief Judge FULD (concurring). I agree that there should be a reversal but on the sole ground that a substantial question of fact has been raised as to whether the clause limiting the time in which to make a claim is "manifestly unreasonable" (Uniform Commercial Code, §1-204) as applied to the type of defect here complained of. In this view, it is not necessary to consider the relevancy, if any, of other provisions of the Uniform Commercial Code (e.g., §§2-302, 2-316, 2-719), dealing with "unconscionable" contracts or clauses, exclusion of implied warranties or limitations on damages.

PROBLEM 31

On November 1, Jack Frost of Portland, Maine, bought a snowmobile from King Cold Recreationland. Jack used the snowmobile to get to work during the week in the winter and for fun on the weekends. The contract that he signed stated that the seller warranted that the vehicle was merchantable, but that, in the event of breach, "the buyer's remedy was limited solely to repair or replacement of defective parts." Moreover, the contract conspicuously stated that the seller was not responsible for "any consequential damages."

One week after he received the snowmobile, Jack noticed a strange rumble in the engine. He took the machine back to the King Cold service department. The machine was returned to him in three days allegedly repaired. These events repeated themselves three times over the next three weeks. Four weeks after he bought the snowmobile, Frost was seriously injured when it blew up while he was riding. The machine, which cost $1,200, was destroyed. Frost temporarily lost the use of his left arm, incurred hospital expenses of $2,500, and lost pay of $1,600. Moreover, when he did return to work, he had to rent a snowmobile for $40 a week until spring (16 weeks—spring is very late in Maine). In addition, a $350 camera he was carrying was also destroyed. Frost brought suit against King Cold. King Cold defended on the ground that its liability was limited to the cost of repair or replacement. Frost argued that the remedy limitation was "unconscionable" and failed of its "essential purpose." All the parties pointed to §§2-316(4), 2-302, 2-719, and 2-715. How should this suit come out? See Beal v. General Motors Corp., 354 F. Supp. 423 (D. Del. 1973); Earl M. Jorgensen Co. v. Mark Constr., Inc., 56 Haw. 466, 540 P.2d 978, 17 U.C.C. Rep. Serv. 1126 (1975).

The New Jersey Supreme Court has produced two leading opinions on the validity of a disclaimer of liability for consequential damages in automobile tire blowout cases. In Collins v. Uniroyal, Inc., 64 N.J. 260, 315 A.2d 16, 14 U.C.C. Rep. Serv. 294 (1974), a consumer was killed in an automobile accident when his right rear tire failed. The tire manufacturer tried to avoid §2-719(3) by saying that its disclaimer of liability for personal injury damages overcame the prima facie presumption of unconscionability because its warranty made a conspicuous statement limiting the remedy for blowout to repair or replacement. The court held that this argument was not "consonant with the commercial and human realities," and added:

> A tire manufacturer warrants against blowouts in order to increase tire sales. Public advertising by defendant relative to these tires stated: "If it only saves your life once, it's a bargain." The seller should be held to realize that the purchaser of a tire buying it because so warranted is far more likely to have made the purchase decision in order to protect himself and the passengers in his car from death or personal injury in a blowout accident than to assure himself of a refund of the price of the

tire in such an event. That being the natural reliance and the reasonable expectation of the purchaser flowing from the warranty, it appears to us patently unconscionable for the manufacturer to be permitted to limit his damages for a breach of warranty proximately resulting in the purchaser's death to a price refund or replacement of the tire.

In a later case, no personal injury occurred, but the car was destroyed when the tire blew. The tire manufacturer argued that since §2-719(3)'s "prima facie unconscionable" language applies only to "injury to the person," the consumer was limited in her recovery to a replacement of the defective tire. The New Jersey Supreme Court, however, still applied §2-719(3) because it found the warranty limitation to be "seriously lacking in clarity." The court stated:

> [T]he booklet presents the owner with a linguistic maze. Throughout the document there is an admixture of terms relating to quality, capacity, and performance, together with disclaimers and exclusions of coverage, as well as limitations and restrictions upon liability and remedies. There are fulsome and repeated references to the term "guarantee," seemingly relating to quality and performance followed by the rather sudden, isolated use of the term "promise," purportedly limiting the entire contractual undertaking to tire replacement. What is thus given to a purchaser is not a simple and straight-forward document defining on the one hand that which constitutes an affirmation of quality or performance and, on the other, the liability which flows from a breach thereof. Rather what is presented is a melange of overlapping, variant, misleading, and contradictory provisions.

Gladden v. Cadillac Motor Car Div., 83 N.J. 320, 333, 416 A.2d 394, 401, 29 U.C.C. Rep. Serv. 369, 380-381 (1980). For a similar result in a commercial setting, see Andover Air Ltd. Partnership v. Piper Aircraft Corp., 7 U.C.C. Rep. Serv. 2d 1494 (D. Mass. 1989) (remedy limitation to repair or replacement held unconscionable where defective and inexpensive bracket caused $100,000 in damages in an airplane crash). Not all courts are this sympathetic to buyers. In NEC Technologies, Inc. v. Nelson, 267 Ga. 390, 478 S.E.2d 769, 31 U.C.C. Rep. Serv. 2d 992 (1996), the Georgia Supreme Court held that a disclaimer of liability for consequential damages was not unconscionable where a TV malfunctioned, burning down the consumer's home but causing no personal injury.

One other point: although §2-719 does not say so, most courts have required that any remedy limitation be *conspicuous* in order to be effective. See, e.g., Stauffer Chem. Co. v. Curry, 778 P.2d 1083, 10 U.C.C. Rep. Serv. 2d 342 (Wyo. 1989) (any other result "absurd"); but see Apex Supply Co. v. Benbow Indus., 189 Ga. App. 598, 376 S.E.2d 694, 9 U.C.C. Rep. Serv. 2d 547 (1988) (conspicuousness not required because a limitation of remedy is not as serious a matter as a disclaimer of warranty).

Pierce v. Catalina Yachts, Inc.

Supreme Court of Alaska, 1999
2 P.3d 618, 41 U.C.C. Rep. Serv. 2d 737

BRYNER, Justice.

I. INTRODUCTION

After finding that Catalina Yachts, a sailboat manufacturer, breached its limited warranty to repair a defect in a boat that it sold to Jim and Karen Pierce, a jury awarded the Pierces monetary damages for the reasonable cost of repair. Before submitting the case to the jury, the trial court dismissed the Pierces' claim for consequential damages, finding it barred by an express provision in the warranty. On appeal, the Pierces contend that they were entitled to consequential damages despite this provision. We agree, holding that because Catalina acted in bad faith when it breached the warranty, the company cannot conscionably enforce the warranty's provision barring consequential damages. Accordingly, we remand for a trial to determine consequential damages.

II. FACTS AND PROCEEDINGS

In June 1992 Jim and Karen Pierce purchased a forty-two-foot sailboat newly built by Catalina Yachts. Catalina gave the Pierces a limited warranty, promising to repair or pay for repair of any below-waterline blisters that might appear in the gel coat—a smooth outer layer of resin on the boat's hull.[26] The warranty expressly disclaimed Catalina's responsibility for consequential damages.

In June 1994 the Pierces hauled the boat out of the water to perform maintenance and discovered gel-coat blisters on its hull and rudder. They promptly notified Catalina of the problem and submitted

---

26. This limited warranty provided, in relevant part: "Catalina will repair or, at its option, pay for 100% of the labor and material costs necessary to repair any below-the-waterline gel coat blisters that occur within the first year after the boat is placed in the water."

a repair estimate of $10,645, which included the cost of removing and replacing the gel coat below the waterline. Catalina refused to accept this estimate, insisting that the hull only needed minor patching. Six months later, after their repeated efforts failed to convince Catalina that the gel coat needed to be replaced, the Pierces sued the company, claiming tort and contract damages. They later amended their complaint to allege a separate claim for unfair trade practices. Before trial, the superior court ruled that the limited warranty's provision barring consequential damages was not unconscionable. Based on this ruling, the court later precluded the Pierces from submitting their consequential damages claim to the jury, restricting the Pierces' recovery on their claim of breach of contract to their cost of repair, as specified in the limited warranty. The jury awarded the Pierces $12,445 as the reasonable cost of repair, specifically finding that the Pierces had given Catalina timely notice of the blister problem, that Catalina breached its gel-coat warranty, that it acted in bad faith in failing to honor its warranty obligations, and that the Pierces could not have avoided any of their losses.

The Pierces appeal, contending that the trial court erred in striking their claim for consequential damages, in excluding evidence supporting their unfair trade practices claim, and in calculating the attorney's fee award. Catalina cross-appeals, also contesting the attorney's fee order.

III. DISCUSSION

A. THE PIERCES ARE ENTITLED TO CONSEQUENTIAL DAMAGES.

The Pierces' consequential damages argument requires us to consider a question of first impression concerning how a warranty provision that creates a limited remedy interacts with another provision that excludes consequential damages: if the limited remedy fails, should the exclusion of consequential damages survive?

Alaska's commercial code addresses these issues in AS 45.02.719. The first paragraph of this provision, subsection .719(a), authorizes limited warranties, allowing parties entering into commercial transactions to "limit or alter the measure of damages recoverable under [chapter 7 of the U.C.C.], as by limiting the buyer's remedies to . . . repair and replacement of nonconforming goods or parts" and to agree that the limited remedy is "exclusive, in which case it is the sole remedy." But when a limited remedy fails, the second paragraph of AS 45.02.719, subsection .719(b), nullifies the warranty's limitation, restoring the buyer's right to rely on any authorized remedy: "If circumstances cause an exclusive or limited remedy to fail of its essential purpose, remedy may be had as provided in the code."

Courts construing U.C.C. subsection 719(b) agree that a limited warranty to repair "fails of its essential purpose," "when the seller is either unwilling or unable to conform the goods to the contract."[27]

The policy behind the failure of essential purpose rule is to insure that the buyer has "at least minimum adequate remedies." Typically, a limited repair/replacement remedy fails of its essential purpose where (1) the "[s]eller is unsuccessful in repairing or replacing the defective part, regardless of good or bad faith; or (2)[t]here is unreasonable delay in repairing or replacing defective components.[28]

Here, by specifically finding that the Pierces' boat experienced gel-coat blisters, that the Pierces gave Catalina timely notice of the problem, that Catalina thereafter breached its obligations under the limited gel-coat warranty, and that the Pierces could not have avoided their damages, the jury effectively determined that the gel-coat warranty had failed of its essential purpose. Under subsection .719(b), then, the Pierces seemingly can pursue any remedy available under the commercial code, including consequential damages.

But the Pierces' right to consequential damages under subsection .719(b) is not as certain as it seems. The last paragraph of AS 45.02.719, subsection .719(c), separately provides that consequential damages may be limited or excluded "unless the limitation or exclusion is unconscionable." By validating consequential damages exclusions subject only to unconscionability, subsection .719(c) casts doubt upon subsection .719(b)'s implied promise that, when a limited remedy fails, the buyer may claim consequential damages because they are a "remedy . . . provided in the code."

The commercial code does not directly resolve this tension between subsections .719(b) and .719(c).[29] When, as here, a limited

27. Chatlos Sys., Inc. v. National Cash Register Corp., 635 F.2d 1081, 1085 (3d Cir. 1980).

28. McDermott, Inc. v. Clyde Iron, 979 F.2d 1068, 1073 (5th Cir. 1993) (internal citations omitted), rev'd on other grounds, McDermott, Inc. v. AmClyde, 511 U.S. 202, 114 S. Ct. 1461, 128 L. Ed. 2d 148 (1994). See also S.M. Wilson & Co. v. Smith Int'l, Inc., 587 F.2d 1363, 1375 (9th Cir. 1978); Liberty Truck Sales, Inc. v. Kimbrel, 548 So. 2d 1379, 1384 (Ala. 1989). See generally Daniel C. Hagen, Sections 2-719(2) & 2-719(3) of the Uniform Commercial Code: The Limited Warranty Package & Consequential Damages, 31 Val. U.L. Rev. 111, 115 (1996).

29. See S.M. Wilson & Co., 587 F.2d at 1375 ("The failure of the limited repair warranty to achieve its essential purpose makes available . . . the remedies 'as may be had as provided in this code.' This does not mean, however, that the bar to recovery of consequential damages should be eliminated.").

repair remedy fails, and a separate provision of the warranty bars consequential damages, the code fails to say whether a court should apply subsection .719(b) by restoring the buyer's right to seek consequential damages, or whether it should instead apply subsection .719(c) by enforcing the bar against consequential damages "unless . . . unconscionable."

Courts addressing this dilemma in other jurisdictions have come to differing conclusions. Some have found the two subsections to be dependent, ruling that when a warranty fails, subsection .719(b)'s command to restore all available remedies trumps subsection .719(c)'s approval of a specific clause that bars consequential damages, regardless of whether that clause might itself be unconscionable. [Citations omitted.] Other courts have applied a case-by-case analysis. [Citations omitted.] But the majority of jurisdictions view these subsections to be independent, ruling that when a warranty fails, a separate provision barring consequential damages will survive under subsection .719(c) as long as the bar itself is not unconscionable. [Citations omitted.]

We believe that the majority approach best serves the Uniform Commercial Code's underlying purposes "to simplify, clarify and modernize the law governing commercial transactions; to permit the continued expansion of commercial practices through custom, usage and agreement of the parties; [and] to make uniform the law among the various jurisdictions."[30] Moreover, this approach balances the purposes of subsections .719(b) and (c) by allowing parties latitude to contract around consequential damages, while protecting buyers from unconscionable results.[31] We therefore adopt the independent approach as the most sensible rule in light of precedent, reason, and policy.

Courts applying this approach recognize that contractual provisions limiting remedies and excluding consequential damages shift the risk of a limited remedy's failure from the seller to the buyer; they examine the totality of the circumstances at issue—including those surrounding the limited remedy's failure—to determine

[handwritten margin note: Q 5 / po/t 2. / 719(b) / doesn't / trumph / 719(c)]

30. U.C.C. §1-102(2) (1996).
31. See McKernan v. United Tech. Corp., 717 F. Supp. 60, 71 (D. Conn. 1989). The comments to U.C.C. §2-719 provide that, while "minimum adequate remedies must be available" to the buyer when a contract fails, "parties are left free to shape their remedies to their particular requirements and reasonable agreements limiting or modifying remedies are to be given effect." U.C.C. §2-719 cmt. 1. In discussing subsection 2-719(3), the U.C.C. comments also recognize that clauses limiting consequential damages are "merely an allocation of unknown or undeterminable risks." U.C.C. §2-719 cmt. 3.

whether there is anything "in the formation of the contract or the circumstances resulting in failure of performance that makes it unconscionable to enforce the parties' allocation of risk."[32]

In determining whether an exclusion is unconscionable, courts examine the circumstances existing when the contract was signed, asking whether "there was . . . reason to conclude that the parties could not competently agree upon the allocation of risk."[33] Courts are more likely to find unconscionability when a consumer is involved, when there is a disparity in bargaining power, and when the consequential damages clause is on a pre-printed form; conversely, they are unlikely to find unconscionability when "such a limitation is freely negotiated between sophisticated parties, which will most likely occur in a commercial setting. . . ."[34]

In addition to inquiring into the circumstances at the time of the sale, courts examine the case "[f]rom the perspective of later events," inquiring whether "it appears that the type of damage claimed . . . came within the realm of expectable losses."[35] The reason for the limited warranty's failure affects this analysis:

> Whether the preclusion of consequential damages should be effective in this case depends upon the circumstances involved. The repair remedy's failure of essential purpose, while a discrete question, is not completely irrelevant to the issue of the conscionability of enforcing the consequential damages exclusion. The latter term is "merely an allocation of unknown or undeterminable risks." Recognizing this, *the question . . . narrows to the unconscionability of the buyer retaining the risk of consequential damages upon the failure of the essential purpose of the exclusive repair remedy.*[36]

And in examining why a limited remedy failed of its essential purpose, courts consider it significant if the seller acted unreasonably or in bad faith.

In the present case, the nature of the Pierces' warranty and the circumstances surrounding Catalina's breach weigh heavily against enforcing the consequential damages bar. The contract at issue was a consumer sale, not a commercial transaction between sophisticated

---

32. *Chatlos,* 635 F.2d at 1087.

33. Id. at 1087.

34. *Schurtz,* 814 P.2d at 1114; see also Associated Press v. Southern Ark. Radio Co., 34 Ark. App. 211, 809 S.W.2d 695, 697 (1991); Construction Assocs. v. Fargo Water Equip. Co., 446 N.W.2d 237, 242 (N.D. 1989).

35. *Chatlos,* 635 F.2d at 1087.

36. Id. at 1086-87 (internal citation omitted; emphasis added).

businesses with equivalent bargaining power. Catalina unilaterally drafted the damages bar and evidently included it in a preprinted standard limited warranty. Moreover, the jury's sizable award for the reasonable cost of repairing the boat's gel coat establishes that Catalina's breach deprived the Pierces of a substantial benefit of their bargain. Though some gel-coat blistering might have been foreseeable, a defect of this magnitude does not fit neatly "within the realm of expectable losses."

But the decisive factor in this case is the nature of Catalina's breach, which caused the limited remedy to fail of its essential purpose. The jury specifically found that Catalina acted in bad faith in failing to honor its warranty. This finding virtually establishes a "circumstance[ ] resulting in failure of performance that makes it unconscionable to enforce the parties' allocation of risk." Because the jury found that Catalina consciously deprived the Pierces of their rights under the warranty, the company cannot conscionably demand to enforce its own warranty rights against the Pierces:

> This Court would be in an untenable position if it allowed the defendant to shelter itself behind one segment of the warranty when it has allegedly repudiated and ignored its very limited obligations under another segment of the same warranty, which alleged repudiation has caused the very need for relief which the defendant is attempting to avoid.[37]

Moreover, in light of Catalina's bad faith, allowing the company to enforce the consequential damages bar would conflict with the commercial code's imperative that "[e]very contract or duty in the code imposes an obligation of good faith in its performance or enforcement."[38] Finally, because it is self-evident that the Pierces did not bargain to assume the risk of a bad faith breach by Catalina, enforcing the bar against consequential damages would thwart AS 45.02.719's basic goal of implementing the parties' agreement.

For these reasons, we hold the superior court erred in ruling that it would be conscionable to enforce the warranty's bar against consequential damages and in declining to allow the Pierces to present their consequential damages claim to the jury. We further hold that this error requires us to remand the case for a trial to determine the extent of these damages. . . .

---

37. Jones & McKnight Corp. v. Birdsboro Corp., 320 F. Supp. 39, 43-44 (N.D. Ill. 1970).

38. See AS 47.01.203; U.C.C. §1-203.

IV. CONCLUSION

For these reasons, we VACATE the judgment and REMAND for a trial to determine the amount of the Pierces' consequential damages.

NOTE

The courts are in sharp disagreement on the issue presented in this last case. In a commercial setting, where the buyer is not a consumer, the courts are more likely to uphold the disclaimer of liability for consequential damages even where the limited remedy fails of its essential purpose. See the thoughtful discussion in Kearney & Trecker Corp. v. Master Engraving Co., 211 N.J. Super. 376, 527 A.2d 429, 3 U.C.C. Rep. Serv. 2d 1684 (1987).

D.   Defenses in Warranty Actions

1. Notice

In all warranty actions a buyer loses all UCC rights if there is a failure to give the seller *notice* of the breach within a reasonable period of time after the breach should have been discovered. Read §2-607(3)(a) and Official Comment 4 to that section. The reason for this technical requirement is to preserve for the seller the right to inspect the goods (§2-515) and the right to *cure* (§2-508) and, of course, to facilitate an early settlement of the dispute.

PROBLEM 32

Pearl, a farmer, exhibited to Dave samples of her apples, but said that the bulk of the apples had less color and were one fifth smaller in size than the samples. Dave said, "Bring your apples to my warehouse; such size apples are worth $3.00 a bushel, and I will pay you that for them." Pearl agreed to do so.

The next day Pearl delivered 150 bushels of apples to Dave's warehouse. These apples were not as good, on an average, as the samples and were one third smaller in size than the samples were. Dave, without inspecting the apples, delivered them 10 days later to his commission merchant, who the same day sold them on the market, bringing only $1.50 per bushel.

The commission merchant, immediately upon making the sale, called Dave and informed him of the price brought by the apples. Dave was disgusted and decided to wait until Pearl billed him for the apples, at which time he would give her a piece of his mind. Sixty days later Pearl billed Dave in the amount of $450 for the 150 bushels of apples. Dave refused to pay, telling Pearl that the apples had not measured up to the contract. Pearl sues Dave. Dave contends that Pearl breached an express warranty under the Uniform Commercial Code since a contract of sale by sample was involved. What result? Review §2-313.

PROBLEM 33

Icarus Airlines ordered 40 new airplanes from the Daedalus Aircraft Company. Twenty were to be delivered on May 8 and the rest on November 10. The first shipment actually came on September 9, but Icarus did not complain. The second came on January 12 of the next year. On January 30 the president of Icarus wrote Daedalus that "We are very disappointed by your late shipment, which has caused us much expense and inconvenience." Three months later Icarus sued, claiming some $24 million in damages caused by the delayed deliveries. In its answer Daedalus responded by stating that it had received no notice of the breach as to the first shipment and that the notice concerning the second shipment was defective because it did not announce Icarus's intention to claim a breach as a result of the late delivery. At trial, Icarus countered by stating that no notice is required where, as here, the breach is obvious to the seller. As to the lack of formal notice of breach in the January letter, Icarus pointed to Official Comment 4 to §2-607.

(a) As the trial court judge, how would you rule on the notice issues? See Aqualon Co. v. MAC Equipment, Inc., 149 F.3d 262, 36 U.C.C. Rep. Serv. 2d 99 (4th Cir. 1998).

(b) What if on January 30 Icarus had filed suit against Daedalus rather than waiting three months? Would the notice requirement have been satisfied? See Armco Steel Co. v. Isaacson Structure Steel Co., 611 P.2d 507, 28 U.C.C. Rep. Serv. 1249 (Alaska 1980). In *Armco*, the court held that filing suit was not sufficient notice. However, the dissenting judge said: "[F]iling suit without prior notice may be impolite but it is not deceptive or dishonest and it certainly is no hindrance to 'normal settlement through negotiation.' Often, in fact, serious settlement negotiations do not take place until a lawsuit is filed." See In re Bridgestone/Firestone, Inc. Tires Products Liability Litigation, 155 F. Supp. 2d 1069, 45 U.C.C. Rep. Serv. 2d 516 (S.D. Ind. 2001).

PROBLEM 34

Alonso Quijana invited his good friend Sancho to dinner and served him a pheasant for the meal. The wine specially uncorked for the meal had been bottled by La Mancha Vineyards. It proved to be laced with a poisonous chemical, but only Sancho drank enough to have a serious reaction: it put him in the hospital for eight months. When he was discharged, he hired an attorney and filed suit against La Mancha Vineyards, which defended on the lack of notice required by §2-607(3)(a). How should this come out? Read §2-318 and Official Comment 5 to §2-607. If the person who had been injured had been Alonso Quijana and if he had given notice of breach to the retail seller, Carrasco Liquors, would that preserve his rights against the manufacturer, La Mancha Vineyards? See Annot., 24 A.L.R.4th 277; compare Cooley v. Big Horn Harvestore Sys., Inc., 813 P.2d 736, 14 U.C.C. Rep. Serv. 2d 977 (Colo. 1991).

2. Privity

Because suits on warranties are contract actions, the buyer must establish that there was in fact and in law a contract between the two parties. This "legal connection" is called *privity*. Where a buyer has purchased the goods directly from the retailer who gave the warranty, there is obviously privity between the two parties. Suppose, however, the warranty was made by the manufacturer, who sold to a wholesaler, who sold to a retailer, who sold to the buyer. If the buyer wishes to sue the manufacturer, the issue of lack of privity arises. At common law the manufacturer could successfully maintain a defense based on lack of privity, because the manufacturer did not deal directly with the buyer. The problem of how far back up the distribution chain the buyer can go is said to be an issue of *vertical privity*. To complicate matters, there is a second type of privity called *horizontal privity*. Horizontal privity deals with identifying to whom the retail seller is liable other than the immediate purchaser. The next Problem illustrates the difference.

PROBLEM 35

The Girard Instruments Corporation manufactured a pocket calculator called the Descartes 1000. It bought the paint used on the machine from the Hamilton Paint Company. Girard sold the calculators to the retailer, Leibnitz Department Store, which sold a calculator to Sylvester Cayley. He in turn gave it to his wife as a birthday gift. The Descartes 1000 was a popular gift. Joan Cayley used it all the time, as did the Cayley children (for homework) and even Mr. Gauss, the mailman, who borrowed it one day to compute the distance he walked on his route. After this last use, Mr. Gauss went home, where his dog, Diophantus, eagerly licked his hand and promptly dropped dead of lead poisoning. It turned out that the paint used on the Descartes 1000 had an extraordinarily high lead content. All the Cayleys and Mr. Gauss became very ill and, on recovery, brought suit for their pain and suffering, lost wages, medical expenses, and, in Mr. Gauss's case, the value of his dog. Whom should they sue?

The privity problem looks like the (following) diagram.

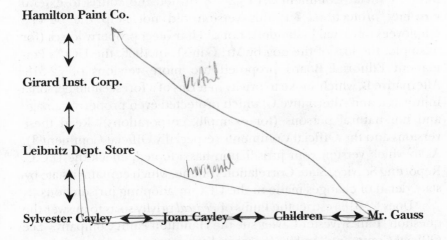

The question "Can Mr. Gauss sue the Leibnitz Department Store?" is a question of horizontal privity. The question "Can Mr. Cayley sue the Hamilton Paint Company?" is a question of vertical privity. The question "Can Mr. Gauss sue the Hamilton Paint Company?" is a question involving both horizontal and vertical privity.

If the Hamilton Paint Company had made express warranties (either in ads or in writings contained in the calculator box), most courts would have had no problem finding a cause of action in contract on the warranty in favor of anyone relying thereon. And if negligence could be proved (the doctrine of res ipsa loquitur helps here), a tort action was possible. Another theory Mr. Cayley (the retail buyer) could have tried, where no express warranty was involved, was that he was a third-party beneficiary of the implied warranties made in the sales between Hamilton and Girard and between Girard and Leibnitz. The other potential plaintiffs might also try the third-party beneficiary argument.

However, all these theories have technical, practical, or historical problems. Even with the doctrine of res ipsa loquitur, negligence can be hard to prove. Contract/warranty actions are bound by centuries of "no privity—no lawsuit" decisions. And, as we have seen, warranty suits have upheld requirements like that in §2-607(3)(a) — *notice* within a reasonable amount of time (a requirement the mailman is not likely to meet even if his attorney remembers it).

The original 1962 version of the UCC had §2-318, which spoke in a limited fashion to the question of how much horizontal privity was excused under the Code. That version (now called Alternative A) protected the retail buyer's family and house guests from personal injury. Official Comment 3 to §2-318 invited the courts to extend warranty protection. But this version did not help the buyer's employees or casual bystanders, nor did it protect property losses (for example, the loss of the dog by Mr. Gauss). In 1966, the UCC's Permanent Editorial Board proposed two more versions of §2-318: Alternative B, which spoke to privity in terms of a foreseeable personal injury test, and Alternative C, which protected even property damage and non-natural persons (for example, corporations). Read these versions and the Official Comments (especially Official Comment 3). As to which version your jurisdiction has adopted, check the U.C.C. Reporting Service, State Correlation volume, which contains a state-by-state detail of changes made in the UCC by adopting jurisdictions.

Does §2-318 restrict the limits of *vertical* privity so as to answer the question "Can Sylvester Cayley sue the Hamilton Paint Company?" See Official Comment 3 to §2-318, second sentence.

3. A Note on Strict Products Liability

About the same time that the UCC drafters were wrestling with §2-318, another legal revolution was occurring: the development of *strict products liability*. See W. Prosser, Torts 692 (5th ed. 1984). This concept has been described by Professor Prosser as "a freak hybrid born of the illicit intercourse of tort and contract." Prosser, The Fall of the Citadel (Strict Liability to the Consumer), 50 Minn. L. Rev. 791, 800 (1966). Basically, strict products liability permits recovery by an injured consumer in a suit against the manufacturer as long as the consumer can prove that the manufacturer distributed into commerce a product that contained a dangerous defect. There is no necessity of proving either negligence or privity.

The primary source of the doctrine is §402A of the Restatement (Second) of Torts:

> §402A. *Special Liability of Seller of Product for Physical Harm to User or Consumer*
>
> (1) One who sells any product in a defective condition unreasonably dangerous to the user or consumer or to his property is subject to liability for physical harm thereby caused to the ultimate user or consumer, or to his property, if
>
> > (a) the seller is engaged in the business of selling such a product, and
> >
> > (b) it is expected to and does reach the user or consumer without substantial change in the condition in which it is sold.
>
> (2) The rule stated in Subsection (1) applies although
>
> > (a) the seller has exercised all possible care in the preparation and sale of his product, and
> >
> > (b) the user or consumer has not bought the product from or entered into any contractual relation with the seller.[39]

Strict products liability as a separate cause of action has been adopted by most (but not all) courts. Starting with Henningsen v. Bloomfield Motors, Inc., 32 N.J. 358, 161 A.2d 69 (1960), and proceeding through landmark opinions such as Greenman v. Yuba Power Prods., Inc., 59 Cal. 2d 57, 377 P.2d 897, 27 Cal. Rptr. 697 (1962); Seely v. White Motor Co., 63 Cal. 2d 9, 403 P.2d 145, 45 Cal. Rptr. 17, 2 U.C.C. Rep. Serv. 915 (1965); State ex rel. Western Seed Prod. Corp. v. Campbell, 250 Or. 262, 442 P.2d 215 (1968); and Kassab v. Central

---

39. In 1997, the American Law Institute published a new Restatement Third, Torts, Products Liability, designed to update the law in this field. The new promulgation answers a host of questions that had been raised under old Restatement §402A, and is a lot more complicated than its predecessor. The primary change made by Restatement Third is that while it retains strict liability for manufacturing defects, it shifts to a negligence standard for design defects and injuries caused by failure to give a proper warning. See Restatement (Third) Torts, Products Liability §2. For a summary of the new Restatement, see David G. Owen, M. Stuart Madden, and Mary J. Davis, 1 Madden & Owen on Products Liability §§5:10-5:12 (2000).

Soya, 432 Pa. 217, 246 A.2d 848, 5 U.C.C. Rep. Serv. 925 (1968), the courts have worked one by one what Prosser has called "the most rapid and altogether spectacular overturn of an established rule in the entire history of the law of torts." W. Prosser, Torts 690 (5th ed. 1984). A cause of action based on strict products liability is very similar to the UCC implied warranty of merchantability ("fitness for ordinary purpose" is only slight degrees away from freedom from "unreasonably dangerous" defects, the §402A test), and some courts have held the two doctrines are to be measured by the same rules as to privity and defenses. See, e.g., Gregory v. White Truck & Equip. Co., 163 Ind. App. 240, 323 N.E.2d 280, 16 U.C.C. Rep. Serv. 644 (1975) (held contributory negligence is not a defense in a §2-315 suit nor in a §402A suit unless it amounts to an assumption of the risk so that plaintiff proceeded to encounter a known danger); see also Annot., 4 A.L.R.3d 501, and Annot., 46 A.L.R.3d 240, on the defense of contributory negligence in warranty/products liability suits.

East River Steamship Corp. v. Transamerica Delaval, Inc.

United States Supreme Court, 1986
476 U.S. 858, 1 U.C.C. Rep. Serv. 2d 609

JUSTICE BLACKMUN delivered the opinion of the Court. In this admiralty case, we must decide whether a cause of action in tort is stated when a defective product purchased in a commercial transaction malfunctions, injuring only the product itself and causing purely economic loss. The case requires us to consider preliminarily whether admiralty law, which already recognizes a general theory of liability for negligence, also incorporates principles of products liability, including strict liability. Then, charting a course between products liability and contract law, we must determine whether injury to a product itself is the kind of harm that should be protected by products liability or left entirely to the law of contracts.

I

In 1969, Seatrain Shipbuilding Corp. (Shipbuilding), a wholly owned subsidiary of Seatrain Lines, Inc. (Seatrain), announced it would build the four oil-transporting supertankers in issue—the T. T. Stuyvesant, T. T. Williamsburgh, T. T. Brooklyn, and T. T. Bay Ridge. Each tanker was constructed pursuant to a contract in which a separate wholly owned subsidiary of Seatrain engaged Shipbuilding. Shipbuilding in turn contracted with respondent, now known as Transamerica Delaval, Inc. (Delaval), to design, manufacture, and supervise the installation of turbines (costing $1.4 million each, see App. 163) that would be the main propulsion units for the 225,000-ton, $125 million, ibid., supertankers. When each ship was completed, its title was transferred from the contracting subsidiary to a trust company (as trustee for an owner), which in turn chartered the ship to one of the petitioners, also subsidiaries of Seatrain. Queensway Tankers, Inc., chartered the Stuyvesant; Kingsway Tankers, Inc., chartered the Williamsburgh; East River Steamship Corp. chartered the Brooklyn; and Richmond Tankers, Inc., chartered the Bay Ridge. Each petitioner operated under a bareboat charter, by which it took full control of the ship for 20 or 22 years as though it owned it, with the obligation afterwards to return the ship to the real owner. See G. Gilmore and C. Black, Admiralty §§4-1, 4-22 (2d ed. 1975). Each charterer assumed responsibility for the cost of any repairs to the ships. Tr. of Oral Arg. 11, 16-17, 35.

The Stuyvesant sailed on its maiden voyage in late July 1977. On December 11 of that year, as the ship was about to enter the Port of Valdez, Alaska, steam began to escape from the casing of the high-pressure turbine. That problem was temporarily resolved by repairs, but before long, while the ship was encountering a severe storm in the Gulf of Alaska, the high-pressure turbine malfunctioned. The ship, though lacking its normal power, was able to continue on its journey to Panama and then San Francisco. In January 1978, an examination of the high-pressure turbine revealed that the first-stage steam reversing ring virtually had disintegrated and had caused additional damage to other parts of the turbine. The damaged part was replaced with a part from the Bay Ridge, which was then under construction. In April 1978, the ship again was repaired, this time with a part from the Brooklyn. Finally, in August, the ship was permanently and satisfactorily repaired with a ring newly designed and manufactured by Delaval.

The Brooklyn and the Williamsburgh were put into service in late 1973 and late 1974, respectively. In 1978, as a result of the Stuyvesant's problems, they were inspected while in port. Those inspections revealed similar turbine damage. Temporary repairs were made, and newly designed parts were installed as permanent repairs that summer.

When the Bay Ridge was completed in early 1979, it contained the newly designed parts and thus never experienced the high-pressure turbine problems that plagued the other three ships. Nonetheless, the complaint appears to claim damages as a result of deterioration of the Bay Ridge's ring that was installed in the Stuyvesant while the Bay

Ridge was under construction. In addition, the Bay Ridge experienced a unique problem. In 1980, when the ship was on its maiden voyage, the engine began to vibrate with a frequency that increased even after speed was reduced. It turned out that the astern guardian valve, located between the high-pressure and low-pressure turbines, had been installed backwards. Because of that error, steam entered the low-pressure turbine and damaged it. After repairs, the Bay Ridge resumed its travels.

II

The charterers' second amended complaint, filed in the United States District Court for the District of New Jersey, invokes admiralty jurisdiction. It contains five counts alleging tortious conduct on the part of respondent Delaval and seeks $3.03 million in damages, App. 73, for the cost of repairing the ships and for income lost while the ships were out of service. The first four counts, read liberally, allege that Delaval is strictly liable for the design defects in the high-pressure turbines of the Stuyvesant, the Williamsburgh, the Brooklyn, and the Bay Ridge, respectively. The fifth count alleges that Delaval, as part of the manufacturing process, negligently supervised the installation of the astern guardian valve on the Bay Ridge. The initial complaint also had listed Seatrain and Shipbuilding as plaintiffs and had alleged breach of contract and warranty as well as tort claims. But after Delaval interposed a statute of limitations defense, the complaint was amended and the charterers alone brought the suit in tort. The nonrenewed claims were dismissed with prejudice by the District Court. Delaval then moved for summary judgment, contending that the charterers' actions were not cognizable in tort.

The District Court granted summary judgment for Delaval, and the Court of Appeals for the Third Circuit, sitting en banc, affirmed. East River S.S. Corp. v. Delaval Turbine, Inc., 752 F.2d 903 (1985). The Court of Appeals held that damage solely to a defective product is actionable in tort if the defect creates an unreasonable risk of harm to persons or property other than the product itself, and harm materializes. Disappointments over the product's quality, on the other hand, are protected by warranty law. Id., at 908, 909-910. The charterers were dissatisfied with product quality: the defects involved gradual and unnoticed deterioration of the turbines' component parts, and the only risk created was that the turbines would operate at a lower capacity. Id., at 909. See Pennsylvania Glass Sand Corp. v. Caterpillar Tractor

Co., 652 F.2d 1165, 1169-1170 (C.A. 3 1981). Therefore, neither the negligence nor the strict liability claims were cognizable. . . .

IV

Products liability grew out of a public policy judgment that people need more protection from dangerous products than is afforded by the law of warranty. See Seely v. White Motor Co., 63 Cal. 2d 9, 15, 403 P.2d 145, 149 (1965). It is clear, however, that if this development were allowed to progress too far, contract law would drown in a sea of tort. See G. Gilmore, The Death of Contract 87-94 (1974). We must determine whether a commercial product injuring itself is the kind of harm against which public policy requires manufacturers to protect, independent of any contractual obligation.

A

The paradigmatic products-liability action is one where a product "reasonably certain to place life and limb in peril," distributed without reinspection, causes bodily injury. See, e.g., MacPherson v. Buick Motor Co., 217 N.Y. 382, 389, 111 N.E. 1051, 1053 (1916). The manufacturer is liable whether or not it is negligent because "public policy demands that responsibility be fixed wherever it will most effectively reduce the hazards to life and health inherent in defective products that reach the market." Escola v. Coca Cola Bottling Co., 24 Cal. 2d, at 462, 150 P.2d, at 441 (concurring opinion).

For similar reasons of safety, the manufacturer's duty of care was broadened to include protection against property damage. See Marsh Wood Products Co. v. Babcock & Wilcox Co., 207 Wis. 209, 226, 240 N.W. 392, 399 (1932); Genesee County Patrons Fire Relief Assn. v. L. Sonneborn Sons, Inc., 263 N.Y. 463, 469-473, 189 N.E. 551, 553-555 (1934). Such damage is considered so akin to personal injury that the two are treated alike. See Seely v. White Motor Co., 63 Cal. 2d, at 19, 403 P.2d, at 152.

In the traditional "property damage" cases, the defective product damages other property. In this case, there was no damage to "other" property. Rather, the first, second, and third counts allege that each supertanker's defectively designed turbine components damaged only the turbine itself. Since each turbine was supplied by Delaval as an integrated package, see App. 162-163, each is properly regarded as a single unit. "Since all but the very simplest of machines have component parts, [a contrary] holding would require a finding of 'property damage' in virtually every case where a product damages itself. Such a holding would eliminate the distinction between warranty and strict products liability." Northern Power & Engineering Corp. v. Caterpillar Tractor Co., 623 P.2d 324, 330 (Alaska 1981). The fifth count also alleges injury to the product itself. Before the high-pressure and low-pressure turbines could become an operational propulsion system, they were connected to piping and valves under the supervision of Delaval personnel. See App. 78, 162-163, 181. Delaval's supervisory obligations were part of its manufacturing agreement. The fifth count thus can best be read to allege that Delaval's negligent manufacture of the propulsion system—by allowing the installation in reverse of the astern guardian valve—damaged the propulsion system. Cf. Lewis v. Timco, Inc., 736 F.2d 163, 165-166 (C.A. 5 1984). Obviously, damage to a product itself has certain attributes of a products-liability claim. But the injury suffered—the failure of the product to function properly— is the essence of a warranty action, through which a contracting party can seek to recoup the benefit of its bargain.

B

The intriguing question whether injury to a product itself may be brought in tort has spawned a variety of answers. At one end of the spectrum, the case that created the majority land-based approach, Seely v. White Motor Co., 63 Cal. 2d 9, 403 P.2d 145 (1965) (defective truck), held that preserving a proper role for the law of warranty precludes imposing tort liability if a defective product causes purely monetary harm. See also Jones & Laughlin Steel Corp. v. Johns-Manville Sales Corp., 626 F.2d 280, 287 and n.13 (C.A. 3 1980) (citing cases).

At the other end of the spectrum is the minority land-based approach, whose progenitor, Santor v. A. and M. Karagheusian, Inc., 44 N.J. 52, 66-67, 207 A.2d 305, 312-313 (1965) (marred carpeting), held that a manufacturer's duty to make nondefective products encompassed injury to the product itself, whether or not the defect created an unreasonable risk of harm.[40] See also LaCrosse v. Schubert, 72 Wis. 2d 38, 44-45, 240 N.W.2d 124, 127-128 (1976). The courts adopting this approach, including the majority of the Courts of Appeals sitting in

40. Interestingly, the New Jersey and California Supreme Courts have each taken what appears to be a step in the direction of the other since *Santor* and *Seely*. In Spring Motors Distributors, Inc. v. Ford Motor Co., 98 N.J., at 579, 489 A.2d, at 672, the New Jersey court rejected *Santor* in the commercial context. And in J'Aire Corp. v. Gregory, 24 Cal. 3d 799, 598 P.2d 60 (1979), the California court recognized a cause of action for negligent interference with prospective economic advantage.

admiralty that have considered the issue, e.g., Emerson G. M. Diesel, Inc. v. Alaskan Enterprise, 732 F.2d 1468 (C.A. 9 1984), find that the safety and insurance rationales behind strict liability apply equally where the losses are purely economic. These courts reject the *Seely* approach because they find it arbitrary that economic losses are recoverable if a plaintiff suffers bodily injury or property damage, but not if a product injures itself. They also find no inherent difference between economic loss and personal injury or property damage, because all are proximately caused by the defendant's conduct. Further, they believe recovery for economic loss would not lead to unlimited liability because they think a manufacturer can predict and insure against product failure. See Emerson G. M. Diesel, Inc. v. Alaskan Enterprise, 732 F.2d, at 1474.

Between the two poles fall a number of cases that would permit a products-liability action under certain circumstances when a product injures only itself. These cases attempt to differentiate between "the disappointed users . . . and the endangered ones," Russell v. Ford Motor Co., 281 Ore. 587, 595, 575 P.2d 1383, 1387 (1978), and permit only the latter to sue in tort. The determination has been said to turn on the nature of the defect, the type of risk, and the manner in which the injury arose. See Pennsylvania Glass Sand Corp. v. Caterpillar Tractor Co., 652 F.2d 1165, 1173 (C.A. 3 1981) (relied on by the Court of Appeals in this case). The Alaska Supreme Court allows a tort action if the defective product creates a situation potentially dangerous to persons or other property, and loss occurs as a proximate result of that danger and under dangerous circumstances. Northern Power & Engineering Corp. v. Caterpillar Tractor Co., 623 P.2d 324, 329 (1981).

We find the intermediate and minority land-based positions unsatisfactory. The intermediate positions, which essentially turn on the degree of risk, are too indeterminate to enable manufacturers easily to structure their business behavior. Nor do we find persuasive a distinction that rests on the manner in which the product is injured. We realize that the damage may be qualitative, occurring through gradual deterioration or internal breakage. Or it may be calamitous. Compare Morrow v. New Moon Homes, Inc., 548 P.2d 279 (Alaska 1976), with Cloud v. Kit Mfg. Co., 563 P.2d 248, 251 (Alaska 1977). But either way, since by definition no person or other property is damaged, the resulting loss is purely economic. Even when the harm to the product itself occurs through an abrupt, accident-like event, the resulting loss due to repair costs, decreased value, and lost profits is essentially the failure of the purchaser to receive the benefit of its bargain—traditionally the core concern of contract law. See E. Farnsworth, Contracts §12.8, pp.839-840 (1982).

We also decline to adopt the minority land-based view espoused by *Santor and Emerson.* Such cases raise legitimate questions about the theories behind restricting products liability, but we believe that the countervailing arguments are more powerful. The minority view fails to account for the need to keep products liability and contract law in separate spheres and to maintain a realistic limitation on damages.

C

Exercising traditional discretion in admiralty, see Pope & Talbot, Inc. v. Hawn, 346 U.S. 406, 409 (1953), we adopt an approach similar to *Seely* and hold that a manufacturer in a commercial relationship has no duty under either a negligence or strict products-liability theory to prevent a product from injuring itself.

"The distinction that the law has drawn between tort recovery for physical injuries and warranty recovery for economic loss is not arbitrary and does not rest on the 'luck' of one plaintiff in having an accident causing physical injury. The distinction rests, rather, on an understanding of the nature of the responsibility a manufacturer must undertake in distributing his products." Seely v. White Motor Co., 63 Cal. 2d, at 18, 403 P.2d, at 151. When a product injures only itself the reasons for imposing a tort duty are weak and those for leaving the party to its contractual remedies are strong.

The tort concern with safety is reduced when an injury is only to the product itself. When a person is injured, the "cost of an injury and the loss of time or health may be an overwhelming misfortune," and one the person is not prepared to meet. Escola v. Coca Cola Bottling Co., 24 Cal. 2d, at 462, 150 P.2d, at 441 (concurring opinion). In contrast, when a product injures itself, the commercial user stands to lose the value of the product, risks the displeasure of its customers who find that the product does not meet their needs, or, as in this case, experiences increased costs in performing a service. Losses like these can be insured. See 10A Couch on Insurance §§42:385-42:401, 42:414-417 (2d ed. 1982); 7 Benedict on Admiralty, Form No. 1.16-7 (7th ed. 1985); 5A Appleman, Insurance Law and Practice §3252 (1970). Society need not presume that a customer needs special protection. The increased cost to the public that would result from holding a manufacturer liable in tort for injury to the product itself is not justified. Cf. United States v. Carroll Towing Co., 159 F.2d 169, 173 (C.A. 2 1947).

Damage to a product itself is most naturally understood as a warranty claim. Such damage means simply that the product has not met the customer's expectations, or, in other words, that the customer has received "insufficient product value." See J. White and R. Summers, Uniform Commercial Code 406 (2d ed. 1980). The maintenance of product value and quality is precisely the purpose of express and implied warranties. See UCC §2-313 (express warranty), §2-314 (implied warranty of merchantability), and §2-315 (warranty of fitness for a particular purpose). Therefore, a claim of a nonworking product can be brought as a breach-of-warranty action. Or, if the customer prefers, it can reject the product or revoke its acceptance and sue for breach of contract. See UCC §§2-601, 2-608, 2-612.

Contract law, and the law of warranty in particular, is well suited to commercial controversies of the sort involved in this case because the parties may set the terms of their own agreements. The manufacturer can restrict its liability, within limits, by disclaiming warranties or limiting remedies. See UCC §§2-316, 2-719. In exchange, the purchaser pays less for the product. Since a commercial situation generally does not involve large disparities in bargaining power, cf. Henningsen v. Bloomfield Motors, Inc., 32 N.J. 358, 161 A.2d 69 (1960), we see no reason to intrude into the parties' allocation of the risk.

While giving recognition to the manufacturer's bargain, warranty law sufficiently protects the purchaser by allowing it to obtain the benefit of its bargain. See J. White and R. Summers, supra, ch. 10. The expectation damages available in warranty for purely economic loss give a plaintiff the full benefit of its bargain by compensating for forgone business opportunities. See Fuller and Perdue, The Reliance Interest in Contract Damages: 1, 46 Yale L.J. 52, 60-63 (1936); R. Posner, Economic Analysis of Law §4.8 (3d ed. 1986). Recovery on a warranty theory would give the charterers their repair costs and lost profits, and would place them in the position they would have been in had the turbines functioned properly.[41] See Hawkins v. McGee, 84 N.H. 114, 146 A. 641 (1929). Thus, both the nature of the injury and the

---

41. In contrast, tort damages generally compensate the plaintiff for loss and return him to the position he occupied before the injury. Cf. Sullivan v. O'Connor, 363 Mass. 579, 584-586, 588, n.6, 296 N.E.2d 183, 187-188, 189, n.6 (1973); Prosser, The Borderland of Tort and Contract, in Selected Topics on the Law of Torts 380, 424-427 (Thomas M. Cooley Lectures, Fourth Series 1953). Tort damages are analogous to reliance damages, which are awarded in contract when there is particular difficulty in measuring the expectation interest. See, e.g., Security Stove & Mfg. Co. v. American Railways Express Co., 227 Mo. App. 175, 51 S.W.2d 572 (1932).

resulting damages indicate it is more natural to think of injury to a product itself in terms of warranty.

A warranty action also has a built-in limitation on liability, whereas a tort action could subject the manufacturer to damages of an indefinite amount. The limitation in a contract action comes from the agreement of the parties and the requirement that consequential damages, such as lost profits, be a foreseeable result of the breach. See Hadley v. Baxendale, 9 Ex. 341, 156 Eng. Rep. 145 (1854). In a warranty action where the loss is purely economic, the limitation derives from the requirements of foreseeability and of privity, which is still generally enforced for such claims in a commercial setting. See UCC §2-715; J. White and R. Summers, Uniform Commercial Code 389, 396, 406-410 (2d ed. 1980).

In products-liability law, where there is a duty to the public generally, foreseeability is an inadequate brake. Cf. Petitions of Kinsman Transit Co., 388 F.2d 821 (C.A. 2 1968). See also Perlman, Interference with Contract and Other Economic Expectancies: A Clash of Tort and Contract Doctrine, 49 U. Chi. L. Rev. 61, 71-72 (1982). Permitting recovery for all foreseeable claims for purely economic loss could make a manufacturer liable for vast sums. It would be difficult for a manufacturer to take into account the expectations of persons downstream who may encounter its product. In this case, for example, if the charterers —already one step removed from the transaction—were permitted to recover their economic losses, then the companies that subchartered the ships might claim their economic losses from the delays, and the charterers' customers also might claim their economic losses, and so on. "The law does not spread its protection so far." Robins Dry Dock & Repair Co. v. Flint, 275 U.S. 303, 309 (1927).

And to the extent that courts try to limit purely economic damages in tort, they do so by relying on a far murkier line, one that negates the charterers' contention that permitting such recovery under a products-liability theory enables admiralty courts to avoid difficult linedrawing. Cf. Ultramares Corp. v. Touche, 255 N.Y. 170, 174 N.E. 441 (1931); State ex rel. Guste v. M/V Testbank, 752 F.2d 1019, 1046-1052 (C.A. 5 1985) (en banc) (dissenting opinion), *cert. pending*, No. 84-1808.

D

For the first three counts, the defective turbine components allegedly injured only the turbines themselves. Therefore, a strict products-liability theory of recovery is unavailable to the charterers. Any warranty claims would be subject to Delaval's limitation, both in time and scope, of its warranty liability. App. 78-89. The record indicates that Seatrain and Delaval reached a settlement agreement. Deposition of Stephen Russell, p.32. We were informed that these charterers could not have asserted the warranty claims. See Tr. of Oral Arg. 36. Even so, the charterers should be left to the terms of their bargains, which explicitly allocated the cost of repairs.

In the charterers' agreements with the owners, the charterers took the ships in "as is" condition, after inspection, and assume full responsibility for them, including responsibility for maintenance and repairs and for obtaining forms of insurance. Tr. of Oral Arg. 11, 16-17, 35; App. 86, 88, 99, 101, 112, 114, 125-126, 127. In a separate agreement between each charterer and Seatrain, Seatrain agreed to guarantee certain payments and covenants by each charterer to the owner. App. 142-156. The contractual responsibilities thus were clearly laid out. There is no reason to extricate the parties from their bargain.

Similarly, in the fifth count, alleging the reverse installation of the astern guardian valve, the only harm was to the propulsion system itself rather than to persons or other property. Even assuming that Delaval's supervision was negligent, as we must on this summary judgment motion, Delaval owed no duty under a products-liability theory based on negligence to avoid causing purely economic loss. Cf. Flintkote Co. v. Dravo Corp., 678 F.2d 942 (C.A. 11 1982); S. M. Wilson & Co. v. Smith International, Inc., 587 F.2d 1363 (C.A. 9 1978). Thus, whether stated in negligence or strict liability, no products-liability claim lies in admiralty when the only injury claimed is economic loss.

While we hold that the fourth count should have been dismissed, we affirm the entry of judgment for Delaval.

It is so ordered.

ECONOMIC LOSS DOCTRINE

This decision has proven very influential in convincing the state courts that the economic loss doctrine should preclude the application of tort theories to commercial matters where the only injury is to the product itself. The chief reason why contracts/commercial law is not utilized in this situation is that the statue of limitations has run on all but the tort claims. Where that is true the injured plaintiff will try the tort theories, but runs afoul of the *East River* doctrine. Courts have even denied tort recoveries in consumer suits; see Clarys v. Ford Motor Co., 592 N.W.2d 573, 39 U.C.C. Rep. Serv. 2d 72 (N.D. 1999) (faulty ignition switch caused automobile to burn in parking lot). Where the injury is not only to the product but to other property as well, most courts will allow the tort theories to go forward, though, as you can imagine, this leads to a lot of fine line-drawing. See, e.g., Wausau Tile, Inc. v. County Concrete Corp., 593 N.W.2d 445, 40 U.C.C. Rep. Serv. 2d 417 (Wis. 1999) (damage by a defective component of an integrated system to other system components is not damage to "other property" which precludes the application of the economic loss doctrine).

Strict products liability suits are largely similar to implied warranty suits, though some courts struggle mightily to draw distinctions between the two causes of action; see Denny v. Ford Motor Co., 87 N.Y.2d 248, 662 N.E.2d 730, 28 U.C.C. Rep. Serv. 2d 15 (N.Y. 1995). Typically, either a suit under §402A or a suit for breach of the implied warranty of merchantability can be a viable legal alternative under the same facts. There are some differences that are immediately visible:

(1) A §402A cause of action does not require notice; a UCC cause of action does. See §2-607(3)(a).

(2) In a §402A cause of action, damages are limited to those for physical injury; the damages in a UCC cause of action are not. See §2-715.

(3) A §402A cause of action has the statute of limitations imposed by state law for tort actions; the UCC action is governed by §2-725. The time periods may differ significantly.

(4) A §402A cause of action is not affected by disclaimers or remedy limitations; a UCC action may be so limited. See §§2-316, 2-719.

(5) Privity is not an issue in §402 suits; privity may be an issue in UCC suits.

(6) Section 402A requires that the product contain a "defect," but a UCC warranty may be breached even if the product is not defective. For example, a perfectly good product may neither fulfill the express warranty nor be fit for the particular purpose for which the buyer needs the goods. See Malawy v. Richards Mfg. Co., 150 Ill. App. 3d 549, 501 N.E.2d 376, 3 U.C.C. Rep. Serv. 2d 511 (1986).

PROBLEM 36

The axle on Monty Python's new car snapped in two while he was driving at a high rate of speed on the interstate. Python's car skidded across the median and ran into a hitchhiker, Thumbs Bystander, killing him instantly. As Bystander's attorney, decide which is the best cause of action: negligence, §402A, or §2-314. Whom should you sue? See Martin v. Ryder Truck Rental, Inc., 353 A.2d 581, 18 U.C.C. Rep. Serv. 870 (Del. 1976).

E. UCC Warranties and the Magnuson-Moss Act

In 1975, Congress passed the Magnuson-Moss Warranty Act,[42] which applies to all consumer products manufactured after July 4, 1975, that are covered by a written warranty. Magnuson-Moss was enacted in response to many years of consumer complaints about warranties—in particular about manufacturers' statements that were labeled warranties, but that upon testing in the courts took away more rights than they gave. The stated purposes of the statute are to improve the adequacy of information available to consumers, to prevent deception, and to improve competition in the marketing of consumer products.[43] For a comprehensive study, see C. Reitz, Consumer Protection Under the Magnuson-Moss Warranty Act (1978).

To apply Magnuson-Moss, the warranty given must fall within its scope. Read Mag.-Moss §101,[44] and answer the following Problems.

PROBLEM 37

Attorney Sam Ambulance formed a professional corporation, Ambulance, L.P.C., under which he practices law. When the corporation buys a company car, is it entitled to the protection of the Magnuson-Moss Warranty Act? See §101(1) and (3).

PROBLEM 38

(a) When Naive Ned bought his car from Sharp Sam's Used Car lot, Sam said, "I refuse to warrant my cars in any way." Is there a possible Magnuson-Moss action? See Mag.-Moss §102(b)(2). Is there a UCC warranty?

(b) When Suspicious Sally bought her car from Sharp Sam, she demanded that he warrant the car. Sam said, "I promise that this car

---

42. The full name of the statute is the Magnuson-Moss Warranty—Federal Trade Commission Improvement Act, 15 U.S.C. §§2301-2312 (1975). Title I deals with consumer product warranties. Title II deals with Federal Trade Commission powers. Only Title I will be discussed in this text.

43. Title I, 15 U.S.C. §2302(a).

44. Citations styled Mag.-Moss §____ refer to 15 U.S.C. §2301 et seq., Magnuson-Moss Warranty—Federal Trade Commission Improvement Act (1975). Note: section enumeration in textbooks is not always consistent with the enumeration in the U.S.C. In some texts, §2301 of the U.S.C. is labeled as §101, §2302 is labeled as §102, etc.

has a sound engine that will last five years." Is there a possible Mag-nuson-Moss action? See Mag.-Moss §102(a). Is there a UCC warranty?

(c) When Clever Carl bought his car from Sharp Sam, he de-manded that Sam write down his warranty. Sam wrote the following: "I guarantee that the only person to ever own this car was a little old lady who only drove it to church every Sunday." If it turns out that in fact the car was owned by Hotdog Harry, a speedway racer, is there a possible Magnuson-Moss action? See Mag.-Moss §101(6). Is there a UCC warranty? See Skelton v. General Motors Corp., 500 F. Supp. 1181 (N.D. Ill. 1981).

(d) When Hardbargain Hannah bought her car from Sharp Sam, she, too, demanded a written warranty. Before the sale Sam took her into his salesroom and pointed out two looseleaf binders. Inside one of the binders under the model name of the car that Hannah desired, Super Z, there was written the following statement:

The Super Z Has a Full Life-Time Guarantee.

Has Sam subjected himself to Magnuson-Moss? See Mag.-Moss §104. Is there a UCC warranty?

(e) Mammoth Motors phones you, its corporate counsel, and says that it has heard that two types of written warranties are possible under Magnuson-Moss: a *Full* (statement of duration, e.g., 1 year or 90 days) *Warranty* and a *Limited Warranty*. It is very proud of the performance of its vehicles and is considering giving the full warranty. What differences are there between the two types? See Mag.-Moss §§103, 104, 105, 108. What do you advise?

The most important intersection between the UCC and the Magnuson-Moss Act lies in the area of implied warranties. Read Mag.-Moss §108.

PROBLEM 39

Fenton Hardy bought a new car from Dixon Motors. The car carried a full three-month warranty, which guaranteed all the parts except the tires as defect-free. The warranty conspicuously stated that "this warranty is in lieu of all other warranties, express or implied, particularly the warranty of merchantability." One day after the three-month period expired, every part in the car (except the tires) malfunctioned. Hardy sued in state court using UCC §2-314 as his theory. Was the warranty disclaimer effective? See Mag.-Moss §108. Would it have been effective had Dixon offered only a "limited warranty"? See Mag.-Moss §108 again. In an action based on §2-314, may Hardy recover his attorney fees? See Mag.-Moss §110(d); Champion Ford Sales, Inc. v. Levine, 49 Md. App. 547, 433 A.2d 1218, 33 U.C.C. Rep. Serv. 108 (1981).

Ventura v. Ford Motor Corp.

New Jersey Superior Court, Appellate Division, 1981
180 N.J. Super. 45, 433 A.2d 801, 31 U.C.C. Rep. Serv. 59

BOTTER, J. Ford Motor Company (Ford) appeals from the final judgment in this action in which plaintiff, the purchaser of a new 1978 Mercury Marquis Brougham, sued Ford's authorized dealer, Marino Auto Sales, Inc. (Marino Auto), and Ford, as manufacturer, for damages due to defects in the vehicle. Marino Auto cross-claimed against Ford for indemnification. The final judgment (a) granted plaintiff rescission of the purchase and damages of $6,745.59 against Marino Auto Sales (representing the purchase price of $7,847.49 less an allowance for plaintiff's use of the car and the sales tax), (b) awarded damages in favor of Marino Auto against Ford on the cross-claim in the sum of $2,910.59 (representing $6,745.59 less the resale value of the car), and (c) awarded counsel fees to plaintiff against Ford in the sum of $5,165. Plaintiff's demands for interest, punitive damages in excess of $2,000,000 and treble damages were denied. The trial court's published opinion was limited to the issue of counsel fees awarded under the Magnuson-Moss Warranty—Federal Trade Commission Improvement Act, 15 U.S.C. §2301 et seq., 173 N.J. Super. 501 (Ch. Div. 1980).

Plaintiff took delivery of the automobile on April 12, 1978. According to the testimony of plaintiff and his wife they experienced engine hesitation and stalling problems early in their use of the car which continued without interruption despite repeated attempts by Marino Auto to cure the problem. Stanley Bednarz, Ford's zone service manager and mechanical specialist who assists dealers in satisfying customers, inspected the vehicle on July 13, 1978 and recommended replacing the exhaust regulator valve. Plaintiff testified that he was told by Bednarz that there was nothing wrong with the car and he would "have to live with this one." Plaintiff also testified that later in July 1978 he returned to Marino Auto intending to ask Mr. Marino to take the car back if it could not be fixed but that he was prevented from doing so and was forcibly removed from the premises. . . .

We reject the contention that, lacking expert proof, plaintiff failed to establish that a defective mechanism for which Ford was responsible caused the engine to hesitate and stall. This conclusion could be reached by inferences from the evidence. [Citations omitted.] The findings that Ford breached its express warranty and that the car was substantially impaired were supported by sufficient credible evidence and must be affirmed on appeal. Rova Farms Resort, Inc. v. Investors Ins. Co. of America, 65 N.J. 474, 483-484 (1974).

At the conclusion of plaintiff's case against Ford the trial judge announced his findings and conclusions that Ford had breached its warranty, that the car was substantially impaired because of persistent and continual stalling and hesitation, but that plaintiff had not proven damages against Ford. He held that the only remedy to which plaintiff was entitled was rescission or revocation of acceptance against Marino Auto, see §2-608; Herbstman v. Eastman Kodak Co., 68 N.J. 1, 9-10 (1975), except that plaintiff would also have a claim for attorney's fees against Ford under the Magnuson-Moss Warranty Act, supra, 15 U.S.C. §2310(d)(2). Various reasons were given for affording plaintiff the right to rescind the purchase and receive a refund of the purchase price from Marino Auto. At one point in his oral decision the trial judge alternatively relied upon the theory of strict liability in tort and breach of an implied warranty of merchantability and fitness. In his written opinion he stated that this result "pierced through the dealership system, granting rescission against the selling dealer Marino, based upon defects in breach of the manufacturer Ford's express warranty." 173 N.J. Super. at 504. He also said: "The only remedy under the Magnuson-Moss Warranty Act for Ford's violation of the act was rescission against the selling dealer Marino"; and he viewed Marino Auto as Ford's "authorized agent to remedy defects. . . ." Id. Punitive damages against Ford were denied because of the absence of "deliberate, willful, malicious fraud or wanton and gross negligence or unconscionable commercial practice. . . ." Thus, the case was continued to permit plaintiff to claim a refund of the purchase price, less an allowance for the use of the car, on a rescission basis against Marino Auto, and to permit Marino Auto to claim indemnification against Ford. Ford was to be afforded the opportunity to defend by establishing Marino Auto's fault in failing properly to repair the auto.

On the next trial date Marino Auto stipulated the sale of the car to plaintiff and seemingly conceded at one point that plaintiff would be entitled to a judgment against Marino Auto based on the finding of

Ford's breach of warranty on the proofs offered by plaintiff against Ford. The issues to be tried, then, were declared to be damages on rescission or revocation of acceptance, §2-608, i.e., the purchase price less the value of the car to be returned to the dealer, minus an allowance for the limited use of the car. (There was evidence that plaintiff was financially compelled to continue to use the vehicle in its imperfect state. Upon the seller's breach the buyer has the right to "cover" by acquiring substituted goods but is not barred from any other remedy if he fails to effect "cover." Sections 2-711 and 712. See also §2-711(3) which gives the buyer a security interest in and the right to retain or resell goods after revocation of acceptance.) The case proceeded on the cross-claim although Ford contended that no claim ever could arise until plaintiff recovered a judgment against Marino Auto. On the assumption that proof of Ford's breach of an express warranty established plaintiff's right to recover against Marino Auto, 173 N.J. Super. at 503-504, the trial judge ordered the trial to proceed on Marino Auto's indemnification claim. Proof of plaintiff's damage claim was also anticipated before a final judgment was to be entered on the complaint and cross-claim.

Proofs were presented by Ford to show that the car was not defective and that there could be other causes for engine hesitation or stalling, such as contaminated fuel. Although Ford contends that Marino Auto was negligent in not checking the fuel system, there was no proof that contaminated fuel was the actual cause of the problem. Thus, there was no proof that the defect in the vehicle would have been discovered but for Marino Auto's lack of reasonable care in attempting to repair the car. Marino Auto cannot be denied indemnification because it failed to successfully diagnose the cause of the problem. Ford's expert could find nothing wrong with the car, and, on the facts of this case the trial judge could properly have rejected Ford's contention that Marino Auto was at fault for not correcting it, regardless of where the burden of proving Marino Auto's negligence was placed.

At the conclusion of this testimony Marino Auto contended that there was no proof of any wrongdoing by Marino Auto and no basis for rescission. However, Marino Auto also claimed indemnification from Ford for any damage award granted to plaintiff against Marino Auto. Ford contended that no judgment should be entered against Marino Auto, that there was no basis for rescission and therefore no need for indemnification. Ford also protested the lack of sufficient notice of plaintiff's complaints about the car's performance.

We have considered the merits of this appeal on the assumption that, although Marino Auto has not appealed the judgment against it,

Ford can contend that no judgment should have been entered against Marino Auto. Ford has an interest in the judgment against Marino Auto since it was the basis for Ford's indemnification obligation. In fact, the trial judge did consider Ford's arguments against Marino Auto's liability to plaintiff.

Our reasoning through the body of law applicable to this commonplace contractual skein, which binds consumers, car dealers and manufacturers together, differs from that of the trial judge. But we affirm plaintiff's recovery. We conclude that, despite Marino Auto's attempted disclaimer of all warranties, plaintiff can recover from Marino Auto for the breach of implied warranty of merchantability. We also uphold the award of counsel fees against Ford pursuant to the Magnuson-Moss Warranty Act.

The contract of sale between Marino Auto and plaintiff conspicuously contained the following legend on its face:

> The seller, MARINO AUTO SALES, Inc., hereby expressly disclaims all warranties, either expressed or implied, including any implied warranty of merchantability or fitness for a particular purpose, and MARINO AUTO SALES, Inc., neither assumes nor authorizes another person to assume for it any liability in connection with the sale of the vehicle.

On the back of this sales order-contract were the following terms which were made part of the contract:

> 7. It is expressly agreed that there are no warranties, express or implied, made by either the selling dealer or the manufacturer on the motor vehicle, chassis or parts furnished hereunder except, in the case of a new motor vehicle the warranty expressly given to the purchaser upon the delivery of such motor vehicle or chassis.
>
> The selling dealer also agrees to promptly perform and fulfill all terms and conditions of the owner service policy.

For the purpose of this opinion we will assume that the disclaimer of implied warranties of merchantability and fitness was effective under the Uniform Commercial Code §2-316. Since the dealer passed on to the purchaser a warranty from the manufacturer, we will not consider whether the attempted disclaimer by Marino Auto should be voided as unconscionable and contrary to public policy under §2-302 even though such disclaimer could foreclose rescission or other remedies against the dealer and, without privity between buyer and manufacturer, rescission has been held ordinarily unavailable under the Code against the manufacturer. Edelstein v. Toyota Motors Distributors, 176 N.J. Super. 57, 64 (App. Div. 1980); see Henningsen v. Bloomfield Motors, Inc., 32 N.J. 358, 372-373, 406-408 (1960); Gladden v. Cadillac Motor Car Div., 83 N.J. 320, 330-331 (1980); Herbstman v. Eastman Kodak Co., supra, 68 N.J. at 9-10; cf. Santor v. A. & M. Karagheusian, Inc., 44 N.J. 52 (1965). Section 2-316(1) provides that "words or conduct tending to negate or limit warranty shall be construed whereever reasonable as consistent with each other; but subject to the provisions of this Chapter on parol or extrinsic evidence (§2-202) negation or limitation is inoperative to the extent that such construction is unreasonable." It may be argued that the dealer's conduct in transmitting Ford's warranty to plaintiff, the reference to such warranty in paragraph 7 on the back of the purchase order-contract, and the undertaking "to promptly perform and fulfill all terms and conditions of the owner service policy," are inconsistent with a disclaimer of all warranties and that such a disclaimer is an unreasonable construction. See Gladden v. Cadillac Motor Car Div., supra, 83 N.J. at 330; Henningsen v. Bloomfield Motors, Inc., supra, 32 N.J. at 407-408; cf. Murray v. Holiday Rambler, Inc., 83 Wis. 2d 406, —, 265 N.W.2d 513, 519 (Sup. Ct. 1978). The contract in the *Henningsen* case contained the identical obligation to perform all terms and conditions of the owner service policy. Id. The combination of the dealer's undertaking and the automobile manufacturer's warranty was interpreted in *Henningsen* to rebut the disclaimer of implied warranty of merchantability by the dealer. The court held that the attempt to limit liability to the replacement of defective parts was contrary to public policy and void with respect to a claim for personal injuries resulting from an accident caused by defects in an automobile. However, we need not explore these issues further because the Magnuson-Moss Warranty Act has solved many of the problems posed by the intricacies confronting consumers under the preexisting law of sales.

The Magnuson-Moss Warranty—Federal Trade Commission Improvement Act, supra, was adopted on January 4, 1975, 88 Stat. 2183. Its purpose was to make "warranties on consumer products more readily understandable and enforceable." Note, 7 Rutgers-Camden L.J. 379 (1976). The act enhances the consumer's position by allowing recovery under a warranty without regard to privity of contract between the consumer and warrantor, by prohibiting the disclaimer of implied warranties in a written warranty, and by enlarging the remedies available to a consumer for breach of warranty, including the award of attorneys' fees. Id. The requirement of privity of contract between the consumer and the warrantor has been removed by assuring consumers a remedy against all warrantors of the product.[45] A consumer is defined in 15 U.S.C. §2301(3) as follows:

> (3) The term "consumer" means a buyer (other than for purposes of resale) of any consumer product, any person to whom such product is transferred during the duration of an implied or written warranty (or service contract) applicable to the product, and any other person who is entitled by the terms of such warranty (or service contract) or under applicable State law to enforce against the warrantor (or service contractor) the obligations of the warranty (or service contract).

A "supplier" is defined as any person engaged in the business of making a consumer product directly or indirectly available to consumers, §2301(4), and a "warrantor" includes any supplier or other person who gives or offers to give a written warranty or who is obligated under an implied warranty. §2301(5). The term "written warranty" is defined in §2301(6) to include:

> (A) any written affirmation of fact or written promise made in connection with the sale of a consumer product by a supplier to a buyer which relates to the nature of the material or workmanship and affirms or promises that such material or workmanship is defect free or will meet a specified level of performance over a specified period of time, or
> (B) any undertaking in writing in connection with the sale by a supplier of a consumer product to refund, repair, replace or take other remedial action with respect to such product in the event that such product fails to meet the specifications set forth in the undertaking.

The Magnuson-Moss Warranty Act provides for two types of written warranties on consumer products, those described as "full" warranties and those described as "limited" warranties. 15 U.S.C. §2303. The nature of the "full" warranty is prescribed by §2304. It expressly provides in subsection (a)(4) that a consumer must be given the election to receive a refund or replacement without charge of a product or part which is defective or malfunctions after a reasonable number of attempts by the warrantor to correct such condition. For the breach of any warranty, express or implied, or of a service contract (defined in 15 U.S.C. §2301(8)), consumers are given the right to sue for damages

---

45. In Miller and Kanter, "Litigation Under Magnuson-Moss: New Opportunities in Private Actions," 13 U.C.C. L.J. 10, 21-22 (1980), the authors discuss the broad definition of a consumer and state that "an assumption is now created that no privity restriction exists."

and "other legal and equitable relief" afforded under state or federal law, 15 U.S.C.A. §2310(d); 15 U.S.C. §2311(b)(1).

Appellant Ford contends that the trial judge improperly invoked section 2304 of the act as a basis for allowing "rescission" in the case since the warranty given by Ford was a limited warranty and not a full warranty. 15 U.S.C. §2303(a)(2) provides that all warranties that do not meet federal minimum standards for warranty contained in §2304 shall be conspicuously designated a "limited warranty." "Limited warranties" protect consumers by prohibiting disclaimers of implied warranties, §2308, but are otherwise not described in the act. Note, supra 7, Rutgers-Camden L.J. at 381. Clearly, Ford's warranty, which is quoted later in this opinion, was a limited warranty.

15 U.S.C. §2308 provides as follows:

(a) No supplier may disclaim or modify (except as provided in subsection (b) of this section) any implied warranty to a consumer with respect to such consumer product if (1) such supplier makes any written warranty to the consumer with respect to such consumer product, or (2) at the time of sale, or within 90 days thereafter, such supplier enters into a service contract with the consumer which applies to such consumer product.

(b) For purposes of this chapter (other than section 2304(a)(2) of this title), implied warranties may be limited in duration to the duration of a written warranty of reasonable duration, if such limitation is conscionable and is set forth in clear and unmistakable language and prominently displayed on the face of the warranty.

(c) A disclaimer, modification, or limitation made in violation of this section shall be ineffective for purposes of this chapter and State law.

We will first consider the application of this act to the dealer, Marino Auto. As quoted above, paragraph 7 of the purchase order-contract provides that there are no warranties, express or implied, made by the selling dealer or manufacturer except, in the case of a new motor vehicle, "the warranty expressly given to the purchaser upon delivery of such motor vehicle. . . ." This section also provides: "The selling dealer also agrees to promptly perform and fulfill all terms and conditions of the owner service policy." Ford contended in the trial court that Marino Auto had "a duty" to properly diagnose and make repairs, that such duty was "fixed both by the express warranty . . . which they passed on . . . and by the terms of [paragraph 7 of the contract with plaintiff]" by which Marino Auto expressly undertook "to perform its obligations under the owner service policy." See 15 U.S.C. §2310(f); 16 C.F.R. §700.4 (1980). The provision in paragraph 7 in these circumstances is a "written warranty" within the meaning of §2301(6)(B) since it constitutes an undertaking in connection with the sale to take "remedial action with respect to such product in the event that such product fails to meet the specifications set forth in the undertaking. . . ." In our view the specifications of the undertaking include, at the least, the provisions of the limited warranty furnished by Ford, namely:

> *LIMITED WARRANTY (12 MONTHS OR 12,000 MILES/19,312 KILOMETRES) 1978 NEW CAR AND LIGHT TRUCK*
> Ford warrants for its 1978 model cars and light trucks that the Selling Dealer will repair or replace free any parts, except tires, found under normal use in the U.S. or Canada to be defective in factory materials or workmanship within the earlier of 12 months or 12,000 miles/19,312 km from either first use or retail delivery.
> All we require is that you properly operate and maintain your vehicle and that you return for warranty service to your Selling Dealer or any Ford or Lincoln-Mercury Dealer if you are traveling, have moved a long distance or need emergency repairs. Warranty repairs will be made with Ford Authorized Service or Remanufactured Parts.
> THERE IS NO OTHER EXPRESS WARRANTY ON THIS VEHICLE.[46]

The record does not contain a written description of the "owner service policy" which the dealer agreed to perform. Nevertheless, since Ford is the appellant here, we take its contentions at trial and documents in the record to establish the dealer's obligation to Ford and to plaintiff to make the warranty repairs on behalf of Ford (subject to the right of reimbursement or other terms that may be contained in their agreement). For the purpose of this appeal we are satisfied that the dealer's undertaking in paragraph 7 constitutes a written warranty

---

46. The warranty also provided:
"TO THE EXTENT ALLOWED BY LAW:
"1. ANY IMPLIED WARRANTY OF MERCHANTABILITY OR FITNESS IS LIMITED TO THE 12 MONTH OR 12,000-MILE/19,312-KM DURATION OF THIS WRITTEN WARRANTY.
"2. NEITHER FORD NOR THE SELLING DEALER SHALL HAVE ANY RESPONSIBILITY FOR LOSS OF USE OF THE VEHICLE, LOSS OF TIME, INCONVENIENCE, COMMERCIAL LOSS OR CONSEQUENTIAL DAMAGES.
"Some states do not allow limitations on how long an implied warranty lasts or the exclusion or limitation of incidental or consequential damages, so the above limitations may not apply to you.
"This warranty gives you specific legal rights, and you also may have other rights which vary from state to state."

within the meaning of 15 U.S.C. §2301(6)(B). Accordingly, having furnished a written warranty to the consumer, the dealer as a supplier may not "disclaim or modify [except to limit in duration] any implied warranty to a consumer. . . ." The result of this analysis is to invalidate the attempted disclaimer by the dealer of the implied warranties of merchantability and fitness. Being bound by those implied warranties arising under state law, §§2-314 and 315, Marino Auto was liable to plaintiff for the breach thereof as found by the trial judge, and plaintiff could timely revoke his acceptance of the automobile and claim a refund of his purchase price. Sections 2-608 and 2-711. Zabriskie Chevrolet, Inc. v. Smith, 99 N.J. Super. 441 (L. Div. 1968). In this connection we note that the trial judge found that plaintiff's attempted revocation of acceptance was made in timely fashion, and that finding has adequate support in the evidence.

As the trial judge noted, 15 U.S.C. §2310(d)(1) provides that a consumer who is damaged by the failure of a warrantor to comply with any obligation under the act, or under a written warranty or implied warranty or service contract, may bring suit "for damages and other legal and equitable relief. . . ." Although the remedy of refund of the purchase price is expressly provided by the Magnuson-Moss Warranty Act for breach of a full warranty, granting this remedy under state law for breach of a limited warranty is not barred by or inconsistent with the act. 15 U.S.C. §2311(b)(1) provides that nothing in the act restricts "any right or remedy of any consumer under State law or other Federal law." See also 15 U.S.C. §2311(c)(2). Thus, for breach of the implied warranty of merchantability, plaintiff was entitled to revoke acceptance against Marino Auto, and a judgment for the purchase price less an allowance for the use of the vehicle was properly entered against Marino Auto. Sections 2-608 and 711. Cf. 15 U.S.C. §2301(12) which defines "refund" as the return of the purchase price "less reasonable depreciation based on actual use where permitted" by regulations.

Plaintiff also could have recovered damages against Ford for Ford's breach of its written limited warranty. Marino Auto was Ford's representative for the purpose of making repairs to plaintiff's vehicle under the warranty. See Henningsen v. Bloomfield Motors, Inc., supra, 32 N.J. at 374; cf. Conte v. Dwan Lincoln-Mercury, Inc., 172 Conn. 112, —, 374 A.2d 144, 149-150 (Sup. Ct. 1976). The limited warranty expressly required the purchaser to return the vehicle "for warranty service" to the dealer or to any Ford or Lincoln-Mercury dealer if the purchaser is traveling or has moved a long distance or needs emergency repairs. Ford contends that it put purchasers on notice that they should advise Ford's district office if they have problems with their cars that a dealer is unable to fix. The record contains a document listing "frequently asked warranty questions" which states:

> The Dealership where you purchased your vehicle has the responsibility for performing warranty repairs; therefore, take your vehicle to that Dealership. . . .
>
> If you encounter a service problem, refer to the service assistance section of your Owner's Guide for suggested action.

We do not read these provisions as requiring notice to Ford as a condition of relief against Ford when Ford's dealer has failed after numerous attempts to correct defects under warranty. . . .

One question posed by this case is whether recovery of the purchase price from the manufacturer was available to plaintiff for breach of the manufacturer's warranty. If the warranty were a full warranty plaintiff would have been entitled to a refund of the purchase price under the Magnuson-Moss Warranty Act. Since Ford's warranty was a limited warranty we must look to state law to determine plaintiff's right to damages or other legal and equitable relief. 15 U.S.C. §2310(d)(1). Once privity is removed as an obstacle to relief we see no reason why a purchaser cannot also elect the equitable remedy of returning the goods to the manufacturer who is a warrantor and claiming a refund of the purchase price less an allowance for use of the product. See Seely v. White Motor Co., 45 Cal. Rptr. 17, —, 403 P.2d 145, 148 (Sup. Ct. 1965); Durfee v. Rod Baxter Imports, Inc., supra, 262 N.W.2d at 357-358, where the Minnesota Supreme Court held as a matter of state law that lack of privity does not bar a purchaser of a foreign car from revoking acceptance and recovering the purchase price from the distributor of such cars as distinguished from the local dealer. The decision was made without regard to the Magnuson-Moss Warranty Act.

We are dealing with the breach of an express contractual obligation. Nothing prevents us from granting an adequate remedy under state law for that breach of contract, including rescission when appropriate. Under state law the right to revoke acceptance for defects substantially impairing the value of the product (§2-608) and to receive a refund of the purchase price (§2-711) are rights available to a buyer against a seller in privity. Where the manufacturer gives a warranty to induce the sale it is consistent to allow the same type of remedy as against that manufacturer. See Durfee v. Rod Baxter Imports, Inc., supra; cf. Seely v. White Motor Co., supra. Only the privity concept, which is frequently viewed as a relic these days, Koperski v. Husker

Dodge, Inc., 208 Neb. 29, —, 302 N.W.2d 655, 664 (Sup. Ct. 1981); see Kinlaw v. Long Mfg. N.C., Inc., 298 N.C. 494, 259 S.E.2d 552 (Sup. Ct. 1979), has interfered with a rescission-type remedy against the manufacturer of goods not purchased directly from the manufacturer. If we focus on the fact that the warranty creates a direct contractual obligation to the buyer, the reason for allowing the same remedy that is available against a direct seller becomes clear. Although the manufacturer intended to limit the remedy to the repair and replacement of defective parts, the failure of that remedy, see §2-719(2); Goddard v. General Motors Corp., 60 Ohio St. 2d 41, 396 N.E.2d 761 (Sup. Ct. 1979); Seely v. White Motor Co., supra, and the consequent breach of the implied warranty of merchantability which accompanied the limited warranty by virtue of the Magnuson-Moss Warranty Act, make a rescission-type remedy appropriate when revocation of acceptance is justified. Durfee v. Rod Baxter Imports, Inc., supra, 262 N.W.2d at 357.

Lastly, we consider Ford's contention that a counsel fee was improperly granted to plaintiff since no judgment was entered in favor of plaintiff against Ford and Ford contends it was not given adequate notice of the defects in the car. 15 U.S.C. §2310(d)(2) provides that a consumer who "prevails in any action brought [in any court] under paragraph (1) of this subsection . . . may be allowed by the court to recover as part of the judgment . . . expenses (including attorneys' fees based on the actual time expended). . . ." This section is subject to the provisions contained in §2310(e). Subsection (e) provides that, with certain exceptions, no action based upon breach of a written or implied warranty or service contract may be prosecuted unless a person obligated under the warranty or service contract "is afforded a reasonable opportunity to cure such failure to comply." Here that opportunity was given to Ford's designated representative to whom the purchaser was required to bring the car. A direct employee of Ford, Bednarz, also met with plaintiff or his wife and was made aware of some difficulty with the car. We are not certain of the extent of Ford's knowledge of those difficulties. However, in our view the opportunities given to Marino Auto to repair the vehicle satisfied the requirements of 15 U.S.C. §2310(e) in this case.

As noted, Ford also contends that a counsel fee could not be awarded against Ford because plaintiff did not recover a judgment against Ford. The Magnuson-Moss Warranty Act permits a prevailing consumer to recover attorney's fees "as part of the judgment." The trial judge found that Ford had breached its warranty and that the car's value was substantially impaired. He entered no damage judgment against Ford. However, in the absence of proof of actual damages, plaintiff was entitled to a judgment against Ford for nominal damages. Ruane Dev. Corp. v. Cullere, 134 N.J. Super. 245, 252 (App. Div. 1975); Ench v. Bluestein, 52 N.J. Super. 169, 173-174 (App. Div. 1958); Winkler v. Hartford Accident and Indem. Co., 66 N.J. Super. 22, 29 (App. Div.), *cert. den.*, 34 N.J. 581 (1961); Packard Englewood Motors, Inc. v. Packard Motor Car Co., 215 F.2d 503, 510 (3d Cir. 1954). Ford was not prejudiced by the failure of the trial judge to enter a judgment for nominal damages to which the award of attorney's fees could be attached. See Nobility Homes, Inc. v. Ballentine, 386 So. 2d 727, 730-731 (Sup. Ct. Ala. 1980). The award of counsel fees fulfills the intent of the Magnuson-Moss Warranty Act. Without such an award consumers frequently would be unable to vindicate warranty rights accorded by law.

As to the amount of counsel fees allowed by the trial judge, we find no abuse of discretion. The allowance was for actual time spent at an hourly rate of $75.00. Consideration could properly be given to the fact that plaintiff's attorney undertook this claim on a contingency basis with a relatively small retainer. D.R. 2-106(A)(8). The normal breach of warranty case ought not require four separate appearances before the trial court. To some extent this was not in the control of plaintiff's attorney; and plaintiff might have obtained all the relief required against Ford on the first day of trial. But it did not work out that way. In other cases it may be possible to stipulate damages and simplify the issues, thus limiting the cost of this type of litigation for consumers and suppliers alike. But the issues raised in this case were novel in this state, and no one can be faulted for the difficulty and time consumed in this litigation. . . .

Affirmed.

Pursuant to the Act's command, the Federal Trade Commission has promulgated rules to supplement the statute; see 40 Fed. Reg. 60188 (1975), 16 C.F.R. §701 et seq. These regulations have delineated the precise information required for the §102 warranties, provided for presale availability of the warranty through signs or warranty binders to be kept at the place of sale, and specified the makeup and procedure to be followed by entities (called *mechanisms*) engaging in §110's informal settlement of disputes.

F. *Warranties and Article 2A*

The warranty rules for the lease of goods found in Article 2A are, with minor variations, mere carbon copies of the Article 2 rules. There is one major difference, however, which arises in what Article 2A calls a "finance lease."

Colonial Pacific Leasing Corp. v. McNatt Datronic Rental Corp.

Georgia Supreme Court, 1997
268 Ga. 265, 486 S.E.2d 804, 33 U.C.C. Rep. Serv. 2d 1135

BENHAM, Chief Justice. We granted a writ of certiorari to the court of appeals to review its decision in McNatt v. Colonial Pacific Leasing Corp., 221 Ga. App. 768 (472 S.E.2d 435) (1996). We expressed particular concern with whether the "hell or high water" clause in the equipment finance leases at issue insulated the assignees of the lessor from the lessee's claim of fraud allegedly perpetrated by agents of the supplier of the equipment. We conclude that a "hell or high water" clause does not insulate a lessor's assignee from a claim of fraud where an agency relationship can be established between the assignee and the perpetrators of the alleged fraud.

In early 1991, Linda and William McNatt, sole shareholders and president and secretary-treasurer, respectively, of Quick-Trip Printers, Inc., entered into negotiations with representatives of Itex Systems Southeast, Inc., for the acquisition of an Itex computer printing system. The McNatts selected the equipment Quick-Trip Printers desired to obtain from Itex and, on June 10, 1991, executed equipment finance leases with Burnham Leasing Company, whereby Burnham agreed to purchase the equipment chosen by Quick-Trip Printers from the supplier with which Quick-Trip had dealt, and to then lease the equipment to Quick-Trip for a monthly rental payment. Burnham Leasing immediately assigned its interest in the leases to appellants Colonial Pacific Leasing Corporation and Datronic Rental Corporation.[47] Though she did not later recall signing it, Linda McNatt's

---

47. The leases executed by Quick-Trip Printers and Burnham Leasing authorized Burnham to assign its interest in the lease, and stated that any assignee of Burnham would have all of the rights but none of the obligations of Burnham under the lease. Quick-Trip Printers, as lessee, agreed that it would not assert against the assignee/lessor any defense, counterclaim, or set-off that it might have against Burnham.

signature appears on an "Acknowledgment and Acceptance of Equipment by Lessee,"[48] dated June 11, 1991. Linda McNatt also purportedly executed a personal guaranty of the lease agreement on June 10, 1991.[49]

Quick-Trip Printers experienced problems with the equipment, and the assignee/lessors delayed payment to Itex. While Itex was ultimately paid for the equipment, Quick-Trip Printers never made a lease payment to the assignee/lessors because the equipment never performed as the Itex agents led the McNatts to believe it would. The lessors repossessed the equipment and, four months after it signed the leasing documents, Quick-Trip Printers filed suit against the equipment supplier, the manufacturer, and the lessors, seeking, among other things, rescission of the leases. In an amended pleading, Quick-Trip Printers sought damages for the assignee/lessors' alleged negligent release of funds to Itex. Colonial Pacific and Datronic each filed a counterclaim seeking payment pursuant to the leases assigned to them. The trial court granted summary judgment in favor of the assignee/lessors on the main claims, relying on Quick-Trip Printers' disclaimer of all warranties concerning the suitability of the equipment,[50] and a finding that lessee Quick-Trip Printers had authorized

48. In that document, Quick-Trip acknowledged that the specified equipment had been received "in good condition and repair, has been properly installed, tested, and inspected, and is operating satisfactorily in all respects for all of Lessee's intended uses and purposes." The document went on to state that "Lessee hereby accepts unconditionally and irrevocably the Equipment" and "specifically authorizes and requests Lessor to make payment to the supplier of the Equipment." Just above the signature line, in upper-case letters, was the lessee's acknowledgment and agreement "THAT LESSEE'S OBLIGATIONS TO LESSOR BECOME ABSOLUTE AND IRREVOCABLE AND LESSEE SHALL BE FOREVER ESTOPPED FROM DENYING THE TRUTHFULNESS OF THE REPRESENTATIONS MADE IN THIS DOCUMENT."

49. While acknowledging that the signature on the personal guaranty looked like her signature, Mrs. McNatt questioned whether she had signed the document, noting that she was not acquainted with the person who purportedly witnessed her signature. The witness, an employee of Burnham Leasing, executed an affidavit in which she stated she had witnessed Mrs. McNatt sign the personal guaranty.

50. Prominently displayed on the front page of both leases signed by Quick-Trip was Burnham Leasing's disclaimer of warranties and claims:

"THERE ARE NO WARRANTIES BY OR ON BEHALF OF LESSOR. Lessee acknowledges and agrees by his signature below as follows: (a) LESSOR MAKES NO WARRANTIES EITHER EXPRESS OR IMPLIED AS TO THE CONDITION OF THE EQUIPMENT, ITS MERCHANTABILITY, ITS FITNESS OR SUITABILITY FOR ANY PARTICULAR PURPOSE, ITS DESIGN, ITS CAPACITY, ITS QUALITY, OR WITH RESPECT TO ANY CHARACTERISTICS OF THE EQUIPMENT; . . . (e) If the Equipment is not properly installed, does not operate as represented or warranted by the supplier or manufacturer, or is unsatisfactory for any reason, regardless of cause or consequence, Lessee's only remedy, if any, shall be against the supplier or manufacturer of the Equipment and not against Lessor."

the release of the funds. The trial court also granted the assignee/
lessors summary judgment on their counterclaims, "pursuant to the
terms of their respective equipment leases."[51]

The court of appeals reversed the trial court's judgment on the
main claims, finding issues of material fact on Quick-Trip's assertion of
failure of consideration and on Quick-Trip's claim that the assignee/
lessors negligently released funds to the equipment supplier. The
appellate court reversed the grant of summary judgment to the
assignee/lessors on their counterclaim for the unpaid rent, holding
that the leases' requirement that the rental payments be made even if
the equipment were damaged, defective, or unfit could not be
enforced when it was alleged that employees of the equipment vendor,
Itex, had fraudulently induced Quick-Trip to acquire the equipment.
That is to say, the "hell or high water" clauses in the leases requiring
payment to the assignee/lessors were of no moment where the lessee
alleged the lease was procured by the fraudulent misrepresentations of
the vendor's agents.

1. The leases in question are classic examples of "lease financing,"
described by one commentator as possibly "'the most important single
source of funds to support business expenditures for capital
equipment.' [Cit.]" Amelia H. Boss, The History of Article 2A: A
Lesson for Practitioner and Scholar Alike, 39 Ala. L. Rev. 575, 577
(1988). The tax laws, rulings of the Comptroller of the Currency, as
well as amendments to the Bank Holding Company Act and government regulations have fueled the trend toward equipment leasing.
Edwin E. Huddleson III, Old Wine in New Bottles: UCC Article 2A—
Leases, 39 Ala. L. Rev. 615, 616, n.1 (1988). As of 1992, it was estimated
that 30 percent of capital equipment in the United States was acquired
through leasing. Robert D. Strauss, Equipment Leases under U.C.C.
Article 2A—Analysis and Practice Suggestions, 43 Mercer L. Rev. 853,
854 (1992). Most finance lessors view the "hell or high water" clause at

---

51. In each lease, Quick-Trip Printers "acknowledge[d] and agree[d]" that "NO
DEFECT, DAMAGE OR UNFITNESS OF THE EQUIPMENT FOR ANY PURPOSE
SHALL RELIEVE LESSEE OF THE OBLIGATION TO PAY RENT OR RELIEVE
LESSEE OF ANY OTHER OBLIGATION UNDER THIS LEASE." It further agreed to
pay the total rent, that it would not "abate, set off, deduct any amount, or reduce any
payment for any reason," that the lease was not cancelable or terminable by Quick-
Trip, and that it would not "assert against the [lessor's] assignee any defense, counterclaim, or setoff that [Quick-Trip] may have against [Burnham Leasing]." The requirement that the lessee continue to make payments regardless of the condition of the
equipment and that the lessee not assert against the assignee/lessors defenses
assertable against the original lessor is commonly referred to as a "hell or high water"
clause.

issue in the cases at bar as sacrosanct. Huddleson, supra, 39 Ala. L. Rev. at 666.

A "finance lease" involves three parties—the lessee/business, the finance lessor, and the equipment supplier. The lessee/business selects the equipment and negotiates particularized modifications with the equipment supplier. Instead of purchasing the equipment from the supplier, the lessee/business has a finance lessor purchase the selected equipment, and then leases the equipment from the finance lessor.

> Traditionally, a finance lessor has been thought of as a passive lessor, whose transactions remain functionally the equivalent of an extension of credit. It is typically the lessee, not the lessor, who selects the goods in a "finance lease." Moreover, a finance lessor often has neither the opportunity nor the expertise to inspect the goods in order to discover defects in them. Given the limited function of the lessor, the lessee relies almost entirely on the supplier for representations, covenants, and warranties.

Huddleson, supra, 39 Ala. L. Rev. at 660.

> In effect, the [lessee/business] is relying upon the [supplier] to provide the promised goods and to stand by its promises and warranties; the [lessee/business] does not look to the [finance lessor] for these. The [finance lessor] is only a finance lessor, and deals largely in paper, rather than goods. In that situation it makes no sense to treat the [finance lessor] as a seller to the [business/lessee] with warranty liability, nor does it make any sense to free the [supplier] from liability for breach of promises and warranties that it would have given in an outright sale to the [business/lessee]. Usually, the [finance lessor] expects to be paid, even though the [equipment] might prove to be defective or totally unsuitable for the [lessee/business's] particular business.

2 J. White & R. Summers, Uniform Commercial Code, §13-3(a) (4th ed. 1995).

2. In Georgia, all lease contracts for "goods," including finance leases, first made or first effective on or after July 1, 1993, are governed by Article 2A of the Uniform Commercial Code. OCGA §11-2A-101 et seq.; Ga. L. 1993, p.633, §5. Because the leases at issue were executed prior to the effective date of Article 2A, we must look to the Georgia law relating to the lease of personal property that Article 2A supplanted—"a hybrid of the law of bailment, contract, UCC Article 2 (Sales of Goods), UCC Article 9 (Secured Transactions), together with common law principles concerning personal property and real estate

leases." Sarah B. King, Commercial Code, Leases: Provide Regulations Relating to Leases of Goods, 10 G.S.U. L. Rev. 34 (1993).

Under pre-Article 2A Georgia law, the conduct of the parties to a lease finance transaction is governed by the terms of the lease. Citicorp Industrial Credit v. Rountree, 185 Ga. App. 417, 420 (364 S.E.2d 65) (1987). Georgia case law generally upholds the bargains struck by parties, as long as the contract is not the product of fraud (OCGA §13-4-60), or is not violative of the public policy of this State. Emory Univ. v. Porubiansky, 248 Ga. 391, 393 (282 S.E.2d 903) (1981). A finance lessor's disclaimer of warranties expressed clearly and unambiguously is not prohibited by law or public policy (Petroziello v. United States Leasing Corp., 176 Ga. App. 858, 860 (338 S.E.2d 63) (1985)), and a finance lease may authorize a lessor to assign its rights in the contract free from claims and defenses which the lessee might have against the original lessor. Short v. General Electric Credit Corp., 113 Ga. App. 476 (148 S.E.2d 450) (1966). A contractual requirement that the lessee make its rental payments is valid in the absence of fraud on the part of or imputed to the finance lessor. Woods v. Advanta Leasing Corp., 201 Ga. App. 844(1) (412 S.E.2d 607) (1991). See Holcomb v. Commercial Credit Svcs. Corp., 180 Ga. App. 451 (349 S.E.2d 523) (1986).

The inclusion of a "hell or high water" clause, however, does not resolve the issue in favor of the assignee/lessors. In Doss v. Epic Healthcare Mgt. Co., 901 S.W.2d 216 (Mo. App. 1995), the Court of Appeals of Missouri held that the clause did not protect an assignee who knew at the time of assignment that the agreement was in default, that the lessee no longer possessed the chattel, and that the agreement had been terminated. In Louisiana, the clause may not be enforced when the lessee withholds payment because the assignee lessor has not provided the lessee with peaceful possession of the equipment for the term of the lease. Angelle v. Energy Builders Co., 496 So. 2d 509 (La. App. 1986). Most recently, the Kansas Court of Appeals concluded that the clause did not preclude a lessee from asserting equitable estoppel. Toshiba MasterLease v. Ottawa Univ., 927 P.2d 967 (Kan. App. 1996).

Each of the leases in the cases at bar clearly exclude warranty and promissory liability of the finance lessor and its assignees to Quick-Trip Printers, each states that Quick-Trip agreed to pay the full amount of the rental agreement to assignee/lessors, regardless of defect, damage, or unfitness of the equipment for any purpose, and each states that the lessee agreed not to assert against the assignee lessors defenses it could assert against the original lessor. Thus, the contract precludes the business lessee from asserting the fraud of or imputable to the original finance lessor as a defense against the assignee lessors' claim for payment.

However, the business lessee in the case at bar did not wait until it was sued by the assignee/lessors to allege fraud. Instead, Quick-Trip Printers took the offensive, filing suit in an effort to enforce its statutory right (OCGA §13-4-60) to rescind its lease contracts with the assignee/lessors on the ground that the equipment supplier's employees fraudulently induced Quick-Trip to enter into the equipment lease contracts with the original finance lessor. In order for the purported fraud of the employees of the equipment supplier to authorize rescission of the finance lease, their actions must somehow be imputed to the assignee lessors through the finance lessor. Although the finance leases clearly stated that Quick-Trip acknowledged that the employees of the equipment supplier were not the agents of the finance lessor, such a contractual statement is "not necessarily conclusive as to the non-existence of such a relationship." Potomac Leasing Co. v. Thrasher, 181 Ga. App. 883 (1) (354 S.E.2d 210) (1987). In *Potomac,* evidence that the supplier's employees were trained with regard to completing the finance leasing documents and were authorized by the finance lessor to negotiate a finance lease for the finance lessor was sufficient to defeat the finance lessor's motion for directed verdict. However, the supplier's employee who merely submitted a business/lessee's credit application to the finance lessor for review and decision is not, as a matter of law, an agent of the finance lessor. Gulf Winds v. First Union Bank, 187 Ga. App. 383 (1) (370 S.E.2d 508) (1988).

In the cases at bar, appellee William McNatt testified on deposition that the equipment supplier's employees who purportedly made the fraudulent statements to the McNatts wanted the McNatts to sign a lease and told Mr. McNatt the monthly leasing costs. Mr. McNatt provided a financing statement to the supplier's employees as part of the effort to secure a finance lease, and the lease documents were presented to the McNatts by the supplier's employees. Mr. McNatt stated unequivocally on deposition that the equipment supplier's employees never represented themselves as being agents of the finance lessors, and Mrs. McNatt, who was also deposed, stated that the employees of the equipment supplier never discussed being employees of the finance lessors. We conclude from our review of the record that the equipment supplier's employees acted only as a conduit of information between the business lessee and the finance lessor; there is no evidence that the finance lease was negotiated by the supplier's employees pursuant to authorization given them by the finance lessor.

In other words, there is no evidence of a relationship pursuant to which the purported fraud of the supplier's employers could be imputed to the finance lessor and vitiate the contracts executed by Quick-Trip with the finance lessor. Woods v. Advanta Leasing Corp., supra, 210 Ga. App. 844; Holcomb v. Commercial Credit Svcs., supra, 180 Ga. App. 451. Contrary to the holding of the Court of Appeals, there is no material issue of fact concerning the imputation of fraud to the assignee/lessors and whether Quick-Trip was entitled to rescission of the assigned leases. As there is no evidence of fraud imputable to the assignee/lessors, the leases are not rescindable under §13-4-60, and the "hell or high water" clauses contained in the lease are viable.

3. Quick-Trip Printers cited failure of consideration as a defense to the assignee/lessors' counterclaims for the unpaid rent. In light of its contractual agreement not to assert against the assignee/lessors any defense it might have against the original lessor, Quick-Trip is estopped to assert failure of consideration as a defense to the assignee/lessors' counterclaims. Furthermore, in the absence of fraud, a lessee is precluded from asserting the defense of failure of consideration against the assignee/lessors of a contract in which the lessee waived all express and implied warranties. United States Leasing Corp. v. Jones Pharmacy, 144 Ga. App. 26 (240 S.E.2d 300) (1977). As was discussed in Division 2, supra, there is no evidence of fraud imputable to the finance lessors. The court of appeals, citing its decision in Granite Equip. Leasing Corp. v. Folds, 133 Ga. App. 856 (212 S.E.2d 490) (1975), concluded that the contractual waiver of warranty was not effective against Quick-Trip since Quick-Trip asserted that the equipment received was not as orally promised by the supplier's employees (the alleged fraud which permeates these cases), and the serial numbers on the equipment received did not match the serial numbers contained in the leasing contract. In *Granite,* the court of appeals held that the lessee's defense of failure of consideration had not been waived by the disclaimer of warranty because the disclaimer applied to the *type* of machine for which the contract called, "a 'factory rebuilt' press," and not to that which was actually delivered—"a 'reconditioned' press." (Emphasis supplied.) See also Avery v. Key Capital Corp., 186 Ga. App. 712 (1) (368 S.E.2d 364) (1988) (disclaimers in lease applicable to 1984 vehicle described therein, but not to 1983 model delivered). Linda McNatt testified in her deposition that the equipment listed in the lease agreements was delivered to Quick-Trip. Her husband did not dispute that the pieces received were the type of machine for which the contract called. He testified only that he noted discrepancies between the serial numbers listed on the contract for

individual pieces, and the serial numbers of the parts actually delivered. There being no discrepancy in the type of equipment contractually promised and that actually delivered, the contractual waiver of warranty was effective and defeated Quick-Trip's defense of failure of consideration.

4. Lastly, we address Quick-Trip's contention that the assignee lessors are liable to Quick-Trip for the negligent release of funds to Itex. Despite having an "Acknowledgement and Acceptance of Equipment by Lessee" which authorized the assignee/lessors to pay the equipment supplier, the assignee/lessors withheld payment from the supplier due to the business lessee's verbal notification, in response to inquiries made by the assignee/lessors, that the equipment was defective. According to the assignee/lessors, the funds were released to the supplier upon notification from the business lessee that the equipment problems had been resolved. The business lessee disputes the assignee/lessors' version of the facts. As there appears to be a genuine issue of material fact concerning the claim that the assignee/lessors negligently released the funds to the equipment supplier, we agree with the Court of Appeals that summary judgment in favor of the assignee/lessors on the business lessee's claim was inappropriate.

Judgment affirmed in part and reversed in part.

PROBLEM 40

Chemicals of Tomorrow Corp. decided that the safest way to work with hazardous materials was through the use of an advanced robot. It persuaded Aurora Robotics, Inc., to design a robot that would meet its needs. To finance the purchase of the robot, Chemicals of Tomorrow went to Octopus National Bank, which bought the robot from Aurora Robotics and then leased it to Chemicals of Tomorrow. The robot was subject to both express and implied warranties, which became important when the robot ran amuck in one of Chemicals of Tomorrow's laboratories and caused extensive damage. Answer these questions:

(a) Is this a "finance lease"? What factors do and do not influence this decision? See §2A-103(1)(g) and its Official Comment (g). As the leasing officer for the bank, what steps would you have recommended to make sure that a court would hold that this lease so qualified?

(b) What name does Article 2A give to Aurora Robotics in this situation? See §2A-103(1)(x).

(c) Does Chemicals of Tomorrow Corp. have the benefit of whatever warranties Aurora gave to Octopus National? See §2A-209 and its Official Comment.

(d) Is Octopus National Bank responsible for breach of the implied warranty of merchantability? See §2A-212.

(e) If Octopus National's leasing officer had told Chemicals of Tomorrow's president, "We have investigated this robot, and I guarantee you it will cause you no trouble," must the lessor then respond in a warranty lawsuit to a claim for damages? See §2A-210 and Official Comment (g), third paragraph, to §2A-103.

(f) The lease between Octopus National Bank and Chemicals of Tomorrow contained a clause stating that the lessee had to pay the lessor even if the goods did not work, a "hell or high water" clause, so-called because the lessee binds itself to pay the lessor no matter what happens in connection with the performance of the leased goods. After the robot ruins the laboratory, must Chemicals of Tomorrow nonetheless pay Octopus National Bank? See §2A-407 and its Official Comment. Would we reach the same result if the lessee were a consumer?

G. *Warranties in International Sales*

The warranty provisions of the CISG for the international sale of goods are very similar to the UCC rules. The major difference is not one of substance, but one of terminology: the treaty drafters, wanting to write on a clean slate, eschewed use of the term "warranty" and all the historical baggage that comes with it. Read Articles 35 to 44 of the Convention, and see if you can nevertheless find within them counterparts to the following:

(a) a warranty of title;

(b) express warranty liability; and

(c) implied warranties of merchantability and/or fitness for a particular purpose.

How are warranties disclaimed under the treaty? See Articles 6 and 35.

Chapter 4

TERMS OF THE CONTRACT

I. FILLING IN THE GAPS

In the nineteenth and early twentieth centuries, if the parties left a major term out of the contract, the courts typically found no legally enforceable agreement. Judges declared themselves powerless to "make a contract for the parties." In more recent years the courts were more willing to save the contract by implying reasonable terms where possible. The drafters of the Code fueled practice by giving the courts statutory guidance in their gap-filling role. Glance through §§2-305 to 2-311.

PROBLEM 41

Edwin Drake wrote to the Watsons Flat Motor Oil Company and said that he wanted to buy 100 cases of its motor oil, some cases to be Type A (the expensive oil) and some to be Type B (a cheaper kind). He said he would let the company know later how much he wanted of each type. The company told him that Type B was selling for $30 a case, but that since the price of Type A was fluctuating, the sale price would have to be set by the company at the time of delivery. Drake agreed. The parties signed a written contract for the delivery of 100 cases, types to be specified by Drake one week prior to the delivery date, which was set for April 8. On April 1, the agent of the oil company called Drake to ask how much he would take of each type. Drake said, "April Fool! I'm not taking any," and hung up the phone. The company calls you, its attorney, for advice. In the past dealings that it has had with Drake, he always has ordered 100 cases and has taken 50 to 65 percent in Type A and the rest in Type B. The usual price for Type A has been $50 a case, but due to a Middle East oil situation, the price has now jumped to $125 a case. What should the company do? See §§2-305, 2-311, 1-205. If this were an international sale of goods under the CISG, what result? See Article 65.

What if Drake had simply said, "April Fool!" and hung up? Is this a definite repudiation? See §§2-610, 2-611. What action can the oil company take to clear up Drake's ambiguous statement? Read §2-609 and its Official Comment; see Pittsburgh-Des Moines Steel Co. v. Brookhaven Manor Water Co., 532 F.2d 572, 18 U.C.C. Rep. Serv. 931 (7th Cir. 1976).

Landrum v. Devenport

Texas Court of Civil Appeals, Texarkana, 1981
616 S.W.2d 359, 32 U.C.C. Rep. Serv. 8

CORNELIUS, J. James N. Landrum brought this action against Joe W. Devenport and William Donald Devenport, d/b/a Devenport Chevrolet, to recover damages for breach of contract and certain alleged violations of the Texas Deceptive Trade Practices—Consumer Protection Act, Tex. Bus. & Comm. Code Ann. §17.41 et seq. The case went to trial before a jury, but after Landrum presented his evidence the trial court granted Devenport's motion for instructed verdict and rendered a take nothing judgment.

The question to be decided is whether Landrum produced some probative evidence tending to support each element of his cause of action. If so, he was entitled to go to the jury with his case and an instructed verdict was improper unless some defense was conclusively established by law or by the evidence. In determining the question, we must view the evidence in the light most favorable to the party against whom the verdict was instructed, giving him the benefit of every reasonable inference which may legitimately be drawn from that evidence. Considering the evidence from that perspective, the following facts are found in the record: the only witness produced by Landrum was his son, Jimmy Landrum, who conducted all dealings with Devenport. The elder Landrum is a collector of automobiles. He is in poor health and seldom leaves his home. His son Jimmy lives with him and helps him maintain his automobile collection. In the Fall of 1977 Landrum became interested in purchasing three Chevrolet Corvettes Z78 Indy Pace Cars. These cars were a limited edition. General Motors made approximately 6,500 of them in 1978. The Devenports conduct business in Wolfe City, Texas, under the name Devenport Chevrolet. On January 25, 1978, Jimmy Landrum contacted Joe Devenport by phone and informed him that he was interested in buying the Indy Pace Car which the Devenports would be receiving from General Motors. On January 26, 1978, Jimmy drove to Wolfe City, talked to Joe Devenport and selected the options he wanted on the car. Jimmy and Devenport then signed a purchase order for the car. The price was left blank. Jimmy testified that Devenport told him that the price would be the car's sticker price which the parties estimated would be between $14,000.00 and $18,000.00. Jimmy said that the reason the price term on the purchase order was not filled in was because he felt it would be rude to require him to write down the window sticker price, since he considered that they had an agreement. Jimmy gave Devenport $100.00 in cash as a deposit on the car and received a receipt. The car arrived in May of 1978 and carried a sticker price of $14,688.21. By the time the car was delivered the demand for the Pace Cars had increased to the point where the market value exceeded the sticker price. Devenport demanded $22,000.00 for the car. The Landrums offered to pay the sticker price which was refused. Jimmy Landrum could find no other Pace Cars in the market. Landrum's attorney sent a letter to Devenport stating that he intended to pursue all of his legal rights and remedies under Texas law if the tender of the sticker price was refused. Devenport's reply was that the price was $22,000.00 and that he had others willing to pay that price. Landrum subsequently purchased the car at the $22,000.00 price.

Jimmy Landrum testified that the car was purchased "Under protest of the papers," referring to the letter written by his attorney.

The reasons given by the trial court for granting the instructed verdict were that no valid contract had ever been entered into because the price had not been expressed in the contract and there was no showing that Jimmy Landrum was acting as his father's agent; the parties entered into a new contract or a novation for the higher price; Landrum renegotiated the trade at the higher price and thus ratified the transaction or waived or is estopped from claiming a breach or violation; that no deceptive trade practice was committed; and that Landrum suffered no damage. We have concluded that the instructed verdict was improperly granted, and accordingly will reverse the case and remand it for a new trial.

The essential elements of a suit for breach of contract are (1) the existence of a valid contract; (2) that the plaintiff performed or tendered performance; (3) the defendant breached the agreement; and (4) the plaintiff was damaged as a result of the breach.

The evidence at least raised a fact issue on the existence of a valid contract. Joe Devenport testified that the agreed price was to be the market value of the car at the time of delivery, but Jimmy Landrum testified that the agreed price was to be the car's sticker price, and the jury could reasonably have found that to be the fact. If both parties agreed on a price, the failure to insert that agreed price in the written contract did not invalidate the agreement under the circumstances present here. Uniform Commercial Code §2-204. See Magnolia Warehouse & Storage Co. v. Davis & Blackwell, 108 Tex. 422, 195 S.W. 184 (1917); M.C. Winters, Inc. v. Cope, 498 S.W.2d 484 (Tex. Civ. App. —Texarkana 1973, *no writ*); Hardin v. James Talcott Western, Inc., 390 S.W.2d 517 (Tex. Civ. App.—Waco 1965, *writ ref'd n.r.e.*); Watson v. Magnolia Petroleum Co., 81 S.W.2d 138 (Tex. Civ. App.—Dallas 1935, *no writ*); 23 Tex. Jur. 2d Evidence §§385, 386. Neither did the parol evidence or integration rule prohibit proof of the actual price. When a writing appears obviously incomplete, as when it is silent on a point which would normally be expressed, it may be completed by extrinsic proof of the omitted term. Magnolia Warehouse & Storage Co. v. Davis & Blackwell, supra; M.C. Winters, Inc. v. Cope, supra; Hardin v. James Talcott Western, Inc., supra; Olan Mills, Inc. v. Prince, 336 S.W.2d 186 (Tex. Civ. App.—Texarkana 1960, *no writ*); 2 R. Ray, Evidence §1632, p.359, et seq. Even if the price was not agreed upon the agreement may still constitute a valid and binding contract if both parties intended to be bound and there is a reasonably certain basis for giving an appropriate remedy. Section 2-204(3), §2-305. In such a case the law will imply that a reasonable price was intended; §2-305(1)(a); Bendalin v. Delgado, 406 S.W.2d 897 (Tex. 1966); Paschal v. Hart, 105 S.W.2d 337 (Tex. Civ. App.—Waco 1937, *no writ*); Burger v. Ray, 239 S.W. 257 (Tex. Civ. App.—Dallas 1922, *writ dism'd*); 13 Tex. Jur. 2d Contracts §164, p.351. The fact that both parties here signed the agreement, which was complete in all respects except specification of the price, is some evidence that they intended to be bound. The question of price then, whether a specific figure or a reasonable price, was a question for the jury upon the evidence.

There was also probative evidence that Jimmy Landrum executed the contract as his father's agent. Jimmy so testified and there was also circumstantial evidence confirming the fact. The rule that an agent's declarations or acts are inadmissible to prove agency applies only to out of court declarations. An agent may testify in court to the fact of agency the same as to any other fact within his knowledge. Cook v. Hamer, 158 Tex. 164, 309 S.W.2d 54 (1958).

Fact issues were raised on the other essential elements of Landrum's case as well. It was undisputed that Landrum tendered performance on the basis of the price he testified was the agreed price. If that was the agreed price, Devenport's refusal to sell the car to Landrum at that price would constitute a breach of the contract. If there was such a breach, Landrum's damages would be established at the difference between the agreed price and the price he actually paid.

The trial court, however, concluded that certain defenses to Landrum's cause of action had been conclusively established. That conclusion was based upon the fact that after Devenport refused to accept the sticker price Landrum paid the higher price of $22,000.00 as demanded by Devenport. But there is evidence that Landrum paid the higher price under protest in order to avoid a loss of the unique product, and that he never intended to acquiesce in Devenport's repudiation of the alleged agreement. He had his attorney write Devenport demanding that the sticker price be accepted and warning that he would pursue all of his rights under the contract if Devenport failed to comply. In addition, he testified that he paid the higher price under protest and without any intention to make a new agreement or waive his rights under the original contract. Intent is an essential element of both novation and waiver. Novation is the voluntary replacement of an old obligation with a new one. It requires that both parties intend for the new arrangement to be substituted for the old one. Allstate Insurance Company v. Clarke, 471 S.W.2d 901 (Tex. Civ. App.—Houston [1st Dist.] 1971, *writ ref'd n.r.e.*); Ridgleawood, Inc. v. White, 380 S.W.2d 766 (Tex. Civ. App.—Waco 1964, *no writ*). Waiver is the voluntary relinquishment of a known right, and its existence is largely dependent upon the intention of the party possessing the right. Ford v. Culbertson, 158 Tex. 124, 308 S.W.2d 855 (1958); 60 Tex. Jur. 2d Waiver §1, p.182. Intention is usually a question of fact, and in view of Landrum's testimony, his attorney's letter, and the other circumstances surrounding the transaction, neither novation nor waiver was established as a matter of law, but were issues for the jury.

Neither did the evidence establish ratification as a matter of law. The rule we applied in B. & R. Development, Inc. v. Rogers, 561 S.W.2d 639 (Tex. Civ. App.—Texarkana 1978, *writ ref'd n.r.e.*), does not apply to the situation we have here. It is true that a person who, with full knowledge of a fraud perpetrated on him, voluntarily renegotiates the transaction or renews his obligation will be held to have ratified the fraud. B. & R. Development, Inc. v. Rogers, supra, and cases there cited. But the basis of that rule is not ratification in the strict sense, but simply that fraud has been eliminated from the transaction and there is no longer any deception. B. & R. Development, Inc. v. Rogers, supra. That is not the situation which is revealed here. Here there was a disagreement as to what was the contractual price. If Landrum did not intend to make a new agreement, but only out of necessity in order to avoid a loss of his bargain paid the higher price under protest and while insisting upon his rights, his act would not amount to a ratification or waiver. Intention to ratify or waive cannot be inferred from acts where, under the exigencies of the case, the party had no satisfactory alternative. See: §1-207; Jon-T Farms, Inc. v. Goodpasture, Inc., 554 S.W.2d 743 (Tex. Civ. App.—Amarillo 1977, *writ ref'd n.r.e.*); Mayhew & Isbell Lumber Co. v. Valley Wells Truck Growers' Assn., 216 S.W. 225 (Tex. Civ. App.—San Antonio 1919, *no writ*); 13 Tex. Jur. 2d Contracts §330, pp.594, 595; 17 Am. Jur. 2d Contracts §395, pp.840, 841. Thus, ratification was a question of fact depending largely upon Landrum's intention and the surrounding circumstances of the transaction.

Estoppel was not established conclusively. Estoppel arises when a representation or act by one party causes the other to do an act which would operate to his detriment if the first party is allowed to complain, or where a party recognizes the validity of a transaction and accepts benefits from it and then attempts to repudiate it. 22 Tex. Jur. 2d Estoppel §1, p.660; §11, pp.674-676. See also Empire Gas & Fuel Co. v. Albright, 126 Tex. 485, 87 S.W.2d 1092 (1935). Neither situation is conclusively established by the facts here.

For largely the same reasons as are stated hereinbefore, it appears that Landrum also raised issues of fact on his alleged cause of action under the Texas Deceptive Trade Practices Consumer Protection Act.

For all the reasons stated, the judgment of the trial court is reversed and this cause is remanded for a new trial.

NOTE

The court at one point cites to §1-207 without explaining how it is relevant. If Jimmy Landrum had called you for advice when he was about to pay the higher price Devenport demanded at delivery, how might he have used §1-207?

II. UNCONSCIONABILITY

The opposite of the incomplete contract is the one that contains too much. In the name of *freedom of contract, caveat emptor,* and the *duty to read,* courts have permitted some rapacious merchants to insulate themselves in legally formidable contracts that have bordered on fraud and were filled with "I win—you lose" provisions. Early attacks on these *adhesion contracts* (so called because the lesser party had to adhere to the will of the stronger) were made in well-known articles like Friedrich Kessler's Contracts of Adhesion—Some Thoughts About Freedom of Contract, 43 Colum. L. Rev. 629 (1943). Later, the chief reporter for the UCC, Karl Llewellyn, proposed this famous "true answer" to the problem:

> The answer, I suggest, is this: Instead of thinking about "assent" to boiler-plate clauses, we can recognize that so far as concerns the specific, there is no assent at all. What has in fact been assented to, specifically, are the few dickered terms, and the broad type of the transaction, and but one thing more. That one thing more is a blanket assent (not a specific assent) to any not unreasonable or indecent terms the seller may have on his form, which do not alter or eviscerate the reasonable meaning of the dickered terms. The fine print which has not been read has no business to cut under the reasonable meaning of those dickered terms which constitute the dominant and only real expression of agreement, but much of it commonly belongs in.

K. Llewellyn, The Common Law Tradition: Deciding Appeals 370 (1960).

The UCC tackled the problem in §2-302. This provision caused whole forests to be stripped to supply the paper for scholarly analysis on a grand scale. The redoubtable Professor Arthur Leff set the tone in a celebrated article attacking §2-302 and its unconscionability principle as "an emotionally satisfying incantation" having "no reality referent"; see Leff, Unconscionability and the Code—The Emperor's New Clause, 115 U. Pa. L. Rev. 485 (1967). Professor Leff's chief contribution to the analysis of §2-302 was his division of "unconscionability" into two types: unfair conduct in the formation of the contract (called *procedural unconscionability*), and unfairness in the terms of the resulting bargain (called *substantive unconscionability*). It was Leff's idea that both are required before a court can make a finding of §2-302 unconscionability.

Read §2-302 and its Official Comment, and then answer the following questions.

QUESTIONS

1. Is *unconscionability* defined in the Code? If asked, how would you define the meaning to a judge?

2. Is the unconscionability issue one for the judge or the jury? What is the policy reason for the Code drafters' decision on this matter?

3. Is the §2-302(2) hearing mandatory as a technical step prior to a finding of unconscionability? See Haugen v. Ford Motor Co., 219 N.W.2d 462, 15 U.C.C. Rep. Serv. 92 (N.D. 1974), holding that the hearing *is* mandatory and that summary judgment is inappropriate without such a hearing.

4. Would the answers to these questions change if this were a lease of goods to a consumer? See §2A-108.

PROBLEM 42

Professor Chalk went into the Swank Boating Company and inquired about the possibility of buying a sailboat. He told the salesman that he knew nothing about sailboats, but had always wanted to get into sailing. The salesman showed him a boat, a handsome catamaran, costing $3,150. Chalk, delighted, signed a contract. On his way home from the store, he passed another boat showplace and saw the same type of sailboat advertised at a price of $1,000. Subsequent investigation proved that the highest price any other store was asking for the boat was $1,200. Chalk, who had done no comparison shopping, had not known this. Does §2-302 permit Chalk to avoid the sale? See Morris v. Capitol Furniture & Appliance Co., 280 A.2d 775 (D.C. 1971); Jones v. Star Credit Corp., 59 Misc. 2d 189, 298 N.Y.S.2d 264 (Sup. Ct. 1969); Annot., 38 A.L.R.4th 25. For a historical viewpoint, see Hamilton, The Ancient Maxim Caveat Emptor, 40 Yale L.J. 1133 (1931). See also Ellinghaus, In Defense of Unconscionability, 78 Yale L.J. 757 (1969).

III. IDENTIFICATION OF THE GOODS

The Code's provisions on risk of loss, casualty to goods, damages, and other matters frequently draw distinctions based on whether the goods have been *identified* as the specific goods to which the contract refers. Read §2-501, and note the general policy favoring early identification found in Official Comment 2; see Rivera, Identification of Goods and Casualty to Identified Goods Under Article Two of the UCC, 13 Ind. L. Rev. 637 (1980).[1]

PROBLEM 43

Decide if *identification* per §2-501 has occurred in the following situations.

(a) Seller, a fisherman, contracts to sell his entire catch for the coming season. Does identification occur on the making of the contract, on the catching of the fish, or on their packaging with a label indicating they belong to this particular buyer? See Official Comment 6.

(b) Three Ring Circus contracted to sell the unborn calf of the circus's elephant Nancy as soon as the calf was born; the contract was made when Nancy was two months pregnant. Does the identification occur on the date of contracting, on the calf's birth, or when the calf is marked for shipment?

---

1. Secured Transactions (cross-reference): §9-203(b)(3) provides that a security interest attaches, inter alia, when "the debtor has rights in the collateral." Where the collateral consists of Article 2 type goods and the *debtor* referred to is a buyer, §2-501 would give the buyer a *special property* interest in the goods on their *identification*, thus dating the Article 9 *attachment* from that moment if the other elements of §9-203 were met.

(c) Farmer Carl agreed to sell to Breakfast Cereals, Inc., one-half of the grain he had stored in Rural Silo, where Farmer Carl's grain was mixed with that of other farmers. Does identification occur on contracting or on segregation of the grain? Read Official Comment 5. See §§2-105(3), 2-105(4).

(d) Wonder Widgets contracted to sell 5,000 widgets to a buyer. Its warehouse contained 2 million widgets, all alike. Does identification occur on contracting or when the goods are picked out and marked as pertaining to this contract? See §1-201(17).

IV.   RISK OF LOSS: NO BREACH

A.   General Rules

Under the old Uniform Sales Act, risk of loss stayed with the person having technical title to the goods and passed to the buyer only when *title* to the goods switched to the buyer. The UCC expressly states that its rules as to who bears the risk of loss have nothing to do with who has technical title (§2-401(1)). This astounded Samuel Williston, the original drafter of the Uniform Sales Act, who called this abandonment of title the "most iconoclastic" idea in the Code; in a famous and rather sad article, he vainly argued against the adoption of the UCC. See Williston, The Law of Sales in the Proposed Uniform Commercial Code, 63 Harv. L. Rev. 561 (1950). Compare Corbin, The Uniform Commercial Code—Sales; Should It Be Enacted?, 59 Yale L.J. 821 (1950), in which Professor Arthur Corbin announced his enthusiastic endorsement of the Code. The general Code rule on the transfer of the risk of loss is that, absent contrary agreement, (1) where the seller is a *merchant*, the risk of loss passes to the buyer on the buyer's actual *receipt* of the goods; and (2) where the seller is not a merchant, risk of loss passes to the buyer when the seller tenders delivery. See §2-509(3).

PROBLEM 44

William College bought a car from Honest John, the friendly car dealer. He paid the price in full, and Honest John promised delivery on the next Monday. On Monday the car was ready, and Honest John phoned College and said, "Take it away." College said he was busy and that he would pick it up the next day, to which Honest John agreed. That night the car was stolen from the lot due to no fault of Honest John, who had taken reasonable precautions against such a thing. Who had the risk of loss? See §2-509(3) and Official Comment 3. Ramos v. Wheel Sports Center, 96 Misc. 2d 646, 409 N.Y.S.2d 505, 25 U.C.C. Rep. Serv. 156 (Civ. Ct. 1978). Might Honest John claim he was a *bailee* so that §2-509(2) applies? See White & Summers §5-3; Galbraith v. American Motor Home Corp., 14 Wash. App. 754, 545 P.2d 561, 18 U.C.C. Rep. Serv. 914 (1976).

PROBLEM 45

Non-merchant

Janice Junk decided to hold a garage sale to clean up her home and get some extra cash. In the course of the sale, which was a huge success, her neighbor, Barbara Bargain, offered Junk $200 for her piano, and the two women shook hands. Junk said to Bargain, "Take it away. It's yours." Bargain replied that she would come to get it the next day with four strong friends and a truck. That night Junk's home burned to the ground, and the piano was destroyed. Did the risk of loss pass from Junk to Bargain? See §2-503. If Bargain never picked up the piano and if it was destroyed in a fire *six months* after the sale, what result? See §2-709(1)(a).

Section 2-509(3) applies only when §2-509(1) or §2-509(2) does not. In many contracts, where the goods are in an independent warehouse, the seller must arrange for the warehouse company (bailee) to change its records to show the buyer as the new owner. Subsection (2) of §2-509 sets out the rules as to when the risk of loss passes to the buyer in such a situation. In essence, the risk of loss rests on whoever has control over the bailee. Read §2-509(2).

Since understanding Subsection (2) of §2-509 depends in large part on understanding the nature of warehouse receipts and delivery orders, both negotiable and non-negotiable, risk of loss under §2-509(2) will be covered in greater depth later in the book, in the Article 7 chapter.

In some contracts the seller is required to ship the goods by independent carrier to the buyer. Such transportation contracts are governed by §2-509(1). Read that section. Note that in transportation contracts the test as to when the risk passes depends on whether the contract requires the seller to "deliver [the goods] at a particular destination." How do you know whether the contract requires the seller to deliver the goods to the buyer or merely to see that they are delivered to the carrier? The next section deals with that problem.

B. Delivery Terms

In sales contracts the parties often agree that the seller need only get the goods to the carrier and then the buyer will take the risk of loss. This type of contract is called a *shipment contract*. On the other hand, the parties may agree that the goods must be delivered by the carrier before the risk passes from seller to buyer. Such a contract is called a *destination contract*. According to Official Comment 5 to §2-503, the presumption made by Article 2 is in favor of a shipment contract. Read that Comment. Where the contract is silent on risk of loss, the courts have enforced this presumption that a shipment contract was intended; Windows, Inc. v. Jordan Panel Systems Corp., 177 F.3d 114, 38 U.C.C. Rep. Serv. 2d 267 (2d. Cir. 1999).

Through the years, merchants have developed a set of *delivery terms* like F.O.B. (free on board), F.A.S. (free along-side), C.I.F. (cost, insurance, freight), C. & F. (cost and freight), and ex-ship (off the ship), which are shorthand methods of stating whether the sale calls for a shipment or a destination contract. These terms (and similar ones) are defined and their legal implications stated clearly in §§2-319 through 2-324. Not only are these terms *delivery* terms, defining the passage of the risk of loss, but also they are *price* terms that inform the buyer that the price quoted includes freight paid to the point indicated. Thus, if the seller is in New York and the buyer is in Chicago, a *$2,000 F.O.B. New York* term means that the risk of loss passes on delivery to the carrier and that the price quoted includes only delivery to the carrier (the buyer must pay the freight charges to get the goods to Chicago). Remember:

(1) C.I.F. and C. & F. always indicate a *shipment* contract. C.I.F. means that the price stated includes the *cost* of the item, the *insurance* premium, and the *freight* charge. The law merchant concluded the C.I.F. was obviously a shipment contract (where the buyer takes the risk of loss during shipment) because the buyer agreed to pay insurance as part of the price. If the buyer did not have the risk of loss, why would insurance be needed? C. & F. is the same as C.I.F. without the buyer's agreeing to pay the insurance. Therefore, one might think that C. & F. should indicate a destination contract. It does not for two reasons. First, the buyer frequently asks for a C. & F. price because a blanket insurance policy already covers goods the buyer owns. Second, the law

merchant regarded C. & F. as a shipment term, and businesses have arranged their affairs accordingly ever since. Read §2-320.

(2) F.A.S. and ex-ship are delivery terms used in connection with ships. Read §§2-319(2) and 2-322, and use them in answering Problem 47 below.

(3) F.O.B. can indicate *either* a shipment or a destination contract. In a contract it is always followed by a named place (like F.O.B. Pittsburgh). The risk of loss passes *at the named place.* Thus, if the named place is the seller's warehouse, the F.O.B. term calls for a shipment contract; if it is the buyer's store, a destination contract results. Read §2-319.

PROBLEM 46

Seller in New York City contracted to sell 80 boxes of clothing to buyer in Savannah, Georgia. The delivery term was "$1,800 F.A.S. S.S. Seaworthy, N.Y.C." Seller delivered the 80 boxes to the dock alongside the S.S. Seaworthy and received a bill of lading from the ship as a receipt. Before the boxes could be loaded, the dock collapsed, and everything thereon disappeared into the water. Under §2-319(2) must buyer pay the $1,800 anyway? What if the delivery term had been "Exship S.S. Seaworthy, Savannah," and the boxes had been properly unloaded just before the dock collapsed? Would §2-322 make the buyer pay?

PROBLEM 47

Seller in Detroit, Michigan, contracted to sell and ship 50 automobiles to buyer in Birmingham, Alabama. Assume lightning strikes, destroying the vehicles *after* the carrier has received them but before they are loaded on board the railroad car that was to take them to Birmingham. Who had the risk of loss if (a) the contract said, "F.O.B. Detroit" (see §2-319(1)(a)); (b) the contract said, "F.O.B. railroad cars Detroit" (see §2-319(1)(c)); or (c) the contract said, "C.I.F. Birmingham" (see §2-320)?

PROBLEM 48

The dispatcher for Perfect Pineapples, Inc., had just finished loading five boxcars of the company's product on board the cars of an independent railroad carrier when he received a notice from PPI's sales department that the company had agreed to sell one boxcar load to Grocery King Food Stores "F.O.B. seller's processing plant." The dispatcher agreed to divert one of the boxcars to Grocery King, but before he could do so, a hurricane destroyed all five boxcars and their contents. Who bears the risk of loss? See Official Comment 2 to §2-509 and §2-501.

Cook Specialty Co. v. Schrlock

United States District Court, Eastern District of Pennsylvania, 1991
772 F. Supp. 1532, 16 U.C.C. Rep. Serv. 2d 360

WALDMAN, J. Defendant Machinery Systems, Inc. ("MSI") contracted to sell plaintiff a machine known as a Dries & Krump Hydraulic Press Brake. When the machine was lost in transit, plaintiff sued defendants to recover for the loss. Presently before the court is plaintiff's motion for summary judgment and defendant MSI's cross-motion for summary judgment. . . .

II. FACTS

The pertinent facts are not contested and are as follow.

Plaintiff entered into a sales contract with defendant MSI for the purchase of a Dries & Krump Press Brake in August of 1989 for $28,000. The terms of the contract were F.O.B. MSI's warehouse in Schaumburg, Illinois. Defendant R.T.L., also known as Randy's Truck Lines, ("the carrier") was used to deliver the press brake from the defendant's warehouse to the plaintiff in Pennsylvania. MSI obtained a certificate of insurance from the carrier with a face amount of $100,000 and showing a $2,500 deductible. (See dfdt. ex. D.)

On October 20, 1989, the carrier took possession of the press brake at MSI's warehouse. While still in transit, the press brake fell from the carrier's truck. The carrier was cited by the Illinois State Police for not properly securing the load. Plaintiff has recovered damages of $5,000 from the carrier's insurer, the applicable policy limit for this particular incident. The machine was worth $28,000.[2]

---

2. Plaintiff, who also sued for certain consequential damages, asserts a claim for a total of $81,000.

III.   DISCUSSION

This dispute is governed by the Uniform Commercial Code ("U.C.C.") provisions regarding risk of loss. The parties agree that there is no meaningful distinction between the pertinent law of Pennsylvania and Illinois, both of which have adopted the UCC.

The term "F.O.B., place of shipment," means that "the seller must at that place ship the goods in the manner provided in this Article (§2-504) and bear the expense and risk of putting them into the possession of the carrier." 13 Pa. C.S.A. §2319. Thus, MSI bore the expense and risk of putting the machine into the carrier's possession for delivery. At the time the carrier takes possession, the risk of loss shifts to the buyer. The UCC provides:

> Where the contract requires or authorizes the seller to ship the goods by carrier
>> a) if it does not require him to deliver them at a particular destination, the risk of loss passes to the buyer when the goods are duly delivered to the carrier. . . .

13 Pa. C.S.A. §2509.

Goods are not "duly delivered" under §2-509, however, unless a contract is entered which satisfies the provisions of §2-504. See 13 Pa. C.S.A. §2509, Official Comment 2. Section 2-504, entitled "Shipment by Seller" provides that:

> Where the seller is required or authorized to send the goods to the buyer and the contract does not require him to deliver them at a particular destination, then unless otherwise agreed he must a) put the goods in the possession of such a carrier and make such a contract for their transportation *as may be reasonable having regard to the nature of the goods* and other circumstances of the case.

13 Pa. C.S.A. §2504 (emphasis added).

Plaintiff argues that the contract MSI made for the delivery of the press brake was not reasonable because defendant failed to ensure that the carrier had sufficient insurance coverage to compensate plaintiff for a loss in transit. Plaintiff thus argues that the press brake was never duly delivered to a carrier within the meaning of §2-509 and accordingly the risk of loss never passed to plaintiff.

Plaintiff relies on two cases. In the first, La Casse v. Blaustein, 93 Misc. 2d 572, 403 N.Y.S.2d 440 (Civ. Ct. 1978), the defendant seller shipped calculators to the plaintiff buyer, a college student, in two cartons by fourth class mail. The buyer authorized the seller to spend up to $50 for shipping and insurance. The seller spent only $9.98 and insured each carton, valued at $1,663, for $200. The seller wrongly addressed one of the cartons, and inscribed a theft-tempting notation on it. The New York County Civil Court held that the defendant had improperly arranged for transportation of the calculators.

La Casse is the only reported case which suggests that a seller's failure to obtain adequate insurance may breach his duty to make a reasonable contract for shipment under §2-504. The dearth of support for plaintiff's position is instructive. A leading UCC authority has remarked: "Under this subsection [§2-504], what constitutes an 'unreasonable' contract of transportation? *Egregious* cases do arise." See J. White and R. Summers, Uniform Commercial Code §5-2 (1988). The only such "egregious case" identified by White and Summers is *La Casse,* where "the package was underinsured, misaddressed, shipped by fourth class mail, and bore a 'theft-tempting' inscription." White and Summers, supra, at §5-2.

The actions taken by the defendant in *La Casse* were utterly reckless. Moreover, unlike the defendant in that case, MSI did not undertake the responsibility to insure the shipment, and did not ship the press brake at a lower cost than the plaintiff expressly authorized it to pay.

Plaintiff also relies on Miller v. Harvey, 221 N.Y. 57, 116 N.E. 781 (1917). This pre-Code case is inapplicable. In *Miller,* by failing to declare the actual value of goods shipped on a form provided for that purpose, the seller effectively contracted away the buyer's rights against the carrier. Official Comment 3 to §2-504 states:

> [i]t is an improper contract under paragraph (a) for the seller to agree with the carrier to a limited valuation below the true value and thus cut off the buyer's opportunity to recover from the carrier in the event of loss, when the risk of shipment is placed on the buyer.

Thus, a contract is improper if the seller agrees to an inadequate valuation of the shipment and thereby extinguishes the buyer's opportunity to recover from the carrier. That is quite different from a seller's failure to ensure that a carrier has sufficient insurance to cover a particular potential loss, in which case the carrier is still liable to the buyer.

Plaintiff's focus on a single sentence of Official Comment 3 ignores the explicit language of the statute which defines reasonable in the context of "having regard to the nature of the goods," 13 Pa. C.S.A. §2504, and the portion of the Comment which states:

Whether or not the shipment is at the buyer's expense the seller must see to any arrangements, *reasonable in the circumstances,* such as refrigeration, watering of live stock, protection against cold . . . and the like. . . .

Id., Official Comment 3.

The clear implication is that the reasonableness of a shipper's conduct under §2-504 is determined with regard to the mode of transport selected. It would be unreasonable, for example, to send perishables without refrigeration. See Larsen v. A.C. Carpenter, Inc., 620 F. Supp. 1084, 1119 (E.D.N.Y. 1985). No inference fairly can be drawn from the section that a seller has an obligation to investigate the amount and terms of insurance held by the carrier.

The court finds as a matter of law that MSI's conduct was not unreasonable under §2-504. MSI obtained from the carrier a certificate of insurance and did nothing to impair plaintiff's right to recover for any loss from the carrier.[3] Accidents occur in transit. For this reason, the UCC has specifically established mercantile symbols which delineate the risk of loss in a transaction so that the appropriate party might obtain insurance on the shipment. The contract in this case was "F.O.B." seller's warehouse. Plaintiff clearly bears the risk of loss in transit.

There are no material facts in dispute and MSI is entitled to judgment as a matter of law.

Rheinberg-Kellerei GmbH v. Vineyard Wine Co.

North Carolina Court of Appeals, 1981
53 N.C. App. 560, 281 S.E.2d 425, 32 U.C.C. Rep. Serv. 96

Plaintiff, a West German wine producer and exporter, instituted this action to recover the purchase price of a shipment of wine sold to defendant and lost at sea en route between Germany and the United States. Subsequent to a hearing, the court, sitting without a jury, made the following findings of fact.

---

3. Plaintiff's argument that because the carrier used an allegedly unprofessional sounding name, Randy's Truck Line, and inelegant stationery, MSI was on notice that the carrier was unreliable is untenable. The Philadelphia telephone directory alone lists dozens of moving companies bearing the name, often just the first name, of an individual. Moreover, plaintiff has made no showing that the carrier, which is a party defendant, does not in fact have the means to satisfy a judgment in the amount sought.

Plaintiff is a West German corporation engaged in the business of producing, selling, and exporting wine. Defendant, a North Carolina corporation, is a distributor of wine, buying and selling foreign and domestic wines at wholesale. Frank Sutton, d/b/a Frank Sutton & Company and d/b/a The Empress Importing Company, and other names, of Miami Beach, Florida, is a licensed importer and seller of wines. During 1978-1979 Sutton served as an agent for plaintiff and was authorized to sell and solicit orders for plaintiff's wine in the United States. During 1978 and early 1979, Randall F. Switzer, then of Raleigh, North Carolina, was a broker soliciting orders of wine on behalf of several producers and brokers, including Sutton, on a commission basis.

During the summer of 1978, Switzer, on behalf of Frank Sutton, began to solicit orders from prospective customers in North Carolina for wines produced by plaintiff. He contacted Bennett Distributing Company in Salisbury, North Carolina and the defendant in Charlotte, North Carolina, soliciting orders for sale through Sutton of wine produced by plaintiff to be shipped from West Germany consolidated in one container. Switzer, in late August 1978, called the office of Sutton in Miami Beach, Florida, reporting that he had secured orders from Bennett Distributing Company and defendant for 625 cases and 620 cases, respectively, of plaintiff's wines. Switzer then mailed to Sutton a copy of the proposed orders. Switzer also left a copy of the proposed order by defendant with the defendant's sales manager.

On 25 August 1978, the office of Sutton prepared a written confirmation of the orders and mailed them to defendant. Defendant received the written confirmation of orders, but never gave written notice of objection to the contents thereof to plaintiff or plaintiff's agent, Sutton. Written confirmation of the orders together with "Special Instructions" which reflected the instructions to plaintiff regarding the proposed consolidated shipment, were mailed to the plaintiff in West Germany on or about 25 August 1978.

According to the stated prices for the wine, the purchase price of the 620 cases of wine ordered by the defendant was 15.125,00 German marks. On 15 September 1980, the rate of exchange of German marks to United States dollars was such that one German mark equals $.57. Therefore, the purchase price of the 620 cases of wine, 15.125,00 German marks, equals $8,621.25.

Between August and December 1978, defendant's president, Cremilde D. Blank, and Switzer made telephone inquiries to Sutton concerning the status of the wine orders, but were not furnished any information concerning when and how the wine would be shipped or when and where it would arrive. On or about 8 November 1978, Mrs. Blank telephoned Sutton's office and obtained certain details concerning the consolidated order and then wrote to Bennett Distributing Company. Thereafter, in November 1978, Bennett Distributing Company informed Mrs. Blank that it had cancelled its order with the plaintiff, and Switzer thereafter attempted to resell Bennett's share of the order.

On or about 27 November 1978, plaintiff issued notice to Sutton giving the date of the shipment, port of origin, vessel, estimated date of arrival and port of arrival. Sutton did not give any of such information to defendant or to Switzer and did not notify defendant of anything. There was never any communication of any kind between plaintiff and defendant, and defendant was not aware of the details of the shipment.

Plaintiff delivered the wine ordered by defendant, consolidated in a container with the other wine, to a shipping line on 29 November 1978, for shipment from Rotterdam to Wilmington, North Carolina, on board the M.S. Munchen. Defendant did not request the plaintiff to deliver the wine ordered to any particular destination, and plaintiff and its agent, Sutton, selected the port of Wilmington for the port of entry into the United States. The entire container of wine was consigned by plaintiff to defendant, with freight payable at destination by defendant.

After delivering the wine to the ocean vessel for shipment, plaintiff forwarded the invoice for the entire container, certificate of origin and bill of lading, to its bank in West Germany, which forwarded the documents to Wachovia Bank and Trust Company, N.A., in Charlotte, North Carolina. The documents were received by Wachovia on 27 December 1978. The method of payment for the sale was for plaintiff's bank in West Germany to send the invoice, certificate of origin and bill of lading, to Wachovia whereupon defendant was to pay the purchase price to Wachovia and obtain the shipping documents. Wachovia then would forward payment to plaintiff's bank, and defendant could present the shipping documents to the carrier to obtain possession.

Wachovia mailed to defendant on 29 December 1978, a notice requesting payment for the entire consolidated shipment, by sight draft in exchange for documents. The notice was not returned by the Post Office to the sender.

On or about 24 January 1979, defendant first learned that the container of wine had left Germany in early December 1978 aboard the M.S. Munchen, which was lost in the North Atlantic with all hands and cargo aboard between 12 December and 22 December 1978.

Defendant did not receive any wine from plaintiff and did not pay Wachovia for the lost shipment. Plaintiff released the sight draft documents to Frank Sutton. Defendant was not furnished with any copy of said documents until receiving some in March and April 1979 and the others through discovery after this action was filed.

The order and "Special Instructions," mailed by Sutton to plaintiff, but not to defendant, provided inter alia: (1) "Insurance to be covered by purchaser"; (2) "Send a 'Notice of Arrival' to both the customer and to Frank Sutton & Company"; and (3) "Payment may be deferred until the merchandise has arrived at the port of entry."

Based upon the foregoing findings of fact, the trial court made the following pertinent conclusions of law:

> 2. The defendant agreed to purchase 620 cases of wine from the plaintiff through its agent or broker, Frank Sutton, in late August 1978.
>
> 3. Plaintiff failed to comply with §2-504, which provides:
>
> "Where the seller is required or authorized to send the goods to the buyer and the contract does not require him to deliver them at a particular destination, then unless otherwise agreed he must . . .
>
> "(c) promptly notify the buyer of the shipment."
>
> 4. The purpose of such notification requirement is so the buyer (as defendant in this instance would have been) may make necessary arrangements for cargo insurance and otherwise to protect itself against any ensuing loss.
>
> 5. The plaintiff failed to deliver any such notice to defendant herein prior to the sailing of the ship and the ensuing loss. While plaintiff gave such notice to its agent, Frank Sutton did not pass such information on to defendant, so defendant was unaware of details vital to securing cargo insurance or otherwise protecting itself against loss in transit. The mailing of documents after shipment to Wachovia Bank & Trust Company, N.A. to collect the invoice amount plus freight and charges from defendant by sight draft, of which defendant was unaware until some weeks after the loss of the ship was not prompt notice to the defendant as required by the above statute.
>
> 6. Risk of loss of the wine therefore did not pass from the plaintiff to defendant upon delivery of the container of wine to the carrier, as provided in §2-509(1)(a).
>
> 7. Plaintiff is not entitled to recover any amount from the defendant due to such lack of notice.

From judgment in favor of the defendant, dismissing plaintiff's action, both plaintiff and defendant have appealed. . . .

WELLS, J. The first question presented by plaintiff's appeal is whether the trial court was correct in its conclusion that the risk of loss for the wine never passed from plaintiff to defendant due to the failure of plaintiff to give prompt notice of the shipment to defendant. Plaintiff made no exceptions to the findings of fact contained in the judgment and does not contend that the facts found were unsupported by the evidence. Our review on appeal is limited to a determination of whether the facts found support the court's conclusions and the judgment entered. Rule 10(a), N.C. Rules of Appellate Procedure; Swygert v. Swygert, 46 N.C. App. 173, 180-81, 264 S.E.2d 902, 907 (1980).

All parties agree that the contract in question was a "shipment" contract, i.e., one not requiring delivery of the wine at any particular destination. See J. White & R. Summers, Uniform Commercial Code §5-2, at 140-42 (1972). The Uniform Commercial Code, as adopted in North Carolina, dictates when the transfer of risk of loss occurs in this situation. Section 2-509(1)(a) provides, in pertinent part:

> Risk of loss in the absence of breach.—(1) Where the contract requires or authorizes the seller to ship the goods by carrier (a) if it does not require him to deliver them at a particular destination, the risk of loss passes to the buyer when the goods are duly delivered to the carrier even though the shipment is under reservation (§2-505). . . .

Before a seller will be deemed to have "duly delivered" the goods to the carrier, however, he must fulfill certain duties owed to the buyer. In the absence of any agreement to the contrary, these responsibilities, set out in §2-504, are as follows: [the court quoted §2-504].

The trial court concluded that the plaintiff's failure to notify the defendant of the shipment until after the sailing of the ship and the ensuing loss, was not "prompt notice" within the meaning of §2-504, and therefore, the risk of loss did not pass to defendant upon the delivery of the wine to the carrier pursuant to the provisions of §2-509(1)(a). We hold that the conclusions of the trial court were correct. The seller is burdened with special responsibilities under a shipment contract because of the nature of the risk of loss being transferred. See W. Hawkland, 1 A Transactional Guide to the UCC §1.2104, at 102-107 (1964). Where the buyer, upon shipment by seller, assumes the perils involved in carriage, he must have a reasonable opportunity to guard against these risks by independent arrangements with the carrier. The requirement of prompt notification by the seller, as used in §2-504(c), must be construed as taking into consideration the need of a buyer to be informed of the shipment in sufficient time for him to take action to protect himself from the risk of damage to or loss of the goods while in transit. But see J. White & R. Summers, Uniform Commercial Code §5-2, fn. 12 (1972). It would not be practical or desirable, however, for the courts to attempt to engraft onto §2-504 of the U.C.C. a rigid definition of prompt notice. Given the myriad factual situations which arise in business dealings, and keeping in mind the commercial realities, whether notification has been "prompt" within the meaning of UCC will have to be determined on a case-by-case basis, under all the circumstances. See W. Hawkland, 1 A Transactional Guide to the U.C.C. §1.2104, at 106 (1964).

In the case at hand, the shipment of wine was lost at sea sometime between 12 December and 22 December 1978. Although plaintiff did notify its agent, Frank Sutton, regarding pertinent details of the shipment on or about 27 November 1978, this information was not passed along to defendant. The shipping documents were not received by defendant's bank for forwarding to defendant until 27 December 1978, days after the loss had already been incurred. Since the defendant was never notified directly or by the forwarding of shipping documents within the time in which its interest could have been protected by insurance or otherwise, defendant was entitled to reject the shipment pursuant to the term of §2-504(c). . . .

In the plaintiff's appeal, the judgment is affirmed.

In the defendant's appeal, the appeal is dismissed.

PROBLEM 49

The University of Beijing in China ordered video equipment to be shipped from Applied Technology, Inc., in San Jose, California. If nothing is said about the subject, as a matter of international law, will this create a shipment or a destination contract? See CISG Articles 67 and 69. If the parties had been negotiating for the purchase of this equipment but had not gotten around to signing the contract until the goods were already on board an airplane crossing the Pacific Ocean, does the buyer have the risk of loss only from the moment of the signing of the contract or from the delivery of the equipment to the air carrier? See Article 68.

PROBLEM 50

Dime-A-Minute Rent-A-Car rented a new sports car to Joseph Armstrong. Due to a snafu at the rental office, Armstrong did not sign a rental agreement. As he was leaving the rental car lot, the car was struck by a city bus due to no fault of Armstrong (who was unhurt). The sports car was totaled. Dime-A-Minute demanded that Armstrong look to his insurance to replace the car. Did he have the risk of loss here? See §2A-219. If he had signed a rental agreement making him responsible for the car, would that agreement be valid? See §§1-102(3) and 2A-108.

The above discussion of risk of loss, both under the UCC and under the CISG, presupposes that neither of the parties is in breach of their agreement at the moment when the risk would normally pass. If this is not true (for instance, when the seller is in breach because the goods do not conform to the warranties made in the contract), §2-509 does not apply (and neither does Article 67 of the CISG); the relevant risk of loss section is §2-510 (§2A-220 for leases and Articles 66 and 70 in the CISG). Before considering §2-510, we need to explore the UCC's definition of *breach,* and that brings us to the standards of performance set by the Code.

Chapter 5

PERFORMANCE OF THE CONTRACT

Section 2-301 states that the seller's basic obligation is "to transfer and deliver" and the buyer's is "to pay in accordance with the contract." Thus, the seller must tender (offer to deliver) conforming goods, and the buyer must pay for them. Read and compare §2-507(1) with §2-511(1). They appear to be conflicting, don't they? The conflict disappears when the sections are considered in light of the technical/procedural snarl that they are designed to unravel. It is this: in any contract action, the plaintiff loses unless it can be shown that the other party is in breach. Where a sale of goods is involved, it is frequently true that the parties contemplated a contemporaneous swap of money for the goods. If at the appointed time neither party shows up, the buyer is not in breach because the seller did not tender, and vice versa. If the parties did not intend a contemporaneous swap, but instead contracted so that one or the other's performance was to come first, then either §2-507(1) or §2-511(1) will not apply, since the parties will have "otherwise agreed." When, for example, the parties agree that buyer is to be given six months after delivery in which to pay, failure of the seller to deliver on time is a breach, and the seller may be sued without the buyer's having to allege a §2-511(1) tender of payment.

Knowing that the seller's basic duty is to tender conforming goods, and that the buyer's duty is to pay for them, leaves unanswered a host of legal questions. What does the seller's *tender* entail? (Answer: §§2-503 and 2-504.) What does *conforming* mean? (Answer: §2-106(2).) What means of payment can the buyer use? (Answer: §§2-511(2) and 2-511(3).) These and other questions are the subject of this portion of the book.

I.   INSTALLMENT ~~SALES~~ DELIVERY

At common law, successful plaintiffs in contract actions were generally required to prove *substantial performance* (as opposed to technically perfect performance) of the terms of the contract. From your contracts course you may remember Judge Cardozo's opinion in Jacob & Youngs Inc. v. Kent, 230 N.Y. 239, 129 N.E. 889 (1921), the so-called *Reading Pipe* case. The court held that the construction contract was substantially performed even though the contractor installed a different but similar brand of pipe instead of the Reading brand called for under the explicit terms of the contract.

In installment contracts, defined in §2-612(1), substantial performance is still the law. The seller is entitled to payment even where the tender of the goods fails to conform exactly to the contract as long as it "substantially" conforms. Read §2-612. For a good discussion of this section (and many others), see Ellen A. Peters, Remedies for Breach of Contracts Relating to the Sale of Goods Under the Uniform Commercial Code: A Roadmap for Article Two, 73 Yale L.J. 199, 223-229 (1963).

PROBLEM 51

Travis Galleries developed a market in copies of famous statues. It ordered monthly shipments of the statues from Ersatz Imports, agreeing to take 12 shipments of 20 statues each over the coming year. The first month all of the statues arrived upside down in their cartons. The manager of Travis Galleries was amazed that most had survived the trip in this condition. Only one was broken, and a phone call to Ersatz Imports resulted in a promise to ship a replacement at once. The next month the statues were again packaged upside down, and half of them were broken. Does §2-612 permit rejection for this reason? Assume that Ersatz replaced the broken statues within a week, but that the next month the shipment contained no statues at all. Instead, Ersatz had mistakenly shipped Travis poor copies of 20 French Impressionist paintings. Travis Galleries called you, its attorney. May it reject this shipment? Under what theory? May it now cancel the remainder of the Ersatz contract?

Cherwell-Ralli, Inc. v. Rytman Grain Co.

Connecticut Supreme Court, 1980
433 A.2d 984, 29 U.C.C. Rep. Serv. 513

PETERS, J. This case involves a dispute about which of the parties to an oral installment contract was the first to be in breach. The plaintiff, Cherwell-Ralli, Inc., sued the defendant, Rytman Grain Co., Inc., for the nonpayment of moneys due and owing for accepted deliveries of products known as Cherco Meal and C-R-T Meal. The defendant, conceding its indebtedness, counterclaimed for damages arising out of the plaintiff's refusal to deliver remaining instalments under the contract. The trial court, Bordon, J., trial referee, having found all issues for the plaintiff, rendered judgment accordingly, and the defendant appealed.

The trial court's unchallenged finding of fact establishes the following: The parties, on July 26, 1974, entered into an instalment contract for the sale of Cherco Meal and C-R-T Meal on the basis of a memorandum executed by the Getkin Brokerage House. As modified, the contract called for shipments according to weekly instructions from the buyer, with payments to be made within ten days after delivery. Almost immediately the buyer was behind in its payments, and these arrearages were often quite substantial. The seller repeatedly called these arrearages to the buyer's attention but continued to make all shipments as requested by the buyer from July 29, 1974 to April 23, 1975.

By April 15, 1975, the buyer had become concerned that the seller might not complete performance of the contract, because the seller's plant might close and because the market price of the goods had come significantly to exceed the contract price. In a telephonic conversation between the buyer's president and the seller's president on that day, the buyer was assured by the seller that deliveries would continue if the buyer would make the payments for which it was obligated. Thereupon, the buyer sent the seller a check in the amount of $9825.60 to cover shipments through March 31, 1975.

Several days later, on April 23, 1975, the buyer stopped payment on this check because he was told by a truck driver, not employed by the seller, that this shipment would be his last load. The trial court found that this was not a valid reason for stoppage of payment. Upon inquiry by the seller, the buyer restated his earlier concerns about future deliveries. Two letters, both dated April 28, 1975, describe the impasse between the parties: the seller again demanded payment, and the buyer, for the first time in writing, demanded adequate assurance of further deliveries. The buyer's demand for assurance was reiterated in its direct reply to the seller's demand for payment. The buyer, however, made no further payments, either to replace the stopped check or otherwise to pay for the nineteen accepted shipments for which balances were outstanding. The seller made no further deliveries after April 23, 1975, when it heard about the stopped check; the buyer never made specific requests for shipments after that date. Inability to deliver the goods forced the seller to close its plant, on May 2, 1975, because of stockpiling of excess material.

The trial court concluded, on the basis of these facts, that the party in breach was the buyer and not the seller. The court concluded that the seller was entitled to recover the final balance of $21,013.60, which both parties agreed to be due and owing. It concluded that the buyer could not prevail on its counterclaim because it had no reasonable grounds to doubt performance from the seller and had in fact received reasonable assurances. Further, the buyer had presented no reasonably accurate evidence to establish the damages it might have sustained because of the seller's failure to deliver.

The buyer on this appeal challenges first the conclusion that the buyer's failure to pay "substantially impaired the value of the whole contract" so as to constitute "a breach of the whole contract," as is required by the applicable law governing instalment contracts. U.C.C. §2-612(3). What constitutes impairment of the value of the whole contract is a question of fact; Graulich Caterer, Inc. v. Holterbosch, Inc., 101 N.J. Super. 61, 75, 243 A.2d 253 (1968); Holiday Mfg. Co. v. B.A.S.F. Systems, Inc., 380 F. Supp. 1096, 1102 (D. Neb. 1974). The record below amply sustains the trial court's conclusion in this regard, particularly in light of the undenied and uncured stoppage of a check given to comply with the buyer's promise to reduce significantly the

amount of its outstanding arrearages. See Frigiking, Inc. v. Century
Tire & Sales Co., 452 F. Supp. 935, 938 (N.D. Tex. 1978).

The buyer argues that the seller in an instalment contract may
never terminate a contract, despite repeated default in payment by the
buyer, without first invoking the insecurity methodology of §2-609.
That is not the law. If there is reasonable doubt about whether the
buyer's default is substantial, the seller may be well advised to tem-
porize by suspending further performance until it can ascertain
whether the buyer is able to offer adequate assurance of future
payments. Kunian v. Development Corporation of America, 165 Conn.
300, 312, 334 A.2d 427 (1973); Dangerfield v. Markel, 252 N.W.2d 184,
192-93 (N.D. 1977). But if the buyer's conduct is sufficiently egregious,
such conduct will, in and of itself, constitute substantial impairment of
the value of the whole contract and a present breach of the contract as
a whole. An aggrieved seller is expressly permitted, by §2-703(f), upon
breach of a contract as a whole, to cancel the remainder of the contract "with respect to the whole undelivered balance." See Frigiking,
Inc. v. Century Tire & Sales Co., supra. Nor is the seller's remedy to
cancel waived, as the buyer argues, by a lawsuit seeking recovery for
payments due. While §2-612(3) states that a contract is reinstated if the
seller "brings an action with respect *only* to past installments" (emphasis added), it is clear in this case that the seller intended, as the
buyer well knew, to bring this contract to an end because of the buyer's
breach.

The buyer's attack on the court's conclusions with respect to its
counterclaim is equally unavailing. The buyer's principal argument is
that the seller was obligated, on pain of default, to provide assurance of
its further performance. The right to such assurance is premised on
reasonable grounds for insecurity. Whether a buyer has reasonable
grounds to be insecure is a question of fact. AMF, Inc. v. McDonald's
Corp., 536 F.2d 1167, 1170 (7th Cir. 1976). The trial court concluded
that in this case the buyer's insecurity was not reasonable and we agree.
A party to a sales contract may not suspend performance of its own for
which it has "already received the agreed return." At all times, the
buyer had received all the goods which it had ordered. The buyer
could not rely on its own nonpayments as a basis for its own insecurity.
The presidents of the parties had exchanged adequate verbal assurances only eight days before the buyer itself again delayed its own
performance on the basis of information that was facially unreliable.
Contrary to the buyer's argument, subsequent events proved the
buyer's fears to be incorrect, since the seller's plant closed due to a
surplus rather than due to a shortage of materials. Finally, it is fatal to

the buyer's appeal that neither its oral argument nor its brief addressed its failure to substantiate, with probative evidence, the damages it alleged to be attributable to the seller's nondeliveries.

There is no error.

In this opinion the other judges concurred.

II. THE PERFECT TENDER RULE

The substantial performance rule has never (at least in theory) applied to single-delivery contracts between merchants. Learned Hand once stated that "There is no room in commercial contracts for the doctrine of substantial performance." Mitsubishi Goshi Kaisha v. J. Aron & Co., 16 F.2d 185, 186 (2d Cir. 1926). To prevail in a single-delivery sale, the seller must make a *perfect tender*, one that complied with all of the terms of the contract, and then show that the buyer refused to take the goods. The reason for this higher standard in single-delivery sales is that in such cases the buyer does not have the same bargaining position a buyer would have in installment sales (where the seller needs to keep dealing with the buyer on repeated occasions and therefore must, as a business matter, keep the buyer happy).

The Code's perfect tender rule is found in §2-601. Read it. (*Commercial unit* is defined in §2-105(6).)

PROBLEM 52

Stella Speculator, a wealthy investor, signed a contract with Swank Motors to buy five new cars. All five were to be delivered on October 1. When the cars arrived, she test drove each of them and then returned two of them, saying she would keep the other three. She rejected the two cars because the audio system did not work in one of them (she was a great music lover) and the carpeting in the trunk of the other was ripping. Swank Motors offered to repair both defects. When Speculator refused to permit repair, Swank sued. Answer these questions:

(a) Does the common law doctrine *de minimis non curat lex* ("the law does not notice small defects") survive §2-601? If so, in spite of the tiny defects, the cars would be conforming. See Official Comment 2 to §2-106; see also Gindy Mfg. Corp. v. Cardinale Trucking Corp., 111

N.J. Super. 383, 268 A.2d 345 (1970) ("Some defects do not justify rejection by the buyer but can be cured by replacement or repair"); D.P. Technology Corp. v. Sherwood Tool, Inc., 751 F. Supp. 1038, 13 U.C.C. Rep. Serv. 2d 686 (D. Conn. 1990) (where goods specially manufactured, buyer not in good faith in rejecting because of insubstantial delay in delivery); Nordstrom §102.

(b) A seller has a right to *cure* in some circumstances; see §2-508. Is this section of use to Swank Motors? See Wilson v. Scampoli, 228 A.2d 848, 4 U.C.C. Rep. Serv. 178 (D.C. 1967), reprinted below.

(c) Suppose Swank can demonstrate that it is common for car sellers to correct small defects. Will Swank succeed if it argues that such correction is a *usage of trade* (§1-205) and thus either that the goods are *conforming* or that because of this usage of trade, the parties have impliedly agreed that a §2-601 perfect tender is not required? See §§1-102(3), 1-102(4), 1-201(3).

III.   CURE

If the seller has not made a *perfect* tender, and as a result the buyer has rejected the goods, the seller has the right in some circumstances to *cure* the defective performance. The key section is §2-508. Read it and its Official Comments. For an annotation on the subject, see Annot., 36 A.L.R.4th 544.

PROBLEM 53

On August 8, Francis and Sophie Ferdinand ordered a new car from Princip Motors for $22,000. The car was scheduled for delivery "no later than September 1" (it had special accessories that had to be installed at the factory). On August 15, Princip Motors told the Ferdinands that the car was ready, so they picked it up. Halfway home (three miles from the car dealer), the engine blew up without warning. The Ferdinands were not hurt, but the engine was destroyed. On being informed that the Ferdinands wanted their money back, Princip made the following responses:

(a) Princip offered to take an engine out of a car of the same model and install it in the original automobile (which was otherwise undamaged).

(b) Princip refused to refund the money; instead, it claimed a right to give the Ferdinands a new car to be delivered fresh from the factory on August 20.

Does §2-508 require the Ferdinands to accept either of these cure offers?

In resolving Problem 54, it may help you to know about the *Shaken Faith Doctrine*, developed in a similar situation by the court in a leading case (worth reading):

> For a majority of people the purchase of a new car is a major investment, rationalized by the peace of mind that flows from its dependability and safety. Once their faith is shaken, the vehicle loses not only its real value in their eyes, but becomes an instrument whose integrity is substantially impaired and whose operation is fraught with apprehension. The attempted cure in the present case was ineffective.

Zabriskie Chevrolet, Inc. v. Smith, 99 N.J. Super. 441, 458, 240 A.2d 195, 205, 5 U.C.C. Rep. Serv. 30, 42 (1968).

And, in the words of one pedant, "The court should be willing to take judicial notice of what all modern day consumers 'know': things that do not work well at the start are not likely to work well in the future unless the original defect is minor in nature." Whaley, Tender, Acceptance, Rejection and Revocation—The UCC's "TARR-Baby," 24 Drake L. Rev. 52, 58 (1974).

Wilson v. Scampoli

District of Columbia Court of Appeals, 1967
228 A.2d 848, 4 U.C.C. Rep. Serv. 178

MYERS, J. This is an appeal from an order of the trial court granting rescission of a sales contract for a color television set and directing the return of the purchase price plus interest and costs.

Appellee purchased the set in question on November 4, 1965, paying the total purchase price in cash. The transaction was evidenced by a sales ticket showing the price paid and guaranteeing ninety days' free service and replacement of any defective tube and parts for a period of one year. Two days after purchase the set was delivered and uncrated, the antennae adjusted and the set plugged into an electrical outlet to "cook out."[1] When the set was turned on, however, it did not

---

1. Such a "cook out," usually over several days, allows the set to magnetize itself and to heat up the circuit in order to indicate faulty wiring.

function properly, the picture having a reddish tinge. Appellant's delivery man advised the buyer's daughter, Mrs. Kolley, that it was not his duty to tune in or adjust the color but that a service representative would shortly call at her house for that purpose. After the departure of the delivery men, Mrs. Kolley unplugged the set and did not use it.[2]

On November 8, 1965, a service representative arrived, and after spending an hour in an effort to eliminate the red cast from the picture advised Mrs. Kolley that he would have to remove the chassis from the cabinet and take it to the shop as he could not determine the cause of the difficulty from his examination at the house. He also made a written memorandum of his service call, noting that the television "Needs Shop Work (Red Screen)." Mrs. Kolley refused to allow the chassis to be removed, asserting she did not want a "repaired" set but another "brand new" set. Later she demanded the return of the purchase price, although retaining the set. Appellant refused to refund the purchase price, but renewed his offer to adjust, repair, or, if the set could not be made to function properly, to replace it. Ultimately, appellee instituted this suit against appellant seeking a refund of the purchase price. After a trial, the court ruled that "under the facts and circumstances the complaint is justified. Under the equity powers of the court I will order the parties put back in their original status, let the $675 be returned, and the set returned to the defendant."

Appellant does not contest the jurisdiction of the trial court to order rescission in a proper case, but contends the trial judge erred in holding that rescission here was appropriate. He argues that he was always willing to comply with the terms of the sale either by correcting the malfunction by minor repairs or, in the event the set could not be made thereby properly operative, by replacement; that as he was denied the opportunity to try to correct the difficulty, he did not breach the contract of sale or any warranty thereunder, expressed or implied. [The court quoted §2-508.] A retail dealer would certainly expect and have reasonable grounds to believe that merchandise like color television sets, new and delivered as crated at the factory, would be acceptable as delivered and that, if defective in some way, he would have the right to substitute a conforming tender. The question then resolves itself to whether the dealer may conform his tender by adjustment or minor repair or whether he must conform by substituting brand new merchandise. The problem seems to be one of first

2. Appellee, who made his home with Mrs. Kolley, had been hospitalized shortly before delivery of the set. The remaining negotiations were carried on by Mrs. Kolley, acting on behalf of her father.

impression in other jurisdictions adopting the Uniform Commercial Code as well as in the District of Columbia.

Although the Official Code Comments do not reach this precise issue, there are cases and comments under other provisions of the Code which indicate that under certain circumstances repairs and adjustments are contemplated as remedies under implied warranties. In L & N Sales Co. v. Little Brown Jug, Inc., 12 Pa. D. & C. 2d 469 (Phila. County Ct. 1957), where the language of a disclaimer was found insufficient to defeat warranties under §§2-314 and 2-315, the court noted that the buyer had notified the seller of defects in the merchandise, and as the seller was unable to remedy them and later refused to accept return of the articles, it was held to be a breach of warranty. In Hall v. Everett Motors, Inc., 340 Mass. 430, 165 N.E.2d 107 (1960), decided shortly before the effective date of the Code in Massachusetts, the court reluctantly found that a disclaimer of warranties was sufficient to insulate the seller. Several references were made in the ruling to the seller's unsuccessful attempts at repairs, the court indicating the result would have been different under the Code.

While these cases provide no mandate to require the buyer to accept patchwork goods or substantially repaired articles in lieu of flawless merchandise, they do indicate that minor repairs or reasonable adjustments are frequently the means by which an imperfect tender may be cured. In discussing the analogous question of defective title, it has been stated that:

> The seller, then, should be able to cure [the defect] under subsection 2-508(2) in those cases in which he can do so without subjecting the buyer to any great inconvenience, risk or loss. [Hawkland, Curing an Improper Tender of Title to Chattels: Past, Present and Commercial Code, 46 Minn. L. Rev. 697, 724 (1962).]

See also Willer & Hart, Forms and Procedures under the U.C.C., §24.07[4]; D.C. Code §28:2-608(1)(a) (Supp. V, 1966).

Removal of a television chassis for a short period of time in order to determine the cause of color malfunction and ascertain the extent of adjustment or correction needed to effect full operational efficiency presents no great inconvenience to the buyer. In the instant case, appellant's expert witness testified that this was not infrequently necessary with new televisions. Should the set be defective in workmanship or parts, the loss would be upon the manufacturer who warranted it free from mechanical defect. Here the adamant refusal of Mrs. Kolley, acting on behalf of appellee, to allow inspection essential to the determination of the cause of the excessive red tinge to the picture defeated any effort by the seller to provide timely repair or even replacement of the set if the difficulty could not be corrected. The cause of the defect might have been minor and easily adjusted or it may have been substantial and required replacement by another new set but the seller was never given an adequate opportunity to make a determination.

We do not hold that appellant has no liability to appellee,[3] but as he was denied access and a reasonable opportunity to repair, appellee has not shown a breach of warranty entitling him either to a brand new set or to rescission. We therefore reverse the judgment of the trial court granting rescission and directing the return of the purchase price of the set.

Reversed.

QUESTIONS

1. Is the court following the perfect tender rule here? See §2-601.
2. What portion of §2-508 is relevant to this case?
3. In this case the buyer rejected the goods but refused to return them to the seller. Is this permissible? See §2-711(3).

IV. REJECTION AND ACCEPTANCE

When the seller makes a tender of the goods, the buyer must choose between two possible legal responses: rejection (§2-602) and acceptance (§§2-606 and 2-607). A buyer cannot do both since rejection and acceptance are mutually exclusive actions. Failure to act results in a technical *acceptance*, since rejection must come within a reasonable period of time after delivery of the goods. Read §2-602. The definition of *acceptance* is found in §2-606, and its legal consequences are spelled out in §2-607. Note two important things about these

---

3. Appellant on appeal has renewed his willingness to remedy any defect in the tender, and thus there is no problem of expiration of his warranties. He should be afforded the right to inspect and correct any malfunction. If appellee refuses to allow appellant an opportunity to do so, then no cause of action can lie for breach of warranty, express or implied, and the loss must be borne by appellee.

sections as you read them: (1) a buyer is entitled to a reasonable *trial-use* period to see if the goods conform (this is phrased in the Code as a "reasonable opportunity to inspect"; see §2-513), and (2) on acceptance, the burden of proof as to defects shifts to the buyer (§2-607(4)). Prior to acceptance, the seller must prove that a perfect tender was made under §2-601.

PROBLEM 54

Midwestern Seafoods, headquartered in Iowa, ordered 50 live lobsters from Maine Exports, "F.O.B. Portland." On September 1, Maine Exports loaded the lobsters on board an airplane in Portland, from where they were flown to Boston and then to Des Moines. Maine Exports failed to notify Midwestern Seafoods of the date of the flight until two days later, when Midwestern's purchasing agent called to inquire. He then made a few calls and located the lobsters in Des Moines, where they had been sitting for a day. Midwestern signed a receipt and picked the lobsters up. Twenty of them were clearly dying (15 due to bad handling by Maine Exports before they were handed over to the airline and 5 due to damage in transit); the other 30 were fine. Midwestern decided, for reasons that are unclear, that it wanted none of the lobsters.

(a) Is the seller's failure to notify Midwestern of the shipment a ground for rejection? See §2-504. •

(b) May Midwestern reject because of the 20 defective lobsters? See §§2-601, 2-503, 2-509(1), 2-510(1).

(c) How quickly must Midwestern act if it wishes to reject? What technical steps is it required to take? See §§2-602, 1-201(26), 1-204.

(d) Must Midwestern reship the goods to Maine Exports if the latter offers to pay the freight? See §2-602(2) with its Official Comment 2; §§2-603, 2-604.

(e) If Midwestern decides to keep 30 of the lobsters for resale, is this allowed? See §§2-602(2)(a), 2-606; cf. §§2-601, 2-105(6); Annot., 67 A.L.R.3d 363.

(f) If Midwestern rejects the goods, must it give its reasons in the notice of rejection? What penalty is there for not doing so? See §2-605 and its Official Comment 2.

(g) If Midwestern gives a valid notice of rejection within a reasonable period of time after the lobsters are delivered, what should it then do with the lobsters? See §2-602(2).

Ramirez v. Autosport

New Jersey Supreme Court, 1982
88 N.J. 277, 440 A.2d 1345, 33 U.C.C. Rep. Serv. 134

POLLOCK, J. This case raises several issues under the Uniform Commercial Code ("the Code" and "UCC") concerning whether a buyer may reject a tender of goods with minor defects and whether a seller may cure the defects. We consider also the remedies available to the buyer, including cancellation of the contract. The main issue is whether plaintiffs, Mr. and Mrs. Ramirez, could reject the tender by defendant, Autosport, of a camper van with minor defects and cancel the contract for the purchase of the van.

The trial court ruled that Mr. and Mrs. Ramirez rightfully rejected the van and awarded them the fair market value of their trade-in van. The Appellate Division affirmed in a brief per curiam decision which, like the trial court opinion, was unreported. We affirm the judgment of the Appellate Division.

I

Following a mobile home show at the Meadowlands Sports Complex, Mr. and Mrs. Ramirez visited Autosport's showroom in Somerville. On July 20, 1978, the Ramirezes and Donald Graff, a salesman for Autosport, agreed on the sale of a new camper and the trade-in of the van owned by Mr. and Mrs. Ramirez. Autosport and the Ramirezes signed a simple contract reflecting a $14,100 purchase price for the new van with a $4,700 trade-in allowance for the Ramirez van, which Mr. and Mrs. Ramirez left with Autosport. After further allowance for taxes, title and documentary fees, the net price was $9,902. Because Autosport needed two weeks to prepare the new van, the contract provided for delivery on or about August 3, 1978.

On that date, Mr. and Mrs. Ramirez returned with their checks to Autosport to pick up the new van. Graff was not there so Mr. White, another salesman, met them. Inspection disclosed several defects in the van. The paint was scratched, both the electric and sewer hookups were missing, and the hubcaps were not installed. White advised the Ramirezes not to accept the camper because it was not ready.

Mr. and Mrs. Ramirez wanted the van for a summer vacation and called Graff several times. Each time Graff told them it was not ready for delivery. Finally, Graff called to notify them that the camper was ready. On August 14, Mr. and Mrs. Ramirez went to Autosport to accept delivery, but workers were still touching up the outside paint.

Also, the camper windows were open, and the dining area cushions were soaking wet. Mr. and Mrs. Ramirez could not use the camper in that condition, but Mr. Leis, Autosport's manager, suggested that they take the van and that Autosport would replace the cushions later. Mrs. Ramirez counteroffered to accept the van if they could withhold $2,000, but Leis agreed to no more than $250, which she refused. Leis then agreed to replace the cushions and to call them when the van was ready.

On August 15, 1978, Autosport transferred title to the van to Mr. and Mrs. Ramirez, a fact unknown to them until the summer of 1979. Between August 15 and September 1, 1978, Mrs. Ramirez called Graff several times urging him to complete the preparation of the van, but Graff constantly advised her that the van was not ready. He finally informed her that they could pick it up on September 1.

When Mr. and Mrs. Ramirez went to the showroom on September 1, Graff asked them to wait. And wait they did—for one and a half hours. No one from Autosport came forward to talk with them, and the Ramirezes left in disgust.

On October 5, 1978, Mr. and Mrs. Ramirez went to Autosport with an attorney friend. Although the parties disagreed on what occurred, the general topic was whether they should proceed with the deal or Autosport should return to the Ramirezes their trade-in van. Mrs. Ramirez claimed they rejected the new van and requested the return of their trade-in. Mr. Lustig, the owner of Autosport, thought, however, that the deal could be salvaged if the parties could agree on the dollar amount of a credit for the Ramirezes. Mr. and Mrs. Ramirez never took possession of the new van and repeated their request for the return of their trade-in. Later in October, however, Autosport sold the trade-in to an innocent third party for $4,995. Autosport claimed that the Ramirez' van had a book value of $3,200 and claimed further that it spent $1,159.62 to repair their van. By subtracting the total of those two figures, $4,159.62, from the $4,995.00 sale price, Autosport claimed a $600-700 profit on the sale.

On November 20, 1978, the Ramirezes sued Autosport seeking, among other things, rescission of the contract. Autosport counterclaimed for breach of contract.

II

Our initial inquiry is whether a consumer may reject defective goods that do not conform to the contract of sale. The basic issue is whether under the UCC, adopted in New Jersey as N.J.S.A. 12A:1-101 et seq., a seller has the duty to deliver goods that conform precisely to the contract. We conclude that the seller is under such a duty to make a "perfect tender" and that a buyer has the right to reject goods that do not conform to the contract. That conclusion, however, does not resolve the entire dispute between buyer and seller. A more complete answer requires a brief statement of the history of the mutual obligations of buyers and sellers of commercial goods.

In the nineteenth century, sellers were required to deliver goods that complied exactly with the sales agreement. See Filley v. Polk, 115 U.S. 213, 29 L. Ed. 372, 373 (1885) (buyer not obliged to accept otherwise conforming scrap iron shipped to New Orleans from Leith, rather than Glasgow, Scotland, as required by contract); Columbian Iron Works & Dry-Dock Co. v. Douglas, 84 Md. 44, 34 A. 1118, 1120-1121 (1896) (buyer who agreed to purchase steel scrap from United States cruisers not obliged to take any other kind of scrap). That rule, known as the "perfect tender" rule, remained part of the law of sales well into the twentieth century. By the 1920's the doctrine was so entrenched in the law that Judge Learned Hand declared "[t]here is no room in commercial contracts for the doctrine of substantial performance." Mitsubishi Goshi Kaisha v. J. Aron & Co., Inc., 16 F.2d 185, 186 (2d Cir. 1926).

The harshness of the rule led courts to seek to ameliorate its effect and to bring the law of sales in closer harmony with the law of contracts, which allows rescission only for material breaches. LeRoy Dyal Co. v. Allen, 161 F.2d 152, 155 (4th Cir. 1947). See 5 Corbin, Contracts §1104 at 464 (1951); 12 Williston, Contracts §1455 at 14 (3d ed. 1970). Nevertheless, a variation of the perfect tender rule appeared in the Uniform Sales Act. N.J.S.A. 46:30-75 (purchasers permitted to reject goods or rescind contracts for any breach of warranty); N.J.S.A. 46:30-18 to -21 (warranties extended to include all the seller's obligations to the goods). See Honnold, "Buyer's Right of Rejection, A Study in the Impact of Codification Upon a Commercial Problem," 97 U. Pa. L. Rev. 457, 460 (1949). The chief objection to the continuation of the perfect tender rule was that buyers in a declining market would reject goods for minor nonconformities and force the loss on surprised sellers. See Hawkland, Sales and Bulk Sales Under the Uniform Commercial Code, 120-122 (1958), cited in N.J.S.A. 12A:2-508, New Jersey Study Comment 3.

To the extent that a buyer can reject goods for any nonconformity, the UCC retains the perfect tender rule. Section 2-106 states that goods conform to a contract "when they are in accordance with the obligations under the contract." Section 2-601 authorizes a buyer to reject goods if they "or the tender of delivery fail in any respect to conform to the contract." The Code, however, mitigates the harshness of the perfect tender rule and balances the interests of buyer and seller. See Restatement (Second), Contracts, §241 comment (b) (1981). The Code achieves that result through its provisions for revocation of acceptance and cure. N.J.S.A. 2-608, 2-508.

Initially, the rights of the parties vary depending on whether the rejection occurs before or after acceptance of the goods. Before acceptance, the buyer may reject goods for any nonconformity. N.J.S.A. 2-601. Because of the seller's right to cure, however, the buyer's rejection does not necessarily discharge the contract. N.J.S.A. 2-508. Within the time set for performance in the contract, the seller's right to cure is unconditional. Id., subsec. (1); see id., Official Comment 1. Some authorities recommend granting a breaching party a right to cure in all contracts, not merely those for the sale of goods. Restatement (Second), Contracts, ch. 10, especially §§237 and 241. Underlying the right to cure in both kinds of contracts is the recognition that parties should be encouraged to communicate with each other and to resolve their own problems. Id., Introduction p.193.

The rights of the parties also vary if rejection occurs after the time set for performance. After expiration of that time, the seller has a further reasonable time to cure if he believed reasonably that the goods would be acceptable with or without a money allowance. N.J.S.A. 2-508(2). The determination of what constitutes a further reasonable time depends on the surrounding circumstances, which include the change of position by and the amount of inconvenience to the buyer. N.J.S.A. 2-508, Official Comment 3. Those circumstances also include the length of time needed by the seller to correct the nonconformity and his ability to salvage the goods by resale to others. See Restatement (Second), Contracts, §241 comment (d). Thus, the Code balances the buyer's right to reject nonconforming goods with a "second chance" for the seller to conform the goods to the contract under certain limited circumstances. N.J.S.A. 2-508, New Jersey Study Comment 1.

After acceptance, the Code strikes a different balance: the buyer may revoke acceptance only if the nonconformity substantially impairs the value of the goods to him. N.J.S.A. 2-608. See Herbstman v. Eastman Kodak Co., 68 N.J. 1, 9 (1975). See generally, Priest, "Breach and Remedy for the Tender of NonConforming Goods under the Uniform Commercial Code: An Economic Approach," 92 Harv. L. Rev. 960, 971-973 (1978). This provision protects the seller from revocation for trivial defects. Herbstman, supra, 68 N.J. at 9. It also prevents the buyer from taking undue advantage of the seller by allowing goods to depreciate and then returning them because of asserted minor defects. See White & Summers, Uniform Commercial Code, §8-3 at 391 (2d ed. 1980). Because this case involves rejection of goods, we need not decide whether a seller has a right to cure substantial defects that justify revocation of acceptance. See Pavesi v. Ford Motor Co., 155 N.J. Super. 373, 378 (App. Div. 1978) (right to cure after acceptance limited to trivial defects) and White & Summers, supra, §8-4 at 319 n.76 (open question as to the relationship between §§2-608 and 2-508).

Other courts agree that the buyer has a right of rejection for any nonconformity, but that the seller has a countervailing right to cure within a reasonable time. Marine Mart Inc. v. Pearce, 480 S.W.2d 133, 137 (Ark. 1972). See Intermeat, Inc. v. American Poultry, Inc., 575 F.2d 1017, 1024 (2d Cir. 1978); Moulton Cavity & Mold, Inc. v. Lyn-Flex Industries, 396 A.2d 1024, 1027 n.6 (Me. 1979); Uchitel v. F.R. Tripler & Co., 434 N.Y.S.2d 77, 81, 107 Misc. 2d 310 (App. Term 1980); Rutland Music Services, Inc. v. Ford Motor Co., 422 A.2d 248, 249 (Vt. 1980). But see McKenzie v. Alla-Ohio Coals, Inc., 29 U.C.C. Rep. 852, 856-857 (D. D.C. 1979).

One New Jersey case, Gindy Mfg. Corp. v. Cardinale Trucking Corp., suggests that, because some defects can be cured, they do not justify rejection. 111 N.J. Super. 383, 387 n.1 (Law Div. 1970). Accord, Adams v. Tremontin, 42 N.J. Super. 313, 325 (App. Div. 1956) (Uniform Sales Act). But see Sudol v. Rudy Papa Motors, 175 N.J. Super. 238, 240-241 (D. Ct. 1980) (§2-601 contains perfect tender rule). Nonetheless we conclude that the perfect tender rule is preserved to the extent of permitting a buyer to reject goods for any defects. Because of the seller's right to cure, rejection does not terminate the contract. Accordingly, we disapprove the suggestion in *Gindy* that curable defects do not justify rejection.

A further problem, however, is identifying the remedy available to a buyer who rejects goods with insubstantial defects that the seller fails to cure within a reasonable time. The Code provides expressly that when "the buyer rightfully rejects, then with respect to the goods involved, the buyer may cancel." N.J.S.A. 2-711. "Cancellation" occurs when either party puts an end to the contract for breach by the other. N.J.S.A. 2-106(4). Nonetheless, some confusion exists whether the equitable remedy of rescission survives under the Code. Compare Ventura v. Ford Motor Corp., 173 N.J. Super. 501, 503 (Ch. Div. 1980) (rescission under UCC) and Pavesi v. Ford Motor Corp., supra, 155 N.J. Super. at 377 (equitable remedies still available since not specifically superseded, §1-103) with Edelstein v. Toyota Motors Dist., 176 N.J. Super. 57, 63-64 (App. Div. 1980) (under UCC rescission is revocation of acceptance) and Sudol v. Rudy Papa Motors, supra, 175 N.J. Super. at 241-242 (under UCC, rescission no longer exists as such).

The Code eschews the word "rescission" and substitutes the terms "cancellation," "revocation of acceptance," and "rightful rejection." N.J.S.A. 2-106(4); 2-608; and 2-711 & Official Comment 1. Although neither "rejection" nor "revocation of acceptance" is defined in the Code, rejection includes both the buyer's refusal to accept or keep delivered goods and his notification to the seller that he will not keep them. White & Summers, supra, §8-1 at 293. Revocation of acceptance is like rejection, but occurs after the buyer has accepted the goods. Nonetheless, revocation of acceptance is intended to provide the same relief as rescission of a contract of sale of goods. N.J.S.A. 2-608 Official Comment 1; N.J. Study Comment 2. In brief, revocation is tantamount to rescission. See Herbstman v. Eastman Kodak Co., supra, 68 N.J. at 9; accord, Peckham v. Larsen Chevrolet-Buick-Oldsmobile, Inc., 99 Idaho 675, —, 587 P.2d 816, 818 (1978) (rescission and revocation of acceptance amount to the same thing). Similarly, subject to the seller's right to cure, a buyer who rightfully rejects goods, like one who revokes his acceptance, may cancel the contract. N.J.S.A. 2-711 & Official Comment 1. We need not resolve the extent to which rescission for reasons other than rejection or revocation of acceptance, e.g. fraud and mistake, survives as a remedy outside the Code. Compare N.J.S.A. 1-103 and White & Summers, supra, §8-1, p.295, with N.J.S.A. 2-721. Accordingly, we approve *Edelstein* and *Sudol,* which recognize that explicit Code remedies replace rescission, and disapprove *Ventura* and *Pavesi* to the extent they suggest the UCC expressly recognizes rescission as a remedy.

Although the complaint requested rescission of the contract, plaintiffs actually sought not only the end of their contractual obligations, but also restoration to their pre-contractual position. That request incorporated the equitable doctrine of restitution, the purpose of which is to restore plaintiff to as good a position as he occupied before the contract. Corbin, supra, §1102 at 455. In UCC parlance, plaintiffs' request was for the cancellation of the contract and recovery of the price paid. N.J.S.A. 2-106(4), 2-711.

General contract law permits rescission only for material breaches, and the Code restates "materiality" in terms of "substantial impairment." See Herbstman v. Eastman Kodak Co., supra, 68 N.J. at 9; id. at 15 (Conford, J., concurring). The Code permits a buyer who rightfully rejects goods to cancel a contract of sale. N.J.S.A. 2-711. Because a buyer may reject goods with insubstantial defects, he also may cancel the contract if those defects remain uncured. Otherwise, a seller's failure to cure minor defects would compel a buyer to accept imperfect goods and collect for any loss caused by the nonconformity. N.J.S.A. 2-714.

Although the Code permits cancellation by rejection for minor defects, it permits revocation of acceptance only for substantial impairments. That distinction is consistent with other Code provisions that depend on whether the buyer has accepted the goods. Acceptance creates liability in the buyer for the price, N.J.S.A. 2-709(1), and precludes rejection. N.J.S.A. 2-607(2); N.J.S.A. 2-606, New Jersey Study Comment 1. Also, once a buyer accepts goods, he has the burden to prove any defect. N.J.S.A. 2-607(4); White & Summers, supra, §8-2 at 297. By contrast, where goods are rejected for not conforming to the contract, the burden is on the seller to prove that the nonconformity was corrected. Miron v. Yonkers Raceway, Inc., 400 F.2d 112, 119 (2d Cir. 1968).

Underlying the Code provisions is the recognition of the revolutionary change in business practices in this century. The purchase of goods is no longer a simple transaction in which a buyer purchases individually-made goods from a seller in a face-to-face transaction. Our economy depends on a complex system for the manufacture, distribution, and sale of goods, a system in which manufacturers and consumers rarely meet. Faceless manufacturers mass-produce goods for unknown consumers who purchase those goods from merchants exercising little or no control over the quality of their production. In an age of assembly lines, we are accustomed to cars with scratches, television sets without knobs and other goods with all kinds of defects. Buyers no longer expect a "perfect tender." If a merchant sells defective goods, the reasonable expectation of the parties is that the buyer will return those goods and that the seller will repair or replace them.

Recognizing this commercial reality, the Code permits a seller to cure imperfect tenders. Should the seller fail to cure the defects, whether substantial or not, the balance shifts again in favor of the buyer, who has the right to cancel or seek damages. N.J.S.A. 2-711. In general, economic considerations would induce sellers to cure minor defects. See generally Priest, supra, 92 Harv. L. Rev. 973-974. Assuming the seller does not cure, however, the buyer should be permitted to exercise his remedies under N.J.S.A. 2-711. The Code remedies for consumers are to be liberally construed, and the buyer should have the option of cancelling if the seller does not provide conforming goods. See N.J.S.A. 1-106.

To summarize, the UCC preserves the perfect tender rule to the extent of permitting a buyer to reject goods for any nonconformity.

Nonetheless, that rejection does not automatically terminate the contract. A seller may still effect a cure and preclude unfair rejection and cancellation by the buyer. N.J.S.A. 2-508, Official Comment 2; N.J.S.A. 2-711, Official Comment 1.

III

The trial court found that Mr. and Mrs. Ramirez had rejected the van within a reasonable time under N.J.S.A. 12A:2-602. The court found that on August 3, 1978, Autosport's salesman advised the Ramirezes not to accept the van and that on August 14, they rejected delivery and Autosport agreed to replace the cushions. Those findings are supported by substantial credible evidence, and we sustain them. See Rova Farms Resort v. Investors Ins. Co., 65 N.J. 474, 483-484 (1974). Although the trial court did not find whether Autosport cured the defects within a reasonable time, we find that Autosport did not effect a cure. Clearly the van was not ready for delivery during August, 1978, when Mr. and Mrs. Ramirez rejected it, and Autosport had the burden of proving that it had corrected the defects. Although the Ramirezes gave Autosport ample time to correct the defects, Autosport did not demonstrate that the van conformed to the contract on September 1. In fact, on that date, when Mr. and Mrs. Ramirez returned at Autosport's invitation, all they received was discourtesy.

On the assumption that substantial impairment is necessary only when a purchaser seeks to revoke acceptance under N.J.S.A. 2-608, the trial court correctly refrained from deciding whether the defects substantially impaired the van. The court properly concluded that plaintiffs were entitled to "rescind"—i.e., to "cancel"—the contract.

Because Autosport had sold the trade-in to an innocent third party, the trial court determined that the Ramirezes were entitled not to the return of the trade-in, but to its fair market value, which the court set at the contract price of $4,700. A buyer who rightfully rejects goods and cancels the contract may, among other possible remedies, recover so much of the purchase price as has been paid. N.J.S.A. 2-711. The Code, however, does not define "pay" and does not require payment to be made in cash. . . .

For the preceding reasons, we affirm the judgment of the Appellate Division.

QUESTIONS

1. Did the defendant's grounds for cure fit within §2-508?
2. Is the court creating a right to cure outside of §2-508?

PROBLEM 55

Ulysses Sinon ran a dude ranch in Troy, Colorado. He decided to erect a statue of a giant horse near the entrance to the ranch as a tourist attraction. The horse was specially manufactured by Epeius of Paris and arrived in six boxes to be assembled by Sinon. When the horse was put together, Sinon was displeased with the appearance of the tail. The horse had been designed by Epeius, and the scale model Sinon had seen when he decided to buy the horse had had a different tail. Sinon removed the tail and substituted one of his own design. He returned the original to Epeius along with a letter of rejection. In the meantime, Sinon painted the rest of the horse black (in the delivered state it was white) and used it extensively in advertising for the ranch. The horse failed to attract new business to the ranch. After three months of display, Sinon took it down and shipped it back to Epeius with a letter of rejection that stated that the problem with the tail made the horse unattractive and unusable. Epeius sues. Did Sinon make a rejection or an acceptance? If the tail did not conform to the model, is that a ground for rejection? See §2-601. If Sinon had made a technical acceptance, does that fact preclude a suit for breach of warranty? See §2-607(2). What steps should Sinon take to preserve his legal rights? See §2-607(3)(a). What reasons lie behind the notice requirement? See §§2-508, 2-515.

Plateq Corp. of North Haven v. Machlett Laboratories, Inc.

Connecticut Supreme Court, 1983
189 Conn. 433, 456 A.2d 786, 35 U.C.C. Rep. Serv. 1162

PETERS, J. In this action by a seller of specially manufactured goods to recover their purchase price from a commercial buyer, the principal issue is whether the buyer accepted the goods before it attempted to cancel the contract of sale. The plaintiff, Plateq Corporation of North Haven, sued the defendant, The Machlett Laboratories, Inc., to recover damages, measured by the contract price and incidental damages, arising out of the defendant's allegedly wrongful cancellation of a written contract for the manufacture and sale of two lead-covered steel tanks and appurtenant stands. The defendant denied liability and counterclaimed for damages. After a full hearing, the trial court found for the plaintiff both on its complaint and on the defendant's counterclaim. The defendant has appealed.

The trial court, in its memorandum of decision, found the following facts. On July 9, 1976, the defendant ordered from the plaintiff two lead-covered steel tanks to be constructed by the plaintiff according to specifications supplied by the defendant. The parties understood that the tanks were designed for the special purpose of testing x-ray tubes and were required to be radiation-proof within certain federal standards. Accordingly, the contract provided that the tanks would be tested for radiation leaks after their installation on the defendant's premises. The plaintiff undertook to correct, at its own cost, any deficiencies that this post-installation test might uncover. The plaintiff had not previously constructed such tanks, nor had the defendant previously designed tanks for this purpose. The contract was amended on August 9, 1976, to add construction of two metal stands to hold the tanks. All the goods were to be delivered to the defendant at the plaintiff's place of business.

Although the plaintiff encountered difficulties both in performing according to the contract specifications and in completing performance within the time required, the defendant did no more than call these deficiencies to the plaintiff's attention during various inspections in September and early October, 1976. By October 11, 1976, performance was belatedly but substantially completed. On that date, Albert Yannello, the defendant's engineer, noted some remaining deficiencies which the plaintiff promised to remedy by the next day, so that the goods would then be ready for delivery. Yannello gave no indication to the plaintiff that this arrangement was in any way unsatisfactory to the defendant. Not only did Yannello communicate general acquiescence in the plaintiff's proposed tender but he specifically led the plaintiff to believe that the defendant's truck would pick up the tanks and the stands within a day or two. Instead of sending its truck, the defendant sent a notice of total cancellation which the plaintiff received on October 14, 1976. That notice failed to particularize the grounds upon which cancellation was based.

On this factual basis, the trial court, having concluded that the transaction was a contract for the sale of goods falling within the Uniform Commercial Code, General Statutes §§2-101 et seq., considered whether the defendant had accepted the goods. The court determined that the defendant had accepted the tanks, primarily by signifying its willingness to take them despite their non-conformities, in accordance with General Statutes §2-606(1)(a), and secondarily by failing to make an effective rejection, in accordance with General Statutes §2-606(1)(b). Once the tanks had been accepted, the defendant could rightfully revoke its acceptance under General Statutes §2-608 only by showing substantial impairment of their value to the defendant. In part because the defendant's conduct had foreclosed any post-installation inspection, the court concluded that such impairment had not been proved. Since the tanks were not readily resalable on the open market, the plaintiff was entitled, upon the defendant's wrongful revocation of acceptance, to recover their contract price, minus salvage value, plus interest. General Statutes §§2-703; 2-709(1)(b). Accordingly, the trial court awarded the plaintiff damages in the amount of $14,837.92.

In its appeal, the defendant raises four principal claims of error. It maintains that the trial court erred: (1) in invoking the "cure" section, General Statutes §2-508, when there had been no tender by the plaintiff seller; (2) in concluding, in accordance with the acceptance section, General Statutes §2-606(1), that the defendant had "signified" to the plaintiff its willingness to take the contract goods; (3) in misconstruing the defendant's statutory and contractual rights of inspection; and (4) in refusing to find that the defendant's letter of cancellation was occasioned by the plaintiff's breach. We find no error.

Upon analysis, all of the defendant's claims of error are variations upon one central theme. The defendant claims that on October 11, when its engineer Yannello conducted the last examination on the plaintiff's premises, the tanks were so incomplete and unsatisfactory that the defendant was rightfully entitled to conclude that the plaintiff would never make a conforming tender. From this scenario, the defendant argues that it was justified in cancelling the contract of sale. It denies that the seller's conduct was sufficient to warrant a finding of tender, or its own conduct sufficient to warrant a finding of acceptance. The difficulty with this argument is that it is inconsistent with the underlying facts found by the trial court. Although the testimony was in dispute, there was evidence of record to support the trial court's findings to the contrary. The defendant cannot sustain its burden of establishing that a trial court's findings of fact are clearly erroneous; Practice Book §3060D; Pandolphe's Auto Parts, Inc. v. Manchester, 181 Conn. 217, 221-22, 435 A.2d 24 (1980); by the mere recitation in its brief of conflicting testimony entirely unsupported by reference to pages of the transcript. Practice Book §3060F(b). There is simply no fit between the defendant's claims and the trial court's finding that, by October 11, 1976, performance was in substantial compliance with the terms of the contract. The trial court further found that on that day the defendant was notified that the goods would be ready for tender the following day and that the defendant responded to this notification by promising to send its truck to pick up the tanks in accordance with the contract.

On the trial court's finding of facts, it was warranted in concluding, on two independent grounds, that the defendant had
accepted the goods it had ordered from the plaintiff. Under the
provisions of the Uniform Commercial Code, General Statutes §32a-2-
606(1) "[a]cceptance of goods occurs when the buyer (a) after a
reasonable opportunity to inspect the goods signifies to the seller . . .
that he will take . . . them in spite of their nonconformity; or (b) fails
to make an effective rejection."

In concluding that the defendant had "signified" to the plaintiff its
willingness to "take" the tanks despite possible remaining minor defects, the trial court necessarily found that the defendant had had a
reasonable opportunity to inspect the goods. The defendant does not
maintain that its engineer, or the other inspectors on previous visits,
had inadequate access to the tanks, or inadequate experience to
conduct a reasonable examination. It recognizes that inspection of
goods when the buyer undertakes to pick up the goods is ordinarily at
the seller's place of tender. See General Statutes §§42a-2-503, 42a-2-
507, 42a-2-513; see also White & Summers, Uniform Commercial Code
§3-5 (2d ed. 1980). The defendant argues, however, that its contract, in
providing for inspection for radiation leaks after installation of the
tanks at its premises, necessarily postponed its inspection rights to that
time. The trial court considered this argument and rejected it, and so
do we. It was reasonable, in the context of this contract for the special
manufacture of goods with which neither party had had prior experience, to limit this clause to adjustments to take place after tender
and acceptance. After acceptance, a buyer may still, in appropriate
cases, revoke its acceptance, General Statutes §42a-2-608, or recover
damages for breach of warranty, General Statutes §42a-2-714. The trial
court reasonably concluded that a post-installation test was intended to
safeguard these rights of the defendant as well as to afford the plaintiff
a final opportunity to make needed adjustments. The court was
therefore justified in concluding that there had been an acceptance
within §42a-2-606(1)(a). A buyer may be found to have accepted goods
despite their known nonconformity; [citations omitted].

The trial court's alternate ground for concluding that the tanks
had been accepted was the defendant's failure to make an effective
rejection. Pursuant to General Statutes §42a-2-606(1)(b), an acceptance occurs when, after a reasonable opportunity to inspect, a buyer
has failed to make "an effective rejection as provided by subsection (1)
of section 42a-2-602." The latter subsection, in turn, makes a rejection
"ineffective unless the buyer reasonably notifies the seller." General
Statutes §42a-2-605(1)(a) goes on to provide that a buyer is precluded

from relying, as a basis for rejection, upon unparticularized defects in his notice of rejection, if the defects were such that, with reasonable notice, the seller could have cured by making a substituted, conforming tender. The defendant does not question the trial court's determination that its telegram of cancellation failed to comply with the requirement of particularization contained in §2-605(1). Instead, the defendant argues that the plaintiff was not entitled to an opportunity to cure, under General Statutes §2-508, because the plaintiff had never made a tender of the tanks. That argument founders, however, on the trial court's finding that the seller was ready to make a tender on the day following the last inspection by the defendant's engineer and would have done so but for its receipt of the defendant's telegram of cancellation. The trial court furthermore found that the defendant's unparticularized telegram of cancellation wrongfully interfered with the plaintiff's contractual right to cure any remaining post-installation defects. In these circumstances, the telegram of cancellation constituted both a wrongful and an ineffective rejection on the part of the defendant. See Uchitel v. F.R. Tripler & Co., 107 Misc. 2d 310, 434 N.Y.S.2d 77, 81-82 (Supreme Court 1980); White & Summers, supra, §8-3, p.315.

Once the conclusion is reached that the defendant accepted the tanks, its further rights of cancellation under the contract are limited by the governing provisions of the Uniform Commercial Code. "The buyer's acceptance of goods, despite their alleged nonconformity, is a watershed. After acceptance, the buyer must pay for the goods at the contract rate; General Statutes §2-607(1); and bears the burden of establishing their nonconformity. General Statutes §2-607(4)." Stelco Industries, Inc. v. Cohen, 182 Conn. 561, 563-64, 438 A.2d 759 (1980). After acceptance, the buyer may only avoid liability for the contract price by invoking the provision which permits revocation of acceptance. That provision, General Statutes §2-608(1), requires proof that the "nonconformity [of the goods] substantially impairs [their] value to him." See Superior Wire & Paper Products, Ltd. v. Talcott Tool & Machine, Inc., 184 Conn. 10 (42 C.L.J. 44, pp.4, 6), 441 A.2d 43 (1981); Conte v. Dwan Lincoln-Mercury, Inc., 172 Conn. 112, 120-21, 374 A.2d 144 (1976). On this question, which is an issue of fact; Superior Wire & Paper Products, Ltd. v. Talcott Tool & Machine, Inc., supra, 6-7; Conte v. Dwan Lincoln-Mercury, Inc., supra, 121; the trial court again found against the defendant. Since the defendant has provided no basis for any argument that the trial court was clearly erroneous in finding that the defendant had not met its burden of proof to show that the goods were substantially nonconforming, we can find no error in the conclusion that the defendant's cancellation constituted an unauthorized and hence wrongful revocation of acceptance.

Finally, the defendant in its brief, although not in its statement of the issues presented, challenges the trial court's conclusion about the remedial consequences of its earlier determinations. Although the trial court might have found the plaintiff entitled to recover the contract price because of the defendant's acceptance of the goods; General Statutes §§2-703(e) and 2-709(1)(a); the court chose instead to rely on General Statutes §2-709(1)(b), which permits a price action for contract goods that cannot, after reasonable effort, be resold at a reasonable price. Since the contract goods in this case were concededly specially manufactured for the defendant, the defendant cannot and does not contest the trial court's finding that any effort to resell them on the open market would have been unavailing. In the light of this finding, the defendant can only reiterate its argument, which we have already rejected, that the primary default was that of the plaintiff rather than that of the defendant. The trial court's conclusion to the contrary supports both its award to the plaintiff and its denial of the defendant's counterclaim.

There is no error.

V.   REVOCATION OF ACCEPTANCE

Having made a technical acceptance, a buyer may still bring a breach of warranty action provided that a proper §2-607(3)(a) notice has been given. If the buyer wins, damages based on §§2-714 and 2-715 will be awarded, and the buyer will still have the goods. If the buyer does not want the goods, but wants the return of the price, the proper UCC method is called *revocation of acceptance*. Read §2-608. At common law this action was called *rescission*. However, revocation of acceptance differs from common law rescission because the buyer not only recovers the price, but may recover consequential damages as well. See Official Comment 1 to §2-608; cf. §§2-711(1), 2-715 (also note Official Comment 1 to §2-715).

In both rejection and revocation of acceptance, the buyer in essence disclaims the goods. The standards under which a buyer can revoke acceptance are more difficult to meet than are the standards for rejection. In rejection, a buyer can in theory reject if the goods "fail in any respect"; however, to revoke an acceptance, the buyer must show that the defect "substantially impairs the value" of the goods. See Annot., 98 A.L.R.3d 1183.

Rester v. Morrow

Mississippi Supreme Court, 1986
491 So. 2d 204, 1 U.C.C. Rep. Serv. 2d 751

ROBERTSON, J.

I

This case presents twin questions regarding the rights of the purchaser and duties of the seller of an automobile which turned out to be a lemon. First, what must the purchaser show before he may revoke his acceptance of the automobile and recover the purchase price? Second, by reference to the standard to be given in answer to the first question, what quantum of proof must the purchaser offer before he has created a jury question on his right to revoke his acceptance?

Norman L. Rester (Rester) appeals from a directed verdict judgment in favor of the defendants Tommy Morrow A.M.C., Inc. (Morrow), Martin Motor Sales (Martin), Mississippi corporations, and American Motor Sales Corp. (AMC), a foreign corporation, in the Circuit Court of Forrest County. Rester had sued these defendants alleging his right under the Mississippi Uniform Commerical Code (UCC) to revoke his acceptance of a demonstrator Renault automobile, and recover the purchase price.

We are of the view that the trial judge erred in holding that Rester failed to make out a jury issue on the question of whether he was entitled to revoke his acceptance and, for the reasons explained below, we reverse and remand.

II

On April 13, 1981, Rester purchased a demonstrator 1981 model Renault series 18i with 2,915 miles from Morrow in Hattiesburg, paying $8,800 cash. He then financed the car through a local bank. The car carried AMC manufacturer's limited warranty against defects for the first occurring of 12,000 miles or 12 months.

While driving the car preparatory to purchase, a piece of chrome trim about one inch square fell off the windshield in heavy traffic. Rester did not stop to pick it up, and Morrow promised to replace it.

Just after his purchase, Rester drove the car to Florida on vacation, and was gone ten or eleven days. He reported to Morrow the following defects he had found in the car:

(1)   When the hazard light (flasher signals) were turned on, the radio also came on.

(2)   There was a gasoline odor in the car, noticeable mainly while driving without the air conditioner on. The odor could be detected in the trunk.

(3)   When operating the air conditioner leaked heavily on the right side of the car.

(4)   The car was equipped with a gauge which indicated the oil level, which Rester called the oil indicator gauge (not to be confused with an oil pressure gauge). This oil indicator gauge was not working.

About two weeks later the car was taken to Morrow's shop for repair. The hazard flasher/radio problem was fixed. The air conditioner started leaking again when Rester got home. Rester's main complaint at that time was Morrow did not replace the piece of chrome or fix the oil indicator gauge.

He telephoned Morrow that the air conditioner had started leaking again, and Morrow told him to bring the car in. After being in the shop the second time, Rester noticed the low speed fan motor of the air conditioner was not working. Morrow told him this was a problem with these cars, and the dealers had been directed by the manufacturer to put a new wiring harness on air conditioners having these problems, but he would have to order the part. When the parts came in and Rester took the car to the shop, he told the mechanic the oil indicator gauge was not working, either, and the mechanic promised to order another gauge.

Rester then changed jobs, and had to drive back and forth from his home in Carriere to New Orleans.

He noticed the air conditioner leaking again. He took the car to Morrow's on a Monday, Morrow told Rester that the mechanic had quit. Rester told Morrow he wanted another oil gauge, and Morrow told him if he could get another mechanic he would do so; otherwise, Rester would have to take the car to another local dealer. Rester did get his car on the following Friday afternoon, and the air conditioner had been fixed. He drove the car from Hattiesburg to his home, and approximately a week later he drove to Baton Rouge to a fire school he was attending. Rester said the air conditioner went out of control while he was attending school in Baton Rouge; when the air conditioner was turned off it still ran. If the heater was turned on, the air conditioner ran instead. Rester said he could still smell gas in the car if the car was running, the windows were down, and the air conditioner was off. He said the air conditioner and gas fumes were a real annoyance, aside from the delay factor.

Rester left Baton Rouge for New Orleans. While in New Orleans late one night, after he had filled the gas tank, Rester drove for some distance with the car running smoothly, and then the lights began to get dimmer and dimmer, the battery progressively weaker. Finally, the car went dead, and Rester had to tow it to a friend's house. Rester telephoned Morrow and told him he wanted his money refunded on the car's purchase. Morrow replied he had sold his agency to Martin.

Morrow told Rester to take the car to a New Orleans dealer, who Rester called, and the car was picked up on a Thursday. On the next day he got his car, and was informed by the shop personnel he had left his wipers on intermediate and run the battery down. They had charged the battery. Rester told them more than simply a dead battery was causing the problems, but was again told there was no electrical problem. Rester paid the agency $49 for towing, checking the electrical system, and charging the battery. He returned home in the car, and a week later drove it back to New Orleans. For the next month he had no problems with the car.

One night after he returned to New Orleans, Rester went to a night club in Metairie, Louisiana. As he was leaving around midnight, the car had no power. There were no lights, it would not crank. Rester telephoned Morrow around 12:30 A.M., who gave him the name of Ron Foshee, the factory representative of AMC, and who lived in Georgia.

Morrow also called Rester later and told him to take the car to a New Orleans dealer. Rester called the same New Orleans dealer who had the car for repair the first time, and was told to get a Metairie dealer, which he did. When he got his car from the Metairie dealer, he was charged $119.00. Part of the charge was for a new battery.

Rester telephoned Foshee and told him what was wrong with the car, that the air conditioner was all messed up. Foshee told him he would order the parts and send them to Martin's. Rester told Foshee he did not want a Martin or Morrow mechanic working on the car, and was promised by Foshee that he would bring the parts to Hattiesburg, and also his own mechanic from Stone Mountain, Georgia, to fix the car.

In September, while he was waiting on his car to be repaired, it stalled twice. Rester also smelled gas fumes. When he drove the car home, he could hear the "battery frying." When he opened the hood, the car was burning the battery up, and Rester thought the alternator was charging too much.

When he later met with Foshee at Martin's in Hattiesburg, Rester reported to Foshee the following problems with the car:

1.   The air conditioner was worse than ever.
2.   The piece of chrome was still missing.
3.   The carpet was bad from water leaking on it.
4.   A problem had developed in the rachet adjusting in the passenger seat.
5.   Gas fumes could still be detected.
6.   The fuse panel had fallen from under the dash.
7.   The oil indicator gauge was not working.
8.   The stalling problem.
9.   The battery smelled like it was burning up.

At one time Morrow had drilled a hole in the gasoline cap, but this still did not stop the odor. They told him to cut some apples and put them in the trunk, but this still did not stop the odor.

As for the battery sizzling problem, Foshee informed Rester when he examined the car that the dealer who installed the new battery put in too small a battery. Foshee also told Rester that part of his problem was the close proximity of the battery to the catalytic converter, which would be repaired by simply putting a shield between them, which they would install.

Rester said he was promised the car would be ready for delivery the next afternoon. He also said, "I loved the car as far as performance, the ride was excellent in the car, the handling was excellent, it was just this nick-pick stuff, and the car was not fitting up to the demands of transportation." He said while you could expect a car to quit every now and then, his had stalled twice in a month.

Two days later, Rester inquired by telephone about his car, and was told by the Martin service manager that they had discovered something wrong with the alternator, and had ordered parts from California, which would take about seven days delivery.

Rester told the service manager he needed a car for transportation 300 miles away or he would lose his job. He then called Foshee and told him if they did not fix the car he was going to see a lawyer.

On the following Friday Rester called Martin's who told him they had the parts but could not put them in because they had no mechanic. This was fourteen days after he had delivered the car. Rester called Foshee again, who was apologetic and said he would call back. Foshee did not call back, however.

Rester bought a 1980 model Oldsmobile, paying $4,900 for it. It was needed in order to have transportation to work.

Approximately 21-22 days after his delivery of the car to Martin's, they telephoned Rester's home and left a message the car was ready.

When Rester returned home from his job and learned the car was ready, he drove to Hattiesburg for it. When he got to Martin's and looked at the car, he noticed the fuse panel was still out from under the dash, the carpet was still soiled, and the chrome was still missing. He had at this time also received a recall notice from AMC, about which he testified.

> With the fuel odor problem. Not actually the fuel odor problem, but it has a recall notice to the fact stating that you might be driving the car and it would have a problem as though it would run out of gas and it was something about the gasoline was eating up the glue or whatever the line was put together in the fuel line and causing it to stop up or contaminance [contaminants] to get in the gas and causing it to die and it had done this to me on two occasions already and I was told by Tommy Morrow and them that I had just let it run out of gas one of the occasions and on the other occasion I didn't even bring it up.

Rester talked to the service manager about the recall notice, who told Rester he would check it out. Rester then told the service manager he would not need the car that day. He also told the service manager the fuse panel was still hanging, and the chrome was still off, according to Rester, "just a couple of little nick-nack details." Rester then told the service manager to fix these defects and attend to the recall defect, and he would come back and get the car later.

The service manager then told Rester that Foshee had told them not to fix anything else, even the oil indicator gauge.

Rester then testified he got irate, and asked if Foshee had worked on the car with his mechanic. The service manager replied Foshee had not brought anybody. Then Rester got angrier because Foshee not only had not brought a mechanic, but had left it with the same mechanic who never fixed the car in the first place, and without determining whether the repairs had been made. Rester testified as follows:

> I said, "Well, if this other yo-yo worked on it and couldn't fix it the first time, there's no way in the world I'll accept the car. He's worked on it this time and he couldn't fix the air conditioner, what's to guarantee him to fix the electrical condition or anything." So I refused the car. . . .

inspection

Rester made only a visual inspection before rejecting the car, from which he determined the fuse panel had not been replaced, the carpet was still soiled and the chrome was still missing. He never attempted to ascertain if, in fact, the other repairs had been made.

It was some time in September when Rester took the car for the last time to the dealer's in Hattiesburg, some five months after his purchase. He had driven the car some 11,000 miles, and had taken it in for repairs a total of five or six times.

Rester employed an attorney, who wrote Morrow and Martin on November 23, 1981, that the car had proved defective, that the return of the car was intended to be a "recision" of the sales contract, and demanded a return of the purchase price, interest, plus $4,000 in damages.

After Rester had employed counsel, he received a January 26, 1982, notice from AMC which stated the following defect:

recall notice

> American Motors Sales Corporation had determined that a defect which relates to motor vehicle safety exists in some 1981 Renault 18i vehicles. Some of these vehicles may have been assembled with a fuel line that could develop a leak near the engine, resulting in a fuel odor or an underhood engine compartment fire. Should you notice a fuel odor, the vehicle should be stopped and not driven until repaired.

On March 18, 1982, Rester brought suit in the Circuit Court of Forrest County against Morrow, Martin and AMC. His testimony was as above set forth. Also testifying was an employee of the local bank. When Rester rested, the defendants moved for a directed verdict. See Rule 50(a), Miss. R. Civ. P.

The trial judge sustained the motion, primarily because of his view that the only defects Rester noted were not substantial impairments of the value of the car, and that Rester had offered no proof as to the others not being repaired, but had abandoned the car at the dealer's. The trial judge stated that clearly Rester would be entitled to damages of some kind for failure to make the repairs, but was obligated to show the defects remained.

From an adverse final judgment, Rester has appealed to this court. We reverse and remand.

III

Norman L. Rester purchased a 1981 Renault on April 13, 1981, and encountered repeated difficulties through and including September 15, 1981, at which time he abandoned the vehicle back to its seller.

The ultimate issue is whether the automobile failed to conform to the seller's contractual and legal obligations incident to the sale and whether such nonconformity substantially impaired the value of the automobile to Rester. Miss. Code Ann. §75-2-608(1) (1972). The resolution of such a question of ultimate fact may be taken from the jury only in conformity with our familiar rule emanating from Paymaster Oil Mill Co. v. Mitchell, 319 So. 2d 652, 657 (Miss. 1975) and progeny. Because the evidence on the substantial impairment issue is quite disputed, the trial judge committed error when he sustained the seller's motion for directed verdict.

Without question, Rester had accepted the automobile, not necessarily on April 13, 1981, but when he failed to make an effective rejection after having had a reasonable opportunity to inspect it. Miss. Code Ann. §75-2-606(1)(b) (1972). Rester's acceptance was reasonably induced by the difficulty of discovery of defects before acceptance and by the seller's assurances. Miss. Code Ann. §75-2-608(1)(b) (1972). Cf. J.L. Teel Company, Inc. v. Houston United Sales, Inc., — So. 2d —, — (Miss. No. 54,448, dec. May 14, 1986) (not yet reported).

Rester then attempted to revoke his acceptance. This revocation occurred when he returned the automobile to the seller on September 15, 1981. The ultimate question, as indicated above, becomes whether on the facts of this case he was entitled to revoke. The outcome determinative question on this appeal is, in the present state of the record, to what decision-making authority—the trial judge or the jury—has our law committed the making of the factual determinations whether the Renault "non-conformed" and whether that non-conformity substantially impaired its value to Rester.

IV

There are two fundamental errors in the trial judge's approach to this case, the first having to do with the UCC conception of substantial impairment and the second, as indicated, having to do with when that issue may be taken from the jury. First, the trial judge seems to have considered that the only bases for rejection are the specific complaints of Rester the day he returned the automobile to his seller. On that occasion Rester pointed out a soiled carpet, an unrepaired fuse panel and an unreplaced piece of chrome. Unquestionably, these are minor defects.

Rester's entitlement to revocation, however, turns upon whether, under the totality of the circumstances—temporally and structurally—the automobile failed to be what the seller was by private and public law obligated to provide Rester and whether that aggregate noncon-formity substantially impaired the value of the automobile to Rester. In Accord Zoss v. Royal Chevrolet, Inc., 11 U.C.C.R.S. 527 (Ind. Super. Ct. 1972). Put another way—and having in mind the testimony in this case, the seller has a right to attempt cure. Cf. Miss. Code Ann. §75-2-508 (1972). But our law does not allow a seller to postpone revocation in perpetuity by fixing everything that goes wrong with the automobile. There comes a time when enough is enough—when an automobile purchaser, after having to take his car into the shop for repairs an inor-dinate number of times and experiencing all of the attendant incon-venience, is entitled to say, "That's all," and revoke, notwithstanding the seller's repeated good faith efforts to fix the car. Welch v. Fitzgerald-Hicks Dodge, Inc., 430 A.2d 144 (N.H. 1981); Durfee v. Rod Baxter Imports, Inc., 262 N.W.2d 349, 354 (Minn. 1977).

The Florida case of Orange Motors of Coral Gables v. Dade Coun-ty Dairies, 258 So. 2d 319 (Fla. App. 1972) made the point this way:

> The buyer of an automobile is not bound to permit the seller to tinker with the article, indefinitely in the hope it may ultimately be made to comply with the warranty . . . [citations omitted]. At some point in time, if major problems continue to plague the automobile, it must become obvious to all people that a particular vehicle simply cannot be repaired or parts replaced so that the same is made free of defect.

258 So. 2d at 321.

Among the legion cases to like effect are Seekings v. Jimmy GMC of Tucson, Inc., 130 Ariz. 596, 638 P.2d 210, 218 (1981); Conte v. Dwan Lincoln-Mercury, Inc., 172 Conn. 112, 374 A.2d 144, 149 (1976); and Tiger Motor Company v. McMurtry, 284 Ala. 283, 224 So. 2d 638, 647 (1969). . . .

The trial judge—and the seller on this appeal—concentrate only upon the straw said to have broken the camel's back. In our view, the whole camel—including its performance over the five month period Rester's use of the Renault—is relevant to the question of whether Rester had the right to revoke. . . .

Our law tells a buyer such as Rester that he may revoke only if there is substantial impairment of the value of the car "to him." Miss. Code Ann. §75-2-608(1) (1972). J.L. Teel Company, Inc. v. Houston United Sales, Inc., — So. 2d —, — (Miss. No. 54,448, dec. May 14, 1986) (not yet reported); Volkswagen of America v. Novak, 418 So. 2d 801, 804 (Miss. 1982). Substantial impairment is determined by reference to the particular needs of the buyer, even though the seller may have no advance knowledge of those needs and even though those needs may change after acceptance of the automobile. White & Summers, Uniform Commercial Code, §8-3, p.308 (2d ed. 1980). UCC Official Comment 2; but see Douglas Whaley, Tender, Acceptance, Rejection and Revocation—The UCC's "Tarr Baby," 24 Drake L. Rev. 52, 76 (1974).

While the statute imports a subjective standard of nonconformity and impairment, we regard that it nevertheless contains an important objective component. The "to him" language in the statute requires that courts proceed by reference to the unique circumstances of the buyer. Once those circumstances have been determined, we proceed to an objective determination of whether the nonconformity would substantially impair the value of the automobile to a reasonable person in the circumstances of the buyer.

Rester's circumstances are set forth adequately above. They involve considerable regular travel. Those circumstances suggest an unequivocal need for a properly functioning automobile. When one pays for a car what Rester paid for the Renault, he is entitled to frills as well as essentials that are relatively troublefree. . . .

The judgment of the Circuit Court is reversed and this case is remanded for a new trial on all issues.

Reversed and remanded.

QUESTIONS

1. In this case the buyer returned the car to the seller at the time he gave a notice of revocation. Need he have done so? Read carefully §§2-711(3) and 1-201(37); cf. §2-706. See Mobile Home Sales Management, Inc. v. Brown, 562 P.2d 1378, 21 U.C.C. Rep. Serv. 1040 (Ariz. App. 1977) ("when the buyer has a security interest in the goods and the seller makes no request for their return, the buyer should not be penalized by making tender back a prerequisite to revocation of acceptance"). See also Deaton, Inc. v. Aeroglide Corp., 99 N.M. 253, 657 P.2d 109, 35 U.C.C. Rep. Serv. 130 (1982). What if the buyer did not have a security interest in the car? See §§2-608(3), 2-602.

2. Should the court when allowing revocation make an allowance for the use the buyer got from the car? Is the seller entitled to a setoff for the amount of benefits the purchaser received? See §1-103; compare Barco Auto Leasing Corp. v. House, 202 Conn. 106, 520 A.2d 162, 3 U.C.C. Rep. Serv. 2d 122 (1987), with Moore v. Howard Pontiac-American, Inc., 492 S.W.2d 227, 12 U.C.C. Rep. Serv. 676 (Tenn. App. 1973).

3. If the buyer keeps the car after revoking acceptance, may the buyer keep driving it without negating the effectiveness of the revocation of acceptance? See §§2-606(1)(c), 2-602(2)(a)(b). Compare Computerized Radiological Serv. v. Syntex Corp., 786 F.2d 72, 42 U.C.C. Rep. Serv. 1656 (2d Cir. 1986) (use of CAT scanner for 22 months after sending letter of revocation constituted acceptance), Wadsworth Plumbing & Heating Co., Inc. v. Tallycraft Corp., 277 Ore. 433, 560 P.2d 1080, 21 U.C.C. Rep. Serv. 502 (1977) ("such use would appear to be an 'act inconsistent with the seller's ownership'"), and Fecik v. Capindale, 54 Pa. D. & C.2d 701, 10 U.C.C. Rep. Serv. 1391 (1971) (post-revocation use destroys buyer's §2-608 suit), with Deere & Co. v. Johnson, 271 F.3d 613, 46 U.C.C. Rep. Serv. 2d 433 (5th Cir. 2001) (farmer's continued use of combine excused where replacement cost high); Stroh v. American Recreation & Mobile Home Corp. of Colo., 35 Colo. App. 196, 530 P.2d 989, 16 U.C.C. Rep. Serv. 726 (Colo. App. 1975) (continued use of mobile home after revocation was not acceptance, but seller could recover damages for buyer's post-revocation use), Fargo Mach. & Tool Co. v. Kearney & Trecker Corp., 428 F. Supp. 364 (E.D. Mich. 1977) ("in 'exceptional circumstances' subsequent use is permissible"), and Garfield v. Lehman Floor Covering Co., 60 Misc. 2d 72, 302 N.Y.S.2d 167, 6 U.C.C. Rep. Serv. 915 (D. Ct. 1969) (use of rejected carpet excused where unavoidable). In a leading case involving vehicles, the Kansas Supreme Court permitted post-revocation use (with a setoff to seller for the benefit buyer received thereby): Johnson v. General Motors Corp., 233 Kan. 1044, 668 P.2d 139, 36 U.C.C. Rep. Serv. 1089 (1983) ("Here buyers were placed in a position where if they stored the truck . . . they would not have had a vehicle for transportation. . . . With little or no low-cost public transportation available to the public, private transportation has changed from a luxury to a necessity."). The Massachusetts Supreme Judicial Court has agreed with this, stating that a jury should be instructed to consider a number of circumstances in deciding the reasonableness of the buyer's actions: the seller's instructions to the buyer after revocation of acceptance; the degree of economic and other hardship that the buyer would suffer if he or she discontinued using the defective goods; the reasonableness of the buyer's use after revocation as a method of mitigating damages; the degree of prejudice to the seller; and whether the seller acted in bad faith; Liarikos v. Mello, 418 Mass. 669, 639 N.E.2d 716, 27 U.C.C. Rep. Serv. 2d 136 (1994).

Given this, if your client tells you, the attorney, that it is necessary to continue to use the goods following rejection/revocation, what do you advise? Cf. §2-714.

NOTE: LEMON LAWS

A number of states have enacted so-called *Lemon Laws* that resolve some of the disputes we have been exploring when they arise in connection with a consumer's purchase of an automobile. For example, the issue addressed in the last question is specifically covered by many of these statutes. New York General Business Law §198a says that a refund from the defendant may be reduced by "a reasonable allowance for the consumer's use of the vehicle in excess of the first 12,000 miles of operation and a reasonable allowance for any damage not attributable to normal wear or improvements." For an exploration of what the various states have done, see Annot., 51 A.L.R.4th 872.

PROBLEM 56

The day after Alice Bluegown bought her new car, the right rear fender fell off. May she use §2-608 or must she give the car dealer a right to cure? Pretend she is sitting in your office expecting an immediate answer; glance at §2-608 and decide. The next day she took the car back to have the fender repaired; this made her late for work. The dealer fixed it, and the fender gave her no more trouble. However, the first time it rained all the paint washed off the car. May she revoke now? She took the car back to the dealer when the rain stopped and rode the bus to work (late again). The car dealer did a nice job repainting the car. Two weeks later the engine quit on her when she was in the middle lane of a superhighway at rush hour. The car had to be towed to the car dealer, and Alice missed an important sales meeting. The car dealer fixed the engine. Now Alice is back in your office. The car's trunk will not open. Must she permit them to fix it, or can she revoke? See Foss, The Seller's Right to Cure When the Buyer Revokes Acceptance: Erase the Line in the Sand, 16 S. Ill. U. L.J. 1 (1991). She has missed enough work to worry about hurting her career. She's also concerned that the car is going to keep breaking down right through and past the warranty period. What do you advise? Is §2-609 of use to her? If she decides to revoke acceptance and if the court agrees that this is allowed, would it also permit her to recover for the cost of a rental car used as substitute transportation while she was attempting to purchase a new car? See McGinnis v. Wentworth Chevrolet Co., 295 Ore. 494, 668 P.2d 365, 37 U.C.C. Rep. Serv. 130 (1983). If she goes out and buys a *new* car, can she make the first car dealer pay for it? See §2-712.

PROBLEM 57

Suppose in the last Problem the contract between the dealer and Bluegown explicitly limits the remedy for breach to repair or replacement of defective parts. The dealer argues that all defects have been promptly and successfully repaired and that the remedy of revocation of acceptance is therefore unavailable to Bluegown. See §2-719(2); Durfee v. Rod Baxter Imports, Inc., 262 N.W.2d 349, 22 U.C.C. Rep. Serv. 945 (Minn. 1977); see also Andover Air Ltd. Partnership v. Piper Aircraft Corp., 7 U.C.C. Rep. Serv. 2d 1494 (D. Mass. 1989).

PROBLEM 58

Arthur Author ordered an expensive computer (the ION #740) from ION Business Machines. ION sent him model #745, a newer and better version of the machine he had ordered, at the same price. When he saw the computer, he liked it and wrote them a letter of acceptance, enclosing a check in payment. However, when he began to use it, he was horrified to learn that the computer was turned on by a hidden switch under the front panel. Arthur Author's father had lost a finger when he reached under a machine to activate it. Arthur had witnessed the accident as a child. Arthur sent a notice of revocation of acceptance to ION, stating that the #740 had a visible switch and explaining that the hidden switch on the #745 brought back childhood memories that kept him from wanting the computer. Does §2-608 permit him to revoke for this reason? See Official Comment 2. Is §2-508(2) relevant? How would you advise ION to respond to Arthur Author's letter? See Annot., 98 A.L.R.3d 1183.

PROBLEM 59

After his car had broken down with the same defect six times, Zack Taylor decided to revoke acceptance and return the car to Fillmore Motors, the dealership that had sold him the vehicle but that had been unable to repair it. To Zack's dismay, he discovered that Fillmore Motors had gone bankrupt and was out of business. Zack is now in your office with this issue: may he revoke acceptance against the *manufacturer* of the car (which had covered its product with a limited warranty)? Compare Fode v. Capital RV Center, Inc., 575 N.W.2d 682, 36 U.C.C. Rep. Serv. 2d 696 (N.D. 1998), with Hardy v.

Winnebago Industries, 34 U.C.C. Rep. Serv. 2d 1007 (Md. Ct. Spec. App. 1998). Note that the Magnuson-Moss Warranty Act might help consumers in this situation. Section 110(d) of the Act allows a civil action against the warrantor that includes both legal and *equitable* relief.

Just as the United Nations CISG treaty does not use the value-loaded word *warranty*, it substitutes the word *avoidance* for concepts such as rescission, rejection, and revocation of acceptance, while keeping much of the substance. The concept of avoidance under the treaty is the subject of the next Problem.

PROBLEM 60

Jeans of the World, a retail clothing outlet in Helsinki, Finland, ordered 20 boxes of jeans from Grey Goods of Manhattan in New York, to be delivered September 1. Use the CISG to answer these questions:

(a) If the goods arrive on July 20, must Jeans of the World take them? See Article 52(1).

(b) If the goods arrive on the appointed date, but there are only 18 boxes, must Jeans of the World accept them? See Articles 35, 49, 51, and 25. Can the buyer get the other two boxes? See Article 46. If the buyer avoids the contract, can the seller reinstate it by delivering the missing two boxes? See Articles 48 and 49.

(c) When the 18 boxes arrived on September 1, Jeans of the World phoned Grey Goods and stated that it would give the seller two weeks in which to come up with the other two boxes. Can Jeans of the World now change its mind and avoid the contract before the two weeks are up? See Article 47.

(d) If a flood causes water damage to the boxes before Jeans of the World tries to avoid the contract, does this affect its ability to do so? See Article 82.

PROBLEM 61

Ambiance Hotel decided to acquire 10 horse-carriages to be specially designed to carry its guests around the tourist areas of the scenic city in which it is located. It had the plans for the carriages transmitted to Buggies, Inc., a carriage manufacturer, which assured

Ambiance that there would be no problem with the creation of the carriages. Ambiance financed this transaction by having Octopus National Bank purchase the carriages from Buggies, Inc., and then lease them to Ambiance for a 10-year period. Assume that this transaction qualifies as a finance lease; see §2A-103(1)(g).

(a) If the carriages are delivered to the hotel and Ambiance rejects them because they are the wrong color, must Ambiance pay the lease amounts to Octopus National Bank? (You may assume that the finance lease contained a "hell or high water" clause.) See §§2A-407(1), 2A-515.

(b) If the hotel accepts the carriages, but becomes upset when they constantly break down, can it revoke its acceptance and refuse to pay the lessor? See §§2A-407, 2A-516 and its Official Comment, 2A.

VI. RISK OF LOSS: BREACH

The Code's general rules on risk of loss are found in §2-509, but that section applies only where neither party has breached the sales contract. If a breach has occurred, §2-510 is the relevant section. Read it.

Jakowski v. Carole Chevrolet, Inc.

New Jersey Superior Court, 1981
180 N.J. Super. 122, 433 A.2d 841,
31 U.C.C. Rep. Serv. 1615

NEWMAN, J. Plaintiff seeks summary judgment on Count I alleging breach of a new car sales contract by the defendant, Carole Chevrolet.

The essential facts are not in dispute. On March 8, 1980 plaintiff, Jakowski, (hereinafter referred to as buyer), entered into a contract of sale with defendant, Carole Chevrolet, (hereinafter referred to as seller), calling for the purchase by plaintiff of one brand new 1980 Chevrolet Camaro. The parties also agreed that the car would be both undercoated and that its finish would have a polymer coating. While there is some disagreement as to exactly when the buyer ordered the coatings, it is undisputed that prior to delivery the seller agreed to deliver the car with the coatings applied. Likewise, it is undisputed that the car in question was delivered to the buyer without the required coatings on May 19, 1980.

The next day, May 20, 1980, the seller contacted the buyer and informed him that the car delivered to him lacked the coatings in question and seller instructed buyer to return the car to seller so that the coatings could be applied. On May 22, 1980, the buyer returned the auto to the seller for application of the coatings. Sometime during the evening of the 22nd or the morning of the 23rd the car was stolen from seller's premises and it was never recovered. Seller has refused to either provide a replacement auto to buyer or to refund the purchase price. Buyer remains accountable on the loan, provided through GMAC, for the purchase of the car.

The narrow question thus presented is upon whom, as between buyer and seller, this loss should fall. In UCC terminology, on May 22, 1980, which party bore the risk of the car's loss.

Seller argues that the risk of loss passed to the buyer upon his receipt of the auto. This is consistent with U.C.C. §2-509(3) pursuant to which the risk of loss passes to the buyer upon his receipt of the goods. Section 2-509(4), however, expressly provides that the general rules of §2-509 are subject to the more specific provisions of §2-510 which deals with the effect of breach upon risk of loss.

Buyer relies upon §2-510(1) which provides:

> Where a tender or delivery of goods so fails to conform to the contract as to give a right of rejection the risk of their loss remains on the seller until cure or acceptance.

Application of this section to the instant facts requires that three questions be answered. First, did the car "so fail to conform" as to give this buyer a right to reject it? If so, did the buyer "accept" the car despite the non-conformity? Finally, did the seller cure the defect prior to the theft of the auto?

The first question must be answered in the affirmative. The contract provided that the car would be delivered with undercoating and a polymer finish and it is undisputed that it was delivered without these coatings. The goods were thus clearly non-conforming and despite seller's assertion to the contrary, the degree of their non-conformity is irrelevant in assessing the buyer's concomitant right to reject them. Section 2-106 is clear in its intent to preserve the rule of strict compliance; that is, the "perfect tender" rule (2-601)

> Goods . . . are "conforming" or conform to the contract *when they are in accordance with* the obligations under the contract. [Section 2-106(2). (Emphasis supplied.) See also Comment 2 to §2-106.]

The language of §2-510(1), "so fails to conform," is misleading in this respect: no particular quantum of non-conformity is required where a single delivery is contemplated. The allusion is to §2-612 which substitutes a rule of substantial compliance where, *and only where,* an installment deal is contemplated. White & Summers, Uniform Commercial Code (2d ed. 1980), §5.5 at 187-188.

Secondly, did buyer "accept" the auto by taking possession of it? This question was presented in Zabriskie Chevrolet, Inc. v. Smith, 99 N.J. Super. 441 (Law Div. 1968). In *Zabriskie* it was held that the mere taking of possession by the purchaser is not equivalent to acceptance. Before he can be held to have accepted, a buyer must be afforded a "reasonable opportunity to inspect" the goods. *Zabriskie*, supra, at 452-453; §2-606.

Seller's actions in this matter preclude analysis in conventional "acceptance" terms. Buyer had no opportunity, indeed, no reason, to reject given seller's own communication to buyer shortly after delivery, to the effect that the goods did not conform and that the seller was exercising its right to cure said non-conformity. See §2-508 (seller's right to cure). This communication, in effect an acknowledgment of non-conformity, obviated the need for a formal rejection on buyer's part, if, indeed, §2-510(1) imposes such an obligation. Put another way, it precluded the buyer from rejecting the car. Consistent with this analysis, I find as a matter of law that there was no acceptance by buyer of this non-conforming auto.

As to the final question of whether the seller effected a cure, there is no evidence, in fact defendant does not even contend, that cure was ever effected.

Given the undisputed facts the operation of §2-510(1) is inescapable. The goods failed to conform, the buyer never accepted them and the defect was never cured. Accordingly, the risk of loss remained on the seller and judgment is granted for plaintiff.

A further note on the law is in order. It is possible to conjure up a host of hypotheticals leading to seemingly perverse results under §2-510. The section has been the subject of some scholarly criticism. See, e.g., White & Summers, supra, §5.5 at 187. Williston, "The Law of Sales in the Proposed Uniform Commercial Code," 63 Harv. L. Rev. 561, 583 (1950).

The fact is, however, that those courts considering it have had little difficulty in applying it as written. See, e.g., United Airlines, Inc. v. Conductron Corp., 69 Ill. App. 3d 847, 26 Ill. Dec. 344, 387 N.E.2d 1272 (Ill. App. 1979) (Flight trainer destroyed in fire after delivery to buyer); Southland Mobile Home v. Chyrchol, 255 Ark. 366, 500 S.W.2d 778 (Ark. Sup. 1973) (Mobile home destroyed in fire after delivery to buyer); Graybar Elec. Co. v. Shook, 283 N.C. 213, 195 S.E.2d 514 (N.C. Sup. 1973) (Non-conforming cable stolen while in buyer's possession); Wilkie v. Cummins Diesel Eng. Inc., 252 Md. 611, 250 A.2d 886 (Md. Ct. App. 1969) (Engine block frozen while in buyer's possession).

The rule is simple enough: under §2-510(1) where goods fail to conform to the contract of sale, the risk of loss remains on the seller until the buyer accepts the goods or until the seller cures the defect. In the aforecited cases, such was the result even though in all of them the goods were still in the *buyer's* possession at the time of their destruction.

For present purposes it is adequate to hold simply that where a seller obtains possession of the goods in an effort to cure defects in them so as to comply with his end of the bargain, he is under a contractual duty to redeliver them to the buyer. In failing to do so, he has breached the contract.

Pursuant to §2-711 buyer is entitled to a refund of so much of the purchase price as has been paid to seller. Included in the cost of the automobile are the finance charges incurred by the buyer who secured financing from GMAC pursuant to a retail installment sales contract entered into with the seller. There is no dispute about including these charges in the purchase cost and the buyer, as of March 30, 1981, indicated the total amount due on any judgment to be $9,398.75. However, since this case was first heard some additional time has passed and a current pay off figure should be obtained for inclusion in this judgment. Plaintiff is directed to submit an appropriate order.

PROBLEM 62

The Lamia Museum's director, Mandrake Griffin, ordered three new pieces for the museum: an Egyptian sphinx, an Old World gargoyle, and an Etruscan statue of a centaur. These objets d'art were purchased under separate contracts from Empusa Exports of London, England. All were to be shipped "F.A.S. S.S. Titanic" on or about April 9, on their way to the museum, which was located in New Jersey. The parties agreed that New Jersey law would apply. Prior to April 9, Empusa Exports received a call from Griffin cancelling the purchase of the centaur statue. Empusa protested the cancellation, but agreed to ship the other two pieces. Empusa's manager discovered that the sphinx was a phony, but kept her mouth shut and shipped it anyway. She also discovered that the gargoyle's condition was such that it could not survive the exposure to sea air, so she decided to send it by air in spite of the contract's F.A.S. Titanic term. This decision proved wise since the Titanic encountered an obstacle on its sea voyage and foundered, taking the sphinx with it. The gargoyle arrived in good condition, and Griffin wrote a letter to Empusa accepting the gargoyle and enclosing the museum's check. A week later Griffin learned that the gargoyle was not from the "Old World," but instead had been cast in Hoboken many years ago and had somehow found its way to Europe. He sent Empusa a letter demanding that the museum's money be returned and stating that he canceled the sale. Before Empusa could respond, two things happened: the museum burned to the ground, and the centaur statue was stolen from Empusa's warehouse (through no fault of Empusa, which was not negligent in guarding it). Both the museum and Empusa were fully insured. Answer these questions:

(a) By shipping the other two objects after the museum refused to take the centaur statue, did Empusa waive its right to sue for the repudiation? See §§2-209(1), 2-106(3), 2-106(4). Would §1-207 have helped Empusa? What should it have done to use this section?

(b) Which party took the risk of loss on
   (1) the centaur?
   (2) the sphinx?
   (3) the gargoyle?

(c) When Empusa shipped the gargoyle by air instead of by sea, could Lamia have treated this as an imperfect tender and rejected the gargoyle for that reason? See §§2-503(1), 2-503(2), 2-504, 2-614.

(d) The Lamia Museum's insurance policy with the Pegasus Insurance Company contains two clauses relevant to §2-510. One provided that on payment of a claim the insurance company was subrogated to any claim its insured had against any other person. The other stated that the policy should not be deemed to provide protection for any claim where the risk of loss rested with another person. What is the effect of these provisions? See Official Comment 3 to §2-510; Nordstrom §§135, 136; White & Summers §§5-6 and 5-7 (Practitioners edition only).

VII. IMPOSSIBILITY OF PERFORMANCE

The Code has four provisions designed to straighten out the legal tangles created by those unexpected events of life that make the performance of a contract impossible or (the UCC equivalent) *commercially impracticable*. By creating a new standard of commercial impracticability, the Code drafters intended to broaden the common law concept of *impossibility*. Many commentators believe that the courts have essentially ignored the drafters' intentions and treated commercial impracticability as synonymous with common law impossibility. See Annot., 93 A.L.R.3d 584.

Read §§2-613 to 2-616, and work through the Problems below.

PROBLEM 63

Virgil Escapement had always wanted a sundial for his garden, and he ordered one for $250 from Horology Timepieces, Inc. The latter had 12 sundials of the type Escapement ordered in its storage room when an earthquake shook the building. All 12 fell over, and all but three were smashed. The remaining three were slightly damaged. Escapement, on being informed of the problem, insisted on the right to look over the three remaining sundials and to select one for his purchase, possibly at a reduced price due to the damage. Horology comes to you. Is §2-613 or §2-615 relevant? Must it let Escapement pick out a sundial, and must it offer to let him purchase at a reduced price, or can it simply cancel without fear of legal liability? For the test for impossibility of performance in international sales, see CISG Article 79; cf. Articles 71 and 72.

PROBLEM 64

Suppose the following, using the basic facts of the last Problem. When Horology received Virgil's order, one of their salespersons immediately put a red tag on one of the sundials. It said, "Hold for Virgil Escapement." Then the earthquake occurred, and miraculously only Virgil's sundial was destroyed. The other 11 sundials, all exactly like Virgil's, were undamaged. When Virgil demanded his sundial, Horology pleaded §2-613. Will that section excuse them? See Valley Forge Flag Co. v. New York Dowel & Molding Import Co., 90 Misc. 2d 414, 395 N.Y.S.2d 138, 21 U.C.C. Rep. Serv. 1320 (Civ. Ct. 1977).

Arabian Score v. Lasma Arabian Ltd.

United States Court of Appeals, Eighth Circuit, 1987
814 F.2d 529, 3 U.C.C. Rep. Serv. 2d 590

WOLLMAN, J. Beating dead horses is the sport of appellate judges, a generally harmless pastime painful only to the readers of appellate opinions. Paying for the promotion of dead horses can be an expensive proposition, however, as the facts of this case make abundantly clear.

Arabian Score (Arabian), a Minnesota limited partnership, appeals from the district court's orders granting summary judgment in favor of Lasma Arabian Ltd. (Limited), a Florida limited partnership, and Lasma Corporation (Lasma), an Arizona corporation. We affirm.

On October 27, 1983, Arabian entered into an agreement to purchase from Limited an Arabian colt named Score. The agreement, which the parties agreed would be governed by and construed in accordance with the laws of Arizona, provided that Arabian would pay Limited $1 million "for the purchase of Score and the performance by Lasma of various services in the promotion of Score." The contract required Lasma to spend $250,000 for the performance of those services which consisted of advertising and promoting Score as a 2 Star Stallion under a license agreement with Lasma Star Stallion, Inc., a separate corporation that is not a party to this lawsuit.

Paragraph 4 of the agreement provided that for a period of five years after the date of his purchase, Score would be a 2 Star Stallion, as defined by the Star Stallion license agreement, with the result that Score's foals would be eligible for nomination to all Lasma-sponsored sales open to the get of Lasma stallions.[4] If Lasma Star Stallion, Inc., in its sole discretion, determined that Score was not eligible to participate in the Star Stallion Program, Lasma would, at Arabian's option, replace Score with an eligible stallion or refund to Arabian the unused portion of the money Lasma would otherwise be required to spend promoting Score pursuant to the terms of the paragraph 5 of the agreement.

Paragraph 5 of the agreement provided that for five consecutive calendar years commencing with 1984, Lasma would implement a complete annual program for the promotion of Score as a 2 Star Stallion. Lasma was to pay $70,000 for the 1984 program and $45,000 for each of the remaining four annual programs. The annual programs were to "include advertising in various trade publications, direct mail programs and the training, boarding, conditioning and showing of SCORE by Lasma."

Pursuant to paragraph 6 of the agreement, Lasma guaranteed that Score was not infertile.

4. As near as we can tell from the materials presented to the trial court, the Star Stallion program is to the ranking of Arabian horses what the Mobil Guide is to the ranking of restaurants. This may not be a totally accurate description, but it will do for the purposes of this case.

Paragraph 9 of the agreement provided: "Except as provided by paragraphs 4 and 6 above, the Partnership accepts SCORE *AS IS,* all implied warranties being excluded. Risk of loss passes upon closing. All incidental and consequential damages are excluded."

On February 8, 1984, Arabian obtained a mortality insurance policy from Transit Casualty Company insuring Score for his actual cash value. Alas—memento mori—Score went to his reward within the year, dying on September 11, 1984, having sired two foals during his brief life. Misfortune compounding, Transit Casualty Company (its name bespeaks its character) went broke. Lasma having expended only $52,891.14 for the promotion of Score, Arabian brought suit against Lasma and Limited, seeking recovery of the $197,108.86 not expended from the $250,000 that the purchase agreement allocated for the promotion of Score.

Count I of Arabian's complaint (later dismissed by stipulation) alleged that Lasma and Limited had breached the contract by not promoting Score. Count II sought recovery of the unspent portion of the $250,000 on the ground of impossibility of performance. Count III sought recovery under paragraph 4 of the purchase agreement.

The district court ruled that because Score's death was a foreseeable risk that was assumed by Arabian by the terms of the purchase agreement, neither the doctrine of impossibility nor of commercial frustration was applicable. Likewise, because the unrebutted evidence established that it is not unusual for Lasma Star Stallions, Inc. and Lasma to promote deceased horses, it was not an arbitrary, capricious, or irrational exercise of discretion by Lasma to determine that Score was still eligible postmortem to participate in the Star Stallion Program.

As provided by the agreement, we look to Arizona law to resolve the issues presented by Arabian's complaint.

In Garner v. Ellingson, 18 Ariz. App. 181, 501 P.2d 22 (1972), the Arizona Court of Appeals defined commercial frustration as circumstances beyond the control of the parties which render performance of the contract impossible and exonerate the party failing to perform. The court did not limit the doctrine to strict impossibility but included impracticability caused by extreme or unreasonable difficulty or expense. Id. at 23. The court did require, however, proof that the supervening frustrating event was not reasonably foreseeable. Id. at 24.

In Mohave County v. Mohave-Kingman Estates, 120 Ariz. 417, 586 P.2d 978, 983 (1978), the Arizona Supreme Court stated that "while Arizona recognizes the doctrine of commercial frustration . . . we do not see fit to interpret it as general absolution whenever performance under the contract becomes difficult or expensive. Proper application of this doctrine requires us to examine whether the allegedly frustrating event was reasonably foreseeable." In that case, the court refused to apply the doctrine where a zoning change had affected the economic feasibility of a contract to buy and develop land. The court reasoned that "the doctrine of commercial frustration does not apply to the instant case because the risk of change in the zoning ordinances was an event properly foreseeable by the defendants, and one which they would have contracted against." Id. at 984.

Arizona rejects the application of the commercial frustration doctrine when a party assumes the risk of the frustrating event. Kintner v. Wolfe, 102 Ariz. 164, 426 P.2d 798 (1967). In *Kintner,* the Arizona Supreme Court rejected a commercial frustration claim by a guarantor who had agreed to remain liable for the rent due on a liquor license lease "without respect to future changes in conditions." A change in law made renting liquor licenses illegal, but the court required the guarantor to pay, stating: "If the parties to a contract have agreed in express or implied terms that the risk of loss shall fall upon one or the other of the parties, full effect is given to such provision." Id. at 803.

We conclude that the trial court was correct in holding that the commercial frustration doctrine is inapplicable in this case, both because Score's death was foreseeable, as evidenced by Arabian's purchase of insurance, and because Arabian assumed the risk that Score might die prematurely. Moreover, the doctrine of impossibility/commercial frustration is not applicable because the party obligated to perform—Lasma—does not contend that it is unable or unwilling to complete its duty to promote Score.

Arabian further contends that by virtue of his death Score is no longer eligible to participate in the Star Stallion Program; consequently, paragraph 4 of the agreement obligates Lasma to return any unspent portion of the funds earmarked for promotional purposes.

As indicated earlier, Lasma Star Stallion, Inc. is not a party to this lawsuit, and there are no findings by the district court that Lasma or Limited controls Lasma Star Stallion, Inc. in the exercise of its discretion. Because Lasma Star Stallion, Inc. has not declared Score to be ineligible for the Star Stallion Program, the condition precedent to Lasma's obligation under paragraph 4 of the agreement has not been satisfied.

Even if it were within Lasma's discretion to declare Score ineligible to participate in the Star Stallion Program, we could not say that the decision that Score is still eligible for the program was an arbitrary or capricious abuse of discretion.

Arabian argues that the decision to promote a dead horse is per se arbitrary.[5] As indicated above, however, Lasma's unrebutted evidence shows that Lasma Star Stallion, Inc. and Lasma regularly promote deceased horses. This is done to enhance the owning entity's reputation and to increase the value of the stallion's progeny. Further, the language of paragraph 4 was not intended to cover the risk of death but of ineligibility for other reasons, such as infertility or substandard offspring.

It is with some reluctance that we affirm the district court's grant of summary judgment. That reluctance stems from the thought that spending $197,108.86 to promote a dead horse borders on the bizarre. The parties to this agreement were sophisticated and, we assume, well-heeled businesspersons, however, and that which we find to be somewhat unusual may be commonplace to those who inhabit the wealthy world of the horsey set.

The judgment dismissing Arabian's complaint is affirmed.

PROBLEM 65

In the mid-1960s, in an effort to boost sales of its nuclear reactors, Westinghouse Corporation agreed to sell 27 utility companies 80 million pounds of uranium over the next 20 years. The average sale price per pound was $10. When Westinghouse made the sale, it actually owned only 15 million pounds of uranium. By the mid-1970s, the price of uranium had risen to $40 a pound. In late 1975, Westinghouse announced that it would not honor its contract. The utilities sued. Westinghouse argued that the best evidence in the late 1960s and early 1970s indicated uranium prices would be stable over the long term. The Corporation claimed that the price rise was unforeseeable and that the contracts were excused under §2-615 as "commercially impracticable." In particular, Westinghouse blamed the 1973 oil embargo and worldwide price fixing for the "unpredictable" price rises. See Official Comments 4 and 5 to §2-615. How should the dispute be resolved? See Publicker Indus. v. Union Carbide Corp., 17 U.C.C. Rep. Serv. 989 (E.D. Pa. 1975); Eagan, The Westinghouse Uranium Contracts: Commercial Impracticability and Related Matters,

---

5. At oral argument, counsel for Arabian asked, rhetorically we assume, "How are you going to show a dead horse?" Considerations of judicial decorum and a due regard for the financial loss suffered by Arabian dissuaded us from suggesting the construction of a mausoleum—an equestrian Lenin's Tomb, if you will.

18 Am. Bus. L.J. 281 (1980). If you could advise Westinghouse on how to avoid this problem in the future, what would you suggest? See §2-305.

Louisiana Power & Light Co. v. Allegheny Ludlum Industries, Inc.

United States District Court, Eastern
District of Louisiana, 1981
517 F. Supp. 1319, 32 U.C.C. Rep. Serv. 847

GORDON, J. This breach of contract case is before the court on plaintiff's motion for summary judgment. The material facts which are not in dispute are as follows:

Plaintiff, Louisiana Power & Light Company (hereinafter referred to as "LP & L"), entered into a contract with defendants, Allegheny Ludlum Industries, Inc. and Allegheny Ludlum Steel Corporation (hereinafter referred to collectively as "Allegheny,") in which Allegheny agreed to supply condenser tubing to LP & L for use at LP & L's Waterford 3 nuclear power plant. The contract was awarded to Allegheny Ludlum Steel Corporation, then a division of Allegheny Ludlum Industries, Inc., after the solicitation of bids by LP & L's agent, Ebasco Services, Incorporated. The contract, dated February 8, 1974, was accepted by Allegheny in mid-March of 1974.

Pursuant to the terms of the contract Allegheny undertook to furnish, fabricate and deliver to LP & L stainless steel condenser tubing in accordance with the specifications of LP & L's agent, Ebasco. Equal shipments of the tubing were to be made on June 1, 1976; June 15, 1976, and July 1, 1976, for a total price of $1,127,387.82. The contract also provided that if LP & L delayed shipment beyond August 31, 1976, but not later than January 31, 1977, the contract price would be increased by three percent (3%). A further adjustment at the rate of ten percent (10%) would take place if LP & L delayed shipment beyond January 31, 1977, but not later than January 31, 1978. No other escalation clauses were included in the contract.

On May 19, 1975, Allegheny sent a letter to LP & L seeking "additional compensation" for performance under the contract. Allegheny informed LP & L that subsequent to the formulation of the contract its "costs [had] risen at such a high rate that escalators built into our contracts have in no way adequately compensated for them. For example, since March of 1974 the price of electrolytic nickel has increased 24%, low carbon ferrochrome 185% and labor 21%." Allegheny sought the opportunity to meet with representatives of LP & L in order to discuss

Allegheny's price increases and possible solutions to Allegheny's problem. Allegheny suggested a renegotiation of the contract price, but LP & L chose not to meet with Allegheny to discuss the matter.

In October of 1975, LP & L, through Ebasco, advised Allegheny that it considered Allegheny's price increases to be business risks which must be absorbed by Allegheny. On November 4, 1975, Allegheny informed LP & L, by letter from C. R. Hastings, General Manager of Allegheny's Wallingford Tubular Products Division, that a "[c]urrent review of this matter suggests that Allegheny Ludlum might be well advised not to perform under the contract." On November 19, 1975, Ebasco wrote to Allegheny's Wallingford Tubular Products Division, and demanded written assurances within thirty days, pursuant to §2-609 of the New York Commercial Code,[6] that Allegheny would fully and properly perform under the contract.

As of January 19, 1976, LP & L had not received any such written assurance of performance from Allegheny and on January 30, 1976, LP & L notified Allegheny by letter that it considered the contract repudiated by Allegheny. Thereafter, on February 17, 1976, C. R. Hastings at Allegheny wrote to LP & L informing it that Allegheny was willing to "make delivery under the subject purchase order at $1.80 per lb. . . . [Allegheny's] full cost of producing the material. . . ."

LP & L rejected Allegheny's offer to supply the tubing at Allegheny's cost and through its agent, Ebasco, LP & L solicited bids from other vendors for supply of the requisite condenser tubing. LP & L steadfastly rejected the offer of Allegheny to supply the tubing at Allegheny's cost, a price higher than that specified in the LP & L/Allegheny contract. On June 16, 1976, LP & L, through Ebasco, entered into a contract with Trent Tube Division of Crucible, Inc. for the purchase of condenser tubing at a price of $1,729,278.

Allegheny intended that the condenser tubing which was the subject of its contract with LP & L would be supplied by its Wallingford Tubular Products Division at Wallingford, Connecticut. C. R. Hastings, General Manager of the Wallingford Tubular Division, stated in his deposition that performance under the terms of the LP & L/Allegheny contract would have caused Allegheny to sustain a projected loss of $428,500 on the contract. Hastings indicated that such a loss would have reduced the planned profit for 1976 at the Wallingford plant from $1,018,000 to $589,500.

---

6. The contract between LP & L and Allegheny stated that the contract was to be governed by the laws of the State of New York, hence the invocation of §2-609 of the New York Commercial Code.

Plaintiff seeks by way of its lawsuit to recover from Allegheny the costs of its "cover," the monetary difference between the LP & L/Allegheny contract and the LP & L/Trent Tube contract, plus the expenses which it incurred in the re-solicitation of bids for the tubing. Allegheny has defended this action on four principal bases: commercial impracticability, mutual mistake, unconscionability and alleged bad faith conduct by LP & L. Plaintiff's claim and Allegheny's defenses will be considered in accord with the appropriate standards for summary judgment motions.

LP & L claims that Allegheny breached its contract to supply condenser tubing to LP & L. The first evidence which LP & L received that indicated that Allegheny would not perform under the contract as written was Allegheny's letter of May 19, 1975 to LP & L in which Allegheny sought "additional compensation" for supplying the condenser tubing. In response to that submission, LP & L sent a letter to Allegheny, invoking the provisions of §2-609 of the New York Uniform Commercial Code and requesting assurance from Allegheny that it would perform under the contract.

The pertinent provisions of §2-609 of the UCC, invoked by LP & L, provide:

§2-609.   *Right to Adequate Assurance of Performance*
(1) A contract for sale imposes an obligation on each party that the other's expectation of receiving due performance will not be impaired. When reasonable grounds for insecurity arise with respect to the performance of either party the other may in writing demand adequate assurance of due performance. . . .
(4) After receipt of a justified demand failure to provide within a reasonable time not exceeding thirty days such assurance of due performance as is adequate under the circumstances of the particular case is a repudiation of the contract.

The letter which LP & L received from Allegheny requesting "additional compensation" provided LP & L with a reasonable basis for insecurity as to Allegheny's performance under the contract. LP & L's letter of November 19, 1975, to Allegheny constituted an adequate demand on Allegheny for an assurance of performance. When LP & L failed to receive such an assurance by January 19, 1976, it was justified in characterizing the contract as repudiated. LP & L notified Allegheny of that fact on January 30, 1976. Subsequently, Allegheny indicated to plaintiff that it would perform under the contract for added compensation. Such a belated and qualified offer of performance cannot, however, be viewed as an assurance of performance under §2-609 of the U.C.C. Allegheny's failure to supply an assurance of performance within the allotted time period operated as a repudiation of the contract.

The UCC provides that:

> When either party repudiates the contract with respect to a performance not yet due the loss of which will substantially impair the value of the contract to the other, the aggrieved party may . . . (b) resort to any remedy for breach (Section 2-703 or Section 2-711). . . . [Uniform Commercial Code §2-610.]

One available remedy in the event of a breach is for the buyer to obtain a "cover" by purchasing goods in substitution for the goods due from the seller. A buyer and non-breaching party may then seek to recover from the seller and breaching party the price of such substituted goods plus incidental and consequential damages. See U.C.C. §2-711 and §2-712. It is just such a claim that plaintiff is making in the instant case. Based on the undisputed facts in this case, plaintiff is entitled to recover on that claim, unless Allegheny prevails on one of its defenses.

COMMERCIAL IMPRACTICABILITY

The first of Allegheny's defenses to be considered is that of commercial impracticability. The Uniform Commercial Code provides that performance under a contract may be excused if performance under the contract is commercially impracticable. Section 2-615 of the UCC, upon which Allegheny relies in its defense of commercial impracticability, states in pertinent part:

> §2-615.   *Excuse by Failure of Presupposed Conditions*
> Except so far as a seller may have assumed a greater obligation and subject to the preceding section on substituted performance:
>   (a) Delay in delivery or non-delivery in whole or in parts by a seller who complies with paragraphs (b) and (c) is not a breach of his duty under a contract for sale if performance as agreed has been made impracticable by the occurance of a contingency the non-occurance of which was a basic assumption on which the contract was made. . . .

In reliance upon that rule of law Allegheny argues that its performance under the contract with LP & L was rendered commercially impracticable because of a "severe shortage of critical raw materials and an increase in the cost of labor, an unexpected contingency which caused a dramatic increase in the price of those raw materials and the condenser tubing. The non-occurrence of such was a basic assumption on which the contract was founded and altered the essential nature of performance."

There are three conditions which must be met pursuant to §2-615 before performance under a contract can be excused because of commercial impracticability: "(1) a contingency must occur, (2) performance must thereby be made 'impracticable' and (3) the non-occurrence of the contingency must have been a basic assumption on which the contract was made." Neal-Cooper Grain Co. v. Texas Gulf Sulphur Co., 508 F.2d 283, 293 (7th Cir. 1974).

The rule has also been stated as "excus[ing] delay or nondelivery when the agreed upon performance has been rendered 'commercially impracticable' by an unforeseen supervening event not within the contemplation of the parties at the time the contract was entered into." Eastern Air Lines, Inc. v. McDonnell Douglas Corp., 532 F.2d 957, 988 (5th Cir. 1976). The rationale behind the doctrine of commercial impracticability is that when an event occurs which renders performance so "vitally different" from that which is anticipated, the contract cannot be reasonably considered to govern and performance under that contract is excused. Eastern Air Lines, Inc., supra, at 991.

The burden of proof on a claim of commercial impracticability rests with the party making the claim, in this case the defendants. Allegheny must meet its burden as to each of the requisite three elements in order to be successful in this defense. See Eastern Air Lines, Inc. v. Gulf Oil Corp., 415 F. Supp. 429, 438 (S.D. Fla. 1975), citing Ocean Air Tradeways, Inc. v. Arkay Realty Corp., 480 F.2d 1112, 1117 (9th Cir. 1973).

The undisputed facts in this case show that Allegheny has not and cannot meet its burden of proof as to this defense because it is unable to show that performance under the contract was commercially impracticable. Allegheny contacted LP & L in May of 1975 and informed LP & L that between March of 1974 and May of 1975, its costs for electrolytic nickel had risen by 24%, for low carbon ferrochrome had risen by 185%, and that its labor costs had risen by 21%. C. R. Hastings, General Manager of Allegheny's Wallingford Tubular Division stated in his deposition that had Allegheny performed under the contract as written, it would have sustained a loss of $428,500 on the contract and that the planned profitability of the Wallingford plant would have been reduced to an overall profit of $589,500 for the year of performance.

There are no facts which indicate that Allegheny's costs increased by more than the amount indicated to LP & L in the Allegheny letter of May 19, 1975. Moreover, there are no facts which indicate that Allegheny would have sustained a greater loss than that attested to by C. R. Hastings had it performed under the contract. There are also no facts which indicate that Allegheny would have been unprofitable during 1976 in either its overall corporate structure or in its Wallingford Tubular Division had it performed under the contract as written. Hastings testified in his deposition that a profit was anticipated for the Wallingford plant even had Allegheny been required to perform under the contract's terms. The material facts in this regard are clear, simple and undisputed. When viewed in the context of a claim of commercial impracticability, as that term has been interpreted in the case law, it must be said that performance under the contract was not commercially impracticable.

The mere fact that performance under the contract would have deprived Allegheny of its anticipated profit and resulted in a loss on the contract is not sufficient to show commercial impracticability. Rather, ". . . [t]he party seeking to excuse his performance must not only show that he can perform only at a loss but also that the loss will be especially severe and unreasonable." Gulf Oil Corp. v. Federal Power Commission, 563 F.2d 588, 600 (3d Cir. 1977), *cert. denied,* 434 U.S. 1062 (1978), *petition for cert. dismissed,* 435 U.S. 911 (1978).

Allegheny's loss by performance would not have been especially severe and unreasonable in this case. On the contrary, by Allegheny's own estimate its costs of performance under the contract increased only 38% over the original contract price of $1,127,387.82. While no seller desires to be called upon to perform under a contract when performance will result in a financial loss, such are the realities of commercial life. Whereas the law quite properly provides relief for situations in which performance can only be had at an excessive and unreasonable cost, see Transatlantic Financing Corp. v. United States, 363 F.2d 312 (D.C. Cir. 1960), Allegheny's cost of performance did not increase to the extent necessary to excuse its performance under the doctrine of commercial impracticability.[7]

Eastern Air Lines, Inc. v. Gulf Oil Corp., 415 F. Supp. 429, 438 (S.D. Fla. 1975) is instructive:

---

7. When consideration is given to Allegheny's anticipated profitability in 1976, it becomes more apparent that this was not a situation wherein performance under the contract would have been especially severe and unreasonable.

The modern U.C.C. §2-615 doctrine of commercial impracticability has its roots in the common law doctrine of frustration or impossibility and finds its most recognized illustrations in the so-called "Suez Cases," arising out of the various closings of the Suez Canal and the consequent increases in shipping costs around the Cape of Good Hope. Those cases offered little encouragement to those who would wield the sword of commercial impracticability. As a leading British case arising out of the 1957 Suez closure declared, the unforeseen cost increase that would excuse performance "must be more than merely onerous or expensive. It must be positively unjust to hold the parties bound." Ocean Tramp Tankers v. V/O Sovfracht (The Eugenia), 2 Q.B. 226, 239 (1964). To the same effect are Tsakiroglou and Co. Ltd. v. Noblee Thorl G.m.b.H., 2 Q.B. 348, (1960), *aff'd*, A.C. 93 (1962), and Caparanoyoti & Co., Ltd. v. E. T. Green, Ltd., 1 Q.B. 131, 148 (1959). These British precedents were followed by the District of Columbia Circuit, which gave specific consideration to UCC §2-615, Comment 4, in Transatlantic Financing Corp. v. United States, 124 U.S. App. D.C. 183, 363 F.2d 312, 319 (1966).

In *Transatlantic Financing Corp.,* supra, Judge J. Skelly Wright considered a claim of commercial impracticability and impossibility in connection with a suit seeking additional compensation for transport of a cargo of wheat around the Cape of Good Hope. The plaintiff was forced to abandon its customary route through the Suez Canal when Egypt obstructed the canal and closed it to traffic. Plaintiff argued that it was subjected to an additional expense of $43,972.00 above the contract price of $305,842.92 because of the longer journey necessitated by the closing of the canal. The court stated:

> . . . While it may be an overstatement to say that increased cost and difficulty of performance never constitute impracticability, to justify relief there must be more of a variation between expected cost and the cost of performing by an available alternative than is present in this case, where the promisor can legitimately be presumed to have accepted some degree of abnormal risk, and where impracticability is urged on the basis of added expense alone. [363 F.2d at 319.] The court affirmed the dismissal of the plaintiff's action because performance under the contract had not been rendered legally impossible.

In a similar case resulting from the closure of the Suez Canal, it was held that extra expense of 31.6% of the contract price, incurred in bringing the vessel around the Cape of Good Hope, was not sufficient to constitute commercial impracticability. American Trading and Production Corp. v. Shell International Marine, Ltd., 453 F.2d 939 (2d Cir. 1972). In discussing the degree of increase in costs that would constitute impossibility or commercial impracticability, it was stated that:

> Mere increase in cost alone is not a sufficient excuse for non-performance (Restatement of Contracts §467 (1932)). It must be an "extreme and unreasonable" expense (Restatement of Contracts §454 (1932)). While in the *Transatlantic* case supra, the increased cost amounted to an increase of about 14% over the contract price, the court did cite with approval the two leading English cases Ocean Tramp Tankers Corp. v. V/O Sovfracht (The Eugenia), [1964] 2 Q.B. 226, 233 (C.A. 1963) (which expressly overruled Societe Franco Tunisienne D'Armement v. Sidemar S.P.A. (The Messalia), [1961] 2 Q.B. 278 (1960), where the court had found frustration because the Cape route was highly circuitous and involved an increase in cost of approximately 50%), and Tsakiroglou & Co. Ltd. v. Noblee Thorl G.m.b.H., [1960] 2 Q.B. 318, 348, *aff'd*, [1962] A.C., 93 (1961) where the House of Lords found no frustration though the freight costs were exactly doubled due to the Canal closure. [453 F.2d at 942.]

In Iowa Electric Light and Power Company v. Atlas Corp., 467 F. Supp. 129 (N.D. Iowa, 1978) the court held that an increase in seller's costs by 52.2%, resulting in the seller's loss of approximately $2,673,125.00, failed to constitute commercial impracticability thereby precluding judicial adjustment or discharge of the contract for supply of uranium concentrate. In making such a determination, the court noted that cost increases of 50-58 percent had generally not been considered of sufficient magnitude to excuse performance under a contractual agreement.

As the jurisprudence indicates, Allegheny's performance under the contract was not commercially impracticable. Even if Allegheny were to show that its increased costs constituted a contingency, the non-occurrence of which was a basic assumption on which the contract was made, it still could not show that performance had been rendered commercially impracticable as a result. Allegheny bears the burden of proof as to each of the requisite three elements on its claim of commercial impracticability. Being unable to prove all three elements, its defense must fall.

Allegheny has suggested that claims of commercial impracticability are inherently insusceptible of resolution by summary judgment. That position is incorrect. While great care should be exercised in granting summary judgment motions in cases of this sort, the mere invocation of the term "commercial impracticability" is not a talisman behind which a defaulting seller may hide and be guaranteed a trial in the absence of a dispute as to the material facts in the matter. Were that the case, every seller or buyer caught in a burdensome position under a contract would find it hard to resist the natural temptation to compel renegotiation of unprofitable contracts by threatening to invoke a claim of commercial impracticability, knowing that it would be assured of a trial on the merits and knowing that even if it lost at trial, it would be required to do no more than fulfill its obligation under the contract. Such a rule of law would constitute a misuse of the protections afforded by the doctrine of commercial impracticability, particularly in cases of this sort where the facts are clear and undisputed and in which the seller in breach has been unable to cite a case wherein a claim of commercial impracticability has been upheld under similar factual circumstances.[8]

The clear undisputed facts require resolution of the commercial impracticability defense in plaintiff's favor. Allegheny is unable to meet its burden of proof. . . .

UNCONSCIONABILITY

Section 4 of the Supplementary Terms and Conditions of the LP & L/Allegheny contract provides that:

4.   Provision for Cancellation
At any time after the acceptance of this Order the Purchaser shall have the absolute right to cancel the entire Order upon the payment to the Seller for all disbursements and expenses which the Seller has incurred or become obligated for prior to date of notice of cancellation, less the reasonable resale value of equipment which shall have been obtained or ordered to become an integral part of the Equipment plus a sum as profit bearing the same ratio to the profit that the Seller would have received upon completing the Work as that portion of Work done bears to the entire amount of Work to be done by the Seller under this Order.

---

8. In Aluminum Company of America v. Essex Group, Inc., 499 F. Supp. 53 (W.D. Pa. 1980), a claim of commercial impracticability was upheld. The facts surrounding the claim of commercial impracticability in *Alcoa* are, however, distinguishable from those in the instant case. Plaintiff stood to lose $60,000,000.00 in *Alcoa* if its performance under the contract was compelled while the defendant stood to gain a concomitant "windfall profit." There are no comparable facts in the instant case. Allegheny stood to lose $428,500 on a $1,127,387.82 contract. It cannot be said that LP & L would be the beneficiary of a "windfall profit" like that in *Alcoa*.

Allegheny argues that the aforementioned cancellation provision is unconscionable, that it taints the contract in its entirety and that as a result the contract is unenforceable. Accordingly, Allegheny urges that LP & L be barred from any recovery for damages.

The unconscionability which Allegheny suggests is rooted in the alleged one-sidedness of the provision which provides a right of cancellation to LP & L with no concomitant right given to Allegheny. The defendants submit that until production commenced, LP & L could cancel its order with impunity and would only be required to pay a penalty for cancellation "if Allegheny would be making a profit on the order, which LP & L now knew it would not. . . ."

Section 2-302 of the U.C.C., which is the basis for Allegheny's claim of unconscionability states: [the court quoted §2-302].

Comment 1 to U.C.C. §2-302 sets forth the standards to be used in making a determination on an unconscionability claim. "The basic test is whether in the light of the general commercial background and the commercial needs of the particular trade or case, the clauses involved are so one-sided as to be unconscionable under the circumstances existing at the time of the making of the contract. . . . The principle is one of the prevention of oppression and unfair surprise . . . and not of disturbance of allocation of risks because of superior bargaining power."

Allegheny's allegation of unconscionability presents a question of law to be decided by the court. It is not a jury issue. U.C.C. §2-302. W. L. May Co., Inc. v. Philco-Ford Corp., 543 P.2d 283 (Or. 1975). However, plaintiff's claim that the cancellation clause and the contract were unconscionable entitles the parties to "a reasonable opportunity to present evidence as to . . . commercial setting, purpose and effect to aid the court in making . . . [its] determination." U.C.C. §2-302(2). The unconscionability claim is not susceptible of resolution by summary judgment. The court's determination of the issue cannot be made without a hearing. Zicari v. Joseph Harris Co., 304 N.Y.S.2d 918 (N.Y. 1969). Accordingly, plaintiff's motion for summary judgment must be denied in this regard.

BAD FAITH

Allegheny also asserts that bad faith conduct by LP & L serves as a defense to LP & L's claim for breach of contract. The basis of Allegheny's allegation of bad faith is that LP & L refused to meet with it in a timely fashion to discuss renegotiation of the contract. Allegheny argues that its bad faith allegation must be resolved at trial by the finder of fact.

The Uniform Commercial Code imposes an obligation of good faith on the performance or enforcement of contracts under the Code. U.C.C. §1-203. "Good faith" is defined as "honesty in fact and the observance of reasonable commercial standards of fair dealing in the trade." U.C.C. §2-103(1)(b).

Allegheny's defense of bad faith based on LP & L's failure to engage in timely renegotiation of the contract is without merit. There is no obligation imposed under law which would have required LP & L to engage in renegotiation or even discuss renegotiation of its contract with Allegheny. See Missouri Public Service Company v. Peabody Coal Co., 583 S.W.2d 721, 725 (Mo. App. 1979), *cert. denied*, 444 U.S. 865. Allegheny has not attempted to show any requirement for renegotiation. Allegheny's claim that LP & L was in bad faith for failure to do what it had no obligation to do cannot withstand scrutiny. It cannot survive the test of plaintiff's summary judgment motion.

Insofar, however, as Allegheny makes a claim of bad faith conduct in connection with LP & L's purchase of goods in substitution for those due from Allegheny, the "cover" under U.C.C. §2-712(1), that defense relates to the damages portion of LP & L's lawsuit. The issue awaits resolution with LP & L's claim for damages.

In that regard, this court cannot now say that there are no genuine issues of material fact surrounding LP & L's claim for damages. The facts surrounding the obtaining of a "cover," timeliness, mitigation of damages, good faith and costs cannot be decided at this time. Unlike the liability portion of plaintiff's claim and consideration of certain of Allegheny's defenses, the issue of LP & L's damages awaits resolution at trial.

CONCLUSION

Based on the foregoing authorities and analysis, the court hereby grants the motion of Louisiana Power & Light Co. for summary judgment on the issue of liability and Allegheny's defenses of commercial impracticability, mistakes of fact and bad faith. The motion for summary judgment must be denied insofar as Allegheny's defense of unconscionability and the issue of LP & L's damages are concerned.

Chapter 6

REMEDIES

I. SPECIAL REMEDIES

The 2-700s of the U.C.C. are the basic remedy provisions (though some remedies, such as rejection and revocation of acceptance, which we covered earlier, are found in other parts of Article 2). The 2-700s may be further divided into two parts: the seller's remedies when the buyer is in breach (§§2-703 to 2-710) and the buyer's remedies when the seller is in breach (§§2-711 to 2-717). These two areas will be discussed below; but before getting to them, pedagogical tidiness calls for a quick look at some special situations.

A. Remedies on Insolvency

When one contracting party becomes insolvent while in possession of goods that have been identified to the contract, the other may in some circumstances elect to forgo damages and try to get the goods themselves. This action is called *reclamation*. The key Code sections are §§2-502 and 2-702; read them. Section 2-702 is very important and much litigated. Quite often a battle develops between a party (buyer or seller) seeking to reclaim the goods and either a secured creditor of the party with the goods or a trustee in bankruptcy. The battle between the secured creditor and the reclaiming party is governed by meshing Article 2 with Article 9, not always an easy task. The leading case is In re Samuels & Co., 510 F.2d 139 (5th Cir. 1975), *rev'd on other grounds*, 526 F.2d 1238 (5th Cir. 1976), *cert. denied*, 429 U.S. 834 (1976), where the secured creditor wins over an unpaid cash seller. If the battle is between the reclaiming party and the trustee in bankruptcy, a section of the Bankruptcy Reform Act was designed to protect a seller's reclamation right from the trustee's avoiding powers in most situations where the seller would win under §2-702; see 11 U.S.C.A. §546(c) (1978).

B. Liquidated Damages

At common law, if the parties put a liquidated damages clause in their contract, it was upheld by the courts only if the parties truly intended the figure named to be compensatory and had made in good faith an attempt to pre-estimate the damages. The courts struck the clause and made the aggrieved party prove actual damages if the courts decided that the parties had intended the liquidated figure to be a penalty amount to be forfeited in the event of breach. See Equitable Lumber Co. v. IPA Land Dev. Corp., 38 N.Y.2d 516, 344 N.E.2d 391, 381 N.Y.S.2d 459, 18 U.C.C. Rep. Serv. 273 (1976); J. Calamari & J. Perillo, Contracts §§14-31, 14-32 (3d ed. 1987).

The Code's liquidated damages provision is §2-718(1). It makes little change from the common law rules except that it provides that the validity of the liquidated damages clause is to be tested, in part, against the *actual* harm caused by the breach (a criterion of no importance at common law). See Note, A New Standard for Liquidated Damage Provisions Under the Uniform Commercial Code?, 38 Ohio St. L.J. 437 (1977); see also Annot., 98 A.L.R.3d 586. Interestingly enough, the liquidated damages provision in Article 2A no longer refers to actual damages, specifically allows a *formula* to be used to compute damages, and drops all reference to the effect of an unreasonably large liquidated damages clause. Read §2A-504 and its Official Comment. Would this section permit the parties to contract for an outrageous amount (obviously a penalty) in the event of lessee default?

See Benfield, Lessor's Damages Under Article 2A After Default by the Lessee As to Accepted Goods, 39 Ala. L. Rev. 915, 953 (1988).

C. The Breaching Buyer's Restitution

PROBLEM 66

The zoo officials for the Minerun (West Virginia) Zoo contracted to buy an elephant from the zoo in White Cliffs, Delaware. The terms of the deal were that the West Virginia zoo would deliver a black bear worth $300 as a down payment and pay $100 a month for 20 months, at the end of which time the Delaware zoo would deliver the elephant. The bear was tendered and accepted. The West Virginia zoo duly made its $100 payments for 15 months before it ran out of money and could pay no more. The West Virginia zoo comes to you. Can it recover the $1,500 it has paid? The bear? Look at §§2-718(2), 2-718(3), and 2-718(4). Assuming the bear was and is still worth $300, calculate the amount that the West Virginia zoo is likely to recover in a restitution action.

II. SELLER'S REMEDIES

The plan of the 2-700s is to describe briefly the seller's remedies in §2-703 and the buyer's in §2-711 and then to flesh out these brief descriptions in the sections immediately following. All of these remedies sections are to be read in light of the Code's guiding remedial principle, §1-106(1):

> The remedies provided by this Act shall be liberally administered to the end that the aggrieved party may be put in as good a position as if the other party had fully performed but neither consequential or special nor penal damages may be had except as specifically provided in this Act or by other rule of law.[1]

Now read §2-703 and its Official Comment.

1. The Wyoming Supreme Court has read this section as prohibiting punitive damages awards in suits alleging fraud; Waters v. Trenckmann, 503 P.2d 1187, 11 U.C.C. Rep. Serv. 712 (Wyo. 1972). Other courts have disagreed; see the discussion in Seaton v. Lawson Chevrolet-Mazda, Inc., 821 S.W.2d 137, 16 U.C.C. Rep. Serv. 2d 1070 (Tenn. 1991).

A. Accepted Goods

The seller's recovery of damages is measured by §2-709 (Action for the Price) if the buyer has made a technical *acceptance* of the goods or if the goods are destroyed within a commercially reasonable period of time after the risk of loss shifts to the buyer. In effect, §2-709 is the equivalent of a specific performance remedy for the seller. As discussed below, if the seller still has possession of the goods (or had the risk of loss at the time of their destruction), damages are measured by other sections in the 2-700s. For now, read §2-709. This section is annotated in 90 A.L.R.3d 1141.

PROBLEM 67

Backslappers Auto Sales sold a new blue sports car to Dwane Diletante on credit. He accepted the car and drove it for a month. He then sent Backslappers a notice of revocation of acceptance and gave as his reason the recent repainting of his garage in a color that clashed with the blue car. The notice stated that Diletante had parked the car down the block from his home (away from the clashing garage) and that Backslappers should come and get it. Dwane also refused to make any more car payments. Three days after Backslappers received the notice, the car disappeared and has never been found. May the seller recover the price under §2-709? Who had the risk of loss? See §§2-608(1) and (3), 2-606(1), 2-510; note Official Comment 5 to §2-709. There are good discussions of this problem in White & Summers §7-3 and Nordstrom §178. Would it make a difference if Diletante had *rejected* the goods for the same reason?

B. Unaccepted Goods

When the buyer repudiates before delivery or rejects the goods, the relevant Code section is §2-706 if the seller resells the goods to someone else. If no resale occurs, damages are measured under §2-708. Other relevant sections are cited in the following Problems.

PROBLEM 68

Lannie Light was the sole proprietor of Light's Bulbs, a lighting fixtures business in Austin, Texas. She contracted to sell 80 neon light fixtures to Signs, Inc., a firm in San Antonio. The price was $1,500 "F.O.B. Austin," and the shipment date was to be March 15. On March 5, Signs, Inc., phoned Light and told her that the deal was off, but Lannie refused to agree to a cancellation. She went to her warehouse and picked 80 of the fixtures from her large stock. Then she posted a notice on the bulletin board near the cash register in her store, stating that 80 of the fixtures would be sold to the person making the best offer. Carl Customer (who was always buying these types of items) saw the sign and offered Light $1,000 for the fixtures. Light sold Customer the goods and took payment. Now Light comes to you. She tells you that on March 5 the fixtures were selling on the open market at $800 for 80 and that on March 15 the price for 80 such fixtures was $900 in Austin and $800 in San Antonio. Answer these questions:

(a) Does the UCC permit Light to select goods from the warehouse *after* the buyer repudiates? See §2-704.

(b) Was the resale proper? See §2-706 and Official Comment 2.

(c) If Light's damages are measured under §2-708(1), what amount may she collect? What amount under §2-706?

(d) Does Light have the choice between the §2-706 (Resale) computation and the §2-708 (Repudiation) computation? See Official Comment 1 to §2-703; White & Summers §7-7.

PROBLEM 69

Fun in the Sun, Inc., sells swimming pools. Its president comes to your law office with this problem. A customer named Esther Swimmer ordered one of the standard above-ground pools, retailing for $2,000. The pool's components are purchased by Fun in the Sun at a wholesale price of $800 and are assembled into the finished product. The assembly process costs the seller $400. Swimmer has now repudiated the contract, and Fun in the Sun wants to sue. The current market price is $2,000 for such a pool. Fun in the Sun is sure it can find another buyer at that price if it resells the pool. Does it have damages? How are they measured? See §2-708(2), along with Official Comment 2. See also White & Summers §§7-8 to 7-13; Nordstrom §177.

The problem with sellers in Fun in the Sun's position (sellers having an unlimited supply of goods) is that if the law forces them to measure damages under §2-706 or §2-708(1), they lose the profit they would have made from the sale to the second customer. A seller in such a position is called a *lost volume seller*. The drafters meant for §2-

708(2) to rescue such a seller from this dilemma, but the actual mechanics of the operation of the section are not clear. The problem arises in part from the undefined phrase "profit (including reasonable overhead)," which contains accounting terms having no fixed legal meaning. For an analysis of their import, see Speidel & Clay, Seller's Recovery of Overhead Under U.C.C. Section 2-708(2): Economic Cost Theory and Contract Remedial Policy, 57 Cornell L. Rev. 681 (1972). See also Scott, The Case for Market Damages: Revisiting the Lost Profits Puzzle, 57 U. Chi. L. Rev. 1155 (1990).

Teradyne, Inc. v. Teledyne Industries, Inc.

United States Court of Appeals, First Circuit, 1982
676 F.2d 865, 33 U.C.C. Rep. Serv. 1669

WYZANSKI, J. In this diversity action, Teradyne, Inc. sued Teledyne Industries, Inc. and its subsidiary for damages pursuant to §2-708(2) of the U.C.C. Teledyne does not dispute the facts that it is bound as a buyer under a sales contract with Teradyne, that it broke the contract, and that Teradyne's right to damages is governed by §2-708(2). The principal dispute concerns the calculation of damages.

The district court referred the case to a master whose report the district court approved and made the basis of the judgment here on appeal.

The following facts, derived from the master's report, are undisputed.

On July 30, 1976 Teradyne, Inc. ["the seller"], a Massachusetts corporation, entered into a Quantity Purchase Contract ["the contract"] which, though made with a subsidiary, binds Teledyne Industries, Inc., a California corporation ["the buyer"]. That contract governed an earlier contract resulting from the seller's acceptance of the buyer's July 23, 1976 purchase order to buy at the list price of $98,400 (which was also its fair market value) a T-347A transistor test system ["the T-347A"]. One consequence of such governance was that the buyer was entitled to a $984 discount from the $98,400 price.

The buyer canceled its order for the T-347A when it was packed ready for shipment scheduled to occur two days later. The seller refused to accept the cancellation.

The buyer offered to purchase instead of the T-347A a $65,000 Field Effects Transistor System ["the FET"] which would also have been governed by "the contract." The seller refused the offer.

After dismantling, testing, and reassembling at an estimated cost of $614 the T-347A, the seller, pursuant to an order that was on hand prior to the cancellation, sold it for $98,400 to another purchaser [hereafter "resale purchaser"].

Teradyne would have made the sale to the resale purchaser even if Teledyne had not broken its contract. Thus if there had been no breach, Teradyne would have made two sales and earned two profits rather than one.

The seller was a volume seller of the equipment covered by the July 23, 1976 purchase order. The equipment represented standard products of the seller and the seller had the means and capacity to duplicate the equipment for a second sale had the buyer honored its purchase order.

(seller)

Teradyne being of the view that the measure of damages under §2-708(2) was the contract price less ascertainable costs saved as a result of the breach—see Jericho Sash and Door Company, Inc. v. Building Erectors, Inc., 362 Mass. 871, 872, 286 N.E.2d 343 (1972) [hereafter "*Jericho*"]—offered as evidence of its cost prices its Inventory Standards Catalog ["the Catalog"]—a document which was prepared for tax purposes not claimed to have been illegitimate, but which admittedly disclosed "low inventory valuations." Relying on that Catalog, Teradyne's Controller, McCabe, testified that the *only* costs which the seller saved as a result of the breach were:

direct labor costs associated with production	$ 3,301
material charges	17,045
sales commission on one T-347A	492
expense	1,800
Total	$22,638

McCabe admitted that he had not included as costs saved the labor costs of employees associated with testing, shipping, installing, servicing, or fulfilling 10-year warranties on the T-347A (although he acknowledged that in forms of accounting for purposes other than damage suits the costs of those employees would not be regarded as "overhead"). His reason was that those costs would not have been affected by the production of one machine more or less. McCabe also admitted that he had not included fringe benefits which amounted to 12% in the case of both included and excluded labor costs.

During McCabe's direct examination, he referred to the 10-K report which Teradyne had filed with the SEC. On cross-examination McCabe admitted that the 10-K form showed that on average the seller's revenues were distributed as follows:

profit	9%
"selling and administrative" expense	26%
interest	1%
"costs of sales and engineering" (including substantial research and development costs incidental to a high technology business)	64%

He also admitted that the average figures applied to the T-347A.

Teradyne contended that the 10-K report was a better index of lost profits than was the Catalog. The master disagreed and concluded that the more appropriate formula for calculating Teradyne's damages under §2-708(2) was the one approved in *Jericho,* supra—"'gross profit' including fixed costs but not costs saved as a result of the breach." He then stated:

> In accordance with the statutory mandate that the remedy "be liberally administered to the end that the aggrieved party may be put in as good a position as if the other party had fully performed," MGL c106 §1-106(1), I find that the Plaintiff has met its burden of proof of damages, and has established the accuracy of its direct costs and the ascertainability of its variable costs with reasonable certainty and "whatever definiteness and accuracy the facts permit." Comment 1 to §1-106(1) of the U.C.C.

In effect, this was a finding that Teradyne had saved only $22,638 as a result of the breach. Subtracting that amount and also the $984 quantity discount from the original contract price of $98,400, the master found that the lost "profit (including reasonable overhead)" was $74,778. To that amount the master added $614 for "incidental damages" which Teradyne incurred in preparing the T-347A for its new customer. Thus he found that Teradyne's total §2-708(2) damages amounted to $75,392.

The master declined to make a deduction from the $75,392 on account of the refusal of the seller to accept the buyer's offer to purchase an FET tester in partial substitution for the repudiated T-347A.

At the time of the reference to the master, the court, without securing the agreement of the parties, had ordered that the master's costs should be paid by them in equal parts.

Teradyne filed a motion praying that the district court (1) should adopt the master's report allowing it to recover $75,392, and (2) should require Teledyne to pay all the master's costs. The district court, without opinion, entered a judgment which grants the first

prayer and denies the second. Teledyne appealed from the first part of the judgment; Teradyne appealed from the second part.

1. The parties are agreed that §2-708(2) applies to the case at bar. Inasmuch as this conclusion is not plain from the text, we explain the reasons why we concur in that agreement.

Section 2-708(2) applies only if the damages provided by §2-708(1) are inadequate to put the seller in as good a position as performance would have done. Under §2-708(1) the measure of damages is the difference between unpaid contract price and market price. Here the unpaid contract price was $97,416 and the market price was $98,400. Hence no damages would be recoverable under §2-708(1). On the other hand, if the buyer had performed, the seller (1) would have had the proceeds of two contracts, one with the buyer Teledyne and the other with the "resale purchaser" and (2) *it seems* would have had in 1976-7 one more T-347A sale.

A literal reading of the last sentence of §2-708(2) — providing for "due credit for payments or proceeds of resale" — would indicate that Teradyne recovers nothing because the proceeds of the resale exceeded the price set in the Teledyne-Teradyne contract. However, in light of the statutory history of the subsection, it is universally agreed that in a case where after the buyer's default a seller resells the goods, the proceeds of the resale are not to be credited to the buyer if the seller is a lost volume seller[2] — that is, one who had there been no breach by the buyer, could and would have had the benefit of both the original contract and the resale contract.[3]

Thus, despite the resale of the T-347A, Teradyne is entitled to recover from Teledyne what §2-708(2) calls its expected "profit (including reasonable overhead)" on the broken Teledyne contract.[4]

2. The term "lost volume seller" was apparently coined by Professor Robert J. Harris in his article A Radical Restatement of the Law of Seller's Damages: Sales Act and Commercial Code Results Compared, 18 Stan. L. Rev. 66 (1965). The terminology has been widely adopted. See Famous Knitwear Corp. v. Drug Fair Inc., 493 F.2d 251, 254 n.5 (4th Cir. 1974); Snyder v. Herbert Greenbaum & Assoc. Inc., 38 Md. App. 144, 157, 380 A.2d 618, 624 (1977); Publicker Industries, Inc. v. Roman Ceramics Corp., 652 F.2d 340, 346 (3d Cir. 1981). See Restatement (Second) Contracts §347 Comment f; J. White and R. Summers, Uniform Commercial Code, 2d ed. (1980) [hereinafter "White and Summers"] §7-9, particularly p.276 first full paragraph.

3. Famous Knitwear Corp. v. Drug Fair Inc., supra, 493 F.2d 254 n.7; Snyder v. Herbert Greenbaum & Assoc. Inc., supra, 380 A.2d 625-626; Neri v. Retail Marine Corp., 30 N.Y.2d 393, 399, 285 N.E.2d 311, 314 (1972). See White and Summers, §7-13, particularly 284-285.

4. Ibid. White and Summers at pp.284-285 give the following suppositious case which parallels the instant case. Boeing is able to make and sell in one year 100

2. Teledyne not only "does not dispute that damages are to be calculated pursuant to §2-708(2)" but concedes that the formula used in Jericho Sash & Door Co. v. Building Erectors Inc., 362 Mass. 871 (1972), for determining lost profit including overhead—that is, the formula under which direct costs of producing and selling manufactured goods are deducted from the contract price in order to arrive

---

airplanes. TWA contracts to buy the third plane off the assembly line, but it breaks the contract and Boeing resells the plane to Pan Am which had already agreed to buy the fourth plane. Because of the breach Boeing sells only 99 aircraft during the year. White and Summers say that the right result, despite the words of §2-708(2), is that Boeing recovers from TWA both the net profit and the overhead components of the TWA contract price, no credit being given for any part of the proceeds Boeing received from its sale to Pan Am.

We do not agree with the third sentence in the following Comment f to Restatement (Second) Contract §347 insofar as it indicates that a volume seller like Teradyne may recover from a defaulting buyer only the lost net profit on the original contract.

> f. Lost volume. Whether a subsequent transaction is a substitute for the broken contract sometimes raises difficult questions of fact. If the injured party could and would have entered into the subsequent contract, even if the contract had not been broken, and could have had the benefit of both, he can be said to have "lost volume" and the subsequent transaction is not a substitute for the broken contract. The injured party's damages are then based on the *net* profit that he has lost as a result of the broken contract. Since entrepreneurs try to operate at optimum capacity, however, it is possible that an additional transaction would not have been profitable and that the injured party would not have chosen to expand his business by undertaking it had there been no breach. It is sometimes assumed that he would have done so, but the question is one of fact to be resolved according to the circumstances of each case. See illustration 16. See also Uniform Commercial Code §2-708(2)." [Emphasis added.]

> Limiting the volume seller's recovery to lost net profit does not permit the recovery of reasonable overhead for which provision is specifically made in the text of §2-708(2). The reason for the allowance of overhead is set forth in Vitex Mfg. Corp. v. Caribtex Corp., 377 F.2d 795, 799 (3d Cir. 1967) [hereinafter "Vitex"]:

>> . . . as the number of transaction[s] over which overhead can be spread becomes smaller, each transaction must bear a greater portion or allocate share of the fixed overhead cost. Suppose a company has fixed overhead of $10,000 and engages in five similar transactions; then the receipts of each transaction would bear $2000 of overhead expense. If the company is now forced to spread this $10,000 over only four transactions, then the overhead expense per transaction will rise to $2500, significantly reducing the profitability of the four remaining transactions. Thus, where the contract is between businessmen familiar with commercial practices, as here, the breaching party should reasonably foresee that his breach will not only cause a loss of 'clear' profit, but also a loss in that the profitability of other transactions will be reduced. Resolute Ins. Co. v. Percy Jones, Inc., 198 F.2d 309 (C.A. 10, 1952); Cf. In re Kellett Aircraft Corp., 191 F.2d 231 (C.A. 3, 1951). . . .

Vitex represents the law of Massachusetts. F.A. Bartlett Tree Expert Co. v. Hartney, 308 Mass. 407, 412 (1941); Roblin Hope Industries Inc. v. J.A. Sullivan Corp., Mass. App. Ct. Adv. Sh. [1980] 2229, 2232.

at "profit (including reasonable overhead)" as that term is used in §2-708(2) — "is permissible provided all variable expenses are identified."

What Teledyne contends is that all variable costs were not identified because the cost figures came from a catalog, prepared for tax purposes, which did not fully reflect all direct costs. The master found that the statement of costs based on the catalog was reliable and that Teledyne's method of calculating costs based on the 10-K statements was not more accurate. Those findings are not clearly erroneous and therefore we may not reverse the judgment on the ground that allegedly the items of cost which were deducted are unreliable. Fed. R. Civ. P. 52(a); Merrill Trust Co. v. Bradford, 507 F.2d 467, 468 (1st Cir. 1974); Van Alen v. Dominick & Dominick, Inc., 560 F.2d 547, 551 (2d Cir. 1977).

Teledyne's more significant objection to Teradyne's and the master's application of the *Jericho* formula in the case at bar is that neither of them made deductions on account of the wages paid to testers, shippers, installers, and other Teradyne employees who directly handled the T-347A, or on account of the fringe benefits amounting in the case of those and other employees to 12 per cent of wages. Teradyne gave as the reason for the omission of the wages of the testers, etc. that those wages would not have been affected if each of the testers, etc. handled one product more or less. However, the work of those employees entered as directly into producing and supplying the T-347A as did the work of a fabricator of a T-347A. Surely no one would regard as "reasonable overhead" within §2-708(2) the wages of a fabricator of a T-347A even if his wages were the same whether he made one product more or less. We conclude that the wages of the testers, etc. likewise are not part of overhead and as a "direct cost" should have been deducted from the contract price. A fortiori fringe benefits amounting to 12 per cent of wages should also have been deducted as direct costs. Taken together we cannot view these omitted items as what *Jericho* called "relatively insignificant items." We, therefore, must vacate the district court's judgment. In accordance with the procedure followed in Publicker Industries, Inc. v. Roman Ceramics Corp., 603 F.2d 1065, 1072-3 (3d Cir. 1979) and Famous Knitwear Corp. v. Drug Fair, Inc., 493 F.2d 251, 255-256 (4th Cir. 1974), we remand this case so that with respect to the omitted direct labor costs specified above the parties may offer further evidence and the court may make findings "with whatever definiteness and accuracy the facts permit, but no more." *Jericho,* p.872.

There are two other matters which may properly be dealt with before the case is remanded to the district court.

3. Teledyne contends that Teradyne was required to mitigate damages by acceptance of Teledyne's offer to purchase instead of the T-347A the FET system.

That point is without merit.

The meaning of Teledyne's offer was that if Teradyne would forego its profit-loss claim arising out of Teledyne's breach of the T-347A contract, Teledyne would purchase another type of machine which it was under no obligation to buy. The seller's failure to accept such an offer does not preclude it from recovering the full damages to which it would otherwise be entitled. As Restatement (Second) Contracts, §350 Comment c indicates, there is no right to so-called mitigation of damages where the offer of a substitute contract "is conditioned on surrender by the injured party of his claim for breach." "One is not required to mitigate his losses by accepting an arrangement with the repudiator if that is made conditional on his surrender of his rights under the repudiated contract." 5 Corbin, Contracts 2d (1964) §1043 at 274. Acc. Campfield v. Sauer, 189 F. 576 (6th Cir. 1911); Stanspec Corp. v. Jelco, Inc., 464 F.2d 1184, 1187 (10th Cir. 1972). Teradyne acted in a commercially reasonable manner in refusing to accept Teledyne's offer. . . .

The district court's judgment is vacated and the case is remanded to the district court to proceed in accordance with this opinion.

QUESTIONS

1. Exactly who qualifies as a "lost volume seller"? If a college student advertises his guitar for sale in the campus newspaper, he contracts to sell it to a caller, the caller then backs out, and the student sells the guitar to someone else, can the student qualify as a lost volume seller?

2. Why does the court draw a distinction between overhead costs and variable expenses (which the court calls "direct costs")? Which was which here?

3. Section 2-708(2) specifically requires a subtraction of the "proceeds of resale." Doesn't this language always defeat the lost volume seller, who will typically have resold the unaccepted goods? See R. E. Davis Chem. Corp. v. Diasonics, Inc., 826 F.2d 678, 4 U.C.C. Rep. Serv. 2d 369 (7th Cir. 1987).

4. The lost volume concept also applies to lessors of goods. See §2A-529's Official Comment 2 and C.I.C. Corp. v. Ragtime, Inc., 319 N.J. Super. 662, 726 A.2d 316, 38 U.C.C. Rep. Serv. 2d 21 (N.J. App. 1999).

PROBLEM 70

Milo Veep, sales agent for the Complex Computer Corporation (CCC), negotiated a contract whereby his company was to design and manufacture a special computer that would regulate the timing of subway trains for the City of Plantation, Mississippi. The price was $20,000 F.O.B. CCC's plant in Atlanta, Georgia. When the computer was half completed, the City of Plantation underwent a change of administration, and the new city leaders decided to dump the subway renovations. They phoned CCC and canceled the computer order. Now Veep phones your law office for advice. To help in your decision, Veep states that as scrap the computer and its components are now worth $5,000. Veep has heard that three other cities have subway systems similar to Plantation's, and if the computer is finished, they might be enticed to buy it at a price between $15,000 and $20,000. On the other hand, it will cost CCC $9,000 to complete the computer.

(a) Should CCC stop the manufacture of the computer and sell it for scrap or complete manufacture and then try to resell it? See §2-704(2) and its Official Comment 2.

(b) If CCC completes manufacture and then, after a good faith effort, is unable to find a new buyer for the computer, can it make Plantation pay for the finished product? See §2-709(1)(b); Official Comment 1 to §2-704.

The remedies provided for the parties in a lease of goods by Article 2A have been slavishly copied from the corresponding provisions in Article 2. For the most part this does no harm, but the Article 2A equivalent to §2-709's "Action for the Price" has generated a lot of discord. Read §2A-529, "Lessor's Action for the Rent."

PROBLEM 71

Lawyer Portia Moot decided to rent a computer from Machines Unlimited and use it in her office. The computer arrived, and Portia found it most satisfactory, but her struggling practice made it difficult for her to make the lease payments on time. After she had missed two payments in a row, Machines Unlimited sent a goon to her office to repossess the computer. Portia was not there at the time, but her loyal secretary protested mightily when the goon grabbed the machine—at one point blocking the door with her body—but she was shoved aside and the computer was taken. The lease still had a year to run, with payments of $100 due each month. Machines Unlimited sued Portia for $1,200.

(a) Was Machines Unlimited's repossession valid? See §2A-525. What remedy does Portia have if it was not?

(b) Assuming there was no problem with the repossession, is the lessor required to try to mitigate damages by re-leasing the machine? See §2A-529 and its Official Comment.

(c) Could the lessor avoid any possible duty to mitigate by so stipulating in the lease agreement? See §§1-102(3), 2A-503; Kripke, Some Dissonant Notes About Article 2A, 39 Ala. L. Rev. 792, 795-796 (1988).

III. BUYER'S REMEDIES

The general list of the buyer's remedies is found in §2-711. This section also gives the buyer a right to cancel and recover the price if the buyer has already paid. In most circumstances, the buyer has further recoverable damages, as identified in other sections. All the sections are designed to follow §1-106's admonition that the Code's goal is to put the aggrieved party in as good a position as performance would have. As for which sections are appropriate in a given case as far as monetary damages are concerned, the answer depends on whether the buyer has *accepted* the goods or not.

A. Accepted Goods

If a technical §2-606 acceptance of the goods has been made and is not later revoked, the buyer may still sue for breach of warranty (or other breach of contract) if a notice of the defect has been given to the seller within a reasonable time after the defect should have been discovered; §2-607(3)(a). Damages are then measured by §§2-714 and 2-715. Read those sections. See Annot., 96 A.L.R.3d 299.

PROBLEM 72

The world-famous pianist Bart Cristofori made $50,000 a year giving concerts. Recently he decided to experiment with some new sounds. He purchased an electric piano for $3,000 from the Silbermann Electronic Music Company. The purchase was negotiated orally; there was no written contract. Cristofori practiced day and night to master the new instrument. After three months of arduous practice, he noticed a strange ringing in his ears. Subsequent medical examination revealed that Cristofori was going deaf. The cause was a high-pitched whine (above the level of human perception) emanating from the electric piano. On learning that the piano had done this to him, Cristofori took an axe and chopped the piano into unrecognizable bits. (This action ended his ability to revoke his acceptance; §§2-608(3), 2-602(2)(b).) When he calmed down, he brought suit against the piano company for breach of warranty. His damages were claimed as $1,755,505, based on the following elements: $3,000 was the cost of the piano, $2,000 was doctor's fees, $500 was paid to experts to examine the piano and determine if it was the cause of the ear problem, $750,000 was lost income for the next 15 years, $1,000,000 was the value of Cristofori's hearing, and $5 was for the axe. Silbermann Electronic Music defended by (1) denying that it had warranted the piano in any way and (2) proving that the whine was harmless to everybody in the world except Cristofori. (The company proved that the accident occurred to him only because of the bone structure of his skull coupled with the fact that he had a metal plate installed in his head as a result of an auto accident in his youth.) Answer these questions:

(a) What warranty, if any, did the Silbermann Company breach? Does the company's care in manufacturing the piano or the freakishness of the injury keep the warranty from being breached?

(b) Which, if any, of Cristofori's damages are recoverable under §2-714?

(c) Which, if any, of the items claimed are *incidental damages* under §2-715(1)?

(d) The §2-715(2)(a) test of consequential damages with its "reason to know" language is a restatement of our old friend Hadley v. Baxendale. Is it relevant here? See Nordstrom §153.

(e) If you were the judge of both the facts and the law, what amount would you award Cristofori, and why?

PROBLEM 73

Sheila Spin made it to the finals of the USA Yo-Yo Championship, where she was widely thought to be a cinch to win the $10,000 first prize. The day of the competition she went into the Smalltime Drug Store owned by her Uncle Mort and told him that she wanted to buy a four-foot nylon yo-yo cord to use in the competition. Mort sold her one for $1.50 (he put it on her bill) and wished her luck. That she did not have. The cord was defective and broke during her first trick, thus eliminating her from the competition. When the bill came from the drug store, Sheila refused to pay it. In fact, she filed suit against Mort, asking for $50,000 consequential damages. Every expert witness who testified stated that Sheila's ability with the yo-yo was the greatest in the world. Mort defended on two grounds: (1) merely knowing about the intended use of the yo-yo in the competition was not enough to impose liability on him unless the parties had agreed to put this risk on him, and (2) her damages were too speculative. Answer these questions:

(a) Does the UCC permit Sheila to refuse to pay the bill? See §2-717. If the buyer feels obligated to pay only part of the bill, what procedure should be followed? See §3-311.

(b) Are the consequential damages for which Sheila asked too speculative? See Official Comment 4 to §2-715; White & Summers §10-4. Cf. Wachtel v. National Alfalfa Journal, 190 Iowa 1293, 176 N.W. 801 (1920) (leading contender in canceled contest entitled to value of the chance of winning).

(c) Is knowledge of the possible consequential damages alone sufficient to impose liability on a seller? Or is Mort right in saying that the liability for consequential damages attaches only if the seller has agreed (expressly or impliedly) to assume the risk? See Official Comment 2 to §2-715; White & Summers §10-4; Beal v. General Motors Corp., 354 F. Supp. 423, 12 U.C.C. Rep. Serv. 105 (D. Del. 1973).

(d) May Sheila recover her attorney fees as consequential damages? See Equitable Lumber Corp. v. IPA Land Dev. Corp., 38 N.Y.2d 516, 344 N.E.2d 391, 381 N.Y.S.2d 459, 18 U.C.C. Rep. Serv. 273 (1976) (may be recovered if the contract so provides, but any specified amount must be valid as a liquidated damages provision); Indiana Glass Co. v. Indiana Michigan Power Co., 692 N.E.2d 886, 37 U.C.C. Rep. Serv. 2d 332 (Ind. App. 1998) (not unless another statute so provides); Modine Mfg. Co. v. North East Indep. Sch. Dist., 503 S.W.2d 833, 14 U.C.C. Rep. Serv. 317 (Tex. Civ. App. 1974) (no, because such fees are penal in nature and the Code does not authorize punitive damages).

PROBLEM 74

Rambo Trucks, Inc., sold Hercules Moving Company a large moving van. The contract of sale limited the buyer's remedy for breach of warranty to replacement or repair only and clearly disclaimed liability for consequential damages. The first day on the job, the truck proved incapable of climbing even small hills, so Hercules Moving Company revoked its acceptance of the truck. It claimed a security interest in the truck pursuant to §2-711(3) and pending sale stored it at a truck depot, which charged it $50.00 a day for storage.

Must Rambo Trucks pay the storage charges, or is the company protected by the disclaimer of consequential damages? See §§2-719(3), 2-715(1); Commonwealth Edison Co. v. Allied Chem. Nuclear Prods., Inc., 684 F. Supp. 1429, 6 U.C.C. Rep. Serv. 2d 380 (N.D. Ill. 1988) (storage charges of $293,000,000!).

B. Unaccepted Goods

Where the seller never delivers the goods or where the buyer rejects or revokes acceptance, §2-711 states that the buyer may recover the price and other damages. These generally include incidental and consequential damages under §2-715. See Official Comment 1 to that section. In addition, the buyer may seek specific performance or replevin under §2-716. Read §2-716 and its Official Comment.

As Comment 1 indicates, the drafters intended to "liberalize" the application of the doctrine of specific performance. Thus, §2-716 provides for the use of specific performance not only when goods are unique, but also "in other proper circumstances." What are "proper circumstances"? See Laclede Gas Co. v. Amoco Oil Co., 522 F.2d 33, 17 U.C.C. Rep. Serv. 447 (8th Cir. 1975), *rev'd on other grounds*, 531 F.2d 942 (8th Cir. 1975) (the court gave the buyer, a distributor of propane gas, a mandatory injunction against the seller, who had promised to supply gas over a long term); Eastern Airlines Inc. v. Gulf Oil Corp., 415 F. Supp. 429, 19 U.C.C. Rep. Serv. 721 (S.D. Fla. 1975) (Gulf Oil was enjoined from breaching its contract with Eastern for jet fuel); Annot., 26 A.L.R.4th 294.

An important buyer remedy is found in §2-712, where the buyer is authorized to *cover*—that is, purchase substitute goods. If a buyer covers properly, the damages are measured by a comparison of the original contract price and the cost of the cover. Read §2-712.

PROBLEM 75

Mr. and Mrs. Transient ordered a 2002 Blocklong model mobile home for $8,000 from the Home on Wheels Sales Corporation, delivery to be made on May 20. The Transients planned on spending an additional $500 to build a foundation that the Blocklong trailer had to have for maximum utility. Due to widespread industry strikes, the price of trailers rose dramatically in the early spring, and on May 10 Home on Wheels informed the Transients that the deal was off. The Transients shopped around and on September 25 bought a 2003 Behemoth model mobile home for $15,000 from another dealer. The Behemoth was larger than the Blocklong model (it had a basement and a laundry room), but it did not require a foundation. The Transients then brought suit. Home on Wheels defended by offering to show that (a) the Behemoth was selling for $10,000 up to September 5 when the price rose to $15,000, and (b) the Behemoth always sells for $2,000 more than the Blocklong since the former is a snazzier trailer. What damages can the Transients get under §2-712? See Official Comment 2 of that section; White & Summers §6-3; Nordstrom §147; Annot., 79 A.L.R.4th 844.

Hughes Communications Galaxy, Inc. v. United States

United States Court of Appeals, Federal Circuit, 2001
271 F.3d 1060, 46 U.C.C. Rep. Serv. 2d 453

RADER, Circuit Judge.

Following a trial on damages for breach of contract, the United States Court of Federal Claims awarded Hughes Communications Galaxy, Inc. $102,680,625. Hughes Communications Galaxy, Inc. v. United States, 47 Fed. Cl. 236 (2000) (*Hughes V*). Because the Court of Federal Claims did not abuse its discretion in calculating damages, this court affirms.

I.

This case has received extensive factual analysis in prior opinions. . . . This appeal addresses only the Court of Federal Claims' breach of contract damage determination in *Hughes IV* and *Hughes V*.

In December 1985, NASA and Hughes entered into a Launch Services Agreement (LSA), which required NASA to use its "best efforts" to launch ten of Hughes' HS-393 satellites on space shuttles. The LSA required NASA to continue using its best efforts to launch Hughes' HS-393s until it launched all ten HS-393s or until September 30, 1994, whichever was earlier. NASA compiled "manifests" of all shuttle payloads scheduled for launch on shuttles. NASA reissued these manifests periodically to account for changed circumstances. The manifests listed commercial payloads in order of their planned or firm launch dates and scheduled a shuttle for each launch. After NASA and Hughes entered the LSA, NASA assigned Hughes' satellites specific slots on a manifest.

In January 1986, the space shuttle Challenger exploded. Following the Challenger explosion, NASA suspended operation of the shuttles until September 1988. Further, in August 1986, President Reagan announced that NASA would no longer launch commercial satellites on shuttles. On July 10, 1986, NASA completed the last manifest before President Reagan's announcement. It projected that NASA would launch eight Hughes satellites on shuttles by September 1994. Thereafter, NASA compiled a new manifest that only included "shuttle unique" and "national security and foreign policy" payloads. That maniest did not list any Hughes satellites. Later NASA informed Hughes that it would almost certainly not launch any Hughes satellites on shuttles.

After 1986, Hughes launched three of its HS-393s on expendable launch vehicles (ELVs), one of which was the JCSAT-1. Hughes also launched several similar satellites on ELVs, including six HS-601 satellites. The HS-601s are similar to the HS-393s, except they are more powerful and better suited for ELV launches. While the ELV launches provided an alternative to shuttle launch services under the LSA, Hughes incurred more costs by launching satellites on ELVs rather than on shuttles.

Hughes sued the United States Government for breach of contract and for taking its property without providing just compensation. The Court of Federal Claims granted summary judgment to the Government on both claims based on the sovereign act defense. *Hughes I*, 26 Cl. Ct. at 144-46. This court reversed that summary judgment and remanded. *Hughes II*, 998 F.2d at 959. On remand, the Court of Federal Claims granted summary judgment for Hughes for breach of contract. *Hughes III*, 34 Fed. Cl. at 634. Before holding a trial on damages, the Court of Federal Claims ruled that the Government could not produce evidence to reduce its damages by the amount Hughes had passed on to its customers in increased prices. *Hughes IV*, 38 Fed. Cl. at 582.

At the damages trial, Hughes sought to prove damages by showing its increased costs in launching satellites on ELVs, rather than on shuttles. Hughes presented two main methods for calculating the increased costs. The first method, the Ten HS-393 Satellites Method, compared the costs of launching ten HS-393s on shuttles under the LSA with the costs of launching ten HS-393s on ELVs. Because Hughes had actually launched only three HS-393s on ELVs, the method based the ELV launch costs on the actual costs of launching the three HS-393s. The second method, the Primary Method, compared Hughes' actual costs of launching ten satellites on ELVs with the costs that Hughes would have incurred by launching ten satellites on shuttles under the LSA. The ten satellites included the three HS-393s, the six HS-601s, and one HS-376.

The Court of Federal Claims used the Ten HS-393 Satellites Method to calculate Hughes' increased costs of "cover." *Hughes V*, 47 Fed. Cl. at 244. However, the court modified the method in several important respects. First, the court found that even using its best efforts, NASA would have only launched five HS-393s under the LSA. Accordingly, the court only awarded Hughes increased costs for five satellites, rather than ten. Id. Second, the court averaged the costs of launching on shuttles the three HS-393s that were actually launched on ELVs and used that average for the fourth and fifth satellites, rather than individually calculating the cost of launching each satellite on a shuttle, as Hughes' expert had done. Id. at 244 n.12. Third, in calculating the ELV launch costs for the fourth and fifth satellites, the court escalated the costs using the midpoint between March 1989 and September 1994, rather than the midpoint between March 1989 and December 1995, as Hughes' expert had done. Id. at 244. Fourth, the court refused to award Hughes prejudgment interest on its damages. Id. at 244-45. Fifth, the court refused to award Hughes reflight insurance costs and increased launch insurance costs for the five satellites. Id. at 245-46.

Based on its modified HS-393 method, the court awarded Hughes $102,680,625 in damages for its increased launch costs. Id. at 247. Hughes and the Government both appeal. This court has jurisdiction under 28 U.S.C. §1295(a)(3) (1994).

II.

"The general rule in common law breach of contract cases is to award damages sufficient to place the injured party in as good a position as he or she would have been had the breaching party fully performed." San Carlos Irrigation & Drainage Dist. v. United States, 111 F.3d 1557, 1562-63 (Fed. Cir. 1997). Thus, "[a] plaintiff must show that but for the breach, the damages alleged would not have been suffered." Id. Moreover, the damages must have been foreseeable at the time the parties entered the contract, which requires that they "be the natural and proximate result of the breach." Locke v. United

— need to be foreseeable
— must be direct damages.
— Buyer allowed to cover

States, 151 Ct. Cl. 262, 283 F.2d 521, 526 (Ct. Cl. 1960). The LSA itself further limits damages to "direct damages only" and excludes consequential damages from any recovery.

The Court of Federal Claims awarded Hughes its increased costs of "cover." If a seller breaches a contract for goods, the buyer may "cover" or, in other words, obtain substitute goods from another seller. U.C.C. §2-712 (1997); E. Allan Farnsworth, Farnsworth on Contracts, §12.11 (2d ed. 1998). Additionally, courts often award an analogous remedy for breach of service contracts such as the LSA. Farnsworth, supra, §12.11. While the cover remedy of the Uniform Commercial Code does not govern this analogous remedy under the LSA, the Uniform Commercial Code provides useful guidance in applying general contract principles. Because both parties and the Court of Federal Claims have referred to this remedy as a "cover" remedy, this court will also use this term to refer to the remedy for Hughes' increased costs of obtaining substitute launch services.

The substitute goods or services involved in cover need not be identical to those involved in the contract, but they must be "commercially usable as reasonable substitutes under the circumstances." U.C.C. §2-712 cmt. 2. Whether cover provides a reasonable substitute under the circumstances is a question of fact. Bigelow-Sanford, Inc. v. Gunny Corp., 649 F.2d 1060, 1065 (5th Cir. 1981) (stating that whether cover is reasonable is a "classic jury issue" (quoting Transammonia Export Corp. v. Conserv, Inc., 554 F.2d 719, 724 (5th Cir. 1977))).

cover Rule

jury question

When a buyer of goods covers, the buyer's remedy for the seller's breach as to those goods equals the difference between the cost of the replacement goods and the contract price plus other losses. U.C.C. §2-712; Farnsworth, supra, §12.11. Similarly, if the seller breaches a contract for services, the buyer's remedy for cover equals the difference between the cost of the substitute services and the contract price plus other losses. Farnsworth, supra, §12.11 (where a building contractor breaches a first contract and the owner obtains substitute performance under a second contract, the owner can recover "any additional amount required by the second contract beyond what the owner would have had to pay under the first").

The Government cross appeals, arguing that Hughes should only be able to recover damages for the three HS-393s that it actually launched. While Hughes did not actually launch the fourth and fifth HS-393s that the Court of Federal Claims used to calculate damages, Hughes did incur costs in launching the HS-601s. The Court of Federal Claims found that Hughes developed the HS-601s to replace the HS-393s because the HS-601s were better suited for ELV launches, and that

Hughes would have launched ten HS-393s on shuttles, given the opportunity. *Hughes V*, 47 Fed. Cl. at 240-41. The Government disputes these findings, asserting that Hughes developed the HS-601s for independent business reasons, specifically, the more powerful HS-601s were more marketable. On this point, however, the Court of Federal Claims specifically credited testimony of Hughes' witnesses that Hughes would not have developed the HS-601 if the Government had not breached the LSA and that Hughes could have designed the HS-393 to accommodate the additional power of the HS-601. Id. at 240. This testimony directly supports the Court of Federal Claims' finding that "the HS-393 could have been used in place of the HS-601" for HS-601 launches during the contract period. *Hughes V*, 47 Fed. Cl. at 240. Thus, the trial court found that the HS-601 launches were reasonable substitutes under the circumstances of this breach.

Additionally, the Court of Federal Claims specifically found that no credible evidence supported the Government's attack on the HS-601 as a reasonable substitute. Specifically, the Government argues that at the time of contracting, the Government could not have foreseen "the demise of the HS-393" as a result of its breach. However, the Court of Federal Claims' damages method does not compensate Hughes for the "demise of the HS-393." Rather it compensates Hughes for increased launch costs. Had Hughes kept using the HS-393s, it would likely have incurred the same damages that the Court of Federal Claims awarded.

In sum, the Court of Federal Claims hinged its determination of this issue on credibility. Such determinations are virtually never clear error. First Interstate Bank v. United States, 61 F.3d 876, 882 (Fed. Cir. 1995). Furthermore, while the damages calculation might have been easier if Hughes had kept launching HS-393s on ELVs, ease of proof in potential future litigation is not sufficient justification to require Hughes to continue launching satellites that were ill-suited for ELV launches. As the victim of the breach, Hughes was within its rights to obtain commercially reasonable substitute launch services even if the substitute services were not identical to those covered by the LSA. The Court of Federal Claims thus did not clearly err in holding that Hughes successfully covered by launching HS-601s on ELVs. Accordingly, this court rejects the Government's cross appeal.

The Court of Federal Claims' use of increased HS-393 launch costs provided reasonable certainty in calculating damages. The trial court compared the costs of launching HS-393s on ELVs with the costs of launching the same HS-393s on shuttles. That comparison provided a basis for assessing Hughes' increased costs in launching the HS-601s. Under this method, the Court of Federal Claims accounted for any measurable difference in value to Hughes between the HS-393 launches and the HS-601 launches. See Farnsworth, supra, §12.11 ("[A]ny measurable difference in quality [of a substitute] can be compensated for by a money allowance."). Accordingly, the Court of Federal Claims used the increased costs for HS-393s as a reasonable approximation of the increased costs incurred by Hughes in launching the substitute HS-601s. Under this method, the trial court did not abuse its discretion. See S.W. Elecs. & Mfg. Corp. v. United States, 228 Ct. Cl. 333, 655 F.2d 1078, 1088 (Ct. Cl. 1981) (the trial court need only "make a fair and reasonable approximation").

The LSA states that damages "shall be limited to direct damages only and shall not include any loss of revenue, profits or other indirect or consequential damages." As discussed above, the increased costs represent direct damages incurred by Hughes in obtaining substitute launch services. Additionally, the damages do not include any lost revenues or profits, only increased costs. Finally, the damages are not consequential. The Uniform Commercial Code is instructive on this point. It allows recovery of the difference between the cost of cover and the contract price "together with any incidental and consequential damages," U.C.C. §2-712 (emphasis added), thereby distinguishing between consequential damages and the direct cost of cover. In sum, the Court of Federal Claims did not abuse its discretion by awarding Hughes damages for its increased costs incurred by obtaining substitute launch services for two HS-601s in addition to the three HS-393s.

Hughes decided to launch the JCSAT-1 satellite, a particular HS-393, on an ELV several months before President Reagan's announcement in 1986 that NASA would no longer launch commercial satellites on shuttles. NASA only breached its best efforts obligation after President Reagan's announcement. *Hughes III*, 34 Fed. Cl. at 630-34; *Hughes V*, 47 Fed. Cl. at 243. However, the LSA is not limited to launching particular satellites, such as the JCSAT-1. Rather, the LSA specifies a particular type of satellite (HS-393) in its preamble, and refers to the ten satellites as "HC-9 through HC-18." Thus, Hughes could have substituted another HS-393 for JCSAT-1, and Hughes still would have launched ten HS-393s on shuttles if NASA had provided those services under the LSA. Accordingly, the Court of Federal Claims did not abuse its discretion by awarding Hughes damages for the increased costs of launching the JCSAT-1.

III.

The Court of Federal Claims found that NASA could have launched five HS-393s during the LSA contract period using its best efforts. The Court of Federal Claims based this finding on the July 1986 manifest, but credited a report by Barrington Consulting Group that unexpected delays beyond NASA's control reduced the number of shuttle launches below the projections in the July 1986 manifest. *Hughes V,* 47 Fed. Cl. at 243. Under the priorities in the July 1986 manifest, the Barrington report concluded that NASA would have launched five HS-393 satellites.

If NASA had given commercial satellites priority over NASA satellites, Hughes asserts, NASA would have launched ten HS-393s. However, before President Reagan's statement, NASA did not elevate commercial launches above its other priorities. NASA did not breach its best efforts obligation before President Reagan's statement. The priorities before President Reagan's statement gave approximately equal priority to commercial and NASA payloads. As the Court of Federal Claims correctly reasoned, Hughes could not have reasonably expected NASA priorities to elevate commercial satellites above other goals for the remainder of the contract period.

Similarly, the LSA's best efforts requirement did not obligate NASA to use the 1984 policy announced in a House sub-committee hearing. In the event of shuttle scheduling conflicts, the 1984 policy gave commercial satellites priority over NASA research and development missions. Under this policy, Hughes asserts, NASA would have launched all ten HS-393s. The LSA itself specifically included a 1982 listing of priorities, but said nothing about the 1984 policy. Without the 1984 policy in the contract, the LSA did not incorporate those priorities into NASA's best efforts obligation.

The Court of Federal Claims also correctly found that circumstances prevented NASA from increasing its launch rates to include all ten HS-393s. In testimony to Congress in 1992, NASA asserted its ability to launch more shuttles than its budget allowed. According to Hughes, the Government chose to limit the number of launches by limiting NASA's budget. The record amply supports the trial court's finding that the post-Challenger investigation and technical problems prevented NASA from launching more shuttles. *Hughes V,* 47 Fed. Cl. at 242-43. The record shows that, in all years except 1994, the Government budgeted for more shuttle launches than NASA was able to launch. In 1994, the Government budgeted for eight launches and NASA actually launched eight. Thus, the Court of Federal Claims did not clearly err in finding that technical obstacles, rather than budget choices, prevented NASA from launching more shuttles during the LSA contract period.

Additionally, Mr. Kiraly, the Government's expert, estimated the number of HS-393s that NASA's best efforts could have launched at between one and six. The variance in this estimate does not undercut the Court of Federal Claims' finding. The Court of Federal Claims relied on the Barrington report, which specifically concluded that NASA's best efforts would have launched five HS-393s. Id. at 243. Thus, the Court of Federal Claims did not clearly err in finding that NASA's best efforts would have produced five HS-393 launches.

IV.

Because Hughes actually launched only three HS-393s, the Court of Federal Claims calculated the average costs of launching those three satellites on shuttles. Then, using the report of Hughes' expert, Mr. Hammer, the trial court applied that average to project the shuttle launch costs of the fourth and fifth satellites. Id. at 244. Hughes asserts that the Court of Federal Claims should have used the shuttle launch costs for each individual satellite shown in Mr. Hammer's report. However, the trial court's method is symmetrical with its calculation of the costs of ELV launches. For ELV launch costs, the trial court averaged the actual ELV launch costs for the three HS- 393s and applied that average to project the ELV launch costs of the fourth and fifth satellites. Id. at 244. Hughes does not disagree with the method of calculating ELV launch costs; the Court of Federal Claims merely did the same thing with the shuttle launch costs. The trial court reasonably exercised its discretion in using this symmetrical approach in calculating damages. . . .

IX.

The Government sought to reduce Hughes' damages by the amount Hughes recouped by increasing prices to customers, in other words, by the amount Hughes "passed through" to its customers. The Court of Federal Claims did not allow the Government to assert this defense at the damages trial. *Hughes IV*, 38 Fed. Cl. at 582. According to the Court of Federal Claims, this type of mitigation is too remote to consider. Id.

Although not in the breach of contract context, the Supreme Court has addressed this issue. In Southern Pacific Co. v. Darnell-Taenzer Lumber Co., 245 U.S. 531, 38 S. Ct. 186, 62 L. Ed. 451 (1918), a railroad overcharge case, the Court addressed the reduction of damages because the damaged party allegedly passed the unreasonable charge on to its customers. The Court stated: "The answer is not difficult. The general tendency of the law, in regard to damages at least, is not to go beyond the first step. As it does not attribute remote consequences to a defendant so it holds him liable if proximately the plaintiff has suffered a loss." Id. at 533-34, 38 S. Ct. 186. In an antitrust case, the Court noted that calculating pass-through damages reductions would present "the nearly insuperable difficulty of demonstrating that the particular plaintiff could not or would not have raised his prices absent the overcharge or maintained the higher price had the overcharge been discontinued." Hanover Shoe, Inc. v. United Shoe Mach. Corp., 392 U.S. 481, 493, 88 S. Ct. 2224, 20 L. Ed. 2d 1231 (1968). Similarly, allowing a pass-through damages reduction in a breach of contract action would destroy symmetry between reduction and escalation of damages. Moreover a standard for pass-through reductions would entail extremely difficult burdens for the trial court. Thus, the Supreme Court's reasoning also applies to this breach of contract action. The Court of Federal Claims did not abuse its discretion by disallowing pass-through damages reductions.

CONCLUSION

Because the Court of Federal Claims did not abuse its discretion in determining Hughes' damages for the Government's breach of the LSA, this court affirms.

Technically, a buyer does not have to cover. If a buyer fails to cover in an appropriate situation, however, consequential damages that could have been avoided are denied. See §2-715(2)(a). If a buyer decides to cover, the legal effect of the steps taken, as well as when cover should be effectuated, is measured against a standard of reasonableness in the given factual situation. Financial inability is an excuse for non-cover. See REB, Inc. v. Ralston Purina Co., 525 F.2d 749, 18 U.C.C. Rep. Serv. 122 (10th Cir. 1975). One practical test by which to gauge the reasonableness of the buyer's covering actions is to ask if the buyer would have made the same arrangements if there was no prospect of a successful suit against the breaching seller. See White & Summers §6-3, at 246.

If the buyer does not cover, damages may be measured under the next section, §2-713, a much criticized provision. See Childres, Buyer's

Remedies: The Danger of Section 2-713, 72 Nw. U. L. Rev. 83?
Read §2-713.

PROBLEM 76

The Student Bar Association (SBA) of the Gilberts Law School decided to hold a mammoth wine- and cheese-tasting party for the students, faculty, staff, and alumni. The SBA ordered the wine from Classy Caterers. They agreed to pay $1,000 for it, the wine to be delivered on March 30, the day of the party. Classy Caterers ordered the wine from Grapes Vineyards in California, "F.O.B. San Francisco" for $750, but Grapes Vineyards went bankrupt on March 25. Classy Caterers was able to find identical wine in its own city for $750, and it bought the wine on March 25 for that amount. On March 25, the price of similar wine in San Francisco was $900. The cost of transporting the wine from San Francisco to the site of the party would have been $100. The SBA paid Classy Caterers $1,000 for the wine. Classy Caterers filed claims for damages in the bankruptcy proceeding of its defaulting supplier.

(a) Compute the damages due Classy for the failure to deliver the wine under §2-712. Now do it under §2-713. See Official Comment 5 to §2-713; White & Summers §6-4.

(b) What role does the $100 transportation cost play in computing damages? Note the definition of "market place" in §2-723.

Tongish v. Thomas

Kansas Court of Appeals, 1992
16 Kan. App. 2d 809, 829 P.2d 916, 18 U.C.C. Rep. Serv. 2d 161,
aff'd on opinion below, 251 Kan. 728, 840 P.2d 471, 20 U.C.C.
Rep. Serv. 2d 936

WALTON, J., assigned. The Decatur Coop Association (Coop) (third-party intervenor/appellant) appeals a breach of contract damages award it received from Denis Tongish (plaintiff/appellee), alleging damages should have been the difference between the market price of sunflower seeds and the contract price under K.S.A. 84-2-713. We agree that the trial court applied the wrong measure of damages. We reverse the damages award and remand with directions that the trial court determine the damages under K.S.A. 84-2-713.

On April 28, 1988, Coop contracted with Denis Tongish to purchase all the sunflower seeds grown by him. The contract required Tongish to plant 160 acres of sunflower seeds but was later reduced to 116.8 acres. The seeds were to be delivered one-third by December 31, 1988, one-third by March 31, 1989, and one-third by May 31, 1989. The price for the seeds was $13 per hundred pounds for large seeds and $8 per hundred pounds for small seeds.

Coop also contracted with Bambino Bean & Seed, Inc., to sell it all the sunflower seeds Coop purchased from the farmers. Bambino paid Coop the same price Coop paid the farmers.

Coop retained a $.55 per hundred pounds handling charge for the seeds it received from the farmers and then delivered the seeds to Bambino. Therefore, Coop had no risk on fluctuating market prices in its contract with Tongish. The only profit anticipated by Coop was the handling fees for the seeds.

In October and November, Tongish delivered sunflower seeds to Coop as the contract required. In January, a disagreement occurred between Tongish and Coop over the amount of dockage[5] found in the seeds Tongish delivered. Coop readjusted the amount and paid Tongish an extra $222.33.

By January the market price of sunflower seeds had doubled from the Tongish-Coop contract price. On or about January 13, 1989, Tongish informed Coop that he was not going to honor the contract. In May 1989, Tongish delivered 82,820 pounds of sunflower seeds to Danny Thomas for a price of $14,714.89. After dockage, the price was about $20 per hundred pounds. Tongish testified that if he sold all of these seeds to Coop under the contract price for large seeds, he would receive about $9,561.76. Therefore, Tongish would receive $5,153.13 more from Danny Thomas than he would by performing under the contract with Coop.

Tongish filed a petition against Danny Thomas to collect the balance due from their sunflower seed sale. Thomas paid $7,359.61 into the court and was later dismissed as a party. Coop intervened as a third-party defendant. Coop alleged that Tongish breached their contract and it was entitled to damages.

A trial was held on May 14, 1991. The trial court found that Tongish had breached the contract and there was no basis for that breach. The court also determined that Coop was entitled to damages in the amount of $455.51, the expected profit for handling charges in the transaction. Coop timely appealed.

---

5. [*Dockage* means the removable waste material in grains. —Ed.]

The trial court decided the damages to Coop should be the loss of expected profits. Coop argues that K.S.A. 84-2-713 entitles it to collect as damages the difference between the market price and the contract price. Tongish argues that the trial court was correct and cites K.S.A. 84-1-106 as support for the contention that a party should be placed in as good a position as it would be in had the other party performed. Therefore, the only disagreement is how the damages should be calculated.

The measure of damages in this action involves two sections of the Uniform Commercial Code: K.S.A. 84-1-106 and K.S.A. 84-2-713. The issue to be determined is which statute governs the measure of damages. Stated in another way, if the statutes are in conflict, which statute should prevail? The answer involves an ongoing academic discussion of two contending positions. The issues in this case disclose the problem.

If Tongish had not breached the contract, he may have received under the contract terms with Coop about $5,153.13 less than he received from Danny Thomas. Coop in turn had an oral contract with Bambino to sell whatever seeds it received from Tongish to Bambino for the same price Coop paid for them. Therefore, if the contract had been performed, Coop would not have actually received the extra $5,153.13.

We first turn our attention to the conflicting statutes and the applicable rules of statutory construction. K.S.A. 84-1-106(1) states:

> The remedies provided by this act shall be liberally administered to the end that the aggrieved party may be put in as good a position as if the other party had fully performed but neither consequential or special nor penal damages may be had except as specifically provided in this act or by other rule of law.

If a seller breaches a contract and the buyer does not "cover," the buyer is free to pursue other available remedies. K.S.A. 84-2-711 and 84-2-712. One remedy, which is a complete alternative to "cover" (K.S.A. 84-2-713, Official comment, ¶5), is K.S.A. 84-2-713(1), which provides:

> Subject to the provisions of this article with respect to proof of market price (section 84-2-723), the measure of damages for nondelivery or repudiation by the seller is the difference between the market price at the time when the buyer learned of the breach and the contract price together with any incidental and consequential damages provided in this

article (section 84-2-715), but less expenses saved in consequence of the seller's breach. . . .

The statutes do contain conflicting provisions. On the one hand, K.S.A. 84-1-106 offers a general guide of how remedies of the UCC should be applied, whereas K.S.A. 84-2-713 specifically describes a damage remedy that gives the buyer certain damages when the seller breaches a contract for the sale of goods.

The cardinal rule of statutory construction, to which all others are subordinate, is that the purpose and intent of the legislature governs. [Citations omitted.] When there is a conflict between a statute dealing generally with a subject and another statute dealing specifically with a certain phase of it, the specific statute controls unless it appears that the legislature intended to make the general act controlling. State v. Wilcox, 245 Kan. 76, Syl. ¶1, 775 P.2d 177 (1989). The Kansas Supreme Court stated in Kansas Racing Management, Inc. v. Kansas Racing Commn., 244 Kan. 343, 353, 770 P.2d 423 (1989): "General and special statutes should be read together and harmonized whenever possible, but to the extent a conflict between them exists, the special statute will prevail unless it appears the legislature intended to make the general statute controlling."

K.S.A. 84-2-713 allows the buyer to collect the difference in market price and contract price for damages in a breached contract. For that reason, it seems impossible to reconcile the decision of the district court that limits damages to lost profits with this statute.

Therefore, because it appears impractical to make K.S.A. 84-1-106 and K.S.A. 84-2-713 harmonize in this factual situation, K.S.A. 84-2-713 should prevail as the more specific statute according to statutory rules of construction.

As stated, however, Coop protected itself against market price fluctuations through its contract with Bambino. Other than the minimal handling charge, Coop suffered no lost profits from the breach. Should the protection require an exception to the general rule under K.S.A. 84-2-713? . . .

There is authority for appellee's position that K.S.A. 84-2-713 should not be applied in certain circumstances. In Allied Canners & Packers, Inc. v. Victor Packing Co., 162 Cal. App. 3d 905, 209 Cal. Rptr. 60, 61 (1984), Allied contracted to purchase 375,000 pounds of raisins from Victor for 29.75 cents per pound with a 4% discount. Allied then contracted to sell the raisins for 29.75 cents per pound expecting a profit of $4,462.50 from the 4% discount it received from Victor. 162 Cal. App. 3d at 907-908, 209 Cal. Rptr. 60.

Heavy rains damaged the raisin crop and Victor breached its contract, being unable to fulfill the requirement. The market price of raisins had risen to about 80 cents per pound. Allied's buyers agreed to rescind their contracts so Allied was not bound to supply them with raisins at a severe loss. Therefore, the actual loss to Allied was the $4,462.50 profit it expected, while the difference between the market price and the contract price was about $150,000. 162 Cal. App. 3d at 908-909, 209 Cal. Rptr. 60.

The California appellate court, in writing an exception, stated: "It has been recognized that the use of the market-price contract-price formula under §2-713 does not, absent pure accident, result in a damage award reflecting the buyer's actual loss. [Citations omitted.]" 162 Cal. App. 3d at 912, 209 Cal. Rptr. 60. The court indicated that §2-713 may be more of a statutory liquidated damages clause and, therefore, conflicts with the goal of §1-106. The court discussed that in situations where the buyer has made a resale contract for the goods, which the seller knows about, it may be appropriate to limit §2-713 damages to actual loss. However, the court cited a concern that a seller not be rewarded for a bad faith breach of contract. 162 Cal. App. 3d at 912-914, 209 Cal. Rptr. 60.

In *Allied,* the court determined that if the seller knew the buyer had a resale contract for the goods, and the seller did not breach the contract in bad faith, the buyer was limited to actual loss of damages under §1-106. 162 Cal. App. 3d at 915, 209 Cal. Rptr. 60.

The similarities between the present case and *Allied* are that the buyer made a resale contract which the seller knew about. (Tongish knew the seeds eventually went to Bambino, although he may not have known the details of the deal). However, in examining the breach itself, Victor could not deliver the raisins because its crop had been destroyed. Tongish testified that he breached the contract because he was dissatisfied with dockage tests of Coop and/or Bambino. Victor had no raisins to sell to any buyer, while Tongish took advantage of the doubling price of sunflower seeds and sold to Danny Thomas. Although the trial court had no need to find whether Tongish breached the contract in bad faith, it did find there was no valid reason for the breach. Therefore, the nature of Tongish's breach was much different than Victor's in *Allied.*

Section 2-713 and the theories behind it have a lengthy and somewhat controversial history. In 1963, it was suggested that §2-713 was a statutory liquidated damages clause and not really an effort to try and accurately predict what actual damages would be. Peters, Remedies for Breach of Contracts Relating to the Sale of Goods Under the Uniform Commercial Code: A Roadmap for Article Two, 73 Yale L.J. 199, 259 (1963).

In 1978, Robert Childres called for the repeal of §2-713. Childres, Buyer's Remedies: The Danger of Section 2-713, 72 Nw. U. L. Rev. 837 (1978). Childres reflected that because the market price/contract price remedy "has been the cornerstone of Anglo-American damages" that it has been so hard to see that this remedy "makes no sense whatever when applied to real life situations." 72 Nw. U. L. Rev. at 841-842.

In 1979, David Simon and Gerald A. Novack wrote a fairly objective analysis of the two arguments about §2-713 and stated:

> For over sixty years our courts have divided on the question of which measure of damages is appropriate for the supplier's breach of his delivery obligations. The majority view, reinforced by applicable codes, would award market damages even though in excess of plaintiff's loss. A persistent minority would reduce market damages to the plaintiff's loss, without regard to whether this creates a windfall for the defendant. Strangely enough, each view has generally tended to disregard the arguments, and even the existence, of the opposing view.

Simon and Novack, Limiting the Buyer's Market Damages to Lost Profits: A Challenge to the Enforceability of Market Contracts, 92 Harv. L. Rev. 1395, 1397 (1979).

Although the article discussed both sides of the issue, the authors came down on the side of market price/contract price as the preferred damages theory. The authors admit that market damages fly in the face "of the familiar maxim that the purpose of contract damages is to make the injured party whole, not penalize the breaching party." 92 Harv. L. Rev. at 1437. However, they argue that the market damages rule discourages the breach of contracts and encourages a more efficient market. 92 Harv. L. Rev. at 1437.

The *Allied* decision in 1984, which relied on the articles cited above for its analysis to reject market price/contract price damages, has been sharply criticized. In Schneider, UCC Section 2-713: A Defense of Buyers' Expectancy Damages, 22 Cal. W. L. Rev. 233, 266 (1986), the author stated that Allied "adopted the most restrictive [position] on buyer's damages. This Article is intended to reverse that trend." Schneider argued that by following §1-106, "the court ignored the clear language of §2-713's compensation scheme to award expectation damages in accordance with the parties' price allocation of risk as measured by the difference between contract price and market price on the date set for performance." 22 Cal. W. L. Rev. at 264.

Recently in Scott, The Case for Market Damages: Revisiting the Lost Profits Puzzle, 57 U. Chi. L. Rev. 1155, 1200 (1990), the *Allied* result was called "unfortunate." Scott argues that section 1-106 is "entirely consistent" with the market damages remedy of 2-713. 57 U. Chi. L. Rev. at 1201. According to Scott, it is possible to harmonize sections 1-106 and 2-713. Scott states, "Market damages measure the expectancy ex ante, and thus reflect the value of the option; lost profits, on the other hand, measure losses ex post, and thus only reflect the value of the completed exchange." 57 U. Chi. L. Rev. at 1174. The author argues that if the nonbreaching party has laid off part of the market risk (like Coop did) the lost profits rule creates instability because the other party is now encouraged to breach the contract if the market fluctuates to its advantage. 57 U. Chi. L. Rev. at 1178.

We are not persuaded that the lost profits view under Allied should be embraced. It is a minority rule that has received only nominal support. We believe the majority rule or the market damages remedy as contained in K.S.A. 84-2-713 is more reasoned and should be followed as the preferred measure of damages. While application of the rule may not reflect the actual loss to a buyer, it encourages a more efficient market and discourages the breach of contracts.

The majority rule further permits the parties to measure the expectancy of what might happen if the seller does not perform the contract. The buyer has an option at the beginning of the contract to take actions to protect against an uncertain future. The parties both know that the option is an election that can be exercised by the buyer to protect against future losses. This generates stability in the market by discouraging the seller from breaching the contract when the market fluctuates to his advantage. The rule is further in accord with the rule of statutory construction that a specific statute shall prevail over a conflicting general statute dealing with the same subject matter unless the legislature intended to make the general statute control.

For the reasons stated, we hold that the provisions of K.S.A. 84-2-713 provide the proper measure of damages in this case. We reject the holding in *Allied* that the provisions of §2-713 of the Uniform Commercial Code (K.S.A. 84-2-713) are more of a statutory liquidated damages clause that conflicts with the goal of §1-106 of the U.C.C. (K.S.A. 84-1-106) to mandate the creation of an exception when a buyer protects itself from market price fluctuations through a contract with another.

The damage award is reversed and the case is remanded with directions that the trial court determine and award damages pursuant to the provisions of K.S.A. 84-2-713.

In affirming the above opinion, which it adopted, the Kansas Supreme Court added this paragraph:

> At first blush, the result reached herein appears unfair. However, closer scrutiny dissipates this impression. By the terms of the contract Coop was obligated to buy Tongish's large sunflower seeds at $13 per hundredweight whether or not it had a market for them. Had the price of sunflower seeds plummeted by delivery time, Coop's obligation to purchase at the agreed price was fixed. If loss of actual profit pursuant to K.S.A. 84-1-106(1) would be the measure of damages to be applied herein, it would enable Tongish to consider the Coop contract price of $13 per hundredweight plus 55 cents per hundredweight handling fee as the "floor" price for his seeds, take advantage of rapidly escalating prices, ignore his contractual obligation, and profitably sell to the highest bidder. Damages computed under K.S.A. 84-2-713 encourage honoring of contracts and market stability.

The damages provisions in the CISG for the international sale of goods are modeled after the similar provisions of the UCC and should look reassuringly familiar to you. Read Articles 74 to 78. There are some new words that the treaty has to teach American ears. One is the concept of "fundamental breach," an idea that comes from the civil law. Read Articles 46(2) and 25. Fundamental breach is roughly equivalent to "material breach" (the opposite of "substantial performance.") The Restatement (Second) of Contracts §241 states:

> *Section 241.   Circumstances Significant in Determining*
> *Whether a Failure is Material*
> In determining whether a failure to render or to offer performance is material, the following circumstances are significant:
>   (a) the extent to which the injured party will be deprived of the benefit which he reasonably expected;
>   (b) the extent to which the injured party can be adequately compensated for the part of that benefit of which he will be deprived;
>   (c) the extent to which the party failing to perform or to offer to perform will suffer forfeiture;
>   (d) the likelihood that the party failing to perform or to offer to perform will cure his failure, taking account of all the circumstances including any reasonable assurances;
>   (e) the extent to which the behavior of the party failing to perform or to offer to perform comports with standards of good faith and fair dealing.

Another new concept is *Nachfrist* (German for "extension"). It is illustrated in the following Problem.

PROBLEM 77

Experimental Transportation, Inc., of Los Angeles designed an all-terrain vehicle for rugged hill country travel (called the "Clod Jumper") and agreed to sell one for $30,000 to Dingo Ranch of Australia. Neither party was willing to be bound by the laws of the other's country, so they agreed to adopt the law of the CISG. Experimental Transportation was supposed to deliver the Clod Jumper by December 1, but it had problems with Customs and that date came and went with no activity. Dingo Ranch sent a letter to Experimental Transportation proposing that the date of delivery be moved to February 1. Having sent such a letter, is it now bound to wait until that date before suing? See Article 47. Is it bound to wait even if Experimental Transportation's reply is "Go to hell!"? What if instead of the buyer proposing the *Nachfrist*, the seller, Experimental Transportation, is the one to propose a grace period? Can this be done? Compare Articles 48 and 63. If the machine is delivered and then fails to work, can Dingo Ranch force Experimental Transportation to fix it? See Article 46(3). Is this remedy available in American law? See Uniform Commercial Code §2-716.

The treaty has a strong presumption in favor of specific performance. See Articles 46 and 62. However, Article 28 does not require specific performance if the court that would be asked to grant it would not do so if its own law applied. For example, in the United States there are major limits on equitable remedies (there must be no adequate remedy at law—i.e., damages; the court must not become involved in undue supervision of the resulting performance; etc.), and an American court might use these rules to duck an order for specific performance.

IV. ANTICIPATORY REPUDIATION

Ever since the classic case of Hochster v. De La Tour, 2 El. & Bl. 678, 118 Eng. Rep. 922 (Q.B. 1853), it has been settled that if one party to a contract makes a definite repudiation of the contract before the date set for performance, the other party could treat the repudiation as a breach and sue immediately. But the common law also permitted the innocent party to ignore the repudiation and await the performance date to see if the repudiator would retract the repudiation. As long as the innocent party had not changed position in reliance on the repudiation (say, by covering), the repudiator was free to retract the repudiation, reinstate the contract, and perform as originally agreed.

To what extent has the Code changed these common law rules? Read §§2-610 and 2-611. These sections do not define *repudiation*, which is, of course, their triggering event. A repudiation must be a definite refusal to perform; mere equivocation is not enough. See Official Comment 1 to §2-610; Nordstrom §149, at 451-453; White & Summers §6-2; Copylease Corp. of Am. v. Memorex Corp., 403 F. Supp. 625, 18 U.C.C. Rep. Serv. 317 (S.D.N.Y. 1975). The equivocating party can be forced into performance or repudiation by use of the procedure outlined in §2-609 (Right to Adequate Assurance of Performance).

Unfortunately, in the process of drafting the Code's damages sections, the drafters became careless when dealing with the time for measuring damages in an anticipatory repudiation situation, and the UCC sections simply do not fit together. Both major treatises I have been citing have splendid discussions of the problem and suggest resolutions. Those discussions will not be repeated here, but you are urged to look at White & Summers §6-7 and Nordstrom §149. The following Problem should help you see the difficulty with these sections.

PROBLEM 78

The United States Army contracted with the Hawaiian Cattle Company for the purchase of 1,000 pounds of beef. Delivery was set six months later, on October 8, the agreed price to be $5,000. Shortly thereafter, the price of beef rose sharply, and Hawaiian Cattle repudiated the contract on July 10, when the price was $6,000. The Army's procurement officer scrambled around and on July 15 discovered it was possible to cover by buying similar cattle from Texas at a cost of $7,000. Instead, the Army sent Hawaiian Cattle a telegram stating that it did not accept or recognize the repudiation and expected performance on October 8. By October 8 the price had risen to $8,000. The Army decided not to cover at all and instead served the troops beans. As general counsel for the Army, advise the Army of the amount it can recover from Hawaiian Cattle. Read §§2-610, 2-713, and 2-723(1). Does it help reconcile these sections to know that the drafters of §2-713 were thinking of a buyer who learns of the repudiation *after* the date set for the original performance, not (as in this Problem) before the due date?

V. THE STATUTE OF LIMITATIONS

The Code drafters decided that it was important to have a uniform statute of limitations for transactions in goods, and they chose four years "as the most appropriate to modern business practice. This is within the normal commercial record keeping period." Official Comment to §2-725. Read §2-725, and note that the four-year period begins to run at the *accrual* of the cause of action (the moment a suit could be brought). The parties may reduce the period by agreement down to one year, but they may not extend it beyond four. One court has decided that an agreement so reducing the limitation period need not be conspicuous to be enforced. Jandreau v. Sheesley Plumbing & Heating Co., 324 N.W.2d 266, 34 U.C.C. Rep. Serv. 785 (S.D. 1982). In most jurisdictions the statute of limitations is an affirmative defense and is waived if not pleaded and proved. See, e.g., Mysel v. Gross, 70 Cal. App. 3d 10, 138 Cal. Rptr. 873, 21 U.C.C. Rep. Serv. 1338 (1977).

PROBLEM 79

Four years and two days after delivery of his new car, Joe Cloudburst came out of his house to discover he had a flat tire. He changed it and, for the first time, put on the spare tire. That afternoon as he was driving on the interstate, the tire burst due to a manufacturing flaw. Joe was killed. Has the statute of limitations run under these situations?

(a) The tire warranty read: "These tires are merchantable." If this were a lease of goods, would Article 2A reach a different result? See §2A-506.

(b) The tire warranty read: "These tires have a lifetime guarantee." See Annot., 93 A.L.R.3d 690.

(c) The sales material said with regard to the tires: "Many tires are still on the road after five years." See Jones & Laughlin Steel Corp. v. Johns-Manville Sales Corp. v. Brown & Kerr, Inc., 460 F.2d 276, 29 U.C.C. Rep. Serv. 1184 (3d Cir. 1980) (a statement of future performance is "explicit" if it does not arise by implication, but is instead "distinctly stated; plain in language; clear; not ambiguous; express; unequivocal").

(d) The tire warranty read: "These tires are warranted for seven years from date of purchase." If a tire first malfunctioned at the beginning of the third year, when would the statute of limitations expire? See Joswick v. Chesapeake Mobile Homes, Inc., 765 A.2d 90, 43 U.C.C. Rep. Serv. 2d 479 (Md. 2001).

(e) There were no express warranties given with regard to the tires; there were also no warranty disclaimers. See Note, When Does the Statute of Limitations Begin to Run on Breaches of Implied Warranties?, 30 Baylor L. Rev. 386 (1978).

Poli v. DaimlerChrysler Corp.

Superior Court of New Jersey, 2002
349 N.J. Super. 169, 793 A.2d 104, 47 U.C.C. Rep. Serv. 2d 260

SKILLMAN, P.J.A.D.

The primary issue presented by this appeal is whether a cause of action for breach of a seller's agreement to repair any product defect that occurs during a warranty period accrues upon delivery of the product or only after the seller fails to perform the agreed repairs. We conclude that such a cause of action does not accrue until the seller fails to perform the required repair within a reasonable period of time. We reach the same conclusion with respect to a warranty claim under the Magnuson-Moss Warranty Act.

On March 23, 1993, plaintiff purchased a new 1992 Dodge Spirit manufactured by defendant DaimlerChrysler Corporation. When he made this purchase, plaintiff elected to obtain a seven-year, seventy-thousand-mile "powertrain" warranty from defendant.

Plaintiff's claims arise out of a series of repairs and replacements of the "engine timing belt," which was one of the parts covered by the powertrain warranty. On December 16, 1993, after the car had been driven 16,408 miles, plaintiff had the timing belt replaced. More than three years later, on March 21, 1997, after the car had been driven 36,149 miles, plaintiff had the belt repaired. Plaintiff then had to have the belt replaced on May 16, 1997, January 5, 1998 and July 6, 1998. According to plaintiff, the timing belt again failed on July 31, 1998, causing the destruction of the "short block" of the engine, which the dealer took six months to repair. All of these timing belt repairs and replacements were purportedly performed by defendant in accordance with the seven-year, seventy-thousand-mile powertrain warranty obtained by plaintiff when he purchased the car.

On December 15, 1998, plaintiff brought this action against defendant for breach of the seven-year, seventy-thousand-mile power-train warranty. Plaintiff also asserted claims under the Lemon Law, N.J.S.A. 56:12-29 to - 49, the Magnuson-Moss Warranty Act, 15 U.S.C.A. §§2301-2312, and the Consumer Fraud Act, N.J.S.A. 56:8-1 to -106.

Defendant moved for summary judgment on the ground that plaintiff's complaint and supporting exhibits did not state a claim under the Lemon Law and that plaintiff's other claims were barred by the statute of limitations. In his response, plaintiff indicated that he was not pursuing his claim under the Consumer Fraud Act.

The trial court granted defendant's motion as to plaintiff's other claims and dismissed the complaint. The court held that plaintiff's claim under the Lemon Law was barred because he had not given defendant notice and an opportunity to correct the alleged defect within the first 18,000 miles of operation. The court dismissed plaintiff's warranty and Magnuson-Moss Act claims as untimely because they were not brought within four years after delivery of the car. The court rejected plaintiff's argument that his warranty and Magnuson-Moss claims were timely because the seven-year, seventy-thousand-mile powertrain warranty was "a guarantee of performance" which defendant breached by failing to properly repair the timing belt.

Plaintiff appeals. We affirm the dismissal of plaintiff's Lemon Law claim, but reverse the dismissal of his warranty and Magnuson-Moss Act claims. . . .

We turn next to the trial court's conclusion that plaintiff's claim for breach of defendant's seven-year, seventy-thousand-mile powertrain warranty was not filed within the four-year limitation period established by the Uniform Commercial Code (UCC) for breach of warranty claims. The powertrain warranty applies to all "parts, assemblies and components that together provide the power to [the] car." During the term of this warranty, which is "7 years or 70,000 miles, whichever occurs first, counted from the vehicle's Warranty Start Date," defendant is obligated to "cover [ ] the cost of all parts and labor needed to repair or adjust any Chrysler supplied item . . . that proves defective in material, workmanship or factory preparation."[6] Defendant acknowledges that the engine timing belt is covered by this warranty.

6. Although the warranty states that defendant is obligated "to cover [ ] the cost of all parts and labor needed to repair" the vehicle, it also states "[e]xcept in emergencies, you MUST bring your vehicle to an authorized Chrysler Dealer for warranty

The limitations period under the UCC for an action for breach of a sales contract is "four years after the cause of action has accrued." N.J.S.A. 12A:2-725(1). The UCC further provides that "[a] cause of action accrues when the breach occurs, regardless of the aggrieved party's lack of knowledge of the breach[,]" and that "[a] breach of warranty occurs when tender of delivery is made[.]" N.J.S.A. 12A:2-725(2). However, the UCC provides an exception to this general rule if "a warranty explicitly extends to future performance of the goods and discovery of the breach must await the time of such performance[.]" Ibid. If a seller has provided this form of warranty, "the cause of action accrues when the breach is or should have been discovered." Ibid.

Defendant contends that the powertrain warranty given to plaintiff was an ordinary sales warranty, and that plaintiff therefore had only four years after the delivery of the car on March 23, 1993, to bring an action for any breach of the warranty. If this view of the powertrain warranty were correct, plaintiff's claim for breach of the warranty would be time barred because he did not file this action until December 15, 1998, which was more than four years after delivery of the car. On the other hand, plaintiff contends that the powertrain warranty was a warranty of future performance, which defendant did not breach until 1998, when it failed to properly repair the timing belt, thus causing plaintiff recurrent problems with the operation of the car. Under this view of the warranty, plaintiff's action was filed well within the four-year period allowed under N.J.S.A. 2A:2-725(1).

In Docteroff v. Barra Corp. of Am., Inc., 282 N.J. Super. 230, 241-43, 659 A.2d 948 (App. Div. 1995), we held that a "guarantee" by a seller of roofing materials that it would "maintain the roof . . . [i]n a watertight condition . . . for (5) five years[,]" and would repair or replace any defects that arose during that period, constituted a promise of future performance, and that the four-year UCC statute of limitations did not begin to run until the seller's breach was or should have been discovered. In reaching this conclusion, we noted that a seller's agreement to repair or replace defects in parts that become evident during a specified period "fit[s] within the modern concept of warranty." Id. at 242, 659 A.2d 948 (quoting Nationwide Ins. Co. v. General Motors Corp., 533 Pa. 423, 625 A.2d 1172, 1177 (1993)).[7] We

---

services and repairs." Therefore, as a practical matter, defendant's obligation to cover the costs of repair is generally an obligation to perform the repairs.

7. Compare Spring Motors Distribs., Inc. v. Ford Motor Co., 191 N.J. Super. 22, 47, 465 A.2d 530 (App. Div. 1983) (holding that "the words 'your vehicle has been designed to give long reliable service with the simplest and least costly maintenance requirements possible' do not make any explicit guarantee as to the vehicle's perfor-

also noted that "[s]uch a warranty . . . 'cannot be characterized as a mere representation of the product's condition at the time of delivery rather than its performance at a future time.'" Ibid. (quoting Commissioners of Fire Dist. No. 9 v. American La France, 176 N.J. Super. 566, 573, 424 A.2d 441 (App. Div. 1980)).

The seven-year, seventy-thousand-mile warranty that defendant gave plaintiff was similar to the warranty involved in *Docteroff.* Although defendant did not describe the warranty as a "guarantee" of future performance, it was not "a mere representation of the [car's] condition at the time of delivery" but rather a promise relating to "its performance at a future time [,]" 282 N.J. Super. at 242, 659 A.2d 948, that is, as in *Docteroff,* an enforceable agreement that if a covered defect arose at any time during the period of the warranty, defendant would repair that condition. Therefore, we conclude that a claim for breach of this warranty did not accrue at the time of delivery of the car but rather when defendant allegedly breached its duty to repair the defect.

The correctness of this conclusion is clearest in a case such as this, where the term of the warranty is longer than the four-year limitations period provided in N.J.S.A. 12A:2-725(1). If we adopted defendant's view that its powertrain warranty is an ordinary sales warranty, and consequently that a buyer must bring an action for breach of that warranty within four years of delivery, this would mean that the buyer would be unable to enforce defendant's warranty obligations for any breach that occurred beyond or even near the end of that four-year period, even though by its terms the warranty extends for as long as seven years. We are unwilling to construe N.J.S.A. 12A:2- 725(2) in a way that could lead to such an unreasonable result. See State v. Gill, 47 N.J. 441, 444, 221 A.2d 521 (1966).

This conclusion is also supported by decisions in other jurisdictions. In Nationwide Ins. Co. v. General Motors Corp., supra, the Pennsylvania Supreme Court held that a "12 month/12,000 mile 'New Car Limited Warranty' promising 'repairs and needed adjustments' to correct manufacturing defects is a warranty that 'explicitly extends to future performance of the goods' for purposes of determining when a cause of action for breach of that warranty accrues" under section 2-725(2) of the UCC:

> [W]e do not read the words "explicitly extends to future performance of the vehicle" to require that the warranty make an explicit promise regarding how the goods will perform in the future. We believe that the

mance over or after a stated period of time"), *rev'd on unrelated grounds,* 98 N.J. 555, 489 A.2d 660 (1985).

focus of §2725 is not on what is promised, but on the duration of the promise—i.e., the period to which the promise extends. . . . Therefore, we agree with Appellant that the phrase "explicitly extends to future performance" can be interpreted to include a promise that, by its terms, comes into play upon, or is contingent upon, the future performance of the goods. . . . Logically, a promise to repair or adjust defective parts within the first 12 months or 12,000 miles after delivery cannot be breached until the vehicle requires repair or adjustment, and "discovery of the breach must await the time of [future] performance." . . .

Furthermore, we will not permit [General Motors] and other sellers who draft similar documents to escape the consequences of presenting them to the consumer as "extended warranties." There can be little question that the consumer will consider the length of any warranty offered in determining whether to purchase a particular vehicle: The consumer naturally would believe that the longer the warranty, the greater the protection, and hence, the better the value, he or she is receiving. If [General Motors] position were to prevail, the protection afforded the buyer during the latter part of a warranty approaching four years would be largely illusory, as the buyer would have a very short period of time in which to bring a cause of action for breach. Moreover, the longer-term protection afforded by a warranty extending beyond four years would be completely illusory.

[625 A.2d at 1173, 1176-78 (citations omitted).]

See also Wienberg v. Independence Lincoln-Mercury, Inc., 948 S.W.2d 685, 690 (Mo. Ct. App. 1997) ("[W]here a warranty expressly extends to future performance of the goods, repair or replacement language does not necessarily nullify the future performance warranty."); Krieger v. Nick Alexander Imports, Inc., 234 Cal. App. 3d 205, 285 Cal. Rptr. 717, 724 (1991) ("A promise to repair defects that occur during a future period is the very definition of express warranty of future performance[.]").

There are other jurisdictions which hold that the kind of repair warranty involved in this case is not "a warranty [that] explicitly extends to future performance of the goods," N.J.S.A. 12A:2-725(2), but that a cause of action for breach of such a warranty does not accrue upon delivery because "the promise to repair is an independent obligation that is not breached until the seller fails to repair." Cosman v. Ford Motor Co., 285 Ill. App. 3d 250, 220 Ill. Dec. 790, 674 N.E.2d 61, 68 (1996), *appeal denied*, 172 Ill. 2d 549, 223 Ill. Dec. 194, 679 N.E.2d 379 (1997); see also Versico, Inc. v. Engineered Fabrics Corp., 238 Ga. App. 837, 520 S.E.2d 505, 509-10, *cert. denied* (Ga. 1999); Nationwide Ins. Co. v. General Motors Corp., supra, 625 A.2d at 1179-81 (Zappala, J., dissenting). The rationale for this view is that [such a] warranty does not promise a level of performance. It warrants only that the dealer will repair, replace, or adjust defects if parts of the powertrain in fact do malfunction. It does not warrant the quality of the powertrain or its performance. . . . A promise to repair parts of the powertrain for six years is a promise that the manufacturer will behave in a certain way, not a warranty that the vehicle will behave in a certain way. . . .

It does not fit within the definition of warranty under the Commercial Code. Although it is a warranty made as part of the sale of the goods in the sense that it promises something associated with the sale, it does not "warrant" the quality of the vehicle or its performance.

[*Cosman*, supra, 674 N.E.2d at 66-67.]

This is also the view taken of some scholarly commentaries. For example, Anderson on the Uniform Commercial Code states:

A warranty of future performance differs from a covenant to repair or replace. The future performance warranty expressly provides some form of guaranty that the product will perform as required during the specified time. The obligation to repair or replace merely imposes a duty to repair or replace when a defect exists within the required period of time. . . . .

Although . . . courts [that treat a covenant to repair or replace as a warranty of future performance] are sound in their conclusion that the statute of limitations should not commence until the seller has breached its promise to repair or replace the goods or any defective parts, it makes more sense to view the seller's failure to do so as a breach of contract, rather than as a breach of warranty. By so doing, the buyer's cause of action does not arise until the seller has refused to repair or replace the goods rather than upon the tender of delivery.

[Lary Lawrence, Lawrence's Anderson on the Uniform Commercial Code §2-725:129 at 332-33 (3d ed. 2001).]

Moreover, this is the view the National Conference of Commissioners on Uniform State Laws has taken in a draft revision of the UCC, which treats a "promise by the seller to repair or replace the goods or to refund all or part of the purchase price upon the happening of a specified event" as a "remedial promise." Amendments to Uniform Commercial Code, Article 2—Sales (Annual Meeting 2001 Draft) §2-103(1)(m). Under this proposed revision, a promise by a seller to repair or replace a defective part during a specified warranty period "is not a warranty at all and therefore is not subject to either the time of tender [rule of 725(1)] or [the] discovery rule [of 725(2)]." Amendments to Uniform Commercial Code, supra, preliminary comment to §2-103(1)(m). Instead, a cause of action for breach of a remedial promise would accrue "when the remedial promise is not performed when due." Amendments to Uniform Commercial Code, supra, §2-725(2)(c).

We have no need to decide whether defendant's seven-year/ seventy-thousand-mile powertrain warranty constituted a warranty of future performance within the intent of N.J.S.A. 12A:2-725(2) or an independent promise to repair defects in the powertrain that appear during the term of the warranty because, under either view, plaintiff's cause of action would not have accrued when the car was delivered in 1993 but rather when persistent problems in the engine timing belt appeared in 1997 or when defendant was allegedly unable to repair this defect in a timely manner in July 1998, and thus plaintiff's complaint was timely filed in December 1998.

III

The Magnuson-Moss Warranty Act (the Act) does not require any consumer product to be warranted. 15 U.S.C.A. §2302(b)(1)(B)(2). However, if a manufacturer or other supplier warrants a product, the Act imposes specific obligations on the warrantor, which include compliance with minimum federal standards for warranties. 15 U.S.C.A. §2304(a). If a warrantor violates any of those obligations, a buyer may bring an action in federal or state court for damages and equitable relief. 15 U.S.C.A. §2310(d).

The Act does not contain any express limitations period for actions brought under its provisions. Where a federal statute creates a cause of action, but does not establish a limitations period for that action, the courts will apply the state statute of limitations governing the state cause of action most closely analogous to the federal action. DelCostello v. International Bhd. of Teamsters, 462 U.S. 151, 158-60, 103 S. Ct. 2281, 2287-89, 76 L. Ed. 2d 476, 485-86 (1983).

The statutory cause of action that is most analogous to a claim under the Act is a breach of warranty claim under the UCC, which is governed by the limitations provisions of N.J.S.A. 12A:2-725. Furthermore, even though, as previously discussed, there is some debate as to whether the kind of repair warranty involved in this case is "a warranty [that] explicitly extends to future performance of the goods" within the intent of section 2-725(2), see supra pp.109-110, it is clear that such a warranty is a warranty of future performance under the more expansive definition of warranty contained in the Act. The term "written warranty" is defined under the Act to mean not only "(A) any written affirmation of fact or written promise made in connection with the sale of a consumer product . . . which relates to the nature of the material or workmanship and affirms or promises that such material or workmanship is defect free or will meet a specified level of performance over a specified period of time," but also (B) any undertaking in writing . . . by a supplier of a consumer product to refund, repair, replace, or take other remedial action . . . in the event that such product fails to meet the specifications set forth in the undertaking." 15 U.S.C.A. §2301(6). Even if the powertrain warranty that defendant gave to plaintiff did not constitute an "affirmation of fact or written promise" that the "material [and] workmanship" of the covered parts were "defect free," it nonetheless constituted an "undertaking in writing . . . by a supplier of a consumer product to refund, repair, replace, or take other remedial action . . . in the event that such product fails to meet the specifications set forth in the undertaking." Therefore, plaintiff's claim under the Act did not accrue until defendant allegedly breached its obligation to repair the defect in plaintiff's engine timing belt.

This conclusion is supported by Cosman, discussed earlier in this opinion, which states:

> [T]he federal definition of "written warranty" under the Magnuson-Moss Act includes promises to repair within the concept of warranty. . . .
>
> A breach of the promise to repair cannot occur until Ford refuses or fails to repair the powertrain if and when it breaks. . . .
>
> Under this analysis plaintiffs should have the right to sue for a failure to repair at any time within the life of the warranty and within four years after the breach. The result we reach here does the least violence to two legislative acts—the Uniform Commercial Code and the Magnuson-Moss Act—drafted without an eye on the other. It preserves a four year statute of limitations for promises that are part of a contract for the sale of goods, while recognizing that the Magnuson-Moss remedy for breach of a promise to repair cannot ripen until the promise is broken and has nothing to do with the inherent quality of the goods or their future performance.

[674 N.E.2d at 67-68.]

See also Keller v. Volkswagen of Am., Inc., 733 A.2d 642, 644 (Pa. Super. Ct. 1999).

Accordingly, we affirm the dismissal of plaintiff's Lemon Law claim, but reverse the dismissal of his breach of warranty and Magnuson-Moss Act claims.

PROBLEM 80

Jane Jinx bought a new car on April 1, 2002. The written warranty that came with the car read: "The manufacturer will replace any part found to be defective in the first five years." Three years and 358 days after Jane purchased the car, the steering wheel came off in her hands. Luckily she was able to brake in time, and both she and the car were uninjured. She had the car towed to the dealer's place that same day. The dealer kept the car for three months, promising each week that it would be repaired. At the end of that period, the dealer told her to come and get the car. On the way home the steering wheel again came off in her hands. This time Jane was not lucky, and she was killed. You are the attorney for her estate. Answer these questions:

(a) When did the cause of action accrue with regard to the defective steering wheel? With the delivery of the car? On the 358th day of the fourth year? On the day of the fatal accident? See Standard Alliance Indus., Inc. v. Black Clawson Co., 587 F.2d 813, 25 U.C.C. Rep. Serv. 65 (6th Cir. 1978).

(b) Was the statute tolled during the three months that the car was in the shop? See Gus' Catering, Inc. v. Menusoft Systems, 762 A.2d 804, 43 U.C.C. Rep. Serv. 2d 1163 (Vt. 2000); Hydra-Mac, Inc. v. Onan Corp., 450 N.W.2d 913, 10 U.C.C. Rep. Serv. 2d 740 (Minn. 1990).

(c) If the manufacturer of a vehicle sold it to the dealership, and the dealership then resold the vehicle to a consumer, would the four-year period on the manufacturer's *implied* warranty start running on the date of delivery to the dealership or on the date of the sale to the ultimate consumer? See Wilson v. Class, 605 A.2d 907, 17 U.C.C. Rep. Serv. 2d 1166 (Del. Super. 1992). Would we reach the same result on an *express* warranty given by the manufacturer?

(d) Should the courts draw a distinction as to when the cause of action accrues based on whether the injury is to person or to property? See Ogle v. Caterpillar Tractor Co., 716 P.2d 334, 42 U.C.C. Rep. Serv. 1668 (Wyo. 1986); In re Hawaii Federal Asbestos Cases, 854 F. Supp. 702, 26 U.C.C. Rep. Serv. 2d 364 (D. Haw. 1994) (warranty suit based on exposure to asbestos barred four years after delivery of product even if impossible to know of personal injury in that period).

PART 2

PAYMENT

_____ Chapter 7
NEGOTIABILITY

I. INTRODUCTION

There is not, of course, enough money to go around, and what money is available is frequently too physically awkward to be moved easily. Human civilization has been able to create additional sources of money in the form of transferable contractual debt. Thus, one can borrow money and give the lender a written promise to repay it (a promissory note) and in this way realize early expected future prosperity. We solved the problem of the awkwardness of the physical transfer of money, and the concomitant possibility of its theft while in transit, by putting the money in the hands of a guarded depository (typically a bank) and then issuing written orders (drafts) for the money's transfer to various people.

In time, complicated things began to happen to these pieces of paper. For one thing, they were transferred (negotiated) through many hands before being presented for payment. If payment was then refused for some reason (the goods proved defective, the maker was financially embarrassed, the bank failed to open its doors one morning), rules had to be invented to straighten out who owed what to whom and to establish which defenses would be good against the person demanding payment and which would not. Similarly, if the instrument was stolen or forged, rules had to be established to put the risk of loss on somebody. Article 3 (Negotiable Instruments) and Article 4 (Bank Deposits and Collections) of the Uniform Commercial Code are designed to supply these rules.

Article 3 replaces its widely adopted predecessor, the Negotiable Instruments Law (hereinafter the NIL), and Article 4 replaces the not-so-widely adopted Bank Collection Code. Article 8 (Investment Securities), discussed in Chapter 14 of this book, deals with similar problems raised by the transfer of stocks and bonds. A more recent addition to the Uniform Commercial Code is Article 4A, which addresses legal issues arising from wire transfers of funds; it, along with similar issues arising under the Electronic Fund Transfer Act, is explored in Chapter 13.

Articles 3 and 4 of the Code were written in the 1950s and promulgated in their most widely adopted version in 1962. The rules contained in these Articles varied but little from ones codified in the NIL (first proposed in 1896). But nineteenth-century law serves poorly in a society now living in the twenty-first century, particularly for banking matters, where computers have replaced paper and have made compliance with many of the old rules impossible. In 1990 the American Law Institute and the National Conference of Commissioners on Uniform State Laws promulgated revised versions of Articles 3 and 4 for adoption by the states. These versions modernize the rules, replace archaic language in the original articles, and answer a host of questions raised by the case law and by commentators over 30 years of litigation. All citations that follow are to the revised versions of Articles 3 and 4.

II. TYPES OF NEGOTIABLE INSTRUMENTS

There are many types of negotiable instruments in the world. *Money* itself is technically a negotiable instrument. A dollar *bill* is a *bill of exchange*—that is, a *draft* (defined below) drawn on the United States Treasury. The Code deals with investment securities (stocks and bonds) in Article 8, and with wire transfers in Article 4A, these matters being specifically excluded from the coverage of Article 3 by §3-102(a).

The types of negotiable instruments that Article 3 does cover can *note* be divided into two basic categories: *notes* and *drafts*.

A *note* is a written promise to pay money. If the note is created by a *bank*, it is called a *certificate of deposit* (or CD for short). Read §3-104(j). Investors buy CDs because they pay higher rates of interest than a normal savings account, but CDs have the disadvantage that the investor is not able to reclaim the money until the CD *matures* (comes due).[1] The typical note is not made by a bank but is the promissory note signed by those who borrow money or make credit purchases.

A *draft* is a written order by one person (the *drawer*—see §3-103(a)(3)) to another (the *drawee*, §3-103(a)(2)), directing the latter to *draft* pay money to a third person (the *payee*). The most common situation involving drafts arises when someone deposits money in a checking account and then writes checks addressed to the bank, ordering it to pay out the account money to those nominated. In this situation, the bank's customer is the drawer, the bank is the *drawee*, and the nominee (the electric company, the book club, the IRS, etc.) is the *payee*. A draft written on a bank and payable on demand is called a *check*; read §3-104(f). If the check is drawn by the bank on itself (the bank is both the drawer and the drawee), the instrument is called a *cashier's check*; see §3-104(g). If one bank draws a draft on another or makes the draft "payable through" another bank, the instrument is called a *teller's check*; see §3-104(h).[2]

PROBLEM 81

When law student Portia Moot went to buy a used car from a man who sold it through the newspaper, the seller told her he refused to take her personal check, demanding instead a cashier's check payable to his order. Portia went to Octopus National Bank and paid the bank the amount required, and the bank then issued the cashier's check, with Portia's car seller being named as payee. The bank gave the check

---

1. If a certificate of deposit states that it is non-negotiable, then Article 3 would not apply (though Article 8 on Investment Securities might). In re Isaacson, 508 So. 2d 1131, 4 U.C.C. Rep. Serv. 2d 103 (Miss. 1987).

2. Section 3-104 also contains a definition of a *traveler's check* in §3-104(i) and a *money order* in §3-104(f), and their legal significance is described in Official Comment 4 to that section.

$360.00

to Portia, and she in turn handed it over to the payee. What is the name that the Code gives to Portia in this situation? See §3-103(a)(11).

If the drawee on a draft is *not* a bank, Article 3 still applies, but the instrument no longer meets the technical definition of a check (which requires that the drawee be a bank). The most common situation in which non-bank drafts are written occurs in the sale of goods. Seller in Boston contracts to sell 100 boxes of goods to buyer in San Francisco, buyer agreeing to pay $5000 one month after receipt of the goods. Seller ships the goods, but decides that it would be nice to get the money now before, for instance, going bankrupt. Seller sits down and draws up a $5000 draft with *buyer as drawee,* leaving the payee line blank. Seller then goes down to a bank and asks the bank if it would be willing to buy the draft at a discount—say, $4750. The bank investigates buyer's credit rating and, finding it good, buys the draft from seller for $4750, having seller fill in the payee line with the bank's name. At the end of one month the bank presents the draft to buyer for payment and receives $5000, thus making a $250 profit on the deal. Buyer doesn't care who gets the payment as long as the debt to seller is discharged; seller, getting the money early, doesn't mind losing $250. Everybody is happy (unless buyer discovers the goods are defective and refuses to pay the draft when the bank re-presents it; more on that later).[3]

Thus, a negotiable instrument containing a *promise* to pay money is a note and one containing an *order* to pay money is a draft. Read §3-104(e).

III. THE NEGOTIABILITY CONCEPT

Whenever the word *negotiable* is applied to any type of paper, the concept always means this: if the paper is technically *negotiable* (which

---

3. Drafts, then called bills of exchange, originated in Europe in the Middle Ages and were used to transfer money during travels. Merchants wishing to journey from City A to City B in the year 1220 faced the very real possibility of robbery en route. They solved this problem by going to a banking company in City A and there exchanging their money for a letter addressed to a corresponding banking company in City B, telling it to give a like amount of money to the merchants on arrival. In an era of rampant illiteracy, this bill of exchange was a lot easier to slip past the brigands than were coins of the realm.

refers to its form), it is technically *negotiated* (which refers to the transfer process) and reaches the hands of a purchaser for value who has no knowledge of problems with the transaction giving rise to the paper's creation (such a person is called a *holder in due course*); then the later purchaser becomes *super-plaintiff*[4] and can sue the parties to the instrument who are not (with certain exceptions) permitted to defend the lawsuit; the defendants simply lose and pay up.

Before the rules of Article 3 apply to an instrument, regardless of whether it is a note or a draft, the instrument must be technically *negotiable* within the rigid definitional requirements of §3-104(a). Every element specified therein must be met, or the instrument is *non-*negotiable, and Article 3 does not apply, except by analogy; see §3-104(b). Read §3-104(a) carefully; it is almost (but not quite) worth memorizing, since the first issue an attorney should explore when dealing with a problem involving commercial paper is this: "Is the instrument technically *negotiable?*"

The question is also important because negotiable instruments pass more freely in commerce than do non-negotiable ones. The transferee of negotiable paper, if qualifying as a holder in due course, has the protection of the rule mentioned above, and the original maker and all other parties to the paper will have to pay it at maturity, even if they have defenses arising from the transactions in which they signed the paper. This rule promotes the desirability of buying *negotiable* instruments. If the paper is non-negotiable, its transfer is nothing more than the assignment of a contract right, and, as is the basic rule of contracts law, later holders (assignees) of a contract take subject to *all* defenses arising from the underlying transaction. As Lord Mansfield, the father of many concepts of negotiable instruments law, said in Peacock v. Rhodes, 2 Douglas 633, 99 Eng. Rep. 402 (K.B. 1781):

> The holder of a bill of exchange, or promissory note, is not to be considered in the light of an assignee of the payee. An assignee must take the thing assigned, subject to all the equity to which the original party was subject. If this rule applied to bills and promissory notes, it

---

4. The designation "Super-Plaintiff" to describe a holder in due course is taken from J. White & R. Summers, Uniform Commercial Code 14-1 (5d ed. 2000) [hereinafter White & Summers; the authors also publish a multi-volume edition of this work for practitioners, but unless indicated, all references are to the one-volume student version]. For a more specialized treatise, see B. Clark, The Law of Bank Deposits, Collections, and Credit Cards (revised edition, updated quarterly).

would stop their currency. The law is settled, that a holder, coming fairly by a bill or note, has nothing to do with the transaction between the original parties; unless, perhaps, in the single case, (which is a hard one, but has been determined) of a note for money won at play.

It follows then that it is important for everyone to know without question whether or not any given instrument is negotiable as soon as it is examined. In situations in which the deviation from the Code's requirements for negotiability is small, pleas are sometimes made to extend Article 3 by analogy to permit the non-complying instruments to be deemed negotiable. The courts are usually deaf to such entreaties:

> Because the prerequisites to negotiability are formal, it is both simple and necessary to comply with them. To hold that [the notes in question] are negotiable would certainly preserve the integrity of these notes and in that limited sense serve the interests of commerce; however, it would reward shoddy drafting and introduce unnecessary doubt into the formalities of negotiability. The reason for employing formalities in legal rules is to preclude the kinds of arguments that the banks offer to circumvent them here. It will not do to argue that the goal of promoting the expansion of commerce with predictably negotiable paper is served by artful reconstruction of the formalities set up initially to serve that same goal.

In re Boardwalk Marketplace Sec. Litig., 668 F. Supp. 115, 122, 4 U.C.C. Rep. Serv. 2d 1464, 1474 (D. Conn. 1987).

Each element of the negotiability requirements listed in §3-104(a) and related sections is discussed below.

A. *"Writing"*

A negotiable instrument cannot be oral (how could it be transferred around?), and the definitions of both *promise* and *order* in §3-103(a) require a "written" instruction or undertaking. However, there is no requirement that the writing be on a piece of paper. See Sir Alan Herbert's article, The Negotiable Cow, reprinted in A.P. Herbert, More Misleading Cases 117 (1930). Banks must sometimes cope with instruments written on odd surfaces (and frequently balk at doing so). The IRS is sometimes the payee of a negotiable shirt.

B. *"Signed"*

Section 3-103(a)'s definitions of both "promise" and "order" require that the instrument be "signed." This is an obvious requirement, but it has interesting wrinkles.

PROBLEM 82

Texas millionaire Howard Chaps signs all of his checks with a small branding iron that prints a fancy "X" on the signature line. Are his checks negotiable? See §1-201(39); cf. Official Comment 39.

PROBLEM 83

Walter Capitalist is the sole proprietor of the Capitalist Company. He signs all of the store's checks by writing "Capitalist Company" on the drawer's line, but the checks are drawn on his personal checking account at the Octopus National Bank. Can the bank treat the check as if Walter had signed his own name? See §3-401(b).

C. *"Unconditional Promise or Order"* S ᴛᴀʀᴛ

A promissory note must contain an unconditional *promise* to pay; a draft must contain an unconditional *order* to the drawee requiring payment. See §3-104(a). The rule that the promise or order be *unconditional* is obviously a necessity if negotiable paper is to circulate without question. If conditional paper were negotiable, prospective holders of the paper would not feel safe in taking it until they had checked to see if the condition had occurred. See First State Bank v. Clark, 91 N.M. 117, 570 P.2d 1144, 22 U.C.C. Rep. Serv. 1186 (1977); Annot., What Constitutes an Unconditional Promise, 88 A.L.R.3d 1100. To prevent this kind of worry, the Code requires that the promise or order be unconditional, or the paper will be technically non-negotiable. Nonetheless, certain conditions are permitted in the instrument without destroying negotiability. Read §3-106 carefully. (The plan of the §§3-100s, which deal generally with negotiability, is to set out all of the requirements in §3-104(a), and then, section by section, to elaborate on them. Section 3-106 is the first elaboration.)

1. Implied Conditions

The fact that it is possible to think up things that *might* happen to destroy the maker's liability on the instrument does not destroy negotiability unless the instrument makes itself *expressly* conditional as to these matters. For example, if Joanie Singer leases a theater from Music Hall, Inc., and gives the lessor the following signed note, "(Date), I have this day rented a theater from Music Hall, Inc., and I promise to pay $800 to the order of Music Hall, Inc.," the possibility that the theater may burn down prior to Joanie's use of it does not make the note conditional (and therefore non-negotiable); this condition is only implied. On the other hand, if the note had said, "I promise to pay $800 to the order of Music Hall, Inc., *only if* the theater does not burn down before I use it," the note would have been non-negotiable, since it would then be subject to an *express* condition. See §3-106(a)(i).

Triffin v. Dillabough

Supreme Court of Pennsylvania, 1998
552 Pa. 550, 716 A.2d 605, 36 U.C.C. Rep. Serv. 2d 255

NEWMAN, Justice. Appellant American Express Travel Related Services Company, Inc. (American Express) asks this Court to decide whether certain of its money orders are negotiable instruments pursuant to the Pennsylvania version of the Uniform Commercial Code, 13 Pa. C.S. §1101, et seq. (Commercial Code), and if they are, whether appellee Robert J. Triffin (Triffin) has the rights of a holder in due course who may recover the face value of those money orders from American Express. We hold that the money orders in question are negotiable instruments and Triffin has the rights of a holder in due course, entitling him to recover the value of the money orders from American Express.

FACTS & PROCEDURAL HISTORY

American Express, among other endeavors, sells money orders through its authorized agents. In a typical transaction, an agent collects an amount of cash from the purchaser, also known as the sender, equal to the face value of the money order plus a small fee. The sender receives a partially completed money order embossed with the amount of the money order and blank spaces for the sender to fill in his or her own name and address, the name of the payee and the date.

On an unknown date, three American Express money orders were stolen from the premises of one of its agents, Chase Savings Bank. In an apparently unrelated incident, one hundred American Express money orders were stolen while being shipped to another agent, I. W. Levin & Company. When they were stolen, all of the money orders contained the pre-printed signature of Louis Gerstner, then Chairman of American Express, but they were blank as to amount, sender, payee and date.

On December 11, 1990, Stacey Anne Dillabough (Dillabough) presented two American Express money orders for payment at Chuckie Enterprises, Inc. (Chuckie's), a check cashing operation in Philadelphia. The money orders were in the amounts of $550.00 and $650.00, respectively, and listed Dillabough as the payee and David W. (last name indecipherable) of 436 E. Allegheny Avenue as the sender. On February 25, 1991, Robert Lynn (Lynn) presented one American Express money order at Chuckie's in the amount of $200.00, which listed himself as payee and Michael C. Pepe as the sender. In each instance, Charles Giunta (Giunta), the owner of Chuckie's, recognized Dillabough and Lynn from their previous visits to Chuckie's. Dillabough and Lynn provided photographic identification to Giunta and properly endorsed their money orders. Giunta paid the face amounts of the money orders to Dillabough and Lynn, less his standard 2 percent fee.

Giunta was unaware the American Express money orders that he cashed had been stolen. The two Dillabough money orders were stolen from the premises of Chase Savings Bank and the Lynn money order was stolen from the shipment to I. W. Levin and Company. After being cashed at Chuckie's, the money orders traveled the regular bank collection routes and were presented for payment at the United Bank of Grand Junction, Colorado. Because American Express had noted on its "fraud log" that the money orders were stolen, they were returned to Chuckie's bearing the stamp "REPORTED LOST OR STOLEN. DO NOT REDEPOSIT." American Express refused to pay Chuckie's the face amounts of the money orders. Chuckie's then sold the Dillabough and Lynn money orders to Triffin, a commercial discounter.[5] Pursuant to written agreements, Chuckie's assigned all of its right, title and interest in the money orders to Triffin.

---

5. Triffin testified that he regularly purchases various types of choses in action from members of the check cashing industry. Although a law school graduate, Triffin is not a member of the Pennsylvania Bar and he is proceeding *pro se* in this appeal.

Triffin filed separate complaints in the Court of Common Pleas of Philadelphia County (trial court) against Dillabough and American Express in July 16, 1992, and against Lynn and American Express on August 20, 1992, seeking payment of the money orders. The trial court consolidated the two actions. Triffin obtained default judgments against Dillabough and Lynn and proceeded to a non-jury trial with American Express. The trial court found that the money orders were not negotiable instruments and entered a verdict in favor of American Express. On appeal, the Superior Court reversed and trial court and held that the money orders were negotiable instruments and Triffin had the status of a holder in due course, entitling him to recover the face amount of the money orders from American Express. We granted American Express' Petition for Allowance of Appeal from the Order of the Superior Court, and we now affirm.

DISCUSSION

When this Court entertains an appeal originating from a non-jury trial, we are bound by the trial court's findings of fact, unless those findings are not based on competent evidence. Thatcher's Drug Store v. Consolidated Supermarkets, Inc., 535 Pa. 469, 636 A.2d 156 (1994). The trial court's conclusions of law, however, are not binding on an appellate court because it is the appellate court's duty to determine if the trial court correctly applied the law to the facts. Id.

1. NEGOTIABILITY

The Superior Court has described the purpose of negotiable instruments and the Commercial Code as follows:

> A negotiable instrument is an instrument capable of transfer by endorsement or delivery. Negotiability provides a means of passing on to the transferee the rights of the holder, including the right to sue in his or her own name, and the right to take free of equities as against the assignor/payee. [Citations omitted.] The purpose of the Commercial Code is to enhance the marketability of negotiable instruments and to allow bankers, brokers, and the general public to trade in confidence. [Citations omitted.] As a matter of sound economic policy, the Commercial Code encourages the free transfer and negotiability of commercial paper to stimulate financial interdependence.

Manor Bldg. Corp. v. Manor Complex Assocs., 435 Pa. Super. 246, 252-53, 645 A.2d 843, 846 (1994) (en banc). With these principles in mind, we turn to a discussion of the American Express money orders at issue here.

The threshold question is whether the money orders qualify as *Issue* negotiable instruments under Division Three of the Commercial Code, 13 Pa. C.S. §3101, et seq., which governs negotiability.[6] Both parties agree that if the money orders are not negotiable instruments then Triffin's claims against American Express must fail. Initially, we note that the Commercial Code does not specifically define the term "money order," nor does it provide a descriptive list of financial documents that automatically qualify as negotiable instruments. Instead, 13 Pa. C.S. 3104(a) sets forth the following four part test to determine if a particular document qualifies as a negotiable instrument:

> (A) Requisites to negotiability—Any writing to be a negotiable instrument within this division must: (1) be signed by the maker or drawer; (2) contain an unconditional promise or order to pay a sum certain in money and no other promise, order, obligation or power given by the maker or drawer except as authorized by this division; (3) be payable on demand or at a definite time; and (4) be payable to order or to bearer.

4 part Test

13 Pa. C.S. §3104(a).

The Superior Court described the face of the money orders in question as follows:

> Prior to being stolen[,] the American Express money orders read: "AMERICAN EXPRESS MONEY ORDER... CHASE SAVINGS BANK... DATE (blank). PAY THE SUM OF (blank), NOT GOOD OVER $1,000, TO THE ORDER OF (blank). Louis V. Gerstner, Chairman. SENDER'S NAME AND ADDRESS (blank). Issued by American Express Travel Related Services Company, Inc., Englewood, Colorado. Payable at United Bank of Grand Junction, Downtown, Grand Junction, Colorado." The two Dillabough instruments were in this form. The third Lynn instrument was identical, except it did not bear an authorized agent's name, e.g., Chase Savings Bank, and was not good for over $200.

Triffin v. Dillabough, 448 Pa. Super. 72, 82, 670 A.2d 684, 689 (1996). When presented at Chuckie's, the sections for date, amount, payee and sender had been completed.

6. On July 9, 1992, the Pennsylvania General Assembly enacted amendments to the Commercial Code, effective July 9, 1993. All of the transactions in this case occurred before the effective date of the 1992 amendments, and therefore, the Commercial Code as it existed before the 1992 amendments controls this case. References in this Opinion to the Commercial Code are to the Act of November 1, 1979, P.L. 255, No. 86, §1, unless otherwise noted. Although the Commercial Code has been revised, its basic provisions survived the 1992 amendments. We expect that this Opinion will provide guidance for transactions conducted pursuant to the Commercial Code as amended in 1992.

The first requisite of negotiability, a signature by the drawer or maker, "includes any symbol executed or adopted by a party with present intention to authenticate a writing." 13 Pa. C.S. §1201. "Authentication may be printed, stamped or written; it may be by initials or by thumbprint. . . . The question always is whether the symbol was executed or adopted by the party with present intention to authenticate the writing." 13 Pa. C.S. §1201, Comment 39. Additionally, section 3307(a)(2) states that when the effectiveness of a signature is challenged, it is presumed to be genuine or authorized unless the signer has died or become incompetent. 13 Pa. C.S. §3307(a)(2). Here, the drawer, American Express, affixed the pre-printed signature of Louis Gerstner, its then Chairman, to the money orders in question before forwarding them to its agents. American Express does not argue that Gerstner's signature was affixed to the money orders for any reason other than to authenticate them. Accordingly, the money orders satisfy the first requisite for negotiability.

The second requisite, American Express argues, is lacking because the money orders do not contain an unconditional promise or order to pay. Specifically, American Express claims that a legend it placed on the back of the money orders qualifies an otherwise unconditional order on the front directing the drawee to "PAY THE SUM OF" a specified amount "TO THE ORDER OF" the payee. The legend provides as follows:

IMPORTANT
DO NOT CASH FOR STRANGERS

THIS MONEY ORDER WILL NOT BE PAID IF IT HAS BEEN ALTERED OR STOLEN OR IF AN ENDORSEMENT IS MISSING OR FORGED. BE SURE YOU HAVE EFFECTIVE RECOURSE AGAINST YOUR CUSTOMER.

PAYEE'S ENDORSEMENT

According to American Express, this legend renders the order to pay conditional on the money order not being altered, stolen, unendorsed or forged and destroys the negotiability of the instrument.

We disagree. In a factually similar case, the Louisiana Court of Appeal construed a legend on the bank of an American Express money order similar to the one at issue here. Hong Kong Importers, Inc. v. American Express Co., 301 So. 2d 707 (La. App. 1974). The legend there stated "CASH ONLY IF RECOURSE FROM ENDORSER IS AVAILABLE. IF THIS MONEY ORDER HAS NOT BEEN VALIDLY ISSUED OR HAS BEEN FRAUDULENTLY

NEGOTIATED, IT WILL BE RETURNED." Id. at 708. The money order also had the following language printed on its face: "KNOW YOUR ENDORSER CASH ONLY IF RECOURSE IS AVAILABLE." Id. The Louisiana Court held that the legend on the back and the language on the front did not convert the money order into a conditional promise to pay, but merely operated as a warning to the party cashing the money order to protect himself against fraud. Although *Hong Kong* was decided before Louisiana adopted the Uniform Commercial Code, we find its rationale to be persuasive and applicable to 13 Pa. C.S. §3104.

American Express attempts to distinguish *Hong Kong* by asserting that the legend in this case is more specific because it explicitly conditions payment on the money orders not being altered, stolen, unendorsed or forged. This argument misses the point. "Any writing which meets the requirements of subsection [(a)] and is not excluded under Section [3103] is a negotiable instrument, and all sections of this [Division] apply to it, *even though it may contain additional language beyond that contemplated by this section.*" 13 Pa. C.S. §3104, Comment 4 (emphasis added). An otherwise unconditional order to pay that meets the section 3104 requirements is not made conditional by including implied or constructive conditions in the instrument. 13 Pa. C.S. §3105(a)(1). Moreover, purported conditions on an otherwise negotiable instrument, that merely reflect other provisions of the law, do not vitiate negotiability. State v. Phelps, 125 Ariz. 114, 608 P.2d 51 (App. 1979); see also Falk's Food Basket, Inc. v. Selected Risks Ins. Co., 214 Pa. Super. 522, 257 A.2d 359 (1969); 4 William D. Hawkland & Larry Lawrence, Uniform Commercial Code Series §3-105:03 (Clark Boardman Callaghan) (1994). Here, the alleged conditions on the back of the money orders are nothing more than a restatement of American Express's statutory defenses against payment because of alteration, 13 Pa. C.S. §3407, theft, 13 Pa. C.S. §3306(4), absence of signature, 13 Pa. C.S. §3401, and forgery, 13 Pa. C.S. §3404. Contrary to American Express's claims, expressing those statutory defenses in a legend with the conditional phrase "THIS MONEY ORDER WILL NOT BE PAID IF . . ." does not elevate the legend to a condition for the purposes of 13 Pa. C.S. §3104(a) because it is merely a restatement of the defenses present in the Commercial Code. See 13 Pa. C.S. §3104, Comment 4; Phelps. The legend is simply a warning that American Express has reserved its statutory defenses. Whether these defenses are effective against Triffin is a separate question to be answered after resolving the issue of negotiability. See 13 Pa. C.S. §3104, Comment 4. We hold, therefore, that the money orders contain an unconditional order to pay, and satisfy the second requisite of negotiability.

The third requisite, that the writing be payable on demand or at a definite time, and the fourth requisite, that the writing be payable to order or bearer, are clear from the face of the money orders and are not disputed by the parties. Thus, the American Express money orders qualify as negotiable instruments pursuant to 13 Pa. C.S. §3104. . . .

[The court then found that Triffin had the rights of a holder in due course, so as to be free of American Express's defense of non-issue. As to this, see §3-105 of the Revision, and its Official Comment 2.]

American Express further contends that even if Triffin qualifies as a holder in due course, the money orders are still not enforceable because the legend on their backs limits the "tenor" of the instruments. Pursuant to 13 Pa. C.S. §3413(a), American Express claims that it is only obligated to pay an instrument "according to its tenor." The 1979 Commercial Code does not define "tenor." The 1992 amendments to section 3413(a), however, substitute the word "terms" for the word "tenor." 13 Pa. C.S. §3413(a) (1992). The Comments accompanying the 1992 amendments to section 3413 indicate that new subsection (a) is consistent with its predecessor. Therefore, it appears that no substantive change was intended by the substitution of the word "terms" for the word "tenor" and we will treat these words synonymously. Thus, American Express is essentially arguing that each money order should be enforced according to its terms, which state that the money order "WILL NOT BE PAID IF IT HAS BEEN ALTERED OR STOLEN OR IF AN ENDORSEMENT IS MISSING OR FORGED."

As previously discussed, the legend on the back of the money orders is merely a warning that restates American Express's defenses against persons other than holders in due course in the event of alteration, theft, lack of endorsement or forgery. These defenses are ineffective against a holder in due course. 13 Pa. C.S. §3305; 13 Pa. C.S. §3407(c). Because Triffin has attained holder in due course status through the assignment of the money orders from Chuckie's, American Express cannot enforce the defenses against him. Accordingly, American Express is liable to Triffin for the face value of the money orders.

The Order of the Superior Court is affirmed and this matter is remanded to the trial court for the entry of an order consistent with this Opinion.

CASTILLE, Justice, dissents.

The majority concludes that appellee Robert J. Triffin ("appellee") is entitled to recover the value of the money orders at issue because the money orders were negotiable instruments and because appellee was a holder in due course of those negotiable instruments. However, since the money orders at issue contained express conditional language which precluded negotiability under the relevant statute, I must respectfully dissent from the majority's conclusion. . . .

At issue here is the second of the four statutory prerequisites to negotiability, the requirement of an "unconditional" promise or order. Regarding this prerequisite, section §3105 provides:

> (A) Unconditional promise or order.—A promise or order otherwise unconditional is not made conditional by the fact that the instrument: (1) is subject to implied or constructive conditions; . . .

The comment to section 3105 states:

> 1. . . . Nothing in [paragraph (a) subsection (1)] is intended to imply that language may not be fairly construed to mean what it says, but implications, whether the law or fact, are not to be considered in determining negotiability.

Thus, the statute clearly distinguishes between language which creates an implied condition and language which creates an express condition. The latter renders a promise or order non-negotiable while the former does not. This conclusion derives further support from the revised §3106(a), which provides that ". . . a promise or order is unconditional unless it states (1) an express condition to payment. . . ."

Here, the operative language in the money orders at issue clearly created an "express" condition and thereby rendered the money orders non-negotiable. [Reprints language on the money order.]

This language explicitly conditions payments on the money orders' not being altered or stolen and the endorsements' not being missing or forged. The use of the word "if" renders the condition an express one, since "if" by definition means "on *condition* that; in case that; supposing that." Webster's New World Dict., 2d College ed. (Emphasis added.)

Furthermore, the official comment to revised section 3106 explains what the code intends by drawing the distinction between implied and express conditions: If the promise or order states an express condition to payment, the promise or order is not an instrument. For example, a promise states, "I promise to pay $100,000 to the order of John Doe if he conveys title to Blackacre to me." The promise is not an instrument because there is an express condition to payment. However, suppose a promise states, "In consideration of John Doe's promise to convey title of Blackacre I promise to pay $100,000 to the order of John Doe." That promise can be an instrument *if* [section 3104] is otherwise satisfied. 13 Pa. C.S. §3106 (1992 amended version) (emphasis added). Accordingly, the use of the word "if" creates an express condition which otherwise might be lacking, and thereby precludes a money order from being a negotiable instrument under the statute. The language at issue in this case created the same type of express condition which is embodied in the Comment; consequently, the language precludes the money orders from being negotiable instruments.[7]

The reasons proffered by the majority to justify its departure from this seemingly inescapable statutory logic are strained. First, the majority cites a case, decided by the Louisiana Court of Appeal in 1974, in which a condition incorporating the word "if" was construed not to bar negotiability. In that case, the Louisiana Court did not evaluate the significance of the word "if" or the significance of the condition which that word introduced. Moreover, in 1974, Louisiana had not yet adopted Article III of the Uniform Commercial Code ("UCC"). Hence, it appears that the Louisiana decision was decided against the backdrop of the Code of Napoleon. See 9 to 5 Fashions, Inc. v. Petr L. Spurney, 538 So. 2d 228, 233 (La. 1989) (discussing roots of Louisiana's civil code in the Napoleonic code). Pennsylvania, on the other hand, has adopted Article III of the UCC, which speaks directly to the issue presented in this case, as explained supra. A decision by an intermediate Louisiana appellate court interpreting French legal principles should not override the explicit statutory guidance furnished by the Pennsylvania legislature on an issue of Pennsylvania law.

The majority also seizes on Comment 4 to 13 Pa. C.S. §3104, which states that "any writing which meets the requirements of subsection [(a)] and is not excluded under Section [3103] is a negotiable instrument, and all sections of this [Division] apply to it, *even though it may contain additional language beyond that contemplated by this section*" (emphasis added by majority). Since, as explained supra, the money orders contained language which precluded them from satisfying subsection (a), the quoted language from Comment 4 does not further the majority's argument.

Finally, the majority attempts to support its conclusion by referring to the principle that "purported conditions on an otherwise negotiable

---

7. Additionally, I note that if there was any doubt about this conclusion, the doubt would be resolved against negotiability. See United States v. Gonzalez, 797 F.2d 1109, 1113 (1st Cir. 1986) ("when a writing is ambiguous with respect to negotiability, the conclusion to be reached is that it is *not negotiable*") (emphasis added) (other citations omitted).

instrument, that merely reflect other provisions of the law, do not vitiate negotiability." Op. at 609 (citations omitted). The majority contends that the language at issue amounts merely to a restatement of appellant's statutory defenses against payment where there has been alteration (13 Pa. C.S. §3407), theft (3306(4)), absence of signature (3401) and forgery (3404). The majority overlooks the fact that all of these statutory defenses are, by their own terms, ineffective against holders in due course. On the other hand, the language at issue here —which categorically states that the money order will not be paid if it was stolen—is operative even against holders who have taken in due course. As noted in the Comment to section 3105(a)(1), conditional language may be fairly construed to mean what it says. By its plain terms, the language at issue here sweeps beyond the scope of appellant's statutory defenses, and therefore does more than simply "reflect other provisions of the law."

In sum, the statute at issue in this case is devoid of ambiguity, and the application of that statute to these facts compels a conclusion contrary to that reached by the majority. Consequently, I respectfully dissent.

CAPPY, J. joins this dissenting opinion.

2. Consideration Stated

In the previous example, the note mentioned that it was given in return for the leasing of the theater—that is, it stated exactly what the consideration was that caused the note to be written. Section 3-106 permits the instrument to mention the details of the underlying contract without destroying negotiability as long as payment of the note is not made "subject to" the performance of that contract. Section 3-106(a)'s last sentence clearly permits a *reference* to the underlying contract, though an incorporation of the terms of that contract (without restating them in the note itself) would be fatal to negotiability. The reason is that the prospective holder should never be required to investigate whether all is well with the original agreement; if the instrument requires the current holder to check on this, it is non-negotiable. Holly Hills Acres, Ltd. v. Charter Bank, 314 So. 2d 209, 17 U.C.C. Rep. Serv. 144 (Fla. Dist. App. 1975) (clause stating "the terms of said mortgage are by reference made a part hereof" rendered the promissory note non-negotiable). Another reason is that the separate agreement might contain terms placing a condition on payment; the requisites of *negotiability* will not even entertain such a possibility. The holder must be able to determine the negotiability of an instrument from within its own four corners alone.

PROBLEM 84

Are the following notes negotiable?

(a) "(Date), I promise to pay bearer $500, subject to the contract I signed with Honest John today, (Signature)." See Official Comment 1, second paragraph, to §3-106.

(b) "(Date), I promise to pay bearer $500 as per contract I signed today with Honest John, (Signature)." Cf.§3-117, which says that a separate agreement affects only the parties thereto and not a subsequent holder in due course.

(c) "(Date), I promise to pay bearer $500 on January 1, 2010. For rights as to prepayment and acceleration, see the contract signed September 25, 2005, between the maker and the payee. (Signature)." See §3-106(b)(i).

PROBLEM 85

Whenever it mails out a check, the Adhesion Insurance Company marks it "Void After 90 Days." Is such an instrument technically negotiable?

PROBLEM 86

The promissory note contained this clause: "The collateral for this note is a security interest in the maker's art collection; for rights and duties on default, see the security agreement signed this day creating the security interest." Does this clause destroy negotiability? See §3-106(b)(i) and its Official Comment 1, third paragraph.

D. *"Fixed Amount of Money"*

It is elementary that an instrument will be non-negotiable if one cannot look at it and readily calculate the *amount* that the maker or drawer has promised to pay.

PROBLEM 87

The promissory note stated that the rate of interest was "2% above the prime rate as of the date of maturity." The prime rate is the interest charged by banks to their best customer and can be ascertained by reference to financial publications. Does the fact that the holder of the note has to consult sources outside of the instrument in order to calculate the interest due destroy negotiability? See §3-112.

"I promise to pay 100 bales of cotton to bearer" is a non-negotiable promise; a negotiable instrument must promise or order payment in *money*. This requirement then raises this amusing question: what is money? If in Borneo a note is made payable with "50 boar's teeth," is the note negotiable? Section 1-201(24) defines *money* as the "medium of exchange authorized or adopted by a domestic or foreign government as a part of its currency." The Official Comment to that section states that the "test adopted is that of the sanction of government . . . which recognizes the circulating medium as a part of the official currency of that government."

Note that *money* does not mean only U.S. currency. According to §3-107 an instrument payable in foreign currency is presumed to be payable in either that currency or the U.S. dollar equivalent on the date due *unless the instrument limits payment to the foreign currency*. As a test in statutory reading, read §3-107 and answer this question: if an instrument states that it is payable only with French francs, is it or is it not negotiable? See §3-107's Official Comment.

E. *"Courier Without Luggage" Requirement*

Pennsylvania's Chief Justice John Gibson once said that a negotiable instrument must be a "courier without luggage." Overton v. Tyler, 3 Pa. 346, 347 (1846). This oft-repeated description means that the instrument must not be burdened with anything other than the simple and clean unconditional promise or order; it cannot be made to truck around other legal obligations. If the maker of a note adds any *additional* promises to it, the note becomes non-negotiable because the prospective holder is then given notice that the note is or may be conditioned on the performance of the other promise. Section 3-104(a)(3) specifies the few additional items that may be mentioned in an instrument without destroying its negotiable character; read it and then do Problem 88.

PROBLEM 88

Do the following clauses in an otherwise negotiable promissory note destroy negotiability?

(a) "Maker agrees that signing this note also indicates acceptance of the contract of sale for which it is given."

(b) "Maker agrees and promises that if the holder of this note deems himself insecure at any time, he may so inform the maker, who will then supply additional collateral in an amount and kind to be specified by the holder."

(c) "Maker agrees to let the holder select an attorney for the maker; at any time the holder directs, said attorney is hereby given the authority to confess judgment against the maker in any appropriate court."

(d) On the front of a check: "By cashing this check, the payee agrees that the drawer has made payment in full of the debt drawer owed payee as a result of the purchase of a 2002 Ford, made on January 24, 2002." The revised version of Article 3 drops any discussion of the effect of this language on negotiability, but §3-311 regulates the contractual result of such a restriction.

(e) "Maker hereby grants the payee a security interest in the collateral described below."

The following case, like most of those in this part of the book, was decided before the effective date of the revised version of Articles 3 and 4 of the Uniform Commercial Code, but the rule of law it states has not changed. The court cites the original numbering of Article 3; you need look only at the new version of §3-104(a).

Woodworth v. The Richmond Indiana Venture

Ohio Court of Common Pleas, 1990
13 U.C.C. Rep. Serv. 2d 1149, 1152

JOHNSON, J. This matter is before the court on plaintiff's motion for partial summary judgment and defendant Signet Bank's motion for summary judgment. On December 18, 1987, plaintiff executed a promissory note in which he promised to pay to the order of The Richmond Indiana Venture, A Limited Partnership or holder the sum of $655,625.00. The promissory note was given to pay part of the deferred portion of plaintiff's investment in the partnership. The promissory note was subsequently assigned or negotiated to defendant,

Signet Bank. Plaintiff is in default on the promissory note having failed to make payments that fell due on July 1, 1989 and July 1, 1990. Plaintiff filed this action on November 2, 1989.

The standard for granting summary judgment is clear. On a motion for summary judgment, the moving party bears the burden of demonstrating that no genuine issue of material fact exists and that it is entitled to judgment as a matter of law. Adickes v. S.H. Kress and Co. (1970), 398 U.S. 144; Harless v. Willis Day Warehousing Co. (1978), 54 Ohio St. 2d 64, 66. The court will construe the evidence most strongly in favor of the party against whom the motion for summary judgment is made. *Harless,* 54 Ohio St. 2d at 66.

In order to be negotiable, a promissory note must be a signed, unconditional promise to pay a sum certain in money which is payable on demand or at a definite, stated time. The note must be payable to order or bearer and contain no other promise, order, obligation, or power given by the maker except as authorized by §§3-101 to 3-805, inclusive, of the Revised Code. UCC §3-104.

The policy under pre-Code law was that instruments should be as concise as possible and free from collateral engagements. Akron Auto Finance Co. v. Stonebraker (1941), 66 Ohio App. 507. As noted above, the Code continues this policy by mandating that the unconditional promise to pay not be cluttered by other promises, orders, obligations, or powers unless otherwise authorized.

The promissory note at issue contains the following term:

> The undersigned agrees that, in the event any payment due pursuant to the terms of this note be not timely made, at the option of the Partnership, the undersigned shall retroactively lose any interest in the Partnership from the date hereof and the Partnership shall have no obligation to account for any payments theretofore made by the undersigned, and that this remedy is in addition to other remedies afforded by the Partnership Agreement.

This term is clearly a promise by the maker resulting in a forfeiture of his partnership interest and payments in the event of default. The term is more than a mere reference to the partnership agreement, a recitation of security, or an agreement to protect collateral; it is a forfeiture provision in addition to other remedies under the referenced partnership agreement.

In Pacific Finance Loans v. Goodwin (1974), 41 Ohio App. 2d 141, the court held that the requirement of an unconditional promise to pay is contravened by a term providing for the repossession of collateral by a seller without judicial process. The case sub judice is analogous since the term at issue is a forfeiture without resort to judicial process.

Nothing in R.C. §3-104 or §3-112 authorizes the forfeiture term at issue. Based on the above analysis, the court finds that the negotiability of this promissory note is doubtful. Where there is doubt, the decision should be against negotiability. Official Code Comment 5 to UCC §3-104. Since the promissory note is not negotiable, defendant Signet Bank cannot claim the status of a holder in due course and is subject to ordinary contract defenses that plaintiff may assert.

Rule: if doubtful then the note is not negotiable

HAVING CONSIDERED THE PLEADINGS AND
MEMORANDA FILED HEREIN, THE COURT FINDS
THAT PLAINTIFF HAS FULFILLED HIS BURDEN.
ACCORDINGLY, PLAINTIFF'S MOTION IS SUSTAINED.
DEFENDANT'S MOTION IS DENIED. COUNSEL FOR
PLAINTIFF SHALL PREPARE AN APPROPRIATE ENTRY. . . .

MOTION FOR RECONSIDERATION

This matter is before the court on defendant's motion for reconsideration. Upon consideration of the memoranda filed herein, the court affirms its decision of September 19, 1990.

The court finds persuasive the fact that the forfeiture provision may be exercised at the option of the *partnership*, not the holder of the instrument. The provision does not require that the holder must declare a default before the partnership may exercise its option. Instead, the partnership may declare a forfeiture if payments are not timely made. A situation could develop, by mistake or otherwise, wherein the partnership exercises its option before the holder declares a default. In such case, the maker might well decline to cure an overdue payment or to make future payments because of the forfeiture. This exemplifies the reason why negotiable instruments may contain no other promise, order, obligation, or power except as authorized by statute.

The forfeiture provision at issue is not, as defendant suggests, analogous to collateral. It is a basic maxim of law that collateral follows the debt; here the option to declare a forfeiture remains with the partnership and the benefit of its exercise flows to the partnership, not the holder of the instrument.

This case is distinguishable from Standard Premium Plan Corp. v. Hirschorn (N.Y. Sup. Ct., 1968), 5 U.C.C. Rep. Serv. 163. In *Hirschorn*, the payee or assignee, in the event of default, could cancel an underlying insurance policy and apply returned premiums against the unpaid balance. Here the forfeiture flows to the partnership, not the holder and the forfeited interest is not applied to the unpaid balance on the instrument.

Any deleterious effects upon the flow of commercial instruments can be avoided by confining forfeiture provisions such as this one to the partnership agreement. Including such provision in the instrument clutters the unconditional promise to pay and thereby makes the commercial viability of this instrument less certain. . . .

. . . Counsel for plaintiff shall prepare an appropriate entry.

F. *"Payable on Demand or at a Definite Time"*

A holder of an instrument must be able to tell when it comes due, or the instrument is non-negotiable; however, there is no requirement that the instrument be dated. An undated instrument that specifies no time of payment is treated as an instrument payable on demand by the holder. Read §§3-108 and 3-113.

PROBLEM 89

Do the following clauses in a promissory note destroy negotiability?

(a) "Payable 30 days after sight."

(b) "Payable in eleven successive monthly installments of $2,414.92 each and in a final payment of $2,415.03 thereafter. The first installment being payable on the ____ day of ____, 20__, and the remaining installments on the same date of each month thereafter until paid." The blanks were not filled in. See Barclays Bank PLC v. Johnson, 129 N.C. App. 370, 499 S.E.2d 768, 37 U.C.C. Rep. Serv. 2d 338 (1998).

(c) "Payable on November 8, 2010, but the holder may demand payment at any time prior thereto if he deems himself insecure." Cf. §1-208 (Option to Accelerate at Will).

(d) "Payable when the sun comes up tomorrow."

(e) "Payable on November 8, 2010, but if my potato crop fails that year, payment shall be extended until November 8 of the following year."

(f) "Payable on November 8, 2010, but the maker hereby reserves the option to extend the time of payment until he can pay without serious financial hardship."

(g) "Payable 120 days after my rich uncle Al dies." Such notes are called *post-obituary* notes.

(h) "Payable 100 years from today, but if my rich uncle Al dies before this note is due, it shall become payable 10 days after distribution of his estate is made to his heirs." See Smith v. Gentilotti, 371 Mass. 839, 359 N.E.2d 953, 20 U.C.C. Rep. Serv. 1222 (1977).

(i) "Payable on my next birthday."

G. "Payable to Bearer or to Order"

The early English common law courts would not permit a subsequent holder of a contract to sue one of the original parties to it; the courts said that there was no *privity* (connection) between the plaintiff and the defendant. These cases were frustrating to the merchants of the day because they recognized the desirability of permitting a direct suit by a remote transferee against the original promisor. These merchants and their attorneys devised two clever ways of establishing privity between the original creator of the paper and the later holder.

The first way was to make the original promise or order payable to *bearer*—that is, payable to the holder of the paper and not to any specific person. In this way, privity passed with the physical delivery of the instrument. The only problem with bearer paper, which is still with us, is that it is too negotiable; it is a little bit too much like money for safety. In Miller v. Race, 1 Burr. 452, 97 Eng. Rep. 398 (K.B. 1758), Lord Mansfield was faced with the problem of a bearer note that had been stolen from the mails and negotiated to plaintiff by one "who had the appearance of a gentleman." Lord Mansfield held that title to bearer paper passes with the instrument since negotiable paper is to be "treated as money, as cash." Plaintiff, a holder in due course, took free of the defense of theft, and defendant had to pay the note.

The second means of establishing privity was to have the creator of the instrument make it payable to a specified person or to whomever that person further ordered the paper paid; thus, notes were made payable to "John Smith or Order" or John Smith or his assigns." This means the person to whom Doe ordered payment acquired privity, since the original promise ran directly to the assignee. This order paper today simply says "Pay to the order of John Smith," meaning that the instrument will be paid to John Smith or to whomever he orders as his nominee. Until John Smith makes some sort of *order*, the instrument cannot be validly transferred. He usually does this by writing his order on the back of the instrument and then signing his own name.

Section 3-104(a)(1) of the Code continues this ancient requirement that the maker or drawer use either bearer or order language (*words of negotiability*) on an instrument before it is technically negotiable. These special words have become so associated with negotiable instruments that they now serve as one means of easily identifying contracts that are meant to be negotiable, and thus warn people that they may be creating paper having the legal consequences of negotiable transfer (loss of defenses on the underlying contract). Read §3-109.

PROBLEM 90

Do the following clauses in a promissory note create bearer paper?

(a) "Pay to John Smith." See Sunrizon Homes, Inc. v. American Guar. Inv. Corp., 782 P.2d 103, 7 U.C.C. Rep. Serv. 2d 796 (Okla. 1988).

(b) "Pay to the order of John Smith or bearer." See Official Comment 2 to §3-109.

(c) "Pay to bearer."

(d) "Pay to the order of Cash."

(e) "Pay to a Merry Christmas."

PROBLEM 91

Do the following clauses create order or bearer paper, or do they make the instrument non-negotiable for failure to create either?

(a) "Pay to the order of (blank)." See §3-115 and Official Comment 2.

(b) "Pay to John Doe's estate." See §3-110(c)(2)(i).

(c) "Pay to the order of the President of the United States." See §3-110(c)(2)(iv).

(d) The drawer of a check drew a line through the words "the order of" that were printed on the check prior to the space for the payee's name. Is the check, as altered, negotiable? See §3-104(c). If the drawer of a check or the maker of a promissory note wants to destroy negotiability, what should be done? See §3-104(d). Why would this ever be desirable?

H.   Consumer Notes

Because the creation of a negotiable instrument deprives a maker of the usual contract defenses, most commentators have argued that it is unwise to permit consumers to sign promissory notes. Many state consumer statutes forbid a seller or a lessor to take a negotiable instrument (other than a check) as part of a consumer sale or lease. These statutes do not typically destroy the negotiability of such an instrument, however, and if a consumer note were to get into the hands of a holder in due course, the consumer would still be unable to assert contract defenses when the holder in due course demanded payment. See Circle v. Jim Walter Homes, Inc., 535 F.2d 583, 19 U.C.C. Rep. Serv. 158 (10th Cir. 1976); see also Jefferson v. Mitchell Select Furniture Co., 56 Ala. App. 259, 321 So. 2d 216, 18 U.C.C. Rep. Serv. 431 (1975) ("Of course, it is difficult to conceive how one could be a holder of a negotiable instrument which showed that it was taken in the credit sale of consumer merchandise with retention of title and a purchase money security interest, without knowledge that it arose from [a violation of the statute]"). The Uniform Consumer Credit Code §3.404(1) (1974 text) does preserve a consumer's defenses even if the instrument is owned by a holder in due course.

The Federal Trade Commission has promulgated a regulation, 16 C.F.R. part 433, requiring that all promissory notes and contracts taken in consumer sales or *purchase money loans* (defined as loans made to purchase goods or services from a seller who refers the consumer to the lender or who is affiliated with the lender by common control, contract, or business arrangement) contain the following language:

NOTICE

ANY HOLDER OF THIS CONSUMER CREDIT CONTRACT IS SUBJECT TO ALL CLAIMS AND DEFENSES WHICH THE DEBTOR COULD ASSERT AGAINST THE SELLER OF GOODS OR SERVICES OBTAINED PURSUANT HERETO OR WITH THE PROCEEDS HEREOF. RECOVERY HEREUNDER BY THE DEBTOR SHALL NOT EXCEED AMOUNTS PAID BY THE DEBTOR HEREUNDER.

The regulation applies to all such notes or contracts signed after May 14, 1976. See White & Summers §14-9. Failure to include the required statement violates §5 of the Federal Trade Commission Act (forbidding Unfair and Deceptive Practices), and §9-404(d) of the

Uniform Commercial Code automatically adds the missing statement to all consumer transactions that should carry it.[8]

QUESTION

Does the required FTC language destroy negotiability? See §3-106(d).

---

8. The proposed 2002 amendments to Article 3 of the Uniform Commercial Code would also automatically add the FTC language to all documents which should contain it, thus bringing Article 3 in line with the same rules in Article 9; see new §3-305(e).

Chapter 8
NEGOTIATION

I. SOME TECHNICAL TERMS

A. Parties

Those whose names appear on a negotiable instrument are given definite labels, with specific legal consequences varying according to the label attached.

A promissory note in its most pristine state is a two-party instrument. The person who issues the instrument and promises to pay is called the *maker* According to §3-412, the legal duty of the issuer of a promissory note is to "pay the instrument (i) according to its terms at the time it was issued . . . , or (ii) if the issuer signed an incomplete instrument, according to its terms when completed."[1] The person to whom the note is made payable is the

---

1. The issuer of a cashier's check assumes the same liability according to §3-412.

payee. If the note is made payable to *bearer*, there is no specific payee, and whoever has possession of the paper is presumptively entitled to payment by the maker.

A draft (or check) is always a three-party instrument. The person who creates the draft and orders the drawee to pay is called the *drawer.* Though the courts, and others who should know better, frequently do so, be careful that you do not confuse a *drawer* with a *maker;* there are important differences between their legal responsibilities. A *drawer* creates a *draft,* a *maker* creates a *note.* According to §3-414(b), by drawing a draft, the drawer engages that upon dishonor of the draft by the drawee the drawer will pay the amount of the draft. The *drawee* is the person to whom the drawer addresses the order of payment. On a check, the drawee is the bank at which the drawer has an account.[2] The *payee* of a draft is the person specified by the drawer as entitled to receive payment. As with notes, if the draft is payable to bearer, there is no specific payee, and any holder is entitled to payment from the drawee. If a check is drawn payable to the order of a specific person, that person is the *payee* and may further transfer (*negotiate*) the check in the manner described below.

B. Negotiability vs. Negotiation

Be careful not to confuse these two very similar terms. The question "Is an instrument negotiable?" asks if the instrument is in the proper form to meet the technical requirements of negotiability found in §3-104(a). The question "Has the instrument been negotiated?" asks about the legal validity of the attempted transfer of the instrument. Thus, negotiability refers to *form,* negotiation to *transfer.*

II. TRANSFER AND NEGOTIATION

A negotiable instrument goes through three stages in its life. The first stage is called *issuance.* Read §3-105. Skipping for a mo-

---

2. As we shall see when we get to bank collection, in Article 4 of the Code the drawee is referred to as the *payor bank.* See §4-105(3).

ment the middle stage, the final stage in the existence of a negotiable instrument is its *presentment* for payment. Read §3-501(a). We will consider the legal ramifications of both issuance and presentment elsewhere. For now, we focus on the middle stage: the *transfer* of the instrument, meaning every legally significant movement of the paper between issuance and presentment.

It was a basic rule at common law and is now a statutory rule, §3-203(b), that the physical transfer of an instrument (whether or not it is also a technical *negotiation*) vests in the transferee whatever rights the transferor had in the instrument. Under the Code, if the physical transfer is done in such a manner as to make the transferee a technical *holder*, then the transfer is called a *negotiation*. This is important because no one can become a *holder in due course* unless that person is first a holder, and becoming a holder is tied up with proper negotiation.[3] Carefully read §1-201(20), defining *holder*, and §3-201, discussing *negotiation*. Think of it this way: a proper negotiation confers holder status on the transferee, with all the benefits holder status carries (including the possibility of becoming a holder in due course). Without a valid negotiation, the transferee is not a holder and has much more limited rights.

The negotiation of order paper is accomplished by (a) the indorsement by the proper person (who thereby becomes an *indorser*) and (b) the delivery of the instrument to the transferee (who thereupon qualifies as a *holder*). An *indorsement* is a signature placed on an instrument by the payee or any later transferees. Glance at §3-204(d), which deals with a wrong or misspelled payee's name and should settle a problem you may have worried about for years. The negotiation of bearer paper needs no indorsement; delivery to the transferee is all that is required for the transferee to qualify as a holder. Read all of §3-201.

III. SPECIAL AND BLANK INDORSEMENT

If the instrument is made payable to the order of a specific payee, that payee will be required to indorse the instrument to

---

3. The issuance of the instrument to the first taker also creates *holder* status in that person without a negotiation having occurred. A named payee becomes a holder on getting possession of the instrument, and if the instrument is payable to bearer, anyone in possession of it is automatically a holder.

transfer it to another. A drawee bank, as a matter of course, will require the payee's indorsement before it makes payment. §3-501(b)(2)(iii). There are two different ways the payee can indorse the instrument. The payee can simply sign the back of the instrument. Such a signature is called a *blank indorsement* and has the legal effect of converting the instrument into bearer paper. If the payee wishes to preserve the *order* character of the instrument, the original payee may specify a new payee by writing "Pay (name of new payee)" above the indorsement. Such an indorsement is called a *special indorsement* and has the legal effect of making the instrument the sole property of the new payee, who becomes a *holder* as soon as the instrument is delivered. Further, the common law always provided that, until that moment, the original payee can strike out the special indorsement and do anything with the instrument.

No further order language is necessary as part of the special indorsement; the negotiability of an instrument is not affected by language written on the instrument during the course of negotiation. Read §3-205.

PROBLEM 92

David Hansen banked with the Mechanical National Bank. Hansen owed $50 to William Egger and decided to pay him by writing out a check for $50, using one of the checks Mechanical furnished him when he opened his account. He gave the check to Egger, who wrote his name on the back of the check. Egger gave the check to his wife, Cynthia, who took it down to the Cornucopia Grocery and asked the manager to cash it. The manager paid Cynthia $50 and then took the check and wrote "Pay to the Cornucopia Grocery" just above William Egger's signature. When Billy Speed, the Check Collection Service's messenger, came by, the manager gave the check to him for delivery to the Octopus National Bank, where the grocery had an account. Speed delivered the check to Octopus National Bank, where the bank's check processing machine merely stamped the words "Octopus National Bank" on the back of the check. Octopus National Bank then forwarded the check to the Mechanical National Bank. Answer the following questions:

(a) To which parties should these labels be attached: drawer, drawee, payee, or depositary bank (defined in §4-105(2))?

(b) Did the following people qualify as *holders*: David Hansen, William Egger, Cynthia Egger, the manager of Cornucopia Grocery,

Cornucopia Grocery, Billy Speed, Octopus National Bank, and Mechanical National Bank?

(c) If William Egger had failed to indorse the check, but simply deposited it in his account with Octopus National Bank, would the bank have been a *holder?* See §4-205.

(d) What was the legal effect of the language written on the check by the grocery store manager?

(e) Which of the parties are properly called *indorsers?* See §3-204.

PROBLEM 93

A check was made payable to "Mary and Donald Colpitts." Must both payees indorse it in order to negotiate the instrument? What if the check were payable to "Mary or Donald Colpitts"? Must both payees indorse now? Finally, what if it simply is payable to "Mary Colpitts, Donald Colpitts" with no connecting word? Are two indorsements needed here? To answer all these questions, see §3-110(d) and its Official Comment 4.

PROBLEM 94

When Portia Moot received her first paycheck from the law firm that recently hired her, she was annoyed to discover that it was made out to "Portia Mort." When she took the check to her bank to cash it, she mentioned the problem to the bank clerk, who promptly called you, the bank's attorney. What steps would you suggest the bank follow in this situation? See §3-204(d) and its Official Comment 3.

In the original version of Article 3, only a *holder* has the right to sue on an instrument to enforce payment, but §3-301 in the revised version would allow owners who are non-holders to sue in some circumstances, replacing the original word *holder* with the more inclusive *person entitled to enforce the instrument.* This term generally means a holder, but it also includes certain parties to whom other sections of the Code give similar rights (matters we will explore later). Read §3-301. To qualify as a holder under §1-201(20), a person must meet two requirements: (a) possession of the instrument and, for non-bearer instruments, (b) be the *person identified* in the instrument (either as payee or special indorsee). Failure to establish *holder* status because of defects in negotiation can be legally fatal.

PROBLEM 95

Desert Paradise, Inc., initiated a scam in which hundreds of middle-class people signed promissory notes in order to invest in the supposed development of a retirement community to be built in the Southwest. Desert Paradise, the payee on all these notes, sold them in bulk to Octopus National Bank (ONB). Rather than indorsing its name hundreds of times on each of the notes, Desert Paradise had its indorsement printed on a separate sheet of paper, which it then folded into each promissory note, not connecting it in any way other than the fold. Desert Paradise's officials then absconded with the money and left the desert land untouched. Octopus National Bank demanded payment from the makers of the notes, and when they tried to raise defenses of breach of contract and fraud, ONB claimed to be a holder in due course, so as to take free of these defenses. Is ONB even a holder? See §3-204(a) and the last paragraph in its Official Comment 1. For a case with somewhat similar facts, see Adams v. Madison Realty & Dev., Inc., 853 F.2d 163, 6 U.C.C. Rep. Serv. 2d 732 (3d Cir. 1988) ($19.5 million involved). A separate paper used for indorsements is called an *allonge*, and the last sentence of §3-204(a) says that it must be affixed to the instrument. What does "affixed" mean? Would a paper clip do the trick? A staple? See Lamson v. Commercial Credit Corp., 187 Colo. 382, 531 P.2d 966, 16 U.C.C. Rep. Serv. 756 (1975) ("Stapling is the modern equivalent of gluing or pasting. Certainly as a physical matter it is just as easy to cut by scissors a document pasted or glued to another as it is to detach the two by unstapling.").

IV. FORGERY OF THE PAYEE'S NAME

Understanding the following rule is crucial to an appreciation of many of the issues we will study in this course.

If an instrument is payable to the *order* of a named payee, only that payee can become a *holder*, and even this status is not con-

ferred until the payee gets possession of the instrument. Thereafter no one can qualify as a *holder* until the payee indorses the
instrument; without the payee's valid indorsement, no later transferees will have taken by a valid *negotiation* of the instrument, which
remains the payee's property. An unauthorized signature (i.e., a
forgery or a signature by a non-agent) is *not* effective to negotiate
the instrument, so following a forgery of the payee's name, no later
transferee (no matter how innocent, no matter how good the forgery, no matter how far down the line the taker is, etc.) can qualify
as a holder.

PROBLEM 96

When Laura Lawyer's briefcase was stolen, it contained her
monthly paycheck from the law firm for which she worked, made
payable to her order. She had not indorsed it. The thief who stole
the briefcase forged her name to the back of the paycheck and
transferred it to an innocent party, Cornucopia Grocery. When the
latter tried to cash the check at the drawee bank, the bank alerted
Laura, and she arrived at the bank immediately. Can she retrieve the
check from Cornucopia Grocery? See §3-306.

PROBLEM 97

Assume that on receiving her paycheck, Laura Lawyer (from
Problem 96) had signed her name to the back of the instrument,
which then was blown out a window and landed at the feet of a
criminal, Harry Thief. Harry took the check down to Cornucopia
Grocery and told the manager that he (Harry) was Lance Lawyer,
Laura's father, and asked the manager to cash it for him. The manager made Harry indorse the instrument (reason: to make Harry
contractually liable thereon (§3-415(a)), so Harry wrote "Lance
Lawyer" under Laura's indorsement. Is Cornucopia Grocery a
holder?

PROBLEM 98

Assume that Laura (from Problem 96) wanted to indorse the
instrument over to her mother, so on the back she wrote "Pay to

Lilly Lawyer" and then signed her own name. Thus indorsed, the instrument was blown out a window, and Harry Thief found it. He indorsed "Lilly Lawyer" under Laura's name and transferred the check to Cornucopia Grocery. Is Cornucopia Grocery now a holder? See §3-205(a).

The rule here is that any unauthorized indorsement of the payee's name or any special indorsee's name is not a valid negotiation and gives subsequent transferees no legal rights in the instrument no matter how innocent they are or how far removed from the forgery. The same rule applies to missing indorsements of the payee or special indorsee; later possessors of the instrument do not qualify as holders. BUT once an instrument becomes bearer paper, subsequent unauthorized signatures have no effect on the holder status of later takers, since valid indorsements are not required to negotiate bearer paper (§3-201(b)).

PROBLEM 99

Laura (again from Problem 96) never had a course in commercial paper, so when she received her paycheck, she simply wrote her name on the back and mailed the check to her mother. Her mother (who had had a commercial paper course) needed for some reason to hold onto the check for a week before cashing it, so she wrote "Pay to Lilly Lawyer" *above* Laura's indorsement. Has the check now become order paper requiring the mother's indorsement for further negotiation? See §3-205(c).

Chapter 9
HOLDERS IN DUE COURSE

I. ACQUIRING HOLDER IN DUE COURSE STATUS

If you remember the rule that a holder in due course takes free of most of the defenses the parties to the original transaction have against one another, it is easy to see why it is important to determine if the person currently possessing the instrument qualifies as a holder in due course. The basic definition is found in §3-302(a), which you should read carefully.

Official Comment 4 to §3-302 makes it clear that the *payee* can qualify as a holder in due course in some rare situations. Normally, the payee is so involved in the underlying transaction that he or she has notice of problems affecting payment obligations, and thus cannot be a holder in due course. But the examples given in

Official Comment 4 describe fact patterns where the payee is innocent of such knowledge and can therefore qualify for the
protection given to holders in due course. See also Eldon's Super
Fresh Stores, Inc. v. Merrill Lynch, Pierce, Fenner & Smith, Inc.,
296 Minn. 130, 207 N.W.2d 282, 12 U.C.C. Rep. Serv. 490 (1973),
for an example of the payee as a holder in due course.

Subsection (c) gives a list of extraordinary transactions—
creditors seizing instruments by judicial process, the sale of an
inventoried business (a "bulk transaction"), or the appointment of
the administrator of an estate containing negotiable instruments
—in which the transferee is statutorily denied holder in due
course status.[1]

A. "Holder"

Note first of all that in order to be a holder in due course the
possessor of the instrument must qualify as a *holder*. This means
that the instrument must be technically *negotiable* and must have
been technically *negotiated* into the hands of its current possessor
(however, the named payee becomes a holder on issuance of the
instrument without the necessity of a negotiation, as does anyone
to whom a bearer instrument is issued). No one can be a holder in
due course of a non-negotiable instrument, nor even of a negotiable instrument if there is some defect in the transfer (negotiation) process.

One technical point: the drawee bank on which a check is
drawn, taking the check for payment, does not qualify as a "holder." The reason is that an instrument must be *negotiated* to a holder,
and the process by which the drawee bank acquires the instrument
is not a negotiation, it is a mere surrender for payment (a "present-

1. In spite of §3-302(c), which would seem to reach the opposite result, the
federal courts have held that federal agencies such as the FDIC when taking over
failed financial institutions acquire holder in due course status as a matter of
federal law. Campbell Leasing, Inc. v. FDIC, 901 F.2d 1244, 12 U.C.C. Rep. Serv.
2d 138 (5th Cir. 1990); but see DiVall Insured Income Fund Ltd. Partnership v.
Boatmen's First National Bank, 69 F.3d 1398, 28 U.C.C. Rep. Serv. 2d 589 (8th
Cir. 1995). However, the federal courts have made it clear that the FDIC cannot
be a holder in due course for *non-negotiable* instruments; Sunbelt Savings, FSB,
Dallas, Texas v. Montross, 923 F.2d 353, 13 U.C.C. Rep. Serv. 2d 792 (1991).

ment"). Thus the drawee bank is not a holder, and consequently not a holder in due course.

B. *"Value"*

It is important to emphasize that whether or not someone qualifies as a holder in due course is measured at the moment he or she gave value for the instrument (assuming there has been a valid negotiation so as to create holder status). Things that happen after value is given (such as receiving notice of problems with the instrument) do not destroy holder in due course status once achieved.

What is "value"?

First of all, the *gift* of an instrument will never create holder in due course status in the donee (though the donee may get similar rights under the *shelter* rule, discussed below). The confusing part of the value requirement is that giving value is not the same thing as giving *consideration.* Read §3-303's Official Comment 1, first paragraph. The drafters of the Code decided that one gives value only to the extent that the holder has performed the consideration or made some irrevocable commitment in connection with it. If all that has been exchanged for the instrument is an unexecuted promise and then a problem arises, the holder has the self-help remedy of refusing to perform and does not need the extraordinary status of holding in due course; thus, the holder has not given *value* under the Code. This is true even though the promise would be sufficient consideration at common law. Read §3-303 and its Official Comment and then resolve the Problems that follow.

PROBLEM 100

Joe Lunchpail arrived home one day to find a note from his wife stating that she was divorcing him and that he should get a lawyer. Since he had just been paid that day, he took his paycheck down to the law office of Nathan Novice and indorsed it over to Nathan in return for the latter's promise to represent Joe in his divorce. Later that evening, Joe's wife sent the sheriff to seize his paycheck. Joe laughingly referred the sheriff to his attorney. Can the sheriff succeed in wresting the check from Nathan's hands? See

§§3-306, 3-303; Carter & Grimsley v. Omni Trading, Inc., 306 Ill. App. 3d 1127, 716 N.E.2d 320, 39 U.C.C. Rep. Serv. 2d 484 (1999).

PROBLEM 101

Zach Taylor bought a car for his business from Fillmore Motors, signing a promissory note for $23,000 payable to Fillmore. Fillmore sold the note to the Pierce Finance Company for $22,800, a $200 discount. The car fell apart, and Zach refused to pay. Is the finance company (assuming good faith and lack of notice) a holder in due course for $23,000 or $22,800? See Bankers Guar. Title & Trust Co. v. Fisher, 2 Ohio Misc. 18, 204 N.E.2d 103 (C.P. 1964). If Millard Fillmore, the owner of Fillmore Motors, owed his mother $21,000 and gave her the note with the understanding that the extra $2,000 was a Mother's Day gift, would the mother be a holder in due course for the full amount? See §3-303.

PROBLEM 102

Tom Winker tricked old Mrs. Nodding into writing a check payable to Tom (she thought he was the agent for a local charity). The check for $1,000 was drawn on her bank, the First County Bank. Tom took the check to his bank, the Last National Bank, and, after indorsing it, put it in his checking account. Last National Bank sent the check to the First County Bank for payment, but by the time it got there Mrs. Nodding had stopped payment so that the check was dishonored and returned to Last National. Is Last National Bank a holder in due course? This question will be important if Tom has skipped town and Last National decides to sue Mrs. Nodding under §3-414.

The bank's major problem in situations like Problem 102 is proving that it *paid* value for the check. Is the bank out of pocket anything? If so, the Code will permit the bank to recover. Thus, if the bank had permitted Tom to get the money *before* the check cleared through the drawee bank, the Last National Bank would be a holder in due course. Article 4 of the UCC (which deals with bank collection) sets out special rules for this kind of value. Section 4-211 provides that for purposes of determining its holder in due course status, a bank gives *value* whenever it has a security interest in the instrument. The situations in which this occurs are spelled out in §4-210(a). Read these sections, and consider the following case.

Falls Church Bank v. Wesley Heights Realty, Inc.

District of Columbia Court of Appeals, 1969
256 A.2d 915, 6 U.C.C. Rep. Serv. 1082

HOOD, J. The sole issue on this appeal is whether and under what circumstances, may a depositary bank achieve the status of holder in due course of negotiable paper deposited with it by a customer. The facts are undisputed.

The appellees drew a check for $1,400.00, payable to the order of a customer of appellant bank. The customer deposited this check in his account with the bank and was given a provisional credit of this amount. The customer was permitted to withdraw $140.00 from this account prior to the bank's discovering that appellees had stopped payment on the $1,400.00 check. When the check was returned to the bank dishonored, the bank's customer had "skipped," leaving no credits in his account on which to charge the $140.00. The bank, thereupon, made demand on appellees for that amount and when appellees refused, this action was brought.

At trial appellees moved for, and were granted, judgment on grounds that the bank "was an agent for collection only and did not have a security interest and was not a holder in due course for value."

We reverse. The Uniform Commercial Code, which controls in this case, expressly provides that a bank acquires a security interest in items deposited with it to the extent that the provisional credit given the customer on the item is withdrawn. UCC §4-208 [§4-210 in the revised version of Article 4—Ed.]. It further provides that, for purposes of achieving the status of holder in due course, the depositary bank gives value to the extent that it acquires a security interest in the item in question. UCC §4-209 [§4-211 in the revision—Ed.].

We agree that appellant bank is deemed by the Uniform Commercial Code to be an agent of its customers (§4-201) but under the scheme of the Code, a "bank may be a holder in due course while acting as a collecting agent for its customer." Citizens Bank of Booneville v. National Bank of Commerce, 334 F.2d 257, 261 (10th Cir. 1964). See also cases collected at 18 A.L.R.3d 1388-1391.

As a holder in due course as to $140.00, appellant's claim cannot be defeated except by those defenses set out in UCC §3-305(2), none of which are herein alleged. The judgment below is accordingly reversed with instructions to enter judgment for appellant.

PROBLEM 103

Same situation as Problem 102 except that when Tom deposits the $1,000 check in his account, the account contains $500. Later that afternoon he withdraws $500. Is the bank a holder in due course for any amount? See §4-210(b) (the FIFO rule: First In, First Out). What result if he withdraws $750?

C. *"Good Faith" and "Notice"*

To become a holder in due course, the owner of the instrument must be, in effect, a bona fide purchaser—that is, the owner must have given value for the instrument in *good faith* (defined in §1-201(19) as "honesty in fact in the conduct or transaction concerned," but redefined in §3-103(a)(4) to include not only "honesty in fact" but also "the observance of reasonable commercial standards of fair dealing"), thus making the test one that is both subjective and objective. Read Official Comment 4 to §3-103. The holder must also be without *notice* that there are problems with the instrument.

These latter two concepts—good faith and notice—are inevitably intertwined: if, at the time value is given for the instrument, a person has *notice* of a defense the maker of a note has against the payee, the holder cannot be said to take the note with the good faith expectation that it should be paid in spite of the defense. See Annot., 36 A.L.R.4th 212. In the cases that follow, you should note how often the court fails to separate these two issues.[2]

2. Incidentally, more cases than usual appear in this segment of the book. Whether or not the holder took in good faith and without notice is largely a factual question; its resolution calls for the kind of detailed analysis only full court opinions can give. The FTC Holder in Due Course Regulation would now settle many of these cases, and all of them were decided before the revised

General Investment Corp. v. Angelini

New Jersey Supreme Court, 1971
58 N.J. 396, 278 A.2d 193, 9 U.C.C. Rep. Serv. 1

FRANCIS, J. The trial judge sitting without a jury, held that plaintiff was a holder in due course of a note signed by defendants Anthony V. Angelini and Dolores H. Angelini and consequently in this action brought thereon was immune from certain defenses sought to be asserted by them. Therefore, he entered judgment against defendants in the amount of $5,363.40 plus interest. The Appellate Division affirmed the judgment in an unreported opinion. We granted defendants' petition for certification. 57 N.J. 238 (1970).

On December 10, 1966, defendants Anthony and Dolores Angelini, husband and wife, entered into a contract with Lustro Aluminum Products, Inc. for certain repair work on their home at 689 Clark Avenue, Ridgefield, N.J. It provided that Lustro, "a home repair contractor, duly licensed under the New Jersey Home Repair Financing Act, Chapter 41, Laws 1960," would

> Supply & Install Gold Bond Plasticrylic Avocado Siding with Grey Sills & Trim. Apply Heavy Quilted Breather Foil on all wall areas around complete house. Corner posts to be green, all mullions to be fabricated in grey aluminum. Supply & install 2 anodized storm doors (Rear & Side Entrances). All overhangs & trim to be covered with special Marine Paint in grey color (as close as possible to Oxford grey trim).
>
> This will include cleaning up job.

The cash price for the work was fixed at $3,600 but the time payment price was $5,363.40, payable in 84 monthly installments of $63.85 each. Payments were to commence "60 days after completion" of the work. The agreement provided also that the Angelinis would "execute a note and application for credit, and any other appropriate instrument for the purpose of financing. . . ." On the same date as the contract, they did sign a note in the principal sum of $5,363.40, promising to pay that amount to the order of Lustro in equal consecutive monthly installments of

---

version of Article 3 took effect, so their citations are to that version. However, the cases are all still good law, with one point only being different: the revision now adds an *objective* component to the test of good faith, so that holders must also behave in a *commercially reasonable* fashion to achieve holder in due course status. The test is no longer purely subjective, as it was when these cases were decided.

$63.85 each "commencing February 19, 1967, with interest after maturity at the highest rate." According to defendants, at the time they signed the note it was not dated and the date of commencement of payment was not set forth. Anthony Angelini testified that he was told by Lustro's representative that the payments would not begin until he was completely satisfied with the job. The trial court found as a fact that when the note was executed it bore "no dates."

Plaintiff General Investment Corp. is a home improvement contract financier. It deals with 300 contractors and arranges approximately 1,800 home improvement loans per year. Approximately 10 percent of its volume came from Lustro. General Investment's representative testified that the Angelini note was purchased for value from Lustro on the day of its alleged execution, December 19, 1966. It was endorsed without recourse, except that the endorser-contractor warranted as part of the endorsement that it "has furnished and installed all articles and materials and has fully completed all work which constitutes the consideration for which this note was executed and delivered by the maker." When the note was endorsed and delivered by Lustro plaintiff required the home improvement contract to accompany it. The two documents were separate pieces of paper but it was obvious from the contract form that they were interrelated parts of a single transaction. Plaintiff's agent read the contract before discounting the note, and he conceded, in any event, that his experience with the nature of Lustro's operation made him fully familiar with the terms of the contract and the note. Defendants' contract and note to his knowledge were in the form customarily used by Lustro. He said also that in cases involving home improvement notes one of the requisites of the transaction was to obtain a copy of the work contract. Having obtained it as part of the note-discounting event, both documents were kept as part of plaintiff's records. Thus, General Investment knew that under Lustro's method of operation the homeowner's obligation to commence payments did not come into being until 60 days after the home improvements were completed. It had to know also by inescapable implication that "60 days after completion" were not just words, but that they meant after completion in a workmanlike manner.

When plaintiff's representative received the note and contract and discounted the note, he did not inquire of the Angelinis if the work had been completed prior to or on December 19, the ostensible execution date of the note, nor did he ask Lustro for a certificate of completion signed by defendants. See N.J.S.A. 17:16-

66, L.1960, c.41, §5, which provides that "[n]o home repair contractor shall request or accept a certificate of completion signed by the owner prior to the actual completion of the work to be performed under the home repair contract." This quoted section is part of the Home Repair Financing Act of 1960 under which plaintiff knew Lustro was licensed to do business. N.J.S.A. 17:16C-93; 17:16C-77. If a request had been made by General Investment for a certificate of completion, it would have learned immediately that the work had not been completed. Instead plaintiff chose to accept the representation in the printed form of endorsement, appearing on the back of the note and above Lustro's signature, that the work had been "fully completed" in the 10 days between the contract date, December 10, 1966 and December 19, the ostensible but false date of execution of the note.

According to Anthony Angelini's undenied testimony, Lustro began work on his house on December 15. After working on that one day nothing further was done for several days. It never did complete the work and the part performance neither conformed to the contract nor met reasonable workmanlike standards. Ultimately Lustro became insolvent and, according to the Angelinis, the contract was never fulfilled.

The plaintiff's testimony is to the effect that when it discounted the note, the payment commencement date appeared therein as February 19, 1967. As already noted, the trial court found as a fact that the places for dates thereon were blank at the time of its execution. At any rate, on or about December 24, 1966 the Angelinis received from plaintiff an installment payment coupon book which called for the first payment to be made on February 19, 1967. Defendants promptly returned the book to plaintiff with the advice that the contract called for payments to begin 60 days after completion of the work and that it had not been completed. Defendants also sent a copy of their letter to Lustro. Moreover, it appears that plaintiff wrote Lustro about defendants' complaint stating that it "would appreciate your immediate adjustment of same." This letter was a printed form, thus indicating that plaintiff was prepared for such complaints. In spite of some further correspondence and the Angelinis' assurance that they would begin payments as soon as the work was completed, Lustro failed to perform. Some months later plaintiff filed this suit.

Plaintiff took the position in the trial court and here that it has the status of a holder in due course of defendants' negotiable note, and as such it is immune from the defense of failure of consideration. A holder in due course is defined in the Uniform Commercial Code, §3-302 as

> (1) . . . a holder who takes the instrument
>   (a) for value; and
>   (b) in good faith; and
>   (c) without notice . . . of any defense against or claim to it on the part of any person.

If the plaintiff is not such a holder it is subject to the defense of failure of consideration on the part of Lustro. Unico v. Owen, 50 N.J. 101, 109 (1967).

As we said in *Unico*:

> In the field of negotiable instruments, good faith is a broad concept. The basic philosophy of the holder in due course status is to encourage free negotiability of commercial paper by removing certain anxieties of one who takes the paper as an innocent purchaser knowing no reason why the paper is not as sound as its face would indicate. It would seem to follow, therefore, that the more the holder knows about the underlying transaction, and particularly the more he controls or participates or becomes involved in it, the less he fits the role of a good faith purchaser for value; the closer his relationship to the underlying agreement which is the source of the note, the less need there is for giving him the tension free rights considered necessary in a fast-moving, credit-extending commercial world. [Id. at 109-110.]

Good faith is determined by looking to the mind of the particular holder. New Jersey Study Comment 1B to N.J.S.A. 12A: 3-302, at p.134, §1-201(19). The test is neither freedom from negligence in entering into the transaction nor awareness of circumstances calculated to arouse suspicions either as to whether the instrument is subject to some defense not appearing on its face or whether the promise to pay is not as unconditional as it appears therein. Joseph v. Lesnevich, 56 N.J. Super. 340, 348 (App. Div. 1959). However, evidence of circumstances surrounding the negotiation of the note which excite question as to whether the obligation it represents is really dependent upon performance of some duty by the payee is of probative value if it provides some support for a finding of a bad faith taking by the holder. Id. at 348. Of course in evaluating the circumstances, we recognize that the unique policy considerations attendant upon consumer home repair transactions, ... require us to closely scrutinize the existence of good faith in these situations. Ordinarily where the note appears to be negotiable in form and regular on its face, the holder is under no duty to inquire as to possible defenses, such as failure of consideration, unless the circumstances of which he has knowledge rise to the level that the failure to inquire reveals a deliberate desire on his part to evade knowledge because of a belief or fear that investigation would disclose a defense arising from the transaction. Id. at 349; First Natl. Bank of Blairstown v. Goldberg, 340 Pa. 337, 17 A.2d 377, 379 (1941). And, in this connection, once it appears that a defense exists against the payee, the person claiming the rights of a holder in due course has the burden of establishing that he is in all respects such a holder. N.J.S.A. §3-307 [§3-308 in the Revision — Ed.].

In this case, as already noted, plaintiff required that the underlying home improvement contract be submitted with the note at the time it was discounted. Plaintiff therefore knew that the February 19, 1967 date appearing in the note as the date of commencement of the installment payments meant that the owner agreed they were to begin as the contract said, "60 days after completion" of the work. The only sensible meaning of the agreement obviously is that the Angelinis' liability to commence payments was dependent upon completion of the improvement in a good and workmanlike manner 60 days prior to February 19. In spite of the substantial nature of the work to be performed under the contract, the fact that the note was being discounted only 10 days after execution of the contract, that the contractor's duty was to complete the work 60 days before the first payment became due, and the knowledge that under the statute, N.J.S.A. 17:16C-66, the contractor could obtain from the owner and submit to the finance company a certificate of completion if the work had been completed, plaintiff neither demanded such a certificate nor inquired of the owner as to completion. Instead it chose to accept the contractor's representation in the note endorsement form that he had fulfilled his contractual obligation. Such conduct justifies a strong inference that plaintiff wilfully failed to seek actual knowledge on the subject of completion because of a belief or a fear that an inquiry would disclose a failure of consideration of the note. Absence of inquiry under the circumstances amounts to an intentional closing of the eyes and mind to any defects in or defenses to the transaction. In our judgment the evidence in its totality and the inferences fairly drawn therefrom establish convincingly that plaintiff did not acquire the note in "good faith" and cannot claim the status of a holder in due course. Consequently it holds the instrument as an assignee and is subject to the defense of failure of consideration. The trial court's holding to the contrary is so opposed to the weight of the evidence as to constitute a manifest injustice. . . .

The judgment is reversed. . . .

PROBLEM 104

The corporate treasurer of the Business Corporation was having major troubles paying his personal bills, so finally he decided to embark on a life of crime. He used a corporate check to pay his American Express bill, making the check out to "Amerex Corp., 770 Broadway, N.Y., N.Y. 10003" (the actual address of American Express). On the corporate check requisition form he wrote a phony explanation that this check represented shipping expenses. This caused no suspicions at Business Corporation and, thus encouraged, he did it every month for two years. When Business Corporation finally figured out what had happened, it sued American Express in quasi-contract for all the money it had received in this fashion. American Express replied that it was a holder in due course of these checks and, as such, was not amenable to this suit. Business Corporation pointed to the suspicious circumstances and to UCC §§3-302(a) and 3-307 (arguing that the corporate treasurer was a fiduciary). How should this be resolved? See Hartford Accident & Indem. Co. v. American Express Co., 74 N.Y.2d 153, 542 N.E.2d 1090, 544 N.Y.S.2d 573, 8 U.C.C. Rep. Serv. 2d 865 (1989).

Winter & Hirsch, Inc. v. Passarelli

Illinois Appellate Court, 1970
122 Ill. App. 2d 372, 259 N.E.2d 312, 7 U.C.C. Rep. Serv. 1210

McCORMICK, J. This appeal is taken from an order denying a motion to vacate a judgment by confession. The judgment was entered against the defendants, Dominic and Antoinette Passarelli, on behalf of the plaintiff, Winter & Hirsch, Inc. Defendants made a motion before the trial court to vacate the judgment; the motion was denied, and from that order of the trial court this appeal is taken. The questions before this court are: 1) whether the loan entered into between the parties provided for a usurious rate of interest, and 2) whether the plaintiff was a holder in due course of the note evidencing the loan in question.

The defendants first contacted the Equitable Mortgage & Investment Corporation (hereinafter referred to as Equitable), attempting to secure a loan. Equitable is a brokerage firm which makes its profit by selling loan contracts to finance companies at a discount. In this case Equitable was to lend the defendants $10,000. Of the several provisions in the note, we will consider the following: 1) a provision whereby the defendants agreed "for value received" to repay a total of $16,260 over a period of 60 monthly payments of $271 each; and 2) a confession of judgment clause. The promissory note signed by the defendants provided for payment to the bearer and was secured by a trust deed.

The maximum legal rate of interest which could have been charged the defendants was exceeded by Equitable, and it is uncontested that Equitable charged a usurious rate of interest. The question to be resolved by this court, however, is whether the defense of usury is available for use against the plaintiff, who claims to be holder in due course of the promissory note and therefore claims to have taken it free from the defense of usury. In the trial court the defense of usury was rejected and judgment was entered against the defendants based on the court's conclusion that the plaintiff was a holder in due course of the promissory note.

In this appeal the defendants pray that the trial court's order be reversed and that the loan be held to be usurious. Defendants further ask that the trial court be directed to enter an order allowing them twice the rate of interest, plus attorney's fees and court costs. They seek this relief based on Ill. Rev. Stat. 1965, c.74, 6. At the time of the original transaction that section allowed one aggrieved by the imposition of a usurious rate of interest to be freed of the obligation to pay any interest at all, but an amendment to the statute, in effect at the time of trial, granted one the right to a penalty in the amount of double the usurious interest charged, plus attorney's fees and court costs.

Defendants defaulted on the note and the plaintiff obtained a judgment by confession. At the trial the defendants attempted to show that before the plaintiff purchased the note it knew of the usurious interest being charged, and consequently could not have become a holder in due course. Defendants point out that the loan application which the defendants filled out on January 7,

1963, has on it the name of the plaintiff. They also call attention to the testimony of Dominic Passarelli that he had been told by an agent of Equitable that Winter & Hirsch might give them $10,000. By the terms of the promissory note the monthly payments were to be made at the office of Ralph E. Brown, an attorney for plaintiff.

The most compelling fact presented to the court is that plaintiff issued a check to Equitable for $11,000 on February 18, 1963, with the notation on the stub that the funds were for "the Passarelli deal," but the defendants did not receive the $10,000 until February 28, 1963, ten days later. In other words, the plaintiff had extended the money to Equitable for the Passarelli loan prior to the time the defendants executed the note which plaintiff claims to have bought from Equitable. This fact renders inapposite an entire series of cases upon which plaintiff relies. Those cases hold that a loan may be discounted at more than the usury rate if the purchaser is without knowledge that the note was originally tainted with usury. Stevenson v. Unkefer, 14 Ill. 103; Sherman v. Blackman, 24 Ill. 345; Colehour v. State Sav. Institution, 90 Ill. 152. The critical factual distinction between those cases and the one before us is that the plaintiff in the instant case provided the money for the usurious loan before the loan was actually made, whereas in the cited cases the party claiming to be the innocent holder of the usurious note had purchased it subsequent to its execution.

On oral argument counsel for plaintiff argued that there must have been a clerical error in the dates, and that no loan company would have given out money without the loan contract in its possession. The insurmountable difficulty with counsel's argument is that the date of the check issued to Equitable (February 18) and the date of the note executed by the defendants (February 28) are clearly established through the admission into evidence, without objection, of the check issued to Equitable and the note signed by the defendants. This court must accept those dates as accurate.

From these dates it appears that the plaintiff was a co-originator of the note since it advanced the funds for the usurious loan before the loan was formalized. As a co-originator it is charged with the knowledge of the terms of the loan, and that knowledge includes information regarding anticipated return on its investment. Such information should have made it clear that a usurious rate of interest was being charged the defendants; nevertheless, the plaintiff still elected to consummate the transaction, and it must now accept the consequences.

We note, however, that the plaintiff has argued that it did not give the $11,000 to Equitable until after it saw the loan contract; in other words, that it was a purchaser of the note after it had already been executed. Although the facts do not sustain this contention because of the respective dates on which the check to Equitable was issued and the note signed by the defendants, even if that version were correct, we would hold for the defendants.

If the note was seen, as alleged by plaintiff, prior to its giving Equitable $11,000, then the plaintiff also saw that the defendants had signed a note promising to repay $16,260. From the face of the note one cannot ascertain the principal amount the defendants had received; it can only be known that "for value received" the defendants agreed to repay $16,260. We feel, however, that as reasonable businessmen, assuming arguendo that plaintiff did not know the truth, it should have raised the question of why Equitable was willing to sell a $16,260 note for $11,000. The difference between what the plaintiff was paying Equitable and the amount of the note was a charge beyond that permitted under the usury statute, and plaintiff should, therefore, have inquired how much money the defendants were receiving. We cannot permit parties to intentionally keep themselves in ignorance of facts which, if known, would defeat their unlawful purpose. The Uniform Commercial Code (Ill. Rev. Stat. 1965, c.26, §3-304(1)) provides that when an instrument is so incomplete as to call its validity into question, a purchaser of that instrument is on notice of the possibility of a claim against it [in the Revision see §3-302(a)(1) —Ed.]. In this case we feel that the instrument, without the information as to the principal sum of the loan extended to the defendants, was "so incomplete" as to call its validity into question after plaintiff learned that it was able to buy it for only $11,000.

In Springer v. Mack, 222 Ill. App. 72, the court said at p.75:

> The question of usury was discussed exhaustively and the authorities reviewed in the case of Clemens v. Crane, 234 Ill. 215, where it was held in substance, that in determining whether the essential elements of usury are present in a particular case, the intention of the parties, as the same appears from the facts and circumstances of the case, may be considered in connection with other evidence. The court also said, p.230:
> "The form of the contract is not conclusive of the question. The desire of lenders to exact more than the law permits and the willingness of borrowers to concede whatever may be demanded to

obtain temporary relief from financial embarrassment have resulted in a variety of shifts and cunning devices designed to evade the law. The character of a transaction is not to be judged by the mere verbal raiment in which the parties have clothed it, but by its true character as disclosed by the whole evidence. If, when so judged, it appears to be a loan or forbearance of money for a greater rate of interest than that allowed by law, the statute is violated and its penalties incurred, no matter what device the parties may have employed to conceal the real character of their dealings."

By failing to include the principal amount loaned to the borrower on the face of the loan contract or note, a subsequent purchaser of that contract is able to say "I had no idea that usury was involved. I simply bought the paper because it was a good buy." If the principal amount were shown, however, all subsequent purchasers would be put on notice if usury were involved, and they could not avoid their own involvement in the charging of a usurious rate by the purchase of such paper.

We feel we are justified in saying that where it appears from the facts and circumstances of the particular transaction under review that a reasonably prudent businessman would have found the purchase suspicious, he should inquire as to the truth. One should become suspicious when, as here, he is himself able to purchase paper at a price which is in itself so far below the amount to be repaid from the borrower that because of that differential the contract would have been usurious had it been the original transaction. The suspicion should be all the more compelling when the paper is bought from a broker or other company that is in the business of selling such paper. Since brokers are in the business of selling loan contracts for a profit, they are likely to have loaned out less than the amount for which they are willing to sell the contract to another. Thus, if one is able to buy a loan contract from a broker for $11,000, it is more than likely that the broker had loaned some figure less than the $11,000, and the broker's profit then becomes the difference between the amount he actually loaned and that for which he sold the contract. It would then appear likely that when this difference is itself usurious, the original transaction was also. Stevenson v. Unkefer, 14 Ill. 103, and similar cases do not dictate a contrary result. . . .

Under the circumstances, if the plaintiff was a purchaser, as it claims to be, it was on notice of a defense, since section 3-304 [in the Revision, §3-302(a)(1)—Ed.], chapter 26 of Ill. Rev. Stat. 1965 provides:

(1) The purchaser has notice of a claim or defense if
(a) the instrument is so incomplete, bears such visible evidence of forgery or alteration, or is otherwise so irregular as to call into question its validity, terms or ownership or to create an ambiguity as to the party to pay. . . .

This code provision is consistent with the earlier definition of "notice" found in section 1-201(25), chapter 26, providing:

A person has "notice" of a fact when . . .
(c) from all the facts and circumstances known to him at the time in question he has reason to know that it exists.

The intendment of these provisions would seem to be an attempt to prevent those dealing in the commercial world from obtaining various rights when, from a reasonable inquiry into the true facts that person would have discovered that a fact existed which prevented him from obtaining the rights which he was seeking. Under the circumstances in the present case, it is fair to say that the plaintiff had "reason to know" there was a good defense against the note in question. Even the earlier cases point out that notice of usury destroyed one's rights in the note. . . .

The judgment of the Circuit Court is reversed, and the cause is remanded with directions to enter a judgment for defendants and for further proceedings in conformity with this opinion.

Reversed and remanded with directions.

LYONS, J. concurs. [The dissenting opinion of BURKE, J., is omitted.]

QUESTION

Would the Federal Trade Commission holder in due course rule (see page 350) apply to the promissory note signed in this case if the transaction had taken place after May 14, 1976 (the effective date of that rule)?

PROBLEM 105

Fred wrote a check on January 5, 2008, but mistakenly put down "2007" as the year. He saw his error, crossed out the last digit, and wrote "8" above it. Can anyone become a holder in due course of this instrument?

PROBLEM 106

Ace Finance Company was the payee on a promissory note signed by John Maker. On its face the note calls for John to make 12 monthly interest payments before the note matures. Ace sold the note at a discount to Big Town Bank (BTB). If the note has written on it, in big letters, a penciled notation, "Missed Paying First Install-ment," can BTB ever qualify as a holder in due course? See §3-304(b) and (c) and its Official Comment 2.

PROBLEM 107

Dan Drawer wrote a check dated April 30 to Dr. Paine, his dentist, for $80, in payment for services rendered. Dr. Paine was not aware that the check fell to the floor behind his desk, where it lay until the end of August, when the janitor found it. Dr. Paine then indorsed the check over to his local grocery store on August 31, and it bounced on September 3, when the drawee bank in-formed the manager of the grocery store that Dan had stopped payment because the dental work had been done badly. Is the grocery store a holder in due course? See §3-304(a)(2).

PROBLEM 108

When Ellen Brown found out that the computer she had pur-chased didn't work, she was furious and decided not to pay the promissory note she had signed. The note stated that it was "payable at Busy State Bank" (which in this case means that the bank would pay the note when presented and then expect reim-bursement from the maker; cf. §4-106(b)). Harold Slow, the head cashier at the bank, took Ellen's phone call and promised not to pay the note when it was presented. Four months went by, and, on one hectic afternoon, the bank paid the note by accident. Slow said he had forgotten the request not to pay. The bank now demands payment, claiming to be a holder in due course. Is it?

Problem 108 involves the *forgotten notice doctrine*, which under the NIL permitted a holder to *forget* notice and thus become a holder in due course if sufficient time passed between the notice and the acquisition of the instrument. See First Natl. Bank of Odessa v. Fazzari, 10 N.Y.2d 394, 179 N.E.2d 493, 233 N.Y.S.2d 483

(1961) ("[W]e think that the doctrine should be applied with great caution in the case where a simple promissory note is involved. A lapse of memory is too easily pleaded and too difficult to controvert to permit the doctrine to be applied automatically irrespective of the circumstances surrounding each transaction and the relationship of the parties."). Does the UCC retain the *forgotten notice doctrine?* See §1-201(25), and in particular the last sentence and Official Comment 25 thereto; McCook County Natl. Bank v. Compton, 558 F.2d 871, 21 U.C.C. Rep. Serv. 1360 (8th Cir. 1977).

PROBLEM 109

Giant Earthmovers bought some machinery from Tractors, Inc., and in payment executed a promissory note payable to the order of Tractors for $2,000. Tractors sold the note without indorsement to the Friendly Finance Company for $1,500. The maker of the note refused to pay the note when it matured, stating that the machinery did not operate properly. Friendly decided to sue Giant Earthmovers, and the day before the lawsuit was filed, Friendly's lawyer noticed that the note had never been indorsed by Tractors, Inc. He had Tractors' president specially indorse the note over to Friendly right away, and then the suit was filed. Is Friendly a holder in due course? See §3-203(c) and its Official Comment 3, and Case #4 in Official Comment 4; Ballengee v. New Mexico Fed. Sav. & Loan Assn., 109 N.M. 423, 786 P.2d 37, 11 U.C.C. Rep. Serv. 2d 124 (N.M. 1990).

Jones v. Approved Bancredit Corp.

Delaware Supreme Court, 1969
256 A.2d 739, 6 U.C.C. Rep. Serv. 1001

HERRMANN, J. The dispositive question in this appeal is whether the plaintiff finance company is a holder in due course of the defendant's note. We hold that the finance company was not a holder in due course under the party-to-the-transaction rule.

I

The relevant facts are undisputed for present purposes.

The defendant, Myrtle V. Jones, owned a lot of land in Delaware and wished to have a house built on it. She responded to a newspaper advertisement by Albee Dell Homes, Inc. (hereinafter "Dell"), a sales agency for pre-cut homes in Elkton, Maryland. After selecting a type of house from various plans presented, Mrs. Jones signed a purchase order contract and credit application and made a deposit. Several weeks later, Dell's representative presented to Mrs. Jones for signature a series of documents evidencing an obligation of $3,250,[3] to be paid by Mrs. Jones in monthly installments over a period of years for the house. The documents evidencing the obligation included the following papers: a mortgage; a judgment bond and warrant; a promissory note; a construction contract; a request for insurance; an affidavit that the masonry work and foundation were completed and paid for (when in fact none of the work had been commenced); and an affidavit that no materials were delivered or work started as of the date of the mortgage.

Mrs. Jones demurred to the signing of the mass of documents thus placed before her and stated that she would like to consult her attorney before signing because she did not understand the documents. Dell's representative objected, stating that it was not necessary for Mrs. Jones to have an attorney; that it would be a waste of money to do so; that he would advise her. Although Mrs. Jones reiterated her wish for an attorney several times, Dell's representative insisted upon her signing the papers then and there, stating that it was necessary to do so if the work was to start seasonably. He assured her that Dell would take care of the entire situation to her satisfaction. Mrs. Jones finally acquiesced and signed all the documents. Immediately thereafter, the paper was endorsed and assigned by Dell to the plaintiff Approved Bancredit Corp. (hereinafter "Bancredit") which paid Dell $2,250.00 for the $3,250.00 note.

During the construction, an employee of the builder drove a bulldozer into the side of the partially completed house and knocked it off its foundations. Thereafter, the builder refused to go forward with the work. Dell disclaimed responsibility on the ground that the damage to the structure was a result of a "cave-in" and was "a work of God." The structure was left in a dangerous condition with the water-filled basement constituting an attractive nuisance to children. The County authorities demanded that this unsafe condition be rectified. Mrs. Jones consulted an attorney

---

3. The principal amount of the obligation was $2,500. The balance consisted of "charges."

who notified Dell and Bancredit that Mrs. Jones would be obliged
to remove the remnants of the building and fill the basement, in
order to make the area safe, unless another satisfactory course of
action was suggested. There was no reply and the demolition was
accomplished at Mrs. Jones' expense. Later, Dell closed its office
and terminated its business except for the servicing of certain
contracts through a representative in Delaware.

Thereafter, Bancredit brought this action against Mrs. Jones,
seeking foreclosure on the mortgage and collection of an unpaid
balance of $2,560.23, with interest. Mrs. Jones interposed several
defenses, mainly that of fraud by Dell. During pretrial proceedings,
the action developed into a suit upon the promissory note, which
Bancredit contended was secured by the mortgage and was negotiable in its hands as a holder in due course by assignment of Dell.
Thereupon, Bancredit moved for summary judgment on the
ground that the defenses claimed against Dell were not available
against it as a holder in due course. The Superior Court denied
summary judgment, stating that Mrs. Jones should have the
opportunity to "demonstrate the precise relationship" between
Dell and Bancredit. Thereafter, depositions were taken and the
following facts, inter alia, appeared regarding that relationship:

Dell and Bancredit were both wholly owned subsidiaries of
Albee Homes, Inc. (hereinafter "Homes"). The business of the
parent corporation was to process pre-cut lumber and sell pre-cut
homes. It had between 50 and 70 sales agencies in 19 states. Dell
was its Maryland sales agency. Ninety-nine percent of Bancredit's
business came from Dell and the other wholly owned sales agency
subsidiaries of Homes; it was organized for this purpose. Bancredit
examined into the laws of the various states in which the sales
agencies operated and prescribed the forms of contracts and financing documents to be used by each agency, including Dell, in
concluding a transaction. Homes and Bancredit had the same
officers and directors; Homes named the directors and officers of
Dell. Checks of Bancredit, issued to consummate a financing
transaction like that entered into by Mrs. Jones and Dell, were
countersigned by Homes. During the construction of a house,
Bancredit routinely requested and received progress reports.
Specifically, the manager of Bancredit testified on deposition that
Bancredit was a "finance department" of Homes; that each
transaction of Dell, like the transactions of each of the other sales
agencies, was approved in advance by Bancredit; that the first
paper received was the application of the purchaser for extension

of credit which was reviewed and passed upon in advance by Bancredit, with directions back to Dell as to any special condition to be imposed upon the purchaser in connection with the loan under consideration. Bancredit had the exclusive power of approval, condition, or rejection of a transaction tendered by the sales agency.

As the result of a pretrial conference, the trial judge stated that with a full understanding of the evidence to be adduced by each side at trial, he had concluded that a directed verdict in favor of Bancredit must necessarily result because, in his opinion, Bancredit was a holder in due course and the defenses sought to be interposed by Mrs. Jones were not available to it. Each of the parties then made a detailed offer of proof on the record and, thereupon, the Superior Court entered judgment for Bancredit on the ground that it was a holder in due course. Mrs. Jones appeals.

II

The question before us has not been heretofore answered by this court. It is a difficult question, as to which the authorities are in sharp conflict.

In dealing with the holder in due course status, a basic problem has been recognized by the courts in cases involving the financing of installment sales, especially of consumer goods and household improvements. The problem arises from the increasingly apparent need for a balancing of the interest of the commercial community in the unrestricted negotiability of commercial papers, on the one hand, against the interest of the installment buyers of the community, on the other hand, in the preservation of their normal remedy of withholding payment whenever there has been misrepresentation, failure of consideration, or other valid reason for refusal to pay. This problem and this need have given rise to this concept: The more the holder knows about the underlying transaction which is the source of the paper, the more he controls or participates in it, the less he fits the role of good faith purchaser for value, and the less justification there is for according to him the protected status of holder in due course considered necessary for the free flow of paper in the commercial world.

The rule, balancing the needs of the installment-buying community and the commercial community, has evolved in various ways. Many courts have solved the problem by denying holder in due course status to the finance company where it maintains a close business relationship with the dealer whose paper it buys; where the financier is closely connected with the particular credit transaction under scrutiny; or where the financier prescribes to the dealer the forms of the papers, the buyer signs the purchase agreement and the note concurrently, and the dealer endorses the note and assigns the contract immediately thereafter. In such situations, many courts look upon the transaction as a species of tripartite transaction; and the tenor of the cases is that the finance company, in such situation, should not be permitted to hide behind "the fictional fence" of the UNIL or the UCC and thereby achieve an unfair advantage over the purchaser. See Unico v. Owen, 50 N.J. 101, 232 A.2d 405 (1967); Buffalo Industrial Bank v. DeMarzio, 162 Misc. 742, 296 N.Y.S. 738 (1937).

The rule of balance thus evolved is exemplified by Mutual Finance Co. v. Martin, 63 So. 2d 649 (Fla. 1953). There a finance company was held not to be a holder in due course where it appeared that the finance company furnished to the payee electrical appliance dealer the form of conditional sales contract and promissory note with its name imprinted thereon; that before the sales transaction occurred the finance company had investigated the purchaser's credit standing, had approved the proposed terms and agreed to purchase the contract and note in the event the transaction was consummated; that over a period of years immediately prior to the transaction, the finance company had provided much financing for the dealer in other transactions. In holding that, under those circumstances, the finance company was sufficiently a party to the transaction to deprive it of holder in due course status, the Supreme Court of Florida stated:

> . . . It may be that our holding here will require some changes in business methods and will impose a greater burden on the finance companies. We think the buyer — Mr. & Mrs. General Public — should have some protection somewhere along the line. We believe the finance company is better able to bear the risk of the dealer's insolvency than the buyer and in a far better position to protect his interests against unscrupulous and insolvent dealers. . . .
>
> If this opinion imposes great burdens on finance companies it is a potent argument in favor of a rule which will afford protection to the general buying public against unscrupulous dealers in personal property. . . .

Another leading case supporting the rule of balance is Commercial Credit Co. v. Childs, 199 Ark. 1073, 137 S.W.2d 260 (1940), wherein the automobile sales contract, note, and assignment forms were attached together, were furnished by the finance company, and were all executed on the same day. The Supreme Court of Arkansas there stated:

> We think appellant was so closely connected with the entire transaction or with the deal that it can not be heard to say that it, in good faith, was an innocent purchaser of the instrument for value before maturity. . . . Rather than being a purchaser of the instrument after its execution it was to all intents and purposes a party to the agreement and instrument from the beginning. . . .

See also Commercial Credit Corporation v. Orange County Machine Works, 34 Cal. 2d 766, 214 P.2d 819 (1950), where the Supreme Court of California held:

> When a finance company actively participates in a transaction . . . from its inception, counseling and aiding the future vendor-payee, it cannot be regarded as a holder in due course. . . .

And in Unico v. Owen, 50 N.J. 101, 232 A.2d 405 (1967), wherein the finance company was formed expressly to handle the financing of sales by the dealer exclusively, the Supreme Court of New Jersey summarized its position on the question before us as follows:

> For purposes of consumer goods transactions, we hold that where the seller's performance is executory in character and when it appears from the totality of the arrangements between dealer and financier that the financier has had a substantial voice in setting standards for the underlying transaction, or has approved the standards established by the dealer, and has agreed to take all or a predetermined or substantial quantity of the negotiable paper which is backed by such standards, the financier should be considered a participant in the original transaction and therefore not entitled to holder in due course status. . . .

The factual situation in the *Unico* case is especially analogous to the instant case.

The divergent line of cases, reflecting an underlying conflict in policy considerations, accords determinative importance to the maintenance of a free flow of credit. These cases protect the finance company from purchaser defenses on the ground that this is an overriding consideration in order to assure easy negotiability of commercial paper and the resultant availability of the rapid financing methods required by our present-day economy. The cases of both lines of authority are collected at Annots., 128 A.L.R. 729 (1940), 44 A.L.R.2d 8, 134-157 (1955), 4 A.L.R.2d Later Case Serv. 929 (1965). See also Swanson v. Commercial Acceptance Corporation (9th Cir.), 381 F.2d 296 (1967); 39 S. Cal. L. Rev. 48, 68-74 (1966); 10 Vill. L. Rev. 309 (1965); 65 Colum. L. Rev. 733 (1965); 53 Harv. L. Rev. 1200 (1940); 1958 Wash. U.L.Q. 177; 35 U. Chi. L. Rev. 739 (1968); 939 Minn. L. Rev. 775 (1954).

Under the totality of facts and circumstances of this case, we hold that the rule of balance should be adopted and applied; that it should operate in favor of the installment buyer for the reason that, in our opinion, Bancredit was so involved in the transaction that it may not be treated as a subsequent purchaser for value. By reason of its sister corporation relationship to Dell and the established course of dealing between them, Bancredit was more nearly an original party to the transaction than a subsequent purchaser of the paper; and, for the reasons of fairness and balance stated in the foregoing authorities, Bancredit should be denied the protected status of holder in due course which would prevent Mrs. Jones from having her day in court on the defenses she would have otherwise had against Dell.

The rule we here adopt must be applied carefully because of the delicate balance of the interests of the installment buying community and the commercial community. But the need for special care in application should not foreclose the adoption of the rule and its application in a proper case. In this day of demonstrated need for emphasis upon consumer protection and truth in lending, special consideration must be given to preventing the misuse of negotiable instruments to deprive installment purchasers of legitimate defenses. In a proper case, such as the one before us, this becomes the controlling consideration.

For the reasons stated, we conclude that the Superior Court erred in holding that Bancredit was a holder in due course. Accordingly, the judgment below is reversed and the cause remanded for further proceedings consistent herewith.

This decision is typical of a large number of cases in which the courts have held that the buyer-transferee of the paper is too "closely connected" with the seller-transferor to be permitted to obtain holder in due course status. The doctrine has been chiefly of benefit to consumers, but it has been applied in purely commercial settings. See, e.g., St. James v. Diversified Commercial Fin. Corp., 102 Nev. 23, 714 P.2d 179, 1 U.C.C. Rep. Serv. 2d 121 (1986). Following are some of the tests the courts use to assess the connection.

(1) Is the buyer-transferee the alter ego of the seller-transferor? Do they have the same officers, same personnel, same location?

(2) Who drafted the original promissory note?

(3) Is the buyer-transferee mentioned in the note?

(4) Does the seller-transferor sell paper to other buyers, or is the buyer-transferee the only market?

(5) Did the buyer-transferee get involved in the transaction by which the note was created? Did it, for instance, conduct a credit investigation of the maker?

(6) Did the buyer-transferee have some knowledge of the seller-transferor's poor past performance of similar contracts?

If the court concludes that the buyer-transferee is too *closely connected* to the seller-transferor, the court has a variety of ways to deny holder in due course status to the plaintiff. It can say that the plaintiff was not acting in *good faith*, that the plaintiff had notice of underlying defenses, or that the plaintiff is the same entity as the seller-transferor and can stand in no better situation.

In light of this problem, what would you advise Bancredit to do in the future to become a holder in due course of notes that pass through the hands of payees like Dell?

Lest you get the idea that in promissory note lawsuits the finance company always loses (which is not even vaguely true), read the following case. It makes the important point that knowledge of the underlying transaction is not the same thing as notice of a claim or a defense arising out of that transaction.

Sullivan v. United Dealers Corp.

Kentucky Court of Appeals, 1972
486 S.W.2d 699, 11 U.C.C. Rep. Serv. 810

REED, J. The sole issue presented is whether appellee, United Dealers Corporation, a finance company, was a holder in due course of a promissory note executed and delivered by appellants, James Earl Sullivan and Norma Jean Sullivan, his wife, in payment for building materials and labor furnished by Memory Swift Homes, Inc., the payee of the note.

Memory Swift Homes, Inc., contracted with the Sullivans to construct a prefabricated dwelling house for them. The contract was dated March 26, 1963, and on April 9, 1963, the Sullivans executed and delivered to Memory Swift, the contractor, their promissory negotiable note in the sum of $18,224.64 secured by a mortgage on the real property and the improvement to be located thereon. On the same day, the contractor negotiated the note and assigned the mortgage to the finance company.

On June 25, 1963, the finance company negotiated the note to a bank which took the instrument with right of recourse. After the negotiation of the note to the finance company but prior to its negotiation by the finance company to the bank, the Sullivans delivered written statements to the finance company that the foundation of the house had been properly installed and also certified that all framing members in the house were properly and sufficiently nailed to make it a sound and sturdy structure and that all work had been performed in a workmanlike manner.

Beginning in August 1963, the Sullivans made several monthly payments according to the terms of the note but then defaulted. The last monthly payment was made in April 1966, but this covered the monthly installment due in August 1965. On April 25, 1966, the bank transferred the note back to the finance company, for value, without recourse. The finance company then instituted action against the Sullivans for collection of the note and foreclosure of the mortgage. The Sullivans pleaded that the finance company was not a holder in due course of the note and that the contractor had constructed the house in an unworkmanlike manner by reason of which they had been damaged; they sought to assert their claim against the contractor as a defense against the finance company. The parties to the action failed to demand a jury trial and, with their consent, the factual issues were tried by the court without a jury.

The trial court found from the evidence that the finance company was a holder in due course of the note; therefore, the defenses arising from the alleged breaches of contract by the contractor and payee of the note were held nonassertable against the finance company. Judgment was entered for the unpaid balance of the note and foreclosure of the mortgage was ordered.

The Sullivans appeal and argue the single proposition that the finance company did not become a holder in due course at the time the note was transferred and negotiated to it by the payee. We affirm the judgment of the circuit court.

The entire case for the Sullivans may be summarized by the following quotation from the brief filed on their behalf:

> The testimony shows that the appellee [the finance company] was cognizant and knew about this contract. The appellee [the finance company] had done around $500,000 with Memory Swift Homes, Inc., over a period of a number of years beginning in 1951. The appellee also knew at the time they purchased this note and mortgage that no work had been performed on the construction of the house. The appellee [the finance company] knowing about this contract, they were put on notice that there *might be* a defense on the note because of the faulty construction of the dwelling house and is, therefore, not a holder in due course and did not take the instrument in good faith—that is the note and mortgage. [Parenthetical expressions and emphasis supplied.]

Notice, in order to prevent one from being a bona fide holder under the law merchant, or a holder in due course under the NIL or the Commercial Code, means notice at the time of the taking or at the time the instrument is negotiated, and not notice arising subsequently. The time when value is given for the instrument is decisive. The moment value is given without notice the status as a holder in due course generally is definitely and irrevocably fixed. The Commercial Code, which has been adopted in Kentucky, provides that to be effective notice to a purchaser must be received at such time and in such manner as to give a reasonable opportunity to act on it. K.R.S. §3-304(6) [in the Revision see §3-302(f) —Ed.]. See 11 Am. Jur. 2d, Bills and Notes, §428, pp.458, 459.

Where a close business association between the payee and one who purchases an instrument from him implies the knowledge of such facts as to show bad faith or renders himself a participant in the transaction between the payee and the maker, a finding that such purchaser is not a holder in due course has been regarded as supportable. See 44 A.L.R.2d 154. In Massey-Ferguson v. Utley, Ky., 439 S.W.2d 57 (1969), we discussed several aspects of the basic problem. Therein we expressed the thought that the policy of the Commercial Code was to encourage the supplying of credit for the buying of goods by insulating the lender from lawsuits over the quality of the goods. The insulation provided, however, appears intended primarily for finance institutions acting independently to supply credit, rather than to protect a manufacturer who finances his own sales either in his own name or by a dominated and controlled agency.

In the case before us, there is no allegation of fraud involving the payee of the note and the finance company. There is no claim any fact existed that the finance company could have discovered at the time of the transfer of the instrument and that would have indicated any deficiency or defect. The maker of the note represented that the state of facts at that time was one of compliance by the contractor with the duties imposed by the contract. The evidence failed to demonstrate any direct connection between the contractor and the finance company except a frequent course of dealing between them. In short, the evidence failed to demonstrate any bad faith on the part of the finance company at the time of the negotiation and transfer of the note to it. All of the evidence demonstrated a complete lack of notice to the finance company that would justify a finding that it failed to acquire the status of a holder in due course.

The judgment is affirmed.

All concur.

D.   The Shelter Rule

It has always been a basic rule of the common law that the unqualified transfer of a chose in action places the transferee in the transferor's shoes and gives the transferee all the rights of the transferor. This rule is codified in §3-203(b), where it is made clear that even holder in due course rights can pass to a person not otherwise entitled to them. Because the transferee of a holder in due course takes shelter in the status of the transferor, §3-203(b) is called the *shelter rule*. Read §3-203(b) and its Official Comments, paying particular attention to Comment 4 and the examples therein. (Similar shelter rules abound throughout the UCC: for sales of goods, see §2-403(1); for documents of title, see §7-504(1); and for investment securities, see §8-301(1).)

PROBLEM 110

Happy Jack, the used car salesman, sold Manny a lemon car, taking in payment a promissory note for $2,000 made payable to the order of Happy Jack. Jack discounted the note with Alfred, a local licensed money broker, who paid him $1,700 and took the note without knowledge of the underlying transaction. Alfred's daughter Jessica had a birthday shortly thereafter, so Alfred indorsed the note in blank and gave it to her as a present. When the note matured, Manny refused to pay it to Jessica—the car had fallen apart and he felt that he shouldn't have to pay for a pile of junk. Is Jessica a holder in due course?

PROBLEM 111

If in the above Problem Jessica had thereafter made a gift of the note to her husband, Lorenzo, would Lorenzo have holder in due course rights? Does it matter if Lorenzo, prior to the gift, knows of Manny's problems with the car? If Manny won't pay, is Alfred liable to Lorenzo? See §§3-305(a)(2) and 3-303.

PROBLEM 112

After Lorenzo (from the last Problem) acquired the note, he sold it for $1,800 to Portia, a local attorney. She had no notice of problems with the instrument. When she presented it to Manny for payment, he refused to pay and instead filed for bankruptcy. May she recover from Alfred? See §3-305(b). If she does and prevails, Alfred will reacquire the instrument. Does the shelter rule give him Portia's holder in due course rights? Does Alfred reacquire his *original* holder in due course status when he gets the instrument back? Could he sue Jessica or Lorenzo? See the following discussion.

Reacquisition of an instrument. If Alfred is forced to pay Portia, he will get the instrument back into his possession. In such a case, §121 of the now-repealed NIL provided that on reacquisition a holder "is remitted to his former rights as regards all prior parties." See Chafee, The Reacquisition of a Negotiable Instrument by a Prior Party, 21 Colum. L. Rev. 538 (1921).[4] Thus, if Alfred used to be a holder in due course, on reacquiring the instrument he would get that status back vis-à-vis parties prior to his first holding. Al-

---

4. Section 3-207 discusses reacquisition, but the rules therein are not relevant to the issues raised by the preceding Problems.

though the UCC never expressly states the same rule, the idea is implicit throughout the Code, and the NIL rule is therefore still the law. As to the issue of whether Alfred can sue Jessica and Lorenzo, we will explore the liability of an indorser in the next chapter.

Section 3-207 provides that when a previous holder reacquires the instrument, he or she has the power to strike the intervening indorsements. As one court explained:

> Intervening indorsements simply vanish from the chain of title when called by a reacquirer. That concept is the obvious product of the principle that permits the current holder of a negotiable instrument to sue its predecessor in the indorsement chain, in which event that party can in turn look to its own predecessor. If those lawsuits up the chain would ultimately lead back to the current holder, that pointless circular process is best avoided by the cancellation of the intervening indorsements and the discharge of those intermediate parties from liability.

Resolution Trust Corp. v. Juergens, 965 F.2d 149, 154, 18 U.C.C. Rep. Serv. 2d 484, 491 (7th Cir. 1992).

Triffin v. Somerset Valley Bank

New Jersey Superior Court, Appellate Division, 2001
343 N.J. Super. 73, 777 A.2d 993, 44 UCC Rep. Serv. 2d 1200

CUFF, J.A.D.

This case concerns the enforceability of dishonored checks against the issuer of the checks under Article 3 of the Uniform Commercial Code (UCC), as implemented in New Jersey in N.J.S.A. 12A:3-101 to 3-605.

Plaintiff purchased, through assignment agreements with check cashing companies, eighteen dishonored checks, issued by defendant Hauser Contracting Company (Hauser Co.). Plaintiff then filed suit in the Special Civil Part to enforce Hauser Co.'s liability on the checks. The trial court granted plaintiff's motion for summary judgment. Hauser Co. appeals the grant of summary judgment. It also argues, for the first time, that plaintiff lacked standing to file suit against Hauser Co. We affirm.

In October 1998, Alfred M. Hauser, president of Hauser Co., was notified by Edwards Food Store in Raritan and the Somerset Valley Bank (the Bank), that several individuals were cashing what appeared to be Hauser Co. payroll checks. Mr. Hauser reviewed the checks, ascertained that the checks were counterfeits and contacted the Raritan Borough and Hillsborough Police Departments. Mr. Hauser concluded that the checks were counterfeits because none of the payees were employees of Hauser Co., and because he did not write the checks or authorize anyone to sign those checks on his behalf. At that time, Hauser Co. employed Automatic Data Processing, Inc. (ADP) to provide payroll services and a facsimile signature was utilized on all Hauser Co. payroll checks.

Mr. Hauser executed affidavits of stolen and forged checks at the Bank, stopping payment on the checks at issue. Subsequently, the Bank received more than eighty similar checks valued at $25,000 all drawn on Hauser Co.'s account.

Plaintiff is in the business of purchasing dishonored negotiable instruments. In February and March 1999, plaintiff purchased eighteen dishonored checks from four different check cashing agencies, specifying Hauser Co. as the drawer. The checks totaled $8,826.42. Pursuant to assignment agreements executed by plaintiff, each agency stated that it cashed the checks for value, in good faith, without notice of any claims or defenses to the checks, without knowledge that any of the signatures were unauthorized or forged, and with the expectation that the checks would be paid upon presentment to the bank upon which the checks were drawn. All eighteen checks bore a red and green facsimile drawer's signature stamp in the name of Alfred M. Hauser. All eighteen checks were marked by the Bank as "stolen check" and stamped with the warning, "do not present again." Each of the nine payees on the eighteen checks are named defendants in this case.

Plaintiff then filed this action against the Bank, Hauser Co., and each of the nine individual payees. Plaintiff contended that Hauser Co. was negligent in failing to safeguard both its payroll checks and its authorized drawer's facsimile stamp, and was liable for payment of the checks.

The trial court granted plaintiff's summary judgment motion, concluding that no genuine issue of fact existed as to the authenticity of the eighteen checks at issue. Judge Hoens concluded that because the check cashing companies took the checks in good faith, plaintiff was a holder in due course as assignee. Judge Hoens also found that because the checks appeared to be genuine, Hauser Co. was required, but had failed, to show that plaintiff's assignor had any notice that the checks were not validly drawn. . . .

As to the merits of the appeal, Hauser Co. argues that summary judgment was improperly granted because the court failed to properly address Hauser Co.'s defense that the checks at issue were invalid negotiable instruments and therefore erred in finding plaintiff was a holder in due course. . . .

As a threshold matter, it is evident that the eighteen checks meet the definition of a negotiable instrument. N.J.S.A. 12A:3-104. Each check is payable to a bearer for a fixed amount, on demand, and does not state any other undertaking by the person promising payment, aside from the payment of money. In addition, each check appears to have been signed by Mr. Hauser, through the use of a facsimile stamp, permitted by the UCC to take the place of a manual signature. N.J.S.A. 12A:3-401(b) provides that a "signature may be made manually or by means of a device or machine . . . with present intention to authenticate a writing." It is uncontroverted by Hauser Co. that the facsimile signature stamp on the checks is identical to Hauser Co.'s authorized stamp.

Hauser Co., however, contends that the checks are not negotiable instruments because Mr. Hauser did not sign the checks, did not authorize their signing, and its payroll service, ADP, did not produce the checks. Lack of authorization, however, is a separate issue from whether the checks are negotiable instruments. Consequently, given that the checks are negotiable instruments, the next issue is whether the checks are unenforceable by a holder in due course, because the signature on the checks was forged or unauthorized.

N.J.S.A. 12A:3-203 and N.J.S.A. 12A:3-302 discuss the rights of a holder in due course and the rights of a transferee of a holder in due course. Section 3-302 establishes that a person is a holder in due course if:

> (1) the instrument when issued or negotiated to the holder does not bear such apparent evidence of forgery or alteration or is not otherwise so irregular or incomplete as to call into question its authenticity; and
> (2) the holder took the instrument for value, in good faith, without notice that the instrument is overdue or has been dishonored or that there is an uncured default with respect to payment of another instrument issued as part of the same series, without notice that the instrument contains an unauthorized signature or has been altered, without notice of any claim to the instrument described in 12A:3-306, and without notice that any party has a defense or claim in recoupment described in subsection a. of 12A:3-305.

Section 3-203 deals with transfer of instruments and provides:

a. An instrument is transferred when it is delivered by a person other than its issuer for the purpose of giving to the person receiving delivery the right to enforce the instrument.

b. Transfer of an instrument, whether or not the transfer is a negotiation, vests in the transferee any right of the transferor to enforce the instrument, including any right as a holder in due course, but the transferee cannot acquire rights of a holder in due course by a transfer, directly or indirectly, from a holder in due course if the transferee engaged in fraud or illegality affecting the instrument.

The official comment to N.J.S.A. 12A:3-203 adds that in situations where a transferee does not take the instrument by indorsement (as in this case), the transferee still assumes the rights of the transferor, so long as the transferee can show that the transferor had valid rights to the instrument, and that the transferee acquired the instrument in accordance with section 3-203's requirements. Specifically, Comment 2 reads:

Subsection (b) states that transfer vests in the transferee any right of the transferor to enforce the instrument "including any right as a holder in due course." *If the transferee is not a holder because the transferor did not indorse, the transferee is nevertheless a person entitled to enforce the instrument under Section 3-301 if the transferor was a holder at the time of transfer. Although the transferee is not a holder, under subsection (b) the transferee obtained the rights of the transferor as holder. Because the transferee's rights are derivative of the transferor's rights, those rights must be proved.* Because the transferee is not a holder, there is no presumption under Section 3-308 that the transferee, by producing the instrument, is entitled to payment. The instrument, by its terms, is not payable to the transferee and the transferee must account for possession of the unindorsed instrument by proving the transaction through which the transferee acquired it. Proof of a transfer to the transferee by a holder is proof that the transferee has acquired the rights of a holder. At that point the transferee is entitled to the presumption under Section 3-308.

Under subsection (b) a holder in due course that transfers an instrument transfers those rights as a holder in due course to the purchaser. The policy is to assure the holder in due course a free market for the instrument.

[N.J.S.A. 12A:3-203, Comment 2 (emphasis added).]

The record indicates that plaintiff has complied with the requirements of both sections 3-302 and 3-203. Each of the check cashing companies from whom plaintiff purchased the dishonored checks were holders in due course. In support of his summary judgment motion, plaintiff submitted an affidavit from each company; each company swore that it cashed the checks for value, in good faith, without notice of any claims or defenses by any party, without knowledge that any of the signatures on the checks were unauthorized or fraudulent, and with the expectation that the checks would be paid upon their presentment to the bank upon which the checks were drawn. Hauser Co. does not dispute any of the facts sworn to by the check cashing companies.

The checks were then transferred to plaintiff in accordance with section 3-203, vesting plaintiff with holder in due course status. Each company swore that it assigned the checks to plaintiff in exchange for consideration received from plaintiff. Plaintiff thus acquired the check cashing companies' holder in due course status when the checks were assigned to plaintiff. See N.J.S.A. 12A:3-203, Comment 2. Moreover, pursuant to section 3-203(a)'s requirement that the transfer must have been made for the purpose of giving the transferee the right to enforce the instrument, the assignment agreements expressly provided plaintiff with that right, stating that "all payments [assignor] may receive from any of the referenced Debtors . . . shall be the exclusive property of [assignee]." Again, Hauser Co. does not dispute any facts relating to the assignment of the checks to plaintiff.

Hauser Co. contends, instead, that the checks are per se invalid because they were fraudulent and unauthorized. Presumably, this argument is predicated on section 3-302. This section states a person is not a holder in due course if the instrument bears "apparent evidence of forgery or alteration" or is otherwise "so irregular or incomplete as to call into question its authenticity." N.J.S.A. 12A:3-302(a)(1).

In order to preclude liability from a holder in due course under section 3-302, it must be apparent on the face of the instrument that it is fraudulent. The trial court specifically found that Hauser Co. had provided no such evidence, stating that Hauser Co. had failed to show that there was anything about the appearance of the checks to place the check cashing company on notice that any check was not valid. Specifically, with respect to Hauser Co.'s facsimile signature on the checks, the court stated that the signature was identical to Hauser Co.'s authorized facsimile signature. Moreover, each of the check cashing companies certified that they had no knowledge that the signatures on the checks were fraudulent or that there were any claims or defenses to enforcement of the checks. Hence, the trial court's conclusion that there was no apparent evidence of invalidity was not an abuse of discretion and was based on a reasonable reading of the record.

To be sure, section 3-308(a) does shift the burden of establishing the validity of the signature to the plaintiff, but only if the defendant specifically denies the signature's validity in the pleadings. The section states:

> In an action with respect to an instrument, *the authenticity of, and authority to make, each signature on the instrument is admitted unless specifically denied in the pleadings.* If the validity of a signature is denied in the pleadings, the burden of establishing validity is on the person claiming validity, but the signature is presumed to be authentic and authorized unless the action is to enforce the liability of the purported signer and the signer is dead or incompetent at the time of trial of the issue of validity of the signature.

[N.J.S.A. 12A:3-308(a) (emphasis added).]

Comment 1 explains that a specific denial is required

> to give the plaintiff notice of the defendant's claim of forgery or lack of authority as to the particular signature, and to afford the plaintiff an opportunity to investigate and obtain evidence. . . . In the absence of such specific denial the signature stands admitted, and is not in issue. Nothing in this section is intended, however, to prevent amendment of the pleading in a proper case.

[N.J.S.A. 12A:3-308, Comment 1.]

> Examination of the pleadings reveals that Hauser Co. did not specifically deny the factual assertions in plaintiff's complaint.

Even if Hauser Co.'s general denial was sufficient, the presumption that the signature is valid still remains, unless Hauser Co. satisfies the evidentiary requirements of N.J.S.A. 12A:3-308. Comment 1 to that section explains that even when the defendant has specifically denied the authenticity of a signature, the signature is still presumed to be authentic, absent evidence of forgery or lack of authorization. Comment 1 states:

> The burden is on the party claiming under the signature, *but the signature is presumed to be authentic and authorized* except as stated in the second sentence of subsection (a). *"Presumed" is defined in Section*

1-201 and means that until some evidence is introduced which would support a finding that the signature is forged or unauthorized, the plaintiff is not required to prove that it is valid. The presumption rests upon the fact that in ordinary experience forged or unauthorized signatures are very uncommon, and normally any evidence is within the control of, or more accessible to, the defendant. *The defendant is therefore required to make some sufficient showing of the grounds for the denial before the plaintiff is required to introduce evidence.* The defendant's evidence need not be sufficient to require a directed verdict, but it must be enough to support the denial by permitting a finding in the defendant's favor. Until introduction of such evidence the presumption requires a finding for the plaintiff.

[N.J.S.A. 12A:3-308, Comment 1 (emphasis added).]

Here, Hauser Co. has not provided any evidence of the invalidity of the signature. Hauser Co.'s reliance on conclusory statements does not constitute such a "sufficient showing." *See Coupounas v. Madden,* 401 Mass. 125, 514 N.E.2d 1316, 1320 (1987) (defendant disputing validity of notes "had to do more than 'call into question' the 'integrity' of the notes").

In addition, as a matter of summary judgment, Hauser Co.'s reliance on its answer, amended answer and Mr. Hauser's affidavit as material, disputed facts is inadequate. In order to defeat a motion for summary judgment, a party must show that there are genuine issues of material fact. *Brill, supra,* 142 N.J. at 540, 666 A.2d 146. "Bare conclusions in the pleadings, without factual support in tendered affidavits, will not defeat a meritorious application for summary judgment." *United States Pipe and Foundry Co. v. American Arbitration Ass'n,* 67 N.J. Super. 384, 399-400, 170 A.2d 505 (App. Div. 1961); *see also Brae Asset Fund v. Newman,* 327 N.J. Super. 129, 134, 742 A.2d 986 (App. Div. 1999). Hauser Co. provided no factual evidence tending to disprove the authenticity of the signature, relying instead on self-interested and conclusory statements. Consequently, the trial court did not err in finding that Hauser Co. had failed to provide any evidence of the invalidity of the checks.

In conclusion, we hold that Judge Hoens properly granted summary judgment. There was no issue of material fact as to: (1) the status of the checks as negotiable instruments; (2) the status of the check cashing companies as holders in due course; (3) the status of plaintiff as a holder in due course; and (4) the lack of apparent evidence on the face of the checks that they were forged, altered or otherwise irregular. Moreover, Hauser Co.'s failure to

submit some factual evidence indicating that the facsimile signature was forged or otherwise unauthorized left unchallenged the
UCC's rebuttable presumption that a signature on an instrument
is valid. Consequently, the trial court properly held, as a matter of
law, that plaintiff was a holder in due course and entitled to
enforce the checks.

Affirmed.

It may seem unfair to give holder in due course status to non-
purchasers and those who take with notice of defenses, but on
reflection the unfairness disappears. If the rule were otherwise, the
current holder would simply pass the instrument back up the
chain until it reached a former holder in due course, who would
then reacquire that status, sue the instrument's creator, and prevail. The shelter rule accomplishes the same result without all
these maneuvers and has the further benefit of promoting commercial confidence in the soundness of the instrument once it has
floated through the hands of multiple purchasers.

II.   REAL AND PERSONAL DEFENSES/CLAIMS

A.   Defenses Against a Holder in Due Course

Holder in due course status has as its primary attribute the
ability to enforce the instrument free from the usual legal excuses
that could be raised in an ordinary contracts action. The key
Uniform Commercial Code section reaching this extraordinary
result is §3-305, to which we now turn.

Section 3-305 is difficult to read, primarily because a number
of the concepts therein are complicated to sort out. Let's take it a
point at a time.

First of all, the *obligor* mentioned throughout §3-305 is the
party to the instrument who is being sued by the holder of the instrument. Thus, the obligor could be the drawer of a draft, the
maker of a note, or someone who indorsed the instrument. In the
next chapter, we shall discuss the nature of the obligations these
parties incur by virtue of having signed the instrument in one of
the above capacities.

A "defense," of course, is the legal excuse the obligor may have to avoid paying the obligation. Subsection (b) tells us that a holder in due course takes subject to the defenses listed in subsection (a)(1), meaning that these defenses, if true, defeat the right of the holder in due course to enforce the instrument. Defenses that are good against a holder in due course are commonly called *real defenses*, a label you might wish to write next to §3-305(a)(1). Subsection (b) tells us that a holder in due course is not subject to the defenses raised in subsection (a)(2), the so-called *personal defenses*.

Subsection (b) also states that a holder in due course holds free of "claims in recoupment" per §3-305(a)(3), but what does that mean? Recoupment is the legal ability to *subtract* from any payment due the amount the person trying to collect the debt (or that person's predecessor) happens to owe the debtor. For example, if I owe you $500 pursuant to our contract, and, as a result of your breach of that same contract, you have caused me $200 worth of damages, my claim in recoupment permits me to subtract those damages and only pay you $300. A claim in recoupment is so similar to a defense that the original version of Article 3 seemed to lump it in with the other personal defenses, but the revised version of Article 3 gives it its own special treatment (leading to awkward references throughout to a "defense or claim in recoupment"). Read Official Comment 3 to §3-305.

PROBLEM 113

Stephen Maturin bought a sailboat from Jack Aubrey, paying $500 down and signing a $1,000 promissory note for the balance due. Maturin loved everything about the boat except its color, and he promptly repainted it his favorite color, black. Prior to the sale Aubrey had told Maturin that the boat was constructed so that it wouldn't sink even in the roughest weather. This proved to be untrue when the sailboat went down in the first storm that came along, and it cost Maturin $300 to have it dredged from the bottom and restored. In the meantime, Aubrey had given the promissory note to his father as a birthday gift, and the father presented it to Maturin for payment at maturity. May Maturin assert his damages against the father's demand for payment? Same result if the boat never sank, but Aubrey's dog bit Maturin on the leg one week after the delivery of the sailboat, and Maturin incurred $100 in medical bills as a consequence? See Zener v. Velde, 135 Idaho 352, 17 P.3d 296, 42 UCC Rep. Serv. 2d 1073 (Idaho App. 2000).

Federal Deposit Insurance Corp. v. Culver

United States District Court, District of Kansas, 1986
640 F. Supp. 725, 1 U.C.C. Rep. Serv. 2d 1585

O'CONNOR, J. This matter comes before the court on defendant's motion to dismiss for lack of personal jurisdiction, on plaintiff's motion for summary judgment, and on defendant's motion for leave to file a demand for jury trial out of time. After reciting the material facts (construed most favorably to defendant), we will address these pending motions.

In 1984, defendant entered into a business arrangement with a Mr. Nasib Ed Kalliel. Kalliel was to assume control over the financial aspects of defendant's farm, while defendant was to manage the farming operation—receiving both a salary and a share of the profits. In July or August of that year, defendant informed Kalliel that he urgently needed money in order to stave off foreclosure. One week later, $30,000.00 was wire-transferred from the Rexford State Bank in Rexford, Kansas, to defendant's bank in King City, Missouri. Although defendant knew that the money had come from the Rexford State Bank, he thought that Kalliel would be responsible for its repayment.

About one week later, defendant was approached by a Mr. Jerry Gilbert, whom defendant believed was working for Kalliel. Gilbert told defendant that "Rexford State Bank wanted to know where the $30,000.00 went, . . . for their records." Gilbert presented defendant with a document and asked defendant to sign it. Apparently, Gilbert either told defendant, or at least led him to believe, that the document was merely a receipt for the $30,000.00 he had received. In any event, defendant signed the document without thereby intending to commit himself to the repayment of any money.

The document defendant signed was a preprinted promissory note form. As might be expected, the form contained a number of blanks into which the parties were expected to insert terms specific to their own transaction. At the time defendant signed the document, none of those blanks had been completed. Thus, the note contained no execution date, no maturity date, no principal amount, and no interest rate. The name of the payee, "THE

REXFORD STATE BANK, Rexford, Kansas," was printed on the note at that time. Moreover, the note did provide that the principal and accrued interest were to be paid to the payee "at its offices."

Although defendant assumed that the figure $30,000.00 would eventually be written on the document, some unknown individual completed the note as follows:

(1) The principal amount was shown as $50,000.00;

(2) the execution date was shown as August 2, 1984;

(3) the maturity date was shown as February 2, 1985; and

(4) the interest rate was shown as 14½ percent per annum until maturity, and 18½ percent per annum thereafter.

Although defendant received only $30,000.00, the Rexford State Bank did deposit the full $50,000.00 in an account controlled by Kalliel. The $30,000.00 apparently came from that account.

Eventually, the note was returned to the Rexford State Bank. When that bank became insolvent, the Federal Deposit Insurance Corporation ["FDIC"] was appointed as its receiver. In its *corporate* capacity, the FDIC then purchased a number of the bank's assets from the receiver—including the note at issue here. At that time, the FDIC had no actual knowledge of the events that had transpired prior to its purchase of the note. As of yet, defendant has made no payment of either principal or interest.

Other than receiving the $30,000.00 wire-transfer from the Rexford State Bank, and then signing the note naming the bank as payee, defendant has had no other relevant contact with the state of Kansas. . . .

II. PLAINTIFF'S MOTION FOR SUMMARY JUDGMENT

. . . Recognizing that "[t]here is no doubt that state and federal law provide the Federal Deposit Insurance Corporation with holder in due course status in the instant litigation" (Defendant's Brief of May 2, 1986, at 11), defendant concedes that the "personal" defenses of fraud in the inducement, estoppel, and failure of consideration would be ineffective against plaintiff's claim. See F.D.I.C. v. Vestering, 620 F. Supp. 1271 (D. Kan. 1985). Accordingly, defendant seeks to assert the "real" defense of fraud in the factum. See K.S.A. 84-3-305(2)(c) [in the Revision see §3-305(a)(1)(iii)—Ed.]. Plaintiff denies that the facts as alleged by defendant constitute fraud in the factum. Alternatively, even assuming that defendant can establish the elements of fraud in the factum, plaintiff contends that such a defense is ineffective against the FDIC because of the doctrine enunciated in D'Oench, Duhme & Co. v. F.D.I.C., 315 U.S. 447 (1942), and codified at 12 U.S.C. §1823(e). Because we conclude that defendant cannot demonstrate fraud in the factum, we do not reach plaintiff's arguments regarding *d'Oench, Duhme* and section 1823(e).

The "fraud in the factum" defense is codified at K.S.A. 84-3-305(2)(c) [in the Revision see 3-305(a)(1)(iii)—Ed.], which provides as follows:

> Rights of a holder in due course. To the extent that a holder is a holder in due course he takes the instrument free from . . .
> (2) all defenses of any party to the instrument with whom the holder has not dealt *except* . . .
> (c) such misrepresentation as has induced the party to sign the instrument with neither knowledge nor reasonable opportunity to obtain knowledge of its *character* or its *essential terms.*

(Emphasis added.) As suggested by our factual summary, defendant contends that he signed the note under the misapprehension that it was merely a receipt. He thus denies having knowledge of the document's "character" at the time he signed it. Moreover, because the note's execution date, maturity date, principal amount and interest rate were all blank at the time he signed it, defendant contends that he had neither knowledge nor reasonable opportunity to obtain knowledge as to the note's "essential terms."

To determine whether these facts fit the definition of fraud in the factum, we look elsewhere in the Kansas Uniform Commercial Code. For instance, Official UCC Comment 7 to §3-305 provides this advice:

> Paragraph (c) of subsection (2) is new. It follows the great majority of the decisions under the original Act in recognizing the defense of "real" or "essential" fraud, sometimes called fraud in the essence or fraud in the factum, as effective against a holder in due course. The common illustration is that of the maker who is tricked into signing a note in the belief that it is merely a receipt or some other document. The theory of the defense is that his signature on the instrument is ineffective because he did not intend to sign such an instrument at all. Under this provision the defense extends to an instrument signed with knowledge that it is a negotiable instrument, but without knowledge of its essential terms.

> *The test of the defense here stated is that of excusable ignorance of the contents of the writing signed.* The party must not only have been in ignorance, but must also have had no reasonable opportunity to obtain knowledge.   *Rule*

(Emphasis added.) A portion of the 1983 Kansas Comment to this same section offers guidance as to the proper construction of the term "excusable ignorance." The Comment provides as follows:

> Kansas decisional law would seem to be in accord on the possibility of fraud in the factum as a real defense, the decision in Ort v. Fowler, 31 Kan. 478, 2 P. 580 (1884), being a good example of facts not satisfying the defense because of the failure of the maker to satisfy a standard of conduct comparable to that required by this subsection.

Given this Kansas Comment's reference to *Ort*, an examination of the facts and the holding in that case should be useful in determining whether defendant showed "excusable ignorance" in mistaking the note at issue here for a receipt.

In *Ort*, a farmer was working alone in his field. A stranger came up to him and represented himself to be the state agent for a manufacturer of iron posts and wire fence. After some conversation, the stranger persuaded the farmer to accept a township-wide agency for the same manufacturer. The stranger then completed two documents which he represented to be identical versions of an agency contract. Because the farmer did not have his glasses with him and, in any event, "could not read without spelling out every word," 31 Kan. at 480, the stranger purported to read the document to the farmer. No mention was made of any note. Both men signed each document, with the farmer not intending to sign anything but a contract of agency. Ultimately, it was established that at least one of those documents was a promissory note. A bona fide purchaser of that note brought suit against the farmer, and the farmer attempted to defend the action on the basis of fraud in the factum. After the trial court rejected that defense, the farmer appealed.

The Kansas Supreme Court, in an opinion by Justice David Brewer (later a United States Supreme Court Associate Justice), phrased the issue on appeal as follows: "A party is betrayed into signing a bill or note by the assurance that it is an instrument of a different kind. Under what circumstances ought he to be liable thereon?" 31 Kan. at 482. Three alternative answers were then suggested:

1) never intended
2) look at Tuf
3) they must find guilty of neg.

One view entertained is, that as he never intended to execute a bill or note, it cannot be considered his act, and he should not be held liable thereon any more than if his name had been forged to such an instrument. A second view is, that it is always a question of fact for the jury whether under the circumstances the party was guilty of negligence. A third is the view adopted by the trial court, that as [a] matter of law, one must be adjudged guilty of such negligence as to render him liable who, possessed of all his faculties and able to read, signs a bill or note, relying upon the assurance or the reading of a stranger that it is a different instrument.

Id. Defendant herein would obviously prefer either the first or second alternative. The court, however, made its preference clear:

> *We approve of the latter doctrine.* It presents a case, of course, of which one of two innocent parties must suffer; but the bona fide holder is not only innocent, but free from all negligence. He has done only that which a prudent, careful man might properly do, while on the other hand the maker of the note has omitted ordinary care and prudence. A party cannot guard against forgery; but if in possession of his faculties and able to read, he can know the character of every instrument to which he puts his signature; and it is a duty which he owes to any party who may be subsequently affected by his act, to know what it is which he signs. By his signature he invites the credence of the world to every statement and promise which is in the instrument he has subscribed; and he is guilty of negligence if he omits to use the ordinary means of ascertaining what those provisions and statements are. If he has eyes and can see, he ought to examine; if he can read, he ought to read; and he has no right to send his signature out into the world affixed to an instrument of whose contents he is ignorant. If he relies upon the word of a stranger, he makes that stranger his agent. He adopts his reading as his own knowledge. What his agent knows, he knows; and he cannot disaffirm the acts of that agent done within the scope of the authority he has intrusted to him.

Id., 31 Kan. at 482-483 (emphasis added). Although *Ort* is of rather ancient vintage, this aspect of the decision has been cited with approval as recently as 1966. See Mid Kansas Federal Savings & Loan Assn. v. Binter, 197 Kan. 106, 110, 415 P.2d 278, 282 (1966).

It is obvious from reading defendant's deposition that he is able to read and understand the English language. Thus, under the rule announced in *Ort*, defendant was negligent in relying on Gilbert's assurance that the note was only a receipt. Given the 1983 Kansas Comment referring to the *Ort* absence-of negligence standard as "comparable to that required by [K.S.A. 84-3-305(2)(c)]," we must also conclude that defendant has failed to show the "excusable ignorance" necessary to establish fraud in the factum. In the words of the statute, we conclude as a matter of law that defendant had a "reasonable opportunity to obtain knowledge of [the document's] character" before he signed it.

Defendant's second argument, assuming that we reject his contention that he neither knew nor had reasonable opportunity to know the "character" of the document he signed, is that he had no such opportunity to learn of the note's "essential terms." Because the note's execution date, maturity date, principal amount and interest rate were all blank when defendant signed the note, he asserts that he had no (let alone a reasonable) opportunity to learn of those terms. On its face, this argument has great appeal; but defendant's reliance thereon is foreclosed by other Code provisions.

Questions arising from incomplete instruments and material alterations are governed by K.S.A. 84-3-115 and -407, respectively. The former provides as follows:

> (1) When a paper whose contents at the time of signing show that it is intended to become an instrument is signed while still incomplete in any necessary respect it cannot be enforced until completed, but when it is completed in accordance with authority given it is effective as completed.
>
> (2) *If the completion is unauthorized the rules as to material alteration apply (section 84-3-407).*

K.S.A. 84-3-115 (emphasis added). Because defendant claims not to have authorized anyone to complete the note as it now reads, we are referred by part (2) of this section to K.S.A. 84-3-407. The latter statute provides, in part, as follows:

> (3) A subsequent holder in due course may in all cases enforce the instrument according to its original tenor, *and when an incomplete instrument has been completed, he may enforce it as completed.*

K.S.A. 84-3-407(3) (emphasis added). As a holder in due course, plaintiff is thus entitled to enforce this note as it was eventually completed—and not merely as defendant would have authorized it to be completed.

The fraud allegedly committed by Gilbert does not affect this conclusion. We learn from Official UCC Comment 4 to K.S.A. 84-3-

407 that "this result is intended even though the instrument was stolen from the maker or drawer and completed after the theft." In other words, one who signs an instrument before all essential terms have been completed creates a "blank check" that may be enforced by a subsequent holder in due course according to any terms that are completed by an intervening holder. See K.S.A. 84-3-305, Kansas Comment 1983. That was precisely what happened here. Defendant executed the note in blank; an intervening holder completed the note as it reads today; and plaintiff, as a holder in due course, is entitled to enforce the note according to its present terms. Defendant's only legal recourse is against the intervening holder who actually completed the note without defendant's authorization. As between the parties now before the court, we must grant plaintiff's motion for summary judgment. . . .

See Annot., Fraud in the Factum, 78 A.L.R.3d 1020.

PROBLEM 114

When Ronald Rube, newly rich, moved to New York City, he was impressed by the Brooklyn Bridge when first he saw it. Simon Mustache, a con man, told Rube that he was the owner of the bridge (a lie, of course), and offered to sell it to Rube for $2,000,000 (described as "a bargain"). Rube paid $20,000 cash as a down-payment and signed a promissory note, payable to Mustache, for the rest. Mustache negotiated the note to a finance company, which claimed to be a holder in due course. When Rube discovered that Mustache lacked title to the bridge, he refused to pay the note. Does he have a real defense of fraud here?

PROBLEM 115

A child prodigy, Thomas Minor, had been playing the piano since he was three and making professional tours of the world since he was twelve. He looked much older than his seventeen years. He signed a promissory note for $800 payable to the order of Merry Music Company as payment for a piano, planning to tour with it. The company was unaware of Minor's age. The payee indorsed the

note over to the Big National Bank for $725. When the first pay-
ment came due, Minor refused to pay. He told the bank to come
pick up the piano—he was disaffirming the sale. Who wins?

PROBLEM 116

Childe Harold, also age 17, received a check for $1,000 from
his employer and decided to use it to buy a car from Byron Auto
Sales, a used car dealership. He picked out the car he wanted,
indorsed the check in blank, and handed it over to the salesman.
Byron Auto Sales indorsed the check on the back and cashed it at
its own bank, the Crusaders National Bank. Before this bank could
present the check to the drawee bank, Childe Harold decided to
buy a horse instead of an automobile, so he returned the car to the
dealer and asked for the check back. Informed that the bank had it,
Childe Harold called up the bank and informed it of his rescission
of the contract. When the bank refused to return the check to
Childe Harold, he filed suit, asking the court to restrain the bank
from presenting the check to the drawee and to order replevin of
the check. How should the court rule? It is clear that a holder in
due course takes subject to the defense of infancy, but does he take
subject to a claim to the instrument based on infancy? See §§3-202,
3-305(a) and (b), and 3-306.

Mental incapacity. Notes signed by those who are mentally
incompetent are *void* or *voidable* depending on the equities of the
situation (i.e., the knowledge of the person dealing with the
incompetent, the benefit received by the incompetent, the degree
of incompetency, etc.). If someone has been judicially declared
incompetent, his or her instruments are more likely to be declared
void (hence a nullity) than if no adjudication has taken place. See
Annot., Insanity as Defense Against Holder in Due Course, 24
A.L.R.2d 1380.

Sea Air Support, Inc. v. Herrmann

Nevada Supreme Court, 1980
613 P.2d 413, 29 U.C.C. Rep. Serv. 918

PER CURIAM. Ralph Herrmann wrote a check for $10,000
payable to the Ormsby House, a hotel-casino located in Carson

City, Nevada, and exchanged it for three counter checks he had written earlier that evening to acquire gaming chips. The Ormsby House was unable to collect the proceeds from the check because Herrmann had insufficient funds in his account. The debt evidenced by the check was assigned to Sea Air Support, Inc., dba Automated Accounts Associates, for collection. Sea Air also was unsuccessful in its attempts to collect and, therefore, filed this action against Herrmann to recover $10,567.

The district judge dismissed the action on the ground that Sea Air's claim is barred by the Statute of Anne. Sea Air appeals the dismissal. We are asked to reconsider the long line of Nevada cases refusing to enforce gambling debts. We refuse to do so, and affirm the dismissal.

Nevada law incorporates the common law of gambling as altered by the Statute of 9 Anne, c.14, 1, absent conflicting statutory or constitutional provisions. N.R.S. 1.030; West Indies v. First National Bank, 67 Nev. 13, 214 P.2d 144 (1950); Burke v. Buck, 31 Nev. 74, 99 P. 1078 (1909). The Statute provides that all notes drawn for the purpose of reimbursing or repaying any money knowingly lent or advanced for gaming are "utterly void, frustrate, and of none effect." Despite the fact that gambling, where licensed, is legal in Nevada, this court has long held that debts incurred, and checks drawn, for gambling purposes are void and unenforceable. Corbin v. O'Keefe, 87 Nev. 189, 484 P.2d 565 (1971); Wolpert v. Knight, 74 Nev. 322, 330 P.2d 1023 (1958); Weisbrod v. Fremont Hotel, 74 Nev. 227, 326 P.2d 1104 (1958); West Indies, 67 Nev. at 31; Burke, 31 Nev. at 80; Evans v. Cooke, 11 Nev. 69 (1876); Scott v. Courtney, 7 Nev. 419 (1872).

In this case, Herrmann's $10,000 check clearly was drawn for the purpose of repaying money knowingly advanced for gaming. See Craig v. Harrah, 66 Nev. 1, 201 P.2d 1081 (1949). The check is void and unenforceable in this state. If the law is to change, it must be done by legislative action.

Sea Air seeks to avoid the defense that the check is void and unenforceable because of gaming purpose by claiming to be a holder in due course, immune to most defenses. N.R.S. 3-305. "A holder in due course is a holder who takes the [negotiable] instrument (a) For value; and (b) In good faith; and (c) Without notice that it is overdue or has been dishonored or of any defense against or claim to it on the part of any person." N.R.S. 3-302(1). Sea Air promised to take "such legal action as may be necessary to enforce collection" of the $10,000. The promise to perform services in the future does not constitute taking for value under N.R.S. 3-303. Anderson, 2 Uniform Commercial Code (2d ed.) §3303:3. In addition, Sea Air had at least constructive notice of a defense against collection because the check was payable to a casino, and Sea Air knew the check had been dishonored. Consequently, Sea Air is not a holder in due course. The action was properly dismissed.

Affirmed.

QUESTION

If Sea Air had been a holder in due course, would it have been able to enforce the check? See §3-305(a); Casanova Club v. Bisharat, 189 Conn. 591, 458 A.2d 1, 35 U.C.C. Rep. Serv. 1207 (1983). It should be noted that following the decision in *Sea Air Support,* the Nevada legislature amended its gaming laws to permit casinos to sue on credit instruments received in payment of gambling debts. Nev. Rev. Stat. 463.368.

Kedzie & 103rd Currency Exchange, Inc. v. Hodge

Illinois Supreme Court, 1993
156 Ill. 2d 112, 619 N.E.2d 732, 21 U.C.C. Rep. Serv. 2d 682

FREEMAN, J. We consider here whether a holder in due course of a check is precluded from payment as against the drawer where the check was given in exchange for contract services for which the provider was required to be, but was not, a licensed plumber. We conclude such a claim is not precluded.

BACKGROUND

Pursuant to a written "work order," Fred Fentress agreed to install a "flood control system" at the home of Eric and Beulah Hodge of Chicago for $900. In partial payment for the work, Beulah Hodge drafted a personal check payable to "Fred Fentress —A-OK Plumbing" for $500 from the Hodges' joint account at Citicorp Savings.

The system's components were not delivered to the Hodges' home as scheduled. And, when Fentress failed to appear on the date set for installation, Eric Hodge telephoned him to announce the contract "cancelled." Hodge also told Fentress that he would order Citicorp Savings not to pay the check Fentress had been given.

Records of Citicorp Savings confirm acknowledgment of a stop-payment order entered the same day.

Nevertheless, Fentress presented the check at the Kedzie & 103rd Street Currency Exchange (Currency Exchange), endorsing it as "sole owner" of A-OK Plumbing, and obtained payment. However, when the Currency Exchange later presented the check for payment at Citicorp Savings, payment was refused in accordance with the stop-payment order.

The Currency Exchange, alleging it was a holder in due course (see Ill. Rev. Stat. 1989, ch. 26, par. 3-302), then sued Beulah Hodge, as drawer of the check, and Fentress for the amount stated. Hodge, in turn, filed a counterclaim against Fentress. Hodge also moved to dismiss the Currency Exchange's action against her (see Ill. Rev. Stat. 1989, ch. 110, par. 2-619). The disposition of Hodge's motion gives rise to this appeal.

Hodge asserted a defense provided by §3-305 of the Uniform Commercial Code (UCC) (Ill. Rev. Stat. 1989, ch. 26, par. 3-305). Under that section, the claim of a holder in due course of a negotiable instrument may be barred based on "illegality of the transaction." (Ill. Rev. Stat. 1989, ch. 26, par. 3-305(2)(b).)[5] Hodge contended Fentress was not a licensed plumber as was required under the Illinois Plumbing License Law (see Ill. Rev. Stat. 1989, ch. 111, pars. 1101 through 1140). The director of licensing and registration of the Chicago department of buildings and the keeper of plumbing licensing records of the Illinois Department of Public Health provided affidavits supporting that contention. Hodge asserted that, because Fentress was in violation of the Illinois Plumbing License Law, his promised performance under the contract gave rise to the requisite "illegality" to bar the Currency Exchange's claim for payment.

The circuit court granted the motion and dismissed the Currency Exchange's action against Hodge. The appellate court, with one justice dissenting, affirmed. (234 Ill. App. 3d 1017.) Pursuant to Supreme Court Rule 315(a) (134 Ill. 2d R. 315(a)), we allowed the Currency Exchange's petition for leave to appeal.

DISCUSSION

. . . The Illinois Plumbing License Law requires that all plumbing, including "installation. . .or extension" of "drains," be per-

5. [Now §3-305(a)(1)(ii) —Ed.]

formed by plumbers licensed under the Act. (Ill. Rev. Stat. 1989, ch. 111, pars. 1102(5), (8), 1103.) The affidavits establish that Fentress was not licensed either by the City of Chicago or the State of Illinois. That failure is a violation of the Illinois Plumbing License Law and is punishable as a misdemeanor. Ill. Rev. Stat. 1989, ch. 111, pars. 1103, 1128. . . .

. . . The concern is whether noncompliance by Fentress with the Illinois Plumbing License Law gives rise to "illegality of the transaction" with respect to the contract for plumbing services so as to bar the claim of the Currency Exchange, a holder in due course of the check initially given Fentress.

The issue of "illegality" arises "under a variety of statutes." (Ill. Ann. Stat., ch. 26, par. 3-305, Uniform Commercial Code Comment, at 66 (Smith-Hurd Supp. 1992).) In view of the diverse constructions to which statutory enactments are given, "illegality" is, accordingly, a matter "left to the local law." (Ill. Ann. Stat., ch. 26, par. 3-305, Uniform Commercial Code Comment, at 66 (Smith-Hurd Supp. 1992).) Even so, it is only when an obligation is made "entirely null and void" under "local law" that "illegality" exists as one of the "real defenses" under §3-305 to defeat a claim of a holder in due course. (Ill. Ann. Stat., ch. 26, par. 3-305, Uniform Commercial Code Comment, at 66 (Smith-Hurd Supp. 1992).) In effect, the obligation must be no obligation at all. If it is "merely voidable" at the election of the obligor, the defense is unavailable. Ill. Ann. Stat., ch. 26, par. 3-305, Uniform Commercial Code Comment, at 66 (Smith-Hurd Supp. 1992).

Historically, this court has recognized "illegality" to arise only in view of legislative declaration affecting both the underlying contract or transaction and the instrument exchanged upon it. (Pope v. Hanke (1894), 155 Ill. 617, 628-30; Town of Eagle v. Kohn (1876), 84 Ill. 292, 295-96.) A contract or transaction which is void must certainly negate the obligation to pay arising from it as between the contracting parties. (Pope, 155 Ill. at 626; Kohn, 84 Ill. at 296.) But, unless an instrument memorializing the obligation is also made void, an innocent third party who has no knowledge of the circumstances of the initial contract or transaction may yet claim payment of it against the drawer or maker. Pope, 155 Ill. at 626; Kohn, 84 Ill. at 296.

Thus, "illegality" has been held to defeat the claims of holders in due course in cases involving contracts of a gaming nature or for retirement of gambling debts. [Citations omitted.] Owing to a deep-seated hostility toward nongovernmental-sanctioned gambling, our legislature has declared that any instrument associated with such activity is void, independent of the status of who may possess it. [Citations omitted.] The absence of similar legislative declaration as for an instrument given upon a usurious contract must account, in part, for the conclusion that usury has not been held to give rise to "illegality" as a defense against a holder in due course. [Citations omitted.]

That the existence or absence of legislative declaration controls the issue was recognized by our appellate court in McGregor v. Lamont (1922), 225 Ill. App. 451, a case involving circumstances similar to those here. John T. Lamont was the maker of a note used to pay for shares of stock issued by the Corn Belt Farmers' Cooperative Association (Association). Lamont's note subsequently came into the possession of Robert Roy McGregor, a holder in due course. When Lamont failed to pay on the note, McGregor filed suit and obtained a judgment against him.

Lamont moved to vacate the judgment. Lamont asserted that the purchase of the shares of stock was void under the Illinois Securities Law because the Association had not complied with its requirements. Because the transaction was void, Lamont concluded, the note given in payment must also be void despite McGregor's status as a holder in due course.

The appellate court noted that the Illinois Securities Law did, indeed, make transactions for the sale of shares of stock void based on noncompliance with the Law's requirements. (*McGregor*, 225 Ill. App. at 453-454, 455.) But the court noted that only the "sale and contract of sale" of shares of stock were expressly made void, not instruments exchanged upon such contracts. (*McGregor*, 225 Ill. App. at 455.) Absent legislative declaration making such instruments void, the court declined to recognize a defense to McGregor's action for payment on the note. *McGregor*, 225 Ill. App. at 455.

The same rule obtains in New Jersey. In New Jersey Mortgage & Investment Corp. v. Berenyi (App. Div. 1976), 140 N.J. Super. 406, 356 A.2d 421, a holder in due course of a note was permitted to maintain a claim for its payment even though the note had been initially obtained by a corporation in a transaction which violated an injunctive order. No statute rendered the note void, and the holder in due course had no knowledge or notice of the injunction. (*Berenyi*, 140 N.J. Super. at 408, 356 A.2d at 423.) But in Westervelt v. Gateway Financial Service (Ch. Div. 1983), 190 N.J. Super. 615, 464 A.2d 1203, the "illegality" defense was held to bar the claim of a holder in due course of a secondary mortgage and note because New Jersey's Secondary Mortgage and Loan Act speciically made void "[a]ny obligation on the part of the borrower arising out of a secondary mortgage loan." (*Westervelt*, 190 N.J. Super. at 620, 464 A.2d at 1205.) *Westervelt* involved what *Berenyi* did not: applicability of a direct statutory expression that an instrument, itself, arising from a particular contract or transaction was void. *Westervelt*, 190 N.J. Super. at 623, 464 A.2d at 1207.

Several other jurisdictions also find reason to draw a distinction between the voidness of a negotiable instrument and the underlying contract or transaction upon which it is exchanged. (See Annot., 80 A.L.R.2d 465, 472-476 (1961) (summarizing several state decisions in which holders in due course were permitted to claim payment of instruments executed in favor of foreign corporations doing business in states without complying with local licensing requirements).) Although recognition of that distinction is not universal (see Columbus Checkcashiers v. Stiles (1990), 56 Ohio App. 3d 159, 565 N.E.2d 883; Wilson v. Steele (1989), 211 Cal. App. 3d 1053, 259 Cal. Rptr. 851 (holding that "illegality" need only be present in the underlying contract between an unlicensed contractor and the drafter of a negotiable instrument to bar the claim of a holder in due course)), we are convinced it remains the better rule.

A plaintiff is precluded from recovering on a suit involving an illegal contract because the plaintiff is a wrongdoer. (See Bankers Trust Co. v. Litton Systems, Inc. (2d Cir. 1979), 599 F.2d 488, 492 (citing the Restatement of Contracts and Restatement (Second) of Contracts).) Enforcement of the illegal contract makes the court an indirect participant in the wrongful conduct. See *Litton*, 599 F.2d at 493.

But a holder in due course is an innocent third party. (*Litton*, 599 F.2d at 492-493.) Such a holder is without knowledge of the circumstances of the contract upon which the instrument was initially exchanged. (Ill. Rev. Stat. 1989, ch. 26, par. 3-302(1)(c) (defining a holder in due course, in part, as a holder who is "without notice . . . of any defense against or claim to [the instrument] on the part of any person").) The same rationale that precludes recovery by a wrongdoing plaintiff is inapplicable in determining such a holder's right to claim payment. (*Litton*, 599 F.2d at 492-493.) Enforcement of that claim does not sully the court. *Litton*, 599 F.2d at 492-493.

The holder in due course concept is intended to facilitate commercial transactions by eliminating the need for "elaborate investigation" of the nature of the circumstances for which an instrument is initially exchanged or of its drafting. (*Litton,* 599 F.2d at 494.) If "illegality" means simply negation of the initial obligation to pay, a holder in due course enjoys no more protection than a party to the original contract or transaction. The "real" defense of "illegality" is reduced to a "personal" one. See Vedder v. Spellman (1971), 78 Wash. 2d 834, 839-840, 480 P.2d 207, 210 (Neill, J., concurring).

It is, therefore, not enough simply to conclude that the initial obligation to pay arising from a void contract or transaction is void. Negation of that obligation as between the contracting parties has little bearing on whether a holder in due course of an instrument arising from the contract or transaction should nevertheless be permitted to make a claim for payment.

The "local law" (Ill. Ann. Stat., ch. 26, par. 3-305, Uniform Commercial Code Comment, at 66 (Smith-Hurd Supp. 1992)) of this state has been formulated upon this court's recognition, in cases predating the UCC, of legislative prerogative regarding negotiable instruments. In adopting the UCC and, in particular, §3-305, our legislature chose to confer upon a holder in due course of a negotiable instrument considerable protection against claims by persons to it. Our legislature also continues to declare certain obligations void because of the circumstances of the agreements from which they arise and without regard to the status of who may claim ownership. (Ill. Rev. Stat. 1989, ch. 38, par. 28-7(b) (subjecting "[a]ny obligation" made void by reason of gambling to be "set aside and vacated" by any court).) The selective negation of obligations reflects a legislative aim to declare what will and will not give rise to "illegality" in cases now governed by the UCC. As legislative direction indicates which obligations are always void, legislative silence indicates when the protection afforded a holder in due course must be honored.

We therefore reaffirm, today, the view this court has consistently recognized in cases predating the UCC. Unless the instrument arising from a contract or transaction is, itself, made void by statute, the "illegality" defense under §3-305 is not available to bar the claim of a holder in due course.

CONCLUSION

To determine whether Hodge is entitled to a judgment of dismissal, we need not engage in an analysis aimed at characterizing the contract between Fentress and the Hodges. Whether the underlying contract should be considered void because Fentress was not licensed as required by the Illinois Plumbing License Law is not dispositive of the Currency Exchange's right, as a holder in due course, to claim payment of the check. It is relevant only to determine whether the Illinois Plumbing License Law provides that any obligation arising from a contract for plumbing services made in violation of its requirements is void. It does not.

For the reasons stated, the judgments of the appellate and circuit courts are reversed, and the cause is remanded to the circuit court for further proceeding. Judgments reversed; cause remanded.

BILANDIC, J., dissenting. . . .

The plain language of §3-305 and the comments to §3-305 make it clear that where the illegality of a transaction renders the obligation of the maker of an instrument a nullity, the illegality of the transaction can be raised as a defense by the maker of the instrument, even against a holder in due course. Section 3-305 does not state that illegality is a defense only where the instrument arising from a contract or transaction has been expressly declared void by the legislature due to the illegality of the transaction. Had the legislature intended for illegality to be a defense only where it had expressly declared an instrument void due to the illegality of the underlying transaction, it could easily have said so in §3-305. It did not say so, however.

The only inquiry necessary to resolve the issue presented in this case, then, is whether the contract between Hodge and Fentress is void on the grounds of illegality. The comments to the UCC instruct that one must look to Illinois statutory and case law to determine whether the underlying contract was illegal and, as a result of that illegality, void. (Ill. Ann. Stat., ch. 26, par. 3-305. Uniform Commercial Code Comment, at 66 (Smith-Hurd Supp. 1992).) An examination of the statute providing for the licensing of plumbers, the public policy behind that statute, and Illinois case law concerning the illegality of contracts made in contravention of professional licensing laws establishes that the contract between Hodge and Fentress is illegal and void.

The Illinois Plumbing License Law (Ill. Rev. Stat. 1989, ch. 111, par. 1101 et seq.) specifically prohibits the performance of plumbing work by nonlicensed plumbers. Pursuant to the Act, "all plumbing shall be performed only by plumbers licensed under the

provisions of this Act." (Ill. Rev. Stat. 1989, ch. 111, par. 1103(1).)
The Act imposes criminal penalties on anyone performing plumbing services without a license. (Ill. Rev. Stat. 1989, ch. 111, par.
1128.) The rationale behind the prohibition of plumbing work by
nonlicensed plumbers is set forth in the Plumbing License Law.
The portion of the Law setting forth its purpose and underlying
policy states:

> It has been established by scientific evidence that improper
> plumbing can adversely affect the health of the public. . . . Faulty
> plumbing is potentially lethal and can cause widespread disease and
> an epidemic of disastrous consequences.
>
> To protect the health of the public it is essential that plumbing
> be installed by persons who have proven their knowledge of the
> sciences of pneumatics and hydraulics and their skill in installing
> plumbing.
>
> Consistent with its duty to safeguard the health of the people
> of this State, the General Assembly therefore declares that in-
> dividuals who plan, inspect, install, alter, extend, repair and main-
> tain plumbing systems shall be individuals of proven skill. . . . [T]his
> Act is therefore declared to be essential to the public interest. (Ill.
> Rev. Stat. 1989, ch. 111, par. 1101.)

Here, the contract between Hodge and Fentress presents the
kinds of dangers the Illinois Plumbing License Law was intended
to guard against. Affidavits attached to Hodge's §2-619 motion to
dismiss, which were not contradicted by the plaintiff, establish that
Fentress was not a licensed plumber. The affidavits also establish
that Hodge and her husband, Eric, believed that Fentress was a
licensed plumber at the time they contracted with him for
plumbing services. Had Fentress performed the work required of
him pursuant to the contract with Hodge, it is likely that his work
would not have conformed to acceptable plumbing standards and
would have posed the kinds of dangers which the Plumbing
License Law was intended to prevent. . . .

The majority asserts that to bar recovery by the Currency Exchange in this case would be unfair because the Currency Exchange is an innocent third party which had no knowledge of the
circumstances of the contract between Hodge and Fentress.
However, section 3-305 clearly provides that the general policy
favoring free negotiability is not absolute. There is a competing
policy disfavoring certain transactions, such as those involving
infancy, duress, illegality or misrepresentation as to the true nature

of an instrument (i.e., fraud in the factum). (Ill. Rev. Stat. 1989, ch. 26, par. 3-305.) Pursuant to §3-305, the Currency Exchange takes a check subject to these and certain other real defenses. The Illinois legislature has provided that, by definition, a holder in due course is one who does not have notice of any of the real defenses listed in §3-305. (See Ill. Rev. Stat. 1989, ch. 26, par. 3-302(1)(c).) By statute, the innocence of the holder in due course cannot defeat *any* of the real defenses listed in §3-305, including illegality. Accordingly, the argument that the Currency Exchange could not have known that the underlying transaction was illegal is simply misplaced. Such reasoning would lead to the conclusion that all of the defenses listed in §3-305 should be unavailable to defeat the claim of a holder in due course, a conclusion obviously contrary to the provisions of §3-305.

For the above reasons, I dissent. I would affirm the judgment of the appellate court which affirmed the circuit court's dismissal of the Currency Exchange's action against Hodge.

PROBLEM 117

When she heard her creditors fighting over priorities on her doorstep, Elsie Maynard knew that she had no choice but bankruptcy. Among the debts that she reported to the bankruptcy court was the loan she had taken from Point National Bank, which was evidenced by a promissory note she had signed. In due course the bankruptcy proceeding culminated in the judge's ordering that Elsie be discharged from all her scheduled debts. Two years later, the promissory note surfaced in the possession of Shadbolt State Bank, which claimed quite convincingly to be a holder in due course. Must Elsie pay? See §3-305(a)(1) and (b).

A little lecture on Discharge as a Real Defense. Subsection (b) to §3-302 tells us that:

> Notice of discharge of a party, other than discharge in an insolvency proceeding, is not notice of a defense under subsection (a), but discharge is effective against a person who becomes a holder in due course with notice of the discharge. . . .

What does this mean? Well, first of all, as the above Problem illustrates, discharge in bankruptcy *is always a real defense*, regardless of what the subsequent holder knows or doesn't know at the time of acquisition of the instrument. Any other discharge that the Code or common law creates is not effective against a holder in due course *unless* that holder, at the time of acquisition, knew of the discharge, in which case the discharge is, in effect, a real defense and assertable against the holder in due course. For example, suppose that there are four sureties who have signed their names as indorsers on a promissory note. The current holder of the note decides to excuse one of them from future liability, and so draws a line through that surety's name, thus discharging that person from all liability (see §3-601 and its Official Comment). Even a later holder in due course of the note, seeing the line drawn through the former surety's name, would know that that surety is no longer liable on the note, and therefore could only enforce it against the other obligors.

PROBLEM 118

Malvolio, a traveling salesman, bought a new car from Valentine Auto Sales, signing a note for $18,000. The payee discounted the note for $16,800 to the Orsino Finance Company, which notified Malvolio that he should make all future payments to them. Malvolio immediately sent them a check for the outstanding balance (he had come into some money when his aunt died). He asked for the note back, but Orsino was evasive. A week later Malvolio received a note from the Olivia Finance Company saying that his note had been assigned to them and that he should direct his payments to their office. When Malvolio protested, they made holder in due course noises and became quite nasty. Malvolio, worried, comes to you for advice. What should he do? See §3-501(b)(2); read §§3-601 and 3-602.[6] Does Malvolio have remedies outside the Code? Think back to your course in Contracts.

B. *A Special Note on Forgery*

Forgery creates very complicated problems under the Code, and these will be dealt with later. The important issue for now is whether forgery is a real defense under the Code, so that it can be

---

6. The proposed 2002 amendments to Article 3 of the Uniform Commercial Code would solve this problem by amending §3-602 so that those paying off notes would be discharged if they paid the original holder of the note, unless notified that the note had been transferred to another.

raised against a holder in due course, or a personal defense, so that it cannot. The answer to this question lies in §3-401(a): "A person is not liable on an instrument unless (i) the person signed the instrument . . . " and in §3-403(a):

> Unless otherwise provided in this Article or Article 4, an unauthorized signature is ineffective except as the signature of the unauthorized signer in favor of a person who in good faith pays the instrument or takes it for value. . . .

Consider the following Problem.

PROBLEM 119

Jimmy Slick, an expert con man, went into John's Jewelers and told John, the owner, that he was Milton Money, the richest man in town. John was too awed to ask for identification. Slick then picked out several very expensive pieces of jewelry and signed Money's name to a promissory note to pay for them. Slick skipped town with the jewelry. When the note matured, the Tenth National Bank (a holder in due course to whom John has negotiated the paper) presented it to Milton Money for payment. May Money refuse to pay a holder in due course?

The answer to this Problem is obviously that Money is not liable, but as an attorney how do you get away from the all encompassing language of §3-305(a) and (b)? Read §3-305(a) and (b) again and see if you can determine how Money's forgery defense fits into the statute.

Additionally, if the forgery is of a name necessary to a valid negotiation, there can be no holder in due course following the forgery because no later transferee will qualify as a *holder*. See the discussion supra at pages 358-360.

PROBLEM 120

When Barbara Shipek was off to Las Vegas for a fun weekend, she bought a traveler's check for $3,000 from Octopus National Bank (ONB). The payee line on the traveler's check was blank, but the bank had her sign a line on the check indicating the name of the remitter (see §3-103(a)(11)). The check contained another blank for a countersignature, under which was printed a statement that the bank would pay the traveler's check only if the remitter re-signed the check on this blank at the time of negotiation to the payee. On Ms. Shipek's first night in Las Vegas a thief stole her purse, getting the traveler's check as part of the booty. The thief apparently forged Ms. Shipek's name on the countersignature line and negotiated the check to Vegas Check-Cashing City, an entity listed as payee when the check was presented by Vegas Check-Cashing City to ONB for payment, by which time Ms. Shipek had phoned the bank and told them what had happened. You are the attorney for the bank. Should it pay the traveler's check to Vegas Check-Cashing City? See §§3-104(i) and 3-106(c) with its Official Comment 2.

C. Procedural Issues

One does not have to be a holder in due course in order to sue on the instrument; a "person entitled to enforce the instrument," a phrase defined in §3-301, may do so. Generally a "person entitled to enforce the instrument" means the *holder* of the instrument (someone in possession pursuant to a valid negotiation), though the phrase does include some non-holders—namely, someone who gets holder rights under the shelter rule (or a depositary bank per §4-205), the rightful owner of a lost instrument (§3-309), or the defendant in a successful restitution action (§3-418(d), yet to be discussed). Only if a defense or claim to the instrument arises will the holder's due course status become relevant, at which time the holder has the burden of establishing the position as a holder in due course. Read §3-308(b).

As mentioned above, and elaborated on later in the forgery discussion, a holder must take through a chain of indorsements that is free of forgeries affecting the title. When the genuineness of signatures becomes an issue, §3-308(a) allocates the procedural burdens. Read it.

Virginia National Bank v. Holt

Virginia Supreme Court, 1975
216 Va. 500, 219 S.E.2d 881, 18 U.C.C. Rep. Serv. 440

COMPTON, J. . . . In May 1974, the plaintiff, Virginia National Bank, filed a motion for judgment against the defendants, Edgar

M. Holt and Gustava H. Holt, his wife, jointly and severally, seeking recovery of the face amount of a "Homestead Waiving Promissory Note," plus interest and attorney's fees. The instrument, payable to the order of the Bank and allegedly made by the Holts to evidence an indebtedness, was dated December 12, 1973, was due 90 days after date, and was in the amount of $6,000.

Edgar M. Holt was duly served with process, but failed to appear on file pleadings in response. A default judgment in the amount sued for was entered against him in August 1974.

In her pleadings, Gustava H. Holt generally denied liability and specifically denied that the instrument was signed by her. On November 20, 1974, judgment was entered on a jury verdict in her favor and we granted the Bank a writ of error.

The dispositive issue is whether the evidence relating to the genuineness of Mrs. Holt's signature on the instrument presented a question of fact to be decided by the jury. We hold that it did not and reverse.

We will summarize only the evidence pertinent to the issue we decide. Testifying for the Bank was one of its commercial loan officers, who did not handle the Holt transaction but through whom the instrument in question was introduced into evidence, and two other witnesses, one of whom was an expert in handwriting analysis, whose statements supported the Bank's position that the signature on the note was in fact the defendant's.

Mrs. Holt did not appear at the trial, but her attorney endeavored to show that his client did not execute the instrument. During cross-examination, the loan officer, over the Bank's objection based on the hearsay rule, was required to answer whether he was present during the taking of Mrs. Holt's discovery deposition in July 1974 when she "denied that she signed the note." The record shows that the witness responded, "Yes, I was. Somewhat surprised." No other statement was elicited by defendant's counsel from any of the Bank's witnesses which would support the defendant's claim that she did not sign the writing.

The only evidence offered in the defendant's behalf was a set of answers previously filed by the Bank to six interrogatories propounded by her attorney. Those responses indicated that the Bank did not know of any witness who saw the defendant sign the note or who heard her admit that she signed it. They further indicated that the Bank had no information that she ever authorized her husband to sign her name to any promissory note or that she ever ratified any act of his in signing her name to such a writing.

By a motion to strike at the conclusion of the evidence, and again by a motion to set aside after the verdict, the Bank moved for judgment in its favor contending, as it does on appeal, that the foregoing hearsay testimony on cross-examination was erroneously admitted and, in the alternative, that even if such evidence was properly received, the defendant had failed, as a matter of law, to overcome the presumption established by §3-307 [§3-308 in the Revision—Ed.] that her signature was genuine and authorized. The trial court, in refusing to sustain the motion to strike and in overruling the motion to set aside, ruled that the question of whether the signature was genuine was for the jury. This was error.

Section 3-307, inter alia, sets out the burden of proof in an action which seeks recovery upon an "instrument" and deals with issues arising, in such a suit, from a challenge of the genuineness or authorization of signatures. 2 R. Anderson, Uniform Commercial Code §3-307:3 (2d ed. 1971). Under that section, each signature on an instrument is admitted unless, as in this case, the "effectiveness" of the signature is put in issue by a specific denial. The burden of establishing the genuineness of the signature is then upon the party claiming under the signature and relying on its "effectiveness," but such party is aided by a presumption that it is genuine or authorized. In this context, "presumption" means that "the trier of fact must find the existence of the fact presumed unless and until evidence is introduced which would support a finding of its nonexistence." Code §1-201(31).

The effect of the presumption is to eliminate any requirement that the plaintiff prove the signature is authentic until some evidence is introduced which would support a finding that the signature is forged or unauthorized. §3-307, Official Comment 1. It is based upon the fact that in the normal course of events forged or unauthorized signatures are very uncommon, and that evidence of such is usually within the defendant's control or more accessible to him. Id. Therefore, under §3-307, the party denying a signature must make some sufficient showing of the grounds for the denial before the plaintiff is put to his proof. The evidence need not be sufficient to require entry of summary judgment in the defendant's favor, "but it must be enough to support his denial by permitting a finding in his favor." Id. "Until the party denying the signature introduces such sufficient evidence, the presumption requires a finding for the party relying on the effectiveness of the signature." §3-307, Virginia Comment. See 2 F. Hart & W. Willier,

Commercial Paper Under the Uniform Commercial Code §2.07(2) (1975).

An application of the foregoing analysis of the statute to the facts of this case demonstrates that the Bank was entitled to entry of summary judgment in its favor at the conclusion of all the evidence, since no material issue of fact requiring resolution by a jury was presented. Rule 3:18.

The defendant's specific denial put the genuineness of the defendant's signature in issue. Because of the foregoing presumption, the signature, which appeared to be that of Gustava H. Holt, was presumed to be genuine and the defendant was thus required to present "sufficient evidence" in support of the denial of genuineness. This she failed to do. We will assume, but not decide, that the disputed answer during cross-examination was properly admitted in evidence. Nonetheless, we conclude that this bit of testimony is insufficient to sustain a finding that the signature was forged or unauthorized. Furthermore, the answers to interrogatories furnish no support to the defendant's claimed defense. A forgery or an unauthorized signature may not be shown by merely demonstrating the plaintiff's apparent lack of evidence on that issue.

We hold, therefore, that the defendant has failed, as a matter of law, to make a sufficient showing to support a finding that she, or her authorized representative, did not in fact write her name on the instrument. The presumption then requires a finding that the signature on the instrument is genuine and effective. Accordingly, production of the instrument entitled the Bank to recover, because the defendant established no defense, §3-307(2), and it was error to submit the case to the jury. For these reasons, the judgment in favor of Gustava H. Holt will be reversed and final judgment will be entered here in favor of the Bank.

Reversed and final judgment.

QUESTION

Would it have been sufficient to overcome the presumption if Mrs. Holt had taken the stand and denied the signature? See Metropolitan Mortgage Fund v. Basiliko, 407 A.2d 773, 28 U.C.C. Rep. Serv. 100 (Md. App. 1979); Freeman Check Cashing, Inc. v. State, 97 Misc. 2d 819, 412 N.Y.S.2d 963, 26 U.C.C. Rep. Serv. 1186 (Ct. Cl. 1979); Bates & Springer, Inc. v. Stallworth, 56 Ohio App. 2d 223, 382 N.E.2d 1179, 26 U.C.C. Rep. Serv. 1181 (1978).

D.   Defenses Against a Non-Holder in Due Course

Read §§3-305(a) and (b) and 3-306 carefully. Note the legal result: all *claims* and both real and personal *defenses* may be asserted against anyone who does not qualify as a holder in due course. The only claim a non-holder in due course takes free of is a perfected security interest in non-negotiable instruments, and then only if they are purchased for value in the ordinary course of business without notice of the security interest (§9-330). The most common personal defenses are *want of consideration* (no consideration) and *failure of consideration* (breach of contract, called a *claim in recoupment* in the Revision).

Herzog Contracting Corp. v. McGowen Corp.

United States Court of Appeals, Seventh Circuit, 1992
976 F.2d 1062, 18 U.C.C. Rep. Serv. 2d 1170

POSNER, Circuit Judge. The district judge granted summary judgment in favor of Herzog Contracting Corporation in its diversity suit to enforce two promissory notes, aggregating $400,000, against the issuer, McGowen Corporation. The appeal raises a tangle of jurisdictional and substantive questions, the latter governed, the parties agree, by Indiana Law. . . .

The next jurisdictional issue requires us to delve into the facts. In 1989 Herzog, the plaintiff, bought the assets of Tru-Flex Metal Hose Corporation from McGowen, the defendant, and formed a wholly owned subsidiary of Herzog (also called Tru-Flex) to hold them, to which Herzog assigned the asset purchase agreement. The agreement called for annual payments from Tru-Flex to McGowen of $500,000 for five years. The two promissory notes, both demand notes, were issued by McGowen to Tru-Flex later in 1989. The parties have radically different positions on the purpose of the notes. Herzog claims that it loaned McGowen $400,000 and the notes are McGowen's promises to repay the loan. McGowen acknowledges having received the $400,000 but denies that it was a loan, contending instead that it was partial prepayment of the next year's installment due under the asset purchase agreement and that the only purpose of the notes that it gave Tru-Flex was to enable it (that is, McGowen) to postpone the realization of taxable income to the following year by making the $400,000 payment look like a loan.

The parties soon fell to squabbling and Herzog refused to make further payments under the asset purchase agreement, precipitating a suit by McGowen against Herzog in an Indiana state court for breach of contract that remains pending. At about the same time that the state court suit was brought, Tru-Flex assigned McGowen's promissory notes to Herzog, which shortly afterward brought this suit to enforce them. . . .

We come to the merits. The case was decided on summary judgment and there has been no determination of the truth of McGowen's claim that the promissory notes were never intended to be presented for payment. So we must assume that the claim is true. The question is whether, as the district judge held, solely on the basis that the notes are "clear and unambiguous," they are enforceable regardless of what the parties actually intended.

They would be if enforcement were being sought by a holder in due course, UCC §3-305, Ind. Code §26-1-3-305, but Herzog concedes that it is not that. It places its case on the parol evidence rule. The promissory notes are unambiguous—they promise Herzog a specified sum of money on demand—and their terms cannot be varied by extrinsic evidence. At first glance Herzog's argument seems a complete nonstarter. A holder of a promissory note who is not a holder in due course takes the note subject to "all defenses of any party which would be available in an action on a simple contract," UCC §3-306(b) [§3-305(b) in the Revision—Ed.], and one of those defenses, notwithstanding the parol evidence rule, is that the parties did not intend to create an enforceable contract. 2 E. Allan Farnsworth, Farnsworth on Contracts §7.4, at p.212 (1990); James J. White & Robert S. Summers, Handbook of the Law under the Uniform Commercial Code §2-10, at p.78 (1980). "It is well settled that whatever the formal documentary evidence, the parties to a legal transaction may always show that they understood a purported contract not to bind them; it may, for example, be a joke, or a disguise to deceive others." In re H. Hicks & Son, Inc., 82 F.2d 277, 279 (2d Cir. 1936) (L. Hand, J.); see also Nice Ball Bearing Co. v. Bearing Jobbers, Inc., 205 F.2d 841, 845 (7th Cir. 1953). The deceived others may, of course, be able to object to the attempt to prove the contract a sham, as in Central States, Southeast & Southwest Areas Pension Fund v. Gerber Truck Service, Inc., 870 F.2d 1148 (7th Cir. 1989) (en banc), and FDIC v. O'Neil, 809 F.2d 350 (7th Cir. 1987), but that is not a factor here. More to the point, a minority of jurisdictions "have refused to admit such evidence [i.e., that the purported contract was a joke, a disguise, in short a sham of some sort] where the purpose of the sham agreement was offensive to public policy." 2 Farnsworth, supra, §7.4, at p.212 n.4; see Annot., "Admissibility of Oral Evidence to Show That a Writing Was a Sham Agreement Not Intended to Create Legal Relations," 71 A.L.R.2d 382, 393-397 (1960); 67 A.L.R.2d Later Case Service 555 (1984), and for an illustrative case Kergil v. Central Oregon Fir Supply Co., 213 Or. 186, 323 P.2d 947 (1958).

We prefer the majority rule, illustrated by our decision in Nice Ball Bearing Co. v. Bearing Jobbers, Inc., supra, so will apply it here in default of any Indiana cases on the question. Apart from the fact that the minority rule rewards a party to the sham agreement and imposes a punishment that may be disproportionate to the promisor's misconduct, it invites a collateral inquiry into the character of the alleged "sham." Here the party accused of shamming by his fellow shammer was angling for a tax advantage. Did that make the transaction a "sham"? Despite the doctrine of tax law that substance prevails over form, Gregory v. Helvering, 293 U.S. 465 (1935); Yosha v. Commissioner, 861 F.2d 494 (7th Cir. 1988), many transactions that would strike a nonspecialist as contrived purely to avoid taxes are entirely lawful. Must we therefore, to resolve this case, decide whether McGowen's effort to postpone its tax liability for the sale of Tru-Flex was one of them? We trust not.

But we are not done. In the face of the principle that any defenses to a contract are available in a suit on a promissory note unless the plaintiff is a holder in due course, some courts enforce the parol evidence rule more broadly in such suits than in suits to enforce ordinary contracts. Annot., "Admissibility of Parol Evidence to Show That a Bill or Note Was Conditional, or Given for a Special Purpose," 54 A.L.R. 702, 717-718 (1928). In Perez-Lizano v. Ayers, 695 P.2d 467, 469 (Mont. 1985), for example, the court refused to allow the admission of parol evidence to show that the note was a sham. One of the cases in this line is an Indiana case, Highfield v. Lang, 394 N.E.2d 204, 206 (Ind. App. 1979). But it is readily distinguishable from our case; and we have found two recent cases from other jurisdictions in which courts admitted parol evidence to show that a promissory note was not intended to be enforceable. American Underwriting Corp. v. Rhode Island Hospital Trust Co., 303 A.2d 121, 125 (R.I. 1973); Simpson v. Milne, 677 P.2d 365, 368 (Colo. App. 1983). The second was a case of a sham; the parol evidence was that the notes in suit "were executed as a fiction to satisfy plaintiff's wife, who was near death, and who strongly felt that [the defendant and his wife] still owed [the plaintiff and his wife] money from prior business transactions." Id.

Despite these last two cases and despite UCC §3-306(b), the parties have tacitly agreed that the applicability of the parol evidence rule to this case is governed not by general contract law but by a special doctrine that allows parol evidence to show, against a plaintiff who is not a holder in due course, that the delivery of the negotiable instrument that he is suing to collect was "for a special purpose." Brames v. Crates, 399 N.E.2d 437, 441 (Ind. App. 1980); UCC §3-306(c); Ind. Code §26-1-3-306(c). This approach is understandable though not inevitable. While §3-306(b) subjects the nonholder in due course to "all defenses" that the original promisor would have had, implicitly including the defense that the promise was not intended to create enforceable rights, §3-306(c) deals with some of these defenses in greater detail. This could be taken to imply that the defense that no enforceable rights were intended to be created is to be analyzed in accordance with the "special purpose" doctrine that predates the Code, though a likelier inference is that the draftsmen wanted simply to make sure that no defense was overlooked.

However this may be, Herzog argues that the special-purpose doctrine is limited to allowing the promisor (McGowen here) to defend by showing that his obligation to make good on the note was subject to a condition precedent, which is not the case here. For it is McGowen's contention not that something had to happen before Herzog could demand payment, but that Herzog could never demand payment. Parol evidence is always admissible to prove a fraud, Franklin v. White, 493 N.E.2d 161, 165 (Ind. 1986); In re Estate of Fanning, 333 N.E.2d 80, 85 (Ind. 1975); Kruse Classic Auction Co. v. Aetna Casualty & Surety Co., 511 N.E.2d 326, 330 (Ind. App. 1987), but McGowen does not contend that when Herzog agreed to the scheme for making the prepayment of the purchase installment look like a loan it intended to double-cross McGowen by demanding payment of the notes. If there was a *special purpose doctrine*. fraud, it was against the Internal Revenue Service, though no one is arguing this. With fraud out of the picture and the scope of the parol evidence rule applicable to promissory notes conceded by McGowen to be governed by §3-306(c) rather than §3-306(b), McGowen is left with the special-purpose doctrine and Herzog concludes that a sham case is outside that doctrine, which, as we have noted, he believes to be limited to conditions precedent.

There are cases, none from Indiana, on both sides of the question whether "delivery for a special purpose" is limited to conditions precedent, although the majority view is that it is not. Compare Perez-Lizano v. Ayers, supra, 695 P.2d at 469-470, with American Underwriting Corp. v. Rhode Island Hospital Trust Co., supra, 303 A.2d at 125. Text and history can help us choose between these positions, though history more than text. Section 3-306(c) expressly recognizes a defense of "nonperformance of any condition precedent," making the "special purpose" defense redundant on Herzog's construal of it. But redundancy is built into §3-306(c), as we have seen, and maybe this is another example of it. So let us turn to history.

Until sometime after the middle of the nineteenth century, courts were highly reluctant to admit parol evidence, in suits on promissory notes, for any purpose other than to prove fraud or mistake. John Barnard Byles, A Treatise on the Law of Bills of Exchange 169 note I (4th Am. ed. 1856). A little later, they were allowing such evidence in three additional types of case: delivery of the note together with a mortgage deed, with the note as additional security for payment of the mortgage; delivery of the note to escrow; and delivery contingent on the satisfaction of a condition precedent. Id. at 112-113 (14th ed. 1885). Some courts also allowed the admission of parole evidence "to show that a contract signed and delivered was never intended to be the real contract between the parties." Id. at 113 note o. One case—oddly enough it is factually similar to ours—used the term "special purpose" to describe the defense in a "no obligation" or "sham" case. Juilliard v. Chaffee, 92 N.Y. 529, 534 (1883). And when the English codified their law of negotiable instruments in 1882, they expressly allowed evidence (other than against a holder in due course) that delivery had been "conditional *or* for a special purpose only, *and not for the purpose of transferring the property in the bill.*" James W. Eaton & Frank B. Gilbert, A Treatise on Commercial Paper and the Negotiable Instruments Law 697 (1903). The meaning brought out by the words that we have italicized seems unmistakable: the "special purpose" defense encompassed all cases in which the negotiable instrument had not been intended to create an enforceable obligation. Byles, supra, at 122 (17th ed. 1911).

The American Negotiable Instruments Law—the first statute drafted by the National Conference of Commissioners on Uniform State Laws—copied the English provision word for word. Joseph Doddrige Brannan, The Negotiable Instruments Law Annotated

129 (4th ed. 1926); see also id. at 135-41. Later, however, darkness descended, and we find some authorities distinguishing among condition cases, no-obligation cases, and special-purpose cases. Annot., "Admissibility of Parol Evidence to Show That a Bill or Note Was Conditional, or Given for a Special Purpose," 20 A.L.R. 421, 490, 498-502 (1922); 4 William D. Hawkland & Lary Lawrence, Uniform Commercial Code Series 3-306:07, at p.481 (1990). This proliferation of unhelpful distinctions was abetted by the fact that the Uniform Commercial Code, in recodifying negotiable instruments law, dropped the explanatory phrase "and not for the purpose of transferring the property in the bill" from the formulation of the special purpose defense. But this was done without any intention of changing the meaning of the defense as it had appeared in the Negotiable Instruments Law. "Notes and Comments to Tent. Draft No. 2—Art. III," 3 Uniform Commercial Code: Drafts 186-187 (Elizabeth Slusser Kelly ed. 1984). Certainly nothing in the history of the Uniform Commercial Code suggests a purpose of abolishing the "no obligation" defense and returning to the law as it existed before the Civil War. The tendency of our law for almost a century has been to relax strict rules, perhaps because of growing (though possibly misguided and even sentimental) confidence in the ability of judges and juries to resolve factual questions (such as, What was the purpose of McGowen's notes?), with reasonable accuracy and at reasonable cost, by sifting testimony. The legal realists who, led by Karl Llewellyn, drafted the Uniform Commercial Code were leaders in the movement to soften the contours of strict common law rules. See, e.g., UCC §§2-103(1)(b), 2-204, 2-205.

It hardly matters whether the no-obligation cases are subsumed under the special-purpose defense or set off by themselves or, as seems simplest and therefore—no other values being at stake so far as we can see—preferable, assimilated to the general contract doctrine that allows parol evidence to show that a contractual-looking document was not intended to be binding. The office of the parol evidence rule is to prevent parties to a written contract from seeking to vary its terms by reference to side agreements, or tentative agreements reached in preliminary negotiations. 2 Farnsworth, supra, §7.2, at p.197. In the case of a condition precedent the promisor is not trying to vary the terms, but to deny the enforceability of the promise by pointing to some condition that has not been fulfilled. The distinction may seem fine-spun and even arbitrary, but it has been deemed consistent with the policy behind the parol evidence rule, or at least a tolerable qualification of it. 2 id., §7.4, at pp.211-215. Two points can be made on behalf of the distinction. The weaker, as it seems to us, is that without such an exception the rule would work dramatic forfeitures, by preventing a party from showing not merely that the terms were somewhat different from what they appeared to be but that he had never agreed to do or pay anything. The stronger point is that the parol evidence rule, properly understood, is not a rule imposed on contracting parties from without but merely an inference, drawn from the language of the document, that the parties intended it to be the complete statement of their agrement, extinguishing any agreements that might have emerged from the preliminary negotiations. Patton v. Mid-Continent Systems, Inc., 841 F.2d 742, 745 (7th Cir. 1988); 2 Farnsworth, supra, §§7.2, 7.3, at pp.197-198. The document is unlikely to reveal whether the parties intended it to be taken seriously, and if it does not, there is no basis for applying the rule. In re H. Hicks & Son, Inc., supra, 82 F.2d at 279.

At all events, to allow parol evidence to expose a sham case such as this is alleged to be would make no greater inroads into the parol evidence rule than the cases on conditions precedent do. McGowen is not trying to change the terms in the promissory notes, but to show that the notes were not in fact intended to create a legally enforceable obligation. They were, not to put too fine a point on it, intended to fool the Internal Revenue Service. Herzog, perhaps fearing that it will be found to have been a party to this little deception, does not argue that McGowen's unclean hands should forfeit its right to make a sham-transaction defense, if there is such a defense, and we think there should be because we can think of no principled distinction between it and the condition-precedent defense that Herzog concedes is valid.

The policy of the law is to facilitate negotiability by allowing assignees of negotiable instruments to take free of defenses not obvious on the fact of the note. Northwestern National Ins. Co. v. Maggie, No. 92-1037 (7th Cir. Sept. 23, 1992). But that policy is expressed in the doctrine of holders in due course. Id. Herzog made no effort to discount the notes to one who would have been such a holder and therefore could have enforced the notes against McGowen regardless of the oral agreement not to enforce them on which McGowen relies in this suit.

The judgment is reversed and the case remanded for further proceedings consistent with this opinion.

QUESTION

How would this case be decided under the Revision? See §§3-117 and 3-105(b), plus the latter's Official Comment 2.

E. *Jus Tertii*

It is a basic rule of law that litigants must succeed or fail on the basis of their *own* rights and not the rights of others. The rights of another, called *jus tertii*, are available to other litigants only in special circumstances. Sureties, called "accommodation parties" in the Code, are permitted, with some exceptions, to raise the defenses of their principals (called "accommodated parties"); see §3-305(d). And, as we shall see when we get to the issue of restrictive indorsements, §3-206(f) permits an obligor to refuse payment if doing so would violate the terms of a restrictive indorsement.

The Code's general prohibition against using jus tertii is found in §3-305(c), which you should now read. Note two important things about it. The first is that the claims of another may always be asserted if that person joins the lawsuit. The second is that §3-305(c)'s last sentence permits one jus tertii to be asserted against a non-holder in due course: the instrument has been lost or stolen so that the current possessor is not the true owner. If this latter jus tertii could not be raised, then the obligor would be exposed to the possibility of double payment when the true owner showed up.

PROBLEM 121

Craig Covey was the maker of the following promissory note, which he signed:

I, Craig Covey, promise to pay to bearer the sum of $5,000, on demand. I also promise to buy the bearer lunch on the date of presentment.

He signed an order to buy a computer. The note was given to his uncle, who had loaned him the money for the computer. The uncle sold the note to the Stonewall Finance Company in return for a check for $4,500. Stonewall Finance Company's check bounced, and the uncle was very angry. He went down to the finance company's office and found that there was a sign on the door saying "GONE OUT OF BUSINESS." The next day the note was stolen from the office of the Stonewall Finance Company and later surfaced in the hands of Jane Eleanor, an innocent purchaser for value, who presented it to Craig for payment. In the meantime both his uncle and the Stonewall Finance Company had contacted Craig and asked him to refrain from paying the instrument, the uncle pointing to the bounced check and Stonewall to the fact that the note had been stolen from it. Is Jane a holder in due course? If not, can Craig raise the suggested jus tertii against her? If Craig wants to pay Jane, can his uncle stop him? See §3-602.

F.   Conclusion

Reference has already been made to special statutes and rules (such as the FTC regulation) that restrict the holder in due course doctrine in consumer transactions. But these statutes do not cover the whole consumer field; for example, a couple signing a promissory note to a bank for a home improvement loan can still lose a lawsuit to a holder in due course. Should the doctrine be wiped out completely in consumer transactions? In commercial ventures? Professor Grant Gilmore, one of the original drafters of the Uniform Commercial Code, has commented:

> The "holder in due course" concept was worked out by Lord Mansfield and his successors in the late eighteenth and early nineteenth centuries against a business background in which bills of exchange and promissory notes did in fact circulate and could be expected to pass through a number of hands before being retired. As the modern banking system developed, instruments gradually ceased to circulate. In this century nothing is rarer than a true negotiation to a third party purchaser for value—the use of negotiable notes which pass from dealer to finance company in the attempt to carry out consumer frauds is hardly a "true negotiation." The whole "holder in due course" concept could usefully have been abolished when negotiable instruments law was codified at the end of the nineteenth century. In fact it was preserved like a fly in amber both in the N.I.L. and in its successor, Article 3 of the Uniform Commercial Code. Indeed our codifications typically preserve once vital but now obsolete concepts in much the same way that our museums preserve the ancient artifacts of bygone civilizations.

G. Gilmore, The Death of Contract 108 n.18 (1974). Professor Gilmore developed this idea more fully in a fascinating article: Gilmore, Formalism and the Law of Negotiable Instruments, 13 Creighton L. Rev. 441 (1979). A leading article containing the same theme is Rosenthal, Negotiability—Who Needs It?, 71 Colum. L. Rev. 375 (1971).

QUESTION

If Article 3 were amended to eliminate the concept of holding in due course, commercial paper would legally resemble nothing more than simple contracts. Would we then need Article 3 at all?

Chapter 10

THE NATURE OF LIABILITY

Once a negotiable instrument is created and enters commerce, the parties thereto are automatically locked into relationships that may lead to legal liability. When a problem arises in connection with one of these instruments, the knowledgeable lawyer (and the wise student facing an exam question) asks four preliminary questions:

(1) What negotiable instrument labels (*drawer, payee, drawee, maker, indorser, guarantor,* etc.) do the parties bear?
(2) What causes of action (contractual obligation, warranty, conversion, suits "off the instrument") are available to each party?
(3) What defenses are possible?
(4) Can liability be passed to someone else?

The basic labels applied to the original parties to notes and drafts have been discussed. You will recall that a promissory note is initially a two-party instrument involving a *maker* and a *payee*. If the payee signs the instrument, whether a blank or special indorsement, he or she becomes an *indorser*. Anyone who thereafter signs his or her name to the instrument is also presumed to be an indorser (§3-204(a)). A draft always begins as a three-party instrument. A *drawer* orders the *drawee* to make payment to the order of the *payee*. If the draft is a check drawn by Carl Consumer on the Big Bank to the order of the Gas Company, the parties are, respectively, the drawer, the drawee, and the payee. If the Gas Company places its name on the back of the check, it will become an indorser, as will anyone else who signs the back of the check prior to its payment by the drawee. The labels that can be applied to other parties to the instrument (*acceptor, accommodation party, guarantor*) will be explained as they come up below.

The remainder of this segment of the book will discuss the different causes of action (legal theories) that one party can bring against another. Negotiable instruments law draws on the basic fields of contract (§§3-412 to 3-415, 4-401), property (that is, warranty rights, §§3-416, 3-417, 4-207, 4-208), and tort (primarily conversion, §3-420) to provide the three possible legal theories on which parties can sue under the Code. In addition, of course, the parties frequently have rights against each other that arise outside of the scope of Articles 3 and 4. There is no way to catalogue all the possible non-commercial paper suits here, but the discussion immediately below introduces the most obvious one.

I.   THE UNDERLYING OBLIGATION

The most common lawsuit connected with negotiable instruments, but not created by Articles 3 and 4, is a suit on the *underlying obligation* that generated the instrument. If a corporation mails a dividend check to one of its stockholders and the check is lost in the mail, the stockholder can sue on the underlying obligation (in this case, the agreement to pay the dividend) and ignore whatever rights negotiable instruments law would give.

Does this mean that in addition to the negotiable instruments suits described below, a party may always bring suit on the underlying obligation? The answer has to be "No," and the following Problem illustrates why.

PROBLEM 122

Aunt Fran was unable to pay the annual rent on her hat shop, so she asked the landlord, Simon Mustache, to accept instead a promissory note from her to him for the amount of the rent, the note to be due three months in the future. Simon took the note and immediately discounted it with a local bank. A week later (and before the note matured), Simon brought suit against Aunt Fran for non-payment of the rent (the underlying obligation being the lease agreement). Can she defend by saying that the note somehow suspended his right to sue on the underlying obligation?

The answer is "Yes." The common law doctrine of *merger* stated that once an instrument was offered and accepted in satisfaction of an underlying obligation, the obligation merged with the instrument, and until the instrument was dishonored the underlying obligation was suspended (unavailable as a cause of action). This doctrine is codified in §3-310(b), which you should read carefully. Note that under §3-310(b)(1) and (2) payment of a check or a note discharges the underlying obligation, but until then that obligation is suspended. Once the instrument is dishonored, subsection (b)(3) divorces the underlying contract from the instrument and separate causes of action then exist for both.

PROBLEM 123

Suppose in the last Problem Aunt Fran had paid her rent by giving a cashier's check to Simon. The check was drawn by Octopus National Bank (ONB) on itself (the very definition of a cashier's check—see §3-104(g)). Simon took the check down to ONB and was dismayed to discover that the bank had failed and was now closed. He returned to Aunt Fran and demanded the rent money. What should she tell him? See §3-310(a).

PROBLEM 124

When Aunt Fran (from Problem 122) told Simon that she was not liable for the rent as long as the note was outstanding, he got it back from the bank and tore it up. May he now sue her for the rent even though the note has not yet matured? See §§3-604, 3-310(b)(4), 3-309; Peterson v. Crown Fin. Corp., 661 F.2d 287, 32 U.C.C. Rep. Serv. 497 (3d Cir. 1981) (creditor's subjective intent irrelevant). See also Annot., 59 A.L.R.4th 617. If the cancellation had been a clerical error, what result? See G.E. Capital Mortg. Services, Inc. v. Neely, 135 N.C. App. 187, 519 S.E.2d 553, 39 UCC Rep. Serv. 2d 1170 (1999).

Ward v. Federal Kemper Insurance Co.

Maryland Court of Appeals, 1985
62 Md. App. 351, 489 A.2d 91, 40 U.C.C. Rep. Serv. 753

ADKINS, J. The issue posed to us by appellant, Aaron Ward, is whether appellee, Federal Kemper Insurance Company, properly cancelled an insurance policy for nonpayment of a premium. The question is whether Ward owed the premium at the time of cancellation. The answer to this seemingly simple question is complicated by a problem in the law of negotiable instruments: in whose hands are the funds represented by a check that the drawer (Federal Kemper) has mailed to the payee (Ward) but that is never paid by the drawee bank because never negotiated by the payee? The facts are undisputed.

On May 19, 1981, Federal Kemper issued an automobile liability policy to Ward and his then wife (hereinafter "Ward"). Ward paid the premium in full. By its terms, the policy was to expire on November 17, 1981. On August 4, because of a change of vehicles owned by Ward, Federal Kemper sent him a check (payable to him) in the amount of $12.00, and drawn on The Citizens National Bank of Decatur, Illinois. This represented a refund of overpaid premium. Ward received the check but never negotiated it.

Soon after sending the check, Federal Kemper discovered that the proper refund should have been $4.50, rather than $12.00. On August 18, it billed Ward the difference of $7.50. Ward did not recall receiving the bill. In any event Ward never paid the $7.50, and pursuant to provisions of the policy, Federal Kemper mailed Ward a notice of cancellation effective October 11. On November 15 Ward was involved in an accident while driving the insured vehicle. The accident resulted in personal injury and property damage to him, his vehicle, and to the persons and properties of others involved in the accident. Federal Kemper declined to provide coverage.

Ward sued the insurance company in the Circuit Court for Baltimore City, seeking a declaratory judgment as to coverage. There were cross-motions for summary judgment. Because he believed that summary judgment is inappropriate in a declaratory judgment action, the hearing judge treated the proceedings as a hearing on the merits. No one objected. The judge concluded that "at the time the bill was sent . . . in the amount of $7.50, that amount was not due Kemper." He thought that "until the negotiable instrument is negotiated and paid by the drawee back [bank] Kemper has suffered no debit." Nevertheless, he went on to opine:

> I . . . conclude that Kemper proceeded properly on an assumption that its bill was being ignored in moving for cancellation. As a matter of fact, the negotiable instrument which it had issued to Mr. Ward was still outstanding and perfectly valid on its face for a period of six months by its very terms. It is not required under the statutory provisions dealing with cancellation to wait for the expiration of the six month period of the draft before seeking its set off amount due. I conclude from the stipulated facts that cancellation was proper on October 11, 1981. That being so, there was no insurance coverage . . . by Kemper . . . at the time of the accident on November 15. . . .

He granted judgment in favor of Federal Kemper.

In this court Ward contends that unless a premium is actually due and unpaid, an insurer may not cancel a policy for its nonpayment, citing Art. 48, §234A(a) to the effect that "[n]o insurer . . . shall cancel . . . a particular insurance risk . . . for any arbitrary, capricious, or unfairly discriminatory reason." Whatever the precise reach of §234A(a), Lumbermen's Mutual Casualty Co. v. Insurance Commissioner, — Md. —, — A.2d —, —, No. 161, September Term, 1982 (filed February 11, 1985), we agree that an insurer may not cancel a policy for nonpayment of premium unless the premium is in fact due. See Government Employees Co. v. Insurance Commissioner, 273 Md. 467, 483, 330 A.2d 653 (1975). To put this self-evident point more directly:

Where the propriety of the cancellation of a policy depends upon the nonpayment of a premium it necessarily follows that there is no effective cancellation when in fact the premium has been paid. For if a premium has been paid, the insurer cannot cancel for non-payment of such premium [citations omitted].

M. Rhodes, Couch Cyclopedia of Insurance Law §67.74 (rev. 2d ed. 1983).

Federal Kemper does not dispute these propositions. The parties agree that the real issue is who had the $7.50 premium due balance that was included in the unnegotiated $12.00 check. If this money was Ward's by virtue of his possession of the check and his ability to negotiate it, then Ward owed Federal Kemper the $7.50 and the cancellation was proper. If, on the other hand, the $7.50 was still under Federal Kemper's control, because the check has not been negotiated when the policy was cancelled, the cancellation was improper. To resolve this question we must turn to the Uniform Commercial Code rather than to Art. 48A.

Ward points to §3-409(1) of the Commercial Law Article (§3-409(1) of the UCC [§3-408 in the Revision—Ed.]) which provides that:

> A check or draft does not of itself operate as an assignment of any funds in the hands of the drawee available for its payment, and the drawee is not liable on the instrument until he accepts it.

Because of this rule, he argues, his mere possession of the $12.00 check did not have the effect of transferring the $12.00 to him. Federal Kemper could have stopped payment or, for that matter, closed its account at the drawee bank prior to presentment of the check. In either of these events, he would have had nothing more than a claim against Federal Kemper for the $4.50 in fact due him; the $7.50 overpayment would at all times have remained under the insurer's control, as it in fact did. He cites Malloy v. Smith, 265 Md. 460, 290 A.2d 486 (1972), in which the Court of Appeals, by way of dictum, observed that a personal check cannot be the subject of a gift causa mortis. Referring to §3-409(1), the court explained:

> The point is, of course, that when the donor uses his own check to make the gift, there is no assignment of funds because he does not relinquish control of the sum which the check represents. A consequence of this is that a valid delivery alone will not complete the gift. To perfect the gift the check must be presented by the donee and accepted by the drawee, because the donor could

stop payment, withdraw from his account the very funds which the check represents, or die before payment is made, any one of which would revoke the gift. 265 Md. at 463.

Federal Kemper counters that by virtue of §3-413 [§3-414 in the Revision—Ed.] the drawer of a check "engages that he will pay the instrument according to its tenor . . . " and further "engages that upon dishonor [as through a stop payment order] and any necessary notice of dishonor or protest he will pay the amount of the draft to the holder. . . ." According to Federal Kemper, a stop payment order may be effective to prevent payment of a check by the drawee, but that does not affect the drawer's liability to a holder in due course. Section 3-305. Had Ward negotiated the $12.00 to a holder in due course, thereby receiving value for it, Federal Kemper would have been liable to the holder in due course despite any stop payment order. First National Bank of Trinity, Texas v. McKay, 521 S.W.2d 661 (Tex. Civ. App. 1975). When Federal Kemper billed Ward for the $7.50 and when it issued the cancellation notice, it had no way of knowing whether a holder in due course had entered the picture. Thus, the argument continues, by issuing the check to Ward, Federal Kemper obligated itself to pay $12.00. And since the obligation was $7.50 more than its actual premium refund debt to Ward, Ward was obligated to pay Federal Kemper the difference. Therefore, Ward owed Federal Kemper a premium of $7.50, a sum that has never been paid.

We think Federal Kemper misapprehends the nature of a check and the relationships of the parties to it. A check is a draft or bill of exchange—an order by a drawer (Federal Kemper) to a drawee (Citizens National Bank of Decatur) to pay money to a payee (Ward). Section 3-104. B. Clark, The Law of Bank Deposits, Collections and Credit Cards Par 1.1[1] (rev. ed. 1981) (hereinafter "Clark"). As between drawer and drawee, the relationship is one of creditor and debtor. The drawer does not "own" the funds it has on deposit with the drawee. Its balance on the drawee's books represents a debt owed the drawer by the drawee. The funds are "owned" by the drawee. Id. par 2.1.

When the drawer draws a check on the drawee and delivers the check to the payee, the check ordinarily is regarded as only a conditional payment of the underlying obligation. Merriman v. Sandeen, 267 N.W.2d 714, 717 (Minn. 1978). H. Bailey, Brady on Bank Checks §1.8, 4.5 (5th ed. 1979 & 1984 Cum. Supp.) (hereinafter "Bailey"). See also Moore v. Travelers Indemnity Ins. Co., 408 A.2d 298 (Del. Super. 1979). The conditions are that the check be presented and honored. Until those conditions are met, no one is directly liable on the check itself; Clark, par 1.3. The underlying obligation represented by the check is similarly suspended until those conditions are met; §3-802(1)(b). If they are not met (if, for example, the check is dishonored), an "action may be maintained either on the [check] or the obligation. . . ." Id.

The point is that the drawer is only secondarily liable on the check when he issues it. Stewart v. Citizens and Southern Natl. Bank, 225 S.E.2d 761 (Ga. App. 1976); Clark, par 1.3; §§3-122(3) and 3-413(2). As Ward correctly asserts, the delivery of Federal Kemper's check did not operate as an assignment to him of any funds in the hands of the drawee; §3-409(1). Clark, par 3.1[1]. Ward, when he received the check acquired no proprietary interest in the fund on deposit. Bailey §4.1.

The $12.00 check involved in this case was, of course, never dishonored. Thus, Federal Kemper never became liable directly on the check, nor was its underlying obligation (to refund $4.50 to Ward) ever actually discharged. The check was never presented to the drawee and, therefore, never paid, so the funds it represented were never transferred to Ward. In point of fact, those funds remained (and so far as we know, still remain) in the Citizens National Bank of Decatur, subject to Federal Kemper's control. Under these circumstances, we do not think that Ward owed any premium to Federal Kemper. See Owl Electric Co. v. United States Fidelity and Guaranty Co., 268 N.E. 493 (Ill. App. 1971). See also Klein v. Tabatchnik, 459 F. Supp. 707, 715-716 (S.D.N.Y. 1978), aff'd (as to relevant issue), 610 F.2d 1043, 1049 (2d Cir. 1979) and In re Sportsco, 12 B.R. 34 (Bkr. Ct., D. Ariz. 1981).

It is perfectly true that when Federal Kemper billed Ward, and when it sent the cancellation notice, there might have been a holder in due course lurking in the wings. That is a business risk Federal Kemper took when it proceeded as it did. The policies underlying the protections given a holder in due course, Lawrence & Minan, The Effect of Abrogating the Holder in Due Course Doctrine on the Commercialization of Innovative Consumer Products, 64 B.U. L. Rev. 325, 327-330 (1984), do not affect the underlying relationships between Ward and Federal Kemper, especially when, as here, there was no holder in due course. When Federal Kemper attempted to cancel the policy the entire premium was in its bank account; Ward owed it nothing at that time.

Accordingly, we hold that the Circuit Court for Baltimore City correctly concluded that "at the date the [premium due] bill was

sent in the amount of $7.50 on August 18, 1981, it was not due."
That being so, Federal Kemper could not lawfully have cancelled
Ward's policy for nonpayment of that premium. Ward is entitled to
a declaratory judgment to the effect that his Federal Kemper pol-
icy was in full force and effect when the accident occurred. See
Jennings v. Government Employees Ins. Co., — Md. —, — A.2d
—, No. 27, Sept. Term, 1983 (filed February 22, 1985).

Judgment reversed.

Case remanded for entry of declaratory judgment consistent
with this opinion. Appellee to pay the costs.

II.   LIABILITY ON THE INSTRUMENT

As soon as someone places a signature on a negotiable instrument, an *implied contractual obligation* is automatically made promising to pay the instrument when it matures (unless in the meantime
a defense, real or personal, develops). The original version of Article 3 actually called these obligations "contracts," but the name was
misleading because the legal responsibility imposed thereby did
not depend on the intention of the relevant party. The so-called
contract was imposed as a matter of law whether or not the contracting party understood the fact or extent of liability.

In the Revision these promises are called *obligations* and not
contracts, but the basic idea is the same. Putting one's signature on
a negotiable instrument in anything other than an innocuous
capacity ("witness," for example) leads to a promise *implied in law*
(actual intent being irrelevant) to pay the instrument under certain circumstances. This obligation is sometimes described as
liability *on the instrument*—that is, as a result of signing the instrument, and the person who could enforce that liability was the
current holder of the instrument.

Before the nature of this liability in contract is explored further, let me emphasize the basic rule found in §3-401(a): "A person is not liable on an instrument unless (i) the person signed the
instrument. . . ." This means that no contractual liability arises on a
negotiable instrument until and unless a signature is placed
thereon. What is a signature? Read the definition of *signed* in §1-
201(39) and the description of signatures in 3-401(b). If you now

review Problems 82 and 83, you should have this concept well under control.[1]

A. The Maker's Obligation

The maker of a promissory note is absolutely liable on the instrument; a maker's liability has no technical implied conditions to
it. The same thing is true of a bank that issues a cashier's check.
This "primary" liability is codified in §3-412 (where both the maker
of a promissory note and the bank issuing a cashier's check are
lumped together as *issuers*).[2] If there is more than one maker,
those who sign are presumed to be jointly and severally liable to
the rest of the world (meaning that they can be sued individually
or as a group), but they have a right to contribution from their co-
makers if they are forced to pay more than their share.

PROBLEM 125

Winkin, Blinkin, and Nod signed the following promissory
note:

Oct. 1, 2010 $3,000

On or after six months from date, we promise to pay to the
order of *Grimms National Bank, the sum of three thousand dollars
($3,000).* We, along with all sureties and subsequent indorsers,
waive all rights to presentment, notice of dishonor, and protest, and
all parties hereto agree to any extension of time granted by the
holder to the makers.

Wilber Winkin
Barney Blinkin
Harry Nod

---

1. If a forger places your name on a check, does the forgery operate as your
signature? The answer is found in §3-403(a), which states that an unauthorized
signature is "ineffective" as that of the person whose name is signed, but it does
operate as if the forger had signed his or her *real* name. We will come back to this
issue in the section on forgery.
2. Section 3-105(c): "Issuer" means a maker or drawer of an instrument.

Grimms National Bank indorsed the note in blank and discounted it to Andersen Finance Co. When the note matured, Andersen sued only Winkin, demanding the entire amount. May he defend on the basis that Andersen should have sued all three of them, since the note contains the words "we promise to pay"? If Andersen wins, can Winkin sue Blinkin for $2,000? $1,000? See §3-116; Ghitter v. Edge, 118 Ga. App. 750, 165 S.E.2d 598, 5 U.C.C. Rep. Serv. 1253 (1968).

B. The Indorser's Obligation

Once the payee signs the back of the instrument, the payee automatically incurs the obligation the law imposes on an *indorser.* In fact, per §3-204(a), *anyone* who signs an instrument in an ambiguous capacity is conclusively presumed to assume this liability. This obligation is described in §3-415, which you should read carefully. Note that unlike the obligation of a maker, the indorser's obligation is *secondary* in that there are certain technical conditions that must be met before the indorser can be sued on the §3-415 obligation: the instrument must have first been *presented* to the maker (if it is a note) or to the drawee (if it is a draft), there must have been a *dishonor* (by the maker or drawee), and in certain circumstances §3-503 requires that the indorser be given *notice of dishonor.*

These three rights (presentment, dishonor, and notice of dishonor) are discussed ad nauseam in the 3-500 sections of the Code. It is unfortunate, but unavoidable, that we must explore these sections at some time, but let's postpone that until after we've established the drawer's liability on a draft. For now it is sufficient if you remember that an indorser is not liable until the person primarily liable has dishonored the instrument and the indorser has been so notified. Section 3-415 settles other problems, too, as illustrated by the following Problems.

PROBLEM 126

Billy Bigelow wrote out a check payable to the order of Enoch Snow to pay for some carnival equipment. Snow cashed the check at Bascombe Drug Store, indorsing his name on the back. Bascombe Drug Store then indorsed the check and deposited it in its account at Jordan State Bank. This bank also indorsed the check and then presented it to the drawee bank, Rodgers National Bank, which dishonored it because Bigelow had no money in his account, marking it "NSF" ("Not Sufficient Funds"). The check was returned to Jordan State Bank. You are the bank's attorney, and it calls you with three questions:

(1) Bascombe Drug Store has suddenly gone out of business and there is no money in its account. Can Jordan State Bank sue Enoch Snow and, if so, on what theory? Read §3-415(a) carefully.

(2) If Jordan State Bank sues Snow, may he raise his defenses (say, that the drugstore had failed to pay him any money when he indorsed it over to them), or is the indorser liability found in §3-415 strict liability?

(3) If the bank does recover from Snow, will he have to pay the whole amount or do the indorsers divide up the indorsement liability and share it proportionately? Cf. §§3-116, 3-205(d).

PROBLEM 127

Charlie Brown wanted to borrow $10,000 from the Peanuts National Bank, but the bank told him that it would not loan him the money unless his note was indorsed by four responsible people. Charlie explained his problem to his friend Lucy, and she signed her name to the back of the instrument. Charlie then took the note to another friend, Schroeder, who not only signed, but also persuaded his friend Pig Pen to add his name below Schroeder's. Finally, Charlie Brown had Peppermint Patty sign her name, at which point he took the note back to the bank, and it loaned him the money. When the note came due, the bank made a presentment of it to Charlie Brown and demanded payment. He had used the money in a business venture that, predictably enough, was a moral but not a financial success, and so he was unable to pay the note (a dishonor). The Peanuts National Bank gave notice of dishonor to all four indorsers, but demanded payment of Peppermint Patty alone. She resisted, claiming she was liable at most for only one-fourth of the amount ($2,500). Look at §3-415 and decide:

(a) Is she right?

(b) If she pays $10,000, can she sue Pig Pen for the entire amount or only for part? Once again look at §§3-116, 3-205(d).

(c) If she is sued, can she bring the other indorsers into the lawsuit? See §3-119 (explaining the so-called "vouching in" notice).

(d) If Charlie Brown comes back into the chips, can she sue him? On what theory?

Co-Suretyship vs. Sub-Suretyship. The common law presumed, unless the sureties agreed otherwise, that those signing later in time could get complete reimbursement from those signing prior in time, and this was called the presumption of *subsuretyship.* If the sureties have agreed, expressly or impliedly, to share the liability, then they are *co-sureties* and have a right of partial contribution from each other. Where the parties have made what §3-205(d) calls an *anomalous* indorsement (one made by a non-holder—i.e., a surety), §3-116 changes the common law and now presumes that the parties are co-sureties, and hence must share the liability among themselves proportionately. See Official Comment 5 to §3-415.

Indorsers and Sureties. Whether the indorser intends it or not, the imposition of a §3-415 obligation makes the indorser an unintentional surety for the parties who have signed the instrument prior to the indorser, and the Code generally gives indorsers all the rights it gives to voluntary sureties, whom it calls *accommodation parties.*

Qualified Indorsements. How can the indorser avoid incurring the §3-415 obligation? The answer is by writing the words "without recourse" next to his or her name, preferably above it. In this manner the indorsement (technically called a *qualified* indorsement) operates to negotiate the instrument, but does not create any contractual liability. See §3-415(b).

PROBLEM 128

Marian Melody, a professional pianist, bought a piano from the Ivory Keys Music Company, signing a promissory note payable to the company for $3,000. The day after the piano was delivered, the music company discounted the note to the Friendly Loan Company for $2,700, indorsing it on the back, "Pay to the Friendly Loan Company, *Ivory Keys Music Company (Without Recourse)*." The piano fell apart, and Melody refused to pay the note when it came due. Friendly Finance sued both Melody and the Ivory Keys Music Company. What is its cause of action against each? What defenses can each defendant raise?

Practical Note. When a lawsuit is settled, the losing side will frequently send the victorious attorney a check on which the attorney and the attorney's client are joint payees. This is done to protect the attorney's lien and to help the attorney get payment from the client. When the attorney indorses such a check, the indorsement should be "without recourse." This makes it clear that the indorsement is made only to negotiate the check and that the attorney assumes no §3-415 obligation. There is no reason why the attorney (or the client for that matter) should make an unqualified indorsement and become, in effect, a surety for the drawer of the check, already known to be a loser.

C.   The Surety's Obligation

This section must of necessity be a long one, not because the concepts herein are particularly complex, but because there is a great deal of suretyship law that one must gulp down and digest before the Code's suretyship provisions look friendlier.[3] In a negotiable instruments setting, suretyship problems come up whenever, as in the Charlie Brown Problem above, the maker must get others to "lend their names" to the maker's basic obligation. Suretyship matters can arise even in connection with checks. If you are the payee on a check drawn on Bank *A*, just see how easy it is to cash the check at Bank *B* if you do not have an account there. Bank *B* will probably not take the check unless one of its customer-depositors is willing to sign (become a surety) along with you.

It is an awesome thing to become surety for someone else, but people nonetheless do it, often with very little thought about the consequences, thus becoming the so-called "fool with a pen" (the Bible has a similar thought: "A man void of understanding . . . becometh surety in the presence of his friend"—Proverbs 17:18). In the desire to help out a friend or relative who is temporarily financially embarrassed (and who often assures the prospective surety "I guarantee you that you really won't have to pay"), the surety co-signs and, like it or not, understand it or not, takes on liability for

---

3. The following brief outline of some of the basic rules of the suretyship can and should be supplemented by the two leading treatises: Stearns, Suretyship (4th ed. 1951), and Simpson, Suretyship (1950). See also the Restatement (Third) of Suretyship and Guaranty.

the debt. To alert potential sureties to the nature of their undertaking, both the Federal Trade Commission and the Federal Reserve Board have issued regulations requiring consumer debts to carry a notice to co-signers (defined for these purposes as natural persons who are uncompensated) in the following manner:

Notice to Co-Signer
You are being asked to guarantee this debt. Think carefully before you do. If the borrower doesn't pay the debt, you will have to. Be sure you can afford to pay if you have to, and that you want to accept this responsibility.

You may have to pay up to the full amount of the debt if the borrower does not pay. You may also have to pay late fees or collection costs, which increase this amount. The creditor can collect this debt from you without first trying to collect from the borrower.

The creditor can use the same collection methods against you that can be used against the borrower, such as suing you, garnishing your wages, etc. If this debt is ever in default, that fact may become a part of your credit record.

This notice is not the contract that makes you liable for the debt.

See F.T.C. Trade Regulation Rule Concerning Credit Practices, 16 C.F.R. part 444.3, effective March 1, 1985, and F.R.B. Reg. AA, 12 C.F.R. part 227, effective January 1, 1986.

In any true surety setting, there are three basic contracts involved. The first contract is the underlying obligation between the principal and the creditor. The second contract is the promise of the surety to back up the underlying obligation and see that the creditor loses nothing as a result of accepting the principal's promise on the first contract. The third contract is the promise of the principal to *reimburse* the surety if the surety is forced to pay off on the surety's promise to the creditor.[4] The contract of reimbursement is frequently implied, as where a sister co-signs for her brother and expects to lose no money from the transaction; when a professional surety's liability is obtained, the contract of reimbursement will be spelled out in a multi-page, fine-print document.

---

4. This contract of reimbursement is one of the theories for Peppermint Patty's suit against Charlie Brown in Problem 127.

PROBLEM 129

Frank Family wanted to move out of his apartment and into his dream house. He hired Quickie Contractor to build the house on land Family had purchased, requiring Quickie to get a performance and payment bond guaranteeing that Quickie would do the work and pay its laborers and suppliers. Quickie got Big Bank to issue the bond guaranteeing these matters. Quickie went bankrupt halfway through the job, and Family called on Big Bank to finish the work. Which of these parties is the surety? Which the principal? Which the creditor? Identify the three contracts.

Sureties have several remedial rights in addition to the right of reimbursement. These include the rights of exoneration, subrogation, and contribution, and the principle of *strictissimi juris*.

1. Exoneration

This is an equitable right by which the surety, at maturity, can compel the principal to perform instead of the surety. That is, by a bill in equity, the surety can prevent the need for a later suit for reimbursement. The basis for this right is said to be the implied duty that every principal owes to the surety to perform at the earliest moment and exonerate the surety from liability.

2. Subrogation

If the surety is forced to pay off the creditor, the surety is subrogated to whatever rights the creditor had. Put another way, the surety steps into the shoes of the creditor and is said to take an "equitable assignment" of the creditor's rights. This may be important if the creditor possesses rights the surety can take advantage of—for instance, a lien, a security interest in collateral, a priority in bankruptcy, a power to confess judgment, etc. In effect, by paying off on the second contract, the surety's right of subrogation permits the surety to become a party to the first contract and enforce it *as if the surety were the creditor.*

3. Contribution

This is a right of partial reimbursement that co-sureties have against each other for proportionate shares of the debt. If X, Y, and Z each sign M's note for \$9,000 agreeing to be co-sureties, the payee may enforce the entire obligation against any one of the three, and the right of contribution will then permit that one to sue the other two for their shares.

4. *Strictissimi Juris*

The following is a discussion of the common law rules only; as we shall see, the revision of Article 3 has drastically changed the rules.

A surety, particularly an uncompensated surety, is a *favorite of the law,* so that at common law the surety's obligation is to be construed *strictissimi juris* (of the *strictest law*), and thus the surety prevails if possible. Since the surety has agreed to back up only the first contract, the courts have held that an agreement between the creditor and the principal that changes that contract *in any detail* operates to discharge and release the non-consenting surety from further liability. Restatement of Security 128 (1941). Why? Because the modification of the first contract converts it into a new contract to which the surety did not consent. The courts even go so far as to say that a surety is discharged by a modification of the first contract that *benefits* the surety by lessening the principal's obligation. See Merchants Natl. Bank v. Blass, 282 Ark. 497, 669 S.W.2d 195, 394 U.C.C. Rep. Serv. 242 (1984) (new note given by maker containing a higher interest rate discharged surety on original note); First Natl. City Bank v. Carbonaro, 9 U.C.C. Rep. Serv. 700 (N.Y. Civ. Ct. 1971) (surety who agreed to back loan of \$4,176 discharged when promissory note filled in with only \$1,656 as the amount).

Moreover, if the creditor agreed by a binding commitment to excuse the principal from liability or to give the principal extra time to pay the first contract, the Restatement (Third) of Suretyship and Guaranty would hold that a non-consenting surety is discharged unless the creditor warns the principal that this agreement works a "preservation of recourse" by the surety against the principal, meaning that the agreement in no way affects the rights of the surety against the principal.

There are theoretical reasons for these rules. By extending the time without the surety's consent, the creditor is thought to prejudice the surety's right of subrogation, but if the creditor expressly states that the surety's right of recourse is unimpaired, supposedly no prejudice occurs to the subrogation rights because the principal debtor is then alerted to the fact that the creditor's promise is conditional on the surety's rights (including subrogation) being preserved intact. The surety who dislikes this modified agreement can ignore it and exercise the usual rights, including exoneration, reimbursement, and even subrogation to the creditor's premodification position. For our purposes it is easier to memorize this black letter rule:

Common Law Rule:

> If the creditor releases the principal debtor from liability on the first contract or gives the debtor a binding extension of time in which to pay, the surety is discharged *unless* (1) the surety consents, or (2) the creditor informs the principal of the preservation of the surety's rights against the principal.

Notice that the non-consenting surety is discharged only by a binding extension of time. There is all the (legal) difference in the world between the following two hypotheticals:

(1) The note comes due, and the principal does not pay it; the creditor waits a month before suing.
(2) The note comes due, and the creditor and principal *agree* to wait a month to enforce it, with the principal agreeing to pay an extra month's worth of interest.

In the first hypothetical the surety is not discharged even if thereby an extra month's worth of interest is added to the obligation.[5] The creditor and the principal have not *agreed* to change the original contract, and surely the surety cannot object if the creditor does not declare an immediate forfeiture. But in the second hypothetical, the surety is discharged by the new agreement unless the surety consents or the creditor adds to the agreement the *preservation of secondary obligator's recourse clause.* The Restatement (Third) of Suretyship and Guaranty, which calls the creditor the "obligee," the principal the "principal obligor," and the surety the "secondary obligor," puts it this way:

---

5. However, if the surety is also an indorser, a delay in presentment (discussed later in the book) may result in a discharge under §3-415(e).

§129. Preservation of Secondary Obligor's Recourse

(1) When an obligee releases the principal obligor from, or agrees to extend the time for performance of, a duty to pay money pursuant to the underlying obligation, the release or extension effect a "preservation of the secondary obligor's recourse" with respect to that duty if the express terms of the release or extension provide that:

(a) the obligee retains the right to seek performance of the secondary obligation by the secondary obligor; and

(b) the rights of the secondary obligor to recourse against the principal obligor (§§21-31) continue as though the release or extension had not been granted.

(2) When the obligee effects a preservation of the secondary obligor's recourse in conjunction with a release or extension, the principal obligor's duties of performance and reimbursement and the secondary obligor's rights of restitution and subrogation continue as though the release or extension did not occur.

There are other important rules of suretyship (for instance, a surety's promise—the second contract—must be in writing to be enforceable under the Statute of Frauds), but these rules play little part in negotiable instruments law. Section 3-419(b), for instance, completely does away with the Statute of Frauds defense as far as negotiable instruments are concerned. Instead, our study will focus on how the above rules have been varied in the law of negotiable instruments.[6]

5. The Accommodation Party

The Uniform Commercial Code in §3-419 reserves special suretyship rights for those who deliberately lend their names to an instrument to accommodate another. These sections spell out the obligation incurred by the Code's sureties. Section 3-419 applies to an *accommodation party,* defined in subsection (a) as a party who "signs the instrument for the purpose of incurring liability on the instrument without being a direct beneficiary of the value given for the instrument." Read Official Comment 1 to §3-419. Subsection (b) informs us that the accommodation party may sign in any capacity (as maker, drawer, acceptor, or indorser), but is "obligated to pay the instrument in the capacity in which the accommodation

---

6. For an excellent article on sureties and the UCC, see Peters, Suretyship Under Article 3 of the Uniform Commercial Code, 77 Yale L.J. 833 (1968).

party signs." This means that the surety (accommodation party) has the same liability as a maker if the surety signs as a maker, but the surety signing as an indorser is liable only in that capacity (and has the rights of an indorser: presentment, notice of dishonor, etc.); in addition, of course, the surety gets both statutory and common law suretyship rights.

PROBLEM 130

Consider the following promissory note:

FRONT: December 23, 2010

I, *Mary Maker*, promise to pay *$4,000* to the order of *Paul Payee* on December 25, 2012, with interest at 8 percent per annum from date.

/s/ George Generous

/s/ Mary Maker

BACK:

Pay to *Ace Finance* /s/Paul Payee

Ace Finance comes to you early in 2013 and tells you that the note is in default, but that it failed to give notice of dishonor—a right that indorsers have but makers do not—to George Generous.

(a) May George Generous establish his status as surety against a holder in due course? See §3-419(c) with its Official Comment 3, §§3-205(d), 3-605(h).

(b) May George defend on the basis that he received no consideration for his undertaking? See §3-419(b) and its Official Comment 2.

(c) Is George an accommodation maker or an accommodation indorser? See §§3-116(a), 3-204(a); cf. Philadelphia Bond & Mortgage Co. v. Highland Crest Homes, Inc., 221 Pa. Super. 89, 288 A.2d 916, 10 U.C.C. Rep. Serv. 668 (1972) ("Thus by long established practice judicially noted or otherwise established, a signature in the lower right hand corner of an instrument indicates an intent to sign as the maker of a note or the drawer of a draft.").

It should be emphasized that Article 3's rules apply only to accommodation parties who *sign the instrument*. If the accommodation party signs a *separate* suretyship agreement but not the note itself, common law rules, not the Code, govern the result. See Official Comment 3, last paragraph, to §3-419; Uniwest Mortgage Co. v. Dadecor Condominiums, Inc., 877 F.2d 431, 9 U.C.C. Rep. Serv. 2d 577 (5th Cir. 1989).

A *guarantor* is a surety who adds words of guaranty to his or her signature ("I hereby guarantee this instrument," for example), but words of guaranty add nothing to the suretyship obligation unless the surety has specifically guaranteed *collection* only, in which case the guarantor is given the extra protections described in §3-419(d), which you should now read.

PROBLEM 131

Suppose in the prior Problem George Generous had written the word *Guarantor* after his name. Would Ace Finance have had to sue Mary Maker first or not? See §3-419(d).

Floor v. Melvin

Illinois Appellate Court, 1972
5 Ill. App. 3d 463, 283 N.E.2d 303,
11 U.C.C. Rep. Serv. 109

ALLOY, J. The action in the present case was instituted by Marjorie Irene Floor in the Circuit Court of LaSalle County to recover money alleged to be due on a promissory note. On motion of defendant Mildred B. Melvin, executrix of the estate of Charles W. Melvin, deceased, an order was entered dismissing the claim for failure to state a cause of action. Claimant, Majorie Irene Floor, seeks reversal of the order on the theory that the deceased Charles W. Melvin was a guarantor of payment.

On April 14, 1959, Melco, Inc., an Illinois corporation, acting through its president, Charles W. Melvin, made and issued its negotiable promissory note in the principal amount of $12,000.00, payable to the order of Majorie Irene Floor. On the back of the note the following language appears: "For and in consideration of funds advanced herein to Melco, Inc., we irrevocably guarantee Majorie Irene Floor against loss by reason of nonpayment of this note." The signature of Charles W. Melvin, as well as others, appeared below such statement.

The complaint of plaintiff in this case does not allege prosecution of her claim to judgment as against the principal obligor on the note and it, also, does not allege the insolvency of the obligor, Melco, Inc. The only issue, therefore, before the court is whether, with respect to the undertaking on the back of the note, plaintiff is required to prosecute her claim against the maker of the note as a pre-condition to making a valid claim as against the estate of Charles W. Melvin.

[The court quoted §3-416, the precursor to §3-419(d)—Ed.]

The quoted subsection in the portion marked as "(1)" codifies the rule of several Illinois cases including Beebe v. Kirkpatrick, 321 Ill. 612, 152 N.E. 539, and Weger v. Robinson Nash Motor Co., 340 Ill. 81, 172 N.E. 7. In the *Weger* case referred to, the guaranty contract that had been executed read (at page 85, 172 N.E. at page 9):

> We, the undersigned directors and stockholders of the Robinson Nash Motor Company, do hereby guarantee the *payment of notes* of said company given the Robinson State Bank of Robinson, Illinois, and hereby agree to be personally liable therefore and to all the conditions and requirements written in said notes . . . [emphasis ours].

The court in construing said language said, at page 90, 172 N.E. at page 11:

> A contract guaranteeing the payment of a note is an absolute contract, and by it the guarantor undertakes for a valuable consideration, to pay the debt at maturity if the principal debtor fails to do so, and upon it, if the debt is not paid at maturity, the guarantor may be sued at once. Guarantors must be regarded as original promisors, who bound themselves to pay the notes when they matured, and their duty was, on their maturity, to go to the holder and take them up, and their liability was not to depend upon the prosecution of suit against the maker.

In Beebe v. Kirkpatrick, 321 Ill. 612, 152 N.E. 539, the question was with respect to construction of the words "I hereby guarantee this loan." In support of its holding that the cited language was absolute in nature, the Supreme Court stated (at page 616, 152 N.E. at pages 540-541):

In this state contracts of guaranty of negotiable instruments are of two kinds: Contracts guaranteeing the collection of the notes, and contracts guaranteeing the payment of the notes. A contract guaranteeing the collection of a note or debt is conditional in its character, and the guarantor thereby undertakes to pay the debt upon condition that the owner thereof shall make use of the ordinary legal means to collect it from the debtor with diligence but without avail. A contract guaranteeing the payment of a note or a debt is an absolute contract, and by it the guarantor undertakes, for a valuable consideration, to pay the debt at maturity if the principal debtor fails to do so, and upon it, if the debt is not paid at maturity, the guarantor may be sued at once.

Other cases, such as Dillman v. Nadelhoffer, 160 Ill. 121, 43 N.E. 378, treat the language of subsection (2) referring to "collection guaranteed." In the *Dillman* case the language before the court was "for a valuable consideration, we do hereby guarantee the collection of the within note at its maturity . . . " (at page 124, 43 N.E. at page 378). In construing this language, the Supreme Court stated that "the guaranty is not a guaranty of the payment of the note, but a guaranty of the collection of the note." The court stated (at page 125, 43 N.E. at page 379) that a contract guaranteeing the collection of a note or debt is conditional in its character and the guarantor thereby undertakes to pay the debt, "upon condition that the owner thereof shall make use of the ordinary legal means to collect it from the principal debtor with diligence, and without avail."

In the cause before us, the primary contention made by plaintiff is that the language of defendant's guarantee presents an absolute undertaking and is, therefore, a guarantee of payment within purview of subsection (1) of the statute in question. In support of that contention, Beebe v. Kirkpatrick, 321 Ill. 612, 152 N.E. 539, Hance v. Miller, 21 Ill. 636, and Empire Sec. Co. v. Berry, 211 Ill. App. 278, are cited as authority. We have indicated that in the *Beebe* case, the court found that the language "I hereby guarantee this loan" presented a guarantee of payment and not collection. The *Hance* case involved construction of language which read "For value received I guarantee payment of the within note at maturity." Consistently, the court had no difficulty in construing that language to be a guarantee of payment. In the *Berry* case, the guarantor had agreed to pay the note if the maker did not "retire" it at maturity. The court found that the word "retire" as used in the context meant "pay" and, therefore, that the guarantee was of payment and not of collection.

The language involved in each of the cases referred to by plaintiff is clearly in conformity with the law in Illinois regarding guaranty contracts. We believe, however, that plaintiff draws an erroneous analogy between guarantees appearing in those cases and that which we have under consideration in the cause before us. In our opinion, the terms of the guarantee in the instant case are made conditional upon collection of the note. While it is true that the word "collection" has not been used, in our view the guarantee as against "loss" is in effect a guarantee of collection rather than payment. At least one case of another jurisdiction, Michelin Tire Co. v. Cutter, 116 Or. 217, 240 P. 895 (1925), involved language similar to that in the instant case. There the defendant agreed to indemnify plaintiff against "any loss on account of any monies" which a certain party may owe from time to time. The court had no difficulty in concluding that the guarantee involved was of collection and not of payment in that case. . . .

A final contention made by plaintiff is that subsection "(3)" of the Illinois statute quoted earlier in our opinion to the effect that where words of guaranty do not otherwise specify, the guarantee [is] of payment could be controlling in such case. We cannot agree with such analysis since it is apparent that the use of subsection "(3)" is limited to instances where no conditional language of the type we find in the present case has been used.

We, therefore, conclude that it is apparent that the instant guarantee is one of collection and not of payment. Since plaintiff does not allege that her claim was prosecuted to judgment and execution thereon returned unsatisfied or that the maker was insolvent, she has not complied with Section 3-416(2) of the Uniform Commercial Code (Illinois Revised Statutes, Ch. 26). The trial court's dismissal of the action was, therefore, proper, and should be affirmed.

Affirmed.

STROUDER, J., and DIXON, J., concur.

To recap: the Uniform Commercial Code's *accommodation maker, accommodation indorser, and guarantor*—known to non-lawyers as *co-signers*—are nothing more than common law sureties dressed up with new labels, their rights partially codified. The common law

rights of subrogation and reimbursement are codified in §3-
419(e), which states that an "accommodation party who pays the
instrument is entitled to enforce the instrument against the accommodated party. An accommodated party who pays the instrument has no right of recourse against, and is not entitled to
contribution from, an accommodation party."

PROBLEM 132

When Portia Moot graduated from law school, she moved to a
new city and needed to borrow money but discovered that her
credit rating was so bad no one would lend her the money. She appealed to her mother, Margaret Moot, a successful doctor, and Margaret agreed to help her out. Margaret borrowed $5,000 from
Octopus National Bank (ONB), signing a promissory note as maker
with the bank as payee. Margaret had Portia indorse the note on the
back before it was handed over to ONB in return for the money.

(a) If Margaret Moot is forced to pay this note when it matures,
can she sue Portia, the indorser? Normally the maker of the note
has no cause of action against indorsers, whose §3-415(a) obligation runs to "a person entitled to enforce the instrument," defined
in §3-301 as the holder (itself defined in §1-201(20) as the person
identified in the instrument as the person to whom it is payable,
which would not include the maker).

(b) If ONB recovers its money from Portia at maturity, can
Portia sue her mother, whose maker's obligation, §3-412, does run
to indorsers such as Portia?

In the above Problem, Portia has made what is called an
anomalous indorsement, §3-205(d), one that is put on the instrument
by a non-holder, and that can only mean that she signed for accommodation. Anyone looking at this note should know that
Portia is a surety; she is not named as the payee, but is the first person to indorse the note and must therefore have signed for some
reason other than negotiation. This means that (if it had been
relevant) in the above Problem the bank is conclusively presumed
to know that Portia is entitled to be treated as a surety. The mere
fact that the bank is presumed to know of Portia's accommodation
status does not, however, keep the bank from becoming a holder
in due course. A surety may prove accommodation status against a
knowledgeable holder in due course or against a non-holder in

due course, but if a holder in due course has no reason to know that a party is a surety, the holder in due course will take free of the suretyship defenses. See §3-605(h).

6.   Tender of Payment

Read the "tender of payment" rule (§3-603), which has meaning beyond suretyship problems; indeed, you may skip the last sentence of §3-603(c), which deals with an issue to be considered later. For an excellent article on point, see Comment, Tender of Payment Under UCC §3-604: A Forgotten Defense?, 39 Ohio St. L.J. 833 (1978). Use §3-603 to solve the following Problem.

PROBLEM 133

When Saul Panzer needed to borrow money, his friend Rex Stout agreed to loan him $10,000 if Saul could get a co-signer. Saul talked Orrin Cather into signing Saul's promissory note as co-maker. The note was payable to the order of Rex Stout, who loaned Saul the $10,000 and took the note in return for the money. Stout indorsed the note and sold it at a discount to Archie Goodwin.

(a) On the date the note matured, knowing that Saul Panzer, the maker, was in financial trouble and wanting to stop the running of interest,[7] Orrin Cather, the co-signer, went to Archie Goodwin, the current holder, and offered to pay the note, planning to seek reimbursement from Saul. Goodwin replied, "Let's give poor Saul a chance to pay it off himself." A month later Saul went bankrupt, and Goodwin demanded that Cather pay the initial amount due plus interest for the extra month. Cather refused, and Goodwin sued, adding a claim for attorney's fees. To what is he entitled, if anything? See §3-603(c)'s first sentence.

(b) On the due date Saul went to Goodwin and offered to pay, but Goodwin said, "Look, I know you need the money for your other bills—pay me next month." A month later Saul went bankrupt. Can Goodwin now recover from Cather? From Stout, the payee/indorser? See §3-603(b).

(c) Instead of the above, assume that on the maturity date Orrin Cather went to Goodwin and offered to pay the debt, to which Goodwin made the same reply. A month later Saul went bankrupt,

7. Section §3-112, requires the instrument to specify an interest rate or it has none.

and Orrin Cather filed for bankruptcy at the same time. Is Stout, the payee/indorser, liable to Goodwin? Cf. §3-415(a).

7. Section 3-605—*Strictissimi Juris* Again

Sureties are the beneficiaries of a number of common law maxims, among them that a "surety is a favorite of the law" and that "security follows the debt." The former you must remember to quote to the court should your client be a surety. The latter refers to the collateral (*security*) given to the creditor by the principal and means that on paying off the creditor and thereby acquiring the negotiable instrument (*debt*), the surety is also entitled to that collateral.

It follows that the surety has an interest in the creditor's handling of the collateral. Both at common law and under §3-605(e), (f), and (g), the non-consenting surety is discharged, up to the value of the collateral, if the creditor (holder) fails to protect the collateral and if it is thereby unavailable to pay the debt.

PROBLEM 134

When Butch Byrd borrowed $10,000 from Octopus National Bank, the bank not only made him get a surety, but also demanded that the inventory of Butch's feed store stand as collateral. Butch talked his brother Arnold into signing the promissory note as a guarantor and signed the necessary papers for the bank to get an Article 9 security interest in the inventory. Unfortunately, the bank failed to file the Article 9 financing statement in the correct place, so when Butch had financial difficulties, other creditors prevailed over the bank's attempt to claim the inventory. The inventory was worth $6,000. What is the effect of the bank's Article 9 difficulties on Arnold's liability? See §3-605(e) and (g).

Chemical Bank v. Pic Motors Corp.

New York Supreme Court, Appellate Division, 1982
87 A.D.2d 447, 452 N.Y.S.2d 41, 34 U.C.C. Rep. Serv. 219, *aff'd on the opinion below*, 58 N.Y.2d 1023, 448 N.E.2d 1349, 462 N.Y.S.2d 438, 35 U.C.C. Rep. Serv. 1190

FEIN, J. Pic, an established car dealership, entered into an inventory financing agreement with plaintiff Bank, pursuant to

which the Bank agreed to lend funds to Pic periodically under an established line of credit on the security of Pic's inventory of automobiles as collateral. Under this form of agreement, known as floor plan financing, the borrower draws upon the line of credit for the purpose of financing the purchase of automobiles for sale. The Bank extends loans within the credit limit based on the value of the vehicles purchased by the borrower. Upon the sale of any vehicle, the borrower pays back the portion of the loan that was granted based on the value of that vehicle. Thus, the bank loan always remains secured. Sales to purchasers in the ordinary course of business are made free of the Bank's lien. As a matter of practice, the Bank conducted periodic inspections of Pic's inventory to determine whether the financed vehicles were owned by Pic and whether the loan was reduced by an appropriate payment upon sale of a financed vehicle. The Bank also followed a curtailment policy under which any loan was proportionately reduced and finally paid in full for inventory remaining unsold over specified periods of time.

Siegel had been director, president and principal stockholder of Pic for many years and had personally guaranteed the loans in writing. In 1978 Siegel sold his interest in the company to defendant Manfred Robl and resigned as an officer and director of Pic. However, it is undisputed that his guaranty continued, as agreed, during all the relevant periods of time. The guaranty reads, in pertinent part, as follows:

> NOW, THEREFORE, in consideration of the premises and of other good and valuable consideration and in order to induce the Bank from time to time, in its discretion, to extend or continue credit to the Borrower, *the undersigned hereby guarantees, absolutely and unconditionally,* to the Bank *the payment of all liabilities of the Borrower to the Bank of whatever nature, whether now existing or hereafter incurred,* whether created directly or acquired by the Bank by assignment or otherwise, whether matured or unmatured and whether absolute or contingent (all of which are hereinafter collectively referred to as the "Liabilities of the Borrower"). . . .
>
> The undersigned hereby consents that from time to time, before or after any default by the Borrower or any notice of termination hereof, *with or without further notice to or assent from the undersigned, any security* at any time held by or available to the Bank for any obligation of the Borrower, or any security at any time held by or available to the Bank for any obligation of any other person secondarily or otherwise liable for any of the Liabilities of the Bor-

rower, *may be exchanged, surrendered or released* and any obligation of the Borrower, or of any such other person, *may be changed, altered, renewed, extended, continued, surrendered, compromised, waived or released in whole or in part,* . . . and *the Bank* . . . *may extend further credit in any manner whatsoever to the Borrower,* and generally deal with the Borrower or any such security or other person as the Bank may see fit; *and the undersigned shall remain bound under this guaranty notwithstanding any such exchange, surrender, release, change, alteration, renewal, extension, continuance, compromise, waiver, inaction, extension of further credit or other dealing.*

The undersigned thereby waives (a) notice of acceptance of this guaranty and of extensions of credit by the Bank to the Borrower; (b) presentment and demand for payment of any of the Liabilities of the Borrower; (c) protest and notice of dishonor or default to the undersigned or to any other party with respect to any of the Liabilities of the Borrower; (d) all other notices to which the undersigned might otherwise be entitled; and (e) any demand for payment under this guaranty.

This is a guaranty of payment and not of collection. . . .

. . . [N]or in the event shall any modification or waiver of the provisions of this guaranty be effective unless in writing nor shall any such waiver be applicable except in the specific instance for which given. [Emphases added.]

In July 1979 the Bank informed Siegel that Pic was "out of trust." More than 50 percent of the inventory was unaccounted for. Pursuant to an understanding with the Bank, Siegel arranged for the sale of the remaining inventory and partial repayment was made. Following demand, the Bank instituted suit for the balance against Pic and the individual guarantors, including Siegel. Siegel appeals from the summary judgment granted against him as guarantor.

By way of defense, Siegel asserts that the deficiency was caused by the failure of the Bank to conduct regular inspections and to enforce its curtailment policy. He further alleges that two of the Bank's employees, either negligently or in complicity with Robl, submitted incorrect or false inventory reports and approved loans on nonexistent automobiles. Siegel asserts that he was assured, as a condition of his continuing guaranty upon his sale to Robl, that regular inspections and enforcement of the curtailment policy would continue. He asserts that the activities of the Bank and its employees impaired the value of the collateral, thus relieving him from liability.

Siegel argues there is a triable issue as to whether the Bank was obligated to conduct regular inspections and enforce the curtailment program, and whether the dishonesty or negligence of the Bank's employees operated to impair the collateral and thus discharge his obligation as guarantor.

It is undisputed that there is no provision in the inventory financing agreement or in the guaranty obligating the Bank to conduct inspections or to maintain the curtailment policy. The guaranty is a fully integrated unambiguous contract which by its terms could not be modified or varied by parol or by an alleged course of conduct. The guaranty expressly provides, in pertinent part:

> This is a guaranty of payment and not of collection and the undersigned further waives any right to require that any action be brought against the Borrower or any other person or to require that resort be had to any security. . . .
>
> No delay on the part of the Bank in exercising any rights hereunder or failure to exercise the same shall operate as a waiver of such rights; no notice to or demand on the undersigned shall be deemed to be a waiver of the obligation of the undersigned or of the right of the Bank to take further action without notice or demand as provided herein; nor in any event shall any modification or waiver of the provisions of this guaranty be effective unless in writing, nor shall any such waiver be applicable except in the specific instance for which given.

Thus neither the alleged prior course of conduct nor the alleged promise that it would be continued could modify the obligation of Siegel as guarantor of payment (General Phoenix Corp. v. Cabot, 300 N.Y. 87, 92; General Obligations Law §15-301, subd. 1).

Siegel expressly consented that the

> security at any time held by or available to the Bank . . . may be exchanged, surrendered or released . . . and the undersigned [defendant Siegel] shall remain bound under this guaranty notwithstanding any such . . . release, . . . compromise, . . . inaction, extension of further credit or other dealing.

It is plain that the Bank had the right to release the collateral without discharging the guarantor. If so, the negligence or dishonesty of the Bank's employees in so doing is irrelevant.

As Special Term ruled, the negligence or dishonesty of plaintiff's employees patently would not be deemed within the scope of their authority. Siegel was an unconditional guarantor of payment, not of collection, and the guaranty was not dependent upon any condition precedent other than the non-payment of the indebtedness.

The dissent relies upon Uniform Commercial Code §3-606, which provides in part:

> (1) The holder discharges any party to the instrument to the extent that without such party's consent the holder . . .
>   (b) unjustifiably impairs any collateral for the instrument given by or on behalf of the party or any person against whom he has a right of recourse.

That section applies to commercial paper, negotiable instruments, not to a guaranty such as that here involved (UCC §3-102[1][e]); Indianapolis Morris Plan Corp. v. Karlen, 28 N.Y.2d 30, 32. Moreover, as that case holds respecting consent to release of collateral:

> Consent may be given in advance, and is commonly incorporated in the instrument, or it may be given afterward. It requires no consideration, and operates as a waiver of the consenting party's right to claim his own discharge. (28 N.Y.2d at p.34, quoting the Official Comment to UCC §3-606.)

In *Indianapolis Morris Plan Corp.*, supra, the lender consented to the substitution of gas consuming equipment for the mortgaged electrical cooking equipment. The debtor failed and the gas company repossessed the substituted equipment on which it had a seller's lien. The collateral security was dissipated by the substitution and the repossession of the substitute. The consent to release of security provided for in the promissory note operated to prevent the discharge of the sureties although they had no notice of these events and had not consented thereto.

Our case stands on the same footing. The consent to release of security was broad and all encompassing so as to preclude discharge of the guarantor. Under the terms of this guaranty there was no obligation to preserve and protect the collateral. The dissent's reliance upon Executive Bank [of Fort Lauderdale] v. Tighe (66 A.D.2d 70) is misplaced. That case holds only that pursuant to UCC §3-606, a guarantor's waiver of the obligation not to impair collateral will not excuse the creditor's failure properly to file the security instrument as required by law, unless the waiver expressly so provides. That issue is not here involved. (See Lafayette Bank & Trust Co. of Suffern v. Silver, 58 Misc. 2d 891.)

Similarly, Federal Deposit Insurance Corp. v. Frank L. Marino Corp., 74 A.D.2d 620, relied upon by the dissent, is not applicable. In that case the collateral was in the possession of the creditor who negligently failed to liquidate it upon the guarantor's demand. The guarantor could not be chargeable with the decline in value of the collateral. In our case the collateral was in the possession of the debtor, not the creditor, and Siegel, as guarantor, was afforded the opportunity to liquidate it, which he did.

For the same reason, Sterling Factors Corp. v. Freeman (50 Misc. 2d 715), relied upon by the dissent, is inapposite. In that case the creditor had replevied the collateral and purchased it at a price far less than its worth, without notice to the guarantors. It then proceeded to sell the collateral at a higher price without giving credit to the guarantors. This was a blatant fraud, held to preclude any recovery against the guarantors. This has nothing to do with our case, where the Bank never had possession of the collateral.

Under the express terms of the guaranty here involved, the Bank could release or surrender the collateral without notifying or discharging Siegel. It could also extend further credit to Pic on an unsecured basis without notifying or releasing Siegel. Hence the complained of actions of the Bank's employees are of no aid to Siegel. We must "take the guaranty as we find it as the surest way of determining the rights of these parties." (Corn Exchange Bank Trust Co. v. Gifford, 268 N.Y. 153, 158.)

Nothing in the agreements or in the Uniform Commercial Code provides for the release of Siegel as unconditional guarantor of payment under the circumstances. In the face of the guaranty as written there was no duty upon the creditor to preserve or protect the collateral. Where the collateral is in the possession of the debtor, inaction by the creditor, negligent or otherwise, does not release a guarantor who has executed such a waiver. A surety may waive any obligation upon the part of a creditor, including the obligation of the creditor not to impair the security (Indianapolis Morris Plan Corp. v. Karlen, supra). The parties, by agreement, may determine the standards by which the fulfillment of the rights and duties of the secured party may be measured (UCC §9-501[3]).

Accordingly, the order of the Supreme Court, New York County (Helman, J.), entered on August 12, 1980 granting plaintiff summary judgment against defendant Aaron Siegel in the sum of $189,717.17 should be affirmed with costs.

[All concur except BLOOM and MILONAS, J., who dissent in an opinion by MILONAS, J.]

MILONAS, J. (dissenting). I would reverse and remand for further proceedings. . . .

Under the express terms of the agreement between Siegel and the bank, the undersigned purportedly undertook to remain bound regardless of any compromise to the security. However, where the bank's negligence has, in contravention of UCC §9-207, resulted in a breach of its duty to preserve and protect the collateral, a waiver "will not be enforced so as to bar a viable setoff or counterclaim sounding in fraud . . ." or where "based upon the creditor's negligence in failing to liquidate collateral upon the guarantor's demand . . ." (Federal Deposit Insurance Corp. v. Frank L. Marino Corp., 74 A.D.2d 620, at p.621). As the court therein explained, to enforce such a waiver provision when there is a triable issue of fact as to the creditor's negligence would enable a creditor to shield itself from its own tortious conduct.

"The holder of security [here the inventory] is not at liberty to do any affirmative act which would impair the security and so deprive the guarantors of the benefit they might derive on a proper liquidation or upon their payment under their guaranty . . . " (Sterling Factors Corporation v. Freeman, 50 Misc. 2d 715, at p.720). In the instant case, whether the bank can be held liable for the tortious acts of its employees presents a clear issue of fact such as to render summary judgment inappropriate. To maintain that a guarantor will always be bound on the underlying obligation, notwithstanding any negligent, fraudulent or tortious conduct on the part of the creditor, simply by the expedient of the creditor's inserting a clause to that effect in the agreement is to undermine completely the spirit of the UCC and is, in my opinion, contrary to public policy.

Order filed.

PROBLEM 135

George and Martha Washington borrowed $10,000 from the Mt. Vernon Finance Company, both signing a promissory note for the amount borrowed. To secure the note, the bank took a mortgage on Martha's vineyard, but failed to file its mortgage in the proper place. Before the note matured, Martha filed for bankruptcy, and the bankruptcy creditors were able to get the vineyard free and clear of the bank's mortgage. Is George discharged in whole or in part by §3-605(e)? By §3-605(f)? If Martha had not filed for bankruptcy, but the vineyard was still lost when the state seized it because she hadn't paid her taxes, is *she* discharged by the bank's failure to perfect its interest in the vineyard? As to all this, see Official Comment 7 to §3-605.

You will recall that at common law any change in the basic contract discharged the surety unless the surety consented. In addition, a binding agreement by the creditor not to sue the principal or to give the principal extra time to pay released the non-consenting surety unless the creditor "preserved rights" against the surety. These issues are treated very differently in the revised version of Article 3, which permits certain agreements between the creditor (the current holder of the instrument) and the principal (the accommodated party) without a discharge of the surety/indorser.[8] Look at §3-605 to answer the following Problem.[9]

PROBLEM 136

When Jack Point borrowed $75,000 from Yeomen National Bank to start up his carnival business, the bank made him sign a promissory note in its favor and get a surety. Point talked his good friend Wilfred Shadbolt into signing as an accommodation maker. Is Shadbolt discharged by any of the following agreements between Yeoman National and Point?

8. One major change under the Revision is that the "preservation of secondary obligor's recourse" doctrine (it used to be called the "reservation of rights" doctrine) has been abolished; see Official Comment 3 to §3-605. For an argument that this is a mistake, and for a complete discussion of all the suretyship rules in the Revision, see Cohen, Suretyship Principles in the New Article 3: Clarifications and Substantive Changes, 42 Ala. L. Rev. 595 (1991).

9. The proposed 2002 amendments to Article 3 of the Uniform Commercial Code dramatically change the rules of §3-605. Under the new version, the surety, now called a "secondary obligor" (which includes indorsers), is still liable no matter what agreements the holder makes with the primary obligor unless the surety can prove loss by the modification, which also binds the surety unless the modification agreement provides otherwise. An impairment of the collateral, however, would still discharge non-consenting sureties up to the value of the collateral lost. The idea behind the changes is to bring §3-605 in line with the common law rules espoused in the Restatement of the Law (Third) of Suretyship and Guaranty (1996). The new Official Comments have a good description of the changes and give examples of how the section is meant to work.

(a) When the note matured, Point told Yeomen National that his business had gone bust and that he was thinking about filing a bankruptcy petition. Worried that it would get nothing in the bankruptcy distribution, Yeomen National persuaded him to pay all he could, a mere $5,000, and then signed an agreement with Point excusing him from having to pay the rest of the debt. The bank then demanded that Shadbolt pay the amount still due. Does Shadbolt owe it? See §3-605(b). Does the accord and satisfaction agreement between the bank and Point also bind Shadbolt, or may the latter still seek complete reimbursement from Point? See §3-419(e) and Official Comment 3 to §3-605.

(b) Assume instead that when the note matured Point went to the bank and asked for more time in which to pay. The bank did this, giving Point an extra six months. No one notified Shadbolt of this extension. At the end of the six-month period, Point filed for bankruptcy instead of paying the note. Was Shadbolt discharged by the bank's actions? Would your answer change depending on whether or not Point ever had the money to pay the note at any relevant period? See §3-605(c) and its Official Comment 4. Who has the burden of proof on the issues? Could Shadbolt, had he known of the extension agreement, have ignored it, paid the note, and then sued Point for reimbursement?

(c) Assume instead that when the note was signed the bank also made Point put up 100 shares of stock as collateral for the debt. Before the note matured Point went to the bank and asked to have the stock back, saying he needed to take advantage of a stock split the issuing corporation was offering. The bank returned the stock to him, but made him agree to pay a higher rate of interest. The original note contained a clause by which the surety automatically agreed in advance to any impairment of the collateral. Has Shadbolt nonetheless been discharged? Who has the burden of proof here? See §3-605(d) and its Official Comment 5.

(d) Is there a simple way that the bank could have avoided all these issues *ab initio*? See §3-605(i) and its Official Comment 2.

London Leasing Corp. v. Interfina, Inc.

New York Supreme Court, 1967
53 Misc. 2d 657, 279 N.Y.S.2d 209, 4 U.C.C. Rep. Serv. 206

CRAWFORD, J. The fundamental question presented on this motion is whether a corporate officer (president) who makes a note on behalf of his corporation and, also, personally endorses that note is discharged from *personal* liability on the note by an agreement between the payee and the corporate maker, by its said president, which extends the corporate maker's time to pay the note.

This is a motion pursuant to C.P.L.R. 3213 for summary judgment against defendants Interfina, Inc., and its president, Fredrick J. Evans. On May 3, 1966, Interfina made and delivered to plaintiff a promissory note in the sum of $52,000, signed by Fredrick J. Evans, as president of Interfina, and also personally endorsed by Fredrick J. Evans. The note was not paid on its due date, August 2, 1966, and thereafter, on August 3, 15 and 19, Interfina, by its president, entered into letter agreements with the plaintiff extending the time for payment of the note. Fredrick J. Evans signed the agreements, but only in his corporate capacity.

The sum of $19,500 is due on the note and as against defendant Interfina there is no question that summary judgment should be granted.

In opposition to the motion as against him, defendant Evans contends that the extension agreements, which were not signed by him in his personal capacity, as a matter of law discharged him from personal liability on the note because he did not personally consent to the extension.

[The court quoted §3-606, the original version of what is now §3-605—Ed.]

The Code does not explicitly define the meaning of the term "consent." However, the Official Comment to §3-606 states:

> 2. Consent may be given in advance, and is commonly incorporated in the instrument, or it may be given afterward. It requires no consideration, and operates as a waiver of the consenting party's right to claim his own discharge. . . .

In the pre-Code case of National Park Bank v. Koehler (204 N.Y. 174), the court explained the rationale which underlies the rule that an endorser is discharged by the maker's agreement with the payee entered into without the endorser's consent to extend the maker's time to pay a note. The court said at pages 179-180:

> . . . It is a rule, long recognized, that an accommodation indorser, or surety, is entitled to have the engagement of the principal debtor preserved, without variation in its terms, and that his *assent* to any change therein is essential to the continuance of his obligation. The

reason of the rule is that his right must not be affected, upon the maturity of the indebtedness, to make payment and, by subrogation to the creditor's place, to, at once, proceed against the principal debtor to enforce repayment. Therefore it is that any agreement of the creditor, which operates to extend the time of payment of the original debt and suspends the right to immediate action, is held to discharge the non-assenting indorser, or surety; as the law will presume injury to him thereby. The creditor may arrange with his debtor, in any way, which does not result in effecting either of these results. He may take, as collateral to the old note, new security, or other notes, and, if time is not given to the debtor, the indorser, or surety, will not be discharged. To prevent such a result, the agreement must expressly reserve all the remedies of the creditor against the indorser, or surety; in which case the latter will be in a position to pay immediately and, then, to proceed against the principal debtor. . . .

In the absence of a clear Code definition of "consent," this court is guided by the statement in Stearns Law of Suretyship (5th ed., §6.13):

> Parties to a contract may always alter it by mutual agreement and this is true of suretyship contract as others. Accordingly, if the creditor and principal modify their contract, and the surety consents thereto, he will not be discharged. Such consent need not be expressly given, *but may be implied from the surrounding circumstances or from his conduct*. [Emphasis supplied.]

The Court in In re Grottola's Estate (124 N.Y.S.2d 85) was also guided by this principle. The court stated, at page 88:

> . . . Thus the voluntary release or surrender of security by the creditor without the consent of the surety will discharge the latter to the extent of the value of the property so released. Stearns Law of Suretyship, Elder's Revision, 5th Edition, §6.46; Cohen v. Rossmoore. If, however, the surety consents to a modification of the contract between the principal debtor and the creditor he will not be discharged. Stearns Law of Suretyship, supra, sec. 6.13. The author states at page 129: "Such consent need not be expressly given, but may be implied from the surrounding circumstances or from his conduct." *Here the deceased endorser was the president and the principal stockholder of Ventura Acres, Inc., the maker of the note. Subsequent to the death of the accommodation endorser the executrix of his will, or her attorney, solicited and secured from the creditor the release of mortgage and*

satisfaction thereof in question. The court holds that such action on the part of the endorser's legal representative constituted a consent to the satisfaction of the mortgage held by the creditor as security for the loan in question. Vose v. Florida Railroad Co., Stearns Law of Suretyship, supra. . . . [Emphases supplied.]

The application of this principle to the present question mandates a holding that defendant Evans consented to the extension. As a matter of fact he applied for, negotiated, signed in his corporate capacity, and received the agreements extending the time for payment. While mere knowledge or acquiescence is not, in and of itself, sufficient to prevent discharge, the defendant's conduct here far exceeded these limits and, under the special circumstances here presented, constituted consent.

Accordingly, the motion for summary judgment in the sum of $19,500 is granted as against both defendants. Submit order.

8.   New Notes for Old

PROBLEM 137

In 2009 Rex Lear borrowed $5,000 from the Kent Lending Corporation and gave them his promissory note due June 8, 2012. Rex had his daughter Cordelia sign as accommodation maker. Early in 2012 Rex defaulted on the installment payments and in return for mercy by the lending company, he signed a new promissory note dated January 11, 2012, payable to the company September 25, 2012, for the same amount but with additional collateral. The Kent Lending Corporation kept the first note as security for the payment of the second. Cordelia never signed the second note. Answer these questions:

(a) Can the payee sue on the *first* note prior to September 25, 2012? See §3-310(b)(2).

(b) If Lear does not pay the second note when it matures, can Kent sue on the *first* note, or has it been paid and discharged by the second note? See §3-310(b)(2).

(c) Assume that Cordelia can prove that the failure of the lender to enforce its rights on the first note caused her major damages in that Lear's financial situation deteriorated drastically between January 11 and September 25, 2012, and the collateral became worthless during the same period. Is Cordelia still liable on the first note? See §3-605(c).

PROBLEM 138

Sam Selachii was the surety on a promissory note that Marty Make had given to the Dogfish Loan Company along with a pledge of 100 shares of Titanic Telephone stock to secure the loan for $800. Shortly after receiving the loan, Marty asked for the stock back, saying that he wanted to sell it and buy other stock that he would repledge as collateral. Dogfish gave him back the stock, which Marty sold. He used the proceeds to finance a bad day at the races. A week later Dogfish transferred the note for value to the Hammerhead Loan Company, a bona fide purchaser. Assume that Sam has been discharged under §3-605(e) (impairment of the collateral). Is he still liable to Hammerhead? See §§3-305(b), 3-601(b), and 3-302(b).

D. The Drawer's Obligation

One of the happiest things about the revised version of Article 3 is its de-emphasis of the technical rules of presentment, notice of dishonor, and protest, all described below. Under the original version of Article 3 these were complicated matters, but they are now of much less importance. We will consider them in connection with both the obligation incurred by the drawer of a draft and that undertaken by an indorser.

The drawer of a draft incurs the obligation specified in §3-414, which you should read now. It is sometimes said that the drawer's liability is *secondary* because the draft must first be presented to the drawee for payment and dishonored by the drawee before the drawer has a legal obligation to pay the instrument (unlike the liability of a maker of a note, which is *primary* since it is not subject to these conditions precedent). Why should the drawer's liability be different from that of a maker? The answer is that, with a draft, it is the understanding of all the parties that the payee will first attempt to secure payment from the drawee (a *presentment*) and only look to the drawer if the drawee refuses to pay (makes a *dishonor*). Consider, for example, that if I owe you money and give you a check for the amount due, common sense tells you that you must first try to collect the check from my bank. Only if my bank refuses to pay the check can you expect me to make the check good. Similarly, with a sales draft drawn by the seller on the buyer, the seller is not liable until the draft is dishonored by the buyer/drawee.

What are these technical rights of presentment, dishonor, and protest? They are discussed exhaustively in the 3-500 sections of the Code.

1. Presentment and Dishonor

Presentment is the demand for payment made to the maker of the note or, for drafts, to the drawee. Read §3-501 (defining and describing *presentment*). Under the NIL the holder was required to exhibit the instrument at the moment of presentment (NIL 74), but the Code is more flexible—exhibition is required only if the presentee demands it. Read §3-501(b)(2), which sets out other rights of the presentee.

Dishonor is the refusal of the presentee to pay. Read §3-502.

PROBLEM 139

Archibald Grosvenor finally paid off an old debt to Reginald Bunthorne by giving him a check drawn on the Patience National Bank. Bunthorne took the check to the bank and demanded payment. The bank asked him to sign his name on the back, but Bunthorne refused, saying, "I will never put my name on any check Grosvenor has touched." If the bank declines to pay the check, has a technical dishonor occurred? See §§3-501(b)(3)(i), 3-501(b)(2)(iii). This may be important because Grosvenor's §3-414 obligation is conditioned on a dishonor, and he can no longer be sued on the underlying obligation that is suspended until dishonor by §3-310.

PROBLEM 140

When Grosvenor gave Bunthorne a check to pay off an old debt, Bunthorne negligently lost it behind the sofa and didn't find it for eight months. The bank it was drawn on refused to pay it because it was suspiciously old (see §4-404). Is Grosvenor still liable on this check? See §3-414(f). Would he be if the drawee bank had

folded five months after the check was written but before it was
presented? If Bunthorne had indorsed the check the day after it was
issued to him and then cashed it at the corner drugstore and the
drugstore mislaid it for five months before the drawee bank dishonored it, is Bunthorne still liable to the drugstore? See §3-415(e).

Messing v. Bank of America, N.A.

Maryland Court of Special Appeals, 2002
143 Md. App. 1, 792 A.2d 312, 47 U.C.C. Rep. Serv. 2d 301

KRAUSER, Judge.

This appeal focuses on one of the most expressive parts of the
human body—the thumb: "thumbs up" (approval), "thumbs
down" (disapproval), "thumbing one's nose" (defiance), and
"thumbing a ride" (requesting transport).[10] Notwithstanding all of
the things we ask of this unassuming two-jointed digit, appellee,
Bank of America, adds one more task—personal identification.
The thumbprint, if Bank of America has its way, will now be one
more means by which the identity of a non-account check holder is
expressed and confirmed. This idea has of course not met with
universal approval, and that is why this matter of first impression is
now before us.

Specifically, we are presented with the question of whether
Bank of America's practice of requiring non-account check holders
to provide a thumbprint signature before it will honor a check is
lawful. Appellant, Jeff E. Messing, claims that it is not and filed a
complaint for declaratory judgment in the Circuit for Baltimore
City, requesting a declaration that the practice is illegal and an order requiring its cessation. In reply, appellee filed a motion for
summary judgment. That motion was granted; appellant's complaint was dismissed; and this appeal followed.

In addition to the question of the legality of appellee's thumbprint signature program, appellant also raises questions as to
whether appellee "accepted," "dishonored," or "converted" appellant's check upon presentment. . . .

---

10. Not to mention, we should add: "thumbing through" (perusing a document), "all thumbs" (clumsiness), and "under one's thumb" (dominance and
control).

BACKGROUND

On August 3, 2000, appellant attempted to cash a check for $976 at the Light Street branch office of appellee in Baltimore City. That check was made out to appellant and drawn on a Bank of America customer checking account.

Upon entering the bank, appellant handed the check to a teller. The teller then confirmed the availability of the funds on deposit, and placed the check in a computer validation slot. After "validating" the availability of those funds, the computer stamped the time, date, account number, and teller number on the back of the check. It also placed a hold on $976 in the drawer's account.

The teller then gave the check back to appellant to endorse. After he had endorsed the check, the teller asked appellant for identification. In response, appellant presented his driver's license and a major credit card. The identification information on the license and credit card was then transferred by the teller to the back of the check.

During this transaction, the teller asked appellant if he was a Bank of America customer. When he said "no," the teller returned the check to appellant and requested that he place his "thumbprint signature" on the check in accordance with appellee's thumbprint signature policy for "non-account holders." That policy, which is posted at each teller's station, requires a non-account holder, seeking to cash a check drawn on a Bank of America customer account, to provide a thumbprint signature.

The provision of such a signature is neither messy nor time consuming. A thumbprint signature is created by applying one's right thumb to an inkless fingerprinting device that leaves no ink stain or residue. The thumbprint is then placed on the face of the check between the memo and signature line.

After requesting appellant's thumbprint signature, the teller counted out $976 in cash from her drawer anticipating that appellant would comply with that request. When he refused to do so, the teller indicated that the bank would not be able to complete the transaction without his thumbprint. Appellant then asked to see the branch manager, and the teller referred him to a "Mr. Obrigkeit," the branch manager.

Upon entering the branch manager's office, appellant demanded that the check be cashed despite his refusal to place his thumbprint on the check. The branch manager examined the check and returned it to appellant explaining that because appellant was not an account holder, Bank of America would not cash the check without his thumbprint on the instrument. The requirement of a thumbprint signature from non-account holders was in accordance with the deposit agreement that Bank of America has with each of its account holders. That agreement states that Bank of America is permitted "to establish physical and/or documentary requirements" of payees or other holders who seek to cash an item drawn on a Bank of America customer's account.

Appellant then requested that the branch manager provide him with a copy of the Bank's thumbprint policy. The branch manager contacted appellee's regional headquarters and was informed that no such information was available for public distribution. After the branch manager conveyed that information to appellant, appellant left the bank. Moments later, the teller released the hold on the customer's funds, voided the transaction in the computer, and placed the $976 in cash back in her drawer.

Indignant over the bank's policy, appellant filed a complaint . . . . Appellant also requested that the circuit court order appellee to cease and desist from requiring thumbprint signatures in Maryland. . . . [W]e conclude, for the reasons set forth below, that the circuit court was legally correct in granting appellee's motion for summary judgment and dismissing with prejudice appellant's complaint.

DISCUSSION

I.

Appellant contends that the circuit court erred in construing the "reasonable identification" requirement of C.L. §3-501(b)(2) to include a thumbprint signature if demanded by appellee, notwithstanding appellant's proffer of his driver's license and a credit card. C.L. §3-501(b)(2) provides:

> Upon demand of the person to whom presentment is made, the person making presentment must (i) exhibit the instrument, (ii) give *reasonable identification* and, if presentment is made on behalf of another person, reasonable evidence of authority to do so, and (iii) sign a receipt on the instrument for any payment made or surrender the instrument if full payment is made. (Emphasis added.) . . .

While the phrase "reasonable identification" under former U.C.C. §3-505(1)(b), now codified in Maryland as C.L. §3-501(b)(2), has been addressed by the other state courts in other contexts, what constitutes "reasonable identification" under C.L. §3-501(b)(2) —particularly whether a " thumbprint signature" does—is a question that has not been addressed by any federal or state court, at least not in any reported opinion.

Appellee's thumbprint requirement is a form of "reasonable identification" for a number of reasons. First, a thumbprint signature has been accepted by the drafters of the Maryland U.C.C. as an effective, reliable, and accurate way to authenticate a writing on a negotiable instrument."In accord with the systematic presentation of the UCC and its use of consistent terminology," U.C.C. §1-201 sets forth "46 basic terms" to be used throughout the Code to "offer a starting point for the interpretation of many Code sections." 1 William D. Hawkland, Uniform Commercial Code Series, §1-201:1 (1998). The term "signed" is defined in C.L. §1-201(39) (1975, 1997 Repl. Vol.) as "any symbol executed or adopted by a party with present intention to authenticate a writing," and that definition applies throughout the Maryland U.C.C. As to what "signed" means, the Official Comment to C.L. §1-201(39) states:

> The inclusion of authentication in the definition of "signed" is to make clear that as the term is used in this Act a complete signature is not necessary. Authentication may be printed, stamped or written; it may be by initials or by *thumbprint*.

C.L. §1-201, Official Comment 39 (1975, 1997 Repl. Vol.) (emphasis added). . . .

Second, the process that a non-account holder goes through to provide a thumbprint signature is not unreasonably inconvenient. As noted, non-account holders seeking to cash a check are asked to apply their right thumb to an inkless fingerprinting device to create a "thumbprint signature." Unlike fingerprinting— which has repeatedly been upheld as an "unobtrusive" form of identification—thumbprint signatures do not require application of ink nor do they require the participation of more than one digit. In fact, appellant's thumbprint signature program uses an inkless fingerprinting device that leaves no ink stains or residue.

And third, this procedure is a reasonable and necessary answer to the growing incidence of check fraud. The American Bankers Association has reported that check fraud losses have grown, between 1995 and 1997, at an average rate of 17.5 percent. Carreker-Antinori, Provide Your Bank with a Shield of Protection against

Check Fraud, Thompson Financial Publishing, at http://www.tfp. com/text/Fraudlink.pdf. "Industry estimates based on survey data show that actual losses from check fraud amounted to $512.3 million in 1997, a 5.2 percent increase over the $487.1 million estimated for 1995." Id.

As a result of the rising level of check fraud, thumbprint programs, as appellee notes, "have been endorsed by the American Bankers Association and more than thirty (30) state bankers associations including Arizona, Maryland, Missouri, Oregon, Texas, Utah and Virginia." Testifying before the United States House of Representatives as to the effectiveness of these programs, Charles L. Owens, former Chief of the Financial Crimes Section of the FBI, stated:

> We have supported implementation of inkless fingerprint policies which have been adopted by over 20 State bankers associations for non-bank customers negotiating checks. Where implemented, these procedures have successfully reduced negotiation of stolen and counterfeit checks by as much as 50 percent.

Computer Generated Check Fraud, Subcommittee on Domestic and International Monetary Policy, Committee on Banking and Financial Services, U.S. House of Representatives, May 1, 1997; see also Perkey v. Department of Motor Vehicles, 42 Cal. 3d 185, 228 Cal. Rptr. 169, 721 P.2d 50, 53 (1986) (stating that the fingerprint requirement is one of the few non-invasive reliable means of combating rampant fraud).

Finally, appellant's contention that a thumbprint does not serve the purposes of the Act is unpersuasive. We agree with appellant that a thumbprint cannot be used, in most instances, to confirm the identity of a non-account checkholder at the time that the check is presented for cashing, as his or her thumbprint is usually not on file with the drawee at that time. We disagree, however, with appellant's conclusion that a thumbprint signature is therefore not "reasonable identification" for purposes of C.L. §3-501(b)(2). . . .

III.

ARGUES DISHONORED BY BANK

Appellant further asserts that the circuit court erred in holding that the appellee did not dishonor the check under C.L. §3-502(d)(1). That section provides that "if the draft is payable on demand, the draft is dishonored if presentment for payment is duly made to the acceptor and the draft is not paid on the day of presentment." Because the check "presented to [appellee] was payable on demand" and because appellee "accepted the check on August 3, 2000, but did not make payment on that date," appellant concludes that appellee "dishonored the check."

C.L. §3-502(d)(1), however, is not relevant to the instant case because the check in question, as we concluded earlier, was never accepted by appellee. In other words, appellant cites the wrong section of the U.C.C. The section that appellant should have cited is C.L. §3-502(b)(2), as it applies to dishonored "unaccepted" checks.

That section provides that if an unaccepted "draft is payable on demand . . . the draft is dishonored if presentment for payment is duly made to the drawee and the draft is not paid on the day of presentment." C.L. §3-502(b)(2). There is no dishonor, however, if presentment fails "to comply with the terms of the instrument, an agreement of the parties, or other applicable law or rule." C.L. §3-501(b)(3). In the words of one authority:

> If the presentment is not proper, payment or acceptance may be refused by the presentee and this refusal does not constitute a dishonoring of the instrument. This provision comes into play if the presentment does not comply "with the terms of the instrument, an agreement of the parties, or other applicable law or rule."

6B Anderson on the Uniform Commercial Code [Rev.] §3-501:15 (3d Ed. 1998).

It is undisputed that appellee had the authority to refuse payment in accordance with the deposit agreement it had with each account holder, including with the drawer of the check in question. Pursuant to that agreement, appellee was permitted to set "physical and/or documentary requirements" for all those who seek to cash a check with appellee. And because appellee had the authority to refuse payment by agreement with its customer under C.L. §3-501(b)(2)(ii) unless "reasonable identification" was presented, appellant's failure to provide his thumbprint rendered the presentment ineffective and did not result in a dishonor of the check when appellee returned it to him. . . .

CASE REMANDED TO THE CIRCUIT COURT FOR FURTHER PROCEEDINGS CONSISTENT WITH THIS OPINION.

2. Notice of Dishonor

Indorsers are also entitled to notice of the dishonor after it occurs (but drawers are entitled to notice of dishonor only if a non-bank acceptor refuses payment of the draft; §3-414(d)). *Notice of dishonor* is defined in §3-503, which you should read.[11] Note that subsection (c) of §3-503 requires notice of dishonor to be given very quickly to be effective.

3. Protest

Protest is a technical ritual in which an official, normally a notary public, makes a formal presentment of a draft to the drawee and, upon dishonor, draws up, signs, and seals an official statement (called a *protest*) of what happened. The protest may also mention to whom notice of dishonor is given. Read §3-505(b). This ritual is no longer required, but is nonetheless sometimes done because it simplifies proof of these matters. See §3-505(a).

4. Excuse

Under some circumstances—spelled out in detail in §3-504, which section you should examine carefully—these technical requirements (presentment, dishonor, notice of dishonor) can become either temporarily or completely unnecessary. For the lawyer whose client has failed to take these technical steps, §3-504 can be a bonanza—the treasure chest from which is pulled the excuse that saves the case.

These technical rights must in some situations give way to the exigencies of life. In an early case, Polk v. Spinds, 5 Cold. (45 Tenn.) 431 (1868), the advent of the Civil War made it "difficult" for the Northern holder of a promissory note signed by a Tennessee maker to make a presentment to the maker until the war ended. The Supreme Court of Tennessee held the presentment and delayed notice of dishonor excused, stating a test that is still often quoted:

> Obstacles of the kind which will excuse, need not be of the degree or extent which make travel, intercourse, presentment, impossible. It is enough if they be of the degree and character which

---

11. *Practice Pointer.* A good attorney advises clients to give notice of dishonor to all prior parties immediately on finding out the check is being returned. See §3-503(b).

deter men of ordinary prudence, energy and courage, from encountering them in prosecution of business, in respect of which they
owe an active and earnest duty, and feel an active and earnest interest.

Id. at 433.

In reading §3-504, note that subsection (c) talks about when
delay in taking one of these steps is excused (but the step must still
be taken), and subsections (a) and (b) address themselves to situations in which the step becomes completely unnecessary.

PROBLEM 141

A promissory note contains a clause stating, "All parties to this
note hereby waive all rights to presentment, notice of dishonor, and
protest. . . ." Is a clause like this buried in the fine print on the front
side of a note sufficient to deprive indorsers of their right to notice
of dishonor? See §3-504(a)(iv) and (b)(ii).

PROBLEM 142

Frank Fortune was walking along the street, his pockets stuffed
with money and checks he had won with a dazzling display of his
prowess in the game of stud poker, when he was stopped by a
creditor, one Mr. Holdit. Holdit demanded payment of a long-due
$50 obligation, and Fortune was glad to indorse over to him a
check for that amount that Fortune had won from Dan Deuces; Fortune was named as payee on the check. After giving the check to
Holdit, Fortune thought better of the whole transaction so he contacted Dan Deuces, the drawer, the next day and persuaded him to
stop payment on the check. Holdit held onto the check for six
weeks and then took it to his bank, the Creditors National, and
cashed it. Creditors National presented the check to the drawee
bank, which dishonored it, whereupon Creditors National reclaimed its money from Mr. Holdit. Holdit, now very mad, sued
Fortune on his indorser's obligation. Was Frank Fortune discharged
by the delay in presentment? See §3-415(e). Was the presentment
delay excused within the meaning of §3-504(a)(iv)? See Harik v.
Harik, 861 F.2d 139, 7 U.C.C. Rep. Serv. 2d 807 (6th Cir. 1988).

Makel Textiles, Inc. v. Dolly Originals, Inc.

New York Supreme Court, 1967
4 U.C.C. Rep. Serv. 95

SPIEGEL, J. This is an action by the plaintiff to recover $8,000 on promissory notes executed by defendant Dolly Originals, Inc., on certain of which the names of defendants Nathan Goldberg, Richard L. Lewis, and Fred Kushner appear as endorsers.

Dolly Originals, Inc., originally borrowed $40,000; $30,000 was repaid to the plaintiff. Thereafter a promissory note in the sum of $10,000 (Pl. Ex. 1) was made to the order of the plaintiff by Dolly Originals, Inc., by Nathan Goldberg, president, and also bore the purported signature of Richard L. Lewis. The signature of Nathan Goldberg and the purported signature of Richard L. Lewis, as endorsers also appear on the back of said note. This note was not paid. Thereafter two notes each in the sum of $5,000 (Pl. Exs. 2A and 2B) were executed to the order of the plaintiff by Dolly Originals, Inc., through its president, Nathan Goldberg, and purportedly by Richard L. Lewis. The endorsement on the back of these two notes, which were given in lieu of the $10,000 note, bears the signatures of Nathan Goldberg and Fred Kushner. Five checks, each in the sum of $2,000 (Pl. Exs. 3A-3E), to the order of the plaintiff, were executed simultaneously with the two $5,000 notes and bore the signature of Nathan Goldberg, president of Dolly Originals, Inc., and the name of Richard L. Lewis. One of these checks was deposited and returned unpaid (plaintiff's exhibit 4A). None of the other four checks was deposited. No names of any endorsers appear on the back of these checks. Thereafter two other corporate checks for $2,000 were given by Dolly Originals, Inc., to the plaintiff. One of these was paid. The balance of $8,000 is now the subject of this suit.

After the trial of this action the complaint was dismissed as against the defendant Richard L. Lewis after proof that his signature was not genuine, and judgment was rendered against Dolly Originals, Inc., which offered no defense to the action. There remains only the determination of liability of the individual defendants, Nathan Goldberg and Fred Kushner, the endorsers on the notes.

The said defendants moved to dismiss the complaint at the end of the trial on the ground that the promissory notes of the corporation had never been presented for payment and thus the obligation of the endorsers was discharged; further, that subsequent checks given after the endorsement on the previous notes were taken by the plaintiff in payment of this obligation relieved the defendants of any further liability on this debt. The latter contention has no merit. A check given in payment of an obligation is merely a conditional payment and does not relieve the endorser of his liability on the obligation if the check is unpaid (Uniform Commercial Code §3-802 [§3-310(b) in the Revision— Ed.] . . .).

From all the evidence adduced upon the trial of this action, it appears that the defendant Nathan Goldberg was the president and principal officer of the defendant Dolly Originals, Inc. As such president, he executed the promissory notes and signed the corporate checks hereinabove mentioned. The promissory notes were also endorsed by him as an individual. By virtue of his active participation in the affairs of Dolly Originals, Inc., it is obvious that the defendant Nathan Goldberg well knew that the notes could not be and were not paid from corporate funds. Under these circumstances the obligation to serve Goldberg with notice of dishonor and non-payment must be deemed unnecessary, at least impliedly, within the meaning of the Uniform Commercial Code. Plaintiff's failure to present the notes for payment and give the said defendant notice of non-payment could not and did not injure nor prejudice his rights in any way. Formal notice of presentment and dishonor to Mr. Goldberg would be merely a useless gesture of advising him of a fact with which he was most familiar (UCC §§3-507, 3-511 [§3-504 in the Revision—Ed.]; J.W. O'Bannon Co. v. Curran, 129 App. Div. 90; William S. Chemical Co. v. Root, 152 N.Y.S. 368; Nemser v. Goldman, 145 N.Y.S.2d 841).

The defendant Fred Kushner was an endorser only, on each of two notes for $5,000 (Pl. Exs. 2A and 2B) above mentioned. As to said defendant Kushner, the record is void of any testimony, or proof of notice of presentment and dishonor as required under the Uniform Commercial Code. Nor is there any evidence of any activity or participation in the affairs of the corporation so as to excuse presentment or notice of dishonor.

Accordingly, the defendant Fred Kushner may have judgment against the plaintiff dismissing the complaint, and the plaintiff may have judgment against the defendant Nathan Goldberg in the sum of $8,000 with interest thereon from May 12, 1965. . . .

E.   The Drawee's Obligation

PROBLEM 143

After he brought a successful Truth in Lending action against Octopus National Bank (ONB), attorney Sam Ambulance made the mistake of continuing to bank at ONB. At a time when his bank balance greatly exceeded that amount, Sam wrote an alimony check for $3,000 and gave it to his ex-wife, Sue. Because similar checks had bounced in the past, Sue hurriedly walked the check directly into the bank and presented it across the counter. The teller who took the check alerted the bank's manager, who laughed evilly as he threw it back across the counter at Sue, informing her that Sam's business was no longer welcome at ONB and that it refused to pay any more of his checks, even though there was money in the account sufficient to meet the check. You are the attorney who handled Sue's divorce, so she calls you and asks what she should do. See §§3-408, 3-401(a), 3-414, 4-402.

If you worked through all of those citations diligently, you should arrive at this conclusion: the drawee, not having signed the draft, is not liable on it. The drawee, having signed nothing, incurs no contractual obligation (though it may still be liable to the drawer under §4-402).

So far, when we have mentioned *drafts*, we have really been talking only about drafts drawn on banks (checks); the drawee we have been discussing is a bank administering a checking account. But the business community makes much use of the non-bank draft in the purchase and sale of goods, particularly when the parties are in different cities.

Consider the following hypothetical.

The seller agrees to ship buyer 10,000 widgets at $20 each, "payment against sight draft." This means that the seller will draw a draft on the buyer payable on "sight" (when the buyer first sees it). Such a procedure permits the seller to discount the draft with the seller's bank, which will indorse the draft over to a collecting bank in the buyer's city. The collecting bank will make a formal presentment to the buyer-drawee. The parties frequently arrange it so that the collecting bank has control over the goods and will turn them over to the buyer at the moment when the latter pays the draft.

Thus, at the moment of payment, buyer receives the goods. No one need trust anyone else.

In the hypothetical, the seller is the drawer, and the buyer is the drawee. The payee on the draft could be any of a number of people—the seller itself, the seller's bank, or simply "bearer." The two banks that transfer the draft will presumably sign it, and as soon as they do so, they will become indorsers. If the buyer dishonors the draft on presentment, the collecting bank will send out the required notices of dishonor and then request payment on the basis of the obligations (indorser and drawer) of the prior parties.

1. The Non-Bank Acceptor

Sometimes in the sales transaction described above, the buyer will ask for time in which to pay the draft after receiving the goods. In such a case the seller will probably want the buyer to assume liability on the instrument, so the seller will require the buyer to sign the instrument when it is presented and thus become primarily responsible for its payment. The drawee who places a signature on a draft is said to have *accepted* it, and he or she incurs the obligation of an *acceptor*. See §3-413. *Acceptance* is defined in §3-409(a) as the "drawee's signed agreement to pay a draft as presented." Read §3-409.

Norton v. Knapp

Supreme Court of Iowa, 1884
64 Iowa 112, 19 N.W. 867

SEEVERS, J. Because of the statements contained in an amended abstract, we are required to set out the petition as follows:

> That the plaintiffs sold and delivered to the defendant, about February 17, 1882, a certain flaxseed-cleaner mill, at the agreed price of eighty dollars, no part of which had been paid, and that the same was then due.
> That on or about April, 1882, plaintiffs drew a sight draft on defendant for the agreed price of said mill, which was in words and figures as follows:

$80   La Crosse, Wis., April 18, 1882.

At sight pay to the order of *Exchange Bank of Nora Springs, Iowa, eighty dollars,* value received, and charge the same to the account of

NORTON & KELLER.

To Miles Knapp, Nora Springs, Ia.

—Which was accepted by said Miles Knapp in written words and figures, on the back thereof, as follows: "Kiss my foot. MILES KNAPP." Also alleging "that said draft was still the property of plaintiff, due and unpaid, and claiming judgment for eighty dollars, interest, and costs." . . .

The amount in controversy being less than $100, the court has certified certain questions upon which the opinion of this court is desired. In substance, two of them are whether the words "kiss my foot," on the back of the draft, signed by the drawee, is a legal and valid acceptance, and whether such acceptance can be introduced in evidence without showing it was the intention to accept the draft. The rule upon this subject is thus stated in 1 Pars. Bills & Notes, 282:

> If a bill is presented to a drawee for the purpose of obtaining his acceptance, and he does anything to or with it which does not distinctly indicate that he will not accept it, he is held to be an acceptor, for he has the power, and it is his duty, to put this question beyond all possibility of doubt. . . .

The rule we understand to be, if the drawee does anything with or to the bill, or writes thereon anything, which does not clearly negative an intention to accept, then he can or will be charged as an acceptor. The question, then, is, what construction should be placed on the words "kiss my foot," written on the bill and signed by him? They cannot be rejected as surplusage. Such language is not ordinarily used in business circles or polite society. But by their use the defendant meant either to accept or refuse to accept the bill. It cannot be he meant the former; therefore, it must be the latter. It seems quite clear to us that the defendant intended by the use of the contemptuous and vulgar words above stated, to give emphasis to his intention not to accept or have anything to do with the bill or with the plaintiff. We understand the words, in common parlance, to mean and express contempt for the person to whom the words are addressed, and when used as a reply to a request, they imply, and are understood to mean, decided, unqualified, and contemptuous refusal to comply with such request. In such sense they were undoubtedly used when the defendant was requested to accept the bill. The question asked upon this point must be answered in the negative. Whether parol evidence is admissible to show the intent of the defendant, we have no occasion to determine, because no such evidence was offered, and our rule is not to determine mere abstract propositions. . . .

If the seller has agreed to give the buyer a credit period prior to payment—say, 60 days—a sight draft similar to this one is drawn:

> To Betty Buyer
>
> Sixty (60) days after sight, pay to the order of *Scott Seller $10,000.*
>
> *Scott Seller*

The seller will then discount the draft with his local bank, indorsing it over to the bank. The bank will forward it to a collecting bank in the buyer's city that will make a "presentment for acceptance" to the buyer and, if she accepts, will see that she gets the goods. When the buyer accepts, she will sign her name, usually diagonally across the face of the instrument, and the instrument will be dated, to start the 60-day period running, and returned to the collecting bank. During the 60-day period the draft (now called a "trade acceptance") may be further negotiated; it is now legally the same as an unmatured promissory note, the acceptor incurring an obligation almost identical to that of a maker. At the end of the 60 days, the holder of the draft will make a second presentment to the drawee (acceptor), this time a "presentment for payment." If the acceptor now dishonors, she can be sued on her §3-413 obligation, or the holder can proceed, after giving notice of dishonor, against the drawer and prior indorsers on their contracts. Note that if the drawee had dishonored the first presentment, the one for acceptance, she would not have been liable on the instrument because at that point she had incurred no §3-413 liability.

When a sight draft gives the drawee time for payment after sight, the holder *must* make a presentment for acceptance in order to start the running of the credit period. Read §3-502(b)(4) and the last paragraph of its Official Comment 4.

2. Checks

When the draft is a *check*, so that the drawee is a bank, the same rules apply. The drawer's writing of the check does not, absent unusual circumstances, create any immediate rights in the checking account funds, and the drawee bank has no liability to the holder of the check until it accepts it. Of course, the drawee bank is bound by the terms of its checking account agreement with its customer, the drawer. This checking account agreement is analogous to the contract of sale in the non-bank drawee situation discussed above. But the checking account agreement is a private contract between the bank and its customers and confers no rights on other parties. Read §3-408.

Galyen Petroleum Co. v. Hixson

Nebraska Supreme Court, 1983
213 Neb. 683, 331 N.W.2d 1, 35 U.C.C. Rep. Serv. 1221

COLWELL, J., Retired. Plaintiff, Galyen Petroleum Company (Galyen), appeals a summary judgment in favor of the Commercial Bank (Bank) of Bassett, Nebraska, in a suit to recover on three checks personally presented to drawee Bank by payee Galyen, upon which payment was refused, although the drawer had funds on deposit to pay some of the checks.

Galyen was a wholesale supplier of fuels to the defendant, Norman J. Hixson, who had an account in and owed Bank more than $7,000 on promissory notes. On October 1, 1975, Hixson issued check No. 2287, $3,763.25, to Galyen, which was presented through channels to drawee Bank for collection and returned unpaid for insufficient funds. On October 15, 1975, Hixson issued check No. 2304, $2,740.88, to Galyen, which was likewise presented and returned. On November 1, 1975, Hixson issued check No. 2324, $378.94, to Galyen, which was likewise presented and returned. On November 12 and 13, 1975, Galyen personally presented the three checks to Bank during regular banking hours at Bassett, Nebraska; upon each presentment, Bank unconditionally refused payment of all three checks and forthwith returned them to Galyen. Bank's records and the evidence show that at the close of business on November 10, 1975, Hixson's account had a credit balance of $3,048.46. There was no account activity on November 11, 1975. On November 12, three deposits were made to the account, $209.27, $92.90, and $443.17. After Galyen presented the checks for collection on November 12, Bank set off Hixson's account for two items of $1,006.75 and $2,700 that were credited to Hixson's note account, leaving a balance of $87.05. The credited notes were not then due. The printed part of the notes recites in part:

> Payee shall have at all times a security interest in and right of setoff against any deposit balances of the maker(s) . . . and may at the time, without notice, apply the same against payment of this note . . . whether due or not. . . .

Bank had a financing statement and security agreement from Hixson dated March 7, 1975. Hixson did not object to the setoffs. Galyen filed its petition on August 23, 1976. Hixson was discharged as a bankrupt on December 7, 1976, and dismissed as a party defendant.

Galyen claims that summary judgment was not a proper remedy here for the reason there were genuine issues of material fact concerning Bank's transactions on November 12 and 13.

Galyen assigns as error that Bank unlawfully refused payment of the checks on presentment and that it had no authority to make a setoff to credit Hixson's promissory notes where (1) the notes were not due and (2) the setoffs were exercised after presentment.

Neb. UCC §3-409(1) [§3-408 in the Revision—Ed.] (Reissue 1980) provides:

> A check or other draft does not of itself operate as an assignment of any funds in the hands of the drawee available for its payment, and the drawee is not liable on the instrument until he accepts it.
>
> The authorities are agreed . . . that a check, of itself, and in the absence of special circumstances, is neither a legal nor an equitable assignment or appropriation of a corresponding amount of the drawer's funds in the hands of the drawee, and that therefore, in and of itself, it gives the holder of the check no right of action against the drawee and no valid claim to the fund of the drawer in its hands, even though the drawer has on deposit sufficient funds to pay it. It creates no lien on the money which the holder can enforce against the bank. [10 Am. Jur. 2d Banks §563 at 532-533 (1963).]

There are no special circumstances or agreements claimed here. The only evidence was the hearsay statement of Richard W. Galyen that Hixson told him that he had telephoned Bank and that the checks were good.

Summary judgment was a proper procedure here, and Galyen had no standing or cause of action against Bank on account of the dishonor of any of the three checks. It did have a remedy against the drawer. Neb. UCC §3-507(2) (Reissue 1980). We do not get to the question of setoffs. The summary judgment was properly granted.

Affirmed.

Section 3-408 does not mean that under no circumstances can the drawee bank become liable to the holder prior to acceptance. It was the common law rule that by special agreement the drawer could work an immediate assignment of bank-held funds so as to give the holder of the check a claim against the drawee bank prior to acceptance. See Fourth Natl. v. Yardley, 165 U.S. 634 (1897) (special agreement between drawer and payee); Ballard v. Home Natl. Bank, 91 Kan. 91, 136 P. 935 (1913) (special agreement between drawer and drawee). In Union Bank v. Safanie, 5 Ariz. App. 342, 427 P.2d 146 (1967), an oral statement by a bank officer to the payee that the drawer's check would clear when presented was held to create liability in fraud, and in Faulkner v. Hillside Bank & Trust Co., 526 S.W.2d 274 (Tex. Civ. App. 1975), a bank that told an enquirer that a stolen cashier's check was good was held liable in an action for negligence. In a similar situation, the Nebraska Supreme Court used promissory estoppel to create liability in the drawee bank. Bigger v. Fremont Natl. Bank, 215 Neb. 580, 340 N.W.2d 142, 37 U.C.C. Rep. Serv. 809 (1983). In one major UCC case finding such a special contractual liability in the drawee bank, the check was payable out of a special loan fund and was issued by the drawer after consultation with the bank, which immediately marked the account to show that the check was outstanding; this was held to create an immediate right in the payee to reach the funds, so that a stop payment order by the drawer came too late. See MidContinent Cas. Co. v. Jenkins, 2 U.C.C. Rep. Serv. 1164 (Okla. 1965). In Graybar Elec. Co. v. Brookline Trust Co., 39 U.C.C. Rep. Serv. 1721 (Boston Mun. Ct., App. Div. 1984), a bank that issued a personal money order in return for cash was required to pay it even though no signature of the bank appeared thereon; the court reasoned that the fact of issuance was an implied promise to pay the personal money order when it was presented. These causes of action would all be preserved as possibilities by §1-103.

3.   Certification

The drawee bank's *acceptance* of a check is called *certification.* All of the Code sections on acceptance apply equally to certification. Read §§3-409(d), 3-411, and 3-413.

PROBLEM 144

George Generous gave a check for $5,000 to the Grapes of Wrath Church as part of the church's drive to get money for a planned new building. The church did not want to cash any checks it received until it had at least $20,000 worth of pledges. On the other hand, the church didn't want contributors to be able to back out and stop payment either, so the church's lawyer advised the church directors to have all large checks certified. This, the lawyer knew, would have the effect of making the certifying bank primarily liable on the check (§3-413(a)). The church treasurer took George's check down to the drawee bank and asked to have it certified, a presentment for acceptance. The drawee bank refused, saying that its practice was never to certify gift checks.

(a) Is that a dishonor so that the church should give George notice of dishonor? See §3-409(d) and its Official Comment 4.

(b) What should the church's lawyer advise it to do now?

(c) If the bank had certified the check but later refused to pay it, could the church sue George on his drawer's obligation? See §3-414(c). Same result if George had donated a certified check that the bank later dishonored? See Official Comment 3 to §3-414; cf. §3-411.

F.   *Signature by an Agent*

Section 3-402(a) generally defers to the common law governing an agent's signing of a contract on behalf of the principal. Thus, the agent's authority to sign the principal's name may be real (express or implied) or even apparent. See Senate Motors, Inc. v. Industrial Bank of Wash., 9 U.C.C. Rep. Serv. 387 (D.C. Super. 1971). The cited section also answers another question the original version of Article 3 had muddied.

PROBLEM 145

When tycoon J.B. Biggley wanted to borrow money for a business venture, he had his agent, J. Pierpont Finch, negotiate the loan from Wickets National Bank. When Finch signed the promissory note payable to the bank, he simply wrote his name as "J. Pierpont Finch, Agent," and failed to mention the name of his principal, J.B. Biggley. Is Biggley bound on this note? See §3-402 and Official Comment 1.

We shall leave the question of the scope of the agent's authority to other courses and instead concentrate on this question: when has the agent signed in so careless a fashion as to become personally liable? For instance, does the signature

Money Corporation, John Smith

make John Smith personally liable on a promissory note? Can he even introduce parol evidence to show that he is the president of the corporation and as such meant to sign only in his official capacity?

The smart way for an authorized agent to sign the instrument so as to avoid personal liability is for the agent to be careful to do two things: name the principal and unambiguously indicate that the agent is signing only in a representative capacity. See §3-402(b)(1). If the agent does one of these two things but not the other, the agent is liable to a holder in due course taking the instrument without notice that the agent was not intended to be liable, but otherwise the agent may prove that the original parties did not intend for the agent to incur liability. Official Comment 2 says that a holder in due course should be able to resolve any ambiguity against the agent.

Look at §3-402, digest the above paragraph, and then test your ability to read and comprehend a statute by resolving the Problems below.

M 146

ıe last Problem would Finch himself be liable to a holder in due course? To Wickets National Bank?

Mundaca Investment Corp. v. Febba

New Hampshire Supreme Court, 1999
727 A.2d 990, 38 U.C.C. Rep. Serv. 2d 464

BROCK, C.J. The defendants, Doris M. Febba, Thomas G. Scurfield, and Linda L. Kendall, appeal the Superior Court's (Smith, J.) grant of summary judgment in favor of the plaintiff, Mundaca Investment Corporation (Mundaca), holding the defendants personally liable for amounts due on two promissory notes. We reverse and remand. The defendants served as trustees of the L.T.D. Realty Trust (trust). On July 28, 1987, they purchased two condominium units for the trust. To finance this transaction, the defendants executed two promissory notes, secured by two mortgages, payable to the order of Dartmouth Savings Bank (bank). At the end of both notes below the signature line, the name of each defendant was typewritten beside the preprinted term "Borrower." Following their signatures, each of the defendants handwrote the word "Trustee." While both promissory notes state that they are secured by a mortgage, the trust is not identified on the face of the notes. The trust, however, is identified as the "Borrower" in both mortgages.

On August 19, 1993, Mundaca acquired the two notes from the Federal Deposit Insurance Corporation as receiver for the bank. By letters dated October 28, 1994, Mundaca notified defendants Scurfield and Febba that the two promissory notes were in default. Mundaca foreclosed on the condominium units and filed suit against the defendants individually for the remaining amount due on the notes. Both Mundaca and the defendants moved for summary judgment. The defendants' motion for summary judgment was denied. In granting Mundaca's motion for summary judgment, the trial court ruled that the form of the defendants' signatures—"[defendant's signature], Trustee"—did not show unambiguously that the defendants were signing in a representative capacity. See RSA 382-A:3-402(b) comment 2 (1994). The trial court then ruled that the defendants failed to meet their burden of proving that Dartmouth Savings Bank did not intend to hold them personally liable. See RSA 382-A:3-402(b)(2) (1994). This appeal followed.

On appeal, the defendants argue that reading the notes and mortgages together shows unambiguously that they signed in a representative capacity for the trust as the identified principal, and therefore they are not personally liable under RSA 382-A:3-402(b)(1) (1994). Alternatively, the defendants contend that the trial court erred in granting Mundaca's motion for summary judgment because there was a genuine issue of material fact regarding whether the original parties intended the defendants to be personally liable. See RSA 382-A:3-402(b)(2).

The trial court applied RSA 382-A:3-402 [UCC Revised §3-402 —Ed.] (1994), and the parties do not dispute that this version of the statute governs the defendants' liability. Accordingly, we will assume for purposes of this appeal that this version of the statute applies. But see, e.g., Barnsley v. Empire Mortgage Ltd. Partnership V, 142 N.H. 721, 723, 720 A.2d 63, 64 (1998). RSA 382-A:3-402 (1994) provides in pertinent part:

> (b) If a representative signs the name of the representative to an instrument and the signature is an authorized signature of the represented person, the following rules apply:
>
> (1) If the form of the signature shows unambiguously that the signature is made on behalf of the represented person who is identified in the instrument, the representative is not liable on the instrument.
>
> (2) Subject to subsection (c), if (i) the form of the signature does not show unambiguously that the signature is made in a representative capacity or (ii) the represented person is not identified in the instrument, the representative is liable on the instrument to a holder in due course that took the instrument without notice that the representative was not intended to be liable on the instrument. With respect to any other person, the representative is liable on the instrument unless the representative proves that the original parties did not intend the representative to be liable on the instrument.

The defendants argue that under RSA 382-A:3-402(b)(1), the handwritten term "Trustee" appearing next to their signatures on the notes shows unambiguously that the signatures were made in a representative capacity. Further, the defendants argue that while the promissory notes did not explicitly identify the trust, the notes and mortgages read together reveal that the term "Borrower" is identified as the trust. Accordingly, the defendants argue that they are not personally liable.

RSA 382-A:3-402(b)(1) requires that the form of the representative's signature show unambiguously that the signature is made on behalf of the represented person who is identified *in the instrument.* The defendants concede that the instruments in this case are the two promissory notes. The defendants, however, argue that fundamental contract law requires that the notes and mortgages be read together to interpret the contracting parties' intentions. General principles of contract law only apply to negotiable instruments if not displaced by the Uniform Commercial Code. See RSA 382-A:1-103 (1994). Accordingly, we hold that because the represented person, in this case the trust, is not identified in the *instrument* as required by RSA 382-A:3-402(b)(1), this case falls squarely under RSA 382-A:3-402(b)(2).

Pursuant to RSA 382-A:3-402(b)(2), the defendants could be personally liable in two situations: (1) to a holder in due course who takes the instrument without notice that the defendants did not intend to be personally liable; and (2) to any other party unless the defendants prove that the original parties did not intend them to be personally liable. While the trial court did not address the first situation, it ruled that the defendants failed to meet their burden of proving that the original parties did not intend them to be personally liable. The defendants contend, however, that summary judgment was inappropriate because there was a genuine issue of material fact as to the intent of the original parties. We agree. . . .

Our review of the record reveals a disputed issue of material fact as to the intent of the original parties, i.e., Dartmouth Savings Bank and the defendants. While the notes do not explicitly identify the trust as the represented party, the mortgages show that the defendants signed in a representative capacity and identify the trust as the "Borrower." See RSA 382-A:3-402(b)(1). Furthermore, the record contains conflicting affidavits by the defendants and Heidi Postupack, the bank's loan officer who handled this transaction. The defendants' affidavits claim that they intended to sign the notes as representatives of the trust. Conversely, Postupack's affidavit states that she understood that the bank intended the defendants to be personally liable, jointly and severally, on the notes. Considering this evidence in the light most favorable to the defendants, see *Barnsley*, 142 N.H. at 723, 720 A.2d at 64, we conclude that a genuine issue of material fact exists as to the bank's intent regarding the defendants' personal liability on the notes.

As noted earlier, the trial court did not address whether Mundaca was a holder in due course who took without notice that the defendants did not intend to be personally liable on the notes. See RSA 382-A:3-402(b)(2). Because the record before us is silent on this matter, we leave this issue for the trial court on remand.

The defendants also argue that the mortgages act as a defense to their alleged personal liability on the notes. This argument is without merit. The mortgages only provide a defense to the defendants' alleged personal liability on the notes to the extent that the mortgages modify, supplement, or nullify their obligation on the notes. See RSA 382-A:3-117 [UCC Revised §3-117—Ed.] (1994). The defendants argue that it is clear that the mortgages modify and supplement the notes. We disagree. What is clear is that the mortgages were issued as collateral for the notes. What is unclear by reading the notes and the mortgages is the identity of the "Borrower." We have already held that the identity of the "Borrower" is a material issue of fact in dispute.

Accordingly, we reverse the grant of summary judgment and remand this case to the trial court for further proceedings consistent with this opinion.

Reversed and remanded.

All concurred.

PROBLEM 147

The president of Money Corporation was John Smith. He signed three corporate promissory notes as follows:

(1) "John Smith." Money Corporation was not mentioned in the note.
(2) "Money Corporation, John Smith."
(3) "Money Corporation, John Smith, President."

In each case is he personally liable to a holder in due course of the instrument?

PROBLEM 148

Kit Fielding was the corporate president of Francis Racing Stables. The corporate checks had the words "Francis Racing Stables"

printed prominently in the upper left-hand corner of the checks, but
when Fielding went to sign the checks on the drawer's line, he simply signed his name and did not sign the name of the company or
in any way indicate that he was signing as an agent. If the check is
negotiated to a holder in due course and then dishonored by the
drawee bank, may the holder in due course successfully impose
personal liability on Fielding? See §3-402(c) and its Official Comment 3.

Nichols v. Seale

Texas Court of Civil Appeals, 1973
493 S.W.2d 589, 12 U.C.C. Rep. Serv. 711

GUITTARD, J. In this appeal from a summary judgment on a
promissory note, the principal questions are (1) whether as between the original parties extrinsic evidence is admissible to show
that the signer acted for a corporation rather than for himself, although the note does not show his representative capacity and
contains only an assumed name under which the corporation was
doing business, and (2) whether a statement in his affidavit that he
was acting on behalf of the corporation rather than for himself is
competent summary judgment proof or an inadmissible conclusion. We hold that the evidence is admissible and raises a fact issue.

The note is on a printed form beginning "I, we or either of
us," and is signed as follows:

THE FASHION BEAUTY SALON
Carl V. Nichols [typewriting]
Carl V. Nichols [handwriting]

The payee sued Carl V. Nichols "individually and doing business as
The Fashion Beauty Salon." Nichols filed a sworn answer denying
that he signed the note in question in his individual capacity and
alleging that he signed on behalf of a corporation, Mr. Carls Fashion, Inc. In response to plaintiff's motion for summary judgment,
defendant Nichols filed the following affidavit:

> My name is Carl V. Nichols, and I served as President of Mr.
> Carls Fashion, Inc., a Texas Corporation, doing business as The
> Fashion Beauty Salon at 2115 Sherry Lane, Dallas, Texas, from the

date of its incorporation, January 14, 1960, and I signed the promissory note attached to Plaintiff's Original Petition and marked Exhibit "A" in the capacity of officer of such corporation and in behalf of such corporation and not in my personal capacity.

The trial court rendered summary judgment against Nichols · on the note. We first consider whether we must affirm that judgment on the ground that the form of the signature makes Nichols individually liable as a matter of law under §3-403(2), which provides: [the court quoted the section].

Plaintiff contends that Nichols is personally obligated under subsection (1) because the note neither "names" the corporation nor shows that Nichols "signed in a representative capacity." Admittedly, the note does not show that he "signed in a representative capacity," because it does not describe him as a corporate officer or agent or use any other language, such as "by," indicating that he was acting for someone other than himself. Neither does it "name the person represented" unless "The Fashion Beauty Salon" can be taken as naming the corporation "Mr. Carls Fashion, Inc."

We hold that use of an assumed name does "name the person represented" within the meaning of the code. This section must be read along with §3-401(2), which expressly authorizes use of an assumed name in a negotiable instrument: "A signature is made by use of any name, including any trade or assumed name, upon an instrument. . . ." The official interpretation of this section includes the following comment concerning a signature on commercial paper: "It may be made in any name, including any trade name or assumed name, however false and fictitious, which is adopted for the purpose. Parol evidence is admissible to identify the signer, and when he is identified the signature is effective." This rule applies as well when the person using the assumed name is a corporation, since corporations are expressly permitted to use assumed names by Tex. Bus. Corp. Act Ann. art. 2.05 (1956) VATS, and may sue on contracts made in assumed names. Davis v. Tex-O-Kan Flour Mills Co., 186 F.2d 50 (5th Cir. 1950), W. B. Clarkson & Co. v. Gans S.S. Line, 187 S.W. 1106 (Tex. Civ. App., Galveston 1916, *writ ref'd*). Consequently, extrinsic evidence was admissible to show that "The Fashion Beauty Salon" was an assumed name for "Mr. Carls Fashion, Inc." This conclusion is supported by Weeks v. San Angelo Natl. Bank, 65 S.W.2d 348 (Tex. Civ. App., Austin 1933, *writ ref'd*), in which a note was signed "Weeks Drug Store No. 4 by Jno. A. Weeks." The court held that this signature was ambiguous and that parol evidence was admissible to show the party's intention that the note should be the obligation of "Weeks Drug Store No. 4, Inc.," a corporation not yet organized.

Since, as we have held, a corporation is "named" within §3-403(2) by use of its assumed name, that section does not forbid extrinsic evidence to show further, as between the original parties, that the signer was not personally obligated. Such proof may be admissible, not to vary terms of the instrument or to show a mistake, but rather to explain an ambiguity with respect to the capacity of the signer. An instrument which "names the person represented but does not show that the representative signed in a representative capacity," may be ambiguous with respect to the capacity in which he signed, since, in the absence of explanatory evidence, the signature may be interpreted either as his individual signature, or as a signature on behalf of the person represented. We find the present signature to be ambiguous for that reason. Directly in point here is Canton Provision Co. v. Chaney, 70 N.E.2d 687 (Ohio App. 1945), in which checks signed "Finer Foods, Jack Chaney" were held to be ambiguous so that parol evidence was admissible to show that Chaney signed as agent for another individual doing business as "Finer Foods." See also First State Bank v. Smoot-Curtis Co., 121 S.W.2d 667 (Tex. Civ. App., Fort Worth 1938, *writ dism'd by agr.*) and Norman v. Beling, 33 N.J. 237, 163 A.2d 129 (1960), both holding that a note signed with the name of a corporation and an officer, without showing his representative capacity, is ambiguous so that the representative capacity of the individual may be shown by parol evidence. In our opinion, the ambiguity in the present note is not removed by Nichols' name in typewriting, which, whether above or below his signature, may have been used only to identify the signer in case his handwriting was not legible. Moreover, it seems to us that the conventional printed language, "I, we or either of us" only serves to increase the ambiguity. . . .

Appellant's motion for rehearing is granted, our former opinion is withdrawn, and the cause is reversed and remanded.

NOTE

On appeal, the Texas Supreme Court reversed for a procedural reason:

> Texas law provides that in order for an agent to avoid liability
> for his signature on a contract, he must *disclose* his intent to sign as a

representative to the other contracting party. Uncommunicated intent will not suffice. Heinrichs v. Evins Personnel Consultants, Inc., No. One, 486 S.W.2d 935 (Tex. 1972); Mahoney v. Pitman, 43 S.W.2d 143 (Tex. Civ. App., Amarillo 1931, *writ ref'd*).

Again viewing Nichols' affidavit broadly, it states that he signed the note as president of the corporation, thus clearly indicating his subjective intent to sign as an agent. However, nowhere does Nichols say that he disclosed his intent to Seale. Nor does his statement that " . . . I signed the promissory note . . . in the capacity of officer of such corporation and in behalf of such corporation and not in my personal capacity," intimate that this intended capacity was communicated to Seale. This is his burden in the context of the summary judgment proceedings. Consequently, Nichols has not effectively raised a fact issue upon his alleged affirmative defense of representation and Seale's motion for summary judgment must be granted.

Seale v. Nichols, 505 S.W.2d 251, 255, 14 U.C.C. Rep. Serv. 457, 461 (Tex. 1974). See also Rotuba Extruders, Inc. v. Ceppos, 46 N.Y.2d 223, 385 N.E.2d 1068, 413 N.Y.S.2d 141, 25 U.C.C. Rep. Serv. 765 (1978).

III. OTHER THEORIES OF LIABILITY

In commercial paper law, contractual obligations arise from the voluntary act of putting one's signature on a negotiable instrument. But the Code also establishes a host of other theories imposing liability.

The next chapter explores the legal relationship between a bank and its customer, and, as we shall see, these parties may sue each other for violations of the rules arising from that relationship, primarily the "properly payable" rule of §4-401 and the wrongful dishonor rule of §4-402.

In Chapter 12 we will look closely at the legal snarls following forgeries and alterations of negotiable instruments and shall there encounter causes of action based on warranty and conversion.

Chapter 11
BANKS AND THEIR CUSTOMERS

Article 4 of the Uniform Commercial Code covers Bank Deposits and Collections, matters inextricably entwined with the rules of Article 3 on Negotiable Instruments. Section 4-102(a) provides that whenever the provisions of Article 3 conflict with those of Article 4, the latter control. This can be important in warranty actions discussed in the next chapter; §§4-207 and 4-208 will prevail over §§3-416 and 3-417 if both are arguably applicable. Another matter of concern is terminology. In addition to a general definitions section, §4-104, the complicated nomenclature of Article 4 banks is laid out in §4-105. Under these definitions, a bank can bear more than one label. In §4-105, which you should examine, the Article 3 drawee bank gets a new name and becomes known as the payor bank (or, in the federal regulations on check collection, the paying bank; 12 C.F.R. §229.2(z)). The depositary bank is the first bank to which an item is transferred for collection; it could also be the payor bank in situations where the drawer and the holder do their banking at the same institution. Any bank in the collection process, except the payor bank, can be called a collecting bank; this includes the depositary bank.

I. THE CHECKING ACCOUNT

Whenever anyone opens a checking account with a bank, two legal relationships spring into being: debtor/creditor and principal/agent. The good news is that the depositor is the creditor and the bank the debtor; further, the bank is an agent for payment of the principal's drafts and other instructions. The opening of the account creates a contract; the force of centuries imbues it with these characteristics. Its other details may be implied—see §1-205—or may be the subject of a detailed contract. See, e.g., David v. Manufacturers Hanover Trust Co., 59 Misc. 2d 248, 298 N.Y.S.2d 847, 6 U.C.C. Rep. Serv. 504 (App. Div. 1969) (waiver of jury trial hidden in fine print of signature card upheld against charge of unconscionability). Read §4-103.

A. *"Properly Payable" Rule*

The basic contract between drawer and drawee, whether detailed or implied, always has at its nucleus this basic understanding: the bank may pay out the customer's money *only* if it follows his or her orders exactly. If it does not do so, it must recredit the account. Article 4 backs up this understanding in §4-401, wherein it is stated that the bank may charge the account if the item is *properly payable*. What does *properly payable* mean here? Section 4-401(a) tells us that an "item is *properly payable* if it is authorized by the customer and is in accordance with any agreement between the customer and bank." It is easiest to understand this if you think of a check as if it were a letter addressed to the bank telling it what to do with the customer's money. The check is "properly payable" only if the bank follows the instructions of the customer *exactly*. If the bank makes a mistake and pays a check in a manner not instructed by the customer, it must put the money back in the account.[1] Read §4-401.

1. Of course, there are exceptions, situations where the bank may violate the properly payable rule and live to tell about it. The bank may be able to escape liability

The typical situations in which the bank might violate the "properly payable" rule are explored next.

PROBLEM 149

When Portia Moot paid off a debt she owed to her law school roommate, she gave her a postdated check, dating it one week later (planning to cover it with the paycheck she would receive before that date). The roommate deposited the check in her own bank immediately, and that bank presented it to the payor bank before the date of the check. Portia's bank paid the check even though this created an overdraft (for which Portia was charged). Was the check properly payable before its date? See §4-401(c). If Portia had phoned the bank and warned it that she had written this postdated check, would it have still been properly payable? See Vincene Verdun, Postdated Checks: An Old Problem with a New Solution in the Revised U.C.C., 14 U. Ark. Little Rock L.J. 37 (1991).

PROBLEM 150

Jack Point lost his checkbook. A month later his bank, Yeomen National, returned his canceled checks, including one payable to W. Shadbolt for $1,000, to which Jack's name was forged as drawer. He notified Yeoman National Bank promptly. Was this check *properly payable*? See §§3-401, 3-403. If Jack had called Yeomen National immediately on finding out that his checkbook was missing, could the bank have made him stop payment on all those blank checks and also pay a good hefty stop-payment fee on each one? See Official Comment 1 to §4-401.

---

by using any one of a number of defenses (customer negligence, subrogation, etc.), to be discussed later.

What should a bank do if the check is ambiguous because, say, the written amount is not the same as the numbers on the dollar sign line? UCC 3-114 states that:

> If an instrument contains contradictory terms, typewritten terms prevail over printed terms, handwritten terms prevail over both, and words prevail over numbers.

PROBLEM 151

The Widow Douglas gave a check for $10.00 to Ben Rogers in return for the latter's mowing her lawn. Rogers' friend Joe Harper stole the check from Rogers, raised the amount to $1,000 by erasing the decimal point and cleverly altering the writing, and forged Rogers' signature to the back of the check. Harper presented the check for payment to the drawee bank, Clemens State Bank, which paid Harper $1,000. This reduced the balance in the Widow Douglas' account to zero and caused four other checks she had sent to her creditors to bounce. The Widow Douglas sued her bank, arguing as follows:

> Section 4-401 says that the bank may charge my account only when the item is *properly payable*. On this check I ordered the bank to pay out $10 of my funds to Ben Rogers or his order. But since Ben Rogers never signed it, he never ordered it paid to anyone, and therefore the bank did not pay in accordance with my instructions and must recredit my account. Whatever payment it made was out of the bank's own funds.

Clemens State Bank replied:

> All we are required to do is make sure that the item is apparently *properly payable,* that is, that it *appears* to contain the proper chain of indorsements. We must also, of course, act in good faith, which we have done. Mrs. Douglas paid Rogers, and if Rogers carelessly lost the check, why should that act as a windfall to Mrs. Douglas? If Mrs. Douglas is permitted to win here, she will have gotten a free lawnmowing job, and we will be out $1,000. In the alternative, even if we improperly charged this account with the entire amount, surely §4-401(d)(2) permits us to take $10 out of the account.

Which argument would prevail if you were the judge? As to the bank's "at least $10" argument, notice the word *holder* in §4-401(d). What effect does it have on the resolution of this dispute? If the bank decides to recredit the account, it will be able to recoup its loss by using the warranty theories explored in the next chapter.

Whenever a bank wrongfully takes money out of the account of its customer, it is very tempting for the customer's attorney to sue in conversion because the bank's misappropriation certainly sounds like an act of conversion. Technically, however, conversion will not lie. The reason is that when a customer puts money in the bank, that money is

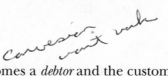

on *loan* to the bank; the bank becomes a *debtor* and the customer is a *creditor.* The bank cannot convert its own property any more than any debtor converts property by failing to repay the debt. Instead, the proper cause of action is for violation of §4-401 (the "properly payable" rule) or is simply an action in contract or quasi-contract (money had and received).

PROBLEM 152

You are the attorney for Octopus National Bank, and the bank has presented you with the following problem: it recently paid a check drawn on a customer's account, and there was no drawer's signature on the check. The payee on the check was a telemarketing firm that had apparently called the bank's customer, sold him some product over the phone, had the customer read off the magnetically encoded numbers at the bottom of the check,[2] and then created the check, including the magnetically encoded line. In lieu of the drawer's signature, the check is stamped "drawer's signature on file." The customer has now called and complained, apparently suffering from "buyer's remorse," and wants the account recredited with the amount of the check. There are a lot of these "pre-authorized drafts" (or "telechecks") now being created. Is the payor bank doing wrong when it honors them?

PROBLEM 153

Lemuel Gulliver opened an account with the Swift State Bank. After using the account for several years, he was away on a sea voyage for a long period of time. When he returned, a check that he had written (and dated) eight years ago was presented and paid against his

---

2. The information magnetically encoded across the bottom of checks is printed in what are called magnetic ink character recognition (MICR—pronounced "micker") symbols so that the line can be read by automated check-processing machines. The MICR line reflects the account number of the drawer, a number representing the drawee bank, and certain other routing information. If you look at one of your canceled checks, you will also notice that at some point (normally done by the depositary bank) someone put MICR numbers in the lower right-hand corner of the check, reflecting the amount of the check. This is done, of course, so that the check-processing machines can read the amount. Section 4-209 creates a warranty that this information has been correctly encoded.

account, creating an overdraft.[3] Gulliver protested the payment. Will this argument succeed? As to the old check, see §§4-401, 4-404; White & Summers §18-3; compare Granite Equip. Leasing Corp. v. Hempstead Bank, 68 Misc. 2d 350, 326 N.Y.S.2d 881, 9 U.C.C. Rep. Serv. 1384 (Sup. Ct. 1971), with New York Flame-Proofing Co. v. Chemical Bank, 15 U.C.C. Rep. Serv. 1104 (N.Y. Civ. Ct. 1974), and Charles Ragusa & Son v. Community State Bank, 360 So. 2d 231, 24 U.C.C. Rep. Serv. 725 (La. App. 1978). Did the creation of an overdraft situation keep the check from being properly payable? See §4-401(a). Does the language of that section mean that a bank must pay overdrafts? See §4-402(a). How quickly must Gulliver file suit? See §4-111; the statute of limitations for actions arising in Article 3 of the Code is found in §3-118.

B. *Wrongful Dishonor*

Whenever a bank makes an improper payment from an account, this debit may cause other checks written by the customer to be wrongfully dishonored. The customer may recover all actual damages whenever the bank makes a *wrongful* (which includes *mistaken*) dishonor of a check that is properly payable from the account. Read §4-402 and its Official Comment.

Twin City Bank v. Isaacs

Arkansas Supreme Court, 1984
263 Ark. 127, 672 S.W.2d 651, 39 U.C.C. Rep. Serv. 35

STEELE HAYS, J. Twin City Bank has appealed from a judgment entered on a jury verdict against it in favor of Kenneth and Vicki Isaacs for damages sustained from the bank's wrongful dishonor of the Isaacs' checks resulting in a hold order against their account for a period of approximately four years.

---

3. A bank that pays overdrafts and charges a greater amount than is charged for returning these checks has imposed a finance charge on the transaction. If this is done pursuant to written agreement with the customer, the bank will need to give a Truth in Lending statement to its consumer customers, or there is a good argument that it will violate the federal Truth in Lending Act. See Regulation Z §226.4(b)(2) and (c)(3).

On Sunday, May 13, 1979, the Isaacs discovered that their check-book was missing. They reported the loss to Twin City promptly on Monday, May 14, and later learned that two forged checks totalling $2,050 had been written on their account and honored by the bank on May 11 and 12. The sequence of events that followed is disputed, but the end result was a decision by the bank to freeze the Isaacs' checking account which had contained approximately $2,500 before the forgeries occurred. A few checks cleared Monday morning before a hold order was issued leaving the balance at approximately $2,000. Mr. Isaacs had been convicted of burglary and the initial hold on the account was attributable to the bank's concern that the Isaacs were somehow involved with the two forged checks. The individual responsible for the forgeries was charged and convicted soon after the forgeries occurred and on May 30, 1979 the police told the bank there was nothing to connect the Isaacs with the person arrested. Two weeks later the police notified the bank a second time they could not connect the Isaacs to the forgeries. The bank maintains it continued to keep the account frozen on the advice of its attorneys. However that may be, the Isaacs were denied their funds for some four years. The Isaacs filed suit in mid-June of 1979 for wrongful dishonor of their checks and wrongful withholding of their funds.

The jury awarded the Isaacs $18,500 in compensatory damages and $45,000 in punitive damages. The bank made a motion for a new trial pursuant to A.R.C.P. Rule 59, which was denied. From that denial the bank brings this appeal contending error on three grounds: 1) Misconduct of a juror at trial, 2) the trial court's refusal to give two requested instructions, and 3) jury error in assessing excessive damages contrary to the evidence and the law. . . .

On the issue of damages, the bank maintains there was insufficient evidence to support the $18,500 award for mental anguish, for loss of credit and loss of the bargain on a house, that the award of punitive damages should not have been given at all as there was not only insufficient proof of actual damages but insufficient evidence of malice or intent to oppress on the part of the bank. The bank does not challenge the sufficiency of the evidence of its wrongful dishonor, but contends only that there was no evidence to support an award of damages. These arguments cannot be sustained.

The statute upon which this suit was based is Ark. Stat. Ann. §85-4-402.

[The court quoted §4-402.—Ed.]

The jury was instructed that if they found the bank liable they were to fix the amount of money which would compensate the Isaacs "for any of the following elements of damage sustained which were proximately caused by the conduct of Twin City Bank: 1) Any amounts of money wrongfully held by the defendant and remaining unpaid, 2) any mental anguish and embarrassment suffered by the plaintiffs, 3) any financial losses sustained by the [Isaacs]."

Initially, there can be no serious question as to certain losses, the $2,000 wrongfully withheld by the bank for four years, and the value of two vehicles repossessed because the Isaacs did not have access to their funds, resulting in a loss of approximately $2,200. Additionally, after the account was frozen the bank continued to charge the account a service charge and overdraft fees on checks written before the forgeries but presented after the account was frozen. The bank does not refute these damages but argues there is no showing of any financial deprivation from loss of credit or loss of the bargain on a house the Isaacs wanted to buy, and insufficient proof of mental anguish. We find, however, that in addition to the losses previously mentioned, there was sufficient evidence to sustain damages for mental suffering, loss of credit, and sufficient demonstration of some loss attributable to the inability to pursue the purchase of a home.

Mental suffering under §4-402 of the Uniform Commercial Code is relatively new and has not been frequently addressed by other courts, but of those a majority has allowed recovery. Morse v. Mutual Federal Savings and Loan, 536 F. Supp. 1271 (Mass. 1982); Farmers & Merchants State Bank of Krum v. Ferguson, 617 S.W.2d 918 (Tex. 1981); Northshore Bank v. Palmer, 525 S.W.2d 718 (Tex. 1975); Kendall Yacht Club v. United California Bank, 50 Cal. App. 3d 949, 123 Cal. Rptr. 848 (1975); and see White & Summers, Uniform Commercial Code (1980 2d ed.) §17-4, p.675. In general, the type of mental anguish suffered under §4-402 does not need to rise to the higher standard of injury for intentional infliction of emotional distress. Wrongful dishonors tend to produce intangible injuries similar to those involved in defamation actions. See State Bank of Siloam Springs v. Marshall, 163 Ark. 566, 260 S.W. 431 (1924). Damages of this kind are more difficult to assess with exactness. In Wasp Oil v. Arkansas Oil and Gas, 280 Ark. 420, 658 S.W.2d 397 (1983) we noted the general rule that damages may not be allowed where they are speculative, resting only upon conjectural evidence, or the opinions of the parties or witnesses, but there are instances where damages cannot be proven with exactness. In *Wasp* we recognized a different rule applies when the cause and existence of damages have been established by the evidence, that recovery will not be denied merely because the damages cannot be determined with exactness. We went on to say the plaintiff in the case at bar was not trying to prove the latter sort of damage such as *mental anguish* as a result of defamation, but loss of income.

Decisions upholding recovery for mental suffering under the code have found injury resulting from circumstances comparable to this case. In Northshore Bank v. Palmer, supra, for example, a $275 forged check was paid from Palmer's account. After the bank knew or should have known the check was forged, it charged Palmer with the $275 check and later wrongfully dishonored other checks. Part of the actual damages awarded was attributed to mental suffering for the "embarrassment and humiliation Palmer suffered from having been turned down for credit for the first time in his life."

In Morse v. Mutual Federal Savings and Loan, supra, $2,200 was awarded for "false defamatory implications arising from temporary financial embarrassment." And in Farmers & Merchants State Bank of Krum v. Ferguson, supra, the plaintiff's account in the amount of $7,000 was frozen for apparently one month for reasons not stated. The plaintiff was awarded $25,000 for mental anguish, $3,000 for loss of credit based on a denial of a loan, $5,000 for loss of time spent making explanations to creditors, and $1,500 for loss of use of his money. The court justified the mental suffering award because the dishonor was found to be with malice—the bank had failed to notify Ferguson that the account was frozen, some checks were honored while others were not, and the bank continued to withdraw loan payments due it during the entire time.

In this case, prior to the forgery incident the Isaacs' credit reputation with Twin City Bank was described by the bank as "impeccable" and the freezing of their funds had a traumatic effect on their lives. They obviously lost their credit standing with Twin City, and were unable to secure credit commercially at other institutions because of their status at Twin City. The Isaacs had to borrow from friends and family, and were left in a precarious position financially. They did not have use of their $2,000 for four years. The allegation relative to the loss of a house resulted from the dishonor of an earnest money check for a home they were planning to buy, ending prospects for the purchase at that time. Though there may have been insufficient proof of loss of the bargain on the house, as the bank argues, nevertheless this evidence was admissible as an element of mental suffering. The denial of credit contributed to some monetary loss as occurred in *Ferguson*, supra, in addition to its being a reasonable element of mental suffering as was found in *Palmer*, supra. There was also testimony that the financial strain contributed to marital difficulties leading at one point to the filing of a divorce suit. The suit was dropped but there was testimony that the difficulties caused by the bank's action caused substantial problems in the marriage. Finally, the Isaacs lost equities in two vehicles repossessed as a result of the withholding of their funds. One of these, a new van, was repossessed by Twin City in June, 1979, before a five-day grace period for a current installment had expired.

We believe there was substantial evidence to support the verdict. The jury heard the evidence of the amount wrongfully withheld, the loss of two vehicles, credit loss through loan denials, loss of the use of their money for four years, the suffering occasioned by marital difficulties, the inability to acquire a home they wanted, and the general anxieties which accompanied the financial strain. We recognize that our holding today presents some conflict with pre-code law by allowing recovery without exactness of proof as to damages. In State Bank of Siloam Springs v. Marshall, supra, a suit based on the predecessor to §4-402, we stated that the plaintiff must show the facts and circumstances which occasioned the damage and the amount thereof. However, *Marshall* itself recognized the nature of the damages in this action, and §4-402, although similar to its predecessor, has additional language which impliedly recognizes mental suffering and other intangible injuries of the type noted in *Wasp*, supra, as recoverable under this statute. See White & Summers, supra, §17-4, p.675. To the extent that exactness in proof is not required, the law as stated in *Marshall* is displaced by §4-402.

The bank's objection to the award of punitive damages is threefold: a) The instruction on punitive damages was in accordance with A.M.I. 2217, which is intended for use in negligence cases and not applicable here; b) there was no evidence that the bank acted intentionally or with malice; and c) the verdict of $45,000 was excessive. However, we address only the question of the excessiveness of the verdict, as the other points were not raised in the trial court by objection to the instruction. Crowder v. Flippo, 263 Ark. 433, 565 S.W.2d 138 (1978); Dodson Creek Inc. v. Walton, 2 Ark. App. 128, 620 S.W.2d 947 (1981); A.R.C.P. Rule 51. . . .

The judgment is affirmed.

PROBLEM 154

Stella and Harry Squabble, after many years of constant fighting, decided to separate and seek a divorce. Stella's attorney filed the proper papers and then, to preserve Harry's financial assets in the status quo, sent a *lis pendens* (notice of litigation) to the bank in which

Harry maintained an account for the barber shop he owned. The bank was uncertain what to do about the lis pendens notice, but the bank's attorney was a conservative type and advised the bank to freeze Harry's account until the divorce matter was settled. Fourteen of the barber shop's checks bounced as a result of this decision, and Harry's ulcer acted up and put him in the hospital. Harry filed suit against his bank, asking for $100,000 in damages. At trial he proved only the above facts but offered no evidence as to damages. Should the trial judge grant the defendant's motion for a directed verdict? See White & Summers §18-4.

PROBLEM 155

When Archie Goodwin received his paycheck from Nero Wolfe, his employer, he walked it into New York Metropolitan National Bank, the drawee, and presented it across the counter. The teller asked him if he had an account of his own with the bank. When he replied that he did not, the bank told him that it was the bank's policy not to pay across-the-counter checks drawn on it unless the payee had an account at the bank. Is this a wrongful dishonor? See Your Style Publications, Inc. v. Mid Town Bank & Trust Co. of Chicago, 150 Ill. App. 3d 421, 501 N.E.2d 805, 3 U.C.C. Rep. Serv. 2d 675 (1986); Buckley v. Trenton Savings Fund Society, 216 N.J. Super. 705, 524 A.2d 886, 4 U.C.C. Rep. Serv. 2d 166 (1987). Could the bank solve this problem by putting a clause in the checking account agreement stating that the customer would permit the bank to refuse to pay checks presented across the counter unless the presenter had an account with the bank? See §4-103.

C. Death or Incompetence of Customer

The common law rule that death or incompetence of a principal revokes the authority of an agent to act used to play havoc with checking accounts. It was a sure thing that the drafters of Article 4, among them representatives of the banking industry, would enact a solution to the problem. Read §4-405 and its Official Comment.

PROBLEM 156

Howard Mortus dropped dead while walking back to his house from the corner mailbox in which he had just deposited the month's

bill payments. His widow phoned the payor bank the next day and
informed the bank of Howard's death. She mentioned the mailed
checks and specifically asked the bank manager to keep the account,
which was in Howard's name only, open to pay them. The bank
manager said that the bank would pay the checks for nine more days.
Later that same day, Crazy Nelly, the Mortuses' next-door neighbor,
somehow got the idea that Howard had left her all his money (he
didn't leave her a cent—he barely knew her) and called up the bank.
She explained she was the Mortuses' neighbor and was "sure to be an
heir to the estate," so she ordered the bank to stop paying checks on
Howard's account. The bank consulted its attorney. Must it stop paying
checks, or may it still continue to do so? If it returns checks, will it
have made a dishonor? Cf. §3-502. Is it a *wrongful* dishonor so as to
subject the bank to §4-402 damages?

D. Bank's Right of Setoff

In the late 1700s there developed a common law lien by which a
bank could unilaterally debit the account of a depositor in order to pay
a debt owed to itself. This common law right, which is in existence in
virtually all states today, is called the bank's right of *setoff* because
one obligation (the customer's to the bank) is offset against another
(the bank's to the customer). Prior to the advent of the Fair Credit
Billing Act (chapter four of the Truth in Lending Act, 15 U.S.C.
§§1601 et seq., effective October 28, 1975), a consumer who had a
checking account with the same bank that issued him or her a credit
card might be the victim of a non-notification setoff on failing to make
a payment. Section 169 of the Fair Credit Billing Act now prohibits
this practice in most instances involving customer credit card debts.[4]

---

4. This section is supplemented by §226.12(d) of the Federal Reserve Board's
Regulation Z, 12 C.F.R. part 226, which explains the rules in more detail. Regulation Z
§226.12(d):

(1) A card issuer may not take any action, either before or after termination of
credit card privileges, to offset a cardholder's indebtedness arising from a consumer
credit transaction under the relevant credit card plan against funds of the cardholder
held on deposit with the card issuer.

(2) This paragraph does not alter or affect the right of a card issuer acting under
state or federal law to do any of the following with regard to funds of a cardholder held
on deposit with the card issuer if the same procedure is constitutionally available to
creditors generally: obtain or enforce a consensual security interest in the funds; attach
or otherwise levy upon the funds; or obtain or enforce a court order relating to the
funds.

Setoff[5] is recognized in the UCC in several sections that mention it in passing (§§4-201(a), 4-215(e), and 4-303), although the Code neither establishes the right nor regulates its terms. It has been argued that non-notification setoff may be unconstitutional under principles similar to those enunciated in Sniadach v. Family Finance Corp., 395 U.S. 337 (1969) (garnishment without prior hearing held to violate Fourteenth Amendment) and also that setoff is a *security interest*, disclosure of which is required under the federal Truth in Lending Act and the Uniform Consumer Credit Code. See Note, Banking Setoff: A Study in Commercial Obsolescence, 23 Hastings L.J. 1585 (1972). The constitutional challenge has been rejected to date. Kruger v. Wells Fargo Bank, 11 Cal. 3d 352, 521 P.2d 441, 113 Cal. Rptr. 449 (1974); Allied Sheet Metal Fabricators v. Peoples Natl. Bank, 10 Wash. App. 530, 518 P.2d 734, 14 U.C.C. Rep. Serv. 432 (Wash. App. 1974). The Truth in Lending Act argument also apparently fails. See Note, Bank Credit Cards and the Right of Setoff, 26 S.C. L. Rev. 89 (1974).

Setoff may be had only against general accounts (such as checking and savings accounts) of the depositor. When the depositor has created a *special* account for a limited purpose, the bank may not set off against it non-related debts of the depositor. See Filosa v. Pecora, 44 Ill. App. 3d 912, 358 N.E.2d 1213 (1976) (setoff not permitted against escrow account). The given reason is that for special accounts the bank is a bailee and not a debtor. See Mid-City Natl. Bank v. Mars Bldg. Corp., 33 Ill. App. 3d 1083, 339 N.E.2d 497 (1975). A bank owes a duty of fair and honorable dealing to its customers. When a bank exercises the right of setoff in an improper fashion, the courts are quick to protect the customer. See Wells v. Washington Heights Fed. Sav. & Loan Assn., 63 Misc. 2d 424, 312 N.Y.S.2d 236 (Cir. Ct. 1970).

---

(3) This paragraph does not prohibit a plan, if authorized in writing by the cardholder, under which the card issuer may periodically deduct all or part of the cardholder's credit card debt from a deposit account held with the card issuer (subject to the limitations in §226.13(d)(1)).

The Official Commentary to this section requires that the "consensual security interest" mentioned in subsection (2) be a separately signed writing stating that the account will be used as collateral for the credit card debt, and not merely be a clause in the credit card contract; Official Commentary .11, Comment 12(d)(2). Further, this Commentary requires that the security interest in the consumer's account be open (as a matter of state law) to other creditors or the card issuer cannot claim an interest therein either. The final thing to note is that the existence of the security agreement must be disclosed in the Truth in Lending statement itself.

5. Bankers, perversely, insist on calling setoff *offset*. The bankers may have won this logomachy; the Fair Credit Billing Act calls this subtraction process *offset*.

Walter v. National City Bank of Cleveland

Ohio Supreme Court, 1975
42 Ohio St. 2d 524, 330 N.E.2d 425

This is an action in civil conversion, involving claims of priority of right to a commercial bank account of Ritzer of Austria, Inc. In the fall of 1969, Ritzer opened a commercial account with The National City Bank of Cleveland, appellant herein. On April 14, 1971, Ritzer executed a 90-day promissory note to appellant in the amount of $3,600, although Ritzer's balance sheet, as of March 31, 1971, showed the company to be insolvent. On May 11, 1971, Robert A. Walter, appellee herein, recovered a judgment against Ritzer in the Euclid Municipal Court for $6,831.95. The following day, the appellant bank was served by mail as garnishee with an order in aid of execution. At the time of service, Ritzer had on deposit with appellant the sum of $3,651.75. The unmatured debt on appellant's promissory note totalled $3,626.25, including interest accrued. On May 24, 1971, appellant sent a letter to the Euclid Municipal Court stating that it was setting off the amount of its loan, leaving a balance of $25.50. Appellant mailed its check for the balance to the Euclid Municipal Court on July 22, 1971.

Appellee brought this action in the Court of Common Pleas of Cuyahoga County. Both parties moved for summary judgment, and judgment was granted for appellee. The Court of Appeals affirmed.

STERN, J. The appellant bank claims a right of equitable setoff of an unmatured indebtedness of its depositor, as against a judgment creditor seeking to reach the depositor's account by an order in aid of execution. Appellant concedes that it has no statutory right of setoff under R.C. 2309.19.

Setoff, both at law and in equity, is that right which exists between two parties, each of whom under an independent contract owes a definite amount to the other, to set off their respective debts by way of mutual deduction. Witham v. South Side Bldg. & Loan Assn. of Lima (1938), 133 Ohio St. 560, 562, 15 N.E.2d 149.

As a general rule, the courts have held that a bank may set off a bank account against the matured indebtedness of its depositor, although the bank has been garnished at the instance of a creditor of the depositor. Schuler v. Israel (1887), 120 U.S. 506, 7 S. Ct. 648, 30 L. Ed. 707; Bennett v. Campbell (1889), 189 Pa. 647, 42 A. 373; Annotation, 106 A.L.R. 62. In Bank v. Brewing Co. (1893), 50 Ohio St. 151, 33 N.E. 1054, it was held that a bank could set off the amount of an insolvent depositor's checking account against an unpaid and overdue note, without the knowledge or consent of the depositor, and that the bank could refuse payment of a check drawn on the account. The theory of these cases is that a bank stands in the relationship of debtor to its depositor, and has the right to apply the deposit to payment of the depositor's matured debts or obligations held by the bank, in the same way that another debtor might assert setoff as a defense to an action on the debt. Holloway v. First Natl. Bank of Pocatello (1928), 45 Idaho 746, 265 P. 699.

In fact, the exercise of setoff by a bank is often quite different from the case of a usual debtor-creditor relationship. A bank account is a debt, but one which is ordinarily subject to demand withdrawal at any time, and one which imposes clear responsibilities upon the bank depending upon the nature of the account. Historically, the bank's right to setoff derives from the bank lien of the law merchant, and that right still possesses some of the characteristics of a lien, since it permits the bank by self-help to take priority over others claiming a right to the funds on deposit.[6] Whereas, in the case of an ordinary debtor, setoff is available as an equitable and statutory defense, in the case of a bank, setoff becomes a means by which the bank, because of its position as a commercial middleman, acquires a priority of right whenever it acts as creditor for a depositor.

The courts have generally held that the bank does not have a priority of right in equity where the bank seeks to set off an unmatured indebtedness. United Bank & Trust Co. v. Washburn & Condon (1930), 37 Ariz. 223, 292 P. 1025; Gerseta Corporation v. Equitable Trust Co. of New York (1926), 241 N.Y. 418, 150 N.E. 501; Stockyards Natl. Bank of Presnall (1917), 109 Tex. 32, 194 S.W. 384. Cf. Valley National Bank of Arizona v. Hasper (1967), 6 Ariz. App. 376, 432 P.2d

6. "It is said to be a well-settled rule of the law merchant, that a bank has a general lien on all the funds of a depositor in its possession for any balance due on general account, or other indebtedness contracted in the course of their dealings, and may appropriate the funds to the payment of such indebtedness. The right to make such appropriation, it is held, grows out of the relation of the parties, as debtor and creditor, and rests upon the principle that, 'as the depositor is indebted to the bank upon a demand which is due, the funds in its possession may properly and justly be applied in payment of such debt, and it has therefore a right to retain such funds until payment is actually made.' Falkland v. Bank, 84 N.Y. 145. Though this right is called a 'lien,' strictly it is not, when applied to a general deposit, for, a person cannot have a lien upon his own property, but only on that of another; and, as we have seen, the funds of general deposit in a bank are the property of the bank. Properly speaking, the right, in such case, is that of set-off, arising from the existence of mutual demands. The practical effect, however, is the same. The cross demands are satisfied, so far as they are equal, leaving whatever balance that may be due on either as the true amount of the indebtedness from one party to the other." Bank v. Brewing Co. (1893), 50 Ohio St. 151, 158 n.59, 33 N.E. 1054, 1055 n.59.

924. An unmatured debt is not presently due or collectible and is not available for setoff, since setoff would alter the contract made by the parties.

An exception to this rule has been made in cases where the depositor is insolvent. In Schuler v. Israel, supra (120 U.S. 506, 7 S. Ct. 648, 30 L. Ed. 708), the court noted that a defense in equity was available to a bank-debtor to prevent an insolvent depositor-creditor from obtaining payment of his debt, where an unmatured obligation was available as setoff and would be lost due to the insolvency.

The same equities do not apply in the case at bar. Here, the negotiation of a 90-day promissory note to Ritzer occurred after the date upon which, the bank itself asserts, Ritzer's balance sheet showed the company to be insolvent. In sum, the bank made a loan for a definite term to an insolvent depositor, and now claims that as a matter of equity it is entitled to priority of right to its depositor's account because of the insolvency. We disagree. The extension of credit to an insolvent was a voluntary act, whether negligent or merely lacking in sound banking practice. In the present case, no equity appears which would require granting priority to the bank's unmatured obligation over the judgment of the appellee.[7]

Lack of maturity is not always permitted to defeat the right of setoff where that right is the only way to prevent clear injustice, and the courts have frequently applied equitable principles in cases of insolvency. "Where insolvency has intervened, a court will not be limited to a strict application of statutory set-off but will apply the doctrines of equity." Union Properties v. Baldwin Brothers Co. (1943), 141 Ohio St. 303, 47 N.E.2d 983 (paragraph nine of the syllabus). But no equity accrues where insolvency did not "intervene" but occurred prior to the voluntary granting of the loan sought to be set off.

The bank also claims a contractual right of setoff based upon its rules and regulations. These rules read, in part, ". . . Bank also reserves the right to apply any balance in the account to the payment of any

---

7. A banker's right of setoff also raises new equitable questions in situations where the bank may have several types of accounts with a depositor, including savings passbook and checking accounts and long-term certificates of deposit, and may also be a creditor for mortgage loans, installment loans, credit card, and other forms of indebtedness. It has been suggested that the setoff of a customer's indebtedness without notice or regard to his protests is not equitable and in conflict with due process and legislation protecting consumers' rights. Comment, Banking Setoff: A Study in Commercial Obsolescence, 23 Hastings L.J. 1585. See also Olsen, The Appropriation of Deposits for Debt: Levies, Liens, and Setoffs, 90 Banking L.J. 827 (1973).

indebtedness, direct or indirect, absolute or contingent, due or to become due and howsoever evidenced, of depositor to bank."

The signature card, signed by the corporate officers of Ritzer in 1969, states that the "depositor acknowledges receipt of a copy of the rules and regulations . . . relative to commercial accounts and agrees to be bound thereby and by any amendments and additions thereto hereafter made." The bank's claim is, in effect, that it could at any time apply any part of the funds deposited in the commercial account to the payment of the 90-day promissory note, even before the note was due, and that the garnisheeing creditor stands in the shoes of the depositor.

The 90-day promissory note executed by Ritzer in favor of the bank contains no statement that it was made upon the security of the commercial account, and contains no provision for acceleration, other than for lack of performance by the debtor. The note was secured by a security agreement in machinery and equipment,[8] but no security agreement was made with respect to the commercial account.

If the language of the bank's rules and regulations is taken to mean that the bank could at any time apply the balance of the commercial account to the promissory note, those rules are in direct conflict with the contract embodied in that note. They would have the effect of converting a note payable at a definite time to one payable on demand. In this case, the later, specific terms of the promissory note control over the general language of the rules. The primary intent of the parties in executing the 90-day note was that it become due in 90 days, not upon demand, and to the extent that the earlier, general language of the rules conflicts with that intent, it must be taken to have been superseded. See 3 Corbin on Contracts, 172 n.178, Section 547; 4 Williston on Contracts (3d ed.), 816, 822, Section 624.

". . . [I]n the construction of any written instrument the primary duty of the court is to determine and give effect to the intention of the parties." United States Fire Ins. Co. v. PhilMar Corporation (1965), 166 Ohio St. 85, 87, 139 N.E.2d 330, 332.

The contract embodied in the promissory note was that the debt would become due and payable in 90 days, and the bank had no

---

8. That agreement defines "liabilities" in almost the exact terms of the rules and regulations, to include "indebtedness . . . due or to become due. . . ." It is clear that under a security agreement the rights of a secured party to enforce his security interest do not accrue until after default by the debtor. UCC §9-501.

contractual right to treat the note as a demand note and set off the commercial account against the debt before maturity.

For the foregoing reasons, the judgment of the Court of Appeals is affirmed.

Judgment affirmed.

_____

Bankruptcy and Setoff. According to §362(a)(7) of the Bankruptcy Code, the filing of a petition in bankruptcy creates an automatic stay against creditor collection activity, specifically including the exercise of the right of setoff. Individuals injured by a violation of the automatic stay may sue under §362(h) of the Bankruptcy Code and recover "actual damages, including costs and attorney fees, and, in appropriate circumstances, may recover punitive damages." Of course, the bank may apply to the bankruptcy court for relief from the stay, §362(d), and on getting it may exercise the right of setoff; see §553. In 1995 the United States Supreme Court granted some relief to banks by ruling that an *administrative freeze* on a checking account is *not* the same as a setoff and does not violate the automatic stay; Citizens Bank of Maryland v. Strumpf, 516 U.S. 16 (1995). This means that a bank could freeze the account on learning of a bankruptcy, not allowing the customer to reach the funds involved, but not taking the money for itself either, thus preserving the status quo while the bankruptcy court is asked to straighten out what is to become of the monies in the account.

E. Customer's Right to Stop Payment

1. Ordinary Checks

The key section on the right to stop payment is §4-403, which you should read. Official Comment 1 states:

> The position taken by this section is that stopping payment or closing an account is a service which depositors expect and are entitled to receive from banks notwithstanding its difficulty, inconvenience and expense. The inevitable occasional losses through failure to stop or close should be borne by the banks as a cost of the business of banking.

Parr v. Security National Bank

Oklahoma Court of Appeals, 1984
680 P.2d 648, 38 U.C.C. Rep. Serv. 275

REYNOLDS, J. We are called upon to decide whether Security National Bank had a reasonable opportunity to stop payment on a check when the description received is exact in all respects except for a single digit error in the check amount. This issue has not been decided by an Oklahoma court.

Parr wrote check number 949 to Champlin Oil. She dated and mailed it September 14, 1981. The amount of the check was $972.96. On September 15, 1981, Parr ordered payment stopped by telephone. Parr gave the bank her account number, the check number, the date, the payee and the amount of the check. A 50-cent error was made in identifying the amount of the check. Parr went to the bank on September 16th or 17th and executed a written stop order dated September 15, 1981. The written stop order was also in error. Security National paid check number 949 on September 17, 1981.

Parr brought suit against Security National seeking recovery for the amount of the check, 12-percent interest on that amount, reasonable attorney's fees and costs. Security National defended by showing their computers were programmed to stop payment only if the reported amount of the check were correct. They argued Parr's 50-cent error relieved them of liability. Timeliness of notice was not an issue.

[The court then quoted §4-403(1) and the Official Comment 1 paragraph reprinted prior to the case—Ed.]

Security National contends that whether a stop payment order has been received "in such manner as to afford the bank a reasonable opportunity to act" should be determined *after* examining how the defendant bank handles stop orders. This interpretation has found favor among highly respected legal authorities, but not among the majority of courts that have addressed this issue.

Both groups acknowledge §4-403(1) has not changed the common law rule that a stop payment order must identify the check with "reasonable accuracy." It is from this premise that courts have determined whether the description is reasonably accurate without consideration of the defendant/bank's computer program. In Elsie Rodriguez Fashions, Inc. v. Chase Manhattan Bank, 23 U.C.C. Rep. 133 (N.Y. Sup. Ct. 1978), the customer gave the bank the correct payee, check number and date but made a 10-cent error in the amount of the check. The court determined the check had been described with sufficient accuracy to allow the bank to stop payment. The opinion makes no mention of the bank's computer program. In accord with this approach on similar facts are the New York cases of Pokras v. National Bank of North America, 30 U.C.C. Rep. 1089 (N.Y. App. Term 1981), and Thomas v. Marine Midland Tinkers National Bank, 86 Misc. 2d 284, 381 N.Y.S.2d 797 (N.Y. Civ. Ct. 1976). A different result was reached by a New York court where the customer was told by the bank the stop order would not be effective unless she provided the exact amount of the check. Poullier v. Nacua Motors, Inc., 108 Misc. 2d 913, 439 N.Y.S.2d 85 (N.Y. Sup. Ct. 1981). Security National does not contend they gave notice to Parr that any discrepancy in the check amount would prevent compliance with her stop payment order.

In Delano v. Putnam Trust Co., 33 U.C.C. Rep. 635 (Conn. Super. Ct. 1981), a single-digit error in the amount of $100.00 did not prevent recovery where customer supplied bank with the correct check number, date, payee, and account number of the check. The bank's computer program required an exact match of check amount before it would stop payment. Court held bank had received sufficient information to allow it a "reasonable opportunity to act" on the stop payment order. Court stated the bank had a duty to inform its customer of the need for precision in reporting the amount before it could rely on customer's error to relieve it of liability.

The Supreme Court of Alabama denied customer's recovery in Sherrill v. Frank Morris Pontiac-Buick-GMC, Inc., 366 So. 2d 251 (Ala. 1979). Customer gave bank three descriptive elements of the check, check amount, payee and date. The check was not numbered. Two of the three pieces of information were incorrect. Court determined the check was not described with reasonable accuracy, therefore the bank was not afforded a "reasonable opportunity to act" on the stop payment order.

In FJS Electronics, Inc. v. Fidelity Bank, 431 A.2d 326 (Pa. Super. Ct. 1981), court allowed customer to prevail even though its 50-cent error in check amount prevented bank's computer from acting on stop payment order. The bank asserted §4-403 "should be read to require compliance with the procedures of a particular bank, regardless of what they are and regardless of whether the customer has been made aware of them." Id. at 328. Court determined that the drafter's policy stated in Comment 2 to §4-403 precluded such an interpretation. They reasoned:

> Fidelity made a choice when it elected to employ a technique which searched for stopped checks by amount alone. It evidently found benefits to this technique which outweighed the risk that an item might

be inaccurately described in a stop order. This is precisely the type of inevitable loss which was contemplated by the code drafters and addressed by the comment quoted above. The focus of §4-403 is the service which may be expected by the customer, and a customer may expect a check to be stopped after the bank is given reasonable notice. A bank's decision to reduce operating costs by using a system which increases the risk that checks as to which there is an outstanding stop payment order will be paid invites liability when such items are paid.

We find this analysis, as well as that in *Delano*, supra, persuasive. We hold Parr described her check with reasonable accuracy, and Security National had a reasonable opportunity to act on the stop payment order.

We are aware of the burden this may place on Oklahoma banks. However, the industry has two alternatives to avoid liability if banking procedures necessitate an exact description of an item: (1) notify the customer at the time a stop order is given, or (2) seek a legislative amendment to §4-403.

We recognize Parr received the benefit of having her debt paid to Champlin Oil and will recover from Security National for failure to stop payment. To avoid this possibility of unjust enrichment, §4-407(b) subrogates the payor bank [Security National] to the rights of the payee [Champlin] against the maker [Parr]. In such a suit, an award of attorney's fees and costs to Security National would be proper under 12 O.S. 1981 §936, as Champlin would have been suing Parr on an open account if Security National had stopped payment on the check.

Trial court is reversed and this cause remanded for award of $972.96 plus reasonable attorney's fees and costs consistent with this opinion.

Reversed and remanded.

PROBLEM 157

Julio Perez, newly arrived in New York from Puerto Rico, was tricked into buying a $50 refrigerator for $280. He paid the seller, Honest Juan, by check and took the appliance home in his truck. His brother saw the refrigerator, told Julio that he had been had, and advised him to call the bank to stop payment on the check. Julio phoned his bank and said, "This is Julio Perez. You must stop—do not give Honest Juan money for my check." The bank clerk who took the call asked, "Which check?" Julio replied, "Today—refrigerator check" and hung up. The bank failed to stop payment on the check, and the next day it was presented by Honest Juan and paid. Julio demanded that the money be replaced in his account, and when the bank refused, Julio retained Juanita Martinez, a lawyer, who filed suit on his behalf, contending that the check was not "properly payable" per §4-401. The complaint set out only the facts of the stop-payment order and the payment in spite of it. As a judge, how would you rule on each of the following issues raised by the bank?

(a) The stop-payment order did not give enough information to be effective. See §4-403(a); Sherrill v. Frank Morris Pontiac-Buick-GMC, Inc., 366 So. 2d 251, 25 U.C.C. Rep. Serv. 757 (Ala. 1978); White & Summers §18-5; Annot., 35 A.L.R.4th 985; Annot., 29 A.L.R.4th 228. Official Comment 5 to §4-403 says that in "describing the item, the customer, in the absence of a contrary agreement, must meet the standard of what information allows the bank under the technology then existing to identify the item with reasonable certainty."

(b) The contract of deposit that Julio initially signed stated: "Customer agrees that no oral stop-payment order shall be effective; stop-payment orders must be in writing to be effective." The bank argues that fully one-half of its customers are Spanish-speaking Americans and that oral stop-payment orders are a nightmare to try to decode. See §4-103(a); White & Summers §18-2.

(c) The contract of deposit also contained this clause: "Customer agrees that the bank shall not be liable if it mistakenly pays an item on which payment has been stopped." See Official Comment 7 to §4-403.

(d) The bank's rules require that a stop-payment order be accompanied by a $15 stop-payment fee, and Julio failed to tender such a fee. See Official Comment 1 to §4-403. Compare Opinion of Attorney General, 30 U.C.C. Rep. Serv. 1626 (Mich. 1981), with Opinion of Attorney General, 33 U.C.C. Rep. Serv. 1445 (Mich. 1981).

(e) Plaintiff's complaint is defective in that it fails to allege any loss to plaintiff as a result of the bank's alleged wrongful payment, and plaintiff carries this burden under §4-403(c). For all the bank knows, plaintiff has revoked his acceptance of the refrigerator and avoided the sale on grounds of unconscionability. See Cicci v. Lincoln Natl. Bank & Trust Co., 46 Misc. 2d 465, 260 N.Y.S.2d 100, 2 U.C.C. Rep. Serv. 1093 (City Ct. 1965) (which found this argument persuasive); contra Thomas v. Marine Midland Tinkers Natl. Bank, 86 Misc. 2d 284, 381 N.Y.S.2d 797, 18 U.C.C. Rep. Serv. 1272 (Sup. Ct. 1976); see White & Summers §18-6.

If the bank accidentally pays over the stop-payment order and re-credits the account, it can use another important section of the Code,

§4-407 (the Subrogation Rule), to step into the shoes of its customer
and sue any party he or she could have sued (Honest Juan, in the
above Problem). Read §4-407(3) carefully. This principle of subrogation can also help the bank out in the following situations.

PROBLEM 158

After he had purchased a new car from Flash Motors, Thomas
Crandall got the car home and discovered that it clashed with the color
of his garage. He couldn't stand this, of course, so he phoned his bank,
Octopus National, and placed an oral stop-payment order on the
check he had written for the car. Negligently, the bank paid the check
anyway. Must the bank recredit the account? See §4-407(2).

Canty v. Vermont National Bank

Vermont Superior Court, 1994
25 U.C.C. Rep. Serv. 2d 1184

KATZ, J. Plaintiff Joseph Canty had a checking acount with
Vermont National Bank and a problem with the Internal Revenue
Service. When the Internal Revenue asked him for canceled checks to
document his payment of certain obligations, he forwarded the checks.
The Internal Revenue redeposited those canceled checks, and Vermont National Bank paid them a second time, withdrawing the funds
from plaintiff's account. Not surprisingly, plaintiff took the position
that he should pay each check once, but not twice. He therefore sues,
and now seeks summary judgment, asserting the Bank must recredit his
account for the funds improperly withdrawn to make the second
payments.

In the words of the Uniform Commercial Code, the payor bank
has "paid an item under circumstances giving a basis for objection by
the drawer or maker." 9A V.S.A. Sec. 4-407. It is fairly implicit in U.C.C.
Sec. 4-401(1) that if an item is not properly payable, the bank may not
charge the customer's account, and if it has done so, it must recredit
the account. Siegel v. New England Merchants Nat. Bank, 386 Mass.
672, 437 N.E.2d 218, 221 (1982); J. White and R. Summers, Uniform
Commercial Code Sec. 17-3 at 657 (2d ed. 1980). Although recrediting
may constitute the usually required response, the law does permit a
bank to refuse to recredit its customer's account after wrongful pay-

ment of an item by subrogating itself to the rights of the presenter of
the improperly paid instrument. Id., at 660. . . .

Although a drawer bank can improperly pay on an item in several
ways, its right to subrogation is inextricably entwined with its liability to
its customer for improper payment. White and Summers, at 683. The
customer's realization of his claim may produce unjust enrichment.
Even when an item is not properly payable, for any of several reasons,
the bank's payment may discharge a legal obligation of the customer,
or create a right in the customer's favor against the payee. Siegel v.
New England Merchants, 437 N.E.2d at 221. If the customer were
permitted to retain such benefits, and recover the amount of the check
as well, he would profit at the bank's expense. Id. Although plaintiff
here argues that there can be no subrogation until his account is first
recredited, that appears contrary to the provisions of §4-407, which
permit a bank to be subrogated to the rights of a payee, against the
drawer or maker—its own customer. Manufacturer's Hanover Trust
Co. v. Ava Industries, Inc., 414 N.Y.S.2d 425 (Sup. Ct. 1978) (Bank may
pursue its own customer upon both subrogation and possible unjust
enrichment; 4-407, comments 2 and 3). Siegel v. New England
Merchants points out that the subrogation rights of 4-407 refer to those
existing prior to the bank's wrongful payment of the item. 437 N.E.2d
221, n.5. Indeed, a bank may invoke subrogation under 4-407 in spite
of a settlement agreement between its customer (the drawer) and
payee. Swiss Credit Bank v. Balink, 614 F.2d 1269, 28 U.C.C. Rep. 479
(10th Cir. 1980). The bank may assert its subrogation rights de-
fensively, when its depositor brings an action for wrongful debit. Siegel,
437 N.E.2d at 222; Chute v. Bank One of Akron, N.A., 460 N.E.2d 720,
38 U.C.C. Rep. 949 (Ohio App. 1983).

On the theory that one form of improper payment is functionally
no different than another, the *Siegel* court analogizes the customer's
right to be recredited to that existing for payment in the face of a
proper stop order, which is governed by 4-403. The issue of injust
enrichment is common to both. The rule of 4-403(3) is that a depositor
bears the burden of proving the fact and amount of any loss.
Kupersmith v. Manufacturer's Hanover Trust Co., 15 U.C.C. Rep. 696
(N.Y. Civ. Ct. 1974). Section 4-403(3) simply protects the bank against
the need to prove events familiar to the depositor, *Siegel*, 437 N.E.2d
222, in this case his account status with the Internal Revenue.

Clearly there is a difference between a check which has never
been paid and one which has already been paid. In the first instance,
the drawer has indicated an intent to pay the payee a stated sum,
presumably a voluntary and justified decision. In the second, the

drawer has already made payment, and thereby satisfied his debt to the amount paid. But among payees, the Internal Revenue must be considered sui generis. One's account with the Internal Revenue is never closed. Even death does not bring immediate finality. Plaintiff argues that he "did not owe any liability to the I.R.S. *for the tax quarters to which his [ill-fated] checks related.*" (Emphasis altered.) But the scope of inquiry, in application of the equitable doctrine of subrogation, is not limited to some particular payment and its due date. Rather, given the purpose of avoiding unjust enrichment, the inquiry must be whether plaintiff depositor actually suffered any loss by the admittedly improper payment. If he did not, he may not recover, for to do so would be to enrich him twice, once on his Internal Revenue account and once on his satisfied judgment.

The purpose of most presumptions is to aid trial by shifting the burden of going forward to the party who has the best access to the facts, or who has the notably less probable side of a common question. Reporter's Notes, Rule 301, V.R. Ev. Lang v. Chase Manhattan Bank, 6 U.C.C. Rep. 1259 (N.Y. App. Div. 1969), reversed a grant of summary judgment against the bank, which was deemed not absolutely liable to its customer for paying in the face of a stop payment order, when the issue of actual loss to the customer "turns upon evidence peculiarly within the knowledge of" the customer and her auto dealer. In this unfortunate situation, plaintiff customer has both the best access to the facts of his accounts with the I.R.S. and has the less probable side of the question, namely that a neutral government agency took his money without giving him any credit for it.

Given the difficulty of the bank securing information from the Internal Revenue about the account of another, the presumed regularity of its proceedings, 1 J. Weinstein and M. Berger Weinstein's Evidence, Par. 301[03] at 301-53 (1994), citing, inter alia, Welch v. Helvering, 290 U.S. 111, 115 (1933), and the fact that we all continue to accrue liability with the Internal Revenue, we conclude that the proper disposition of this most unusual case must require plaintiff actually to prove his loss.

Saratoga Polo Assn., Ltd. v. Adirondack Trust Co., 460 N.Y.S.2d 712, 36 U.C.C. Rep. 251 (Sup. Ct. 1983), and Mitchell v. Republic Bank & Trust Co., 239 S.E.2d 867 (N.C. App. 1978), hold that a customer initially establishes a prima facie case by showing that an item was improperly paid. Thereupon the bank, exercising its subrogation rights under 4-407, has the burden of coming forward and presenting evidence of an absence of actual loss to the customer. When the bank meets the burden of coming forward with such evidence, the customer must then sustain the ultimate burden of proof. We hold that when the improperly paid item was paid to the Internal Revenue Service, we will presume an absence of actual loss to the customer; the bank has therefore met its burden of coming forward with such evidence.

We reject plaintiff's contention that the Bank must first recredit his account, before earning any right to subrogation. Such a rule would tend to see the funds disappear while the case was ongoing. While presumably not so in this case, many of this class of cases—improperly paid checks—arise out of fraud. Requiring subrogated banks to first recredit the funds would tend to put those funds back into the hands of the miscreant, at a time when the court is still in a difficult position to know whether fraud has been practiced in the particular case at hand. Requiring recrediting as a threshold to subrogation would always arise as an interlocutory order, as there is no final judgment until all claims have been resolved. Rule 54, V.R.C.P. The effect would therefore be that the bank would have no appeal, and that the mere filing of a complaint would require the defendant to grant plaintiff the money he seeks, as a price for even litigating an affirmative defense to such recrediting. Requiring threshold recrediting of funds is not supported by Siegel v. New England Merchants. Moreover, a bank's 4-407 right of subrogation has been elevated above any duty to adjust its customer's account, Sunshine v. Bankers Trust Co., 34 N.Y.2d 404, 314 N.E.2d 860, 866 (N.Y. 1974), which threshold duty the New York Court of Appeals labeled a "technical mechanical requirement of common-law subrogation." As the right of subrogation has "particular approval" under our law, Lopez v. Concord Genl. Mut. Ins. Group, 155 Vt. 320, 324, 583 A.2d 602 (1990), we conclude that its value should not be diluted by requiring banks to first recredit accounts in order to gain the benefits of this venerable doctrine of equity. This is in accord with the U.C.C's intent that 4-407 was intended to provide a broad, liberal remedy that incorporated and is based upon the common law equitable principles of unjust enrichment and restitution. Swiss Credit Bank v. Balink, 28 U.C.C. Rep. at 482.

We therefore deny plaintiff's motion for summary judgment. Partial summary judgment is accorded to defendant Vermont National Bank; unless plaintiff can show actual loss by the improper second payment of his canceled checks, his claims shall be dismissed. We shall allow plaintiff 60 days to marshall his evidence regarding actual loss, and then expect either a joint status report to the clerk, a request for a pretrial conference, or a further motion for summary judgment, depending on the proof available to plaintiff.

We also grant defendant's motion to dismiss the punitive damage claims. First, we find considerable merit in the defenses raised by the bank. Second, to accept plaintiff's argument would be to telescope into one case both the merits of that case and the "malicious defense" claim inherent in the punitive damage theory. In malicious prosecution, Vermont law has always required a successful outcome in the underlying litigation before supporting punitive damages for the tort of wrongful litigation. Anello v. Vinci, 142 Vt. 583, 587, 458 A.2d 1117 (1983).

PROBLEM 159

Rupert Signer gave his fiancee, Maggie Lee, a check for $1,000 as a birthday gift. She took the check, thanked him politely, and then told him that she was getting ready to marry his best friend Charlie and "this is good-bye." Rupert left in a huff and went straight to his bank, the Careless State Bank, where he filled out a written stop-payment order on the check he had given to Maggie Lee. In the meantime, Maggie Lee indorsed the check over to Computer City in payment for a $1,000 software package she purchased there. When Computer City presented the check to Careless State Bank for payment, the bank paid it without a murmur. Rupert sued when the bank refused to recredit his account, alleging a $1,000 loss because he had tried to revoke a gift promise on which the bank now made him liable. Are either of these defenses by the bank good?

(a) Computer City was a holder in due course of Rupert's check, and he could not have refused to pay Computer City if it had presented the check to him. See Official Comment 7 to §4-403. Under §4-407, the bank is subrogated to the rights of any holder in due course of the check. Does this help the bank? See Official Comment 1 to §4-407.

(b) Same argument that Computer City was a holder in due course and that Rupert would eventually have had to pay Computer City if the bank had been able to remember to stop payment. This being true, Rupert has really suffered no loss by the wrongful payment, so he cannot recover. Cf. §4-403(c); see Seigel v. Merrill Lynch, Pierce, Fenner & Smith, Inc., 745 A.2d 301, 40 U.C.C. Rep. Serv. 2d 819 (D.C. App. 2000).

PROBLEM 160

Same fact situation, except that Maggie Lee takes the check and deposits it in her checking account with Octopus National Bank. The balance in the checking account prior to the deposit was $.07. Later that same day, Maggie wrote a check for $1,000.07 and cashed it at her bank, thereby withdrawing all the money from her account. Octopus National Bank sent the check to the payor bank, Careless State Bank, which negligently paid the check over the stop-payment order. Can Careless State still use the above two defenses when Rupert sues? See §§4-211, 4-210(a); Universal C.I.T. Credit Corp. v. Guaranty Bank & Trust Co., 161 F. Supp. 790, 1 U.C.C. Rep. Serv. 305 (D. Mass. 1958).

2. Cashiers, Tellers, and Certified Checks

At common law and under prior statutes there was much confusion surrounding the question of whether a customer could stop payment on a check that had been certified. The Code now makes it clear that the answer is "No." A customer has no right to stop payment on a certified check. See Official Comment 4 to §4-403. The reason is that once the check is certified, the payor bank itself is the primary obligor on the instrument, §3-413(a), and the drawer has no right to require the bank to breach its acceptor's contract.[9] The same thing is true of a cashier's check (a check on which the bank is both drawer and drawee) and of a bank check (a check drawn by one bank on another, also called a *teller's check*); see §3-104(g) and (h).[10]

PROBLEM 161

Harry Flashman agreed to sell his sports car to Tom Brown if the latter paid with a cashier's check (see §3-104(g)) for $15,000, issued by Fraser National Bank. Tom purchased such a cashier's check from the bank; it was payable to the order of Harry Flashman (in such a situation, a person in Tom's position is called a *remitter*; §3-103(a)(11)). After Tom handed the check over to Harry, the latter told him that the

9. The so-called Four Legals section, §4-303(a)(1), discussed later in this chapter, states that a customer loses his or her right to stop payment once the bank accepts or certifies an item. In actuality, when a check is certified by the drawee, an amount of money sufficient to pay the check when it is presented is taken from the account and held pending the second presentment; in this way the drawee bank protects itself as it undertakes the primary liability of an acceptor (§3-413).

10. Remember that the giving of an instrument on which a bank is primarily liable is an absolute payment of the underlying obligation and discharges the underlying obligor unless he or she is liable on the instrument. See §3-310(a).

car was parked at an address Harry gave him. Tom went to the address and found it was an automobile dump. The sports car had been wrecked and was worthless. He phoned Fraser National Bank and demanded that the bank not pay the check. Should the bank do this? See §3-411 and its Official Comment; see also §3-305(c). What can Tom do if the bank refuses to help him? See §3-202 and Official Comment 2 to §3-201.

In 1991, the drafters of the Uniform Commercial Code proposed an addition to Article 3 that not all states having the revised version of that Article have adopted; it is §3-312. It provides an elegant solution to the problem of stopping payment on lost, destroyed, or stolen cashier's checks, teller's checks, or certified checks. In this procedure, the person who lost possession files with the issuing bank a *declaration of loss*, and for 90 days after the date of the check the issuing bank must pay it if it is presented by a person entitled to enforce it, but after the 90-day period has passed, the issuing bank should pay the amount of the check to the person filing the declaration of loss.

PROBLEM 162

Portia Moot agreed to buy a car from her uncle who lived in another state, but the uncle demanded a cashier's check in payment. Portia obtained such a check for the correct amount from Octopus National Bank (which took a corresponding amount from her bank account), making the check payable to the order of Portia Moot. Portia signed her name to the back of the check and mailed it to her uncle. The uncle denied receiving the check (a lie), and Portia went down to Octopus National and filled out a declaration of loss on March 1. Having heard nothing during the next 90 days, on June 1, the bank refunded the money to Portia. Meantime, the uncle cashed the check at his local bank on May 25th. Assume that the local bank qualifies as a holder in due course. What should ONB do when the local bank presents the check on June 2 and demands payment? See §3-312(b)(2) and Official Comment 3 (second paragraph). If ONB won't pay, what should the local bank do? See §§3-312(c); 3-415.

Losing a negotiable instrument of whatever kind is always unfortunate. Section 3-309 provides a mechanism whereby the true owner of the check can go to court and, in effect, judicially re-create it, having to post bond or give other adequate protection for the entity that will then pay the instrument. In states adopting §3-312, explored above, the two procedures are alternative possibilities; see §3-312(d) and Official Comment 1 to §3-312.

F. Bank Statements

The original version of §4-406, the Bank Statement Rule, presumed that banks were always returning canceled checks with the monthly bank statement, and this presumption proved awkward once banks moved to automation. As the next part of this chapter discusses, banks have instituted a range of measures to speed up check collection, including *check truncation* systems, in which the check itself is photographed shortly after deposit and then destroyed. In place of the check, an electronic signal describing it is forwarded through the system to the payor bank. Since the payor bank never receives the check, it can hardly return it to the customer along with the bank statement, as the original §4-406 arguably required.

Subsection (a) of the new version requires only that the bank return "sufficient information" about the check in the bank statement but does not mandate return of the check. *Sufficient information* is then defined in §4-406(a)'s last sentence as "item number, amount, and date of payment" (these being things either in the payor bank's records or magnetically encoded on the check and hence readable by computers and check processing equipment). Official Comment 1 opines that with this much information customers (at least those with accurate records) will have enough to be able to locate the check in their records and figure out the missing matters (payee, date, etc.). Of course, nothing forbids the bank from returning the check itself if available, but the three terms required by (a) — item number, amount, and date of payment—provide what Official Comment 1 calls a "safe harbor rule," the absolute minimum the bank can provide and escape liability. Under (b) for seven years the payor bank must be able to furnish its customer with either the check itself or a legible copy thereof.

PROBLEM 163

When she got the ominous letter from the IRS telling her that she was scheduled for an audit, Portia Moot phoned her bank and told the employee with whom she spoke that she needed copies of the 172 checks she had written during the last calendar year. The bank employee replied that the bank would gladly furnish her with these copies but that the charge was $25.00 per copy. Can they do this to her? See Official Comment 3 to §4-406. How quickly must the bank come up with the copies? See §4-406(b). What is Portia's remedy if the bank neglects to produce the promised copies?

After the customer gets the bank statement, the law imposes a duty of examination for unauthorized signatures or alterations and requires prompt reporting of these matters. If the customer does not receive the actual check or a photo thereof but instead is furnished only the information required by the safe harbor rule, how can the customer discover forgeries or alterations? There is no discussion of this in the Comments, but §4-406(c) imposes a customer reporting duty only if "the customer should reasonably have discovered the unauthorized payment."

PROBLEM 164

When Joe Armstrong opened a checking account with Last National Bank, he signed an account agreement authorizing the bank to destroy the checks and return to him only a list of checks paid from the account identified only by check number, amount, and date of payment. The first time he received a statement it reflected the following:

Check Number	Date Paid	Amount
101	6-1-09	$132.45
102	6-1-09	$84.00
103	6-2-09	$1,204.00
104	6-3-09	$50.00
105	6-4-09	$2,000.00

Two things bothered Joe about this: (1) his records show that check 103 was written for $204.00 only, and (2) he has written no more than four checks on this account since he opened it. Looking in his checkbook, he discovered that check 105 was missing. Does §4-406(c) require Joe to report all this to his bank? yes

The rest of §4-406 is so related to the forgery and alteration rules addressed in the next chapter that further discussion of the Bank Statement Rule awaits you there.

II.   BANK COLLECTION

The transfer of an item (*check*) from the depositary bank to the payor bank and the remittance of the proceeds inevitably lead to legal difficulties. To facilitate the handling of the huge number of checks passed around each year, there exists a sophisticated network of banks, federal agencies, and local clearinghouses that generally make up the bank collection system. In addition to Article 4's statutory regulation, the system is governed by a federal statute on point, plus Federal Reserve regulations and clearinghouse contractual agreements, all of which are permitted to vary the rules of Article 4. See §4-103(b).

For decades the law on this subject was contained in two enactments: Article 4 of the Uniform Commercial Code and the Federal Reserve Board Regulation J on Collection of Checks and Other Items and Wire Transfer of Funds by Federal Reserve Banks, 12 C.F.R. Part 210 (which applies only if the check clears through the Federal Reserve System). But, effective September 1, 1988, a federal statute— the Expedited Funds Availability Act, 12 U.S.C. §§4001-4010, 248a [hereinafter EFAA]—superseded many of the UCC rules and resulted in an amendment to Regulation J as well. The federal statute is also supplemented by a Federal Reserve Board regulation having the force of law, Regulation CC, 12 C.F.R. 229, which will also be explained in the materials that follow (indeed, any reference to a section beginning with the numerals "229" is a reference to Regulation CC). Regulation CC is elaborated on in an official Federal Reserve Board Commentary, which is contained in Appendix E to the Regulation itself; the Commentary also has the force of law. Regulation CC should be in your statute book, likely identified as "Availability of Funds and Collection of Checks."

Thus a lawyer wanting to understand the rules of check collection must compare the rules of the EFAA (which is almost impenetrable— it reads as if it were badly translated from the German), Regulation CC (which, being drafted by the Federal Reserve, is much more readable, if soporific), and the Official Commentary in Appendix E to the regulation (which is very user-friendly, with very helpful examples included).

The EFAA and Regulation CC do not completely do away with the Uniform Commercial Code rules on check collection, which still apply in any situation not covered by federal rules, and, of course, those rules were written with the UCC as a backdrop. So we begin our coverage of check collection with the Uniform Commercial Code and then look at the variations worked thereon by the EFAA and Regulation CC.

A. Funds Availability

It is important to appreciate that the rules that follow, both state and federal, set outside time limits on the period that banks can hold deposited funds, but they do not prohibit the depositary bank from allowing the customer *earlier* access to those funds, should the bank so decide. Earlier access is a business decision. The discussion below looks at the question of when as a *matter of legal right* the customer is entitled to the funds.

We begin with the issue of how quickly the depositor can get back money from the bank in which items are deposited. It is easiest to understand the whole process if approached from a personal point of view. So—presuming that you have had some experience with a checking account—let's use the Code to answer the basic questions.

1. Cash

If you deposit cash in your account, how quickly can you take it out again? Answer: on the next banking day. See §4-215(f).[11] The "subject to any right of the bank" language in §4-215(f) refers to the bank's right of setoff.

Banking day is defined in §4-104(a)(3) as that part of the day when the bank is "open to the public for carrying on substantially all of its banking functions."[12] As to this, see §4-108, which further refines *banking day* so as to permit a bank to establish a cutoff hour in the early afternoon and to pretend that items received after that hour were received on the next banking day. Thus, if that bank's banking day ends at 2:30 P.M., a check received at 2:31 P.M. on Friday is treated as if it were received early Monday morning (assuming neither is a holiday and the bank is not open on Saturday and Sunday). The purpose of such a rule is stated in §4-108(a).[13]

11. Section 603(a)(1) of the EFAA has the same requirement. The Federal Reserve Board has stated that UCC §4-215(f) is *not* preempted by the adoption of Regulation CC. 53 Fed. Reg. 32,354 (Aug. 24, 1988).

12. If a bank has a teller window open on Saturday, is this a banking day? Probably not, since the bank is not open for carrying on "substantially all of its banking functions," the statutory test. See Merrill Lynch, Pierce, Fenner & Smith, Inc. v. Devon Bank, 832 F.2d 1005, 8 U.C.C. Rep. Serv. 2d 79 (7th Cir. 1987) (where main lobby closed, Saturday not a banking day).

13. The same rule for a cutoff hour is found in Regulation CC, except that for automated teller machines (ATMs) a bank may establish 12:00 noon as the cutoff hour for the receipt of deposits (§229.19(a)). However, Regulation CC draws a distinction not in the UCC between "business day," meaning days other than Saturdays, Sundays,

2. Checks

a. Across-the-Counter Presentments. If someone gives you a check and you (the payee) walk into the drawee bank and present it across the counter, how quickly must the bank pay or dishonor it? Answer: before the close of business. When an over-the-counter presentment for payment is made, §3-502(b)(2) requires the bank to make a decision that same day.

b. "On Us" Items. If someone gives you a check and you deposit it in your own account, how quickly may you take it out? Answer: as soon as your bank will let you, though, as discussed below, for certain kinds of checks federal law regulates this issue. If the amount is not great and you are a good customer, your bank may permit you to write checks on the deposited amount immediately, particularly if the drawer is well known and solvent (e.g., a large corporation). The real question is this: when do you have a legal *right* to draw checks on the deposited amount?

If, by coincidence, you (the payee) and the drawer each maintain an account at the same bank (that is, the depositary and payor banks are one and the same—the bankers call this an "On Us" item), §4-215(e)(2) permits you to remove the money at the opening of the *second banking day* following receipt of the item, unless, of course, in the meantime the check is dishonored, in which case you will be so notified (§§4-202(a)(2) and 3-503(c)). In this period of time, the bank, acting as the drawee-payor, will sort the check into a stack of "On Us" items and then examine the drawer's account and decide whether to pay the check.

The EFAA here makes its first major change. It speeds things up one day by requiring the depositary bank to make same-bank checks available for withdrawal on *the business day after the business day of deposit* (this is commonly referred to as "next day availability"). EFAA §603(a)(2)(E); Regulation CC §229.10(c)(1)(vi). For "On Us" items, the bank must now make its decision to pay or dishonor overnight.

---

and federal holidays, and "banking day," meaning business days on which a bank is open for carrying on substantially all of its banking functions. Saturday could never be a "banking day" for Regulation CC purposes under these definitions, though it might be a "banking day" under the UCC if the bank were open for business on Saturdays. 12 C.F.R. §229.2(f) and (g).

c. **"Transit" Items.** If the depositary bank and the payor (drawee) bank are *not* the same, then the check is a "transit" item and must go through some sort of multi-bank collection machinery. This can be as simple as exchanging checks with the bank across the street or as complicated as sending the check to the payor bank in Japan, so of course the rules are more complicated. As soon as your bank (the depositary bank) begins this process, it is called a *collecting bank.* During the process it acts as your agent (§4-201(a)).

PROBLEM 165

When his son was in Japan as an exchange student, Professor Chalk decided to give him a $1,000 check as a birthday present. He mailed the check to his son, who in turn mailed it, unindorsed, to his own bank back in the United States for deposit. This bank stamped its own indorsement on the back of the check in the spot where depositary banks are supposed to indorse and then forwarded the check for collection. Two things happened before the check was presented: (1) Professor Chalk and his son had a phone conversation that ended so angrily that Chalk stopped payment on the check, and (2) the depositary bank offset against all of the son's bank account to pay a debt the son owed it. When the check was returned to the depositary bank, it threatened to sue Chalk unless he made the check good; see §3-414(b). He responded that the bank did not take pursuant to a valid negotiation (no payee's signature) and was not a "person entitled to enforce the instrument"; see §3-301. In any event, Chalk added, he had a defense based on the fact that he received no consideration for his drawer's obligation. How does this come out? See §4-205 and its Official Comment.

If the depositary bank and the payor bank are in the same small town, they will typically arrange to exchange checks drawn on each other once each day. At the appointed time, they will present checks to one another in a bundle. Must the banks decide which checks to pay and which to dishonor before the close of the business day, as in §3-502 above? No, because Article 4 has a special rule for interbank collection presentments, and Article 4 overrides Article 3 where they conflict; §4-102(a).

The two banks will probably maintain accounts with each other and, by contract, will agree to permit the depositary bank to debit the account of the payor bank for the amount of the deposited check, subject to the right of the payor bank to dishonor the check later and have the account recredited. Such a contract results in a *provisional settlement* (*provisional* because the so-called settlement is subject to revocation). Thus, at the time the banks exchange the checks each day, they will have already debited each other's accounts with the amounts of the presented checks. If, after receiving the checks drawn on it, the payor bank decides to dishonor one or more, it simply returns the check, and the provisional settlement for that check is wiped out (technically, *charged back*).

Suppose that Mary Depositor deposits a check on which she is the payee in her bank, which we shall call Depositary Bank. Depositary Bank will mark her account with a *provisional settlement* for the amount of the item—in effect a bookkeeping entry reflecting the hope that the check will be paid by the payor/drawee bank. During the time that the check is traveling (called the "float period" by bankers), Depositary Bank may or may not allow Mary access to the money (more about that below), but even if it lets her withdraw it, if the check is later properly returned, she will have to repay any amounts provisionally withdrawn; §4-214 (Charge Back, also discussed in detail in this chapter).

The check collection system works through computers, so the check must be magnetically *encoded* so that all the computers it will pass through can read it. The little fractional number in the upper right-hand corner of the check is the routing symbol of the drawee bank. This routing symbol, along with the drawer's account number, is already encoded across the bottom of the check on the left-hand side. The amount of the check will be encoded on the bottom right-hand side.[14]

If Depositary Bank and the payor bank are located in the same large city, they will probably make the provisional settlements and check exchanges through a central *clearinghouse,* which can be loosely defined as an association of local banks that has drawn up regulations and procedures to effectuate the exchange of checks. Clearinghouse rules are allowed to change the rules of the Uniform Commercial Code, including all the deadlines discussed in this chapter. That means a lawyer for a bank that is a member of a clearinghouse would be well advised to read the clearinghouse rules, with thoughts of malpractice providing the incentive to wade through them carefully.

If Depositary Bank and the payor bank are not located close to one another, Depositary Bank will send the check to the first inter-

14. The Revision provides for a warranty of proper encoding; §4-209. The courts have had no problem finding liability for misencoding checks; see the cases cited in Official Comment 2 to §4-209.

mediary bank, typically a Federal Reserve Bank, established by the federal government. The United States is divided into 12 Federal Reserve districts, and in the center of each district sits a Federal Reserve Bank. These Superbanks have only banks as customers (a bank for banks) and permit member banks to open accounts therein and use the efficient cross-country check collection machinery operated by the Federal Reserve Banks. In return, member banks must observe Federal Reserve Board regulations. The Federal Reserve Banks each maintain accounts with one another, which they will debit or credit as they receive checks or payment (*remittances*) from member banks.

As the check passes from one bank to another, the presenting bank will give itself a provisional settlement for the amount of the check in the account it carries with the bank to which it forwards the check (the Federal Reserve Banks do this too). Each bank has two banking days in which to pass the item on to the next bank; §4-202(b). If the payor bank pays the check, all the provisional settlements (those bookkeeping entries) along the check collection route are said to "firm up," and now *final settlement* occurs. When this happens, Mary has a legal right to the money at her end.[15]

The Uniform Commercial Code reaches this result in a section that is difficult to read—§4-215(e). The beginning two small-case roman numerals refer, respectively, to (i) the superior command of federal law (i.e., the EFAA and Regulation CC), and (ii) the bank's own right of setoff. Subsection (2) discusses the rule for "On Us" items (see above), so subsection (1) is the relevant part that covers the transit item rules described in the last few paragraphs. Read it carefully, remembering that provisional settlements become final settlements when the payor bank pays the check at issue.

---

15. Under Regulation CC, as we shall see, checks may or may not be returned along the same route they took in forward collection. For this reason the Official Commentary to Regulation CC §229.36(d) states that the Regulation now eliminates the whole concept of "provisional" and "final" settlement in the check collection process, all settlements being final when made. Technically this may be true, but to my mind it is a misstatement of the actual result. First of all, as between the depositary bank and its customer, any crediting of the account remains provisional until the deposited check is finally paid; §4-214. Second, Regulation CC §229.35(b) and its Commentary provide that when the check is returned but the depositary bank fails to refund payment as required, liability flows back along the return route to the payor bank and from there back along the original collection route used for forward collection until liability rests with the first bank to take the check from the depositary bank. In practice, then, until the check is paid by either the payor bank or the depositary bank, any bookkeeping entries must of necessity be considered in some sense "provisional."

PROBLEM 166

You are chief counsel for Octopus National Bank. The bank officials tell you that the bank earns a lot of money off of the float period,
so it wants the float period to be as long as possible when it is
collecting checks. The officials have two questions. First, is it okay to
send the check on a circuitous route, much longer than is necessary, in
order to inflate the float? See §4-204. Second, if Mary Depositor
deposits a check on May 1 and the check is drawn on a bank in
another state, so that by the fastest collection route the check will pass
through two intermediary banks before getting to the payor bank, and
come back the same route if dishonored, on what date in May (or later,
if possible) must Depositary Bank allow Mary to withdraw the money?
You should know that under the *final payment* rules discussed below
the payor bank will also have two banking days to hold the check
while it is considering whether or not to pay it. See §4-215(e)(1).

d. The Federal Availability Rules.   Customers objected to holds
for long float periods, pointing out that of the 68 billion checks written
every year, 99 percent are honored on first presentment, and the most
of the rest on second presentment (or are made good by the depositor). Customers also highlighted the facts that the banks have the
use of the funds during the float period (because the bank has been
given a provisional credit during collection), and that the banks were
estimated to earn approximately $290 million each year from this
practice.

A number of states responded to this problem by passing statutes
regulating the hold on deposited funds or, at least, requiring clear disclosure of the bank's policies on the issue. New York, Illinois, California, and Massachusetts, for example, required immediate credit for
small checks and for those issued by the government or banks, and
specified the float periods for checks that travel various distances from
the depositary bank. In 1987, the federal government got into the act,
passing the EFAA and Regulation CC, and preempting the state laws
(except to the extent they are better for depositors than the federal
rules, see Appendix F to Reg. CC).

The federal rules in most cases completely displace §4-215(e)(1),
which you have just read, and have concrete answers to how long the
hold for the float period can be.

(i) Next Day Availability of Special Items.   The EFAA availability
rules are designed to strike a balance between the customer's need for

the funds and the risks of non-collection faced by the banks in which these funds are deposited. Congress decided that there should be *next banking day* availability[16] for items that are not likely to be dishonored, and the EFAA (§602)and Reg. CC (see §229.10) have a list of such items:

(1) Government checks: checks issued by any branch of government, federal, state, or local;

(2) Bank checks: checks on which a bank is primarily liable (cashier, teller, and certified checks); and

(3) Wire transfers: electronically sent payment orders of the sort covered by Article 4A of the Uniform Commercial Code, and covered by Chapter 13 of this book.

There is one more addition to this list: the *$100 Availability Rule,* Reg. CC §229.12(c)(vii). The rule is based on the idea that even for riskier checks we ought to allow the customer access to a small amount immediately. Thus federal law requires the bank to make the following computation: take the aggregate of the day's deposits, from that amount subtract items already requiring next day availability, and give the customer $100 of the amount remaining.

(ii) Availability of Ordinary Checks. To understand the federal availability rules for ordinary checks you need first to master the difference between "local" checks and "non-local" checks, as those terms are used in Regulation CC. In order to process checks, the Federal Reserve has drawn lines across the map of the United States to create 48 different check processing regions. Banks are said to be "local" to one another if they are physically located in the same Fed check processing region; if not, they are "non-local." For obvious reasons, the rules give the banks a longer float period for non-local checks than for local ones. The rules also vary depending on whether the depositor wants to take out *cash* or simply write *checks* against the deposited amounts, since checks by their very nature have a built-in float period for collection, but cash is cash and gone immediately.

The following rules, from Reg. CC §229.12, may have more interest for you if you remember that they govern how fast you are allowed to make withdrawals based on checks that you deposit in your own account that are drawn on other banks. You should remember however, that even if these rules require your bank to give you access to the deposited funds, if a check is properly returned after you have

16. If these items are deposited in an automated teller machine (ATM), the bank is given an extra day, and the items must be available for withdrawal on the *second* day after deposit; see Regulation CC §§229.10(a)(2) and 229.10(c)(2).

taken out the money, you will still be required to repay your own bank for the amount withdrawn, under the charge-back rules yet to be discussed.

First of all, the $100 availability rule allows you immediate access to the first $100 deposited in any one day, whether you want it in cash or by check.

Secondly, if the depositary bank and the payor bank are local to one another (both in the same Fed check processing region), the entire amount above $100 must be available for check writing purposes on the second banking day following the date of deposit. However, if the customer wants to take out cash, he or she can only get to $400 of the amount of the check on the second banking day (with the rest of the amount available for cash withdrawal on the day following).

Finally, the same rules apply for non-local checks, except that the period of availability is on the fifth banking day following the day of deposit, not the second.

For a graphic depiction of these rules, see the very helpful chart promulgated by the Federal Reserve as part of Reg. CC, which is reprinted on pages 544-545. To understand the chart, look in the upper right hand corner, which explains the geometric shapes. The circles indicate the amount of deposit, the triangles the amount available for check-writing purposes, and the rectangles the amount of cash that can be withdrawn. The dotted line through the middle of the chart separates the two transactions covered; in the top part the banks are *local* to one another, and below the line they are *non-local*. The footnotes at the bottom explain the rules described above.

Congress, ever alert, recognized that the early availability sched- ules described above could be misused by some bank customers, so it gave the banks a few escape valves:

(1) New Accounts. During the first 30 days of the existence of a new account, there must be next day availability for cash or wire deposits, for government checks, and for bank-generated checks (cashier's checks, etc.). If the government check or the bank-generated checks exceeds $5000, the depositary bank may put a hold on the amount that exceeds the $5000 for up to nine business days. There are no rules that describe the time period for the availability of local or nonlocal checks, so the usual UCC rules would apply—see UCC §4-215(e)(1). See EFAA §604(a) and Regulation CC §229.13(a). There is no require- ment of $100 next day availability for new accounts; Regulation CC §229.13(a)(iii).

(2) Large Checks. According to Regulation CC §229.13(b) and (h), only the first $5,000 of a day's deposit is subject to the normal availability rules. The excess may be held for an *additional reasonable period of time* (and five business days is presumed to be reasonable for local checks, six business days for nonlocal checks; for longer periods the bank must carry the burden of establishing the period is reasonable). Deposits by cash or electronic payment are not subject to this exception for large deposits.

(3) Redeposited Checks. The normal availability rules are extended by an extra reasonable period of time (with the same five/six business days presumption) in the case of redeposited checks, unless the announced reason for the return was a missing indorsement or because the check was post-dated, and these problems have been cleared up at the time of redeposit; Regulation CC §229.13(c) and (h).

(4) Repeated Overdrafts. The normal availability rules are extended by an extra reasonable period of time (with the same five/six business days presumption) for six months after the account or any combination of a customer's accounts has been repeatedly overdrawn. As to whether an account is considered to be repeatedly overdrawn, there is a two-prong test and if either prong is met, the bank may hold deposited checks for the extra period of time. Under these tests, the account is considered repeatedly overdrawn if the account balance is negative (or would have been negative if all checks or other charges to the account had been paid) on six or more banking days within the preceding six months, *or* if on two or more banking days within the preceding six months the account balance is negative (or would have been negative if all checks or other charges to the account had been paid) in the amount of $5000 or more. See Regulation CC §229.13(d) and (h).

(5) The "Reasonable Cause" Exception. Under EFAA §604(c), if the bank has "reasonable cause" to believe that a check is uncollectible, then it may ignore the usual rules if it gives the notice to the customer, described below, telling him or her when the funds will be made available. A bank has "reasonable cause," according to the statutory language, whenever there exist "facts which would cause a well-grounded belief in the mind of a reasonable person." Such reasons must be included in the notice. The Board has elected not to expand upon the statutory language, though the Commentary does give examples of proper use of the exception. These include the fact that

Permanent Funds Availability

Illustrates availability of different types of checks deposited the

MONDAY (Day 0)	TUESDAY (Day 1)	WEDNESDAY (Day 2)	THURSDAY (Day 3)	FRIDAY (Day 4)

1 The first $100 of a day's deposit must be made available for either cash withdrawal or check writing purposes at the start of the next business day, §229.10(c)(1)(vii).

2 Local checks must be made available for check writing purposes by the second business day following deposit, §229.12(b).

3 Nonlocal checks must be made available for check writing purposes by the fifth business day following deposit, §229.12(c).

Schedules

same day, under the permanent schedules.

MONDAY (Day 5)	TUESDAY (Day 6)	WEDNESDAY (Day 7)	THURSDAY (Day 8)
		◯ **Deposit** ☐ **Cash Withdrawals** △ **Check Writing**	
△ 3 $900 ↕ ☐ 4 $400	☐ 5 $500		

4    $400 of the deposit must be made available for cash withdrawal no later than 5:00 p.m. on the day specified in the schedule. This is in addition to the $100 that must be made available in the business day following deposit, §229.12(d).

5   The remainer of the deposit must be made available for cash withdrawal at the start of business the following day, §229.12(d).

bank has received a notice that the check is being returned, the fact that the check is stale (more than six months old when deposited), or that check kiting is suspected. If the bank is going to invoke this "reasonable cause" exception for cashier's, teller's, or certified checks or those drawn on a Federal Reserve Bank or those deposited at an ATM, it must use the usual time periods plus a later reasonable time (presumed to be five/six days, as above). See Regulation CC §229.13(e) and (h).

(6) Emergency Conditions. Regulation CC §229.13(f) has a rule modeled on UCC §4-109 (described at the end of this chapter in the section called "Delays") that excuses compliance with the normal availability rules due to emergencies beyond the bank's control.

(7) The Notice. Except in the "new accounts" situation, where a bank plans to take advantage of either the "large check," "redeposited check," "repeated overdrafts," or "reasonable cause" exceptions, the depositor must be notified as soon as possible of the date the funds will be made available. Appendix C to the Regulation contains model forms, including a model form of Notice of Exception to the usual availability rules. Since reliance on this form insulates the bank from any civil liability, its use is the better part of wisdom. The Federal Reserve is very insistent that banks follow whatever availability policy they disclose and not deviate from it unless the right to do so has also been disclosed.

(8) Civil Liability. Under §611 of the Act, the bank that does not follow the statute or the regulations promulgated thereunder by the Federal Reserve Board can be sued by the injured customer for his or her actual damages, punitive damages (not greater than $1000, nor less than $100, though in a class action the upper figure is the lesser of $500,000 or 1 percent of the net worth of the bank), plus costs of suit and attorney's fees. The suit may be brought in federal or state court within one year after the occurrence of the violation.

Variation by agreement from the rules of Regulation CC is permitted only for the check return rules of Subpart C, and such agreements only bind the specific parties to the agreement. No variation is permitted from the funds availability and disclosure requirements.

Check Truncation. To avoid the mountains of checks that must be moved around each day, some banks are asking their depositors to sign agreements so that the banks can indulge in a process called *check truncation*. Where this is done, the depositary bank simply keeps the deposited check and forwards only a description of it through the bank collection process. Specific provision is made for electronic present- ment and warranties connected with same; see §§4-110 and 4-209(b). In such a check truncation system, the customer never gets the check back, although it is reflected on the bank statement. The payor bank must maintain the ability to furnish the customer with legible copies of the truncated check for seven years; §4-406(b). The advantage of check truncation to the banks is obvious; customers needing canceled checks for any reason will have to live with the problems check truncation creates.

B. Final Payment

A signal legal moment in the check collection rules of both Article 4 of the Uniform Commercial Code and the EFAA is the moment that a payor bank engages in *final payment* of a check. This moment is important because it fixes many of the legal rights arising under Articles 3 and 4. Following final payment, the payor bank is "account- able" for the amount of the check according to the language of §4- 302(a), which means that it has lost the right to dishonor the check and must pay it to the person entitled to enforce it. If the check is properly payable (§4-401) from the drawer's account, well and good. If not, the payor bank is in a spot. The only legal theories in its favor that survive final payment are breach of presentment warranties (these have to do with forgeries and alterations, rarely at issue, discussed in the next chapter) and common law restitution, codified in §3-418, against villainous parties (who are hard to find or are often judgment proof). Hence this rule: following final payment, the payor bank bears the risk of any mistaken payment not covered by one of these theories, which almost never help. Read §4-302(b).

When does final payment occur? The key section is §4-215. This section, which you should read carefully, states the events that make a payor bank "accountable" (§4-302(a)) for the item, whether it means to be or not. See Annot., 23 A.L.R.4th 203. The final payment of a check destroys the check as a cause of action. All of the Article 3 im- plied obligations (§§3-414, 3-415, 3-419, etc.) are at an end because the check has been paid and these obligations, being secondary, are con- ditioned on *dishonor* by the drawee. Once the drawee makes final payment, dishonor is no longer possible, and the drawer and indorsers are off the hook.

PROBLEM 167

Harold Sure walked into Octopus National Bank and made a presentment of a $12,000 check drawn on the bank to the head cashier, Christopher Coin, who was staffing one of the teller's windows. Coin asked Sure (who was the check's payee) to indorse the check on the back and then tapped the computer's memory bank to check on the state of the drawer's account. The computer replied that the account contained "one thousand dollars," but Coin misread the display and thought it said "one hundred thousand dollars." He went back to the teller's window and counted out the money thoughtfully. When he was done, a nagging doubt about his vision overcame him, and—passing the money to Sure—he said, "Excuse me a minute," and rechecked the computer. This time he read the amount correctly and rushed back to his window to discover Sure still standing there, slowly recounting the money in front of him. Coin snatched the money out of Sure's hands, saying, "I'm sorry, we must dishonor the check." Sure protested, but in vain. If Sure sues, will he win? Had the bank made *final payment*? See §4-215(a)(1).

The Problem above is an elaboration of the fact situation in a famous case, Chambers v. Miller, 13 C.B. (N.S.) 125, 143 Eng. Rep. 50 (1862). (Judge Byles, writing in this case, said, "I think it would be extremely dangerous, and would create a great sensation in the city of London, if it were held in Westminster Hall, that after a check had been regularly handed over the banker's counter and the money received for it, and in the act of being counted, the banker might treat the check as unpaid because he had subsequently ascertained that the state of the customer's account was unfavorable.")

PROBLEM 168

Sally Phillips was the payee on a $1,000 check given to her by Joseph Armstrong. She and Joe both banked at the same bank, Octopus National Bank. Sally took Joe's check to the bank and filled out a deposit slip for her checking account, putting $800 of the check in her account and taking the other $200 in cash across the counter (this is called a *split deposit*). Two hours later, while posting the check, the bank clerk discovered that Joe's account was overdrawn. Can the bank now dishonor the whole check? $800 worth? Does §4-215(a)(1) apply here? See Kirby v. First & Merchants Natl. Bank, 210 Va. 88, 168 S.E.2d 273, 6 U.C.C. Rep. Serv. 694 (1969).

PROBLEM 169

Sally Phillips was the payee on a $1,000 check given to her by Joseph Armstrong. She walked it into Octopus National Bank, on which the check was drawn, and presented it across the counter, asking for a $1,000 cashier's check payable to her order as the method of payment. The bank gave her such a check; see §§3-104(g) and 3-412. She indorsed the check over to one of her creditors, but when Octopus National Bank failed and closed its doors before the check could be presented and paid, the creditor returned the cashier's check to her and demanded payment. Must she repay the creditor? See §3-310(a). If she does repay the creditor, may she sue Joseph Armstrong either as drawer of the check, §3-414, or on the original obligation, §3-310(b)(1)? See §§4-215(a)(2) and 4-213(c).

The second method of making final payment is settling for a check and not having the legal right to revoke the settlement; §4-215(a)(2). "Settle" is defined in §4-104(a)(11) as meaning "to pay in cash, by clearing-house settlement, in a charge or credit or by remittance, or otherwise as agreed. A settlement may be either provisional or final." If there exists a right to revoke the settlement, §4-215(a)(2) does not apply. Section 4-215(a)(2) is deliberately worded vaguely since the drafters wanted to encompass all possible methods of making payment that a bank might employ: wire transfer, netting of outstanding accounts, tapping of an account, etc. As long as the bank uses one of these methods and does not reserve the right to change its mind, final payment has occurred and the payor bank is accountable for the amount of the check.

The final (and most common) method of making final payment is contained in §4-215(a)(3). Almost all checks are not presented over the counter, but come into the payor bank when presented by another bank, which will have already made a provisional settlement in its own favor for the item. In that case, final payment is made by simply holding onto the check past the deadline for returning it. Read §4-215(a)(3). What is this deadline? The answer depends on what arrangements the payor bank has made with the presenting bank. If their agreement is that presented items must be returned by 4:00 P.M. on the day following the day of presentment, then that agreement prevails. If the check is presented through a local clearinghouse, the clearinghouse rules will govern the required time of return. Absent such agreements, the "statute" mentioned in §4-215(a)(3) is the Uniform Commercial Code itself, which requires return before expiration of the midnight deadline. The "midnight deadline" referred to is not midnight of the date of presentment, as it sounds, but instead is defined thusly in UCC §4-104(a)(10):

> (10) Midnight deadline: with respect to a bank is midnight on its next banking day following the banking day on which it receives the relevant item or notice or from which the time for taking action commences to run, whichever is later.

PROBLEM 170

What is the latest the payor bank can return a check before expiration of its midnight deadline, assuming: the bank has established a cut-off hour[17] of 2:00 P.M., it is not open on Saturdays (nor, of course, on Sundays), Monday is a holiday, and the Federal Reserve Bank presents a check for $1,000,000 on Friday at 4:00 P.M.?

Bankers must be ever alert to the possible expiration of the midnight deadline because once it has passed for a check, the check may not be dishonored and returned. When the customer of the bank is pleading for more time to cover a check overdrawing the account, the midnight deadline should be uppermost in the thoughts of a banker who is making decisions. The following is the leading case on the legal meaning of missing this deadline.

Rock Island Auction Sales, Inc. v. Empire Packing Co.

Illinois Supreme Court, 1965
32 Ill. 2d 269, 204 N.E.2d 721, 2 U.C.C. Rep. Serv. 319

SCHAFFER, J., delivered the opinion of the court: This case presents issues concerning the construction and validity of section 4-302 of the Uniform Commercial Code.

17. See §4-108.

The facts were admitted or stipulated. On Monday, September 24, 1962, the plaintiff, Rock Island Auction Sales, Inc., sold 61 head of cattle to Empire Packing Co., Inc. and received therefor Empire's check in the sum of $14,706.90. The check was dated September 24, 1962, and on that day the plaintiff deposited it in the First Bank and Trust Company of Davenport, Iowa. It was received by the payor bank, Illinois National Bank and Trust Company of Rockford, Illinois, on Thursday, September 27, 1962. Empire's balance was inadequate to pay the check, but the payor bank, relying upon Empire's assurances that additional funds would be deposited, held the check until Tuesday morning, October 2, 1962. It then marked the check "not sufficient funds," placed it in the mail for return to the Federal Reserve Bank of Chicago and sent notice of dishonor by telegram to the Federal Reserve Bank. The depositary bank, the First Trust and Savings Bank of Davenport, received the check on October 4, 1962. The check was never paid. On November 7, 1962, bankruptcy proceedings were instituted against Empire and on December 13, 1962, it was adjudicated a bankrupt.

On February 15, 1963, the plaintiff instituted this action against Illinois National Bank and Trust Company of Rockford, Empire Packing Co., Inc., and Peter Cacciatori, the officer of Empire who had signed the check. Cacciatori was not served with process, and no further action was taken against Empire after a stay order was issued by the United States District Court in the Bankruptcy proceeding. The plaintiff's case against Illinois National Bank and Trust Company of Rockford (hereafter defendant) rests squarely on the ground that as the payor bank it became liable for the amount of the check because it held the check without payment, return or notice of dishonor, beyond the time limit fixed in section 4-302 of the Uniform Commercial Code. . . .

[The court quoted §§4-302 and 4-104(a)(10).—Ed.]

The important issues in the case involve the construction and validity of section 4-302. The defendant argues that the amount for which it is liable because of its undenied retention of the check beyond the time permitted by section 4-302 is not to be determined by that section, but rather under section 4-103(5) which provides that "[t]he measure of damages for failure to exercise ordinary care in handling an item is the amount of the item reduced by an amount which could not have been realized by the use of ordinary care. . . . " To support this argument it points out that other provisions of Article 4 use the words "liable," "must pay," and "may recover." Its position is that the word "accountable" in section 4-302 means that "the defendant must account for what it actually had (which is zero because there were no funds on deposit sufficient to pay the check) plus the damages (as measured by section 4-103(5)) sustained by the plaintiff as the result of the failure to meet the deadline, but for no more."

But the statute provides that the bank is accountable for the amount of the item, and not for something else. "Accountable" is synonymous with "liable" (Webster's New Twentieth Century Dictionary Unabridged, Second Edition, Webster's Dictionary of Synonyms), and section 4-302 uses the word in that sense. The word "accountable" appears to have been used instead of its synonym "liable" in order to accommodate other sections of Article 4 of the Code which relate to provisional and final settlements between banks in the collection process, and to bar the possibility that a payor bank might be thought to be liable both to the owner of the item and to another bank. The circuit court correctly held that the statute imposes liability for the amount of the item.

This construction does not create an irrational classification and so cause the statute to violate constitutional limitations. Defendant's contention to the contrary is based upon the proposition that section 4-302 is invalid because it imposes a liability upon a payor bank for failing to act prior to its midnight deadline that is more severe than the liability which section 4-103(5) imposes upon a depositary bank or a collecting bank for the same default. Of course there are no such separate institutions as depositary, collecting and payor banks. All banks perform all three functions. The argument thus comes down to the proposition that the failure of a bank to meet its deadline must always carry the same consequence, regardless of the function that it is performing.

But the legislature may legitimately have concluded that there are differences in function and in circumstance that justify different consequences. Depositary and collecting banks act primarily as conduits. The steps that they take can only indirectly affect the determination of whether or not a check is to be paid, which is the focal point in the collection process. The legislature could have concluded that the failure of such a bank to meet its deadline would most frequently be the result of negligence, and fixed liability accordingly. The role of a payor bank in the collection process, on the other hand, is crucial. It knows whether or not the drawer has funds available to pay the item. The legislature could have considered that the failure of such a bank to meet its deadline is likely to be due to factors other than negligence, and that the relationship between a payor bank and its customer may so influence its conduct as to cause a conscious disregard of its statutory duty. The present case is illustrative. The defendant, in its position as a payor bank, deliberately aligned itself with its customer in order to protect that customer's credit and consciously disregard the duty imposed upon it. The statutory scheme emphasizes the importance of speed in the collection process. A legislative sanction designed to prevent conscious disregard of deadlines cannot be characterized as arbitrary or unreasonable, nor can it be said to constitute a legislative encroachment on the functions of the judiciary. . . .

Judgment affirmed.

A payor bank that misses its midnight deadline is *strictly liable* for the amount of the check involved. It is no defense that other parties, such as the depositary bank, were negligent or did not suffer a provable loss. See First Nat. Bank In Harvey v. Colonial Bank, 898 F. Supp. 1220, 28 U.C.C. Rep. Serv. 2d 290 (N.D. Ill. 1995); Los Angeles National Bank v. Bank of Canton, 280 Cal. Rptr. 831, 14 U.C.C. Rep. Serv. 2d 848 (Cal. App. 1991); Hanna v. First Nat. Bank of Rochester, 87 N.Y.2d 107, 637 N.Y.S.2d 953, 28 U.C.C. Rep. Serv. 2d 417 (N.Y. 1995). A payor bank that tries to return a check on which it has already made final payment is said to be making a "late return," which, of course, is not allowed. Regulation CC creates a *warranty of timely return* for checks, so that if a bank is guilty of making a late return it has to respond in damages; Reg. CC §229.34.

When the Federal Reserve was drafting Regulation CC, it decided to make a major alteration to the midnight deadline rule to stop the following practice. Under the Uniform Commercial Code a payor bank was required to "send" the check back before the expiration of the midnight deadline. Suppose that late in the second banking day, shortly before midnight, a payor bank made a last minute decision to dishonor a check. The fastest way to get the check back to the presenting bank would be to wait until the armored courier could take it back the next day, but the statute did not allow that delay. "Send," as it happens, is defined in the Uniform Commercial Code to include "deposit in the mail" (see §1-201(38)), and the Federal Reserve discovered that that is what the banks were doing with the checks: putting them in an envelope and then into a mailbox before midnight. Who knew when the check would actually get back to the presenting bank, but the payor bank had nonetheless complied with the law. To change this awkward procedure, Reg. CC now provides that a payor bank is permitted to miss its midnight deadline as long as it is able nonetheless to return a check to the presenting bank before the close of that bank's next banking day, in effect giving the banks an extra day to return the check.

First National Bank of Chicago v. Standard Bank & Trust

United States Court of Appeals, Seventh Circuit, 1999
172 F.3d 472, 38 U.C.C. Rep. Serv. 2d 1

FLAUM, Circuit Judge. First National Bank of Chicago, known at the time relevant to this suit as NBD Bank ("NBD"), brought an action for declaratory judgment alleging that Standard Bank & Trust ("Standard Bank" or "Standard") failed to return certain checks to NBD in a timely fashion under the Expedited Funds Availability Act, 12 U.S.C. §4010(d) & (f) ("EFAA"). Finding that the checks were returned in a timely fashion, the district court granted summary judgment to the defendant Standard Bank, and awarded it prejudgment interest on the returned checks. Standard claimed it was entitled to the average prime rate for the relevant time period. However, the district court used the three-month Treasury Bill rate—4.9241%—compounded quarterly. Both sides appeal. For the reasons set out below, we affirm the district court's decision that the checks were properly returned, but vacate the award of interest, and remand for entry of the proper measure of prejudgment interest.

BACKGROUND

This litigation revolves around which party—Standard or NBD—should absorb the losses resulting from a check-kiting scheme perpetrated against both of these banks in November, 1993. On November 18, 1993, an individual presented to NBD checks with an aggregate value of $3,997,406.75, drawn on customer accounts maintained at Standard Bank, which NBD initially accepted. That day, the same person deposited $4,025,000.00 in checks at Standard, drawn on NBD customer accounts.

The following day, Friday, November 19, 1993, NBD presented the checks it received to Standard, and vice versa. LaSalle Bank, in its capacity as the collecting bank, charged both banks' accounts for the checks drawn on them, and provisionally credited each bank for the amount presented to them. On the next business day (Monday, November 22, 1993), NBD opted not to honor the checks, and returned all of the checks, totaling $4,025,000.00, to Standard Bank. Standard received notice of NBD's decision on Tuesday morning, November 23. That afternoon, Standard attempted to dishonor the checks it had received. Three of its bank officers dashed off to NBD's Operations Processing Center carrying checks totaling $3,785,441.35. The checks were received by NBD at 3:58 P.M. that day, but NBD did not credit Standard's account for that sum. On November 30, 1993, NBD filed suit, seeking a declaration that Standard Bank's return of the checks was not timely, because it neither met the "midnight deadline," nor any of the deadline's exceptions laid out in Federal Reserve Board ("the Board") Regulations appurtenant to EFAA. Standard Bank defended by arguing that its return was proper, and it counterclaimed for prejudgment interest.

On a motion for judgment on the pleadings, the district court originally found for NBD, but reversed its decision in light of a clarifying amendment[18] to the relevant Federal Reserve Regulations. The district court also decided that prejudgment interest was appropriate, but did not award the prime rate. Instead it chose a lower rate (the average T-bill rate) because of the absence of bad faith on NBD's part, and because this was a "close case." Each side appealed portions of the decision below.

I.

NBD's appeal from the district court's order granting Standard Bank's motion for judgment on the pleadings is reviewed by this court de novo. Rooding v. Peters, 92 F.3d 578, 579-80 (7th Cir. 1996).

A.

The legal question at issue is whether Standard Bank's return of the checks comports with Federal Reserve Board Regulation CC sec. 229.30(c)(1), 12 C.F.R. Part 229 ("Regulation CC"). Regulation CC's language states:

> (c) Extension of deadline. The deadline for return or notice of nonpayment under the U.C.C. or Regulation sec.229.36(f)(2) of this part is extended:

---

18. When we refer to Regulation CC, we refer to the pre-clarification version of that rule. The amended version is referred to as "postclarifying amendment Regulation CC."

(1) If a paying bank, in an effort to expedite delivery of a returned check to a bank, uses a means of delivery that would ordinarily result in the returned check being received by the bank to which it is sent on or before the receiving bank's next business day following the otherwise applicable deadline; this deadline is extended further if a paying bank uses a highly expeditious means of transportation, even if this means of transportation would ordinarily result in delivery after the receiving bank's next banking day.

As the text notes, Regulation CC extends the UCC's deadline, known in the vernacular as the "midnight deadline."[19] Under the UCC, a paying bank may dishonor or revoke its provisional settlement of a check before midnight on the next business day after it received the check. UCC sec. 4-301(a)(1); Hanna v. First Nat'l Bank of Rochester, 87 N.Y.2d 107, 637 N.Y.S.2d 953, 661 N.E.2d 683, 686 n.2 (N.Y. 1995). While the Board favored the UCC's emphasis on expeditiously dealing with dishonored checks, it was concerned that the midnight deadline might unintentionally retard the return of checks. It noted "[b]ecause the return process must begin by midnight, many paying banks return checks by mail when a courier leaving after midnight would be faster." 52 Fed. Reg. 47119, 47123 (Dec. 11, 1987). Thus, the Board enacted the extension to the midnight deadline.

NBD argues that the Board's extension of the midnight deadline does not apply here. It primarily points to a number of statements in Regulation CC's legislative history indicating that use of the extension is limited to banks which regularly use couriers services to return checks. However, NBD is putting the cart before the horse—before we delve into the Board's commentary on Regulation CC, we must first examine its language's plain meaning.

Administrative rules are subject to the same well-known maxims of construction as legislative statutes. Alabama Tissue Ctr. v. Sullivan, 975 F.2d 373, 379 (7th Cir. 1992). As we recently noted, in statutory construction cases, "the beginning point must be the language of the statute, and when a statute speaks with clarity to an issue, judicial inquiry into the statute's meaning, in all but the most extraordinary circumstances, is finished." United States v. Kirschenbaum, 156 F.3d

---

19. The statute Regulation CC was promulgated under, the EFAA, granted the Board the power to "supersede any provision of [state law] including the Uniform Commercial Code as in effect in [any state], which is inconsistent with this [Act] or such regulations." 12 U.S.C. sec. 4007(b).

784, 789 (7th Cir. 1998) (quoting Estate of Cowart v. Nicklos Drilling Co., 505 U.S. 469, 475, 112 S. Ct. 2589, 120 L. Ed. 2d 379 (1992)). If we can decipher Regulation CC's meaning on its face, there is no need to examine legislative history absent extraordinary circumstances. United States v. Hudspeth, 42 F.3d 1015, 1022 (7th Cir. 1994).

There is little in the text of the statute that supports NBD's argument that the extension is only available to banks which regularly or ordinarily use expedited delivery. Regulation CC extends the deadline when a paying bank "expedite [s] delivery of a returned check..." and we note the singular "a returned check" rather than the plural "returned checks." See Metropolitan Stevedore Co. v. Rambo, 515 U.S. 291, 295, 115 S. Ct. 2144, 132 L. Ed. 2d 226 (1995). Although it is not dispositive, this use of the singular suggests that Regulation CC may apply to one-time single check transactions. Far more conclusive is the structure of the second clause, which allows a bank to extend the deadline when it "uses a means of delivery that would ordinarily result in the returned check being received by the bank to which it is sent on or before the receiving bank's next business day following the otherwise applicable deadline." NBD argues, implausibly, that this mandates that a bank ordinarily or routinely use a means of expedited delivery in order to avail itself of the extension. For "ordinarily" to have such meaning, however, it would have to modify the verb "uses," causing the sentence to read: "a bank may extend the deadline if it ordinarily uses a means of delivery that would result in the returned check being received. . . ." Of course, in the actual regulation, "ordinarily" modifies the verb "would result," denoting that the bank's means of delivery must ordinarily result in return by the applicable deadline. Any other reading, including the one NBD proposes, is contrary to the clear import of the second clause.

NBD also points to Regulation CC's first clause, which allows banks to use the extension "in an effort to expedite delivery of a returned check to a bank." It argues that Standard Bank's efforts were not in "an effort to expedite delivery" of the dishonored checks. We disagree. There is no doubt that Standard Bank's executives drove the checks to NBD's processing center in order to speed up delivery.

This interpretation squares with a leading commentary on the UCC by Professors White and Summers. Analyzing the plain language of Regulation CC (before the clarifying amendment) White and Summers posed—and answered—the following hypothetical:

> Assume that the payor bank received a $100,000 check on Monday morning and that it discovers on Wednesday morning that it failed to

send the check back by Tuesday midnight (the midnight deadline), but it now wishes to dishonor the check. Under the UCC the midnight deadline would have passed, and unless it had an unusual defense, payor would be liable for the $100,000. *Regulation CC* changes that. If the bank can somehow get the check back to the depositary bank before that bank's close of business on Wednesday, it escapes liability under the UCC. That appears to be the meaning of the first sentence of [Regulation CC sec. 229.30(c)].

James J. White & Robert F. Summers, Uniform Commercial Code, at 325 (4th ed. 1995) (emphasis added). Although NBD brings other scholarly points of view to our attention, those positions appear less faithful to Regulation CC's actual text than White & Summers.

We only look past the express language of a regulation when it is ambiguous or where a literal interpretation would lead to an "absurd result or thwart the purpose of the overall statutory scheme." United States v. Hayward, 6 F.3d 1241, 1245 (7th Cir. 1993). We see no ambiguity in Regulation CC which admits of the meaning NBD presses upon us. Also, a literal interpretation does not lead to an "absurd result"—there is nothing absurd about extending the midnight deadline irrespective of whether a bank avails itself of the extension once or repeatedly. Moreover, the reading we adopt does not thwart the purpose of the rule, which promoted the speedy return of dishonored checks over the postmark conscious "midnight deadline." See 52 Fed. Reg. 47112, 47140 (Dec. 11, 1987) (noting that Regulation CC "removes the constraint of the midnight deadline if the check reaches either the depositary bank or the returning bank to which it is sent on the banking day following the expiration of the midnight deadline or other applicable time for return.").

We briefly examine the rule's regulatory history for any signs that our decision would thwart the Board's intent. United States v. Mueller, 112 F.3d 277, 281 (7th Cir. 1997) (where statute is clear, examining legislative history useful to "determine if it reflects a clearly expressed legislative intention" contrary to plain meaning) (citation omitted). Regulation CC's regulatory history is not quite as clear as the text. Both sides present evidence from the available sources to support their statutory interpretations. Among other references, NBD points to Regulation CC's Official Commentary, which lists two circumstances in which the midnight deadline may be extended, one not relevant here. The putatively relevant circumstance is where "a West Coast paying bank . . . ship[s] a returned check by air courier directly to an East Coast depositary bank even if the check arrives after the close of the depositary bank's banking day." Official Commentary sec. 229.30, 12

C.F.R. Part 22, App. E (1997). This does suggest that the intent of the regulation may not have been as broad as its wording indicates. On the other hand, the commentary notes that the West Coast/East Coast bank scenario is an "example" of a highly expeditious means of delivery. 12 C.F.R. part 229, App. E. The history also states that Regulation CC "pertains primarily to air courier arrangements from West Coast banks to East Coast banks." 53 Fed. Reg. 19372, 19418 (May 27, 1988). "Pertains primarily" suggests that other exceptions exist too, and that an overly constricted reading of when the extension applies would be inappropriate. After examining the relative regulatory history, we believe it is a wash. This works to NBD's detriment, because its inability to coax strong support from the regulatory history means that it cannot overcome the clear import of Regulation CC's words. Oneida Tribe v. Wisconsin, 951 F.2d 757, 761 (7th Cir. 1991).

B.

Although our reading of Regulation CC finds little ambiguity, the Board issued a self titled "Clarifying Amendment" in 1997 to remove any doubt as to whether the midnight deadline applies to checks returned to avoid a kite. Assuming that our interpretation of the pre-clarification rule was incorrect—an assumption without which this analysis is superfluous—Standard argues that the Clarifying Amendment has retroactive effect. It was on this ground that the district court found for Standard Bank. NBD argues that the "Clarifying Amendment" was actually a legislative rule, and as such has no retroactive effect under Bowen v. Georgetown University Hospital, 488 U.S. 204, 208, 109 S. Ct. 468, 102 L. Ed. 2d 493 (1988).

The Clarifying Amendment expunged the words "in an effort to expedite delivery of a returned check to a bank" from Regulation CC sec. 229.30(c)(1). 62 Fed. Reg. 13801, 13805 (March 24, 1997). This was done to remove any doubt as to whether an inquiry into the returning bank's motives was appropriate. Id. . . .

Based on our analysis, even if the original Regulation CC did not allow Standard Bank to return the checks, we find that the 1997 Clarifying Amendment retroactively permitted the extension of the midnight deadline. Thus, the district court's finding that NBD should have honored the checks Standard delivered in the amount of $3,785,441.35 was correct. . . .

CONCLUSION

While we Affirm the judgment on the pleadings in favor of Standard Bank, the district court's grant of prejudgment interest is

Vacated and we Remand with instructions to enter an award of prejudgment interest consistent with the average prime rate for the appropriate time period.

Regulation CC §229.30(c)(1) also creates another situation where the bank may miss its midnight deadline: "the deadline is extended further if a paying bank uses a highly expeditious means of transportation." For example, says the Commentary, "a west coast bank may use this further extension to ship a returned check by air courier directly to an east coast depositary bank even if the check arrives after the close of the depositary bank's banking day." Regulation CC has detailed rules concerning the return of checks, discussed in the next section.

PROBLEM 171

Octopus National Bank, which has branches throughout the state, has one central processing center where it makes all decisions about whether to pay checks drawn on the branches. The canceled checks are returned to the branches two days after the processing center decides to pay them. Is the moment of presentment to the payor bank the moment of presentment to the processing center or the moment when the check is returned to the individual branch? See Regulation CC §229.36(b)(4).

C. Check Return

The major thrust of the EFAA is to require depositary banks to give customers quick access to funds represented by deposited checks. This has the effect, however, of putting the depositary banks at risk. The customer might withdraw the funds under the EFAA rules, and then the check, for whatever reason, might still be returned. The customer is required to repay the money after the check is charged back to the account (§4-214, explored later in this chapter), but all too often the money is gone and cannot be retrieved. Regulation CC therefore has a number of provisions designed to make the check collection machinery operate very quickly to forward checks for collection and return them if they are dishonored.

The Federal Notice for Large Check Return. On checks of $2,500 or more, depositary banks take the biggest risks unless they are alerted to the fact that the check is being dishonored by the payor bank. Section 229.33 of Regulation CC therefore requires the payor bank to send a direct notice to the depositary bank any time it decides not to pay a check in the amount of $2,500 or more. The notice must include the name and routing number of the paying bank, the name of the payee, the amount, the reason for return, the date of the indorsement of the depositary bank, the account number of the depositor, the branch where the item was first deposited, and the trace number on the item of the depositary bank, unless these matters cannot be reasonably determined from an examination of the item itself. Failure of the payor bank to send the required notice makes it liable for actual damages caused (up to the amount of the item) and, if the payor bank failed to act in good faith, for other consequential damages.

How quickly must the notice be given? Regulation CC §229.33(a), in relevant part, states: "If a paying bank determines not to pay a check in the amount of $2,500 or more, it shall provide notice of nonpayment such that the notice is received by the depositary bank by 4:00 P.M. (local time) on the second business day following the banking day on which the check was presented to the paying bank. . . ." Notice may be provided by any reasonable means, including physical return of the check, a writing (which includes a copy of the check), telephone, Fedwire, telex, or other form of telegraph.

Historically, returned checks had not been handled with any great speed, and had taken far longer to get back to the depository bank than checks being forwarded for collection traveling the same route. Regulation CC, Subpart C, has a number of provisions designed to speed up check returns, requiring what the Reg. calls "expeditious return." Section 229.30 requires the payor bank to return checks in a manner that is as fast or faster than that which would be used to dispatch forward collection were the depositary and payor banks reversed in function, or in lieu of using this "forward collection" test, the payor bank is deemed to act expeditiously if it returns the check in such a manner that it would normally be received by the depositary bank not later than 4:00 P.M. on the second business day following the original presentment to the payor bank. This period is extended to *four* business days if the payor bank is "non-local" to the depositary bank, meaning that they are not physically located in the same geographical region served by a Federal Reserve processing center (there are 48 such regions).

Regulation CC allows returns directly to the depositary bank (thus skipping over any collecting banks), use of a route different from the one the check traveled originally, and the sending of the check through the Federal Reserve System. The reason for the return of the check must be stamped on the check itself.

D. Charge Back

These rules about final payment apply only to the actions of the payor (drawee) bank. If that bank dishonors the check and returns it to the depositary bank, the latter will expect reimbursement from its depositor no matter how many days elapsed since the check was first deposited. The bank has three ways to justify its demand for repayment: the initial contract agreement signed when the account was opened, the indorser's obligation (§3-415), and the statutory right of charge back.

Read §4-214.

PROBLEM 172

Damon owed $500 to his friend Pythias and in payment gave him a check for that amount drawn on the Bulfinch National Bank, which Pythias deposited in his account with the Dionysius State Bank on Monday, July 8. On July 11, not having heard anything, Pythias assumed that final payment had occurred and wrote checks against the augmented balance. On July 10 the check reached the Bulfinch National Bank and was marked "NSF" and returned to Dionysius State Bank the next day. Dionysius State Bank took $500 out of Pythias' account without notice, causing several other checks of his to bounce on July 15.

(a) Can Pythias sue Dionysius State Bank under §4-402 for wrongful dishonor of these later checks? See §§4-215(d), 4-215(e)(1), 4-214; Salem Natl. Bank v. Chapman, 64 Ill. App. 3d 625, 381 N.E.2d 741, 25 U.C.C. Rep. Serv. 234 (1978).

(b) Since Dionysius State Bank has failed to give a proper charge-back notice, is it liable for the amount of the item? See §4-214(a)'s second sentence.

(c) If it had given Pythias notice of dishonor, could Dionysius State Bank have recovered the $500 even if it had let Pythias withdraw all the money from his account prior to the return of the check from the payor bank? See §4-214(d)(1).

(d) Would your answer to the first question be the same if Dionysius State were both the depositary and the payor bank? See §§4-215(e)(2), 4-302; and Regulation CC §229.10(c)(vi).

(e) If the check had been returned by Bulfinch National Bank to Dionysius State Bank on September 25, could Dionysius have still charged back? See §4-214(a)'s final sentence.[20]

(f) Assume that when the check is first returned to Dionysius, the bank does not charge it back against Pythias' account, but instead again sends the check through for re-presentment, hoping this time there will be money in the drawer's account and the check will be paid. If this hope proves fruitless and the check is returned by Bulfinch a second time, does §4-214 allow Dionysius to charge back, assuming that it does so immediately on learning of the second return? See also Leibson, Handling Re-Presented Checks—Risky Business for Collecting and Payor Banks, 72 Ky. L.J. 549 (1983-1984).

Gordon v. Planters & Merchants Bancshares, Inc.

Arkansas Supreme Court, 1996
326 Ark. 1046, 935 S.W.2d 544,
31 U.C.C. Rep. Serv. 2d 636

ANDREE LAYTON ROAF, Justice. The appellant, Ashel Gordon, sued his bank, the appellee, Planters & Merchants Bancshares, Inc. ("Planters"), for wrongful charge-back of a check he deposited into his account. Gordon alleged that Planters violated Ark. Code Ann. §4-4-213 (1987) and acted maliciously, intentionally, and in bad faith; he sued for the amount of the check, plus interest and punitive damages.

---

20. The rule here is actually simpler than it looks. Charge-back is allowed only for *provisional* settlements. If the payor bank made final payment on a check, all the provisional settlements "firmed up" and became final. Charge-back is not allowed to undo final settlements, and §4-214(a)'s final sentence states such a rule. When the payor bank tries to undo final payment by making a late return, the depositary bank should not accept the check back, since it has lost its right of charge-back. How does the depositary bank (or any collecting bank) know whether the payor bank has made timely return? It doesn't, and in all but the rarest situation will assume that the payor bank has acted properly so that the depositary bank's right of charge-back still exists. If that assumption is wrong—the payor bank did make a late return—Regulation CC §229.34 creates a *warranty of timely return* by the payor bank, which, having been breached, provides the needed remedy to the depositary bank.

This court reversed the trial court's previous dismissal of Gordon's action under Ark. R. Civ. P. 12(b)(6) in Gordon v. Planters & Merchants Bancshares, Inc., 310 Ark. 11, 832 S.W.2d 492 (1992), and held that a collecting bank's right to charge back an account terminates when settlement for a check becomes final. On remand, during a jury trial, the trial court granted a directed verdict to Planters on the issue of punitive damages, after which Planters conceded liability for compensatory damages for the wrongful charge-back. The trial court awarded Gordon the amount of the check, plus interest and $335 in attorney's fees. On appeal, Gordon contends that the trial court erred in granting Planters a directed verdict as to punitive damages and the amount of attorney's fees awarded. We agree that the trial court erred in directing a verdict on punitive damages and reverse and remand for a new trial.

Ashel Gordon and Lloyd Wallace were partners for approximately three years in a farming business known as "Gordon Wallace Farms." In 1982, the partnership ended when Wallace decided to take a job with Planters Bank. Pursuant to a dissolution agreement, Gordon paid Wallace $67,000 for what Gordon believed was the right to all assets formerly belonging to the partnership.

In September, 1990, Gordon received a $2,494.21 check issued by Stuttgart Cooperative Buyers' Association ("Co-op"), drawn on the First National Bank of Stuttgart ("First National"), and made payable to Gordon Wallace Farms. The check was for patronage dividends which accrued during the operation of the partnership. Gordon endorsed the check "Gordon Wallace Farms" and deposited it on September 24, 1990 into his personal account at Planters where Wallace, Gordon's former partner, was working as a loan officer. The next day, First National made final settlement with Planters for the amount of the check, Planters completed the posting process, and credited Gordon's account for the amount of the check.

On September 26, just two days after the check was deposited, Wallace phoned the Gordon home and inquired whether Gordon Wallace Farms had received a check from the Co-op. It is not clear whether Wallace acquired knowledge of the check through his employment with Planters or through some other source. Gordon's wife told Wallace that the check had been received and deposited. When Wallace inquired whether he was entitled to one-half of the check, Mrs. Gordon instructed him to call back later and speak to Mr. Gordon; Wallace did not do so.

Instead, on September 27, Wallace called the Co-op to determine whether the check to Gordon Wallace Farms had been cleared. The Co-op officer manager called Wallace back at his office phone number at Planters and informed him that the check had been cleared. Wallace did not identify himself as an officer of the bank, or tell the Co-op manager that he was calling from his office phone.

Wallace then called Jack Barber, a friend of his who was a loan officer at First National. Wallace told Barber that Gordon Wallace Farms no longer existed, that he had been a member of the partnership, and that the check had been improperly endorsed. Barber passed this information on to the Co-op and to a customer service manager at First National. The First National service manager called the Co-op manager on two consecutive days, October 1 and October 2, obtained return of the canceled check from the Co-op after the second call, and returned it to Planters.

On October 3, a bookkeeper at Planters received from First National the check which was marked "Return to Maker." The bookkeeper consulted Wallace, her supervisor, who instructed her to charge-back the check against Gordon's account.

Planters did not contact Gordon about the charge-back of the check, and Gordon was not aware of the debit to his account until he received a notice of overdraft approximately eight days after the check had been deposited at Planters. Gordon immediately went to Planters and spoke with Larry Bauer, the bank president. Bauer told Gordon that the charge-back was a personal matter between him and Wallace, and that Gordon would have to resolve the dispute with Wallace. Bauer did not investigate the matter or offer to assist Gordon in the resolution of the dispute.

Gordon brought suit against Planters alleging that the bank was strictly liable under Ark. Code Ann. §4-4-213 (1987) (now codifed as Ark. Code Ann. §4-4-215 (Repl. 1991) [1990 Official Text]) when it charged-back the check after final settlement. In addition, Gordon sued for punitive damages on the basis that Planters, through Wallace, acted maliciously and in bad faith. The trial court dismissed the action under Ark. R. Civ. P. 12(b)(6) for failure to state a claim on which relief could be granted.

Gordon appealed the dismissal to this court in Gordon v. Planters & Merchants Bancshares, Inc., 310 Ark. 11, 832 S.W.2d 492 (1992) ("Gordon I"). In Gordon I, this court held that under Ark. Code Ann. §4-4-213 (1987), a collecting bank's right to charge-back an account terminates when a settlement for the check becomes final. Id. Therefore, the facts, as alleged by Gordon, were sufficient to state a cause of action, and the case was remanded for trial. Id.

At trial, the judge granted Planters' motion for a directed verdict as to punitive damages. At that point, Planters conceded liability for compensatory damages for the wrongful charge-back. Accordingly, Gordon was granted a judgment of $2,494.21 in compensatory damages plus costs and interest, and $335 in attorney's fees. Planters was given credit for one-half of the amount of the check which represented the funds that Gordon had received in a settlement of his dispute with Wallace. On appeal, Gordon challenges the directed verdict on punitive damages and the amount of attorney's fees awarded.

1. PUNITIVE DAMAGES

Planters admitted that it wrongfully charged-back Gordon's account; thus, the only issue on appeal is whether Gordon has sufficiently pled and submitted evidence to support an award of punitive damages. In order to reverse the trial judge's ruling, this court must find that: 1) punitive damages are permissible under §4-4-4215(d) [UCC Revised §4-215(d)]; 2) there was sufficient evidence to allow the issue to be submitted to the jury; and 3) Planters Bank may be held vicariously liable for Wallace's wrongful actions.

A. PUNITIVE DAMAGES UNDER §4-4-215(d)

This issue of whether punitive damages are recoverable under the wrongful charge-back provision of the Uniform Commercial Code ("UCC"), Ark. Code Ann. §4-4-215(d) (Repl. 1991), is an issue of first impression in Arkansas. We also have not found that other jurisdictions have considered this question. Therefore, it is necessary to review the general provisions in the UCC regarding the appropriate measure of damages, and cases in which we and other states have addressed the award of punitive damages under other UCC provisions. The introductory article to the UCC instructs that:

> The remedies provided by this subtitle shall be liberally administered to the end that the aggrieved party may be put in as good as position as if the other party had fully performed but neither consequential or special nor penal damages may be had except as specifically provided in this subtitle or by other rule of law.

Ark. Code Ann. §4-1-106(1) (Repl. 1991) (emphasis supplied). There are three different ways that courts have interpreted this language. William D. Hawkland, UCC Series §1-106:04 (1982).

Some jurisdictions take a broad view of this section and find that it is permissible to impose consequential, special, or punitive damages unless they are specifically prohibited by a particular section of the Code. Id. Courts following this approach rely on the mandate at the beginning of the paragraph that remedies under the UCC are to be "liberally administered." Id.

Other courts take the opposite, or narrow approach, and hold that consequential, special, and punitive damages are allowable only when specifically authorized by the Code. Id. These jurisdictions find that as a general principle of law courts should not go beyond the Code for answers to problems that are not specifically addressed therein. Id. Instead, "gaps in the Code are usually best filled through the use of analogy and extrapolation" rather than resort to common law. Id. However, the commentators note that this narrow approach appears "contrary to the plain meaning of subsection 1-106(1)" which specifically refers to "other rules of law." Id.

The third, and final approach is an intermediary or neutral interpretation of the section. Id. According to this view, §1-106 neither provides for nor prevents the imposition of special, consequential, or punitive damages. Id. Instead, the court must look to the common law to supplement the Code as provided in §1-103. Id. The commentators state that:

> This theory seems sound, because subsection 1-106(1) states quite plainly that it does not authorize the imposition of consequential, special or penal damages and that such damages are unavailable to the aggrieved party unless "specifically provided in this Act *or by other rule of law.*"

Id. (emphasis in the original).

Arkansas has not specifically adopted any of these three approaches. However, regardless of the approach, other jurisdictions have held that punitive damages are allowable under the UCC whenever a wrongdoer acts in a willful or malicious manner. See, e.g., Fedders Corp. v. Boatright, 493 So. 2d 301 (Miss. 1986) (finding that punitive damages are allowable under the UCC when there is a breach of "gross magnitude"); First Nat'l Bank v. Twombly, 689 P.2d 1226 (Mont. 1984) (holding that punitive damages are recoverable under the UCC when "the Bank's conduct is sufficiently culpable").

As to damages under Article 4 of the UCC, the general provision on damages in this article declares:

> (a) The effect of the provisions of this chapter may be varied by agreement, but the parties to the agreement cannot disclaim a bank's responsibility for its lack of good faith or failure to exercise ordinary care or limit the measure of damages for the lack or failure. However, the parties may determine by agreement the standards by which the

bank's responsibility is to be measured if those standards are not manifestly unreasonable. . . .

(e) The measure of damages for failure to exercise ordinary care in handling an item is the amount of the item reduced by an amount that could not have been realized by the exercise of ordinary care. *If there is also bad faith, it includes any other damages the party suffered as a proximate consequence.*

Ark. Code. Ann. §4-4-103 [UCC Revised §4-103] (Repl. 1991) (emphasis added). From this provision, it is clear that Article 4 provides for the imposition of "other" damages when a bank acts in bad faith when dealing with its customers.

Moreover, we have recognized the imposition of punitive damages in wrongful dishonor cases which, like wrongful charge-back cases, are governed by Article 4 of the UCC. City Nat'l Bank v. Goodwin, 301 Ark. 182, 783 S.W.2d 335 (1990); Twin City Bank v. Isaacs, 283 Ark. 127, 672 S.W.2d 651 (1984).

When *Goodwin* and *Isaacs* were decided, the UCC provision on damages allowable for wrongful dishonor provided in part:

> A payor bank is liable to its customers for damages proximately caused by the wrongful dishonor of an item. *When the dishonor occurs through mistake, liability is limited to actual damages* proved. If so proximately caused and proved damages may include damages for an arrest or prosecution of the customer *or other consequential damages.*

Ark. Code Ann. §4-4-402 (1987) (emphasis supplied). As with Ark. Code Ann. §4-4-215, the wrongful dishonor provision was silent as to punitive damages. In addition, §4-402 specifically included limiting language as to the types of damages awardable, and only provided for actual and consequential damages.

In *Goodwin,* this court said that punitive damages were allowable when a bank dishonors a check based on an "erroneous belief that it had a legal right to do so" or in bad faith "deliberately or willfully dishonors a check," but that only actual damages were recoverable when the dishonor occurred through a mistake. *Goodwin,* supra. Although reference to dishonor through mistake was deleted from §402(b) in the revised uniform law in 1990, which Arkansas has adopted, *Goodwin* remains evidence of this court's rejection of the narrow approach in determining the amount of damages allowable under the UCC.

Furthermore, in Citizen's Bank v. Chitty, 285 Ark. 55, 684 S.W.2d 814 (1985), we addressed the question of damages in the context of a wrongful charge-back by a bank to its customer's account. Chitty's complaint alleged that his bank was negligent in the breach of a fiduciary duty owed to its depositor. Id. Although we held that Chitty was not entitled to consequential damages because there was not even an implication that the bank acted in bad faith, we stated:

> Ark. Stat. Ann. §85-4-103(1) (Add. 1961) states that a bank may not disclaim its responsibility for failure to exercise ordinary care or . . . limit the measure of damages for such lack or failure . . . "The measure of damages for failure to exercise ordinary care in handling an item is the amount of the item reduced by an amount which could not have been realized by the use of ordinary care, *and where there is bad faith it includes other damages, if any, suffered by the party as approximate consequence."* Ark. Stat. Ann. 85-4-103(5). Thus it may be seen that the amount of recovery is limited to the amount of the item[s] *in the absence of bad faith.*

Id. (citing Ark. Stat. Ann. 85-4-103 which is now codified as Ark. Code Ann. §4-4-103 (Repl. 1991)) (emphasis added).

Because we have allowed the imposition of punitive damages when the pertinent wrongful dishonor provision did not specifically provide for them, it is clear that we have not adopted a narrow interpretation of §1-106. Moreover, in Goodwin, this court stated that punitive damages were recoverable under *both* the claim of wrongful dishonor and conversion, although we found no substantial evidence to support a punitive-damage award on either cause of action in that instance. *Goodwin,* supra. Consequently, this court has indicated that punitive damages can be awarded for Article 4 violations where the statute does not specifically prohibit them without the necessity that an alternative, common law tort be pled. Thus, Gordon's failure to assert a claim for conversion is not fatal to his claim for punitive damages.

There is a further reason that punitive damages should be allowed in this case. Arkansas Code Annotated §4-1-203 (Repl. 1991) clearly provides that, "*Every* contract *or duty within this subtitle* imposes an obligation of good faith in its performance or enforcement." (Emphasis added.) As previously mentioned, Planters had a clear duty under Ark. Code Ann. §4-4-215 to refrain from charging-back the check against Gordon's account once payment had become final. Planters' breach of this duty, under the circumstances presented by this case, could have been construed to be an exercise of bad faith which is strictly prohibited by §1-203. Moreover Gordon sufficiently apprised the trial court of this issue when he alleged in his complaint that Planter's actions were "taken in bad faith," and that Planters "violated and exploited its fiduciary relationship" with him.

Although we have not specifically addressed whether punitive damages are recoverable for a breach of the duty of good faith under §1-203 of the UCC, in Adams v. First State Bank, 300 Ark. 235, 778 S.W.2d 611 (1989), we declared that the issue could have gone to the jury under a subjective test if the plaintiff had simply alleged sufficient facts to avoid summary judgment. Moreover, other jurisdictions have recognized that punitive damages are recoverable for a breach of the duty of good faith imposed by §1-203. See, e.g., *Twombly,* supra (finding that punitive damages are recoverable under the UCC when there is a breach of "gross magnitude"); Commercial Cotton v. United Cal. Bank, 209 Cal. Rptr. 551 (Cal. App. 4th Dist. 1981) (holding that punitive damages are recoverable where the bank breached the duty of good faith and fair dealing towards its depositor). Consequently, Planters' argument that punitive damages may not be allowed because Gordon's case is based in contract, as opposed to negligence or intentional tort, does not defeat Gordon's right to punitive damages pursuant to the duty of good faith imposed by §1-203 of the UCC.

B.   SUBSTANTIAL EVIDENCE

In order to avoid a directed verdict and reach the jury on the issue of punitive damages, Gordon must have presented substantial evidence that the defendant acted "wantonly in causing the injury or with such conscious indifference to the consequences that malice may be inferred." Stein v. Lukas, 308 Ark. 74, 823 S.W.2d 832 (1992). We find that Gordon satisfied this burden, and thus the issue should have been submitted to the jury. See *Goodwin,* supra.

On September 26, Wallace notified Gordon that he thought he was entitled to half of the check made payable to "Gordon Wallace Farms" which Gordon had deposited into his personal bank account. Instead of pursuing the matter with Gordon or an attorney, Wallace abused his position at Planters Bank to have the check charged-back against Gordon's account with Planters.

The testimony with regard to the handling of this check is pertinent to the resolution of the issue of punitive damages and it is accordingly summarized in detail. The Co-op manager, Virginia Woodward, testified that she did not dispute the check, that the Co-op did not have any problems with the endorsement, and that the check would not have been sent back "but for the intervention of whoever it was there at the bank in Stuttgart." Woodward was sufficiently concerned about this incident that she prepared a memo approximately one week after she returned the check. This memo recited the three phone calls she received from Wallace and Harr and the request from Harr to return the check because of a disputed endorsement.

Jack Barber, Gordon's friend at First National, testified that he did not determine that the negotiation of the check was unlawful, that he never saw the check, did not check the endorsement, and that he called the Co-op simply to relate information to his customer. Donna Harr, the manager at First National, testified that the reason for return which was stamped on the check was "other" and that "refer to maker" was also written on it at her direction. Harr could not explain why the endorsement box was not checked. She stated that the "customer [the Co-op] is the one that asked us to return the check, at our request." Harr further testified that she thought the Co-op asked that the check be returned "because of the endorsement," and that she made the decision that the endorsement was insufficient because the check was not signed by an authorized partner or party. She further stated that First National returned the check to Planters and the Co-op's account was credited with the funds.

Bonnie Wilbanks, the bookkeeper for Planters, testified that she discovered the returned check sitting in a basket by itself at the end of the work day on October 3. Wilbanks explained that the endorsement box was not checked, and that according to the bank's policy, "Gordon Wallace Farms" was a proper endorsement. When she inquired about the check, Wilbanks was instructed to speak with Wallace. According to Wilbanks, Wallace told her that there was a problem with the check and that it should be returned. Wilbanks further testified that Larry Bauer, the president of Planters, was in the room when she discussed the check with Wallace.

We think that there is substantial evidence that Wallace knew the effect of his actions and intentionally did them to achieve his personal ends. Thus, there is substantial evidence that it was Wallace's intentional and malicious purpose to have the check, in which he had a personal, pecuniary interest, charged-back against Gordon's account. At the very least, Wallace's behavior amounted to a conscious disregard for the consequences of his actions. Hence, we hold that there was sufficient evidence to present the issue of punitive damages to the jury.

C.   AGENCY RELATIONSHIP

Finally, to allow the jury to impose punitive damages on Planters, we must find that an agency relationship existed between Wallace and Planters when Wallace caused the check to be charged-back against Gordon's account.

Under the doctrine of respondeat superior, an employer may be held liable for punitive damages for the acts of his employee if the employee was acting within the scope of his or her employment at the time of the incident. J.B. Hunt Transp., Inc. v. Doss, 320 Ark. 660, 899 S.W.2d 464 (1995). Whether the employee's action is within the scope of the employment is not necessarily dependent upon the situs of the occurrence, but on whether the individual is carrying out the "object and purpose of the enterprise," as opposed to acting exclusively in his own interest. Id.

Planters asserts correctly that Wallace's personal, pecuniary interest motivated him to cause the charge-back of Gordon's check. However, Wallace utilized his position at the bank to achieve the purpose. Wallace further utilized his banking connections with Jack Barber of First National to start the charge-back procedure. Finally, Wallace was clearly acting within his supervisory capacity when he instructed Planters' bookkeeper to charge-back Gordon's check. Consequently, we find that Wallace was acting within the scope of his employment when he caused the charge-back of the account.

In addition, Planters may be held liable for punitive damages based on the conduct of Larry Bauer, the president of Planters. Specifically, Bauer refused to assist Gordon with the charge-back to his account, and instead, instructed Gordon to resolve the matter with Wallace. With this response, Bauer demonstrated his awareness of Wallace's actions, and more importantly, his "conscious indifference" to the charge-back on Gordon's account. See, Stein v. Lucas, 308 Ark. 74, 823 S.W.2d 832 (1992). We find that Planters Bank may be held liable for punitive damages based on Wallace's and/or Bauer's conduct.

Furthermore, Bauer's behavior may be construed as a ratification of Wallace's conduct. In Brady v. Bryant, 319 Ark. 712, 894 S.W.2d 144 (1995), we said:

> It is well settled in Arkansas law that when the principal has knowledge of the unauthorized acts of his agent, and remains silent . . . he cannot thereafter be heard to deny the agency but will be held to have ratified the unauthorized acts. . . . It has been said that the affirmance of an unauthorized transaction may be inferred from the failure to repudiate it, or from receipt or retention of benefits of the transaction with knowledge of the facts.

(citing Arnold v. All American Assurance Co., 255 Ark. 275, 496 S.W.2d 861 (1973)). Although *Brady* involved an agent's unauthorized entrance into a settlement agreement on behalf of the principal, the principle of ratification also applies when the agent's actions are tortious, and ratification may bind the principal for punitive damages. Restatement (Second) of Agency §§217(c) & 218 (1957).

Because there was sufficient evidence to allow the jury to decide whether Gordon was entitled to punitive damages based on Wallace or Bauer's conduct, we reverse the directed verdict and remand for retrial.

2. ATTORNEY'S FEES

Because we reverse and remand this case for retrial, we do not reach the issue of the award of attorney's fees to Gordon. However, we note that in an affidavit submitted to the court Gordon claimed he was entitled to $11,248.95 in attorney's fees for eighty-seven billable hours at $120 an hour and $800 for depositions. The trial judge awarded Gordon's attorney only $335, which does not even cover the cost of the depositions in this case involving a difficult issue of first impression in Arkansas.

Reversed and remanded.

CORBIN, J., and Special Justices ROBERT S. SHAFER and K. LEANNE DANIEL dissent. DUDLEY and BROWN, JJ., not participating.

DON CORBIN, Justice, dissenting. So much for the old adage that cheaters never prosper. After the majority's opinion today, it is apparent that not only do they prosper, but they may be entitled to punitive damages in addition to all the prosperity. There was no substantial evidence presented at trial to support an award of punitive damages to Appellant Ashel Gordon. To the contrary, there was evidence presented to the jury, including Gordon's own admissions, which demonstrated that Gordon was not entitled to the entire proceeds of the check and that this cause of action resulted only because Gordon's former partner, Wallace, happened to catch Gordon while he was attempting to keep the proceeds of the check all to himself. The trial judge said it best when he stated:

> [M]y conscience tells me that Mr. Gordon is trying to make—is already doubling his money on this deal. And to—to allow for him to shoot for punitive damages on top of that, after he has been frustrated in his attempt to possibly avoid his liability to Mr.—Mr. Wallace, that I can't in good conscience go with that.

The majority opinion mischaracterizes the trial testimony when it states that substantial evidence existed to present the issue of punitive damages to the jury. The majority is correct that both Gordon and his wife testified that it was their understanding that the partnership had been bought out by Gordon, and that, at the time, Wallace was not entitled to half of the money. The majority neglects to point out, however, that during the trial, on cross-examination, Gordon testified that ultimately he agreed that the check did not belong entirely to him. There was a further admission by Gordon that the Co-op had in the interim paid one-half of the proceeds of the check to him and the other half to Wallace. Thus, the trial judge was correct in his observation that Gordon had already gained all that he was rightfully entitled to when the Co-op paid him his share of the proceeds. The fact that he received the other half of the proceeds of the check when Planters moved for a directed verdict against itself demonstrates that Gordon had in fact gained twice the amount to which he was ever entitled. . . .

For all of the above reasons, I respectfully dissent.

[The other dissenting opinion of ROBERT S. SHAFER, Special Justice, who searched the Uniform Commercial Code in vain to find an authorization for punitive damages in this situation, is omitted.]

NOTE

For a commentary on this case, see Casenote, 51 Ark. L. Rev. 611 (1998).

PROBLEM 173

Octopus National Bank, as a depositary bank, took a check on which its customer, Stefanie Cochran, was the payee and allowed her to deposit it in her account. Since it was drawn on a nearby bank, ONB placed a hold on the deposited amount for two additonal banking days and then permitted her to withdraw the entire amount when that period expired. The very next day the check was returned NSF by the bank on which it was drawn. Is it too late to charge back the amount of the check to Stefanie's account?

E. Undoing Final Payment

While UCC rights *off* the instrument (such as the right to sue for breach of the presentment warranties) survive final payment, the instrument itself is canceled by final payment, thus ending all Article 3 suits on the implied obligations created there, and the payor bank, now itself *accountable* for the check, must pay over the check's amount to the presenter. One issue that refuses to go away is whether the payor bank may resist payment, using common law theories such as mistake.

PROBLEM 174

Sandra Shirker and Frank Foxholer, two commercial law students, learned about the Midnight Deadline Statutes and decided to see if they could use them to create money out of thin air. Shirker, who had a checking account at the Busy National Bank, withdrew all the money in the account and, by agreement with the bank, closed it. She then wrote a $5,000 check on the account payable to Foxholer, who deposited the check in his own bank account with a different bank. At the same time, Shirker called up her old bank and talked to the vice president in charge of check payment. Shirker told him that a $5,000 check would be presented against the closed-out account but that there was "something funny" about it and Shirker would appreciate it if the vice president would call her when it came in. The vice president did so when the check came in late in the banking day, and Shirker told him that it was important that they meet. Shirker promised to come down to the bank the next day.

The following morning Shirker called the bank and said that she was delayed but was still coming and the vice president should wait. Shirker never showed up and eventually the vice president went home. On the second banking day following receipt, the Busy National Bank marked the check "Account closed" and returned it to the depositary-presenting bank, which passed it on to Foxholer, the payee. Foxholer sued the payor bank, claiming final payment had been made under §4-215(a)(3) in that the provisional settlement had not been revoked within the time allowed by §4-301, so the bank was accountable for the check under §4-302(a). Assume that Foxholer has not breached one of the §4-208 presentment warranties. All right-thinking people would agree that Foxholder should lose this suit; the only question is as to what defense the Code permits. Read §§4-302(b) and 3-418; cf. §1-203.

PROBLEM 175

When the police department of Rome, Wisconsin, opened the box of new police radios it had ordered, it was dismayed to learn that the radios were not the correct size specified in the contract. Since the police department had already sent a check in payment to Voice of Japan, Inc., the seller, it immediately stopped payment on the check by so notifying its bank, Kelly National Bank. Negligently, Kelly National paid the check and, when the police department complained that the check was not properly payable, recredited the account.[21] You are the counsel for the bank, and the head of Checking Services calls you wanting to know whether the bank can recover the amount of the check from Voice of Japan. Look at §3-418 and its Official Comment and give your answer.

If the bank is successful in its restitution action against Voice of Japan, the latter is entitled to get the check back for use in its dispute with the police department. Even if the check is unavailable (it has been destroyed en route by a check truncation system or was returned to the drawer, who refuses to surrender it), §§3-418(d) and 3-301(iii) give Voice of Japan the status of a "person entitled to enforce the instrument" so as to enable Voice of Japan to sue the police department on the §3-414(b) obligation of the drawer of a draft (which runs to a "person entitled to enforce the draft"). Of course, when the §3-414(b) suit is brought, the police department may raise its breach of warranty defense (Voice of Japan is not a holder in due course), which, if valid, would enable it to prevail.

F. Restrictive Indorsements and Banks

Section 4-203 establishes the rule that only the collecting bank's transferor can give it binding instructions and the collecting bank need not examine the document to see whether other instructions or restrictions are contained in it. This is the *chain of command* theory of bank collection. See the Official Comment to §4-203.

PROBLEM 176

Nina Needy received her state welfare check and immediately made the following indorsement:

> For deposit only
> /s/Nina Needy

---

21. The subrogation rule of §4-407 is not likely to help the bank here because the payee, Voice of Japan, is guilty of breach of warranty, and so it is useless for the bank to subrogate itself to the payee's legal position.

On her way to the bank, her purse was snatched by Max Runner, who escaped and then examined the purse's contents. He found the check and wrote his own name below that of Nina. Max then took the check to his bank, Pursesnatchers National, and had the bank cash it. Pursesnatchers National stamped its indorsement on the check and forwarded it to the Innocent State Bank, which also indorsed the check and presented it to the drawee, the Welfare Payor Bank, which held the check past its midnight deadline. In the meantime, Nina Needy reported her loss to the state (the check's drawer), but by the time the state investigated the matter, the check had been paid. Nina consulted a lawyer. Can she sue the depositary, collecting, and drawee banks in conversion, arguing that by paying in violation of her express instruction (the restrictive indorsement "for deposit only"), the banks converted her check? Or can the banks use the chain of command sections cited above to escape liability? See §3-206(c).

People frequently place restrictive language above their signatures, and the effect of this is to create a *restrictive indorsement*. Read §3-206. A famous case, similar in its facts to the above Problem, Soma v. Handrulis, 277 N.Y. 233, 14 N.E.2d 46 (1938), held that all three banks (depositary, intermediary, and payor) had *converted* the check by paying it in obvious violation of a restrictive indorsement. The country's bankers were horrified by the decision; they knew that, as a practical matter, it is impossible for the banks involved in the check collection process to take the time to read and investigate all the restrictive indorsements on the backs of instruments. The Code's solution is stated first in §3-206(c): of the banks involved, *only the depositary bank* faces liability for non-compliance with the terms of a restrictive indorsement. Only at the depositary bank is the check likely to be examined by a human being (the teller). The computers that process the check thereafter cannot even read the restrictive indorsements. Read §3-206.

G. Delays

Back to bank collection—and the following true story.

PROBLEM 177

In the early 1970s, a Boise, Idaho, bank's janitor mistakenly placed a box full of 8,000 unprocessed checks on a table reserved for trash. The operator of the bank's paper shredder dutifully fed the checks into his machine, turning them into quarter-inch strips. About $840,000 worth of checks underwent this ordeal. The next morning the error was discovered, and the bank hired 50 temporary employees to work six hours a day for two months to paste the checks back together (puzzle lovers were particularly welcome). At the moment of the shredding, many of the checks involved were bound to be in the process of collection. For some of the checks the bank would be a depositary or collecting bank, and for others it would be the payor-drawee. Collecting banks are required to take action before their midnight deadline following receipt, §4-202(b), and, of course, the payor bank becomes absolutely accountable for a check not returned before the expiration of the midnight deadline. §§4-215(a)(3), 4-301, 4-302. Should the Boise bank just close down, or is there hope in §4-109(b) (Delays)? See Port City State Bank v. American Natl. Bank, 486 F.2d 196, 13 U.C.C. Rep. Serv. 423 (10th Cir. 1973); Sun River Cattle Co. v. Miners Bank, 164 Mont. 237, 521 P.2d 679, 14 U.C.C. Rep. Serv. 1004 (1974). Regulation CC §229.13(f) has a similar exemption for emergency conditions.

H.   Priorities in the Bank Account: The Four Legals

The final bank collection problem we have left is the question of priority: what gets paid first? Bankers must constantly deal with four events—notice (for instance, of a depositor's death), stop-payment orders, service of legal process (garnishment, etc.), and the bank's right of setoff—and decide whether the happening of one of these events, which bankers call *the four legals*, has priority over the payment of a check. The issue is now resolved by §4-303(a), which states in essence that the four legal events come too late, as to any given check, if that check has either been certified or the bank has taken the steps that lead to final payment of the check. Further, the four legal events are too late if they arrive after the time periods described in (a)(5). Read §4-303(a) and consider these matters.

PROBLEM 178

Joseph Armstrong had $4,000 in his checking account with the Antitrust National Bank on the afternoon of October 5 at the moment when he filed a voluntary petition in bankruptcy with the local federal district court. Early in the morning of October 6, the bank received three checks drawn on the account. One for $1,000 was presented in person by the payee and paid over the counter. Another for $500, which had been presented by another bank, was posted against the account, marked "Paid," and placed in the drawer's statement file. A third, which had also been presented by another bank on October 6, was for $3,000, and the bank was unsure what to do with it, so it placed it in a "hold pending consultation with drawer" file. At noon, Armstrong ran into Vivian Visor, the bank's head teller, while eating in the same restaurant, and since they were friends, Armstrong told Visor that the day before he had filed the bankruptcy petition. Visor expressed sympathy. At one o'clock, just as Visor walked back into the bank, another teller made an over-the-counter payment of $500 on a fourth check. At two o'clock the bankruptcy trustee phoned the bank and made a formal demand that the bank freeze the account. On receiving this notice, Robert Startup, a bank vice president, checked the bank's records, found that Armstrong owed the bank $75 on a home improvement loan, and told the bank clerk to deduct this amount from Armstrong's account. Subsequently, the bank reported to the trustee that the account contained $1,925, as follows:

Oct. 5	$4,000
Oct. 6	
First Check	− 1,000
	3,000
Second Check	− 500
	2,500
Fourth Check	− 500
	2,000
Home Improvement Loan	− 75
	$1,925

The third check was marked "Not Sufficient Funds" and was returned to the presenting bank early in the morning of October 8.

Answer these questions:

(a) Can the trustee in bankruptcy claim that the filing of a voluntary petition in bankruptcy on October 5 automatically froze the account of $4,000 so that the bank owes the bankruptcy estate that amount? In 1966 the U.S. Supreme Court held that the bank was protected until it had notice of the bankruptcy proceeding. Bank of Marin v. England, 385 U.S. 99 (1966). This result was subsequently codified in the Bankruptcy Reform Act of 1978, 11 U.S.C. §542(c), although the trustee can usually recover the money from the payee. See Bankruptcy Code §549(a).

(b) At what moment did the bank have notice of the bankruptcy: when Armstrong told Visor, when Visor returned to the bank, or when the phone call was received? The answer to this question will determine the validity of the payment of the fourth check. See §§1-201(25), 1-201(26), and 1-201(27), all defining *notice* and *knowledge*.

(c) Was the home improvement loan payment effective against the trustee? See Bankruptcy Code §553 (setoff permitted on getting relief from the automatic stay of §362(a)(7)).

(d) If you are the attorney representing the bank that presented the third check, what legal theory, if any, might attract your attention?

PROBLEM 179

The newly established Embryo State Bank hires you as counsel to the bank. After a month's operations, the bank calls you up with the following dilemma. One of its customers is Thomas Crandall, whose account currently contains $5,000. This morning at 9:00 A.M. the bank received a bundle of checks from the bank across the street, and the bundle contained five checks drawn against Crandall's account payable to different payees and totaling $1,258. At 9:05 A.M., the bank received a bundle of checks from the nearest Federal Reserve Bank, and this bundle contained one check drawn on Crandall's account for $4,986. The dilemma: should the bank dishonor the one big check or the five little ones? Three of the little checks are dated prior to the big check and two after. The bank is afraid that if it dishonors the big one, Crandall will quickly be sued by a major creditor. On the other hand, if it dishonors the little ones, five creditors, not just one, will think Crandall is a bum. The bank is afraid it will face §4-402 damages for wrongful dishonor. Without looking at the Code, what would you advise the bank to do? Now look at §4-303(b) and its Official Comment; see Hill v. St. Paul Fed. Bank, 768 N.E.2d 322, 47 UCC Rep. Serv. 2d 26 (Ill. App. 2002); Smith v. First Union Nat. Bank of Tennessee, 958 S.W.2d 113, 35 U.C.C. Rep. Serv. 2d 1309 (Tenn. App. 1997).

Chapter 12
WRONGDOING AND ERROR

This course does not get involved with the substance of the crimes one might possibly commit using a negotiable instrument. Suffice it to say that it is a crime in all jurisdictions to write a check against an account known to be insufficient (or non-existent), to forge a signature to a check, or to pass (*utter*) an instrument known to be forged. It is also illegal to try to use the delay period of bank collection, the float, to create money on empty accounts. This process, known as *check kiting*, in its simplest form involves opening two bank accounts in distant locations and writing and depositing checks on the other account in each bank, increasing the amount and using the slowness of the bank collection process to create the false appearance of assets.[1]

---

1. I hesitate, for some reason, to elaborate on the how-to's of check kiting; let me note that bankers have devised methods of detecting many check-kiting schemes in their early stages.

Ignoring the commercial paper crimes, this section of the book explores the legal tangles that follow in the wake of such nefarious activity.

I. FORGERY OF THE PAYEE'S NAME

A. Some Basic Ideas

It is important that you go back and review two concepts that we have already covered and make sure that they are still part of your repertoire.

The first of these was the principle explored at the end of Chapter 2 (Negotiation): the forgery of the payee's name (or of a special indorsee's name) means that no valid negotiation takes place, and therefore no one taking the instrument thereafter can qualify as a *holder.*

PROBLEM 180

When she graduated from law school, Portia Moot received a $500 check signed by her grandmother. She put it in her personal papers when she packed up to move to a new city, where she planned on using it to open a checking account there. When her car, containing all her belongings, was stolen en route, the check went with it. The thief, Harry Villain, forged Portia's name to the back of the check and then signed his own name below hers. He deposited the check in the account he carried with Careless State Bank. Before the check was presented, Portia had her grandmother stop payment on the check, so it was dishonored and returned to Careless State Bank. By this time Harry had withdrawn the money and fled the jurisdiction. Careless State phoned its attorney. Since it gave value for the check, isn't it a holder in due course and, as such, can't it enforce the check against the grandmother per §3-414(b)? See §3-201.

As we saw at the end of Chapter 2, if a check is payable to the order of a named individual, only that person can be a holder, a status postponed until the payee acquires possession; see §1-201(20). Without a valid indorsement by the payee, no later person can qualify as a holder (much less a holder in due course), and this is true no matter how many times the instrument is thereafter transferred, no matter how good the forgery appears to be, no matter how innocent the later takers or how much value they paid. Indeed, the check is still the property of the payee whose name was forged and that person could replevy it from the current transferee.

We would get a completely different result if this check were either made out to bearer or if the payee had indorsed it in blank before the check was stolen. In that case, anyone in possession of the check would be a holder and, if otherwise qualifying, a holder in due course.

The second concept to review is the meaning of the phrase "a person entitled to enforce the instrument." Section 3-301 defines the phrase, and you should reread it now. The primary definition is that of *holder* (i.e., someone who takes pursuant to a valid negotiation), but the phrase also includes some others the law thinks worthy of protection. Subsection (ii) speaks of "a nonholder in possession of the instrument who has the rights of a holder." What does this mean? Consider the following.

PROBLEM 181

Assume from the last Problem that when Portia was leaving the city she owed $500 to her former roommate, Helen Midlaw, so she gave her the graduation check but forgot to indorse it. Is Helen a "holder"? When she discovers that Portia forgot to indorse the check, could she force Portia to do so? See §3-203.

Helen qualifies as a non-holder with the rights of a holder pursuant to the shelter rule of §3-203(b), and is therefore a person entitled to enforce the instrument. Another example of such a person is a depositary bank. Suppose that Portia took the check from her grandmother and deposited it, unindorsed, in the bank account she opened in the new city to which she moved. Section 4-205 gives the depositary bank Portia's holder rights and makes it a person entitled to enforce the instrument in spite of the lack of payee indorsement.

Return to the definition of "person entitled to enforce the instrument" in §3-301. There are two other possible entities that qualify per subsection (iii). The first of these is someone who has lost the instrument but who has the right to go to court to re-create it pursuant to §3-309. Consider this possibility: Portia's cat chews up the check while stuck in the car when Portia is driving across country. Portia no longer is a holder—there is nothing to hold. But she has the right to use the mechanism of §3-309 and is therefore still a person entitled to enforce the instrument. The final person so qualifying is the person described in §3-418(d); see the text following Problem 175 at page 576.

B. Warranty Liability

After the forger plies his or her trade, the other parties dealing with the check must adjust their responsibilities vis-à-vis each other. There are three primary theories: the properly payable rule of §4-401, the warranties rules discussed next, and the ability of certain parties to sue in conversion (covered later in the chapter).

PROBLEM 182

Portia Moot owed $400 to her landlord, John Clark, so she handed him a check on the first of the month when they met in the lobby. John thought he had put it in his pocket, but in reality it had fluttered to the floor, where it was discovered by Harry Villain, another tenant of the building. Harry took the check down to Tower Drug Store and asked the manager to cash it for him, pretending to be John Clark, whose name he had forged to the back of the check. The manager then gave Harry $400, stamped "Tower Drug Store" under the forgery, and deposited the check in the account Tower Drug carried at Merchants Bank. Merchants Bank presented the check to Octopus National Bank, the drawee bank, and was paid. A week later John Clark searched everywhere for the check. Finally he went back to Portia and told her he had lost it. By this time the check had been returned to Portia by Octopus National Bank as part of her monthly bank statement. Portia showed it to John, and he positively declared that his signature on the back of the check was a forgery. Portia, a law student with a good grasp of the forgery rules of the Uniform Commercial Code, knew just what to do. She wrote him another check and then went down to Octopus National Bank.

(a) Can she make Octopus National Bank recredit her account? What is her theory? See §4-401.

(b) Octopus National Bank has made final payment on this check, and, as we saw in the last chapter, that ends its ability to dishonor the check. However, §4-302(b) provides that final payment does not prevent warranty liability from giving relief to the bank, specifically referring to §4-208. Read that section and answer these two questions: (1) which warranty described therein was breached, and (2) who breached it?

Both Articles 3 and 4 contain warranty sections, and they are virtually identical as a matter of substance. Sections 3-417 and 4-208 both describe *presentment* warranties, and §§3-416 and 4-207 cover *transfer* warranties. The Article 3 warranties control until the check is taken for deposit, at which point the Article 4 warranties take over. This usually has no practical significance, given that the warranty liability is the same in both articles, but if an attorney needs to file a complaint, it is important that the correct article be cited.

What is the difference between *presentment* and *transfer*? The answer is easiest to understand if you think of a negotiable instrument as having three stages in its life: issuance, transfer, and presentment. Issuance (§3-105) is the creation of the instrument and its handing over to the first taker. There are no warranties made on issuance. Skipping for a moment the middle stage (transfer), the final stage in the life of the instrument is presentment: its surrender to the drawee for either acceptance or payment.[2] At that moment presentment warranties are made by not only the entity physically making presentment but also all prior transferors (this giving the drawee a choice of defendants). Every other movement of the instrument for consideration between issuance and presentment is a *transfer* of the instrument and gives rise to the transfer warranties. Warranty suits are said to be suits "off the instrument" because they do not require possession of the instrument as a prerequisite to suit.

PROBLEM 183

Return to the facts of the last Problem. Assume that Octopus National Bank successfully recaptured its money from Merchants Bank under a theory of breach of a presentment warranty. Now Merchants Bank calls in its attorney and asks for legal advice. Can it sue the drugstore using §4-208(a) (note the word *drawee* in subsection (a))? How does it get legal relief? See §4-207(a). What warranties have been breached? Must it give notice to the drugstore within any given period

---

2. If the instrument is a promissory note, presentment is made to the maker of the note, in which case the only presentment warranty is that described in §3-417(d).

of time? See §4-207(d). If the drugstore refuses to pay, how quickly must suit be commenced? See §4-111; cf. §3-118.

PROBLEM 184

Still using the facts of the above Problems, now assume that you are the attorney for the drugstore. To what relief is it entitled, assuming it can find Harry Villain in a solvent condition?

When a forgery of a payee's name occurs, it is the policy of our law to use warranty theories, first presentment and then transfer, to pass the loss back to the wrongdoer (or the first person to trust the wrongdoer). Note that the drugstore was always in the best position to discover the forgery by making Harry produce identification when he tried to cash the check.

As for damages for breach of warranty, the relevant sections in both Articles 3 and 4 are identical with, for example, §3-416(b) providing for a recovery of "the loss suffered as a result of the breach, but not more than the amount of the instrument plus expenses and loss of interest incurred as a result of the breach."

Using the original version of these sections, some courts allowed the injured party, particularly a payor bank, to recover its attorney's fees. See Bagby v. Merrill Lynch, Pierce, Fenner & Smith, Inc., 491 F.2d 192, 13 U.C.C. Rep. Serv. 1069 (8th Cir. 1974); First Virginia Bank-Colonial v. Provident State Bank, 582 F. Supp. 850, 38 U.C.C. Rep. Serv. 561 (D. Md. 1984); and Provident Natl. Bank v. National Bank of N. Am., 17 U.C.C. Rep. Serv. 486 (N.Y. Civ. Ct. 1975); *contra* Riedel v. First Natl. Bank, 287 Or. 285, 598 P.2d 302, 27 U.C.C. Rep. Serv. 503 (1979) (no matter what the Code appears to say, Oregon's judicial policy does not permit the award of attorney's fees). In the Revision, all the warranty sections in both Article 3 and Article 4 authorize the recovery of "expenses," and the Official Comments to all these sections —for example, Official Comment 6 to §3-416—have this to say:

> There is no express provision for attorney's fees, but attorney's fees are not meant to be necessarily excluded. They could be granted because they fit within the phrase "expenses . . . incurred as a result of the breach." The intention is to leave to other state law the issue as to when attorney's fees are recoverable.

Since in most jurisdictions attorney's fees are not recoverable in the typical lawsuit, this language is likely to exclude them in Article 3 and Article 4 warranty suits brought under the Revision. So far no courts have allowed attorneys fees as damages; see *Christensen Aviation, Inc. v. State Bank, N.A.*, 20 P.3d 170, 44 U.C.C. Rep. Serv. 2d 213 (Okla. App. 2001).

C. Conversion Liability

Conversion is the civil action for misappropriation of another's property. There are many ways a negotiable instrument can be converted.

PROBLEM 185

Your employer gives you your paycheck, drawn on the employer's bank, Octopus National. You take the check down to the bank and present it across the counter. The teller takes it, walks away from the window and comes back a few minutes later empty-handed. "Yes?" she asks, looking at you blankly. "The check?" you ask. "Sorry," she says, "we are not going to pay it." "Then I want it back," you reply, planning to use it to pursue your employer on the drawer's obligation (§3-414(b)). "Sorry," she says, "we are also keeping the check." Do they have the right to do that?

PROBLEM 186

Mr. Aristotle Wellborn was walking along the street when he was surreptitiously relieved of his wallet by Art Dodger. In the wallet was a check made out to Wellborn, who had already indorsed it. Is Dodger guilty of conversion?

The original language of the conversion section in the prior version of Article 3 was so poorly written that it did not appear to cover all the situations where a conversion action should lie, and the courts were forced to fill in the gaps. The Revision handles this difficulty by simply incorporating the common law of conversion as applicable to negotiable instruments (see the first sentence of §3-420(a)), and that should permit the courts to find conversion liability in both of the last Problems.

Only the person whose property rights are adversely affected may sue for conversion. For negotiable instruments the *holder* is the owner

...trument and is the person with the property rights therein. ... at the outset only the payee can be the holder of an order ...strument, only the payee has a sufficient property interest to become the plaintiff (or if the payee has negotiated the instrument to another, only that person can be the *holder* having a property interest in the instrument). Since the instrument, once delivered, gives the payee these property rights, the payee can take a number of different possible courses of action whenever the check is stolen, his or her name is forged thereon, and the instrument is paid by the drawee bank:

(1) *Conversion.* The payee can sue the drawee bank, or anyone taking the check after the forgery, in conversion. If the drawee is forced to pay the payee, the drawee will sue the check's presenter for breach of the presentment warranty that he or she was a "person entitled to enforce the instrument"; §4-208(a)(1). That person can then sue the transferee for breach of transfer warranties; §3-416(a)(1), (2), and (4). Thus, the loss will pass back up the chain until it reaches the forger or, if the forger has departed for parts unknown, the first person to trust the forger. The cases are collected in Annot., 23 A.L.R.4th 855.

(2) *Drawer's Obligation.* Since the check is still the property of the payee, he or she can replevy it from its current possessor (probably the drawer, who will have it among the canceled checks), cross off the forged indorsement, sign it, and present it to the drawee bank for payment. If the drawee pays it, well and good. If not, a dishonor will have occurred, and the payee may then sue the drawer on the drawer's obligation, §3-414(b), or, certainly now, the underlying obligation.

(3) *Quasi-Contract.* Most courts considering the issue will permit the quasi-contractual action by the payee for money had and received, a cause of action that typically has a longer statute of limitations than does conversion. See Peerless Ins. Co. v. Texas Commerce Bank, 791 F.2d 1177, 1 U.C.C. Rep. Serv. 2d 622 (5th Cir. 1986).

(4) *Negligence.* Most courts considering the issue have not allowed either a common law negligence claim against banks handling forged checks, finding that the statutory scheme of Article 3 of the Uniform Commercial Code preempts all common law theories; see Lee Newman, M.D., Inc. v. Wells Fargo Bank, 87 Cal. App. 4th 73, 104 Cal. Rptr. 2d 310, 43 UCC Rep. Serv. 2d 912 (2001). There are a minority of decisions allowing the common law to supplement the Code; Racso

Diagnostic, Inc. v. Community Bank of Homestead, 735 So. 2d 519, 38 U.C.C. Rep. Serv. 2d 486 (Fla. App. 1999).

The common law had always provided that payment on a forged indorsement was conversion—see Restatement (Second) of Torts §241A—but that statement leaves a lot of substantive law to be explored. The original conversion section did not answer a host of questions that §3-420 now settles. These matters are explored by the following Problems.

PROBLEM 187

When Portia Moot learned that the check she had given to her landlord had been stolen from him, his name forged as payee, and the check had been paid by her bank, she sued her bank in conversion. Is she the proper plaintiff in this lawsuit? If not, (1) who is, and (2) what relief does the law give her? See §§3-420(a) and 4-401(a).

PROBLEM 188

After he won the lottery, Tim Isle decided to pay off the mortgage on his home. He mailed a check for $80,000 to Octopus National Bank (ONB), the mortgagee, but it was stolen from the mail by an unknown person, who forged "Octopus National Bank" on the back and cashed the check at Sleepy Hollow State Bank, which then collected it from the drawee bank. Since ONB, the payee, never received possession of the check, does it have sufficient property rights therein to succeed in a conversion action against Sleepy Hollow State Bank or the drawee? See §3-420(a). What can the bank do? See §3-310(b).

Leeds v. Chase Manhattan Bank, N.A.

New Jersey Superior Court, Appellate Division, 2000
752 A.2d 332, 42 U.C.C. Rep. Serv. 2d 195

WECKER, J.A.D.

Plaintiffs William Leeds and Carol Leeds, a mother and son, (collectively "plaintiff" or "Leeds"), hired Louis Egnasko, Esq.[3] to represent

___

3. Egnasko has since been disbarred by both New York and New Jersey. Matter of Egnasko, 151 N.J. 506, 701 A.2d 701 (1997); Matter of Egnasko, 223 A.D.2d 317, 646 N.Y.S.2d 698 (App. Div. 1996).

them in connection with a mortgage foreclosure action, as well as the purchase and resale of the property in East Orange, New Jersey on which they held the mortgage. After plaintiff bought the property at the foreclosure sale, they entered into a contract to sell the property. Egnasko closed the sale and accepted a settlement check for $87,293.56 on plaintiff's behalf. The settlement check payable to William Leeds, Carol Leeds, and Isabel Gibbs,[4] was a United Jersey Bank teller's check drawn at that bank's Hackensack, New Jersey branch. Summit Bank is the successor-in-interest to United Jersey Bank (hereinafter "Summit").

Following the closing, and unknown to Leeds, Egnasko altered the settlement check by typing "* * *Louis Egnasko, as attorney for* * *" above the payee line, so that the check then read:

* * *LOUIS EGNASKO AS ATTORNEY FOR* * *
* * *WILLIAM LEEDS, CAROL LEEDS, ISABEL GIBBS* * *

Egnasko alone endorsed the check "for deposit only, 067003443" and deposited the check into his attorney trust account at Chemical Bank. Chemical Bank stamped the back of the check "Endorsement guaranteed." Defendant Chase Manhattan Bank is the successor-in-interest to Chemical Bank (hereinafter "Chase"). Chase presented the check for collection in the ordinary course, and Summit honored its own teller's check. The check was negotiated between May 8 and May 16, 1996.

On June 6, 1996, Egnasko drew a check for $92,050 payable to William and Carol Leeds from an attorney trust account he held at the Trust Company of New Jersey (Trustco). This check apparently covered the proceeds of the sale of the home. Trustco honored the check drawn to Leeds, and Leeds received payment on that check. However, Egnasko's Trustco account also contained funds that Egnasko had obtained by similarly altering and depositing a check payable to Shrewsbury State Bank ("Shrewsbury"), which was intended to pay off a mortgage loan in an unrelated real estate transaction. Instead of delivering that check to Shrewsbury, Egnasko again inserted

4. Gibbs had been a record owner with the right of survivorship of an undivided one-third share of the East Orange property along with Grace Livingston and Louise Bevans, to whom Leeds made a mortgage loan. Gibbs apparently died intestate. Although Leeds alone received a deed from the Sheriff, the buyer required that Gibbs be named as a contract seller, and issued the check payable to Leeds and Gibbs, as described. The record reveals no claim by Gibbs' estate to the proceeds of the sale, and the estate is not involved in this appeal.

his own name, "Louis Egnasko as attorney," above the payee's name and deposited the check into his Trustco attorney trust account. Egnasko thus used funds that belonged to Shrewsbury to pay Leeds.

Facing a claim for conversion by Shrewsbury, Trustco filed suit against Egnasko and Leeds in New York, seeking repayment of monies traceable to Egnasko's fraud. Leeds filed an answer and crossclaim in the New York action on December 5, 1997, admitting receipt of the Trustco check from Egnasko, but denying that "William and Carol Leeds owe [Trustco] the traceable converted proceeds of the check delivered to William Leeds with interest. . . ."

On December 24, 1997, Leeds filed this action alleging strict liability for payment on the altered settlement check against both Chase, the depository bank, and Summit, the drawer/drawee/payor bank. In support of their motion for summary judgment, defendants argued that (1) Leeds had been paid and therefore suffered no damages; (2) Leeds would only be ordered to return that payment in the Trustco action if Leeds were found to have accepted payment with knowledge that the funds were stolen; and (3) if Leeds knowingly accepted stolen monies, the equitable doctrine of unclean hands would bar recovery against the banks. . . .

Leeds argued in opposition to summary judgment and in support of his cross-motion that Chase, as the depository bank, is strictly liable for conversion under N.J.S.A. 12A:3-420, including damages related to the cost of defending the New York suit. The motion judge granted summary judgment in favor of both Chase and Summit dismissing plaintiff's complaint. . . .

We first address Leeds' cause of action in conversion against Chase. The applicable provision of the Uniform Commercial Code (UCC), N.J.S.A. 12A:3-420a, states:

> The law applicable to conversion of personal property applies to instruments. *An instrument is also converted if* it is taken by transfer, other than a negotiation, from a person not entitled to enforce the instrument *or a bank makes or obtains payment with respect to the instrument for a person not entitled to enforce the instrument or receive payment.* An action for conversion of an instrument may not be brought by the issuer or acceptor of the instrument or a payee or indorsee who did not receive delivery of the instrument either directly or through delivery to an agent or a co-payee. [Emphasis added.]

Although the check was not actually delivered to Leeds, it was delivered to Egnasko as Leeds' attorney, with intent that title be transferred to Leeds, the payee. Thus Leeds is entitled to bring this action for conversion as one who "receive[d] delivery of the instrument . . . through delivery to an agent. . . . " N.J.S.A. 12A:3-420a. . . . It is undisputed that Egnasko was not authorized by Leeds to indorse the check and had no right to receive or enforce payment on that check.

Section 3-420a does not explicitly refer to "forgery" or "alteration," but instead addresses a class of persons who are "not entitled to enforce the instrument or receive payment." However, there can be no question that because the Summit teller's check payable to Leeds was altered by Egnasko, he was not "entitled" to payment on the instrument. Such an alteration constitutes a forgery under the Code and the common law. See N.J.S.A. 12A:3-407a . . . . By crediting Egnasko's trust account with the face amount of the check, Chase paid the check to "a person not entitled to . . . receive payment." N.J.S.A. 12A:3-420a.

As a depository bank under the Uniform Commercial Code, see N.J.S.A. 12A:4-105b, Chase is strictly liable for conversion on a forged or stolen instrument. See N.J.S.A. 12A:3-420, comment 1. Therefore, Chase is strictly liable on Leeds' claim for conversion under N.J.S.A. 12A:3-420a, because Chase "[made or obtained] payment with respect to the instrument for a person not entitled to enforce the instrument or receive payment." See New Jersey Lawyers' Fund, 303 N.J. Super. at 224, 696 A.2d 728.

The justification for strict liability upon the depository bank is that "the loss should normally come to rest upon the first solvent party in the stream after the one who forged the indorsement. . . ." 2 James J. White & Robert S. Summers, Uniform Commercial Code §18-4 at 209-10 (4th ed. 1995). See also Uniform Commercial Code, comment 3 to N.J.S.A. 12A:3-420:

> The depositary bank is ultimately liable in the case of a forged indorse-ment check because of its warranty to the payor bank under Section 4-208(a)(1) and it is usually the most convenient defendant in cases involving multiple checks drawn on different banks. There is no basis for requiring the owner of the check to bring multiple actions against the various payor banks and to require those banks to assert warranty rights against the depositary bank.

We are therefore convinced that the motion court improperly entered summary judgment against Leeds and in favor of Chase. We are also convinced that Chase is not entitled to summary judgment based upon the defense of payment, in light of Leeds' continuing exposure to the New York action, until that action has been resolved. If Leeds is not required in that action to disgorge the payment received from Egnasko, Chase will be entitled to set off that payment against its liability for conversion. Cf. County Concrete Corp. v. Smith, 317 N.J. Super. 50, 61-62, 721 A.2d 34 (App. Div. 1998). Leeds cannot be allowed a double recovery. If Leeds is required to disgorge, we will then address Chase's "unclean hands" defense on a complete record. That Leeds' damage claim may be limited (or even dismissed) in the future does not affect our determination of Chase's liability here and now.

We next address Leeds' cause of action in conversion against Summit. Summit is the drawer, the drawee, and the payor bank on the altered check under the Code definitions. A drawee bank is also strictly liable for conversion when it pays on a forged endorsement. . . . In Gast v. American Cas. Co. of Reading, Pa., 99 N.J. Super. 538, 541, 240 A.2d 682 (1968), we said:

> As both drawer and drawee defendant had the responsibility to make payment to the named payees on the instrument. . . . The statute [the former UCC §§3-419] created an absolute right to recover in favor of plaintiffs . . . upon proof that the draft was paid on the forged indorsements. Plaintiffs' indorsements were concededly forged. It follows that defendant, having paid the draft, was rendered liable for the conversion in the face amount.

However, N.J.S.A. 12A:3-420c limits damages for conversion against

> [a] representative, other than a depository bank, who has in good faith dealt with an instrument or its proceeds on behalf of one who was not the person entitled to enforce the instrument . . . [for any more than] the amount of any proceeds that it has not paid out.

Summit is not a depositary bank in this case. Summit has paid out the entire face amount of the forged check and is not alleged to have acted other than in good faith; it therefore cannot be liable to Leeds for conversion under §3-420. Whether Summit could have been found liable for negligence, as a result of its failure to detect the alteration on its own teller's check, is not before us. Plaintiff has not pled or argued a negligence cause of action against Summit. Summary judgment is therefore affirmed in favor of Summit. . . .

We affirm summary judgment dismissing the complaint against Summit, reverse summary judgment in favor of Chase, and remand for entry of partial summary judgment on liability against Chase. A determination of damages must abide the outcome of the New York action.

PROBLEM 189

The drawer made the check out to "John and Mary Doe" in order to pay a debt owed to them both. John got the check first, signed his name alone as indorser, and deposited the check in his individual checking account. His bank presented the check to the drawee bank and was paid. The issue: is a missing signature treated the same as a forged one? Has the presenting bank breached the warranty that it is a person entitled to enforce the check? Could Mary Doe sue the banks in conversion? See §§3-110(d) and 3-420(a).

Finally, you should remember that payment in violation of the terms of a restrictive indorsement ("For Deposit Only," for example) also gives rise to a cause of action in conversion; see §3-206(c) (a matter discussed in Subsection II.F of Chapter 11).

II. FORGERY OF THE DRAWER'S NAME

When a forger forges the *drawer's* name (as opposed to that of the payee), the law reaches a completely different result from what we saw in the last section. The basic rule, the rule of Price v. Neal (below), coming to us from 1762, is that the drawee who pays or accepts a draft takes the risk of a forged drawer's signature. Later cases, however, then established the rule that the drawee does not take the risk of a forged *indorser's* signature. Canal Bank v. Bank of Albany, 1 Hill 287 (N.Y. 1841). This dichotomy still exists in our law.

Vital to an understanding of the Code's position on forgery is a grasp of the famous English case of Price v. Neal, reprinted below. Students have been telling me for years that the fact situation is too complicated to follow and, as a consequence, Lord Mansfield's opinion is meaningless. The reason for this confusion is that several key facts are unreported in the decision and have to be guessed at before the decision makes sense. To aid you in this endeavor, I have prepared my own interpretation of the facts, which you may compare with those reported in the decision.

The Facts of Price v. Neal. John Price had agreed with one Benjamin Sutton to accept and pay any drafts that Sutton drew on Price; the drafts were called *bills of exchange.* Sutton became involved in business dealings with two other men, Rogers Ruding and Thomas Ploughfor, the upshot of which was that Sutton apparently drew up two drafts on Price payable to Ruding. Both drafts were indorsed by several people before coming into the hands of Edward Neale.[5] The first draft (bill of exchange), for 40 pounds, Neale presented to Price (the drawee) for payment, and Price, via his servant, paid the draft. The second draft, also for 40 pounds, was presented for acceptance, and Price wrote on it: "Accepted, John Price," adding an order on the back to his bankers, Messieurs Freame and Barclay, telling them to pay the draft for him when it was presented for payment. We are not told who made the presentment of the second draft for acceptance, but after Price had accepted it, the draft was returned to the presenter, who indorsed it over to Neale. The latter obtained payment from Price's bankers. Subsequently, Price learned that Sutton had not really signed the drafts; his name as drawer had been forged to the instruments by a man named Lee. Price brought suit against Neale for "money had and received," demanding a return of the mistaken payments.

Price v. Neal

King's Bench, 1762
3 Burr. 1354, 97 Eng. Rep. 871

This was a special case reserved at the sittings of Guildhall after Trinity term 1762, before Lord Mansfield.

It was an action upon the case brought by Price against Neal; wherein Price declares that the defendant Edward Neale was indebted to him in 80£ for money had and received to his the plaintiff's use: and damages were laid to 100£. The general issue was pleaded; and issue joined thereon.

It was proved at the trial, that a bill was drawn as follows "Leicester, 22d November 1760. Sir, six weeks after date pay Mr. Rogers Ruding or order forty pounds, value received for Mr. Thomas Ploughfor, as advised by, sir, your humble servant Benjamin Sutton. To Mr. John Price in Bush-Lane Cannon-Street, London"; indorsed "R. Ruding, Antony Topham, Hammond and Laroche. Received the contents, James Watson and Son, witness Edward Neale."

5. I've always worried about the "e" at the end of Neale's name—it doesn't appear in the case style.

That this bill was indorsed to the defendant for a valuable consideration; and notice of the bill left at the plaintiff's house, on the day it became due. Whereupon the plaintiff sent his servant to call on the defendant, to pay him the said sum of 40£, and to take up the said bill: which was done accordingly.

That another bill was drawn as follows—"Leicester, 1st February 1761. Sir, six weeks after date pay Mr. Rogers Ruding or order forty pounds, value received for Mr. Thomas Ploughfor; as advised by, sir, your humble servant Benjamin Sutton. To Mr. John Price in Bush-Lane, Cannon-Street, London." That this bill was indorsed, "R. Ruding, Thomas Watson and Son. Witness for Smith, Right and Co." That the plaintiff accepted this bill, by writing on it, "Accepted John Price:" and that the plaintiff wrote on the back of it—"Messieurs Freame and Barclay, pray pay forty pounds for John Price."

That this bill being so accepted was indorsed to the defendant for a valuable consideration, and left at his bankers for payment; and was paid by order of the plaintiff, and taken up.

Both these bills were forged by one Lee, who has been since hanged for forgery.

The defendant Neale acted innocently and bona fide, without the least privity or suspicion of the said forgeries or of either of them; and paid the whole value of those bills.

The jury found a verdict for the plaintiff; and assessed damages 80£ and costs 40s. subject to the opinion of the Court upon this question—

> Whether the plaintiff under the circumstances of the case, can recover back, from the defendant, the money he paid on the said bills, or either of them.

Mr. Stowe, for the plaintiff, argued that he ought to recover back the money, in this action; as it was paid by him by mistake only, on supposition "that these were true genuine bills"; and as he could never recover it against the drawer, because in fact no drawer exists; nor against the forger, because he is hanged.

He owned that in a case at Guild-Hall, of Jenys v. Fawler et Al', (an action by an indorsee of a bill of exchange brought against the acceptor), Lord Raymond would not admit the defendants to prove it a forged bill, by calling persons acquainted with the hand of the drawer, to swear "that they believed it not to be so": and he even strongly inclined, "that actual proof of forgery would not excuse the defendants against their own acceptance, which had given the bill a credit to the indorsee."

But he urged, that in the case now before the Court, the forgery of the bill does not rest in belief and opinion only; but has been actually proved, and the forger executed for it.

Thus it stands even upon the accepted bill. But the plaintiff's case is much stronger upon the other bill which was not accepted. It is not stated "that this bill was accepted before it was negotiated"; on the contrary, the consideration for it was paid by the defendant, before the plaintiff had seen it. So that the defendant took it upon the credit of the indorsers, not upon the credit of the plaintiff; and therefore the reason, upon which Lord Raymond grounds his inclination to be of opinion "that actual proof of forgery would be no excuse," will not hold here.

Mr. Yates, for the defendant, argued that the plaintiff was not entitled to recover back this money from the defendant.

He denied it to be a payment by mistake: and insisted that it was rather owing to the negligence of the plaintiff; who should have inquired and satisfied himself "whether the bill was really drawn upon him by Sutton, or not." Here is no fraud in the defendant; who is stated "to have acted innocently and bona fide, without the least privity or suspicion of the forgerys and to have paid the whole value for the bills."

Lord Mansfield stopt him from going on; saying that this was one of those cases that could never be made plainer by argument.

It is an action upon the case, for money had and received to the plaintiff's use. In which action, the plaintiff can not recover the money, unless it be against conscience in the defendant, to retain it; and great liberality is always allowed, in this sort of action.

But it can never be thought unconscientious in the defendant to retain this money, when he has once received it upon a bill of exchange indorsed to him for a fair and valuable consideration, which he had bona fide paid, without the least privity or suspicion of any forgery.

Here was no fraud: no wrong. It was incumbent upon the plaintiff, to be satisfied "that the bill drawn upon him was the drawer's hand," before he accepted or paid it: but it was not incumbent upon the defendant, to inquire into it. Here was notice given by the defendant to the plaintiff of a bill drawn upon him: and he sends his servant to pay it and take it up. The other bill, he actually accepts; after which acceptance the defendant innocently and bona fide discounts it. The plaintiff lies by, for a considerable time after he has paid these bills; and then found out "that they were forged" and the forger comes to be hanged. He made no objection to them, at the time of paying them.

Whatever neglect there was, was on his side. The defendant had actual encouragement from the plaintiff himself, for negotiating the second bill, from the plaintiff's having without any scruple or hesitation paid the first: and he paid the whole value, bona fide. It is a misfortune which has happened without the defendant's fault or neglect. If there was no neglect in the plaintiff, yet there is no reason to throw off the loss from one innocent man upon another innocent man: but, in this case, if there was any fault or negligence in any one, it certainly was in the plaintiff, and not in the defendant.

Per Cur'. Rule—That the postea be delivered to the defendant.

This, then, is the rule of Price v. Neal: if the *rule* drawee pays or accepts the draft, it cannot pass the risk of the drawer's signature being forged off onto prior good faith parties. Moreover, the rule has been expanded by judicial application to place on the drawee the risk of *any* mistaken payment not covered by a presentment warranty, so that, for example, the bank's payment of a check drawn against insufficient funds is a legal fait accompli (but see §4-401(a)). It is interesting to note that the finality rule of Price v. Neal has been unpopular in the courts. See, e.g., Citizens Bank v. Blach & Sons, 228 Ala. 246, 153 So. 404 (1934). It has also been criticized by lawyers such as John R.H. Kimball, an attorney for the Federal Reserve Bank of Boston, *viz*: "The rule of Price v. Neal has, I believe, outlived its rationalizations, particularly with respect to large dollar checks," Check Collection for the 21st Century, 32 U.C.C. L.J. 3, 10 (1998), and by legal commentators, both recent, White & Summers §16-2 (2d ed.), at 617 ("In conclusion we may ask whether Price v. Neal is worth the agony it causes lawyers and law students"), and in earlier times, Morse, Banks & Banking §464 (6th ed. 1928) ("This doctrine is fading fast into the misty past, where it belongs. It is almost dead, the funeral notices are ready, and no tears will be shed, for it was founded in misconception of the fundamental principles of law and common sense."). Morse's prediction proved too hasty; Price v. Neal is firmly imbedded in the UCC and is apparently alive and well for decades yet to come. The rule is reflected in Article 4's *final payment* statute, §4-302, which makes the payor bank *accountable* for an item that has been finally paid. In Article 3 the key section is §3-418, a *finality* rule, which is said to be a codification of Price v. Neal. Read carefully §3-418 and its Official Comments. Note that §3-418(b) also applies the finality rule to the analogous situation of makers who have paid notes on which their own signatures have been forged.

Ordinarily the rules of the Uniform Commercial Code do not control the federal government, since the UCC is a state statute. However, as a matter of federal common law, the federal courts, including the United States Supreme Court, have applied the rule of Price v. Neal to checks drawn on the Federal Treasury and paid through the Federal Reserve System. If the government subsequently discovers that the checks are forgeries and not truly signed by the appropriate federal official, the government cannot recover its money from the banks that presented the checks. See extended discussion in ABN Amro Bank v. United States, 34 Fed. Cl. 126, 1995 WL 539779 (1995). For more on the relationship of federal law and check forgery, see page 615.

The policy reasons for the finality rule are unclear. Lord Mansfield at one point in his decision said that the drawee was guilty of "neglect" if he failed by "fault or negligence" to recognize the drawer's signature. But surely if the forgery is very skillful, the "fault," if any, is minimal. Another reason often given is that at some point it is highly desirable to *end* the transaction and have the liabilities of the parties defined and not subject to change.

Decibel Credit Union v. Pueblo Bank & Trust Co.

Colorado Court of Appeals, 2000
996 P.2d 784, 43 U.C.C. Rep. Serv. 2d 941

Opinion by Judge RULAND.

This case requires us to address which party must bear the loss for amounts paid on forged checks. Defendant, Pueblo Bank & Trust Company, appeals from the summary judgment awarded to plaintiff, Decibel Credit Union. We reverse and remand the case for further proceedings.

A thief stole blank checks furnished by Decibel to one of its checking account customers. During a period of approximately 40 days, the thief forged the signature of the customer on a series of 14 checks totaling $2,350. Each of the checks was cashed at Pueblo Bank where the thief had a bank account.

On some of the days during the 40-day period, the thief cashed more than one check per day. At no time during this period did either the thief's checking account or his ready reserve account have sufficient funds to cover the checks that were being cashed.

Pueblo Bank processed all 14 checks through the Federal Reserve System to Decibel, and Decibel timely paid the checks. Decibel's customer discovered the forgeries when he received his bank statement. The customer immediately notified Decibel. Decibel then made demand upon Pueblo Bank for reimbursement. Pueblo Bank declined, and this litigation followed.

After the complaint was filed, both parties filed motions for summary judgment. Based upon those submissions, the trial court entered judgment for Decibel.

First, the trial court concluded that Decibel had given timely notice to Pueblo Bank as soon as the forgery was discovered by its account holder. Next, the trial court determined that in submitting the checks to Decibel for payment, Pueblo Bank had triggered its responsibility under the Colorado version of the Uniform Commercial Code for both presentment and transfer warranties. The court finally determined that a breach of these warranties had occurred and that Decibel was entitled to reimbursement. This appeal followed.

I

For purposes of the Colorado Uniform Commercial Code, Decibel was the "drawee" bank in these transactions. See §4-3-103(2), C.R.S. 1999. Pueblo Bank was the "presenting bank." See §4-4-105(6). . . .

The parties also agree on most of the legal principles from the Uniform Commercial Code that apply. Generally, a drawee bank is liable to its checking account customer for payment of a check on which the customer's signature has been forged. See §4-3-418, C.R.S. 1999; Travelers Indemnity Company v. Stedman, 895 F. Supp. 742 (E.D. Pa. 1995). Further, when the drawee bank honors the forged instrument, the payment is deemed final for a person who or an entity which takes the instrument in good faith and for value. See Bank of Glen Burnie v. Loyola Federal Savings Bank, 336 Md. 331, 648 A.2d 453 (1994); North Carolina National Bank v. Hammond, 298 N.C. 703, 709, 260 S.E.2d 617, 622 n.1 (1979). . . .

II

Pueblo Bank asserts that under the circumstances of this case, there were no presentment or transfer warranties made to Decibel and that the trial court erred in ruling to the contrary. We agree.

A

Presentment warranties in the Colorado version of the Uniform Commercial Code appear in §4-4-208(a), C.R.S. 1999, as follows: [The court quoted §4-208(a).].

As noted in the Official Comment to a similar section
C.R.S.1999, the warranty in subsection (a)(1) is only a w
there are no unauthorized or missing endorsements on
Further, subsection (a)(2) does not apply because there was
alteration to the checks. Finally, there is no claim that Pueblo Bank
had actual knowledge of the forged signatures, and thus subsection
(a)(3) does not apply.

Indeed, as the court noted in Payroll Check Cashing v. New
Palestine Bank, 401 N.E.2d 752 (Ind. App. 1980), if the warranty that
all signatures were genuine applied to a bank in the position of Pueblo
Bank, the final payment doctrine contained in §4-3-418 would be
meaningless. This doctrine is of great importance in banking commerce because it creates certainty relative to which institution must
bear the loss and thus avoids time consuming and expensive litigation.
See Travelers Indemnity Company v. Stedman, supra, at 747 n.9.

Accordingly, we hold that Pueblo Bank did not extend any
presentment warranty to Decibel by returning the checks to it through
the Federal Reserve System. Hence, the trial court erred in concluding
that presentment warranties applied for the benefit of Decibel under
the circumstances of this case.

B

The term "transfer" is defined in §4-3-203(a), C.R.S. 1999, as
delivery by a party other than the maker of an instrument for the
purpose of giving that party the right to enforce the check. And, §4-4-
207, C.R.S. 1999, contains Colorado's version of the transfer warranties
of the Uniform Commercial Code. That section provides:

> (a) A customer or collecting bank that transfers an item and
> receives a settlement or other consideration warrants to the trans-
> feree . . . that:
>> (1) The warrantor is a person entitled to enforce the item;
>> (2) All signatures on the item are authentic and authorized;
>> (3) The item has not been altered;
>> (4) The item is not subject to a defense or claim in recoup-
> ment . . . ;
>> (5) The warrantor has no knowledge of any insolvency proceed-
> ing commenced with respect to the . . . drawer.

Even if we assume that a transfer is involved here, it is well established that a transfer warranty as to the genuineness of the drawer's
signature does not apply for the benefit of the drawee bank. See Bank
of Glen Burnie v. Loyola Federal Savings Bank, supra, 336 Md. at 344,

648 A.2d at 459 n.6; see also 5 W. Hawkland, J.F. Leary & R. Alderman, Uniform Commercial Code Series §4-207:1 n.6 (1999). Hence, the trial court erred in relying on this section to enter judgment for Decibel.

To the extent that Decibel relies upon Vectra Bank v. Bank Western, 890 P.2d 259 (Colo. App. 1995) as support for the judgment, we conclude that this case does not apply. Consistent with prior interpretations of the Uniform Commercial Code in other jurisdictions, the division in *Vectra* correctly applied the transfer warranties in a case involving forged endorsements. Here, however, the signatures of the maker have been forged. . . .

The judgment is reversed, and the cause is remanded for further proceedings consistent with the views expressed in this opinion.

Judge CASEBOLT and Judge ROY concur.

PROBLEM 190

Harry Villain climbed into the window of Portia Moot's house when she was not home and stole her checkbook. When he was alone in the quiet of his own apartment, Harry wrote out one of her checks to himself and signed her name to the drawer's line. He then cashed the check at the local drugstore, which passed it on to Merchants Bank. Merchants then presented the check to and was paid by Octopus National Bank, the drawee. When Portia got this check back in her next monthly statement, she was very upset. She immediately demanded that the bank replace the money in her account, saying the check was not properly payable without her valid signature; §4-401(a). The bank recredited her account and then called you, its attorney. Who can it sue and under what theory? See §§4-208(a) and 3-418.

For years I have wandered around the country lecturing bankers on the law of checking accounts. It has amazed me that banking usage of trade ignores the rule of Price v. Neal. Over and over I have been told by bankers that when the payor bank, having made final payment and then discovering the drawer's name was forged, demands repayment from the depositary bank, the latter simply coughs up the money. "We always do it that way," I am told. "Stop that!" I reply. "You have no right to give away your customer's money without authority, and the next time a payor bank demands its money back, ask it to specify the legal theory for its recovery." That will end that.

PROBLEM 191

Unhappy with being told that the depositary bank did not violate §4-208(a)(3), Octopus National Bank now asks you if the depositary bank violated §4-208(a)(1). Did it?

The answer is no, but it is a rather complicated no. Start by reading §3-403. Subsection (a) contains the basic idea that the forgery acts as if the forger had signed his or her *own* name instead of the name forged. Were that true in the above Problems, Harry Villain would be the true drawer of this check. In that case we would have a check drawn by Harry Villain, payable to the order of Harry Villain, properly indorsed by the payee, and then properly negotiated by the drugstore and the depositary bank. The depositary bank *was* a "person entitled to enforce the draft" of Harry Villain. In effect, the payor bank here paid the draft of a non-customer payee. That isn't the draft they thought they were paying, but the rule of Price v. Neal puts that risk squarely on the drawee; there was nothing wrong with the negotiation. The age-old saying is that "the drawee must know the drawer's signature as a mother must know her child," and making a mistake on this cannot pass the loss back to innocent parties.

PROBLEM 192

In Problem 152 of the last chapter a drawee bank paid a check with no drawer's signature at all because the check had been created over the telephone by the telemarketing payee. When we did this Problem the last time, the relevant question was whether the check was properly payable from the drawer's bank account under §4-401 (the "properly payable" rule), and the answer (as yet unaddressed by the courts) is highly likely to be "no." Thus the drawee bank must replace the money in the drawer's account (unless the subrogation rule of §4-407 can be brought into play to protect the bank). Having done so, the bank now calls you, its attorney. It wants to pass the liability back to the depositary bank. Can this be done, and, if so, under what theory? Compare §§4-208(a) and 3-418; Interbank of New York v. Fleet Bank, 2001 WL 950196, 45 U.C.C. Rep. Serv. 2d 167 (N.Y. Civ. 2001).[6]

What steps do banks take to protect themselves from the vicious bite of Price v. Neal? In an era of check truncation and electronic presentment, many payor banks don't recapture their drawers' checks and have no opportunity to compare drawers' signatures with the signature cards. Others, for economic reasons, engage in a practice called "bulk filing," in which the banks don't physically examine the checks at all if they are below a certain amount but simply file them away in bulk. If a check proves forged and the forger cannot be found, these banks recredit the drawers' accounts and look to their forgery insurance. Of course, some banks religiously examine all checks and return those with forged drawers' signatures before final payment occurs, but such banks are a dwindling number.

QUESTION

If the drawer's signature is forged, but the bank pays the check anyway, the rule of Price v. Neal puts the loss on the payor bank. However, if the payee's name is forged, the loss tends to fall on the depositary bank. Are these results merely whimsical, or is there a rational reason for the two different placements of liability?

III. VALIDATION OF THE FORGERY

Both Price v. Neal and the rule that the forged indorsement is ineffective to negotiate the instrument put a heavy burden on the drawee bank, which must frequently bear the forgery loss (or insure against it). To militate against the harshness of these rules, the basic forgery rule, §3-403(a), has an escape clause in the words "Unless otherwise provided in this Article or Article 4" and "an unauthorized

---

6. The proposed 2002 Amendments to Article 3 of the Uniform Commercial Code would solve this problem by adding both new presentment and transfer warranties in consumer transactions that the owner of the account did authorize the transaction, thus allowing the liability to be passed back to the first bank to deal with the creator of the unsigned check. See new §§3-416(a)(6), 3-417(a)(4), and 4-208(a)(4).

signature may be ratified." This means that under some circumstances the forged signature will be treated as genuine. What are these circumstances that validate a forgery?

Ratification, a doctrine coming to us from agency law, for negotiable instrument purposes occurs when the party in question, with full knowledge of the forgery or alteration, accepts the benefits thereof or actively assents to the wrongful activity. See Rakestraw v. Rodrigues, 8 Cal. 3d 67, 500 P.2d 1401, 104 Cal. Rptr. 57, 11 U.C.C. Rep. Serv. 780 (1972); cf. Salsman v. National Community Bank, 102 N.J. Super. 482, 246 A.2d 162, 5 U.C.C. Rep. Serv. 779 (1968), *aff'd*, 105 N.J. Super. 164, 251 A.2d 460, 6 U.C.C. Rep. Serv. 168 (1969); Bank of Hoven v. Rausch, 382 N.W.2d 39, 42 U.C.C. Rep. Serv. 1359 (S.D. 1986).

PROBLEM 193

George learned that his wife, Martha, had been forging his name to business checks received in his business on which he was the named payee. Except for this peccadillo, she was a model wife, and it was a good marriage, so he said nothing rather than embarrass her. Two years later his extramarital affair caused a divorce, so he decided to recover the money by bringing a conversion action against the banks that had paid money on the forged indorsements. Will his suit succeed?

Ratification of supposed agency status can also occur, as where the non-agent has apparent authority due to the alleged principal's actions or inactions. See §3-402(a) and its Official Comment 1; Fulka v. Florida Commercial Banks, Inc., 371 So. 2d 521, 26 U.C.C. Rep. Serv. 1198 (Fla. Dist. App. 1979) (payee estopped to bring conversion action where she knew a business associate was forging her name to checks, but kept silent); Annot., 82 A.L.R.3d 625. The major UCC case is Senate Motors, Inc. v. Industrial Bank of Washington, 9 U.C.C. Rep. Serv. 387 (D.C. Super. 1971). For pre-Code cases finding apparent authority in an agent to cash the alleged principal's checks, see Corbett v. Kleinsmith, 112 F.2d 511 (6th Cir. 1940); Commercial Cas. Ins. Co. v. Isabell Natl. Bank, 223 Ala. 48, 134 So. 810 (1931); Arcade Realty Co. v. Bank of Commerce, 180 Cal. 318, 181 P. 66 (1919); Rosser-Moon Furn. Co. v. Oklahoma State Bank, 192 Okla. 169, 135 P.2d 336 (1943). It is important to appreciate that the courts are slow to presume such authority. See, e.g., Taylor v. Equitable Trust Co., 269 Md. 149, 304 A.2d 838, 12 U.C.C. Rep. Serv. 922 (1973).

A.   Common Law Validation

Hutzler v. Hertz Corp.

Court of Appeals of New York, 1976
39 N.Y.2d 209, 347 N.E.2d 627, 383 N.Y.S.2d 266,
18 U.C.C. Rep. Serv. 1089

JASEN, J. In this action against defendant tortfeasor arising out of
the compromise of a personal injury and wrongful death claim made
with the tortfeasor by plaintiff's attorney with the consent of the
plaintiff, we are asked to decide whether defendant tortfeasor was
discharged from liability where its settlement draft, naming plaintiff
and her attorney as payees, was negotiated by the attorney on plaintiff's forged indorsement and the proceeds of the draft appropriated.
For the reasons which follow, we hold that the tortfeasor's liability was
discharged upon payment of the settlement draft by the drawee bank,
the forgery notwithstanding, and that the claimant may not thereafter
recover against the tortfeasor.

The parties are in agreement as to the basic facts. On June 1,
1966, Christina Hutzler was granted limited letters of administration by
the Surrogate of Queens County on the estate of her husband who had
perished on October 4, 1965, in an automobile accident. Through her
attorney, Daniel D. Yudow, she commenced an action against Hertz
Corporation to recover damages for the personal injuries and wrongful
death of her husband. After some time Yudow succeeded in settling
the action with Hertz and on November 23, 1970, in consideration of
that settlement, Mrs. Hutzler, after obtaining permission of the Surrogate's Court to compromise the action, executed a general release in
Hertz' favor. On December 11, 1970, Hertz issued and mailed to
Yudow two checks totalling $11,500, the amount of the settlement, both
of which were drawn on the Manufacturers Hanover Trust Company.
One of these with which we are not concerned, was in the sum of $571,
made payable to "The State Insurance Fund c/o Daniel D. Yudow."
The second check was for $10,929, the balance of the settlement, and
was payable to "Christina Hutzler Individually And As Administratrix of
the Estate of Michael E. Hutzler and Daniel D. Yudow as attorney." On
December 14, 1970, Yudow, having indorsed this check with his own
signature and with the forged signature of Mrs. Hutzler, deposited it in
an account in his name at Manufacturers Hanover. Four months later,
in April 1971, he closed the account. In the meantime, Mrs. Hutzler
attempted to obtain her share of the proceeds of the settlement, but
was unsuccessful in locating Yudow until June, 1973. In the interim she

learned that he had closed his office and was no longer in practice.[7]
Thereafter she retained her present counsel who made oral and
written demand for payment on Hertz in June, 1973. Hertz produced a
copy of its settlement draft and refused payment. Upon examination of
the indorsements, the forgery was at once apparent to Mrs. Hutzler,
and both Hertz and Manufacturers Hanover were immediately
apprised of this fact. Since no satisfactory resolution could be made,
Mrs. Hutzler, a short time later, commenced this action against Hertz
and Manufacturers Hanover to recover the amount of the settlement
check. She alleged one cause of action against Hertz for negligence in
not comparing the forged signature with her signature on the
settlement agreement, and two causes of action against Manufacturers
Hanover, one for conversion of the check and its proceeds and the
other for breach of warranty.

On cross-motions for summary judgment, Special Term granted
Mrs. Hutzler judgment against Hertz for the amount of the check, and
denied Hertz' motion for summary judgment. Summary judgment was
also granted to the defendant bank on which the check was drawn, but
no appeal was taken by the plaintiff from this part of the judgment and
order. On Hertz' appeal, a divided Appellate Division modified the
judgment and order "by adding to each of them a provision that the
amount of plaintiff's recovery against defendant The Hertz Corporation be reduced by the amount of the lien that attorney Yudow,
had he not engaged in misconduct with respect to the settlement
check, and not converted the proceeds thereof, would have been entitled to for professional services," and remitted the case for a determination of the amount of that lien. (47 A.D.2d 839.) Special Term
thereupon determined the amount of the lien, and amended its earlier
judgment accordingly. Hertz now appeals directly, as of right, from this
amended judgment, bringing up for review with it the prior non-final
order of the Appellate Division. (C.P.L.R. 5601, subd. [d].) Mrs.
Hutzler cross appeals, also as of right (C.P.L.R. 5601, subd. [a], par.
[iii]), claiming that the Appellate Division erred in reducing the
amount of her judgment by the amount of her former attorney's lien
for services rendered.

At the outset, we note that the courts of other jurisdictions have
divided on the question now before us and it seems as though no
majority rule can be stated. (See generally Annot., Forgery by Debtor's

7. We are informed that the records of the First Department indicate that
Yudow's name was stricken from the Roll of Attorneys and Counselors-at-Law, on
consent, on March 22, 1972.

Agent Discharge, 49 A.L.R.3d 843, 846.) Indeed, the cases of this state have been characterized as representing in microcosm this division of authority, with no definitive statement of our rule possible. (Id., at pp.847, 859.)

As we view this case, we are concerned with two separate sets of legal relationships. The first involves a plaintiff and a tortfeasor, and the tortfeasor's payment to the plaintiff's attorney in settlement of the tort action. Reference must be made to principles of agency law in analyzing the rights and duties which arise from this set of relationships. The second concerns the relationships created when payment is made by a negotiable instrument. The rights and duties growing out of this set of relationships evolve from the law of negotiable instruments embodied principally in the Uniform Commercial Code. Only by keeping in mind that we are dealing with two separate bodies of law can we properly resolve this controversy.

We start with agency considerations. An attorney retained to collect a debt, or as here, to recover damages for personal injuries and wrongful death, normally also has at least apparent authority to receive payment from the debtor or tortfeasor once a settlement has been reached or a judgment entered. (McCoy v. Barclay, 250 App. Div. 682, 684; Moss v. Standard Brands, 68 Misc. 2d 625, 627; 2 Mechem, Agency 2180, p.1762.) This is clearly the rule, at least where payment is in cash. (See 7 Am. Jur. 2d, Attorneys at Law 102; 7 C.J.S., Attorney and Client 106, subd. c.) Having made such a payment to the creditor's or claimant's attorney, the debtor or tortfeasor can be assured that he has been discharged from liability. If the attorney absconds with the cash without paying it over to his client, the client may not thereafter compel the debtor or tortfeasor to pay a second time. (See Morrison v. Chapman, 155 App. Div. 509, 514; Burstein v. Sullivan, 134 App. Div. 623, 625.) He must instead look to the defalcating attorney.

An analogous situation develops where payment is made to the attorney for a claimant by means of a check made payable solely to the attorney. Payment by check, sometimes referred to as "conditional payment," is not, by itself, payment of the underlying obligation. (Chatham Securities Corp. v. Williston & Beane, 41 Misc. 2d 817, 821, aff'd, 22 A.D.2d 260, aff'd without op., 16 N.Y.2d 1016; Mansion Carpets v. Marinoff, 24 A.D.2d 947; Uniform Commercial Code §3-802, Official Comment 3 [now §3-310(b) —Ed.].) Only when the drawee bank pays on the check is payment actually effected. Thus, once the drawee bank has paid on the check the debtor or tortfeasor is discharged from the underlying obligation as fully as though he had paid the attorney cash. As where payment is in cash, if the agent appropriates the proceeds of a check for himself, the claimant may not seek repayment from the debtor or tortfeasor.

The situation becomes somewhat more complicated where the check is made payable only to the creditor or claimant, or, as here, to the claimant and attorney jointly. It is at this juncture that the agency principles just described and certain principles of the law of negotiable instruments would seem to come into conflict. Indeed, Mrs. Hutzler argues that the forged indorsement by Yudow was "wholly inoperative as that of the person [Mrs. Hutzler] whose name is signed" (Uniform Commercial Code §3-404 subd. (1)) and that Hertz' liability was therefore not discharged by its settlement draft. This argument, if accepted, would require Hertz to pay a second time.

Long ago the rule developed in this state that debtor's liability is discharged when a check payable to the creditor is wrongfully indorsed by the creditor's agent and is paid by the drawee bank, and the proceeds converted by the agent. (Sage v. Burton, 84 Hun. 267; Allen v. Tarrant & Co., 7 App. Div. 172; Morris v. Hofferberth, 81 App. Div. 512, aff'd, 180 N.Y. 545.) The basis for this rule is that the drawer's only obligation to the payee, upon issuance of the check, is to "see that funds are in the bank." (Sage v. Burton, supra, at p.270.) The drawer thereafter has no obligation to examine the check for forged indorsements. (See National Surety Co. v. Manhattan Co., 252 N.Y. 247, 254.) Since checks and drafts are the usual and ordinary means of transferring money in the transaction of business, a contrary rule would add an unnecessary element of risk and uncertainty where payment is made by check to an authorized agent. Because of the time factors involved in processing a check through the depositary bank, intermediate collecting banks and the drawee bank, the discovery of the forgery by the drawer, even if possible, would often be of little practical value to the payee. Moreover, as indicated above, if a check is payable solely to the agent, there is no question that the obligation would be discharged upon payment by the drawee bank. By making the check payable to the creditor, the drawer has given the creditor a measure of protection by requiring the agent to expose himself to criminal prosecution by forging an indorsement before converting the proceeds. (See Burstein v. Sullivan, 134 App. Div. 623, 625, supra.) Therefore, as between the creditor and the drawer of the check, the party who should be required to bear the loss under such circumstances is the creditor. It is the creditor, after all, who selected a dishonest person to represent him, and he, not the drawer, should bear the risk of his unauthorized acts, having placed him in a position to perpetrate the wrong. (Sage v. Burton, 84 Hun. 267, 270, supra, Morrison v. Chapman, 155 App. Div. 509, 512, 514, supra.) The fact that the agent acted in excess of his authority in forging the indorsement is, of course, no more helpful to the creditor than is the fact that the agent who absconds with a cash payment also acts in excess of his authority. (Morrison v. Chapman, supra, at p.514.). . .

We note that this resolution squares with the position taken by the American Law Institute in the Restatement Second of Agency.[8] We expressly approve of that provision and hold that it correctly states the law of this state.

Returning to considerations of the law of negotiable instruments, we conclude that our holding today, in the context of the kind of relationship involved, is consistent with §3-404 of the Uniform Commercial Code [now §3-403(a)—Ed.], despite the apparent conflict noted earlier. Subdivision (1) of that section provides in part that "[a]ny unauthorized signature is wholly inoperative as that of the person whose name is signed unless he ratifies it or is precluded from denying it. . . ." Since our resolution of the issue before us is based primarily upon the principles of agency, we would hold that a person whose name is forged on an instrument by his agent is, by his unwise selection of this agent, estopped or "precluded from denying" the unauthorized signature.

Finally, we note that this rule is not unduly harsh on a person who has been defrauded in this manner by a dishonest agent. To be sure, the unfaithful agent is an unpromising defendant, and often there is little likelihood of recovering from him. However, generally the creditor could pursue an action for conversion against the drawee bank.

---

8. The relevant section is as follows:

> §178. Agent Authorized to Collect a Debt . . .

> (2) If an agent who is authorized to receive a check payable to the principal as conditional payment forges the principal's endorsement to such a check, the maker is relieved of liability to the principal if the drawee bank pays the check and charges the amount to the maker.

> This subsection is discussed in Comment c:

> > If a debtor, having an account at a solvent bank sufficient to pay a check, gives to an authorized agent a check payable to the principal in accordance with business customs as conditional payment, he has performed his obligation, and any loss caused by delay because of the conduct of the agent is at the creditor's risk. Thus, if the drawee bank cashes the check after a forgery and embezzlement by the agent and charges the amount to the debtor, the latter is relieved of his debt. The creditor then would be subrogated to the right of the debtor against the bank. If, in the meantime, the bank becomes insolvent, it is the creditor and not the debtor who loses.

(Henderson v. Lincoln Rochester Trust Co., 303 N.Y. 27, 31; Spaulding v. First Natl. Bank, 210 App. Div. 216, 217, *aff'd without op.*, 239 N.Y. 586; Uniform Commercial Code §3-419, subd. [1], par. [c] [now §3-420(a)—Ed.].) Unfortunately, that rule does little for the plaintiff in this case as no appeal was taken from the order dismissing her conversion action against Manufacturers Hanover. Our compassion for the plaintiff cannot, however, serve as a basis for granting her relief against Hertz.

Accordingly, the amended judgment should be reversed and Hertz' motion for summary judgment granted and the complaint dismissed.

Judgment reversed, without costs, the motion by defendant The Hertz Corporation for summary judgment granted and the complaint dismissed. All concur.

QUESTION

Could the plaintiff sue the drawee bank? What would be her cause of action? See §3-420(a); Florida Bar v. Allstate Ins. Co., 391 So. 2d 238, 30 U.C.C. Rep. Serv. 1054 (Fla. Dist. App. 1980).

PROBLEM 194

Donna Drawer gave her check to Paul Payee, who lost it before he indorsed it. The finder was an evil person, identity unknown, who forged "Paul Payee" to the back of the check and received payment from the drawee, Octopus National Bank (ONB). Is ONB liable to Paul Payee? See §3-420(a). If ONB pays Paul, is it also liable to Donna? See §§4-401, 4-407.

The common law handled this double liability problem by saying that it is always a defense to a negotiable instruments action to show that the money got where it was supposed to go, and, thus, the plaintiff has no damages. See Ambassador Fin. Serv., Inc. v. Indiana National Bank, 605 N.E.2d 746, 19 U.C.C. Rep. Serv. 2d 1121 (Ind. 1992); Tonelli v. Chase Manhattan Bank, N.A., 41 N.Y.2d 667, 363 N.E.2d 564, 394 N.Y.S.2d 858, 21 U.C.C. Rep. Serv. 1344 (1977); Middle States Leasing Corp. v. Manufacturers Hanover Trust Co., 62 A.D.2d 273, 404 N.Y.S.2d 846, 23 U.C.C. Rep. Serv. 1215 (1978). Whether approached under this idea or under §4-407's subrogation rule, the result is the same: a successful conversion action by the payee destroys the drawer's §4-401 not *properly payable* suit against the drawee.

The four Uniform Commercial Code sections that validate the wrongdoing in certain circumstances are §3-404 (the Impostor Rule), §3-405 (the Employee Indorsement Rule), §3-406 (the Negligence Rule), and §4-406 (the Bank Statement Rule). They come up next, one by one.

B. The Impostor Rule[9]

An "impostor" is someone pretending to be someone else. The Impostor Rule in the Uniform Commercial Code validates the forgery of the *payee's* name (and only the payee's name) in the situations described in §3-404. In each of these situations the drawer or maker has been duped by either an outsider or a trusted employee into creating an instrument on which the name of the payee is highly likely to be forged, and it is proper to put the resulting liability on the drawer/maker rather than on non-negligent parties, such as the indorsers or banks involved in collecting or paying the checks.

PROBLEM 195

Old and rich Amy Altruism was well known for her charitable contributions. One day she answered her door to find Sandra Sting, a woman whose photograph was at that moment decorating the post offices of the country, standing on the front stoop. Sandra told Amy that she was Hilda Humane, the founder of Humane's Home for Homeless Dogs, Inc., and that she wished to solicit a contribution for this worthy cause, which she described in much detail. Amy was taken in by this story, and while weeping copiously over the plight of the canine element of the world, she wrote a check for $5,000 payable to "Hilda Humane." Sandra pocketed the check, thanked her warmly, and left her quickly. She went straight to the drawee bank where, after signing "Hilda Humane" to the back of the check, she received payment. If Amy discovers that there is no such thing as Humane's Home for Homeless Dogs, Inc., can she successfully demand that her

_____

9. The word *impostor* is one of the most frequently misspelled words in the English language. Note the "or" at the end.

account be recredited on the theory that the check was cashed on an improper signature (not "properly payable")? See §3-404(a).

PROBLEM 196

Mrs. Walter Heartstrong wrote the Methuselah Life Insurance Company telling them, "I want to discontinue my life insurance policy. Please cancel it and mail me the cash surrender value. I hereby certify that I have lost the policy (#T12-011Z) itself or misplaced it some-where, (signed) Walter Heartstrong." The company mailed a check to the order of "Walter Heartstrong." Mrs. Heartstrong got to the mailbox first, obtained the check, forged her husband's name on the back, and cashed the check at the Smalltown State Bank. The latter presented it to the drawee, Octopus National, which cashed it without a murmur. When Walter sues the insurance company and they call you, what would you advise? See Hicks v. Northwestern Mut. Life Ins. Co., 166 Iowa 532, 147 N.W. 883 (1914); cf. Franklin Natl. Bank v. Shapiro, 7 U.C.C. Rep. Serv. 317 (N.Y. Sup. Ct. 1970).

To understand §3-404(b) you need to conquer the concept of the "person whose intent determines to whom an instrument is payable" in §3-110(a) and (b). Generally it means the person who signed the instrument, though for check-writing machines it means the person who supplied the name of the payee, whether or not authorized to do so. Apply §3-404(b) to the following Problem.

PROBLEM 197

One day it occurred to the corporate treasurer of the Business Corporation that his personal situation would be easier if he started adding fictitious employees to the payroll and took their checks each month for deposit into accounts opened under the phony names. Are such checks properly payable from the account Business Corporation has with its bank? See §3-404(b). Would the result be different if the treasurer padded the payroll with the names of real former employees and then did the same thing with these checks? If the depositary banks that took these checks were negligent in allowing the treasurer to open the accounts, would that change the result? See §3-404(d).[10]

---

10. There are similar comparative fault sections in each of the validation sections; see §§3-405(b), 3-406(b), and 4-406(e).

PROBLEM 198

Lawyer Sam Ambulance was sitting in his office when his secretary brought him his checkbook. The secretary informed him that he owed $1,500.00 to John Creditor on a debt, so he wrote out a check for that amount to John. As it turned out, Sam really didn't owe any money to John Creditor, and the secretary forged John's name to the check and pocketed the proceeds. Is this check properly payable from Sam Ambulance's account? See §3-110(a). Does it make any difference whether or not John Creditor is a real person?

C. The Employee Indorsement Rule

In the last Problem §3-404(b) offers no relief because it is Sam Ambulance's intent that controls under §3-110(a), since he is the drawer of the check. Now do the Problem again, this time looking at §3-405.

Official Comment 1 to this section explains the policy here:

> Section 3-405 is based on the belief that the employer is in a far better position to avoid the loss by care in choosing employees, in supervising them, and in adopting other measures to prevent forged indorsements on instruments payable to the employer or fraud in issuance of instruments in the name of the employer. If the bank failed to exercise ordinary care, subsection (b) allows the employer to shift loss to the bank to the extent the bank's failure to exercise ordinary care contributed to the loss. "Ordinary care" is defined in Section 3-103(a)(7). The provision applies regardless of whether the employer is negligent.

PROBLEM 199

When a check for $800,000 came into Business Corporation to pay a bill owed to it by one of its buyers, the amount dazzled Lucille Larceny, the head of the bookkeeping department. She promptly forged the indorsement "Business Corporation" as payee on the back of the check, and then negotiated it through an account she opened in that name at a bank. Lucille had no authority to indorse the company name, though she was generally in charge of the handling of checks. Does §3-405 make the employer responsible for employees' forgeries where the employer is itself the *payee* (as opposed to the issuer) of the instrument? See Official Comment 1 to §3-405. Would that section

reach a different result if the forgeries were done by Brad Byte, ~~ℕ𝒪~~
who had found a blank corporate check behind the computer he ℕ𝒪
was repairing as part of his job as corporate computer maintenance
specialist?

The Official Comments to both §§3-404 and 3-405 have a number
of "case" studies giving examples of fact patterns in which these rules
either apply or don't, and you should read these case studies to make
sure you appreciate what the drafters intended. If these fact patterns
show up in actual cases, the courts are highly likely to reach the same
results as those in the Comments.

NOTE ON FEDERAL COMMERCIAL PAPER LAW

The Uniform Commercial Code is a *state* statute, and the federal
government does not feel bound thereby. In an actual case, you may
discover that, for example, the Midnight Deadline statutes and other
rules of bank collection are much altered when a check is drawn on
the Treasury of the United States. So it is with the padded payroll part
of the Impostor Rule. While the U.S. Supreme Court decisions to date
preclude the use of §§3-404(b) and 3-405, the part of these sections
that deals with a true *impostor*, §3-404(a), *has* been adopted as a federal
rule by lower federal courts, the Supreme Court having expressed no
opinion on the issue; see Bank of Am. Natl. Trust & Sav. Assn. v.
United States, 552 F.2d 302, 21 U.C.C. Rep. Serv. 812 (9th Cir. 1977);
see also Comment, Federal Commercial Paper and the Common Law,
14 Tulsa L.J. 208 (1978). In United States v. Kimbell Foods, 440 U.S.
715, 26 U.C.C. Rep. Serv. 1 (1979), the Supreme Court adopted Article
9 of the Uniform Commercial Code as a matter of federal common
law. This has given hope of the Court's possible federal incorporation
of Articles 3 and 4 the next time the issue arises. See Official Comment
4 to §3-102 and Official Comment 1 to §4-102.

PROBLEM 200

Peter Shopper left his checkbook lying on a department store
counter, and it was picked up by "Fingers" McGee. McGee wrote out a
check for $100 payable to the order of "John Doe," a name he rather
imaginatively made up; then he forged Shopper's name to the drawer's
line. He indorsed the check "John Doe" and "Fingers McGee" and
deposited the check in his own account with the Fence State Bank. The

latter was paid $100 by the drawee, the Antitrust National Bank. Shopper complained to the drawee about the forgery, and the bank reluctantly recredited his account. It now wants to pass the loss on to the presenting bank, claiming that it breached the warranty that it was a person entitled to enforce the draft because of the forged indorsement of "John Doe." Has that warranty been breached, or did Fence State somehow become a *holder*? See §3-404(b), and remember the rule of Price v. Neal.

D. *The Negligence Rule*

Another situation in which a party may be estopped to complain about a forgery occurs when the person's own negligence substantially contributed to the creation of the forgery. (The same rule applies to the creation of alterations of the instrument.) The leading case establishing this negligence-as-estoppel principle is the 1827 English case, Young v. Grote, 4 Bing. 253 (Common Pleas). The Problem below is based on the facts in that case.

PROBLEM 201

Young decided to go abroad for a while, so he signed five checks and left them with his wife. After he had been gone a week, one of Young's employees, Worcester, a clerk, showed Mrs. Young how to fill out the check so as to pay employees' wages for 50 pounds. She filled out the check as directed and gave it to Worcester to cash. He inserted the numeral 3 on the check in the blank he had had Mrs. Young leave in writing the amount and cashed the check for 350 pounds with the drawee, Grote & Co. When Young returned, he sued Grote & Co. for wrongly paying that amount. In the actual case the court gave a sexist explanation for its result, deciding that Young's negligence was in trusting a woman with a business matter (remember this was 1827): "If Young, instead of leaving the check with a female, had left it with a man of business, he would have guarded against fraud in the mode of filling it up. . . . " In our century, is it enough negligence that a space was left on the amount line to which a numeral could be added? See Official Comment 1 to §3-406.

Note that the language of §3-406 uses the doctrine of negligence only as a defense, not as a separate affirmative cause of action. The

Code does not authorize an affirmative cause of action based on negligence. Read Official Comment 1, last paragraph, to §3-406, which explains why not. Affirmative negligence actions must be brought outside the Code (see §1-103) and judged by common law standards. See, e.g., Faulkner v. Hillside Bank & Trust Co., 526 S.W.2d 274 (Tex. Civ. App. 1975) (bank telling an inquirer that a stolen cashier's check was good held liable in negligence).

PROBLEM 202

Arena Auto Auction (AAA) by coincidence dealt with two customers named Plunkett Auto Sales, one in Illinois and the other in Alabama. AAA sold a car for the Alabama customer, but AAA's secretary mistakenly mailed a check to Plunkett Auto Sales in Illinois. The surprised owner of the Illinois Plunkett operation promptly cashed the check with his own bank, Park State, which forwarded the check to the drawee bank. The latter dishonored the check at AAA's request—AAA had stopped payment when it learned about its secretary's error. The Illinois Plunkett skipped the state, and the Park State Bank was left holding the check. Park State sued AAA on its drawer's obligation, §3-414(b), and the latter tried to raise the defense of mistake. Does §3-406 apply? See Official Comment 3, Case No. 2. The actual case is Park State Bank v. Arena Auto Auction, Inc., 59 Ill. App. 2d 235, 207 N.E.2d 158, 2 U.C.C. Rep. Serv. 903 (1965).

(" *Bank* ")   (" *Citizens* ")
The Bank/First Citizens Bank v. Citizens and Associates

Court of Appeals of Tennessee, 2001
44 U.C.C. Rep. Serv. 2d 1072

FRANKS, J.
Drawer of checks and Bank failed to exercise ordinary care in transactions under Tenn. Code Ann. §47-3-406. Drawer was assessed 80% of fault and Bank 20%. Drawer appeals. We affirm, as modified.

In this action, Citizens and Associates ("Citizens"), claim against The Bank/First Citizens Bank ("The Bank"), resulted in the Court finding Citizens 80% at fault for the loss, and The Bank 20% at fault. Citizens has appealed.

The basis of this action is that Frieda Gray, a branch manager for Allied Mortgage Capital Corporation ("Allied"), received three checks from Citizens which totaled $50,000.00, and were made payable to

Allied. Gray deposited these checks in her personal account, with an endorsement which reads "Allied Mortgage Company # 259" or "Allied Mortgage Branch # 259."

At trial, Bill Wilburn testified that he was President of Wilcore, Inc., that Wilcore is a partner in Citizens, and that the checks in question were written by him. He testified that he learned of Gray through business associates, and that she had opened an office for Allied in Cleveland, Tennessee. He testified that he and the other partner and principal Mathis Bush went to Cleveland and observed the operation, finding Allied's name on the door and with Gray as the Branch Manager. Based upon the explanations of Gray, they decided to purchase a franchise and Wilburn testified he wrote a check for $25,000.00 payable to Allied. Wilburn testified that when he wrote the check he called Gray for the mailing address. She volunteered to "overnight" it for him to Texas, because she had a package going out anyway. Someone on Gray's behalf picked up the check from his office. The first check was dated February 10, 1997, and subsequently another check in the amount of $16,666.68 dated March 6, 1997 and a check dated March 7, 1997 in the amount of $8,333.34 were issued, payable to Allied, and picked up in Knoxville by Gray. However, the checks were not forwarded to Allied's office, but deposited by Gray in her personal account in the names of herself and her husband. The Bank, after receiving the three checks, delivered them to the First Tennessee Bank for credit of the funds deposited into Gray's account, and First Tennessee paid over the money and debited the same from Citizens' account. . . .

[The court quoted §3-406.]

The Trial Court found this section applicable to the facts in this case, and found that Citizens failed to exercise ordinary care by engaging in negligent or careless business practices, and that The Bank also failed to exercise ordinary care in accepting the checks and allowing them to be deposited in Gray's personal account, and that The Bank's failure substantially contributed to the loss suffered by Citizens. The Court then allocated the loss 80% to Citizens and 20% to The Bank. The evidence does not preponderate against this allocation. Cross v. City of Memphis, 20 S.W.3d 642 (Tenn. 2000).

Citizens insists that it was not negligence, and that even if it was, the negligence did not substantially contribute to the forgery, nor did The Bank take the items in good faith. Tenn. Code Ann. §47-3-406 requires The Bank to prove that Citizens failed to exercise ordinary care. Ordinary care is defined in Tenn. Code Ann. §47-3-103(a)(6) as "observance of reasonable commercial standards, prevailing in the area in which the person is located, with respect to the business in which the person is engaged."

The record reveals that Wilburn is a very experienced business-man, making investments and loans over the last 37 years, and also possessed a realtor's license. Likewise, the proof showed Bush was an experienced businessman with a realtor's license.

Given the experience of these individuals, we agree with the Trial Court that they failed to exercise ordinary care by delivering the checks to Gray without having any written documentation and without ever verifying her authority or the terms of the alleged agreement with Allied. In fact, she acted as their agent for purposes of delivering the check and not as an agent of Allied in processing the application. There is no evidence that Gray had any authority to accept and process applications for franchises. Wilburn admitted that had he made one phone call to Allied before writing the checks, this would have been avoided. Numerous cases have addressed a drawer's negligence or failure to exercise ordinary care such as entrusting a third party to deliver a check to the payee, and failing to adequately investigate the transaction, as is present here. See Thompson Maple Products, Inc. v. Citizens National Bank, 234 A.2d 32 (Pa. 1967); Fidelity and Deposit Co. v. Chemical Bank New York Trust Co., 318 N.Y.S.2d 957 (N.Y.A.D. 1970); Union Bank & Trust Co. v. Elmore County Nat'l Bank, 592 So. 2d 560 (Ala. 1991).[11] The evidence does not preponderate against the Trial Court's finding that Citizens engaged in negligent and careless business practices.

Aside from the change in the Code, if Ms. Gray had fraudulently endorsed and deposited a check sent in by a customer to pay his mortgage at Allied per the usual custom, then the . . . Bank, under current law, would likely be charged 100% at fault. Rather, Citizens gave the checks to Gray without any checking on her authority, which is unlike a customer paying a monthly bill, but was instead a $50,000.00 investment in a new venture.

Where a drawer negligently issues an instrument so as to contribute to its alteration or forgery, he must be judged by the comparative fault test set forth in Tenn. Code Ann. §47-3-406. See Official Comment 1. The loss suffered by Citizens was foreseeable, given Citizens lack of care in the handling of the transaction. See 6 William D. Hawkland & Lary Lawrence, Uniform Commercial Code

---

11. All cases cited in this Opinion and the dissenting opinion were decided before the current version of UCC-3-406 which was adopted in Tennessee in 1995. Thus comparative fault was not addressed.—Ed.

Series §3-406:6 (1999), citing Keeton, Dobbs, Keeton & Owen, Prosser and Keeton on the Law of Torts at 169-173 (5th Ed. 1984).

Next, Citizens argues that even if found negligent, the negligence did not contribute to the forged endorsement, as required by Code section. "Substantially contributes" has been defined as less stringent than a direct and proximate cause test, and is found where the conduct is a contributing cause and a substantial factor in bringing it about. Tenn. Code Ann. §47-3- 406, Official Comment 2.

Citizens was negligent in issuing the checks without verification and negligent in delivering them to Gray. The evidence further shows that this negligence substantially contributed to Gray's forgery, because the checks were put at her disposal. Thus Citizens's negligence contributed to her ability to forge the endorsement, and was a substantial factor in bringing it about. The evidence does not preponderate against the Trial Court's finding on this issue.

Citizens insists that The Bank did not pay the checks in good faith and therefore the Code section is inapplicable. Citizens seems to confuse good faith with ordinary care. The Trial Court found The Bank failed to exercise ordinary care in accepting the checks for deposit in Gray's personal account, and was properly assessed fault in this transaction pursuant to the comparative fault analysis in the Code section. The Trial Court's determination that The Bank failed to exercise ordinary care and this failure substantially contributed to the loss was not raised on appeal. Moreover, the failure to exercise ordinary care is not same as a lack of good faith.

"Good faith" is defined in Tenn. Code Ann. §47-1-201(19) as "honesty in fact in the conduct or transaction concerned."[12] There has been no showing in this case that The Bank did not take the checks in good faith, or that there was any dishonesty or collusion involved in the transaction. Again, we conclude the Code section was properly applied to the facts of this case by the Trial Judge. . . .

We affirm the Judgment of the Trial Court, as modified, and remand with cost of the appeal assessed 80% to Citizens and Associates and 20% to The Bank/First Citizens Bank.

CHARLES D. SUSANO, Jr., J., concurring in part and dissenting in part.

I concur in so much of the majority opinion as holds that Citizens is precluded from raising an issue on appeal as to the dismissal of First

---

12. [Actually, in Article 3, there is a special definition of "good faith," which includes *both* "honesty in fact and the observance of reasonable commercial standards of fair dealing"; §3-103(a)(4)—Ed.]

Tennessee Bank. I disagree, however, with the majority's conclusion that the facts do not preponderate against the trial court's finding that Citizens was 80% at fault for the loss occasioned by Frieda Gray's forgery. In my judgment, Citizens did not engage in negligent conduct that substantially contributed to the forgery, as that concept is embodied in T.C.A. §47-3-406. Accordingly, I would hold that the Bank, who was clearly negligent in allowing checks made payable to a business to be deposited directly into an individual's bank account, was 100% at fault for the loss.

The majority, upon finding that Wilburn and Bush, as representatives of Citizens, were "very experienced" businessmen, concludes that Citizens was negligent in delivering the checks to Gray "without having any written documentation and without ever verifying her authority or the terms of the alleged agreement with Allied." The majority supports its conclusion by stating that "[n]umerous cases have addressed a drawer's negligence or failure to exercise ordinary care such as entrusting a third party to deliver a check to the payee, and failing to adequately investigate the transaction, as is present here." In my judgment, the cases cited by the majority do not support its decision in the instant case.

In Thompson Maple Products, Inc. v. Citizens National Bank, 234 A.2d 32 (Pa. Super. Ct. 1967), the drawer was a logging company, whose employees had entrusted blank sets of delivery slips to an independent log hauler who regularly made deliveries to the company on behalf of local suppliers. The hauler filled in the blank slips to show fictitious deliveries of logs from the suppliers. The hauler then delivered the slips to the company bookkeeper, who prepared checks payable to the suppliers and entrusted the hauler to deliver them. The hauler then forged the endorsements of the payees and cashed the checks. The Superior Court of Pennsylvania found that the drawer conducted its business affairs "in so negligent a fashion as to have 'substantially contributed'" to the forgeries. Id. at 34-35. In so holding, the court noted that the company's regular practice of making blank delivery slips readily available to haulers and entrusting haulers with completed checks to be delivered to third parties, along with the company's other lax business practices, were sufficient to support a finding that the company's negligence substantially contributed to the making of the unauthorized signatures. Id. at 35-36.

In Fidelity and Deposit Co. v. Chemical Bank New York Trust Co., 318 N.Y.S.2d 957 (N.Y. App. Div. 1970), a representative of a brokerage firm received a call from a friend stating that he had recently met two people who wished to sell securities through the firm. The friend advised the representative to verify that the securities were transferable. The representative made unsuccessful attempts to do so, but made no attempt to verify the identities of the purported sellers or whether in fact they owned the securities at issue. Nevertheless, the firm sold the securities and issued checks for payment to the sellers. The securities were later discovered to have been stolen. The court, finding that the brokerage firm had failed to follow the "know your customer" rule, a well-established custom in the business, concluded that the firm was negligent and that its negligence substantially contributed to the issuance of the checks for the stolen securities. Id. at 959.

In the third case cited by the majority, Union Bank & Trust Co. v. Elmore County National Bank, 592 So. 2d 560 (Ala. 1991), the drawer was a bank that approved a car loan based upon a forged bill of sale. Without verifying the purchase with the car dealership, the bank issued to the forger a check payable to the forger and the car dealership's title agent as joint payees. The forger fraudulently endorsed the name of the title agent on the check and deposited the money in his own account at the defendant bank. The drawer bank sued the defendant bank for breach of duty to authenticate the endorsement and breach of implied warranty. The Supreme Court of Alabama reversed the grant of summary judgment to the defendant bank, noting that "[a]lthough the trial court discussed a number of facts that indicated negligence on the part of [the drawer bank], and although those facts might be found to have proximately caused the making of the forgery, these facts cannot establish the defense under Ala. Code 1975, §7-3-406, as a matter of law." Id. at 563. The case was thus remanded for a trial on the merits. Id.

In my opinion, the authorities relied upon by the majority are not dispositive of the case before us because none of these cases involve the delivery of an instrument to an agent of the payee. In *Thompson Maple Products*, the drawer was found to be negligent in entrusting the forger with checks payable to third parties. In *Fidelity and Deposit Co.*, the brokerage firm was found to be negligent because it failed to verify the identities of the payees and whether they in fact owned the securities at issue. In *Union Bank & Trust Co.*, the drawer delivered to the forger a check payable to the forger and the title agent as joint payees. These cases involve the delivery of an instrument to a party when another entity, unrelated to the party who received the instrument, is, in fact, the payee. That is not the case here. Gray was, without question, an employee of Allied and was authorized to receive documents and checks for her employer. The instant case is more factually similar to Society National Bank v. Capital National Bank, 281 N.E.2d 563 (Ohio Ct. App. 1972). In that case, Rzepka, a customer of Society National Bank, drew two checks payable to the ABS Company and delivered them to Mishler, a selling agent of ABS. Mishler forged ABS's endorsements on the checks, signed his own name, and obtained from Society National Bank two cashier's checks payable to ABS. Mishler again forged the endorsements and deposited them in his account. The defendants argued that Rzepka was negligent in issuing the checks to Mishler. The Ohio Court of Appeals disagreed:

> Appellants claim negligence on the part of the drawer Fred Rzepka. We find none. He drew a check to his creditor, the ABS Co., and delivered it to William Mishler, an acknowledged agent of the payee with whom Rzepka had previously dealt.

Id. at 566. Although UCC §3-406 was not implicated in *Society National Bank*, the rationale of that case is nevertheless relevant to the instant case. Gray was "an acknowledged agent of the payee." See 281 N.E.2d at 566. In fact, she was more than just a lower-level employee or agent; she was the branch manager of Allied's Cleveland office, and Wilburn and Bush had observed her there in that capacity. Based upon the evidence of her employment and her authority as a branch manager with the company, I do not find that Citizens acted unreasonably in expecting Gray, as an agent of Allied, to deliver the checks to her employer. I therefore would not find that Citizens failed to exercise ordinary care when it delivered the checks to her.

In addition to concluding that Citizens was negligent in delivering checks to Gray "without ever verifying her authority," the majority finds that Citizens was negligent in that it delivered the checks (1) without any written documentation and (2) without verifying the terms of the agreement with Allied. I believe this analysis misconstrues the issue in this case. The issue is not, as the majority seems to believe, whether Gray had the apparent authority to bind Allied to a contract to sell Citizens a franchise for upper East Tennessee; nor is the issue whether such a contract ever came into existence. Furthermore, the issue is not whether Allied is liable for the forgery of Gray. Were any of these issues before us, I would not hesitate to find them adverse to Citizens. However, the finding of negligent conduct on the part of Citizens vis-à-vis the franchise contract is not the same as a finding of negligence that substantially contributed to the forgery.

In my judgment, the real issue in this case is whether Citizens acted reasonably in expecting an identified branch manager of Allied to deliver a check intended for Allied, and made payable to it, to the branch manager's principal, i.e., Allied. To find that Citizens acted negligently, one has to find fault in its belief that it was secure in giving an admitted agent a check that, in order to be properly negotiated, had to be endorsed by the principal. It seems clear to me that Gray's status as a branch manager was sufficient indicia of her authority to warrant giving her a check for delivery to her principal. Citizens had absolutely no reason to suspect that an admitted agent, whose identity was well known to both Citizens and Allied, and whose whereabouts were apparently well known in Cleveland, would commit such a brazen criminal act. This is not a situation where a drawer gives a check to a stranger with the hope that he or she will deliver the check to the payee.

In the context of T.C.A. §47-3-406, I do not find in Citizens' conduct the type of "failure to exercise ordinary care" that I feel is contemplated by that statute, nor do I find the requisite nexus to the forgery. Accordingly, I respectfully dissent from so much of the majority opinion as pertains to Citizens' suit against the Bank. I would reverse the trial court's judgment and render judgment in Citizens' favor against the Bank.

PROBLEM 203

Lucille Larceny, corporate treasurer of Business Corporation, had the authority to indorse the corporate name to checks coming into the corporation. Over a period of months she took a number of such checks, stamped the corporate name as payee, then indorsed her own name below the corporate stamp and deposited the checks in her personal account at Busy National Bank. Is it negligent for the depository bank to allow her to do this? See §3-307(b)(2); Al Sarena Mines, Inc. v. Southtrust Bank, 548 So. 2d 1356, 9 U.C.C. Rep. Serv. 2d 1290 (Ala. 1989); In re Lou Levy & Sons Fashions, Inc., 785 F. Supp. 1163, 17 U.C.C. Rep. Serv. 2d 820 (S.D.N.Y. 1992), aff'd, 988 F.2d 311 (2d Cir. 1993).

PROBLEM 204

It was the practice of Octopus National Bank to treat checks payable to the bank as if they were payable to bearer. It did this because many check drawers made the same assumption. Whenever Business Corporation wanted to put money into a special account reserved for the payment of taxes, it wrote a check for the requisite amount, payable to the order of "Octopus National Bank," and, by use of a deposit slip with the tax account number on it, made the deposit. Lucille Larceny, the corporate treasurer of Business Corporation, wrote out a check for $250,000, payable to the order of "Octopus National Bank," cooking the books so that it appeared this amount was going into the tax account but in reality putting it into her own personal account, using a deposit slip with her account number on it. When the check cleared, Lucille disappeared with the money. Business Corporation protested to the bank and, when the bank refused to recredit its account, sued, arguing that these checks were not "properly payable" under §4-401 of the UCC. Was the bank negligent? See Olean Area Camp Fire Council, Inc. v. Olean Dresser Clark Fed. Credit Union, 142 Misc. 2d 1049, 538 N.Y.S.2d 905 (Sup. Ct. 1989) ("In charity we will withhold characterizing such conduct as 'abject stupidity' and call it merely negligence of the grossest kind"); Govoni & Sons Const. Co. v. Mechanics Bank, 51 Mass. App. 35, 742 N.E.2d 1094, 43 U.C.C. Rep. Serv. 2d 1058 (2001); Master Chemical Corp. v. Inkrott, 55 Ohio St. 3d 23, 563 N.E.2d 26, 13 U.C.C. Rep. Serv. 2d 14 (1990); but see Trail Leasing, Inc. v. Drovers First American Bank, 447 N.W.2d 190, 10 U.C.C. Rep. Serv. 2d 145 (Minn. 1989) (bank is a holder in due course and takes free of the defenses of the drawer[13] For an Annotation on the subject, see 69 A.L.R.4th 778. If the corporation were also found to be negligent in not better supervising Lucille, how does that affect the result?

PROBLEM 205

When Edwin Dennis died, he left all of his property in trust to his minor son, Patrick, whose guardianship was given over to Edwin's sister, Mame, who was named as trustee. One of the assets thus transferred was a $10,000 certificate of deposit, changed after Edwin's

13. This decision seems terribly wrong to me. What possible value does the bank give? It is merely releasing the customer's money and parting with none of its own. Furthermore, the bank is hardly in good faith and without notice (requirements to become a holder in due course) when it is behaving this carelessly. For a case saying that the bank cannot be a holder in due course in this situation, see Mutual Service Cas. Ins. Co. v. Elizabeth State Bank, 265 F.3d 601, 45 U.C.C. Rep. Serv. 2d 281 (7th Cir. 2001).

death so that it was payable to "Mame Dennis, as guardian and trustee for Patrick Dennis, a minor." When Mame decided to open her own catering business, she took the CD down to Babcock National Bank and pledged it as collateral for an $8,000 loan to her personally, and the bank took possession of the CD and put it in its vault. When Patrick came of age he consulted you, a former schoolmate and newly licensed attorney, and asked if he can get the CD back from the bank without having to repay the loan. See §3-307.

If Mame had used the Patrick Dennis Trust Account carried at Babcock National Bank, on which she was the named trustee, to write herself a check to pay her salary as trustee, would that be a suspicious circumstance giving rise to a claim in Patrick's favor to recover the money? See §3-307(b)(3) and its Official Comment 4.

E.   *The Bank Statement Rule*

In the earlier discussion of the bank and its customer, we covered §4-406, which establishes the rule that the customer must examine the bank statement or be estopped from asserting unauthorized signatures or material alterations that could have been discovered. That section, which you should read again, is nothing more than an extension of §3-406, the Negligence Rule; it establishes a specific act of negligence, failure to examine bank statements, which leads to an estoppel.

PROBLEM 206

While repairing a furnace in Rhonda Rivers' home, John Burly took advantage of her absence to sneak to her desk and tear out a blank check from the back of her checkbook. On March 25, this check cleared through Rhonda's checking account with her name forged thereto; the amount was $500. This check was returned to Rhonda on April 1. She failed to balance her checkbook until August 1 of that year, when she discovered and reported the forgery. Must the bank recredit her account? See §4-406(d)(1). Would it help or hurt the bank's position if John Burly had also had an account at the bank and had had $500 or more in this account at all times up until the end of July?

PROBLEM 207

Lucille Larceny was secretary to Howard Head, CEO of Business Corporation. Over a period of three years she stole 87 blank corporate checks from Head's checkbook, made the checks out to her brother, forged Head's name as drawer, and (with the help of her equally wicked brother) managed to take $378,000 out of the corporate account before she was caught and she and her brother, both penniless, went to jail. You are the corporate counsel for Business Corporation. How much, if anything, can it make its bank recredit? See §4-406(c), (d), (e), and (f).

Falk v. Northern Trust Co.

Appellate Court of Illinois, 2001
763 N.E.2d 380, 46 U.C.C. Rep. Serv. 2d 302

Presiding Justice HALL delivered the opinion of the court:

The plaintiff, Ralph Falk, II, filed a multicount complaint against the defendant, The Northern Trust Company (the Bank), seeking damages and an accounting based upon the Bank's failure to investigate and alert the plaintiff to fraudulent transactions involving his accounts with the Bank.

The trial court granted the Bank's motion to dismiss the plaintiff's second amended complaint, finding that the plaintiff's action was time-barred under section 4-406(f) of the Uniform Commercial Code-Bank Deposits and Collections (UCC) (810 ILCS 5/4-406(f) (West 1992))....

For over 13 years, the plaintiff employed Patricia Podmokly as his personal assistant. Her duties for the plaintiff included paying his personal bills, handling his bookkeeping, reporting to his accountants, and communicating with his investment advisors. In 1984, in order to carry out her duties, Ms. Podmokly was made a signatory on the plaintiff's demand accounts at the Bank. Ms. Podmokly held a position of a fiduciary with respect to the plaintiff, a fact which was known to the Bank.

In 1993, Ms. Podmokly began misappropriating funds from the plaintiff's accounts at the Bank for her own personal benefit. The misappropriation included drawing large amounts from the plaintiff's accounts through checks payable to cash which Ms. Podmokly used to pay her personal obligations, such as loans she had at the Bank and obligations of her business associates and friends at the Bank. Between

1993 and 1997, Ms. Podmokly misappropriated over $2,000,000 of the plaintiff's funds.

According to the plaintiff, the Bank ignored clear evidence of Ms. Podmokly's misappropriation of his funds and allowed her to continue her misappropriations well into 1997.

The plaintiff alleged that the Bank was placed on notice of Ms. Podmokly's misappropriation of the plaintiff's funds by the number of changes and irregularities in the plaintiff's account activity at the Bank, beginning in 1993 and continuing into 1997. In addition, in 1995, the Bank accepted an unsigned $2,000 check drawn on the plaintiff's account for payment of Ms. Podmokly's personal equity credit line at the Bank.

The Bank was also placed on notice of Ms. Podmokly's misappropriations, since she maintained her own accounts at the Bank, including her mortgage and equity line of credit. Because the Bank made loans to her and, in connection with those loans, reviewed her tax returns and other personal information, the Bank was aware that her income was insufficient to support the account and loan activity she was generating.

In his second amended complaint, the plaintiff requested an accounting and alleged causes of action against the Bank in negligence; under the Fiduciary Obligations Act (the Act) (760 ILCS 65/7, 8 (West 1992)); and under the UCC-Negotiable Instruments (810 ILCS 5/3-101 *et seq.* (West 1992)).

On May 5, 2000, the Bank . . . maintained, *inter alia,* that the second amended complaint should be dismissed in its entirety . . . because the plaintiff's claims are barred under the provisions of section 4-406(f) of the UCC . . . which required him to notify the Bank within one year after receiving his bank statement of any unauthorized signature or alteration or be precluded from bringing an action against the Bank based on those facts.

On May 24, 2000, the plaintiff filed his response to the Bank's motion to dismiss. The plaintiff argued that section 4-406(f) was inapplicable to his claim against the Bank because section 4-406(f) did not apply to claims based upon "actual knowledge" or "bad faith" on the part of the Bank.

On July 26, 2000, the trial court entered an order dismissing the plaintiff's second amended complaint with prejudice based upon the plaintiff's failure to comply with section 4-406(f) of the UCC. On August 15, 2000, the plaintiff filed a timely notice of appeal. . . .

Prior to January 1, 1992, section 4-406 of the UCC provided that when a bank sent a statement to a customer accompanied by items paid in "good faith," the customer must exercise reasonable care and promptness to examine the statement and promptly notify the bank of an unauthorized signature or alteration. . . . Section 4-406 further provided that a customer had one year from the time the statement and items were made available to him to report his unauthorized signature or alteration, or he was precluded from asserting the unauthorized signature or alteration against the bank, regardless of the care or lack of care on the part of either the bank or the customer. A customer had three years to report an unauthorized endorsement. . . .

In 1992, section 4-406 was amended and re-numbered. Section 4-406(1) became section 4-406(a). Sections 4-406(a) and 4-406(b) now provided that in order for banks to impose on their customers the duty to examine their statements and report unauthorized signatures or alterations, the statement that the Bank sends to its customer must contain sufficient information to allow the customer to identify the items paid, and that the bank must retain items or copies thereof for seven years. . . .

Eliminated from section 4-406(a) was the requirement contained in section 406(1) that the items be paid in "good faith." Section 4-406 goes on to provide that the customer is precluded from asserting the customer's unauthorized signature or any alteration of an item if the customer failed to examine the bank statement with reasonable promptness. . . . The "preclusion" is treated differently depending upon the bank's conduct. If the bank "failed to exercise ordinary care" in paying the item, then the customer and the bank share the loss. However, if the customer proves that the bank did not pay the item in "good faith," the preclusion under subsection (d) does not apply. . . .

Whether the time limitation set forth in section 4-406(f) bars an action against a bank where the bank is alleged to have paid items in bad faith is a case of first impression in Illinois.

Prior to the 1992 amendments to section 4-406, the Court of Appeals for the Seventh Circuit held that where the plaintiff alleged that the bank acted in bad faith in allowing the plaintiff's fiduciary to cash checks and make withdrawals from her accounts with forged endorsements or no endorsements at all, the time limitation in section 4-406(4) did not apply because section 4-406(1) required that the bank pay the items in "good faith." See *Appley v. West*, 832 F.2d 1021, 1032 (7th Cir. 1987).

The Bank maintains that the decision in *Appley* is not controlling because the 1992 amendments to section 4-406 eliminated the requirement in section 4-406(1) that the items be paid in "good faith" by the bank. . . . The Bank also maintains that the decision in *Appley* has no precedential value in light of this court's decision in *Euro Motors, Inc. v. Southwest Financial Bank and Trust Co.*, 297 Ill. App. 3d 246, 231 Ill. Dec. 415, 696 N.E.2d 711 (1998).

In *Euro Motors, Inc.*, the plaintiff's checking account required two signatures for any check drawn over $30,000. In 1994, Southwest paid two checks over $30,000, both with only the signature of the plaintiff's president. The president was removed in 1995. In 1996, the plaintiff sued Southwest for breach of contract and conversion seeking to recover the face value of the checks. Southwest moved for summary judgment alleging, *inter alia,* that the plaintiff had not timely notified it of the unauthorized signatures and, therefore, section 4-406(f) barred the plaintiff's suit. The trial court granted summary judgment, and the plaintiff appealed.

This court held that the plaintiff's suit was time-barred by section 4-406(f). This court first found that section 4-406(f) was not a statute of limitation, but a statutory prerequisite of notice and therefore not subject to the discovery rule. We then determined that the provisions of section 4-406(f) evidenced a public policy in favor of imposing on customers the duty of prompt examination of their bank accounts and the notification to banks of forgeries and alterations and in favor of reasonable time limitations on the responsibility of banks for payment of forged, altered or unauthorized items. *Euro Motors, Inc.*, 297 Ill. App. 3d at 253, 231 Ill. Dec. 415, 696 N.E.2d at 716. This court then stated as follows:

> Both the breach of contract claim and the conversion claim asserted in Euro Motors' complaint are time-barred by section 4-406(f). This provision bars any untimely claims, whether under the UCC or under common law. [Citation.] The time limit imposed by UCC section 4-406 is applicable without regard to the theory on which the customer brings his or her action. [Citations.] Moreover, the commercial certainty doctrine and the purposes of the UCC are compelling regardless of the theory underlying the lawsuit.

Euro Motors, Inc., 297 Ill. App. 3d at 254, 231 Ill. Dec. 415, 696 N.E.2d at 716.

The present case is more akin to *Appley* than to *Euro Motors, Inc.*, since the latter case did not deal with the issue of bad faith on the part of Southwest in paying the checks in question. While *Appley* is a federal case and decisions of the federal court are not binding on this court, . . . a federal court's interpretation of Illinois law is persuasive unless it runs contrary to previously decided state cases which, if correctly reasoned, will not be overturned. . . .

In addition, the court in *Euro Motors, Inc.* did not address the decision in *Appley*, which further compels the decision that *Euro Motors, Inc.* did not encompass the scenario in which a bank acted in bad faith by paying an item. In fact, using the reasoning of the court in *Euro Motors, Inc.*, regardless of the type of suit brought, the public policy behind placing the burden of discovering an authorized signature or alteration on the customer is hardly served where the bank is an active or passive partner in the scheme to defraud the customer.

Therefore, we conclude that *Euro Motors, Inc.* does not control the result in this case. We must now examine the statute to determine if the 1992 amendments require a result different than the one reached in *Appley*.

In interpreting a statute, the primary rule of statutory construction to which all other rules are subordinate is to ascertain and give effect to the true intent and meaning of the legislature. . . . In order to determine the legislative intent, courts must read the statute as a whole, all relevant parts must be considered, and each section should be construed in connection with every other section. . . . Courts should look to the language of the statute as the best indication of legislative intent, giving the terms of the statute their ordinary meaning. . . . Where the statutory language is clear, courts should give effect to the statute as enacted without considering extrinsic aids for construction. . . .

Our own examination of section 4-406, as amended, in its entirety convinces us that section 4-406(f) does not bar suits brought beyond the time limitation set forth in that section, where the customer alleges that the bank acted in "bad faith" in paying the items that are the subject of the suit.

As we previously noted, while prior to the 1992 amendments, section 4-406(1) required the bank to have paid the items in "good faith" before the time limitation in section 4-406(4) would run, the 1992 amendments eliminated the term "good faith" from section 4-406(a), section 4-406(1)'s amended counterpart. However, while prior to the 1992 amendments, section 4-406(3) provided that the customer was not precluded from asserting against the bank an unauthorized signature or alteration if the customer could establish that the bank did not use "ordinary care," its amended counterpart, section 4-406(e), requires the bank and the customer to share the loss where the customer establishes that the bank did not use "ordinary care" in paying the item. In addition, section 4-406(e) now allows a customer to avoid preclusion entirely, if the customer can prove that the bank did not pay the item in "good faith." . . .

Finally, under amended section 4-406(f), the bank escapes liability regardless of the "care" or lack thereof exercised by it or the customer, if the unauthorized signature or alteration is not reported to the bank within one year of the customer's receipt of the statement from the bank. Unlike section 4-406(e), however, section 4-406(f) does not refer to "good faith."

> We believe that the legislature's use of the term "care" in section 4-406(f) cannot be read to include "good faith." The fact that, in other parts of section 4-406, the legislature drew a distinction between "ordinary care" and "good faith" in describing the consequences suffered clearly indicates that the legislature did not intend to limit a bank's liability when it acted in "bad faith" as opposed to acting with a lack of care when paying an item.

In addition, we agree with the plaintiff that under the UCC every contract or duty contains an obligation of "good faith" in its performance or enforcement, therefore, the Bank was required to pay the items in "good faith.". . .

In summary, we conclude that section 4-406(f) requires that a bank act in "good faith" when paying the items on the statement in order to claim the protection of the prerequisite of notice requirement contained in that section. As we stated previously, the public policy behind placing the burden on the customer to determine unauthorized signatures or alterations is not served when the bank is a party, either actively or passively, to a scheme to defraud the customer.

However, a plaintiff may not avoid dismissal by merely reciting the words "actual knowledge" and "bad faith." *County of Macon v. Edgcomb*, 274 Ill. App. 3d 432, 438, 211 Ill. Dec. 136, 654 N.E.2d 598, 602 (1995). We must determine whether, taking all well-pleaded facts and reasonable inferences as true, the plaintiff has set forth sufficient facts to support his claim that the Bank acted in "bad faith."

In this case, the plaintiff alleged that the Bank was placed on notice of Ms. Podmokly's misappropriations from his accounts at the Bank based upon certain facts, such as the increased activity in his accounts during Ms. Podmokly's tenure as his personal assistant along with specific transactions, and that the Bank's failure to take action upon such notice amounted to "bad faith." Section 3-307 of the UCC provides in pertinent part as follows:

> "(b) If (i) an instrument is taken from a fiduciary for payment or collection or for value, (ii) the taker has knowledge of the fiduciary status of the fiduciary, and (iii) the represented person makes a claim

to the instrument or its proceeds on the basis that the transaction of the fiduciary is a breach of fiduciary duty, the following rules apply: * * *

(4) If the instrument is issued by the represented person or the fiduciary, as such, to the taker as payee, the taker has notice of the breach of fiduciary duty if the instrument is *(i) taken in payment of or as security for a debt known by the taker to be the personal debt of the fiduciary, (ii) taken in a transaction known by the taker to be for the personal benefit of the fiduciary, or (iii) deposited to an account other than an account of the fiduciary, as such, or an account of the represented person.*" (Emphasis added.)

The second amended complaint alleged that the Bank had actual knowledge of the fiduciary relationship between Ms. Podmokly and the plaintiff. It further alleged that the Bank had accepted checks drawn by Ms. Podmokly on the plaintiff's account for payment of her loans at the Bank, for payment on her personal equity credit line at the Bank and for deposit into her own personal account at the Bank.

Based upon the above allegations, the Bank was on notice that Ms. Podmokly was acting in breach of her fiduciary duties to the plaintiff. Given the number of years and the numerous transactions alleged by the plaintiff, the Bank's failure to investigate in light of its knowledge of the breach of fiduciary duty constitutes more than a lack of care for which it would be protected by section 4-406(f). See *Edgcomb*, 274 Ill. App. 3d at 436, 211 Ill. Dec. 136, 654 N.E.2d at 601 (an example of bad faith is where the taker suspects that the fiduciary is acting improperly and deliberately refrains from investigating in order that he may avoid knowledge that the fiduciary is acting improperly). As the court stated in *Appley*,

In determining whether the bank acted with bad faith, "courts have asked whether it was commercially unjustifiable for the payee to disregard and refuse to learn facts readily available." [Citation.] At some point, obvious circumstances become so cogent that it is "bad faith" to remain passive. [Citation.]

Appley, 832 F.2d at 1031.

We conclude that the plaintiff has set forth sufficient facts to establish that the Bank acted in bad faith rather than with a lack of care when it permitted Ms. Podmokly's check writing activities to continue without conducting an investigation in light of the fact that it was on notice that she was in breach of her fiduciary duties to the plaintiff.

The judgment of the circuit court of Cook County is reversed and the cause is remanded for further proceedings in accordance with the views expressed in this opinion.

WOLFSON, J., concurs.

Justice CERDA dissenting:

I respectfully dissent. . . .

I believe that the legislature could have inserted "good faith" if it had wanted to do so. Since "good faith" was not included in section 4-406(f), I do not believe that we can require the bank to pay the items in "good faith" in order for the one-year period to apply. . . .

In this case, the plaintiff did not discover and report unauthorized actions by Ms. Podmokly to the bank within the one-year period; therefore, he is precluded from making any claim against the Bank in this case. That includes claims of "bad faith" or lack of "good faith" in paying the unauthorized checks. The burden falls on the customer to examine the bank statements. I would affirm.

PROBLEM 208

Original National Bank engaged in the practice of "bulk filing," meaning that the bank did not examine checks for forgeries if they were written for amounts less than $5,000. The bank justified this practice as necessary for economic reasons. It therefore paid a series of $3,500 checks on which a customer's signature as drawer was forged and sent them over a period of months to its customer as part of his monthly statement. The customer negligently failed to report the forgeries of his name until seven months after the first one was returned to him. When he did complain, the bank pointed to §4-406(c) and (d). The customer replied that §4-406(e) requires the bank to share the loss since it did not observe ordinary care. As to the meaning of *ordinary care,* see §4-103(c) and a definition of the term in §3-103(a)(7) that should prove very interesting to the bank's attorney. Who prevails here?

PROBLEM 209

When the law firm of Factory, Factory & Money (F.F. & M.) opened a checking account with Octopus National Bank (ONB), the firm members signed a deposit contract, stating that they would report all irregularities in their bank statements within 10 days of their receipt. Failure to do so resulted in a waiver of any problems with the statement. Two years later LeNore Ledger, F.F. & M.'s bookkeeper, wrote three checks to herself, each for $5,000, and forged the necessary F.F. & M. signatures to the drawer's line. The first check cleared through the bank in time to be returned with the bank statement that arrived at the law office on December 10. Ledger burned the statement and then took off for parts unknown. On January 23, Amos Factory, a senior partner, notified ONB that he could not find the December statement. When a duplicate was furnished to F.F. & M., they pointed out the first $5,000 check. By this time the other two checks had cleared through F.F. & M.'s account and were ready to be sent out in the February statement. The bank declined to recredit F.F. & M.'s account with any of the $15,000, pointing to the 10-day notice requirement in the deposit contract and to §4-406(d). F.F. & M. sued under §4-401's *properly payable* rule and argued that §4-103 invalidated the 10-day notice provision. How should this come out? See Coine v. Manufacturers Hanover Trust Co., 16 U.C.C. Rep. Serv. 184 (N.Y. Sup. Ct. 1975). Cf. White & Summers 18-2, at 653-655; State ex rel. Gabalac v. Firestone Bank, 46 Ohio App. 2d 124, 346 N.E.2d 326, 19 U.C.C. Rep. Serv. 219 (1975). In J. Sussman v. Manufacturers Hanover Trust, 2 U.C.C. Rep. Serv. 2d 1605 (N.Y. Sup. Ct. 1986), a 14-day period was allowed; in Stowell v. Cloquet Co-op Credit Union, 557 N.W.2d 567, 31 U.C.C. Rep. Serv. 2d 623 (Minn. 1997), a 20-day period was permitted; and in Qassemzadeh v. IBM Poughkeepsie Employees Fed. Credit Union, 561 N.Y.S.2d 795, 13 U.C.C. Rep. Serv. 2d 833 (N.Y. Sup. Ct. 1990), a 30-day period was approved. Would it make a difference if Ledger's forgeries were very badly done? See §4-406(e).

PROBLEM 210

When Octopus National Bank found out about the rule of Price v. Neal (making the drawee liable for forgeries of the drawer's name unless the wrongdoer could be found), it asked its attorney what could be done to avoid this liability. The bank's attorney had the bank add a clause to the checking account agreement as follows: "Customer understands and agrees that the bank is no longer examining checks written for amounts less than $5,000, and also agrees that if the drawer's signature on such checks shall be unauthorized, the checks shall nonetheless be properly payable from the bank account, with the

customer having the sole duty to pursue legal remedies against others."
Is this clause valid? See §§4-103, 4-401(a), and 3-103(a)(7).

PROBLEM 211

Maximilian Money was not only very rich but also very lazy. He
let the Investors National Bank handle all his affairs, the least of which
was to act as drawee of his checking account. So as to save time, he
signed all of his checks with a little rubber signature stamp when he
first received his checkbook. Though the bank regularly sent him
monthly statements, he never even opened them. At income tax time
his tax lawyer discovered that his bank account was $4,000 short due
to a check that had been stolen from Max and filled in to "Cash" for
$4,000 over two years ago. The lawyer, as Max's agent, demanded that
the account be replenished with this amount. The bank, to which
$4,000 was a small matter in comparison to its income as trustee of
Max's affairs, instantly complied. The $4,000 was not, however, so
small a matter that it could be forgotten, so the Investors National Bank
demanded repayment from the presenting bank, the Fallguy State Bank,
charging breach of the §4-208(a)(2) warranty of no alteration. What
result if Fallguy State refuses and suit is brought? See §4-406(f)'s last
sentence and §4-208(c).

PROBLEM 212

Bertrand Balance was the payroll clerk for Tentacles Corporation,
and one day in a moment of weakness he drew up 107 extra
paychecks payable to phony names. He signed the payees' names to
the back of every check and cashed each of the checks at various local
depositary banks over the period of one month. As soon as the last one
had been cashed, Balance hurriedly left the state, leaving behind only
an apologetic letter explaining what he had done. The corporation
immediately demanded that the money be recredited to its payroll
account. The bank comes to you for advice. Tentacles Corporation is
one of the bank's largest depositors, and the bank doesn't want to lose
it. If it recredits the account, can it sue the depositary banks for breach
of presentment warranties?

Note that (c) of §4-208 (and the corresponding (c) in Article 3's
presentment warranty section, §3-417) permits the entity making

presentment warranties to raise the various validation rules to avoid warranty liability. This is as it should be. If the payor bank did make proper payment in spite of the forgery/alteration because these irregularities are validated by one of the sections we have studied, then the payor bank should not be permitted to ignore the validation and pass the loss on to innocent parties such as the presenting bank. Of course, the payor bank may be reluctant to offend its wealthy depositors, as in the above Problems, and, as a business matter, may elect to eat the loss itself rather than lose their trade, but if it is going to be this nice to its customers, any damages caused thereby are self-inflicted. Any time anyone has a valid defense and fails to raise it, that person has shot himself in the foot. The proximate cause of this loss is the unwillingness to raise the defense, not the technical breach of a presentment warranty.

IV. ALTERATION

PROBLEM 213

Earnest Innocent went into the Mafia Loan Company and asked to borrow $100 to finance the repair of a broken tooth. The loan company advanced him the money after he signed a promissory note for this amount plus eight percent interest per annum, payable to the order of the Mafia Loan Company on demand. After Innocent left the office, the loan officer took out his special chemicals and used them to erase the original typewritten amount ($100). In its place he typed in $9,500. The Mafia Loan Company discounted the paper for $100 to Michael Schmidt, a self-employed commercial factor, who always bought the company's altered paper. Schmidt presented the note to Innocent for payment, and when Innocent protested, Schmidt's "collectors" broke both his arms. They said they would return the following month and would expect him to have the money ready then. Assuming Innocent can get police protection against Schmidt's "self-help" collection procedures, what legal defenses does he have? Read §3-407 carefully.

Note that §3-407(b) states that a fraudulent alteration completely *discharges* any non-negligent person whose negotiable instruments contract is changed by the alteration. The alteration in the above Problem is technically said to be a *raising* of the amount.

PROBLEM 214

George Johnson owed around $50 to Marmaduke Brown and, while making out checks to his creditors, decided to write out a check to Brown. Unfortunately, he couldn't remember how to spell Brown's name or the exact amount owed, so he simply signed his name to the drawer's line while making a mental note to fill in the rest later. He put the check in his wallet, and it was stolen along with the wallet when he was mugged the following night. The check, made out to "Cash" for $150, cleared through his checking account the next week. Johnson brought suit against his bank, demanding that the bank recredit his account since the amount was not *properly payable*. He argues that this was an alteration under §3-407 and that he was discharged by the alteration. What reply should the bank's attorney make? See §§3-115, 3-407, 3-406, and 4-401(d).

PROBLEM 215

Joseph Goodheart was the owner and manager of the Goodheart Home for the Aged. He was also the payee of a promissory note for $1,000 given him by Nick Nephew to pay for three months' care Goodheart had given to Nephew's elderly aunt, Strange Molly. One day Strange Molly, who was not responsible for her actions, sneaked into Goodheart's empty office and ransacked his files. She found her nephew's promissory note and took a pen and deftly changed the amount to $1,000,000. Does this operate, under §3-407, to discharge Nephew from his maker's obligation? What would be the result if Strange Molly had torn up and eaten the note? See §3-309 and its Official Comment.

PROBLEM 216

Lloyd Smith mailed a check for $5.00 to his friend, David Rouge, as a birthday gift. Rouge cleverly raised the amount to $500.00 and cashed it at his own bank, Octopus National Bank, which then obtained payment from the drawee bank. When Smith received his bank statement, he immediately complained to his bank about the alteration of the check. Assuming he was not negligent in writing the check, can Smith make the bank recredit the account for $500.00, or only $495.00? See §§3-407, 4-401(d). Is the bank without a remedy? See §4-208(a).

Chapter 13
ELECTRONIC
BANKING

In recent years, books on commercial law typically have included chapters speculating on a future *checkless* society. Some authors, while agreeing that radically new payment systems are evolving, feel that checks are likely to be in major use for some time yet and so refer to a coming *less-check* society. But as employers begin depositing paychecks directly into employees' bank accounts, the Treasury Department does the same thing for Social Security and other checks, bills are paid by phone, and banking can be done at automated teller machines (ATMs) or right at the merchant's checkout counter at the point of sale (POS), and mountains of money move from bank to bank as electronic signals only, then the *checkless* society is here, and future shock engulfs the law.

Elimination of the tons of checks that daily must be carted around the world is of obvious benefit to the banks involved. (Similar concerns in connection with investment securities led to the redrafting of Article 8 of the Code so as to permit corporations to issue securities that are recorded in a computer and are not evidenced by pieces of paper.) The benefits to some of the banks' customers are more questionable. As electronic fund transfers (EFTs) replace checks, the consumer drawer at least faces loss of control over the account and the evidentiary nightmare of proving that computers are in error.

Our study in this chapter is divided into two parts. The first concerns the rights and duties of the parties when a consumer is permitted (or required) to use electronic fund transfers to move monies in and out of the consumer's bank account. The second looks at the wire transfers of funds between banking institutions. Both areas of EFT law are changing fast (faster than pleases casebook writers).

I. THE ELECTRONIC FUND TRANSFER ACT

In the beginning, since no law obviously applied to these transactions, the banks regulated the inevitable disputes by contract terms, which were fair or not, depending on the bank. Some 35 percent of the banks made their customers agree to bear complete liability for all unauthorized transfers, at least until the customer notified the bank of the loss. See Taffer, The Making of the Electronic Fund Transfer Act: A Look at Consumer Liability and Error Resolution, 13 U.S.F.L. Rev. 231, 233 n.14 (1979). States began passing statutes on point, and in 1978 Congress enacted the Electronic Fund Transfer Act (EFTA), 15 U.S.C. §§1693 et seq. In this book, citations will be to Regulation E, promulgated by the Federal Reserve Board to implement the EFTA. However, before we examine the EFTA, it is necessary first to consider related legislation.

In 1968, after a decade of attempts, Congress passed the comprehensive Consumer Credit Protection Act, 15 U.S.C. §§1600 et seq. (1976). This much-amended statute is divided into titles: Title I is the Truth in Lending (TIL) Act, Title VII is the Equal Credit Opportunity Act, etc. Most of these titles authorize a federal agency, typically the Federal Reserve Board (FRB), to issue regulations having the force of law. These regulations then implement and supplement the statute and are "explained" in frequent pronouncements, official and unofficial, by the agency involved. Thus, the Truth in Lending Act's statutory provisions are the bare bones on which the FRB has hung its Regulation Z, 12 C.F.R. §226, which is the primary reference for resolving TIL disputes. Both TILA (part of the Consumer Credit Protection Act) and Regulation Z should be in your statute book. The Truth in Lending Act and Regulation Z are relevant to our discussion because they cover three related matters: credit card liability, available defenses to credit card bills, and procedures for resolving billing disputes. Detailed exploration of these provisions awaits you in a consumer law course, but a brief look at each follows.

A. Credit Cards

PROBLEM 217

When his sister Alice went off to California to "find herself," Clark Consumer loaned her his bank charge card. She promised to charge no more than $200 worth of purchases. Now Clark, who lives in Ohio, hasn't heard from her in months, but she has so far run up $1,800 in charges, and the charge slips mount each day. Octopus National, the bank that issued the card, says Clark is liable for all her charges until he can find her and reclaim his card. Is he? See Martin v. American Express, Inc., 361 So. 2d 597 (Ala. Civ. App. 1978); Walker Bank & Trust Co. v. Jones, 672 P.2d 73 (Utah 1983). If the EFTA applied to the kind of credit card involved, what result? See Regulation E §205.2(m), which should be in your statute book, perhaps called "Electronic Fund Transfer Regulations."

In the above Problem, the use of the card was *authorized*, at least at its inception, and the consumer usually must pay the resulting bills. Where, however, the use is *unauthorized* (because, for instance, the credit card was stolen), §226.12 of Regulation Z limits the cardholder's liability to $50 (or whatever lesser amount has been charged before the cardholder notifies the issuer of the loss), and the cardholder is not even liable for this amount unless the card issuer has notified the cardholder of the rights, the card identifies the user, and the card issuer has provided the cardholder with a means of notifying the card issuer of the loss (a telephone number, for example).

B.   Asserting Defenses Against the Credit Card Issuer

PROBLEM 218

Linda Liable lived in Newark, New Jersey. One year she took a trip to San Francisco. While there, she charged her hotel bill using her bank credit card issued by Octopus National Bank in Newark, but she protested to the hotel manager that the bill was twice the amount it should have been. The hotel manager refused to listen. On her return to Newark, Linda refused to pay ONB's credit card bill for this charge; she also refused to pay for other charges: an $80 suitcase she had purchased in New York City that fell apart on the trip (the New York seller is now bankrupt) and a $25 art print ordered from Florida that had never arrived (ONB had included promotional literature on these Florida artworks in its last credit card billing). Is she liable to ONB?

To resolve this issue, see Regulation Z §226.12(c):

> (c) Right of cardholder to assert claims or defenses against card issuer.
>
> (1) *General rule.* When a person who honors a credit card fails to resolve satisfactorily a dispute as to property or services purchased with the credit card in a consumer credit transaction, the cardholder may assert against the card issuer all claims (other than tort claims) and defenses arising out of the transaction and relating to the failure to resolve the dispute. The cardholder may withhold payment up to the amount of credit outstanding for the property or services that gave rise to the dispute and any finance or other charges imposed on that amount.
>
> (2) *Adverse credit reports prohibited.* If, in accordance with paragraph (c)(1) of this section, the cardholder withholds payment of the amount of credit outstanding for the disputed transaction, the card issuer shall not report that amount as delinquent until the dispute is settled or judgment is rendered.
>
> (3) *Limitations.* The rights stated in paragraphs (c)(1) and (2) of this section apply only if:
>
> (i) The cardholder has made a good faith attempt to resolve the dispute with the person honoring the credit card; and
>
> (ii) The amount of credit extended to obtain the property or services that result in the assertion of the claim or defense by the cardholder exceeds $50, and the disputed transaction occurred in the same state as the cardholder's current designated address or, if not within the same state, within 100 miles from that address.

At the end of this section Regulation Z adds an explanatory footnote:

> The limitations stated in paragraph (c)(3)(ii) of this section shall not apply when the person honoring the credit card: (1) is the same person as the card issuer; (2) is controlled by the card issuer directly or indirectly; (3) is under the direct or indirect control of a third person that also directly or indirectly controls the card issuer; (4) controls the card issuer directly or indirectly; (5) is a franchised dealer in the card issuer's products or services; or (6) has obtained the order for the disputed transaction through a mail solicitation made or participated in by the card issuer.

Regulation Z §226.12(c) n.26.

C. Billing Errors

Under §226.13 of Regulation Z, if the cardholder complains to the issuer of a billing error, the card issuer must acknowledge the complaint within 30 days, conduct a good faith investigation of the problem, and resolve the difficulty one way or the other within 90 days of the complaint (or within two billing cycles, whichever is less). During the interim the issuer must not treat the disputed amount as overdue or report it adversely to credit reporting agencies. Failure to honor the consumer's rights under this provision leads to the card issuer's forfeiture of up to $50 of the disputed amount and to additional liability, including attorney's fees, under §130 of the Truth in Lending Act. These penalties can be collected even if the consumer was in error and the bank was right all along.

D. Electronic Fund Transfers and the Consumer

The applicability of Regulation Z to EFTs was unclear until Congress solved the problem by passing the Electronic Fund Transfer Act, 15 U.S.C. §§1693 et seq., making it the new Title IX of the Consumer Credit Protection Act of 1968. Section 904 of the Act authorized the FRB to prescribe regulations to carry out the purposes of the Act, and the Board has responded with Regulation E, 12 C.F.R. part 205. Both can be found in your statute book. You should also know that the Federal Reserve Board has published an Official Staff Commentary on Regulation E, 12 C.F.R. part 205, which explains the rules in detail and gives examples. This Commentary (which is not in your statute book) has the force of law and should therefore be consulted when difficult questions arise in practice.

PROBLEM 219

Electra Smith was employed as a clerk for the Business Corporation. One day it informed her that henceforth all her paychecks would automatically be deposited in the local bank of her choice. She chose Octopus National Bank (ONB), her usual bank. Could she have demanded a check and refused the EFT?[1]

ONB informed Electra that she could pay all her bills by phone and that many creditors would be willing to set up an automatic monthly payment plan whereby ONB would pay routine bills unless she instructed otherwise. Electra signed such a contract with her landlord, to whom ONB agreed to transfer $300 on the first day of each month as rent. What details does ONB have to explain to her? See Regulation E §205.7. (The FRB has promulgated model forms for this purpose, and the bank is well advised to use them since such use shields the bank from arguments about disclosure errors. See §915(d)(2) of the Act.) Consider these issues:

(a) One day ONB's computer malfunctioned and for no apparent reason deducted $1,000 from Electra's checking account and credited it to an account designated "Computer Maintenance." Several of her checks bounced as a result. Is the computer's deduction an "electronic fund transfer" under Regulation E §205.3(b)? If so, is it also an "unauthorized electronic fund transfer" under §205.2(m)? Is the bank liable under §910? Under UCC §4-401(a)? (Note UCC §4-104(a)(9).) Are there common law theories that she might use? As to the bounced checks, see UCC §4-402 (Wrongful Dishonor).

(b) ONB failed to pay Electra's rent on the first of January because the computer got backlogged with the huge Christmas volume. Can her landlord evict her? See §912. When she is evicted and sues ONB over §910, can the bank defend using §910(b)(1)? Cf. Blake v. Woodford

---

1. This issue is resolved by §913 of the EFTA, reprinted below:
    Section 913. Compulsory Use of Electronic Fund Transfers
  No person may—
    (1) condition the extension of credit to a consumer on such consumer's repayment by means of preauthorized electronic fund transfers; or
    (2) require a consumer to establish an account for receipt of electronic fund transfers with a particular financial institution as a condition of employment or receipt of a government benefit.

Bank & Trust Co., 555 S.W.2d 589, 21 U.C.C. Rep. Serv. 383 (Ky. Ct. App. 1977) (a case deciding a similar issue under UCC §4-109).

(c) One month Electra had a dispute with her landlord, so she phoned ONB and told them not to pay the next month's rent due to be transferred four days later. Is oral notice sufficient? Is her notice timely? See §907(a); Regulation E §205.10(c). If the bank fails to stop payment, what remedy does she have? See §910. What damages does she have? Can she recover her attorney's fees? Compare §910(c) and §915(a).

(d) If Linda Liable in the last Problem had made purchases with point of sale (POS) EFTs, would she be able to assert her defenses against her bank under the EFTA?

PROBLEM 220

Jane Austen owned a bookstore and handled the store's financial affairs through a checking account with Octopus National Bank (ONB). If ONB grants the store an ability to pay its debts by EFTs, does the EFTA apply? See §903(2); Regulation E §205.2(b).

PROBLEM 221

The first time Arthur Greenbaum used his *access card* at an all-night automated teller machine, he told the machine to give him $50 from his checking account, and it promptly did so. At the same time the ATM deducted $500 from Arthur's account and reported that Arthur had withdrawn this amount. It gave Arthur no written statement.

(a) At the end of the month Arthur's bank sent him a statement showing the status of his checking account. Should it reflect this transaction? How? See §906; Regulation E §205.9(b). May it be combined with the statement required by UCC §4-406? See §906(c).

(b) If Arthur does not examine this statement for one year, does the EFTA cause him problems? Note §§909(a), 903(11), and 915(g). Does UCC §4-406(f) cause problems?

(c) If Arthur examines the statement promptly and discovers the error, what should he do? See §908(a); Regulation E §205.11(b). The bank received Arthur's notice on May 1. By what date need it act? Need it put the money back in his account during its investigation? See §§908(a), 908(c); Regulation E §205.11(c).

(d) Who bears the burden of proof as to whether the ATM gave Arthur $50 or $500? See §909(b); cf. Gramore Stores, Inc. v. Bankers

Trust Co., 93 Misc. 2d 112, 402 N.Y.S.2d 326 (Sup. Ct. 1978) (dispute over deposit made in a bank's night depository).

(e) What liability does the bank have simply because it never programmed the ATM to hand out written statements? See §906(a), 915; Regulation E §205.9(a). If the ATM had been so programmed but failed to give the statement to Arthur due to mechanical failure, is this a defense? See §915(c). Is it a defense that the ATM growled at Arthur when he walked up to it, so that he should have known it wasn't working, and thus he assumed the risk of the resulting error? Cf. §910(b)(2).

(f) After receiving Arthur's complaint (and also the complaint of every single person using that particular ATM), the bank's investigation consisted solely of having a computer printout made of the transaction and mailing it to Arthur. Similar documentation was sent to each complainant. Does this satisfy §908? Note particularly §908(e).

If the customer agrees to make EFTs, the bank will frequently give the customer a method of identifying himself or herself when ordering the debit or credit to the account. Typically, either a bank card (called an *access* or *debit card*) is used or the customer is assigned a secret number (a *personal identification number* or PIN) or both. Like all credit cards, this access card and/or the PIN must be guarded by the customer, or life can become difficult even if the customer prevails in the resulting legal disputes. Read §909 and Regulation E §205.6, which follows.

§205.6   *Liability of Consumer for Unauthorized Transfers*

(a) *Conditions for liability.* A consumer may be held liable, within the limitations described in paragraph (b) of this section, for an unauthorized electronic fund transfer involving the consumer's account only if the financial institution has provided the disclosures required by §205.7(b)(1), (2), and (3). If the unauthorized transfer involved an access device, it must be an accepted access device and the financial institution must have provided a means to identify the consumer to whom it was issued.

(b) *Limitations on amount of liability.* A consumer's liability for an unauthorized electronic fund transfer or a series of related unauthorized transfers shall be determined as follows:

(1) Timely notice given. If the consumer notifies the financial institution within two business days after learning of the loss or theft of the access device, the consumer's liability shall not exceed the lesser of $50 or the amount of unauthorized transfers that occur before notice to the financial institution.

(2) Timely notice not given. If the consumer fails to notify the financial institution within two business days after learning of the loss or theft of the access device, the consumer's liability shall not exceed the lesser of $500 or the sum of:

(i) $50 or the amount of unauthorized transfers that occur within the two business days, whichever is less; and

(ii) The amount of unauthorized transfers that occur after the close of two business days and before notice to the institution, provided the institution establishes that these transfers would not have occurred had the consumer notified the institution within the two-day period.

(3) Periodic statement; timely notice not given. A consumer must report an unauthorized electronic fund transfer that appears on a periodic statement within 60 days of the financial institution's transmittal of the statement to avoid liability for subsequent transfers. If the consumer fails to do so, the consumer's liability shall not exceed the amount of the unauthorized transfers that occur after the close of the 60 days and before notice to the institution, and that the institution establishes would not have occurred had the consumer notified the institution within the 60-day period. When an access device is involved in the unauthorized transfer, the consumer may be liable for other amounts set forth in paragraphs (b)(1) or (b)(2) of this section, as applicable.

(4) Extensions of time limits. If the consumer's delay in notifying the financial institution was due to extenuating circumstances, the institution shall extend the times specified above to a reasonable period.

(5) Notice to financial institution.

(i) Notice to a financial institution is given when a consumer takes steps reasonably necessary to provide the institution with the pertinent information, whether or not a particular employee or agent of the institution actually receives the information.

(ii) The consumer may notify the institution in person, by telephone, or in writing.

(iii) Written notice is considered given at the time the consumer mails the notice or delivers it for transmission to the institution by any other usual means. Notice may be considered constructively given when the institution becomes aware of circumstances leading to the reasonable belief that an unauthorized transfer to or from the consumer's account has been or may be made.

(6) Liability under state law or agreement. If state law or an agreement between the consumer and the financial institution imposes less liability than is provided by this section, the consumer's liability shall not exceed the amount imposed under the state law or agreement.

PROBLEM 222

Ebenezer Scrooge owned a bank credit card issued by Dickens National Bank, the same bank with whom he maintained a checking account. One day the mail contained a letter assigning Scrooge a PIN and explaining to him that by inserting his credit card in an ATM and punching in the PIN, he could receive immediate cash withdrawals from his checking account.

(a) Has Dickens National violated the EFTA? See §911; Regulation E §205.5.

(b) Scrooge threw the PIN letter in the wastebasket, from which it was removed by his employee Bob Cratchit, who stole Scrooge's card and extracted $100 from the ATM in order to buy crutches for his crippled son. Is Scrooge liable for this withdrawal? See §§909(a), 903(1); Regulation E §205.6.

PROBLEM 223

While Carl Consumer was asleep one day, his sister Nancy sneaked into his bedroom and stole his bank card. She knew his PIN because he had once loaned her the card and authorized her to make a small series of withdrawals, but this time it was an out and out theft.[2] She took the card on April 30 and used it to take $500 from his account with Original National Bank on that same day. He missed the card when he woke up, and he rightly guessed that Nancy had taken it. Rather than notify the bank, he tried to track her down and retrieve the card. On May 5, she used the card to remove $800 from his bank account, and then she left the state. Heartsick at her perfidy, Carl slumped into a depression so severe that he could not leave his bed. On May 31, the bank sent Carl the usual bank statement; it reflected all of these transactions. On June 10, Nancy returned to the state and used the card to take $3,000 from Carl's account. A lawsuit followed. Resolve it, using §205.6 of Regulation E, reproduced above.

PROBLEM 224

When Joseph Armstrong walked up to the ATM, someone stepped into line behind him. While Armstrong was taking his debit card from

---

2. For a case saying that disclosure of the PIN for one authorized use does not make subsequent uses authorized as well, see Vaughan v. United States National Bank, 79 Ore. App. 172, 718 P.2d 769 (1986).

his wallet, the person behind him stuck a gun in his back and ordered him to withdraw the maximum amount. Is this an "unauthorized" EFT, so that his liability is limited to $50? See the Federal Reserve Board's Official Staff Commentary on Regulation E, 12 C.F.R. 205, EFT-2 Q2-28. If Armstrong lost his wallet and it contained his debit card, on which he had negligently written his PIN, would his liability for unauthorized use increase? See the same Staff Commentary at Q6-6.5.

One real burden facing the bank's customer in an EFT world is uncertainty as to the daily bank balance. This problem is sure to arise unless the customer keeps accurate account of all checks, charges, ATM and POS transactions, preauthorized EFTs, bank service fees, and telephonic EFTs. Furthermore, when the monthly statement arrives, the customer must be very organized to do an accurate reconciliation within the EFTA's 60-day period. The lack of documentation that is one of the benefits of EFTs for banks is going to make the customer's life more difficult. The inevitable solution is that the customer, too, is going to have to get a computer, although some are experimenting with the so-called *smart card*, a debit card that has an internal memory of each transaction for which it has been used so that the card itself can do all of the consumer's record keeping. O brave new world, that has such machines in it!

II. WIRE TRANSFERS

The safe and efficient movement of money is now accomplished electronically through a host of systems devised by bankers and implemented by government action (the Federal Reserve System) or private agreement. Consider the advantage to the federal government of electronic payment of Social Security debts: mountains of paper (paper that can be lost or stolen) need not move clumsily through the mails. Instead, electronic signals do all the work quickly and with fewer errors. Similarly, imagine the benefits to a national retailer if the movement of money to and from its thousands of outlets can be accomplished efficiently at the end of every business day by the mere electronic adjustment of funds.

Until 1990 there was no organized body of law to deal with such transfers, though the Federal Reserve had promulgated its Regulation J, 12 C.F.R. §210, to resolve disputes internal to transfers through the

Federal Reserve System.[3] But there was no guidance to resolve a host of disputes likely to occur: bank failure, computer hackers mugging the system to steal electronic dollars, glitches whereby the computer sent out duplicate order after duplicate order, etc. Nor is this a small matter; each day's wire transfers in the United States averaged $3,000,000,000,000 (that's $3 trillion; yes, *trillion*). This number is, of course, growing.

The Federal Reserve System's wire transfer mechanism is called *Fedwire*. It electronically moves funds from one Federal Reserve bank to another at the instruction of the sending institution to the receiving institution, both of which will maintain accounts at Federal Reserve banks. These wholesale wire transactions are enormous in scale. The average Fedwire transfer is $2 million (compared with a $600 average for checks).

The international transfer of money is accomplished through a New York-based system called CHIPS (for "Clearinghouse Interbank Payments System," run by the New York Clearinghouse Association). Its transfers are made in U.S. dollar amounts converted from foreign currencies. The sender instructs its bank to make the wire transfer to a designated payee's account at a different receiving bank. The sending bank informs the CHIPS computer to make the transfer and then sends a verification of the proposed transfer. At the end of the banking day, settlement must occur when CHIPS informs all banks involved of their net position for the day. At this point wire transfers through the New York Federal Reserve Bank are made to adjust the accounts of all participants. CHIPS transfers are also of fantastic amounts, averaging close to $7 million a day.

The advantages of wire transfers are their speed and safety. Typically, a receiving bank allows its non-bank customer immediate access to the funds even though settlement (and thus the actual transfer of the money) will not occur until the end of the day. If, for one reason or another (bank failure, for example), settlement never happens, the receiving bank faces the very real risk of being unable to recapture the funds.

Since many wire transfers occur in the computers before the funds are actually exchanged, all participating banks at some point during the banking day face exposures often greater than the bank's assets. If settlement is made at the end of the day, fine, but in the meantime there is a situation called *daylight overdraft,* and the rules of the various

___

3. In 1991, the Federal Reserve Board amended Regulation J so that its rules are in accordance with those of Article 4A.

wire transfer systems may limit the amount of exposure by imposing a *debit cap*—a limit on the daylight overdraft that a participating bank may incur.[4]

An *automated clearinghouse*, or ACH, is, as its name suggests, a mechanism for the electronic transfer of recurring debits and credits between participants, typically for low-dollar/high-volume batched messages such as payrolls. There are a number of such privately created ACHs in the United States, typically linking the transfers through a Federal Reserve bank.[5] Transfers utilizing ACHs are now more than $1 billion annually, with the bulk being transfers by the federal government to pay its routine debts (social security, veteran's benefits, employee paychecks, etc.). Transfers through the ACH are accomplished by telephone, electronic communication, or manual delivery to the ACH of a computer program containing all the relevant payment or debit instructions. The actual transfer of funds typically occurs on the day *after* the ACH receives the sender's instructions (or, by agreement, even later).

With new systems and private associations being created constantly (and old ones dropping by the wayside, their usefulness spent), the law is sorely pressed to keep up with the technology. Many of the legal disputes are resolved by contract between the participants, though a body of electronic fund transfer law is developing. We have already considered the Electronic Fund Transfer Act, which protects consumers. Non-consumer wire transfers are regulated in part by Regulation J, promulgated by the Federal Reserve Board to govern transfers using the federal system, and in part by the Uniform Commercial Code's Article 4A, "Funds Transfers." This article has now been adopted by all the states, and Regulation J has been amended so that its rules are virtually identical, thus producing one area in which we have a happy coincidence of both state and federal law.

A. Scope of Article 4A

While Article 4A is largely concerned with wholesale wire transfers, it is not limited to transfers by wire alone. It includes any *payment order*, whether the instruction is to be transmitted orally, electronically, or in writing; §4A-103(a)(1). A payment order *pushes* funds of the

---

4. Sometimes called the *bilateral net credit limit*.

5. The National Automated Clearing House Association (NACHA) is an organization of such clearinghouses that regulates ACH activities through a comprehensive set of rules, now amended to incorporate Article 4A for electronic credit transfers.

person giving the order (the *sender*) out of his or her bank account and into the bank account of the payee (the *beneficiary*). Article 4A does not cover payment instructions, such as checks, that involve the efforts of the payee to *pull* funds from the payor's bank account into the bank account of the payee. A payment order requires an electronic *credit*, not an electronic *debit*.

PROBLEM 225

Big Department Store was a national operation, the largest retailer of goods in the United States. Every month it paid its employees by electronic transfer of funds (through an ACH) to their bank accounts throughout the country. Every Friday it received the weekly receipts from its thousands of retail stores by instructing Big Department Store's bank to transfer to itself all the monies the retail outlets had deposited in their *Friday Receipts* accounts. Are the payroll ACH transfers *payment orders*? Are the Friday remittances? See §4A-103(a)(1); Official Comment 4 to §4A-104.

The courts have consistently held that Article 4 of the Uniform Commercial Code does not govern electronic transfers.[6] If electronic debits are not within the scope of Article 4A, what body of law covers them? Until a comprehensive law is enacted, the matter will likely be covered by Operating Letters of the Federal Reserve Banks or private agreements such as those reflected in the rules of the National Automated Clearing House Association.

PROBLEM 226

When Sheridan Whiteside, a resident of New York, agreed to buy the Mesalia Journal, a newspaper in Mesalia, Ohio, from Bert Jefferson, its current owner, he instructed his bank, New York Metropolitan National Bank (NYMNB), to wire $1 million to Jefferson's Bank, the Mesalia County Bank (MCB). The bank did so through Fedwire, having the Federal Reserve Bank of New York (N.Y. Fed) debit this amount

---

6. Sinclair Oil Corp. v. Sylvan State Bank, 254 Kan. 836, 869 P.2d 675, 22 U.C.C. Rep. Serv. 2d 961 (1994). However, Article 4 does govern an electronic presentment if the item began as a check and then a truncation system stopped its physical movement and simply presented its relevant information by electronic means (called a *presentment notice*); see §4-110.

from NYMNB's account with it and crediting the same amount to itself. The N.Y. Fed used Fedwire to transfer the $1 million to the account it carried with the Federal Reserve Bank of Cleveland (Clev. Fed). Since the Mesalia County Bank did not have an account with Clev. Fed, Clev. Fed transferred the money to the account of the Lake Erie State Bank (LESB), which did, and LESB credited the $1 million into the account that MCB carried with it. MCB, in turn, placed the money into Bert Jefferson's account. All this happened in one day.

(a) Look at §§4A-103, 4A-104, and 4A-105, and put the appropriate labels on the parties: *originator, originator's bank, sender, intermediary bank, receiving bank, beneficiary, and beneficiary's bank.* Which of these parties gave a *payment order* as that phrase is defined in §4A-103?

(b) At what exact moment does Bert Jefferson have a legal right to the money? See §4A-404(a). Must MCB notify Jefferson that the money is in his account? See §4A-404(b). Can MCB impose a charge against Jefferson for its actions in accepting the funds transfer? See §4A-406(c) and Official Comment 5.

(c) MCB believed that Jefferson owed it $40,000 on a loan it made to him last year, so it told him that it was allowing him access to only $960,000. He protested, telling the bank that he had repaid the entire loan two weeks ago (this was true) and that he needed the $40,000 to pay off the newspaper's creditors so that the sale to Whiteside could go through. Does the bank have a right of setoff for legitimate debts that its customer owes it? See §4A-502(c)(1). If the newspaper sale collapses because Jefferson failed to pay off the creditors, what damages can he recover from MCB? See §4A-404(a).

Most funds transfers are completed on the day that the sender gives the originating payment order to his or her bank. However, in ACH transfers, as mentioned above, the usual arrangement is that the funds become available to the beneficiary on the day after the transfer is completed. You should also remember that the Expedited Funds Availability Act (see page 541) requires next business day availability for wire transfers. EFAA §603(a); Regulation CC §229.10(b).

B. Acceptance of Payment Orders

A key concept in Article 4A is *acceptance* of a payment order. If a receiving bank makes a technical acceptance of such an order, it cannot change its mind and reverse the acceptance; there is no right of *charge-back* simply because a bank fails to receive payment.[7] If the receiving bank does not want to make an acceptance, it must *reject* the payment order.

It is important to appreciate this: Article 4A itself *never* requires any bank to make an acceptance of a payment order. A bank, therefore, is always free to reject the payment order unless it has made a separate agreement otherwise. If the bank does make an agreement to accept a payment order and then wrongfully refuses to do so, the law of contracts, not Article 4A, governs its liability. See §4A-212.

If the payment order specifies a payment date,[8] no *acceptance* can occur until that date, even if the banks have made provisional settlements with each other prior to that time; §4A-209(d). A receiving bank (other than the beneficiary's bank) makes acceptance by *executing* the payment order (passing it on). The beneficiary's bank makes acceptance in one of four ways, whichever occurs first: (1) payment of the amount of the order to the beneficiary, (2) notification to the beneficiary that the amount is available for withdrawal, (3) receipt itself of full payment of the order, or (4) failure of the beneficiary's bank to reject the payment order within the time limits set forth in §4A-209(b)(3).[9] Following acceptance of the payment order, the beneficiary's bank must notify the beneficiary of the receipt of the order before midnight of the next funds-transfer business day following the payment date.

Before acceptance, any credit in the beneficiary's account is provisional only (see Official Comment 2 to §4A-502). The way that a beneficiary's bank avoids liability to the beneficiary is by delaying *acceptance* of the payment order in one of the ways specified above

---

7. However, for ACH transfers, §4A-405(d) does permit provisional payment, revocable if the beneficiary's bank does not receive full payment from the sender. In such a case the beneficiary must be warned of this possibility and agree to it. If so, any acceptance of the payment order by the beneficiary's bank can be nullified.

8. Some do, some don't. If none is specified, the payment date is the date of receipt by the beneficiary's bank; §4A-401.

9. These time limits are as follows: the opening of the next funds-transfer business day following the order's payment date if the beneficiary's bank has received payment or the sender's account is fully covered by a withdrawable credit balance, *unless* the beneficiary's bank rejects the order before that time, or within one hour of that time, or within one hour after the opening of the sender's next business day if the sender was not immediately available to receive rejection.

Funds-transfer business day is defined in §4A-105(a)(4) as "the part of a day during which the receiving bank is open for the receipt, processing, and transmittal of payment orders and cancellations and amendments of payment orders." Section 4A-106(a) permits the bank to establish a cut-off time for the funds-transfer business day, and treat payment orders and other Article 4A communications received after the cut-off time as if received on the next funds-transfer business day.

(typically saying nothing to the beneficiary until payment is received). Once acceptance occurs, the beneficiary has a right to the funds, and the debt between the originator and the beneficiary is paid. If the beneficiary's bank accepts the payment order and then, for whatever reason, fails to make payment to the beneficiary, it is liable to the beneficiary for the amount of the payment (plus interest thereon) and for any consequential damages (say, for example, the failure of the beneficiary's business) of which it was made aware, unless the beneficiary's bank proves it did not pay because of a reasonable doubt concerning the right of the beneficiary to payment; §4A-404(a).

PROBLEM 227

During the great bank collapse of 2013, wire transfer completion became a major concern. You are the chief counsel for Octopus National Bank. If it receives a payment order from a bank whose financial status is either shaky or unknown, how can it protect itself from liability to its customers in the event that the sender fails to forward the funds (or settle at the end of the business day)? See §§4A-403, 4A-405(e) (the "doomsday" rule), 4A-209 (and its Official Comment 8). For a practical guide to the law and the steps lawyers might recommend to their bank clients, see Patrikis, Baxter, & Bhala, Article 4A: The New Law of Funds Transfers and the Role of Counsel, 23 U.C.C. L.J. 219 (1991).

PROBLEM 228

Octopus National Bank (ONB) made its customers sign an agreement providing that even though the bank had informed them that they were the beneficiaries of a wire transfer, no acceptance was final unless the bank itself actually received the funds. Any withdrawal of the funds prior to the bank's receipt was merely a loan by ONB to its customers, to be repaid either by receipt of the funds or, failing that, by customer repayment. Is this agreement enforceable? See §§4A-209(b)(1) (and its Official Comment 5), 4A-405(c).

C. Transmission Errors

Mistakes will happen, of course, and there are many kinds: wrong dollar amount, duplicate orders, misidentified beneficiary, etc. Fraud might also be at work: some crook might send an unauthorized payment order to sender's bank telling it to make payment to the account of the crook at another bank. Who bears the loss in these situations?

Grain Traders, Inc. v. Citibank, N.A.

United States District Court,
Southern District of New York, 1997
960 F. Supp. 784, 33 U.C.C. Rep. Serv. 2d 220

CHIN, District Judge. Plaintiff Grain Traders, Inc. ("Grain Traders") brings this diversity action under Article 4-A of New York's Uniform Commercial Code (the "U.C.C.") and principles of common law seeking the refund of money it alleges it lost in the process of an electronic funds transfer. The funds transfer—which was to "pass" through several banks—was not completed, allegedly because defendant Citibank, N.A. ("Citibank") froze an account of one of the banks in question. Grain Traders claims that Citibank acted improperly by accepting $310,000 for a funds transfer and then failing to forward the funds in accordance with instructions, and contends that Citibank instead took the funds as a set-off against a debt owed to Citibank by one of the intermediary banks.

On the record before the court, however, no reasonable factfinder could conclude that Citibank engaged in any conduct that would form the basis for liability under the U.C.C. or the common law. Rather, Citibank did all that it was required to do: it debited one account $310,000, credited another account $310,000, and forwarded payment instructions to the bank whose account it credited. That bank was supposed to carry out the next step in the funds transfer, but it was unable to do so because of apparent financial problems that eventually caused it to cease doing business. Likewise, the final bank in the chain also was suffering from financial problems that forced it to go out of business. Both banks were chosen by Grain Traders, not Citibank, and it was those choices—rather than any wrongdoing by Citibank—that led to the apparent loss of the $310,000.

Grain Traders's principal argument is that Citibank should not have accepted the payment order. Rather, Grain Traders argues that because Citibank knew or should have known that the next bank in the chain was experiencing financial problems, Citibank should have exercised its judgment to reject the payment order. Grain Traders's arguments, however, do not make sense and they are inconsistent with the concept of funds transfers as well as the letter and spirit of Article 4-A.

Funds transfers are high-speed means of moving large sums of money at a low cost. As the Prefatory Note to Article 4-A observes:

> There are a number of characteristics of funds transfers covered by Article [4-A] that have influenced the drafting of the statute. The typical funds transfer involves a large sum of money. Multimillion dollar transactions are commonplace. The originator of the transfer and the beneficiary are typically sophisticated business or financial organizations. High speed is another predominant characteristic. Most funds transfers are completed on the same day, even in complex transactions in which there are several intermediary banks in the transmission chain. A funds transfer is a highly efficient substitute for payments made by the delivery of paper instruments. Another characteristic is extremely low cost. A transfer that involves many millions of dollars can be made for a price of a few dollars. Price does not normally vary very much or at all with the amount of the transfer. This system of pricing may not be feasible if the bank is exposed to very large liabilities in connection with the transaction. . . .

U.C.C. Art. 4-A, Prefatory Note, p.38 (McKinney Supp. 1997). Because of these characteristics—high speed and low cost—one could not expect an intermediary bank in the funds transfer to engage in due diligence to verify the creditworthiness of subsequent banks in the chain, particularly when those banks were designated by the originator itself. Indeed, in such circumstances, the risk of loss must be borne by the originator, for it was the originator's choice of an intermediary bank that led to the loss.

Grain Traders's motion for summary judgment on its claims under Article 4-A of the U.C.C. is denied and Citibank's cross-motion for summary judgment dismissing Grain Traders's claims is granted. The complaint is dismissed.

BACKGROUND

A.   THE FACTS

On December 22, 1994, Grain Traders initiated a funds transfer (the "Funds Transfer") to effectuate the payment of $310,000 to Claudio Goidanich Kraemer ("Kraemer"). (Pl. Rule 3(g) Statement ¶3). The Funds Transfer was designed to move money from Grain Traders to Kraemer in one day. The payment order issued by Grain Traders to its bank, Banco de Credito Nacional ("BCN"), stated as follows:

WE HEREBY AUTHORIZE YOU DEBIT OUR ACCOUNT NR 509364 FOR THE AMOUNT OF US$ 310,000.00 AND TRANSFER TO: BANQUE DU CREDIT ET INVESTISSEMENT LTD ACCOUNT 36013997 AT CITIBANK NEW YORK IN FAVOUR OF BANCO EXTRADER S.A. ACCOUNT NR 30114 BENEFICIARY CLAUDIO GOIDANICH KRAEMER UNDER FAX ADVISE TO BANCO EXTRADER NR 00541-312 0057/318-0124 AT. DISTEFANO/M. FLIGUEIRA.

(Pargana Aff. ¶3 & Ex. C). Thus, the funds transfer was to proceed as follows: (1) Grain Traders's account at BCN was to be debited $310,000; (2) the $310,000 was then to be "transferred" to Banque Du Credit Et Investissement Ltd.'s ("BCI") at Citibank by way of a debit to BCN's Citibank account and a corresponding credit in that amount to BCI's Citibank account; (3) the $310,000 was in turn to be "transferred" from BCI to Banco Extrader, S.A. ("Extrader") by way of an unspecified transaction between BCI and Extrader; and (4) the $310,000 was finally to be transferred to Kraemer by way of a credit to his account at Extrader.

After the payment order was issued by Grain Traders to BCN, the Funds Transfer initially proceeded as expected. BCN's account at Citibank was debited $310,000 and BCI's account at Citibank was credited $310,000. At the same time, BCN sent instructions to Citibank, directing Citibank to instruct BCI to instruct Extrader to credit $310,000 to Kraemer. (Patrickakos Aff. ¶6 & Ex. 1). Citibank in turn sent instructions to BCI on the same day, notifying BCI that Citibank had credited its account with $310,000 and instructing BCI to instruct Extrader to credit this amount to Kraemer. (Patrickakos Aff. ¶7 & Ex. 2).

Either just before or just after BCI's account at Citibank was credited with the $310,000, however, the BCI account was placed by Citibank on "hold for funds" status. (Pl. Rule 3(g) Statement ¶19). The "hold for funds" status, which was put into place because BCI's account with Citibank was overdrawn by more than $12 million, prevented BCI from making any further withdrawals from the account. (Id. ¶¶19, 22).

Kraemer apparently never received a credit to his Extrader account for the $310,000. Kraemer's affidavit, submitted by Grain Traders, states that on December 28, 1994, just six days after the attempted Funds Transfer, the government of Argentina ordered Extrader to suspend payments and that Extrader became insolvent "[s]ometime later." (Kraemer Aff. ¶5). Likewise, BCI, a Bahamian bank, ceased making payments in January 1995; it was closed by supervisory authorities in the Bahamas on July 31, 1995. (Def. Rule 3(g) Statement ¶10-12).

B. PRIOR PROCEEDINGS

Grain Traders commenced this action against Citibank in November 1995. The complaint asserts four causes of action: (1) for a refund under U.C.C. §4-A-402; (2) for a refund as well as reasonable expenses and attorneys' fees under U.C.C. §§4-A-209, 4-A-301, and 4-A-305; (3) for breach of the obligation to deal in good faith under U.C.C. §1-203; and (4) for conversion and money had an received under common law.

These motions followed . . .

DISCUSSION . . .

B. FUNDS TRANSFERS AND ARTICLE 4-A

Funds transfers, also commonly referred to as wire transfers, are a specialized "method of payment in which the person making the payment (the 'originator') directly transmits an instruction to a bank," generally through electronic means, "to make payment to the person receiving payment (the 'beneficiary') or to instruct some other bank to make payment to the beneficiary." §4-A-104, Official Comment 1. A funds transfer consists of one or more payment orders each instructing the next party in line as to the steps it must follow to carry out the funds transfer. Id. Hence, funds are "transferred" through a series of debits and credits to a series of bank accounts. Most often, funds transfers are used as an inexpensive and efficient method of discharging an "underlying payment obligation which arose through earlier commercial dealings between the originator . . . and the beneficiary." Sheerbonnet, Ltd. v. American Express Bank, Ltd., 905 F. Supp. 127, 130 (S.D.N.Y. 1995).

In the present case, Grain Traders was the originator of a funds transfer intended to pay $310,000 to Kraemer, the beneficiary. Grain Traders requested a series of payment orders that would "transfer" the funds from its bank, BCN, through two "intermediary" banks, Citibank and BCI and, finally into Kraemer's account at his bank, Extrader. Grain Traders asserts that Citibank did not carry out the Funds Transfer as directed and instead improperly used the funds it received as a set-off against debt owed to Citibank by BCI.

1. §4-A-402

In its first cause of action, Grain Traders claims that it is entitled to a refund of the $310,000 from Citibank under the "money back guarantee" of §4-A-402. Section 4-A-402 states:

(3) . . . With respect to a payment order issued to a receiving bank other than the beneficiary's bank, acceptance of the order by the receiving bank obliges the sender to pay the bank the amount of the sender's order. . . . The obligation of that sender to pay its payment order is excused if the funds transfer is not completed. . . .

(4) If the sender of a payment order pays the order and was not obliged to pay all or part of the amount paid [because the funds transfer was not completed], the bank receiving payment is obliged to refund payment to the extent the sender was not obliged to pay.

§4-A-402(3), (4).

Grain Traders argues that its obligation to pay BCN, and BCN's obligation to pay Citibank, was excused because the Funds Transfer was not completed. Grain Traders therefore asserts that it is entitled to a refund of its payment—pursuant to §4-A-402—from Citibank. Citibank, however, argues that Grain Traders has sued the wrong party. Citibank claims that §4-A-402 only allows a party to a funds transfer to obtain a refund from the next party or bank in line. Hence, Grain Traders may only seek a refund—if at all—from BCN. For at least four reasons, I agree with Citibank's interpretation of §4-A-402.

(i) *Plain Language of §4-A-402.*   First, the plain language of §4-A-402 and other provisions of Article 4-A make it clear that a party to a funds transfer is only entitled to a refund from the specific party to which it made payment. Article 4-A treats a funds transfer as a series of individual transactions, each of which involve two parties dealing directly with each other. This notion is embodied in the very definition of a "funds transfer" as set forth in §4-A-104(1):

> "Funds transfer" means the series of transactions, beginning with the originator's payment order, made for the purpose of making payment to the beneficiary of the order. The term includes *any* payment order issued by the originator's bank or an intermediary bank intended to carry out the originator's payment order.

§4-A-104(1) (*emphasis added*). Thus, Article 4-A approaches each funds transfer not as a single payment order, but rather as a series of transactions each of which involves only the parties to the individual payment order.

After establishing this structure, Article 4-A proceeds to define the rights and duties of each bank involved in a funds transfer. First, §4-A-402(3) states that the bank that sent the payment order must pay the bank that received the payment order when the payment order is accepted. §4-A-402(3). Thus, the obligation of payment runs only from the sender bank—the bank that sent the payment order—to the bank that received the payment order. Id. This subsection further provides that the sending bank's obligation to pay the receiving bank is excused if the funds transfer is not completed. Id.

Then, §4-A-402(4) provides that when a sending bank that is not required to pay—because the funds transfer has not been completed —has already paid, the sending bank is entitled to a "refund" from the receiving bank. §4-A-402(4). Thus, these sections do not create an obligation to pay or refund a payment with respect to all the parties to a fund transfer, but instead only create an obligation between the sending bank and the receiving bank pursuant to each individual payment order making up the funds transfer. This conclusion is supported by the fact that the singular form of "bank," as opposed to the plural "banks," is used when §4-A-402 provides that "the *bank* receiving payment is obliged to refund" the payment. §4-A-402 (*emphasis added*). Thus, the plain language of §4-A-402 makes it clear that a right of refund lies only with respect to parties to a specific payment order and not as to all the parties to a funds transfer.

(ii) *Official Comment to §4-A-402.*   Second, the Official Comment to §4-A-402 further underscores the intent of Article 4-A's drafters to limit the right of refund under §4-A-402 to the parties to a specific payment order. The Comment states as follows:

> The money-back guarantee [of §4-A-402(4)] is particularly important to Originator if noncompletion of the funds transfer is due to the fault of an intermediary bank rather than Bank A [the Originator's bank]. In that case Bank A must refund payment to Originator, and Bank A has the burden of obtaining refund from the intermediary bank that it paid.

§4-A-402, Official Comment 2. Thus, as the Comment explains, the originator is entitled to a refund from the bank to which it issued its payment order, and the originator's bank must then look to the intermediary bank—the bank to which it issued a payment order—to get a refund.

Accordingly, the Comment shows that Article 4-A's drafters intended the "money back guarantee" to apply only as between the parties to a payment order and not the parties to the funds transfer as a whole. Applied to the facts of this case, the originator—Grain Traders —would be entitled to a refund under §4-A-402(4) from its bank, BCN, but not from Citibank.

   (iii)   *Right of Subrogation.*   Third, the subrogation language of §4-A-402(5) demonstrates that the originator does not, as a general matter, have a right to sue all the parties to a funds transfer. Subsection (5) deals with a situation where an intermediary-receiving bank cannot give a refund to its sending bank because the intermediary bank "suspends payment." In that case, §4-A-402(5) relieves the sending bank of its obligation to refund the payment it received. Instead, §4-A-402(5) provides that:

> [t]he first sender in the funds transfer that issued an instruction requiring routing through that intermediary bank [i.e., the one that "suspends payment"] is subrogated to the right of the bank that paid the intermediary bank to [a] refund.

   Hence, the first sender to designate the defaulting bank (the bank that suspended payments) is the one that, by virtue of the subrogation, has the burden of seeking recovery.

   What subsection (5) makes clear is that under §4-A-402(4) no right to a refund otherwise exists between the originator and an intermediary bank. This is evident because there would be no need for the subrogation language of subsection (5) if the originator (as the first sender) already had a right to assert a refund claim directly against all intermediary banks.

   The Official Comments to §4-A-402 confirm that when it is the originator who chooses an intermediary bank that is unable, for financial reasons, to complete its part of the funds transfer, it is the originator, and not any other bank in the funds transfer, who bears the risk of loss. Comment 2 gives the following example:

> Suppose Originator instructs Bank A to pay to Beneficiary's account in Bank B and to use Bank C as an intermediary bank. Bank A executes Originator's order by issuing a payment order to Bank C. Bank A pays Bank C. Bank C fails to execute the order of Bank A and suspends payments. Under subsections [(3) and (4)], Originator is not obliged to pay Bank A and is entitled to a refund from Bank A of any payments that it may have made. Bank A is entitled to a refund from Bank C, but Bank C is insolvent. Subsection [(5)] deals with this case. *Bank A was required to issue its payment order to Bank C because Bank C was designated as an intermediary bank by Originator.* Section [4-A-302(1)(a)]. *In this case Originator takes the risk of insolvency of Bank C.* Under subsection [(5)], Bank A is entitled to payment from Originator and Originator is subrogated to the right of Bank A under [subsection (4)] to refund of payment from Bank C.

§4-A-402, Official Comment 2 (emphasis added).

Subsection (5) may not be precisely applicable here because it applies to a situation where an intermediary bank suspends payments and it is unclear from the record when BCI suspended payments. Nonetheless, the reasoning of subsection (5) supports the conclusion that in the present case Grain Traders must bear the risk of loss, for it was Grain Traders that chose BCI and Extradere to carry out the funds transfer. Grain Traders thus may not turn to Citibank to recovery the loss suffered as a result of Grain Traders's choice of BCI and Extrader to complete the transfer.

(iv) *Creation of Explicit Cause of Action by Originator Against Intermediary Bank.* Finally, Citibank's argument that it owes no refund to Grain Traders finds support from the working of §4-A-305. Section 4-A-305(2) provides that a "receiving bank" is liable to the "originator" for interest and expenses under certain circumstances. §4-A-305(2). Grain Traders points to this section as proof that all intermediary-receiving banks are liable directly to the originator for a refund. However, this section shows just the opposite. Section 4-A-305(2), which has no relationship to the refund provisions of §4-A-402, demonstrates that when the drafters of Article 4-A wanted to give the originator the right to bring a cause of action against any bank in the funds transfer chain, they knew how to make that clear. Thus, had the drafters of Article 4-A intended to allow the originator to seek a refund from any bank in the funds transfer chain, they could have made that clear also.

Accordingly, I hold that Grain Traders may not, as a matter of law, assert a claim against Citibank under §4-A-402 and hence summary judgment is granted in favor of Citibank on Grain Traders's first claim for relief.

2. §§4-A-209 and 4-A-301

Grain Traders's second claim for relief is premised on §§4-A-209 and 4-A-301, which govern "acceptance" and "execution" of a payment order, respectively. Grain Traders alleges that because Citibank intended to use the $310,000 as a set-off to the debt owed to Citibank by BCI, Citibank did not intend to carry out the payment order received from BCN. Grain Traders argues that because of Citibank's misplaced intent, the payment order issued by Citibank of BCI did not constitute the "execution" or "acceptance" of BCN's payment order under §4-A-209 or §4-A-301. See §4-A-301 ("A payment order is 'executed' by the receiving bank when it issues a payment order

intended to carry out the payment order received by the bank.")
(emphasis [sic] added). Grain Traders thus concludes that Citibank is
liable for its failure to properly execute BCN's payment order. I
disagree.

As a threshold matter, the record shows unequivocally that
Citibank properly executed the payment order that it received. It
debited BCN's account $310,000; it credited BCI's account $310,000;
and it forwarded instructions to BCI to instruct Extrader to credit
Kraemer with $310,000. That was all that it was required to do. As §4-A-
302 makes clear, an intermediary bank that accepts a payment order "is
obliged to issue . . . a payment order complying with the sender's order
and follow the sender's instructions concerning . . . any intermediary
bank. . . ." Here, Citibank accepted a payment order from BCN that
instructed it to instruct BCI to instruct Extrader to credit $310,000 to
Kraemer. Citibank followed these instructions, thereby meeting its
obligations, as it relayed the appropriate instructions to the next
intermediary bank, BCI.

Moreover, even if Grain Traders were able to prove that Citibank
failed to execute or accept BCN's payment order, it would nevertheless
not be entitled to prevail on its second claim for relief. This is because
neither §4-A-209 nor §4-A-301 provides a remedy for the failure to
carry out a payment order. Rather, these two sections simply define the
terms "acceptance" and "execution" as those terms are used in the rest
of Article 4-A. If a funds transfer is not completed because one of the
parties involved in the funds transfer fails to either "accept" or
"execute" a payment order, the only remedy to which the originator is
entitled is a refund—pursuant to §4-A-402—of any payment it made.
Thus, Grain Traders's second claim for relief simply leads us back to
the same place as its first claim—i.e., a claim for a refund under the
"money back guarantee" of §4-A-402. Accordingly, Grain Traders's
second claim for relief is dismissed for the same reasons as its first
claim for relief.

C.   U.C.C. §1-203

In its third claim for relief, Grain Traders asserts that Citibank's
actions violated §1-203. Section 1-203 imposes an obligation of good
faith and fair dealing on a party's performance or enforcement of any
contract or duty within the ambit of the Uniform Commercial Code.
N.Y.U.C.C. §1-203. Grain Traders alleges that it is entitled to damages
because Citibank violated this section. For two reasons, I disagree.

First, §1-203 only imposes an obligation of good faith and fair
dealing on the performance of a "contract or duty." Id. In this case,

Grain Traders has not alleged that any contract existed between Citibank and itself. Thus, Grain Traders must be relying on a statutory duty as the predicate for its third claim for relief. The only statutory duty that applied in this case, however, is Article 4-A and, for the reasons I have already discussed, Grain Traders has failed to state a claim under that Article. Thus, there is no contract or statutory duty to which Grain Traders can argue that its good faith claim under §1-203 applies.

Second, to the extent that Grain Traders is asserting that a violation of §1-203 gives rise to an independent cause of action, its assertion is without merit, for §1-203 does not give rise to an independent cause of action. See, e.g., Super Glue Corp. v. Avis Rent A Car System, Inc., 132 A.D.2d 604, 517 N.Y.S.2d 764, 766 (2d Dep't 1987) ("the Code does not permit recovery of money damages for not acting in good faith where no other basis of recovery is present"). The Official Comment to §1-203 supports this conclusion:

> This section does not support an independent cause of action for failure to perform or enforce in good faith. . . . [T]he doctrine of good faith merely directs a court towards interpreting contracts within the commercial context in which they are created, performed, and enforced, and does not create a separate duty of fairness and reasonableness which can be independently breached.

§1-203, Official Comment, at Supp. p.13. Accordingly, Grain Traders's third claim for relief is dismissed.

D.   COMMON LAW CLAIMS

Grain Traders's fourth claim for relief relies on the common law torts of "conversion" and "money had and received." Grain Traders's tort claims, however, must be dismissed because Grain Traders has failed to present evidence to support either of those claims.

To prevail on either of its common law claims, Grain Traders must prove that at the time it alleges Citibank improperly kept the $310,000, Grain Traders still had a possessory interest in the funds. Lind v. Vanguard Offset Printers, Inc., 857 F. Supp. 1060, 1066 (S.D.N.Y. 1994) (under New York law, conversion "requires a showing . . . that the plaintiff had an ownership interest or an 'immediate superior right to possession of property'"); Aaron Ferer & Sons Ltd. v. Chase Manhattan Bank, 731 F.2d 112, 125 (2d Cir. 1984) (to state a claim for money *had and received* under New York Law, the plaintiff must show that "defendant received money belonging to plaintiff") (*emphasis added*). Grain Traders, however, did not have possession of the funds at the time Citibank credited them to BCI's account. This is because a depositor loses title to money deposited in a general account at the moment those funds are deposited. Peoples Westchester Savings Bank v. FDIC, 961 F.2d 327, 330, 332 (2d Cir. 1992); Swan Brewery Co. Ltd. v. United States Trust Co., 832 F. Supp. 714, 718 (S.D.N.Y. 1993). Moreover, the cases cited by Grain Traders in support of its fourth claim for relief are inapposite. See, e.g., Raymond Concrete Pile Co. v. Federation Bank & Trust Co., 288 N.Y. 452, 43 N.E.2d 486 (1942) (dealing with a trust account rather than a general deposit account); Daly v. Atlantic Bank, 201 A.D.2d 128, 614 N.Y.S.2d 418 (1st Dep't 1994) (dealing with funds held by an agent as fiduciary for third parties); Manufacturers Hanover Trust Co. v. Chemical Bank, 160 A.D.2d 113, 559 N.Y.S.2d 704 (1st Dep't 1990) (dealing with case where bank deposited funds in wrong account and then seized funds).

Citibank did not convert any funds, nor, in fact, did it receive any funds. Rather, it debited one account $310,000 and credited another account $310,000, and it forwarded the appropriate payment instructions. That was all it was required to do. BCI should have carried out those instructions, but it was unwilling or unable to do so.

CONCLUSION

For the foregoing reasons, Grain Traders's motion for summary judgment is denied and Citibank's cross-motion for summary judgment is granted. Accordingly, the Clerk of the Court shall enter judgment in favor of Citibank dismissing the complaint with prejudice and without costs.

So ordered.

PROBLEM 229

Saul Sender agreed to buy Betty Beneficiary's business from her for the amount of $1 million, the deal to be off unless he made payment of this amount to her account (12345) at Merchants Bank on September 25. On September 24, Saul ordered his bank, Original National Bank (ONB), to wire $1 million from his account with ONB to Betty Beneficiary, Account #12345, at Merchants Bank, with a payment date of the next day. ONB executed this payment order by issuing an identical payment order to Merchants Bank, but unfortunately, it mistakenly gave the account number as 12346, though it correctly identified Betty by name. Merchants Bank notified Harry Innocent, the holder of Account #12346, that $1 million had been deposited in his account and was available for withdrawal as of September 25. Harry, delighted, withdrew the money and lit out for parts unknown. When Betty didn't receive the money, she phoned Saul on September 26 and told him that the deal was off and that she was selling the business to her brother. Saul, furious, sued his bank. Who bears what liability here?

The drafters of Article 4A discovered that the usage of trade in wire transfers was for all banks involved to look only at the account number and ignore the actual name of the beneficiary, and rather than trying to change the practice, they decided to give it statutory blessing. Thus, §4A-207 deals with misdescription of the beneficiary and provides that the beneficiary's bank may ignore the name specified in the payment order and deal only on the basis of the given account number (unless it was actually aware of the discrepancy, in which case it is responsible for seeing that the correct beneficiary gets the funds). Thus, Merchants Bank is off the hook in this situation even though it put the money in the wrong account. Original National Bank made the mistake and must go after Harry Innocent in order to recover the money.[10] ONB is liable to its customer, Saul, though he has a duty to discover and report the problem within 90 days after his bank sends him notification of the payment or be responsible for whatever loss the bank can prove it suffered because of his delay in reporting; §4A-304. Any time a bank does not properly execute the payment order, the originator must be made whole; Official Comment 2 to §4A-402 calls this the "money-back guarantee." ONB is liable for Saul's expenses, the $1 million and interest thereon, but the bank is not liable for any consequential damages (for example, the loss of the chance to buy Betty's business) unless a written agreement between Saul and ONB provides that the bank will bear this greater loss; §4A-305 (which also provides that in certain circumstances the bank may have to pay Saul's attorney's fees—see (e)).

Corfan Banco Asuncion Paraguay v. Ocean Bank

Florida District Court of Appeal, 1998
715 So. 2d 967, 35 U.C.C. Rep. Serv. 2d 1320

SORONDO, J. Corfan Banco Asuncion Paraguay, a foreign banking corporation (Corfan Bank), appeals the lower court's entry of a Final Summary Judgment in favor of Ocean Bank, a Florida bank.

---

10. Its cause of action is common law restitution; §4A-207(d).

On March 22, 1995, Corfan Bank originated a wire transfer of $72,972 via its intermediary Swiss Bank to the account of its customer, Jorge Alberto Dos Santos Silva (Silva), in Ocean Bank. The transfer order bore Silva's name as the recipient and indicated that his account number was 0100702 10400 (in fact, this was a nonexistent account). Upon receipt of the wire transfer, Ocean Bank noticed a discrepancy in this number and before depositing the money, confirmed with Silva that his correct account number was 0100762 16406.[11] Ocean Bank did not, however, inform Corfan Bank or Swiss Bank of the error. Once the correct number was confirmed by Silva, Ocean Bank accepted the wire transfer and credited Silva's account.

The next day, Corfan Bank became aware of the account number discrepancy and, without first checking with either Silva or Ocean Bank, sent a second wire transfer of $72,972 to Silva's correct account number at Ocean Bank. The second transfer order did not indicate that it was a correction, replacement or amendment of the March 22nd transfer. Because the information of the transfer was correct, it was automatically processed at Ocean Bank and was credited to Silva's account. Several days later, Corfan Bank inquired of Ocean Bank regarding the two transfers, maintaining that only one transfer was intended. By that time, Silva had withdrawn the proceeds of both wire transfers. When Ocean Bank refused to repay $72,972 to Corfan Bank, this litigation ensued. Corfan Bank proceeded on two claims, one based on the §670.207, Florida Statutes (1995), which codifies as Florida law §4A-207 of the Uniform Commercial Code (UCC), and one based on common law negligence. Ocean Bank answered denying liability under the statute and also contending that the negligence claim was precluded by the preemptive statutory scheme.

The trial court, emphasizing that Florida's adoption of the UCC sections concerning wire transfers did not abrogate the basic tenets of commercial law, found that Ocean Bank had not contravened §670.207 by crediting the erroneous March 22nd wire transfer to Silva's account. Finding that Corfan Bank was the party best situated to have avoided this loss, the court held that Corfan Bank must bear that loss and, therefore, the court granted Ocean Bank's motion for summary judgment as to count one (the UCC count). Additionally, the court dismissed count two (the negligence count).

We begin with a review of the exact language of §670.207(1), Florida Statutes:

---

11. As indicated by the italicized numbers, the three sixes in the account number had been replaced with zeros on the transfer order.

(1) Subject to subsection (2), if, in a payment order received by the beneficiary's bank, the name, bank account number, or other indentification of the beneficiary refers to a nonexistent or unidentifiable person or account, no person has rights as a beneficiary of the order and acceptance of the order cannot occur.

Corfan Bank argues that this language is clear and unambiguous, where a name *or* bank account number, *or* other identification refers either to a nonexistent or unidentified person or a nonexistent account, the order *cannot* be accepted. Ocean Bank responds that such a "highly technical" reading of the statute is "contrary to commercial and practical considerations and common sense." It suggests that we look to the legislative intent and conclude that the "or" in the statute should be given conjunctive rather than disjunctive effect. We respectfully decline Ocean Bank's invitation to look behind the plain language of the statute and conclude that given its clarity it must be read as written.

In Capers v. State, 678 So. 2d 330 (Fla. 1996), the Florida Supreme Court stated:

> [T]he plain meaning of statutory language is the first consideration of statutory construction. St. Petersburg Bank & Trust Co. v. Hamm, 414 So. 2d 1071, 1073 (Fla. 1982). Only when a statute is of doubtful meaning should matters extrinsic to the statute be considered in construing the language employed by the legislature. Florida State Racing Comm'n v. McLaughlin, 102 So. 2d 574, 576 (Fla. 1958). . . .

In the present case, although the payment order correctly identified the beneficiary, it referred to a nonexistent account number. Under the clear and unambiguous terms of the statute, acceptance of the order could not have occurred. As the Florida Supreme Court stated in [State v. Jett, 626 So. 2d 691 (Fla. 1993)]:

> We trust that if the legislature did not intend the result mandated by the statute's plain language, the legislature itself will amend the statute at the next opportunity.

Jett, 626 So. 2d at 693.

As indicated above, the trial court dismissed count two of the complaint which sounded in negligence. The court concluded that the statutory scheme preempts the common law remedy of negligence. It is not clear whether the adoption of Article 4A of the UCC abrogated the common law cause of action for negligence relating to a wire transfer, as raised in count two of the complaint. The Uniform Commercial

Code Comment following §670.102, Florida Statutes (1995), which delineates the subject matter for chapter 670, provides in part:

> In the drafting of Article 4A, a deliberate decision was made to write on a clean slate and to treat a funds transfer as a unique method of payment to be governed by unique rules that address the particular issues raised in this method of payment. A deliberate decision was also made to use precise and detailed rules to assign responsibility, define behavioral norms, allocate risks and establish limits on liability, rather than to rely on broadly stated, flexible principles. In the drafting of these rules, a critical consideration was that the various parties to funds transfers need to be able to predict risk with certainty, to insure against risk, to adjust operational and security procedures, and to price funds transfer services appropriately. This consideration is particularly important given the very large amounts of money that are involved in funds transfers.
>
> Funds transfers involve competing interests—those of the banks that provide funds transfer services and the commercial and financial organizations that use the services, as well as the public interest. These competing interests were represented in the drafting process and they were thoroughly considered. *The rules that emerged represent a careful and delicate balancing of those interests and are intended to be the exclusive means of determining the rights, duties and liabilities of the affected parties in any situation covered by particular provisions of the Article.* Consequently, resort to principles of law or equity outside of Article 4A is not appropriate to create rights, duties and liabilities inconsistent with those stated in this Article.

(Emphasis added.) See U.C.C. §4A-102 cmt. (1977); see also, 19A Fla. Stat. Ann. 15 (U.C.C. cmt. 1995) (emphasis added). This comment suggests the exclusivity of Article 4A as a remedy. Although the commentary to the UCC is not controlling authority, see Solitron Devices, Inc. v. Veeco Instruments, Inc., 492 So. 2d 1357, 1359 (Fla. 4th DCA 1986); 1 Ronald A. Anderson, Anderson on the Uniform Commercial Code, §1-102:34-:37 (1995 Revision), we are persuaded by the expressed intent of the drafters.

In addressing this issue we restrict our analysis to the pleadings and facts of this case. In pertinent part, count two reads as follows:

> Ocean Bank owed Corfan Bank a duty of care to follow the accepted banking practice of the community, and to return the funds from the first transfer to Corfan Bank upon receipt due to the reference in the first transfer to a non-existent account number.

The duty claimed to have been breached by Ocean Bank in its negligence count is exactly the same duty established and now governed by the statute. Under such circumstances we agree with the trial judge that the statutory scheme preempts the negligence claim in this case and affirm the dismissal of count two.[12] We do not reach the issue of whether the adoption of Article 4A of the UCC preempts negligence claims in all cases.

We reverse the Final Summary Judgment entered by the trial court in favor of Ocean Bank as to count one of the complaint and affirm the dismissal of count two. We remand this case for further proceedings consistent with this opinion.

LEVY, J., concurs.

NESBITT, J., dissenting. I respectfully dissent. I would affirm final summary judgment for Ocean Bank. In my view, the trial court's well-reasoned and pragmatic approach to the interpretation of §670.207, Florida Statutes (1995), was the best solution to the disagreement between these parties. Corfan Bank itself was negligent in handling the wire transfer in question. Corfan Bank incorrectly listed Silva's account number on the first wire transfer order and, compounding that error, Corfan sent the second wire transfer order with no indication that it was a correction of the first. These errors caused Corfan's loss.

More important, the language of §670.207 does not proscribe the actions taken by Ocean Bank. Section 670.207 precludes acceptance of a wire transfer order only if "the name, account number, or other identification of the beneficiary refers to a nonexistent or unidenti-fiable person or account." Considering this section in its entirety as statutory construction requires, see Fleischman v. Department of Professional Regulation, 441 So. 2d 1121, 1123 (Fla. 3d DCA 1983), it seems apparent that the part of the statute that permits the receiving

---

12. We note that allowing a negligence claim in this case would "create rights, duties and liabilities inconsistent" with those set forth in §670.207. In a negligence cause of action, Ocean Bank would be entitled to defend on a theory of comparative negligence because Corfan Bank provided the erroneous account number which created the problem at issue and then initiated the second transfer without communicating with Ocean Bank. Section 670.207 does not contemplate such a defense. (Oddly enough, allowing Corfan Bank's negligence claim in this case might actually inure to Ocean Bank's benefit.) As explained in the comment, one of the primary purposes of the section is to enable the parties to wire funds transfers to predict risk with certainty and to insure against risk. The uniformity and certainty sought by the statute for these transactions could not possibly exist if parties could opt to sue by way of pre-Code remedies where the statute has specifically defined the duties, rights, and liabilities of the parties.

bank to look to "other identification" surely allows more flexibility than the majority here would permit.

In my view, the statute question should neither be construed in the disjunctive or the conjunctive. As stated above, the construction of a statute that will reject part of it should be avoided. See Snively Groves, Inc. v. Mayo, 135 Fla. 300, 184 So. 839 (1938); or, as sometimes stated, "A court should avoid reading the statute so that it will render part of the statute meaningless." Unruh v. State, 669 So. 2d 242, 245 (Fla. 1996). There are segments of this statute that plainly permit a receiving bank to look at other identification, thus affording the receiving bank more flexibility in making the correct identification than the court recognizes today.

Ocean Bank's actions seem to better comport with the overall statutory scheme relating to funds transfers than the avenue supported by the court. The primary purpose of using a wire transfer of funds is to enable the beneficiary to get the funds quickly. Indeed, commercial or contract deadlines may be adversely impacted if the wire transfer does not go through quickly, as anticipated. We should recognize that the importance of speed in a wire transfer becomes even more critical in transactions involving different countries with, perhaps, different time zones. For example, if transmitting back Corfan was closed by the time the funds were received by Ocean Bank, Ocean Bank would not have been in a position to rectify the error until the next business day —which might well render the entire reason for the transfer moot.

Ocean Bank chose to use the beneficiary's name (which was properly included on the first wire transfer order) and "other identification of the beneficiary"—the fact that the account number given was similar to that of the beneficiary, as well as verification that the beneficiary was expecting the transfer in order to accept the wire transfer and properly credit the beneficiary's account. Ocean Bank decided that there was enough information in the first wire transfer order for it, after verification, to credit the transfer to the beneficiary's account. The order contained the beneficiary's name and account number, with a few zeros replacing the correct "6"s. This information referred not to a "nonexistent or unidentifiable person or account" but rather to an existing customer—the intended beneficiary—and to an identifiable (through "other identification") account.

I can find no common sense reason to prohibit Ocean Bank or other banks from accepting the responsibility that goes with choosing to use "other identification" in order to deposit funds into a customer's account. Basically, by verifying with Silva that he was the intended beneficiary, Ocean Bank was correcting Corfan Bank's error. Ocean

Bank was seeking to aid its customer, the intended beneficiary of the funds, in getting the funds in an expeditious manner. Had Ocean Bank erroneously deposited the funds into the wrong account, it would have to face the liability associated with that decision. However, it should not face liability because it deposited the funds into the correct account—the intended beneficiary's account. Indeed, it was only because of Ocean Bank's actions that the intended beneficiary, Mr. Silva, received the funds from the first transfer.

Moreover, as the trial court emphasized, Florida's enactment of the U.C.C. did not abrogate other common law principles applicable to commercial transactions. A longstanding equitable tenet of Florida law is that, as between two innocent parties, the party best suited to prevent the loss caused by a third party wrongdoer must bear that loss. See Exchange Bank of St. Augustine v. Florida Nat'l Bank of Jacksonville, 292 So. 2d 361, 363 (Fla. 1974) ("[I]f one of two innocent parties is to suffer a loss, it should be borne by the one whose negligence put in motion the flow of circumstances causing the loss.") See also In re International Forum of Florida Health Benefit Trust, 607 So. 2d 432, 437 (Fla. 1st DCA 1992) ("if two innocent parties are injured by a third party, either by negligence or fraud, the one who made the loss possible must bear legal responsibility"); Cheek v. McGowan Electric Supply Co., 483 So. 2d 1373, 1377 (Fla. 1st DCA 1986) ("as between . . . [two] innocent parties, the responsibility for [a third party's fraud] rests with . . . the party who was in the better position to protect himself. . . .") . . . .

Here, Corfan put in issue the question of the correlative negligence of its and Ocean's actions. It is undisputed that Corfan was initially negligent in transmittal of the first wire transfer. It realized its mistake the following business day, and sent a second wire transfer with no indication it was a correction of the former. It was entirely unnecessary to transmit additional funds merely to correct the previous day's error. If it had not sent the additional funds, it is unlikely there would ever have been a dispute bringing the matter before us. Simply, Corfan Bank was in a better position to prevent the loss and, indeed, Corfan's negligence played a "substantial role" in that loss. These facts should prevent its recovery from Ocean Bank. . . .

For the above-mentioned reasons, I would affirm.

PROBLEM 230

Same facts as the last Problem, except that Saul is the one that gave his bank the incorrect account number, though he correctly listed the beneficiary's name. What result? See §4A-207(c) (and its Official Comment 3). What practical step does this section suggest to the bank?

Bank of America N.T.S.A. v. Sanati

California Court of Appeal, 1992
14 Cal. Rptr. 2d 615, 19 U.C.C. Rep. Serv. 2d 531

JOHNSON, J. In an action for unjust enrichment, money had and received, conversion, and declaratory relief, the trial court granted plaintiff's motion for summary judgment, finding that defendants had no defense to plaintiff's request for restitution for an erroneous fund transfer. Defendants appeal from the adverse judgment, claiming the trial court erroneously applied the common law pertaining to checks and negotiable instruments instead of the law specifically pertaining to funds transfers. We affirm.

FACTS AND PROCEEDINGS BELOW

In 1963 Hassan and Fatane Sanati were married in Tehran, Iran. They lived in Iran until Mrs. Fatane Sanati moved with their two children to Los Angeles in 1983. Between 1983 and 1987 Mr. Sanati spent nearly half his time living in Los Angeles. In 1987 Mr. Sanati permanently left the United States.

When Mr. Sanati left, he arranged for payments to be made to Mrs. Sanati in Los Angeles. He instructed Bank of America in London to send interest, as it accrued monthly from an account held in his name only, to an account he held jointly at Bank of America with Mrs. Sanati in Tarzana, California.

The amount of each interest payment was between $2,000 and $3,000.

On April 30, 1990, Bank of America in London erroneously sent the principal of Mr. Sanati's bank account as well as the accrued interest to the joint Sanati account in Tarzana, California. The amount of the erroneous fund transfer was $203,750. The next day Mrs. Sanati authorized her children to withdraw $200,000 from this account. These funds were then deposited into various bank accounts under Mrs. Sanati's and her children's names.

Bank of America (bank) immediately realized its error and requested reimbursement for the erroneous payment. Mrs. Sanati and her children, Babek and Haleh Sanati (collectively Sanatis or defendants) refused the bank's requests.

In July 1990, the bank filed a complaint against the Sanatis seeking restitution for the amount of the erroneous payment. Eventually Mr. Sanati's bank account in London was re-credited the amount of the principal transferred without his authority and he was dismissed as a defendant in the action. The remaining parties stipulated the funds from the erroneous transfer would be placed in a blocked account at Bank of America pending resolution of the litigation.

The bank then moved for summary judgment. The trial court denied the bank's motion to allow the defendants to depose Mr. Sanati to determine whether he had altered his payment instructions to Bank of America London in this instance. The trial court allowed an additional 90 days' continuance for this purpose. When 90 days elapsed and Mr. Sanati had not been deposed, the bank again moved for summary judgment, claiming it was entitled to judgment as a matter of law because the Sanatis had no defense to the bank's claim for restitution.

The trial court granted the bank's motion and this appeal followed.

DISCUSSION

I. REVIEW OF THE COMMON LAW GOVERNING ERRONEOUS FUND TRANSFERS

At the time of the fund transfer in this case the law controlling the risks and liabilities of banks, beneficiaries and originators was general common law and equitable principles. Courts often borrowed concepts from Articles 3 and 4 of the Uniform Commercial Code governing commercial paper and negotiable instruments as well. This sometimes resulted in inconsistent decisions and was generally determined to be an unsatisfactory method of allocating risks and responsibilities in these widely used transactions generally involving large sums of money. Ultimately the American Law Institute developed section 4A of the Uniform Commercial Code to specifically deal with fund transfers. In 1990 the California Legislature adopted Article 4A of the Uniform Commercial Code as Division 11 of the California Uniform Commercial Code.

However, as stated, under the law in effect at the time of the fund transfer in this case, the general common law and equitable principles controlled. Under the law as it then existed, the bank was entitled to restitution from the beneficiaries for the amount of the unauthorized transfer despite its negligence under general legal principles of mistake and unjust enrichment. (Rest., Restitution, Sec. 59, com. a, p.232;

American Oil Service, Inc. v. Hope Oil Co. (1965) 233 Cal. App. 2d 822, 830; Frontier Refining Co. v. Home Bank (1969) 272 Cal. App. 2d 630, 634; Aebli v. Board of Education (1944) 62 Cal. App. 2d 706, 724-725; see also Annot., Recovery by Bank of Money Paid Out to Customer by Mistake (1981) 10 A.L.R.4th 524 Secs. 6-7 and cases collected.)

This rule, however, was subject to certain defenses. The most widely acknowledged defense to a claim for restitution for an erroneous transfer of funds was detrimental reliance by an innocent beneficiary. (Rest., Restitution Sec. 142, com. c; 1 Witkin Summary of Cal. Law (9th ed. 1987) Contracts, Sec. 94, pp.124-125; Doyle v. Matheron (1957) 148 Cal. App. 2d 521, 522.)

A less widely acknowledged defense to a claim for restitution was the "discharge for value" rule. (Rest., Restitution, Sec. 14.) This defense arises where there is a preexisting liquidated debt or lien owed to the beneficiary by the originator of the payment. If the originator or some third party erroneously gives the beneficiary funds at the originator's request, and the beneficiary in good faith believes the funds have been submitted in full or partial payment of that preexisting debt or lien and is unaware of the originator's or third party's mistake, the originator or third party will not be entitled to seek repayment from the beneficiary of the erroneously submitted funds. (1 Witkin (9th ed. 1987) Contracts, Secs, 94, 100, 102, pp.124, 129-130.) . . .

. . . Thus, under existing law the bank was entitled to seek restitution for the overpayment to defendants despite its negligence, unless defendants had detrimentally relied on the additional payment without notice of the mistake or unless the defendants had applied in good faith the additional erroneous payment to a preexisting debt or lien owed to them from Mr. Sanati.

II.   THE BANK WAS ENTITLED TO JUDGMENT EVEN IF THE
        STATUTORY PROVISIONS GOVERNING ERRONEOUS FUND
        TRANSFERS CONTROLLED

On appeal defendants vigorously argue the trial court erred in applying to a fund transfer case the general common law pertaining to commercial paper and negotiable instruments.

They argue the court should have applied Division 11 of the California Uniform Commercial Code [UCC Article 4A] which governs the consequences of an erroneous execution of a payment order. Defendants also suggest that had the court applied the new law, summary judgment would have been inappropriate because there would have been a triable issue of material fact whether defendants believed in good faith the additional erroneous payment was sent in satisfaction or discharge of a preexisting debt or lien from Mr. Sanati.

Defendants' argument fails for two reasons. First, the trial court did not err in failing to apply the new fund transfer provisions of Division 11 of the California Uniform Commercial Code [UCC Article 4A]. The Legislature expressly stated that division only applied to fund transfers in which the originator's payment order was transmitted on or after January 1, 1991. (Stats. 1990, c. 125, Sec. 3.) The payment order in the present case was transmitted in April of 1990. Thus, by its terms the new fund transfer provisions of the California Uniform Commercial Code did not apply to the transfer in this case.

Secondly, even if the new fund transfer provisions were applied to this case, we conclude defendants have failed to create a triable issue of material fact whether Mr. Sanati owed them a preexisting debt or lien even assuming their good faith.

Section 11303 of the California Uniform Commercial Code [UCC §4A-303] discusses the effect of an erroneous transfer. That section merely restates existing law governing such errors and provides in pertinent part:

> (a) A receiving bank that (i) executes the payment order of the sender by issuing a payment order in an amount greater than the amount of the sender's order, . . . is entitled to payment of the amount of the sender's order. . . . The bank is entitled to recover from the beneficiary of the erroneous order the excess payment received to the extent allowed by the law governing mistake and restitution.

The comment to the Uniform Commercial Code which was incorporated into the comments in the California Uniform Commercial Code provides examples illustrating how this section should operate. The effect of the comment explicating this section is to expressly adopt the "discharge for value" rule found in §14 of the Restatement of Restitution.

The relevant comment [2] provides:

> Subsections (a) and (b) deal with cases in which the receiving bank executes by issuing a payment order in the wrong amount. If Originator ordered Originator's Bank to pay $1,000,000 to the account of Beneficiary in Beneficiary's Bank, but Originator's Bank erroneously instructed Beneficiary's Bank to pay $2,000,000 to Beneficiary's account, subsection (a) applies. If Beneficiary's Bank accepts the order of Originator's Bank, Beneficiary's Bank is entitled to receive $2,000,000 from Originator's Bank, but Originator's Bank is entitled to receive only

$1,000,000 from Originator. Originator's Bank is entitled to recover the overpayment from Beneficiary to the extent allowed by the law governing mistake and restitution. Originator's Bank would normally have a right to recover the overpayment from Beneficiary, but in unusual cases the law of restitution might allow Beneficiary to keep all or part of the overpayment. For example, if Originator owed $2,000,000 to Beneficiary and Beneficiary received the extra $1,000,000 in good faith in discharge of the debt, Beneficiary may be allowed to keep it. In this case Originator's Bank has paid an obligation of Originator and under the law of restitution, which applies through section 1-103, Originator's Bank would be subrogated to Beneficiary's rights against Originator on the obligation paid by Originator's Bank.[13]

Thus, under this section defendants would be entitled to retain the erroneously sent funds if in good faith they believed the funds were sent to them in satisfaction of or in discharge of a valid preexisting debt or lien.

Toward this end, Fatane Sanati asserted she had a quasi community property interest in Mr. Sanati's London bank account as well as in all other property accumulated during their marriage. In an affidavit offered in opposition to the bank's motion for summary judgment Mrs. Sanati declared:

> . . . 3. I was married to Hassan Sanati, ("husband") on September 7, 1963 in Tehran, Iran where we resided until I came to Los Angeles with our two children.
>
> 4. My husband and I lived with our children, also defendants in this action, in Los Angeles since 1983. My husband was travelling in and out of the United States and until November of 1987, he had collectively spent 22 months in California during that period.
>
> 5. During our marriage we accumulated a substantial amount of money and real property, most of which was located in Iran and England.
>
> 6. My husband has always kept all of the bank accounts and most of the real property, wherever situated, in his own name.
>
> 7. Since he left in November, 1987, my children and I have been receiving interest monthly from our bank account in London, England

13. Thus, under both the common law and the new statutory provisions, the money used to effect the transfers, and the money erroneously overpaid to defendants in this case, is deemed to belong to the bank. (Cooper v. Union Bank (1973) 9 Cal. 3d 371, 377; Basch v. Bank of America NT&SA (1943) 22 Cal. 2d 316, 321.) Thus, the real issue in this case is not whether defendants could properly claim a community property interest in the bank's money but whether, and under what circumstances, the defendants could be allowed to retain the bank's money erroneously sent them as a result of the bank's lack of due care.

to our account . . . at Bank of America, Tarzana branch. The account in London was opened by my husband with funds derived from our bank accounts and real property in Iran.

8. I had asked my husband on numerous occasions to transfer the London account to me in Los Angeles. Although he had agreed to do so on several occasions he had never done it.

9. My children and I have been virtual prisoners here and completely at my husband's mercy with regard to financial matters. For the last twenty-five years, my husband has always exercised complete control over all of our marital community assets worldwide.

. . . 11. In May, 1990, the Bank of America in London transferred the monthly interest and the entire principal of the account to my and my husband's account in Bank of America in Tarzana.

12. I used some of these funds for the family and I removed the remainder to accounts under my control.

. . . 17. Since the London account was transferred to our joint account in California, I have spoken to my husband via telephone. On several occasions, he agreed to keep the transferred money in our joint account under both our names. However, to this date, he has not done so.

. . . 19. I have filed a petition for Dissolution of Marriage at the Los Angeles Superior Court on July 2, 1990. . . . The Summons and Complaint were personally served upon my husband, in Tehran, Iran, by Rosy Shahbodaghi, on September 24, 1990. I have instructed my counsel to enter his default therein. . . .

Thus, Mrs. Sanati's declaration raises a reasonable inference of a potential quasi community property interest in the funds in the London bank account held in Mr. Sanati's name alone. However, this evidence does not raise a reasonable inference of a preexisting debt or lien at the time of the transfer of the type recognized in those decisions applying the "discharge for value" rule.

For example, in Banque Worms v. Bank America International (S.D.N.Y. 1989) 726 F. Supp. 940, aff'd, (2d Cir. 1991) 928 F.2d 538, the case upon which defendants primarily rely, the debt was a bank loan. In that case the originator had an outstanding loan for $2,000,000 from Banque Worms. On the day before the erroneous transfer, Banque Worms notified the originator it was calling the loan. The next day Banque Worms received a wire transfer for $2,000,000 from Security Pacific International Bank (SPIB), the originator's bank, and applied it to the originator's outstanding loan balance.

Shortly thereafter Banque Worms received a second wire transfer from the originator's bank for $1,974,267.97 which was the amount the originator actually requested to be sent. Because it only had instructions for the latter payment, SPIB could not debit the originator's bank account for the first erroneous payment. Because Banque Worms received the payment in the good faith belief it was in response to their demand for repayment of the loan, the court held SPIB had to suffer the loss for the mistaken payment under the "discharge for value" rule.

Examples in the Restatement of Restitution describing the "discharge for value" rule describe debts that are liquidated, concrete and preexisting, not merely probable and undetermined. (E.g., Rest., Restitution, Sec. 14, com. b, illus. facts 1 [no restitution for proceeds erroneously used to pay existing mortgage on real estate]; illus. 2 [no restitution from city for property taxes paid on property not actually owned]; illus. 3 [no restitution where bank erroneously cashes customer's check given to payee in payment for services rendered]; illus. 4 [no restitution from judgment creditor for execution of judgment of wrong person's property].) No decision we are aware of has applied the discharge for value rule where the debt or lien in question was anything less than an objectively verifiable, preexisting, liquidated obligation. (See Rest., Restitution (append.), Sec. 14 and cases collected.) Indeed, allowing the rule to apply to debts or obligations any less substantial would risk destroying the certainty of the rule and allow the exception to control its application.

Consequently, it does not appear the "discharge for value" rule can be properly invoked in a case such as this where the alleged preexisting debt or lien is at best a probable yet undetermined interest in a portion of the funds in Mr. Sanati's bank account in London.[14]

The defendants do not contend they changed their position to their detriment in reliance on the erroneously transmitted funds. Nor do the defendants' opposition papers raise any other potential defense to the bank's action for restitution. Thus, in the absence of any viable defense, the bank was entitled to restitution from the beneficiaries for the erroneously transmitted funds. We therefore conclude the trial court did not err in finding the bank was entitled to judgment as a matter of law.

DISPOSITION

The judgment is affirmed. Each side to bear its costs of appeal.

14. This case would raise entirely different issues if, for example, there was a preexisting judgment dividing the parties' marital assets decreeing a sum certain of $200,000 or more in cash to be transferred to Mrs. Sanati as part of the settlement and that this amount was due and owing to her at the time of the erroneous wire transfer. But those are not the facts of this case. In fact, Mrs. Sanati did not file for dissolution of marriage until several months after the erroneous fund transfer.

PROBLEM 231

Business Corporation paid all of its bills by funds transfers through its bank, Original National Bank (ONB). These two entities signed an agreement providing that funds transfers could be made only if the originator included in the payment order a secret code number, which would change daily according to the number assigned by a computer program accessed by both the corporation and the bank. The Business Corporation employee in charge of approving its payment orders was John Smith, and he was so proud of his new job that he described it in detail (including how to access the secret code) to his wife, Mary. Mary, who was the owner of her own computer repair business, became curious whether, from the safety of her own home, her skills as a computer hacker would permit her to access Business Corporation's files, issue phony payment orders, and have ONB execute them. She was amazed how easy it all was, and by the end of the day she had ordered ONB to transfer $830,756 to the account of her business at another bank. The next morning she withdrew the money from that account, left her husband a "Dear John" letter, and has not been heard from since. Can Business Corporation demand that ONB recredit its account for the amount she stole? See §§4A-201, 4A-202(b), 4A-203.

PROBLEM 232

Suppose, in the last Problem, the security procedure between the parties had one other wrinkle: if the amount transferred was above $500,000, the secret code had to begin with the letter "A," but the secret code itself did not tell senders this. Mary didn't know about it either (John had forgotten to mention this extra step), so when she transferred the $830,756 to her bank account, she failed to put the "A" in front of the secret code. ONB accepted the payment order anyway when it made the funds transfer to Mary's bank. Now what? See §4A-205(a)(1).

As a general rule, Article 4A tends to place liability for erroneous payment orders on the entity that made the mistake; §4A-303.

D. Conclusion

Section 4A-501(a) contains an important rule for banks: "Except as otherwise provided in this Article, the rights and obligations of a party to a funds transfer may be varied by agreement of the affected party." If you, as counsel for the bank, don't like the results explained above, negotiate a contract with those involved that reaches a happier conclusion. Be warned, however, that in various places throughout Article 4A, the sections do restrict the right of the parties to change the Code's rules by agreement. For example, §4A-404(c) provides: "The right of a beneficiary to receive payment and damages as stated in subsection (a) may not be varied by agreement or a funds-transfer system rule." Thus, the contract negotiated by the bank must be checked against Article 4A carefully to ensure that it does not attempt impermissible variations.[15]

Banks do not charge much for the execution and acceptance of payment orders, and the system would collapse if the banks faced enormous exposure for wire transfer mishaps. Article 4A recognizes this and is animated by a spirit of bank protection. See, e.g., Official Comment 2 to §4A-305. In the event of bank insolvency, banks that have accepted payment orders but not received payment must bear the loss unless a funds-transfer system (such as CHIPS) has adopted a plan for loss-sharing and the plan fails, in which case §4A-405(e) (the "doomsday" rule) provides that the payment is undone even though acceptance had occurred. Many funds-transfer systems have loss-sharing plans (typically providing for the creation of a "settlement kitty"), and they should help ease the problem of bank exposure.

---

15. There is a strong presumption in favor of the effectiveness of a rule adopted by a funds-transfer system; §4A-501(b). Such systems are particularly encouraged to adopt rules making payments provisional, and plans for the sharing of losses in the event of bank insolvency; see §4A-405(d) and (e).

Chapter 14

INVESTMENT SECURITIES

Article 8 on investment securities is something of a stepchild to the rest of the Uniform Commercial Code. White and Summers do not even cover it in their hornbook, and it is embarrassing how often the issues it addresses are litigated without Article 8 even once being cited. To avoid malpractice in this field, you should know something about its scope and general area of regulation.

The original version of Article 8 was created at a time when all investment securities were evidenced by the issuance of pieces of paper labeled as stocks or bonds (now called *certificated securities*). As corporate and government issuers moved from paper to registration of the investors' interest at the issuer's headquarters or some other central location, Article 8 was rewritten in 1978 to deal with these so-called *uncertificated securities*. But developments in the world of stocks and bonds made the 1978 version obsolete rather quickly because investors began holding their investments merely as bookkeeping entries on the records of their brokers, and often the brokers themselves did not hold the paper certificates either but instead had similar accounts at clearing corporations. The 1978 Article 8 did not deal with these investment rights, leaving the law in limbo. In 1994 a new version of Article 8 made its appearance and is in the process of being rapidly adopted by the various jurisdictions.[1] The 8-100s to the 8-400s deal with certificated and uncertificated securities, doing little to change the prior law, but a new part, the 8-500s, now regulates the rights that investors have in security accounts (calling these rights *security entitlements*). A wonderfully detailed "Prefatory Note" (included in most statute books reprinting Article 8) explains the evolution of the law in this area and examines the business background for investment securities and securities holding systems. The chapter that follows deals with the 1994 version of Article 8.

I. TERMINOLOGY

Article 8 of the Code (Investment Securities) deals with the rights and liabilities created by the issuance and transfer of stocks and bonds. These items, called *securities* in the Code, are defined in §8-102(a)(15). Under §8-103(d) all securities are governed by Article 8, not by Article 3, even if the security is technically negotiable under §3-104(a).

Essential to your comprehension of Article 8 is an understanding of the meaning of some of the technical terms, such as *registered owner*. What follows is a brief sketch of the basic business transaction that results in the creation of Article 8 paper.

Corporate securities can be divided into two main classes: *debt* securities (generally bonds or debentures and the interest coupons attached thereto), which represent the obligation of the corporation to pay the holder a specified sum, and *equity* securities (such as preferred or common shares of stock), which represent an ownership interest in the corporate enterprise. A corporation, hereinafter called the *issuer*, will make use of both types of securities to provide financing for its activities.

1. Even better, the Department of the Treasury has adopted the Revised Article 8 as a matter of federal law; see 31 C.F.R. §8-357.

If the issuer is offering the securities to the public (making a *public offering*), it frequently must register them with the Securities and Exchange Commission pursuant to the Securities Act of 1933, 15 U.S.C. §§77a et seq. When printed, the securities are either signed manually, which is quite a task in the issue of, say, 100,000 shares of stock, or by facsimile (printed) signature. Debt securities are almost always placed under the control of an independent trustee, frequently a bank, called the *authenticating trustee,* who signs the securities manually, thereby expressly certifying that the item signed is one of the securities intended as part of the offering.

Debt securities may be made payable to the *bearer* or to a named person, the *registered owner* (so called because the owner's name is registered on the corporation's books as the record owner). Equity securities in this country are always issued in registered form; the registered owner then has voting rights, rights to dividends, etc. If the security is in registered form, the issuer need recognize these rights only in the registered owner. Section 8-207(a) provides:

> Before due presentment for registration of transfer of a certificated security in registered form or of an instruction requesting registration of transfer of an uncertificated security, the issuer or indenture trustee may treat the registered owner as the person exclusively entitled to vote, receive notifications, and otherwise exercise all the rights and powers of an owner.

If the registered owner sells the security, the purchaser will want to have the corporate records changed to show the purchaser as the new registered owner. To do this, the registered owner (transferor) *indorses* the instrument, by writing either on it or on a separate sheet of paper, over to the new owner, and the instrument is presented to the *transfer agent,* who may be either an employee of the corporation or a separate entity. The registered owner may simply indorse the instrument in blank, naming no transferee. This is frequently done when the registered owner is selling the security through a broker and the name of the eventual purchaser is unknown.

Prior to seeking a new registration, a blank instrument is filled in with the name of the purchaser and then submitted to the transfer agent. Of course, instruments indorsed in blank give rise to a situation that can easily become exciting when the security falls into the hands of an individual whose respect for other people's property is minimal. For this reason it has become common for registered owners who wish to sell their securities on the market to indorse them over to their brokers, who then register the security in the brokers' names.

Securities registered to a broker are said to be *street name* securities (so called because of the broker's connection with New York's Wall Street). When the selling broker finds a purchaser, the broker submits the security to the transfer agent so that the records can be changed to switch the registered ownership from the broker (the street name) to the purchaser. As mentioned above, in today's world the actual certificate may be held only by a clearing corporation, and rights therein are passed down to lower tiers of owners by bookkeeping entries. In these indirect holding situations, the beneficial owner of the security is said to have a *security entitlement* in a *securities account* held with a *security intermediary*, who one instructs by giving an *entitlement order* (read §8-102(a)), in which all these terms are defined in more detail (*securities account* is defined in §8-501(a)).

To facilitate a change in the registered ownership, a typical security has printed on the back a transfer form more or less similar to the following language that I copied off a debenture:

> For value received, _____ hereby sell, assign and transfer unto _____ the within registered debenture and do hereby irrevocably constitute and appoint _____ my attorney to transfer the said registered debenture on the books of the within named company with full power of substitution in the premises.
>
> Dated: _____
> Signed: _____
> In the presence of: _____

The filling in of the third blank in the above form gives a power of attorney to the person named (frequently a broker). If no transferee is named, the transfer agent will register the security to whomever the attorney nominates; this procedure is sometimes used in lieu of the additional steps involved in registering the security in the street name. If no attorney is named and only the transferee blank (the second one above) is filled in, then the transfer agent will register the security in the name of the transferee. "Where both the name of a transferee and that of an attorney are filled in, the same person should be designated in both blanks. Otherwise, even registration in the name of the specified transferee will require instructions from, if not further indorsement by, the specified attorney." E. Guttman, Modern Securities Transfers 7-11 (3d ed. 1987). You will note that the power of attorney gives the attorney full power to substitute a new transferee. Cf. §8-308.

Another entity sometimes involved in Article 8 problems is the *registrar*. A registrar—normally, though not always, a separate entity from the issuer—has the duty to inspect proposed transfers to determine whether they will result in the issuer's having outstanding more stock than it is authorized to have, a situation called *overissue*. In effect, the registrar is an auditor of the corporate capacity of the transfer. The registrar may also be the transfer agent, the entity keeping the records and performing the physical process involved in the transfer. See Hollywood Natl. Bank v. International Bus. Machs. Corp., 38 Cal. App. 3d 607, 113 Cal. Rptr. 494, 14 U.C.C. Rep. Serv. 782 (1974); E. Guttman, Modern Securities Transfers, ch. 9 (3d ed. 1987).

The practice of issuing shares of stock that are registered with the issuing company but that are not represented by a physical piece of paper results in what are called *uncertificated securities*. With uncertificated securities the owner's interest is registered in the issuer's computer, and only an initial *transaction statement* is sent to the purchaser to evidence that purchaser's right to the security. Thereafter, transfers of the uncertificated security are accomplished by the current owner's issuing an *instruction* to the issuer, telling it to whom the security now belongs. Read §§8-102(a)(12) and 8-305.

II. OVERISSUE

Read §8-210 carefully.

PROBLEM 233

Colossus Corporation was authorized to issue 100,000 shares of stock at a par value of $1; it had 150,000 printed up, and the extra 50,000 were saved for the purpose of replacing the old pieces of paper as they became worn. The company sold 100,000 shares. The extra 50,000 shares were stolen by a clever thief, who negotiated them to a bona fide purchaser (BFP). Can the BFP require the corporation to recognize the 50,000 shares as valid? What remedy does §8-210 give to the BFP?

III.   THE ISSUER AND THE HOLDER

Read §§8-201 through 8-206, 8-208, and 8-407, which explain the duties of the issuer and its agents.

As for §8-204, the most common restriction on transfer is the following, which is frequently printed on securities:

> The shares represented by this certificate have been exchanged exclusively with the Corporation's shareholders and have not been registered under the Securities Act of 1933. These shares may not be pledged or hypothecated and may not be sold or transferred in the absence of an effective Registration Statement under the Securities Act of 1933 or an opinion of counsel to the Corporation that registration is not required under the said Act.

Another common restriction is that the corporation itself is to be given the right of first refusal when sale of the stock is contemplated.

Sections 8-205, 8-208, and 8-406 deal with the responsibilities of the issuer and its agents. Look at these sections in light of the following quote. Guttman's Modern Securities Transfers, supra, states, at pages 10-11:

> Where the issuer relies on the manual signatures of its officers, "John Beta," who is an employee of the issuer might sign the name of "Richard Gamma, President," who is in fact the only officer authorized to sign. The security . . . is clearly not "genuine" under the Code definition and the issuer need not recognize it.

Do you agree? Consider the following case.

First American National Bank v. Christian Foundation Life Insurance Co.

Arkansas Supreme Court, 1967
242 Ark. 678, 420 S.W.2d 912, 4 U.C.C. Rep. Serv. 287

SMITH, J. This is a suit brought by one of the appellees, Christian Foundation Life Insurance Company, for a declaratory judgment with respect to the validity of certain duplicate bearer bonds ostensibly issued by the First Methodist Church of Mena. That duplicate bonds were outstanding was due to the fraud of the late Lawrence Hayes, former president of Institutional Finance Company, which handled the bond issue as fiscal agent for the church. Parties to the suit include the rival owners of the duplicate bonds, the church and its trustees, the Union Bank of Mena, which acted as paying agent for the bonds, the estate of Hayes, the receiver for Institutional Finance, and the corporate surety upon Institutional Finance's qualifying bond as a securities dealer. . . .

We need state the facts only in broad outline. On January 19, 1964, the church adopted a resolution authorizing a $90,000 bond issue for the construction of a new church and employing Institutional Finance as its fiscal agent to market the bonds. On the same day the church treasurer, Bettie Jean Montgomery, in the presence of the pastor and a trustee of the church, affixed her signature to a blank sheet of paper and delivered it to Joe B. Springfield, executive vice-president of Institutional Finance, for use as a facsimile signature upon the bonds.

Two days later Springfield requested a printing company to print the bonds, which were numbered from 1 to 188 and totaled $94,000. (The record does not explain why an extra $4,000 of bonds was printed.) On January 30 the printer delivered the bonds to Springfield. They bore the facsimile signatures of Springfield and Mrs. Montgomery, with no provision for an authenticating manual signature.

Institutional Finance sold $45,000 of the bonds to members of the church but had trouble in finding buyers for all the rest of the issue. On July 3, 1964, Hayes personally borrowed $25,000 from First American National Bank and pledged as collateral, along with other securities, $27,000 (later increased to $28,800) of the Mena church bonds. There is no sound basis for questioning the bank's standing as a good faith purchaser for value, as those terms are defined in the Uniform Commercial Code. Ark. Stat. Ann. §85-1-201 (Add. 1961). Hayes had borrowed money from the bank on a number of occasions. The bank's president, who handled this loan, understood Hayes to be an employee of a Texas dealer in church bonds and was unaware of his connection with Institutional Finance. Nothing in the transaction warned the bank that Hayes did not own the bonds.

On February 1, 1965, Hayes fraudulently ordered the printer to print $25,000 of numbered bonds that included duplicates of some of those pledged to the bank. Later in the month, Hayes, in order to complete a sale to Christian Foundation Life, had printed additional bonds in certain larger denominations requested by that insurance company. The duplicate bonds now held by Richards and Christian Foundation Life are among those obtained by Hayes in the two supplemental printings.

We find no merit in the appellant's insistence that its adversaries were not purchasers in good faith because they bought the bonds at discounts of 10 and 15 percent. We have held that the price paid for a negotiable instrument may be so grossly inadequate as to support a finding of bad faith, Hogg v. Thurman, 90 Ark. 93, 117 S.W. 1070, 17 Ann. Cas. 383 (1909), but there is no proof in this record to indicate that the discounts offered to the appellees were so great as to arouse suspicion. Nor is there evidence to sustain the appellant's argument that the purchasers of the duplicates should have been put upon inquiry by the church's apparent inability to market the entire bond issue within a period of about a year.

Hayes' dishonesty finally became known when duplicate interest coupons were presented to the Mena bank for payment. The paying agent refused to honor the coupons until their validity had been established. Hence this suit.

We think the chancellor should have found all bonds held by bona fide purchasers to be binding obligations of the church. It is plain enough that the church was careless in entrusting its treasurer's facsimile signature to Institutional Finance and in failing to take the precaution of requiring authentication of the bonds by a manual signature. By contrast, the holders of the bonds acquired them in the ordinary course of business and in circumstances entitling them to the protection afforded to bona fide purchasers.

The case is controlled by the pertinent provisions of the Uniform Commercial Code. Before the adoption of the Code the church might have been held liable by contract to one purchaser and in damages to the other, but the draftsmen of the Code point out in their Comment to our §8-205 that the Code simply validates most defective securities in the hands of innocent purchasers, refusing to prefer one such purchaser over another.

Specifically, this controversy falls within §8-205, which provides that an unauthorized signature is effective in favor of an innocent purchaser when the signing is done either by a person entrusted by the issuer with the signing of the security or by an employee of such a person or of the issuer itself. By resolution the church employed Institutional Finance as its fiscal agent to handle the sale of the bonds. The first line of the printed prospectus for the bond issue identified that concern as the issuer's fiscal agent. There can hardly be any serious contention that Hayes's wrongful use of the treasurer's facsimile signature did not fall within the purview of the Code. . . .

Reversed and remanded.

JONES, J. (dissenting). I do not agree with the conclusion reached by the majority in this case, nor do I agree with the decision of the chancellor.

Our Uniform Commercial Code §8-202(3) [now §8-202(c) —Ed.] is as follows:

> Except as otherwise provided in the case of certain unauthorized signatures on issue (Section 8-205), lack of genuineness of a security is a complete defense even against a purchaser for value and without notice.

Just what constitutes the genuineness of a security is not set out in chapter 8 of the Code on investment securities, but §1-201 contains 46 numbered general definitions, one of which is as follows: "(18) 'Genuine' means free of forgery or counterfeiting." . . .

It is my view that the duplicate bonds printed without authority and certainly with the apparent intent to defraud, were forged counterfeits of the original bonds and lacked the genuineness of the original authorized bonds, and that their lack of genuineness was a complete defense even against Christian Foundation and Reverend C.R. Richards. . . .

Under the majority holding in this case, once authority is given to an unscrupulous agent to print and sell a limited number of bonds over a facsimile signature, the principal or issuer has no further protection from being bound by such individual. A revocation of authority, or even confinement in the penitentiary, would offer no protection. Such agent or ex-agent, would be able to bind his former principal, or the issuer of bonds, for as long as such agent could find innocent purchasers and access to a printing press.

I would reverse the chancellor in this case and hold that the original bonds held by First American are genuine and legal bonds, but that the duplicates sold to Christian Foundation and Reverend Richards are forged counterfeits of the originals and are not genuine but are void as binding obligations of First Methodist.

PROBLEM 234

Titanic Telephone Company (TTC), Inc. called up the Pronto Printing Corporation (PPC) and asked Felix Pronto (founder and president) if PPC would run off 100 more of the $100 TTC bearer bonds PPC had printed in the past. PPC had previously printed 1,000 of these bonds and still had the plates. The bonds had the facsimile signatures of the TTC president, secretary, and authenticating trustee already printed on them. Felix agreed and called up Happy Clatter, the chief printer, and told him to run off 100 more of the bonds and send them by messenger to TTC. Happy ran off 200 of the bonds. He sent 100 by messenger to the offices of TTC, and he sent the other 100 as a Christmas present to his mother in Twin Falls, Idaho. Eventually the latter bonds turned up as the property of Bing, Bong & Bell Brokerage, a purchaser for value without notice of anything unusual, which presented the bonds to TTC for payment of the interest due that year. Titanic Telephone comes to you for advice. It doesn't know whether it should treat the bonds as valid or not and is afraid that if it pays the interest, TTC's stockholders will bring suit against TTC's officers for misusing corporate funds. Give TTC your opinion as to whether the law requires TTC to honor the bonds, noting carefully §§8-202(c) and 8-205.

IV. TRANSFERS BETWEEN PURCHASERS

The proper transfer of a registered security is a three-step process: indorsement by the owner, delivery to the purchaser, and registration with the corporation in the name of the new owner. The effective transfer of a bearer security requires *only* delivery. Read §§8-304, 8-108(f), and 8-307.

The Article 8 equivalent of Article 3's holder in due course is called a *protected purchaser* (see §8-303), and he or she takes free of adverse claims in both direct and indirect holding systems. Section 8-303(a)(3) requires that the protected purchaser obtain *control* over the security, and while *control* is defined extensively in §8-106, the requirements are nicely summarized in Official Comment 3 to §8-303, which you should now read. It should be noted that *purchase* is defined so broadly in §1-201(32) that, incredibly enough, it includes taking by *gift*. See Rogers v. Rogers, 271 Md. 603, 319 A.2d 119, 14 U.C.C. Rep. Serv. 1211 (1974). *Notice* is defined in §8-105. Read it.

Note that Article 8 has a shelter rule very similar in effect to §3-203(b) in Article 3. See §8-302. Thus, even a person with notice of an adverse claim can get the rights of a protected purchaser by taking from one.

Warranties. On transfer to a purchaser for value, the seller makes the warranties listed in §8-108. A *broker* (defined in §8-102(a)(3)) makes the warranties in §8-108(i). As in Articles 3 and 4, warranty theories are frequently used to pass liability from one person to another.

PROBLEM 235

Lynn Brown was the registered owner of 20 shares of Regional Telephone Company when the stock was stolen from her by a clever thief who forged her indorsement on the shares and sold them to Bing, Bong & Bell (B.B. & B.), stockbrokers, who purchased the shares for the brokerage firm. B.B. & B. then had the stock reregistered by Regional Telephone to its own (street) name and thereafter sold the shares to Barbara Shipek, a wealthy client who was trying to buy up all the shares of Regional Telephone that she could. When Lynn found that the shares were missing, she contacted Barbara and demanded the return of her stock. Must Barbara surrender the shares? Would B.B. & B. have had to surrender the shares if Lynn had made a demand to do so before B.B. & B. had the shares reregistered? After? See §§8-106(b), 8-108(f) (and its Official Comment 3), 8-303 (and particularly its own Official Comment 3). Who is obviously liable to Lynn here? See §8-404.

V. REGISTRATION

When a transfer of a registered security occurs between purchasers, the transfer is *complete* upon delivery to the purchaser (§8-304(c)). But the new owner will want to have the security registered on the company's books in his or her name.[2] The impetus to registration is that until the corporate records are changed, the issuer can send dividend checks, etc., to the record owner (§8-207(a)). The seller must supply the documentation needed to register, §8-307, but does not in any way warrant that the issuer will honor the security, §§8-304(f) and 8-305(b).

On presenting the security for registration, the presenter makes the warranties stated in §8-108(f). The issuer is under a legal *duty* to register the transfer if the requirements of §8-401, which you should

---

2. The company, once it decides to change the registration, cancels the old certificate and issues a new one to the new registered owner.

now read, are met. If any of these requirements has not been satisfied, the issuer can refuse the registration.

PROBLEM 236

Professor Chalk was the registered owner of 50 shares of the Beaten Path Mousetrap Corporation, and he wanted to sell. The shares bore a restrictive legend like the one on page 690, stating that no SEC registration had occurred and that no transfer could take place unless a registration was filed with the Securities Exchange Commission (SEC) or the owner could supply the written opinion of counsel that such a registration was unnecessary. Professor Chalk wrote the SEC and received a *No Action* letter, which is a non-binding recommendation by an SEC staff counsel that states that the counsel will not recommend that any action be taken by the Commission in connection with the transfer. He then submitted this letter to Beaten Path Mousetrap's transfer agent along with the stock and requested registration to his buyer. The transfer agent refused, claiming non-compliance with the restriction. While the dispute was going on, Beaten Path Mousetrap Corporation went bankrupt. Professor Chalk sued. Who should win? See §§8-401, 8-407; Kenler v. Canal Natl. Bank, 489 F.2d 482, 13 U.C.C. Rep. Serv. 905 (1st Cir. 1973).

The Guarantee of Signature. The transfer blanks on securities frequently contain a place for the signature of a *guarantor.* Consider the following quotations from Guttman, Modern Securities Transfers, supra, at 2-4, 2-5:

> The legal responsibility of the transfer office was construed for over a century in extremely stringent terms. That office was and remains today fully responsible for the genuineness of the signature of the "member" purporting to transfer his interest. This responsibility is absolute. Good faith, even the highest degree of diligence and care, does not relieve the issuer from liability where the signature was not in fact genuine or authorized. . . .
>   . . . To mitigate the issuer's absolute liability in respect of genuineness of a necessary signature, commercial practice developed a working solution, the guarantee of signature. That guarantee remains today the cornerstone of the structure and the essential lubricant of the transfer process.

Read §8-306, ignoring subsections (c) and (d). Do you understand why Professor Israels (one of the drafters of Article 8) once stated that if lawyers discover that their broker clients have rubber stamps reading "Indorsement guaranteed," they should see that the stamps are jettisoned immediately? Israels, How to Handle Transfers, 19 Bus. Law. 90, 98 (1963). Note that an issuer may not *require* a guarantee of an *indorsement*; a guarantee of *signature* is required as a matter of course. Read §8-402 carefully.

Jennie Clarkson Home for Children v. Missouri, Kansas & Texas Railway

Court of Appeals of New York, 1905
182 N.Y. 47, 74 N.E. 571

HAIGHT, J. This action was brought to recover four registered bonds, of the par value of $1,000 each, payable in gold, in the year 1990, with 4 percent interest coupons attached, numbered respectively 8,872, 8,873, 8,874, and 8,875, issued by the defendant Missouri, Kansas and Texas Railway Company, and secured by first mortgage on the property of the company, or bonds of like amount and value, or, in default thereof, to recover the value of such bonds. The trial resulted in a judgment for the plaintiff substantially for the relief demanded in the complaint, which has been affirmed in the Appellate Division. The facts are without substantial dispute. The plaintiff, the Jennie Clarkson Home for Children, is a domestic corporation organized under the laws of this state for charitable purposes. It was the owner of the bonds in question, which by their terms were not transferable after registration, unless made on the books of the railway company by the registered holder, or by his attorney duly authorized, and noted on the bonds. They were kept in a safe deposit vault in one of the banks in the city, the president and the treasurer of the plaintiff each having a key thereto. On or about the 11th day of March, 1902, George W. Lessels, treasurer of the plaintiff, without the knowledge or consent of any of the officers or directors of the plaintiff corporation, took the bonds in question from the safe deposit vault where they were stored, for the purpose of converting them to his own use, and thereupon he took them to the office of Robert Gibson, who was a member of the stock exchange, doing business as stockbroker under the name of the limited partnership of H. Knickerbacker & Co., and asked that they be sold. The cashier of the defendant Gibson, seeing that the bonds were registered in the name of the plaintiff corporation, informed Lessels that, before the bonds could be sold, the registration must be so altered that they would be payable to bearer. Lessels asked how that could be done and he was then instructed to take them to the transfer office of the defendant railway company, and that there he could find out what was to be done in order to effect the change. Upon application to the railway company he was advised, in substance, that it would be necessary to have a resolution of the board of directors of the plaintiff corporation passed, authorizing a transfer of the bonds, and the furnishing of the company with a copy authenticated by the certificate of the secretary, under the seal of the corporation, to the effect that the copy presented was a true and correct copy of the resolution of the board and that a power of attorney would have to be executed by the corporation, authorizing the transfer of the bonds to bearer, the signature of which must be witnessed by some stock exchange house. Thereupon Lessels returned to the office of H. Knickerbacker and Co., and had the power of attorney drawn, and signed it in the name of the plaintiff, the Jennie Clarkson Home for Children, George W. Lessels, treasurer, and underneath is the statement that it was signed and acknowledged in the presence of John F. Busch, who was the cashier for H. Knickerbacker & Co., and by H. Knickerbacker & Co., which was signed by Gibson. At the same time Lessels presented to H. Knickerbacker & Co. a paper purporting to be a copy of the resolution of the board of directors, authorizing a sale of the bonds, with the certificate of the secretary, under seal, attached. But the resolution was never passed by the board of directors, the certificate of the secretary was never signed by him, and the seal affixed thereto was not the seal of the corporation. All of these papers had been forged. Upon their presentation to defendant Gibson, he caused them to be transmitted to the office of the railway company and there the bonds were changed and made payable to bearer; and then they were returned to the defendant Gibson, who sold them and paid the proceeds over to Lessels, who converted the money to his own use and subsequently absconded.

[The court then quoted Story on Agency to the effect that a principal is not bound by the actions of an agent done beyond the scope of his employment, and concluded that the treasurer was not acting within the scope of his employment while carrying out his defalcation.]

The plaintiff was the owner of the bonds in question. They had been registered by the defendant railway company. That company undertook to keep a registry of such bonds, and not to transfer them, except upon the books of the company by the direction of the owner or by his duly authorized attorney. It is deemed to have undertaken to pay the interest accruing upon these bonds, and the principal, when due, to such registered owner. The purpose of such registration was to save the owner from loss resulting from larceny or destruction of the bonds. Being registered, they could not be sold. If presented to the railway company for payment of the interest or principal by other than the registered owner, payment would be refused. They were only property in the hands of the registered owner. The bonds having been stolen from the plaintiff, it had the right to follow them and recover them wherever found. If they could not be found, it had the right to recover their value from those who had been instrumental in changing them from registered to negotiable bonds. Pollock v. National Bank, 7 N.Y. 274, 57 Am. Dec. 520. The defendant railway company knew that the bonds belonged to the plaintiff, and that it had no right to cancel the registration thereof without the authority of the plaintiff. In cancelling such registry and making them payable to bearer, thus enabling them to be sold in the market, it violated its agreement with the plaintiff, and it cannot be relieved from the effect of such violation by reason of the fact that its transfer agent was deceived by the forgeries of Lessels. So, also, did the defendant Gibson know that the bonds belonged to the plaintiff, and that they were registered, and could not be sold until the registration was changed. To some extent he assisted Lessels in procuring the registration to be changed. He advised Lessels how to obtain the information to make the change. After the requisite information had been obtained, he assisted him in drawing the power of attorney, and took part in its execution, becoming a witness thereto. He had been furnished with copies of what purported to be a resolution of the board of directors, with the false signatures of the president and secretary attached, which he transmitted, with the bonds, to the transfer agent of the railway company, to procure the change in the registry. Even after that change had been made, he still knew that the bonds belonged to the plaintiff, and that he had no right to sell them without its authority. And the fact that he was deceived by the fraudulent misrepresentations of Lessels did not relieve him from the responsibility of his acts with reference to depriving the plaintiff of them. The bonds had been traced into his hands, and the plaintiff had the right to seek them there and recover them if they were still in his possession, or if he had sold them and misappropriated the proceeds, knowing that they were the plaintiff's, to recover the value thereof from him. . . .

After the complaint in this action had been served upon the defendant railway company, it served an answer upon the defendant Gibson, in which it demanded relief as against him to the effect that, in case it was compelled to restore the bonds or pay plaintiff's claim, it should have a judgment for the amount so compelled to be paid over as against Gibson. We thus have an issue raised as between the defendants, in which the plaintiff is not interested. Under the provisions of the bonds, they may be registered in the books of the company, and, if so registered, they will thereafter be transferable only upon the books of the company by the owner in person or by attorney duly authorized. It therefore became necessary, in order to change the registry of the bonds, to have a power of attorney executed by the plaintiff. This power of attorney, as we have seen, was drawn in the office of the defendant Gibson, and executed in his presence and that of his cashier, by Lessels signing the name of the corporation thereto, and underneath his own name with the word "treasurer." It was then witnessed by Gibson and by his cashier. Both Gibson and the transfer agent of the railway company were members of the stock exchange. The trial court found as a fact "that in and by the custom among the members of the New York Stock Exchange and of railway transfer agencies in the city of New York the signature of a stock exchange house or a member thereof upon a power of attorney to transfer securities was, during all the times mentioned in the complaint, a guaranty of the correctness of the signature of the parties purporting to execute it." This finding is based upon the rule of the exchange and the testimony of the witness. The rule is as follows: "An indorsement by a member of the exchange, or a firm represented by the exchange, on a certificate is considered a guaranty of the correctness of the signature of the party in whose name the stock stands. In all cases where powers of substitution are used, the original assignment and power of attorney, and each power of substitution, must be guaranteed by a member, or a firm represented in the exchange, resident or doing business in New York." James L. Carter was sworn as a witness on behalf of the defendant railway company, and testified that he was employed by the banking house of J.P. Morgan & Co., that they were transfer agents for about 150 companies, and that there was an established custom as to the requirements upon the transfer of bonds in the city of New York, and that was to require the guaranty of a stock exchange house, or a member of the stock exchange, on the power of attorney on which the transfer is made.

As we have seen, Gibson not only witnessed the power of attorney authorizing the transfer of the bonds on the books of the railway company, but he also transmitted the bonds accompanied by such power of attorney, and with what purported to be the resolution of the board of directors, to the transfer agent of the defendant railway company to have the change of the registration made. The transfer agent, in making the change in the bonds, acted upon the papers so forwarded from defendant Gibson's house. Gibson was a member of the stock exchange in good standing, acquainted with Lessels, his customer, and he must be deemed to have become a witness to the power of attorney under the custom in force. As we have seen, the bonds stood in the name of the Jennie Clarkson Home for Children. Lessels had no power or authority to sell or transfer the bonds or to sign the plaintiff's name as attorney or agent authorizing the transfer of the bonds. The power of attorney was not, therefore, signed by the genuine or the correct signature of the corporation. Under these circumstances the courts below have held that the defendant Gibson was liable over to the defendant railway company. . . .

This much is conceded. But it is contended on behalf of Gibson that he did not, by becoming a witness, undertake to guaranty that Lessels had authority to sign the name of the corporation. This presents the real question in the case, and it really becomes one of construction as to the meaning of the rule of the stock exchange which is the basis of the custom found by the trial court. Under the rule, an indorsement by a member of the exchange on a certificate is considered "a guaranty of the correctness of the signature of the party in whose name the stock stands." If stock is held by an individual who is executing a power of attorney for its transfer, the member of the exchange who signs as a witness thereto guarantees not only the genuineness of the signature affixed to the power of attorney, but that the person signing is the individual in whose name the stock stands. With reference to stock standing in the name of a corporation, which can only sign a power of attorney through its authorized officers or agents, a different situation is presented. If the witnessing of the signature of the corporation is only that of the signature of a person who signs for the corporation, then the guaranty is of no value, and there is nothing to protect purchasers of the companies who are called upon to issue new stock in the place of that transferred from the frauds of persons who have signed the names of corporations without authority. If such is the only effect of the guaranty, purchasers and transfer agents must first go to the corporation in whose name the stock stands and ascertain whether the individual who signed the power of attorney had authority to so do. This will require time, and in many cases will necessitate the postponement of the completion of the purchase by the payment of the money until the facts can be ascertained. The broker who is acting for the owner has an opportunity to become acquainted with his customer, and may readily before sale ascertain, in case of a corporation, the name of the officer who is authorized to execute the power of attorney. It was therefore, we think,

the purpose of the rule to cast upon the broker who witnesses the signature the duty of ascertaining whether the person signing the name
of the corporation has authority to so do, and making the witness a
guarantor that it is the signature of the corporation in whose name the
stock stands. . . .

The judgment should be affirmed, with costs.

Official Comment 2 to §8-306 quotes extensively from this very
case, so it still accurately states the law. The New York markets require
that the guarantor be either a member of an exchange in New York
(individual or corporate) or a commercial bank or trust company
either located in New York or having a correspondent in New York. See
N.Y.S.E. Rule 209, A.S.E. Rule Sr-47, N.Y.S.T.A. Rule 20. In theory any
person may guarantee a signature. Read Official Comment 2 to §8-402.

PROBLEM 237

Maude Raisin was 80 years old and the registered owner of 100
shares of IBM stock. Her faithful companion of 15 years was Charleyne
Rikki, who, one day after being turned down for a raise, took the stock
and forged Ms. Raisin's signature to it. She took the stock to Bing, Bong
& Bell (B.B. & B.), stockbrokers, and asked them to sell it. B.B. & B. did
so, guaranteeing the Raisin signature as part of the registration process.
Maude discovered the loss, Charleyne went to jail, and Maude sued
B.B. & B. on their signature guarantee. Should she prevail? See §8-
306(h). Would a common law suit for conversion prevail? See §8-115
and its Official Comment 3. Whom should she sue? See §8-404 and its
Official Comment; Scott v. Ametek, Inc., 277 A.2d 714, 9 U.C.C. Rep.
Serv. 723 (Del. Ch. 1971).

PROBLEM 238

Assume in the last Problem that Maude Raisin realizes that the
stock had been taken and immediately contacts the issuer of the stock
and alerts the issuer to the theft. When the stock is presented to the
issuer later in the week, what duties does it have? See §§8-403 and 8-
404. Does Maude have a duty to notify the issuer promptly? Read §8-
406. If the issuer gives her a replacement for her missing stock and

then the original shares turn up in the hands of a protected purchaser, what are the issuer's rights? See §8-405.3[3]

VI. SECURITY ENTITLEMENTS

Part 5 of Article 8 deals with security entitlements in indirect holding systems. Use the §8-500s to solve the following Problem.

PROBLEM 239

Mr. Goldbury, an investor, told his broker, Bing, Bong & Bell (B.B. & B.), to buy him 100 shares of Utopia, Ltd. stock. The broker placed the order by having this number of shares transferred to the account it carried with Clearing Corporation. B.B. & B. then marked its books to reflect that Mr. Goldbury owned 100 shares of Utopia, Ltd.

(a) Using the definitions in §8-102, who are the *entitlement holder* and the *securities intermediary*, and what is the *security entitlement*? Who has a *securities account* as that phrase is defined in §8-501(a)?

(b) If the former owner of the 100 shares Mr. Goldbury purchased claims that they were stolen from her and somehow traces them to the account B.B. & B. has with Clearing Corporation, will she succeed in reclaiming the stock? See §8-502 and its Official Comment. If Mr. Goldbury decides to sell his stock, can the former owner announce her ownership rights to the world and thereby give such notice that no one could be free from her adverse claim? See §8-510(a) and (b).

(c) B.B. & B. has many creditors itself. Can a creditor of B.B. & B. seize the rights Mr. Goldbury has in the 100 shares of Utopia, Ltd. stock if B.B. & B. does not pay its debts to that creditor? See §8-503(a); Nathan V. Drage, P.C. v. First Concord Securities, Ltd., 184 Misc. 2d 92, 707 N.Y.S.2d 782, 41 U.C.C. Rep. Serv. 2d 673 (Sup. Ct. 2000).

3. Under §17(f) of the Securities Act of 1934, 15 U.S.C. §78q(f) (1967), and S.E.C. Rule, 17 C.F.R. §240.17f-1, brokers and others regularly dealing with securities must comply with rigorous notification procedures for lost securities. See Pillero, Ilkson, & Yadley, Does SEC Rule 17f-1 Destroy Bona Fide Purchaser Status Under the UCC?, N.Y. L.J., Dec. 13, 1976, at 46. For a case denying protected purchaser status to a bank that failed to check with the Securities Information Center computer before buying stolen bonds, see First Natl. Bank of Cicero v. Lewco Sec. Corp., 860 F.2d 1407, 7 U.C.C. Rep. Serv. 2d 10 (7th Cir. 1988).

(d) B.B. & B. became insolvent. Mr. Goldbury discovered that he was not the only owner of Utopia, Ltd. stock held by B.B. & B. but that Mr. Blushington also supposedly owned 100 shares of the same stock, according to B.B. & B.'s records. However, in violation of §8-504(a), B.B. & B. only had 50 shares of this stock in its account with Clearing Corporation. Mr. Goldbury's transaction with B.B. & B. occurred two days before Mr. Blushington's. Does that mean that he gets the entire 50 shares? See §8-503(b).

Powers v. American Express Fin. Advisors, Inc.

United States Court of Appeals, Fourth Circuit, 2000
238 F.3d 414, 43 U.C.C. Rep. Serv. 2d 425

PER CURIAM

Amy Powers and Michael D'Ambrosia, who lived together, had a joint investment account with American Express Financial Advisors (American Express). On the instructions of D'Ambrosia alone, American Express transferred all of the funds ($86,836.79) in the investment account to a bank account in the couple's joint name. After D'Ambrosia took all of the money, Powers sued American Express, claiming that its transfer to the bank account was ineffective because the signature of both owners of the investment account was required for a transfer of more than $50,000. The district court granted summary judgment to Powers and awarded her damages of $86,836.79, together with prejudgment interest. We affirm.

I.

Powers and D'Ambrosia began living together in 1983. On July 28, 1994, the couple opened an investment account, as joint tenants with right of survivorship, with American Express. The account was initially funded with a $15,000 transfer from the couple's joint bank account. Additions to the account were to come from D'Ambrosia's earnings. D'Ambrosia agreed to the joint account because Powers provided him with "domestic needs" and because she had contributed to improvements made to the couple's residence. To open the American Express account, Powers and D'Ambrosia filled out an investment application. In Section C of the application, Powers and D'Ambrosia checked the box next to the "Joint Tenant" provision, which reads:

First and second clients have right of Survivorship. This is not the same as tenants-in-common. The first client's home or mailing address will be used for account-related purposes. You understand that only one signature is required for redemption requests up to $50,000.

The couple's application also directed American Express to place their money in four separate mutual funds.

On August 4, 1997, Powers and D'Ambrosia parted ways. By that time their American Express account was valued at over $80,000. Both of them contacted American Express and asked it to freeze the account. Later, in a letter dated September 26, 1997, D'Ambrosia and Powers authorized a release of the freeze and directed American Express to transfer the funds to a Prudential Securities account. There is a dispute about whether Powers actually signed the September 26 letter. Powers asserts that her signature was forged, but American Express contends that there is a genuine issue of fact about whether that is the case. The forgery issue is not material, however.[4]

On October 15 and 16, 1997, D'Ambrosia sent American Express two separate faxes. The first, on October 15, contained a memo signed by D'Ambrosia, a copy of D'Ambrosia and Powers's statement of account at American Express, and a copy of the September 26 letter. D'Ambrosia's memo, included in the fax, changed the instructions in the September 26 letter. The memo directed American Express to close the couple's account and to mail the proceeds to D'Ambrosia and Powers's former residence in Columbia, MD. The second fax, dated October 16, also contained a memo from D'Ambrosia, a statement of the couple's account at American Express, and a copy of the September 26 letter. The memo attached to this fax again changed the instructions in the September 26 letter. The memo, signed only by D'Ambrosia, directed American Express to transfer the funds to a joint bank account held by Powers and D'Ambrosia at FCNB Bank. After receiving both faxes, American Express ignored the September 26

---

4. American Express contends that a genuine issue of material fact exists as to whether Powers's signature on the September 26 letter was forged. We disagree. Although the district court devoted some attention to the September 26 letter, its decision did not depend on the validity or invalidity of Powers's signature on that letter. Rather, the court's decision turns on the fact that Powers never authorized a transfer of funds to the FCNB account. The September 26 letter directed American Express to send the funds to a Prudential Securities account. The only entitlement order requesting a transfer to the FCNB account was the October 16 fax memorandum that Powers never signed. Thus, the district court's ultimate conclusion that Powers never authorized or ratified the transfer to the FCNB account is based on facts that are not contradicted.

letter and followed the instruction in D'Ambrosia's October 16 fax memo. The company wired $86,836.79 to Powers and D'Ambrosia's FCNB joint account, and within a few days, D'Ambrosia absconded with the money.

When Powers discovered what had happened, she filed this action against American Express to recover the money. Both parties moved for summary judgment. Powers claimed that American Express transferred the funds in contravention of section 8-507(b) of Maryland's Commercial Code. See Md. Com. Law (U.C.C.) §8- 507(b). Under U.C.C. §8-507(b), a "securities intermediary," like American Express, which transfers funds pursuant to an "ineffective entitlement order," is liable to an "entitlement holder" for any damages caused by the improper transfer. Powers contended that the faxes were ineffective entitlement orders because Section C of the investment application required both signatures for redemption requests over $50,000. Thus, as an entitlement holder, Powers claimed that American Express was liable to her for acting on D'Ambrosia's fax requests of October 15 and 16, 1997, which she did not sign. American Express claimed that Powers's authorization was not necessary. It claimed that D'Ambrosia's faxes constituted an effective entitlement order because, under U.C.C. §8-107(b)(1), D'Ambrosia was an "appropriate person" to order the transfer of the couple's funds.

The district court agreed with Powers that the faxes received by American Express constituted an "ineffective entitlement order." Powers v. American Express Fin. Advisors, Inc., 82 F. Supp. 2d 448, 452 (D. Md. 2000). The court recognized that Powers and D'Ambrosia were "entitlement holders" because as co-owners of the American Express account, "they were identified in the records of the securities intermediary (American Express) as having a security entitlement against the intermediary." Id. at 451. Because D'Ambrosia was an entitlement holder, the court acknowledged American Express's contention that D'Ambrosia was an "appropriate person" to give an entitlement order to American Express under U.C.C. §8-107. Id. at 451-52. The court also noted that when an "appropriate person" issues an entitlement order to a securities intermediary, the intermediary has a duty to execute the order under U.C.C. §8- 507(a)(2). Id. at 452. The court decided, however, that section 8- 507(a)(2) cannot be read in a vacuum because Section C of the couple's investment application with American Express requires the signatures of both investors for any redemption request above $50,000. The district court held that Section C's joint signature requirement was valid under U.C.C. §1-103. See id. at 453. Section 1-103 states that "the principles of law and equity . . .

shall supplement [the U.C.C.]." Thus, "when an intermediary has agreed that the 'appropriate person' to make an order is both owners of a joint account, both owners must make the order." Id. Because Powers did not authorize or otherwise ratify the transfer of the $86,836.79 to an the account at FCNB, the district court concluded that the transfer was ineffective. See id. at 452.

The district court also rejected American Express's assertion that the $50,000 threshold only applied to transfers from a single mutual fund account. See id. at 454. Because Powers and D'Ambrosia did not have more than $50,000 in any one of their four mutual funds, American Express asserted that two signatures were not required for the $86,836.79 redemption. The district court held, however, that American Express's interpretation was contrary to the plain language of Section C which states that "only one signature is required for redemption requests up to $50,000." Because the language of Section C refers to redemption requests generally and not to redemption requests out of individual funds, the district court concluded that two signatures were required for any transfer greater than $50,000. See id.

The district court summarily rejected American Express's remaining contentions. American Express claimed that Powers was barred from seeking damages under U.C.C. §8-115. According to U.C.C. §8-115, a securities intermediary is not liable to an individual who has an adverse claim to an asset that a securities intermediary transfers at the direction of a customer. The district court held that Powers was not an adverse claimant for the simple reason that she was one of two entitlement holders with respect to the account. See id. at 453.

Finally, the district court rejected American Express's request that the court impress the funds in the FCNB account with a constructive trust on behalf of D'Ambrosia's former employer, Signal Perfection Limited. See id. D'Ambrosia had been an accountant at Signal Perfection. Around December 1997 or January 1998, Signal Perfection discovered that D'Ambrosia had been embezzling money from the company for some time. In late January of 1998 D'Ambrosia and Signal Perfection signed a settlement agreement disposing of all claims the company had against D'Ambrosia. In exchange for the release D'Ambrosia assigned to Signal Perfection his interest in certain accounts, including the FCNB joint account. American Express argued that the district court should impose a constructive trust on the FCNB account because D'Ambrosia allegedly had deposited the converted American Express funds in that account. The district court denied American Express's request, holding that American Express did not have standing to seek a constructive trust on behalf of Signal Perfection and that, in any event, American Express had failed to demonstrate that it could trace the converted funds. See id.

Based on this reasoning, the district court granted Powers's motion for summary judgment and concluded that she was entitled to damages caused by American Express's improper transfer of the funds from the joint investment account. See id. at 454. The district court subsequently entered judgment against American Express in the amount of $86,836.79, together with prejudgment interest. See id. at 457-58. American Express appeals.

II.

After considering the joint appendix, the briefs, and the oral arguments of counsel, we are persuaded that the district court reached the correct result. We therefore affirm substantially on the reasoning of the district court. See Powers v. American Express Fin. Advisors, Inc., 82 F. Supp. 2d 448 (D. Md. 2000).

AFFIRMED.

PART 3

PAYMENT IN DOCUMENTED SALES

Chapter 15

DOCUMENTS
OF TITLE

Article 7 of the Code deals with the legal problems created by *documents of title* (defined in §1-201(15))—pieces of paper issued for the purpose of actually representing title to goods. The two primary types of documents of title are bills of lading (§1-201(6)) and warehouse receipts (§1-201(45)).[1]

The creation of paper representing the right of ownership of the goods became inevitable as soon as merchants wanted to borrow money and pledge goods that they owned as collateral. If the goods were large enough to store in a warehouse, the money lender was normally unwilling to take physical possession of the goods. The money lender was also normally unwilling to give the borrower possession of

---

1. For treatises on point, see W. Towle, Warehousing Law (1988), and R. Henson, Documents of Title Under the Uniform Commercial Code (2d ed. 1990).

the collateral for fear the goods would be sold to someone else or taken by the buyer's other creditors. The solution to the problem was to store the goods with a bailee and have the bailee issue a paper stating that the goods belonged to the owner of the paper. In this fashion, the paper, representing the obligation of the bailee to deliver the goods to the holder, could be freely transferred, discounted, and rediscounted without the necessity of moving the goods into the physical control of each new owner. Any holder of the paper could surrender it and require the bailee (*issuer*) to turn over the goods.

Read §7-403 carefully. Note that under subsection (3) the person claiming the goods *must* (except in the §7-503 situation discussed later) surrender the negotiable document of title for cancellation in order to receive the goods. If the document has been lost, the holder can get the goods only by procuring a court order directing the bailee to turn over the goods. Read §7-601.

Documents of title are negotiable or non-negotiable depending on whether they contain order or bearer language (§7-104). Since under §7-403(3) the bailee can demand only the surrender of negotiable paper, only negotiable documents of title truly represent absolute ownership of the goods. Non-negotiable paper simply evidences the contract between the bailor and the bailee, which is to do whatever the contract says. Non-negotiable documents normally state exactly to whom the bailee will deliver the goods and under what conditions. Therefore, for reasons of safety, lenders prefer to loan money against negotiable documents. With non-negotiable documents, lenders run the risk that there has already been a delivery of the goods to someone else.

I.   WAREHOUSE RECEIPTS

A.   Form

The front of a *negotiable* warehouse receipt states the name of the warehouse that is issuing the receipt and states in large type that:

> This is to certify that we have received in storage for the account of _____ in apparent order, except as noted hereon (contents, condition, and quality being unknown), the following described property, subject to all of the terms and conditions on the front or back of this contract,

such property to be delivered to _____ or order, upon payment of all storage, handling and other charges and the surrender of this Warehouse receipt properly endorsed.

Following this statement usually there are the following:

1. a space for listing the goods stored,
2. a statement of the warehouse company's intention to claim a lien against the goods until the storage charges are paid,
3. a statement as to the amount of the storage charge, and
4. the official signature of the warehouse company.

The back of the warehouse receipt contains a space in which the agent of the warehouse can note *partial* deliveries to the holder of the document (later holders can claim only the amount of goods the document shows were not delivered to prior holders). The back also has the *standard contract terms* in small print (these standard terms were adopted by a 1926 conference of experts and approved by the Department of Commerce); the terms cover the fact that the storage is on a month-to-month basis and spell out in detail the warehouse company's position as to insurance, limitation of liability, right to move the goods, etc.

A non-negotiable warehouse receipt looks substantially the same except:

1. It is not made deliverable to anyone. The warehouse engages to deliver the goods as per instructions received from the person storing the goods (the bailor). *Order* language is not used.

2. There is no space on the back for notation of partial deliveries. This is because surrender of the document is not required to take out all or part of the goods. Section 7-403(3) applies only to *negotiable* documents.

Negotiable warehouse receipts normally have the word NEGOTIABLE stamped across their face in large letters (and the documents tend to have fancy and ornate borders, designed to make counterfeiting more difficult). Non-negotiable documents have NON-NEGOTIABLE stamped on the front.

Glance through §7-202.

As can be seen from the above, the warehouse receipt plays three roles: it is (1) a *receipt* for the goods, (2) a *contract* for storage, and (3) if negotiable, *a physical embodiment* of the concept of *title* to the goods.

B. Basic Bailment Law

All document-of-title situations start with the bailment of the goods and the issuance of a receipt by the bailee. Bailment law is relevant to fill in the gaps in Article 7 and the federal statutes. The most important bailment concept needed to supplement the Code is that the bailee is required to make proper delivery of the goods to the bailor when the bailment ends or is to be responsible for non-delivery. Section 7-403(1) gives very few excuses for non-delivery. An *unauthorized* delivery of the goods by a bailee is conversion. Restatement (Second) of Torts §234; cf. §7-601(2). Read §7-404. A "bailee is absolutely liable for misdelivering cargo, unless his mistake as to the person entitled to receive the goods was induced by the bailor." David Crystal, Inc. v. Cunard Steam-Ship Co., Ltd., 339 F.2d 295, 298 (2d Cir. 1964); Met-Al, Inc. v. Hansen Storage Co., 828 F. Supp. 1369, 21 U.C.C. Rep. Serv. 2d 1107 (E.D. Wis. 1993) ("Equitable defenses to allegations of misdelivery are disfavored."); Singer Co. v. Stott & Davis Motor Express, Inc., 79 A.D.2d 227, 463 N.Y.S.2d 508, 31 U.C.C. Rep. Serv. 658 (App. Div. 1981) ("Once a plaintiff establishes delivery of goods and the failure of the bailee to return them on demand, a prima facie case of negligence is made and the burden of coming forward with evidence tending to show due cause shifts to the bailee. . . ."). These principles are best illustrated by one of the cases rising out of the famous *Salad Oil* scandal.

Procter & Gamble Distributing Co. v. Lawrence American Field Warehouse Corp.

New York Court of Appeals, 1965
16 N.Y.2d 344, 213 N.E.2d 897, 266 N.Y.S.2d 765,
3 U.C.C. Rep. Serv. 157, 21 A.L.R.3d 1320

VAN VOORHIS, J. This is an action against a warehouse corporation based upon the nondelivery of the merchandise for which it issued its warehouse receipts. The theory of action is conversion. Plaintiff (hereafter called P & G) asserts that in the absence of any explanation of the disappearance of these goods, the defendant (hereafter called Field) is liable for the market value of this merchandise at the times when it was delivered to the warehouse. Plaintiff is correct in these contentions, we have concluded, and is entitled to summary judgment in this amount. We agree with the Appellate Division that no triable issue is presented concerning the liability of defendant, but consider that the Appellate Division erred in directing an assessment of damages and in not awarding to plaintiff the undisputed market value of the merchandise delivered to defendant at the time of its delivery, which was as high as at any subsequent time or times prior to notification to plaintiff of its disappearance. The basic issue is simple, but it has been encrusted with a complex of fact and legal argument which makes it necessary to discuss the case in more detail.

Allied Crude Vegetable Oil Refining Corp. (hereinafter called Allied) is not a party to this action, but this cause of action against defendant arose through a course of dealings between plaintiff and Allied, which traded in vegetable oils manufactured by various producers including plaintiff. Originally plaintiff sold such merchandise outright on sight draft with bill of lading attached. In the early Fall of 1962, however, in order more fully to utilize its working capital, Allied persuaded plaintiff to engage in a practice known as field warehousing. Allied had leased oil storage tanks at Bayonne, New Jersey, formerly owned by the Tidewater Associated Oil Company. These were sublet to Field, a wholly owned subsidiary of American Express Company (hereafter called Amexco), which thereupon operated as an independent warehouse company. When Allied purchased vegetable oils from plaintiff, and other producers, as it did f.o.b. seller's plant or warehouse, Bayonne, New Jersey, the oil would be shipped to Bayonne to the seller's order, and stored for the seller's account in Field's warehouses. Down payments were made, described in the contract as "Margin Requirements on Consigned Shipments," amounting to about 20% of the purchase price, at the time of receipt of the oil at Field's warehouse, and the balance by sight draft with bill of lading attached, or cash in advance of shipment to buyer, as Allied disposed of the oil.

In accordance with this procedure, plaintiff shipped 9,206,740 pounds of fully refined soybean oil under bills of lading to plaintiff itself as consignee at Bayonne, New Jersey, which was delivered for storage and safe keeping to Field at said warehouse for plaintiff's account. Field, the defendant, issued five warehouse receipts for this oil dated March 22, April 1 and April 9, 1963. Each warehouse receipt recited the number of the bill of lading for the tank car in which it had been contained, amounting in total to 151 tank carloads. Not only was the presence of this oil in defendant's tanks attested by these nonnegotiable receipts issued in plaintiff's name, but also by a series of month-end statements, issued by defendant indicating that the oil was in the warehouse. Both the warehouse receipts and these month-end statements, based on defendant's books, are evidence that the oil was received by defendant at its tank warehouse in Bayonne, New Jersey. In the absence of any evidentiary facts showing that defendant did not receive the oil in the suit, its warehouse receipts, month-end statements and books of account are conclusive against defendant on this point. Mere suspicion that the oil was stolen before reaching defendant's tanks is not sufficient to overcome this documentary evidence. . . . The usual measure of damage, in event of non-delivery of goods by a bailee, is the market value on the date of the conversion . . . not the date when the bailor learns of the loss or presents his warehouse receipt and demands his merchandise. Where, as here, the date of the conversion has not been identified, the Appellate Division has held that the value should be fixed as of the date when the bailor received notice of the loss. This, we think, was error. The circumstances regarding the loss of bailed property are more likely to be known by the bailee than by the bailor, and, where the time and manner of the loss is unknown, it ought not lie in the power of the bailee to choose the date for determining market value by electing when to notify the bailor that the goods have disappeared and cannot be accounted for. The rule that the loss is to be measured as of the time of the conversion, when the conversion date is known, should not be reshaped to designate the date when the bailor is notified of the conversion if the conversion date is unknown. That would place the bailee in a better legal position by pleading ignorance of the circumstances of the loss than if he knew or revealed the circumstances. . . .

[I]t follows that the bailor should be awarded damages measured by the highest value of the property between the date when the bailment commenced and the date when the bailor has received notice that the property has been lost. . . .

On its appeal defendant (Field) contends that there is a triable issue respecting whether it exercised reasonable care as bailee of this oil. Defendant points to section 7-204 of the Uniform Commercial Code, in effect in New Jersey at the time, providing that a warehouseman is liable for damages for loss or injury to the goods "caused by his failure to exercise such care in regard to them as a reasonably careful man would exercise under like circumstances but unless otherwise agreed he is not liable for damages which could not have been avoided by the exercise of such care." Section 7-403 of the same statute provides that the bailee must deliver the goods to a person under the document unless and to the extent that the bailee established "damage to or delay, loss or destruction of the goods for which the bailee is not liable."

These sections of the Uniform Commercial Code appear not to have altered for present purposes the prior law . . . that a warehouseman shall not be liable for loss or injury to the goods which could not have been avoided by the exercise of reasonable care, and section 8 (General Business Law, former §95), like section 7-403 of the Uniform Commercial Code, stated that a warehouseman is liable for nondelivery of bailed goods "in the absence of some lawful excuse provided by this article." Citing these sections, the Appellate Division correctly stated . . . that a warehouseman "has the burden of explanation for any loss or disappearance of the property bailed. . . . It is not enough to assert that care was taken, describing the practices used, when the disappearance of the oil remains wholly unexplained." . . . In the opinion by the present Chief Judge the rule applicable here was stated in the form of a quotation from Claflin v. Meyer (75 N.Y. 260, 264):

> If he [the bailor] proves the demand upon the warehouseman and his refusal to deliver, these facts unexplained are treated by the courts as prima facie evidence of negligence; but if, either in the course of his proof or that of the defendant, it appears that the goods have been lost by theft, the evidence must show that the loss arose from the negligence of the warehouseman. . . .

The Appellate Division well said that it is self-contradictory for a warehouseman simultaneously to assert due care and total lack of knowledge of what happened, and that it would establish an unwise rule to place a bailee in better position to be excused if he knew less about the disappearance of the goods than if he knew more. That is the underlying reason for the time-honored law of New York and New Jersey requiring a warehouseman to make an explanation of injury or loss in the case of bailed merchandise, which has been continued and not abolished by the Uniform Commercial Code.

The other points raised on the appeal by defendant Field merit but passing mention. One is that plaintiff should be obliged to accept a proportionate share of the conglomerate found on hand in the tanks of these subsidiaries of Amexco. This consisted mostly of acid soap stock, fish oil and water. These mixed fluids were not the edible fully refined vegetable oil delivered to Field by plaintiff. An argument is made that the warehouse receipts showed plaintiff's refined vegetable oil to be fungible, and granted permission to mix it with similar oil owned by other depositors. From that it is said that a warehouseman need do no more than take the word of other customers concerning the nature of the fluids which are being placed in the tanks of the warehouseman, and that if it be soap acid or fish oil then that is plaintiff's misfortune. It is a sufficient answer to that contention that plaintiff is not required to acquit the warehouse in whole or in part by taking in return a commodity or blend of commodities of a different nature from that which was deposited. . . .

———————————

No one has ever discovered exactly what happened to the missing salad oil (which was the collateral for millions of dollars worth of loans). N. Miller, The Great Salad Oil Swindle (1965).

As this case indicates, a warehouse company that issues a warehouse receipt is liable to good faith holders even if the warehouse never received the goods. Read §7-203. It is also liable if the goods are incorrectly described. A warehouse is required to keep goods separate unless they are fungible. See §7-207. If the goods are fungible, a "buyer in the ordinary course of business" can purchase the goods and get good title even though there is an outstanding negotiable warehouse receipt (§7-205).

A bailee's duty of care is that which "a reasonably careful man would exercise under the circumstances." Read §7-204 and the following case.

Dunfee v. Blue Rock Van & Storage, Inc.

Delaware Superior Court, New Castle, 1970
266 A.2d 187, 7 U.C.C. Rep. Serv. 1344

PER CURIAM. Plaintiff sued defendant in negligence for loss of her goods by fire while they were stored in defendant's warehouse. Defendant answered, pleading non-liability by reason of arson by a public enemy. It is undisputed that the loss occurred during civil disorders in Wilmington immediately following the assassination of Martin Luther King, Jr. on April 4, 1968. Following completion of the usual pretrial discovery procedures, trial by jury commenced on February 10, 1970. On February 12, 1970, the jury returned a verdict for plaintiff in the amount of $5,500.00.

On February 10, 1970, the morning when the jury trial began, the defendant moved to amend his answer, pleading a limitation of liability by virtue of a warehouse receipt, signed by the plaintiff when her chattels were picked up, and establishing the maximum liability of the warehouseman at $1,000.00. Plaintiff objected upon the grounds that (1) limitation of liability is an affirmative defense which must be specifically raised in the pleadings to avoid surprise, and (2) the alleged warehouse receipt upon which defendant relies is insufficient in that it fails to conform to the requirements of such a receipt as set forth in section 7-202 of the Uniform Commercial Code. . . .

The evidence disclosed that the plaintiff knew and understood that defendant's coverage was limited to $1,000.00 and, based upon that information she purchased an additional separate $4,000.00 insurance policy to cover the loss of her chattels. The warehouse receipt, signed by the plaintiff at the time her goods were picked up, limited liability to ".60 per pound, per article." Plaintiff's goods weighed 4,340 pounds. . . . [The court quoted §7-204, which you have just read.]

Plaintiff argues that the language employed in the receipt and contract in this case, ".60 per pound, per article" fails to measure up to the specific requirements set forth in the statute, a limitation "by article or item, or value per unit of weight." It is plaintiff's contention that the limitation in this receipt is by weight and by article rather than by weight or article. The Court finds the plaintiff's argument to be without merit.

This section of the Code was adopted to specify that a bailee could, in fact, limit his liability for loss of goods without impairing his obligation of reasonable care.

Where the storage contract fairly spells out the limitation of liability and contains a provision for increased charges and additional insurance where an excess value is declared, there is substantial compliance with the requirements of the statute. The Court cannot read the statute to intend that a monetary limitation must be based upon either item or weight, without any possibility of using both, even though circumstances might so require. The limitation was clearly stated, the plaintiff understood its significance, and she availed herself of the opportunity to secure additional protection. All parties understood that the limitation of liability, despite items, articles or weight, would not exceed $1,000.00. Insofar as the storage contract limited the warehouseman's liability for loss it complied with the requirements of Section 7-204(2), of the Uniform Commercial Code (Title 5A, Delaware Code, §7-204(2)).

[Defendant was permitted to amend its answer, and plaintiff was limited to the relief stated.]

QUESTIONS

1. Would the court have reached the same result if Ms. Dunfee had not known of the limitation of liability, it being buried in the fine print on the receipt? See Keefe v. Bekins Van & Storage Co., 540 P.2d

1132, 17 U.C.C. Rep. Serv. 1286 (Colo. App. 1975) (limitation effective even though not called to customer's attention); Sanfisket Inc. v. Atlantic Cold Storage Corp., 347 So. 2d 647, 21 U.C.C. Rep. Serv. 1155 (Fla. Dist. App. 1977) (inconspicuous limitation held effective).

2. Could the bailee depend on a clause in the receipt that completely disclaimed liability for its own negligence? See §1-102; Blue Valley Co-op. v. National Farmers Organization, 600 N.W.2d 786, 39 U.C.C. Rep. Serv. 2d 633 (Neb. 1999) (disclaimer in crop storage); Gonzalez v. A-1 Self Storage, Inc., 795 A.2d 885, 411 U.C.C. Rep. Serv. 2d 1119 (N.J. Super. 2000) (disclaimer in consumer goods storage).

3. If the bailee here were a carrier that had issued a bill of lading, would we reach a different result? See §7-309; Downstate Medical Ctr. v. Purolator Courier Corp., 138 Misc. 2d 714, 525 N.Y.S.2d 120, 6 U.C.C. Rep. Serv. 2d 1544 (Civ. Ct. 1988).

C. Bailee's Lien

All bailees (including warehousemen and carriers) are given a statutory lien in the bailed goods to the extent of the charges for storage and expenses incident to the bailment contract (expenses necessary to preserve the goods, for instance). For warehouses, this lien is described in §§7-209 and 7-210; for carriers, §§7-307 and 7-308. These bailee's liens are possessory liens only; the bailee loses its lien if it voluntarily surrenders the goods (or wrongfully refuses to surrender them). See Darby v. Baltimore & Ohio Ry. Co., 259 Md. 493, 270 A.2d 652, 8 U.C.C. Rep. Serv. 375 (1970). If the bailor does not pay the bailee's charges, the latter may foreclose its lien by public or private sale (the rules of which are described in the above-named sections). The Code primarily requires the foreclosure sale to be held in a "commercially reasonable manner." For a case exploring the details of a bailee lien foreclosure on stored household goods, see Bradford v. Muinzer, 498 F. Supp. 1384, 29 U.C.C. Rep. Serv. 1597 (N.D. Ill. 1980).

Following Supreme Court decisions such as Fuentes v. Shevin, 407 U.S. 67, 10 U.C.C. Rep. Serv. 913 (1972), constitutional (due process) attacks have been made on these bailee lien enforcement sections. In 1978 the Supreme Court settled the issue in Flagg Bros., Inc. v. Brooks, 436 U.S. 149, 23 U.C.C. Rep. Serv. 1105 (1978). In that case a warehouse company had sold goods under the power of §7-210(2). The Court held that the sale was not "properly attributable to the State of New York," hence there was no "state action." Without state action the sale did not do violence to the due process requirements of the

Fourteenth Amendment. Nonetheless, §7-210 was later declared unconstitutional by the New York Court of Appeals as a matter of *state* constitutional law. See Svendsen v. Smith's Moving & Trucking Co., 54 N.Y.2d 865, 429 N.E.2d 411, 444 N.Y.S.2d 904, 32 U.C.C. Rep. Serv. 275 (1981). This in turn led to a 1982 amendment to New York's §7-210 and the creation of a new §7-211, designed to cure the constitutional objections by adding both notice and a court hearing to the lien enforcement procedure.

D. Delivery Orders

You will remember that if the goods are stored under a non-negotiable warehouse receipt, the bailee can deliver the goods without requiring surrender of the warehouse receipt. Many non-negotiable warehouse forms state that delivery will be made "on *detached* written authority *without* the return of this receipt." When the owner (bailor) wants the order delivered, the owner simply sends a letter (called a *delivery order*) to the bailee, explaining to whom the goods are to be delivered.

Storing goods in bulk under a non-negotiable warehouse receipt and then breaking them up into smaller units by separate delivery orders is a convenient way to merchandise commodities. The delivery orders, which need take no particular form, can be negotiable or non-negotiable. A delivery order is negotiable if it directs the bailee to deliver the goods to someone, "or his order," or "to bearer"; otherwise, it is non-negotiable. In many ways a delivery order is directly analogous to an Article 3 draft, only it is an order to deliver goods instead of to pay money. Like a draft, it imposes no liability on the bailee until the bailee *accepts* the order (no liability to the holder of the delivery order, that is; the bailee who refuses to accept a delivery order may be in breach of the bailment contract and, if so, is liable to the bailor). See §7-502(1)(d), especially the last sentence.

All of this ties in with how a seller of bailed goods makes *tender* to the buyer under Article 2 of the Code. Read §§2-509(2) and 2-503(4) carefully. Where a *negotiable* document of title is involved, both §§2-509(2) and 2-503(4)(a) make it clear that the risk of loss shifts to the buyer on delivery of the document if the goods conform to the contract (if not, §2-510 applies). However, these sections do *not* apply to negotiable delivery orders, which are lumped in with the rules governing non-negotiable documents in §§2-509(2)(c) and 2-503(4)(b) ("written direction to deliver" means a delivery order). Where no documents are involved (say, a pet dog is boarded at a kennel and then sold), §2-509(2)(b) passes the risk of loss to the buyer on the bailee's acknowledgment of the buyer's right to possession. See Whately v. Tetrault, 29 Mass. App. Dec. 112, 5 U.C.C. Rep. Serv. 838 (1964).

PROBLEM 240

Fred Bandanna, a farmer, took two truckloads of his cotton to Rural Warehouse for storage. The first truckload of 80 bales he stored under a negotiable warehouse receipt issued by Rural. For the second truckload of 80 bales, he obtained a non-negotiable warehouse receipt. Fred took the documents to the offices of Harold Fastbuck, a commodity merchant. Harold bought both the negotiable receipt covering the first truckload and the non-negotiable receipt covering the second truckload of cotton from Fred. Harold asked, however, that Fred divide the 80 bales represented by the non-negotiable receipt into two equal lots so that Harold could resell them more easily. Fred sat down and wrote out two delivery orders addressed to Rural, each requiring the warehouse to turn over 40 bales to "Harold Fastbuck or order." As soon as Fred left his office, Harold sold one of the delivery orders to another commodity merchant, Sue Fourthparty. He endorsed on the back of the delivery order "Deliver to Sue Fourthparty or order, (signed) Harold Fastbuck." Sue phoned Rural Warehouse and said that she was the owner of 40 bales of the Fred Bandanna cotton under a delivery order. The warehouse agent agreed that Sue could pick up the bales the next day. That night lightning struck the warehouse, and all the cotton burned. Who took the risk of loss as to each segment of the cotton?

E.   Terminology: The Issuer

Under the Code, the person primarily liable on a document of title is the *issuer* of the document. Since the *bailee* (warehouse or carrier) is almost always the person who *issues* (creates) the document, there is a temptation to think of *issuer* as synonymous with *bailee*. This would be correct except for the fact that the issuer of a delivery order (which *is* a document of title according to §1-201(15)) is the *bailor*. Read §§7-102(1)(d) and 7-102(1)(g). This fact will become important later on when we get to talking about *due negotiation* and the duties of the issuer. Question: who was (were) the issuer(s) in Problem 240?

II.   BILLS OF LADING

Just as warehouses issue negotiable or non-negotiable receipts for bailed goods, carriers (such as railroads, airlines, ocean liners, and trucking firms) issue similar documents on the receipt of goods for transportation across the country or the world. These documents, called *bills of lading,* may be negotiable or non-negotiable (depending on whether order or bearer language is used). As with warehouse receipts, the bill of lading is, simultaneously, a receipt for the goods, a contract of transportation, and tangible evidence of ownership of the bailed goods.

A.   Federal Law

Article 7 of the Code covers only *intra*state shipments. If the goods are to cross state lines, the documents issued by the carrier are governed by the Federal Bills of Lading Act (the Pomerene Act of 1916), 49 U.S.C. §81 et seq. If the goods are to cross water, they will be governed by a host of federal statutes including the Shipping Act, 46 U.S.C. §801 et seq.; the Intercoastal Shipping Act, 46 U.S.C. §843 et seq.; and (most important) the Carriage of Goods by Sea Act, 46 U.S.C. §1300 et seq. (For those of you who will have commercial bailees as clients, note at this point that all interstate carriers and warehouses are subject to federal regulation of their trade. The Federal Aviation Administration, for example, formulates rules and regulations for the airlines involved in interstate and foreign air carriage. The Department of Agriculture regulates warehouses storing agricultural products. See the United States Warehouse Act, 7 U.S.C. §241 et seq. There will also be special state statutes and regulations that deal with warehouses and carriers.)

Fortunately, the basic law set out in the Federal Bills of Lading Act is more or less the same as that in Article 7, and unless the wording is particularly crucial, language of the federal act will not be mentioned. What is important is that you remember that Article 7 does *not* apply (except by analogy) to any bill of lading issued for goods that are to leave the state. For such a bill you need to refer to the exact language of the relevant federal statutes.

B.   The Basic Idea

Do not confuse *shipper* with *carrier* or *issuer.* The *shipper* is the original owner (bailor) of the goods who turns them over to the carrier for transportation. The *carrier* then issues a bill of lading (thus becoming an *issuer*) to the shipper. If the bill is negotiable, the carrier (issuer) will not turn over the goods at the destination until the negotiable bill of lading is surrendered (§7-403(3) applies to carriers as well as warehouses). This means that the shipper must mail the bill of lading to the person who is to receive the goods (normally the buyer) before the latter can get possession of the goods. Often the shipper will not surrender the bill of lading to the buyer until the latter has paid for the goods (or has *accepted* a draft drawn on it; see the discussion below); this is called requiring *payment against documents.* As soon as the buyer pays the seller (or seller's agent), the buyer gets possession of the negotiable bill of lading and can claim the goods from the carrier. A carrier that delivers the goods to the buyer without demanding surrender of an outstanding negotiable bill of lading has converted the goods and is liable to the holder of the negotiable bill. See Rountree v. Lydick-Barmann Co., 150 S.W.2d 173 (Tex. Civ. App. 1941) (decided under the Uniform Bills of Lading Act, Article 7's predecessor). See also Koreska v. United Cargo Corp., 23 A.D.2d 37, 258 N.Y.S.2d 432, 2 U.C.C. Rep. Serv. 789 (1965).

Review §7-403(3), and read §§7-404 and 7-601(2).

BII Finance Co. v. U-States Forwarding Services Corp.

California Court of Appeals, 2002
115 Cal. Rptr. 2d 312, 46 U.C.C. Rep. Serv. 2d 827

Mosk, J.

Introduction

Defendant U-States Forwarding Services Corp. (U-States), appeals a judgment against it in favor of plaintiff BII Finance Company Ltd. (BII) in the amount of $74,060.76, plus costs in the amount of $7,069.57 and attorneys' fees in the amount of $30,222.07. Judgment was entered following a court trial. The parties waived the statement of decision. BII, the shipper's assignee, prevailed on its claim that U-States, the shipping carrier, was liable for delivering goods without requiring surrender by the purchaser of the original bills of lading. In this case, the purchaser had not paid for the goods. The judgment was also entered against Primaline, Inc. (Primaline), the shipping carrier's agent, pursuant to a default. Primaline does not appeal.

A bill of lading that is consigned "To Order," without designating a named person, arguably may not be a negotiable document under California Uniform Commercial Code section 7104, subdivision (1). If it is not, the bill of lading nonetheless should be treated as a negotiable document under California Uniform Commercial Code section 7104, subdivision (3) in this case. The trial court correctly found that U-States was liable to BII, the holder by due negotiation of the bills of lading at issue, because U-States delivered the goods covered by those bills at the instruction of a party who was not such a holder, to a party who also was not such a holder. In addition, there was substantial evidence to support the trial court's finding that BII's acceptance of partial payment from the party that received the goods did not relieve U-States of liability for the remainder of the amount owed. Accordingly, we affirm the judgment.

BACKGROUND

On June 5 and 6, 1997, Primaline, a shipping company that acted as agent for U-States (a California corporation), issued four bills of lading in favor of Shineworld Industrial Limited (Shineworld), a Hong Kong manufacturer and exporter of garments. Although the goods covered by the bills of lading (cartons of jackets) were to be shipped to the buyer, Jacobs & Turner, Ltd. (Jacobs & Turner) in Glasgow, Scotland, the goods were consigned simply "TO ORDER," without specifying any name or person.

Jacobs & Turner agreed to pay by letter of credit approximately U.S. $200,000 for the goods covered by the bills of lading. (The amounts at issue were in Hong Kong dollars. Here, the amounts are specified in United States dollars because the parties did so. Those amounts are expressed in approximations, also because the parties did so—presumably due to fluctuating exchange rates.) Shineworld assigned each bill of lading to BII, a commercial Hong Kong bank, for a loan of approximately U.S. $200,000.

The goods were placed on a vessel in early June 1997 and arrived in the United Kingdom in July 1997. While the goods were in transit, BII sent the shipping documents (including the bills of lading) to Jacobs & Turner's bank, Clydesdale Bank PLC, in Glasgow, Scotland, and requested payment under the letter of credit. On June 25, 1997, Clydesdale Bank gave notice to BII that because the bank had found discrepancies between the letter of credit and the shipping documents sent to it by BII, the bank would not release the funds to BII until the buyer, Jacobs & Turner, consented to a waiver of the discrepancies. BII then notified Shineworld of the claimed discrepancies, and Shineworld responded that it would contact Jacobs & Turner about the matter.

Shineworld apparently did not have any further communications with BII about the shipment. Sometime later, in September 1997, BII learned that the goods had been released to Jacobs & Turner at Shineworld's direction, even though BII had not been paid for the goods. In fact, on July 15, 1997, Shineworld had inexplicably sent a letter to Primaline requesting that it release the goods to Jacobs & Turner without requiring surrender of the original bills of lading. This request or instruction was not noted on the bills of lading because Shineworld had already transferred them to BII.

As a result of the communication from Shineworld, U-States (by its agent, Primaline) released the goods to Jacobs & Turner on July 15, 1997 without the surrender of the original bills of lading. There is no indication that Jacobs & Turner had waived the claimed discrepancies under the letter of credit or had paid for the goods.

U-States had no knowledge that Shineworld had assigned the original bills of lading to BII at the time U-States released the goods to Jacobs & Turner. BII did not know of Shineworld's letter instructing U-States to release the goods to Jacob & Turner until September 1997, after the goods had been released, and had not authorized the release of the goods.

BII could not recover from Shineworld because Shineworld had no ascertainable assets. BII claimed against Jacobs & Turner, which party asserted that the goods were defective, although there was a certificate from the inspector of the goods at the place of delivery that the goods were not defective. BII and Jacobs & Turner agreed that, as a settlement between them, Jacobs & Turner would pay to BII 65 percent of the goods' total agreed price, and that amount was paid.

After BII was told by U-States that Primaline had no authority to issue bills of lading as U-States' agent, BII brought an action in Hong Kong against Primaline. That action was dismissed based on evidence produced by Primaline that indicated that Primaline acted as agent for U-States. BII then sought the unpaid amount of the original contract price from U States in this case.

Alleging causes of action for breach of contract and conversion, BII asserted that U-States' delivery of the goods to Jacobs & Turner without the surrender of the original bills of lading was a misdelivery for which U-States is liable in damages to BII. BII relied on the bills of lading that were consigned "TO ORDER" and on what it deemed to be the applicable law. U-States contended that the bills of lading should be read to have permitted the delivery it made. U-States also argued that the payment from Jacobs & Turner constituted an accord and satisfaction, in effect, releasing U-States from any liability.

The trial court found that Primaline acted as agent for defendant U-States (U-States concedes this on appeal), that Primaline—and therefore U-States—misdelivered the goods, that BII made proper efforts to mitigate its damages, and that therefore the unpaid portion of the obligation was not extinguished. The trial court rendered a judgment in favor of the plaintiff for the unpaid amount, plus costs and attorneys' fees.

U-States appeals from the judgment.

DISCUSSION

On appeal, U-States argues that it is not liable to BII for delivering the goods to Jacobs & Turner without requiring surrender of the original bills of lading because the bills of lading should be interpreted to give U-States the option to require or not require such surrender without liability to the holder of the original bills of lading. U-States also argues that BII's acceptance from Jacobs & Turner of 65 percent of the agreed price of the goods constituted an accord and satisfaction and extinguished any obligation for the unpaid portion of the agreed price. . . .

The trial court's decision that there was a misdelivery for which U-States is liable is not dependent on conflicting evidence. Therefore, we review that legal determination independently. We review the trial court's decision that there was no accord and satisfaction on the basis of whether there was substantial evidence to support that conclusion.

THE TRANSACTION

Bills of lading have long been used in international sales transactions as one means to protect the interests of sellers, who want assurance of being paid for goods shipped by a carrier, and buyers, who do not want to pay for goods until they arrive. They also are used as a means to facilitate credit arrangements and to reflect title in goods being shipped by a carrier. (See Gilmore & Black, The Law of Admiralty (2d ed. 1975) §§3-1, 3-4.)

The bill of lading constitutes a receipt for the goods shipped, a contract for their carriage, and a document of title. (Pioneer Fruit Co. v. Southern Pac. Co. (1920) 47 Cal. App. 44, 46, 190 P. 50; Internatio, Inc. v. M/V Yinka Folawiyo (E.D. Pa. 1979) 480 F. Supp. 1245, 1251; see also Dolan, The Law of Letters of Credit (rev. ed. 1999) ¶1.07[1][c]; Colinvaux, Carver's Carriage by Sea (13th ed. 1982) ¶¶1596, 1623-

1624; Gilmore & Black, supra, at §3-1.) It describes the goods shipped, identifies the shipper (or consignor) and the buyer (consignee) and directs the carrier to deliver the goods to a specified location or person. As a contract of carriage drafted by the carrier, a bill of lading is strictly construed against the carrier. (See C-ART, Ltd. v. Hong Kong Islands Line America, S.A. (9th Cir. 1991) 940 F.2d 530, 532, and cases cited therein.)

A negotiable bill of lading, in effect, requires delivery to the bearer of the bill or, if to the order of a named person, to that person. (A person includes an individual or an organization. Cal. U. Com. Code, §1201, subd. (30).) A nonnegotiable bill of lading is one in which the consignee is specified. (See 3 White & Summers, Uniform Commercial Code (4th ed. 1995) §29-4, p.354; Met-Al Inc. v. Hansen Storage Co. (E.D. Wis. 1993) 828 F. Supp. 1369, 1375; see also, 2 Schoenbaum, Admiralty and Maritime Law (3d ed. 2001) §10-11, at p.62.) If the bill of lading is negotiable, the holder of the original bill can negotiate it by indorsing and delivering it to another or, when it is indorsed in blank or to bearer, by delivery alone. (Cal. U. Com. Code, §7501; Colinvaux, supra, at ¶90.) An indorsee is the holder and, in effect, holds title to the goods covered by the bill. (Cal. U. Com. Code, §7502, subd. (b); *Colinvaux*, supra, at ¶1597.)

In a typical international transaction, once the buyer and seller have agreed on terms, the buyer (in this case, Jacobs & Turner) obtains a letter of credit with its bank (here, Clydesdale Bank in Scotland) in favor of the seller (here, Shineworld). The seller (generally referred to as the shipper) delivers the goods to a carrier (here, U-States through its agent Primaline). The carrier issues a bill of lading, usually in duplicate sets, and gives the original bill of lading to the shipper. (See Dolan, supra, at ¶¶1.01[2]-1.01[3].)

The shipper issues a draft or other document directing the buyer to pay the purchase price to the shipper or the shipper's nominee. The shipper or its nominee then presents the draft and the bill of lading (made to the order of or indorsed to the buyer) to the buyer's bank for payment. (Id.; see also Gilmore & Black, supra, at §3-9.)

The buyer's bank compares the draft and bill of lading against the letter of credit to ensure there are no discrepancies between them. If none is found, the bank pays the shipper or its nominee and forwards the original bill of lading to the buyer, who presents it to the carrier to obtain delivery of the goods. If the bank finds discrepancies between the letter of credit and the shipper's documents, as it did here, the bank notifies the shipper, who may ask the buyer to waive the discrepancies. If the buyer agrees to such a waiver, the bank pays the shipper and forwards the bill of lading to the buyer, who presents it to the carrier for delivery of the goods. If there is no waiver, the original bill of lading is returned to the shipper and the transaction is cancelled. (Dolan, supra, at ¶¶1.07[1][c]; 6.06[2].)

The transaction at issue in this case essentially was initiated as we describe, in that Jacobs & Turner obtained a letter of credit to purchase goods from Shineworld, Shineworld delivered the goods to U-States' agent for shipment to Jacobs & Turner, and U-States (through its agent, Primaline) issued bills of lading and gave them to Shineworld. Shineworld then indorsed the bills of lading to BII in exchange for a loan by BII to Shineworld in the amount that was covered by the amount owed by the buyer, Jacobs & Turner. Therefore, BII, rather than Shineworld, presented the original bills of lading to Clydesdale Bank for payment. When the bank found discrepancies that Jacobs & Turner did not waive, the bank returned the original bills of lading to BII.

LAW APPLICABLE TO BILLS OF LADING

With regard to issues concerning the bills of lading at issue in this case, we apply (as do the parties) California law, in accordance with the terms of the bills of lading that were issued by U-States, a California corporation. (See Cal. U. Com. Code, §1105, subd. (1).) The bills of lading also incorporate by reference the Carriage of Goods by Sea Act (COGSA), Title 46 United States Code section 1300 et seq., and the International Convention for the Unification of Certain Rules of Law Relating to Bills of Lading signed at Brussels, August 25, 1924 as amended by the "protocol" signed at Brussels February 23, 1968 (Visby Rules or Hague-Visby Rules).

Although the Federal Bills of Lading Act (49 U.S.C. §§80101-80116), when applicable, preempts much of the application of Division 7 of the California Uniform Commercial Code (U.S. Const., art. VI, cl. 2; Cal. U. Com. Code §7103), the act applies only to interstate and foreign commerce in which the goods travel through one of the states of the United States. (49 U.S.C. §80102; see also National Union Fire Ins. Co. v. Allite, Inc. (2000) 430 Mass. 828, 831-833, 724 N.E.2d 677, 679-681, citing 3 White & Summers, supra, §29-2, at p.324.) Because the goods in this case did not travel through the United States, the Federal Bills of Lading Act does not supersede California law here.

NEGOTIABILITY OF THE DOCUMENTS

California Uniform Commercial Code section 7104 governs whether a document of title, such as a bill of lading, is negotiable or nonnegotiable. Under subdivision (1), a bill of lading is negotiable:

"(a) If by its terms the goods are to be delivered to the bearer or to the order of a named person; or (b) Where recognized in overseas trade, if it runs to a named person or assigns." (Cal. U. Com. Code, §7104, subd. (1).) Subdivision (2) provides that "[a]ny other document is nonnegotiable." (Cal. U. Com. Code, §7104, subd. (2).) Subdivision (3), however, provides that a nonnegotiable bill of lading "must be conspicuously (Section 1201) marked 'nonnegotiable'," and if it is not so marked, "a holder of the document who purchased it for value supposing it to be negotiable may, at his option, treat such document as imposing upon the bailee the same liabilities he would have incurred had the document been negotiable." (Cal. U. Com. Code, §7104, subd. (3).)

The bills of lading in this case were consigned "TO ORDER." They were not to the order of any specific person or entity; nor did they specifically provide for delivery of the goods to the bearer. Therefore, the bills of lading do not appear to fall within the scope of subdivision (1) as negotiable.

BII argues, however, that the "TO ORDER" bills of lading are negotiable because they may be interpreted as consigned to bearer, citing to California Uniform Commercial Code section 3109, subd. (a). That section, which provides that a "promise or order is payable to bearer if it . . . [d]oes not state a payee," does not apply here.

Section 3109 is found in Division 3 of the California Uniform Commercial Code, which division governs specified commercial paper, rather than in Division 7, which division governs documents of title such as bills of lading. The treatment of commercial paper in Division 3 of the California Uniform Commercial Code does not override Division 7's treatment of documents of title such as the bills of lading in this case. (See Cal. U. Com. Code, com. 2 to §3102.)

Authorities in other jurisdictions suggest that there should be a broad interpretation of negotiability and that documents of title need not contain the exact words specified in Uniform Commercial Code section 7-104 for negotiability. (See Bank of New York v. Amoco Oil Company, (S.D.N.Y. 1993) 831 F. Supp. 254, *affd.* (2d Cir. 1994) 35 F.3d 643; In re George B. Kerr, Inc. (Bankr. D.S.C. 1981) 25 B.R. 2, *affd.* (4th Cir. 1982) 696 F.2d 990.) These authorities are distinguishable because they dealt with situations in which the word "Order" was not used or not used precisely. None of those authorities involved a non-bearer instrument that did not specify the person to whom the "Order" was made.

In one authority, Hawkland, Uniform Commercial Code Series, section 7-104:01, article 7, page 27, it is stated, "subsection 7-104(1) specifies words of negotiability that must be included in the terms of a document of title in order to make the document negotiable. Consequently, a document of title that fails to include words of negotiability in its terms is nonnegotiable." The statutory words of negotiability include that the order be to a "named person."

Despite the specific words of negotiability required by subdivision (1), BII asserts the bills of lading were negotiable because U-States' president testified that a person in possession of an original bill of lading is entitled to possession of the goods it covers. Although it does not appear that the intent of a party bears on negotiability under subdivision (1) (see, e.g., Bank of New York v. Amoco Oil Company, supra, 831 F. Supp. at 264), the parties' intent is relevant under subdivision (3) to the treatment as negotiable of a nonnegotiable bill of lading that is not conspicuously marked "nonnegotiable."

Subdivision (3) is a California addition to the Uniform Commercial Code. (See Cal. U. Com. Code, com. to §7104; Hawkland, Uniform Commercial Code Series, supra, §7-104, Art. 7 page 26.) As noted above, that section provides that, if a nonnegotiable bill of lading is not conspicuously marked "nonnegotiable," a holder who purchased the bill of lading for value "supposing it to be negotiable" may treat the bill of lading as imposing upon the bailee (in this case, U-States) the same liabilities it would have incurred had the document been negotiable. (Cal. U. Com. Code, §7104, subd. (3).) Therefore, even if the bills of lading in this case were not negotiable under subdivision (1), they may be treated as negotiable if BII purchased them for value supposing them to be negotiable, because the bills of lading were not marked "nonnegotiable."

U-States asserts that BII did not purchase the bills of lading for value because it says that the transaction was a "post-shipment financing." Yet, BII advanced monies to the shipper, Shineworld, against the shipping documents, thereby, in effect, purchasing the bills of lading for value. The evidence is that the parties considered the bills of lading to be negotiable, and BII has elected to treat the bills of lading as negotiable. Accordingly, under section 7104, subdivision (3), if the bills of lading are not actually negotiable, U-States has the same liabilities by virtue of the documents it would have incurred had the bills of lading been negotiable.

IMPROPER DELIVERY OF GOODS

The parties do not dispute that U-States delivered the goods to someone who did not surrender the original bills of lading. U States argues that it cannot be held liable for improper delivery based upon its failure to require surrender of the bills of lading because there is no express term requiring surrender as a pre-condition to delivery.

The absence of an express term requiring surrender of the original bill of lading does not absolve U-States of liability. That a bill of lading is negotiable means that under the law, with some exceptions not relevant here, its surrender is required in exchange for the goods covered and shipped by that bill of lading. (See Cal. U. Com. Code, §7403, subd. (3); Cal. U. Com. Code, com. to §7403 ["1. The general and primary purpose of this revision is to simplify the statement of the bailee's obligation on the document. . . . [¶] 5. Subsection (3) states the obvious duty of a bailee to take up a negotiable document . . . and the result of failure in that duty."]; see also Pere Marquette Ry. Co. v. J.F. French & Co. (1921) 254 U.S. 538, 546, 41 S. Ct. 195, 65 L. Ed. 391; Cal. U. Com. Code, §7303; Riegert & Braucher, Documents of Title (3d ed. 1978) §2.4, at p.30 [explaining that when a document is negotiable, "the bailee is under a duty not to deliver the goods without surrender of the document"].) Indeed, the duty of the carrier to "take up" the original negotiable bill of lading in exchange for delivery of the goods it covers is necessary to fulfill the purpose of a bill of lading that is negotiable. (See, e.g., Schaefer, Inc. v. Minneapolis, N. & S. Ry. Co. (1959) 254 Minn. 248, 255 [94 N.W.2d 551, 557].)

U-States contends that the requirement of surrender of the original bills of lading should not be applied in this case because the bills of lading include a provision that states: "If required by the Carrier [U-States] one (1) original Bill of Lading must be surrendered duly endorsed in exchange for the Goods or delivery order." U-States contends this provision gives it the option to require or not require surrender of the original bill of lading as a condition of delivery.

That provision did not eliminate U-States' duty to ensure delivery of the goods to the proper party, i.e., the holder of the original bill of lading or someone to whom the holder directs delivery. The provision simply made clear that U-States may require surrender of the original bill of lading, which requirement allows U-States to protect itself from liability by ensuring that the party to whom it delivers the goods is entitled to them. Because of this provision, U-States did not have to comply with Shineworld's request to deliver the goods to Jacob & Turner without surrender of the original bills of lading. The clause did not absolve U-States of liability for misdelivery to a party not entitled to the goods.

Delivery to a person who is not the holder, without the holder's authorization, constitutes a conversion of the goods and a breach of contract. (Pere Marquette Ry. Co. v. J.F. French & Co., supra, 254 U.S.

at p.546, 41 S. Ct. 195 ["Where the failure to require the presentation and surrender of the bill is the cause of the shipper losing his goods, a delivery without requiring it constitutes a conversion"], and cases cited therein; see also Allied Chemical Internat. Corp. v. Companhia de Navegacao Lloyd Brasileiro (2d Cir. 1985) 775 F.2d 476, 484-485 [carrier that delivered goods to consignee without requiring surrender of bill of lading liable for breach of contract where consignee did not hold bill of lading because it had not yet paid for goods]; Colinvaux, supra, at ¶1593 ["Delivery to a person not entitled to the goods without production of the bill of lading is prima facie a conversion of the goods and a breach of contract [fns. omitted]"].)

U-States relies on Chilewich Partners v. M.V. Alligator Fortune (S.D.N.Y. 1994) 853 F. Supp. 744, in arguing that liability cannot be imposed for misdelivery when the carrier delivers goods at the direction of the shipper without requiring surrender of the original bill of lading. In *Chilewich*, the United States District Court found that the defendant carriers in that case were not liable to the plaintiff shipper when they delivered goods covered by bills of lading to bonded warehouses located at the buyer's factory, without requiring surrender of the original bills of lading. *Chilewich* is distinguishable.

The transaction in *Chilewich* was a type of transaction commonly used in the Korean hide trade, in which the shipper, carrier, and buyer agree in advance that the goods will be delivered to a government-controlled warehouse before payment is made and the original bill of lading surrendered. (Chilewich Partners v. M.V. Alligator Fortune, supra, 853 F. Supp. at pp.748-749, 752-753.) In contrast, in the transaction here, there was no agreement that the goods would be delivered to anyone before payment was made and the bills of lading surrendered. Moreover, unlike the circumstances in *Chilewich*, in which the agreement not to require surrender of the bills of lading was made by the shipper at a time when it was in effect the holder of the bill of lading (id. at pp.749, 752-753, 755), here Shineworld's instruction to deliver without requiring surrender of the bills of lading was made when it no longer was the holder of the bills of lading.

Although a carrier may choose to follow a shipper's instruction to deliver goods covered by a negotiable bill of lading or its equivalent without requiring surrender of the original bill, the carrier does so at its own peril because (as happened in this case) the shipper may have negotiated the bill before giving that instruction. If the carrier delivers to a party not entitled to possession of the goods, that carrier is liable to the holder of the original bill of lading. (See C-ART, Ltd. v. Hong Kong Islands Line America, S.A., supra, 940 F.2d 530; Allied Chemical

Internat. Corp. v. Companhia de Navegacao Lloyd Brasileiro, supra, 775 F.2d 476.)

U-States chose to comply with Shineworld's instruction without determining whether Shineworld was the proper holder of the bills of lading and whether Jacobs & Turner was the party with the right of possession of the goods. Thus, U-States, without requiring the original bills of lading, assumed the risk that neither party had the right to possession and that it would be liable to the holder of the bills of lading by due negotiation. The trial court correctly determined that because BII was the holder of the bills of lading by due negotiation, U States' misdelivery of the goods to Jacobs & Turner renders U States liable to BII.

NO ACCORD AND SATISFACTION

U-States argued at trial that it is not liable to BII for any amount because BII's acceptance of partial payment from Jacobs & Turner constituted an accord and satisfaction. The trial court did not find that there had been an accord and satisfaction, but rather found that the agreement for partial payment by Jacobs & Turner to BII constituted an effort by BII to mitigate its damages. U-States challenges that finding on appeal.

Although U-States did not comply with the requirement that accord and satisfaction be pleaded as an affirmative defense (in fact, U-States first raised this defense in its written closing argument filed several weeks after close of evidence), there is an exception to that requirement. That exception, which is applicable here, allows the defendant to rely on plaintiff's evidence of payment to attempt to establish an accord and satisfaction. (Riskas v. De La Montanya (1956) 145 Cal. App. 2d 636, 639-640, 302 P.2d 821.)

Both U-States and BII rely upon California law in connection with their positions on the issue of an accord and satisfaction. The agreement that U-States contends is an accord and satisfaction was between Jacobs & Turner (in Scotland) and BII (in Hong Kong) involving acts that took place in the United Kingdom—either Southampton or Glasgow. U-States, which seeks to take advantage of the transaction, is a California corporation, and the bills of ladings that are the subject of the dispute contain California choice-of-law provisions. As both parties have asserted that California law should apply because of the choice-of-law clause in the bills of lading, and as there is no indication that the laws of the other jurisdictions are not consistent with California law, we apply California law.

"The question whether an agreement amounts to an accord and satisfaction is one of the intention of the parties and is therefore a question of fact." (Conderback, Inc. v. Standard Oil Co. (1966) 239 Cal. App. 2d 664, 680, 48 Cal. Rptr. 901.) The party asserting this defense bears the burden of establishing the accord and satisfaction. (Rabinowitz v. Kandel (1969) 1 Cal. App. 3d 961, 965, 81 Cal. Rptr. 897.)

A defendant asserting the defense of accord and satisfaction must establish "(1) that there was a 'bona fide dispute' between the parties, (2) that the debtor made it clear that acceptance of what he tendered was subject to the condition that it was to be in full satisfaction of the creditor's unliquidated claim, and (3) that the creditor clearly understood when accepting what was tendered that the debtor intended such remittance to constitute payment in full of the particular claim in issue." (Thompson v. Williams (1989) 211 Cal. App. 3d 566, 571, 259 Cal. Rptr. 518.) U-States failed to present evidence of the terms of the agreement between BII and Jacobs & Turner and therefore did not establish the parties' intent that Jacobs & Turner's payment was to be in full satisfaction of BII's claim under the bills of lading.

There is evidence BII intended that its acceptance of monies was only to mitigate its damages. BII's managing director and chief executive officer testified that when BII accepted the partial payment from Jacobs & Turner, it retained the original bills of lading. BII then sought the remainder of the amount owed under the bills of lading from Primaline and U-States.

Civil Code section 1474 ("performance of an obligation, by one of several persons who are jointly liable under it, extinguishes the liability of all"), is not applicable because there is no showing that Jacobs & Turner performed the entire obligation, which performance is required by that provision to eliminate the whole liability. (See Giordano v. American Fidelity & Cas. Co. (1950) 97 Cal. App. 2d 309, 313, 217 P.2d 444.)

There was substantial evidence to support the trial court's determination that Jacobs & Turner's partial payment did not extinguish BII's claim against U-States.

DISPOSITION

The judgment is affirmed. Costs on appeal are awarded to BII.

C. Form

1. Negotiable

The word *consign* means to send or hand over goods to another. A negotiable bill of lading is called an order bill of lading because the goods are consigned to the "order of _____." In bill of lading terminology, the goods are entrusted to the carrier by the *consignor* (the shipper) for delivery to the *consignee* (the person to whom the goods will belong at the end of their journey, normally the buyer). The consignee is *not* the carrier-bailee. If Sam Seller in Toledo sells goods to Betty Buyer in Atlanta via the Monopoly Railroad, using a negotiable bill of lading issued by the railroad, then Sam is the consignor, Betty is the consignee, and the Monopoly Railroad is the carrier-issuer (the agent of the consignor who carries out the consignment contract). Order (negotiable) bills of lading are yellow in color, as required by Interstate Commerce Commission (ICC) regulations.

An order bill states that the goods have been received in apparent good order, except as otherwise indicated, and states the contract of transportation (including rates), incorporating all the fine print on the back of the contract. On the front is space for describing the goods covered by the document and blanks to be filled in showing, among other things,

1.   shipper's (consignor's) name and address,
2.   to whose order the goods are consigned,
3.   the destination of the goods, and
4.   whom the carrier is to notify when the goods arrive (normally the buyer).

A negotiable bill also contains sentences like this one in large print on the front: "Surrender of this original order bill of lading properly indorsed is required prior to the delivery of the property. Inspection of such property will not be permitted by anyone prior to delivery unless permission is indorsed hereon or given in writing by the consignor." (As to inspection rights, see note §2-513(3), which agrees with this language.)

2. Non-Negotiable

A non-negotiable bill of lading is called a *straight* bill of lading because the goods are delivered straight to the consignee whether or not the non-negotiable bill is surrendered. Straight bills are to be printed on white paper by ICC regulation. The carrier will take the goods to their destination, notify the consignee of their arrival, and await instructions as to whom the goods are to be delivered.

Frequently the consignor consigns the goods to *itself,* thereby making the consignor and the consignee the same entity. This happens on negotiable as well as non-negotiable bills. The reason that this is often done is to make it clear that the consignor is at all times the owner of the goods, and for that reason it is called a "shipment under reservation" (meaning a reservation of *title*). When the buyer pays for them, the seller will indorse a negotiable bill over to the buyer or, if a non-negotiable bill is used, will issue a *delivery order* (the same as with warehouse receipts) to the carrier telling it to deliver the goods to the buyer. In effect, consigning the goods to itself gives the seller a security interest in the goods until the purchase price is paid. The Code recognizes that the *equitable* interest is in the buyer even though the legal title is in the seller. Read §2-505 carefully.

PROBLEM 241

Homer Widget, of South Bend, Indiana, the inventor of the three-dimensional widget, contracted to sell 5,000 widgets to Ned's Novelty Store in Evansville, Indiana. Homer delivered the goods to the Overnight Trucking Company, consigning the goods to himself but writing "Notify Ned's Novelty Store on arrival" on the straight bill of lading. (The carrier keeps a duplicate copy of the bill of lading with the goods; the original is, of course, turned over to the consignor.) Homer mailed the original bill to his cousin Wilbur Widget, who lived in Evansville. Along with the bill he sent a delivery order signed by himself and addressed to the trucking company telling the company to deliver the goods to Ned's Novelty Store. Homer's cover letter to his cousin stated that Wilbur should take the delivery order down to Ned at the store and turn it over to Ned only if Ned paid Wilbur cash for the goods. Wilbur did present the delivery order as Homer directed, but Ned was short on funds and could not pay. Wilbur, confused, mailed all the documents back to Homer with a letter saying Ned would not pay. Meanwhile, the goods arrived at Evansville, and John ("Slow") Burly, the company's truck driver, had to decide what to do with the widgets. Reading the bill of lading, he discovered that the consignee lived in South Bend. By checking the phone book, he learned that Homer Widget had no address in Evansville. Then the truck driver noticed that he was to notify Ned's Novelty Store, which did have an Evansville address, so he delivered the widgets to Ned.

(a) Was the carrier's delivery to Ned improper? Read §7-303 carefully and §7-501(6); see Mistletoe Express Serv. v. Sanchez, 721 S.W.2d 418, 2 U.C.C. Rep. Serv. 2d 1648 (Tex. App. 1986).

(b) If the widgets were destroyed in an auto accident prior to Ned's refusal to pay, who would have had the risk of loss if the contract was "F.O.B. truck South Bend"? See §2-509(1). See also Sternheim v. Silver Bell of Roslyn, Inc., 66 Misc. 726, 321 N.Y.S.2d 965, 9 U.C.C. Rep. Serv. 465 (Cty. Ct. 1971). As to the carrier's duty of care, read §7-309(1).

(c) Would the result with regard to the risk of loss or proper delivery change if the bill of lading had been an order bill? See §§7-403(3), 2-509.

PROBLEM 242

Blue Skies Air Lines was about to deliver a shipment of frozen fish to the buyer to whom it was consigned under a straight airbill (§1-201(6)) when the phone rang. The seller-consignor was on the phone, and she forbade the delivery, telling Blue Skies to return the fish to her, since she had learned that the "buyer is a bum." If Blue Skies returns the goods to the seller, is it risking liability to the buyer? See §§7-303, 2-505, 2-705 (plus Official Comment 1 to §2-705); Clock v. Missouri-Texas R.R., 407 F. Supp. 448, 19 U.C.C. Rep. Serv. 224 (E.D. Mo. 1976).

PROBLEM 243

Jane Pitchfork, a southern Iowa farmer, had an excellent pumpkin crop (1,700 pumpkins) this year. She stored 1,000 pumpkins with the Pumpkin Warehouse, Inc., located in Des Moines, taking a negotiable warehouse receipt for 500 and a non-negotiable receipt for the other 500. She also contracted to sell 700 other pumpkins to Peter P. Pumpkineater, who lived in Sioux City, Iowa. The terms of the contract required her to ship Pumpkineater 700 stemless pumpkins "F.O.B. railroad car Fort Madison, Iowa." Jane was too lazy to cut off the stems, but she thought Pumpkineater really would not care, so she loaded 700 pumpkins on board an Iowa Pacific Railroad car at Fort Madison, Iowa. She received a negotiable bill of lading consigned to her own order and made a proper contract for carriage of the pumpkins to Sioux City. She sold the 1,000 warehouse pumpkins to Mom's Pies, Inc., of Cedar Rapids. She indorsed the negotiable warehouse receipt over to Mom's Pies for the first 500 stored pumpkins and gave them a non-negotiable delivery order for the other 500 stored pumpkins.

Before Mom's Pies could contact the warehouse, the Iowa Pacific Railroad train carrying the pumpkins passed through Des Moines and derailed (due to the negligence of the train's engineer). The train ran off the track and went through the center of the Pumpkin Warehouse, destroying all 1,700 pumpkins. Jane Pitchfork, a dejected woman, comes to you. The railroad is, of course, going to be liable to whoever took the risk of loss as to the pumpkins. Advise Jane as to where the risk of loss is placed for each of the pumpkin transactions. See §§2-503, 2-509, 2-510, 2-601, 2-319.

D. Misdescription

Consider this problem. The bill of lading states that the boxcar contains 42 cartons of widgets. When the goods are delivered to buyer, there are only 32 cartons, or the cartons contain peanuts, or the boxcar (which was loaded and sealed by the shipper) is empty. Is the carrier liable for wrong information (misdescription) on the bill of lading if the shipper furnished the carrier with the information? The problem frequently comes up because carriers (particularly railroads) often permit the shipper to load the goods itself and then to fill out the descriptive section of the bill of lading, which the carrier then signs. Carriers defend this practice by saying that as a practical matter it is impossible for the carrier's agents to police the shipper's loading or to inventory the goods loaded. To guard against possible liability for resulting misdescription, the carrier normally states SHIPPER'S WEIGHT, LOAD, AND COUNT on the bill of lading in order to indicate that the carrier makes no warranties as to these matters. Is this language effective to eliminate the carrier's liability for misdescription? Study §7-301.

The corresponding federal law is the Federal Bills of Lading Act §22, which follows. This section has been much litigated:

> If a bill of lading has been issued by a carrier or on his behalf by an agent or employee the scope of whose actual or apparent authority includes the receiving of goods and issuing bills of lading therefor for transportation in commerce among several States and with foreign nations, the carrier shall be liable to (a) the owner of goods covered by a straight bill subject to existing right of stoppage in transit or (b) the holder of an order bill, who has given value in good faith relying upon the description therein of the goods, or upon the shipment being made upon the date therein shown, for damages caused by the nonreceipt by

the carrier of all or part of the goods upon or prior to the date therein shown, or their failure to correspond with the description thereof in the bill at the time of its issue.

GAC Commercial Corp. v. Wilson

United States District Court, Southern District of New York, 1967
271 F. Supp. 242, 4 U.C.C. Rep. Serv. 772

BRYAN, J. [The St. Lawrence Pulp & Paper Corp. borrowed money from plaintiff G.A.C., which took as collateral straight bills of lading, both interstate and intrastate, issued by defendant Norwood & St. Law. Railroad. The bills of lading indicated that St. Lawrence, as consignor, had shipped various amounts of paper products to different consignees and the plaintiff took the bills with the understanding that the goods had not yet been delivered. Plaintiff loaned St. Lawrence $254,173.42 against the bills of lading, but St. Lawrence went bankrupt anyway. To the great surprise of everyone but some of St. Lawrence's employees, the railroad cars proved to be empty. Plaintiff brought this action against St. Lawrence's officers and the Norwood Railroad.]

The method by which the alleged fraudulent scheme was carried out appears for purposes of this motion to be as follows: the bankrupt St. Lawrence, as part of its facilities in Norfolk, New York, maintained a railroad siding connected with the lines of defendant carrier which had a freight office approximately 1/8th of a mile from the siding. St. Lawrence was permitted to load freight at its spur track in preparation for shipments on defendant's line. The railroad cars were sealed by St. Lawrence with seals provided by the railroad. St. Lawrence also prepared the bills of lading on blanks furnished in quadruplicate by defendant Norwood. The bills thus prepared were then presented to Norwood's agent who signed the original and one copy without inspecting the contents of the cars. No notation such as "contents of packages unknown" or "shipper's weight, load and count" was written on the bills. The signed copies were returned to St. Lawrence and forwarded with the invoices to G.A.C. which made advances on the goods described, which, as it turned out, had not been shipped.

Since sixty of the bills of lading were issued by a common carrier for the transportation of goods in interstate commerce, the issues as to these bills are controlled by the provisions of the Federal Bills of Lading Act, 49 U.S.C. §81. This statute stands as "a clear expression of the determination of Congress to take the whole subject matter of such bills of lading within its control." . . .

Prior to the passage of the Federal Bills of Lading Act "the United States courts held that a carrier was not liable for the act of its agent in issuing a bill of lading for goods where no goods had in fact been received." Josephy v. Panhandle & S.F. Ry., 235 N.Y. 306, 310, 139 N.E. 277, 278 (1923); see, e.g., Clark v. Clyde S.S. Co., 148 F. 243 (S.D.N.Y. 1906). The liability of carriers for acts of their agents was expanded, but not drastically, by the passage of the federal legislation which draws a sharp distinction between order bills of lading and straight bills where in fact the goods are never received for shipment by the carrier. Under §22 of the Act, 49 U.S.C. §102, "[i]f a bill of lading has been issued by a carrier or on his behalf by an agent or employee . . . , the carrier shall be liable to . . . the holder of an order bill, who has given value in good faith, relying upon the description therein of the goods, . . . for damages caused by the nonreceipt by the carrier of all or part of the goods upon or prior to the date therein shown." However, the liability of the carrier for nonreceipt extends only to "the owner of goods covered by a straight bill," provided, of course, he also gives value in good faith in reliance upon the description of goods contained in the bill. See Strohmeyer & Arpe Co. v. American Line S.S. Corp., 97 F.2d 360, 362 (2d Cir. 1938).

It is clear that a party in the position of Norwood is not included within the narrow category of those liable on a straight bill under the federal legislation. In the first place there is no question that the straight bills of lading here involved are non-negotiable. [Citations omitted.] As a consequence plaintiff G.A.C., as apparent transferee of bills and invoices representing accounts receivable under the agreement with St. Lawrence, upon notification to the carrier of the transfer, could only "become the direct obligee of whatever obligations the carrier owed to the transferor of the bill immediately before the notification." 49 U.S.C. §112; see id. §109. Norwood obviously owed St. Lawrence nothing because no goods in fact were received. There was therefore no outstanding obligation to G.A.C. . . .

By no stretch of the imagination does G.A.C. qualify as an "owner of goods covered by a straight bill" who can sue the carrier under §22 of the Federal Bills of Lading Act, 39 U.S.C. §102, for representing that goods in fact had been received. The reason for this is that it is completely illusory to attempt to assign an "owner" to non-existent goods. R. Braucher, Documents of Title 23 (1958); 2 S. Williston, Sales §419a, at 576-77 (rev. ed. 1948). While the consignee is generally deemed to have title to goods shipped under a straight bill of lading, see George F. Hinrichs, Inc. v. Standard Trust & Sav. Bank, 279 F. 382, 386 (2d Cir. 1922), even he cannot sue the carrier for representing in a straight bill

that non-existent goods had in fact been received. Martin Jessee
Motors v. Reading Co., 87 F. Supp. 318 (E.D. Pa.), *aff'd,* 181 F.2d 766
(3d Cir. 1950). The rationale applied in *Martin Jessee Motors*—that the
consignee can prevail against the carrier "only by proving its title to
specific property," 181 F.2d at 767—applies a fortiori to bar the claim
of G.A.C. Plaintiff's interest in the "aggregate face value of the accounts receivable pledged as security" under no conceivable reading of
the statute can be deemed an "[ownership] of goods covered by a
straight bill." G.A.C. is not one of the favored few who can recover
under the Federal Bills of Lading Act. . . .

Plaintiff G.A.C. fares no better with respect to the two bills of
lading representing intrastate shipments in New York. . . . Although the
awkward term "owner" in 49 U.S.C. §102 has been replaced by the
word "consignee" in the Uniform Commercial Code §7-301 . . . the
change is immaterial for purposes of this case. Plaintiff, perhaps an
assignee, transferee or pledgee of the non-negotiable bills, though it
claims not to be, is certainly not a "consignee," which is the only party
protected. 2 Anderson, Uniform Commercial Code 261 n.9 (1961); see
R. Braucher, Documents of Title 23-24 (1958). Contrast U.C.C. §7-203.
Thus, as with the sixty interstate bills, G.A.C. cannot successfully sue on
the two intrastate bills. . . .

It is true that the result dictated by the federal legislation may lead
to some inequities. A straight bill under the Federal Bills of Lading Act
is obviously not a good security risk. Casenote, 63 Harv. L. Rev. 1439,
1440 (1950). The fraud of the shipper by failing to deliver goods to the
carrier can result, as it did here, in misleading statements on the bills
of lading, which operate to the detriment of banks and other commercial financers making advances on the basis of the bills. See Oliver
Straw Goods Corp. v. Osaka Shosen Kaisha, 27 F.2d 129, 134 (2d Cir.
1928) (A. Hand, J.). Moreover, the carrier can readily prevent such a
situation from arising by inserting "in the bill of lading the words,
'Shipper's weight, load, and count,' or other words of like purport" to
"indicate that the goods were loaded by the shipper and the description of them made by him." 49 U.S.C. §101.

But the overriding policy considerations in the Act look the other
way on the issue of liability. First, "[t]here is nothing in the statute to
indicate that the mere omission of the words 'Shipper's weight, load,
and count' in and of itself makes the carrier liable for damages to
goods improperly loaded. The omission of the statutory words merely
serves to shift upon the carrier the burden of proving that the goods
were improperly loaded by the shipper, and that the damage ensued
from that cause." (D.N.J. 1951); see UCC §7-301(4). According to the

allegations the true culprits in this case were the shipper and its agents; there is no reason to saddle defendant Norwood with liability simply because it did not insert the "Shipper's weight, load, and count" language in the bills. In addition, practicality demands loading arrangements such as those here, where the shipper places his goods aboard and seals the railroad car which the carrier has provided. Section 21 of the Act, 4 U.S.C. §101, anticipates that shippers are expected to do much of the counting and loading on their own sidings or spur tracks. The rapid flow of commerce might well be hindered if the carrier in every instance were charged with ascertaining whether in fact there were goods behind every one of its straight bills.

Moreover, denying security value to a straight bill of lading does not work a hardship upon banks and other commercial institutions. G.A.C., as a knowledgeable lender, is fully aware of the risks inherent in straight bills, and could well have required order bills to protect itself. See Chicago & Northwestern Ry. v. Stevens Natl. Bank, 75 F.2d 398 (8th Cir. 1935). It nevertheless chose to rely upon straight bills to lend money to the now bankrupt St. Lawrence at a profitable rate of interest. Wiser now, G.A.C. seeks to shift its loss to Norwood, an undoubtedly solvent defendant. The Federal Bills of Lading Act protects against this type of hindsight by requiring the lender to accept this kind of security subject to the defenses between the carrier and the shipper.

The motion of defendant Norwood for Judgment on the pleadings treated as a motion for summary judgment is granted.

It is so ordered.

Read §7-301.

In the *GAC* case, which involves a straight bill of lading, §22 of the Federal Bills of Lading Act (FBLA) does not protect GAC because there are no goods, and hence there can be no owner. Professor Robert Riegert argues that the protection given owners of straight bills by the FBLA is thus illusory and that Congress did not intend the *GAC* result. See Riegert, Rights of a Transferee of Document of Title Who Is Not Holder by Due Negotiation, 9 Cumb. L. Rev. 27 (1978). The UCC in §7-301 gives protection on a straight bill to the consignee. Is the GAC court right in saying that plaintiff is not protected by §7-301? See §7-102(1)(b).

Both the FBLA and §7-301 protect holders by due negotiation of order bills. Both acts also allow the carrier to disclaim liability under certain circumstances. For a case involving an order bill where the disclaimer did not work, see Chicago & Nw. Ry. Co. v. Stephens Natl. Bank of Fremont, 75 F.2d 398 (8th Cir. 1935). Liability for non-receipt or misdescription under bills of lading, either negotiable or non-negotiable, is a tricky subject. See R. Riegert & R. Braucher, Documents of Title 33-41 (3d ed. 1978).

PROBLEM 244

Harry Thief went to the offices of Monopoly Railroad to see his old prison cellmate, Phillip ("Forger") Copy. Copy, under an assumed name, was currently employed by Monopoly as chief shipping clerk. Harry asked Phillip to make out some phony negotiable bills of lading representing non-existent shipments by Harry to a buyer in California. Harry wanted to sell the bills to a bank and split the money with Phillip. Phillip made out the bills, which Harry discounted at the Octopus National Bank, and the two of them left town. When the bank sued the railroad, the latter defended on the grounds that the phony bills contain the words "Shipper's weight, load, and count." Is this defense good? See §7-301 and its Official Comment 3; Gleason v. Seaboard Air Line Ry. Co., 278 U.S. 349 (1929); cf. Societe Generale v. Federal Ins. Co., 856 F.2d 461, 6 U.C.C. Rep. Serv. 2d 1236 (2d Cir. 1988).

III. DUE NEGOTIATION

A. The Basic Concept

The word *negotiable* in our law always means that if a piece of paper is in the proper form (a typical requirement is that it be made out either to *bearer* or to the *order* of a named individual), is transferred in the proper manner, and reaches the hands of a bona fide purchaser (BFP) who has no knowledge of problems with the paper, then the BFP may enforce the paper as written and does not take subject to the usual claims or defenses. In Article 3 of the Uniform Commercial Code, the BFP who gets these extraordinary rights is called a *holder in due course.* In Article 7 the BFP is given the jaw-breaking designation of a "holder to whom a negotiable document of title has been duly negotiated" (§7-502). Note well that the whole concept only applies to *negotiable* documents and hence excludes non-negotiable warehouse receipts and straight bills of lading. Holders of such documents get no special rights (§7-504).

Negotiation of a negotiable document of title (whether warehouse receipt, bill of lading, or delivery order) is accomplished by indorsement and delivery under rules that are virtually interchangeable with the rules for the negotiation of Article 3 drafts and notes: §§7-501(1), 7-501(2), 7-501(3). "Indorsement of a *non*-negotiable document neither makes it negotiable nor adds to the transferee's rights" (emphasis added); §7-501(5).

A person cannot become a §7-502 holder until the document has been *duly negotiated.* Due negotiation is a term of art. It is defined in §7-501(4), which should be read carefully at this point.

Cleveland v. McNabb

United States District Court,
Western District of Tennessee, 1970
312 F. Supp. 155, 7 U.C.C. Rep. Serv. 1226

BROWN, C.J. The plaintiffs here, Dr. W.B. Cleveland and his wife, Katherine Cleveland, are owners of lands situated in Fayette County, Tennessee. On January 17, 1967, these plaintiffs entered into a written lease with the defendant Jack McNabb which lease provided that, for a period of five years, the tenant McNabb would pay the landlord an annual rental amounting to fifty dollars per acre for all acreage allotted to cotton by the government and ten dollars per acre for all acreage actually planted in soybeans. (This lease is attached to the Amended and Supplemental Complaint as Exhibit A.) In this action the plaintiffs sue the defendant McNabb for rent allegedly due and owing from the 1968 crop year. Further, the plaintiffs sue the defendants TFC Marketing Service, Inc., John S. Wilder and W.W. Wilder, individually and as partners doing business as Longtown Supply Company, the Commodity Credit Corporation and the United States of America to enforce landlord's liens for the value of purchased crops to the extent that such liens are necessary to satisfy any unpaid rent. It is undisputed that each of this group of defendants received crops raised by the defendant McNabb on the plaintiffs' lands. (The United States is named as a defendant because the Commodity Credit Corporation is a branch of the United States Department of Agriculture. The named defendant Ralston Purina Company has by consent been dismissed.) . . .

As stated previously, the plaintiffs also seek in this action to enforce landlord's liens for the value of crops raised on their lands in 1968 to the extent that such liens are necessary to satisfy any unpaid rent. In this connection it is stipulated that the defendant Commodity Credit Corporation made a loan on and later acquired ownership of cotton grown on the plaintiffs' lands in 1968 and that this cotton had a value of $27,155.40. . . .

To support their contention that they are entitled to liens on all crops grown on their lands in 1968, the plaintiffs rely on the Tennessee Crop Liens Statute, T.C.A. §§64-1201 to 64-1214. In particular the plaintiffs rely on the following sections: [The court then quoted the statute which gives landlords a lien on all crops grown on their land to the amount of rent due, and further provides that the landlord can enforce this lien against a purchaser of the crop "with or without notice."].

It is next contended by the defendant United States that the plaintiffs are not entitled to a lien upon crops purchased by the Commodity Credit Corporation because the Commodity Credit Corporation was a good faith purchaser for value of negotiable warehouse receipts. As a result of such negotiation, the United States contends, the Commodity Credit Corporation acquired title to the crops in question free of the plaintiffs' crop lien.

Article Seven of the Uniform Commercial Code, as adopted in Tennessee, provides that, with limited exceptions, a holder to whom a negotiable document of title has been "duly negotiated" thereby acquires title to the goods described in such documents. §7-502. The term "duly negotiated" is defined in the preceding section, §7-501, as follows: [the court quoted §7-501(4)].

In addition, §1-201 provides in part:

> (25) A person has "notice" of a fact when . . . (c) from all the facts and circumstances known to him at the time in question he has reason to know that it exists.

The United States contends that the Commodity Credit Corporation received the warehouse receipts in question "duly negotiated." The plaintiffs, on the other hand, contend that the negotiation in question was not in the regular course of business and that the Commodity Credit Corporation, from all the facts and circumstances known to it, had reason to know of the plaintiffs' lien. Consequently it is the plaintiffs' position that the Commodity Credit Corporation did not acquire title, through due negotiation, to the crops it purchased.

The proof shows that the defendant McNabb delivered the cotton he had raised on the plaintiffs' lands and later sold to Commodity Credit Corporation to a cotton gin. After the cotton was ginned it was taken directly to a warehouse which issued a negotiable warehouse receipt for each bale of cotton it held. McNabb later received these receipts which were issued in his name as producer at the cotton gin and took them to the Agricultural Stabilization and Conservation Service office, which is the government office administrator of the cotton loan program in Somerville, Tennessee. McNabb left the warehouse receipts at this office and in return ultimately received a "loan." [Under the system, if the loan is not paid, the cotton becomes the property of the government.]

A clerk from the ASCS office, Mrs. Sally Pat McNeil, testified that she had made no inquiry as to where the defendant McNabb had grown his cotton. The loan papers executed by this clerk show in the space designated for information concerning liens that there was no lien on the cotton grown by McNabb. Mrs. McNeil testified that she obtained this information from McNabb himself. McNabb testified that a copy of his lease with the plaintiffs was on file in the ASCS office. Further, the proof shows that the warehouse receipts referred to cotton gin tickets which in turn indicate that the cotton delivered by McNabb was grown on the plaintiffs' lands.

On this record we find that the warehouse receipts were not "duly negotiated" to the Commodity Credit Corporation so as to cut off the plaintiffs' lien. First, as the plaintiffs point out, the Department of Agriculture's own regulations, specifically 7 C.F.R. 1427.1364, require that cotton going into the loan program be lien-free. This regulation, we think, indicates that some inquiry is to be made by the local ASCS office to determine if there is a lien on cotton which is to be put into the government loan program. McNabb, as a tenant farmer (albeit a large one) could not reasonably be expected to be fully familiar with the Tennessee Lien statutes and therefore limited inquiry from him alone, even if it might reasonably be assumed that he would give an honest answer, was not sufficient, especially since Mrs. McNeil only asked McNabb whether there was a lien on the cotton he had grown, and not whether his farm land was leased. Also, as indicated, the information that McNabb was a tenant farmer was readily available to the ASCS office. Either the government office disregarded the Tennessee Lien statute or was unfamiliar with it. At any rate, we think from all the facts and circumstances known to it, the Commodity Credit Corporation had reason to know of the plaintiffs' lien. Further, we do not believe that the existence of the above-mentioned custom and usage should lead us to the conclusion that the government through its representatives had no reason to know that the lien existed.

In *McNabb*, Commodity Credit Corp. was denied §7-502 holder status because it "had reason to know." Not all courts agree on the amount of knowledge of a claim or defense that is sufficient to deprive one of the §7-502 status. Compare R.E. Huntly Cotton Co. v. Fields, 551 S.W.2d 472, 21 U.C.C. Rep. Serv. 1157 (Tex. Civ. App. 1977) ("access to information sufficient to put [transferees] on notice of claims . . . is immaterial unless defendants had actual knowledge of facts and circumstances that would amount to bad faith").

Under §7-501, the negotiation must also be in the regular course of business or financing to be a due negotiation. Official Comment 1 to §7-501 provides in part:

> There are two aspects to the usual and normal course of mercantile dealings, namely, the person making the transfer and the nature of the transaction itself. The first question which arises is: Is the transferor a person with whom it is reasonable to deal as having full powers? In regard to documents of title the only holder whose possession appears, commercially, to be in order is almost invariably a person in the trade. No commercial purpose is served by allowing a tramp or a professor to "duly negotiate" an order bill of lading for hides or cotton not his own, and since such a transfer is obviously not in the regular course of business, it is excluded from the scope of the protection of subsection (4).
>
> The second question posed by the "regular course" qualification follows: Is the transaction one which is normally proper to pass full rights without inquiry, even though the transferor himself may not have such rights to pass and even though he may be acting in breach of duty? In raising this question the "regular course" criterion has the further advantage of limiting the effective wrongful disposition to transactions whose protection will really further trade. Obviously, the snapping up of goods for quick resale at a price suspiciously below the market deserves no protection as a matter of policy; it is also clearly outside the range of regular course.
>
> Any notice from the face of the document sufficient to put a merchant on inquiry as to the "regular course" quality of the transaction will frustrate a "due negotiation." Thus irregularity of the document on its face or unexplained staleness of a bill of lading may appropriately be recognized as negating a negotiation in "regular" course.

A §7-502 holder gets the rights listed in that section. The FBLA is similar. Read §7-502 carefully and do the next Problem.

PROBLEM 245

Wonder Warehouse issued a negotiable warehouse receipt to "bearer" which covered 40 drums of oil. The bailor was Bonanza Petroleum Company. The receipt was pledged by Bonanza to the Octopus National Bank as collateral for a $5,000 loan. While in the bank's possession, the receipt was stolen by the bank's credit manager, Claude McStuffy, who gave it to his cousin Al McStuffy, a disreputable oil products salesman. Al presented the receipt at the warehouse, and the new agent on duty delivered the drums to him. The agent, however, also stupidly returned the receipt to Al. Al sold the drums through his business. He then took the old warehouse receipt to the Antitrust National Bank, where he pledged it as collateral for a $5,000 loan. Al and Claude then skipped town. When both banks make demand on the warehouse for the goods, does the warehouse have any defenses? Remember §7-403? Consider it; then read §7-404.

B.   The Section 7-503(1) Owner

Go back to Article 2 (Sales), and read the *entrusting rule* found in §§2-403(2) and 2-403(3); see Simson v. Moon, 137 Ga. App. 82, 222 S.E.2d 873, 18 U.C.C. Rep. Serv. 1191 (1975); Annot., 59 A.L.R.4th 567. An understanding of what constitutes an entrusting is essential to understand the Problem and discussion that follow.

PROBLEM 246

Albert Collector took his favorite antique grandfather clock down to the Antique Clock Store to be cleaned. The proprietor assured him it would be ready on Friday. On Thursday, Betty Shopper wandered into the store, saw the clock, and became entranced by it. She made the proprietor an offer he couldn't refuse, so he sold her the clock and she took it home. Albert Collector was furious. He consults you. Can he replevy the clock from Betty? See Sutton v. Snider, 33 P.3d 309, 47 U.C.C. Rep. Serv. 2d 175 (Okla. App. 2001). Can he sue the proprietor? Using what theory(ies)? If the proprietor had stored the clock in a warehouse, received a negotiable warehouse receipt therefor, and pledged the receipt to Last National Bank in return for a loan, could Albert Collector retrieve the clock from the warehouse? Compare §§7-403, 7-502, and 7-503.

What *real* defenses are available against a §7-502 holder? The only ones that the Code sets out are listed in §7-403(1): proper delivery to a superior claimant, non-negligent destruction of the goods, sale to enforce bailee's lien, and "any other lawful excuse" (not further defined in the Code). Who is the *superior claimant* that §7-403(1) permits to get the goods from the bailee even though there is an outstanding negotiable document of title? The answer: a §7-503(1) owner.

A §7-503(1) owner is a person who had a legal interest or perfected security interest in the goods *prior* to the bailee's issuance of a document of title and who was in no way responsible for the creation of a situation permitting a negotiable document of title to come into existence. Read §7-503(1) carefully along with Official Comment 1. Essentially, §7-503(1) means that if the owner of goods *entrusts* them (or documents covering them) or delivers them to anyone so that that person has the *apparent* authority to deal with the goods, the owner is estopped to assert ownership against a subsequent §7-502 holder. See In re Jamestown Farmers Elevator, Inc., 49 Bankr. 661, 41 U.C.C. Rep. Serv. 578 (Bankr. D.N.D. 1985).

Where the owner has entrusted and is thus estopped, *ownership* becomes a *personal* defense and unassertable against a §7-502 holder. *But* when the owner of goods has had them, in effect, stolen by someone other than the owner's agent, then the owner is the very person §7-503(1) was meant to protect. A §7-503(1) owner has a superior right to the goods even against a §7-502 holder. In this case, ownership is a *real* defense, and the true owner can force the bailee to turn over the goods to the §7-503(1) owner without surrendering the negotiable document (though, as a practical matter, the owner will probably either have to get a court order or sign an indemnity agreement with the bailee before the latter will turn over the goods).

The policy here is that—since one of two innocent parties must bear a loss—if the owner has been even slightly at fault by permitting someone else to have the goods (and therefore apparent authority to ship or store them) or the documents, the owner should bear the loss. The owner must learn not to be so trusting in the future—or to insure against employee defalcation. But if the owner has had the goods stolen by someone not permitted to hold onto the goods, then the owner should be able to trace the goods and recover them even if they are found in the possession of a bailee.

Agricredit Acceptance, LLC v. Hendrix

Unites States District Court, Southern District of Georgia, 2000
82 F. Supp. 2d 1379, 41 U.C.C. Rep. Serv. 2d 242

NANGLE, District Judge.

Before the Court is defendant Hohenberg Bros. Co., Loeb & Company, Inc., Weil Brothers-Cotton, Inc., and the Montgomery Company, Inc.'s (the merchants') motion for summary judgment (Doc. 80). For the reasons that follow, defendants' motion is denied.

I. BACKGROUND

Many of the facts of this case were thoroughly set forth in this Court's Order denying defendants' motion to dismiss dated December 21, 1998 (Doc. 70). Consequently, the background section of that Order; Order dated Dec. 21, 1998 at 1-4; is incorporated herein by reference. Facts specific to the determination of this motion are set forth below.

The defendant merchants buy cotton stored in warehouses and resell it to textile mills. Br. Supp. Defs.' Consolidated Mot. Summ. J. at 1 (Doc. 81). These transactions are generally electronic in nature, involving electronic warehouse receipts (EWRs) maintained in the central operating systems of various EWR providers. Id. at 1-2. The sale typically begins with the merchants' receipt of a recap sheet from a prospective seller, which describes a number of bales being offered for sale by grade, quantity and warehouse in which the bales are stored. Id. at 2. The merchant then telephones the seller and submits an offer involving either a fixed price or an "on call" price which is based on the price of cotton futures on the New York market. Id. Once an agreement is reached between the merchant and the seller, the seller transfers the EWRs for the bales sold into the name of the merchant, and the merchant receives a confirmation of this transaction from the EWR provider. Id. When the EWRs are in the name of the merchant, the merchant is able to obtain a list of the bales by receipt number from the central filing system by downloading the list into the merchant's computers. Id. The sale is completed when the merchant pays the seller for the cotton represented by the EWRs. Id.

These sales can also be accomplished via contract for future delivery. Id. at 5. These contracts involve the seller promising to provide some specific number of bales in the future at a provisional price. After the seller acquires the bales, it transfers the EWRs for the bales into the name of the merchant and the process proceeds as above. Id.

Thomas Hendrix's 1997 cotton crop was financed by a loan from plaintiff Agricredit Acceptance Corporation (AAC). Order dated Dec. 21, 1998, at 2. The loan was secured by the cotton crop. Id. AAC's security interest was properly perfected by filing the Security Agreement in the real estate records of the counties wherein the cotton was grown and with the County clerks' offices. Id. at 3. Sea Island Cotton Trading was designated as a selling agent through which Hendrix would sell the cotton crop, and AAC notified Sea Island of its security interest in accordance with the provisions of the Food Security Act (FSA), 7 U.S.C. §1631. Id. Hendrix's cotton crop was ginned, baled, and stored in various warehouses, including Collins Gin & Warehouse, Candler Gin & Warehouse, Goldkist, Inc., Growers Gin & Warehouse, Inc., and Bulloch Gin. Id.; Br. Supp. Defs.' Mot. Summ. J. at 3. The warehouses issued EWRs for the cotton in the central filing system of the EWR provider to which they were subscribed. Br. Supp. Defs.' Mot. Summ. J. at 3. These receipts were eventually placed in the name of Sea Island. Id. at 4; Order dated Dec. 21, 1998, at 3.

All of the defendant merchants purchased large quantities of cotton from Sea Island in 1997 and 1998, including many bales from Hendrix's 1997 crop. The merchants paid Sea Island for these bales, and the EWRs representing the bales were transferred by Sea Island into the names of the purchasing merchants. Br. Supp. Defs.' Mot. Summ. J. at 4-15. Sea Island never paid AAC or Hendrix for the cotton in violation of its obligations under the FSA notice. Order dated Dec. 21, 1998, at 4. Consequently, plaintiff AAC filed suit against the defendant merchants and others seeking foreclosure of its security interest in the Hendrix cotton, a writ of possession against anyone in possession of the cotton, and a finding of conversion and an award of damages against the cotton merchants, among other things. Id.

The defendant merchants assert that because the EWRs representing the Hendrix cotton were duly negotiated to them by Sea Island and because AAC entrusted the cotton to Hendrix with apparent authority to sell it, the cotton is no longer subject to AAC's security interest. That is, the merchants assert that duly negotiated EWRs have priority over a prior perfected security interest, especially when the secured party entrusts the collateral to the borrower. As this Court found in its Order dated December 21, 1998, the resolution of these issues depends on this Court's interpretation of the Georgia Uniform Commercial Code and its application to the facts of this case. Id. at 13-14.

II. ANALYSIS . . .

In Georgia, a security interest in crops can only be perfected by the filing of a financing statement. O.C.G.A. §11-9-302(1)(h). Generally, a perfected security interest takes priority over other liens, claims or rights to property and to security interests perfected at a later date. O.C.G.A. §§11-9-310 and -312. This general rule is of course subject to exception. For example, a buyer in the ordinary course of business takes free of a security interest created by his seller, O.C.G.A. §11-9-307(1). Furthermore, nothing in Article 9 of the UCC limits the rights of "a holder to whom a negotiable document of title has been duly negotiated . . . and such holders . . . take priority over an earlier security interest even though perfected," O.C.G.A. §11-9-309.

A warehouse receipt is a negotiable document of title if it provides by its terms that the goods are to be delivered to bearer or to the order of a named person. O.C.G.A. §11-7-104(1)(a). These receipts may be in an electronic format. O.C.G.A. §10-4-19(e). A negotiable document running to order is negotiated by indorsement and delivery. O.C.G.A. §11-7-501(1). A negotiable document running to bearer is negotiated by delivery alone. O.C.G.A. §11-7-501(2).

To be duly negotiated, a document of title must be negotiated "to a holder who purchases it in good faith without any notice of any defense against it or claim to it on the part of any person and for value, unless it is established that the negotiation is not in the regular course of business." O.C.G.A. §11-7-501(4). Good faith is defined by reference to O.C.G.A. §11- 1-201(19) as "honesty in fact in the conduct or transaction concerned." "A person has 'notice' of a fact when: (a) He has actual knowledge of it; or (b) He has received a notice or notification of it; or (c) From all the facts and circumstances known to him at the time in question he has reason to know that it exists." O.C.G.A. §11-1-201(25). Finally, in general, a person gives value for rights if he acquires them "in return for any consideration sufficient to support a simple contract." O.C.G.A. §11-1- 201(44). Section 11-7-502 provides that a holder to whom a negotiable warehouse receipt has been duly negotiated acquires title to the document, title to the goods, and the direct obligation of the warehouse to deliver the goods, except as provided in O.C.G.A. §11-7-503.

Section 11-7-503 provides that:

> (1) A document of title confers no right in goods against a person who before issuance of the document had a legal interest or a perfected security interest in [the goods] and who neither:

(a) Delivered or entrusted [the goods] . . . to the bailor or his nominee with actual or apparent authority to ship, store, or sell . . . ; nor

(b) Acquiesced in the procurement by the bailor or his nominee of any document of title.

Neither Article 1 nor Article 7 defines the term "entrusted." This term is used elsewhere in the UCC, however. Section 11-2-403(3) defines it as "any delivery and any acquiescence in retention of possession regardless of any condition expressed between the parties." However, Georgia courts have found that this provision only applies to owners of goods, because one cannot entrust goods one does not own. Sunnyland Employees' Fed. Credit Union v. Fort Wayne Mortgage Co., 182 Ga. App. 5, 354 S.E.2d 645, 647 (1987) (holding that party with security interest in mobile home could not be the entruster of it because party was not the owner of the home); United Carolina Bank v. Sistrunk, 158 Ga. App. 107, 279 S.E.2d 272, 274 (1981) (holding party with security interest in car could not be the entruster of it because party was not the owner of the car); McConnell v. Barrett, 154 Ga. App. 767, 270 S.E.2d 13, 15-16 (1980) (holding that non-owners cannot be entrusters and citing Adams v. City Nat'l Bank & Trust Co., 565 P.2d 26, 29 (Okla. 1977)). Acquiescence is not defined anywhere in the UCC.

C. INTERPRETATION AND APPLICATION OF THE UCC

Defendants' motion for summary judgment is based on two theories: (1) that the EWRs were duly negotiated to the merchants and pursuant to O.C.G.A. §11-9-309, the merchants' interest in the cotton has priority over AAC's interest, Br. Supp. Defs.' Mot. Summ. J. at 16-19; Defs.' Objections to Dep. Testimony Offered by Pl. at 2-4, 6, 7-8 (Doc. 123); and (2) that AAC waived the priority of its security interest by entrusting the cotton to Hendrix pursuant to O.C.G.A. §11-7-503, Br. Supp. Defs.' Mot. Summ. J. at 20; Defs.' Objections to Dep. Testimony Offered by Pl. at 7-8; Defs.' Resp. Opp'n AAC's Objection to Affs. at 9-12 (Doc. 120).

1. Due Negotiation and §11-9-309 [now §9-331—Ed.]

For the EWRs to be duly negotiated to the merchants, the merchants must be purchasers in good faith without notice of claims or defenses to the receipts and for value. O.C.G.A. §11-7-501(4). It is undisputed that the merchants purchased the EWRs for value. Consequently, the Court must determine whether the merchants also purchased the EWRs in good faith and without notice.

Good faith as defined in Article 1 means "honesty in fact." Plaintiff does not dispute that the merchants acted with honesty in fact in this transaction. Rather, relying on an improper definition of good faith, AAC asserts that good faith requires the merchants to perform a lien check on the cotton before purchase. The Court finds that the "honesty in fact" definition does not require the merchants to perform a lien check on the cotton prior to purchase. Consequently, the Court holds that the merchants are purchasers in good faith as a matter of law.

However, this finding does not end the inquiry. The merchants must also be purchasers without notice of any defenses or claims to the EWRs. Plaintiff relies on the third prong of Article 1's definition of notice in arguing that the merchants' experience with the cotton industry and its willful ignorance as to the existence of liens on the cotton constitute reason to know that plaintiff's defense to the EWRs existed. Pl.'s Resp. Opp'n Defs.' Mot. Summ. J. at 22-24 (Doc. 93). While some jurisdictions have required the existence of suspicious circumstances for a finding of "reason to know;" Colin v. Central Penn Nat'l Bank, 404 F. Supp. 638, 640-41 (E.D. Pa. 1975); others hold that willful or deliberate indifference to or ignorance of information is a basis for a finding of "reason to know;" Demoulas v. Demoulas, 428 Mass. 555, 703 N.E.2d 1149, 1167 (1998) ("If a person confronted with a state of facts closes his eyes in order that he may not see that which would be visible and therefore known to him if he looked, he is chargeable with 'knowledge' of what he would have seen had he looked.") (citations omitted); New Bedford Inst. for Savings v. Gildroy, 36 Mass. App. Ct. 647, 634 N.E.2d 920 (1994) ("Further, a holder has no duty to inquire unless 'the circumstances reveal a deliberate desire by the holder to evade knowledge of claims made by the maker.'") (citations omitted).

The Court finds that the evidence in the record indicates that a genuine issue of fact exists concerning the merchants' notice of AAC's claims to the cotton. The merchants testified in deposition that they do not perform lien searches on cotton bought from merchants or gins. Dep. Hohenberg Bros. Co. through John D. Mitchell at 25-27 (Doc. 91); Dep. Weil Brothers-Cotton, Inc. through James A. Wade at 18-19 (Doc. 90); Dep. Loeb & Co., Inc. through James L. Loeb at 24 (Doc. 87); Dep. Montgomery Co. through Jack D. Atkins at 27-28, 42-43 (Doc. 89). However, when buying directly from the producer or when buying in a state with a central lien filing system, most of the merchants do perform lien searches. Dep. Mitchell at 25-26; Dep. Loeb at 24; Dep. Atkins at 28, 42-43. Further, when dealing with sales via contract for future delivery, the merchants include a clause in the contract requiring the seller to warrant that there are no liens on the cotton. Dep. Mitchell at 68-72. These facts imply that the merchants certainly knew of the possibility of the existence of liens. Whether their failure to search for liens amounts to deliberate indifference or ignorance to their existence, however, is less than clear from the facts presently in the record. The Court finds that this issue is one for a jury to decide.

Even if the Court finds that the merchants had no notice of AAC's claims to the cotton, this finding would not automatically provide superiority to the merchants' claims to the cotton. O.C.G.A. §11-9-309 [now §9-331—Ed.] provides that "Nothing in this article limits the rights . . . of a holder to whom a negotiable document of title has been duly negotiated . . . and such holders take priority over an earlier security interest even though perfected." Defendants urge the Court to hold that this Section provides that any duly negotiated EWR automatically trumps a prior perfected security interest in the goods covered by that EWR. Defendants' interpretation of §11-9-309 is in error. Such an interpretation would eviscerate the provisions of O.C.G.A. §11-7-503, which expressly provide that EWRs confer no rights in the goods covered by the EWRs against security interests existing and perfected prior to the issuance of the EWR where there has been no entrustment or acquiescence on the part of the secured party. The proper interpretation of §11-9-309 is that the Section only applies when the negotiable document holder and the secured party are both claiming an interest in the document. Farmers State Bank of Somonauk v. National Bank of Earlville, 230 Ill. App. 3d 881, 172 Ill. Dec. 894, 596 N.E.2d 173, 174-76 (1992). That is, §11-9-309 addresses disputes between competing interests in a negotiable document whereas §11-7-503 covers disputes between competing interests in the underlying goods. Accordingly, even if the EWRs were duly negotiated to the merchants, disposition of the cotton covered by those EWRs depends upon the application of O.C.G.A. §11-7-503.

2. Entrustment

Defendants argue that despite the Georgia courts' interpretation of §11-2-403, this Court is free to find that AAC entrusted the cotton to Hendrix by leaving it in his possession and allowing him to sell it through Sea Island. However, because Article 1 and Article 7 provide no definition for the term "entrusted," this Court must look to the Georgia courts' interpretation of that term as it is used in other sections of the UCC. Banks v. Georgia Power Co., 267 Ga. 602, 481 S.E.2d 200, 202 (1997) (stating that court is required to construe statute with reference to other statutes and decisions of the courts); Poteat v. Butler, 231 Ga. 187, 200 S.E.2d 741, 742 (1973) ("All statutes are presumed to be enacted by the General Assembly with full knowledge of the existing condition of the law . . . and their meaning and effect is to be determined in connection . . . with reference to other statutes and decisions of the courts."). Because the Georgia courts have held in the context of §11-2-403 that a secured party who does not own the goods cannot entrust them; *Sunnyland,* 354 S.E.2d at 647; *United Carolina Bank,* 279 S.E.2d at 274; *McConnell,* 270 S.E.2d at 15-16; this Court must hold similarly in the context of §11-7-503.[2] Consequently, the Court finds that plaintiff did not entrust the cotton to Hendrix as a matter of law.

Plaintiff may, however, have acquiesced in the procurement of a document of title in the cotton (namely the EWRs) pursuant to §11-7-503(1)(b). When a bank knows that a farmer is attempting to sell his collateral and it acquiesces in his procurement of documents of title to that collateral, the bank has waived its right to assert its security interest in the collateral. Mercantile Bank of Springfield v. Joplin Regional Stockyards, Inc., 870 F. Supp. 278, 283 (W.D. Mo. 1994). The evidence presently before the Court is not sufficient to support a ruling on this issue as a matter of law. Consequently, the question of plaintiff's acquiescence is better left to a jury.

III. CONCLUSION

Because genuine issues of material fact exist,

IT IS HEREBY ORDERED that defendants' motion for summary judgment is denied.

C. *Other Transfers*

Section 7-504, which you should read as soon as you finish this paragraph, sets out the rights acquired by a transferee of a document

---

2. This interpretation does not make the use of the term "entrusted" superfluous in the context of §11-7-503. Rather, that Section also applies to any persons with any legal interest in the goods which was created prior to the issuance of the document of title. When such persons are the owners of the goods, the entrustment provision would apply.

when there has been no *due negotiation*. Section 7-505 goes on to provide that the indorser of a document of title does not make any *contract* that the bailee will honor the document, but §7-507 (which you should also glance at) provides that any transferor makes the warranties listed there. In addition, since a sale of goods is involved in the transfer of any document of title, a transferor also makes the Article 2 warranties, discussed in the earlier part of this book.

It is a basic rule of all commercial law that a transferee gets whatever legal rights the transferor had. This rule is called the shelter rule because the transferee is said to take shelter in the status of the transferor. In Article 2 (Sale of Goods) the shelter rule is found in §2-403; read it. In Article 3 (Commercial Paper) the rule turns up in §3-203(b), and in Article 8 (Investment Securities) it is reflected in §8-301. For Article 7 the rule is codified in §7-504(1). Read it, and use it to work the following Problem.

PROBLEM 247

The shipping agent for the King Cotton Manufacturing Company wrongfully took for himself 90 bales of cotton that had come under his control and stored them in the Rural Warehouse, which issued to him a negotiable warehouse receipt. This receipt he took to Octopus National Bank (ONB) and gave as security for a loan. He indorsed the receipt over to ONB. King Cotton discovered the bales were missing and investigated; the shipping agent was arrested. Shortly thereafter, ONB sold the warehouse receipt to Antitrust National Bank (ANB), which bought the document with full knowledge of the above facts. Both ANB and King Cotton made a demand on Rural Warehouse for the cotton. Rural calls you, its attorney, for advice. What do you say? Note §§7-403(3), 7-501 through 7-504, and 7-603.

IV. COLLECTION THROUGH BANKS

A. *"Payment Against Documents"*

If the seller and buyer deal with each other on a face-to-face basis, delivery of the goods and payment of the price normally occur at the same moment, and neither party need trust the other. Where seller and buyer are separated by great distances, a seller must either trust the buyer to live up to the contract (a sale on *open account* with trust on both sides) or figure out a way to make certain that the buyer cannot get the goods until they are paid for. The easiest way to do this would be to have an agent in the buyer's city who could present the bill of lading covering the goods to the buyer but not turn it over to the buyer until cash was paid for the goods. In effect, this is the solution that sellers have adopted. See §2-503(5)(b). The *agent* that sellers use is a bank in the buyer's city. And, instead of a letter of instruction telling the bank-agent what to do, the seller simply draws an Article 3 draft (§3-104(e)) on the buyer (so that the buyer is the drawee) and attaches it to the bill of lading.

A draft is similar to a check; it is an instruction of payment. The seller is the drawer, and the buyer is the drawee. A simple draft will look like this:

                                                  _____
(Date)

To: _____
      (Buyer's Name)   (Amount)

At sight pay to the order of _____
                                (Payee's Name)

_____ dollars and _____ cents.

                                          _____
                                      (Seller's Signature)

The payee will be whomever the seller nominates: the seller's bank, one of the seller's creditors, or even the seller itself. The only difference between this draft and your typical check is that the drawee is the buyer and not a bank.

Now that the seller has created the draft, it is combined with other papers for delivery to the buyer. The papers (which will normally include the bill of lading, a sales invoice, and, occasionally, an inspection certificate) along with the seller's draft on buyer are indorsed over to the seller's local bank for collection. Then the normal bank collection machinery in Article 4 is put into motion. Eventually, a bank in buyer's vicinity makes a formal Article 3 *presentment* of the draft (§3-501), and the buyer must either pay or dishonor. In any event, the buyer cannot get the documents (especially the bill of lading) until payment, so the seller is protected from having to trust a buyer in an arm's length transaction. If the buyer dishonors, the seller is notified by the collecting bank. The seller will then give instructions to the bank as to what to do with the goods when they arrive (the bank will be able to claim them from the carrier because it has the bill of lading. Cf. §7-403(3)).

Any draft accompanied by sales documents like those mentioned above is called a *documentary draft.* See §4-104(a)(6). The normal rules for negotiable instruments in Articles 3 and 4 apply to such drafts, but occasionally the sections make special rules for documentary drafts. E.g., §4-202(a)(2) (providing that after dishonor a collecting bank need not return a documentary draft to its transferor).

Sometimes the seller does not demand that the buyer actually pay prior to receiving the documents. Under some contracts, it is enough that buyer *accept* the draft and incur the obligation of an *acceptor* (§3-413), thus becoming primarily liable on the draft (the draft is now commonly called a *trade acceptance*). Typically, these are *time drafts* (as opposed to *sight drafts,* whereby payment is required as soon as buyer sees the draft) because they require payment in 30, 60, or 90 days after "sight" (presentment to buyer). The business reason why this is frequently done is so that buyer can take the goods during the grace period, by manufacturing transform them into other goods, and resell them. In these transactions the seller sends the draft and documents through the banks and asks the collecting bank to call the buyer and make a presentment for acceptance. Read §4-212. The buyer shows up and accepts by writing the buyer's signature on the draft (if the buyer does not show up, the draft is dishonored). After acceptance, the draft is returned to the presenter and may be further negotiated. On acceptance by the buyer, the bank turns over the documents, and in 30, 60, or 90 days (or whatever time period the draft provides) the buyer is required to pay the draft or is in breach of the acceptor's contract. For an article spelling out *payment against documents* in detail, see Farnsworth, Documentary Drafts Under the Uniform Commercial Code, 22 Bus. Law. 479 (1967).

PROBLEM 248

Sam Seller in Dallas signed a sales contract to sell one ton of tennis balls to Beth Buyer in Indianapolis, "FOB truck in Dallas," $800 to be paid by a 60-day time draft on the buyer. Sam boxed the tennis balls and filled out a packaging invoice describing the goods. He drew a draft as follows:

To: Beth Buyer

Sixty days after sight pay to the order of *Sam Seller* $800.

(signed) *Sam Seller*

He took the tennis balls down to the Texas Trucking Company and asked for a negotiable bill of lading consigned to his own order, with the instructions "notify Beth Buyer on arrival." The trucking company issued the negotiable ("order") bill to Sam.

Sam then took the bill of lading, the invoice describing the goods, and the draft on Buyer down to his local bank, the Lone Star National Bank. He asked Lone Star to collect the draft. On agreeing to the bank's collection charge, Sam indorsed both the draft and the bill of lading over to the bank. Lone Star Bank then forwarded the draft and the documents to the Indianapolis State Hoosier Bank for collection. The Hoosier Bank called Beth Buyer and told her to come by the bank and get the papers. Beth came down that afternoon, wrote her name on the draft (which the bank dated and kept), and received the other documents. Read §2-514. Two days later the Texas Trucking Company showed up with the goods and promptly notified Buyer of their arrival. Buyer went down to the truck depot and surrendered the bill of lading (as required by §7-403(3)), whereupon she received the tennis balls. Now, to see how Article 2 and Article 7 fit together like one glorious puzzle, answer the following questions:

(a) Can Beth Buyer *inspect* the goods? If so, when? See §2-513.

(b) If the tennis balls are defective (Seller has breached one of his Article 2 warranties), can Buyer reject (§2-602) or revoke her acceptance (§2-608) and refuse to pay?

(c) If the cartons are empty (Sam is a crook), can Buyer sue the Texas Trucking Company, since the bill of lading states that the goods shipped are "ONE TON TENNIS BALLS"?

(d) Can Buyer sue the collecting bank because the documents did not conform to the goods shipped? Read §7-508 to answer this one.

B.   Liability of the Collecting Bank

Sometimes a seller in the position of Sam (above) will sell (*discount*) the draft and documents to a local bank. This generally makes no difference in the resulting rights (see, for example, the last sentence of §7-508), but it does give the collecting bank a security interest in the draft and documents (§4-210(a)(3)) and therefore permits it to become a holder in due course (§4-211). Read §2-506.

The last Part of Article 4 contains four sections that deal specifically with the collection of documentary drafts. Read §§4-501 to 4-504 to see how these sections link the sale under Article 2 with the use of Article 7 documents of title.

Rheinberg Kellerei GmbH v. Brooksfield National Bank of Commerce

United States Court of Appeals, Fifth Circuit, 1990
901 F.2d 481, 11 U.C.C. Rep. Serv. 2d 1214

GARZA, J. American bank did not notify German bank of difficulty in payment on international collection order which came due on arrival of goods in Houston; the collection order was eventually dishonored. The district court held that the American bank did not know, and had no duty to inquire, whether goods had arrived, and entered take nothing judgment. Because we find that the American bank was on notice of the possibility of dishonor and should have told the German bank of the problem in collection, we reverse.

FACTS

In January of 1986, J & J Wine, an American company, ordered a shipment of wine from a German firm, Rheinberg Kellerei GmbH, through an importer, Frank Sutton & Co.[3] Payment was to be made through an international letter of collection handled by Edekabank in Germany and Brooksfield National Bank of Commerce Bank in San Antonio ("NBC Bank").[4] On March 27, NBC Bank received the letter

3. The "GmbH" designation means "Gesellschaft mit beschränkter Haftung," or "company with limited liability." GmbH is a common form of corporate organization in Germany and is similar to the "Inc." designation in the American corporate system.
4. In a case like this one, international letters of collection are issued by the seller's bank (Edeka) and sent to the buyer's bank (NBC Bank), which in turn pre-

of collection, bill of lading and invoices from Edeka.[5] The letter of collection noted that payment was due "on arrival of goods in Houston harbor," and called for NBC Bank to notify Sutton "in case of any difficulty of lack payment." The invoices noted an estimated time of arrival: April 2, 1986. NBC Bank then presented the documents to J & J Wine on March 27.

There is some dispute as to what, exactly, J & J Wine told NBC Bank about its financial situation at the time, but it is sure that J & J Wine did not pay the amount due, and instead asked NBC Bank to hold the letter for a time while J & J Wine worked to raise the money for payment. NBC Bank did not notify Edeka or Sutton of J & J Wine's failure to pay on presentment. In fact, NBC Bank did nothing further until early May, when Sutton informed them that the wine was still at the Houston port and NBC Bank cabled Edeka for further instructions.

The wine had arrived in Houston on March 31, but NBC Bank did not receive notice of that. Because J & J Wine had not taken delivery of it, the wine sat, exposed, at Houston harbor in metal containers until it had deteriorated completely. U.S. Customs agents eventually sold it at auction. J & J Wine subsequently went out of business, and Rheinberg Kellerei was never paid for the wine.

Rheinberg Kellerei then brought this suit, alleging that NBC Bank had negligently failed to inform it of J & J Wine's failure to pay, and that because of that negligence, the wine had spoiled at Houston harbor. After a bench trial, the district court entered a take-nothing judgment for NBC Bank. The court reasoned that, because payment was not due until the wine's arrival, and NBC Bank had no notice of that arrival and no duty to inquire further, NBC Bank had no knowledge that J & J Wine was in breach of the payment terms. For that reason, the district court held that NBC Bank could not be held liable for failure to inform Edeka of J & J Wine's default.

Complaining that the district court improperly applied the requirements of the International Rules for Collection (the "Rules") and erred in construing the letter of collection itself, Rheinberg Kellerei brought this appeal.

---

sents the letter and its documents to the buyer. To receive the documents and collect the goods, the buyer pays the amount due to its bank, which then forwards the funds to the seller's bank. Enforcement of these letters is governed by the International Chamber of Commerce's International Rules for Collection.

5. The bill of lading called for notification of Sutton and M.G. Maher & Co., the customs broker, on arrival of the goods in Houston. NBC Bank was not listed on the Bill of Lading or the invoices.

DISCUSSION

I. DUTY TO INFORM

NBC Bank presented the letter of collection and the other documents to J & J Wine for payment on March 27, 1986, before the wine had arrived and before the payment was due. Rheinberg Kellerei argues that, regardless of whether NBC Bank knew when the wine had arrived, once NBC Bank presented the documents, it had a duty to inform Edeka of any problem in collecting J & J Wine's payment. We agree. That duty arises both from the Rules and the collection letter itself.

A. Letter of Collection

The letter, which is the primary source of responsibility in this case, instructs NBC Bank to notify Sutton "in case of any difficulty of lack payment."[6] The district court found that section demanded notice only if there were a "lack of payment or failure to pay." Likewise, NBC Bank emphasizes that the trigger for notice is a *lack* of payment. What the court below and NBC Bank ignore is the word "difficulty." The letter did not instruct NBC Bank to notify Sutton only if there were a default, or a failure to pay, or a lack of payment. Rather, NBC Bank was called on to act also if there were any *difficulty* in collecting payment. And the request that NBC Bank hold the letter while J & J Wine sought financing certainly posed a difficulty in collection. Once NBC Bank knew that J & J Wine had asked for time to come up with the money, it should have notified Sutton in accordance with the letter's instructions.

The Rules specify that any special instructions posted on a letter of collection should be "complete and precise." General Provisions, §C. While the instructions given on this letter could have been in clearer language, they are sufficiently precise to make NBC Bank aware of its duty to notify Sutton once difficulty arose in the collection.

B. International Rules for Collection

Article 20(iii)(c) of the Rules provides that the "collecting bank [NBC Bank] must send without delay advice on non-payment or advice of non-acceptance to the bank from whom the collecting order was received [Edeka]." The court below and NBC Bank submit that section called on NBC Bank to notify Edeka if J & J Wine had not paid on the

6. Sutton was Rheinberg Kellerei's agent in this sale.

letter at the time it came due: on arrival of the goods in Houston harbor. And, they argue, since NBC Bank had no actual notice of the arrival of the goods, it did not breach that duty to notify.

The issue, it seems, is the definition of "non-payment" as it is used in Art. 20(iii)(c). Does it refer to a failure to pay on presentment? Does it require an affirmative statement of intent not to pay? Must the due date have arrived? No court has yet defined the term and its attendant duties, so we must look for guidance elsewhere.

The Rules were adopted to aid in "defining, simplifying and harmonizing the practices and terminology used in international banking." I.C.C. Banking Commission, Statement of Services to Business. They serve, for the international banking community, the same function as the Uniform Commercial Code does for domestic players. There is no reason, then, to ignore the UCC as an advisory source.

Section 4-502 of the UCC governs payment of "on arrival" drafts, such as were presented in our case. Tex. Bus. & Com. Code Ann., §4-502 (Tex. UCC) (Vernon's 1968). Under that section, a bank such as NBC Bank may, but need not, present the documents to the buyer before the goods arrive. But if the buyer does not pay at that time, the bank must notify the seller's bank: "Refusal to pay or accept because the goods have not arrived is not dishonor; *the bank must notify its transferor of such refusal* but need not present the draft again. . . ." UCC §4-502 (emphasis added). The UCC imposes on the presenting bank a duty to notify the seller's bank of any delay or failure to pay on presentment of an "on arrival" draft, *whether or not the draft is yet due.*

If §4-502 were applied to our case, NBC Bank would have a duty to notify Edeka of J & J Wine's failure to pay the letter of collection when it was presented on March 27, even though the goods were not yet in Houston harbor and the payment was not yet due. This is not to say that J & J Wine was in default at that time or had dishonored the letter. Rather, the notice is an act of prudence, an exercise in due care. And, as the aims of the Rules and the UCC are more than consistent, and both demand the exercise of due care, we find that the Rules impose the same duty. NBC Bank should have notified Edeka of J & J Wine's failure to pay at presentment, as that failure constituted a "non-payment" under Art. 20(iii)(c).

NBC Bank and the court below rely heavily on the fact that NBC Bank had no actual knowledge of the wine's arrival in Houston, and had no duty to inquire further. We agree with those premises, but do not feel they affect NBC Bank's duty to notify. That duty arose—under both the Rules and the letter itself—when J & J Wine failed to pay on presentment and asked for time. Arrival of the wine did not trigger it.

And NBC Bank cannot avoid liability by hiding from knowledge of arrival and claiming that ignorance as a defense.

II.   DAMAGES

State law governs the measure of damages in a case such as this one. Gathercrest, Ltd. v. First American Bank & Trust, 805 F.2d 995, 997 (11th Cir. 1986). Tex. Bus. & Com. Code Ann. §2-709(1) (Tex. UCC) (Vernon's 1968) gives the relevant standard: "the seller may recover, together with any incidental damages under the next section, the price (1) of goods accepted or of conforming goods lost or damaged . . . after risk of their loss has passed to the buyer."[7] Risk of loss had passed to J & J Wine when the goods arrived at Houston harbor and were available for J & J Wine to take delivery. Tex. Bus. & Com. Code Ann., §2-509(1)(b) (Tex. UCC) (Vernon's 1968). The district court found that because the wine was exposed for such a long period in Houston harbor, it was "'over cooked' and had deteriorated, lost its original flavor, freshness, was flat and should not be sold into the market that it was intended." Since the goods were so damaged, Rheinberg Kellerei is entitled to the contract price plus the unpaid freight costs, as provided in UCC [§2-709(1)(a)].

NBC Bank is entitled to a credit for the net proceeds of any resale of the damaged wine. UCC §2-709(2). Customs agents sold the wine at auction, but we have no evidence before us of the price paid or the net amount remaining after customs fees, wharfage, and the costs of the auction were paid. For that reason, we remand this case to the district court for the limited purpose of calculating that net amount. After finding that net amount, the district court should enter judgment for Rheinberg Kellerei for the contract price plus freight charges, less the net proceeds of the customs auction.

CONCLUSION

NBC Bank had a duty to notify Edeka or Sutton, which was triggered when J & J Wine failed to pay the letter of collection on presentment and asked for more time. That duty arose from two sources:

---

7. The district court applied, and the parties refer to, UCC §2-708, which figures damages as the difference between market value *at the time and place for tender* and contract price, plus incidental damages. That section is inapposite here, as the wine's market value at the time of tender was destroyed by the long delay at Houston harbor. Section 2-708 is more properly used in cases where resale at a reasonable rate is possible. The wine's ultimate sale price here bears no resemblance to its market price at the time of tender.

the Rules and the letter itself. Though payment was not due until the wine arrived in Houston harbor, that arrival was not a triggering event for the duty to arise, and lack of knowledge of it is no defense. The judgment of the district court is, therefore, reversed, and this cause is remanded for calculation of damages.

It is so ordered.

Up to this point the text has mostly dealt with sales transactions within the United States. To understand sales of goods between sellers and buyers in different countries, Article 5 (Letters of Credit) must now be mastered. In international sales, most sales are carried out through the use of documents of title, with the added complication that letters of credit are also used. International collection of documentary drafts is regulated by Brochure 500 of the International Chamber of Commerce (1993 revision), which the banks regard as "the law." The relevant UCC Articles—4, 5, and 7—are similar to its provisions.

Chapter 16
LETTERS OF CREDIT

There are two primary sources for the law relating to letters of credit: Article 5 of the Uniform Commercial Code and the Uniform Customs and Practice for Documentary Credits, 1993 Revision [Brochure 500 of the International Chamber of Commerce, hereinafter the UCP]. Since the two are not significantly different, we shall look primarily to the Code for study purposes. If you should get involved in a letter of credit case, however, remember to study the UCP carefully —it is recognized as a complete statement of prevailing international banking practices in the field; for the relationship of Article 5 to the UCP, see Official Comment 2 to §5-103. Further, you should be aware that Article 5 was substantially rewritten in 1995, and it is that version that is considered in this chapter (the cases, however, refer to the prior version, and the citations in those cases are updated by editorial notes). The leading treatise on Article 5 is J. Dolan, The Law of Letters of Credit (rev. ed. 1996).

I.   THE BASIC PROBLEM

Assume you are the proprietor of a business in Detroit, Michigan, that makes and sells men's shirts. One day you get a letter from Germany saying: "I want to buy 50,000 shirts at $7 each United States currency, FOB Frankfurt. (Signed) *Hans Goldschnitt.*" Since you have never heard of Hans Goldschnitt, you are reluctant to ship him 50,000 shirts and risk non-payment after the shipping costs are incurred. There are no satisfactory credit bureaus similar to Dun and Bradstreet on an international basis. How can you avoid a credit risk? The answer devised by the law merchant is for you to write Herr Goldschnitt and tell him that you will ship the goods only to a *bank* of international repute that is willing to write a letter to you making itself *primarily* and *irrevocably* liable for the payment of the contract price. If Hans Goldschnitt agrees and you agree on the other contract terms, he will go to a major German bank—say, the National Volksbank of Frankfurt (NVF)—and establish credit with the bank. Shortly thereafter you will receive a letter from the bank more or less in the following form:

NATIONAL VOLKSBANK OF FRANKFURT
Credit No. 829-411
November 20, 2008

Dear Detroit Seller:
 We hereby establish our IRREVOCABLE CREDIT in your favor for the account of Hans Goldschnitt, our customer, up to the aggregate amount of $350,000, U.S. dollars, available by your sight draft on us, to be accompanied by the following documents:
 (1) full set of clean bills of lading issued by German Ocean Lines to the order of National Volksbank of Frankfurt, notify Hans Goldschnitt;
 (2) signed commercial sales invoices describing the goods;
 (3) customs certificates;
 (4) packing lists;
 (5) inspection certificate by Grey Goods Inspection Service of New York.
 Bills of lading must be dated not later than August 1, 2008; drafts must be negotiated within ten days of shipment; all drafts must be marked "Drawn Under Credit No. 829-411." Subject to UCP rules (Brochure 500). We hereby agree with drawers, indorsers, and bona fide holders of drafts drawn under and in compliance with the terms

and conditions of this credit to honor the same on due presentation of draft to the drawee.

Yours very truly,

National Volksbank
of Frankfurt

The German bank will probably forward this letter of credit to you through a local Detroit bank (which has translation facilities and better international commercial paper routing procedures than you do). The Detroit bank will give you the letter and tell you that it is willing to transmit the documents and drafts to the German bank at the proper time. In this situation the Detroit bank is called an *adviser*.

On July 6, 2008, per your contract with Hans Goldschnitt, you draw up the packing lists, invoices, and certificates required by the letter of credit and put the goods on board a German Ocean Lines ship. In return you get a *clean* (free of carrier's notation indicating a defect in the goods or packaging) bill of lading to the order of the German bank and draw a draft payable to yourself on the NVF (that is, the German bank will be the drawee). You clip all these documents together and take them down to the Detroit bank, which forwards them to the German bank and makes an Article 3 presentment for you. If the German bank decides that you have complied with the terms of the letter of credit, it will honor the draft (pay it—the money is then remitted to you by the Detroit bank) and receive all the documents. The German bank then calls Hans Goldschnitt and tells him to come pay if he wants the documents he will need to get the goods off the ship. He does so. When the goods arrive, German Ocean Lines notifies Hans pursuant to instructions on their copy of the bill of lading. He presents the bill of lading and receives the goods.

Several variations on the above are possible. If you are unwilling to wait to get your money, you may be able to sell (*discount*) the drafts to the Detroit bank. Or, as part of your initial contract with the buyer, you may have required him to get a *Detroit bank* to issue the letter of credit to you. He can do this as follows: he establishes credit with the NVF; the NVF issues a letter of credit to you through the Detroit bank and asks the Detroit bank to *confirm* it. If the Detroit bank decides to do so (and it will first investigate the credit reputation of the German bank), it will notify you that the NVF has issued a letter of credit to you and that the Detroit bank "hereby confirms it." This makes the Detroit bank a *confirmer* and liable in exactly the same fashion as the issuer. The confirming letter of credit will state that the Detroit bank will honor

drafts under the letter of credit if accompanied by the listed documents. The transaction then proceeds as above, except the drafts you
draw are drawn on and presented to the Detroit bank for payment.
(*Note:* it is possible to draw a *time* draft on the issuing bank whereby it is
given 30, 60, or 90 days—as determined by contract—following formal
acceptance in which to pay. Such a time draft is commonly called a
banker's acceptance.) The issuing bank may require that the draft be
presented for payment not to itself but to another entity with whom it
has a contractual arrangement (called a *nominated person*—see §5-
102(a)(11), defining the term, and §5-107(b) and its Official Comment
4, explaining the legal status of a nominated person). This is often
done, for example, when the issuer does not carry sufficient amounts
of the currency called for by the credit.

To be distinguished from the above *documentary credit* is the so-
called *standby letter of credit.* A standby credit is issued by a bank to be
honored only if there is default in an unrelated contract. For example,
assume that a contractor agrees to build 50 apartment buildings for the
owner of the lots on which the construction will occur. The owner
might require the contractor to have its bank issue a standby credit in
favor of the owner, to be drawn on only in the event that the contractor does not fulfill its contractual obligation. A standby credit differs
from a documentary credit in that the beneficiary of the credit is not
required to produce documents along with its draft against the letter of
credit; instead, it typically just gives a written notice of breach. Thus, a
standby credit is similar to a surety obligation (though not the same[1]).
Standby letters of credit are much in use nowadays; in 1993 it was
estimated that standby letters of credit in the United States totaled
$250 billion (and double that worldwide).

PROBLEM 249

The U.S. Army wanted to order uniforms for its soldiers from Khaki
Clothing, Inc., agreeing to pay a set amount on delivery. The Army,
however, had had major problems in past dealings with Khaki, which
was always very late at meeting delivery schedules. The purchasing

---

1. It is *ultra vires* for a bank to act as a surety, so the courts have been careful to
draw distinctions between suretyship and the issuance of a standby letter of credit,
typically pointing to the fact that a surety is secondarily liable on the contract between
the principal and the creditor, but that a bank's liability on a standby letter of credit is
an independent obligation. See, e.g., State ex rel. Missouri Highway & Transp.
Commn. v. Morganstein, 703 S.W.2d 894, 1 U.C.C. Rep. Serv. 2d 197 (Mo. 1986).

officer for the Army asked the Army's attorney if the contract could contain a penalty clause, imposing a huge penalty on Khaki if it did not deliver the uniforms by the required date. The attorney, mindful of basic contracts law, opined that penalty clauses (even if disguised as liquidated damages clauses) are invalid as a matter of common law, but then he had an idea. He put a clause in the purchasing contract requiring Khaki to get a standby letter of credit in favor of the Army and requiring the issuing bank to pay a huge penalty sum to the Army in the event that Khaki did not deliver the uniforms on time. Octopus National Bank issued such a credit, but when Khaki missed the delivery deadline and the Army tried to collect the penalty specified in the credit, the bank balked and in its defense pointed to the common law rule forbidding penalty clauses in contracts. Will this succeed? See Balboa Ins. Co. v. Coastal Bank, 42 U.C.C. Rep. Serv. 1716 (S.D. Ga. 1986); Telenois, Inc. v. Village of Schaumburg, 628 N.E.2d 581, 23 U.C.C. Rep. Serv. 2d 862 (Ill. App. 1993); McLaughlin, Standby Letters of Credit and Penalty Clauses: An Unexpected Synergy, 43 Ohio St. L.J. 1 (1982).

II.   DEFINITIONS AND SCOPE OF ARTICLE 5

Section 5-102(a)(9) addresses itself to the question of who can issue a letter of credit. Section 5-104 describes the formal requirements of such a letter (note that electronically generated letters of credit are clearly allowed; see Official Comment 3 to §5-104). Read these sections with this question in mind: is the bank credit card you probably are carrying in your wallet a letter of credit under Article 5? (The question is academic only since credit cards are regulated by the Truth In Lending Act, 15 U.S.C.A. §1642 et seq.)

Letters of credit *not* requiring the presentation of documents are called *clean credits* because normally only drafts are tendered. See Housing Sec. Inc. v. Maine Natl. Bank, 391 A.2d 311, 26 U.C.C. Rep. Serv. 750 (Me. 1978). The most startling use of such a letter of credit occurred in 1963, when the Royal Bank of Canada, the Morgan Guaranty Trust Co., and the Bank of America issued letters of credit totaling $106 million as security for the ransom of prisoners from the Cuban Bay of Pigs invasion. See Business Week, Feb. 9, 1963, at 84-85, which is discussed in Wiley, How to Use Letters of Credit in Financing the Sale of Goods, 20 Bus. Law. 495 (1965).

Now read the definitions in §5-102. In the above hypothetical you were the *beneficiary* of the letter of credit; Hans Goldschnitt was the *applicant* (the former version of Article 5 called Hans the *customer*); the German bank was the *issuer;* and the Detroit bank was the *advisor* or *confirmer*, depending on which part of the hypothetical you are looking at. Read §5-107. Do not get these terms confused.

Now go back and re-read §5-102(a)(10), which defines *letter of credit.* A letter of credit may be either revocable or irrevocable. Article 6 of the UCP *presumes* (if not otherwise stated) that a letter of credit is irrevocable, and so does §5-106(a). Remember this: *no one wants a revocable letter of credit.* To understand why, see §5-106(b); Official Comment 1 to that section comments that "revocable letters of credit offer unhappy possibilities for misleading the parties who deal with them." See Beathard v. Chicago Football Club, Inc., 419 F. Supp. 1133, 20 U.C.C. Rep. Serv. 164 (N.D. Ill. 1976). Article 2 of the UCC decrees that in sale of goods contracts, a clause requiring a letter of credit means an *irrevocable* letter of credit. Read §2-325. Circle the word *irrevocable* in subsection (3).

III.   THE ISSUER—DUTIES AND RIGHTS

When the applicant comes to the issuing bank and asks to establish credit so that the bank will issue a letter of credit to the seller, the bank normally makes the applicant sign an airtight contract absolutely binding the applicant to reimburse the bank *or else.* Cf. §5-108(i)(1). When a bank issues an irrevocable letter of credit, it is under a duty to honor a draft properly drawn thereunder, §5-108(a), so it wants to protect itself. A bank owes corresponding duties to its applicant. Read §5-108 carefully. It is important to understand that if the issuer honors a draft that it should have dishonored, the issuer may not seek reimbursement from its applicant.[2] See Brenntag Intern. Chemicals, Inc. v. Norddeutsche Landesbank GZ, 70 F. Supp. 2d 399, 42

---

2. Failure of the applicant to reimburse the issuer is irrelevant as far as the beneficiary is concerned. In this situation, the beneficiary is not liable to the issuer in quasi-contract under a theory of unjust enrichment. See City Natl. Bank v. Westland Towers Apartments, 152 Mich. App. 136, 2 U.C.C. Rep. Serv. 2d 1623 (1986). The usual explanation is that the beneficiary has not in any way been unjustly enriched; it was paid for goods delivered. Section 5-108(i)(4) clearly bars a restitution action in any situation where the defect was apparent on the face of the documents presented.

U.C.C. Rep. Serv. 2d 1107 (S.D.N.Y. 1999). An issuer in this predicament has a potential remedy in the warranty section, §5-110.

PROBLEM 250

At the request of its applicant, Greenbaum Construction Company, the Last National Bank issued a letter of credit to Latek Steel Company, obligating itself to pay drafts drawn against it, reflecting steel shipped to Greenbaum Construction under "Invoice #0046." Two weeks after the letter of credit was issued, the buyer and seller changed the shipment dates on the underlying contract and issued a new invoice, this one being "Invoice #0060." Latek Steel Company shipped the steel to Greenbaum Construction Company as agreed and was disturbed to learn that the buyer had filed for bankruptcy two days later. However, it was reassured by the terms of the letter of credit. On Friday, March 27, it submitted a draft to Last National, accompanied by Invoice #0060, and was turned down for payment on April 1. Answer these questions:

(a) Label the parties: who is the *issuer*, the *beneficiary*, the *applicant*?

(b) What is the effect of the bank holding onto the presented draft until April 1? See §5-108(b).

(c) Remembering the doctrine of *de minimis non curat lex* ("the law does not notice small defects"), the attorney for Latek Steel argued that it had substantially complied with the letter of credit, so the bank was guilty of wrongful dishonor and ought to respond in damages under §5-111. Is this right? See Dubose Steel, Inc. v. Branch Banking & Trust Co., 72 N.C. App. 598, 324 S.E.2d 859, 41 U.C.C. Rep. Serv. 187 (1985); Dolan, Strict Compliance with Letters of Credit: Striking a Fair Balance, 102 Banking L.J. 18 (1985).

(d) Does the seller have any other remedy? See §2-702; Bankruptcy Code §546(c).

Voest-Alpine Trading Co. v. Bank of China

United States District Court, Southern District of Texas, 2000
167 F. Supp. 2d 940, 46 U.C.C. Rep. Serv. 2d 808

GILMORE, District Judge.

On February 16-17 and 21-23, 2000, a bench trial was held in the above-styled case. Having considered the evidence in this case and the applicable law, the Court enters the following findings of fact and conclusions of law.

On June 23, 1995, Plaintiff Voest-Alpine Trading USA Corporation ("Voest-Alpine") entered into a contract with Jiangyin Foreign Trade Corporation ("JFTC") to sell JFTC 1,000 metric tons of styrene monomer at a total price of $1.2 million. To finance the transaction, JFTC applied for a letter of credit through Defendant Bank of China. The letter of credit provided for payment to Voest-Alpine once the goods had been shipped to Zhangjiagang, China and Voest-Alpine had presented the requisite paperwork to the Bank of China as described in the letter of credit. The letter of credit was issued by the Bank of China on July 6, 1995 and assigned the number LC9521033/95. In addition to numerous other typographical errors, Voest-Alpine's name was listed as "Voest-Alpine USA Trading Corp." instead of "Voest-Alpine Trading USA Corp." with the "Trading USA" portion inverted. The destination port was also misspelled in one place as "Zhangjiagng," missing the third "a." The letter of credit did indicate, however, that the transaction would be subject to the 1993 Uniform Customs and Practice, International Chamber of Commerce Publication Number 500 ("UCP 500").

By the time the product was ready to ship, the market price of styrene monomer had dropped significantly from the original contract price between Voest-Alpine and JFTC. Although JFTC asked for a price concession in light of the decrease in market price, Voest-Alpine declined and, through its agents, shipped the styrene monomer on July 18, 1995. All required inspection and documentation was completed. On August 1, 1995, Voest-Alpine presented the documents specified in the letter of credit to Texas Commerce Bank, the presenting bank. Texas Commerce Bank found discrepancies between the presentation documents and the letter of credit which it related to Voest-Alpine. Because Voest-Alpine did not believe that any of the noted discrepancies would warrant refusal to pay, it instructed Texas Commerce Bank to forward the presentation documents to the Bank of China.

Texas Commerce Bank sent the documents via DHL courier to the Bank of China on August 3, 1995. According to the letter of credit, Voest-Alpine, the beneficiary, was required to present the documents within fifteen days of the shipping date, by August 2, 1995. As the documents were presented on August 1, 1995, they were presented timely under the letter of credit. Bank of China received the documents on August 9, 1995.

On August 11, 1995, the Bank of China sent a telex to Texas Commerce Bank, informing them of seven alleged discrepancies between the letter of credit and the documents Voest-Alpine presented, six of which are the subject of this action. The Bank of China claimed that 1) the beneficiary's name differed from the name listed in the letter of credit, as noted by the presenting bank; 2) Voest-Alpine had submitted bills of lading marked "duplicate" and "triplicate" instead of "original"; 3) the invoice, packing list and the certificate of origin were not marked "original"; 4) the date of the survey report was later than that of the bill of lading; 5) the letter of credit number in the beneficiary's certified copy of the fax was incorrect, as noted by the presenting bank; and 6) the destination was not listed correctly in the certificate of origin and the beneficiary's certificate, as noted by the presenting bank. The telex further stated. "We are contacting the applicant of the relative discrepancy [*sic*]. Holding documents at your risks and disposal."

On August 15, Texas Commerce Bank faxed the Bank of China, stating that the discrepancies were not an adequate basis to refuse to pay the letter of credit and requested that the bank honor the letter of credit and pay Voest-Alpine accordingly. The telex identified Voest-Alpine as the beneficiary in the transaction. Voest-Alpine also contacted JFTC directly in an effort to secure a waiver of the discrepancies but was unsuccessful.

On August 19, 1995, the Bank of China sent another telex to Texas Commerce Bank further explaining what it believed to be discrepancies between the letter of credit and the documentation presented by Voest-Alpine according to the UCP 500. In relevant part, the telex provided: "You cannot say [the discrepancies] are of no consequence. The fact is that our bank must examine all documents stipulated in the credit with reasonable care, to ascertain whether or not they appear, on their face, to be incompliance [*sic*] with the terms and conditions of the credit. According to Article 13 of UCP 500, an irrevocable credit constitutes a definite undertaking of the issuing bank, providing that the stipulated documents are complied with the terms and conditions of the credit according to Article UCP 500. Now the discrepant documents may have us refuse to take up the documents according to article 14(B) of UCP 500."

The Bank of China returned the documents to Voest-Alpine and did not honor the letter of credit.

I.

The commercial letter of credit is a payment device often used in international trade which permits a buyer in a transaction to substitute its financial integrity with that of a stable credit source, usually a bank. Alaska Textile Co., Inc. v. Chase Manhattan Bank, N.A., 982 F.2d 813, 815 (2d Cir. 1992).

"[A letter of credit] transaction usually comprises three separate contracts: '[f]irst, the issuing bank enters into a contract with its customer to issue the letter of credit. Second, there is a contract between the issuing bank and the party receiving the letter of credit. Third, the customer who procured the letter of credit signs a contract with the person receiving it, usually involving the sale of goods or the provision of some service.'" Resolution Trust Corporation v. Kimball, 963 F.2d 820, 820 (5th Cir. 1992) (quoting East Girard Sav. Ass'n v. Citizens National Bank, Etc., 593 F.2d 598, 601 (5th Cir. 1979)). The underlying principle of the letter of credit transaction is the independence of the three contracts. Philadelphia Gear Corp. v. Central Bank, 717 F.2d 230, 235 (5th Cir. 1983). The issuing bank does not verify that all the terms of the underlying contract have been fulfilled and must pay on a draft properly presented by a beneficiary, without reference to the rights or obligations of the parties to the contract. Tex. Bus. & Comm. Code Ann §5.108(a), (f)(1) (Vernon's 2000). The issuing bank need only make a facial examination of the presenting documents to determine whether the beneficiary has complied with the terms of the letter of credit, however, the bank bears the risk of any misinterpretation of the beneficiary's demand for payment. Tex. Bus. & Comm. Code Ann. §5.108(i)(4) (Vernon's 2000).

Prior to the amendments to the Texas Business and Commercial Code in 1999, a beneficiary was not required to make its presentation documents strictly comply with the letter of credit, but to present documents that on their face "appear [ed] to comply" with the letter of credit in order to receive payment. Tex. Bus. & Comm. Code Ann. §5.109(b) [the prior version of Article 5—Ed.] (Vernon's 1998); see also Vest v. Pilot Point Nat'l Bank, 996 S.W.2d 9, 12 (Tex. Civ. App. 1999) (finding that the language in section 5.109 did not mandate strict compliance). The current statutory law requires an issuer to honor a presentation that, as determined by standard practice of financial institutions that regularly issue letters of credit, "appears on its face strictly to comply with the terms and conditions of the letter of credit." Tex. Bus. & Comm. Code Ann. §5.108(a), (e) (Vernon's 2000). Determination of what constitutes standard practice of financial institutions is a "matter of interpretation for the court." Tex. Bus. & Comm. Code Ann. §5.108(e) (Vernon's 2000).

The Uniform Customs and Practices for Documentary Credits, first issued in 1930 by the International Chamber of Commerce and revised approximately once every ten years since, is a compilation of internationally accepted commercial practices which may be incorporated into the private law of a contract between parties. Banco General Runinahui, S.A. v. Citibank Int'l, 97 F.3d 480, 482 (11th Cir. 1996) (citing *Alaska Textile*, 982 F.2d at 816). In this case, the parties expressly adopted the UCP 500 as the governing authority in the letter of credit. Where parties explicitly refer to the UCP 500 in their contracts, the UCP has been interpreted to apply to the transaction. *Vest*, 996 S.W.2d at 15. Accordingly, the Court will look to the UCP for guidance in analyzing whether the actions of the Bank of China were in conformity with "standard practice" of financial institutions.

The Bank of China claims that its August 11, 1995 telex to Texas Commerce Bank constituted notice of refusal under the UCP 500 because it contained the required elements listed in Article 14(d). Voest-Alpine argues that the telex did not constitute notice of refusal because there is no clear statement of refusal and because the portion of the telex that indicated that the Bank of China was contacting JFTC to seek a waiver rendered the communication ambiguous.

Article 14(d) of the UCP 500 provides:

> i. If the Issuing Bank . . . decides to refuse the [presentation] documents, it must give notice to that effect by telecommunication or, if that is not possible, by other expeditious means, without delay but no later than the close of the seventh banking day following the day of receipt of the documents. Such notice shall be given to the bank from which it received the documents, or to the Beneficiary, if it received the documents directly from him.
>
> ii. Such notice must state all discrepancies in respect of which the bank refuses the documents and must also state whether it is holding · the documents at the disposal of, or is returning them to, the presenter.

International Chamber of Commerce, ICC Uniform Customs and Practice for Documentary Credits, ICC Publication No. 500 20 (1993). According to Article 14(d), if the issuing bank elects not to honor the presentation documents, it must provide a notice of refusal within seven banking days of receipt of the documents and the notice must contain any and all discrepancies and state the disposition of the rejected documents. The section requires that if a bank wishes to reject a presentation of documents, it "*must give notice to that effect.*" (Emphasis supplied.)

Here, the Bank of China's notice is deficient because nowhere does it state that it is actually rejecting the documents or refusing to honor the letter of credit or any words to that effect. While it is true that under the UCP 500 the notice must contain a list of discrepancies and the disposition of the documents and the Bank of China's telex of August 11, 1995 does indeed contain these elements, this only addresses the requirements of Article 14(d)(ii). A notice of refusal, by its own terms must actually convey refusal, as specified in Article 14(d)(i). This omission is only compounded by the statement that the Bank of China would contact the applicant to determine if it would waive the discrepancies. As Plaintiff's expert, Professor James Byrne, testified, within the framework of Article 14, this additional piece of information holds open the possibility of acceptance upon waiver of the discrepancies by JFTC and indicates that the Bank of China has not refused the documents.

In the August 19, 1995 telex, the Bank of China stated, "Now the discrepant documents may have us refuse to take up the documents according to article 14(B) of UCP 500" (emphasis supplied). This is the bank's first mention of refusal and it is tentative at best. The use of "now" further indicates that the documents were not previously refused in the August 11, 1995 telex. Even if this second telex was sent as a notice of refusal, it came too late. The Court finds that the evidence establishes that the telex was sent on August 19, 1995. Seven banking days, the refusal period allotted by the UCP 500 Article 14(d), would have expired on August 18, 1995. International Chamber of Commerce, ICC Uniform Customs and Practice for Documentary Credits, ICC Publication No. 500 21 (1993). Accordingly, the Court finds that the Bank of China did not provide a notice of refusal within seven banking days of receipt of the presentation documents as required by Article 14(d) of the UCP 500. The Bank of China's failure to formally refuse the documents before the deadline precludes the bank from claiming that the documents are not in compliance with the terms and conditions of the credit, according to Article 14(e) of the UCP 500. Id. Although the Court could properly conclude its analysis here, the Court will analyze the discrepancies listed by the Bank of China in the August 11, 1995 telex.

II.

Voest-Alpine claims that the six remaining discrepancies cited by the Bank of China are mere technicalities and typographical errors that do not warrant the rejection of the documents. Voest-Alpine argues for a "functional standard" of compliance, contending that if the whole of the documents obviously relate to the transaction covered by the credit, the issuing bank must honor the letter of credit. The

Bank of China argues that the discrepancies were significant and that if the documents contain discrepancies on their face, it is justified in rejecting them and is not required to look beyond the papers themselves.

Section 13(a) of the UCP 500 provides:

> Banks must examine all documents stipulated in the Credit with reasonable care, to ascertain whether or not they appear, on their face, to be in compliance with the terms and conditions of the Credit. Compliance of the stipulated documents on their face with the terms and conditions of the Credit shall be determined by international standard banking practice as reflected in these Articles. Documents which appear on their face to be inconsistent with one another will be considered as not appearing on their face to be in compliance with the terms and conditions of the Credit.

International Chamber of Commerce, ICC Uniform Customs and Practice for Documentary Credits, ICC Publication No. 500 19 (1993).

The UCP 500 does not provide guidance on what inconsistencies would justify a conclusion on the part of a bank that the documents are not in compliance with the terms and conditions of the letter of credit or what discrepancies are not a reasonable basis for such a conclusion. The UCP 500 does not mandate that the documents be a mirror image of the requirements or use the term "strict compliance."

The Court notes the wide range of interpretations on what standard banks should employ in examining letter of credit document presentations for compliance. Even where courts claim to uphold strict compliance, the standard is hardly uniform. The first and most restrictive approach is to require that the presentation documents be a mirror image of the requirements. See Banco General Runinahui, S.A. v. Citibank Int'l, 97 F.3d 480, 483 (11th Cir. 1996) ("This Court has recognized and applied the 'strict compliance' standard to requests for payment under commercial letters of credit. . . . '[T]he fact that a defect is a mere technicality' does not matter.") (quoting Kerr-McGee Chem. Corp. v. FDIC, 872 F.2d 971, 973 (11th Cir. 1989)); Alaska Textile Co. v. Chase Manhattan Bank, 982 F.2d 813, 816 (2d Cir. 1992) (Noting that documents that are nearly the same as those required by the letter of credit are unacceptable for presentation in a letter of credit transaction).

Second, there are also cases claiming to follow the strict compliance standard but support rejection only where the discrepancies are such that would create risks for the issuer if the bank were to accept the presentation documents. See Flagship Cruises Ltd. v. New England Merchants Nat'l Bank of Boston, 569 F.2d 699, 705 (1st Cir.

1978) ("We do not see these rulings as retreats from rigorous insistence on compliance with letter of credit requirements. They merely recognize that variance between documents specified and documents submitted is not fatal if there is no possibility that the documents could mislead the paying bank to its detriment"); Crist v. J. Henry Schroder Bank & Trust Co., 693 F. Supp. 1429, 1433 (S.D.N.Y. 1988) (where a party who has succeeded by operation of law to the rights of the beneficiary of a letter of credit, refusal was improper, even though the terms of the credit provided for payment only to the beneficiary); Bank of Cochin, Ltd. v. Manufacturers Hanover Trust Co., 612 F. Supp. 1533, 1541 (S.D.N.Y. 1985) (even under the strict compliance standard, a variance is permitted between the documents specified in a letter of credit and the documents presented thereunder where "there is no possibility that the documents could mislead the paying bank to its detriment"); *Vest*, 996 S.W.2d at 14 (noting that strict compliance does not demand "oppressive perfectionism").

A third standard, without much support in case law, is to analyze the documents for risk to the applicant. See Int'l Chamber of Commerce, Comm'n on Banking Technique and Practice, Publication No. 511, UCP 500 & 400 Compared 39 (Charles del Busto ed. 1994) (discussion of a standard that would permit "deviations that do not cause ostensible harm" to the applicant); see also Breathless Assoc. v. First Savings & Loan Assoc., 654 F. Supp. 832, 836 (N.D. Tex. 1986) (noting, under the strict compliance standard, "[a] discrepancy . . . should not warrant dishonor unless it reflects an increased likelihood of defective performance or fraud on the part of the beneficiary").

The mirror image approach is problematic because it absolves the bank reviewing the documents of any responsibility to use common sense to determine if the documents, on their face, are related to the transaction or even to review an entire document in the context of the others presented to the bank. On the other hand, the second and third approaches employ a determination-of-harm standard that is too unwieldy. Such an analysis would improperly require the bank to evaluate risks that it might suffer or that might be suffered by the applicant and could undermine the independence of the three contracts that underlie the letter of credit payment scheme by forcing the bank to look beyond the face of the presentation documents.

The Court finds that a moderate, more appropriate standard lies within the UCP 500 itself and the opinions issued by the International Chamber of Commerce ("ICC") Banking Commission. One of the Banking Commission opinions defined the term "consistency" between the letter of credit and the documents presented to the issuing bank as used in Article 13(a) of the UCP to mean that "the whole of the documents must obviously relate to the same transaction, that is to say, that each should bear a relation (link) with the others on its face. . . . " Int'l Chamber of Commerce, Banking Comm'n, Publication No. 371, Decisions (1975-1979) of the ICC Banking Commission R. 12 (1980). The Banking Commission rejected the notion that "all of the documents should be *exactly* consistent in their wording." Id. (emphasis in original).

A common sense, case-by-case approach would permit minor deviations of a typographical nature because such a letter-for-letter correspondence between the letter of credit and the presentation documents is virtually impossible. See Int'l Chamber of Commerce, Comm'n on Banking Technique and Practice, Publication No. 511, UCP 500 & 400 Compared 39 (Charles del Busto ed. 1994) (noting the difficulty in attaining mirror-image compliance). While the end result of such an analysis may bear a strong resemblance to the relaxed strict compliance standard, the actual calculus used by the issuing bank is not the risk it or the applicant faces but rather, whether the documents bear a rational link to one another. In this way, the issuing bank is required to examine a particular document in light of all documents presented and use common sense but is not required to evaluate risks or go beyond the face of the documents. The Court finds that in this case the Bank of China's listed discrepancies should be analyzed under this standard by determining whether the whole of the documents obviously relate to the transaction on their face.

First, the Bank of China claimed that the beneficiary's name in the presentation documents, Voest-Alpine Trading USA, differed from the letter of credit, which listed the beneficiary as Voest-Alpine USA Trading. While it is true that the letter of credit inverted Voest-Alpine's geographic locator, all the documents Voest-Alpine presented that obviously related to this transaction placed the geographic locator behind "Trading," not in front of it. Furthermore, the addresses corresponded to that listed in the letter of credit and Texas Commerce Bank's cover letter to the Bank of China identified Voest-Alpine Trading USA as the beneficiary in the transaction with JFTC. The letter of credit with the inverted name bore obvious links to the documents presented by Voest-Alpine Trading USA. This is in contrast to a misspelling or outright omission. See Beyene v. Irving Trust Co., 762 F.2d 4 (2d Cir. 1985) (listing beneficiary as "Soran" rather than "Sofan" was sufficient basis for refusal); Bank of Cochin, Ltd. v. Manufacturers Hanover Trust Co., 612 F. Supp. 1533 (S.D.N.Y. 1985) (omitting "Ltd." from corporate name justified rejection). In contrast with these cases, the inversion of the geographic locator here does not signify a different corporate entity. The expert testimony of Professor Byrne supports the finding that this is not a discrepancy that warrants rejection of the presentation documents because the UCP 500 does not impose a standard of exact replication.

Second, the Bank of China pointed out that the set of originals of the bill of lading should have all been stamped "original" rather than "original," "duplicate" and "triplicate." It should be noted that neither the letter of credit nor any provision in the UCP 500 requires such stamping. In fact, the ICC Banking Commission expressly ruled that "duplicate" and "triplicate" bills of lading did not need to be marked "original" and that failure to label them as originals did not justify refusal of the documents. Int'l Chamber of Commerce, Banking Comm'n, Publication No. 565, Opinions of the ICC Banking Comm'n 1995-1996 38 (Gary Collyer ed. 1997). While it is true that this clarification by the ICC came after the transaction at issue in this case, it is clear from the face of the documents that these documents are three originals rather than one original and two copies. The documents have signatures in blue ink [*sic* "that"?] vary slightly, bear original stamps oriented differently on each page and clearly state on their face that the preparer made three original bills. Further, one possible definition of duplicate is "[t]o make or execute again" and one definition of triplicate is "[o]ne of a set of three identical things." Webster's II New Riverside University Dictionary 410, 1237 (1994). While the "duplicate" and "triplicate" stamps may have been confusing, stamps do not make obviously original documents into copies.

Third, the Bank of China claimed that the failure to stamp the packing list documents as "original" was a discrepancy. Again, these documents are clearly originals on their face as they have three slightly differing signatures in blue ink. There was no requirement in the letter of credit or the UCP 500 that original documents be marked as such. The ICC's policy statement on the issue provides that, "banks treat as original any document that appears to be hand signed by the issuer of the document." (Int'l Chamber of Commerce, Comm'n on Banking Technique and Practice, The determination of an "Original" document in the context of UCP 500 sub-Article 20(b) July 12, 1999.) http://www.iccwbo.org/home/statementsrules/statements/1999/the-determination-of-an-original-document.asp. The failure to mark obvious originals is not a discrepancy.

Fourth, the Bank of China argues that the date of the survey report is after the bill of lading and is therefore discrepant. A careful examination of the survey report reveals that the survey took place "immediately before/after loading" and that the sample of cargo "to be loaded" was taken. The plain language of the report reveals that the report may have been issued after the bill of lading but the survey itself was conducted before the ship departed. The date does not pose a discrepancy.

Fifth, the Bank of China claims that the letter of credit number listed in the beneficiary's certified copy of [*sic*] fax is wrong. The letter of credit number was listed as "LC95231033/95" on the copy of [*sic*] fax instead of "LC9521033/95" as in the letter of credit itself, adding an extra "3" after "LC952." However, adding the letter of credit number to this document was gratuitous and in the numerous other places in the documents that the letter of credit was referenced by number, it was incorrect only in one place. Moreover, the seven other pieces of information contained in the document were correct. The document checker could have easily looked to any other document to verify the letter of credit number, or looked to the balance of the information within the document and found that the document as a whole bears an obvious relationship to the transaction. Madame Gao, the document checker who reviewed Voest-Alpine's presentation documents for the Bank of China, testified that she did not look beyond the face of this particular document in assessing the discrepancy. The cover letter from Texas Commerce Bank, for example, had the correct number.

Finally, the Bank of China claims that the wrong destination is listed in the certificate of origin and the beneficiary's certificate. The certificate of origin spelled Zhangjiagang as "Zhangjiagng" missing an "a" as it is misspelled once in the letter of credit, making it consistent. The beneficiary's certificate, however, spelled it "Zhanjiagng," missing a "g" in addition to the "a," a third spelling that did not appear in the letter of credit. Madame Gao first considered the discrepancy a "misspelling" rather than an indication of the wrong port, according to her notes. There is no port in China called "Zhangjiagng" or "Zhanjiagng." "Gng" is a combination of letters not found in Romanized Chinese, whereas "gang" means "port" in Chinese. The other information contained in the document was correct, such as the letter of credit number and the contract number, and even contained the distinctive phrase "by courie lukdt within 3 days after shipment," presumably meaning by courier within three days after shipment, as in the letter of credit. The document as a whole bears an obvious relationship with the transaction. The misspelling of the destination is not a basis for dishonor of the letter of credit where the rest of the document has demonstrated linkage to the transaction on its face.

Based on the foregoing, the Court finds in favor of the plaintiff, Voest-Alpine.

NOTE

1. This case was decided under the UCP 500, where the so-called *strict compliance* requirement is less markedly pronounced than it currently is in the Uniform Commercial Code. Read §§5-103(d) and 5-108(a) and the following Official Comments: Official Comment 3 to §5-102 and Official Comment 1 to §5-108. Using the tests therein, would the court in the above case have reached the same result?

2. As to the waiver issue in the above case, see §5-108(c).

3. In letter of credit transactions, it should be emphasized that banks issuing the credits do not charge a great deal and therefore should be exposed to a minimum risk. If a bank is going to dishonor the credit, it should make sure that it is playing fair with all the parties involved so that in any ensuing litigation the commercial reasonableness of its actions will attract the sympathy of the court.

PROBLEM 251

Assume in the last Problem that the letter of credit issued by Last National had required that the bill of lading representing the goods be given not to Greenbaum Construction Company, the applicant, but presented to the bank itself. Assume also that Latek Steel has completely complied with all of the terms of the credit, but Last National, knowing of the applicant's bankruptcy, wrongfully refuses to pay the credit as agreed. You are the attorney for Latek Steel, and the vice president in charge of marketing calls you with some questions. The market for steel is falling rapidly. Must Latek Steel resell the steel involved in this transaction immediately, or may it wait, hoping the bank will change its mind and pay what it owes? If it does resell, does that reduce the amount it can claim as damages from Last National? As to both these matters, see §5-111(a).

PROBLEM 252

At the request of its applicant, Octopus National Bank (ONB) issued an irrevocable letter of credit to Warren Crook, the beneficiary. The credit's terms required a bill of lading showing that the goods were loaded on board the S.S. Titanic by April 1, 2009. Crook cleverly drew up a phony bill of lading supposedly issued by the Titanic and presented it along with a draft on the bank to the issuer. ONB paid the draft. Can it collect from its applicant? See §5-108; also note §§5-110 (warranties on transfer and presentment), 5-111 (presenter's right to damages on wrongful dishonor of a draft), and 5-117 (subrogation rights of the parties). Could the applicant use the §5-110 warranties to sue the beneficiary?

PROBLEM 253

Luddite Technologies, Inc. wanted to build a new company headquarters. It hired Weekend Construction Company to do the job, requiring a standby letter of credit of $80,000 to be paid if Weekend failed to keep to the required schedule for completion of the building. At Weekend's request, Last National Bank issued such a credit in favor of Luddite, payable, according to the terms of the credit, "on default by Weekend Construction Company in meeting the attached completion schedule and the beneficiary's presentation of an affidavit to that effect along with a draft drawn on us for $80,000." Weekend Construction dutifully performed its contractual duties, but the president of Luddite, needing money, sent the required draft and affidavit to Last National, wrongfully asserting that Weekend had missed timely completion of a part of the project. Last National paid the draft without investigating the truth of the assertions in the affidavit and now seeks reimbursement from the applicant, Weekend Construction. Can Weekend resist paying under the theory that Last National did not verify the default as the letter of credit required? See §5-108(g) and its Official Comment 9. White & Summers explain: "Where the documents commit the issuer to assess facts and events outside the documents presented, they disable the independence principle and topple the wall that separates presented documents from beneficiary-applicant disputes"; §26-6 at 156-157 (Practioner Treatise). If Weekend Construction has gone bankrupt since the bank honored the draft, can Last National pursue Luddite Technologies to get its money back? See §§5-108(i)(4), 5-110. How quickly must it act? See §5-115.

Sztejn v. J. Henry Schroder Bank Corp.

New York Supreme Court, 1941
177 Misc. 719, 31 N.Y.S.2d 631

SHIENTAG, J. This is a motion by the defendant, the Chartered Bank of India, Australia and China, (hereafter referred to as the Chartered Bank), made pursuant to Rule 106(5) of the Rules of Civil Practice to dismiss the supplemental complaint on the ground that it fails to state facts sufficient to constitute a cause of action against the moving defendant. The plaintiff brings this action to restrain the payment or presentment of payment of drafts under a letter of credit issued to secure the purchase price of certain merchandise, bought by the plaintiff and his coadventurer, one Schwarz, who is a party defendant in this action. The plaintiff also seeks a judgment declaring the letter of credit and drafts thereunder null and void. The complaint alleges that the documents accompanying the drafts are fraudulent in that they do not represent actual merchandise but instead cover boxes fraudulently filled with worthless material by the seller of the goods. The moving defendant urges that the complaint fails to state a cause of action against it because the Chartered Bank is only concerned with the documents and on their face these conform to the requirement of the letter of credit.

On January 7, 1941, the plaintiff and his coadventurer contracted to purchase a quantity of bristles from the defendant Transea Traders, Ltd. (hereafter referred to as Transea) a corporation having its place of business in Lucknow, India. In order to pay for the bristles, the plaintiff and Schwarz contracted with the defendant J. Henry Schroder Banking Corporation (hereafter referred to as Schroder), a domestic corporation, for the issuance of an irrevocable letter of credit to Transea which provided that drafts by the latter for a specified portion of the purchase price of the bristles would be paid by Schroder upon shipment of the described merchandise and presentation of an invoice and a bill of lading covering the shipment, made out to the order of Schroder.

The letter of credit was delivered to Transea by Schroder's correspondent bank in India, Transea placed fifty cases of material on board a steamship, procured a bill of lading from the steamship company and obtained the customary invoices. These documents describe the bristles called for by the letter of credit. However, the complaint alleges that in fact Transea filled the fifty crates with cowhair, other worthless material and rubbish with intent to simulate genuine merchandise and defraud the plaintiff and Schwarz. The complaint then alleges that Transea drew a draft under the letter of credit to the order of the Chartered Bank and delivered the draft and the fraudulent documents to the "Chartered Bank at Cawnpore, India, for collection for the account of said defendant Transea." The Chartered Bank has presented the draft along with the documents to Schroder for payment. The plaintiff prays for a judgment declaring the letter of credit and draft thereunder void and for injunctive relief to prevent the payment of the draft.

For the purpose of this motion, the allegations of the complaint must be deemed established and "every intendment and fair inference is in favor of the pleading." . . . Therefore, it must be assumed that Transea was engaged in a scheme to defraud the plaintiff and Schwarz, that the merchandise shipped by Transea is worthless rubbish and that the Chartered Bank is not an innocent holder of the draft for value but is merely attempting to procure payment of the draft for Transea's account.

It is well established that a letter of credit is independent of the primary contract of sale between the buyer and the seller. The issuing bank agrees to pay upon presentation of documents, not goods. This rule is necessary to preserve the efficiency of the letter of credit as an instrument for the financing of trade. One of the chief purposes of the letter of credit is to furnish the seller with a ready means of obtaining prompt payment for his merchandise. It would be a most unfortunate interference with business transactions if a bank before honoring drafts drawn upon it was obliged or even allowed to go behind the documents, at the request of the buyer and enter into controversies between the buyer and the seller regarding the quality of the merchandise shipped. If the buyer and the seller intended the bank to do this they could have so provided in the letter of credit itself, and in the absence of such a provision, the court will not demand or even permit the bank to delay paying drafts which are proper in form. . . . Of course, the application of this doctrine presupposes that the documents accompanying the draft are genuine and conform in terms to the requirements of the letter of credit. . . .

However, I believe that a different situation is presented in the instant action. This is not a controversy between the buyer and seller concerning a mere breach of warranty regarding the quality of the merchandise; on the present motion, it must be assumed that the seller has intentionally failed to ship any goods ordered by the buyer. In such a situation, where the seller's fraud has been called to the bank's attention before the drafts and documents have been presented for payment, the principle of the independence of the bank's obligation under the letter of credit should not be extended to protect the unscrupulous seller. It is true that even though the documents are forged or fraudulent, if the issuing bank has already paid the draft before receiving notice of the seller's fraud, it will be protected if it exercised reasonable diligence before making such payment. . . . However, in the instant action Schroder has received notice of Transea's active fraud before it accepted or paid the draft. The Chartered Bank, which under the allegations of the complaint stands in no better position than Transea, should not be heard to complain because Schroder is not forced to pay the draft accompanied by documents covering a transaction which it has reason to believe is fraudulent.

Although our courts have used broad language to the effect that a letter of credit is independent of the primary contract between the buyer and seller, that language was used in cases concerning alleged breaches of warranty; no case has been brought to my attention on this point involving an intentional fraud on the part of the seller which was brought to the bank's notice with the request that it withhold payment of the draft on this account. This distinction between a breach of warranty and active fraud on the part of the seller is supported by authority and reason. As one court has stated: "Obviously, when the issuer of a letter of credit knows that a document, although correct in form, is, in point of fact, false or illegal, he cannot be called upon to recognize such a document as complying with the terms of a letter of credit." Old Colony Trust Co. v. Lawyers' Title & Trust Co., 2d Cir., 297 F. 152 at page 158, *certiorari denied*, 265 U.S. 585, 44 S. Ct. 459, 68 L. Ed. 1192. . . .

No hardship will be caused by permitting the bank to refuse payment where fraud is claimed, where the merchandise is not merely inferior in quality but consists of worthless rubbish, where the draft and the accompanying documents are in the hands of one who stands in the same position as the fraudulent seller, where the bank has been given notice of the fraud before being presented with the drafts and documents for payment, and where the bank itself does not wish to pay pending an adjudication of the rights and obligations of the other parties. While the primary factor in the issuance of the letter of credit is the credit standing of the buyer, the security afforded by the merchandise is also taken into account. In fact, the letter of credit requires a bill of lading made out to the order of the bank and not the buyer. Although the bank is not interested in the exact detailed performance of the sales contract, it is vitally interested in assuring itself that there are some goods represented by the documents. Finkelstein, Legal Aspects of Commercial Letters of Credit, p.238; O'Meara v. National Park Bank of New York, 239 N.Y. 386, 401, 146 N.E. 636, 39 A.L.R. 747, opinion of Cardozo, J., dissenting; Thayer, Irrevocable Credits in International Commerce, 37 C.L.R. 1326, 1335.

On this motion only the complaint is before me and I am bound by its allegation that the Chartered Bank is not a holder in due course but is a mere agent for collection for the account of the seller charged with fraud. Therefore, the Chartered Bank's motion to dismiss the complaint must be denied. If it had appeared from the face of the complaint that the bank presenting the draft for payment was a holder in due course, its claim against the bank issuing the letter of credit would not be defeated even though the primary transaction was tainted with fraud. . . .

Accordingly, the defendant's motion to dismiss the supplemental complaint is denied.

Is *Sztejn* still good law? Read §5-109 and its Official Comments carefully; see Mid-America Tire, Inc. v. PTZ Trading Ltd. Import and Export Agents, 2000 WL 1725415, 43 U.C.C. Rep. Serv. 2d 964 (Ohio App. 2000).

PROBLEM 254

Just as Octopus National Bank was about to honor a draft drawn on it by the beneficiary of its letter of credit, the bank's applicant called and demanded that the bank dishonor the draft because the beneficiary was guilty of "out and out fraud" on the underlying transaction between them. The bank calls you, its attorney, for advice. The documents presented along with the draft exactly match the terms of the credit, and the bank officials are sure that there is no fraud in the documents. Look at §§5-108 and 5-109, and tell the bank what you think it should do. Cf. Emery-Waterhouse Co. v. Rhode Island Hosp. Trust Natl. Bank, 757 F.2d 399, 40 U.C.C. Rep. Serv. 737 (1st Cir. 1985) (punitive damages of $1,397,000 awarded against beneficiary who fraudulently drew against a letter of credit). If ONB dishonors the draft and this causes the beneficiary to lose millions of dollars on the underlying transaction, is ONB ever liable for *more* than the amount of the letter of credit? See §5-111.

In §5-109(a) the bank is given the option to honor or not as it wishes. As you can well imagine, banks tend to pay more attention to the applicant's request to dishonor if his name is Donald Trump than if her name is Jane Doe. If the bank decides to honor the draft, the applicant has two causes of action against the seller-beneficiary: the underlying obligation (normally the contract of sale, see Article 2) and the §5-110(a)(2) warranty.

Intrinsic Values Corp. v. Superintendencia De Administracion Tributaria

Florida Court of Appeals, 2002
806 So. 2d 616, 46 U.C.C. Rep. Serv. 2d 1092

SHEVIN, Judge.

Intrinsic Values Corporation appeals an order denying its motion to dissolve a temporary injunction. We affirm.

Superintendencia de Administracion Tributaria, the Guatemala tax administration agency, entered into a contract with Intrinsic, a Panamanian corporation, for the purchase of automobile license plates, decals and identification cards. At Superintendencia's request, Banco de Guatemala issued irrevocable letters of credit for Intrinsic's benefit; First Union National Bank and Barclays Bank, PLC, were the confirming banks.

Based on Intrinsic's failure to supply the goods, Superintendencia unilaterally canceled the contract, as provided therein. Superintendencia filed an action against Intrinsic in Guatemala, the forum selected in the parties' agreement. The Guatemala court issued an injunction barring Banco de Guatemala from paying on the letters of credit.

Subsequently, in Florida, Superintendencia brought an action pursuant to section 675.109(2), Florida Statutes (2001) to prevent First Union and Barclays from honoring the letter of credit. Superintendencia asserted that it had canceled the contract due to Intrinsic's failure to perform according to contract specifications, that the Guatemalan injunction was in force, and that honor of any presentment by Intrinsic would facilitate a material fraud. Intrinsic was not named in the complaint, nor served with notice. The court entered an agreed-upon injunction. Intrinsic learned of the injunction when it sought payment under the letter of credit. Intrinsic intervened in the action and sought an order dissolving the injunction. Following an evidentiary hearing, the court denied the motion.

The trial court properly denied Intrinsic's motion to dissolve the temporary injunction. In support of its request for a temporary injunction, Superintendencia presented two bases for the injunction: presentment would result in a material fraud; and comity militated in favor of the injunction. The temporary injunction was properly entered on those bases.

Section 675.109(2) provides:

> (2) If an applicant claims that a required document is forged or materially fraudulent or that honor of the presentation would facilitate

a material fraud by the beneficiary on the issuer or applicant, a court of competent jurisdiction may temporarily or permanently enjoin the issuer from honoring a presentation or grant similar relief against the issuer or other persons only if the court finds that:

(a) The relief is not prohibited under the law applicable to an accepted draft or deferred obligation incurred by the issuer;

(b) A beneficiary, issuer, or nominated person who may be adversely affected is adequately protected against loss that it may suffer because the relief is granted;

(c) All of the conditions to entitle a person to the relief under the laws of this state have been met; and

(d) On the basis of the information submitted to the court, the applicant is more likely than not to succeed under its claim of forgery or material fraud and the person demanding honor does not qualify for protection under paragraph (1)(a).

As required under the statute, Superintendencia demonstrated that honoring a presentation would facilitate a material fraud by the beneficiary on the issuer or applicant. The record demonstrates as follows: Intrinsic did not perform in accordance with the contract; Superintendencia had canceled the contract; Superintendencia notified Intrinsic of cancellation, and had obtained an injunction against payment by the issuing bank; and Superintendencia had brought this action to prevent Intrinsic from committing a material fraud by presenting documents for payment of the letter of credit. Superintendencia also demonstrated, more likely than not, that it would succeed on the material fraud claim. Itek Corp. v. First Nat'l Bank of Boston, 730 F.2d 19 (1st Cir. 1984); Rockwell Int'l Sys. v. Citibank, N.A., 719 F.2d 583 (2d Cir. 1983); Touche Ross & Co. v. Manufacturers Hanover Trust Co., 107 Misc. 2d 438, 434 N.Y.S.2d 575 (Sup. Ct. 1980).

The Uniform Commercial Code Comment to section 675.109 addresses the propriety of awarding an injunction under the factual scenario in this case. "Material fraud by the beneficiary occurs only when the beneficiary has no colorable right to expect honor and where there is no basis in fact to support such a right to honor." U.C.C. §5-109 (1999) cmt. 1. Here, Intrinsic was aware that the contract had been canceled prior to presentment. Under these circumstances Intrinsic's demand for payment had "absolutely no basis in fact;" the Guatemala injunction forbid the issuer's payment on letters of credit based on this contract. Thus, the facts demonstrate the possibility of a " 'fraud' so serious as to make it obviously pointless and unjust to permit the beneficiary to obtain the money." U.C.C. §5-109 (1999) cmt. 1 (quoting

Ground Air Transfer, Inc. v. Westates Airlines, Inc., 899 F.2d 1269, 1272-73 (1st Cir. 1990)). Under this scenario, section 675.109 contemplates the issuance of an injunction. We, therefore, hold that the trial court properly denied the motion to dissolve the temporary injunction.

The temporary injunction is also properly granted based on principles of comity. A foreign decree "is entitled to comity, where the parties have been given notice and the opportunity to be heard, where the foreign court had original jurisdiction, and where the foreign decree does not offend the public policy of the State of Florida." Nahar v. Nahar, 656 So. 2d 225, 229 (Fla. 3d DCA), *review denied,* 664 So. 2d 249 (Fla. 1995). Here, the Guatemala court had jurisdiction, in accordance with the parties' contract, to resolve the controversy over Intrinsic's performance vel non, and Intrinsic had notice and opportunity to be heard in that forum. As Florida's jurisdiction and due process requirements had been met, the Guatemala injunction is entitled to comity. Absent the Florida injunction, the confirming banks would be required to honor payment requests under the letter of credit, but the Guatemala injunction would bar reimbursement from the issuing bank. As a result, the trial court properly enjoined payment on the letter of credit to render effective the Guatemala injunction and to preserve the status quo pending a final decree of the Guatemala court. See Cardenas v. Solis, 570 So. 2d 996 (Fla. 3d DCA 1990) (applying comity principles to enforce Guatemala court temporary injunction), *review denied,* 581 So. 2d 163 (Fla. 1991).

Based on the foregoing, the trial court's order denying the motion to dissolve the temporary injunction is hereby,

Affirmed.

PRACTICAL NOTE

In deciding the liability of an issuer who refuses to honor a credit, the courts have placed great emphasis on the "real" reason the issuer wants out. If that reason is that the applicant is bankrupt, so that the issuer fears no reimbursement will be forthcoming, the courts will stretch to hold the issuer liable. After all, fear of applicant insolvency was the very reason the seller wanted a letter of credit in the beginning. On the other hand, where the issuer hesitates because it is afraid that honoring will violate §5-108, and the issuer will lose the right to seek reimbursement from its applicant, the issuer's conduct is more likely to receive favorable treatment from the court. For a fascinating example of these considerations at work, compare the district and appellate court opinions in Courtaulds N. Am., Inc. v. North Carolina

Natl. Bank, 387 F. Supp. 92, 16 U.C.C. Rep. Serv. 1323 (M.D.N.C. 1975), *rev'd*, 528 F.2d 802, 18 U.C.C. Rep. Serv. 467 (4th Cir. 1975).

PROBLEM 255

Octopus National Bank issued a $50,000 letter of credit to Grey Goods of New York, payable to Grey Goods on presentation of a draft and certain documents demonstrating shipment of clothing to Ohio Wholesalers, the bank's applicant. Grey Goods needed money to finance its operations, so it borrowed $30,000 from Midwest State Bank, giving MSB a security interest in the proceeds of the letter of credit, and assigning the right to those proceeds to MSB, which promptly notified ONB of the assignment. Grey Goods had trouble filling the Ohio Wholesalers order, so those two parties agreed to lower the amount shipped and the price to $10,000 worth of clothing, and the letter of credit was amended to reflect this lower amount. When the clothing was shipped and the draft presented under the letter of credit, ONB was only willing to pay $10,000 to MSB. MSB calls you, its attorney. What are its rights here? See §§5-114 and 5-106, and Official Comment 2 to the latter.

Ochoco Lumber Co. v. Fibrex & Shipping Co., Inc.

Oregon Court of Appeals, 2000
994 P.2d 793, 40 U.C.C. Rep. Serv. 2d 530

KISTLER, J.

The trial court ruled that neither the applicant nor the issuer on a standby letter of credit can be subrogated to the beneficiary's claims. The court accordingly granted defendants' motion to dismiss plaintiff's equitable subrogation claims, denied plaintiff leave to replead, and entered judgment on those claims. We reverse and remand.

In 1993, defendant Fibrex & Shipping Co., Inc., entered into an agreement to purchase timber in Montana. To fund the purchase, Fibrex borrowed $3,900,000 from West One Idaho Bank. West One imposed two conditions on the loan. First, it required that Fibrex's sole shareholder, Akira Saheki, and his wife, Saeko Saheki, personally guarantee the loan. Second, "[a]s security for repayment of [Fibrex's] note," West One required a standby letter of credit "in an amount no less than the amount of the principal balance of th[e] note."

Fibrex obtained the letter of credit by entering into an agreement with plaintiff Ochoco Lumber Company. Fibrex agreed to sell and Ochoco agreed to buy up to six and one-half million board feet of harvested ponderosa pine logs. As part of their agreement, Ochoco provided for an irrevocable standby letter of credit for $3,900,000, which First Interstate Bank issued for the benefit of West One. The letter of credit both served as security for Ochoco's performance under its agreement with Fibrex and also "was used by Fibrex to fulfill its obligations under [its loan from West One]."[3]

In 1994 and 1995, Fibrex failed to fulfill its obligations under its agreement with Ochoco. In May 1995, Ochoco and Fibrex renegotiated their agreement. In August 1995, Fibrex, Ochoco, and the persons who owned the timber entered into an amended timber purchase agreement. In September 1996, Fibrex's loan from West One came due. Fibrex failed to pay the loan, and West One drew over two million dollars on First Interstate's letter of credit. Ochoco reimbursed First Interstate Bank in full. Ochoco then demanded repayment from Fibrex. After Fibrex refused to repay Ochoco, Ochoco notified West One that it was subrogated to West One's rights against both Fibrex and the Sahekis, the guarantors of Fibrex's loan.

When West One refused to acknowledge Ochoco's equitable subrogation rights, Ochoco brought an action alleging, among other things, four claims for relief that were based on equitable subrogation. Ochoco sought a declaration that it is subrogated to West One's rights, it sued Fibrex on the note that Fibrex had given West One, and it sued the Sahekis on their guarantee. Ochoco also sought injunctive relief against Fibrex and the Sahekis. Defendants moved to dismiss Ochoco's claims for relief that were based on equitable subrogation. Relying on Tudor Dev. Group, Inc. v. U.S. Fid. & Guar. Co., 968 F.2d 357 (3d Cir. 1992), and Shokai v. U.S. National Bank of Oregon, 126 F.3d 1135 (9th Cir. 1997), defendants argued that equitable subrogation is not available to the parties on a standby letter of credit. The trial court agreed. It dismissed Ochoco's subrogation claims without leave to replead and entered judgment on those claims pursuant to ORCP 67 B.

On appeal, defendants advance two arguments. They argue initially that equitable subrogation is available only to persons who are secondarily liable for a debt. They reason that the issuer's contractual

3. Fibrex agreed to use the funds it received from Ochoco's log purchases to reduce the balance on its loan with West One and thus reduce Ochoco's exposure on the letter of credit.

obligation to pay on a standby letter of credit[4] means that the issuer is primarily, not secondarily, liable. They argue alternatively that, in any event, the particular facts of this transaction make subrogation inappropriate. Ochoco responds that a standby letter of credit is no different from a surety bond or a guarantee in that the issuer's obligation to pay on a standby letter of credit does not arise until there is a default. It follows, Ochoco reasons, that equitable subrogation should be equally available to the parties to a standby letter of credit; the transactions are in substance no different.

We begin with the statutes that govern letters of credit. When First Interstate issued the letter of credit in this case, the Oregon statutes did not address whether equitable subrogation was available on a standby letter of credit. Nothing should be inferred from that omission, however. ORS 75.1020(3) (1991) specifically recognized that "ORS 75.1010 to 75.1170 deal with some but not all the rules and concepts of letters of credit as such rules or concepts have developed . . . or may hereafter develop." It added: "The fact that ORS 75.1010 to 75.1170 state a rule does not by itself require, imply or negate application of the same or a converse rule to a situation not provided for . . . by ORS 75.1010 to 75.1170." ORS 75.1020(3) (1991). The statute thus explicitly left to judicial development those rules that were not codified in ORS chapter 75.

In 1997, the legislature authorized issuers of and applicants for letters of credit to seek equitable subrogation but made the new statute applicable to letters of credit issued on or after January 1, 1998.[5] Or.

---

4. A letter of credit "is an engagement by an issuer, usually a bank, made at the request of the [applicant] for a fee, to honor a beneficiary's drafts or other demands for payment upon satisfaction of the conditions set forth in the letter of credit." Tudor Dev. Group, Inc., 968 F.2d at 360; accord Peter R. Jarvis, Standby Letters of Credit-Issuers' Subrogation and Assignment Rights, 9 UCC LJ 356, 356-60 (1977). There are two major types of letters of credit transactions. A commercial letter of credit is typically used when the seller is unfamiliar or uncertain about the buyer's credit history. Id. The beneficiary of a commercial letter of credit (usually the seller) may draw upon the letter by showing that it has performed and is entitled to the funds. Id. A standby letter of credit, on the other hand, typically requires the production of documents showing that the applicant has defaulted on its obligation to the beneficiary, which triggers the beneficiary's right to draw on the letter. Id.

5. Oregon Laws 1997, chapter 150, section 20 [UCC §5-117], provides:

(1) An issuer that honors a beneficiary's presentation is subrogated to the rights of the beneficiary to the same extent as if the issuer were a secondary obligor of the underlying obligation owed to the beneficiary and of the applicant to the same extent as if the issuer were the secondary obligor of the underlying obligation owed to the applicant.

(2) An applicant that reimburses an issuer is subrogated to the rights of the issuer against any beneficiary, presenter or nominated person to the same extent as if the

Laws 1997, ch. 150, §§20, 27 & 29. The Ninth Circuit has concluded that because Oregon's 1997 law applies prospectively, the Oregon legislature must have believed that prior law did not allow subrogation. See *Shokai*, 126 F.3d at 1136. Defendants find the Ninth Circuit's reasoning "instructive" and urge us to follow it. We decline to do so.

The 1997 Legislature amended many of the provisions in ORS chapter 75 governing letters of credit. See Or. Laws 1997, ch. 150, §§3-20. The fact that the legislature provided that all those amendments would apply prospectively hardly reflects a judgment on the existing state of the law with respect to each or any of them. See Or. Laws 1997, ch. 150, §27. The inference the Ninth Circuit drew is, at best, a weak one and is at odds with the long-standing principle that one legislature's view on an earlier state of the law is entitled to little or no weight. Cf. DeFazio v. WPPSS, 296 Or. 550, 561, 679 P.2d 1316 (1984) ("[t]he views legislators have of existing law may shed light on a new enactment, but it is of no weight in interpreting a law enacted by their predecessors"). Even if, however, the inference that defendants urge were textually permissible, it is not required and the legislative history points in the opposite direction. The Oregon Bankers' Association, which sponsored the 1997 legislation, told the legislature that the courts had not agreed on the availability of equitable subrogation, giving rise to confusion in the law. Testimony, Senate Committee on Business, Law and Government, SB 246, January 22, 1997, Ex H (statement of Frank E. Brawner). Although the legislature sought to clarify the law for letters of credit issued after the effective date of the act, the text, context, and the legislative history of the 1997 act do not suggest that the legislature made any judgment about the parties' right to equitable subrogation for letters of credit issued before the act's effective date. We are accordingly left to resolve that issue under common-law principles.

The court has explained that subrogation is " 'the substitution of another person in place of the creditor to whose rights he succeeds in relation to the debt, and gives to the substitute all of the rights, priorities, remedies, liens and securities of the party for whom he is substituted.' " Maine Bonding v. Centennial Ins. Co., 298 Or. 514, 521, 693 P.2d 1296 (1985) (quoting United States F. & G. Co. v. Bramwell,

---

applicant were the secondary obligor of the obligations owed to the issuer and has the rights of subrogation of the issuer to the rights of the beneficiary stated in subsection (1) of this section.

By its terms, this law applies only to letters of credit issued on or after January 1, 1998. Or. Laws 1997, ch. 150, §§27 & 29.

108 Or. 261, 277, 217 P. 332 (1923)). The purpose of subrogation is to
prevent unjust enrichment. See Barnes v. Eastern & Western Lbr. Co.,
205 Or. 553, 596, 287 P.2d 929 (1955). Simply stated, subrogation is an
equitable device used "'to compel ultimate discharge of a debt by [the
person] who in equity and good conscience ought to pay it. . . .'"
Maine Bonding, 298 Or. at 521, 693 P.2d 1296 (quoting United States
F. & G. Co., 108 Or. at 277, 217 P. 332).

As a general rule, the courts have required that the party seeking
subrogation must have paid a debt for which it was secondarily liable.
Wasco Co. v. New England E. Ins. Co., 88 Or. 465, 469-71, 172 P. 126
(1918); accord *Tudor Dev. Group, Inc.*, 968 F.2d at 361. The party must
not have acted as a volunteer but must have paid to protect its own
interests. Id. Finally, equitable subrogation "will not be enforced where
it will work injustice to those having equal equities." Id. The Oregon
courts have not specifically addressed how these requirements apply to
standby letters of credit. A handful of courts and commentators have
done so, although their decisions have not been uniform. See *Tudor
Dev. Group, Inc.*, 968 F.2d at 361-62 (collecting cases).

The majority and minority views are perhaps best illustrated by the
two opinions in *Tudor Dev. Group, Inc.* The majority in *Tudor* focused
on whether the issuer is primarily or secondarily liable for the debt.
968 F.2d at 362. It reasoned, as a majority of courts have, that the issuer
is primarily liable because a letter of credit imposes an independent
obligation on the issuer to pay. Id. The majority reasoned that the
issuer is "satisfying its own absolute and primary obligation to make
payment rather than satisfying an obligation of its customer." Id. The
majority recognized that the issuer's obligation on a standby letter of
credit is secondary in the sense that it does not arise until the applicant
has defaulted, but it still declined to view an issuer as comparable to a
guarantor.

The dissent in *Tudor* responded that the majority's reasoning
proved too much. A surety also has a contractual obligation to pay, but
that fact neither means that the surety is primarily liable nor prevents it
from seeking equitable subrogation. In the dissent's view, the fact that
there is a contractual obligation to pay provides no basis for saying that
the issuer of a standby letter of credit is not secondarily liable. Rather,
like a surety or guarantor, the issuer of a standby letter of credit only
has an obligation to pay if and when there is a default. In this case, for
example, the note between West One and Fibrex required Fibrex to
obtain a letter of credit as "security for repayment of [Fibrex's] note."

The relevant question, in the dissent's view, was whether allowing
equitable subrogation would defeat the independence principle that

distinguishes letters of credit from guarantees and suretyships. Guarantors generally may assert defenses available to the party whose obligation is guaranteed. *Tudor Dev. Group, Inc.*, 968 F.2d at 366. Under the independence principle, however, the issuer of a standby letter of credit may not assert those defenses. Rather, it must pay if the documents presented by the beneficiary satisfy the conditions set out in the letter of credit. Id.

In the dissent's view, once the issuer has honored the letter of credit, the purpose of the independence principle—ensuring prompt payment on the letter of credit according to its terms—has been satisfied. Id. at 368. The dissent reasoned that denying equitable subrogation after the issuer had paid the letter of credit would not advance the purposes of the one principle that distinguishes letters of credit from guarantees. Id. Rather, in the dissent's view, denying subrogation after payment amounts to "[i]nsistence on . . . pointless formalism." Id. Although the dissent's view has only gained minority support among the courts, it has been generally supported by the commentators. See James J. White & Robert S. Summers, Uniform Commercial Code §26-15 (4th ed. 1995); Peter R. Jarvis, Standby Letters of Credit, Issuers' Subrogation and Assignment Rights, 10 UCC LJ 38 (1977); cf. Task Force on the Study of U.C.C. Article 5, An Examination of U.C.C. Article 5 (Letters of Credit) 21 (Sept. 29, 1989), reprinted in 45 Bus. L. 1527 (1990).

Faced with these two positions, we conclude that the minority view is more persuasive. It recognizes that First Interstate was a de facto surety for Fibrex's obligations and is thus consistent with the long-standing principle in Oregon law that equity looks to the substance of the transaction rather than its form. General Electric Co. v. Wahle, 207 Or. 302, 317, 296 P.2d 635 (1956); Decker v. Berean Baptist Church, 51 Or. App. 191, 199, 624 P.2d 1094 (1981). It is also consistent with the general practice on standby letters of credit—that the issuer's obligation to pay on the letter of credit only arises if there is a default. See Jarvis, 9 UCC LJ at 368-71 (comparing standby letters of credit and guarantees). More importantly, it is consistent with our legislature's recognition that having paid the beneficiary, the issuer (and the applicant if it has reimbursed the issuer) should be able to step into the beneficiary's shoes and assert its rights. Accordingly, we hold that equitable subrogation is available to both the issuer and the applicant on a standby letter of credit.

Defendants advance a second argument. As we understand it, they contend that even if there is no absolute bar to subrogation, the transactions that the parties entered into after First Interstate issued the letter of credit make subrogation inequitable in this case. This case, however, arises on defendants' Rule 21 motion. The parties have not had the opportunity to develop a complete record that would allow either the trial court or this court to weigh the equities. Indeed, at oral argument both parties claimed that there were factual issues not apparent on this record that would bear on that determination. In these circumstances, we decline to reach defendants' second argument. Rather, we remand the case for proceedings consistent with this decision.

Reversed and remanded.

NOTE

The 1995 revision of Article 5 now does address the subrogation issue squarely in §5-117. In reading that section you should know that the Restatement (Third) of Suretyship and Guaranty calls sureties and similar parties "secondary obligors," and has complicated rules explaining under what circumstances they are entitled to subrogation. See the Official Comments to §5-117.

PART 4

SECURED
TRANSACTIONS

Chapter 17
INTRODUCTION TO SECURED TRANSACTIONS

It is understandable that someone extending credit in a sale or loan transaction wants to be sure of repayment. Some debtors are so solvent and/or trustworthy that the creditor demands nothing more than the debtor's promise to pay (sometimes called a "signature" loan); creditors doing this are said to be *unsecured*. In many transactions the creditor is less sanguine about the debtor's ability or desire to repay and may demand that the debtor either obtain a surety (called by various names: a *co-signor*, a *guarantor*, or, in Article 3 of the Uniform Commercial Code, an *accommodation party*) or *secure* the debt by nominating some of the debtor's current or future property as collateral. If the debtor defaults, the collateral may be seized and sold and the proceeds of the sale used to pay the debt.

A basic problem with mastering the law of secured transactions has always been in understanding the terminology: *lien, pledge, perfection, purchase money security interest,* etc. The terminology is complex because historically what we now call *secured transactions* have their source in many separate business devices, each with an individual set of descriptive terms. Additionally, Article 9 of the Uniform Commercial Code places a new and different nomenclature. To understand the pre-Code cases and the Code commentators' references to these pre-Code devices, it is necessary to have some minimal appreciation of how creditors protected their interests prior to the adoption of the UCC.

The core problem is that when a debtor cannot pay the bills, creditors must look to the debtor's property for whatever satisfaction they will get. These creditors must compete with other claimants for the property: donees, buyers, and (if financial death has occurred) the debtor's bankruptcy trustee. Worse yet, the creditors must compete with each other, and the law must somehow provide rules to determine who among all these individuals is to receive the property. As fast as the lawmakers create one set of statutes, those in business and their advisors think up new contractual arrangements that the statutes do not cover, and the law is chaotic until a new group of statutes can be added to those already regulating similar practices.

The original version of Article 9 of the Uniform Commercial Code, dealing with these "secured" transactions, was promulgated in 1962 and has twice been substantially rewritten: in 1972 and most recently in 1999, the version considered in this book. In most states the 1999 revision went into effect on July 1, 2001. The transition rules from the old version to the next can be found in the 9-700s. Official Comment 4 to §9-101 has a concise summary of the changes that the 1999 revision makes to the earlier version of the statute.

We start with some basic definitions.

A *lien* is an interest in the debtor's property given by the law to protect a creditor. If the debtor voluntarily grants such an interest, a *consensual* lien is created. If a consensual lien is taken in the debtor's real property, the lien is called a *mortgage.* A consensual lien in personal property or fixtures is called a *security interest* and is governed by Article 9 of the Uniform Commercial Code. Involuntary liens can also be imposed against the debtor's property. If the lien arises from judicial proceedings (the creditor sues, recovers judgment, and sends the sheriff out to seize the defendant's property), a *judicial lien* is created. A *statutory lien* is one imposed by either a statute or the common law in favor of certain creditors the law deems worthy of protection. Examples are the liens given to landlords, to artisans repairing personal property (the garage mechanic, for example), and to a host of others, such as ostlers, innkeepers, and even attorneys. A mechanic's lien is a statutory lien in favor of those who perform construction work. And if you do not pay your taxes, the federal government will file the awesome federal tax lien, a statutory lien that reaches *all* of the taxpayer's property, a matter we will treat at length in a later chapter.

Although it is impossible to make a categorical statement, generally the prior statutes regulating these matters established a hierarchy of winners in the derby to divide up the debtor's assets. Assuming a claimant qualifies, a "bona fide purchaser [BFP] in the ordinary course of business" was (and still is under Article 9) a favorite in the race. Another current favorite is the bankruptcy trustee, who represents all of the bankrupt's unsecured creditors and to whom the federal bankruptcy statute gives an awesome arsenal of weapons with which to attack the supposed interests that secured creditors assert in the estate's property. Under what is called the *strong arm clause* (§544(a) of the Bankruptcy Code), as of the date of the filing of the bankruptcy petition, the trustee (and all the claims the trustee represents) is conclusively presumed to occupy the legal position of a judicial lien creditor who has levied on all of the bankrupt's property. As we shall see, secured creditors whose security interests are *unperfected* at this moment lose the right to claim the collateral. But if a creditor's claim to the property will survive the attack of the bankruptcy trustee, the creditor's security interest (lien) is said to be *perfected.* Perfection of the security interest then becomes the ultimate goal of any creditor taking an interest in the debtor's collateral. And— again this is a generality—creditors with perfected security interests not only beat out the bankruptcy trustee, but also win over non-BFPs— creditors without perfected security interests, creditors whose security interests were perfected later in time, and creditors with no security interests at all (called, in bankruptcy parlance, *general creditors:* typically, for example, the corner grocer, the family doctor).

How is a creditor's security interest perfected? The answer depends on the nature of the collateral, the technical steps required by the statutes (or the courts if the legislature has not yet acted), and the particular moment in history in which the question is asked. Before embarking on a description of the major pre-Code security devices, there follows a brief outline of the bankruptcy rules against which the validity of these devices (and Article 9) must be viewed.

The leading treatise on the Uniform Commercial Code is written by Professors James J. White and Robert S. Summers (hereafter "White & Summers"). There are two versions: the four-volume Practitioner series (4th edition 1995, with pocket part updates), and the one-volume student hornbook (5th edition 2000). References in this book are to the latter.

I. BANKRUPTCY

The United States Constitution states that Congress shall pass laws pertaining to bankruptcy; the result is the Bankruptcy Reform Act of 1978, 11 U.S.C. §§101 et seq. (hereinafter the Bankruptcy Code). There are four primary types of bankruptcy: Chapter 7, straight bankruptcy (a pure liquidation proceeding); Chapter 11, a reorganization proceeding for businesses; Chapter 12, a reorganization proceeding for farmers; and Chapter 13, a debt repayment plan for individuals. The vast majority of bankruptcies are straight bankruptcies, and over 90 percent of those are filed by individuals, as opposed to businesses. Consequently, the rest of this discussion is a sketch of the proceedings in straight bankruptcy.

To commence bankruptcy, the debtor (a *voluntary* bankruptcy) or the debtor's creditors (an *involuntary* bankruptcy) file a petition with the bankruptcy court. This is a federal court under the direction of the local federal district court. The date on which the petition is filed is important because it is the measuring moment for many of the Bankruptcy Code's sections. Along with the petition the debtor will file lists (called *schedules*), showing assets and creditors. The creditors are then summoned to a meeting (called, not inaptly, the "first meeting of creditors" or, because of its Bankruptcy Code number, a "§341 meeting") at which they elect someone (the *trustee*) to gather up the debtor's property, sell it, and represent the creditors' interests in the distribution of the proceeds. If the debtor's property must be tended to *before* the first meeting of creditors (say, for instance, a circus goes bankrupt—someone must see to it that the menagerie doesn't run loose), a temporary custodian (an *interim trustee*), who acts until the trustee can take over, is appointed.[1]

The trustee collects the debtor's property. This can be a more complicated task than it may seem. If other people claim the property (creditors, a relative who was the recipient of a very generous birthday

---

1. The interim trustee automatically becomes the trustee unless someone else is elected trustee at the first meeting of creditors. Bankruptcy Code §702(d).

gift, or even the bankrupt should there be an argument over *exempt* assets), the trustee may have to litigate the issue either before the bankruptcy judge or in the state or federal courts. Property exempt from bankruptcy under federal or—in some jurisdictions—state law and worthless property (the bankrupt's cat, for example) are returned to the bankrupt. The bankrupt then petitions the bankruptcy judge for a *discharge* (read *forgiveness*) of all the scheduled debts so that the bankrupt's life can be resumed financially unburdened. With certain exceptions, bankrupts usually receive a discharge from most (but not all) debts.[2]

When the trustee gathers the estate's property, either the trustee surrenders the encumbered collateral to the secured creditors, or, if the trustee elects to sell the collateral, creditors with perfected security interests get their debts paid *first* from the proceeds of the sale. The unencumbered assets of the estate are also sold, and those proceeds are used to pay the expenses of the bankruptcy proceeding, wages of the bankrupt's employees, some tax claims, certain other priority claimants, and, finally, the general creditors (who get nothing until all the above are paid in full).

The trustee need not accept the creditor's statement that the creditor has a perfected security interest; the validity (*perfection*) of the security interest is a matter of state law and will be measured by state standards. If the security interest is finally determined to be *unperfected,* the interest is destroyed, and the creditor becomes just another general (*unsecured*) creditor. Not only is the trustee armed (as has been mentioned) with the position of a perfected *lien* creditor coming into existence on the date of the petition filing (Bankruptcy Code §544(a)), but also the trustee occupies the same legal position as any actual existing creditor (Bankruptcy Code §544(b)). Further, the Bankruptcy Code codifies the old common law maxim that a debtor must "be just before he is generous." Section 547 of the Bankruptcy Code condemns as a *preference* the following type of conduct:

> On January 1, Alice owed to Tom, Dick, and Harry $1,000 each for past due loans. On May 1 she paid Tom $1,000, and the next day she filed a voluntary petition in bankruptcy.

Section 547 provides that many payments made by an insolvent debtor to an existing creditor within 90 days of the date of the filing of the petition are void as *preferences*. The trustee can recover the payment

---

2. See §§523 and 727 of the Bankruptcy Code.

from the preferred creditor. (The fairness of §547 to Dick and Harry should be obvious.)

A final practical note worth remembering: in most bankruptcies the unsecured creditors receive NOTHING. For this reason most creditors want security (collateral) for their debts, and they want their lawyers to advise them how they can perfect that security against other creditors and the bankruptcy trustee.

II.   PRE-CODE SECURITY DEVICES

Students who know nothing other than Article 9 (and, as to real property creditor conflicts, know only what they learned in their basic property course) may not appreciate the wide variety of devices the UCC replaced. Such a student may ask why all these devices, particularly those that were very similar, were needed. The answer is historical. Our legal ancestors (lawyers, judges, and legislators) had some rigid ideas about what was transferable property (a diamond ring) and what was not (a right to sue your customer if the bill wasn't paid) and about the propriety of certain business practices that now seem commonplace. We begin our study with a famous case.

Benedict v. Ratner

United States Supreme Court, 1925
268 U.S. 353

BRANDEIS, J. The Hub Carpet Company was adjudicated bankrupt by the federal court for southern New York in involuntary proceedings commenced September 26, 1921. Benedict, who was appointed receiver and later trustee, collected the book accounts of the company. Ratner filed in that court a petition in equity praying that the amounts so collected be paid over to him. He claimed them under a writing given May 23, 1921—four months and three days before the commencement of the bankruptcy proceedings. By it the company purported to assign to him, as collateral for certain loans, all accounts present and future. Those collected by the receiver were, so far as appears, all accounts which had arisen after the date of the assignment, and were enumerated in the monthly list of accounts outstanding which was delivered to Ratner September 23. Benedict resisted the petition on the ground that the original assignment was void under the law of New York as a fraudulent conveyance; that, for this reason, the delivery of the September list of accounts was inoperative to perfect a lien in Ratner; and that it was a preference under the Bankruptcy Act. He also filed a cross-petition in which he asked that Ratner be ordered to pay to the estate the proceeds of certain collections which had been made by the company after September 17 and turned over to Ratner pursuant to his request made on that day. The company was then insolvent and Ratner had reason to believe it to be so. These accounts also had apparently been acquired by the company after the date of the original assignment.

The District Judge decided both petitions in Ratner's favor. He ruled that the assignment executed in May was not fraudulent in law; that it created an equity in the future acquired accounts; that because of this equity, Ratner was entitled to retain, as against the bankrupt's estate, the proceeds of the accounts which had been collected by the company in September and turned over to him; that by delivery of the list of the accounts outstanding on September 23, this equity in them had ripened into a perfect title to the remaining accounts; and that the title so perfected was good as against the supervening bankruptcy. Accordingly, the District Court ordered that, to the extent of the balance remaining unpaid on his loans, there be paid to Ratner all collections made from accounts enumerated in any of the lists delivered to Ratner; and that the cross-petition of Benedict be denied. There was no finding of fraud in fact. On appeal, the Circuit Court of Appeals affirmed the order. 282 Fed. 12. A writ of certiorari was granted by this Court. 259 U.S. 579.

The rights of the parties depend primarily upon the law of New York. Hiscock v. Varick Bank of N.Y., 206 U.S. 28. It may be assumed that, unless the arrangement of May 23 was void because fraudulent in law, the original assignment of the future acquired accounts became operative under the state law, both as to those paid over to Ratner before the bankruptcy proceedings and as to those collected by the receiver; and that the assignment will be deemed to have taken effect as of May 23. Sexton v. Kessler, 225 U.S. 90, 99. That being so, it is clear that, if the original assignment was a valid one under the law of New York, the Bankruptcy Act did not invalidate the subsequent dealings of the parties. Thompson v. Fairbanks, 196 U.S. 516; Humphrey v. Tatman, 198 U.S. 91. The sole question for decision is, therefore, whether on the following undisputed facts the assignment of May 23 was in law fraudulent.

The Hub Carpet Company was, on May 23, a mercantile concern doing business in New York City and proposing to continue to do so. The assignment was made there to secure an existing loan of $15,000, and further advances not exceeding $15,000 which were in fact made July 1, 1921. It included all accounts receivable then outstanding and all which should thereafter accrue in the ordinary course of business. A list of the existing accounts was delivered at the time. Similar lists were to be delivered to Ratner on or about the 23rd day of each succeeding month containing the accounts outstanding at such future dates. Those enumerated in each of the lists delivered prior to September, aggregated between $100,000 and $120,000. The receivables were to be collected by the company. Ratner was given the right, at any time, to demand a full disclosure of the business and financial conditions; to require that all amounts collected be applied in payment of his loans; and to enforce the assignment although no loan had matured. But until he did so, the company was not required to apply any of the collections to the repayment of Ratner's loan. It was not required to replace accounts collected by other collateral of equal value. It was not required to account in any way to Ratner. It was at liberty to use the proceeds of all accounts collected as it might see fit. The existence of the assignment was to be kept secret. The business was to be conducted as theretofore. Indebtedness was to be incurred, as usual, for the purchase of merchandise and otherwise in the ordinary course of business. The amount of such indebtedness unpaid at the time of the commencement of the bankruptcy proceedings was large. Prior to September 17, the company collected from accounts so assigned about $150,000, all of which it applied to purposes other than the payment of Ratner's loan. The outstanding accounts enumerated in the list delivered September 23 aggregated $90,000.

Under the law of New York a transfer of property as security which reserves to the transferor the right to dispose of the same, or to apply the proceeds thereof, for his own uses is, as to creditors, fraudulent in law and void. This is true whether the right of disposition for the transferor's use be reserved in the instrument or by agreement in pais, oral or written; whether the right of disposition reserved be unlimited in time or be expressly terminable by the happening of an event; whether the transfer cover all the property of the debtor or only a part; whether the right of disposition extends to all the property transferred or only to a part thereof; and whether the instrument of transfer be recorded or not.

If this rule applies to the assignment of book accounts, the arrangement of May 23 was clearly void; and the equity in the future acquired accounts, which it would otherwise have created, did not arise. Whether the rule applies to accounts does not appear to have been passed upon by the Court of Appeals of New York. But it would seem clear that whether the collateral consists of chattels or of accounts, reservation of dominion inconsistent with the effective disposition of title must render the transaction void. Ratner asserts that the rule stated above rests upon ostensible ownership, and argues that the doctrine of ostensible ownership is not applicable to book accounts. That doctrine raises a presumption of fraud where chattels are mortgaged (or sold) and possession of the property is not delivered to the mortgagee (or vendee). The presumption may be avoided by recording the mortgage (or sale). It may be assumed, as Ratner contends, that the doctrine does not apply to the assignment of accounts. In their transfer there is nothing which corresponds to the delivery of possession of chattels. The statutes which embody the doctrine and provide for recording as a substitute for delivery do not include accounts. A title to an account good against creditors may be transferred without notice to the debtor or record of any kind. But it is not true that the rule stated above and invoked by the receiver is either based upon or delimited by the doctrine of ostensible ownership. It rests not upon seeming ownership because of possession retained, but upon a lack of ownership because of dominion reserved. It does not raise a presumption of fraud. It imputes fraud conclusively because of the reservation of dominion inconsistent with the effective disposition of title and creation of a lien.

The nature of the rule is made clear by its limitations. Where the mortgagor of chattels agrees to apply the proceeds of their sale to the payment of the mortgage debt or to the purchase of other chattels which shall become subject to the lien, the mortgage is good as against creditors, if recorded. The mortgage is sustained in such cases "upon the ground that such sale and application of proceeds is the normal and proper purpose of a chattel mortgage, and within the precise boundaries of its lawful operation and effect. It does no more than to substitute the mortgagor as the agent of the mortgagee to do exactly what the latter had the right to do, and what it was his privilege and his duty to accomplish. It devotes, as it should, the mortgaged property to the payment of the mortgage debt." The permission to use the proceeds to furnish substitute collateral "provides only for a shifting of the lien from one piece of property to another taken in exchange." Brackett v. Harvey, 91 N.Y. 214, 221, 223. On the other hand, if the agreement is that the mortgagor may sell and use the proceeds for his own benefit, the mortgage is of no effect although recorded. Seeming ownership exists in both classes of cases because the mortgagor is permitted to remain in possession of the stock in trade and to sell it freely. But it is only where the unrestricted dominion over the proceeds is reserved to the mortgagor that the mortgage is void. This dominion is the differentiating and deciding element. The distinction was recognized in Sexton v. Kessler, 225 U.S. 90, 98, 32 S. Ct. 657, where a transfer of securities was sustained. It was pointed out that a reservation of full control by the mortgagor might well prevent the effective creation of a lien in the mortgagee and that the New York cases holding such a mortgage void rest upon that doctrine.

The results which flow from reserving dominion inconsistent with the effective disposition of title must be the same whatever the nature of the property transferred. The doctrine which imputes fraud where full dominion is reserved must apply to assignments of accounts although the doctrine of ostensible ownership does not. There must also be the same distinction as to degrees of dominion. Thus, although an agreement that the assignor of accounts shall collect them and pay the proceeds to the assignee will not invalidate the assignment which it accompanies, the assignment must be deemed fraudulent in law if it is agreed that the assignor may use the proceeds as he sees fit.

In the case at bar, the arrangement for the unfettered use by the company of the proceeds of the accounts precluded the effective creation of a lien and rendered the original assignment fraudulent in law. Consequently the payments to Ratner and the delivery of the September list of accounts were inoperative to perfect a lien in him, and were unlawful preferences. On this ground, and also because the payment was fraudulent under the law of the State, the trustee was entitled to recover the amount. . . .

Reversed.

The evil under attack in Benedict v. Ratner is the *secret lien* that other creditors do not know about. If it is enforced by the courts, the other creditors who were deceived by the debtor's apparently unencumbered prosperity are hurt. But, although the Court in this case ruled against the creditor's security interest, most creditors took comfort from the decision because the Court had indicated methods by which the lien *would* have survived the trustee's attack. By requiring the creditor to *police* the debtor's conduct (record the mortgage, pay over collections to the creditor, etc.), the Court paved the way for increased commercial financing. Once the creditors knew what the rules were, they were more willing to extend the credit.

Did the rule of Benedict v. Ratner survive the enactment of Article 9? Read §9-205 and its Official Comment 2. Article 9 solves the secret lien problem by making sure that the creditor's interest in the debtor's property is obvious so that no later creditors are deceived (typically by the filing of a notice, called a *financing statement,* in the public records, though there are other methods, such as taking possession of the collateral, that serve the same function). Note that in a sale of goods transaction it still is a bad idea for the seller to retain possession of the sold objects for a long period of time after the sale is over; read §2-402(2).

One way around the problems encountered in this famous case was to permit the creditor to have physical possession of the property (a *pledge;* see below), though this is a solution only where the collateral has tangible form, which accounts receivable, of course, do not. Other ways were suggested by the opinion itself. A very brief summary of the major devices follows.

A.   Pledge

In a *pledge*[3] the debtor (called a *pledgor*) gives physical possession of the collateral to the creditor (called the *pledgee*) until the debt is paid. Possession then *perfects* the creditor's interest in the collateral (even against the bankruptcy trustee). Obviously when the creditor has possession of, say, a diamond ring, the whole world is on notice that the creditor has some legal interest therein. Pledging is a superior way to perfect the creditor's security interest, but it has two drawbacks: (1) only tangible objects can be pledged, and a business debtor may want to borrow money against intangible collateral (such as accounts receivable due from existing customers); and (2) for some types of collateral the debtor needs to keep possession (the machines used in manufacturing, for example). It was therefore necessary to create *non-possessory* security interests.

B.   Chattel Mortgage

The debtor could always mortgage land, so why not have something similar for personal property (*chattels*)? And, as with real prop-

---

3. A pledge is sometimes called a *hypothecation.*

erty, the mortgage given by the debtor (the *mortgagor*) to the creditor (the *mortgagee*) was recorded in a designated place and indexed under the name of the debtor so that other potential creditors could check and see whether the collateral was encumbered. Thus, the debtor could have possession, but the secret lien problem so dreaded in Benedict v. Ratner was avoided because the mortgage was (through the recording system) witness to the creditor's very public interest in the property.

C.   Conditional Sale

Here's a surprise. Without first reading the text that follows, form an opinion as to the answer to this Problem.

PROBLEM 256

Honest John sold Nancy Debts a used car for $900, to be paid off in three payments of $300 each. The contract was oral. Nancy missed the second payment, and one of Honest John's employees repossessed the car and returned it to the seller. Nancy sued Honest John for conversion. Who should win? After forming your initial opinion, read §2-702 and see if that has any bearing on your answer.

Most people assume that the unpaid seller always has a right to repossess. THIS IS UNTRUE. The unpaid seller may repossess in only three circumstances: (1) when §2-702 (which you have just read and about which more later) applies; (2) when the buyer has specifically granted the seller a *security interest* in the object sold; and (3) when the seller sues, recovers judgment, and has the sheriff seize the property as part of the execution of the seller's judgment. (When an unsecured creditor sues and acquires a judgment and then sends the sheriff out to levy on the defendant's property, the creditor is called, variously, a *judgment creditor*, a *judicial creditor*, or simply a *lien creditor*.) Of course, prior to the UCC, the seller could take a chattel mortgage in the property sold and file to record this interest, but that was a lot of trouble. Another way was to have a *conditional sale* whereby the buyer got possession of the property, but the seller reserved full and complete title to it until the buyer paid in full (the *condition* in *conditional sale* was this payment before the buyer got any title). A conditional sale has the Benedict v. Ratner problem of the debtor-in-possession and a secret lien in the seller's favor, and the fictitious title retention theory had as short a life here as it did in the real property mortgage situation. The upshot was that in many states the seller's "title" was treated as nothing more than an unperfected security interest, so that the seller lost to later judicial creditors, to creditors who perfected their security interests, and to the buyer's trustee in bankruptcy. That is certainly the result in Article 9; see §9-202. In most states the seller's interest in a conditional sale had to be filed to be perfected.

Some sellers still use *conditional sale* terminology in their contracts. What effect does the seller's retention of title have under the UCC? Read §§2-401(1), second sentence, and 1-201(37), last sentence in the first paragraph.

D. Trust Receipt

A strained use of trust law principles helped the retail automobile dealer finance (*floor plan*) purchases of vehicles from the manu-facturer. In trust receipt financing, the car dealer would ask a bank to buy the cars from the manufacturer. The bank would then turn them over to the dealer after two things happened: (1) the bank filed a notice in the appropriate place announcing its intention to engage in trust receipt financing with this particular dealer; and (2) the dealer signed a *trust receipt* (thereby becoming a *trustee;* the bank was called an *entruster*), acknowledging receipt of the vehicles and granting the bank a security interest therein. As the cars[4] were sold, the bank's interest was paid off, and, when paid in full, the trust receipt was canceled. Various complications could arise, the most common of these being a sale "out of trust," meaning that the dealer failed to remit the proceeds of the car sales as required by the agreement, which often happened if the bank failed to police the debtor's activities. Trust receipt financing rules were codified in the Uniform Trust Receipts Act, a very difficult statute that was adopted in two-thirds of the states.

E. Factor's Lien

The word *factor* originally meant any selling agent (wholesaler or retailer) who helped finance the principal's business. As time went on,

---

4. Trust receipt financing was, of course, used in financing the acquisition of inventory other than automobiles, but was available only where the inventory consisted of easily identifiable separate items—for instance, those having serial numbers.

the factor's selling function died out, and the factor became a financing entity who loaned money against inventory the manufacturer put up as collateral. In return, the factor was granted a lien (a security interest) in the inventory, but this security interest had to be filed to be perfected under most states' factor lien statutes. Most of these statutes contained this drawback: the lien did not extend to new additions to the inventory (*after-acquired property*); that is, it was not a *floating lien* that attached to the changing objects in the inventory. If the after-acquired property in the inventory was to become collateral for the factor, a new security agreement and, typically, a filing of the same were prerequisites to perfection.

F.   Field Warehousing

In Benedict v. Ratner the primary evil was that the debtor was in possession of property that secretly belonged to the creditor. With a pledge, possession of the collateral is in the creditor, and no deception problem arises. If the collateral is too big to be conveniently left in the creditor's possession (say, for instance, the collateral is an inventory of Christmas tree ornaments waiting for the Christmas season), one way of pulling off a pledge was for the debtor to store the goods in a warehouse and have the warehouse company issue a negotiable warehouse receipt made out to *bearer.* Such a warehouse receipt (a *document of title,* now regulated by Article 7 of the UCC) has to be surrendered before the warehouse company will turn over the goods to anyone (§7-403(3)); in effect, this rule makes the warehouse receipt take the place of the goods, and thus the receipt was pledged to the creditor in return for the loan of money. Possession of a negotiable document of title (a warehouse receipt or a bill of lading) perfected the creditor's security interest. A *field warehouse* is the same thing as a normal warehouse with one difference: the warehouse comes to the goods instead of vice versa. If the goods are too bulky to move easily, the field warehouseman goes to the goods, stakes them out in some way, issues a warehouse receipt therefor, and guards them (even the debtor, on whose premises they remain, is not supposed to be able to get to the goods). The receipt is then pledged to a financing agency; when the debt is repaid, the warehouse receipt is returned to the debtor, who presents it to the field warehouseman, who surrenders the goods and then packs up and leaves the debtor's property. (The field warehouseman is frequently only temporarily employed as an agent of the field warehouse company and is actually a regular employee of the debtor. The resulting loyalty conflicts often gave rise to warehouseman misbehavior and, inevitably, lawsuits.)

Article 9 of the Code replaced all these devices (though some of the practices, such as a pledge or field warehousing, live on) with new rules as to creation of the security interest, the collateral to which it can attach, and the steps necessary for perfection. It is meant to be all-inclusive so as to cover all possible security interests in personal property and fixtures (see §9-109(c) and (d) for a list of transactions excluded from Article 9's dominion).

Chapter 18

THE SCOPE OF ARTICLE 9

[text obscured/faded]

I. SECURITY INTEREST DEFINED

Read §1-201(37) (defining *security interest*) and §9-109(a) (Scope of Article).

PROBLEM 257

Assume that a state statute gives someone doing repairs a possessory artisan's lien on the property repaired. Mr. Baker took his car into Mack's Garage for repair, but, being strapped for funds, couldn't pay the full bill, and Mack wouldn't let him have the car back. Is Mack's artisan's lien an Article 9 *security interest*? See §9-

109(d)(2). If, prior to the repair work, Mr. Baker signed a statement giving Mack's Garage a right to repossess the car if the bill wasn't paid, does this agreement create a *security interest* under the Code? See §9-109(a)(1).

PROBLEM 258

To raise money, Farmer Brown's Fresh Vegetables Roadside Stand sold all of its accounts receivable to Nightflyer Finance Company, which notified the customers that henceforth all payments should be made directly to Nightflyer. (Note that this is not a loan from the finance company to the farmer with the accounts put up as collateral; it is an outright sale. If it were a loan, and if the collectible accounts exceeded the amount of the loan, the excess would be returned to Farmer Brown; in an actual sale Nightflyer can keep the surplus. See §9-608(b).) Is this sale nonetheless an Article 9 "security interest"? See §9-109(a)(3). If so, even though Farmer Brown has no further obligations to Nightflyer, he would of necessity be termed an Article 9 "debtor." See §9-102(a)(28)(B). Then Nightflyer would have to file an Article 9 financing statement to perfect its interest against later parties. Why would the Code drafters have brought an outright sale of accounts (and *chattel paper, payment intangibles,* and *promissory notes,* all defined below) under the coverage of Article 9? Remember Benedict v. Ratner? See Official Comment 4 to §9-109; Major's Furniture Mart, Inc. v. Castle Credit Corp., 602 F.2d 538, 26 U.C.C. Rep. Serv. 1319 (3d Cir. 1979).

For the practicing attorney the possibility that a business transaction with no apparent *loan* or *collateral* may still fall within Article 9 is a matter of great concern. If the transaction creates an Article 9 *security interest,* the attorney's client had better have taken whatever steps Article 9 requires for perfection, or the client may lose the property to later creditors. If the attorney has not advised the client of this possibility, the client's thoughts may turn to malpractice actions.

A few of the obviously troublesome areas where Article 9 may or may not apply are discussed next.

II.   CONSIGNMENTS

A true consignment is neither a *sale* nor a *security device;* it is a marketing procedure by which the owner of goods (the *consignor*) sends (*consigns*) them to a retailer (the *consignee*) for sale to the public. The retailer does not *buy* the goods (so no sale takes place when the consignor delivers the goods to the consignee). If the retailer cannot sell them, they are returned to the consignor. In effect, the consignee is the selling agent for the consignor, or, looked at another way, the consignee is a bailee with the ability to sell the bailor's goods. The advantages to the consignor of a true consignment over an outright sale (with reservation of a security interest so the goods can be reclaimed if the retailer does not pay for them) is that the consignor retains control over the terms of the retail sale (and thus can dictate the retail price), and, at least at common law, there is no requirement that the consignor file a notice anywhere announcing that a consignment is going on. (Why, the consignors argue, should they have to notify anyone that they have claimed an interest in their own property?) At common law, this argument tended to prevail, with the consignors able to reclaim the consigned goods from the inventory of the consignee over the objections of the consignee's other creditors; see Ludwigh v. American Woolen Co., 231 U.S. 522 (1913).

Nonetheless, consignments have the Benedict v. Ratner problem: the retailer appears to be the unfettered owner of goods in inventory that actually belong to someone else (the consignor). The retailer's other creditors may wish to extend credit with the inventory as collateral, but there is no place they can go to check whether some or all of the inventory is actually held on consignment.

Further, some consignments are not *true consignments* at all, but are sales on credit (i.e., secured transactions) disguised as consignments in order to escape the filing requirements. If the retailer must pay for the goods whether or not able to resell them, this is not a true consignment, even if called that; it is the creation of a security interest in goods. If a *security interest* is intended, then it is not a true consignment at all; see §9-102(a)(20)(D).[1] Article 9 *must* be complied with (perfection by filing, etc.).

In the end, the drafters of the revised version of Article 9 decided to take some kinds of true consignments and treat them as Article 9 matters, thus requiring the usual steps for perfecting a security interest in someone else's inventory (see Chapter 22—purchase money security interests in inventory), but leaving some true consignments

---

1. This so-called consignment would typically create a purchase money security interest, requiring the steps yet to be discussed for its perfection. Since Article 9 consignments are also given this treatment, this distinction, carefully preserved in the statute, is much ado about nothing.

outside the Code (and thus protected by the common law rule that favored the consignor). Read §9-102(a)(20).

PROBLEM 259

Antiques Are Us was the largest antiques store in the city, well known as a place where antique dealers could hire out space and exhibit their wares, with the store handling the sales and taking a commission on each one, and returning to the dealers items that remained unsold. When the store takes out a loan from Octopus National Bank and uses as collateral "all its property," will the bank's security interest reach the items in the store that belong to the dealers if the dealers have never taken the steps required of consignors under Article 9? See §9-102(a)(20)(A)(iii).

The "not generally known by its creditors to be substantially engaged in selling the goods of others" test from §9-102(a)(20)(A)(iii) is taken from an identical provision in the former language of §2-326, which also exempted such retail transactions from the necessity of compliance with the perfection rules of Article 9. If the consignor failed to take these steps, the consignor would frequently appeal to this factual test as a last resort, but, as the case below indicates, it was slim reed on which to lean.

In re Fabers, Inc.

United States District Court, District of Connecticut,
Bankruptcy Division, 1972
12 U.C.C. Rep. Serv. 126

SEIDMAN, REF. BANKR. The bankrupt is a retail carpet and rug merchant. On May 31, 1971, the petitioner, Mehdi Dilmaghani & Company, Inc. (dealer), shipped oriental rugs to the bankrupt on consignment. Subsequent deliveries of rugs on a similar basis were made on May 5, 1971, October 4, 1971, October 5, 1971, October 7, 1971, December 6, 1971, and December 23, 1971. All of the rugs so shipped had an identifying label attached. On each label was printed "MD. & CO., INC., Reg. No. R.N. 22956, 100% wool pile, No. ___, Quality ___, Size ___, Sq. Feet ___, Made in Iran." The consignment agreement provided that title to the rugs remained in the dealer until fully paid for; that the consignee had the right to sell the rugs in the ordinary course of business and only at a price in excess of the invoice price; that the proceeds of any sale were the property of the dealer and held in trust for the dealer; that the proceeds of any sale were to be remitted to the dealer immediately with a report of the sale; [and] that all rugs were held at the risk of the consignee.

No effort was made to comply with the provisions of the Uniform Commercial Code relating to security interests. The dealer does not assert a security interest in the rugs, claiming only that the rugs are and always were the property of the dealer under a "true consignment" and, therefore, not subject to the provisions of the Code relating to security interests. . . .

The dealer's claim is that the consignment was not intended for security and is, therefore, not subject to the requirements of Article 9. The logic of this argument escapes the court. If the dealer did not want the agreement to provide it with security for either the payment of the rugs or their return, what other purpose could there have been? The agreement describes the rugs as belonging to the dealer, but the risk of loss or damage is on the consignee. This is inconsistent with the liability of a bailee. The proceeds of the sales were to be the property of the dealer but the consignee is described as holding the proceeds in trust. A trustee has *title* to the trust estate. The agreement impliedly permitted the consignee to mingle the proceeds with his own funds before remitting. At any rate, there was no requirement of a separate account. This is inconsistent with a true trust. . . .

The principal claim of the dealer is that the transaction was a true consignment, that at all times the consignee was acting as the agent of the dealer and, therefore, the transaction came under the exception allowed in §2-326. . . . To protect itself from the claims of creditors, the dealer could have complied with the filing provisions of Article 9, §2-326(3)(c), but it admittedly did not. The only other exceptions are compliance with an applicable Connecticut law providing for a consignor's interest by a sign (there apparently is no such law) or establishing that the consignee-bankrupt was generally known by his creditors to be substantially engaged in selling the goods of others.

In support of the latter theory, evidence was submitted that the dealer never dealt in oriental rugs prior to May 1971 and that an advertisement in the local newspapers on October 12, 1971, included a picture of Mr. Mehdi Dilmaghani together with the narrative: "By Special Arrangement, we proudly introduce: A distinctive collection of Mehdi Dilmaghani . . . renown importer of genuine handmade Oriental, India, and Petit-Point Rugs . . . . " This hardly complies with the requirement that the bankrupt "is generally known *by his creditors* to be substantially engaged in selling the goods of others." (Emphasis added.) There was no evidence of any notification to any of the bankrupt's creditors to that effect. In fact, it is found that the contrary was true. The bankrupt was not substantially engaged in selling the goods of others.

The dealer argues that the oriental rugs were not the kind of goods in which the bankrupt dealt. They may not have been of the same quality or price range as the other rugs and carpets sold by the bankrupt, but they were all of the same kind of goods—to wit: floor coverings. The trade name of the bankrupt was "Faber's World of Carpets." Other than the reference to the collection by Dilmaghani in the newspaper advertisement there was nothing to suggest any possible connection with the dealer. In fact, this advertisement is no different from that of a department store advertising a full line of "Frigidaire" appliances, or a collection of Pierre Cardin's new spring line. This is a far cry from the situation in In re Griffin, 1 U.C.C. Rep. Serv. 492, where the bankrupt had a sign in his window advertising used furniture and the court found that under the particular circumstances, this was notice that goods of others were being sold. In the instant case, there was no such notice.

There was evidence that the members of the Oriental Rug Dealers Association usually sold their rugs on consignment. This was well known to the members of the association. There was no evidence that this was the universal invariable practice in the trade, or that the creditors of the bankrupt who apparently did not deal in oriental rugs knew anything about the custom of the members of the Oriental Rug Dealers Association. As between the parties, the transaction was a consignment agreement. As to the creditors, it was a sale or return and bound by the provisions of Section 2-326. Since the petitioner does not come under the exceptions in this section, it was required to comply with the filing provisions of Article 9 to preserve its secured position. Admittedly, this was not done.

It is found that the agreement was intended for security and subject to the requirements of §2-326. There was no perfection of the security interest and the agreement did not come under the exceptions set forth in §2-326(3). Accordingly, it is held that the goods are subject to the claims of creditors, §2-326(2). The reclamation petition is denied, and it is so ordered.

PROBLEM 260

When Luke Skywalker inherited a valuable sword collection from his father, he took it down to Weapons of the World (WOW), a large gun and weapons dealer, which mostly sold items that it either manufactured itself or bought from other dealers around the globe. The collection was appraised as being worth over $25,000. Luke asked WOW to sell the collection for him. Is this an Article 9 consignment so that Luke needs to take Article 9 steps to protect himself from WOW's other creditors who have an interest in the store's inventory?

III. LEASES

A problem similar to the applicability of Article 9 to consignments occurs when the parties disguise a secured sale as a lease.

PROBLEM 261

B.I.G. Machines, Inc. leased a duplicating machine to Connie's Print Shop. The lease was for five years, and the rental payments over this period exactly equaled the current market price of the machine. The lease contract further provided that at the end of the five years Connie's Print Shop might purchase the machine outright by paying B.I.G. Machines $5.00. B.I.G. Machines did not file an Article 9 financing statement. Thereafter Connie's Print Shop borrowed money from the Octopus National Bank and signed a security agreement with the bank granting it an interest in all of the print shop's "equipment." Octopus National duly perfected its security interest by filing a financing statement in the appropriate place. When Connie's Print Shop failed to repay the loan, Octopus National seized all the shop's equipment, including the duplicating machine. In the lawsuit Octopus National Bank v. B.I.G. Machines, Inc., who gets the machine? Read §1-201(37).

Parties may wish to cast a transaction as a lease rather than a sale for many reasons. At various times in the tortured history of tax law (a history that is changing so fast that this writer expresses no opinion as to the current status of the issue under the Internal Revenue Code), rental payments on a *true lease* could be deducted from gross income, but in a *sale* the "lessee" could take only depreciation on the object purchased. Tax lawyers developed much experience wrestling with the distinctions between a true lease and a disguised sale, witness:

At the time of this writing, the use of many millions (and probably billions) of dollars' worth of equipment is being obtained through a medium of tax-oriented leases where the ability of the lessor to take accelerated depreciation and obtain the Investment Tax Credit are so crucial that the lease will not be entered into without a ruling by the Commissioner on this point, or at the very least, an unqualified opinion by tax counsel, who necessarily must err only on the side of caution. Tax counsel and administrators have developed a lore of their own for distinguishing a true lease from a disguised sale. One point of interest is their emphasis upon the necessity for the lessor's retention of a residual of significant and measurable value. Although this element is seldom stressed as such in chattel security literature, it is suggested that if UCC draftsmen ever deem it feasible to devise something better than either old U.S.C.A. section 1(2) or abandoned section 7-403, study should be directed toward the possibility of devising a formula based on the value of the residual to be returned at the end of the lease term. A rule of thumb in tax rulings and in super-cautious opinions of lessors' tax counsel is (1) that the lease must come to an end at a time when at least two years or twenty percent of the useful life of the leased item remains, and (2) that this residual must be valued at not less than 15 percent of the purchase price. The lessor's tax counsel is likely to insist that there be no options, or only an option to purchase at the market value as determined when the option is exercised. This position is based on the premise that risk of an increase or decrease in value of the residual is an incident of the lessor's ownership and that he should, therefore, bear this risk.

P. Coogan, Leases of Equipment and Some Other Unconventional Security Devices: An Analysis of UCC Section 1-207(37) and Article 9, 1973 Duke L.J. 909, 966-967. For other IRS tests, see Rev. Rul. 55-540, 1955-2 Cum. Bull. 39; Rev. Proc. 75-21, 26 C.F.R. §601.201 (1975). The same issue comes up when books must be maintained:

> From an accounting point of view, the true lease has had the advantage to the lessee of providing him with "off balance sheet financing." That is to say, the lease obligates him to pay rent and not to buy goods. Accordingly, the leased property is not shown as an asset on the lessee's balance sheet, and, consistently, the obligation to pay rent is not listed as a liability. This treatment tends to improve the balance sheet ratios commonly used in determining the lessee's financial strength. Additionally, the obligations of a lessee under a true lease usually are not subject to restrictions on the amount of money he may borrow contained in existing loan agreements, corporate charters and so forth.

W. Hawkland, The Proposed Amendments to Article 9 of the UCC— Part 5: Consignments and Equipment Leases, 77 Com. L.J. 108, 113 (1972). The tax/accounting tests tend to focus on the "intention of the parties" and on two other factors: (1) the "equity" the lessee builds in the leased property and (2) the value of the property surrendered to the lessor at the end of the term.

On May 22, 1987, the last of the various organizations involved approved the drafters' final version of Article 2A of the UCC, called "Leases," which deals with the leasing of personal property, and it has been widely adopted (though in some states, notably California, major changes were made to the official text). Since the distinction between a true lease and a disguised sale is of crucial importance in deciding the application of either Article 2A or Article 9, the drafters have given us the complicated definition of *security interest* in §1-201(37), which you have just read in connection with the last Problem.

What are we to make of this definition? The happiest thing about it (despite its formidable size) is that it does draw some bright lines to help attorneys tell leases from secured transactions:

1. If at the end of the lease period the lessee becomes the owner of the property for little or no consideration, a secured transaction and not a lease has been created.
2. If the contract contains a clause that permits the lessee to terminate the lease at any time and return the leased goods, a true lease has resulted. Such a right of termination is not an attribute of a sale of goods.
3. If the lease is for the entire economic life of the leased goods, with or without renewal, a disguised sale has occurred.

Other than that, each lease must be evaluated on its own. It does not necessarily answer the central question if the lessee pays consideration equal to or even greater than the fair market value of the leased goods as long as the lease does not cover the total economic life of the goods. Nor does the lessee's assumption of major duties (taxes, risk of loss, etc.) necessarily indicate a lease or a sale of goods.

Use the definition and the above tests to answer the following Problem.

PROBLEM 262

Business Corporation leased a massive copier from Copies, Inc. for a five-year period. At the outset of the lease the copier had a fair market value of $300,000 and a predicted ten-year useful life. Over the course of the five-year lease the rental payments would total to $330,000. The lease provides that Business Corporation has the option to become the owner of the copier at the end of the five-year period by paying Copies, Inc. the amount of $10,000. Is this a true lease or a secured sale? Would we reach a different result if the copier's useful life were only five years?

In re Architectural Millwork of Virginia, Inc.

United States Bankruptcy Court, W.D. Virginia, 1998
226 B.R. 551, 39 U.C.C. Rep. Serv. 2d 36

WILLIAM E. ANDERSON, Bankruptcy Judge.

The matter before the Court in this Chapter 11 case is the motion of Associates Leasing, Inc., ("Associates") to compel assumption or rejection of leases. A few weeks after that matter was heard and taken under advisement, Associates brought a motion for the payment of leases before the Court. That matter was also taken under advisement at the conclusion of its hearing.

As the outcome of the second motion is tied to the central issue of the first motion regarding whether the transactions in question were, in fact, leases, the Court dispenses with both matters in this memorandum opinion.

FACTS

The debtor filed its Chapter 11 Bankruptcy petition on March 25, 1998. The debtor remains in possession of its assets and is operating its business as a debtor-in-possession pursuant to Bankruptcy Code §1107.

Prior to the filing date, Associates and the debtor entered into an agreement on May 16, 1996, entitled Truck Lease Agreement, providing for the lease of a 1995 Freightliner vehicle (the "Freightliner agreement").[2] Then on August 2, 1996, River Ridge Supply and the debtor entered into a Conditional Sales Contract regarding a Komatsu forklift (the "Komatsu agreement"). Contemporaneous with the execu-

---

2. As discussed later in this opinion, the Court looks beyond the face of the agreement which states the vehicle is to be "leased" in order to determine if this agreement is, in fact, a true lease or a disguised security agreement. The labeling of the agreement as a "lease" and referring to the parties as "lessor" and "lessee" in and of themselves are not controlling. In re Owen, 221 B.R. 56, 62 (Bankr. N.D.N.Y. 1998).

tion of the Komatsu agreement, River Ridge Supply assigned to Associates all of its rights under the agreement.

At the May 16, 1998, hearing on Associates's motion to compel assumption or rejection of leases, the parties put on evidence in support of their positions. Based on the testimony and evidence from the hearing, the Court makes the following additional findings regarding the relevant circumstances surrounding these agreements.

The debtor entered into the Freightliner agreement after Darryl Motley, on behalf of the debtor, visited the Virginia Truck Center ("V.T.C.") in Roanoke, Virginia. Mr. Motley testified that he decided to purchase a new vehicle while at V.T.C. after concluding that it would not be economically feasible to repair his previous truck.

After Mr. Motley selected the Freightliner, he then negotiated a purchase price with V.T.C. Next, Mr. Motley selected and negotiated a price for the appropriate van body to be attached to the Freightliner. Since Mr. Motley elected to finance the vehicle, he met with the credit department at V.T.C. According to Mr. Motley's testimony, it was at that time that he first considered financing the vehicle with a leasing company instead of a bank because he felt that he could more easily obtain credit. The amount that had to be financed, after subtracting the trade in value of the debtor's previous vehicle, is shown on the Freightliner agreement as capitalized costs totaling $38,500.00.

Mr. Motley also testified that the circumstances surrounding the execution of the Komatsu agreement with River Ridge Supply paralleled those of the Freightliner agreement. Specifically, the evidence indicated that the debtor selected the goods without input from Associates, and Associates never inspected the goods before or after the agreements.

At the conclusion of the hearing, Associates argued that the debtor should be compelled to act pursuant to Bankruptcy Code §365, and the debtor, in turn, claimed §365 does not apply because the transactions were not true leases. Thereafter, the parties submitted memoranda for the Court's consideration.

DISCUSSION

The Court's ruling on Associates's motion turns on whether the agreements in question are true leases or, in fact, security agreements, for purposes of Bankruptcy Code §365. Such a determination is made by reference to state law. . . . Accordingly, a careful analysis of the relevant state code provisions is in order.

Virginia has adopted the Uniform Commercial Code. Of particular importance to this case, the first paragraph of Virginia Code §8.1-201(37) reads as follows.

> (37) 1. "Security interest" means an interest in personal property or fixtures which secures payment or performance of an obligation. . . . Whether a lease is intended as security is to be determined by the facts of each case; however, (a) the inclusion of an option to purchase does not of itself make the lease one intended for security, and (b) an agreement that upon compliance with the terms of the lease the lessee shall become or has the option to become the owner of the property for no additional consideration or for a nominal consideration does make the lease one intended for security.

Although this first paragraph of the statute requires the Court to examine the facts of each case in characterizing a transaction, "[t]he plain language of the statute creates a security interest in property as a matter of law if the parties' contract allows the lessee to become the owner of the leased property for nominal or no additional consideration upon compliance with the terms of the lease." C.F. Garcia Enterprises v. Enterprise Ford Tractor, 253 Va. 104, 107, 480 S.E.2d 497 (1997). As discussed later in this opinion, the second paragraph of Virginia Code §8.1-201(37) restates this same proposition.

Applying this rule to the two agreements involved in this case produces mixed results. The Komatsu agreement clearly provides for the option to purchase the forklift for one dollar after all scheduled payments are completed. Consequently, the Court finds that this transaction was, in fact, a security agreement for purposes of Bankruptcy Code §365 and dispenses with that portion of Associates's motion. Although this conclusion is well supported by the law, the Court also notes that neither the evidence submitted by Associates nor the arguments of its memoranda refute or even seriously address the characterization of the Komatsu agreement. Associates has focused on the more difficult issue of the Freightliner agreement.

Although the Freightliner agreement does not provide an option to purchase the equipment for one dollar, the debtor nonetheless argues that the purchase option is for nominal consideration. Associates, in turn, asserts that no option to purchase even exists in the Freightliner agreement. Instead, Associates argues that the agreement includes a final adjustment clause in paragraph 8 that requires the sale of the property at the end of the lease. If the proceeds are more than the residual value set forth in the agreement, then a credit is given to the debtor. If, however, the sale proceeds are less than the residual value, the debtor is charged the difference. See May 16, 1996, Truck Lease Agreement at paragraph 8.

Contrary to Associates suggestion, however, the Court treats the final adjustment clause in this case as simply an option for the debtor to purchase the equipment at the end of the lease at the price set by the residual value, $9,625.00. Not only is this a logical conclusion under the circumstances of this case, but Associates's own representative, Robert Davis, testified at the hearing in this matter that Associates would release title to the debtor, without the need for an actual public or private sale, if the debtor offered the residual value at the conclusion of the lease term. The result, of course, is that an option to purchase is created.

The characterization of the final adjustment clause as an option to purchase, however, is only a step in the process of determining whether the Freightliner agreement is a disguised security agreement and not a true lease. The Court returns to the remaining provisions of Virginia Code §8.1-201(37) to resolve this question.

2. Whether a transaction creates a lease or security interest is determined by the facts of each case; however, a transaction creates a security interest if the consideration the lessee is to pay the lessor for the right to possession and use of the goods is an obligation for the term of the lease not subject to termination by the lessee, and:
(a) The original term of the lease is equal to or greater than the remaining economic life of the goods;
(b) The lessee is bound to renew the lease for the remaining economic life of the goods or is bound to become the owner of the goods;
(c) The lessee has an option to renew the lease for the remaining economic life of the goods for no additional consideration or nominal additional consideration upon compliance with the lease agreement; or
(d) The lessee has an option to become the owner of the goods for no additional consideration or nominal additional consideration upon compliance with the lease agreement.

This section, paragraph 2 of the definition of a security agreement, again instructs the Court to analyze these situations on a case by case basis. Next, the code section sets forth several situations that conclusively indicate a security agreement. As conceded by the debtor, the relevant portions of this statute are found in the main body of paragraph two and in subsection (d). Under this analysis, if (i) the debtor cannot avoid paying Associates the value of the payments due under the lease, and (ii) the debtor can become the owner of the Freightliner for nominal or no consideration upon compliance with the lease terms, then the transaction creates a security interest.

The first of these two conditions exists in this case. While the debtor could terminate the lease early, it cannot avoid or terminate the obligation to pay Associates the value of the consideration due under the agreement, whether payable at the natural end of the lease or upon earlier termination. The Court agrees with the analysis of the debtor on this point as outlined in its initial memorandum. See Initial Brief Debtor at 10 and 11.[3] The Court finds that the Freightliner agreement requires payment to Associates of the present value, upon early termination, of exactly what it would be paid upon the natural termination of the lease. Consequently, the condition outlined in the main body of paragraph 2 of . . . §8.1-201(37) is met in that the debtor could not terminate the obligation to pay the consideration due to Associates under the Freightliner agreement.

Now consider what must be paid if the debtor terminated the lease early. After meeting the technical requirements for lease termination in paragraph 3 of the agreement, the debtor would be required to pay the total of: (i) the full amount of any past due payments, (ii) the present value of any future, unaccrued monthly payments, plus (iii) the present value of the 9,625.00. Again, the same adjustments are made after the sale of the vehicle. Clearly, the agreement requires payment to Associates of the present value, upon early termination, of exactly what it would be paid upon the natural conclusion of the lease. Consequently, the debtor cannot terminate the obligation to pay Associates the value of the consideration under the lease.

Having satisfied the first condition of paragraph 2, the Court looks to the second condition. If any of the four criteria detailed in the subsections (a) through (d) are also met, then the Freightliner agreement is not a true lease. The debtor, of course, asserts that subsection (d) is satisfied. Associates, in contrast, strongly contends that the residual value purchase price of $9625.00 may not be characterized as nominal consideration under subsection (d).

---

3. To paraphrase the debtor's argument, the debtor's obligation is to pay all monthly payments, plus the residual value of $9,625.00. If the debtor pays the $9,625.00 in cash at the conclusion of the monthly payments, then Associates would turn over the title to the vehicle. If no such cash payment were made, then Associates would sell the vehicle. If the sale brought more than the $9,625.00 owed by the debtor, then the excess would be returned to the debtor. If the sale brought less, then the debtor would owe the difference to Associates. Thus the agreement ensures that Associates will be paid all the monthly payments plus $9,625.00.

The Court sides with Associates and finds that this option to purchase for the residual value is not, in fact, for no consideration or for nominal consideration. Although the Court declines to speculate on where the line would be drawn for what constitutes nominal consideration, clearly $9,625.00 does not qualify as such, particularly in light of the agreement's capitalized cost of only $38,500.00. Furthermore, the testimony of both parties indicates that the $9,625.00 residual value was a fair estimate, when made at the time the agreement was executed, of the vehicle's value at the conclusion of the lease payments. Consequently, it is not clear from the evidence before the Court that the parties expected for the debtor to recognize much, if any, equity in the vehicle. Nor is it clear that the only economically sensible course for the debtor would be to exercise the option to purchase the vehicle. In re Dunn Brothers, Incorporated, 16 B.R. 42, 45 (Bankr. W.D. Va. 1981) (describing the economic realities test for determining if a sum is nominal by questioning whether the option is set at such an attractive price that the only sensible course for the lessee is to take it). As a result, the Court finds that the option price in this case is not nominal. Id.; See also In re Aspen Impressions, Inc., 94 B.R. 861, 865 (Bankr. E.D. Pa. 1989) ("The more nominal the purchase option . . . the more likely is the conclusion that the lease was really one intended to accomplish the transfer of a title interest.").

The fact that the transaction in question does not clearly fall under any of the bright line tests for a security agreement outlined in paragraph 2 of Virginia Code §8.1-201(37) does not conclusively determine that the Freightliner agreement is a true lease. It is simply another factor that the court must consider as it carefully analyzes all of the facts of this case to make its decision. For further guidance, the Court looks to paragraph 3 of Virginia Code §8.1-201(37).

3. A transaction does not create a security interest merely because it provides that:
      (a) The present value of the consideration the lessee is obligated to pay the lessor for the right to possession and use of the goods is substantially equal to or is greater than the fair market value of the goods at the time the lease is entered into;
      (b) The lessee assumes risk of loss of the goods, or agrees to pay taxes, insurance, filing, recording, or registration fees, or service or maintenance costs with respect to the goods;
      (c) The lessee has an option to renew the lease or to become the owner of the goods;
      (d) The lessee has an option to renew the lease for a fixed rent that is equal to or greater than the reasonably predictable fair market

rent for the use of the goods for the term of the renewal at the time
the option is to be performed; or

    (e) The lessee has an option to become the owner of the goods
for a fixed price that is equal to or greater than the reasonably
predictable fair market value of the goods at the time the option is to
be performed.

Although this code section states that the existence of any one of
these factors alone does not create a security interest, the Court has
considered each of them in order to decide whether the weight of
evidence in this case requires a determination that the transaction was
a true lease or a security agreement. Of the paragraph 3 factors,
subsections (b) and (c) apply in that the debtor assumed the risk of
loss and insured the vehicle, the debtor paid taxes on the vehicle, the
debtor has paid for all maintenance on the vehicle, and the debtor has
the option to purchase the vehicle. In contrast, Associates strongly
asserts that factors under subsection (b), such as the debtor's responsibility for taxes, registration fees, and insurance, are not inconsistent with a true lease. In re Zaleha, 159 B.R. 581, 584 (Bankr. D.
Idaho 1993).

    The Court weighs less heavily the factors emphasized by the
debtor. As stated in the commentary to the amended U.C.C. definition
of security interest, "courts have relied upon factors that were thought
to be more consistent with sales or loans than leases. Most of these
criteria, however, are as applicable to true leases as to security
interests." See Official Comment Virginia Code §8.1-201(37).

    The Court finds many of the subsection (b) factors to be as
applicable to true leases as to security interests and generally agrees
with the language of Judge Clarkson in Basic Leasing, Inc. v. Paccar,
Inc.: "It makes sense that a lessee would provide insurance on the
property while in possession of it under a lease; it seems perfectly
reasonable for a lessee to agree to undertake some of the risks of loss
or damage while the lessee enjoys possession and use of the property.
The same holds true for taxes and maintenance." 1991 WL 117412
(D.N.J.). . . .

    Of greatest importance to the Court in making this decision, after
exhausting, to no avail, the statutory tests outlined in paragraphs 1 and
2 of Virginia Code §8.1-201(37), are factors such as whether the vehicle
can be purchased for nominal consideration and the anticipated
amount of the lessee's equity in vehicle. In re Bumgardner, 183 B.R.
224, 228 (Bankr. D. Idaho 1995); See also Amvest Funding Co. v. Rex
Group, Inc., 80 B.R. 774, 780 (Bankr. W.D. Va. 1987) ("Any creation of

equity in the lessee has been held to be one of the distinctive characteristics of a lease intended for security.").

These factors are intertwined. "If a lease contains an option to purchase for no or nominal consideration . . . , it suggests that the lessor does not care, in an economic sense, whether or not the option is exercised." In re Zaleha, 159 B.R. 581, 585 (Bankr. D. Idaho 1993). Likewise, if the lessee develops equity in the leased property because the purchase price is low relative to the option price, then the only sensible decision economically for the lessee is to exercise the option. In such case, the lessor did not likely expect the return of the leased goods. Id.

Due to the final adjustment clause in paragraph 8 of the Freightliner agreement, the debtor in this case theoretically has the opportunity to build up equity in the vehicle if its value can be maintained over the lease term at an amount higher than the $9,625.00 option price. The Court's concern, however, is that the evidence indicates that the parties did not expect much, if any, equity to actually accrue for the benefit of the debtor in this transaction. In re Aspen Impressions, Inc., 94 B.R. 861, 868 (Bankr. E.D. Pa. 1989).

As noted previously, the parties' testimony indicated that the $9,625.00 residual value was a fair estimate, when made at the time the agreement was executed, of the vehicle's anticipated value at the conclusion of the lease payments. Again, the Court does not find the resulting option price of $9,625.00 to be nominal consideration under these circumstances. Furthermore, the Court finds that little, if any, equity was anticipated by the parties.

After analyzing the Freightliner agreement and weighing all of the facts and arguments presented by the parties, the Court finds that the Freightliner agreement is a true lease. The Freightliner agreement transferred the right to possession and use of a vehicle to the debtor for a term. The lease included an option to purchase the vehicle; however, that option was for more than just nominal consideration. The equity, if any, created in the lessee in this case is minimal and is therefore of limited significance to the debtor's argument that this lease should be considered as a security agreement.

CONCLUSION

For the reasons set forth above, Associates's Motion to Compel the Assumption or Rejection of Leases is denied with respect to the Komatsu agreement and granted with respect to the Freightliner agreement. In addition, based on the Court's characterizations of the agreements in question, Associates's second Motion for Payments of Leases is granted with respect to the Freightliner agreement and denied with respect to the Komatsu agreement.

In close cases the advising attorney may wish to tell the lessor (or the alleged consignor in quasi-consignment problems) to play it safe and file a financing statement even if it is believed that a true lease/non-consignment has been created. This may create a danger, however, that the Article 9 filing is an admission (for tax/accounting purposes) that only a secured transaction is involved. To avoid this admission problem, the drafters gave us §9-505, which you should read.

IV. OTHER TRANSACTIONS

PROBLEM 263

When Mercy Hospital's administrators decided to build a new addition, they hired a general contractor named Crash Construction Co. and required it to get a surety to guaranty the performance of the construction job and the payment of all the workers and material suppliers (to avoid a mechanic's lien on the hospital). Standard Surety issued such a performance and payment bond covering Crash's obligation to Mercy Hospital. To finance the construction, Crash borrowed money from Octopus National Bank (ONB) and gave as collateral the right to collect the progress payments from Mercy Hospital as they came due. ONB duly filed an Article 9 financing statement. Halfway through the job, Crash went bankrupt, and Standard Surety had to finish and pay off the employees and suppliers. At this point, by virtue of the common law right to *subrogation* (the equitable right given to sureties to step into the legal shoes of persons they have paid), Standard Surety claimed a superior right to unpaid monies retained by Mercy Hospital, which were to be paid to Crash. ONB also claimed this fund, pointed to its filed security interest, and stated that Standard Surety's subrogation right was only an unfiled Article 9 security interest. Who should win? See New Mexico State Highway and Transp. Dept. v. Gulf Ins. Co., 996 P.2d 424, 40 U.C.C. Rep. Serv. 2d 863 (N.M. App. 1999); Comment, Equitable Subrogation

—Too Hardy a Plant to Be Uprooted by Article 9 of the UCC?, 1971 U. Pitt. L. Rev. 580.

V. EXCLUSIONS FROM ARTICLE 9

Read §9-109(c) and (d).

A. Federal Statutes

It is no surprise that the Uniform Commercial Code, a state statute, cannot displace federal law. From the way §9-109(c)(1) is worded, however, note that the UCC *does* apply to the extent that the federal statute does not answer the problem presented. See G. Gilmore, Security Interests in Personal Property, ch. 13 (1965) (hereinafter G. Gilmore); for a list of such statutes, see J. White & R. Summers, Uniform Commercial Code §21-10 (hereinafter White & Summers). With the exception of the federal tax lien statute, Internal Revenue Code §§6321-6325, most federal statutes (for example, the Ship Mortgage Act of 1920 and the Civil Aeronautics Act's provisions on security interests in aircraft) do not cover the field and are constantly supplemented by Article 9 provisions in litigation.

In United States v. Kimbell Foods, 440 U.S. 715, 26 U.C.C. Rep. Serv. 1 (1979), the Supreme Court decided that, as a matter of *federal* law, the relative priority of private consensual liens arising in favor of the U.S. government under various lending programs is to be decided under non-discriminatory state law (i.e., the UCC), unless a federal statute clearly provides otherwise.

For the practitioner, the important thing to remember is that certain matters must be researched on a federal as well as a state level. Ship mortgages, aircraft titles, patents and copyrights,[4] railroad equip-

---

4. Strangely enough, there is great confusion as to whether security interests in various types of intellectual property are to be perfected under federal or state law, though most courts have found that state law governs. See In re Together Development Corp., 37 U.C.C. Rep. Serv. 2d 227 (Bankr. D. Mass. 1998) (trademarks should be filed under Article 9); In re Cybernetic Services, Inc., 252 F.3d 1039, 44 U.C.C. Rep. Serv. 2d 639 (9th Cir. 2001) (patents should be filed under Article 9); In re World Auxiliary Power Co., 244 B.R. 149, 40 U.C.C. Rep. Serv. 2d 1099 (Bkr. N.D. Cal. 1999) (copyrights should be filed under Article 9); Alice Haemmerli, Insecurity Interests: Where Intellectual Property and Commercial Law Collide, 96 Colum. L. Rev.

ment, and some interstate commercial vehicles (such as trucks and buses registered with the Interstate Commerce Commission) are, in part, governed by federal statutes. Creditors (and their attorneys) who simply think an Article 9 filing will perfect their interest in, say, an airplane end up as unsecured creditors whose only cause of action may be against their state-law-minded attorneys. See Feldman v. Chase Manhattan Bank, N.A., 368 F. Supp. 1327, 13 U.C.C. Rep. Serv. 1333 (S.D.N.Y. 1974) (assignment of airplane lease with Article 9 filing not effective against bankruptcy trustee where creditor failed to file with FAA as required by Federal Aviation Act).

Further, certain federal statutes may void some security interests. Section 125 of the Truth in Lending Act, 15 U.S.C. §1635 (1980), for instance, destroys any security interest taken in a consumer's home as part of a credit transaction if the credit seller does not notify the consumer of a three-day right to rescind the contract (and supply the consumer with other truth-in-lending disclosures).

Philko Aviation, Inc. v. Shacket

United States Supreme Court, 1983
462 U.S. 406, 36 U.C.C. Rep. Serv. 1

Justice WHITE delivered the opinion of the Court.

This case presents the question whether the Federal Aviation Act of 1958 (Act), 49 U.S.C. §§1301 et seq., prohibits all transfers of title to aircraft from having validity against innocent third parties unless the transfer has been evidenced by a written instrument, and the instrument has been recorded with the Federal Aviation Administration (FAA). We conclude that the Act does have such effect.

On April 19, 1978, at an airport in Illinois, a corporation operated by Roger Smith sold a new airplane to respondents. Respondents, the Shackets, paid the sale price in full and took possession of the aircraft, and they have been in possession ever since. Smith, however, did not give respondents the original bills of sale reflecting the chain of title to the plane. He instead gave them only photocopies and his assurance that he would "take care of the paperwork," which the Shackets understood to include the recordation of the original bills of sale with

---

1645 (1996). The matter is of some real practical importance. If a UCC filing is all that is required, one filing in the name of the debtor will do it for all the intangible rights he/she owns; if a federal filing is necessary, it will have to be done for *each* patent/copyright/trademark, a much more expensive undertaking. See White & Summers §22-10.

the FAA. Insofar as the present record reveals, the Shackets never attempted to record their title with the FAA.

Unfortunately for all, Smith did not keep his word but instead commenced a fraudulent scheme. Shortly after the sale to the Shackets, Smith purported to sell the same airplane to petitioner, Philko Aviation. According to Philko, Smith said that the plane was in Michigan having electronic equipment installed. Nevertheless, Philko and its financing bank were satisfied that all was in order, for they had examined the original bills of sale and had checked the aircraft's title against FAA records. At closing, Smith gave Philko the title documents, but, of course, he did not and could not have given Philko possession of the aircraft. Philko's bank subsequently recorded the title documents with the FAA.

After the fraud became apparent, the Shackets filed the present declaratory judgment action to determine title to the plane. Philko argued that it had title because the Shackets had never recorded their interest in the airplane with the FAA. Philko relied on §503(c) of the Act, 49 U.S.C. §1403(c), which provides that no conveyance or instrument affecting the title to any civil aircraft shall be valid against third parties not having actual notice of the sale, until such conveyance or other instrument is filed for recordation with the FAA. However, the District Court awarded summary judgment in favor of the Shackets, 497 F. Supp. 1262 (N.D. Ill. 1980), and the Court of Appeals affirmed, reasoning that §503(c) did not preempt substantive state law regarding title transfers, and that, under the Illinois Uniform Commercial Code, Ill. Rev. Stat., ch. 26, §§1-101 et seq., the Shackets had title but Philko did not. 681 F.2d 506 (CA7 1982). We granted certiorari, — U.S. — (1982), and we now reverse and remand for further proceedings.

Section 503(a)(1) of the Act, 49 U.S.C. §1403(a)(1), directs the Secretary of Transportation to establish and maintain a system for the recording of any "conveyance which affects the title to, or any interest in, any civil aircraft of the United States." Section 503(c), 49 U.S.C. §1403(c), states:

> No conveyance or instrument the recording of which is provided for by [§503(a)(1)] shall be valid in respect of such aircraft . . . against any person other than the person by whom the conveyance or other instrument is made or given, his heir or devisee, or any person having actual notice thereof, until such conveyance or other instrument is filed for recordation in the office of the Secretary of Transportation.

The statutory definition of "conveyance" defines the term as "a bill of sale, contract of conditional sale, mortgage, assignment of mortgage, or other instrument affecting title to, or interest in, property." 49 U.S.C. §1301(20) (Supp. V, 1981). If §503(c) were to be interpreted literally in accordance with the statutory definition, that section would not require every transfer to be documented and recorded, it would only invalidate unrecorded title *instruments,* rather than unrecorded title *transfers.* Under this interpretation, a claimant might be able to prevail against an innocent third party by establishing his title without relying on an instrument. In the present case, for example, the Shackets could not prove their title on the basis of an unrecorded bill of sale or other writing purporting to evidence a transfer of title to them, even if state law did not require recordation of such instruments, but they might still prevail, since Illinois law does not require written evidence of a sale "with respect to goods for which payment has been made and accepted or which have been received and accepted." Ill. Rev. Stat., ch. 26, §2-201(3)(c).

We are convinced, however, that Congress did not intend §503(c) to be interpreted in this manner. Rather, §503(c) means that every aircraft transfer must be evidenced by an instrument, and every such instrument must be recorded, before the rights of innocent third parties can be affected. Furthermore, because of these federal requirements, state laws permitting undocumented or unrecorded transfers are preempted, for there is a direct conflict between §503(c) and such state laws, and the federal law must prevail.

These conclusions are dictated by the legislative history. The Senate, House, and Conference committee reports, and the section-by-section analysis of one of the bill's drafters, all expressly declare that the federal statute "requires" the recordation of "every transfer of any interest in a civil aircraft." The Senate report explains: "This section requires the recordation with the Authority of every transfer made after the effective date of the section, of any interest in a civil aircraft of the United States. The conveyance evidencing *each such transfer* is to be recorded with an index in a recording system to be established by the Authority." Thus, since Congress intended to require the recordation of a conveyance evidencing *each transfer* of an interest in aircraft, Congress must have intended to preempt any state law under which a transfer without a recordable conveyance would be valid against innocent transferees or lienholders who have recorded.

Any other construction would defeat the primary congressional purpose for the enactment of §503(c), which was to create "a central clearing house for recordation of titles so that a person, wherever he may be, will know where he can find ready access to the claims against, or liens, or other legal interests in an aircraft." Hearings before the

House Comm. on Interstate and Foreign Commerce, 75 Cong., 3d Sess., p.407 (April 1, 1938) (testimony of F. Fagg, Director of Air Commerce, Dept. of Commerce). Here, state law does not require any documentation whatsoever for a valid transfer of an aircraft to be effected. An oral sale is fully valid against third parties once the buyer takes possession of the plane. If the state law allowing this result were not preempted by §503(c), then any buyer in possession would have absolutely no need or incentive to record his title with the FAA, and he could refuse to do so with impunity, and thereby prevent the "central clearing house" from providing "ready access" to information about his claim. This is not what Congress intended.

In the absence of the statutory definition of conveyance, our reading of §503(c) would be by far the most natural one, because the term "conveyance" is first defined in the dictionary as "the action of conveying," i.e., "the act by which title to property . . . . is transferred." Webster's Third New International Dictionary 499 (P. Gove ed. 1976). Had Congress defined "conveyance" in accordance with this definition, then §503(c) plainly would have required the recordation of every transfer. Congress' failure to adopt this definition is not dispositive, however, since the statutory definition is expressly not applicable if "the context otherwise requires." 49 U.S.C. §1301. Even in the absence of such a caveat, we need not read the statutory definition mechanically into §503(c), since to do so would render the recording system ineffective and thus would defeat the purpose of the legislation. A statutory definition should not be applied in such a manner. Lawson v. Suwannee S.S. Co., 336 U.S. 198, 201 (1949). Accordingly, we hold that state laws allowing undocumented or unrecorded transfers of interests in aircraft to affect innocent third parties are preempted by the federal Act.

In support of the judgment below, respondents rely on Matter of Gary Aircraft Corp., 681 F.2d 365 (CA5 1982), which rejected the contention that §503 preempted all state laws dealing with priority of interests in aircraft. The Court of Appeals held that the first person to record his interest with the FAA is not assured of priority, which is determined by reference to state law. We are inclined to agree with this rationale, but it does not help the Shackets. Although state law determines priorities, all interests must be federally recorded before they can obtain whatever priority to which they are entitled under state law. As one commentator has explained, "The only situation in which priority appears to be determined by operation of the [federal] statute is where the security holder has failed to record his interest. Such failure invalidates the conveyance as to innocent third persons. But recordation itself merely validates, it does not grant priority." Scott, Liens in Aircraft: Priorities, 25 J. Air L. & Com. 193, 203 (1958). Accord, Sigman, The Wild Blue Yonder: Interests In Aircraft under Our Federal System, 46 So. Cal. L. Rev. 316, 324-325 (1973) (although recordation does not establish priority, "failure to record . . . serves to subordinate"); Note, 26 Wash. & Lee L. Rev. 205, 212-213 (1979).

In view of the foregoing, we find that the courts below erred by granting the Shackets summary judgment on the basis that if an unrecorded transfer of an aircraft is valid under state law, it has validity as against innocent third parties. Of course, it it undisputed that the sale to the Shackets was valid and binding as between the parties. Hence, if Philko had actual notice of the transfer to the Shackets or if, under state law, Philko failed to acquire or perfect the interest that it purports to assert for reasons wholly unrelated to the sale to the Shackets, Philko would not have an enforceable interest, and the Shackets would retain possession of the aircraft. Furthermore, we do not think that the federal law imposes a standard with which it is impossible to comply. There may be situations in which the transferee has used reasonable diligence to file and cannot be faulted for the failure of the crucial documents to be of record. But because of the manner in which this case was disposed of on summary judgment, matters such as these were not considered, and these issues remain open on remand. The judgment of the Court of Appeals is reversed, and the case is remanded for further proceedings consistent with this opinion.

So ordered.

Justice O'CONNOR, concurring in part and concurring in the judgment.

I join the opinion of the Court except to the extent that it might be read to suggest this Court's endorsement of the view that one who makes a reasonably diligent effort to record will obtain the protections ordinarily reserved for recorded interests. I would express no opinion on that question, for it is not before us and has not been addressed in brief or in argument or, indeed, in the statute.

NOTE

For the resolution of this case on retrial, see Shackett v. Philko Aviation, Inc., 841 F.2d 166, 5 U.C.C. Rep. Serv. 2d 727 (7th Cir. 1988).

B.   Landlord's Lien and Other Statutory Liens

Subsections (d)(1) and (2) of §9-109 exclude statutory liens (like the one in Problem 257) from Article 9; but what about the following situation?

PROBLEM 264

When Christopher Morley opened his bookshop, the landlord wanted security for the rent. They signed a lease agreement providing that all of the inventory (the books) would be subject to a lien in the landlord's favor and could be seized and sold if Christopher defaulted in the rent payments. Is the landlord's lien required to be perfected under Article 9? See Persky, Shapiro, Salim, Esper, Arnoff & Nolfi Co., L.P.A. v. Guyuron, 2000 WL 1867407, 43 U.C.C. Rep. Serv. 2d 1009 (Ohio. App. 2000).

C.   Wage Assignments

Claims to wages were once a fertile source of collateral, but special statutory regulation has all but killed off wage assignments. Thus, some states absolutely prohibit the assignment of future wages (see, e.g., Ala. Code tit. 39, §201; such assignments are *void*); some permit them in limited circumstances if the employer consents (see, e.g., Del. Code Ann. tit. 5, §2115; N.C. Gen. Stat. §95-31); and some states require the consent of both the employer and the spouse (see, e.g., Ind. Code §22-2-7). Employers always disliked having to bother with direct payments to an employee's creditors (and further disliked the idea that employees had little or no equity left in their own paychecks). The special statutes on the matter survive the enactment of Article 9; §9-109(d)(3).

PROBLEM 265

Carl Jugular was an independent insurance agent who sold policies for many companies, though his primary sales were the life and automobile policies of the Montana Insurance Association (MIA). In order to float a loan to buy a car, Carl gave the lending bank a security interest in "all present and future commissions earned or to be earned" from the MIA. Does Article 9 cover this assignment? See Massachusetts Mut. Life Ins. Co. v. Central Pa. Natl. Bank, 372 F. Supp. 1027, 14 U.C.C. Rep. Serv. 212 (E.D. Pa. 1974).

D. Non-Financing Assignments

The §9-109(d)(4) through (7) exclusions of some transfers of accounts, chattel paper, payment intangibles, and promissory notes is meant to be an exclusion of all such assignments of a non-financing nature. See G. Gilmore §10-5. Generally, as we have seen, such sales would be Article 9 matters, but in the listed situations no one would think to comply with Article 9, and the possibility of the deception of later parties is small.

PROBLEM 266

When Michael Logan sold his lucrative art business to John Pivarski, he sold not only all the tangible assets but his outstanding accounts receivables as well. Must the buyer take the steps required by Article 9 of a secured party? See §§9-102(a)(72)(D) and 9-109(d)(4). If Logan received a commission to paint the portrait of the city's mayor but decided he was too busy to perform the task and (with the mayor's permission) transferred the job (and the right to the payment for it) to another artist, must the new artist take Article 9 steps? See §9-109(d)(6). When one of Logan's clients refused to pay for a delivered painting, Logan sold the account to Trash Collection Agency. Must Trash comply with Article 9? See §9-109(d)(5). Finally, pressed by his art supplies store for payment of his outstanding tab, Logan transferred to the store the money due him from a client whose portrait he had painted the month before. Must the art supplies store take Article 9 steps? See §9-109(d)(7).

E. Real Estate

Except for fixtures, real estate security interests are not covered by Article 9, but what happens when the paperwork creating them (the mortgage itself and the promissory note the debtor signs) are used as security when the mortgagee itself seeks a loan?

PROBLEM 267

Local Loan Company (LLC) needed to borrow money, and Octopus National Bank (ONB) agreed to loan it the requisite amount, taking into ONB's possession as collateral the real property mortgages and accompanying promissory notes given to LLC by its borrowers. Need ONB do anything either in the real property recording office or under the UCC's Article 9 to protect its interest in this collateral? Compare §§9-109(d)(11) and 9-109(b); read Official Comment 7 to §9-109; see the helpful discussion in R. Bowmar, Real Estate Interests as Security Under the UCC: The Scope of Article Nine, 12 UCC L.J. 99 (1979); and see §§9-203(g) and 9-308(e).

F.   Other Exclusions

Section 9-109(d) lists some other items that are excluded from Article 9 coverage in whole or in part (insurance, certain bank accounts, certain tort claims, etc.). We will consider these matters as they arise in other contexts.

Chapter 19

THE CREATION OF A SECURITY INTEREST

I. CLASSIFYING THE COLLATERAL

Article 9 divides *collateral* (defined in §9-102(a)(12)) into many different categories:

Goods (read §9-102(a)(44); cf. §2-105):
  Consumer Goods (read §9-102(a)(23));
  Equipment (read §9-102(a)(33));
  Farm Products (read §9-102(a)(34)); and
  Inventory (read §9-102(a)(48)).

Quasi-Tangible Property (pieces of paper used as collateral):
    Instruments (read §§9-102(a)(47) and 3-104);
        Promissory Notes (read §9-102(a)(65)—these are a
        subcategory of "instruments");
    Investment Property (stocks and bonds and rights to accounts
    containing same) (read §9-102(a)(49));
    Documents (warehouse receipts and bills of lading)
    (read §§9-102(a)(30) and 1-201(15));
    Chattel Paper (read §9-102(a)(11)); and
    Letters of Credit Rights (read §9-102(a)(51).

Intangible Property (property having no significant physical form):
    Accounts (read §9-102(a)(2));
        Health-Care-Insurance Receivables (read §9-102(a)(46)—
        these are a subcategory of "accounts");
    Deposit Accounts (read §9-102(a)(29));
    General Intangibles (read §9-102(a)(42)); and
        Payment Intangibles (read §9-102(a)(61)—these are a
        subcategory of "general intangibles").

Note that *equipment* is defined not only so it has its usual meaning, but also so it is a catchall category for any goods that do not fit into the other three goods categories. Similarly, *general intangibles* include all intangible collateral not falling into another category.

Classification of the collateral is important because many provisions of Article 9 make legal distinctions based on the type of collateral. For example, the technical steps required to *perfect* a security interest in a negotiable instrument, a family car, or a hardware store's inventory are completely different, as we shall explore when we address the issue of perfection.

It is important to note that it is the *debtor's* announced use of the collateral that determines its classification.

PROBLEM 268

Fill in the blanks with the proper classifications of these items of collateral:

(a) A professional pianist's piano: _____ (see In re Symons, 5 U.C.C. Rep. Serv. 262 (Ref. Bankr., E.D. Mich. 1967)).

(b) Cattle fattened by a farmer for sale: _____ (see In re Cadwell, Martin Meat Co., 10 U.C.C. Rep. Serv. 710 (Ref. Bankr., E.D. Cal. 1970)); the farmer's tractor: _____ (see Central Natl. Bank v.

Wonderland Realty Corp., 38 Mich. App. 76, 195 N.W.2d 768, 10 U.C.C. Rep. Serv. 1117 (1972)); the farmer's chickens: _____ United States v. Pete Brown Enter., Inc., 328 F. Supp. 600, 9 U.C.C. Rep. Serv. 734 (N.D. Miss. 1971)); manure from the dairy herd: _____ (see Miller, Farm Collateral Under the UCC: "Those Are Some Mighty Tall Silos, Ain't They Fella?," 20 S.D. L. Rev. 514, 526 (1975)).

(c) A mobile home: _____ (compare §9-102(a)(53)).

(d) A right to sue someone for breach of contract: _____ (see Friedman, Lobe & Block v. C.L.W. Corp., 9 Wash. App. 319, 512 P.2d 769, 13 U.C.C. Rep. Serv. 136 (1973)); a right to sue someone for negligence arising out of an automobile accident: _____ (see §9-109(d)(12)); a right to sue a corporation for wooing away a trusted employee: _____ (see §9-102(a)(13)); a security interest in a lawsuit plaintiff has already won and that has been reduced to a settlement agreement: _____ (see §9-109, Official Comment 15).

(e) Pencils and other stationery supplies used by Sears or a similar large retailer in its credit offices: _____ (see §9-102, Official Comment 4 (a), fourth paragraph).

(f) A liquor license: _____ (see United States v. McGurn, 596 So. 2d 1038, 17 U.C.C. Rep. Serv. 2d 235 (Fla. 1992)); a right to the return of a security deposit held by a landlord: _____ (see United States v. Samel Ref. Corp., 461 F.2d 941, 10 U.C.C. Rep. Serv. 1232 (3d Cir. 1972)); a newspaper carrier's right to payments for papers already delivered: _____; a newspaper carrier's right to payments for papers to be delivered in the future: _____.

(g) Curtains bought by a lawyer for the law office: _____ (see In re Bonnema, 4 U.C.C. Rep. Serv. 894 (N.D. Ohio 1967)). What if after purchasing the curtains the lawyer decides to use them at home? Do they become consumer goods? See §9-507(b) and the next case; cf. In re McClain, 447 F.2d 241, 9 U.C.C. Rep. Serv. 545 (10th Cir. 1971).

(h) Aunt Augusta loaned her nephew $5000 with an oral agreement he would repay the money the following year. If she wants to use this agreement as collateral, how would it be classified?

In re Morton

United States District Court, District of Maine, Bankruptcy Division, 1971
9 U.C.C. Rep. Serv. 1147

CYR, REF. BANKR. Upon his voluntary adjudication in bankruptcy Philip Morton was in possession of a 1968 Ford Bronco subject to the purchase money security interest now under attack by the trustee in bankruptcy. When he purchased the Bronco the bankrupt was employed as an unlicensed surveyor by Knox Mining & Surveying Company. He bought the Bronco to replace an aging Chevrolet station wagon, which had been used primarily for personal and household purposes. Several months after the purchase of the Bronco, Knox Mining & Surveying Company contracted to reimburse the bankrupt on a mileage basis for transporting surveying equipment. Thereafter, the Bronco was used primarily for that purpose, although it was used to a lesser extent for other purposes as well.

When Maine National Bank's security interest attached by virtue of the execution of a valid security agreement between Harold B. Stetson, the seller, and the bankrupt, the bankrupt was residing in Union, Maine. On October 10, 1969, the same day the security agreement was executed, the seller caused a sufficient financing statement to be filed with the Town Clerk of Union.

The court is satisfied, on the basis of the evidence presented, that the bankrupt bought this vehicle primarily for personal and household purposes, but that the actual use to which it was put was of other than a personal, family, or household nature. The Bronco was used primarily in connection with the bankrupt's employment and in furtherance of his employer's surveying business.

CONCLUSIONS OF LAW

The filing of the financing statement in the office of the clerk of the municipality where the debtor resided at the time the security interest attached on October 10, 1969, perfected the Bank's purchase money security interest, providing the collateral constituted consumer goods. In re O'Donnell, 7 U.C.C. Rep. Serv. 888 (D. Me. 1970). But if the vehicle was neither used nor bought for use primarily for personal, family or household purposes, it was incumbent upon the secured party to cause an additional financing statement to be filed in the office of the Secretary of State. Since the bankrupt bought the vehicle primarily for personal purposes, it constituted consumer goods. The filing of a sufficient financing statement with the Town Clerk of Union sufficed to perfect the purchase money security interest, despite the fact that the vehicle was used thereafter primarily for other than personal, family and household purposes.

There is a measure of commercial expediency inherent in gauging compliance with Code perfection requirements by recourse to the *extrinsic circumstances prevailing at the time the security interest attaches.*[1] In re O'Donnell, 7 U.C.C. Rep. Serv. 888 (D. Me. 1970); In re Pelletier, 5 U.C.C. Rep. Serv. 327 (D. Me. 1968). While §9-109(1) seems to restrict the court's determination of the buyer's intended use of the collateral to the time of purchase,[2] it is not so necessarily as concerns the actual use to which the collateral is put. Therefore, serious judicial consideration should be given to applying the collateral use tests prescribed by §9-109(1) and (2) [the definition of *consumer goods* now found in §9-102(a)(23)—Ed.] in the circumstances prevailing *when the security interest attaches.* Cf. In re Pelletier, 5 U.C.C. Rep. Serv. 327 (D. Me. 1968). But cf. Bender's U.C.C. Service, Willier & Hart, U.C.C. Reporter-Digest, §9-401, A20 (Matthew Bender & Co.). In terms of

1. The protection afforded by §9-401(3) [now §9-507(b)—Ed.] precludes a filing made in the proper place from being struck down later because of a change in the collateral's *actual* use. Furthermore, although §9-401(3) makes no reference to the *intended* use of the collateral, subsections (1) & (2) of §9-109 [the definition of *consumer goods* now found in §9-102(a)(23)—Ed.] seem to fix the moment of purchase as the relevant point for inquiry into the buyer's intention. It is difficult to conceive of a circumstance in which the purchase of the collateral will not precede the attachment of the security interest, except as to collateral which was never purchased. Often collateral which was never purchased by the debtor or any predecessor in title will be inventory or farm products, whose classifications do not depend on the application of §9-109(1) & (2). Where it is otherwise, the shortcoming inherent in the statute lies in the use of the phraseology *bought* for use, which seems necessarily to imply the occurrence of a purchase and the presence of a buyer-debtor, neither of which will always be found in any given secured transaction. Provided the moment of the attachment of the security interest is selected as the critical point at which collateral use is tested, there can be no period following the attachment of the security interest in which a change of collateral use could render ineffective a filing accomplished in response to circumstances which existed at the moment of attachment. It is otherwise, of course, if the time of filing is the critical point, since filing may follow by a substantial period but is seldom simultaneous with either the purchase of, or the attachment of a security interest in, the collateral. A more serious problem in terms of the notice function that Code filing is supposed to serve, is that a filing made in contemplation of a security agreement will be insulated by §9-401(3) from later attack regardless how dissimilar the debtor's circumstances were at the time of filing as compared to those which obtained when he acquired rights in the collateral, or possession of the collateral, or granted a security interest in the collateral. The purpose of notice filing is not to notify the world of the debtor's place of residence at the time of filing, but to inform it of the existence of a security interest in collateral which arose while the debtor resided in the place where the filing is made. In re Pelletier, 5 U.C.C. Rep. Serv. 327, 335 (D. Me. 1968).

2. The wording of §9-109(1) could be more precise. The purchase of the collateral will by no means always occur when the security interest attaches. Security interests commonly attach long after the purchase of the collateral. Nor is the debtor always a buyer, in which event the *debtor's intended use* of the collateral could be deemed irrelevant. This combination of possibilities suggests the wisdom of redundant filing on collateral the debtor either does not buy or buys long before or after the security agreement. . . .

facilitating commerce it would be cumbersome to require secured parties to maintain a continuing surveillance of debtors and their collateral beyond the time when the security interest attached. Less awkward collateral policing requirements were thought commercially unacceptable before the advent of the Uniform Commercial Code. It seems doubtful, therefore, that the Code architects intended to inhibit commercial transactions by making filing or the occurrence of some event other than the attachment of the security interest the critical time to apply the collateral use test; however curious it is that neither §9-109 itself nor the Official Comments evidence awareness of the problem.

Accordingly, it is ordered, adjudged and decreed that the purchase money security interest of Maine National Bank be and it is hereby determined perfected, and it is further:

Ordered, adjudged and decreed that the application of the trustee in bankruptcy be and it is hereby dismissed, with prejudice.

QUESTIONS

What will be the result where a car buyer tells the seller he wants the car for personal family use, but is lying and really plans to resell it on his own lot? See Balon v. Cadillac Auto. Co., 113 N.H. 108, 303 A.2d 194, 12 U.C.C. Rep. Serv. 397 (1973). Some creditors contemplating a loan to the debtor require that the debtor fill out an application that explains the intended use of the collateral. Is this legally wise from the creditor's point of view?

PROBLEM 269

Mercy Hospital needs financing and calls you, its attorney, with this question. Many of its patients are members of various health plans and when they come in for treatment they sign paperwork authorizing the hospital to seek payment from their health insurance coverage provider. The hospital always has a large number of such receivables in the process of collection. When the hospital borrows money can it use the monies due it from the various health plans as collateral? See §§9-109(d)(8) and 9-102(a)(46).

PROBLEM 270

Passport Credit Card Company issued millions of credit cards internationally, sending them to cardholders, who then used them in millions of transactions with merchants. The merchants would then send the resulting paperwork to Passport for reimbursement (minus Passport's fee). You are the attorney for Passport. When it needs to borrow money, can it use these credit card transactions as collateral? See §9-102(a)(2). Remember that the outright sale of such property by Passport is also an Article 9 transaction; §9-109(a)(3).

PROBLEM 271

Fill in the blanks with the proper collateral classifications:

(a) Milk in the hands of the farmer: _____; in the hands of the grocery store: _____; in the hands of the grocery store's customer who is buying for consumption: _____. Would your answer to the second question change if "restaurant" were used in place of "grocery store"? See §9-102, Official Comment 4(a), seond paragraph.

(b) A certificate of deposit issued by a bank: _____ (compare §3-104(j), §9-102(a)(47), and Southview Corp. v. Kleberg First Natl. Bank, 512 S.W.2d 817, 15 U.C.C. Rep. Serv. 408 (Tex. Civ. App. 1974)); an *airbill* issued by an airline as a receipt for frozen shrimp shipped by air: _____ (see §1-201(6)); the receipt given to a farmer by a silo operator when the farmer stored grain there: _____.

(c) Rare coins bought by a hobbyist for addition to his collection: _____ (see In re Midas Coin Co., 264 F. Supp. 193, 4 U.C.C. Rep. Serv. 220 (E.D. Mo. 1967), aff'd, 387 F.2d 118, 4 U.C.C. Rep. Serv. 908 (8th Cir. 1968)).

(d) A tax refund: _____ (see In re American Home Furnishings Corp., 48 Bankr. 905, 41 U.C.C. Rep. Serv. 631 (Bankr. W.D. Wash. 1985).

(e) A debenture bond issued by a corporation: _____ (see §§8-102(a)(15) and 9-102(a)(49)); a right to 100 shares of stock recorded on the books of the debtor's stockbroker: _____ (see §8-102(a)(17)).

(f) The checking account you have down at your bank: _____ (see §9-101(a)(29)).

(g) A computer program: _____ (see §9-102(a)(44));

(h) The monthly rental obligations owed to a landlord, who wants to use these obligations as collateral for a loan: _____ (compare §§9-102(a)(2), 9-109(d)(11)); the promissory notes signed for the tenants to pay their rent: _____ (§§9-102(a)(47), 9-109(b)).

Morgan County Feeders, Inc. v. McCormick

Colorado Court of Appeals, 1992
836 P.2d 1051, 180 U.C.C. Rep. Serv. 2d 632

[Neil Allen made an agreement with James McCormick to sell him 56 head of cattle Allen owned. The cattle were subject to a perfected security interest in favor of Morgan County Feeders, Inc., which seized the cattle prior to their delivery to McCormick. Items sold in the "ordinary course of business" (i.e., *inventory*), as we shall see, pass to the buyer free of even perfected security interests; pieces of *equipment* generally do not. After stating the facts and noting that the trial court had ruled in favor of Morgan County Feeds, Judge Rothenberg continued as follows.]

McCormick first contends that the trial court erred in determining that the cattle purchased by Allen were equipment, rather than inventory. We disagree.

Under the Uniform Commercial Code, "goods" are defined as "all things which are movable at the time the security interest attaches. . . ." Section 4-9-105(1)(f), C.R.S. (1991 Cum. Supp.) [now §9-102(a)(44) — Ed.]. Goods are classified under four major types which are mutually exclusive. These include: consumer goods; equipment; farm products; and inventory. . . .

Here, the parties agree that the cattle constitute "goods" under the Uniform Commercial Code. They further agree that the cattle are not "farm products." Thus, the remaining issue surrounding the cattle is whether they should be designated as inventory or equipment. The distinction is important because buyers of inventory in the ordinary course of business take free of perfected security interests. [See §9-320 —Ed.]

Section 4-9-109(2), C.R.S. [now §9-102(a)(33)—Ed.], provides that goods are equipment:

if they are used or bought for use primarily in business (including farming or a profession) . . . or if the goods are not included in the definitions of inventory, farm products, or consumer goods.

In contrast, §4-9-109(4), C.R.S. [now §9-102(a)(48)—Ed.], provides that goods are inventory:

> if they are held by a person who holds them for sale or lease or to be furnished under contracts of service or if he has so furnished them, or if they are . . . materials used or consumed in a business. Inventory of a person is not to be classified as his equipment.

In ascertaining whether goods are inventory or equipment, the principal use of the property is determinative. Section 4-9-109, C.R.S. (Official Comment 2). The factors to be considered in determining principal use include whether the goods are for immediate or ultimate sale and whether they have a relatively long or short period of use in the business. Section 4-9-109, C.R.S. (Official Comment 3); First Colorado Bank & Trust v. Plantation Inn, Ltd., 767 P.2d 812 (Colo. App. 1988).

Goods used in a business are equipment when they are fixed assets or have, as identifiable units, a relatively long period of use. They are inventory, even though not held for sale, if they are used up or consumed in a short period of time in the production of some end product. First Colorado Bank & Trust v. Plantation Inn, Ltd., supra. . . .

At trial, the court determined that the longhorn cattle were "equipment" and not "inventory" because: "Allen did not acquire or hold them for the principal purpose of immediate or ultimate sale or lease. . . . Instead, the cattle were to be used principally for recreational cattle drives. . . . While Allen might have occasionally leased the cattle to other entrepreneurs, it was his intention to utilize the cattle principally in his own recreational business. . . ." Thus, the court concluded that McCormick bought the cattle subject to Morgan County Feeders' security interest.

Although we recognize that the classification of cattle as "equipment," rather than "inventory," is highly unusual, we also recognize that the evidence presented to the trial court disclosed unusual circumstances, and we conclude that the record supports the court's classification.

Allen testified that his purpose for purchasing the longhorn cows was to use them on cattle drives and that these cows have a relatively long period of use in comparison to rodeo calves and feeder cattle. Several other witnesses also testified that Allen had stated his intent to use the longhorn cows for recreational cattle drives. Thus, the trial court was justified in rejecting McCormick's contention that the cattle were purchased only for rodeos. And, it did not err in finding that, under these unique circumstances, the cattle should be classified as "equipment."

In light of this conclusion, we need not address McCormick's additional contention that the trial court erred in finding that McCormick was not a buyer in the ordinary course of business . . . .

The judgment is affirmed.

PROBLEM 272

Sam Ambulance was a lawyer who loved speculative investments. When Elvis Presley died, Ambulance managed to acquire one of the singer's guitars. He decided to keep it for years and let it appreciate in value (he did not himself play the guitar). If Ambulance uses the guitar as collateral for a loan needed to run his law practice, how is the guitar classified?

A Few Words about Chattel Paper.   Chattel paper is an artificial construct of Article 9. Suppose, for example, that you run an automobile dealership and your business successfully sells a lot of cars each month on credit. The purchasers sign promissory notes in your favor and also sign a security agreement giving your dealership a security interest in the sold vehicles so that you (or your assignee) can repossess them in the event of default. This set of papers, taken collectively, is called *chattel paper* (note that it includes an instrument therein). Read §9-102(a)(11).[3] There is a huge market for such paper, so when your dealership needs money it can either sell the chattel paper outright or use it as collateral for a loan from some lending institution. Either way is an Article 9 transaction and will require the purchaser/lending institution to take the steps required by Article 9 to protect its security interest in the paper; §9-109(a).

PROBLEM 273

How would you categorize the car lease contracts that Dime-A-Minute Rental Cars use as collateral when it borrows money from a bank? If Dime-A-Minute so moves into the computer age that it stops

3. This is just one example of chattel paper, which is defined broadly enough to encompass the sale of most security interests from one secured party to another. Since the buying secured party takes possession of the paper, that is usually sufficient to satisfy the Article 9 rules on attachment and perfection.

using paper entirely, can the electronic version of this paperwork be used as collateral? See §9-102(a)(31) and its Official Comment 5(b). Article 9 provides that a secured party will be protected as to such electronic chattel paper if it has "control" over the paper, but, given that there is no actual writing, how could this possibly be done? Read §9-105.

PROBLEM 274

The State of Montana has enacted a statute giving unpaid crop dusters a lien on the crops of the farmer; Montana Statues §71-3-901. This, of course, is a statutory lien (since it arises by statute and is not created by the consent of the debtor—the farmer). Is this nonetheless an Article 9 transaction requiring compliance with the usual Article 9 rules? See §§9-102(a)(5) and 9-109(a)(2) and (d)(2).

II.   TECHNICAL VALIDITY OF THE FORMS

The creation of an Article 9 security interest typically involves two documents: the *security agreement* and the *financing statement*. The security agreement is the *contract* between the debtor and the creditor by which the debtor grants to the creditor (the *secured party*) a security interest in the collateral. See §9-102(a)(73). The financing statement is the *notice* that is filed in the place specified in §9-501 (and indexed under the debtor's name) in order to give later creditors an awareness that the collateral is encumbered. Thus, the purpose of the security agreement is to create property rights between the debtor and the creditor, and the purpose of a financing statement is to create property rights in the creditor against most of the rest of the world.

This section of the book explores the technical requirements for valid security agreements and financing statements. While not inherently interesting in and of themselves, these sections deserve your close attention. Much of the litigation involving Article 9 of the Code could have been avoided if the attorneys had done their job carefully when the documents were created. Imagine that you are a new associate at a major law firm that has just landed a multimillion-dollar account requiring Article 9 compliance. The senior partner confirms that you studied secured transactions in law school (this course) and puts you in charge of making sure that the client's interests are perfected in this big-ticket transaction. The partner tells you, unnecessarily, that the whole firm is trusting you not to make any mistakes. Now read §§9-203(a) and (b), 9-502(a), 9-509(a) and (b), and 9-521. *Record* (a new term in the 1999 revision) is defined broadly in §9-102(a)(69) with the hope that it will encompass all the possible future ways of memorializing legal arrangements.

A.   The Security Agreement

Where the collateral is in the possession of the secured party (a *pledge*), no written security agreement is required by law (though one is probably still desirable for evidentiary reasons). Where, however, the property is to leave the creditor's control, §9-203 becomes relevant and creates technical problems.

If the collateral is not in the secured party's possession or control, the §9-203 security agreement must (a) be authenticated by the debtor (*authenticate* is defined in §9-102(a)(7)) and (b) describe the collateral (plus the land if timber is involved). The security agreement need not be in any particular form or contain any particular words. Cf. §1-201(3), defining *agreement*. It needn't call itself a security agreement. See Official Comment 3 to §9-203 on the admissibility of parol evidence to establish the security nature of apparently absolute transactions.

PROBLEM 275

When Frederick Bean bought a new computer on credit from Centerboro Office Supply, before he could take it home the store made him sign a "Conditional Sale Contract," by which he agreed that title to the computer would remain with the store until he had fully paid for his purchase. The contract described the computer, but nowhere did it mention a security interest. Does the contract qualify as a security agreement under §9-203? See §1-201(37) last sentence of the first paragraph, and 2-401(1), second sentence; Sommers v. International Bus. Machs., 640 F.2d 686, 30 U.C.C. Rep. Serv. 1757 (5th Cir. 1981).

A good security agreement will, of course, spell out much more than §9-203 requires. It should identify the parties, describe the collateral, contain a grant by the debtor to the creditor of a security interest in the collateral, and specify the contractual understandings of the parties—in particular, naming what events will constitute *default* so as to permit the creditor to realize on the security interest by repossessing the collateral. Many more desirable clauses will be suggested by the materials that follow.

B. The Financing Statement

The financing statement—commonly called by its form number, "UCC-1"—is the document filed in the appropriate public office by the creditor (secured party) to *perfect* the creditor's rights in the collateral against later parties. Under the 1999 revision, the requirements for a financing statement have been significantly simplified. Per §9-502(a) it need be signed by no one (though the debtor must have *authenticated* it, which follows automatically from the signing of the security agreement; §9-509), but it must identify the parties and indicate what collateral is covered. If realty interests are involved (timber, fixtures, minerals to be extracted from the ground), §9-502(b) adds other requirements—particularly that it describe the realty and the record owner of the realty (if he or she is not the obligor) and indicate that it be filed in the real property records (so that the filing officer sees that it gets to the right place).

In addition, §9-516 lists other things that need to be in the financing statement before the filing office will accept it. Read that section. Note, however, that if the filing office does take the financing statement not containing these things, the financing statement is effective nonetheless.

The financing statement has as its function the giving of notice to later creditors as to what property of the debtor is encumbered by prior liens. Consequently, the financing statement does not typically contain many details of the underlying transaction. Such things as the amount of the loan, the time periods of repayment, etc., are not required to be described in the financing statement. If later curious parties are to discover these details, they must find them out from the original parties, not the public record. This is facilitated by the fact that the financing statement will have on it the addresses of the debtor and secured party, so that those searching the files know how to contact the original participants and discover the current state of the described encumbrance.

Security agreements and financing statements serve different purposes, but they have several problems in common: who the *debtor* is, what a sufficient *description of the collateral* is, etc. Some of these issues are resolved identically for both documents, and some are not. The most common specific problems are explored next.

C. The Debtor's Identity

When the financing statement is filed (typically in the Secretary of State's office), it will be indexed under the debtor's name. Because later possible creditors will search the records under that name, it is particularly important that it be correct.

PROBLEM 276

Harry Fellini ran a movie theater called "Fellini's Art Theater," but, since he was the sole proprietor, that was a trade name. He gave a security interest in the business's equipment to Sharkteeth Finance Company. The financing statement calls for a listing of the "debtor's name."

(a) Should the parties use the business name or individual name? Read §9-503.

(b) If the theater were run as a partnership, would the partnership's name be used as the debtor's name? See §9-503(4)(A) and its Official Comment 2.

PROBLEM 277

The debtor's correct name was "Raymond F. Sargent, Inc.," but the financing statement listed the debtor's name as "Raymond F. Sargent Co., Inc.," and it was so indexed. Is the financing statement effective? See §9-506; Darrell W. Pierce, Revised Article 9 of the Uniform Commercial Code: Filing System Improvements and Their Rationale, 31 U.C.C. L.J. 16 (1998).

PROBLEM 278

Barbara Song borrowed $50,000 from Octopus National Bank (ONB) in order to start a business called "Barb's Interiors," interior design being her specialty. ONB and Ms. Song signed a security agreement showing her as the debtor and giving ONB an interest in the inventory and equipment. ONB duly filed a financing statement. Subsequently, Ms. Song married Fred Dancer, and she changed her name to Barbara Dancer. She borrowed another $50,000 from the Nightflyer Finance Company, which loaned her the money after searching the records under "Dancer" and finding no prior encumbrances on the business's inventory and equipment. Did ONB lose its security interest because it failed to refile when her name changed? See §9-507(c) and its Official Comment 4.

PROBLEM 279

The Last National Bank filed a financing statement in the proper place to perfect its security interest in the accounts receivable of the American Electronics Store. When the latter ran into financial difficulty, its assets were sold to a new electronics concern, Voice of Japan, which moved into the same retail location. Must Last National refile to keep its security interest perfected in (1) the accounts actually transferred by American Electronics to Voice of Japan or (2) accounts thereafter acquired by Voice of Japan? See §9-507(a) and its Official Comment 3. Do we get the same result if American Electronics Store merges with Voice of Japan and the new entity is called "Voice of Electronics, Inc."? See §§9-102(a)(56), 9-203(d) and (e) and its Official Comment 7, and 9-508. What if the opposite happens, and the debtor remains the same, but Last National assigns its interest in the debtor's accounts to Octopus National Bank? Need the records be changed? Read §§9-310(c) and 9-511. Is Octopus National's interest superior to that of Last National's creditors? Consider that the transfer of the security interest from Last National to Octopus National is itself the transfer of an account or chattel paper; see Official Comment 4, Example 2 to §9-310.

PROBLEM 280

When Robin Oakapple found he could not get a loan unless he had collateral, he got permission from his foster brother, Richard Dauntless, to use Richard's yacht as collateral. Should the lender make both sign the security agreement (only Robin signed the promissory note)? Which of these parties is the "debtor" and which the "obligor"? Compare §§9-102(a)(28)(A) and 9-102(a)(59). Under whose name should the financing statement be filed?

D.   Description of the Collateral

One of the great fears of those opposed to Article 9's original adoption was that it would lead to creditor overreaching in demanding too much collateral.

PROBLEM 281

Peter Poor signed a security agreement and financing statement in favor of the Total Finance Company, giving the company a security interest in "all personal property debtor now owns or ever owns or even hopes to own between now and the end of the world or his death, whichever occurs first." Does this perfect an interest in his guitar? Compare §§9-108 and 9-504. Why would the drafters have drawn this distinction between the description in the security agreement and that in the financing statement?

PROBLEM 282

Polly Travis owned a clothing store that was doing quite well, so she decided to open branches all over the state. She borrowed money to do so from Longhorn State Bank, which took a security interest (according to the filed financing statement) in "all inventory, accounts receivable, equipment, instruments, general intangibles, and personal property." The bank also made her pledge her extensive collection of jewelry to the bank, making her bring it from her home and putting it in the vault. A year later she asked to have the jewelry back so that she could wear it to a social occasion, and the bank gave it to her. Before she could return it to the bank, another creditor seized it by judicial process. You are the lawyer for Longhorn State Bank. Is their interest in the jewelry perfected by the filed financing statement? What will be your argument? See In re Boogie Enter., Inc., 866 F.2d 1172, 7 U.C.C. Rep. Serv. 2d 1662 (9th Cir. 1989); Merchants Natl. Bank v. Halberstadt, 425 N.W.2d 429, 7 U.C.C. Rep. Serv. 2d 202 (Iowa App. 1988).

A much-discussed issue facing the drafters of the Uniform Commercial Code was the wisdom of permitting debtors to encumber not only their current property, but also property that they would acquire in the future. In the end, freedom of contract prevailed, and debtors are allowed (with one exception involving consumer goods, discussed later) to use future as well as current property as collateral for a credit extension. Where this is done, the so-called *floating lien* arises, since the creditor's lien will attach to new property without the signing of any further paperwork. Read §9-204(a).

PROBLEM 283

The security agreement and the financing statement both described the collateral as "inventory." Does this limit the security interest to existing inventory only, or does the security interest extend to replacement for the original collateral? See In re Filtercorp, Inc., 163 F.3d 570, 37 U.C.C. Rep. Serv. 2d 799 (9th Cir. 1998). If the security agreement had said "inventory now owned or after-acquired," but the financing statement had simply mentioned "inventory," does this perfect a security interest in after-acquired inventory? See Official Comment 3 to §9-108 and Official Comment 2 to §9-502; Kubota Tractor Corp. v. Citizens & S. Natl. Bank, 198 Ga. App. 830, 403 S.E.2d 218, 14 U.C.C. Rep. Serv. 2d 1247 (1991) (similar issue where collateral was "all farm equipment"). The same problem arises where the collateral is accounts receivable. See In re Shenandoah Warehouse Co., 202 B.R. 871, 32 U.C.C. Rep. Serv. 2d 573 (Bankr. W.D. Va. 1996).

Section 9-108 (read it along with its Official Comment 2) speaks to the faulty description problem in both the security agreement and the financing statement. The test adopted by the courts is the one from the Official Comment: "whether the description does the job assigned to it, i.e., make possible the identification of the thing described." Marine Midland Bank-Eastern Natl. Assn. v. Conerty Pontiac-Buick, Inc., 77 Misc. 2d 311, 352 N.Y.S.2d 953, 14 U.C.C. Rep. Serv. 814 (Sup. Ct. 1974). Or, since the later potential creditors will be doing the records searching, would a "reasonable person" be put on inquiry as to the identity of the collateral? Ray v. City Bank & Trust Co., 358 F. Supp. 630, 13 U.C.C. Rep. Serv. 355 (S.D. Ohio 1973). The UCC adopts a system of *notice filing*, so that the description in the financing statement must be sufficient to alert the searcher to the necessity for further inquiry. "The description need only inform, it need not educate." *Marine Midland Bank*, supra, at 960; see also Official Comment 2 to §9-502.

PROBLEM 284

The financing statement's description said "Various Equipment, see attached list." No list was attached. Is the statement sufficient to perfect a security interest in the debtor's equipment? See Chase Manhattan Bank v. J. & L. Gen. Contractors, Inc., 832 S.W.2d 204, 18 U.C.C. Rep. Serv. 2d 1286 (Tex. App. 1992).

PROBLEM 285

The security agreement stated that the collateral was "machinery, equipment, furniture and fixtures." To this list the financing statement added "inventory and accounts receivable." The parties are all willing to testify that the loan was intended to be secured by inventory and accounts receivable as well as by the items listed in the security agreement. Other creditors object. Does the secured party's interest reach inventory and accounts receivable? See §9-203(b) and In re Martin Grinding & Mach. Works, Inc., 793 F.2d 592, 1 U.C.C. Rep. Serv. 2d 1329 (7th Cir. 1986).

PROBLEM 286

The loan officer at Octopus National Bank has sent you, the bank's attorney, an email with the following question. The bank is planning to make a loan to Luddite Technology, Inc., and wants to take a security interest in all of the equipment of the debtor. However, Luddite's most important piece of equipment is the very expensive Abacus-12, which makes computer hardware. Should the security agreement be drafted to say that the debtor grants a security interest in "the Abacus-12 plus all other equipment," "all equipment, particularly the Abacus-12," or simply "all equipment"? Or do you have a better phraseology?

PROBLEM 287

The security agreement stated that the tractor buyer granted a security interest to "_____," but the seller forgot to fill in his name. The seller later filed a financing statement showing he had a secured interest in the buyer's tractor. Is the purported document with the blank a §9-203 security agreement? What about the financing statement? What about both? See In re Bollinger Corp., 614 F.2d 924, 28 U.C.C. Rep. Serv. 289 (3d Cir. 1980).

PRACTICAL NOTE

To meet all the above objectives, the wise creditor will:

(a) Make sure all the forms are correctly filled out in all particulars;

(b) Check the debtor's technical legal name now and in the immediate past and make sure it is correctly listed on all the documents;

(c) Refile if the debtor's name changes in any way;

(d) Describe the collateral as accurately and completely as possible in all documents;

(e) Inquire into the source of the debtor's title to ensure that the former owner's creditors have no valid claims.

III. ATTACHMENT OF THE SECURITY INTEREST

Attachment is the process by which the security interest in favor of the creditor becomes effective against the debtor. *Perfection* is the process by which the creditor's security interest becomes effective against most of the rest of the world. The steps involved in attachment are described in §9-203. They are:

(1) a security agreement must be "authenticated in a record";

(2) the creditor must give *value* (defined in §1-201(44) —after all, you shouldn't get a security interest unless you've done something to deserve it); and

(3) the debtor must have some rights in the collateral (one cannot give a security interest in property one does not own or have some legal interest in).

Read both §§9-203 and 9-204.

Thrift, Inc. v. A.D.E., Inc.

Indiana Court of Appeals, 1983
454 N.E.2d 878, 37 U.C.C. Rep. Serv. 545

ROBERTSON, J. Thrift, Incorporated (Thrift) appeals the trial
court's judgment which held that its security interests in three
automobiles had not attached. The trial court ruled the automobiles
were not inventory of a third party, Devers Auto Sales (Devers) and
found in favor of the original seller, A.D.E., Inc. (A.D.E.).

We reverse.

A.D.E. is an Indiana corporation which engages in the sale of
motor vehicles in Indianapolis. Thrift is also an Indiana corporation
and one of its activities includes the financing of motor vehicles
intended for resale. Devers was an automobile dealer in Evansville
involved in the acquisition, purchase, and resale of motor vehicles.

Devers obtained inventory financing from Thrift which perfected
its security interests in Devers's inventory by filing a financing
statement with the Secretary of State pursuant to Article 9 of the Uniform Commercial Code, Ind. Code §§26-1-9-101 et seq. The financing
statement included a security interest in Devers's after acquired
inventory. On February 18, 1981, A.D.E. entered an agreement to sell
three automobiles to Devers. In order to prevent Devers from making a
return trip to Evansville, A.D.E. gave Devers possession of the three
vehicles and Devers agreed to pay A.D.E. $20,335 on February 23, 1981.
Thrift advanced Devers $17,975 and executed a trust receipt agree-
ment which purported to give Thrift a security interest in the motor
vehicles. Devers tendered checks to A.D.E. on February 23, 1981, which
were dishonored for insufficient funds.

The parties stipulated that Devers did not receive express
permission to encumber, use, sell, or dispose of the automobiles until
the sale from A.D.E. was completed. A.D.E. retained title to the
vehicles at all times and did not give Devers any bills of sale or
odometer verification statements regarding the vehicles. Devers mixed
the automobiles with the other vehicles on its lot. There was no
evidence that the vehicles were prepared or offered for sale prior to
Devers's default on its financing agreement with Thrift on March 9,
1981. Upon default, Thrift took possession of Devers's inventory,
including the three automobiles in question. Thrift demanded the
titles of these vehicles from A.D.E., and A.D.E. demanded the return of
the vehicles. This action followed with judgment entered in favor of
A.D.E.

The trial court examined the provisions of Ind. Code §26-1-9-204 and ruled that Thrift's security interests did not attach because Devers did not obtain any rights in the collateral. The trial court found that A.D.E. had a superior interest in the automobiles because it had retained the certificates of title and that Devers was a mere possessor or bailee of the vehicles. The trial court held that the three automobiles did not constitute inventory and thus, perfection of A.D.E.'s security interests had been accomplished by noting a valid lien on the certificates of title. The trial court also found that Thrift failed to inquire about the certificates of title prior to advancing funds to Devers.

The provisions of Ind. Code §26-1-9-302 control when a financing statement is required. This section provides:

> (3) The filing provisions of this Article do not apply to a security interest in property subject to a statute . . .
> (b) of this state which provides for central filing of security interests in such property, or *in a motor vehicle which is not inventory held for sale* for which a certificate of title is required under the statutes of this state if a notation of such a security interest can be indicated by a public official on a certificate or duplicate thereof. (Emphasis added.)

This section indicates the filing provisions of Article 9 are still applicable to motor vehicles which are "inventory held for sale." National Bank and Trust Co. of South Bend v. Moody Ford, Inc., (1971) 149 Ind. App. 479, 273 N.E.2d 757.

A.D.E. does not contest this interpretation of the statute, but argues the trial court correctly concluded that the vehicles did not constitute inventory. The classification of goods is contained in Ind. Code §26-1-9-109, which provides:

> Sec. 109. Goods are—
> (1) "consumer goods" if they are used or bought for use primarily for personal, family or household purposes;
> (2) "equipment" if they are used or bought for use primarily in business (including farming or a profession) or by a debtor who is a nonprofit organization or a governmental subdivision or agency or if the goods are not included in the definition of inventory, farm products or consumer goods;
> (3) "farm products" [not applicable];
> (4) "inventory" if they are held by a person who holds them for sale or lease or to be furnished under contracts of service or if he has so furnished them, or if they are raw materials, work in process or

> materials used or consumed in a business. Inventory of a person is
> not to be classified as his equipment.

An examination of the comments regarding this section is very helpful. Comment 2 states that the classes of goods are mutually exclusive such that the goods can only be characterized as belonging in one of the four classes at the same time by the same person.

A characterization that the automobiles are consumer goods fails because Devers was engaged in the business of buying and selling motor vehicles, and the automobiles were not being used for personal, family, or household purposes. The determination which remains is whether the automobiles held by Devers constituted equipment or inventory. Comment [4] is dispositive of this question because it indicates that the principal test to determine whether goods are inventory is that they are held for immediate or ultimate sale. Although A.D.E. and Devers may have intended that Devers not encumber the vehicles for immediate sale until A.D.E. was paid, the facts clearly indicate that Devers held the automobiles for ultimate sale. Thus, the vehicles constituted inventory.

A.D.E. also argues that Thrift's security interest did not attach. Under the UCC, a party can only claim a security interest in property when the debtor has signed a security agreement, and the agreement contains a description of the collateral. The security interest does not attach to the collateral until there is an agreement that it attach, value is given, and the debtor has rights in the collateral. Cargill, Inc. v. Perlich, (1981) Ind. App., 418 N.E.2d 274. It is not contested that Thrift and Devers had an agreement describing the collateral or that value had been given, but A.D.E. does argue that Devers did not have rights in the collateral.

A.D.E. argues Devers merely had possession of the automobiles and did not have any rights in the collateral because A.D.E. retained the titles. A.D.E. supports its argument with the evidence that Devers did not have permission to sell or encumber the automobiles, nor did Devers receive bills of sale or odometer verification statements. A.D.E. directs our attention to Gicinto v. Credithrift of America, No. 3, Inc., (1976) 219 Kan. 766, 549 P.2d 870, where the opinion distinguished cash sales from credit transactions and found in favor of an automobile dealer who had retained the titles to motor vehicles after transferring the vehicles to another automobile dealer. *Gicinto* is distinguishable from the present situation because the secured party in *Gicinto* stipulated that its security interest was unperfected. Furthermore, the present case does not involve a cash sale as A.D.E. contends. Devers was not obligated to pay A.D.E. until February 23, 1981, which was five days after Devers received the automobiles. In Central National Bank of Mattoon v. Worden-Martin, Inc., (1980) 413 N.E.2d 539, the Appellate Court of Illinois faced similar facts and ruled such an arrangement constitutes a credit sale. While A.D.E. correctly notes that mere possession of goods by a debtor does not establish rights in the collateral, Cain v. Country Club Delicatessen, Inc., (1964) 25 Conn. Supp. 327, 203 A.2d 441, we believe Devers acquired an interest in the three automobiles.

The passage of title pursuant to an Article 2 transaction is contained in Ind. Code §26-1-2-401(1). This section in relevant part provides:

> Any retention or reservation by the seller of the title (property) in goods shipped or delivered to the buyer is limited to a reservation of a security interest.

Moreover, the decision of First National Bank of Elkhart County v. Smoker, (1972) 153 Ind. App. 71, 286 N.E.2d 203, is dispositive on the issue of when the debtor obtains rights in the collateral. The decision held:

> [W]hen the debtor acquires possession of the collateral under a contract, he has acquired such rights in the collateral as to allow the security of his creditor to attach to the collateral, and this is true regardless of who may be deemed to have title to and ownership of such collateral. 153 Ind. App. at 81.

In the present case, Devers acquired an interest in the collateral when it received possession of the automobiles from A.D.E. pursuant to their contract. Thus, Thrift's secured interest attached at that time. This result is in full accord with the holding of Central National Bank of Mattoon v. Worden-Martin, supra, which also found in favor of a secured party where a debtor, an automobile dealer, acquired possession of motor vehicles pursuant to a contract from another automobile dealer who retained the titles to the vehicles.

A.D.E. argues the Smoker decision is distinguishable because Smoker involved cattle and not motor vehicles where priority interests are determined by notation of liens upon the certificates of title. However, as this opinion stated previously, motor vehicles held as inventory are not subject to these provisions. National Bank and Trust Co. of South Bend v. Moody Ford, supra.

A.D.E. also argues the present case is distinguishable because A.D.E. and Devers did not intend for the titles to pass until A.D.E. received payment from Devers. In *Smoker*, the buyer and seller had an oral agreement to delay the passage of title until a specified time after delivery, which was in accordance with the custom and usage of the industry. We rejected this argument and found in favor of the secured creditor, holding that the cattle became a part of the buyer's inventory upon coming into his possession pursuant to a contract. We remain unpersuaded that the present case is distinguishable from *Smoker*.

The final argument A.D.E. presents is that Thrift, with reasonable diligence, could have protected itself by inquiring about the titles to the automobiles. While this assertion is true, it is also quite clear that A.D.E. could have taken precautions to protect its interest. A.D.E., as an automobile dealer, must certainly be aware that other dealers have financing arrangements which are secured by the dealers' inventory. A fundamental policy of Article 9 of the UCC is to discourage secret liens, Matter of Maplewood Poultry Co. (Bankr. D. Me. 1980) 2 B.R. 550. A contrary decision would undercut this fundamental policy.

The judgment is reversed.

PROBLEM 288

Roy Gabriel decided to go into the music business and borrowed $35,000 from Octopus National Bank (ONB) in order to open his shop, named Gabriel's Trumpets. On January 6 he signed a security agreement with the bank, giving ONB an interest in all "existing and after-acquired inventory in the store." That same day he received the money. On January 6 his inventory consisted of four guitars and a pitch pipe. Gabriel did have a contract with Triumphant Trumpet Manufacturing Company (TTMC) to sell him 40 trumpets, which he paid for in advance of the delivery date (March 30). On March 15 TTMC packaged the 40 trumpets and marked them "For Shipment to Gabriel's Trumpet Store." On March 30 TTMC shipped them to Gabriel, who received them that day and displayed them in the store.

(a) On what day or days did the bank's security interest *attach* (that is, become effective) to the guitars, pitch pipe, and trumpets? See §9-203(a) and read §2-501. (Why is it relevant?)

(b) Does your answer change if we add the fact that the bank filed a proper financing statement covering Gabriel's inventory on January 7? Can a financing statement be filed before the security agreement is signed? Attached? See §9-502(d). Why would a creditor wish to file a financing statement before the security interest had attached? See §9-322(a)(1).

(c) If the bank did not advance any money until March 31 (the date the bank actually saw the trumpets in the store), and if the bank did not make any commitment (see §9-102(a)(68)) to advance any money until that date, when did the security interest attach?

In re Howell Enterprises, Inc.

United States Court of Appeals, Eighth Circuit, 1991
934 F.2d 969, 14 U.C.C. Rep. Serv. 2d 1236

ROSENBAUM, J. It all started simply enough. Howell Enterprises, Inc., (Howell) and Tradax America, Inc., (Tradax) both sell rice. A customer, Bar Schwartz Limited (Bar Schwartz), wanted to buy some rice and pay for it with a commercial letter of credit. But Bar Schwartz could not buy rice from Howell because Howell would not accept the commercial letter of credit as payment. This means of payment was acceptable to Tradax, but Bar Schwartz refused to buy rice from Tradax for reasons of its own. So, Howell and Tradax came up with a plan—Tradax would sell its rice to Bar Schwartz under Howell's name. This seemingly simple solution created the complex legal problem now before the court, a problem the parties clearly did not contemplate when the transaction took place.

I. BACKGROUND

Howell is an Arkansas corporation engaged in the business of buying, selling, storing, and milling rice. On June 20, 1986, Howell borrowed $2,100,000 from the First National Bank of Stuttgart, Arkansas, (First National) and granted the bank a security interest in all accounts receivable.

Tradax is a New York corporation engaged in the business of buying and selling rice in the United States and abroad. Tradax transacted business with Howell on a regular basis in 1987. One of those transactions engendered this lawsuit.

On February 25, 1987, a contract was signed in the name of Howell, under which rice would be sold by Tradax to Bar Schwartz. Payment was to be accomplished by a one-year commercial letter of credit. Names were used interchangeably throughout the transaction: Tradax was listed as the owner on some shipping documents and on one bill of lading; Howell was listed on another bill of lading and on the certificate of origin; Tradax prepared the shipper's export declaration, but identified the shipper as Howell; Tradax paid the shipping and loading expenses and the brokerage fees, but sometimes did so under Howell's name.

Critical to this controversy, Howell listed the Bar Schwartz transaction as an account receivable on its books, with a corresponding and equivalent account payable to Tradax. Tradax documented the transaction on its books as a sale to Howell, but did not invoice Howell for a sale.

The rice was successfully, but not uneventfully, delivered to Bar Schwartz.[4] In due course, Howell sent an invoice to Bar Schwartz for the purchase price of the rice. On April 29, 1987, Bar Schwartz arranged for the letter of credit to be issued, naming Howell as beneficiary.

On June 18, 1987, Howell presented the letter of credit and the necessary supporting documents to First National. It was understood that Howell would transfer the proceeds to Tradax when the letter of credit matured, in May, 1988. But on April 4, 1988, before the maturity date, Howell filed for Chapter 11 bankruptcy. Upon the filing of the bankruptcy, First National came forward to claim its perfected security interest in Howell's accounts receivable. The Bar Schwartz letter of credit was swept into the bankruptcy.

Tradax brought this complaint before the bankruptcy court on May 9, 1988, asserting that Bar Schwartz's letter of credit was not one of Howell's accounts receivable and therefore was not subject to First National's security interest. Tradax alternatively argued that the letter of credit was subject to a constructive trust in favor of Tradax.

In an order, entered September 8, 1989, the bankruptcy court ruled that Tradax did have an equitable interest in the letter of credit and its proceeds as beneficiary of a constructive trust. The bankruptcy court then looked to the UCC as adopted in Arkansas to define First National's security interest in "all accounts receivable." Section 4-9-106 of the Arkansas Statutes defines "account" as "any right to payment for goods sold." The bankruptcy court ruled that because the letter of credit could be characterized as a "right to payment," First National had a perfected security interest in the letter of credit. The bankruptcy court, faced with two competing claims to the letter of credit, found

---

4. A short time after the rice was loaded on a barge, Tradax determined that the ship which would carry the rice overseas was delayed. Tradax arranged a swap with Sunrice, another rice trading company, whereby the original barge-load was sold in exchange for a barge-load of rice available at a later date. The second load of rice was loaded aboard the ocean-going vessel on May 26, 1987.

that First National qualified as a bona fide purchaser for value and held an interest superior to Tradax's equitable interest.

Tradax appealed to the district court, which affirmed on April 16, 1990. On appeal, Tradax argues that the district court erred in ruling that the Bar Schwartz letter of credit was an "account" or evidence of a right to payment to Howell, that First National had a security interest in the letter of credit and that First National was entitled to prevail on general equitable principles.

II. DISCUSSION

As the second reviewing court, we review the bankruptcy court's legal conclusions de novo and its factual findings under the clearly erroneous standard. Wegner v. Grunewaldt, 821 F.2d 1317, 1320 (8th Cir. 1987). The parties, in this case, do not dispute the factual findings of the bankruptcy court. This case turns, instead, on the legal characterization of the Bar Schwartz letter of credit. As such, our review is de novo.

Both parties acknowledge that First National had a perfected security interest in Howell's accounts receivable. As the parties would frame the issue, if the letter of credit is an account receivable, First National is entitled to its proceeds; if not an account receivable, the asset goes to Tradax.

The court eschews the parties' categorical inquiry. A letter of credit is an instrument of commerce, which is sui generis.[5] Its unique character is reflected in the fact that Article 5 of the UCC is devoted to letters of credit. The court is disinclined to go beyond the UCC and decide this case on unnecessarily broad grounds. Analysis reveals that the court need not answer whether a letter of credit can ever constitute an account. It is clear that this particular letter of credit was never intended to be an account and was listed as such purely by happenstance.

---

5. Letters of credit are means of guaranteeing payment for sales of goods. Here, the seller did not wish to deliver goods without assurance of payment; likewise the buyer did not want to pay prior to receiving the goods. The letter of credit resolved this difficulty by substituting a stable third party's, here a bank's, credit for that of the buyer. Upon receiving the letter of credit, the seller delivers the requested goods to a common carrier and obtains a payment-authorizing document in return. The seller presents the letter of credit and the required documentation to the issuing bank to collect payment. After honoring the letter of credit, the bank is entitled to reimbursement and a fee from the buyer. Upon reimbursement, the bank gives the bill of lading to the buyer who then can present it to the common carrier and receive the goods. See generally, 2 J. White & R. Summers, Uniform Commercial Code §19-1 (3d ed. 1988).

In this court's view, the primary and relevant inquiry is whether or not First National's undisputed security interest can reach that particular line item in Howell's accounts receivable identified as the Bar Schwartz account. With this inquiry in mind, the court turns to the specific facts of this case.

Arkansas has adopted the UCC secured transactions and letters of credit provisions. Ark. Stat. Ann. §§4-9-101 to 4-9-507; 4-5-101 to 4-5-117. Under Arkansas Statutes, §4-9-203, a security interest cannot attach unless "the debtor has rights in the collateral." The courts below found that Howell had a legal interest in the Bar Schwartz account receivable, subject to Tradax's equitable interest. This court has a less expansive view of Howell's rights.

Howell's only claim to the Bar Schwartz account receivable is by reason of its arbitrarily having elected to record the Bar Schwartz letter of credit on its receivable ledger. Tradax had no opportunity to know of or protest this infelicitous listing. More critically, Tradax had no notice that Howell's accounts receivable were encumbered by First National's security interest. The lower courts determined, as matters of fact, that the only agreement between Tradax and Howell was that Howell would allow Tradax to use its name on pertinent documents. Howell did not, and could not, claim any right in the Bar Schwartz account or the proceeds of the letter of credit, because the rice was always owned by Tradax.

Certainly Howell acquired physical possession of the letter of credit, but mere possession of such a document is insufficient to establish a right to collateral upon which to base a security interest. Rohweder v. Aberdeen Production Credit Assn., 765 F.2d 109 (8th Cir. 1985); Pontchartrain State Bank v. Poulson, 684 F.2d 704, 707 (10th Cir. 1982); Montco, Inc. v. Glatzer, 665 F.2d 36, 40 (2d Cir. 1981). Howell was involved in this transaction for the sole and limited purpose of serving as a conduit for Tradax's sale to Bar Schwartz.

This lawsuit, however, became inevitable when Howell mistakenly attempted to "book" the deal. The court finds this factual occurrence to be of no legal effect; the fact of booking this transaction as an account receivable did not make it an account receivable in law. Howell did not own and could not legitimately encumber any interest in the Bar Schwartz account, regardless of the bookkeeping procedure it chose.

Finally, the court declines to embrace the "equitable" theory referenced by the courts below. Each suggested that Tradax was a "culpable" party and was, perforce, responsible for the legal consequences here. Certainly, Tradax and Howell sought to hide the identity of the true seller from Bar Schwartz. But no legal consequences flow from this fact. Legal arrangements through undisclosed partners, agents, and proxies are not unknown in the marketplace. The court finds no reason, based solely on an undisclosed but legal arrangement, to require Tradax to pay twice, with no hope of recompense, for the same barge of rice by permitting First National to execute its security interest on the Bar Schwartz account. Moreover, while First National was an innocent third party in this transaction, First National has shown no detrimental reliance on Howell's accounting error.

III.   CONCLUSION

For the foregoing reasons we reverse the judgment of the district court and remand the case for entry of judgment in favor of Tradax.

Chapter 20

PERFECTION OF THE SECURITY INTEREST

If a security interest is *perfected,* it is senior to most later creditor interests (especially that of the trustee in bankruptcy should the debtor go bankrupt). Read §9-308 carefully. Note particularly that a security interest must first *attach* before perfection is possible (if you think about it, this is an obvious requirement: a security interest must be effective between the debtor and the creditor before it has legal meaning as to other parties).

The UCC's most common means of perfection is by having the secured party (the creditor) file a financing statement in the appropriate place. In fact, §9-310 presumes that the filing of a financing statement is the usual way of perfecting a security interest in the debtor's property. However, the Code does permit perfection in other ways too. Perfection of security interests in tangible collateral (goods, instruments, documents, and chattel paper) may be accomplished by the creditor's taking physical possession of the collateral (a common law *pledge;* see below). Further, for some types of collateral the security interest is *automatically* perfected without filing *or* possession; attachment is all that is required. Finally, perfection for some types of collateral can be accomplished by achieving "control" over the collateral. The legal steps involved in all these sorts of perfection choices are considered next.

I. PERFECTION BY POSSESSION (PLEDGE)

If the collateral is in the physical possession of the creditor, the world at large is alerted to that creditor's possible interest in the property, and no other notice is therefore required. Obviously, only collateral having physical form can be possessed. Read §9-313 and its Official Comments 2, 3, and 4. The Code drafters did not attempt to define "possession," leaving that to the common law. Professors White & Summers comment that possession "is a notoriously plastic idea"; White & Summers §22-8(b) at 771.

PROBLEM 289

Your client, Archibald Gracie, owns The White Star of England, a famous large diamond currently on display at the Astor Museum in New York. Molly Brown, a wealthy Colorado investor, has agreed to buy the diamond from Gracie, and she has made a substantial down payment, with an agreement to make three more payments before she gets possession. Gracie and Brown have signed the purchase agreement, which contains a clause granting him a security interest in his own diamond until she has made all the required payments. His question to you is this: can he perfect a security interest in the diamond by simply notifying the Astor Museum of the sale and telling the museum to hold it for his benefit until she makes payment in full, thus creating an escow arrangement in which possession is held by the escrow agent? See §9-313(c), (f), and (g).

Sometimes the collateral is so large that possession by the secured party is too awkward. In that case it may be possible to store the goods in a warehouse and get a negotiable warehouse receipt representing the goods. Such a receipt is regulated by Article 7 of the Uniform Commercial Code, where an important provision, §7-403(3), provides that the warehouseman cannot surrender the goods unless the recipient turns over any outstanding warehouse receipt (a *document of title*—the same rule applies to negotiable bills of lading, another kind of document of title). Read §9-312(c). Sometimes, as in the next Problem, it is more convenient for the warehouse to come to the goods instead of vice versa, a practice called *field warehousing*.

PROBLEM 290

Kiddie Delight, Inc., a manufacturer of toys, wanted to borrow money and use its inventory of toys as collateral. It called up Fred's Field Warehouse Company, and Fred's came to the plant, put the inventory in a locked room, and posted a sign on the door saying "Contents of Room Under Control of Fred's Field Warehouse." Fred's then issued a negotiable warehouse receipt deliverable to the order of Kiddie Delight. Fred's hired Mort Menial, the Kiddie Delight janitor, as their local warehouse custodian (Mort was paid $1.00 a week by Fred's to mind the goods; he continued to receive his normal paycheck from Kiddie Delight). Kiddie Delight pledged the warehouse receipt (a *document*) to Mammon State Bank in return for a loan. Kiddie Delight went bankrupt shortly thereafter.

(a) By having possession of this document, did the bank have a perfected security interest in the inventory? See §9-312(c) and Official Comment 3 to §9-313.

(b) If the bank and Kiddie Delight signed a written security agreement covering the warehouse receipt and the inventory it represented and if the bank gave Kiddie Delight the money, does the bank have a perfected security interest in the warehouse receipt even *before* the bank gets possession of it? See §9-312(e) (this is called *temporary perfection*).

(c) If Kiddie Delight (prior to bankruptcy) wanted to get the warehouse receipt back from the bank in order to present it to the warehouseman (Mort), get the goods, clean them, return them to the field warehouse, and get back the receipt for rehypothecation to the bank, will the bank lose its perfection if it turns the document over to the debtor? Read §9-312(f).

(d) If the bank loses its perfection, who would you advise it to sue? See §7-204(1).

PROBLEM 291

Karate, Inc. was a self-defense training school. It pledged 36 of the promissory notes given it by its customers to Nightflyer Finance Company in return for a loan. The parties signed a security agreement, and the finance company took possession of the notes. A month later Karate, Inc.'s president, Arnold Sun, asked Nightflyer to let him have back one of the notes so that he could present it to the customer for payment (an Article 3 *presentment*). The finance company gave him the note on April 6. Sun put it in his desk at the school and forgot about it. On October 12 the karate school went bankrupt. Does the bank have a perfected security interest in any or all of the promissory notes? See §9-312(g) and (h). Could the finance company have protected itself by filing a financing statement as to the promissory notes? See §9-312(a).

NOTE

The primary use of §9-312(e) and (f) occurs in letter of credit transactions (UCC Article 5), wherein the issuing bank receives a bill of lading (a *document*) covering the goods and turns it over to the buyer (*debtor*) so the buyer can get the goods from the carrier, sell them, and reimburse the bank. During the 20-day period the bank's security interest in the document remains perfected even though the document is out of its possession. Under §5-118, a section added to Article 5 by the 1999 revision of Article 9, the issuer of a letter of credit will always have a security interest in bills of lading presented under the letter of credit until the issuer is reimbursed by its customer (the *applicant*).

II. AUTOMATIC PERFECTION

Automatic perfection means that the secured party need only make sure that its security interest has *attached*, and perfection is thereby accomplished without the need for any further steps. The materials below explore the situations in which this occurs.

A. Purchase Money Security Interest in Consumer Goods

The various transactions qualifying for automatic perfection are listed in §9-309. The first of these we will study is the automatic perfection given to purchase money security interests in consumer goods; read §9-309(1). The reason for having an automatic perfection of purchase money security interests in consumer goods without requiring either filing or possession was partly historical (it had always been done that way) and partly practical. Consumer goods are unlikely to be used as collateral *twice*, so there are rarely any later creditors to protect. Filing costs money, and it is simply not worth it for merchants to file to perfect a security interest in every nickel and dime sale (note that there is no automatic perfection for motor vehicles—see §9-311(a)(2); security interests in them require definite steps for perfection, typically notation of the lien interest on the certificate of title once the vehicle leaves the dealer's inventory).

To qualify for automatic perfection under §9-309(1), the security interest in consumer goods must qualify as a *purchase money* interest, a term defined in §9-103. A purchase money security interest (PMSI) is granted to sellers or lenders whose willingness to extend credit permitted the debtor to acquire the collateral. Such creditors obviously have a superior equity in the collateral vis-à-vis other creditors, and the Code therefore frequently affords them special considerations.

PROBLEM 292

Bilko Siding, Inc. put aluminum siding on Mr. and Mrs. Brown's home. They signed a contract on August 4, giving the company a security interest in all their currently owned consumer goods plus those acquired in the future. On September 25, the Browns went to First Finance Company and borrowed $80 for the stated purpose of buying a sewing machine. They signed a security agreement with the finance company, granting it a security interest in the machine. First Finance did not file a financing statement. The Browns bought the machine on October 11. They filed for bankruptcy on October 12. Bilko, First Finance, and their trustee all claim the machine.

(a) Did Bilko's security interest attach to the sewing machine? See §9-204(b); In re Johnson, 13 U.C.C. Rep. Serv. 953 (Bankr. D. Neb.

1973) (creditor's security interest in "all consumer goods" held totally invalid because the bankruptcy judge found the after-acquired property clause overbroad, unconscionable, and unfair since it had an *in terrorem* effect on consumers). What did the bankruptcy judge in this last-cited opinion mean? And why, in the first place, would Bilko want a security interest in a used sewing machine (which, after all, has little resale value)?

(b) Was the loan agreement create a *purchase money security interest* even though First Finance was a lender and not the seller of the machine? See §9-103(a)(2).

(c) Would it have been a purchase money security interest if the Browns had used the $80 to pay a liquor bill and had used $80 from their savings account to buy the sewing machine? How can finance companies protect themselves from the debtor's misuse of the funds advanced? See §3-110(d).

(d) Assuming the $80 was used for the announced purpose, who gets the sewing machine?

Congress thought it was outrageous to allow creditors to take a non-purchase money security interest in consumer goods that the consumer would otherwise want to claim as exempt from creditor process, so §522(f) of the Bankruptcy Code permits the debtor in bankruptcy to avoid such security interests. This has led to a much-litigated issue: if a purchase money transaction has later been renegotiated and either consolidated with other debts or new money loaned, does it retain its purchase money character so as to escape avoidance under Bankruptcy Code §522(f)? The next case illustrates the problem.

In re Short

United States Bankruptcy Court, S.D. Ill., 1994
170 B.R. 128, 24 U.C.C. Rep. Serv. 2d 1020

KENNETH J. MEYERS, Bankruptcy Judge. Debtors Robert and Dawn Short seek to avoid the lien of American General Finance, Inc. ("American") as a nonpossessory, nonpurchase money security interest impairing an exemption claimed by them in household goods. See 11 U.S.C. §522(f)(2). American objects that its lien is a purchase money security interest not subject to avoidance under §522(f)(2) and that its lien retained this status even though the original note granting such interest was consolidated with another obligation of the debtors, with the goods in question serving as collateral for the entire amount. The debtors respond that this refinancing destroyed the purchase money character of American's lien and that the lien, therefore, may be avoided under §522(f)(2).

The facts are undisputed. On June 20, 1992, the debtors entered into a retail installment contract with Anderson Warehouse Furniture for the purchase of bedroom furniture. Under the contract, no interest was charged for one year and no payments were due until June 20, 1993, at which time the entire balance of $2,880.00 became due. The contract, which granted a security interest in the bedroom furniture purchased by the debtors, was assigned to American on the date it was signed. The debtors made no payments under this contract.

On July 16, 1993, the debtors executed a note with American in which they consolidated the June 20 contract obligation with another note to American for $3,642.33 dated June 22, 1992. The July 16 note in the amount of $7,337.30 provided funds to pay off the June 20 and June 22 notes, with the remaining balance applied to pay credit life and disability insurance premiums. The July 16 note, providing for an interest rate of 21.90 percent, was to be paid in monthly installments, with the final payment due in July 1997.

A disclosure statement accompanying the note described the collateral for the July 16 note as a "continued purchase money interest" in the debtors' bedroom furniture and, on a separate line, listed numerous other recreational and household items owned by the debtors. There was no indication that these latter items served as collateral for the June 22 note or that American had a purchase money security interest in them.

The debtors made one payment under the July 16 note of $248.38 and a partial payment of $146.00. On January 4, 1994, the debtors filed their Chapter 7 bankruptcy petition. The debtors then moved to avoid American's lien on household goods, including the bedroom furniture, under §522(f)(2).

DISCUSSION

Section §522(f)(2) allows a debtor to avoid the fixing of a lien on property that would otherwise be exempt if such lien is a nonpossessory, nonpurchase money security interest.[1] The Bankruptcy Code

---

1. Section 522(f)(2) provides in pertinent part:

    (f) [T]he debtor may avoid the fixing of a lien on an interest of the debtor in property to the extent that such lien impairs an exemption to which the debtor would have been entitled . . . if such lien is—
       (2) a nonpossessory, nonpurchase-money security interest in any—

does not define "purchase money security interest" or specify how a lien's purchase money status is affected by refinancing or consolidation with other debt. Reference must be had, therefore, to the state law definition of "purchase money security interest" in §9-107 of the Uniform Commercial Code. See Pristas v. Landaus of Plymouth, Inc. (In re Pristas), 742 F.2d 797, 800 (3d Cir. 1984).

That section provides:

> A security interest is a "purchase money security interest" to the extent that it is
> (a) taken or retained by the seller of the collateral to secure all or part of its price; or
> (b) taken by a person who by making advances or incurring an obligation gives value to enable the debtor to acquire rights in . . . collateral.

810 ILCS 5/9-107 (emphasis added).

Under this definition, a seller obtains a purchase money security interest by retaining a security interest in goods sold. A financing agency, such as American in the present case, obtains a purchase money security interest when it advances money to the seller and takes back an assignment of chattel paper. See Uniform Commercial Code, §9-107, cmt. 1 (1993); Raymond B. Check, The Transformation Rule under §522 of the Bankruptcy Code of 1978, 84 Mich. L. Rev. 109, 126 n.104 (1985) (hereinafter Check, Transformation Rule).

In this case, American clearly had a purchase money security interest in the debtors' bedroom furniture when it accepted an assignment of the debtors' contract on these goods. Debtors contend that this interest was canceled when their original note of June 20 was consolidated with other indebtedness and the note was paid by renewal. American argues, however, that its purchase money lien survived despite this refinancing and that it retained a nonavoidable purchase money security interest in the debtors' bedroom furniture to the extent of the balance remaining on the original note for purchase of the collateral.

There is a split of authority among the circuits concerning whether a purchase money security interest is extinguished when the original purchase money loan is refinanced through renewal or

---

(A) household furnishings . . . that are held primarily for the personal, family, or household use of the debtor. . . .

11 U.S.C. §522(f)(2).

consolidation with another obligation. One line of cases holds that a purchase money security interest is automatically "transformed" into a nonpurchase money interest when the proceeds of a renewal note are used to satisfy the original note. See Matthews v. Transamerica Financial Services (In re Matthews), 724 F.2d 798, 800 (9th Cir. 1984); Dominion Bank of Cumberlands v. Nuckolls, 780 F.2d 408, 413 (4th Cir. 1985); In re Keeton, 161 B.R. 410, 411 (Bankr. S.D. Ohio 1993); Hipps v. Landmark Financial Services of Georgia, Inc. (In re Hipps), 89 B.R. 264, 265 (Bankr. N.D. Ga. 1988); In re Faughn, 69 B.R. 18, 20-21 (Bankr. E.D. Mo. 1986). Because the collateral now secures an antecedent debt rather than a debt for purchase of the collateral or, in the case of a renewal note consolidating debt or advancing new funds, secures more than its purchase price, these courts hold that the resulting lien on the purchased goods no longer qualifies as a "purchase money security interest" under §9-107. Following such refinancing, then, the lien may be avoided in its entirety under §522(f)(2).

The second line of cases, rejecting the "all or nothing" approach of the transformation rule, holds that a lien may be partially purchase-money and partially nonpurchase-money and that the purchase-money aspect of a lien is not automatically destroyed by refinancing or consolidation with other debt. See Billings v. Avco Colorado Industrial Bank (In re Billings), 838 F.2d 405, 409 (10th Cir. 1988); Pristas, 742 F.2d at 801 (3d Cir. 1984); Geist v. Converse County Bank (In re Geist), 79 B.R. 939, 941 (D. Wyo. 1987); In re Hemingson, 84 B.R. 604 (Bankr. D. Minn. 1988); In re Parsley, 104 B.R. 72, 75 (Bankr. S.D. Ind. 1988). This view, referred to as the "dual status" rule, is premised on the language of §9-107, which provides that a lien is a purchase money security interest "to the extent" that it is taken to secure the purchase price of collateral. Accordingly, the purchase money security interest taken under the original note is preserved to the extent of the balance remaining unpaid on the original purchase money loan. See Russell v. Associates Financial Services Co. (In re Russell), 29 B.R. 270, 273-274 (Bankr. W.D. Okla. 1983).

Courts adopting the "dual status" rule note that it gives effect to the substance of the refinancing transaction.

> Though in form the original note is canceled, its balance is absorbed into the refinancing loan. To the extent of that balance, the purchase money security interest taken under the original note likewise survives, because what is owed on the original note is not eliminated[;] it is merely transferred to, and increased in amount by, another obligation. The refinancing changes the character of neither the balance due under the first loan nor the security interest taken under it.

Associates Finance v. Conn (In re Conn), 16 B.R. 454, 459 (Bankr. W.D. Ky. 1982); see *Russell*, 29 B.R. at 273.

The difficulty with the dual status rule lies in determining the extent of the purchase money interest remaining after refinancing. See *Pristas*, 742 F.2d at 801; Coomer v. Barclays American Financial, Inc. (In re Coomer), 8 B.R. 351, 353-54 (Bankr. E.D. Tenn. 1980). When a purchase money loan has been consolidated with nonpurchase money debt and payments have ensued, some method of applying payments between the purchase money and nonpurchase money portions of the refinanced loan is necessary so that the purchase money collateral secures only its own price and does not remain as collateral for the entire obligation. See Mulcahy v. Indianapolis Morris Plan (In re Mulcahy), 3 B.R. 454, 457 (Bankr. S.D. Ind. 1980). This problem has led some courts to find that purchase money status is forfeited if no method of allocation has been supplied, either by the parties' contract or by statute. See *Coomer*, 8 B.R. at 355; *Mulcahy*, 3 B.R. at 457; cf. *Pristas*, 742 at 802 (apportionment formula supplied by statute); Matter of Weigert, 145 B.R. 621, 623 (Bankr. D. Neb. 1991) (parties' agreement provided allocation formula). Other courts have adopted a judicial "first in, first out" method of allocation, under which payments are applied sequentially to purchase money debts in the order in which they were incurred. See In re Clark, 156 B.R. 693, 695 (Bankr. S.D. Fla. 1993); *Parsley*, 104 B.R. at 75; Matter of Weinbrenner, 53 B.R. 571, 579-80 (Bankr. W.D. Wis. 1985); Conn., 16 B.R. at 458; In re Gibson, 16 B.R. 257, 267-268 (Bankr. D. Kan. 1981); see generally Bernard A. Burk, Preserving the Purchase Money Status of Refinanced or Commingled Purchase Money Debt, 35 Stan. L. Rev. 1133, 1144-1146 (1983) (hereinafter Burk, Preserving Purchase Money Status).

Having considered the rationales for both the "automatic transformation" and "dual status" rules, this court finds that the dual status rule more closely adheres to the statutory language of §9-107 while effectuating the policy behind §522(f)(2). The "to the extent" language of §9-107 clearly contemplates that a lien may be partially purchase money and partially nonpurchase money, depending on the circumstances of its creation. Thus, if a lender makes two separate loans— one for the purchase of goods, the other a cash advance—and retains a security interest in the purchased goods for both loans, the resulting lien is both purchase money (for the outstanding balance of the purchase money loan) and nonpurchase money (for the amount remaining on the cash advance loan). No reason appears why the purchase money character of the first loan should disappear if the two loans are later consolidated, so long as the amounts attributable to the two loans may be separated. See Check, Transformation Rule, at 128.

Section 522(f)(2), moreover, with its distinction between purchase money and nonpurchase money liens, was designed to permit debtors to avoid liens attached to household goods already owned by them rather than liens on collateral purchased with the money advanced. See *Russell,* at 274. Congress limited this avoidance option to nonpurchase money interests in order to protect those lenders whose credit enabled the debtor to acquire the collateral in the first place. Check, Transformation Rule, at 127. When a purchase money loan is refinanced, the creditor is not committing the type of overreaching that §522(f)(2) aims to prevent, as the purchased goods remain as collateral for the loan. Thus, application of the dual status rule, with its recognition of the continued existence of the creditor's purchase money interest after refinancing, preserves the legislative balance between debtors' and creditors' rights in exempt property that is the purpose of §522(f)(2). See id.; In re Billings, 838 F.2d at 409-410.

Courts in the Seventh Circuit have not embraced either the transformation or the dual status rule but have, for the most part, taken a case by case approach which examines whether the debtor's obligation has been so changed by the refinanced loan that the resulting lien can no longer be characterized as a purchase money security interest. See In re Hatfield, 117 B.R. 387, 389-390 (Bankr. C.D. Ill. 1990) (quoting from In re Hills, No. 86-72037, slip op. at 4-5 (Bankr. C.D. Ill. July 29, 1987)); In re Gayhart, 33 B.R. 699, 700-701 (Bankr. N.D. Ill. 1983); Matter of Weinbrenner, 53 B.R. at 579-581; Johnson v. Richardson (Matter of Richardson), 47 B.R. 113, 117 (Bankr. W.D. Wis. 1985); but see In re Parsley, 104 B.R. at 75 (applying "dual status" rule). Under this approach, a refinanced loan is determined to be either a renewal of the original purchase money obligation, in which case the purchase money lien survives, or a novation, which extinguishes the purchase money character of the loan, depending upon the degree of change in terms and obligation between the two loans. See *Hatfield,* 117 B.R. at 390 ("the greater the degree of change in obligation . . . , the more likely a novation will be found").

While the "middle of the road" approach of these courts lacks the certainty of a well-defined rule such as the transformation or dual status rule, this approach is not surprising given the diversity of fact situations presented in cases examining the purchase money character of refinanced loans. In the case of a simple refinancing that merely extends the repayment period of a loan—with a reduction in the amount of monthly payments and the same interest rate and security, strict application of the automatic transformation rule works an obvious injustice to the lender who has acted to benefit the borrower. See *Gayhart,* 33 B.R. at 700-01; *Hatfield,* 117 B.R. at 390. At the other end of the spectrum, when a purchase money loan is refinanced for new consideration and the second note involves different security and terms, this change may be seen to evidence the parties' intent to enter into a new obligation that cannot be characterized as a purchase money loan. See *Hills,* slip op. at 5 (refinanced note involving fresh advance of funds constituted a novation). Thus, courts that employ a case by case approach attempt to give effect to the parties' intent as derived from the facts of a particular transaction.

The facts of this case support a finding that American retained a purchase money lien on the debtors' bedroom furniture under either the dual status rule of the Tenth and Third Circuits or the case by case approach of bankruptcy courts in this circuit. As noted above, the problem under the dual status rule is allocating payments between the purchase money and nonpurchase money aspects of a loan following consolidation in order to determine the extent to which the purchase money lien survives refinancing. The problem under the case by case approach is to determine whether the facts evidence the parties' intent to continue the purchase money character of the original loan.

In this case, the debtors had made no payments on the original purchase money loan of June 20 at the time they agreed to consolidate this obligation with another, nonpurchase money note of June 22. Since the entire purchase price of the collateral remained unpaid, it is unlikely the parties intended to extinguish the debtors' obligation under the first note or to change its character. Rather, the purchase money note of June 20, a no-interest note with one annual payment, was essentially "extended" by the consolidation note of July 16 to allow for monthly payments at a commensurately high interest rate. Thus, the July 16 note merely enabled the debtors to pay the original purchase price of the bedroom furniture over a longer period of time. Despite the change in interest rate and repayment terms, the purchase money character of the loan had not become blurred by repeated refinancings, see Slay v. Pioneer Credit Co. (In re Slay), 8 B.R. 355, 358 (Bankr. E.D. Tenn. 1980) ("at some point the number of transactions between the lender and the debtor destroys any claim that the debt is part purchase money"), and the essential character of American's interest in the purchase money collateral remained intact.

The parties' intent to continue the purchase money character of American's lien following consolidation was specifically stated in the documentation for the July 16 note, in which the security was described as a "continued purchase money interest" in the debtors' bedroom furniture. Cf. In re Billings, 838 F.2d at 109 (loan document expressly stating intent to continue the purchase money security interest showed parties did not intend to extinguish the original debt and security interest). While such a statement would not be sufficient, of itself, to preserve purchase money status upon refinancing, it adds weight to the Court's conclusion that the parties considered the new note to be a continuation of the debtors' original purchase money obligation. This statement of intent distinguishes the present case from In re Hills, in which the court found a novation based on the fact that the parties' note consolidating a purchase money obligation with nonpurchase money debt did not identify the purchased goods as collateral and stated that the creditor was "not being given a 'security interest in the goods or property being purchased.'" *Hills*, slip op. at 1. Based on the parties' express statement of intent in this case and the fact that no payments had been made on the original purchase money loan at the time of refinancing, the Court finds that the parties intended to continue the purchase money status of American's lien in the July 16 note consolidating debt.

The problem of determining the extent of American's purchase money lien following consolidation is complicated only slightly by the fact that the debtors made one monthly payment and a partial payment on the consolidated note before their bankruptcy filing. If the debtors had made no payments at all, the purchase money portion of the consolidated debt would be the amount owing on the purchase money debt at the time of the consolidation. See In re Slay, 8 B.R. at 358. The *Slay* court, noting the difficulty of apportioning payments between the purchase money and nonpurchase money parts of a consolidated loan, ruled that normally a creditor's purchase money status is forfeited upon consolidation with nonpurchase money debt. However, the court found an exception to this general rule based on the fact that the debtors in *Slay* had made no payments following consolidation. Id.

It would be ironic if the debtors' payments here of $248.38 and $146.00 on a note that included $2,880.00 in purchase money debt would cause American's lien to lose its purchase money status completely. Neither the parties' contract nor an applicable statute provides a method for allocating payments between the purchase money and nonpurchase money portions of the consolidated debt. However, courts of equity are peculiarly suited to the task of allocating payments, see In re Weinbrenner, 53 B.R. at 580 (citing Luksus v. United Pacific Insurance Co., 452 F.2d 207, 209 (7th Cir. 1971)), and have, in other contexts, supplied an allocation method when the parties failed to do so. See Burk, Preserving Purchase Money Status, at 1160, 1163 n.107 (creditor's burden to prove security interest extends only to production of facts and documents necessary to application of tracing rule). Therefore, in the absence of contractual or legislative direction, the Court will allocate the debtors' payments to determine the amount still owing on the purchase money debt—and, hence, the extent of American's purchase money lien—following consolidation. See In re Conn, 16 B.R. at 458.

Under the "first in, first out" allocation method employed by most courts, payments are deemed applied to the oldest debts first, with the result that purchase money liens are paid off in the order in which the goods are purchased. See *Parsley,* 104 B.R. at 74; *Conn,* 16 B.R. at 458. Once the purchase price of an item has been paid, any security interest remaining in it becomes a nonpurchase money security interest and is avoidable under §522(f)(2). The purchase price includes the cost of the item and any financing charges and sales taxes attributable to that item. *Parsley;* see Burk, Preserving Purchase Money Status, at 1178 (charges that would be considered part of the purchase money obligation of the original sale are accorded similar status after refinancing). In this case, there were no financing charges on the June 20 purchase money loan, as it was interest-free for the one-year term of the loan. The $2,880.00 amount of the loan presumably included sales taxes on the purchase of the bedroom furniture. Accordingly, the debtors' payments of $248.38 and $146.00 will be applied to reduce the unpaid purchase price of $2,880.00, resulting in a continued purchase money lien on the bedroom furniture of $2,485.62. The debtors' motion to avoid lien is granted to the extent of American's remaining nonpurchase money lien on this furniture.

NOTES

1. Why would Congress have enacted §522(f), which permits the debtor to avoid non-possessory, non-purchase money security interests in certain items? What policy is at work to restrict the use of such collateral in lending? Note that Bilko Siding, Inc., in the last Problem, attempted to do this. Since most used consumer goods have little resale value, why would creditors want the debtor to use them as collateral?

2. Both the Federal Trade Commission and the Federal Reserve Board have issued regulations forbidding creditors from taking non-

possessory security interests in household goods unless they are purchase money security interests. See F.T.C. Trade Regulation Rule Concerning Credit Practices, 16 C.F.R. Part 444.2(4), effective March 1, 1985; F.R.B. Reg. AA, 12 C.F.R. Part 227, effective January 1, 1986. These rules should be in your statute book under the heading "FTC Credit Practices Rule."

3. The 1999 revision of Article 9 now provides that in non-consumer goods cases, the "dual status" rule prevails and creates methods of allocating the payments so as to ascertain what portion of the purchase money debt survives. Read §9-103(e) through (g). But these rules do not obtain where the collateral is consumer goods, leaving cases like the one you have just read as arguably good law. Read §9-103(h) and its Official Comment 8. Why did the drafters not extend the statutory change to consumer goods? Surely the lenders here have typically done no evil and therefore ought not to lose their purchase money status in bankruptcy because of a technical misstep. Nonetheless, one of the major compromises made by the drafter of the 1999 Article 9 revision was to exempt consumer goods transactions from most of the Article 9 rules, leaving the resolution of these issues to other statutes or common law decisions.

PROBLEM 293

Facade Motors decided to buy an expensive Oriental rug for its main office. It selected one from the stock of Treasures of Persia, Inc., which let Facade Motors take the rug back to the office to try it out to see if it wanted to buy the rug. All of the equipment of Facade Motors was covered by a perfected floating lien in favor of Octopus National Bank. As soon as Facade gets possession of the rug (and before it makes up its corporate mind whether it wants to buy it) does the bank's lien attach? See §2-326(1) and (2). Facade Motors did decide to purchase the rug, so it signed a contract to do so with Treasures of Persia, Inc., making a down payment at the time it did so. To finance the rest of the installment payments, Facade Motors borrowed the necessary amount from Nightflyer Savings and Loan, giving it a security interest in the rug. Does Nightflyer's security interest qualify as the purchase money kind? See §9-103(a), its Official Comment 3, and the next case.

General Electric Capital Commercial Automotive Finance, Inc. v. Spartan Motors, Ltd.

New York Supreme Court, 1998
246 App. Div. 2d 41, 675 N.Y.S.2d 626, 36 U.C.C. Rep. Serv. 2d 19

FRIEDMANN, J. This appeal arises from a dispute between two automobile finance companies as to which had a superior security interest in two Mercedes Benz cars—part of the inventory of the defendant Spartan Motors, Ltd. (hereinafter Spartan), a now-defunct car dealership. The issue presented is whether by advancing Spartan the funds to purchase the vehicles after Spartan itself had already paid for and received them, the defendant General Motors Acceptance Corporation (hereinafter GMAC) thereby acquired a purchase money security interest in the merchandise that could defeat a previously-perfected security interest in all of Spartan's inventory held by the plaintiff, General Electric Capital Commercial Automotive Finance, Inc. (hereinafter GECC). We conclude that under the circumstances presented here, GMAC has established that its post-purchase advance entitled it to a purchase money security interest in the disputed collateral such that its lien enjoyed priority over GECC's prior "dragnet" lien.

FACTS

On Sept. 28, 1983, a predecessor of GECC entered into an "Inventory Security Agreement" with Spartan in connection with its "floor plan" financing of the dealership's inventory. By assignment of that agreement, GECC acquired a blanket lien (otherwise known as a "dragnet" lien) on Spartan's inventory to secure a debt in excess of $1,000,000. "Inventory" was defined in the agreement as "[a]ll inventory, of whatever kind or nature, wherever located, now owned or hereafter acquired, and all returns, repossessions, exchanges, substitutions, replacements, attachments, parts, accessories and accessions thereto and thereof, and all other goods used or intended to be used in conjunction therewith, and all proceeds thereof (whether in the form of cash, instruments, chattel paper, general intangibles, accounts or otherwise)." This security agreement was duly filed in the Office of the Dutchess County Clerk and with the New York State Secretary of State.

On July 19, 1991, Spartan signed a new Wholesale Security Agreement with GMAC, in which the latter agreed to finance or "floor-plan" Spartan's inventory. According to its terms, Spartan covenanted, inter alia, as follows:

In the course of our business, we acquire new and used cars, trucks and chassis ("Vehicles") from manufacturers or distributors. We desire you to finance the acquisition of such vehicles and *to pay the manufacturers or distributors therefor.*

We agree upon demand to pay to GMAC *the amount it advances or is obligated to advance to the manufacturer or distributor* for each vehicle with interest at the rate per annum designated by GMAC from time to time and then in force under the GMAC Wholesale Plan.

We also agree that to secure collectively the payment by us of *the amounts of all advances and obligations to advance made by GMAC to the manufacturer, distributor or other sellers,* and the interest due thereon, GMAC is hereby granted a security interest in the vehicles and the proceeds of sale thereof ("Collateral") as more fully described herein.

The collateral subject to this Wholesale Security Agreement is new vehicles held for sale or lease and used vehicles acquired from manufacturers or distributors and held for sale or lease. . . .

We understand that we may sell and lease the vehicles at retail in the ordinary course of business. We further agree that as each vehicle is sold, or leased, we will faithfully and promptly remit to you the amount you advanced or have become obligated to advance on our behalf to the manufacturer, distributor or seller (emphasis supplied).

It is not disputed that GMAC's security agreement was duly filed. In addition, by certified letter dated July 17, 1991, GMAC officially notified GECC of its competing security interest in Spartan's inventory, as follows:

This is to notify you that General Motors Acceptance Corporation holds or expects to acquire purchase money security interests in inventory collateral which will from time to time hereafter be delivered to Spartan Motors Ltd. of Poughkeepsie, New York, and in the proceeds thereof.

Such inventory collateral consists, or will consist, of the types of collateral described in a financing statement, a true copy of which is annexed hereto and made a part hereof.

On May 7, 1992, Spartan paid $121,500 of its own money to European Auto Wholesalers, Ltd. to acquire a 1992 600 SEL Mercedes Benz. Six days later, on May 13, 1992, GMAC reimbursed Spartan and the vehicle was placed on GMAC's floor plan.

On July 7, 1992, Spartan paid $120,000 of its own money to the same seller to acquire a second 1992 600 SEL Mercedes. Two days later, on July 9, 1992, GMAC reimbursed Spartan for that amount and placed the second vehicle on its floor plan. The two vehicles remained unsold in Spartan's showroom.

A few months later, on or about Oct. 2, 1992, GECC commenced this action against Spartan, seeking $1,180,999.98, representing money then due to GECC under its agreement with Spartan. Claims were also made against the principals of Spartan, upon their guarantees, as well as against GMAC and Mercedes-Benz of North America, Inc. (hereinafter MBNA), to determine lien priority in the collateral.

After commencement of the litigation, Spartan filed a bankruptcy petition and ceased doing business. GECC, GMAC, and MBNA took possession of and liquidated their respective collateral pursuant to a prior agreement between the parties. Among the assets appropriated and sold by GMAC were the two Mercedes Benz automobiles, which were auctioned for $194,500.

Since commencing this action, GECC has apparently settled its claims against all of the defendants except GMAC, which it has accused of converting the two Mercedes Benz vehicles in violation of GECC's antecedent security interest.

The court granted GECC's motion for summary judgment (and, upon reargument, adhered to its original determination), finding persuasive GECC's argument that a literal reading of GMAC's security agreement with Spartan, in conjunction with the wording of Uniform Commercial Code §9-107(b) [now §9-103(a)(2)—Ed.], required a holding that GMAC had a purchase money secured interest *only* to the extent that it paid funds *directly* to "manufacturers, distributors and sellers" of Spartan's inventory *in advance* of the transfer of the merchandise to the car dealership. The court reasoned that because "[n]owhere in the contracts of adhesion signed by Spartan with GMAC is there an obligation by GMAC to *reimburse* Spartan for funds used to purchase automobiles" (emphasis supplied), GECC's previously-perfected security interest in all of Spartan's inventory should prevail.

We now reverse and, upon searching the record, grant summary judgment to GMAC.

ANALYSIS

A perfected purchase money security interest provides an exception to the general first-in-time, first-in-right rule of conflicting security interests. Thus, a perfected purchase money security interest in inventory has priority over a conflicting prior security interest in the same inventory. . . . However, as the Supreme Court, Dutchess County observed, the purported purchase money security interest must fit within the Uniform Commercial Code definition to qualify for the exception.

Uniform Commercial Code §9-107 [now §9-103—Ed.] defines a "purchase money security interest" as a security interest:

> (a) taken or retained by the seller of the collateral to secure all or part of its price; or
>
> (b) taken by a person who by making advances or incurring an obligation gives value to enable the debtor to acquire rights in or the use of collateral if such value is in fact so used.

The issue here is therefore whether GMAC's payment as reimbursement to Spartan after it had acquired the two Mercedes Benz vehicles on two different occasions qualifies as an "advance" or "obligation" that enabled Spartan to purchase the cars, such that GMAC acquired a purchase money security interest in the vehicles. The arguments against finding a purchase money security interest under these circumstances are basically twofold: Firstly, of the few courts to construe Uniform Commercial Code §9-107(b), many have been reluctant to decide that a purchase money security interest has been created where, as here, title to and possession of the merchandise have passed to the debtor before the loan is advanced. Secondly, the literal wording of the agreement between GMAC and Spartan appears to accord GMAC purchase money secured status only when the finance company paid Spartan's "manufacturer, distributor or other seller" directly. As the supreme court noted, nothing in GMAC's contract with Spartan appears to contemplate any obligation on the part of the financier to "reimburse" the auto dealership for funds that the latter had already expended to purchase merchandise. These two interrelated arguments will be discussed seriatim.

(1) WHETHER AFTER-ADVANCED FUNDS MAY QUALIFY FOR PURCHASE MONEY SECURITY STATUS UNDER UNIFORM COMMERCIAL CODE §9-107(B)

Research indicates that there is no judicial authority in New York construing the application of UCC §9-107(b) vel non, to circumstances such as those presented here. Indeed, there has been little judicial discussion in any jurisdiction of the applicability of UCC §9-107(b) to a creditor's subsequent reimbursement of a debtor for an antecedent purchase of collateral.

Accordingly, it is appropriate to examine the legislative history of UCC §9-107(b), to arrive, if possible, at the intent of the framers.

Professor Grant Gilmore, one of the original drafters of UCC Article 9 (see, MBank Alamo Natl. Assn. v. Raytheon Co., 886 F2d 1449, 1459), has explained that UCC §9-107(b) was enacted at least in part to liberalize the rather rigid traditional rules, e.g., regarding the circumstances under which purchase money secured status could be obtained by a creditor who enables a debtor to acquire new inventory (see, Gilmore, The Purchase Money Priority, 76 Harv L Rev 1333, at 1373 [1963]).

For example, whereas under pre-Code law a person who advanced the purchase price on a buyer's behalf directly to the seller would be found to have a purchase money interest in the items so acquired, no such security interest was guaranteed to the person advancing money to a buyer who then used the funds to pay for merchandise (see, e.g., Manlove v. Maggart, 111 Ind App 398, 41 NE2d 633; Hughbanks, Inc. v. Gourley, 12 Wash 2d 44, 120 P2d 523). Under UCC §9-107(b), however, if a financier can show both that his advance was made for the purpose of enabling the debtor to acquire the collateral and that it was in fact so used, he will be accorded purchase money secured status (Gilmore, The Purchase Money Priority, supra, at 1373).

Similarly, under pre-Code law the *sequence* of the transfers was dispositive. Indeed, as Professor Gilmore noted, even 9-107(b), on its face, seems to assume "the sequence of loan first and acquisition second or . . . that the loan and acquisition take place simultaneously." Where, for example, "the buyer pays the price (or writes a check) on Monday and borrows that amount from the secured party on Tuesday," the secured party is faced with the obvious difficulty of satisfying both the "'to enable'" and the "'in fact so used'" prongs of the statute (Gilmore, at 1374). However, under the Code, "in . . . the hypothetical [case] just put a court could reasonably find that the secured party had acquired a purchase money interest. If the loan transaction appears to be *closely allied* to the purchase transaction, that should suffice. The evident intent of paragraph (b) is to free the purchase money concept from artificial limitations; rigid adherence to particular formalities and sequences should not be required" (Gilmore, at 1374, emphasis supplied; see also, 2 Gilmore, Security Interests in Personal Property, §29.2, at 782; Anderson, Uniform Commercial Code, §9-107:26, at 529; White and Summers, Uniform Commercial Code, §33-5, at 325-326 [Practitioner's 4th ed]).

If under UCC §9-107(b) neither the chronology of the financing nor the configuration of the cash flow is, without more, dispositive (see, e.g., Clark, The Law of Secured Transactions Under the Uniform Commercial Code, §3.09[2][a]), how can we tell if a loan transaction is sufficiently "closely allied" to a purchase transaction to qualify for purchase money status?

One factor that courts have considered is simple temporal proximity—that is, whether the value is given by the creditor "more or less contemporaneously with the debtor's acquisition of the property" (see, e.g., Matter of Brooks, 29 UCC Rep Serv [US Bankr Ct, D. Me]). However, it should be noted that early drafts of UCC §9-107 contained an additional paragraph (c), which envisioned a purchase money interest to the extent of value advanced for the purpose of financing new acquisitions within 10 days of the debtor's receiving possession of the new goods, *even though the value was not in fact used to pay the price.* The paragraph was deleted according to the sponsors, because it extended the purchase money interest too far (see, Gilmore, The Purchase Money Priority, supra, at 1374, n97, citing 1956 Recommendations of the Editorial Board for the Uniform Commercial Code §9-107). It appears, then, that mere closeness in time is but another mechanical circumstance to be considered—a significant clue, but not one dispositive of the relationship between the transactions.

The authorities are agreed that the critical inquiry, as in all contract matters, is into the intention of the parties (see, e.g., Township of Stambaugh v. Ah-Ne-Pee Dimensional Hardwood, 841 F Supp 803; New West Fruit Corp. v. Coastal Berry Corp., 1 Cal App 4th 92 1 Cal Rptr 2d 664, 668; see also, Anderson, Uniform Commercial Code, supra, at 529). "In determining whether a security interest exists, the intent of the parties controls, and that intent may best be determined by examining the language used and considering the conditions and circumstances confronting the parties when the contract was made" (Baldwin v. Hays Asphalt Constr., 20 Kan App 2d 853, 856, 893 P2d 275). In assessing the relationship of the transactions, the test should be whether the availability of the loan was a factor in negotiating the sale, and/or whether the lender was committed at the time of the sale to advance the amount required to pay for the items purchased (see, Matter of Hooks, 39 UCC Rep Serv 332, 341 [US Bankr Ct, M.D. Ga]; Anderson, Uniform Commercial Code, supra, at 529; Clark, The Law of Secured Transactions Under the Uniform Commercial Code, §3.09[2][a] [rev ed 1993]).

Applying these principles to the matter before us: (1) The record establishes that GMAC's reimbursements to Spartan following its two Mercedes Benz purchases were only six and two days apart, respectively. (2) GECC does not dispute GMAC's contention that a post-purchase reimbursement arrangement was common in the trade, as well as routine in Spartan's course of dealing with GMAC and its other financers, depending upon the circumstances of the purchase. For example, GMAC employee Philip Canterino, who handled GMAC's account with Spartan, has averred without contradiction by GECC that although it was customary for GMAC to pre-pay a car manufacturer before it delivered new vehicles to Spartan's showroom, in a case of the sort at issue here—where the vehicles were difficult to obtain from the manufacturer but were readily available from a distributor—it was not uncommon for GMAC to reimburse Spartan after the cars had been delivered to Spartan's showroom, upon Spartan's presentation of proof of clear title. In the language of Uniform Commercial Code §9-107(b): GMAC was committed to give value to enable the car dealership to acquire rights in the collateral. The value so extended was intended to and in fact did enable Spartan to acquire the two Mercedes Benzes, as GECC does not seriously suggest that without GMAC's backing Spartan could have afforded to purchase the expensive vehicles. Accordingly, the literal requirements of Uniform Commercial Code §9-107(b) are satisfied, notwithstanding the inverted purchase-loan chronology (see, e.g., Matter of McHenry, 3 UCC Rep Serv 2d 1545 [US Bankr Ct, N.D. Ohio]; Thet Mah & Assocs. v. First Bank of N. Dakota, 36 UCC Rep Serv 649 [Sup Ct, ND]). Because GMAC's loans were "closely allied" with Spartan's inventory acquisitions, GMAC enjoys a purchase money security interest in the contested merchandise (see, e.g., Matter of Hooks, supra).

Concededly, in making assessments of this sort, courts have considered an important factor to be whether or not title had passed to the borrower before the loan was issued (see, e.g., DeKalb Bank v. Purdy, 205 Ill App 3d 62, 562 NE2d 1223 [purchase money status clear where title to cattle did not pass until creditor advanced payment]; Matter of Hooks, supra [creditor had purchase money security interest where legal ownership in cows was not transferred to the debtor until loan closed]). This is because, where the borrower already possesses all possible rights in the collateral, the value extended by the creditor looks more like a loan procured to satisfy a pre-existing debt than an advance "enabl[ing] the debtor to acquire rights in . . . the . . . collateral" (UCC 9-107[b]). However, it seems ill-advised to create an artificial rule premised upon this circumstance, as there will be cases where a purchase money arrangement will not be established even though title has not passed, and other cases, like the one before us, where the passing of title is irrelevant to the creditor's demonstration that the value he extended was closely allied to the purchase of the collateral. In this regard, it is worthy of note that the *Hooks* court, and to some degree the *DeKalb* court as well, treated the passage of title as merely one element to consider—albeit a significant one—in applying the "closely allied" test to arrive at the parties' intentions (see, e.g., Matter of Hooks, supra, at 340-341; DeKalb Bank v. Purdy, supra, at 1226-1227).

A classic case holding the opposite, North Platte State Bank v. Production Credit Assn. (189 Neb 44, 200 NW2d 1), relied upon by GECC, is distinguishable for many reasons. There, the borrower took a loan from the plaintiff bank approximately one and one-half months after purchasing certain cattle, without informing the bank that the loan was intended for any particular purpose. The North Platte court noted that the debtor had merely borrowed money several weeks after acquiring title to and possession of a herd of cattle in order to discharge an antecedent debt. Although the "closely allied" test was not discussed by the *North Platte* court, which focussed instead on the pre-loan passage to the debtor of all rights in the collateral, the case is in fact an illustration of a failure to meet that test's requirement (see also, e.g., First Interstate Bank of Utah, N.A. v. I.R.S., 930 F2d 1521; Valley Bank v. Estate of Rainsdon, 117 Idaho 1085, 793 P2d 1257; ITT Commercial Finance Corp. v. Union Bank & Trust Co. of N. Vernon, 528 NE2d 1149 [Ind App]; Wade Credit Corp. v. Borg-Warner Acceptance Corp., 83 Or App 479, 732 P2d 76; Matter of Manuel, 33 UCC Rep Serv 691 [US Bankr Ct, D. SC]). In contrast to the matter before us, there was no pretransaction meeting of the minds between debtor and creditor; the bank was not "obligated" to give value to enable the debtor to acquire rights in the collateral; and the purchase and loan transactions were not close in time, but were nearly two months apart. Put somewhat differently, in *North Platte* the availability of the loan was not a factor in the debtor's negotiation of the sale; and the plaintiff bank was not committed at the time of the sale to advance the amount required to pay for the items purchased.

In addition, the *North Platte* court's conclusion that the plaintiff had not acquired a purchase money interest in the debtor's collateral was reinforced by the "even more fundamental" consideration that the plaintiff had neglected to file its security interest within 10 days of the debtor's receiving possession of the merchandise, as required by Uniform Commercial Code §9-312(4) (North Platte State Bank v. Production Credit Assn., 189 Neb 44, 200 NW2d 1, 6; see also, White and Summers, Uniform Commercial Code, supra, at 326). Here, in contrast, it is not disputed that GMAC timely filed its purchase money security interest in Spartan's inventory, and that in July 1991 it notified GECC of that interest.

(2) WHETHER GMAC'S LIEN IS CIRCUMSCRIBED
     BY THE PRECISE LANGUAGE OF ITS AGREEMENT
     WITH SPARTAN

It is well established that the terms of a written security agreement may be amplified by "other circumstances including course of dealing or usage of trade or course of performance" (UCC 1-201[3]; see also, UCC 1-205, 2-208; New West Fruit Corp. v. Coastal Berry Corp., supra). Here, GECC does not deny that, although the written terms of GMAC's contract with Spartan *appeared* to contemplate a single method of inventory-financing (i.e., GMAC's payment to Spartan's sellers in advance of the purchase transaction), *in fact* it was not at all unusual for the parties to pursue the same end by somewhat different means (i.e., GMAC's post-transaction reimbursement to Spartan for its inventory purchases), as GMAC employee Canterino repeatedly explained.

Generally, the express terms of an agreement and a differing course of performance, course of dealing, and/or usage of trade "shall be construed whenever reasonable as consistent with each other" (UCC 1-205[4], 2-208[2]). Only when a consistent construction would be "unreasonable" must express terms control over course of performance, and course of performance prevail over course of dealing and usage of trade. GMAC's election on some occasions to fund Spartan's floor-planning by reimbursing the car dealership for its purchases can hardly be considered inconsistent with its decision on other occasions to accomplish the same goal by following the strict wording of the contract and pre-paying the supplier directly. Rather, it is only reasonable to consider these two methods of financing to be entirely compatible with one another.

In any event, it is well established that a written contract may be *modified* by the parties' post-agreement "course of performance" (UCC 2-208[1], [3]; see, e.g., Farmers State Bank v. Farmland Foods, 225 Neb 1, 402 NW2d 277; see also, Rose v. Spa Realty Assoc., 42 NY2d 338, 343-344; Maynard Ct. Owners Corp. v. Rentoulis, 235 AD2d 867; Indemnity Ins. Co. of N. Am. v. Levine, 168 AD2d 323, 326; Recon Car Corp. of N.Y. v. Chrysler Corp., 130 AD2d 725, 729). In this regard, GECC offered no rebuttal to the testimony and affidavit of GMAC's employee who had handled the financier's account with Spartan, to the effect that it was the custom in the trade, as well as in GMAC's course of dealing with Spartan and others, for the financier to reimburse the debtor following delivery of the merchandise to the debtor's showroom, and upon presentation by the debtor of proof of clear title.

There is no merit to GECC's suggestion that, because Spartan and GMAC had diverged in practice from the literal language of their contract, GECC lacked notice of the inventory covered by GMAC's security interest. . . .

CONCLUSION

Accordingly, the supreme court erred when it found that, having financed the two vehicles at issue here by way of reimbursements—"the very opposite of an advance"—GMAC did not acquire a purchase money security interest pursuant to Uniform Commercial Code 9-107(b). Rather, since GMAC has established—and GECC does not deny—that GMAC was "obligated" to give value to enable Spartan to acquire rights in the two Mercedes Benzes, and the purchase and loan transactions were only days apart, it is clear that Spartan's purchase and GMAC's subsequent reimbursement were sufficiently "closely allied" to give GMAC a purchase money security interest in the subject vehicles. Under these circumstances, we conclude, upon searching the record, that GMAC is entitled to retain the proceeds of the sale of the two contested vehicles and to summary judgment against GECC (see, CPLR 3212[b]). . . .

B.   Certain Accounts and Other Intangibles

Read §9-309(2) and Official Comment 4. The courts have split over whether the major test is "significant part" (a percentage test) or "casual or isolated transaction" (the Official Comment test). See White & Summers §22-7. A creditor is ill-advised to rely on §9-309(2) and not file; it is simply too dangerous to take the chance that a court will find that the section applies. Grant Gilmore, one of the drafters of the original Article 9, concluded that the exemption was meant to protect assignees who don't normally take such assignments and are therefore unlikely to file. Under his test the assignee must be "both insignificant and ignorant." G. Gilmore, Security Interests in Personal Property §19.6 (1965). One court adopted his test and permitted the assignee to establish his "insignificance and ignorance" so as to have a perfected interest without filing, E. Turgeon Constr. Co. v. Elhatton Plumbing & Heating Co., 110 R.I. 303, 292 A.2d 230, 10 U.C.C. Rep. Serv. 1353 (1972).

In re Wood

United States District Court, Western District of New York, 1986
67 Bankr. 321, 2 U.C.C. Rep. Serv. 2d 1098

TELESCA, J. This appeal is from the order of the Bankruptcy Court
holding that the security interest and the accounts assigned to the
plaintiff, Edwin M. Larkin, by the debtors is unsecured due to the lack
of perfection by filing under the Uniform Commercial Code. Specifically, the decision of the court below determined that the transaction
in question did not fall within the exemptions from filing contained in
UCC §9-302(1)(e).

The facts are relatively simple. Both the plaintiff and the defendant are practicing attorneys. They have had a continuing professional and personal relationship spanning a number of years. On or
about March 15, 1977, Mr. Larkin loaned to his friend and attorney,
Robert F. Wood, the sum of $10,000.00. The debtors executed a
demand promissory note at that time including provision for the
payment of interest. No payment was made on the note by either of the
debtors for a period of five years. By letter agreement dated on or
about June 3, 1982, the debtors agreed to pay to Mr. Larkin the sum of
$1,000.00 within ten days of May 28, 1982, to be applied towards the
payment of accrued interest. Subsequent payments would also be
applied first to interest and then to reduction of the principal balance.
In the agreement, the debtors also agreed to a limited assignment of
the proceeds that might be due the debtors from two litigations in
which the debtors were engaged. The litigations provided for contingency fee agreements between Mr. Wood and his clients. The assignment of the contingency proceeds contained restrictions on the
assignee's right to disclose the existence of the assignment to any third
parties, including the clients, or to participate in the prosecution of the
underlying litigations or any settlement negotiations.

On September 9, 1983, the debtors filed voluntary petitions
pursuant to Chapter 11 of the Bankruptcy Code. In this proceeding,
the debtors seek to avoid the security interest of Larkin and the
proceeds subsequently received by the debtors from the settlement of
the litigations.

In reaching its decision, the Bankruptcy Court reviewed numerous
court decisions relating to the interpretation of U.C.C. §9-302(1)(e)
[now §9-309(2) — Ed.]. Relevant language is:

> (1) A financing statement must be filed to perfect all security
> interests except the following. . . .

(e) an assignment of accounts which does not alone or in conjunction with other assignments to the same assignee transfer a significant part of the outstanding accounts of the assignor; . . .

The official Comment 5 to the above section explains the policy as follows:

The purpose of the subsection (1)(e) exemptions is to save from ex post facto invalidation casual or isolated assignments: some accounts receivable statutes have been so broadly drafted that all assignments, whatever their character or purpose, fall within their filing provisions. Under such statutes, many assignments which no one would think of filing might have been subject to invalidation. The subsection (1)(e) exemptions go to that type of assignment. Any person who regularly takes assignments of any debtor's accounts should file. . . .

After reviewing the cases and learned articles on the subject, the Bankruptcy Court concluded that the appropriate standard to be applied in interpreting UCC §9-302(1)(e) is a combination of both the "percentage test" and "casual and isolated transaction test." Both tests need to be reviewed in conjunction with all of the facts and circumstances involved in the relationship between the parties and the transactions in which they are engaged. See, generally, 85 A.L.R.3d at 1050, 1053-1054, 1062. See also, White and Summers, Uniform Commercial Code §23-8.

No hard and fast rule interpreting UCC §9-302(1)(e) can be established in view of the unlimited variety of facts and circumstances present in private lending transactions. A standard utilizing either or both the percentage test and the casual and isolated transaction test ought to be employed. . . .

This court elects to follow the policy stated in In re B. Hollis Knight Company, 605 F.2d 397, 401 (8th Cir. 1979):

Both of the policies underlying the two tests appear to be valid limitations on the scope of UCC §9-302(1)(e). The language of the section would not permit an assignee to escape the filing requirements if he received a large portion of an assignor's accounts whether or not the transaction was an isolated one.

Nor is it unfair to require a secured party who regularly takes such assignments to file, since the comments to UCC §9-302(1)(e) indicate that the section was designed as a narrow exception to the filing requirement—not applicable if the transaction was in the general course of commercial financing.

The Bankruptcy Court correctly determined that the burden of meeting each test is on the assignee. Miller v. Wells Fargo Bank Intl. Corp., 406 F. Supp. 452 (S.D.N.Y. 1975). The court then held that Larkin failed to meet his burden in either test.

This court will not disturb the Bankruptcy Court's finding that the assignee Larkin failed to meet his burden to demonstrate the size of the assignment made by the debtor in this case in relation to the debtor's other outstanding accounts at the time of the assignment was not significant. However, in reviewing the application of the casual and isolated transaction test, the court below incorrectly held that by reason of the fact that Mr. Larkin was an attorney at law, he should be familiar with the importance of perfecting security interests by filing and that this imputed professional knowledge excluded him as one of the members of the class protected under UCC §9-302(1)(e). This was an erroneous interpretation of the casual and isolated transaction test and is not supported by any reported authority.

The casual and isolated transaction test requires the court to examine the circumstances surrounding the transaction, including the status of the assignee, to determine whether the assignment was, in fact, casual and isolated. Architectural Woods, Inc. v. State of Washington, 88 Wash. 2d 406, 562 P.2d 248 (1977). The underlying rationale behind the test is that it would not be unreasonable to require a secured creditor to file if he regularly takes assignments of a debtor's accounts, but it would be unreasonable if this was not a usual practice. However, the authorities are clear that where the assignee is regularly engaged in commercial financing and routinely accepts assignments of accounts, perfection by way of filing under the UCC is required regardless of the actual amount of the accounts assigned. In re B. Hollis Knight Co., supra.

In reviewing the reported authority, the distinguishing fact in determining whether or not the *status* of the assignee required filing for protection turned on whether or not the assignee was involved in commercial lending or regularly took assignment of accounts. The court however cited no authority for the stated proposition that attorneys who accept the security interest in an account are excluded from this exception to the filing requirement, nor has research revealed any. This court is unable to find any authority which characterizes attorneys as a group which are ineligible to engage in casual and isolated assignments of accounts under UCC §9-302(1)(e).

The record in this case clearly establishes that Larkin was not a commercial lender engaged in regularly accepting assignments from debtors. He made one loan to the debtors and subsequently obtained one assignment of the proceeds of two cases as collateral for the repayment of the loan. The record amply supports the conclusion that this was a casual and isolated transaction between two individuals who maintained a personal and professional relationship. That requires a finding that Larkin was not regularly engaged in the business of taking accounts, and therefore, he clearly falls within the exemption from filing under UCC §9-302(1)(e). It was error for the Bankruptcy Court to hold otherwise. . . .

The Bankruptcy Court's holding that plaintiff's claim was unperfected and unsecured is reversed. Plaintiff had a perfected security interest in the two accounts as of June 4, 1982. This case is remanded to the Bankruptcy Court for proceedings not inconsistent with this opinion, including reconsideration of plaintiff's motion for contempt.

So Ordered.

Now read all of §9-309, extending the same automatic perfection to the transfer of a number of types of intangible or quasi-intangible collateral.

PROBLEM 294

Octopus National Bank sold all the promissory notes it was holding in its vault to Last National Bank. Remember that the *sale* of promissory notes is an Article 9 transaction (with the seller being the "debtor" and the buyer the "secured party"—see §9-109(a)(3)). Must Last National file a financing statement or make sure it has possession in order to perfect its security interest in the notes? See §9-309(4).

The sale of debt is big business; there is a huge market for the transfer of payment obligations of all kinds. Often investors will create a trust to buy up debts from others (mortgages, promissory notes, accounts receivable, etc.), and then sell stock in this trust (the whole process is called *securitization*). Similarly credit card companies can sell the credit card account receivables to others, banks making big loans can sell off parts thereof to other bankers (called a *loan-participation* agreement), and banks extend loans to mortgage lenders, taking a security interest in the underlying mortgages (*mortgage warehousing*). The financial world is creating busy creating all sorts of new financing mechanisms and markets for the transfer of debt.

When debts are sold, they are sometimes transferred "with recourse," and sometimes "without recourse." The difference has to do with which party assumes the risk of non-collection. If the sale is "with recourse," then if the underlying obligors do not make full payment of the debts sold, the original seller must make up the deficiency. If the sale is "without recourse," then the buyer of the debt assumes both the risk that the debts won't be paid and gets any surplus if more is collected than the selling price.

It is important to appreciate this: the automatic perfection rules for the sale of some types of debt—§9-309(3) and (4)— apply only if a true *sale* is taking place. If the seller of the debt keeps any of the indicia of ownership, there is an argument that a "sale" has not taken place. In that case, automatic perfection will not work, and the so-called buyer must take the usual steps for perfection (possession, filing a financing statement) in order to prevail over other claimants to the obligations sold. If the transfer was "with recourse," it looks more like merely a loan than an outright sale, so the buyer is arguably not automatically perfected when its interest attaches. In doubtful cases, as always, the smart thing to do is to file a financing statement or take possession of the promissory notes and thus be assured of perfection. See White & Summers §22-7.

PROBLEM 295

When Nightflyer Finance Company loaned $20,000 to Portia Moot to enable her to expand her law practice, she gave the finance company a security interest in her accounts receivable (the monies her client owed her), which Nightflyer promptly perfected by filing a financing statement in the appropriate place. One of these accounts has a surety, the mother of the client, who promised Portia that she would pay the debt if the client did not. What must NFC do to perfect its interest in the surety obligation of the mother? See §§9-102(a)(77), 9-102(a)(71), 9-203(f), and 9-308(d). Note that under the cited definitions, the same rule for automatic perfection extends to letters of credit that support the original transaction.

III.   PERFECTION BY FILING

The basic supposition of §9-310 is that except for the transactions listed therein, the *filing* of a "financing statement" is the exclusive method of perfection of the creditor's security interest.

A.   The Mechanics of Filing

Under the original version of Article 9, the filing rules were quite complicated and often required dual or sometimes even triple filing of financing statements in both local and statewide offices. This made some sense in the pre-computer age, when the state offices were hard to get to and the searches were often done manually by rifling through paper records. The revision mandates central filing (typically in the office of the Secretary of State) for almost all financing statements, with local county filing only for matters having to do with realty: minerals to be extracted from the earth, timber, or fixtures; see §9-501.

PROBLEM 296

Hamlet Corporation borrowed $100,000 from the Elsinore Finance Company and gave it a security interest in the corporation's equipment. The parties properly filled out a financing statement; W. Shakespeare was mentioned on the financing statement as the president of Hamlet Corporation. Elsinore gave the financing statement and the filing fee to a clerk at the Secretary of State's office. The clerk, Ophelia Nunnery, had just announced her intention to quit to her fellow office workers and was not paying attention to her job as she indexed the financing statement under "Shakespeare" instead of "Hamlet." One year later another finance company loaned Hamlet Corporation more money, taking a security interest in the same equipment (the second finance company had checked the records and discovered nothing under "Hamlet Corp."). Since priority of creditors in this situation depends on order of filing (§9-322(a)(1)), did Elsinore "file" first, or did it bear the risk of clerical error? See §§9-516(a), 9-517 (and its Official Comment 2); In re Masters, 273 B.R. 773, 47 U.C.C. Rep. Serv. 2d 398 (Bkr. E.D. Ark. 2002); In re Butler's Tire & Battery Co., 17 U.C.C. Rep. Serv. 1363 (Bankr. D. Or. 1975), *aff'd on opinion below,* 18 U.C.C. Rep. Serv. 1302 (D. Or. 1976) (creditor not protected where creditor's error caused filing official's mistake). Whichever creditor loses should sue the state for negligence. Some states have set aside a fund from the filing fees with which to pay judgments against the filing officer.

PRACTICAL NOTE

When filing financing statements, always pay whatever extra amount is necessary to have duplicate copies of the financing statement made, stamped, and returned to you (or get an acknowledgment of the filed written record). See §9-523(a) for the procedure. That way you can prove what was filed, where it was filed, and when it was filed.

B.   Other Filings

A financing statement is effective for five years and then it lapses unless a continuation statement is filed (*public finance transaction*—defined in §9-102(a)(67) and *manufactured home transactions* — defined in §9-102(a)(53) are effective for 30 years). Read §9-515. The filing office is commanded by statute to keep records of lapsed financing statements for an additional one-year period; see §9-522. If the secured party *assigns* the security interest to another creditor, the two creditors may (it is not compulsory) file an assignment statement; read §9-514. If the debtor and secured party want to free some of the collateral from coverage under a filed financing statement, see the procedure provided for in §9-512.

PROBLEM 297

Octopus National Bank (ONB) had a security interest in the equipment of the Weekend Construction Company for which it filed a financing statement in the proper place on May 1, 2002. Antitrust National Bank took a security interest in the same collateral and filed its financing statement on May 2, 2002, in the same place.

(a) How long is a financing statement effective? See §9-515(a).

(b) If ONB files a continuation statement on May 1, 2006, is its perfected position continued? See §§9-515(d), 9-510(c). Pre-revision decisions called this the problem of "premature renewal."

(c) If ONB never files a continuation statement at all, after May 1, 2007, does it nonetheless retain its priority over ANB (who, after all, always thought of itself as junior to ONB's prior filing and would get a windfall if it suddenly prevails)? See §9-515(c).

(d) If ONB fails to file a continuation statement in time, so that its perfection lapses, but a week later it files another financing statement, is it still senior to ANB?

PROBLEM 298

When Portia Moot paid off her debt to Last National Bank, which had loaned her $3000 to buy a computer for her law office (and taken a purchase money security interest therein, for which it had duly filed a financing statement), she wanted the bank to clear up the records down at the filing office. Does she have this right? See §9-513. What can she do if they stiff-arm her? See §§9-509(d)(2), 9-625(b) and (e)(4).

One happy idea codified in the 1999 revision of Article 9 is called the *open drawer* concept of file searches. What this means is that later searchers are given absolutely everything related to the original financing statement (amendments, assignments, deletions, continuation statements, terminations statements, etc.) when they do a search, so that they have complete information as to the current status of the filed transaction. Note that the definition of *financing statement* includes an original filing and *all related amendments*; §9-102(a)(39). Section 9-519(c) requires the filing office to index the filing under the debtor's name and the file number and associate all related filings to the original filing. Thus, when a later searcher requests the financing statement per §9-523(c), the entire file will be forthcoming. Section 9-522(a) requires the filing office to maintain all filings until at least one year after the filing has lapsed with respect to all secured parties of record; §9-519(g) prohibits the removal of a debtor's name from the index until one year after complete lapse. When you put all this together you have the "open drawer" system where a "drawer" is created for each new financing statement into which all related filings are deposited. Everything stays in the searchable drawer until a year after lapse. That is not to say that everything in the drawer is legally effective. A valid termination may have been filed by all secured parties of record. But note that the effectiveness of the termination (or any other filing, for that matter) cannot be ascertained from the public record, as it needs to have been properly authorized to be effective. For a complete discussion of this and other issues related to the filing system, see Darrell W. Pierce, Revised Article 9 of the Uniform Commercial Code: Filing System Improvements and Their Rationale, 31 UCC L.J. 16 (1998).

PROBLEM 299

When attorney Sam Ambulance handled a divorce for a client, he incurred the wrath of her ex-husband, Andrew Anarchist, president of the Freeman Common Law Movement, a group that did not recognize the authority of the state or federal government. The irate ex-spouse filed 42 phony financing statements in the public records showing that all of Sam's assets were security for various non-existent loans in favor of Anarchist, the secured party of record. What can Sam do to clear up these clouds on his title to his property (which the common law would have regarded as defamation)? See §9-513, its Official Comment 3, §9-518, its Official Comment 3, and §9-625(b) and (e)(4).

IV. PERFECTION BY CONTROL

In addition to the possibility of filing a financing statement, for certain types of collateral the secured party may achieve perfection of the security interest by gaining control over the collateral. Section 9-314(a) provides that a "security interest in investment property, deposit accounts, letter-of-credit rights, or electronic chattel paper may be perfected by control of the collateral under Section 9-104, 9-105, 9-106, or 9-107." *Control* generally means that the secured party has taken the steps described in these sections so it is obvious to anyone investigating the state of the collateral that the secured party has rights therein. We will investigate perfection by control when we take up the issue of priority in Chapter 6.

Chapter 21
MULTI-STATE
TRANSACTIONS

I. GENERAL CHOICE OF LAW RULES

Section 1-105 is the Code's general choice of law provision. It permits *party autonomy,* so that those involved in the transaction may agree to be bound by the law of any state or nation bearing a "reasonable relation" to the transaction. Read §1-105. Article 9 has its own overriding conflicts provisions, chiefly §9-301, and when Article 9 dominates the problem, this section is controlling. The original Article 9 rules had very complicated choice of law provisions, but things are much simplified in the 1999 revision, which primarily adopts a *domicile* approach and looks to the law of the *debtor's location* as the state in which the steps for perfection need to be taken. See §9-301(1). However, if the collateral has physical form, the law of the jurisdiction in which the collateral is located will govern issues involving priority and other Article 9 matters; §9-301(1) and (3). So, the secured party looks to the jurisdiction in which the debtor is located as the place of perfection, but the jurisdiction of the collateral's location as to the effect of perfection.

PROBLEM 300

Mary Bush lived in a home she owned in Cheyenne, Wyoming, but she also wanted to buy a large sailboat in Cleveland, Ohio, and planned to keep the boat there after the purchase. Ohio law provides that whenever a consumer has paid more than 75 percent of a debt secured by consumer goods, the creditor's security interest automatically is stripped from the consumer goods, but Wyoming has no such rule. If a creditor loans Mary money to buy the sailboat and takes a security interest in it, where should the creditor file the financing statement? When Mary has paid 75 percent of the debt, will the creditor's security interest still be attached to the boat?

Sections 9-301 through 9-306 have some special choice of law rules for certain kinds of collateral: minerals to be extracted from the ground (§9-301(4)), agricultural liens (§9-302), goods covered by a certificate of title (§9-303, considered in detail below), deposit accounts (§9-304), investment property (§9-305), and letter of credit rights (§9-306). The provisions of these sections generally choose the law where these types of collateral are located to resolve the relevant issues.

PROBLEM 301

Peripatetic Corporation was organized under the laws of the State of Delaware but has its large retail store outlet in New Jersey. Further, the corporation was really a husband-and-wife type of business, and they did all the corporate paperwork at their home in Baltimore, Maryland (where they also kept the corporate records). Their corporate stationery used their home address. When the corporation borrows money against its accounts receivable, in what state should the financing statement be filed? See §9-307(b) and (e). If the corporation was registered in the Republic of Jahala, a Pacific island nation, where should the financing statement be filed? See §9-307(c).

Section 9-307(a) gives some guidance as to where a debtor's place of business is located, and the courts have developed a number of tests for this issue. In re Mimshell Fabrics, Ltd., 491 F.2d 21, 14 U.C.C. Rep. Serv. 227 (2d Cir. 1974) (principal place is "frequent and notorious" to "probable potential creditors"); In re Carmichael Enter., 334 F. Supp. 94, 9 U.C.C. Rep. Serv. 895 (N.D. Ga. 1971) (the "factual" principal place of business). See also this oft-quoted passage from In re McQuaide, 5 U.C.C. Rep. Serv. 802, 806-807 (Ref. Bankr., D. Vt. 1968):

> "Place of business" is defined in 48 C.J. 1213 §3 as an agency, an office; a place actually occupied, either continually or at regular periods, by a person or his clerks, or those in his employment; a place devoted by the proprietor to the carrying on of some form of trade or commerce; a place where people generally congregate for the purpose of carrying on some sort of traffic, or where people are invited or expected to come to engage in some sort of mercantile transaction; a place where a calling for the purpose of gain or profit is conducted; a place where business is carried on by persons under their control and on their own account; some particular locality, appropriated exclusively to a local business, such as a farm, store, shop, or dwelling place; that specific place within a city or town at which a person transacts business. *An occasional use or occupation of a place for business purposes is not sufficient to constitute it as a place of business.* [Emphasis in original.]

PRACTICAL NOTE

For perfectly obvious reasons, when in doubt, file everywhere.

PROBLEM 302

Factory, Factory & Money is a legal partnership that has its only place of business in Chicago, Illinois, where Octopus National Bank, which has a security interest in the accounts receivable of the firm, had filed its financing statement. If the law firm makes a permanent move to Washington, D.C., on January 1, 2013, does the bank lose its perfection, or does it have a grace period in which to refile in the new jurisdiction? Read §9-316(a). If the law firm *merges* with a law firm in D.C., with the new D.C. firm assuming all the debts of the former one, is the time period the same? See §9-316(a)(3).

PROBLEM 303

Suppose that Factory, Factory & Money, the Chicago law firm in the last Problem, had two creditors before its permanent move to D.C., both of which had a perfected security interest in the firm's accounts receivable—Octopus National Bank, which had filed its financing statement first, and Last National Bank, which had filed second, both creditors filing in Chicago early in the year 2012. When the move occurred on January 1, 2013, Last National promptly refiled in D.C. before the end of March of that year, but Octopus National was careless and didn't realize that the firm had moved until that September. If it files in D.C. in September, will it retain its priority over Last National? See §9-316(b) and its Official Comment 3. Note the definitions of *purchase* and *purchaser* in §1-201(32) and (33).

II.   CERTIFICATES OF TITLE

Grant Gilmore, one of the principal drafters of the original version of Article 9, wrote a famous treatise on its meaning, Security Interests in Personal Property (1965) [hereafter cited as G. Gilmore]. In his treatise he had this to say about automobile financing:

The automobile, in addition to its potentialities as an instrument of destruction and an agent of social change, has been one of the great sources of law in the twentieth century. As the most expensive chattel ever to come into general use, it generated novel methods of secured financing. Its unique mobility, combined with the high resale value of used cars, made theft both easy and profitable.

From a legal point of view there is nothing interesting in the situation where *A*, a thief, steals *B*'s car and sells it to *C*: *A*, if apprehended, will go to jail and *C*, if found, can be forced to return the car to *B*. However, the fact that most automobile purchases are financed under some kind of security device has led to a refined version of automobile theft which is legally much more interesting than the crude business of smash and grab. Under the refined version, *A* buys a car, making the smallest possible down payment and executing a chattel mortgage, a conditional sale contract or an Article 9 security agreement for the balance in favor of *B*. *A*, representing the car to be free from liens, now sells it to *C*, who buys it, we may assume, in good faith and without actual knowledge of *B*'s interest. *C* is typically a used car dealer, so that a further complication is introduced when *C* resells to *D*, who also buys in good faith and without notice. *A*'s behavior is criminal and legally uninteresting; if caught, he will and should go to jail. The sales to *C* and *D*, however, begin to be worth thinking about since *A*, who is a criminal, albeit a refined one, is also in some sense an owner of the car, with some kind of title to it, and our legal system has always sharply distinguished between the lot of the good faith purchaser from a thief without title (who gets nothing) and that of the good faith purchaser from a person with a defective title (who may get perfect title, despite the intervening fraud or crime).

Section 20.1, at 550-551. For the protected status of a good faith purchaser buying from someone with voidable title, read §2-403(1) (and remember that *purchaser* is broadly defined in Article 1 to include any voluntary transferee—creditors and well as buyers).

PROBLEM 304

Lyle Saylor was a trucker who lived and worked in the State of Michigan. When his old rig wore out and he decided to buy a completely new truck, he went to Pennsylvania and purchased a truck on credit from Ringer Truck City. Because the State of Indiana charged a great deal less for licenses and other registration fees, Saylor told the dealership that he lived in Indiana and that the truck would be domiciled there. He gave Ringer Truck City the address of his sister, who did live in Indiana. Indiana law requires that lien interests be noted on the certificate of title, a step that Ringer Truck City duly took when it procured the Indiana Certificate. When Saylor went bankrupt a year later, the trustee in bankruptcy argued that Ringer Truck City was unperfected since it had not gotten a *Michigan* certificate of title and had its lien interest noted thereon, as Michigan law required. Ringer Truck City argued that it was entitled to believe the debtor when he told the company that he lived in Indiana. How should this come out? See §9-303(a); In re Stanley, 249 B.R. 509, 41 U.C.C. Rep. Serv. 2d 1234 (D. Kan. 2000).

PROBLEM 305

On May 10, Holly Tourist, a resident of Dallas, Texas, bought a new car on credit while on vacation in Norman, Oklahoma, from Norman Car Sales (NCS), Inc. Oklahoma law required lien interests to be noted on the certificate of title as a condition of perfection, which NCS did on May 12. On May 14, Holly drove the car to Dallas, and that same day she re-registered the car there and received a Texas certificate. Somehow she was able to do this without surrendering the Oklahoma certificate (though Texas law apparently required her to turn in the old certificate before a new one should have been issued). Texas required lien interests to be noted on the certificate of title as a condition of perfection, but the Texas certificate showed no liens of any kind thereon. On May 26, Holly sold the car to her neighbor, William Innocent, who paid full value therefor without knowledge of NCS's interest. On May 28, learning of the sale to William, NCS arranged for the car to be repossessed from in front of his house. Assuming that her resale of the car was a "default" so as to entitle NCS to repossess, decide which of them is entitled to the car. See §9-303 and its Official Comment 6, §9-316(d) and (e) and its Official Comment 5, and §9-337 and its Official Comment. Note that §9-337 favors nonbusiness buyers; a used car lot buying an out-of-state vehicle is not entitled to the same protection. Why would the drafters have made this distinction?

PROBLEM 306

Joseph Armstrong bought a yacht in a state that did not use certificates of title for boats and that required filing for perfection in such collateral, which step the financing bank, Octopus National Bank (ONB), duly took. Armstrong then moved to a state that required all security interests on boats to be noted on certificates of title issued by that state, but he never took the trouble to get such a certificate. Does ONB's perfection in the second state last as long as its filed financing statement is still effective or for only four months? See §9-316. Suppose that the opposite situation occurs: Armstrong starts in a title state and ONB's interest is duly noted on that state's certificate. Armstrong moves to a state that has no certificates of title at all, ONB never files there, and Armstrong never re-registers the yacht. Now what result? See §9-303 and its Official Comment.

Chapter 22

PRIORITY

I. SIMPLE DISPUTES

When the debtor's financial situation collapses, the creditors all scramble to seize the debtor's assets. The legal issue of *priority* decides which creditor gets what. A basic priority provision is §9-317, which lists the parties prevailing over an *unperfected* security interest (one that has attached but that the creditor has failed to take the steps required for perfection). Read it and work through these Problems.

PROBLEM 307

Epstein's Bookstore borrowed $10,000 from Octopus National Bank (ONB), signing a security agreement giving the bank a floating lien over the store's inventory. ONB, due to negligence, never got around to filing the financing statement. Martin's Travel Service was an unpaid creditor of the bookstore that sued on the debt and recovered a judgment against the store. It then had the sheriff levy on the inventory. ONB learned of this and calls you, ONB's attorney. Does ONB or Martin's Travel Service get paid first when the inventory is sold? See §9-317(a)(2), and the definition of *lien creditor* in §9-102(a)(52). If, instead of a judgment creditor's seizing the goods, Epstein's Bookstore had filed a bankruptcy petition while ONB's lien was still unperfected, what result?

PROBLEM 308

Coke Travel Agency used its accounts receivable as collateral for a loan from the Mansfield State Bank, but the bank failed to file the financing statement that Coke Travel Agency had signed because the bank's attorney lost the statement in the maze of papers on his desk. Six months later, Coke Travel Agency needed another loan and applied for one from the Bentham National Bank, which searched the files, discovered that there were no financing statements recorded for Coke Travel Agency as debtor, and took a security interest in the agency's accounts receivable. Bentham National Bank did file a financing statement in the proper place. Which bank has the superior interest in the collateral? See §9-322(a)(2) and Official Comment 3 to §9-317.

The major Article 9 priority section is §9-322(a)(1), which you should read after you finish this paragraph. Use it to resolve the Problems that follow.

PROBLEM 309

Jay Eastriver ran a clothing store and needed money. He went to two banks, the First National Bank and the Second State Bank, and asked each to loan him money using his inventory as collateral. They each made him sign a security agreement. First National Bank filed its financing statement first, on September 25, but did not loan Eastriver any money (nor did it make any commitment to do so) until November 10. On October 2, Second State both loaned Eastriver the money and filed its financing statement. Eastriver paid neither bank. Answer these questions:

(a) Did both banks have a perfected security interest, assuming they filed in the proper place? That is, is it possible for two creditors to have perfected security interests in the same collateral?

(b) Remembering that attachment is a prerequisite to perfection, §9-308, and that attachment cannot occur until the creditor gives value, decide which bank has the superior right to the inventory. See Example 1 in Official Comment 4 to §9-322.

PROBLEM 310

When First National Bank took a perfected security interest in the inventory of Jay Eastriver's clothing store, the security agreement provided that the inventory would secure not only the current loan, "but all future advances of whatever kind." Six months later First National loaned Eastriver an additional $10,000 and had him sign a new promissory note for that amount. Do the existing filed financing statement and security agreement need to be altered in any way, or are they sufficient as is to protect the bank? See §9-204(c) and its Official Comment 5.

PROBLEM 311

Assume in the last Problem that after First National made Eastriver the first loan and filed its financing statement, he then borrowed more money from Second State Bank, using the same inventory as collateral, and this lender also filed a financing statement in the correct place. Eastriver then paid off the loan to First National completely, but the bank never filed a termination statement. A month later, First National loaned Eastriver more money. The parties signed a new security agreement, but no new financing statement was filed. First National's attorney reasoned that the earlier financing statement would protect the later loan's priority, even though this loan was not contemplated when the first financing statement was filed. Is this right? Second State would prefer that the court rule that the first financing statement was "spent" when the underlying debt was paid off, and could not be used to give a top priority to a later uncontemplated loan. See §9-323(a) and its Official Comment 3, Example 1. Often a security agreement will have in it a clause stating that the collateral protects not only this loan, but all future advances as well; see §9-204(c). If such a future advances clause had *not* been in the original security agreement that Eastriver signed with First National, does that affect the answer at all? See In re K&P Logging, Inc., 272 B.R. 867, 47 U.C.C. Rep. Serv. 2d 731 (Bankr. D. S.C. 2001).

PROBLEM 312

Phillip Philately pledged his valuable stamp collection to the Collectors National Bank (CNB) in return for a loan (he gave CNB an oral security interest in the collateral; no financing statement was signed). The bank put the stamp collection in its vault. Philately later borrowed money from his father, Filbert Philately, and gave him a signed security agreement in the same stamp collection. The father filed a financing statement in the proper place. Answer these questions:

(a) Who has priority between CNB and the father?

(b) If Phillip goes to the bank and takes the collection home so that he can add new stamps but does then return it, does the answer change? At common law the pledgee could return the collateral to the pledgor for a "temporary and limited purpose" without losing its perfection. See G. Gilmore §14.5. Has this doctrine survived the enactment of the Code? See §9-313(d). Is §9-312(f) relevant?

(c) If CNB makes Phillip sign a security agreement and then turns the collection over to him but never files a financing statement, who wins? See §9-308(c). What should CNB have done?

Section 9-204(c) broadly authorizes future advance clauses in the security agreement. Does it also give the drafters' imprimatur to the so-called *dragnet clause*, a clause purporting to expand the security interest to cover unrelated obligations owed by the debtor to the creditor? Professor Gilmore thought not and, in §35.6 of his treatise, proposed that the courts develop a test based on the intention of the parties and a requirement that the later obligation be "related," "similar," or "of the same class" as the original transaction. Under prior versions of Article 9, the courts often followed this recommendation—see the case below. Is it still good law? See Official Comment 5 to §9-204.

PROBLEM 313

Howard "Red" Poll decided to go into the cattle business and borrowed $65,000 from the Brangus National Bank to finance part of the purchase of the initial herd. Poll signed a security agreement using the cattle as collateral for this "and all other obligations now or hereafter owed to the bank." A financing statement covering this transaction was filed in the appropriate place. Two years later Poll received a charge card from the same bank and used it to finance a trip to Australia to look over cattle ranching there. When he failed to pay the credit card bill, the bank repossessed the cattle (even though his payments on the cattle purchase loan were current). Did the bank's security interest in the cattle encompass the credit card obligation? Would it make a difference if he had gone to Australia in search of the perfect wave for surfing? See In re Johnson, 31 U.C.C. Rep. Serv. 291 (Ref. Bankr., M.D. Tenn. 1981) (consumer goods held not to secure future advances of a business nature in spite of dragnet clause); Kimbell Foods, Inc. v. Republic Natl. Bank, 401 F. Supp. 316, 18 U.C.C. Rep. Serv. 507 (N.D. Tex. 1975) ("The true intention of the parties is really the sole and controlling factor in determining whether future advances were covered by the original agreement. . . . [or] would have to be reperfected."); John Miller Supply Co. v. Western State Bank, 55 Wis. 2d 385, 199 N.W.2d 161, 10 U.C.C. Rep. Serv. 1329 (1972) (adopts the Gilmore tests); Note, Future Advances Financing Under the UCC: Curbing the Abuses of the Dragnet Clause, 34 U. Pitt. L. Rev. 691 (1973).

In re Wollin

United States Bankruptcy Court, D. Oregon, 2000
249 B.R. 555, 41 U.C.C. Rep. Serv. 2d 1257

ALBERT E. RADCLIFFE, Chief Judge.

These matters come before the Court on Oregon Federal Credit Union's (OFCU's) objections to confirmation and the debtors' objections to OFCU's proofs of claim.

PROCEDURAL HISTORY:

On June 7, 1999, Steven and Cynthia Moody (Moody) filed their Chapter 13 petition. On that same day, Patricia Wollin (Wollin) also filed a Chapter 13 petition. OFCU filed a secured claim in each case. Both the Moodys and Wollin filed Chapter 13 plans proposing to modify OFCU's secured claim.

In each case, OFCU objected to confirmation and the debtors objected to OFCU's proof of claim. The two cases are factually similar, and share the same legal issues.

At a joint hearing on confirmation and the claims objections, the parties stipulated to the values of certain vehicles securing OFCU's claim. The parties also filed a "Stipulation of Facts." The Chapter 13 Trustee recommended confirmation in both cases. At the hearing's conclusion, the Court took the matters under advisement. Since then, the Court has received correspondence from the Moodys' counsel as to a stipulation reached regarding the disposition of a vehicle representing part of OFCU's collateral.

FACTS:

MOODYS:

On February 7, 1992 OFCU gave Steven Moody a $3,000.00 LoanLiner line of credit. No security, except a $5.00 pledge of credit union shares, was given. On April 26, 1996 OFCU gave the Moodys a $3,900.00 advance pursuant to a "LoanLiner Application and Credit Agreement" and an "Advance Request Voucher and Security Agreement." The loan was to consolidate debts. To secure this loan, the Moodys gave OFCU a security interest in a 1978 Ford Bronco (the Bronco). The Moody's have agreed to surrender the Bronco, and OFCU has waived any deficiency claim.

On July 30, 1996 OFCU gave the Moodys a $31,850.50 advance pursuant to another "LoanLiner Application and Credit Agreement" and "Advance Request Voucher and Security Agreement." This loan was to purchase a 1996 Ford F350 pickup truck (the Pickup). To secure this loan, the Moodys gave OFCU a security interest in the Pickup. The Pickup's replacement value is $23,630.00.

In December, 1998 OFCU issued a visa card to Steven Moody.

WOLLIN:

On April 30, 1988 OFCU gave Wollin a $2,000.00 line of credit. In May, 1988 OFCU issued a visa card to Wollin.

On July 17, 1996 OFCU gave Wollin a $9,000.00 advance pursuant to a "LoanLiner Application and Credit Agreement" and an "Advance Request Voucher and Security Agreement." The loan was to purchase a 1995 Ford Probe (the Probe).[1] To secure the loan, Wollin gave OFCU a security interest in the Probe. The Probe's replacement value is $9,341.00.

COMMON FACTS:

The vehicle loan security agreements all contained identical "dragnet" clauses, discussed below. OFCU maintains a perfected security interest in the vehicles. OFCU did not discuss any cross-collateraliza-

---

1. The July 1996 loan secured by the Probe, as well as the April and July 1996 loans to the Moodys, secured respectively by the Bronco and Pickup, will collectively be referred to as "the vehicle loans." All other loans will be referred to collectively as the "non-vehicle loans."

tion rights with the debtors at the time of any of the above loan transactions. The debtors did not read their loan documents and were unaware of the cross-collateral rights asserted by OFCU at the time of each advance.

When OFCU is asked to release collateral granted by one of its members under loan agreements, like those governing the Moodys' and Wollin's accounts, OFCU reviews whether the member is in default on other loans secured by the collateral. If there is no default, OFCU generally releases the collateral. If one or more of the other loans are in default, OFCU generally does not release the collateral.

ISSUE:

The question presented is whether the vehicles secure the "non-vehicle" loans. In addressing this question, the Court must examine the enforceability of the "dragnet" clause in each "Advance Request Voucher and Security Agreement" as it relates to debt incurred both subsequent and antecedent thereto. State law (here Oregon) controls these issues.

DISCUSSION:

The dragnet clause provides in pertinent part as follows:

> The security interest secures the advance and any extensions, renewals or refinancings of the advance. It also secures any other advances you have now or receive in the future under the LOANLINER Credit Agreement and any other amount you owe the credit union for any reason now or in the future.[2]

A. *Subsequent Loans (VISA charges in Moody):*

OFCU argues the dragnet clause should be enforced under ORS 79.2010[3] according to its plain meaning. Thus, because the Moody VISA charges are "any other amount" owed "in the future," the Bronco and Pickup secure the charges. In the alternative, OFCU argues the VISA charges are of the "same class" as the Bronco and Pickup loans, because they all were consumer debt. Thus, the VISA charges are secured by these vehicles. For the reasons set forth below, the Court rejects both of these arguments.

2. A similar clause is found in each "LoanLiner Application and Credit Agreement" as follows:

> Property given as security under this Plan or for any other loan will secure all amounts you owe the credit union now and in the future.

3. Except as otherwise provided by the Uniform Commercial Code a security agreement is effective according to its terms between the parties. . . .

The law in Oregon is well settled regarding the standard for bringing future debt into a dragnet clause.[4] As stated by the Oregon Supreme Court, "no matter how the clause is drafted, the future advance to be covered must 'be of the *same class* as the primary obligation . . . and so related to it that the consent of the debtor to its inclusion may be inferred.'" Community Bank v. Jones, 278 Or. 647, 666, 566 P.2d 470, 482 (1977) (quoting with approval, National Bank of Eastern Arkansas v. Blankenship, 177 F. Supp. 667 (E.D. Ark. 1959), *aff'd sub nom.*, National Bank of Eastern Arkansas v. General Mills, Inc., 283 F.2d 574 (8th Cir. 1960)) (emphasis added). Thus, the Oregon Supreme Court has clearly rejected the "plain meaning" argument that OFCU proffers.

Concerning debts which meet the "same class" test, at least in the business loan context, the courts have construed the Oregon standard with some variation. Compare *Community Bank,* supra (loan to satisfy overdraft on business checking account was not related to prior floor financing loan in which security was given, even though both loans were for business purposes), with Lansdowne v. Security Bank of Coos County (In re Smith & West Construction, Inc.), 28 B.R. 682 (Bankr. D. Or. 1983) (holding that loans of a business nature, all evidenced by promissory notes, were of the same class).

The Court could find no Oregon authority applying the "same class" standard in the consumer loan context. Other jurisdictions have taken a variety of approaches. Some have held that all consumer debts meet the test. E.g., In re Johnson, 9 B.R. 713 (Bankr. M.D. Tenn. 1981) (applying Tennessee law). Others have held that if the primary loan is for a purchase money transaction, then only subsequent purchase money loans meet the test. E.g., Dalton v. First National Bank of Grayson, 712 S.W.2d 954 (Ky. App. 1986) (applying Kentucky law). Finally, some courts appear to require that each consumer transaction be for the same specific use, and not be evidenced by separate debt instruments. E.g., In re Grizaffi, 23 B.R. 137 (Bankr. D. Colo. 1982) (applying Colorado law).

It appears that the Oregon Supreme Court would apply at least as strict an interpretation of the "same class" test in the consumer context

---

4. Future advances may be swept into security agreements under ORS 79.2040(3), which provides in pertinent part:

Obligations covered by a security agreement may include future advances or other value. . . .

However, as discussed below, the standards for sweeping in future advances are court imposed.

as in the business context.[5] In *Community Bank,* supra, the plaintiff bank, over a period of years, provided inventory flooring financing for defendant Jones' automobile business. Jones gave back a security interest in his inventory, with the collateral securing all "notes." Jones then began issuing overdrafts on his business checking account, which the bank honored for a time. When Jones began experiencing financial difficulties, the bank refused to pay on the overdrafts, having decided it would only pay on collected funds. It did however, give Jones a loan, evidenced by a trust receipt, which was credited directly to Jones' overdrawn checking account. The issue in the case was whether this latter loan was covered by the "notes" language in the inventory security agreement. The Oregon Supreme Court found the reference to "notes" included trust receipts. It held, however, that the "same class" test had not been met, even though both the flooring loans and the trust receipt were business related. It explained:

> The only practical effect of this transaction [the trust receipt] was to reduce a portion of the previously unsecured debt created by the overdrafts against Jones' checking account. Unlike the other monies loaned pursuant to the security agreement, the December 17 transaction gave Jones no financing with which to floor new inventory.
>
> Although this transaction appears in form to conform to the security agreement, we find its substance to be different in kind and not related to the purpose intended by the parties when they entered into the October 28 security agreement. (Parenthesis added.)

Id. at 666, 566 P.2d at 482.

This Court used similar reasoning to enforce a dragnet clause in In Re Bear Cat Logging, Inc., Case # 693-60940-aer11 (Bankr. D. Or. April 18, 1994) (unpublished) (Radcliffe, J.) finding that leases and loans met the standard where they were all for the purpose of enabling the debtor to acquire heavy logging equipment and vehicles to be used in the debtor's business. Under the Community Bank standard, loans of the same general category (i.e., all business loans or all consumer loans) do not necessarily meet the "same class" standard.

This Court also declines to adopt a per se test based on the status of the loans as purchase money transactions. The future transaction must be "so related to" the primary loan "that the consent of the debtor to its inclusion may be inferred." *Community Bank,* supra. Here,

---

5. Some courts have noted that dragnet clauses may be more strictly construed in the consumer context, because of the parties' unequal bargaining position. E.g., Bank of Kansas v. Nelson Music Company, Inc., 949 F.2d 321 (10th Cir. 1991) (applying Kansas law).

the Court cannot find the VISA charges (while presumably purchase money), sufficiently related to the Pickup loan.[6] A loan to purchase a vehicle differs both in scope and solemnity from the miscellaneous charges typical of a VISA account. The Court cannot infer the Moodys' consent to have their vehicles secure the VISA account.

B.   Antecedent Loans: (February 1992 Line of Credit in Moody);
     (April 1988 Line of Credit, and VISA charges in Wollin):

Regarding the loans which were antecedent to the vehicle loans, OFCU again argues that the plain meaning of the dragnet clauses should be applied. The debtors, on the other hand, argue that antecedent loans must be specifically referenced in the dragnet clauses to be enforceable. The Court finds no Oregon authority directly on point. Elsewhere, courts are split. A significant number (perhaps a majority) apply the "plain meaning" test urged by OFCU. E.g., Stannish v. Community Bank of Homewood-Flossmoor, 24 B.R. 761 (Bankr. N.D. Ill. 1982) (applying Illinois law); First National Bank v. First Interstate Bank, 774 P.2d 645 (Wy. 1989) (applying Wyoming law). Others apply the "same class" standard. E.g., Potomac Coal Co. v. $81,961.13 in the Hands of an Escrow Agent, 451 Pa. Super. 289, 679 A.2d 800 (1996) (applying Pennsylvania law). Still others have demanded that the dragnet clause specifically reference any antecedent debt (the "specific reference" standard). E.g., National Bank of Eastern Arkansas v. Blankenship, 177 F. Supp. 667 (E.D. Ark. 1959), aff'd sub nom., National Bank of Eastern Arkansas v. General Mills, Inc., 283 F.2d 574 (8th Cir. 1960) (applying Arkansas law); In re Hill, 210 B.R. 1016 (Bankr. E.D. Wis. 1997) (applying Wisconsin law); Lundgren v. National Bank of Alaska, 756 P.2d 270, 278 (Alaska 1987) (applying Alaska law).

As with future advances, this Court rejects the "plain meaning" test as to antecedent debt. The Oregon Supreme Court has adopted a standard stricter than "plain meaning" for future advances. This Court cannot conclude that it would lessen that standard for antecedent debt, especially in the consumer context. Instead, guided by the policy that dragnet clauses are generally disfavored and strictly construed, this Court adopts the "specific reference" standard as divining the parties' true intent and comporting with sound public policy. As the Alaska Supreme Court notes:

6. Neither can the Court find the VISA charges sufficiently related to the Bronco loan, the purpose of which was to "consolidate debt."

A key rationale underlying these holdings is that since the antecedent debt is already owed by the borrower to the lender, the parties would have had no good reason not to identify it in the subsequent security instrument if they had truly intended the deed of trust or mortgage to cover it. *Lundgren,* supra at 278.

Here, the antecedent debts are not specifically referenced, as such, the vehicles do not secure them.[7]

CONCLUSION:

Based upon the foregoing, OFCU's objections to confirmation should be overruled and the debtors' objections to OFCU's claims should be sustained, an order consistent herewith shall be entered. . . .

PROBLEM 314

Aware of difficulties with cross-collateralization clauses, rancher Howard Poll was always careful to keep his consumer obligations

---

7. One other issue was cryptically briefed and argued by the parties, that is, the enforceability of the cross-collateral clauses in the VISA agreements themselves.

In *Moody,* the VISA cross-collateralization clause provides as follows:

> You grant the Credit Union a Security interest in all existing and future funds of your accounts with the Credit Union to secure advances under the VISA Credit Card Agreement. You further acknowledge that this VISA account is cross collateralized with any Loan Liner subaccount.

Initially, it must be noted that the VISA agreement, both at the top, in the type of account applied for, and at the bottom, in the type of account approved, indicates the card was a "debit" card. Under the agreement the cross-collateral clause only applies to a "credit" card. Thus, it is arguable whether the clause even applies. Assuming it does, the clause cannot be read to identify the vehicles (generically or specifically) as collateral.

In *Wollin,* the VISA cross-collateralization clause, provides:

> To secure your account you grant us a purchase money security interest under the Uniform Commercial Code in any goods you purchase through the account....With respect to this account only, we will not assert any statutory right we may have if you are in default to prevent withdrawal of your unpledged Credit Union shares below the unpaid balance of your account. However *if you have given* us a specific pledge of your Credit Union shares or any other security interests for all your debts, your account will also be secured by your pledged shares and the property described in those other security agreements. (Emphasis added.)

The operative language, "if you have given," denotes past, not future tense. As the Probe loan was executed after the VISA agreement, the clause is ineffective to secure the VISA charges with the Probe.

(from his Visa card, using the objects purchased as collateral) with a different bank than the one that financed his ranching operations (with a traditional loan, using his cattle as collateral). Both banks had him sign security agreements that provided that the collateral nominated for each debt would also protect "any and all debts, now existing or after-acquired" owed to the same creditor. Howard was therefore distressed to learn that when the two banks merged, the new bank's loan officer now insisted that his cattle also protect the debts he owed on his Visa card. Is that right?

II. PURCHASE MONEY SECURITY INTERESTS

A. The Basic Rule

The seller who extends credit to the buyer or the lender who advances the money to enable the buyer to purchase the collateral has a special equity in it in the eyes of the law. If the parties sign a security agreement, the seller/lender gets a *purchase money security interest* (PMSI). Read §9-103. Even though the goods become subject to an existing security interest when they come into the buyer's possession, the purchase money security interest is given priority. This is true in spite of the fact that the purchase money security interest is later in time to earlier perfected interests. Where the collateral is consumer goods, no further steps are required for a purchase money security interest therein to prevail over prior or later interests. See §9-309(1). All other purchase money security interests must be perfected during a 20-day "grace period" following the buyer's possession of the goods in order to take advantage of a relation-back of priority to that date. Read §§9-317(e) and 9-324(a) carefully. Section 9-324(b) has a special rule for purchase money security interests taken in goods that are to become part of the buyer's *inventory,* and §9-324(d) has a similar one for a PMSI in *livestock,* but we'll defer consideration of those rules for a few pages.

PROBLEM 315

When Paramount Homes finished building "Utopia, Ltd.," its newest fancy apartment complex, it had to furnish the clubhouse, so it sent its construction manager, Bill Gilbert, to Sophy's Interiors, a furniture store, where he made $2,000 worth of credit purchases and signed a security agreement on behalf of Paramount Homes in favor of the seller. The agreement was signed on June 8; the goods were delivered that same day. Bill failed to mention that all his employer's equipment was designated as collateral on an existing security agreement and financing statement in favor of Sullivan National Bank. This agreement contained an "after-acquired property" clause, which stated that later similar collateral coming into the buyer's estate would automatically fall under the bank's security interest. (See §9-204(a).) The policy of Sophy's Interiors was not to file financing statements for its credit furniture sales.

(a) Why might it have such a policy? Is it wise here?

(b) On June 10, which creditor will have priority in the furniture? On June 30?

Galleon Industries, Inc. v. Lewyn Machinery Co.

Alabama Court of Civil Appeals, 1973
50 Ala. App. 334, 279 So. 2d 137,
12 U.C.C. Rep. Serv. 1224

WRIGHT, J. Galleon Industries, Incorporated, and Central Bank and Trust Company, Incorporated, were defendants below in an action in detinue. From a verdict and judgment in favor of plaintiff for the property sued for, after denial of motion for new trial, defendants each have appealed. . . .

The facts giving rise to plaintiff's suit are generally as follows: A representative of Lewyn Machinery Company, with offices in Atlanta, Georgia, came to the place of business of Galleon Industries in Pell City, Alabama, and discussed the sale by Lewyn and purchase by Galleon of certain items of equipment. A decision was made as to the items to be purchased subject to arrangement of financing. Upon investigation of Galleon's credit standing, Lewyn notified Galleon that no credit could be extended and that the items could be purchased for cash at Lewyn's office in Atlanta and delivered to Galleon there. Galleon subsequently went to Lewyn's office in Atlanta, paid cash, and accepted delivery of all items except one. This one item was a machine which Lewyn did not have on hand, but which was to be obtained by them from the manufacturer, J. M. Lancaster, located in North Carolina. Galleon was informed that when the machine was received by Lewyn he could return to Atlanta, pay cash, and accept delivery.

The price was to be $2800.00. Through mistake or misunderstanding, the machine was subsequently shipped by the manufacturer, Lancaster, directly to Galleon in Pell City. Lancaster notified Lewyn of the shipment. Lewyn then sent to Galleon an invoice on the machine stating thereon the terms of "net 30 days." Shipment by Lancaster to Galleon was shown to be June 22, 1970. Lewyn's invoice was dated the same day. Actual receipt of the machine by Galleon was apparently about July 5, 1970.

On November 21, 1969, a security agreement had been entered into by Galleon with Central Bank and Trust Company. This agreement included as collateral all equipment and inventory owned or to be thereafter acquired by Galleon. A financing statement was filed thereon on December 1, 1969. On July 13, 1970, the loan of Central being in default, Central foreclosed its security agreement and took possession of Galleon's property, including the machine which is the subject of this suit.

Appellee's testimony was that after notice of shipment by Lancaster to Galleon, Galleon was contacted by phone at least twice and a check for the machine was requested. Such check was promised but did not arrive. After several days the owner of Lewyn Machinery Company came to Pell City and learned of the taking of possession by Central. He retained counsel and brought suit in detinue against Galleon and Central.

Plaintiff, Lewyn, presented his case on the theory that title to the machine did not pass to Galleon until it had been paid for and since Galleon never paid, the title, and thus the right to possession, remained in Lewyn. We consider that the vesting of rights, as required under §9-204 of the Uniform Commercial Code, and not the passing of title (§2-401) is the question to be determined on this appeal. The provisions of §2-401 are explicitly subject to the provisions of Article 9 —therefore, the question being the effect of Central's after-acquired property clause, we will limit our discussion to whether or not sufficient rights did in fact vest in the buyer Galleon, for Central's perfected security interest to attach.

It is without dispute in the evidence that the machine was shipped by the manufacturer to the buyer, Galleon. Lewyn stated that such shipment was by mistake, and that it was orally agreed between Galleon and Lewyn that delivery was not to be made except upon payment. However, after receiving notice of the shipment, Lewyn sent to Galleon an invoice requiring payment "net in 30 days." Thus any prior agreement as to delivery and payment was modified or waived by Lewyn and

Galleon became a credit buyer. We do not decide here the application of §2-201, the Statute of Frauds, to the sales agreement. The effect of delivery, together with the invoice, was to limit any retention of rights or title to an explicit security agreement subject to the provisions of Article 9 of the Uniform Commercial Code as to perfection and priority. Harvey v. Spellman, 113 Ill. App. 2d 463, 251 N.E.2d 265; §2-401, Title 7A, Code 1940, recompiled.

Section 9-202 states "Each provision of this Article with regards to rights, obligations or remedies applies whether title to collateral is in the secured party or in the debtor." It is stated in Anderson, Uniform Commercial Code, 2d Edition, Volume 2, page 26: "If it is the desire of the parties to effect a reservation of title until the purchase price be paid, a secured transaction should be entered into and a proper filing made if required to protect the creditor's interest as against third persons."

Section 9-204 provides for a security agreement covering after-acquired property such as that held by Central. This section also provides the manner in which such security interest shall attach. In the case of the security interest of Central, it attached when the debtor, Galleon, acquired "rights" in the collateral covered by the security agreement. As we have previously stated, the delivery of the machine and the forwarding of the invoice stating "net 30 days" made Galleon a credit buyer. A credit buyer acquires "rights" in the property when possession is received from the seller. In re Ten Brock, 4 U.C.C. Rep. Serv. 712.

Lewyn, if retaining title until payment, by delivery to a credit buyer reserved only a purchase money security interest, such security interest was never perfected by filing as required by §9-302 [now §9-310(a)—Ed.]. Lewyn could have perfected its purchase money security interest and received priority over the perfected security interest of Central by filing a financing statement at the time of delivery, or within 10 days [now 20 days—Ed.] thereafter. Section 9-312(4) [now §9-324(a)—Ed.]. According to the evidence, Lewyn learned of the foreclosure and taking of possession by Central eight days after delivery to Galleon. There still remained two days for perfection of its security interest by filing a financing statement. Such filing would have given it priority over the perfected security interest of Central. Section 9-312(4).

Since sufficient "rights" had passed to Galleon by delivery and the sending of the invoice, the requirements of §9-204 were satisfied and the security interest of Central attached to the machine. The failure of

Lewyn to perfect its security interest by filing within 10 days after delivery gave Central priority. Thus at the time of the filing of the suit in detinue, Central had a superior right to possession.

Reversed and remanded.

PROBLEM 316

Video Wonder, an electronics store, had granted a floating lien over its inventory and equipment to Last National Bank, which perfected its security interest by filing a financing statement in the appropriate place. Needing a guard dog for the store, Video Wonder's manager responded to an ad in the newspaper placed by Agatha Shaw, who was selling her beloved German shepherd, Fang. She had bought him for protection when he was but a pup, but he had proven too much for her, having seriously injured a meter-reader and two mailmen. She checked out the store carefully before agreeing to sell Video Wonder the dog, saying she wanted a good home for Fang. He cost the store $1,200. The manager agreed to send her $100 a month until the dog was paid for, at which time she agreed in writing to sign over Fang's papers. Ms. Shaw and the manager agreed that the store would not get any title to Fang until all the payments had been made. Fang proved to be a fine watchdog for the store, but when Video Wonder stopped making payments to all creditors two months later, Last National Bank seized all of the store's assets, including Fang. Agatha Shaw is upset. She calls you, her attorney. Is there any hope for her? Can she argue that the bank's security interest only attached to Video Wonder's equity in the dog, or that until Video Wonder had paid the entire debt, it had no property interest to which the bank's floating lien could attach? See ITT Indus. Credit Co. v. Regan, 487 So. 2d 1047, 1 U.C.C. Rep. Serv. 2d 274 (Fla. 1986); First Natl. Bank v. Quintana, 733 P.2d 858, 3 U.C.C. Rep. Serv. 2d 773 (N.M. 1987).

PROBLEM 317

Hart Farm Equipment leased a construction backhoe to Farmer Bean for a six-month period with the understanding that Farmer Bean would be given the option to purchase the backhoe at any time during that period, and, in fact, the lease at one point called this a "sale on approval." Farmer Bean's equipment was already subject to a perfected floating lien in favor of Octopus National Bank. Three months after the delivery of the backhoe, Farmer Bean agreed to buy the backhoe, and Hart Farm Equipment filed its financing statement the next day, claiming its purchase money security interest. Who wins in the priority battle between Hart Farm Equipment and Octopus National Bank? See §2-326(2); Official Comment 3 to §9-324.

B. Inventory and Livestock

The inventory financier will have a perfected interest in existing and after-acquired inventory, in effect a floating lien over the mass of changing goods available for sale by the debtor to others. If the debtor buys new inventory and gives the seller a purchase money security interest therein, the original financier is seriously hurt if (a) it does not know of the purchase money interest but instead thinks *all* the inventory is collateral in which it has priority, and (b) the purchase money interest is held to prevail over the already perfected interest in after-acquired inventory. To protect the first creditor, §9-324(b) provides a notification procedure that the purchase money secured creditor must follow in order to take the normal priority. See White & Summers §24-5; G. Gilmore §29.3.

PROBLEM 318

The Merchants Credit Association held a perfected security interest in the inventory of Harold's Clothing Store. Harold went to a fashion showing in New York and contracted to buy $4,000 worth of new clothes for resale; the seller was to be Madame Belinda's Fashions, Inc., which took a purchase money security interest in the clothes on December 10, the date of sale. Madame Belinda herself wrote the Merchants Credit Association on December 11 and informed the credit manager of the sale. He protested but did nothing. Madame Belinda filed on December 11; the goods were delivered to the store on December 12.

(a) Who has priority?

(b) Would your answer change if Madame Belinda's notice wasn't received until December 13?

(c) If the notice was received on December 11, as above, is it sufficient to permit Madame Belinda to keep selling goods to Harold for an indefinite period thereafter or only for this one transaction? See §9-324(b)(3).

How does it help the creditor with the prior perfected interest in the inventory to get notice if that creditor still ends up junior to the purchase money creditor? The Code drafters decided that if the prior creditor has notice, it can take whatever steps are called for to protect its interest. The creditor may not care that the debtor is encumbering the inventory with purchase money security interests, believing that the inventory will sell for enough to make all the creditors happy. Or, if the creditor does care, it can call the loan (or forcefully explain to the debtor the folly of continuing to subordinate the creditor's security interest by such purchases). In any event, alerted by the §9-324(b) notice as to what is going on, the prior creditor must watch out for itself and cannot complain if the purchase money creditor prevails as to the inventory covered by the notice.

Kunkel v. Sprague National Bank

United States Court of Appeals, Eighth Circuit, 1997
128 F.3d 636, 33 U.C.C. Rep. Serv. 2d 943

JOHN R. GIBSON, Circuit Judge. In this appeal two creditors, Hoxie Feeders, Inc. and Sprague National Bank, both claim first priority security interests in the same cattle. The district court affirmed the bankruptcy court's summary judgment for Hoxie holding that Hoxie's purchase money security interest had priority over Sprague's earlier security interest in the cattle. Kunkel v. Sprague Nat'l Bank, 198 B.R. 734, 735 (D. Minn. 1996). As an alternative holding for Hoxie, the district court held that Sprague did not have a security interest in the cattle because the debtor lacked "rights in the collateral," as required by the Uniform Commercial Code. Id. at 739. On appeal, Sprague alleges that the district court erred in interpreting and applying various provisions of the UCC governing sales and secured transactions. We reverse the district court's holding that Sprague did not have a security interest in the cattle but affirm its judgment for Hoxie because Hoxie's security interest is senior to Sprague's security interest.

Beginning in 1990, Sprague made a number of loans to John and Dorothy Morken pursuant to certain loan agreements and promissory notes. The Morkens executed a security agreement in favor of Sprague covering their inventory, farm products, equipment, and accounts receivable presently owned or thereafter acquired. Sprague filed with the Kansas Secretary of State a UCC-1 financing statement regarding the collateral located in Kansas. Sprague contends that the Morkens' debt to Sprague currently exceeds $1.9 million.

Hoxie is in the business of financing and selling cattle and operating a feedlot near Hoxie, Kansas. In five transactions between February and April 1994, John Morken purchased interests in approximately 1900 head of cattle from Hoxie. Hoxie financed Morken's cattle purchases. For each transaction, Morken executed a loan agreement and promissory note in favor of Hoxie and a security agreement granting Hoxie a purchase money security interest (PMSI) in the cattle, which were identified by lot number when the documents were executed. In addition, Hoxie was paid $100 per head by either Morken or a company in which he owned an interest. The invoices for the cattle transactions recited that the cattle were shipped to Morken, Hoxie, or both.

Hoxie did not file a UCC-1 financing statement with the Kansas Secretary of State but instead perfected its security interest by taking possession of the cattle pursuant to feedlot agreements between Morken and Hoxie. The feedlot agreements stated that the cattle belonged to "the Party of the First Part," meaning Morken, and acknowledged that Morken had delivered the cattle to Hoxie, although Morken never had physical possession of the cattle. Under the feedlot agreements, the cattle were to remain on Hoxie's feedlot for purposes of care and feeding. The feedlot and loan agreements authorized Hoxie to sell the cattle in its own name for slaughter, to receive direct payment from the packing house, and to deduct the feeding and purchase expenses from the sale proceeds and then remit the balance to Morken. Hoxie's general manager acknowledged, however, that he needed Morken's authority to sell the cattle, and that Morken determined at what price the cattle would be sold. The loan agreements recited that Morken bore all risk as to the profit or loss generated by feeding and selling the cattle.

On June 10, 1994, Morken and his wife filed a Chapter 11 bankruptcy case under Title 11 of the United States Bankruptcy Code. After the bankruptcy case was commenced, Hoxie sold the cattle to Iowa Beef Processors for slaughter. After deducting amounts owed to Hoxie for the care and feeding of the cattle, approximately $550,000 in sale proceeds remained. It is these funds which are subject of competing claims by Sprague and Hoxie.

After the cattle sales, the Morkens' bankruptcy trustee commenced an adversary proceeding in the bankruptcy court to determine which party—Sprague or Hoxie—was entitled to the net sale proceeds. Hoxie and the trustee subsequently reached a settlement. Hoxie and Sprague filed cross-motions for summary judgment regarding entitlement to the funds.

The bankruptcy court granted Hoxie's motion for summary judgment and denied Sprague's motion. It held that both Sprague and Hoxie had perfected security interests in the cattle but Hoxie's interest had first priority under the Kansas UCC, Kan. Stat. Ann. §84-9-312(3) [now §9-324(b)—Ed.]. This UCC provision gives "superpriority" to a creditor with a PMSI in inventory if certain conditions are met, including the requirement that the creditor must send a specified notification to any competing secured party. The competing secured party must receive the notification within five years before the debtor receives possession of the inventory. Although Sprague [sic—Hoxie] did not send its statutory notification to Hoxie [sic—Sprague] until March 1995, long after the cattle had been sold and slaughtered and the adversary proceeding commenced, the bankruptcy court held that the timing of the notification was nevertheless sufficient because "the Debtor never obtained possession and never will."

Sprague appealed to the district court, which affirmed the bankruptcy court's summary judgment in favor of Hoxie. The district court held that a creditor that has perfected its security interest in inventory through possession, rather than by filing, is not required to provide notification of its PMSI to competing secured creditors to attain "superpriority." According to the district court, the "superpriority" provision presumes that the creditor perfected by filing and that the debtor has possession of the inventory. The court concluded that this presumption was strong evidence that the notification requirement did not apply to a PMSI creditor that perfects by possession. 198 B.R. at 737-738.

As an alternative holding, the district court ruled that Sprague did not even have a security interest in the cattle because delivery of the cattle to Morken had not been completed and, therefore, no "present sale" had occurred. The court explained:

> Under Kansas law, a delivery may be completed although the goods remain in the possession of the seller if the seller's possession "is as an agent or at the request of the buyer under an agreement to store or care for the property, *and nothing further remains to be done by either party to complete the sale.*" Lakeview Gardens, Inc. v. Kansas, 221 Kan. 211, 557 P.2d 1286, 1290-91 (1976) (emphasis added). Here, something further was required, payment to Hoxie under the loan agreement.

Id. at 739. Because the transactions were not a "present sale," the court reasoned that Morken did not have "rights in the collateral," as required by the Kansas UCC, Kan. Stat. Ann. §84-9-203(1)(c), to convey a security interest in the cattle to Sprague. Morken's interest in the cattle was only a "remedial" interest against Hoxie; such an interest was inadequate to support Morken's alleged grant of a security interest to Sprague. Id. at 739-740.

I.

. . . The issues on appeal are: (a) did Sprague have a perfected security interest in the cattle?; (b) did Hoxie have a "superpriority" purchase money security interest which had priority over Sprague's interest in the cattle?; and (c) was Hoxie entitled to the proceeds from the sale of the cattle to IBP?

II.

The district court held that Sprague did not have a security interest in the cattle because Morken did not have "rights in the collateral" sufficient for a security interest to attach. We reverse on this issue.

Under the UCC, a security interest is not enforceable against the debtor or third parties, and does not attach, unless and until the following three requirements are met: (a) either the secured party has possession of the collateral by agreement with the debtor (as is the case here) or the debtor has signed a security agreement; (b) value has been given; and (c) "the debtor has rights in the collateral." Kan. Stat. Ann. §84-9-203(1). Only the last requirement is at issue in this case.

The phrase "rights in the collateral" is not defined in the UCC. "If the debtor owns the collateral outright, it is obvious that the security interest may attach. . . ." B. Clark, The Law of Secured Transactions Under the Uniform Commercial Code ¶2.04[1], at 2-43 (Rev. ed. 1993). It is also well settled, however, that "rights in the collateral" may be an interest less than outright ownership, but must be more than the mere right of possession. See id.; see also 4 J. White & R. Summers, Uniform Commercial Code 126 (4th ed. 1995) ("It follows that almost any 'rights in the collateral' will suffice under 9-203."). The concept of "title" is not determinative. See Kan. Stat. Ann. §84-9-202. "An agreement to purchase can give rise to sufficient rights in the debtor to allow a security interest to attach, regardless of whether the debtor has technically obtained title to the property." United States v. Ables, 739 F. Supp. 1439, 1444 (D. Kan. 1990). Courts consider factors such as the extent of the debtor's control over the property and whether the debtor bears the risk of ownership. See, e.g., Kinetics Tech. Int'l Corp. v. Fourth Nat'l Bank, 705 F.2d 396, 399 (10th Cir. 1983) (debtor's control); Chambersburg Trust Co. v. Eichelberger, 588 A.2d 549, 552-

553 (Pa. Super. Ct. 1991) (debtor had risk of ownership). The debtor need not have possession in order to pledge the property; the UCC expressly contemplates that the secured party may retain possession of the collateral. See Kan. Stat. Ann. §84-9-305 [now §9-313—Ed.].

The district court looked to Article 2 of the UCC, which governs sales, to determine whether Morken had "rights in the collateral." It was appropriate to consider Article 2 principles. "In many cases the secured creditor may turn to Article 2 of the UCC to measure the debtor's 'rights' with respect to collateral." Kan. Stat. Ann. §84-9-203 Kan. cmt. (1996). The district court erred, however, in its interpretation of Article 2 and its conclusion that the cattle transactions did not bestow Morken with "rights in the collateral." As will be seen, the cattle were sold and delivered by Hoxie to Morken and Morken thus acquired "rights in the collateral."

A "sale" is the passing of title from buyer to seller for a price. Kan. Stat. Ann. §84-2-106(1). Where delivery of the goods is made without moving the goods, title passes from buyer to seller at the time parties contracted if the goods are identified at that time. Id. §84-2-401(3)(b). When identification occurs, the buyer acquires a "special property" and, importantly, any title interest retained by the seller is limited to the reservation of a security interest. Id. §84-2-401(1). Physical receipt of the goods by the debtor is not necessary; rather, a sale may take place if the goods are constructively delivered to the buyer through delivery to the buyer's agent or bailee. "Delivery is not required for a 'sale' to take place, and the buyer does not even need any right to possession of the goods in question." B. Clark, The Law of Secured Transactions ¶3.04[2], at 3-48.

In this case, the cattle were identified in the invoices and other transaction documents, and the parties agreed that delivery would be made to Morken by delivering the cattle to Hoxie at its feedlot. The feedlot agreements recited that the cattle belonged to Morken. Morken solely bore the risk that the venture would not generate a profit. Hoxie became a bailee of the cattle because it took "delivery of property for some particular purpose on an express or implied contract that after the purpose has been fulfilled the property will be returned to the bailor, or dealt with as he directs." M. Bruenger & Co., Inc. v. Dodge City Truck Stop, Inc., 675 P.2d 864, 868 (Kan. 1984) (quoting 8 C.J.S. Bailments §1). Even though Hoxie had the right to deduct the costs of purchasing and caring for the cattle from the sale proceeds, the parties viewed Morken as owner of the cattle, and Morken determined when cattle would be sold and at what price. In sum, Morken became the owner of an interest in the cattle, and Hoxie's interest in the cattle was therefore limited to that of a bailee and secured party.

In similar circumstances, other courts have held that the debtor acquired "rights in the collateral" even though the debtor received only constructive delivery of the cattle to a feedlot. See, e.g., The Cooperative Fin. Ass'n, Inc. v. B & J Cattle Co., 937 P.2d 915, 917, 920-921 (Colo. Ct. App. 1997) (debtor acquired rights when cattle were delivered to a third party feedlot; secured creditor prevailed over unpaid cattle seller); O'Brien v. Chandler, 765 P.2d 1165, 1168-1169 (N.M. 1988) (same); see also The Hong Kong & Shanghai Banking Corp. v. HFH USA Corp., 805 F. Supp. 133, 142-143 (W.D.N.Y. 1992) (physical possession of the collateral is not necessary for the debtor to have rights).

Hoxie contends that the sale transactions were not completed because it had the right to stop delivery of the cattle upon discovering Morken's insolvency. See Kan. Stat. Ann. §84-2-702. Hoxie lost its Article 2 right to stop delivery, however, when the cattle were constructively delivered to Morken and Hoxie acknowledged to Morken in the feedlot agreements and other transaction documents that Morken had purchased the cattle and Hoxie was holding them for Morken for feeding and sale purposes. See id. §84-2-705(2)(b); see also Abilene Nat'l Bank v. Fina Supply, Inc. (In re Brio Petroleum, Inc.), 800 F.2d 469, 472 (5th Cir. 1986) ("the Code makes clear that a seller's right to stop goods in transit may continue after delivery and until the buyer is in actual, physical or constructive possession of them"); Ramco Steel, Inc. v. Kesler (In re Murdock Mach. & Eng'r Co.), 620 F.2d 767, 773 (10th Cir. 1980) (same).

Moreover, in some circumstances, the debtor can transfer greater rights in the collateral to a third party than the debtor himself holds. Thus, "[a] person with voidable title has power to transfer a good title to a good faith purchaser for value." Kan. Stat. Ann. §84-2-403(1). "Purchase" includes taking an interest in property by mortgage, pledge, or lien. Id. §84-1-201(32). Therefore, a secured party such as Sprague can be a "good faith purchaser" which can acquire an interest in the collateral greater than the interest of the debtor, Morken, and superior to the interest of an unpaid seller such as Hoxie. The leading case on this point is Stowers v. Mahon (In re Samuels & Co., Inc.), 526 F.2d 1238 (5th Cir.) (en banc) (per curiam), cert. denied, 429 U.S. 834 (1976), pitting a creditor with a security interest in the debtor's cattle against the unpaid seller of the cattle. The court held that the secured creditor's interest was superior to the unpaid seller's interest under

UCC §2-403 which "gives good faith purchasers of even fraudulent buyers-transferors greater rights than the defrauded seller can assert." Id. at 1242. As to whether the debtor had "rights in the collateral," the court reasoned that the UCC's priority scheme of elevating a "good faith purchaser" over an unpaid seller necessarily requires that the debtor had "rights in the collateral" even though it had not paid for the cattle:

> The existence of an Article Nine interest presupposes the debtor's having rights in the collateral sufficient to permit attachment, §9-204(a). Therefore, since a defaulting cash buyer has the power to transfer a security interest to a lien creditor, including an Article Nine secured party, the buyer's rights in the property, however marginal, must be sufficient to allow attachment of a lien.

Id. at 1243. Thus, the debtor had "rights in the collateral," even though it had not paid the seller for those cattle.

In summary, when the dust had settled after each of the five cattle transactions: (a) a sale had occurred; (b) Hoxie had constructively delivered the cattle to Morken and had possession of the cattle on Morken's behalf; (c) Morken had title to and owned the cattle; (d) the only interest retained by Hoxie in the cattle was a security interest and interest as bailee; (e) Hoxie's UCC Article 2 remedy of refusing to deliver the cattle had been cut off; and (f) Morken had "rights in the collateral" sufficient for Sprague's security interest to attach. Accordingly, we hold that Sprague had a perfected security interest in the cattle and reverse the district court on this issue.

III.

Having determined that Sprague held a perfected security interest in the cattle, we now turn to the priority dispute between the two secured creditors, Sprague and Hoxie. We hold that Hoxie attained purchase money security interest "superpriority" under the Kansas UCC, Kan. Stat. Ann. §84-9-312(3), and has priority over Sprague's interest.

Section 9-312 of the UCC sets forth rules for determining priorities among conflicting security interests in the same collateral. See Kan. Stat. Ann. §84-9-312. The general priority scheme is that the first creditor to perfect its security interest beats later perfected security interests. See Kan. Stat. Ann. §84-9-312(5)(a). There is an important exception to this "first-to-perfect" rule for a purchase money security interest. A PMSI in inventory has "superpriority" over an earlier perfected interest if: (a) the PMSI is perfected at the time the debtor receives possession of the inventory; (b) the PMSI creditor gives written notification to all holders of competing security interests which had UCC-1 financing statements on file when the PMSI creditor filed its UCC-1; (c) the competing secured creditor receives the notification within five years before the debtor receives possession of the inventory; and (d) the notification states "that the person giving the notice has or expects to acquire a purchase money security interest in inventory of the debtor, describing such inventory by item or type." Id. §84-9-312(3).

Sprague contends that the §84-9-312(3)'s "superpriority" status cannot be attained by a creditor that has perfected its security interest in inventory by possession, rather than by filing a UCC-1 financing statement. It emphasizes language in this UCC section and its commentary that refers to perfection by filing and the debtor receiving possession of the inventory. See Kan. Stat. Ann. §84-9-312(3) & Official UCC cmt. 3. We observe, however, that there is no language expressly excluding a creditor that has perfected by possession from taking advantage of this UCC section. More importantly, there is no sound policy reason to distinguish between perfection by filing and possession, and to provide the former, but not the latter, the opportunity to attain "superpriority." The common law of pledge—perfection by possession—predates, and was incorporated by, the UCC. In addition, pre-UCC law afforded special priority to purchase money security interests, and this has been carried over into the UCC. See B. Clark, The Law of Secured Transactions ¶3.09[1], at 3-100 ("the purchase money priority . . . breaks up what would otherwise be a complete monopoly on the debtor's collateral"). Thus, the UCC, as it stands today, does not reflect any intent to penalize a PMSI creditor by depriving it of the opportunity to attain "superpriority" simply because of its means of perfection.

We believe that there is a more logical explanation for UCC §9-312(3)'s contemplation that a creditor with a security interest in inventory would likely perfect by filing rather than possession. Inventory are goods "held for immediate or ultimate sale." Kan. Stat. Ann. §84-9-109 [now §9-102(a)(48)—Ed.]. Official UCC cmt. 3. The debtor typically needs its inventory to run its business and is not in a position to allow a third party, such as its lender, to possess the inventory. Therefore, the situation here—in which the creditor has possession of the inventory—will arise only rarely. The fact that the "superpriority" provision of §84-9-312(3) does not expressly refer to perfection by possession does not establish that its scope is limited to perfection by filing. The UCC was not drafted to address every possible factual situation, but, rather, was "intentionally designed to allow room to grow," Kan. Stat. Ann. §84-1-102 Kan. cmt. 1 (1996), and to accommodate the "expansion of commercial practices." Id. Official UCC cmt. 1.

Having concluded that it was possible for Hoxie to use §84-9-312(3) to attain "superpriority," we must now decide whether it did so by fulfilling the statutory requirements. The only requirement at issue here is the timing of Hoxie's PMSI notice, which was received after the cattle were sold and slaughtered and this litigation was commenced. We believe that this issue turns on the meaning of "possession" in the context of §84-9-312(3). As explained above, the UCC treats constructive possession as analogous to actual possession in certain circumstances. If Morken's constructive possession triggered the notification requirement, then Hoxie's notification was untimely because Sprague received the notification after Morken received constructive possession of the cattle. On the other hand, if "possession" is limited to actual possession, Hoxie's notice was timely because Sprague received it before Morken could ever receive actual possession.

Professor Grant Gilmore, the primary drafter of UCC Article 9, provides guidance on the meaning of "receives possession" in §84-9-312(3). Professor Gilmore's treatise Security Interests in Personal Property has been described as "an invaluable source of legislative intent because he is the fountainhead in this area." B. Clark, The Law of Secured Transactions ¶1.01[2][c], at 1-8. In that treatise, Professor Gilmore states that "'[r]eceives possession' is evidently meant to refer to the moment when the goods are physically delivered at the debtor's place of business—not to the possibility of the debtor's acquiring rights in the goods at an earlier point by identification or appropriation to the contract or by shipment under a term under which the debtor bears the risk." II G. Gilmore, Security Interests in Personal Property §29.3, at 787 (1965). In light of Professor Gilmore's comments, we interpret UCC §9-312(3)'s notification requirement to be triggered by actual possession of the inventory by the debtor. Because Sprague received Hoxie's notification within five years before Morken could have received actual possession, that notification was timely.

Sprague complains that the purpose of §84-9-312(3) is frustrated by granting "superpriority" to a PMSI without requiring pre-perfection notification to prior filed secured creditors. It contends that debtors on the brink of insolvency will now have the motive to create "secret liens" to the detriment of prior perfected secured creditors. The notification requirement, however, was not intended to allow other secured creditors veto power over the extension of new credit because the notification does not have to be given before the PMSI is acquired. The notification is required to state "that the person giving the notice *has* or expects to acquire a purchase money security interest in inventory of the debtor, describing such inventory by item or type." Kan. Stat. Ann. §84-9-312(3)(d) (emphasis added). Thus, the PMSI creditor can wait to notify competing secured creditors after it has acquired and perfected its security interest. The Official UCC Comment explains that the notification protects the inventory financier from making additional advances to the debtor in the mistaken belief that it is secured by inventory which, in fact, has been financed by a third party with a PMSI in that inventory. If the inventory financier "has received notification, he will presumably not make an advance; if he has not received notification (or if the other interest does not qualify as a purchase money interest), any advance he may make will have priority." Kan. Stat. Ann. §84-9-312 Official UCC cmt. 3.

Our holding is consistent with this purpose in the context of this case. Sprague did not extend further credit in reliance on the cattle serving as its collateral; in fact, Sprague had not made any loans to Morken since at least a year before Morken acquired an interest in these particular cattle. We stop short, however, of holding, as did the district court, that a PMSI creditor that perfects by possession of inventory does not ever have to send a statutory notification. It is not necessary to reach that issue because Hoxie timely sent its statutory notification. A different fact pattern in another case might justify a different conclusion. See Scallop Petroleum Co. v. Banque Trad-Credit Lyonnais, 690 F. Supp. 184, 192 (S.D.N.Y. 1988) (PMSI creditor was required to send notification even though debtor never had possession of the inventory).

IV.

The "superpriority" of the purchase money security interest extends to inventory and "identifiable cash proceeds received on or before the delivery of the inventory to a buyer." Kan. Stat. Ann. §84-9-312(3). Sprague argues that Hoxie does not have "superpriority" as to the proceeds from the cattle sales to IBP because Hoxie received payment "two or three days" after delivering the cattle to IBP. We hold that Hoxie has priority over Sprague as to the proceeds from the cattle sales.

The "on or before delivery" language in this UCC provision was discussed by the Fourth Circuit in Sony Corp. of America v. Bank One, West Virginia, Huntington NA, 85 F.3d 131 (4th Cir. 1996). The court explained that this language "was meant to distinguish between cash proceeds and accounts proceeds." Id. at 136 (citing UCC §9-312 Official UCC cmt. 3). The court concluded that "[t]he drafters of the U.C.C. decided to protect accounts financers over inventory financers, and they limited the priority of purchase money secured creditors to the cash proceeds of inventory collateral." Id. at 137 (citing UCC §9-312 Official UCC cmt. 8); see also B. Clark, The Law of Secured Transactions ¶3.09[3][c], at 3-121 (describing the drafters' favorable treatment of the account lender over the PMSI creditor). Thus, the issue here turns on whether cattle sales generated an account receivable or cash proceeds.

The answer is found in the Packers and Stockyards Act, 1921, 7 U.S.C. §181-229. The Act provides that for purposes of livestock sales to packers, "a cash sale means a sale in which the seller does not expressly extend credit to the buyer." 7 U.S.C. §196(c) (1976). Even if there is a delay in payment, the transaction is a "cash sale" unless there is an express agreement extending credit from the seller to the buyer. See The First State Bank v. Gotham Provision Co., Inc. (In re Gotham Provision Co., Inc.), 669 F.2d 1000, 1004-1005 (5th Cir. Unit B), cert. denied, 459 U.S. 858 (1982). There was no written credit agreement here; therefore, the cattle transactions between Hoxie and IBP were cash sales and not accounts receivable.

Even if these were cash sales, Sprague argues that PMSI "super-priority" does not extend to the sale proceeds because Hoxie did not receive them "on or before the delivery of the inventory to the buyer." The Fourth Circuit faced a similar issue in Sony Corp., in which payment was received one day after delivery. 85 F.3d at 136. The court refused to construe UCC §9-312(3) to limit the PMSI creditor's "superpriority" in inventory proceeds to only those proceeds received on the same day as delivery because such a construction would lead to arbitrary results. Id. at 137. Instead, the court adopted a "reasonably contemporaneous" standard and held that the creditor had priority in the sale proceeds received one day after delivery. Id.

When cattle are sold on a "weigh and grade" basis, the purchase price is determined after the cattle are slaughtered and the meat is graded and weighed. This explains the delay between delivery and payment. See In re Gotham Provision Co., 669 F.2d at 1005 n.3 (discussing the difference between "grade and yield" and "live weight" purchases). We follow the reasoning of the Fourth Circuit in Sony Corp. and hold that, in the circumstances of the sales here, Hoxie's receipt of the cash proceeds was reasonably contemporaneous with delivery. Accordingly, Hoxie's "superpriority" extends to those proceeds.

In conclusion, we reverse the district court's holding that Sprague did not have a security interest in the cattle, but affirm its judgment that Hoxie's security interest has priority over Sprague's security interest.

This case should continue to be good law even after the 1999 revision is adopted. Official Comment 5 to §9-324 states that if "the debtor never receives possession, the five year period never begins, and the purchase-money security interest has priority even if notification is not given."

The revised version of Article 9 extends the superpriority procedure for gaining a PMSI security interest in inventory to a PMSI in the debtor's livestock (see §9-324(d)), and, in Appendix II to the 1999 revision, states the option to use the same procedure for creditors taking a PMSI in the debtor's future crops (there called a *production money security interest*).

PROBLEM 319

Hans Racing Equipment bought much of its inventory from Standard Auto Wholesales, Inc., which always took a purchase money security interest in the goods sold to Hans and which filed a financing statement on the same day. Hans also borrowed money from the Matching Dishes National Bank (MDNB) to finance the purchase of inventory from wholesalers, part of which was used to pay off Standard Auto. MDNB filed a financing statement, claiming a security interest in Hans's inventory. On March 28, Hans contracted to buy $3,000 in goods from Standard, making a down payment of $1,500 and giving Standard a purchase money security interest in the goods for the rest. On that same day he borrowed the $1,500 down payment from MDNB and also gave the bank a purchase money security interest in the same goods. Both creditors knew of the other, so they both sent written notice to each other. The goods were delivered to Hans on April 2. Which creditor has priority? See §9-324(g) and its Official Comment 13.

Similar problems arise, of course, with consignments. Even true consignors hoping to prevail over perfected interests in the inventory of the consignee must follow a notification procedure of this type. See §9-103(d) and Example 3 in Official Comment 3 of §9-319.

PROBLEM 320

Barbara Shipek was pleased and flattered when Tim Isle, owner of Isle's Fine Art Works, asked her if he could exhibit and sell some of her pottery. She gave him five of her favorite pieces. The next day she took a party of friends down to the store to see the display and was astounded to learn that Octopus National Bank (ONB), which had a perfected floating lien on the store's inventory, had foreclosed and seized everything in the store, including Barb's pottery. Can ONB do this to her? Murphy v. Southtrust Bank of Ala., 611 So. 2d 269, 19 U.C.C. Rep. Serv. 2d 456 (Ala. 1992).

III.   CONTROL AND PRIORITY

The 1999 revision of Article 9 makes much of the idea of *control* as a means of perfection. White & Summers explain the basic concept best by telling us that "'control' is to intangibles as 'possession' is to goods"; White & Summers §22-4 at 757. Taking the steps for control, described below, gives the world some notice at least that the creditor has legal rights in the intangible property that must be respected.

A.   Control Over Investment Property

The 1994 version of Article 8, concerning investment securities, dealt not only with traditional stocks and bonds represented by actual pieces of paper (*certificated securities;* see §8-102((a)(4)), and similar rights against the issuing corporation that are merely registered in a computer at that corporation (*uncertificated securities;* see §8-102(a)(18)), but also with the widespread practice of holding securities in an account with a stockbroker, with the investor's rights reflected merely by a bookkeeping entry in the stockbroker's records (called a *securities entitlement;* see §8-102(a)(17)).[8] Article 9 lumps all of these methods of holding securities, along with similar rights in commodity

---

8. The stockbroker may not itself have possession of the actual certificates either, but may only have rights to an account it carries with a clearing corporation or bank, where the actual certificates are physically located. In this case the broker has a *security entitlement* in the latter account, and its rights pass through to its investor free of the claims of most creditors of either upper-tiered party; see §8-503(a).

contracts and accounts, and names them *investment property*. Read §9-102(a)(49).

How is a security interest taken in investment property? There are two ways: the filing of a financing statement and/or the taking of *control* over the investment property, with the latter trumping the former (that is, a secured party who has control has priority over one who has merely filed; see §9-328(1)). *Control* is defined in §8-106, with similar rules for commodity contracts in §9-106(b). Generally one has control over a certificated security by taking delivery of it along with any necessary indorsements; §§8-106(a), (b) and 8-301(a). The same is true of uncertificated securities (see §8-106(c)), only here *delivery* is artificially defined in §8-301(b) as making sure that the secured party is registered as the stock owner in the records of the issuing corporation. In the context of indirect holding, *control* requires that the secured party take steps to make sure that it can reach the rights of the debtor in the event that it needs to foreclose, as is illustrated in the following Problem.

PROBLEM 321

Mr. Goldbury instructed his stockbroker, Bing, Bong & Bell (B, B & B) to buy 100 shares of Utopia, Ltd. stock and place it in his account at B, B & B. B, B & B bought the shares and kept them in the account it held at Clearing Corporation but marked its records to indicate that Mr. Goldbury was really the owner of this number of shares of the stock. In this case Article 8 would deem Mr. Goldbury an *entitlement holder* who has a *securities entitlement* in a *security account* with a *securities intermediary;* see §8-102, which defines all these terms (*securities account* is in §8-501(a)). Mr. Goldbury went to Octopus National Bank (ONB) and asked to borrow money using the above 100 shares as collateral. You are the counsel for ONB and are in charge of making sure that the bank's security interest is perfected, which means getting "control" over the securities entitlement. Look at §8-106(d) and its Official Comment 4, and advise the bank. Which of the possible methods is the safest for your client?

Then answer these two questions:

(a) If another creditor also gets control over the rights to the 100 shares, which has priority? See §9-328(2).

(b) If Mr. Goldbury borrows money from B, B & B after ONB has control and grants B, B & B a security interest in all stocks held in his account with them, is B, B & B's security interest superior to ONB's? See §9-328(3) and Official Comment 4, Example 5.

For all these issues of control and perfection of security interests in investment property, the Official Comments to both §§8-106 and 9-328 contain a wealth of information, including Examples aplenty, to which you are referred in the event of an actual legal dispute.

B. Control Over Deposit Accounts

Similar rules govern the use of bank accounts as collateral. Prior to the 1999 revision of Article 9 it was unclear whether a bank account could stand as collateral for debts owed to anyone other than the bank in which the account was maintained (and, subject to non-uniform amendments, the prior version of Article 9 excluded deposit accounts from its scope). The revision allows a perfected security interest in such accounts by a creditor obtaining control over the account. Consumer accounts may not be used as collateral for consumer debts (though they could be so used for non-consumer debts); see White & Summers §21-9.

PROBLEM 322

Computer World, Inc. desires to borrow money from Investment Bank of America, which will grant it a revolving line of credit, secured in part by the bank account that Computer World maintains at Last National Bank. You are the attorney for Investment Bank of America. Advise the bank how it can perfect its security interest in this bank account and which of the methods of control specified in §9-104 would be the safest form of security. If Computer World later borrows money from Last National Bank and grants the bank a security interest in the account carried there, would Last National have priority over your client? See §9-327(3) and (4).

C. Control Over Letters of Credit Rights

Letters of credit (the subject of Article 5 of the Uniform Commercial Code) are an increasingly popular means of financing various transactions. If one party does not trust the other to make payment at an agreed-upon time, that party may require that the payment be made directly by a bank of good repute. If this is done, the bank that is persuaded to do so will issue a letter of credit to the person to whom payment is to be made (called the *beneficiary*) specifying the circumstances under which the bank will honor drafts drawn on it by that person. The other party to the transaction who persuades the bank to issue the letter of credit (the bank's customer) is called the *applicant*. The beneficiary may use its rights under the letter of credit as collateral for a different loan with a different creditor, who will then want to perfect its security interest in the rights represented by the letter of credit.

PROBLEM 323

Computer World agreed to sell 10,000 computers to Football University for the sum of $25,000, with Football University agreeing to obtain a letter of credit for this amount in favor of the seller. Shortly thereafter Computer World received a letter of credit from Octopus National Bank (ONB) naming Computer World as the beneficiary and stating that it would honor drafts drawn on the bank in favor of Computer World for the amount of $25,000 on presentation of an invoice showing shipment of the computers to the university by September 25 of that year. Computer World comes to you, its attorney, in February of the same year with the following problem. It needs to borrow $10,000 from some lender in order to finance the construction of the computers by the required deadline. It wants to use the letter of credit as collateral for this loan. How can the new lender obtain a perfected interest in the rights represented by the letter of credit? See §9-107. When Computer World asked ONB if it would agree to an assignment of the proceeds of the letter of credit to Computer World's lender, the bank not only refused but pointed to clauses in the letter of credit that provided a number of things: (1) the right of Computer World to draw drafts on the bank was not transferable; and (2) the letter of credit specifically forbade the beneficiary (Computer World) the right to make an assignment of the proceeds of the letter of credit and *voided* the letter of credit if the beneficiary made such an assignment without the banks' consent. What can Computer World tell potential lenders who might be willing to loan it money if the letter of credit rights could be used as collateral? Remember as you read the cited sections that follow that the obligation from Football University to Computer World is an *account*. See §§9-308(d), 9-102(a)(77), 9-409, and the latter's Official Comments.

IV. BUYERS

Section 9-201(a) states what White & Summers call Article 9's "Golden Rule" (White & Summers §24-12):

> Except as otherwise provided by the Uniform Commercial Code, a security agreement is effective according to its terms between the parties, against purchasers of the collateral and against creditors.

Section 9-320(a) is one of the sections that fit in the "except" language of §9-201; so is §9-317(b), which lists other buyers who win out over the *unperfected* secured party in some circumstances. A corollary to §9-201's "Golden Rule" is §9-315(a)(1):

> (a) Except as otherwise provided in this article and in Section 2-403(2):
>   (1) a security interest or agricultural lien continues in collateral notwithstanding sale, lease, license, exchange, or other disposition thereof unless the secured party authorized the disposition free of the security interest or agricultural lien; . . .

PROBLEM 324

Betty Consumer bought a television set from Distortion TV, Inc., a retail store. A month later Distortion went bankrupt, and a minor functionary from the Octopus National Bank (ONB) showed up on her stoop and asked her to turn over the set. He explained that ONB held a perfected security interest in all of Distortion's inventory and that since Distortion had not paid off its debts to ONB, the bank was repossessing.

(a) What should Ms. Consumer tell the bank's flunky? See §9-320(a).

(b) Would it matter if she had known that ONB had a perfected security interest in Distortion's inventory? See White & Summers §26-13; Official Comment 3 to §9-320.

(c) Would it matter if she bought at a "Liquidation Sale" and was informed by the store's owner that the store planned to file a bankruptcy petition the following week? See In re Fritz-Mair Mfg. Co., 16 Bankr. 417, 33 U.C.C. Rep. Serv. 554 (Bankr. N.D. Tex. 1982).

(d) What if Ms. Consumer had put the TV on "layaway" and had paid 50 percent of the price but permitted Distortion to keep the TV (she signed a contract obligating herself to pay the balance), and then the store filed for bankruptcy? Read §2-502 and its Official Comments. The Bankruptcy Code also offers such consumers some relief in §507(a)(6), which gives layaway buyers a priority payment up to the amount of $900 per individual.

International Harvester Co. v. Glendenning

Texas Supreme Court, 1974
505 S.W.2d 320, 14 U.C.C. Rep. Serv. 837

WILLIAMS, C.J. This appeal is from a take nothing judgment in a suit to recover damages for wrongful conversion of three tractors.

International Harvester Company and International Harvester Credit Corporation (both hereinafter referred to as International) brought this action against Don Glendenning in which it was alleged that International was the holder of a duly perfected security interest in three new International Harvester tractors; that such security agreements had been executed in favor of International by Jack L. Barnes, doing business as Barnes Equipment Company, an International Harvester dealer; that Barnes and Glendenning had entered into a fraudulent conspiracy wherein Glendenning had wrongfully purchased the three tractors from Barnes; that Glendenning was not a buyer in the ordinary course of business; that he did not act in a commercially reasonable manner and did not act honestly, therefore taking the tractors subject to International's security interest. It was further alleged that Barnes and Glendenning had wrongfully conspired to convert the ownership of the tractors and to deprive International, by fraud and deceit, of its ownership of the tractors by virtue of their security interest therein in that (1) Glendenning acquiesced in falsifying a retail order form so that it was made to indicate receipt of $16,000 in cash and the trade-in of two used tractors allegedly worth a total of $8,700, while in fact both Glendenning and Barnes knew that Glendenning had only paid the sum of $16,000 in cash, a sum far below the market value of the tractors; (2) Glendenning, in the furtherance of the conspiracy and unlawful conversion, represented to a representative of International that he, Glendenning, had, in fact, traded certain used tractors to Barnes, which was untrue; and (3) Glendenning removed the new tractors in which International had a security interest to the State of Louisiana where he sold the same and converted the proceeds to his own use and benefit. International sought damages in the sum of $24,049.99 which was alleged to be the reasonable value of the tractors on the date of conversion.

Glendenning answered by a general denial and with the special defense to the effect that he purchased the tractors in the ordinary course of business and that such purchase was made in good faith and without any knowledge of any security interest held by International. The court submitted the case to the jury on one special issue:

> Do you find from a preponderance of the evidence that on the time and occasion in question, the defendant, Don Glendenning, was a buyer in the ordinary course of business?

In connection with this issue the court instructed the jury that the term "buyer in ordinary course of business" means "a person who in good faith and without knowledge that the sale to him is in violation of the ownership rights or security interest of the third party in the goods buys in the ordinary course from a person in the business of selling goods of that kind."

The court instructed the jury that the term "good faith" means "honesty in fact in the conduct or transaction concerned."

The jury answered the special issue "Yes." . . .

[The court quoted §§9-307(1) (the predecesor to §9-320(a)), 1-201(9), and 1-201(19) and noted that "whether a sale is in the ordinary course of business is a mixed question of law and fact."]

The material testimony presented to the court and jury may be summarized, as follows:

At the time of the trial of this case appellee Glendenning was a farmer in Collin County. He described himself as being not only a farmer but a trader. He said that he frequently traded tractors and other farm equipment as well as anything else from which he could make a profit. He has had almost twenty years' experience in the business of buying and selling farm tractors. In the early 1950s he owned an International Harvester dealership in Frisco, Collin County, Texas. From 1956 to 1960 he was a salesman for International Harvester. After leaving International he began trading farm equipment of his own, using some of the implements on his own farm and holding others strictly for resale. For many years he had been familiar with

International Harvester's custom of "floor-planning" tractors and other farm equipment. By this plan International would supply tractors and other equipment to the dealers who, in turn, would give International a note and security agreement to protect International in its investment. When a dealer sold a piece of equipment from the floor he would pay International the amount due. He also testified that he knew that when used tractors were taken as trade-ins by International Harvester dealers such used tractors were also mortgaged or covered by the security agreement to International. He admitted that International Harvester always kept close tabs to see what was wrong with the used tractors and that International always wanted to know what its dealers traded for in connection with new equipment sales. Glendenning acknowledged that any false information contained on a retail order form would provide incorrect information concerning the transactions to International Harvester, or any other lender.

Glendenning said that he had known Jack L. Barnes, an International Harvester dealer, for two or three years and during that time he had bought several tractors from him. In the early part of July 1971 Barnes, and Joe Willard, another friend, came to his home in Collin County and talked to him about buying some tractors. He said that Barnes had eight tractors to sell but that he was only interested in buying three of the machines. Barnes described the tractors and told Glendenning that he wanted $18,500 for the three. Glendenning declined that offer but told Barnes that he would give $16,000 cash for the three. Barnes accepted the offer.

At the time of this transaction Glendenning knew that the three tractors were reasonably worth $22,500. Willard went to Vernon, Texas, and got the tractors and delivered them to Mr. Glendenning's home. Glendenning asked Willard to bring him a bill of sale when he returned with the tractors. Willard received from Barnes an instrument entitled "Retail Order Form" dated July 5, 1971, which recited that Glendenning had purchased from Barnes three tractors for the total price of $24,700 with a cash payment of $16,000 leaving a balance of $8,700. The instrument recited that Glendenning had traded in four tractors with values totaling $8,700 so that the total consideration of $24,700 was shown to have been paid.

Glendenning said that the next day Barnes came to his home to get payment for the tractors. At that time Glendenning requested a "bill of sale" and he watched Barnes fill in another retail order form similar to the one that he had obtained from Willard the day before. This order form stated that Glendenning had traded in four tractors worth $8,700 in addition to payment of $16,000 in cash making a total purchase of $24,700. After Barnes had completed filling out this form and signed the same Glendenning said that he put his signature on the instrument also. He then gave Barnes $16,000.

Concerning the contents of the retail order form Glendenning said that at the time Barnes filled in the blanks indicating that Glendenning was trading in four tractors he knew that he was not trading anything and that he did not question Barnes about the trade-in information contained in the form. He admitted that he did not ask Barnes whether the tractors which he purchased were free and clear nor did he call International to determine whether or not such company had a mortgage on the tractors. Glendenning admitted that he knew that the information contained in the printed form concerning trade-ins and total consideration for the sale of the three new tractors was false; that he knew of this falsification when he signed the order form; and that he also knew that such falsification would mislead any creditors relying on the document such as a dealer, a manufacturer or a bank lending money with the equipment as collateral. He admitted that at the time of the transaction in question Barnes was probably "trying to come out even" or that he did it to make his books balance. Glendenning admitted that he was suspicious of the manner in which Barnes prepared the order form and confessed that his actions amounted to dishonesty. He said that to his knowledge he had never before signed an order form with false trade-ins. He admitted that such action was "unusual."

A few days after the transaction a Mr. McKinney, collection manager for International Harvester Company, and a representative of International Harvester Credit Corporation, telephoned Glendenning concerning the transaction in question. In that conversation Glendenning told McKinney that he had traded four tractors to Barnes in addition to paying $16,000 cash for the three new International tractors. Glendenning testified that he knew that he had lied to Mr. McKinney concerning the trade-ins and that such oral misrepresentation or lie was dishonest.

After receiving the tractors Glendenning removed them to a barn near Alexandria, Louisiana, although it was his usual practice to place equipment on his own premises or at another dealer's place of business. He subsequently sold the three tractors in Louisiana.

As a part of his direct examination Glendenning testified that he considered the deal to be a purchase of three tractors for $16,000; that he had no side agreement with Barnes; that he thought he was making a good deal; and that he was acting in good faith.

At the very beginning of this trial appellee Glendenning confessed the validity of appellant's cause of action against him based upon fraud, conspiracy and conversion, but sought to evade legal liability by assuming, pursuant to Tex. R. Civ. P. 266, the burden of going forward and establishing his sole defense that he was a buyer in ordinary course of business within the meaning of §9.307(a) (1968). This assumption carried with it the additional burden of establishing by competent evidence that Glendenning acted in good faith and without knowledge that the sale to him was in violation of the ownership rights or security interest of a third party. Good faith, as the court correctly charged the jury, means honesty in fact in the conduct or transaction concerned. In an effort to establish this affirmative defense and thereby evade liability, appellee Glendenning testified on direct examination with the broad conclusory statement that he had acted in good faith. However, this subjective and conclusory statement was immediately annihilated by factual evidence falling from the lips of Glendenning himself.

Appellee Glendenning's own testimony immediately removes him from the category of an innocent Collin County farmer who seeks to purchase one or more tractors in the ordinary course of business. By his own testimony he has had many years of experience as a tractor dealer, a salesman and one of the most active traders of farm equipment in Collin County. Based upon this experience he is knowledgeable in the very nature of business done by International by "floorplanning" its equipment. With all of this knowledge and information in his possession he purchased the equipment for considerably less than its value, made no investigation of International's security interest, acquiesced in the falsification of the retail order form showing nonexistent trade-ins, and misrepresented the particulars of the transaction to International's representative by stating that there were, in fact, trade-ins. He confesses that his actions were dishonest.

Thus it is evident to us that Glendenning's own testimony, which is the only material testimony offered, is entirely devoid of honesty in fact and completely negates his contention that he was a buyer in the ordinary course of business within the meaning of the Texas Business & Commerce Code.

While we have been unable to find any Texas authorities decided under this specific provision of the Business & Commerce Code a recent Uniform Commercial Code release notes that the good faith requirement was added "to make it clear that one who buys dishonestly is not within the definition. The 'without knowledge' addition spells out one important type of dishonesty." UCC Release No. 27-1973, 6 Bender's Uniform Commercial Code Service §1-201 at 1-29 (1965).

The complete picture revealed by all of the material testimony in this case reveals a definite pattern of lies, deceit, dishonesty and bad faith. We find no competent evidence in this record to support the jury's answer to the special issue submitted and therefore the same should have been set aside and disregarded by the trial court. . . .

———————

Even where the Code is silent about a "good faith" requirement, §1-203 imposes one. There is a growing body of UCC law that says that good faith is a condition precedent to any protection under the statute. "Bad faith," a phrase not defined in the Code, can alter the usual Article 9 priorities. See Limor Diamonds, Inc. v. D'Oro by Christopher Michael, Inc., 558 F. Supp. 709, 35 U.C.C. Rep. Serv. 1509 (S.D.N.Y. 1983).

PROBLEM 325

Deering Milliken was a textile manufacturer. It routinely sold textiles on credit to Mill Fabrics, a firm that finished the textiles into dyed and patterned fabrics. It was Mill Fabrics' practice to resell the fabrics to Tanbro Fabrics, a wholesaler. While the textiles were still in Deering's warehouse, Mill Fabrics contracted to buy them from Deering, signing a security agreement to that effect and giving Deering a financing statement, which it duly filed. In turn, Mill Fabrics sold the textiles to Tanbro, which paid Mill Fabrics for them, but delayed taking delivery for a few weeks, so that the fabrics remained in Deering's possession. Deals of this kind were common in the textile industry, and all parties knew of the others' interest. Unfortunately, Mill Fabrics became insolvent and never paid Deering for the textiles, and Deering therefore refused to deliver them to Tanbro. The latter sued. Who should prevail? See §9-320(e) and its Official Comment 8.

There is quite a list of qualifications (culled from §9-320(a) and §1-201's definition of "buyer in the ordinary course of business") that a buyer must meet to purchase free of a prior security interest in the purchased property:

(1) He/she must be a buyer in the ordinary course of the seller's business (i.e., buying the seller's inventory in the routine way),

(2) who does not buy in bulk (that is, does not buy an entire inventoried business) and does not take the interest as security for or in total or partial satisfaction of a preexisting debt (that is, the buyer must give some form of "new" value),

(3) who buys from one in the business of selling goods of that kind (that is, cars from a car dealer, i.e., inventory),

(4) who buys in good faith and without knowledge that this purchase is in violation of others' ownership rights or security interests, and

(5) who does not buy farm products from a person engaged in farming operations,

(6) the seller's creditor must part with possession (the issue in the above Problem), and

(7) the competing security interest must be one "created by his seller." The meaning of this cryptic phrase will be explored as we progress in this segment.

PROBLEM 326

Octopus National Bank (ONB) had a perfected security interest in all cars on Smiles Motors' lot. Smiles owed $5,000 in past due insurance premiums to its insurance agent, Howard Teeth, who showed up one morning to buy a new car from Smiles. The president of Smiles first gave Howard a check for $5,000, but Howard endorsed it back over to Smiles when he saw a new car he wanted to buy. Is Howard a §1-201(9) "buyer in the ordinary course of business" so as to take free of ONB's security interest? See Chrysler Credit Corp. v. Malone, 502 S.W.2d 910, 13 U.C.C. Rep. Serv. 964 (Tex. Civ. App. 1973).

First National Bank and Trust Co. of El Dorado v. Ford Motor Credit Co.

Kansas Supreme Court, 1982
231 Kan. 431, 646 P.2d 1057, 34 U.C.C. Rep. Serv. 746

FROMME, J. This controversy is between a bank and a credit company, both claiming prior security interests in three vehicles allegedly sold by a car dealer. The trial court held that the bank's security interests were prior and ordered the vehicles released to the bank. The credit company appeals.

Heritage Ford Lincoln Mercury, Inc., (Dealer) of El Dorado, Kansas, was in the business of selling new cars. On February 18, 1981, it quit business. On February 24, 1981, it voluntarily surrendered its entire new car inventory to the credit company. Vehicle 1 and Vehicle 2 were on the new car lot and were listed in the documents when the cars were surrendered to the credit company.

Ford Motor Credit Company (Credit Company) had entered into an agreement with the Dealer in April, 1978, extending a continuing line of credit by which the Dealer purchased vehicles from the manufacturer. This inventory financing is generally called a floor plan, and under such a plan a car dealer gives a credit company a purchase money security interest in all motor vehicles then owned and thereafter acquired, and in all proceeds from the sale thereof. This was done in the present case. The Credit Company also filed a financing statement with the Secretary of State on May 11, 1978, giving notice that it held a security interest in all new and used motor vehicles held by the Dealer, and in the proceeds.

This floor plan agreement provides:

> 5.   *Dealer's Possession and Sale of Merchandise*
>
> Dealer's possession of the merchandise financed hereunder shall be for the sole purpose of storing and exhibiting the same for sale or lease *in the ordinary course of Dealer's business.* Dealer shall keep such merchandise brand new and subject to inspection by Ford Credit and free from all taxes, liens and encumbrances. Dealer shall not mortgage, pledge or loan any of such merchandise, and shall not transfer or otherwise dispose of the same except by sale or lease *in the ordinary course of Dealer's business.* As used in this paragraph 5, *"sale in the ordinary course of Dealer's business" shall include only (i) a bona fide retail sale to a purchaser for his own use at the fair market value* of the merchandise sold, and (ii) an occasional sale of such merchandise to another dealer at a price not less than Dealer's cost of the merchandise sold, provided such sale is not a part of a plan or scheme to liquidate all or any portion of Dealer's business. [Emphasis supplied.]

Tom Overton was the president of the dealer corporation. Robert Magill was vice-president. Robert Ward is Robert Magill's father-in-law and he had invested upwards of $100,000.00 in the dealership. These three men were more or less active in the dealership and at times drove cars referred to in the business as demonstrators. The dealership was in financial trouble and it may be inferred that Overton and Magill decided to double finance certain new cars held under floor plan to raise operating cash for the business.

As to Vehicle 1, which was a new Lincoln Continental automobile, Tom Overton issued dealer papers to himself and obtained financing at First National Bank and Trust Company of El Dorado (Bank). Overton signed a note and security interest which were issued to and held by the Bank on this vehicle. Notice of security interest was sent in to the Division of Motor Vehicles. The loan proceeds were deposited directly in the dealer account at the Bank. The dealer's wholesale cost of the vehicle was $18,992.27. The Bank loaned $17,992.27 on this vehicle. The retail value was $22,386.00. Overton paid no down payment. The vehicle was not personally licensed by Overton and it remained on the new car lot where it was available at all times for new car sale. The proceeds from this alleged sale were never paid to the Credit Company. The vehicle was on the premises and was turned over to the Credit Company when the Dealer went out of business in February 1981. The Dealer had continued to carry insurance on the vehicle.

As to Vehicle 2, which was also a new Lincoln Continental automobile, Robert Magill issued dealer papers to himself and obtained financing at the Bank. Magill signed a note and security interest which were issued to and held by the Bank. The date of the alleged sale was February 3, 1981. This security interest was never perfected by filing. The loan proceeds were deposited in the Dealer account in the Bank. The Dealer's wholesale cost of Vehicle 2 was $15,394.62. The Bank loaned $15,394.62 on the vehicle. The retail value was $18,052.00. Magill made no down payment and the Credit Company was never paid the proceeds. The car was not licensed in Magill's name. It remained on the Dealer's new car lot where it was available for new car sale until the Dealer went out of business and turned it over to the Credit Company in February 1981. The Dealer had continued to carry insurance on the vehicle.

When the dealership closed its doors and turned over the cars to the Credit Company the Bank immediately filed suit to prevent the removal of these cars from the Dealer's premises and to establish a prior claim thereto. During the course of this action the trial court ordered the three vehicles delivered to the Bank and the Bank sold them and now holds the proceeds. We will set forth additional facts as to Vehicle 3 later in this opinion since the facts and applicable law are dissimilar.

We turn now to the Uniform Commercial Code, K.S.A. 1981 Supp. 9-312 relating to priorities among conflicting security interests in the same collateral. Section 9-312(3) [now §9-324(b) —Ed.] provides:

> A perfected purchase money security interest in inventory has
> priority over a conflicting security interest in the same inventory and

also has priority in identifiable cash proceeds received on or before the delivery of the inventory to a buyer if

> (a) the purchase money security interest is perfected at the time the debtor receives possession of the inventory.

Then follows subparagraphs (b), (c) and (d) as to notice which provisions of the statute are not pertinent to our discussion.

The Credit Company's purchase money security interest in inventory was perfected by filing with the Secretary of State and under the above section is to receive top priority, subject, however, to the rights of certain purchasers in particular sales which are made in ordinary course of Dealer's business and thus are contemplated by the parties in the floor plan agreement. Credit Company held a purchase money security interest within the definition appearing in K.S.A. 9-107(b) [now §9-103—Ed.]:

> A security interest is a "purchase money security interest" to the extent that it is . . .
>
> (b) taken by a person who by making advances or incurring an obligation gives value to enable the debtor to acquire rights in or the use of collateral if such value is in fact so used.

Credit Company paid the manufacturer the Dealer's wholesale cost of these cars when they were first delivered to the Dealer.

Both the floor plan agreement and K.S.A. 1981 Supp. 9-307 [now §9-320-320(a)—Ed.] recognize that a buyer in ordinary course of business will take free of a security interest created by the seller-dealer. K.S.A. 1981 Supp. 9-307 provides:

> (1) A buyer in ordinary course of business (subsection (9) of section 84-1-201) other than a person buying farm products takes free of a security interest created by his seller even though the security interest is perfected and even though the buyer knows of its existence.

A buyer in the ordinary course of business is defined in K.S.A. 1981 Supp. 1-201(9) as follows:

> "Buyer in ordinary course of business" means a person who in good faith and without knowledge that the sale to him is in violation of the ownership rights or security interest of a third party in the goods buys in ordinary course from a person in the business of selling goods of that kind but does not include a pawnbroker.

In the Official Comment 2 under §9-307 it is suggested that by reading §§9-307 and 1-201(9) together, "it results that the buyer takes free if he merely knows that there is a security interest which covers the goods but takes subject if he knows, in addition, that the sale is in violation of some term in the security agreement not waived by the words or conduct of the secured party."

There can be no question in the present case that both Overton and Magill, who were officers in the Dealer corporation, arranged these sham sales in violation of the terms of the floor plan security agreement. There can be little doubt, Overton and Magill were not buyers in ordinary course of business under the above definition. They did not obtain licenses on these cars for personal use and they placed these vehicles on the new car lot where the cars were displayed for sale. These vehicles remained there until the business of the Dealer was closed down. The vehicles were not sold for fair market value as required by the floor plan agreement.

Even Robert Saferite, vice-president of the Bank, by his own testimony, was aware that these cars were not being sold in ordinary course of business. Under questioning by defendant's lawyer he testified:

Q:	All right. On any of the vehicles did you actually ever go through the steps of obtaining a title on any of the vehicles?
A:	No sir, I did not.
Q:	Those vehicles then were used in a short term, is that a correct assumption?
A:	Yes, sir.
Q:	And then would be sold?
A:	Yes sir.
The Court:	I am curious. Were you using them as demonstrators or what—I don't understand?
Mr. Saferite:	They would be used either one—either personal or for demonstrator purposes.
Q:	(By Mr. Hargrove) About how long did Overton or Magill keep one of the vehicles before they paid off their notes?
A:	It varied from a few days to several months.

We wish to emphasize that in this case the Bank is not a buyer, it is a financier of the alleged buyers, and although §9-307(1) would allow a buyer in ordinary course to take free of Credit Company's security interest in the inventory, the Bank has no such rights for it is the financier, not a buyer. See Clark, The Law of Secured Transactions Under the Uniform Commercial Code §3.4[3] n.55 (1980).

The case cited by plaintiff Bank in support of the trial court's judgment establishing priority, has been considered by this court and is not persuasive as to plaintiff's claim.

Plaintiff Bank attempts to distinguish the case of Borg-Warner Acceptance Corp. v. Atlantic Bank, 364 So. 2d 35 (Fla. App. 1978). We find it supports a holding in favor of the floor planner Credit Company in this case. In the *Borg-Warner* case Borg-Warner was the floor planner and perfected the security interest which eventually covered the motor home in question. A dealer named Hill's World held the motor home in inventory. Hill's World then obtained a bank loan from Atlantic Bank. Title certificate was issued by the Department of Motor Vehicles showing Hill's World as owner and Atlantic Bank as lien holder. As to priority of liens between Borg-Warner, the floor planner, and Atlantic Bank, the Florida court determined that since there was no sale to a buyer in the ordinary course of business, judgment should be entered in favor of the floor planner Borg-Warner.

A security interest continues in collateral notwithstanding sale, exchange or other disposition thereof unless the disposition was authorized by the secured party in the security agreement or otherwise, and also continues in any identifiable proceeds. K.S.A. 1981 Supp. 9-306(2) [now §9-315(a)(1)—Ed.]. Under the Official Comment 3 following this section of the statute it is stated:

> In most cases when a debtor makes an unauthorized disposition of collateral, the security interest, under prior law and under this Article, continues in the original collateral in the hands of the purchaser or other transferee. That is to say, since the transferee takes subject to the security interest, the secured party may repossess the collateral from him or in an appropriate case maintain an action for conversion. Subsection (2) codifies this rule. The secured party may claim both proceeds and collateral, but may of course have only one satisfaction.

In the context of the present case the trial court erred in holding the sales of Vehicle 1 and Vehicle 2 were in ordinary course of business. The floor plan security interest continued in those two vehicles and in the proceeds. The trial court wrongfully permitted plaintiff Bank to take possession and to sell the same. On remand, the trial court is directed to determine the amount of proceeds received by the Bank from the sale of these vehicles and enter judgment in favor of defendant for such amounts, together with interest from the date the Bank sold these vehicles. . . .

PROBLEM 327

Arthur Greenbaum bought a new car on credit from Lorri's Car City, which took a purchase money security interest in the vehicle, perfecting same by notation of its lien interest on the certificate of title, as required by state law. Arthur was a used car dealer by profession, but he had purchased the car for his own private use. Nonetheless, he frequently parked the car on his lot, and one day sold it for cash to Ann Matheson, a customer in search of a good used car. Arthur did not mention to her that it was his personal car. When everyone learned what had happened, Ann sued Lorri's Car City, demanding that it release the title. What result? See First Dallas County Bank v. General Motors Acceptance Corp., 425 So. 2d 464, 35 U.C.C. Rep. Serv. 701 (Ala. 1983).

PROBLEM 328

Wonder Spa, Inc., pledged 50 of its promissory notes to the Conservative State Bank and Trust Company (CSBTC) in return for a loan. The bank took possession of the notes. The spa asked to have 10 of the notes back for presentment to the makers for payment, and the bank duly turned over the notes, which Wonder Spa sold (*discounted*) to Octopus National Bank (ONB), a bona fide purchaser without knowledge of CSBTC's interest. This resale was in direct violation of the spa's agreement with CSBTC. Which bank is entitled to the instruments? Read §§9-312(g) and 9-331. Is ONB one of the parties protected by §9-331? See §§3-302 and 3-305.

Subsection (b) to §9-320 appears at first glance to apply to more situations than it really fits. It is meant to cover only a rare transaction: a sale of consumer goods by a consumer to a consumer. White & Summers §24-15; Balon v. Cadillac Auto. Co., 113 N.H. 108, 303 A.2d 194, 12 U.C.C. Rep. Serv. 397 (1973); Everett Natl. Bank v. Deschuiteneer, 109 N.H. 112, 244 A.2d 196, 5 U.C.C. Rep. Serv. 561 (1968). In such a sale the buyer takes free of the seller's creditor's security interest only if the buyer is ignorant of it *and* if there is no financing statement on file.

PROBLEM 329

Andy Audio bought a stereo receiver on credit from Voice of Japan, Inc., an electronics store, giving it a purchase money security interest in the receiver. Voice of Japan did not file a financing statement. Six months later, when Andy still owed Voice of Japan $300, he held a garage sale and sold the receiver to Nancy Neighbor for $200 cash. If Andy stops making payments to Voice of Japan, can it repossess the receiver from Nancy? See §9-320(b) and its Official Comment 5.

PRACTICAL NOTE

Even though a purchase money security interest in consumer goods is automatically perfected on attachment, per §9-309(1), the above Problem is meant to suggest the wisdom of filing a financing statement in big-ticket consumer transactions lest the creditor suffer the same fate as Voice of Japan when the consumer sells the collateral to another consumer.

PROBLEM 330

The Repossession Finance Company had a perfected (filed) security interest in the equipment of White Truck Ice Cream (WTIC), Inc. (the company sold ice cream to children from trucks that traveled through the city's neighborhoods). Though technically a corporation, WTIC was in actuality a family business, and Bill White-Truck himself frequently drove one of the trucks. One day while making his rounds, Bill met Frank Family, a consumer who asked about buying an ice-cream-making machine for his family. Bill promptly sold him one of the machines the company owned, for which Frank paid cash. When WTIC failed to make its payments, the finance company lived up to its name and repossessed all equipment. When Frank refused to turn over the ice cream machine, Repossession sued him for conversion (a tort that does not require *scienter* or guilty knowledge for its commission). Answer these questions:

(a) Does he lose? Compare §§9-201, 9-401(b), and 9-315(a)(1) and Production Credit Assn. v. Nowatzski, 90 Wis. 2d 344, 280 N.W.2d 118, 26 U.C.C. Rep. Serv. 1338 (1979).

(b) Would we get a different result if the bank's interest were unperfected at the time of the sale? See §9-317(b).

(c) Would we get a different result if the bank knew and approved of the sale? Compare §9-315(a)(1).

PROBLEM 331

Paul Pop was a rock singer to whom Octopus National Bank (ONB) loaned $8,000 so he could buy stereo equipment for his road show. On April 2, Paul purchased the equipment, and on April 10, ONB filed its financing statement in the proper place. However, in the interim, on April 8, Paul sold the equipment to Used Stereo Heaven, which bought with no knowledge of the bank's purchase money security interest. Does ONB or Used Stereo Heaven have the superior claim to the equipment? Compare §§2-403, 9-201, and 9-317(e).

PROBLEM 332

When Farmer Bean borrowed a large amount of money from Farmers' Friend Financing Company (FFFC), he was required to sign a security agreement by which he promised not to sell the crop that was the collateral for the loan without the written consent of FFFC. Nonetheless, every year he sold the crop to the same buyer and remitted the proceeds to FFFC without getting its written consent. Does the buyer take free of the security interest of the secured party under §9-320(a)? If FFFC never protested what was going on year after year as the security agreement was violated, can it be said to have *waived* its security interest? Can a security interest be waived? See §9-315(a)(1) and the following famous case.

Clovis National Bank v. Thomas

New Mexico Supreme Court, 1967
77 N.M. 554, 425 P.2d 726, 4 U.C.C. Rep. Serv. 137

OMAN, J. This is a suit by plaintiff-appellant for alleged conversion of cattle by defendant-appellee. The parties operate their respective businesses in Clovis, Curry County, New Mexico, and will be referred to as plaintiff and defendant.

In its capacity as a bank, plaintiff, on March 27, 1963, loaned the sum of $8,800 to a Mr. W. D. Bunch. To evidence and secure the indebtedness he gave plaintiff a promissory note and a security agreement by which he granted a security interest in about 46 head of cattle belonging to him and branded "W D Bar." On April 11, 1963, a further security agreement, granting a security interest in 102 head of cattle, was given by him to plaintiff as additional security for the loan of

March 27, and as security for additional loans to be made to him by plaintiff from time to time.

On July 29, 1963, he deposited $3,507 with plaintiff. This money represented proceeds from the sale by him of 35 head of cattle covered by the security agreements. $3,300 of this amount was applied by plaintiff on the indebtedness then owing by him.

On October 29, 1963, he deposited with plaintiff the sum of $5,613.17, the total amount of which was applied to his indebtedness, and which amount represented proceeds from the sale by him of 56 head of cattle covered by the security agreements. This deposit consisted of two checks given by defendant, who is a licensed commission house and market agency and as such handled the sale of the cattle for him.

Plaintiff admitted to being aware that Mr. Bunch was making sales of cattle covered by the security agreements.

In about September 1963, he made application to plaintiff for an additional loan with which to purchase additional cattle and with which to carry his cattle through the winter. An investigation was made by plaintiff during September, to determine the feasibility of granting this additional loan. Plaintiff approved the loan, and cattle were acquired by him and paid for by drafts drawn on plaintiff. By November 12, 1963, the additional cattle had been acquired.

On November 12, a new note in the principal amount of $21,500 and a new security agreement covering 283 head of cattle branded W D Bar were given by him to plaintiff to evidence and secure his then indebtedness. This indebtedness in the amount of $21,500 represented $2,007.67 still owing on the original note of March 27, $2,743.10 credited to his checking account on November 12, and amounts loaned or advanced to him during the intervening period. The security agreement was duly recorded in both Curry and Quay counties and in part provided:

> DEBTOR FURTHER REPRESENTS, WARRANTS, AND AGREES THAT: . . . .
> Without the prior written consent of Secured Party, Debtor will not sell, . . . or otherwise dispose of the collateral. . . .

Thereafter, cattle covered by the November 12 security agreement were consigned to defendant by Mr. Bunch for sale on his behalf at public auction. The plaintiff had no actual knowledge of these sales and had not given any express consent to Mr. Bunch to make the sales. He remitted no part of the proceeds from these sales to the plaintiff for application on his indebtedness. The sales were of 45 head of cattle on February 20, 1964, 95 head on May 14, 1964, and one head on May 21, 1964. The total value of these cattle was $16,450.34, and plaintiff sought recovery from defendant of this amount under the first cause of action of its complaint.

Mr. Bunch has a son by the name of William D. Bunch, Jr., also known as Bill Bunch, Jr., who will be referred to either by name or as the son. The son was the owner of a brand referred to as "Swastika K." Some time prior to July 15, 1964, at least 90 head of cattle were acquired by either Mr. Bunch or his son and were branded Swastika K. There was some evidence tending to show that these cattle, at least to some extent, were actually property of the father. No security agreement was ever given by either the father or the son by which a security interest in cattle branded Swastika K was granted to the plaintiff, unless in some way it can be held that they were covered by the security agreement of November 12.

On July 15, 1964, plaintiff requested that Mr. Bunch sell the remainder of his cattle, including the Swastika K cattle. On the following day, 90 head of Swastika K cattle were trucked to defendant's place of business for sale and were carried on the defendant's records as belonging to Bill Bunch, Jr. Plaintiff knew the cattle were at defendant's place of business to be sold and told defendant that plaintiff claimed some interest in the cattle. Defendant was not told the nature or extent of the claimed interest of plaintiff in these cattle.

The cattle were sold on July 16. Plaintiff was aware of the sale and advised defendant that it would be "nice" if the check in payment for these cattle could be made payable to one or both of the Bunches and to the plaintiff. At no time did the plaintiff demand payment or request that defendant not make payment to Bill Bunch, Jr.

Bill Bunch, Jr., consulted the local brand inspector and solicited his aid in securing payment from the defendant. The brand inspector advised defendant that the Swastika K brand was recorded in the name of Bill Bunch, Jr., and that insofar as the Cattle Sanitary Board was concerned, payment could be made to him.

An attorney also called defendant on behalf of Bill Bunch, Jr., concerning payment for the cattle, and demand was made by Bill Bunch, Jr., upon defendant to pay him the proceeds from the sale of the cattle. This the defendant did on July 22. This payment was in the amount of $7,777.84, which is the amount of plaintiff's claim against defendant under the second cause of action.

On this same date, plaintiff filed suit against W. D. Bunch and William D. Bunch, Jr., wherein plaintiff sought to recover from the father on the note of November 12, and sought to recover from the son the said sum of $7,777.84. In this proceeding plaintiff filed an affidavit in support of an application for a writ of garnishment, wherein it was asserted that the defendant was indebted to William D. Bunch, Jr. No claim was made that the proceeds from the sale belonged to plaintiff, but rather plaintiff asserted that the proceeds belonged to William D. Bunch, Jr., and, as already stated, tried to reach these proceeds by garnishment, which came too late. The present suit was then filed against defendant on August 31, 1964.

The plaintiff asserts thirteen separate points relied upon for reversal. However, the ultimate conclusions upon which the judgment for defendant rests are (1) the plaintiff consented to the sales of W D Bar cattle covered by the security agreement of November 12, and thus waived any possessory rights it may have had in these cattle, and (2) the plaintiff had no perfected security interest in the Swastika K cattle, and failed to prove an unperfected security interest in these cattle of which defendant had knowledge.

Insofar as the sales of the W D Bar cattle are concerned, the trial court found plaintiff, as a matter of common practice, usage and procedure, permitted Mr. Bunch to sell cattle covered by the security agreements of March 27 and April 11, and consented to receipt of the sale proceeds by Mr. Bunch. It also found that plaintiff, by common practice, custom, usage and procedure, permitted and consented to the sales of W D Bar cattle covered by the security agreement of November 12, and permitted and consented to the receipt by Mr. Bunch of the proceeds from these sales.

The trial court concluded that plaintiff had permitted, acquiesced in, and consented to these sales; that by its conduct, plaintiff had waived any possessory rights it may have had in and to these cattle; that defendant did not wrongfully convert cattle in which plaintiff had an enforceable security interest; and that defendant was not responsible for the debtor's failure to remit the proceeds of the sales to plaintiff.

We agree with the findings and conclusions of trial court. Insofar as consent and waiver on behalf of plaintiff are concerned, in addition to the facts recited above, the plaintiff's officers testified that it was the custom and practice of plaintiff to permit a debtor, who has given cattle as collateral, to retain possession and to sell the collateral without ever obtaining prior written consent of plaintiff, and that at no time in its dealings with Mr. Bunch between the time of the making of the note on November 12, 1963, and the sale of cattle on May 21, 1964, did plaintiff demand of him that he obtain prior written consent before making a sale.

It is true there was some testimony that the collateral was not released from the lien until the debtor actually delivered the proceeds of the sale to plaintiff, but, as testified to by one of the plaintiff's officers, the debtor never contacts the plaintiff and secures permission to make a sale, but the sale is made and plaintiff relies upon the debtor to bring the proceeds to plaintiff to be applied on the indebtedness. This practice is followed because 99% of the people with whom plaintiff deals are honest and take care of their obligations.

The general rule of liability of an auctioneer, who sells, in behalf of his principal, property subject to a mortgage lien, is stated as follows in the annotation at 96 A.L.R.2d 208, 212 (1964):

> According to the overwhelming weight of authority, an auctioneer who sells property on behalf of a principal who has not title thereto, or who holds the property subject to a mortgage or other lien, or who for other reasons has no right to sell such property, is personally liable to the true owner or mortgagee for conversion regardless of whether he had knowledge, actual or constructive, of the principal's lack of title or want of authority to sell, in the absence of facts creating an estoppel or showing acquiescence or consent on the part of the true owner or mortgagee. . . .

The trial court, in addition to holding plaintiff had consented to and acquiesced in the sales and had waived his possessory rights in the cattle, concluded plaintiff was estopped from recovery by reason of its conduct. The plaintiff and the amicus curiae have both made strong attacks on this conclusion. We are inclined to agree that the essential elements of an estoppel are lacking. We do not, however, predicate our decision upon estoppel, but rather upon consent and waiver.

The plaintiff, if not expressly consenting to the questioned sales, certainly impliedly acquiesced in and consented thereto. It not only permitted Mr. Bunch, but permitted all its other debtors who granted security interests in cattle, to retain possession of the cattle and to sell the same from time to time as the debtor chose, and it relied upon the honesty of each debtor to bring in the proceeds from his sales to be applied on his indebtedness.

Plaintiff was fully aware of its right to require its written authority to sell or otherwise dispose of the collateral, but it elected to waive this right. Waiver is the intentional abandonment or relinquishment of a known right. Smith v. New York Life Ins. Co., 26 N.M. 408, 193 Pac. 67; Miller v. Phoenix Assur. Co. Ltd., 52 N.M. 68, 191 P.2d 993.

In Farmers' Natl. Bank v. Missouri Livestock Comm. Co., 53 F.2d 991 (8th Cir. 1931), suit was brought by the holder of chattel mortgages for alleged conversion of cattle by a livestock commission house. Although the facts are dissimilar from those of the present case, that case does stand for the principle that consent may be established by implication arising from a course of conduct as well as by express words, and that consent to a sale operates as a waiver of the lien or security interest. See also Moffet Bros. & Andrews Comm. Co. v. Kent, 5 S.W.2d 395 (Mo. 1928).

In First Natl. Bank & Trust Co. v. Stock Yards Loan Co., 65 F.2d 226 (8th Cir. 1933), the effect of a course of conduct on the part of a mortgagee, such as was followed by the mortgagee in that case and such as was followed by plaintiff in the present case, was stated to be:

> . . . When a mortgagee under a chattel mortgage allows the mortgagor to retain possession of the property and to sell the same at will, the mortgagee waives his lien, and this is true whether the purchaser knew of the existence of the chattel mortgage or not.

The fact that plaintiff may have intended that the proceeds from the sales of cattle covered by the security agreements should be remitted to plaintiff by Mr. Bunch for application on his indebtedness did not change the waiver. When plaintiff consented to the sales and the collection of the proceeds of the sales by him, it lost its security interest in the collateral and was then looking to him personally for payment. . . .

The collateral here in question—livestock, falls within the classification of "farm products," and these products are expressly excluded from the classifications of "equipment" and "inventory." Section 9-109(3), N.M.S.A. 1953. By excluding "farm products" from the classifications of "equipment" and "inventory," and by expressly providing in §9-307(1) [now §9-320(a)—Ed.], N.M.S.A. 1953, that a buyer in the ordinary course of business of farm products from a person engaged in farming operations does not take free of a security interest created by the seller, the draftsmen of the code apparently intended "to freeze the agricultural mortgagee into the special status he has achieved under the pre-code case law." 2 Gilmore, Security Interests in Personal Property 714 (1965).

It would only seem logical and consistent that if the buyer from one engaged in farming operations takes subject to the security interest, then the selling agent is subject to the rights of the secured party in the collateral. This is consistent with the foregoing cited authorities. See also United States v. Union Livestock Sales Co., 298 F.2d 755 (4th Cir. 1962); United States v. Matthews, 244 F.2d 626 (9th Cir. 1957).

Section 9-306(2) [now §9-315(a)(1)—Ed.], N.M.S.A. 1953 provides:

Except where this article otherwise provides, a security interest continues in collateral notwithstanding sale, exchange or other disposition thereof by the debtor unless his action was authorized by the secured party in the security agreement or otherwise, and also continues in any identifiable proceeds including collections received by the debtor.

No section of the code provides otherwise as to farm products. Thus, the holder of the security interest in farm products has the same protection under the code which he had under the pre-code law, and the cattle broker is still liable to the secured party for conversion of the collateral. United States v. Sommerville, 211 F. Supp. 543 (W.D. Pa. 1962), *aff'd on other grounds*, 324 F.2d 712 (3d Cir. 1963), *cert. denied*, 376 U.S. 909 (1964). See also 2 Gilmore, Security Interests in Personal Property 715 (1965).

Also, under the code the secured party may consent to the sale of the collateral, and thereby waive his rights in the same. See Official Comment No. 3, §9-306, and Official Comment No. 2, §9-307 [in the 1998 revision, see Official Comment 2 to §9-315, second paragraph—Ed.]. There being no particular provision of the Code which displaces the law of waiver, and particularly waiver by implied acquiescence or consent, the code provisions are supplemented thereby. Section 1-103, N.M.S.A. 1953. The defendant cannot be held liable for a conversion of the W D Bar cattle, because plaintiff consented to and acquiesced on the sales thereof, and thereby waived its rights in this collateral. . . .

It follows from what has been stated that the judgment should be affirmed. It is so ordered.

CHAVEZ, C.J., and NOBLE and COMPTON, J.J., concur. CARMODY, J. (dissenting). [Omitted.][9]

NOTE

This case and the waiver issue it presents have an uneasy history. The difficulty is created by the rule in §9-320(a) that a buyer in the ordinary course from one selling farm products does not take free of

---

9. The New Mexico legislature responded by amending the UCC to provide that course of dealing or trade usage could not have the effect of waiving a security interest in farm products. The court did not consider the effect of §1-205(4); had it, would the result have changed? Compare Official Comment 2 to §1-205 with §2-208(3). [In the revised version of Article 1, see §1-303.]

the secured party's interest in the products sold. Why would the Code drafters have done this? The answer lies in the special deference always shown to farmers as debtors.

The importance of farming to our society has created any number of rules favoring agricultural borrowers. It is crucial that financial institutions be encouraged to loan money to farmers, and §9-320(a) is an example of a statute that reflects this policy. If the lenders can follow the collateral into the hands of an innocent buyer, they are more secure and therefore more likely to make the original loan to the farmer. In truth, a farmer's sale of the annual crop is more like an Article 6 *bulk sale* (the sale of a large part of the inventory) than the typical retail sale that §9-320(a) usually covers, so the buyer from a farmer ought to be more careful to make sure that everything is squared with the farmer's lender. On the other hand, §9-320(a) catches all buyers, even auctioneers and commission merchants, and involves them in policing the relationship between the farmer and the bank, and these buyers bitterly resented fulfilling this function.

Where the bank was aware that the farmer was routinely ignoring the security agreement's requirement of written consent, the courts were, like in the *Clovis* case, especially likely to find a waiver of the security interest. Later courts generally (though not always) followed *Clovis*. See the case law summary in Anon, Inc. v. Farmers Prod. Credit Assn., 446 N.E.2d 656, 35 U.C.C. Rep. Serv. 1383 (Ind. App. 1983). Some courts developed a "conditional consent" test whereby the waiver was ineffective unless the condition under which it was made (typically payment of the proceeds to the secured party) was complied with. See, e.g., Baker Prod. Credit Assn. v. Long Creek Meat Co., 97 Or. 1372, 513 P.2d 1129, 13 U.C.C. Rep. Serv. 531 (1973). Other courts, noting that the bank's "waiver" was really nothing more than the acceptance of a fait accompli ("I sold the collateral even though I said I wouldn't; here's the money"), did not permit such a "course of dealing" to override the express selling prohibition of the security agreement. See §1-205(4); Wabasso St. Bank v. Caldwell Packing Co., 251 N.W.2d 321, 19 U.C.C. Rep. Serv. 315 (Minn. 1976).[10] For the position of revised

___

10. One other matter: fair or not, it is the rule that no agent of the United States government has actual or apparent authority to waive the government's security interests. United States v. Hughes, 340 F. Supp. 539, 10 U.C.C. Rep. Serv. 697 (N.D. Miss. 1972). Where the federal government is the farmer's creditor, the courts are quick to find conversion despite the buyer's lack of knowledge; FDIC v. Bowles Livestock Commn. Co., 739 F. Supp. 1364, 13 U.C.C. Rep. Serv. 2d 23 (D. Neb. 1990). For an informative discussion of the meaning of *conversion* in Article 9, see Mammoth Cave Prod. Credit Assn. v. Oldham, 569 S.W.2d 833, 25 U.C.C. Rep. Serv. 603 (Tenn. App. 1977).

Article 9 on this issue, see Official Comment 2, second paragraph, to §9-315.

The answer of many states was to enact a statute creating a system whereby a buyer of farm products would take free of the security interest of the farmer's creditor if the buyer first jumped through certain hoops. These statutes proved to be the model for a federal statute that has now replaced them and has completely preempted the farm products exclusion in UCC §9-307(1), §1324 of the Food Security Act of 1985 (hereinafter FSA), 7 U.S.C. §1631. (This statute is in your statute book.) The FSA contemplates the following schema: the security agreement between the farmer and the bank requires the farmer to furnish the bank with a list of prospective buyers of the farm products (see §1631(h)(1)), and the farmer agrees not to sell to anyone else unless the farmer notifies the bank in writing at least seven days before the sale (§1631(h)(2)). The bank then sends a direct notice to the listed buyers informing them of any payment instructions the bank wants to impose; the notice must contain the details mentioned in §1631(e)(1)(A). If the buyers follow the payment instructions, they take free of the bank's security interest (§1631(d) and (e)). In addition to the above, the state may establish a central filing system for the registration of financing statements covering farm products.[11] Buyers then register with the central filing office, which regularly sends them a list of the relevant financing statements concerning the types of farm products they wish to buy. Or the central filing office will respond to buyers' inquiries within 24 hours as to the existence of any financing statements covering farm products they wish to purchase; §1631(c)(2). If the buyers then obtain either a release or a waiver from the secured parties (or follow their instructions as to payments), the buyers take free of the security interests in the farm products. See White & Summers §24-14.

---

11. Nineteen states have central filing systems; see the list at http://www.usda.gov/gipsa/programspsp/cleartitle.htm. The financing statement to be filed in the central filing system must be more detailed than the usual one filed under the UCC. See §1631(c)(4) for the definition of *effective financing statement,* which must include, among other things, the social security number of the debtor, the amount of farm products covered, and their location. See Sanford, The Reborn Farm Products Exception Under the Food Security Act of 1985, 20 UCC L.J. 3 (1987). The central filing system indexes these financing statements by four different categories, including *crop year.* See §1631(c)(2). "Attorneys for agricultural lenders have recently found themselves pondering such questions as: What is the 'crop year' of a pig?" Reiley, State Law Responses to the Federal Food Security Act, 20 UCC L.J. 260 (1988). The regulations adopted pursuant to the Act have shed some light on this and other mysteries; see 9 C.F.R. §205.107 (*crop year* of an animal is the year in which it is born or acquired).

PROBLEM 333

Farmer Bean borrowed money from Octopus National Bank (ONB), which had him sign a security agreement covering his crops. The security agreement forbade him the right to sell his crops without the written consent of the bank. It also required him to give the bank a list of potential buyers of the crop. Farmer Bean did so. The list was of the five buyers to whom he had sold his crop (or parts thereof) in the past. The bank sent a written notice complying with §1631(e)(1) to each of the listed buyers, telling them that all payments for Farmer Bean's crops should be by check made payable to ONB. One buyer not on the list was Rural Silo, Inc., a grain merchant that contracted to buy all of Farmer Bean's 2010 wheat crop. Rural Silo knew that Farmer Bean had borrowed money from ONB and that ONB had filed a financing statement to perfect its security interest (the state had not created an FSA central filing system). It bought the crop from Farmer Bean and paid him cash for it at his request. Is Rural Silo, which after all knew all about ONB's security interest, a *buyer in the ordinary course* as defined in §1631(c)(1)? See Lisco State Bank v. McCombs Ranches, Inc., 752 F. Supp. 329, 13 U.C.C. Rep. Serv. 2d 927 (D. Neb. 1990); Ashburn Bank v. Farr, 206 Ga. App. 517, 426 S.E.2d 63, 20 U.C.C. Rep. Serv. 2d 355 (1992). Does Rural Silo take free of the bank's security interest? See §1631(d). Does the bank have any other remedy here? See §1631(h)(3).

Farm Credit Bank of St. Paul v. F & A Dairy

Wisconsin Court of Appeals, 1991
165 Wis. 2d 360, 477 N.W.2d 357,
16 U.C.C. Rep. Serv. 2d 885

CANE, J. F & A Dairy (the dairy) appeals a judgment in favor of Farm Credit Bank of St. Paul for conversion of secured farm property. The dairy raises four issues on appeal: (1) The trial court erred by basing its decision on §9-307, in contravention of 7 U.S.C. §1631 (1988), which the dairy claims preempts state law; (2) the dairy took free and clear of the bank's security interest because the bank did not meet the notice requirements of §1631; (3) the bank was not in possession or entitled to immediate possession of the secured property and, thus, could not maintain an action for conversion; and (4) the trial court's decision was unfair, inequitable and contrary to the policy behind §1631. . . .

John and Barbara Bonneprise own and operate a dairy farm. The Bonneprises borrowed $300,000 from Farm Credit Bank of St. Paul. As collateral for the loan, the bank obtained and perfected a security interest covering the Bonneprises' milk and all accounts arising from the sale or other disposition of their milk and milk products. The Bonneprises were selling milk to Land O' Lakes Dairy. In return for waiver of its lien, the bank executed an assignment with Land O' Lakes and the Bonneprises whereby Land O' Lakes would pay the bank $4,333 per month from the Bonneprises' milk proceeds.

In August 1988, the Bonneprises switched dairies and began selling their milk to F & A Dairy. After the bank received no payment in August, it found out that the Bonneprises had switched dairies. The Bonneprises refused to make an assignment directing the dairy to make payments to the bank. By letter dated August 22, 1988, the bank notified the dairy of its previous assignment with Land O' Lakes and demanded payments of $4,333 in accordance with the assignment. Also, the bank enclosed a copy of the assignment, a product lien notification statement and a copy of its financing statement filed in accordance with the UCC. Four days later the bank notified the dairy of its perfected security interest in the Bonneprises' milk and all accounts arising from the sale or other disposition of their milk and milk products and enclosed a copy of the security agreement.

The dairy refused to pay the bank $4,333 per month for milk sales during August, September, October and November.[12] The reasons it gave for not paying the bank were that there was no assignment between the bank, the Bonneprises and the dairy, and that John Bonneprise directed it to pay him and not the bank. Each of these months' sales to the dairy exceeded $4,333.

The trial court found that the bank had an effective perfected security interest covering the sale of the Bonneprises' milk to the dairy. It also found that the Bonneprises defaulted on their payments to the bank in August 1988, and, therefore, the bank was entitled to immediate possession of the secured property. The trial court concluded that the dairy bought the Bonneprises' milk subject to the bank's security interest under §1631 because the bank met the §1631 notice requirements. It further concluded that the dairy was guilty of converting the sum of $4,333 per month during September, October, November, and December (constituting proceeds from the August, September, October, and November milk sales), totaling $17,332. The

12. The milk sales from December 1988 and following are not in issue because they were placed in escrow.

trial court entered judgment in the amount plus 5% interest from the date of conversion to the date of judgment, and costs.

PREEMPTION

[The court concluded that 7 U.S.C. §1631 (Food Security Act) preempted what is now §9-320(a).]

APPLICATION OF 7 U.S.C. §1631

Next, we address whether the dairy purchased the Bonneprises' milk subject to or free of the bank's security interest, under §1631. The application of a statute to a particular set of facts is a question of law that we review de novo. Cleaver v. DOR, 158 Wis. 2d 734, 738, 463 N.W.2d 349, 351 (1990).

Section 1631(d) provides that a buyer of farm products takes free of a security interest except as provided in §1631(e). Subsection 1631(e) provides in part:

> *(e) Purchases subject to security interest*
> A buyer of farm products takes subject to a security interest created by the seller if—
>> (1)(A) within 1 year before the sale of the farm products, the buyer has received from the secured party . . . written notice of the security interest organized according to farm products that—
>>> (i) is an original or reproduced copy thereof;
>>> (ii) contains,
>>>> (I) the name and address of the secured party;
>>>> (II) the name and address of the person indebted to the secured party;
>>>> (III) the social security number of the debtor. . . .
>>>> (IV) a description of the farm products subject to the security interest created by the debtor . . . ; and . . .
>>> (v) [contains] any payment obligations imposed on the buyer by the secured party as conditions for waiver or release of the security interest; and
>> (B) the buyer has failed to perform the payment obligations. . . . (Footnote omitted.)

If the bank has met the §1631(e) notice requirements, including notice of any payment obligation, and the dairy failed to perform the payment obligations, it purchased the milk from the Bonneprises subject to the bank's security interest.

Here, the bank sent letters and documents to the dairy containing a copy of the security agreement creating the security interest in the milk and accounts from its sale, the bank's name and address, the Bonneprises' names and address, John Bonneprise's social security number and a reasonable description of the secured property and where it was located. It also demanded the monthly sum of $4,333.

The dairy argues that the bank did not meet the "payment obligation" notice requirement because its payment obligation was ambiguous. We disagree. Under its perfected security interest and by giving proper notice under §1631(e), the bank was entitled to receive all proceeds from the sale of the Bonneprises' milk, not merely the payment amount of $4,333. See Miracle Feeds, Inc. v. Attica Dairy Farm, 129 Wis. 2d 377, 385 N.W.2d 208 (Ct. App. 1986). The requirement of giving notice of "any payment obligations" is merely to allow the bank, if it wishes, to accept a lesser amount of milk sale proceeds and to waive its lien for the balance of the proceeds. The bank's documents and letters sent to the dairy provide sufficient notice that it had a lien on the Bonneprises' milk and proceeds from its sale, and that it demanded payment of $4,333 per month as a waiver of its lien.

The dairy also argues that the bank's payment obligation notice required an assignment from the Bonneprises directing it to pay a specific amount to the bank because the lien notification statement sent to the dairy referred to such an assignment. It further argues that because there was no such assignment, the notice requirements of §1631(e) are not met and it therefore takes free of the bank's security interest.

Subsection (e) does not require an assignment to be filed with the buyer. Although the bank's lien notification statement arguably requires such an assignment, the lack of an assignment does not allow the dairy to take free of the bank's security interest. If we were to view only the lien notification statement without an assignment, arguably the bank would be entitled to all proceeds from the milk sales because there would be no payment obligation for waiver of its lien. However, reviewing the correspondence and documents sent to the dairy, the only reasonable construction is that the bank was demanding payment of $4,333 per month in lieu of receiving the Bonneprises' milk and all proceeds arising from its sale. Thus, we hold that the bank adequately informed the dairy of "any payment obligations . . . as conditions for waiver" under §1631(e).

Section 1631(e) requires that the notice be given within one year before the sale of the farm products. The bank's notice was given in late August. The Bonneprises began selling their milk to the dairy earlier in August. Thus, the notice was given before the September, October, and November sales, but not before the August sales. Consequently, we hold that the bank's notice was timely only as to the September, October, and November milk sales, covering the October, November, and December proceeds. We therefore reverse that portion of the judgment pertaining to the August milk sales and September proceeds.

In addition to proper notice, §1631(e) requires that the buyer failed to perform the payment obligations of the secured party. At no time did the dairy make a payment of $4,333, or any other amount, to the bank. Thus, we conclude that the dairy, having proper notice of the bank's security interest and payment obligations as conditions for waiver for the September, October, and November milk sales, failed to comply with those payment obligations. Consequently, the bank met all the requirements of §1631(e), and the dairy takes subject to the bank's security interest.

CONVERSION

Next, the dairy contends that the bank cannot succeed on its action for conversion because it was not in possession or entitled to immediate possession of the secured property, and because it did not allege in the complaint that the Bonneprises defaulted on their loan. The issue of whether a particular set of facts fulfill a particular legal standard is a question of law that we review de novo. State v. Trudeau, 139 Wis. 2d 91, 103, 408 N.W.2d 337, 342 (1987). An action for conversion is the proper means for a secured party to enforce its security interest against a transferee. United States v. Fullpail Cattle Sales, 640 F. Supp. 976, 980 (E.D. Wis. 1986) (applying state law). Conversion is the wrongful or unauthorized exercise of dominion or control over a chattel. PCA v. Equity Coop Livestock Sales Assn., 82 Wis. 2d 5, 10, 261 N.W.2d 127, 129 (1978). A plaintiff in a conversion action must prove that he was in possession of or entitled to immediate possession of the chattel that was converted. Id.

The bank did not receive the August payment from the Bonneprises' milk sales. Thus, as of August, the Bonneprises were in default on their payments and, under §9-503 [now §9-609—Ed.], the bank had the right to immediate possession of the secured property. The bank established that the Bonneprises had defaulted on their required payments from August through December. Thus, we conclude that the bank was entitled to immediate possession of the

Bonneprises' milk proceeds, and the dairy wrongly exercised control over them by not giving the required proceeds to the bank.

Finally, we reject the dairy's argument that the bank's action for conversion is fatal because the complaint did not allege that the Bonneprises had defaulted. In Wisconsin, a notice pleading state, the complaint is not required to state all ultimate facts constituting each cause of action. Ollerman v. O'Rourke Co., 94 Wis. 2d 17, 24, 288 N.W.2d 95, 98 (1980). The complaint alleged that the bank gave the dairy notice of its secured position, that the dairy received proceeds in excess of its demand for $4,333 per month and that the dairy converted milk proceeds belonging to the bank. Thus, the pleadings were sufficient to allege an action for conversion, and they need not allege specifically that the Bonneprises defaulted.

Because we conclude that 7 U.S.C. §1631 preempts §9-307, and §1631 applies to the facts in this case, we need not consider the dairy's argument that the trial court's decision was contrary to equity, fairness and the policy behind §1631. Therefore, we hold that the bank is entitled to recover the proceeds from milk sales in September, October, and November, plus interest. The matter is therefore remanded to the trial court to modify the judgment consistent with this opinion.

By the Court—Judgment affirmed in part; reversed in part and cause remanded with directions. No costs to either party.

PROBLEM 334

Mr. and Mrs. Halyard purchased a large sailboat with money borrowed from the Boilerplate National Bank (BNB), which took a security interest therein and promptly filed a financing statement in the proper place. The Halyards sold the boat to Oil Slick Boat Sales, Inc., a used boat concern, telling Oil Slick of the bank's interest and of the necessity of making monthly payments to the bank. Oil Slick turned around and resold the boat to Mr. and Mrs. Blink, innocent people who paid full value for the boat believing Oil Slick had clear title. When BNB did not receive its usual monthly payment, it investigated, found the boat, and repossessed it. Has the Blinks' property been converted, or don't they fit into §9-320(a)? What does "created by the buyer's seller" mean in §9-320(a)? See White & Summers §24-13. Does Article 2's "entrusting" rule, §2-403, help the Blinks? What is §2-403's relationship with Article 9? See White & Summers §24-16; Milledgeville Community Credit Union v. Corn, 307 Ill. App. 3d 8, 716 N.E.2d 864, 39 U.C.C. Rep. Serv. 2d 929 (1999). The "created by the buyer's seller" language will often cause trouble for buyers buying goods from a used merchandise dealer. Why would the drafters have favored the original creditor in this situation over a buyer in the ordinary course? If the Blinks lose this lawsuit, whom should they sue, and what is their theory? See §2-312. Can Oil Slick use the same theory against the Halyards?

V. LEASES

In resolving the Problems that follow, it should be noted that according to §2A-103(1)(j) (defining *lease*): "Unless the context clearly indicates otherwise, the term includes a sublease."

PROBLEM 335

The Highbid Construction Company gave a security interest to Octopus National Bank (ONB) in all of its construction equipment "now owned or after-acquired." ONB filed a financing statement in the proper place. Two years later Highbid was in the middle of an enormous construction project at Football University when a number of its key employees quit, leaving it very short-staffed. To avoid breach of contract, it became necessary to farm out the project to someone else, though Highbid had never done this before. The president of Highbid reached an agreement with Newcomer Construction Company, one of its subcontractors on the Football University job, by which Highbid would lease all of its construction equipment to Newcomer for the length of the Football University project so that Newcomer could finish the job for Highbid. Use the rules of Article 2A to answer the following question: Is the lessee subject to ONB's existing security interest in the equipment? See §§2A-307 and 9-321(c).

PROBLEM 336

When the Football University project was completed, the lease described in the last Problem ended, and the machinery was returned by the lessee to Highbid Construction Company. Things were going so well for Highbid that it was able to pay off all of its loans in full and free all of its assets from the security interests that had encumbered them. Highbid's lawyer advised the company that for both tax and accounting reasons it would be better if Highbid leased the new grading machine that it had recently purchased rather than owning it outright. To accomplish this, Highbid's attorney worked out a deal by which Octopus National Bank (ONB) would purchase the grading machine from Highbid and then lease it back to Highbid. The term of the lease was exactly equal to the useful life of the grading machine.

Two months after this arrangement had come into being, Highbid's president absconded with the company's liquid assets, leaving the company in bad financial shape and needing to borrow some money. ONB refused to advance further funds, so Highbid looked elsewhere. The new president of Highbid went to Antitrust National Bank (ANB) and sought a loan, offering the grading machine as collateral. He was able to produce a bill of sale showing that Highbid had purchased the grading machine a mere three months ago when it was involved in the Football University contract. He did not tell ANB about the subsequent sale and leaseback arrangement that Highbid had with ONB. After ANB checked the public records and found no evidence of a security interest in the grading machine, it had Highbid sign the necessary Article 9 documents and a promissory note, loaned the money, and filed its financing statement in the appropriate place.

When Highbid defaulted on its lease payments, ONB repossessed the grading machine, at which point ANB claimed the superior interest therein. ANB's attorney argued that ONB was a party to fraud in that the sale and leaseback helped Highbid create the false appearance of assets.

How does this come out? See §§2A-307, 2A-308(3), and 1-201(37), and compare §2-402(2) in Article 2. Would you reach the same result if the lease agreement between Highbid and ONB provided the lessee with a right of termination at any time?

VI. ARTICLE 2 CLAIMANTS

PROBLEM 337

Jack Gladhand was a traveling salesman. He needed new luggage to carry his samples and bought a set from Alligator Fashions, which reserved a security interest therein and filed a financing statement. A month later, in the middle of a hot sales deal, Jack sold all of his samples *and* the luggage to Mark Impulse, a compulsive buyer. Jack told Mark (who paid cash for the goods) that the luggage was genuine alligator (a lie—he knew it was lizard). When Mark discovered the truth, he revoked his acceptance of the goods pursuant to §2-608 and claimed a security interest in the goods. Read §2-711(3). On learning of Jack's resale to Mark and of the latter's revocation of acceptance, Alligator Fashions decided to call the loan and repossess the luggage. Who is entitled to the luggage? See §9-110.

The rights of an unpaid seller are governed by both Article 2 and Article 9. If the seller gets a security agreement covering the item sold, a purchase money security interest (§9-103) arises, and Article 9 handles the priority in §9-324(a) and (b). If the seller extends credit to the buyer but fails to reserve a security interest, §2-702 applies. Finally, if the buyer gets the goods and pays with a check that is then dishonored ("N.S.F."—"not sufficient funds"), the seller's rights are governed by §§2-403, 2-507, and 2-511 (which you should now read), not by §2-702.

PROBLEM 338

Guy Baldwin was a successful author who decided to self-publish his latest book and market it directly to retailers. He received an order for 200 copies from Cowskin Book Chain, and he shipped off the books immediately, along with an invoice for their price. Two days later he learned that Cowskin was hopelessly insolvent and unable to pay any creditors. What can he do? See §2-702. Suppose that two weeks before he shipped the books, Cowskin had sent him a letter lying about its financial condition; now how long does he have to make his reclamation demand? If he gets the books back, can he sue Cowskin for the wasted shipping costs? See §2-702(3). If Cowskin's inventory was subject to a perfected security interest in favor of a bank, which thereby had a floating lien on the inventory, could he still reclaim the books? See §§2-702(3) and 2-403(1). Note that the definition of a *purchaser* in §1-201(32) and (33) includes any voluntary transferee, which would encompass secured parties. What should Baldwin have done? See §9-324(b).

If, in the last Problem, the buyer had filed a bankruptcy petition shortly before receiving the books, Bankruptcy Code §546(c) might allow him to recover the books from the bankruptcy trustee:

(c) ... [T]he rights and powers of a trustee under sections 544(a), 545, 547, and 549 of this title are subject to any statutory right or common-law right of a seller of goods that has sold goods to the debtor, in the ordinary course of such seller's business, to reclaim such goods if the debtor has received such goods while insolvent, but—

(1) such a seller may not reclaim any such goods unless such seller demands in writing reclamation of such goods before 20 days after receipt of such goods by the debtor; and

(2) the court may deny reclamation to a seller with such a right of reclamation that has made such a demand only if the court—

(A) grants the claim of such a seller priority as a claim of a kind specified in section 503(b) of this title [an administrative expense]; or

(B) secures such claim by a lien.

In re Arlco, Inc.

United States Bankruptcy Court, S.D.N.Y., 1999
239 B.R. 261, 39 U.C.C. Rep. Serv. 2d

ARTHUR J. GONZALEZ, Bankruptcy Judge.

On June 6, 1997, Arley Corporation ("Arley") and Home Fashions Outlet, Inc. ("Home Fashions" and together with Arley, the "Debtors") each filed a petition under chapter 11 of title 11 of the United States Code (the "Bankruptcy Code"). Arley was engaged in the business of manufacturing, importing, and wholesaling home furnishings, window coverings, bedcoverings, and linens which were sold to retailers, one of which was Home Fashions, Arley's wholly-owned subsidiary. Home Fashions operated retail outlet stores in Massachusetts and California. In addition, the Debtors maintained business and corporate offices, a showroom, and a design facility in New York. They also maintained business offices in Massachusetts and manufacturing facilities in Massachusetts, North Carolina, South Carolina, and California.

On September 15, 1997, pursuant to 11 U.S.C. §363, the Court approved an asset purchase agreement for the sale of substantially all of the Debtors' assets as a going concern. The asset purchase agreement included a requirement that the Debtors' change their corporate names contemporaneously with the closing of the sale transaction. Thus, Arley changed its name to Arlco, Inc. and Home Fashions changed its name to HFO, Inc. On August 6, 1998, the Debtors chapter 11 cases were converted to chapter 7. Thereafter, Robert Fisher, Esq. was appointed as chapter 7 trustee (the "Trustee").

Galey & Lord, Inc. ("Galey") is a fabric manufacturer. Prior to the filing of the Debtors' petitions, Galey, in its ordinary course of business, sold textile goods on credit to Arley. On May 16, 1997, Galey sent a letter to Arley by fax, overnight courier, and certified mail (the "May 16th Letter") demanding that Arley return the merchandise it "received during the applicable periods referred to in [§2-702 of the Uniform Commercial Code]" and notifying Arley that "all goods subject to [Galey's] right of reclamation should be protected and segregated by [Arley] and are not to be used for any purpose whatsoever." Subsequently, on May 21, 1997, Galey sent the Debtor an additional notice detailing each invoice issued to Arley within the 10-day period prior to May 16, 1997 for the goods allegedly subject to reclamation. Since early 1995, CIT Group/Business Credit Inc. ("CIT") has held a perfected security interest in substantially all Arley's assets, including accounts receivable and inventory.

On June 9, 1997, prior to the sale of the Debtors' assets, Galey commenced an adversary proceeding against Arley seeking reclamation of the textile goods referred to in the May 16th Letter. On June 11, 1997 Galey filed an Amended Complaint. Currently before the Court are motions for summary judgment filed by Galey and by the Trustee, respectively.

In its summary judgment motion, Galey maintains that it has complied with all the statutory requirements for establishing a valid claim for reclamation. The Trustee refutes Galey's contention and opposes entry of summary judgment in favor of Galey. Rather, the Trustee maintains that his arguments support entry of summary judgment in Arley's favor. The three principal reasons advanced by the Trustee in opposition to Galey's motion and in support of his own motion are that 1) the reclamation notice was legally deficient, 2) Galey failed to prove what goods Arley still had on hand when Galey made its demand, and 3) Galey's right to reclamation is subject to CIT's perfected security interest. In addition, Arley contends that there are factual disputes that preclude entry of summary judgment in favor of Galey.

DISCUSSION

The purpose of 11 U.S.C. §546(c) is to recognize any right to reclamation that a seller may have under applicable nonbankruptcy law. In re Victory Markets Inc., 212 B.R. 738, 741 (Bankr. N.D.N.Y. 1997). Section 546(c) does not create a new, independent right to reclamation but merely affords the seller an opportunity, with certain limitations, to avail itself of any reclamation right it may have under nonbankruptcy law. Id.; Toshiba America, Inc. v. Video King of Illinois, Inc. (In re Video King of Illinois, Inc.), 100 B.R. 1008, 1013 (Bankr. N.D. Ill. 1989). Pursuant to §546(c), a seller may reclaim goods it has sold to an insolvent debtor if it establishes:

(1)   that it has a statutory or common law right to reclaim the goods;

(2)   that the goods were sold in the ordinary course of the seller's business;

(3)   that the debtor was insolvent at the time the goods were received; and

(4)   that it made a written demand for reclamation within the statutory time limit after the debtor received the goods.

Victory Markets, 212 B.R. at 741. The reclaiming seller has the burden of establishing each element of §546(c) by a preponderance of the evidence. *Victory Markets*, 212 B.R. at 741. Thus, in addition to establishing the requirements necessary to obtain reclamation under common law or any statutory right for such relief, the seller seeking reclamation under §546(c) must prove that it sold the goods in the ordinary course of business and it made a written demand within ten days of the receipt of the goods. Pester Refining Co. v. Ethyl Corp. (In re Pester Refining Co.), 964 F.2d 842, 845 (8th Cir. 1992). Moreover, Bankruptcy Code §546(c) limits the definition of insolvency to that found in 11 U.S.C. §101(31). *Video King*, 100 B.R. at 1013.

In addition, to be subject to reclamation, goods must be identifiable and cannot have been processed into other products. Party Packing Corporation v. Rosenberg (In re Landy Beef Co., Inc.), 30 B.R. 19, 21 (Bankr. D. Mass. 1983). It has also been noted that "an implicit requirement of a §546(c) reclamation claim is that the debtor must possess the goods when the reclamation demand is made." Flav-O-Rich, Inc. v. Rawson Food Service, Inc. (In re Rawson Food Service, Inc.), 846 F.2d 1343, 1344 (11th Cir. 1988). . . . However, it is not clear "whether possession is an element under §546(c) of the Bankruptcy Code or in establishing an independent right of reclamation under nonbankruptcy law to be recognized under §546(c)." *Video King*, 100 B.R. at 1014. Logic dictates that, if not possession, the debtor should at least have control over the goods if it is to be required to return them. For the same reason, if the goods are not identifiable, the debtor could not identify or extract the goods to return them to the reclaiming seller. The issue concerning control of the goods or the identifiable nature of the goods would be relevant whether or not the reclaiming seller is seeking the goods in a bankruptcy context. Thus, it appears that these elements are requirements under the "independent right of reclamation under nonbankruptcy law." *Video King*, 100 B.R. at 1014.

Section 546(c) also affords the bankruptcy court broad discretion to substitute an administrative claim or lien in place of the right to reclaim. *Pester*, 964 F.2d at 845. This discretion gives the court needed flexibility and permits it to recognize the reclaiming creditor's rights while allowing the debtor the opportunity to retain the goods in order to facilitate the reorganization effort. Id.

Uniform Commercial Code ("U.C.C.") §2-702, as enacted in various jurisdictions, ordinarily forms the statutory right upon which sellers base their reclamation demand. Thus, as previously noted, the reclaiming seller must establish the requirements of the relevant U.C.C. section and remains subject to its limitations. Pursuant to U.C.C. §2-702(3), the seller's right to reclamation is "subject to" the rights of a good faith purchaser from the buyer. Pester, 964 F.2d at 844. . . . That the right of a reclaiming creditor is subordinate to that of a good faith purchaser does not automatically extinguish the reclamation right. *Pester*, 964 F.2d at 846. Rather, the reclaiming creditor is "relegated to some less commanding station." *Leeds*, 141 B.R. at 268.

Most courts have treated "a holder of a prior perfected, floating lien on inventory . . . as a good faith purchaser with rights superior to those of a reclaiming seller." See Victory Markets, 212 B.R. at 742 [many citations omitted]. Galey argues that the courts that have found parties with secured interests in inventory to be good faith purchasers have merely referred to the definitions of good faith purchaser under the U.C.C. §1-201(19), (32), and (33). Galey contends that because U.C.C. §2-702(3) refers to the reclaiming seller's interest as being subject to the interest of a good faith purchaser "under this Article," only parties acquiring their interests under Article 2 of the U.C.C. are the type of good faith purchasers encompassed within the protection of U.C.C. §2-702(3). Therefore, Galey contends that parties acquiring security interests under Article 9 of the U.C.C. are not included. Galey also points to the Seventh Circuit decision in *In re Reliable Drug Stores, Inc.*, where the court, in dicta, noted that there was room for debate as to whether a party with a security interest qualified as a good faith purchaser. 70 F.3d 948, 949 (7th Cir. 1995).

U.C.C. §2-702(3) provides that the right to reclamation is "subject to the rights of a buyer in ordinary course or other good faith purchaser under this Article (Section 2-403)." However, neither U.C.C. §2-403 nor any other section in Article 2 defines "good faith purchaser." U.C.C. §2-403 is entitled "Power to Transfer; Good Faith Purchase of Goods; Entrusting" and concerns the power certain parties have to transfer goods and the rights of certain parties who acquire those goods. While the section makes reference to these various parties, it does not define who they are. In fact, the only definition provided in U.C.C. §2-403 is of the term "entrusting." To derive the definition of "good faith purchaser," reference must be made to several subsections of U.C.C. §1-201, which provides general definitions applicable to the entire U.C.C. First, "good faith" is defined as "honesty in fact in the conduct or transaction concerned." U.C.C. §1-201(19). This is further refined when dealing with a merchant because U.C.C. §2-103(1)(b) requires the "observance of reasonable commercial standards of fair dealing in the trade." A "purchaser" is defined as one "who takes by purchase," U.C.C. §1-201(33), and "purchase" is defined to include "taking by sale, discount, negotiation, mortgage, pledge, lien, issue or re-issue, gift or any other voluntary transaction creating an interest in property." U.C.C. §1-201(32). Thus, the definition of purchaser is broad enough to include an Article 9 secured party, which then qualifies as a purchaser under U.C.C. §2-403. See *Samuels & Co.*, 526 F.2d at 1242. The reference in U.C.C. §2-702(3) to "the rights of a buyer in ordinary course or other good faith purchaser under this Article (Section 2-403)" does not mean to imply that reclaiming sellers are only subject to interests acquired under Article 2. Rather, the focus is on the rights of the listed parties under Article 2. Under this reading, the purpose for the reference to U.C.C. §2-403 is clear. U.C.C. §2-403 provides, in part, that "[a] person with voidable title has power to transfer a good title to a good faith purchaser for value." As included in the U.C.C. §1-201(44) definition, "value" is considered to be given for rights if they are acquired "as security for or in total or partial satisfaction of a pre-existing claim." Thus, under Article 2—specifically U.C.C. §2-403—the party who qualifies as a "good faith purchaser" as defined under U.C.C. §1-201 and gives "value," as defined in U.C.C. §1-201(44), acquires greater rights than the party transferring the goods to it had. Therefore, U.C.C. §2-403 gives a transferor, even one who has acquired goods wrongfully, the power to transfer the goods "to a Code-defined 'good faith purchaser.'" *Samuels & Co.*, 526 F.2d at 1242. Thus, in the instant case, if CIT qualifies as a good faith purchaser pursuant to U.C.C. §1-201 and gave value pursuant to U.C.C. §1-201(44), then pursuant to U.C.C. §2-403, even if Arley had voidable title to the goods, it could transfer good title under Article 2 to CIT. Further, if CIT obtained the goods in this manner, the demand of a reclaiming seller is subject to CIT's interest. U.C.C. §2-702(3). . . .

Galey also directs the Court's attention to dicta in *Reliable Drug*, 70 F.3d at 949-50, where the court noted that, although there was substantial case law holding that properly perfected lienholders were good faith purchasers, legal scholars debated the issue. The *Reliable Drug* court observed that one view was that "[U.C.C. §2-702)(2)] gives a vendor the rights of a purchase-money security holder for 10 days, and the purchase-money lender undoubtedly beats a creditor with a security interest in after-acquired inventory." Id. at 950 (citing, Thomas A. Jackson & Ellen Ash Peters, Quest for Uncertainty: A Proposal for Flexible Resolution of Inherent Conflicts Between Article 2 and Article 9 of the Uniform Commercial Code, 87 Yale L.J. 907, 965-70 (1977-78)). The law review article is premised on the view that a party with a security interest should only be considered a good faith purchaser for value if it has suffered detrimental reliance by extending new value. The authors of the article acknowledge that a prior secured lender with an after-acquired property interest "meets the apparently literal requirements of a good faith purchaser for value." 87 Yale L.J. at 965. Nevertheless, they argue that the "open-ended" language of U.C.C. §2-403, a comment to the section, and "the pervasive weighing of equities in Article 2" should "justify relying on [a] more flexible approach." 87 Yale L.J. at 966, 968.

However, if the language of a statute is plain, the court's role "is to enforce it according to its terms." U.S. v. Ron Pair Enterprises, Inc., 489 U.S. 235, 241, 109 S. Ct. 1026, 1030, 103 L. Ed. 2d 290 (1989). The Uniform Commercial Code includes "value" as being given for goods if they are acquired "as security for or in total or partial satisfaction of a pre-existing claim." U.C.C. §1-201(44). The state legislature is the appropriate forum to address the issue of whether or not the statute should be amended to allow a reclaiming seller priority against a prior secured lender with an after-acquired property interest who has not advanced new funding. However, this Court is required to interpret the statute as written and, based on our earlier analysis of the relevant sections of the Uniform Commercial Code as currently drafted, a creditor with a security interest in after-acquired property who acted in good faith and for value, which includes acquiring rights "as security for or in total or partial satisfaction of a pre-existing claim," U.C.C. §1-201(44), is a good faith purchaser to whose claim that of a reclaiming seller is subject.

The Court now turns to whether CIT acted in good faith. The U.C.C. definition of good faith is "honesty in fact," U.C.C. §1-201(19), which "for Article Two purposes, is 'expressly defined as . . . reasonable commercial standards of fair dealing.'" *Samuels & Co.*, 526 F.2d 1238 (5th Cir. 1976) (citing, U.C.C. §§1-201, Comment 19; 2-103(a)(2)).

Galey argues that a determination as to CIT's good faith cannot be made on summary judgment because there is a factual issue as to CIT's good faith. However, Galey has not challenged the validity of the lien nor has it asserted that there was any misconduct by CIT. Neither has it alleged that CIT acted in bad faith in its dealings with Arley. Rather, Galey argues that CIT was aware that Arley was having financial problems and stopped advancing funds to Arley without informing Galey of its decision. Therefore it appears that Galey's argument is that Arley was aware that other creditors would be impacted by its decision to stop funding Arley.

However, the secured creditor with a floating lien remains a good faith purchaser even if it terminates funding with knowledge that sums are owed to third parties, as long as the decision concerning the funding was commercially reasonable. *Samuels*, 526 F.2d at 1244. There is no allegation that the contract obligated CIT to advance any additional funds. The "honesty in fact" element does not require a secured creditor to continue to fund a business with enormous debt and continuous losses. Id.; Mitsubishi Consumer Electronics America, Inc. v. Steinberg's, Inc. (In re Steinberg's, Inc.), 226 B.R. 8, 11 (Bankr. S.D. Ohio 1998). Rather, a decision to stop funding such an enterprise is "clearly reasonable." *Samuels*, 526 F.2d at 1244. An entity that advances funds secured by a valid lien on all the borrower's assets is a good faith purchaser absent a showing of misconduct by the secured creditor. Pillsbury Co. v. FCX, Inc. (In re FCX, Inc.), 62 B.R. 315, 320 (Bankr. E.D.N.C. 1986). The burden is on the reclaiming seller to show misconduct by the secured creditor. *FCX, Inc.*, 62 B.R. at 322. Some courts have framed the issue as an absence of bad faith. *Victory Markets*, 212 B.R. at 742 (citing cases). Others as the secured creditor's lack of good faith. *Steinberg's Inc.*, 226 B.R. at 11 (citing cases). Under any formulation, the reclaiming seller bears the burden of proof under §546(c). Id.; *Victory Markets*, 212 B.R. at 741. . . .

Galey's conclusory assertions concerning the absence of good faith by CIT are not sufficient to create the fair doubt required to show that the issue is genuine. Galey makes no allegation of misconduct by CIT in its negotiations with Arley or in its compliance with the terms of the financing agreement with Arley. CIT has not set forth any basis upon which to question CIT's good faith. Thus, there is no genuine issue of material fact concerning whether CIT acted in good faith. Moreover, there is no factual dispute on the issue of whether CIT gave value and qualifies as a good faith purchaser for value, pursuant to the Code's definitions of the various terms. Therefore, the Court grants summary judgment on the issue and finds that CIT qualifies as a good faith purchaser for value.

As previously noted, while a seller's right to reclamation is subject to the rights of a good faith purchaser, the reclamation right is not automatically extinguished. Relying on this principle, Galey argues that, pursuant to §546, it is entitled to either an administrative claim or lien in lieu of its right to reclamation. Galey maintains that if it is denied this relief, its claim effectively is extinguished by the presence of a good faith purchaser. Further. Galey contends that because there will be surplus collateral once CIT has been paid in full, that collateral should be used to pay Galey's reclamation claim and it should get its administrative claim or lien on that surplus.

The Trustee counters that it is not arguing that a reclaiming seller's claim is extinguished. Rather, the Trustee argues that when the goods subject to a reclamation demand are liquidated and the proceeds are used to pay the secured creditor's claim, the reclaiming seller's subordinated right is rendered valueless. The Trustee maintains that once the secured creditor is paid in full, the reclaiming seller is only entitled to reclamation when the surplus collateral remaining consists of the very goods sold by the reclaiming seller or the traceable proceeds from those goods.

Courts differ on the treatment to be afforded reclaiming sellers subject to the superior rights of good faith purchasers. Some courts have awarded a reclaiming seller, who otherwise meets the criteria to qualify as a reclaiming seller but is subject to a superior claim, an administrative claim or replacement lien for the full amount of the goods sought to be reclaimed. *Sunstate Dairy*, 145 B.R. at 345-46; In re Diversified Food Service Distributors, Inc., 130 B.R. 427, 430 (Bankr. S.D.N.Y. 1991). However, the majority view appears to be some method of assuring that the reclaiming seller only receive what it would have received outside of the bankruptcy context after the superior claim was satisfied. *Pester*, 964 F.2d at 847; *Leeds*, 141 B.R. at 269; *Blinn*, 164 B.R. at 448; *Victory Markets*, 212 B.R. at 744. Thus, it is only when the reclaiming seller's goods or traceable proceeds from those goods are in excess of the value of the superior claimant's claim that the reclaiming seller will be allowed either to reclaim the goods or receive an administrative claim or lien in an amount equal to the goods that remain after the superior claim has been paid. . . .

Thus, while the reclaiming seller's claim is not automatically extinguished, the reclaiming seller is also not automatically granted an administrative claim or lien in the full amount sought when it is subject to the rights of the good faith purchaser. *Victory Markets*, 212 B.R. at 743. Rather, the reclaiming seller's right to reclaim depends on the value of the excess goods remaining once the secured creditor's claim is paid or released. Id.

As the bankruptcy filing does not enhance the reclaiming seller's rights, the Court should determine what would have happened to the reclaiming seller's claim in a nonbankruptcy context. The parties concede that under state law the secured creditor would have the option of proceeding against any of its collateral. Therefore, the secured creditor may choose to foreclose on the goods sold by the reclaiming seller if these goods can be readily liquidated. When the secured claim, or a portion of it, is paid out of the goods sought to be reclaimed, the right to reclaim is rendered valueless. *Pester,* 964 F.2d at 847. Thus, "in the non-bankruptcy context, the secured creditor's decision with respect to its security interest in the goods will determine the value of the seller's right to reclaim." *Pester,* 964 F.2d at 847. Here, following the Debtors' filing, CIT decided not to seek relief from the Court to pursue those remedies available to it to secure the immediate liquidation of all the Debtors' assets. Rather, it supported the Debtors' efforts to sell its inventory including any Galey goods in the ordinary course of its business. As a result, all of the goods which Galey sought to reclaim were sold and the proceeds used to pay CIT. Moreover, even after CIT received payment from the sale of the goods, there was still a balance due it. Thus, Galey's reclamation claim was rendered valueless. . . .

Finally, because this Court finds that Galey is not entitled to an administrative claim or replacement lien inasmuch as any right to reclamation it might have was subject to CIT's security interest and was rendered valueless by CIT's interest, it is unnecessary for the Court to reach the issue of whether Galey otherwise complied with all the requirements for a right to reclamation.

CONCLUSION

CIT, as the holder of a perfected security interest in substantially all Arley's assets including accounts receivable and inventory, is a good faith purchaser for value. Galey's interest as a reclaiming seller in the goods it sold Arley is subject to CIT's rights as a good faith purchaser. Galey's reclamation claim was rendered valueless because the proceeds from the disposition of the Galey goods were used to pay CIT's secured claim. Therefore, the value of any right Galey has to an administrative claim or replacement lien, pursuant to §546, is zero. . . .

The Trustee is to settle an Order consistent with this Memorandum Decision.

QUESTION

What could the seller have done is this situation in order to prevail over the floating lien that CIT had on the buyer's inventory? See §9-324(b).

PROBLEM 339

Octopus National Bank (ONB) held a perfected security interest in all the cattle owned by Family Farms of Iowa, Inc. (a Mom and Pop operation). When it became obvious that the farm was failing financially, ONB decided to pull the plug. Before it did so, it wanted to make sure that the cattle were well fed, so the ONB officer in charge of loan management called Cow Chow, Inc., and encouraged it to make another delivery of cattle feed to Family Farms, even though it had not been paid for its last two deliveries. ONB did not mention that it was about to foreclose on the fattened cattle, which it did as soon as they had consumed most of the new delivery (for which Cow Chow billed Family Farms in the amount of $10,000). Cow Chow was an unsecured creditor, which ONB well knew. Is ONB required to give Cow Chow any of the money it realizes from the foreclosure sale? See §§1-103 and 1-203; Ninth Dist. Prod. Credit Assn. v. Ed Duggan, Inc., 821 P.2d 788, 16 U.C.C. Rep. Serv. 2d 853 (Colo. 1991).

VII.   STATUTORY LIEN HOLDERS

Just as the buyer in the ordinary course of business is a favorite of the law, the repairperson in the ordinary course of business is frequently given priority over previously perfected consensual security interests. Read §9-333 and its Official Comments.

PROBLEM 340

The Repossession Finance Company (RFC) had a perfected security interest in Hattie Mobile's car (RFC's lien was noted on the certificate of title as required by state law). The car broke down on the interstate one day, and Hattie had it towed to Mike's Greasepit Garage, where it was repaired. State law gave a possessory artisan's lien to repairpersons. The garage told Hattie it was claiming such a lien, but when she pleaded with the manager, he let her drive the car to work after she assured him that she would return the car to the garage for storage every night (fortunately, she lived across the street). Repossession found out about this practice and, deeming itself insecure (§1-208), accelerated the amount due and repossessed the car from the parking lot in front of Hattie's place of business.

(a) Which creditor has the superior interest in the car under §9-333? Forrest Cate Ford v. Fryar, 62 Tenn. App. 572, 465 S.W.2d 882, 8 U.C.C. Rep. Serv. 239 (1970).

(b) If the car had been in Mike's possession when the conflict arose, would it matter under §9-333 that the finance company never gave its consent to the repairs? See Williamsport National Bank v. Shrey, 612 A.2d 1081, 19 U.C.C. Rep. Serv. 2d 623 (Pa. Super. 1992); Annot., 69 A.L.R.3d 1162.

(c) Once Mike's released the car to Hattie, did its lien reattach whenever she returned it to the garage? See M&I W. State Bank v. Wilson, 172 Wis. 2d 357, 493 N.W.2d 387, 19 U.C.C. Rep. Serv. 2d 615 (Ct. App. 1992).

If the garage's charges are unconscionably high, does the lien still prevail? See §1-203; G. Gilmore §33.5, at 888: "To be entitled to priority under [§9-333] the lienor must have furnished services or materials 'in the ordinary course of his business.' This limitation should be read as tantamount to a requirement of good faith. . . . Section [9-333] is designed to protect the honest lienor and not the crook."

VIII. FIXTURES

Article 9 of necessity had to make special rules for the creation and perfection of a *fixture*—the legal bugaboo that hangs in limbo somewhere between chattel mobility and realty attachment. See, e.g., §9-109(a) ("[T]his Article applies . . . to: (1) any transaction . . . that creates a security interest in personal property *or fixtures*. . . .") and §9-501(a)(1)(B) (directing that fixture filings be made in the real property records).

The Code has only the most limited definition of *fixtures:* "'Fixtures' means goods that have become so related to particular real property that an interest in them arises under real property law,"

§9-102(a)(41), and "A security interest does not exist under this article in ordinary building materials incorporated into an improvement on land," §9-334(a). Obviously pre-Code state law defining *fixtures* is very important. State law tests range from a pure *annexation* test (measured by the difficulty of removal) to an "intention of the parties" test (for which the leading case is Teaff v. Hewitt, 1 Ohio St. 511 (1853)). Moreover, some courts have developed different categories of fixtures. *Trade fixtures* are items of personal property necessary to the conduct of the tenant's business but not permanently affixed to the realty. They remain the tenant's and may be removed when the tenancy ends. Generally, the UCC courts treat a trade fixture as equipment and not as a true fixture, In re Factory Homes Corp., 333 F. Supp. 126, 9 U.C.C. Rep. Serv. 1330 (W.D. Ark. 1971), though the wide-awake lawyer will advise dual filings. A similar idea is the *assembled industrial plant* doctrine, which has it that all items connected with the operation of a going business are fixtures (primarily a Pennsylvania way of thinking; for the doctrine's clash with the UCC, see In re Griffin, 26 U.C.C. Rep. Serv. 2d 670 (Bankr. M.D. Pa. 1995)). For general treatise discussions of the meaning of *fixture,* see R. Powell, Real Property, ch. 57 (Rohan ed. 2000); G. Thompson, Real Property §46.02 (Thomas 1998 ed. 1998); M. Friedman, Contracts and Conveyances of Real Property §1.2(f) (6th ed. 1998); W. Stoebuck & D. Whitman, The Law of Real Property §6.48 (2000); 5 American Law of Property 19.1-19.4 (1952).

George v. Commercial Credit Corp.

United States Court of Appeals, Seventh Circuit, 1971
440 F.2d 551, 8 U.C.C. Rep. Serv. 1315

DUFFY, J. This is an appeal from an order of the District Court affirming the decision of a Referee in Bankruptcy and sustaining a secured creditor's interest in a mobile home.

The question before us for decision is whether appellee's real estate mortgage on his mobile home may prevail against the trustee's claimed interest.

The referee and the District Court upheld the appellee's claim finding that the mobile home had become a fixture under Wisconsin law. The trustee argues that the mobile home was not a fixture, in fact, and secondly, that the law of fixtures does not apply to security interests in mobile homes.

Dale Wallace Foskett owned five acres of land in Jefferson County, Wisconsin. On December 6, 1968, he purchased a Marshfield Mobile

Home, No. 9090, from Highway Mobile Home Sales, Inc. He signed an installment contract and paid $880 on the purchase price of $8,800. Added was a sales tax and interest covering a ten-year period.

Sometime in December 1968, Foskett executed a real estate mortgage to Highway Mobile Home Sales, Inc. The mortgage recites the sum of $14,227.70 and described the real estate in metes and bounds. The mortgage was assigned to Commercial Credit Corporation, the respondent-appellee herein.

The mobile home here in question could not move under its own power. It was delivered to Foskett's real property by Mobile Sales. This mobile home was never again operated on or over the highways as a motor vehicle.

The mobile home here in question was 68 feet in length, 14 feet in width and 12 feet in height. It contained six rooms and weighed 15,000 pounds.

The bankrupt owned no other home and he and his wife occupied the mobile home continuously from December 6, 1968, until forced to vacate same by order of the Trustee in Bankruptcy.

The home was set on cinder blocks three courses high. It was connected with a well. It was hooked up to a septic tank. It also was connected with electric power lines.

The bankrupt never applied for a certificate of title from the Wisconsin Motor Vehicle Department. However, he did apply for a home owner's insurance policy and he asked the seller to remove the wheels from his home. He also applied for a building permit and was told he had to construct a permanent foundation for the home. The permit was granted upon condition that the foundation be constructed within one year. However, within that period, the petition for bankruptcy was filed.

The issue before us can be thus stated: Commercial Credit Corporation argues that the mobile home was a fixture under applicable law and is not personalty. The trustee insists that the mobile home was and still is a "motor vehicle" and is personalty.

The mobile homes industry has grown rapidly in the last few years. There has been a great demand for relatively inexpensive housing by middle income families. In Wisconsin, a distinction is now recognized between mobile homes (those used as homes) and motor homes (those often used as vehicles).

In the recent case of Beaulieu v. Minnehoma Insurance Co., 44 Wis. 2d 437, 171 N.W.2d 348 (1969), the Wisconsin Supreme Court pointed out the unique character of mobile homes: "As indicated by the plaintiff, a mobile home has a dual nature. It is designed as a house; yet, unlike a house, it is also capable of being easily transported. In the instant case, it was employed solely as an economical means of housing. It was never moved, nor was moving contemplated at the time the insurance coverage was procured." (44 Wis. 2d at 439).

We look to state law to determine the applicable standards for determining when personalty becomes affixed to real property.

The Wisconsin law on the question is found in Auto Acceptance and Loan Corp. v. Kelm, 18 Wis. 2d 178, 118 N.W.2d 175 (1962) where the Wisconsin Supreme Court reaffirmed its decision in Standard Oil Co. v. LaCrosse Super Auto Service, Inc., 217 Wis. 237, 258 N.W. 791 (1935). That case held that the three tests for determining whether facilities remain personalty or are to be considered part of the realty are (1) actual physical annexation to the realty; (2) application or adaption to the use or purpose to which the realty is devoted, and (3) intention of the person making annexation to make a permanent accession to the freehold.

In the *Standard Oil Company* case, supra, the court pointed out that "physical annexation" is relatively unimportant and "intention" of the parties is the principal consideration.

In Premonstratensian Fathers v. Badger Mutual Insurance Co., 46 Wis. 2d 362, 175 N.W.2d 237 (1970), the court reaffirmed its adherence to the three-fold test saying, (46 Wis. 2d at p.367) "It is the application of these tests to the facts of a particular case which will lead to a determination of whether or not an article, otherwise considered personal property, constitutes a common-law fixture, and hence takes on the nature of real property."

Viewed in light of these Wisconsin tests, the finding of the referee and the District Court that this mobile home had become a fixture must clearly stand. The bankrupt's actual intention pointed definitely toward affixing the mobile home to the land as a permanent residence, as seen in his application for a building permit (which, by law, required him to erect a concrete slab as a permanent foundation within one year), his purchase of a homeowner's insurance policy, and his requests made to the seller to have the wheels of the home removed. Moreover, the home was clearly adapted to use as the permanent residence of the bankrupt and was never moved off of his five-acre plot.

The fact that it may have been physically possible for this mobile home to have been more securely attached to the ground should not alter our position. Physical attachment did occur by means of cinder blocks and a "C" clamp, while connections for electricity, sewage and natural gas were provided as well. Finally, we note that the very size and difficulty in transporting this mobile home further highlight the fact that this was a vehicle which was intended primarily to be placed in one position for a long period of time and to be used as an intended permanent home. . . .

Our reading of the Wisconsin Statutes is thus consistent with other statutory and common law provisions dealing with the fixture situation, such as §9-334 of the Uniform Commercial Code which takes care to state that the Code does *not* prevent creation of encumbrances upon fixtures or real estate pursuant to the law applicable to real estate. (See also 4A Collier on Bankruptcy, §70.20 pp.283-295.)

In view of our holding that this particular mobile home had become a fixture under Wisconsin law and that the law of fixtures may, by law, be applied to mobile homes in that state, the judgment of the District must be and is

Affirmed.

NOTE

See White & Summers §24-8. Then there is this oft-quoted passage from Strain v. Green, 25 Wash. 2d 692, 695, 172 P.2d 216, 218 (1946):

> [W]e will not undertake to write a Treatise on the law of fixtures. Every lawyer knows that cases can be found in this field that will support any position that the facts of his particular case require him to take. . . . [T]here is a wilderness of authority. . . . Fixture cases are so conflicting that it would be profitless . . . to review . . . them.

In theory, your basic property course taught you to tell fixtures from non-fixtures. Our main concern is resolution of priority disputes between those who have a security interest in the fixture and those who have or acquire an interest in the realty to which the collateral is affixed. Read §9-334 carefully, and then consider these Problems.

PROBLEM 341

Monopoly Railway went to Octopus National Bank (ONB) and asked to borrow money, using as part of the collateral its extensive network of railroad track (rails and ties), which winds through 12 western states. ONB consults you. The track is installed in a total of 117 counties. Must it file a financing statement in each one? See §§9-501(b) and 9-102(a)(80).

PROBLEM 342

Simon Mustache decided to erect an apartment building on a vacant lot he owned, so he borrowed $4 million from Construction State Bank (CSB), to which he mortgaged the real estate "and all appurtenances or things affixed thereto, now present or after-acquired." Simon and CSB signed the mortgage, which contained a legal description of the realty, and the mortgage was filed in the real property recorder's office. Is the mortgage effective as a financing statement? See §9-502(c). During construction of the apartment building, Simon Mustache bought a furnace on credit from Blast Home Supplies, giving Blast a security interest in the furnace that described the real estate. Where should Blast file its financing statement? See §9-501. Is there a technical sentence that needs to be in this financing statement? See §9-502(b)(2). Why would the drafters have added such a requirement? Even if Blast files a proper financing statement in the right place before the furnace is installed, will Blast prevail over CSB? See §9-334(d) and (h), and Official Comment 11. If CSB's interest is not perfected, will Blast prevail? See §9-334(e)(1). What can Blast do to ensure itself of priority? See §§9-334(f)(1), 9-339.

PROBLEM 343

Would your answer to the last Problem's priority disputes change if the object in question were a refrigerator? What if it were a computer that Simon purchased for use in his office (which is located in the apartment building)? (Note: some states would consider the computer a *fixture* under the *industrial plant* doctrine; see the discussion above.) See §9-334(e)(2) and (f)(2), and Official Comment 8.

Lewiston Bottled Gas Co. v. Key Bank of Maine

Maine Supreme Judicial Court, 1992
601 A.2d 91, 17 U.C.C. Rep. Serv. 2d 282

CLIFFORD, J. Plaintiff Lewiston Bottled Gas Company (LBG) appeals from an order of summary judgment entered by the Superior Court (Androscoggin County, Perkins, J.) in favor of defendant Key Bank of Maine in this declaratory judgment action brought to determine the rights of the parties with respect to ninety heating and air-conditioning units installed in the Grand Beach Inn at Old

Orchard Beach. We agree with the Superior Court that Key Bank's mortgage gives it priority over LBG's purchase money security interest in the units and we affirm the judgment.

In July 1986, Key Bank loaned $2,580,000 to William J. DiBiase, Jr. The loan was secured by a mortgage on the real estate owned by DiBiase located on East Grand Avenue in Old Orchard Beach. The mortgage, which covered after-acquired fixtures, was properly recorded in the York County Registry of Deeds. On June 10, 1987, DiBiase incorporated Grand Beach Inn., Inc. (Grand Beach) for the purpose of constructing and operating the Grand Beach Inn on DiBiase's East Grand Avenue property. DiBiase was the president and sole shareholder of Grand Beach and at all relevant times was the owner of the property.

On June 15, 1987, Grand Beach contracted to purchase ninety heating and air-conditioning units from LBG. The contract provided that the units would remain the personal property of Grand Beach notwithstanding their attachment to the real property. On June 16, Grand Beach granted to LBG a purchase money security interest in the ninety units. Financing statements disclosing the security interest and identifying the debtor as "Grand Beach Inn, Inc., William J. DiBiase, Jr., President" and describing the real estate upon which the units were located as "Grand Beach Inn, East Grand Avenue, Old Orchard Beach, ME 04064" were filed with the Secretary of State and also recorded in the York County Registry of Deeds. In each place, they were indexed under the name "Grand Beach Inn, Inc." Nothing, however, was indexed under DiBiase's name. In September and October 1987, the units were installed in the exterior walls of each room in the Inn.

On June 29, 1987, Key Bank made a second loan to DiBiase secured by a second mortgage on the same property, also covering after-acquired fixtures and also properly recorded. The title search undertaken by Key Bank in the York County Registry of Deeds prior to the execution of the mortgage failed to disclose the financing statement and the existence of LBG's security interest in the units because LBG's financing statement was indexed under the name "Grand Beach" even though DiBiase was the record owner of the property at the time.

In May 1989, Key Bank foreclosed on both its mortgages. LBG was not joined as a party-in-interest because Key Bank was unaware of LBG's interest in the units until after the foreclosure was commenced. The parties agreed to allow the foreclosure to proceed and to litigate the issue of title to the heating and air-conditioning units later. Key Bank was the successful bidder at the foreclosure sale. LBG then filed the present complaint against Key Bank seeking a declaratory judgment that its purchase money security interest in the units had priority over the interest of Key Bank. The Superior Court granted summary judgment to Key Bank concluding that the heating and air-conditioning units were fixtures and that Key Bank's properly recorded mortgages had priority over LBG's unperfected security interest. This appeal followed. . . .

II.   UNITS AS FIXTURES

11 M.R.S.A. §9-313(1)(a) [the predecessor to §9-334—Ed.] (1964 & Supp. 1991) provides that "[g]oods are 'fixtures' when they become so related to particular real estate that an interest in them arises under real estate law." That interest arises when the property is (1) physically annexed to the real estate, (2) adapted to the use to which the real estate is put, that is, the personal and real property are united in the carrying out of a common purpose, and (3) annexed with the intent to make it part of the realty. Boothbay Harbor Condominiums, Inc. v. Department of Transp., 382 A.2d 848, 854 (Me. 1978) (citing Bangor-Hydro Elec. Co. v. Johnson, 226 A.2d 371, 378 (Me. 1967)).

The evidence compels a conclusion that, under the first prong of the three-part fixture test, the units were physically annexed to the real estate. The heating and air-conditioning units were installed when the Inn was under construction and are part of the walls of the building. The units are attached by bolts and although they could be removed, their removal would create a large hole in the walls of each room. See Roderick v. Sanborn, 106 Me. 159, 162, 76 A. 263 (1909) (property need not be permanently fastened to realty to be physically annexed).

As to the second prong of the test, it is undisputed that the units, although they are catalogue items and not specially made for the Grand Beach Inn, were adapted to the use of the real estate as the Grand Beach Inn. The real estate was designed and built as an inn to accommodate overnight guests. The heating and air-conditioning units help create a livable atmosphere for those guests by providing heat and cooling to the rooms. The personal and real property, therefore, are united in the carrying out of a common enterprise. See *Bangor-Hydro*, 226 A.2d at 376. The fact that the units are catalogue items, and not custom-made, does not preclude them from being fixtures.

The intent of the person annexing the personal property to the real estate is the third and most important of the three prongs of the fixture test. *Bangor-Hydro*, 226 A.2d at 377. LBG contends that summary judgment was improperly granted to Key Bank because the agreements between DiBiase and LBG granted to LBG a purchase money security interest in the units and expressly stated that the units would remain personal property and therefore demonstrated DiBiase's intent that the units remain personal property. We disagree.

In determining the intent of the parties as to whether a chattel annexed to real estate becomes a fixture, it is not the hidden subjective intent of the person making the annexation that must be considered but rather "the intention which the law deduces from such external facts as the structure and mode of attachment, the purpose and use for which the annexation has been made and the relation and use of the party making it." *Bangor-Hydro*, 226 A.2d at 378. The agreement DiBiase made with LBG to have the heating and air-conditioning units remain personal property cannot be considered against Key Bank on the fixtures issue because Key Bank was not a party to those agreements and was unaware of them. Vorsec Co. v. Gilkey, 132 Me. 311, 314, 170 A. 722 (1934); Gaunt v. Allen Lane Co., 128 Me. 41, 46, 145 A. 255 (1929).

The objective manifestation of intent in this case, as evidenced by the physical annexation of the units to the walls of the building and their adaptation to the use of the real estate as an inn, leaves no genuine dispute that the units are fixtures and part of the Grand Beach Inn real estate.

III. LBG's Failure to Perfect Its Security Interest

Because the heating and air-conditioning units were fixtures and part of the real estate, they became subject to Key Bank's mortgages pursuant to §9-313. Key Bank's first mortgage takes priority over LBG's security interest in the units unless LBG's security interest falls within one of the exceptions found in §9-313. 11 M.R.S.A. §9-313(7) (Supp. 1991). The only relevant exception in this case is §9-313(4)(a) [now §9-334(d)—Ed.], which states:

> (4) A perfected security interest in fixtures has priority over the conflicting interest of an encumbrancer or owner of the real estate where:
> (a) The security interest is a purchase money security interest, the interest of the encumbrancer or owner arises before the goods become fixtures, the security interest is perfected by a fixture filing before the goods become fixtures or within 10 days thereafter, and the debtor has an interest of record in the real estate or is in possession of the real estate.

The security interest of LBG was a purchase money security interest. 11 M.R.S.A §9-107 (1964). The record clearly demonstrates, however, that it was not properly perfected and does not otherwise come within any recognized exception that would give it priority over Key Bank's first mortgage.

A security interest is perfected when it has attached and all of the applicable steps required for perfection have been taken. 11 M.R.S.A. §9-303(1)(1964). To perfect a security interest in a fixture, the secured party must file a "fixture filing." "A 'fixture filing' is the filing in the office where a mortgage on the real estate would be filed or recorded of a financing statement covering goods which are or are to become fixtures and conforming to the requirements of section 9-402, subsection (5)." 11 M.R.S.A. §9-313(1)(b) (Supp. 1991). Section 9-402(5) (Supp. 1991) requires that, in addition to the general requirements for financing statements set forth in §9-402(1) (the name and signature of the debtor, the name and address of the secured party and a description of the collateral), the fixture filing must contain a description of the real estate and, if the debtor does not have an interest of record in the real estate, "the financing statement must show *the name of a record owner.*" 11 M.R.S.A. §9-402(5) (emphasis added).

In this case, LBG's financing statement was correctly filed in the York County Registry of Deeds, identified the debtor as "Grand Beach Inn, Inc., William J. DiBiase, Jr., President," and contained a description of the real estate that we assume is adequate. Because it failed to identify DiBiase as the record owner of the property, however, the financing statement does not comply with §9-402(5).

As a general rule, a financing statement is sufficient if, in all the circumstances, the filing would give a title searcher sufficient notice to justify placing a duty upon the searcher to make further inquiry concerning the possible lien. In the Matters of Reeco Elec. Co., 415 F. Supp. 238, 240 (D. Me. 1976). In this case, the financing statement was indexed under "Grand Beach Inn, Inc." A title searcher would not be expected to check the index for "Grand Beach Inn, Inc." at a time when the property is owned by DiBiase. Because LBG failed to perfect its security interest in the heating and air-conditioning units pursuant to §9-402(5), the rights of Key Bank as mortgage holder of the real estate to which the units are affixed take priority over LBG's unperfected security interest.

The entry is: Judgment affirmed.

All concurring.

PROBLEM 344

Simon Mustache (of the last Problem) failed to pay his attorney, Susan Mean, so she sued him, recovered judgment, and levied on the apartment building and its contents. Will Simon's creditors holding security interests in the fixtures prevail if they have perfected by fixture filings? See §9-334(e)(3). What if those creditors filed financing statements in all the correct places *except* the real estate records? See Official Comment 9 to §9-334; In re Allen, 35 U.C.C. Rep. Serv. 2d 1029 (Bankr. S.D. Ill. 1998).

PROBLEM 345

After the building was complete, Tuesday Tenant moved in. Not liking the refrigerator Simon had installed, she had him remove it, and she bought another refrigerator on time from Easy Credit Department Store, which reserved a security interest therein but never filed a financing statement. Assume state real property laws permit CSB's after-acquired property mortgage to reach fixtures installed by lessees. (If they do not, Easy Credit will always prevail. See §9-334(f)(2).) Will Easy Credit be entitled to priority if it is forced to repossess? See §9-334(e)(2)(C) and Official Comment 8, third paragraph.

PROBLEM 346

Assume Tuesday (last Problem) bought a trash compactor on credit from Easy Credit Department Store and had her kitchen area re-modeled to accommodate it. It was installed on May 5. Easy Credit comes to you on May 7. Is it entitled to automatic perfection of its security interest in consumer goods here? See Official Comment 3 (last sentence) to §9-309. Suppose it has a financing statement indicating the debtor is Tuesday. Should the statement contain Simon Mustache's name too? Why? See §9-502(b)(4). Will Easy Credit prevail over CSB if it files on May 10? See §9-334(d). Will it prevail over Simon's land-lord's lien?

PROBLEM 347

Assume that Blast Home Supplies held a perfected security interest in Simon's furnace and that this interest was entitled to priority over CSB, the real estate mortgagee. If Simon defaults on his payments, what liability does Blast have to CSB if removal (repossession) of the furnace will do $1,000 damage to the building's structure and if to replace it Simon (or CSB) will have to spend $8,000? See §9-604 and its Official Comment 2. What are CSB's rights? See the last sentence of §9-604(d). Is Blast liable to Simon for the damage to the building caused by the furnace's removal?

Maplewood Bank & Trust v. Sears, Roebuck & Co.

New Jersey Superior Court, Appellate Division, 1993
625 A.2d 537, 21 U.C.C. Rep. Serv. 2d 171

COLEMAN, P.J.A.D. This appeal requires us to decide whether a first mortgage lender or a fixture financier is entitled to priority in the funds realized from a foreclosure sale of the mortgaged premises. We hold that a first mortgage is entitled to priority in such funds.

Plaintiff Maplewood Bank and Trust is the holder of a first purchase money mortgage dated September 20, 1988, and recorded on October 5, 1988, on premises owned by defendants Edward and Terre Capers. The original mortgage debt was for $121,000. On May 31, 1989, Sears, Roebuck and Company (Sears) filed a financing statement covering a completely new kitchen, consisting of "new countertops, cabinets, sinks, disposal unit, dishwasher, oven, cooktop and hood," installed in the mortgaged premises at the request of the Capers after they executed a security agreement. The financing statement, known as the UCC-1 form, filed by Sears gave notice that Sears had a security interest in the new kitchen installed in the mortgaged premises in the sum of $33,320.40.

On August 18, 1989, the Capers executed a second mortgage on the previously mortgaged premises to defendant New Jersey Savings Bank for the sum of $34,000. That mortgage was recorded on August 23, 1989.

When the Capers eventually defaulted in the payments due plaintiff and Sears, plaintiff declared the entire unpaid balance on the mortgage was due. Nonpayment of the entire balance plus interest prompted plaintiff to file its complaint for foreclosure on November 5, 1990, and an amended complaint on or about December 6, 1990. Sears filed an answer and a counterclaim. Sears sought a declaration that its debt was "prior to the mortgage of the plaintiff" and, among other things, to compel plaintiff to "pay [Sears] the amount due on its Agreement." The essence of the counterclaim was that under N.J.S.A. 12A:9-313 [now §9-334—Ed.], Sears was entitled to priority over the plaintiff in the funds realized from the anticipated foreclosure sale. Sears' answer and counterclaim were stricken on July 26, 1991, and the matter proceeded as an uncontested foreclosure action. A final judgment in foreclosure was entered on February 28, 1992.

Sears has appealed the dismissal of its counterclaim. It argues that the priority given Sears as a purchase money security interest holder under the Uniform Commercial Code "applies to the proceeds of a judicial sale instituted" by a purchase money mortgagee. This is the same issue Sears raised in Orange Savings Bank v. Todd, 48 N.J. 428, 430 (1967), wherein Sears asserted that it was entitled to priority over the purchase money mortgagee "in the funds realized on foreclosure." Ibid. The Supreme Court concluded that although the briefs raised "interesting and important questions under the secured transactions provisions of the Uniform Commercial Code (N.J.S.A. 12A:9-101 et seq.), we find no present occasion to deal with any of them in view of the position now taken by the parties." Ibid. In the present case, we have considered the contention raised by Sears and conclude that it is unsound and must be rejected.

It is undisputed that the new kitchen Sears installed and financed satisfies the definition of a fixture under N.J.S.A. 12A:9-313(1)(a). It is also undisputed that Sears obtained a purchase money security interest in the fixture to secure full payment. See N.J.S.A. 12A:9-107(a) [now §9-103—Ed.]. Sears perfected its security interest by filing a financing statement (UCC-1) covering the fixtures in the Hunterdon County Clerk's Office where the first mortgage held by plaintiff was recorded. N.J.S.A. 12A:9-313(b) and N.J.S.A. 12A:9-402(5) [now §9-502—Ed.].

The purchase money security interest of Sears attached to the goods or chattels before they became affixed to the realty as fixtures. N.J.S.A. 12A:9-313(4)(a). By perfecting the security interest, Sears was able to make its security interest in the fixtures permanent, or until paid or discharged. The point to be made is that Sears' security interest is limited to the fixtures and does not extend to the realty otherwise.

By statute, Sears' purchase money security interest, when perfected, "has priority over the conflicting interest of an encumbrancer or owner of the real estate." N.J.S.A. 12A:9-334(4). This concept was expressed more clearly in the version of the statute which predated the 1981 amendments. The prior version of N.J.S.A. 12A:9-313(2) provided

"A security interest which attaches to goods before they become fixtures takes priority as to the goods over the claims of all persons who have an interest in the real estate except as stated in subsection (4)." This means the purchase money security interest of Sears in the goods or chattels which became fixtures gives it a "super priority" as to those goods or chattels which became fixtures.

Next we must focus upon the remedies available to a purchase money security interest lienholder upon default by the debtor. Sears contends it should be entitled to receive from the proceeds obtained at the foreclosure sale, the difference between the value of the realty with the new kitchen and the value of the realty after the new kitchen has been removed. We reject this entire approach as an inappropriate remedy absent authorization by statute. The Uniform Commercial Code, as adopted in New Jersey, provides at N.J.S.A. 12A:9-313(8) [now §9-604—Ed.] that:

> When the secured party has priority over all owners and encumbrancers of the real estate, *he may* on default, subject to the provisions of sub-chapter 5, *remove his collateral from the real estate* but he must reimburse any encumbrancer or owner of the real estate who is not the debtor and who has not otherwise agreed for the cost of repair of any physical injury, but not for any diminution in value of the real estate caused by the absence of the goods removed or by any necessity of replacing them. . . . (Emphasis added).

Thus based on the plain language of §9-313(8), Sears has two options: removal of the fixtures or foregoing removal of the fixtures.

New York, the only other jurisdiction which has addressed the issue, rejected Sears' argument. In Dry Dock Savings Bank v. DeGeorgio, 305 N.Y.S.2d 73 (1969), the defense asserted a lien superior to the mortgage by reason of a properly filed fixture financial statement covering aluminum siding on a house which was the subject of a foreclosure action. The mortgage was recorded prior to the time the fixture financial statement was filed.

The court held that under §9-313 the purchase money security interest holder may remove his fixtures from the real estate, but must reimburse any owner or encumbrancer for the cost of repair. Id. at 75. The court observed: "He merely has the right to remove the goods after posting security to repair any damage. This may turn out to be a somewhat Pyrrhic victory, giving the lienor a pile of dubious scrap not worth the labor of getting it off the house, repairing nail holes, etc. . . . [Removal] may hurt the mortgagee without doing the lienor any corresponding good. However, that is something for the parties to consider and beyond the control of the court." Ibid.

In Nu-Way Distributing Corp. v. Schoikert, 355 N.Y.S.2d 475, 14 U.C.C. Rep. Serv. 1058 (N.Y. App. Div. 1974), plaintiff instituted an action to recover the price of fixtures (kitchen cabinets, etc.) sold by plaintiff, after the goods or chattels had been installed in the realty as fixtures. The Appellate Division construed §9-313 "as merely providing the creditor with the statutory right of repossession, provided that he first comply with the security provision of the statute." Id. at 476.

The Appellate Division opined that even if the purchase money security interest holder failed or did not desire to repossess the fixtures upon default, that lienholder was not entitled to maintain an action for the purchase price against a subsequent purchaser of the real property. Ibid. The court further held that the same rule would apply even in cases where the fixtures are custom-made and would be of no use or value should they be repossessed. The underlying rationale for the rule was that such a lienholder as the one involved in *Nu-Way* must be assumed to have known and understood the risk he was taking.

Sears' approach has been adopted only in Louisiana and there it was based on the legislature's definitive modification of §9-313(8) by adding the following language:

A secured party may also demand separate appraisal of the fixtures to fix his interest in the receipts of the sale thereof in any proceedings in which the real estate is sold pursuant to execution upon it by a mortgagee or other encumbrancer. [Uniform Commercial Code §9-313, 3 U.L.A. 332 to 23 (1992) (Action in Adopting Jurisdictions).]

The most compelling authority supportive of Sears' position is an article "An Integrated Financing System for Purchase Money Collateral: A Proposed Solution to the Fixture Problem Under Section 9-313 of the Uniform Commercial Code" by Morris G. Shanker. 73 Yale L.J. 795 (1964). In this article, Professor Shanker states "[w]here the fixture secured debt is not paid, removal of the fixture seems to be the favorite means of foreclosing on the fixture security interest." Id. at 804.

The article goes on to cite certain instances where the fixture secured party may prefer not to exercise his removal rights. For example, if an elevator was designed for a specific building, it would have little or no value apart from that building. Ibid. Other cited examples include situations where a fixture secured party should be required to use judicial foreclosure proceedings even though he has the right of removal. For example, a secured party should not be free to remove a heating system in a large apartment building in the dead of winter, even where the debtor defaulted.

Shanker opines that "the Code, as it now stands, probably authorizes the fixture secured party to employ judicial foreclosure proceedings to enforce his security interest" in lieu of removal of the fixtures. Ibid. He states that limiting the remedy to the right to remove or choosing not to remove, in no way detracts from the fixture secured party's paramount security interest in his collateral; it merely requires him to enforce his security interest in a sensible and equitable fashion. Id. at 805.

We decline to adopt the creative approach articulated by Professor Shanker. Such action, in our view, would be legislating. We prefer the approach followed in Louisiana where the legislature, upon its preference and initiative, provided the innovative remedy sought by Sears. To adopt Sears' argument in the absence of legislation, would mean that a mortgagee's security interest could be impaired substantially without the legislature pronouncing an intention to do so. Any modification of long established fundamental property rights of purchase money mortgagees must be done in some straightforward manner and may not be implied from the existing statute. The fact that fixtures may be custom-made does not require any different result. See *Nu-Way*, supra, 355 N.Y.S.2d at 476.

We are also persuaded that Sears is not entitled to any remedy, other than removal of the fixtures, based on equitable principles. Sears knew its remedy was limited to removal upon default. Indeed, the Retail Installment Contract and Security Agreement prepared by Sears and signed by the Capers provided that the Capers were giving Sears a "security interest under the Uniform Commercial Code in all merchandise purchased under this contract . . . [and] *the security interest allows Sears to repossess the merchandise*" in the event the Capers did not make payments as agreed. (Emphasis added.)

Summary judgment in favor of plaintiff is affirmed.

NOTE

Professor Shanker appears to have prevailed on this issue, since revised Article 9 has very different rules for repossessing fixture creditors in §9-604, and Official Comment 3 to that section specifically states that it was meant to overrule the case you have just read. But what does that mean in the context of the facts of the case? What could Sears do if §9-604 had been the law when the case was decided? See

Timothy R. Zinnecker, The Default Provisions of Revised Article 9 of the Uniform Commercial Code: Part I, 54 Bus. Law. 1113, 1124-1128 (1999).

It should also be noted that a creditor who is repossessing a fixture is bound by all the usual repossession rules that we study will in Chapter 9 (and therefore cannot breach the peace; see §9-609, for example).

PROBLEM 348

Farmer Bean had a filed mortgage on his home in favor of Rural State Bank. The mortgage stated that it extended to the realty and all things "growing on, or attached thereto, now in existence or in the future." When Farmer Bean borrowed money to plant this year's crop, he gave a security interest in the crop to Seeds, Inc., the purchase money lender. If the latter files its financing statement in the appropriate place, will it prevail over Rural State's mortgage lien? See §9-334(i), and its Official Comment 12.

PROBLEM 349

When Farmer Bean bought a doublewide trailer from Traveling Homes, Inc. for $100,000, he had it towed to a vacant lot on his farm with police protection en route, and large WIDE LOAD signs attached. That was the only trip the doublewide made in its life. It was then placed on a foundation that had been built on the vacant lot, attached to various utilities for electricity and water, and Farmer Bean built a fancy deck that he extended out the front door of the trailer. If you are the attorney representing the bank that loaned Farmer Bean the money to buy the doublewide, what steps should be taken to perfect its purchase money security interest in the collateral: a real estate mortgage, a fixture filing under Article 9 of the Uniform Commercial Code, or notation of the bank's interest on a certificate of title issued for the doublewide? See §9-334(e)(4); White & Summers §22-5(5).

IX. ACCESSIONS AND COMMINGLING

When goods are affixed to other goods (as opposed to realty), an *accession* occurs, and the rights of the creditors are regulated by §9-335.

A similar problem arises when goods are so combined with other goods (eggs in a cake mix, for example) that they cannot be recovered. See §9-336 on *commingling*. Article 9's contribution to the solution to these problems can only be completely understood in light of centuries of property law development. A lawyer embroiled in litigation should review the basic common law rules. See G. Thompson, Real Property §13.04(g)(6) (Thomas 1998 ed. 1998); W. Stoebuck & D. Whitman, The Law of Real Property §6.48 (2000).

PROBLEM 350

Victor Valises was a traveling salesman. He owned a Ford in which the Salesmen's Credit Union held a perfected security interest, which was duly noted on the certificate of title. When the tires were worn out, he bought new ones from the Yeti Tire Company, which claimed a purchase money security interest in the tires and filed a financing statement covering them in the appropriate place. Will the credit union or the tire company have priority in the tires? See §9-335(d) and its Official Comment 7; but see Paccar Financial Corp. v. Les Schwab Tire Centers of Montana, Inc., 920 P.2d 977, 31 U.C.C. Rep. Serv. 2d 1197 (Mont. 1996) (easily removable items like tires are not accessions).

X.   FEDERAL PRIORITIES FOR DEBTS AND TAXES

A.   The Federal Priority Statute

Most of the federal statutes concerning secured transactions are registration acts only and say little or nothing about priorities in the collateral. There are two major exceptions: the general federal priority statute, 31 U.S.C. §3713, and the Federal Tax Lien Act, which is part of the Internal Revenue Code (§§6321 to 6323).

The federal priority statute is a broadly worded grant of pre-bankruptcy priority for *all* federal claims (no matter how they arise: as tax matters, contract debts, federal insurance loans, guaranties, etc.), so these claims are paid first when a debtor becomes insolvent.

Priority of Government Claims 31 U.S.C. §3713

(a) (1) A claim of the United States Government shall be paid first when—

(A) a person indebted to the Government is insolvent and—

(i) the debtor without enough property to pay all debts makes a voluntary assignment of property;

(ii) property of the debtor, if absent, is attached; or

(iii) the act of bankruptcy is committed; or

(B) the estate of a deceased debtor, in the custody of the executor or administrator, is not enough to pay all debts of the debtor.

(2) This section does not apply to a case under title 11 [Bankruptcy].

(b) A representative of a person or an estate (except a trustee acting under title 11) paying any part of a debt of the person or estate before paying a claim of the Government is liable to the extent of the payment for unpaid claims of the Government.

The statute makes no exceptions to absolute federal priority, but the courts have subordinated the federal claim to an earlier lien (judicial, statutory, and consensual) if the lien is *choate*. The United States Supreme Court, in a maddening series of cases, has refused to clarify the meaning of *choate*, so it is difficult to predict when an earlier perfected lien will be sufficiently choate to prevail over the federal debt. In Illinois ex rel. Gordon v. Campbell, 329 U.S. 362 (1946), the Court held that a lien is choate (and therefore superior to the federal interest) if the lien is "definite . . . in at least three respects: . . . (1) the identity of the lienor . . . ; (2) the amount of the lien . . . ; and (3) the property to which it attaches." In the *Campbell* case the Court held that a state statutory lien for unemployment contributions that purported to cover "all the personal property . . . used . . . in business" was not choate because the collateral's description was too vague under test number (3), above. In a later case, United States v. Gilbert Assocs., Inc., 345 U.S. 361 (1953), the Court added that a lien was "inchoate" (and thereby lost to a federal claim) where the lien claimant had neither title nor possession. Since the 1946 *Campbell* decision, the Court has never found a lien sufficiently choate to survive a federal challenge, (see United States v. McDermott, 507 U.S. 447 (1993)), though lower federal courts have held that most security interests perfected under Article 9 are sufficiently choate to come ahead of the United States' claim. Pine Builders, Inc. v. United States, 413 F. Supp. 77, 19 U.C.C. Rep. Serv. 306 (E.D. Va. 1976). There is general agreement, however, that a security arrangement claiming a floating lien on after-acquired property or claiming a priority for future advances is inchoate and inferior to the federal claim. G. Gilmore §40.5.

B.   Tax Liens—Basic Priority

A federal tax lien arises on *assessment* and covers all of the taxpayer's property, real or personal, presently owned or after-acquired. It is a secret lien, since it may happen that no one knows of the assessment except the IRS, but the tax lien nevertheless binds the property, and the government wins out over all parties claiming an interest in the property except those listed in §6323(a): "any purchaser, holder of a security interest, mechanic's lienor, or judgment creditor." To prevail over such persons, the federal tax lien must be *filed* in the place designated under state law. See I.R.C. §6323(f).

United States v. Estate of Romani

Supreme Court of the United States, 1998
523 U.S. 517

Justice STEVENS delivered the opinion of the Court.

The federal priority statute, 31 U.S.C. §3713(a), provides that a claim of the United States Government "shall be paid first" when a decedent's estate cannot pay all of its debts. The question presented is whether that statute requires that a federal tax claim be given preference over a judgment creditor's perfected lien on real property even though such a preference is not authorized by the Federal Tax Lien Act of 1966, 26 U.S.C. §6321 et seq.

On January 25, 1985, the Court of Common Pleas of Cambria County, Pennsylvania, entered a judgment for $400,000 in favor of Romani Industries, Inc., and against Francis J. Romani. The judgment was recorded in the clerk's office and therefore, as a matter of Pennsylvania law, it became a lien on all of the defendant's real property in Cambria County. Thereafter, the Internal Revenue Service filed a series of notices of tax liens on Mr. Romani's property. The claims for unpaid taxes, interest and penalties described in those notices amounted to approximately $490,000.

When Mr. Romani died on January 13, 1992, his entire estate consisted of real estate worth only $53,001. Because the property was encumbered by both the judgment lien and the federal tax liens, the estate's administrator sought permission from the Court of Common

Pleas to transfer the property to the judgment creditor, Romani Industries, in lieu of execution. The Federal Government acknowledged that its tax liens were not valid as against the earlier judgment lien; but, giving new meaning to Franklin's aphorism that "in this world nothing can be said to be certain, except death and taxes," it opposed the transfer on the ground that the priority statute gave it the right to "be paid first."

The Court of Common Pleas overruled the Government's objection and authorized the conveyance. The Superior Court of Pennsylvania affirmed, and the Supreme Court of the State also affirmed. 547 Pa. 41, 688 A.2d 703 (1997). That court first determined that there was a "plain inconsistency" between §3713, which appears to give the United States "absolute priority" over all competing claims, and the Tax Lien Act of 1966, which provides that the federal tax lien "shall not be valid" against judgment lien creditors until a prescribed notice has been given. Id., at 45, 688 A.2d, at 705. Then, relying on the reasoning in United States v. Kimbell Foods, Inc., 440 U.S. 715, 99 S. Ct. 1448, 59 L. Ed. 2d 711 (1979), which had noted that the Tax Lien Act of 1966 modified the Federal Government's preferred position in the tax area and recognized the priority of many state claims over federal tax liens, id., at 738, 99 S. Ct., at 1463-1464, the court concluded that the 1966 Act had the effect of limiting the operation of §3713 as to tax debts. . . .

There is no dispute about the meaning of two of the three statutes that control the disposition of this case. It is therefore appropriate to comment on the Pennsylvania lien statute and the Federal Tax Lien Act before considering the applicability of the priority statute to property encumbered by an antecedent judgment creditor's lien.

The Pennsylvania statute expressly provides that a judgment shall create a lien against real property when it is recorded in the county where the property is located. 42 Pa. Cons. Stat. S 4303(a) (1995). After the judgment has been recorded, the judgment creditor has the same right to notice of a tax sale as a mortgagee.[13] The recording in

---

13. The Pennsylvania Supreme Court has elaborated:

> We must now decide whether judgment creditors are also entitled to personal or general notice by the [County Tax Claim] Bureau as a matter of due process of law.
>
> Judgment liens are a product of centuries of statutes which authorize a judgment creditor to seize and sell the land of debtors at a judicial sale to satisfy their debts out of the proceeds of the sale. The judgment represents a binding judicial determination of the rights and duties between the parties, and establishes their debtor-creditor relationship for all the world to notice when the judgment is recorded in a Prothonotary's Office. When entered of record, the judgment also operates as a lien upon all real property of the debtor in that county.

one county does not, of course, create a lien on property located elsewhere. In this case, however, it is undisputed that the judgment creditor acquired a valid lien on the real property in Cambria County before the judgment debtor's death and before the Government served notice of its tax liens. Romani Industries' lien was "perfected in the sense that there is nothing more to be done to have a choate lien— when the identity of the lienor, the property subject to the lien, and the amount of the lien are established." United States v. City of New Britain, 347 U.S. 81, 84, 74 S. Ct. 367, 369, 98 L. Ed. 520 (1954); see also Illinois ex rel. Gordon v. Campbell, 329 U.S. 362, 375, 67 S. Ct. 340, 347-348, 91 L. Ed. 348 (1946).

The Federal Government's right to a lien on a delinquent taxpayer's property has been a part of our law at least since 1865.[14] Originally the lien applied, without exception, to all property of the taxpayer immediately upon the neglect or failure to pay the tax upon demand. An unrecorded tax lien against a delinquent taxpayer's property was valid even against a bona fide purchaser who had no notice of the lien. United States v. Snyder, 149 U.S. 210, 213-215, 13 S. Ct. 846, 847-848, 37 L. Ed. 705 (1893). In 1913, Congress amended the statute to provide that the federal tax lien "shall not be valid as against any mortgagee, purchaser, or judgment creditor" until notice has been filed with the clerk of the federal district court or with the appropriate local authorities in the district or county in which the property subject to the lien is located. Act of Mar. 4, 1913, 37 Stat. 1016. In 1939, Congress broadened the protection against unfiled tax liens to include pledgees and the holders of certain securities. Act of June 29, 1939, §401, 53 Stat. 882-883. The Federal Tax Lien Act of 1966 again broadened that protection to encompass a variety of additional secured transactions, and also included detailed provisions protecting certain secured interests even when a notice of the federal lien previously has been filed. 80 Stat. 1125-1132, as amended, 26 U.S.C. §6323.

In sum, each time Congress revisited the federal tax lien, it ameliorated its original harsh impact on other secured creditors of the delinquent taxpayer.[15] In this case, it is agreed that by the terms of

---

In re Upset Sale, Tax Claim Bureau of Berks County, 505 Pa. 327, 334, 479 A.2d 940, 943 (1984).

14. The post-Civil War Reconstruction Congress imposed a tax of three cents per pound on "the producer, owner, or holder" of cotton and a lien on the cotton until the tax was paid. Act of July 13, 1866, §1, 14 Stat. 98. The same statute also imposed a general lien on all of a delinquent taxpayer's property, see §9, 14 Stat. 107, which was nearly identical to a provision in the revenue act of Mar. 3, 1865, 13 Stat. 470-471. . . .

15. For a more thorough description of the early history and of Congress' reactions to this Court's tax lien decisions, see Kennedy, The Relative Priority of the

§6323(a), the Federal Government's liens are not valid as against the lien created by the earlier recording of Romani Industries' judgment.

The text of the priority statute on which the Government places its entire reliance is virtually unchanged since its enactment in 1797. As we pointed out in United States v. Moore, 423 U.S. 77, 96 S. Ct. 310, 46 L. Ed. 2d 219 (1975), not only were there earlier versions of the statute, but "its roots reach back even further into the English common law," id., at 80, 96 S. Ct., at 313. The sovereign prerogative that was exercised by the English Crown and by many of the States as "an inherent incident of sovereignty," ibid., applied only to unsecured claims. As Justice Brandeis noted in Marshall v. New York, 254 U.S. 380, 384, 41 S. Ct. 143, 145, 65 L. Ed. 315 (1920), the common law priority "[did] not obtain over a specific lien created by the debtor before the sovereign undertakes to enforce its right." Moreover, the statute itself does not create a lien in favor of the United States. Given this background, respondent argues that the statute should be read as giving the United States a preference over other unsecured creditors but not over secured creditors.

There are dicta in our earlier cases that support this contention as well as dicta that tend to refute it. Perhaps the strongest support is found in Justice Story's statement:

> What then is the nature of the priority, thus limited and established in favour of the United States? Is it a right, which supersedes and overrules the assignment of the debtor, as to any property which the United States may afterwards elect to take in execution, so as to prevent such property from passing by virtue of such assignment to the assignees? Or, is it a mere right of prior payment, out of the general funds of the debtor, in the hands of the assignees? We are of opinion that it clearly falls, within the latter description. The language employed is that which naturally would be employed to express such an intent; and it must be strained from its ordinary import, to speak any other.

Conard v. Atlantic Ins. Co. of N.Y., 1 Pet. 386, 439, 7 L. Ed. 189 (1828).

Justice Story's opinion that the language employed in the statute "must be strained" to give it any other meaning is entitled to special respect because he was more familiar with 18th-century usage than judges who view the statute from a 20th-century perspective.

We cannot, however, ignore the Court's earlier judgment in Thelusson v. Smith, 2 Wheat. 396, 426, 4 L. Ed. 271 (1817), or the

---

Federal Government: The Pernicious Career of the Inchoate and General Lien, 63 Yale L.J. 905, 919-922 (1954) (hereinafter *Kennedy*).

more recent dicta in United States v. Key, 397 U.S. 322, 324-325, 90 S. Ct. 1049, 1051-1052, 25 L. Ed. 2d 340 (1970). In *Thelusson,* the Court held that the priority statute gave the United States a preference over the claim of a judgment creditor who had a general lien on the debtor's real property. The Court's brief opinion[16] is subject to the interpretation that the statutory priority always accords the Government a preference over judgment creditors. For two reasons, we do not accept that reading of the opinion.

First, as a factual matter, in 1817 when the case was decided, there was no procedure for recording a judgment and thereby creating a choate lien on a specific parcel of real estate. See generally 2 L. Dembitz, A Treatise on Land Titles in the United States §127, pp.948-952 (1895). Notwithstanding the judgment, a bona fide purchaser could have acquired the debtor's property free from any claims of the judgment creditor. See Semple v. Burd, 7 Serg. & Rawle 286, 291 (Pa. 1821) ("The prevailing object of the Legislature, has uniformly been, to support the security of a judgment creditor, by confirming his lien, except when it interferes with the circulation of property by embarrassing a fair purchaser"). That is not the case with respect to Romani Industries' choate lien on the property in Cambria County.

Second, and of greater importance, in his opinion for the Court in the *Conard* case, which was joined by Justice Washington, the author of *Thelusson,* Justice Story explained why that holding was fully consistent with his interpretation of the text of the priority statute:

---

16. The relevant portion of the opinion reads, in full, as follows:

These [statutory] expressions are as general as any which could have been used, and exclude all debts due to individuals, whatever may be their dignity. . . . The law makes no exception in favour of prior judgment creditors; and no reason has been, or we think can be, shown to warrant this court in making one. . . .

The United States are to be first satisfied; but then it must be out of the debtor's estate. If, therefore, before the right of preference has accrued to the United States, the debtor has made a bona fide conveyance of his estate to a third person, or has mortgaged the same to secure a debt; or if his property has been seized under a fi. fa., the property is devested out of the debtor, and cannot be made liable to the United States. A judgment gives to the judgment creditor a lien on the debtor's lands, and a preference over all subsequent judgment creditors. But the act of congress defeats this preference in favour of the United States, in the cases specified in the 65th section of the act of 1799.

Thelusson v. Smith, 2 Wheat. 396, 425-426, 4 L. Ed. 271 (1817).

In the later *Conard* case, Justice Story apologized for *Thelusson:* "The reasons for that opinion are not, owing to accidental circumstances, as fully given as they are usually given in this Court." Conard v. Atlantic Ins. Co. of N.Y., 1 Pet. 386, 442, 7 L. Ed. 189 (1828).

The real ground of the decision, was, that the judgment creditor had never perfected his title, by any execution and levy on the Sedgely estate; that he had acquired no title to the proceeds as his property, and that if the proceeds were to be deemed general funds of the debtor, the priority of the United States to payment had attached against all other creditors; and that a mere potential lien on land, did not carry a legal title to the proceeds of a sale, made under an adverse execution. This is the manner in which this case has been understood, by the Judges who concurred in the decision; and it is obvious, that it established no such proposition, as that a specific and perfected lien, can be displaced by the mere priority of the United States; since that priority is not of itself equivalent to a lien.

Conard, 1 Pet., at 444, 7 L. Ed. 189.[17]

The Government also relies upon dicta from our opinion in United States v. Key, 397 U.S., at 324-325, 90 S. Ct., at 1051-1052, which quoted from our earlier opinion in United States v. Emory, 314 U.S., at 433, 62 S. Ct., at 322-323: "Only the plainest inconsistency would warrant our finding an implied exception to the operation of so clear a command as that of [§3713]." Because both *Key* and *Emory* were cases in which the competing claims were unsecured, the statutory command was perfectly clear even under Justice Story's construction of the statute. The statements made in that context, of course, shed no light on the clarity of the command when the United States relies on the statute as a basis for claiming a preference over a secured creditor. Indeed, the *Key* opinion itself made this specific point: "This case does not raise the question, never decided by this Court, whether §3466 grants the Government priority over the prior specific liens of secured creditors. See United States v. Gilbert Associates, Inc., 345 U.S. 361, 365-366, 73 S. Ct. 701, 97 L. Ed. 1071 (1953)." 397 U.S., at 332, n.11, 90 S. Ct., at 1056, n.11.

The *Key* opinion is only one of many in which the Court has noted that despite the age of the statute, and despite the fact that it has been the subject of a great deal of litigation, the question whether it has any application to antecedent perfected liens has never been answered definitively. See United States v. Vermont, 377 U.S. 351, 358, n.8, 84 S. Ct. 1267, 1271, n.8, 12 L. Ed. 2d 370 (1964) (citing cases). In his dis-

---

17. Relying on this and several other cases, in 1857 the Attorney General of the United States issued an opinion concluding that *Thelusson* "has been distinctly overruled" and that the priority of the United States under this statute "will not reach back over any lien, whether it be general or specific." 9 Op. Att. Gen. 28, 29. See also Kennedy 908-911 (advancing this same interpretation of the early priority act decisions).

sent in the *Gilbert Associates* case, Justice Frankfurter referred to the Court's reluctance to decide the issue "not only today but for almost a century and a half." 345 U.S., at 367, 73 S. Ct., at 705.

The Government's priority as against specific, perfected security interests is, if possible, even less settled with regard to real property. The Court has sometimes concluded that a competing creditor who has not "divested" the debtor of "either title or possession" has only a "general, unperfected lien" that is defeated by the Government's priority. E.g., id., at 366, 73 S. Ct., at 704-705. Assuming the validity of this "title or possession" test for deciding whether a lien on personal property is sufficiently choate for purposes of the priority statute (a question of federal law, see Illinois ex rel. Gordon v. Campbell, 329 U.S., at 371, 67 S. Ct., at 345-346), we are not aware of any decisions since *Thelusson* applying that theory to claims for real property, or of any reason to require a lienor or mortgagee to acquire possession in order to perfect an interest in real estate.

Given the fact that this basic question of interpretation remains unresolved, it does not seem appropriate to view the issue in this case as whether the Tax Lien Act of 1966 has implicitly amended or repealed the priority statute. Instead, we think the proper inquiry is how best to harmonize the impact of the two statutes on the Government's power to collect delinquent taxes.

IV

In his dissent from a particularly harsh application of the priority statute, Justice Jackson emphasized the importance of considering other relevant federal policies. Joined by three other Justices, he wrote:

> This decision announces an unnecessarily ruthless interpretation of a statute that at its best is an arbitrary one. The statute by which the Federal Government gives its own claims against an insolvent priority over claims in favor of a state government must be applied by courts, not because federal claims are more meritorious or equitable, but only because that Government has more power. But the priority statute is an assertion of federal supremacy as against any contrary state policy. It is not a limitation on the Federal Government itself, not an assertion that the priority policy shall prevail over all other federal policies. Its generalities should not lightly be construed to frustrate a specific policy embodied in a later federal statute.

Massachusetts v. United States, 333 U.S. 611, 635, 68 S. Ct. 747, 760-761, 92 L. Ed. 968 (1948) (Jackson, J., dissenting).

On several prior occasions the Court had followed this approach and concluded that a specific policy embodied in a later federal statute should control our construction of the priority statute, even though it had not been expressly amended. Thus, in Cook County Nat. Bank v. United States, 107 U.S. 445, 448-451, 2 S. Ct. 561, 564-567, 27 L. Ed. 537 (1883), the Court concluded that the priority statute did not apply to federal claims against national banks because the National Bank Act comprehensively regulated banks' obligations and the distribution of insolvent banks' assets. And in United States v. Guaranty Trust Co. of N.Y., 280 U.S. 478, 485, 50 S. Ct. 212, 214, 74 L. Ed. 556 (1930), we determined that the Transportation Act of 1920 had effectively super-seded the priority statute with respect to federal claims against the railroads arising under that Act.

The bankruptcy law provides an additional context in which another federal statute was given effect despite the priority statute's literal, unconditional text. The early federal bankruptcy statutes had accorded to " 'all debts due to the United States, and all taxes and assessments under the laws thereof' " a preference that was "coexten-sive" with that established by the priority statute. Guarantee Title & Trust Co. v. Title Guaranty & Surety Co., 224 U.S. 152, 158, 32 S. Ct. 457, 459, 56 L. Ed. 706 (1912) (quoting the Bankruptcy Act of 1867, Rev. Stat. S 5101). As such, the priority act and the bankruptcy laws "were to be regarded as in pari materia, and both were unquali-fied; . . . as neither contained any qualification, none could be inter-polated." Ibid. The Bankruptcy Act of 1898, however, subordinated the priority of the Federal Government's claims (except for taxes due) to certain other kinds of debts. This Court resolved the tension between the new bankruptcy provisions and the priority statute by applying the former and thus treating the Government like any other general creditor. Id., at 158-160, 32 S. Ct., at 459-460; Davis v. Pringle, 268 U.S. 315, 317-319, 45 S. Ct. 549, 550, 69 L. Ed. 974 (1925).[18]

There are sound reasons for treating the Tax Lien Act of 1966 as the governing statute when the Government is claiming a preference

---

18. Congress amended the priority statute in 1978 to make it expressly inap-plicable to Title 11 bankruptcy cases. Pub. L. 95-598, §322(b), 92 Stat. 2679, codified in 31 U.S.C. §3713(a)(2). The differences between the bankruptcy laws and the priority statute have been the subject of criticism: "as a result of the continuing discrepancies between the bankruptcy and insolvency rules, some creditors have had a distinct incentive to throw into bankruptcy a debtor whose case might have been handled, with less expense and less burden on the federal courts, in another form of proceeding." Plumb, The Federal Priority in Insolvency: Proposals for Reform, 70 Mich. L. Rev. 3, 8-9 (1971) (hereinafter *Plumb*).

in the insolvent estate of a delinquent taxpayer. As was the case with the National Bank Act, the Transportation Act of 1920, and the Bankruptcy Act of 1898, the Tax Lien Act is the later statute, the more specific statute, and its provisions are comprehensive, reflecting an obvious attempt to accommodate the strong policy objections to the enforcement of secret liens. It represents Congress' detailed judgment as to when the Government's claims for unpaid taxes should yield to many different sorts of interests (including, for instance, judgment liens, mechanic's liens, and attorneys' liens) in many different types of property (including, for example, real property, securities, and motor vehicles). See 26 U.S.C. §6323. Indeed, given our unambiguous determination that the federal interest in the collection of taxes is paramount to its interest in enforcing other claims, see United States v. Kimbell Foods, Inc., 440 U.S., at 733-735, 99 S. Ct., at 1461-1462, it would be anomalous to conclude that Congress intended the priority statute to impose greater burdens on the citizen than those specifically crafted for tax collection purposes.

Even before the 1966 amendments to the Tax Lien Act, this Court assumed that the more recent and specific provisions of that Act would apply were they to conflict with the older priority statute. In the *Gilbert Associates* case, which concerned the relative priority of the Federal Government and a New Hampshire town to funds of an insolvent taxpayer, the Court first considered whether the town could qualify as a "judgment creditor" entitled to preference under the Tax Lien Act. 345 U.S., at 363-364, 73 S. Ct., at 703-704. Only after deciding that question in the negative did the Court conclude that the United States obtained preference by operation of the priority statute. Id., at 365-366, 73 S. Ct., at 704-705. The Government would now portray *Gilbert Associates* as a deviation from two other relatively recent opinions in which the Court held that the priority statute was not trumped by provisions of other statutes: United States v. Emory, 314 U.S., at 429-433, 62 S. Ct., at 320-323 (the National Housing Act), and United States v. Key, 397 U.S., at 324-333, 90 S. Ct., at 1051-1056 (Chapter X of the Bankruptcy Act). In each of those cases, however, there was no "plain inconsistency" between the commands of the priority statute and the other federal act, nor was there reason to believe that application of the priority statute would frustrate Congress' intent. Id., at 329, 90 S. Ct., at 1053-1054. The same cannot be said in the present suit.

The Government emphasizes that when Congress amended the Tax Lien Act in 1966, it declined to enact the American Bar Association's proposal to modify the federal priority statute, and Congress again failed to enact a similar proposal in 1970. Both proposals would have expressly provided that the Government's priority in insolvency does not displace valid liens and security interests, and therefore would have harmonized the priority statute with the Tax Lien Act. See Hearings on H.R. 11256 and 11290 before the House Committee on Ways and Means, 89th Cong., 2d Sess., 197 (1966) (hereinafter Hearings); §2197, 92d Cong., 1st Sess. (1971). But both proposals also would have significantly changed the priority statute in many other respects to follow the priority scheme created by the bankruptcy laws. See Hearings, at 85, 198; Plumb 10, n.53, 33-37. The earlier proposal may have failed because its wide-ranging subject matter was beyond the House Ways and Means Committee's jurisdiction. Plumb 8. The failure of the 1970 proposal in the Senate Judiciary Committee—explained by no reports or hearings—might merely reflect disagreement with the broad changes to the priority statute, or an assumption that the proposal was not needed because, as Justice Story had believed, the priority statute does not apply to prior perfected security interests, or any number of other views. Thus, the Committees' failures to report the proposals to the entire Congress do not necessarily indicate that any legislator thought that the priority statute should supersede the Tax Lien Act in the adjudication of federal tax claims. They provide no support for the hypothesis that both Houses of Congress silently endorsed that position.

The actual measures taken by Congress provide a superior insight regarding its intent. As we have noted, the 1966 amendments to the Tax Lien Act bespeak a strong condemnation of secret liens, which unfairly defeat the expectations of innocent creditors and frustrate "the needs of our citizens for certainty and convenience in the legal rules governing their commercial dealings." 112 Cong. Rec. 22227 (1966) (remarks of Rep. Byrnes); cf. United States v. Speers, 382 U.S. 266, 275, 86 S. Ct. 411, 416, 15 L. Ed. 2d 314 (1965) (referring to the "general policy against secret liens"). These policy concerns shed light on how Congress would want the conflicting statutory provisions to be harmonized:

> Liens may be a dry-as-dust part of the law, but they are not without significance in an industrial and commercial community where construction and credit are thought to have importance. One does not readily impute to Congress the intention that many common commercial liens should be congenitally unstable.

E. Brown, The Supreme Court, 1957 Term—Foreword: Process of Law, 72 Harv. L. Rev. 77, 87 (1958) (footnote omitted).

In sum, nothing in the text or the long history of interpreting the federal priority statute justifies the conclusion that it authorizes the equivalent of a secret lien as a substitute for the expressly authorized tax lien that Congress has said "shall not be valid" in a case of this kind.

> The judgment of the Pennsylvania Supreme Court is affirmed.
> It is so ordered.

C. Tax Liens and After-Acquired Property

PROBLEM 351

Octopus National Bank (ONB) had a perfected security interest in the inventory, accounts receivable, instruments, and chattel paper of an automobile dealership named Smiles Motors, to which the bank made periodic loans. Smiles Motors failed to pay its federal taxes, and the IRS filed a tax lien in the proper place on October 1. On the first days of November and December new shipments of cars arrived at Smiles's lot, and all during the year Smiles continued to sell cars on credit, generating chattel paper and accounts receivable. Does the filing of the tax lien cut off ONB's floating lien in whole or in part? Is this issue in any way affected by the bank's knowledge of the tax lien filing?

The answer to Problem 351 is that §6323(c) of the Internal Revenue Code expressly permits *commercial financing security* (defined at the end of the section) to fall under an existing perfected security arrangement and take priority over a filed federal tax lien if the new collateral is acquired by the taxpayer-debtor in the 45 days following the tax lien filing. The statute, like most of the tax code, is written in almost impenetrable language, but that is what it means. While §6323(c)(2)(A) requires that the loan has to be made without knowledge of the tax lien filing, the lender's later discovery of the tax lien filing in no way affects the priority of its floating lien during the 45-day period; see Treas. Reg. §301.6323(c)-1(d) (1976). Section 6323(c) reads:

> (c) Protection for certain commercial transactions financing agreements, etc.
> (1) In general. To the extent provided in this subsection, even though notice of a lien imposed by section 6321 has been filed, such

lien shall not be valid with respect to a security interest which came into existence after tax lien filing but which—

(A) is in qualified property covered by the terms of a written agreement entered into before tax lien filing and constituting—

(i) a commercial transactions financing agreement,

(ii) a real property construction or improvement financing agreement, or

(iii) an obligatory disbursement agreement, and—

(B) is protected under local law against a judgment lien arising, as of the time of tax lien filing, out of an unsecured obligation.

(2) Commercial transactions financing agreement. For purposes of this subsection—

(A) Definition: The term "commercial transactions financing agreement" means an agreement (entered into by a person in the course of his trade or business)—

(i) to make loans to the taxpayer to be secured by commercial financing security acquired by the taxpayer in the ordinary course of his trade or business, or

(ii) to purchase commercial financing security, (other than inventory) acquired by the taxpayer in the ordinary course of his trade or business;

but such an agreement shall be treated as coming within the term only to the extent that such loan or purchase is made before the 46th day of tax lien filing or (if earlier) before the lender or purchaser had actual notice or knowledge of such tax lien filing.

(B) Limitation on qualified property. The term "qualified property," when used with respect to a commercial transactions financing agreement, includes only commercial financing security acquired by the taxpayer before the 46th day after the date of tax lien filing.

(C) Commercial financing security defined. The term "commercial financing security" means (i) paper of a kind ordinarily arising in commercial transactions, (ii) accounts receivable, (iii) mortgages on real property, and (iv) inventory.

To take advantage of this 45-day period, §9-323(b) creates a similar 45-day rule in which advances made by a perfected Article 9 creditor prevail over the intervening interest of a judicial lien creditor.[19]

---

19. Similarly, §9-323(d) creates a 45-day period that protects non-ordinary course buyers from future advances made with knowledge of the purchase or more than 45

Plymouth Savings Bank v. U.S. I.R.S.

United States Court of Appeals, First Circuit, 1999
187 F.3d 203, 39 U.C.C. Rep. Serv. 2d 543

CUDAHY, Senior Circuit Judge.

Jordan Hospital ("Hospital") owed Shirley Dionne ("Dionne") $75,000. Dionne, in turn, was indebted to the Plymouth Savings Bank ("Bank") and the Internal Revenue Service ("IRS"), both of which held valid liens on the money the Hospital owed Dionne. The Hospital deposited the money with the district court, and we must now decide who is entitled to it. The problem is simply to determine which of the two liens has priority. We hold that the Bank's lien may trump the IRS's and therefore reverse the district court's grant of summary judgment in favor of the IRS.

Most of the facts are not in dispute. Dionne owned and operated the Greenlawn Nursing Home, a 47-bed state-licensed facility. On September 22, 1993 and apparently before extending credit, the Bank filed a financing statement with the state of Massachusetts describing and giving notice of its security interest in Greenlawn and other assets of Dionne. On April 13, 1994, Dionne executed an $85,000 promissory note in favor of the Bank. As security for the loan, Dionne granted the Bank a security interest in all of her tangible and intangible personal property individually, as well as in her capacity as a sole proprietor doing business as Greenlawn. Paragraph 2 of the agreement specifically granted the Bank: all cash and non-cash proceeds resulting or arising from the rendering of services by Dionne; all general intangibles including proceeds of other collateral; and all inventory, receivables, contract rights or other personal property of Dionne. On or about December 1, 1994, Dionne defaulted on her $85,000 obligation to the Bank, leaving some $65,465 unpaid.

Dionne's financial troubles did not end there. She failed to make Federal Insurance Contribution Act, 26 U.S.C. §3101, et seq. (FICA), payments of $19,639 for the second quarter of 1994. The IRS assessed liability on September 19, 1994 and filed a federal tax lien in the district court on December 19. Dionne again failed to make FICA payments of $62,767 for the fourth quarter of 1994. Liability was assessed on February 2, 1995 and a lien was filed on February 14.

On March 31, 1995, Dionne signed a contract in which she agreed to help the Hospital obtain a license to operate a skilled nursing

---

days after the purchase. There is an identical rule for leases in §9-323(f). All of this will be explored below in Problem 353.

facility in exchange for $300,000, payable in three installments. Dionne would receive $25,000 when she signed a letter of intent, $200,000 when Massachusetts approved a license and the final $75,000 two years after the license-approval date. With Dionne's assistance, by mid-May 1995 the Hospital had received approval for its license and had paid Dionne the first two installments, totaling $225,000. (In practical effect, it appears that Dionne transferred her Greenlawn license to the Hospital.) The Hospital never paid Dionne the $75,000 balance.

The Bank sued the Hospital in Massachusetts state court to recover the unpaid balance of its loan to Dionne. Considering cross-motions for summary judgment, the state court ruled for the Bank. It found that, pursuant to the contract between Dionne and the Hospital, the $75,000 constituted cash proceeds arising from the rendering of personal services by Dionne. Because the security agreement between the Bank and Dionne expressly covered "proceeds" of services, the court held that the Bank had a secured interest in the money. The court rejected the Bank's argument that the security interest attached to the nursing home license or to proceeds of the transfer of that license. Instead of awarding the $75,000 to the Bank, however, the court directed the Bank to bring a declaratory judgment action to determine whether its interest in the money had priority over that of other lien-holders.

Ever diligent, the Bank brought such an action—this one—which the IRS subsequently removed to the district court. The Hospital, content to let the Bank and the IRS do battle, deposited the $75,000 with the district court and exited from the action. The Bank and the IRS filed cross-motions for summary judgment, each asserting that its lien trumped the other's. The court sided with the IRS. The Bank's right to recover as against the government depended on when Dionne had performed the services required by the contract, the district court stated. And, although the record on the timing of Dionne's performance was sparse, the court determined that it was undisputed that she had not helped the Hospital secure approval of a nursing home license within the 45 days following the tax lien filing as required by the Federal Tax Lien Act, 26 U.S.C. §§6321, 6323(c) (FTLA). See Dis. Ct. Mem. Op. & Order at 18-19. Accordingly, the district court held that the IRS's two liens were superior to the Bank's lien. The Bank appeals this decision, and we review de novo the district court's grant of summary judgment in favor of the government. . . .

When an individual fails to pay her taxes after a demand has been made, the FTLA grants the United States a lien "upon all property and rights to property, whether real or personal, belonging to such person." 26 U.S.C. §6321. The lien also attaches to property acquired by the delinquent taxpayer after the initial imposition of the lien. See, e.g., Glass City Bank v. United States, 326 U.S. 265, 267, 66 S. Ct. 108, 90 L. Ed. 56 (1945). Section 6323 of the FTLA, however, gives certain commercial liens priority over federal tax liens. Pursuant to §6323(a) and as defined in §6323(h), for example, tax liens are subordinate to security interests in a taxpayer's property that is "in existence" before the government files notice of the tax lien. (Subsection 6323(f) details the filing requirements.) And §6323(c) extends the priority of these prior security interests to certain "qualified property" that the taxpayer acquires even after the government has filed a notice of the tax lien. The scope of this safe harbor for after-acquired property under §6323(c) is at issue here. Mindful that we are entering "the tortured meanderings of federal tax lien law, intersected now by the somewhat smoother byway of the Uniform Commercial Code [UCC]," Texas Oil & Gas Corp. v. United States, 466 F.2d 1040, 1043 (5th Cir.1972), we lay out the pertinent provisions with as much specificity as we can apply.

To fall within §6323(c)'s safe harbor for after-acquired property, a security interest must be in "qualified property covered by the terms of a written agreement entered into before tax lien filing," including "commercial transactions financing agreement[s]." 26 U.S.C. §6323(c)(1)(A)(i). The security interest must also be superior, under local law, to a judgment lien arising out of an unsecured obligation. See id. at §6323(c)(1)(B). A "commercial transactions financing agreement" is defined as "an agreement (entered into by a person in the course of his trade or business) . . . to make loans to the taxpayer to be secured by commercial financing security acquired by the taxpayer in the ordinary course of his trade or business," id. at §6323(c)(2)(A)(i), and must be entered into within 45 days of the date of the tax lien filing. See id. at §6323(c)(2)(A). "Commercial financing security" can include, among other things, "paper of a kind ordinarily arising in commercial transactions" and "accounts receivable," id. at §6323(c)(2)(C), and it must be "acquired by the taxpayer before the 46th day after the date of tax lien filing." Id. at §6323(c)(2)(B).

The relevant Treasury regulations include still more definitions. "Paper of a kind ordinarily arising in commercial transactions" means "any written document customarily used in commercial transactions," and includes "paper giving contract rights." 26 C.F.R. §301.6323(c)-1(c)(1). For purposes of the FTLA, a "contract right" is "any right to payment under a contract not yet earned by performance and not evidenced by an instrument or chattel paper." Id. at §301.6323(c)-1(c)(2)(i). "An account receivable is any right to payment for goods sold or leased or for services rendered which is not evidenced by an instrument or chattel paper." Id. at §301.6323(c)-1(c)(2)(ii).

Because Dionne signed the personal service contract with the Hospital exactly 45 days after the IRS filed notice of the second tax lien (February 14-March 31),[20] the fighting issue is whether by so doing she "acquired" rights to the $75,000, the money the Hospital owed Dionne and deposited with the district court. See 26 U.S.C. §6323(c)(2)(B). If, by signing the contract, Dionne acquired rights to the money, then the Bank's lien trumps the IRS's. For, if that is the case, it is undisputed that the Dionne-Hospital contract is commercial financing security within §6323(c)(2)(C) and that the Dionne-Bank agreement is a commercial transactions financing agreement within §§6323(c)(1)(A)(i) & (c)(2). In this scenario, the Bank's security interest is in qualified property, and the $75,000 would fall within the safe harbor for after-acquired property. On the other hand, if Dionne did not acquire the rights to the money when she signed the contract, the IRS's lien takes priority.

The Treasury Department (of which the IRS is a part) has provided an answer. Recall that the potential qualified property here is the contract between Dionne and the Hospital, which granted Dionne certain rights to payments when she performed certain services. Before the 46th day after the tax lien was filed (that is, before April 1, 1995), if Dionne had acquired anything, she could only have acquired a contract right, not an account receivable, because she had yet to perform any services. See 26 C.F.R. §301.6323(c)-1(c)(2)(i) & (ii). The regulations provide that a "contract right . . . is acquired by a taxpayer when the contract is made." Id. at §301.6323(c)-1(d). So, Dionne acquired the right to be paid for services to be rendered in the future at the time she entered into that contract. In statutory terms, the commercial transactions financing agreement (the Dionne-Bank agreement), which was entered into well before the tax lien filing, covers the Bank's loan (the $85,000) to the taxpayer (Dionne). The loan in turn was secured by commercial financing security (the Dionne-Hospital contract). The Dionne-Hospital contract conferred contract rights (the right to be paid $75,000 two years after Massachusetts approved a nursing home license for the Hospital) and was acquired by the taxpayer within 45 days of the tax lien filing. See 26 U.S.C. §6323(c)(2)(A) &

---

20. The Bank does not claim that its lien should take priority over the first tax lien, filed on December 19, 1994. The duel here is between only the second tax lien (filed on February 14, 1995 and covering FICA payments of $62,767 for the fourth quarter of 1994) and the Bank's lien.

(B). The contract, and the rights (even if conditional) under it, are therefore qualified property covered by the Bank's security interest and protected by §6323(c)'s safe harbor.

Of course, the Bank is interested in the money, not the contract right. The regulations again point the way. "Proceeds" are "whatever is received when collateral is sold, exchanged, or collected." 26 C.F.R. §301.6323(c)-1(d). The regulations further provide: "Identifiable proceeds, which arise from the collection or disposition of qualified property by the taxpayer, are considered to be acquired at the time such qualified property is acquired if the secured party has a continuously perfected security interest in the proceeds under local law." Id. Recall that the commercial financing security (the Dionne-Hospital contract and the rights under it) is simply collateral for the loan (the Bank's $85,000 loan to Dionne). So, where the collateral is a contract giving contract rights, the proceeds of those rights, like the rights themselves, are considered to have been acquired at the time the contract was made. This is so even though the right to proceeds under the contract does not become unconditional until the contract is performed. Pursuant to the Treasury regulations, the conditional right to the proceeds relates back to the time the contract was formed and executed. Therefore, Dionne acquired the rights to the proceeds of the contract right on March 31, 1995, exactly 45 days from the date of the tax lien filing.

In this case, however, the proceeds of the contract right are simply an account receivable, the right to payment of $75,000 for services rendered by Dionne. See 26 C.F.R. §301.6323(c)-1(c)(2)(ii). And herein lies the rub. The IRS argues that, pursuant to the regulations, a taxpayer acquires an account receivable "at the time, and to the extent, a right to payment is earned by performance." Echoing the district court, the IRS correctly points out that Dionne did not earn a right to payment before the 45 days. See Appellee's Br. at 18. But the contract and the rights under it, rather than the account receivable, are the qualified property at issue here, and the regulations provide that the proceeds of qualified property are deemed to be acquired at the time the qualified property is acquired. The regulations do not distinguish between forms of proceeds. Well then, the IRS parries, the account receivable cannot be "proceeds" because the contract was not "sold, exchanged, or collected." See 26 C.F.R. §301.6323(c)-1(d). Had Dionne sold the contract, the IRS says, the Bank's lien would reach the proceeds of that sale; but performance (rendering the services) does not amount to a sale. See Appellee's Br. at 18. This ingenious quibble is unconvincing. Dionne's rendering of the contracted-for services effectively "exchanged" her contract right, converting it into an account receivable. See 26 C.F.R. §301.6323(c)-1(d). The IRS has given us no good reason, nor can we find any basis in commercial reality, to distinguish between a "sale" or an "exchange" and a conversion by performance for this purpose. In fact, performance would seem to be necessary for the production of proceeds even if there were a sale or exchange of the contract. We therefore conclude that the account receivable, the right to the $75,000, is the proceeds of the contract right.

To this, the IRS responds by complaining that we have expanded too far §6323(c)'s safe harbor for after-acquired property. It cites legislative history which it claims suggests that Congress intended §6323(c)'s protections to extend only to property that was collected within 45 days of the tax lien filing. See Appellee's Br. at 17 (citing S. Rep. No. 1708, 89th Cong., 2d Sess. (1966), at 2, 8). We find this argument unpersuasive. As an initial matter, this Senate Report does not directly address commercial financing secured by contract rights, the precise issue here. The Report does indicate, however, that the FTLA was "an attempt to conform the lien provisions of the internal revenue laws to the concepts developed in [the UCC]." S. Rep. No. 1708, 89th Cong., 2d Sess., at 2. The Treasury regulations reflect this intent by providing definitions for FTLA terms that closely track UCC definitions of like terms. For example, the FTLA definitions of "contract right" and "account receivable" match the pre-1972 revision definitions of "contract" and "account," compare, e.g., 26 C.F.R. §301.6323(c)-1(c)(i) & (ii) with Mass. Gen. Laws Ann. ch. 106, §9-106 (West 1998) (Official Reasons for 1972 Changes), and the two definitions of the term "proceeds" are almost identical, compare 26 C.F.R. §301.6323(c)-1(d) with Mass. Gen. Laws Ann. ch. 106, §9-306(a) (West 1988) [now §9-102(a)(64)—Ed.] (defining "proceeds" as "whatever is received upon the sale, exchange, collection or other disposition of collateral or proceeds"). Our conclusion that the Bank's security interest in the contract rights covers the proceeds of those rights-even if the proceeds are accounts receivable-is compatible with still other provisions of the UCC. See, e.g., Mass. Gen. Laws Ann. ch. 106, §9-306(2) (West 1980) [now §9-315—Ed.] (providing that security interests extend to the proceeds of all secured property). In all events, whatever Congress intended, the regulations make it clear that, so long as the contract was entered into within 45 days of the tax lien filing, the rights under that contract and all of the proceeds of those rights fall within §6323(c)'s protective bounds.

This conclusion can hardly come as a surprise to the IRS. The IRS has advanced the same arguments which it uses here in cases analogous to this one, and has lost each time (except, of course, below). See Bremen Bank & Trust Co. v. United States, 131 F.3d 1259 (8th Cir. 1997); State Bank of Fraser v. United States, 861 F.2d 954 (6th Cir. 1988); In re National Fin. Alternatives, Inc., 96 B.R. 844 (Bankr. N.D. Ill. 1989). Each of these cases, like this one, turned neither on a clever interpretation of the FTLA nor on a thorough scouring of the Congressional records in an attempt to divine intent, but instead on a plain reading of the regulations. It is that simple: the regulations governing §6323(c) say that contract rights and the proceeds thereof are acquired at the time the parties enter into the contract. It matters not that the proceeds of that contract right might be accounts receivable because the regulations do not distinguish among different kinds of proceeds. The IRS, which promulgates these regulations, has had ample opportunity to rewrite them to better suit its desired interpretation of the statute. (Congress, of course, might yet disagree.) To our knowledge, it has made no such effort.

One issue remains. The IRS, reminding us that we "can affirm a correct judgment on any ground," Appellee's Br. at 20 (citing Levy v. FDIC, 7 F.3d 1054, 1056 (1st Cir. 1993)), argues that Dionne did not enter into the contract with the Hospital "in the ordinary course of [her] trade or business" as required by §6323(c)(2)(A)(i). . . . In this case, not only did the district court fail to address the "ordinary course of business" element, both parties also acknowledge that the record is undeveloped on this point. Because the record is so undeveloped, and because trade-or-business determinations are highly fact-intensive, see, e.g., Higgins v. Commissioner, 312 U.S. 212, 217, 61 S. Ct. 475, 85 L. Ed. 783 (1941); Deputy v. du Pont, 308 U.S. 488, 496, 60 S. Ct. 363, 84 L. Ed. 416 (1940), we decline the IRS's invitation to affirm the district court on this ground. However, the parties are free to develop the factual record on remand to the district court.

These arguments foreshadow the ultimate question in a trade-or-business determination: what constitutes ordinariness? The IRS is arguing, in essence, that the Dionne-Hospital contract, because it resulted in the transfer of Dionne's Greenlawn license, cannot be considered ordinary. The Bank appears to have conceded as much; in its original complaint against the Hospital in Massachusetts state court, it claimed that the "transfer of the license was not in the ordinary course of Shirley Dionne's business." See App. at 24, ¶21. The state court, however, determined that the contract was for personal services, rather than for the sale or transfer of the Greenlawn license. The Bank echoes this characterization—the Dionne-Hospital contract as a personal services contract—and appears to focus its brief arguments on the normality of such contracts in Dionne's business. (And, in response to the IRS's argument, if the $75,000 represented proceeds of a sale or transfer of the license, there is no question that the Bank would have held a prior secured interest, entitling it to the money without having to navigate §6323(c)'s maze of definitions.) Prudence compels us to allow the district court to weigh these fact-specific considerations in the first instance.

Because we find that the Bank's lien may trump the IRS's, we REVERSE the district court's grant of summary judgment in favor of the IRS. The case is REMANDED to the district court for proceedings consistent with this opinion.

PROBLEM 352

Six months after the IRS filed a tax lien against her, Charlene McGee bought a fire extinguisher system for her horse stables. She purchased the system on credit from King Protection Enterprises, which reserved a purchase money security interest in itself and perfected it. Is the IRS's lien superior to King's purchase money security interest? See Rev. Rul. 68-57, 26 C.F.R. §301.6321-1; In re Specialty Contracting & Supply, Inc., 140 Bankr. 922, 18 U.C.C. Rep. Serv. 2d 917 (Bankr. N.D. Ga. 1992).

D.   Tax Liens and Future Advances

After the filing of the tax lien, the taxpayer's financing creditor may make a new loan, expecting it to be secured by an existing perfected interest in the collateral listed in the security agreement. If the secured party is aware of the filed tax lien, it almost certainly will refuse to make the advance, but if the lien is undiscovered and the advance is given, which has priority—the IRS or the lender?

Section 6323(d) of the Internal Revenue Code gives protection to future advances made without knowledge of the tax lien in the 45 days after its filing if the advance is collateralized by a perfected security interest in existing property of the taxpayer, such as equipment. It provides:

> (d) 45-day period for making disbursements.
>   —Even though notice of a lien imposed by section 6321 has been filed, such lien shall not be valid with respect to a security inter-

est which came into existence after tax lien filing by reason of disbursements made before the 46th day after the date of tax lien filing, or (if earlier) before the person making such disbursements had actual notice or knowledge of tax lien filing, but only if such security interest

(1) is in property (A) subject, at the time of tax lien filing, to the lien imposed by section 6321, and (B) covered by the terms of a written agreement entered into before tax lien filing, and

(2) is protected under local law against a judgment lien arising, as of the time of tax lien filing, out of an unsecured obligation.

PROBLEM 353

Marie Medici owned a hat factory. She financed her business through a series of loans from the Richelieu State Bank pursuant to an agreement by which she gave the bank a security interest in all of the factory's equipment, and the bank agreed to loan her money from time to time "as it thinks prudent." A financing statement covering the equipment was filed in the proper place. On August 1 she owed the bank $1,500 (having paid back most of the prior loans). The equipment consisted of two machines: the Habsburg Hat Blocker (worth $7,000) and the Huguenot Felt Press (worth $5,000). On that date the United States filed a federal tax lien against all of Medici's property. On August 31, the bank loaned her another $10,000. Answer these questions:

(a) Assuming the bank did not know of the tax lien on August 31, does the bank or the United States have priority in the equipment, and to what amount? See I.R.C. §6323(d). What if the bank did know?

(b) Assume there is no tax lien, but on August 15 Louis Dupes paid Medici $5,000 cash for the Huguenot Felt Press, and on August 31 the bank loaned her the $10,000. Does the purchase cut off the bank's security interest? Does it matter whether or not the bank knew of the sale prior to the August 31 loan? See §§9-323(d) and (e), 9-102(a)(68).

(c) Instead of buying the machine, as in the last paragraph, assume that Dupes is another creditor of Medici. On August 15 he levied execution on the felt press pursuant to a judgment. If he did this with full knowledge of the bank's security interest and if with notice of his levy the bank still loans Medici the $10,000 on August 31, does Dupes or the Richelieu State Bank have the superior interest in the felt press as to the future advance? See §9-323(b). If the bank did not know of the levy by Dupes on August 15 but loaned Medici an additional $5,000 on October 15, who would have priority as to this advance?

BANKRUPTCY
AND ARTICLE 9

I. THE TRUSTEE'S STATUS

The filing of a bankruptcy petition creates an automatic stay of any further creditor collection activity. Bankruptcy Code §362. Thereafter, creditors must pursue whatever rights they have in the bankruptcy proceeding only.

The trustee in bankruptcy is given a number of useful rights in resisting or attacking creditors' claims. As we have seen, the so-called *strong arm clause* imbues the trustee with the state law status of a hypothetical judicial lien creditor who acquires a lien on all of the debtor's property as of the moment of the filing of the bankruptcy petition. Bankruptcy Code §544(a) (reprinted below). Since state law, here §9-317(a)(2) of the Uniform Commercial Code, allows such a lien creditor to avoid unperfected security interests, the trustee may do so too. In addition, §558 gives the trustee the benefit of whatever defenses the debtor would have had against the creditor's claim, so that, for example, if the debt is barred by the Statute of Frauds or a statute of limitations, the trustee may assert these matters. Under §544(b) of the Bankruptcy Code the trustee is imbued with the rights and position of any unsecured creditor who has a claim against the estate. In the cryptic and often criticized opinion of Moore v. Bay, 284 U.S. 4 (1931), the Supreme Court, per Oliver Wendell Holmes, held, however, that the trustee gets better rights than the creditor represented because the trustee's claim is not limited to the amount of the actual creditor's claim but rather is the size of the entire estate.

§544.   *Trustee as Lien Creditor and as Successor*
to Certain Creditors and Purchasers

(a) The trustee shall have, as of the commencement of the case, and without regard to any knowledge of the trustee or of any creditor, the rights and powers of, or may avoid any transfer of property of the debtor or any obligation incurred by the debtor that is voidable by—

(1) a creditor that extends credit to the debtor at the time of the commencement of the case, and that obtains, at such time and with respect to such credit, a judicial lien on all property on which a creditor on a simple contract could have obtained such a judicial lien, whether or not such a creditor exists;

(2) a creditor that extends credit to the debtor at the time of the commencement of the case, and obtains, at such time and with respect to such credit, an execution against the debtor that is returned unsatisfied at such time, whether or not such a creditor exists; or

(3) a bona fide purchaser of real property, other than fixtures, from the debtor, against whom applicable law permits such transfer to be perfected, that obtains the status of a bona fide purchaser and has perfected such transfer at the time of the commencement of the case, whether or not such a purchaser exists.

(b) The trustee may avoid any transfer of an interest of the debtor in property or any obligation incurred by the debtor that is voidable under applicable law by a creditor holding an unsecured claim that is allowable under section 502 of this title or that is not allowable only under section 502(e) of this title.

PROBLEM 354

Lew Sun, a Korean, moved to Chicago and opened a Korean restaurant called "Seoul Food." He had many unsecured creditors (food sellers, linen services, employees, etc.). On April 17, he applied to the International State Bank for a loan of $10,000, and, signing a security agreement and a financing statement in favor of the bank, secured by an interest in Sun's equipment. On April 18, one hour before the bank filed the financing statement, Sun filed a bankruptcy petition in the federal court.

(a) If no new general creditors came into existence between the loan on April 17 and the petition filing on April 18, can the trustee avoid the bank's security interest under §544(a) of the Code?

(b) What result if the bank had filed its financing statement two seconds before the bankruptcy petition was filed?

(c) If the bank's interest had been a *purchase money security interest,* would the filing of the bankruptcy petition have cut off the usual 10-day grace period? See §546(b) of the Code, which follows.

> §546. *Limitations on Avoiding Powers*
> ... (b) (1) The rights and powers of the trustee under section 544, 545, or 549 of this title are subject to any generally applicable law that—
> (A) permits perfection of an interest in property to be effective against an entity that acquires rights in such property before the date of such perfection; or
> (B) provides for the maintenance or continuation of perfection of an interest in property to be effective against an entity that acquires rights in such property before the date on which action is taken to effect such maintenance or continuation. ...

II. PREFERENCES

A *preference* is a "transfer" (defined in the Bankruptcy Code to include the creation of a security interest in the debtor's property) made or suffered by the bankrupt to pay or secure a pre-existing debt within the 90-day period preceding the filing of the bankruptcy petition,[1] which has the effect of giving the transferee (the creditor) a greater payment than the creditor would get under the usual bankruptcy distribution. The trustee can avoid such preferential transfers under §547 of the Bankruptcy Code, reprinted below, if the

---

1. The preference period is *one year* before the filing of the petition if the transfer is to an *insider,* defined in §101(31) of the Bankruptcy Code to include relatives, partners, and officers of corporations.

debtor was insolvent at the time of transfer, which is presumed in the 90-day period. An Article 9 creditor who delays perfection until the 90 days before bankruptcy is frequently met with a trustee who is wielding §547 as a weapon.

If the creation of a security interest is deemed preferential, the trustee can cancel it, thus turning the preferred creditor into an unsecured (read *unpaid*) one. Other transfers of the debtor's property (for instance, a cash payment) are returned to the bankrupt's estate at the trustee's insistence.

§547. *Preferences*
(a) In this section—
(1) "inventory" means personal property leased or furnished, held for sale or lease, or to be furnished under a contract for service, raw materials, work in process, or materials used or consumed in a business, including farm products such as crops or livestock, held for sale or lease;
(2) "new value" means money or money's worth in goods, services, or new credit, or release by a transferee of property previously transferred to such transferee in a transaction that is neither void nor voidable by the debtor or the trustee under any applicable law, including proceeds of such property, but does not include an obligation substituted for an existing obligation;
(3) "receivable" means right to payment, whether or not such right has been earned by performance; and
(4) a debt for a tax is incurred on the day when such tax is last payable without penalty, including any extension.
(b) Except as provided in subsection (c) of this section, the trustee may avoid any transfer of an interest of the debtor in property—
(1) to or for the benefit of a creditor;
(2) for or on account of an antecedent debt owed by the debtor before such transfer was made;
(3) made while the debtor was insolvent;
(4) made—
(A) on or within 90 days before the date of the filing of the petition; or
(B) between ninety days and one year before the date of the filing of the petition, if such creditor at the time of such transfer was an insider; and
(5) that enables such creditor to receive more than such creditor would receive if—
(A) the case were a case under chapter 7 of this title;
(B) the transfer had not been made; and

(C) such creditor received payment of such debt to the extent provided by the provisions of this title.

(c) The trustee may not avoid under this section a transfer—

(1) to the extent that such transfer was—

(A) intended by the debtor and the creditor to or for whose benefit such transfer was made to be a contemporaneous exchange for new value given to the debtor; and

(B) in fact a substantially contemporaneous exchange;

(2) to the extent that such transfer was—

(A) in payment of a debt incurred by the debtor in the ordinary course of business or financial affairs of the debtor and the transferee;

(B) made in the ordinary course of business or financial affairs of the debtor and the transferee; and

(C) made according to ordinary business terms;

(3) that creates a security interest in property acquired by the debtor—

(A) to the extent such security interest secures new value that was—

(i) given at or after the signing of a security agreement that contains a description of such property as collateral;

(ii) given by or on behalf of the secured party under such agreement;

(iii) given to enable the debtor to acquire such property; and

(iv) in fact used by the debtor to acquire such property; and

(B) that is perfected on or before 20 days after the debtor receives possession of such property;

(4) to or for the benefit of a creditor, to the extent that, after such transfer, such creditor gave new value to or for the benefit of the debtor—

(A) not secured by an otherwise unavoidable security interest; and

(B) on account of which new value the debtor did not make an otherwise unavoidable transfer to or for the benefit of such creditor;

(5) that creates a perfected security interest in inventory or a receivable or the proceeds of either, except to the extent that the aggregate of all such transfers to the transferee caused a reduction, as of the date of the filing of the petition and to the prejudice of other creditors holding unsecured claims, of any amount by which the debt secured by such security interest exceeded the value of all security interests for such debt on the later of—

(A) (i) with respect to a transfer to which subsection (b)(4)(A) of this section applies, 90 days before the date of the filing of the petition; or

(ii) with respect to a transfer to which subsection (b)(4)(B) of this section applies, one year before the date of the filing of the petition; or

(B) the date on which new value was first given under the security agreement creating such security interest;

(6) that is the fixing of a statutory lien that is not avoidable under section 545 of this title; or

(7) to the extent such transfer was a bona fide payment of a debt to a spouse, former spouse, or child of the debtor, for alimony to, maintenance for, or support of such spouse or child, in connection with a separation agreement, divorce decree or other order of a court of record, determination made in accordance with State or territorial law by a governmental unit, or property settlement agreement, but not to the extent that such debt—

(A) is assigned to anther entity, voluntarily, by operation of law, or otherwise; or

(B) includes a liability designed as alimony, maintenance, or support, unless such liability is actually in the nature of alimony, maintenance or support; or

(8) if, in a case filed by an individual debtor whose debts are primarily consumer debts, the aggregate value of all property that constitutes or is affected by such transfer is less than $600.

(d) The trustee may avoid a transfer of an interest in property of the debtor transferred to or for the benefit of a surety to secure reimbursement of such a surety that furnished a bond or other obligation to dissolve a judicial lien that would have been avoidable by the trustee under subsection (b) of this section. The liability of such surety under such bond or obligation shall be discharged to the extent of the value of such property recovered by the trustee or the amount paid to the trustee.

(e)(1) For the purposes of this section—

(A) a transfer of real property other than fixtures, but including the interest of a seller or purchaser under a contract for the sale of real property, is perfected when a bona fide purchaser of such property from the debtor against whom applicable law permits such transfer to be perfected cannot acquire an interest that is superior to the interest of the transferee; and

(B) a transfer of a fixture or property other than real property is perfected when a creditor on a simple contract cannot acquire a judicial lien that is superior to the interest of the transferee.

(2) For the purposes of this section, except as provided in paragraph (3) of this subsection, a transfer is made—

(A) at the time such transfer takes effect between the transferor and the transferee, if such transfer is perfected at, or within 10 days after, such time, except as provided in subsection (c)(3)(B);

(B) at the time such transfer is perfected, if such transfer is perfected after such 10 days; or

(C) immediately before the date of the filing of the petition, if such transfer is not perfected at the later of—

(i) the commencement of the case; or

(ii) 10 days after such transfer takes effect between the transferor and the transferee.

(3) For the purposes of this section, a transfer is not made until the debtor has acquired rights in the property transferred.

(f) For the purposes of this section, the debtor is presumed to have been insolvent on and during the 90 days immediately preceding the date of the filing of the petition.

(g) For the purposes of this section, the trustee has the burden of proving the avoidability of a transfer under subsection (b) of this section, and the creditor or party in interest against whom recovery or avoidance is sought has the burden of proving the nonavoidability of a transfer under subsection (c) of this section.

PROBLEM 355

On June 8, Business Corporation borrowed $80,000 from Octopus National Bank (ONB) and gave the bank a security interest in its equipment (worth $100,000). On July 18, ONB filed a valid financing statement in the proper place. The next day Business Corporation filed its bankruptcy petition. Can the trustee destroy ONB's secured position and turn it into a general creditor under the theory that the delayed perfection is a preference? If ONB *had* perfected on June 8 but the debtor made some extraordinary payments to ONB in the 90-day period before the filing of the petition, could the trustee use §547 to make ONB pay that money back into the estate? See White & Summers §23-4, at 1088. Finally, again assume that ONB had perfected on June 8 but that the collateral was only worth $60,000 (the debt was still $80,000, so the bank is undersecured). Would routine payments made to service this debt be preferential? See §547(c)(2); Union Bank v. Wolas, 502 U.S. 151 (1991).

PROBLEM 356

On November 1 the Piggy National Bank loaned Kermit $1,000 to buy a banjo he wanted for his nightclub act, making him sign a security agreement and a financing statement. He bought the banjo on

November 15, and the bank filed the financing statement in the proper place on November 20. Kermit filed his bankruptcy petition the next day. Is the *transfer* of the security interest in his banjo a preference? See §547(c)(3). If the bank's security interest was not of the *purchase money* variety but was simply a floating lien covering all after-acquired equipment, what result using the same dates? See §547(e)(2); White & Summers §23-5.

PROBLEM 357

In early 2013 John Carter borrowed $1,000 from the Barsoom World Bank; it was a *signature loan* (i.e., no collateral). On September 25, 2013, John made a $500 payment to the bank (assume that this payment is not in the ordinary course), but on October 4 he borrowed $300 more from the bank, giving it a security interest in his sword collection. The bank never filed a financing statement, and John filed a bankruptcy petition on November 8, 2013. How much, if anything, can his bankruptcy trustee recover from the bank? See §§544(a)(2), 547(c)(4); White & Summers §23-5.

III. THE FLOATING LIEN IN BANKRUPTCY

Section 60 of the former Bankruptcy Act condemned as a preference the creation of a security interest within four months of the filing of the bankruptcy petition unless the creditor advanced new money for the collateral as it was acquired. A question of immense concern to creditors who lent against inventory or accounts receivable was whether their security interest in the collateral acquired in that four-month period would be preferential. Even though the UCC clearly permits after-acquired property to be covered automatically by the security interest, the Code is drafted so that the security interest cannot *attach* or be *perfected* until the debtor acquires an interest in the property and, arguably, *that* occurs within the four-month period; §§9-203, 9-308(a). Under both the prior and the current versions of the Bankruptcy Act *perfection* of the security interest is the moment of "transfer" in preference disputes, and thus the argument is that the collateral first falling under the floating lien during the preference period is recoverable by the trustee as a preferential "transfer" securing an old debt.

Everyone crossed their fingers and waited for a federal appellate court to hear a bankruptcy challenge to an Article 9 floating lien. The Seventh Circuit spoke first. In Grain Merchants of Ind., Inc. v. Union Bank & Sav. Co., 408 F.2d 209, 6 U.C.C. Rep. Serv. 1 (7th Cir. 1969), the court upheld the floating lien's validity as to the property falling under it during the preference period, though the court noted that in the case at bar there was both inflow and outgo of collateral during the relevant time period, and the creditor had thus not improved its position by getting an increased amount of collateral prior to bankruptcy.

The Bankruptcy Code's solution to this after-acquired property/ preference issue is found in §547(c)(5). The test found therein, while alarming at first view, is remarkably simple in operation. It commands the courts to compare the debt/collateral ratio at two points: 90 days before the filing of the petition (or the first date within that period where a debt was owed if the loan was made within the 90-day period), and the date of the filing of the petition. There is a preference to the extent that the creditor's position has improved within this period.

PROBLEM 358

The Last National Bank had a perfected security interest in the inventory of the Epstein bookstore, which owed the bank $20,000. On March 1, the inventory was worth $8,000. On May 28, when Epstein filed for bankruptcy, the inventory was worth $20,000 because the store had purchased several new shipments for cash in the interim. What can the trustee do about the bank's claim? What if the bank first loaned Epstein $20,000 on May 1, when the inventory was worth $12,000?

In re Smith's Home Furnishings, Inc.

United States Court of Appeals, Ninth Circuit, 2001
254 F.3d 959

CYNTHIA HOLCOMB HALL, Circuit Judge:
Plaintiff-appellant Michael Batlan ("trustee") appeals the district court's judgment affirming the decision of the bankruptcy court. Batlan filed an action to recover payments made by a chapter 11

debtor to defendant-appellee Transamerica Commercial Finance Corporation ("TCFC"). The bankruptcy court found that the payments were not avoidable transfers under 11 U.S.C. §547(b). We agree with the bankruptcy court and the district court that the trustee did not satisfy his burden of showing that TCFC received a greater amount by virtue of the payments than it would have received in a hypothetical chapter 7 liquidation.

FACTUAL AND PROCEDURAL BACKGROUND

Smith's Home Furnishings, Inc. ("Smith's"), sold furniture, electronic goods, and appliances at 19 stores in Oregon, Washington, and Idaho. TCFC was one of Smith's primary lenders for almost a decade. TCFC financed Smith's purchase of some merchandise (the "prime inventory"), consisting mainly of electronic goods and appliances. TCFC's loans were secured by a first-priority floating lien on the prime inventory and the proceeds from it. Thus, the prime inventory served as collateral for TCFC's loans to Smith's.

Under the loan agreements, TCFC extended credit to Smith's by granting approval to various manufacturers. After receiving approval, the manufacturers shipped merchandise to Smith's. When Smith's sold a product financed by TCFC, it paid TCFC the wholesale price of that product.

Smith's did not segregate its sales receipts. Instead, Smith's deposited all its sales proceeds into commingled bank accounts at the end of each day. First Interstate Bank ("the Bank"), Smith's revolving-line-of-credit financier, swept the accounts daily, leaving the accounts with overnight balances of zero. The next day, the Bank advanced new funds to Smith's if sufficient collateral was available. Smith's then paid its operating expenses and creditors, including TCFC.[2]

During 1994, Smith's suffered substantial losses. Consequently, in March 1995 TCFC reduced Smith's line of credit from $25 million to $20 million. Over the next few months, TCFC reduced Smith's line of credit twice more, down to $13 million by August. During the same period, TCFC required substantial paydowns of Smith's debt; Smith's paid TCFC most of its available cash in a series of 36 payments, totaling more than $12 million, between May 24, 1995, and August 22, 1995.

---

2. Because of these procedures, the allegedly preferential payments, which we will describe below, were not made directly from the proceeds of the sales of TCFC's collateral.

On August 18, 1995, TCFC declared a final default, accelerated the entire debt due from Smith's, and sought a receiver for the company. For the first time, TCFC also sought to require Smith's to segregate the proceeds from its collateral.

Smith's voluntarily initiated bankruptcy proceedings under chapter 11 of the Bankruptcy Code on August 22, 1995 (the "petition date"). As of that date, Smith's owed $10,728,809.96 to TCFC. TCFC took possession of its collateral and liquidated it, receiving $10,823,010.58.

On October 11, 1995, the case was converted to a chapter 7 liquidation and Batlan was appointed as trustee. The trustee discovered the $12,842,438.96 in payments that Smith's had made to TCFC during the 90 days before the petition date (the "preference period"). Believing that the payments were preferential, he asked TCFC to return the money to the bankruptcy estate. When TCFC refused, the trustee initiated this adversary proceeding, seeking to avoid the payments as preferential transfers, under 11 U.S.C. §547(b), and to recover the money for the benefit of other creditors of Smith's, under 11 U.S.C. §550(a).

The parties stipulated that the payments met the first four elements of a preferential transfer under 11 U.S.C. §547(b)(1)-(4). . . . The parties proceeded to trial to determine whether the payments met the fifth element of the preferential transfer statute, 11 U.S.C. §547(b)(5), and whether TCFC could establish an affirmative defense under 11 U.S.C. §547(c)(5).

On September 10, 1998, the bankruptcy court ruled, in a letter opinion, that the trustee had failed to meet his burden of proof in showing that the payments were preferential transfers. The court reasoned that, because the value of the collateral on the petition date ($10,823,010.58) exceeded the amount of TCFC's claim on the petition date ($10,728,809.96), TCFC was oversecured by $94,200.62. As a result, the court concluded that, because TCFC was a floating-lien creditor, the trustee was required to prove that TCFC was under-secured at some time during the preference period in order to avoid the transfers. The court also ruled that TCFC's collateral should be valued at liquidation value ($10,823,010.58) and that liquidation costs should be deducted from the liquidation value in computing the value of the collateral, but that the trustee had failed to present credible evidence of TCFC's liquidation costs. Because the bankruptcy court concluded that the trustee had not proved that the transfers were preferential, the court did not address TCFC's affirmative defense under §547(c)(5).

The trustee filed a motion for reconsideration. In response, the bankruptcy court amended its opinion to correct typographical and computational errors, but otherwise confirmed its judgment. The trustee timely filed an appeal to the district court, raising the same issues that it raises in this appeal. In a published opinion, Batlan v. Transamerica Commercial Finance Corp., 237 B.R. 765, 776 (D. Or. 1999), the district court affirmed the bankruptcy court's decision "in all respects." This timely appeal followed. . . .

DISCUSSION

I.   "GREATER AMOUNT" TEST

This case requires us to interpret two sections of the Bankruptcy Code, 11 U.S.C. §§547(b)(5) and 547(g). 11 U.S.C. §547(b) permits a trustee to "avoid any transfer of an interest of the debtor in property" when certain conditions are met. One of the conditions is that the transfer enable the creditor to receive more than such creditor would receive if:

> (A) the case were a case under chapter 7 of this title;
> (B) the transfer had not been made; and
> (C) such creditor received payment of such debt to the extent provided by the provisions of this title.

11 U.S.C. §547(b)(5). TCFC and the trustee dispute whether the 36 payments made during the preference period enabled TCFC, as a result of the 36 payments, to receive more than if the payments had not been made and TCFC had received payments only pursuant to a Chapter 7 liquidation. Section 547(g) places the burden of proof on the trustee to show all of the conditions of §547(b). Thus, the trustee must show that the creditor received a greater amount than it would have if the transfer had not been made and there had been a hypothetical chapter 7 liquidation as of the petition date. If the trustee shows that TCFC received a greater amount by virtue of the 36 payments, then the payments are avoidable as preferential transfers. See In re Lewis W. Shurtleff, Inc., 778 F.2d 1416, 1421 (9th Cir. 1985). The trustee contends that he satisfied his burden because: 1) the 36 payments plus the amount that TCFC received from the post-petition sale of its collateral is greater than the amount received from the post-petition sale of the collateral standing alone; and 2) TCFC has not traced the source of the allegedly preferential payments to sales of its collateral. We disagree with both of the trustee's arguments.

A.   *The add-back method does not satisfy the trustee's burden when*
     the payments come from collateral secured by a floating lien

The trustee tried to satisfy his burden under §547(b)(5) by adding the amount of the 36 payments to the amount TCFC received as a result of the post-petition sale of its remaining collateral. The trustee then compared this amount to the obviously smaller amount of the post-petition sale by itself and concluded that TCFC must have received a greater amount because of the payments. Some bankruptcy courts have used the same "add-back" method employed by the trustee to determine the status of a creditor on the petition date. See In re Al-Ben, Inc., 156 B.R. 72, 75 (Bankr. N.D. Ala. 1991) (adding alleged preferences to the amount of unpaid balance at the petition date to find the creditor's secured status); In re Estate of Ascot Mortgage, Inc., 153 B.R. 1002, 1018 (Bankr. N.D. Ga. 1993) (adding pre-petition amounts received to what would have been received under a chapter 7 liquidation).

We agree with the bankruptcy court and the district court, however, and conclude that the "add-back" calculation does not satisfy the trustee's burden in this case. Pre-petition transfers to a creditor that is fully secured on the petition date are generally not preferential because the secured creditor is entitled to 100 percent of its claims. See In re LCO Enterprises, 12 F.3d 938, 941 (9th Cir. 1993). This is not a hard and fast rule. As the bankruptcy court in this case noted, payments that change the status of a creditor from partially unsecured to fully secured at the time of petition may be preferential. See Porter v. Yukon Nat'l Bank, 866 F.2d 355, 359 (10th Cir. 1989). Moreover, a transfer may be avoided when the creditor is fully secured at the time of payment, but is undersecured on the petition date. See In re Estate of Sufolla, Inc., 2 F.3d 977, 985-86 (9th Cir. 1993). The trustee failed to show, however, that TCFC was undersecured *at any time* during the preference period. Instead, the evidence submitted showed that as of the petition date, the value of the collateral held by Smith's exceeded its indebtedness to TCFC. If TCFC was never undercollateralized, then TCFC could not have received more by virtue of the 36 payments than it would have received in a hypothetical liquidation without the payments.

It is important to understand that TCFC did not loan one fixed amount to the debtor; instead, TCFC held a "floating lien." A floating lien is a financing device where the creditor claims an interest in property acquired after the original extension of the loan and extends its security interest to cover further advances. The floating lien is a lien against a constantly changing mass of collateral for a loan value that will change as payments are received and further advances are made. See 3 Norton Bankr. L. & Prac. 2d §57.23. The cases the trustee cites applying the "add-back" method do not deal with floating liens. It is not correct to assume that the 36 payments gave TCFC more than it would have received if the payments had not been made. Instead, under a floating lien arrangement, those payments are used to liquidate part of the debtor's debt. Then, new credit under the floating lien is extended and is secured by new collateral. It is not enough for the trustee to show that the 36 payments plus the amount received upon dissolution exceeded the amount of TCFC's secured claim as of the petition date. Since collateral and indebtedness changed throughout the preference period, these values do not prove that TCFC received more by virtue of the payments than it would have received without them. Under §547(b)(5), the trustee must show that the amount of indebtedness under the floating lien was greater than the amount of collateral at some point during the 90-day period. See In re Schwinn Bicycle Co., 200 B.R. 980, 992-93 (Bankr. N.D. Ill. 1996) ("At no point in time did the collateral value fall below the outstanding debt, and therefore TIFCO was not preferenced in having received payments on its secured debt.").

The trustee contends that the existence of the floating lien means that the burden is shifted to TCFC under §547(c)(5). Section 547(c)(5) provides an affirmative defense for creditors when the trustee has successfully demonstrated that the creditor received more from the payments than under a hypothetical liquidation. Section 547(c)(5) insulates the transfer of a security interest in after-acquired property, i.e., a floating lien, provided that the creditor does not improve its position during the preference period. In effect, the trustee contends that the existence of a floating lien means that he does not have to prove that the creditor was undersecured at some point during the 90-day period and therefore received more by virtue of the payments than the creditor would have if the creditor had waited for a chapter 7 liquidation.

We reject the trustee's argument. A floating lien does not shift the burden of showing avoidability to the creditor. The trustee still has to satisfy his burden under §547(b)(5). The Tenth Circuit has addressed the question of what needs to be shown by a trustee to avoid a transfer financed by the sale of inventory subject to a floating lien. See In re Castletons, 990 F.2d 551 (10th Cir. 1993). In *Castletons*, the creditor held a floating lien on the debtor's inventory, accounts receivable, and proceeds. The trustee sought to avoid the payments given by the debtor to the creditor during the preference period. The Tenth Circuit affirmed the district court's holding that the trustee failed to show that the creditor received more from the challenged payments than it would have received in a chapter 7 liquidation. It explained:

> [A]ll payments to [the creditor] came from assets already subject to its security interest. It is further uncontested that the nature of [the creditor's] security interest in debtor's assets was never altered during the preference period. Under these circumstances, it cannot be said, as §547(b)(5) requires, the transfers enabled [the creditor] to receive more on its debt than would be available to it in a Chapter 7 distribution.

Id. at 555. Essential to the court's holding was its recognition that the creditor held a floating lien:

> "While the identity of individual items of collateral changed because of sales and subsequent acquisitions of new collateral, the overall nature of [the creditor's] security interest remained the same."

Id. at 556.

It is true that other courts have evaluated floating lien cases by proceeding directly to the §547(c)(5) affirmative defense without a discussion of the requirements of §547(b)(5). See In re Wesley Indus., 30 F.3d 1438, 1443 (11th Cir. 1994); In re Lackow Bros., Inc., 752 F.2d 1529, 1530-31 (11th Cir. 1985). But in those cases, the parties had stipulated or the bankruptcy court had found that the creditor was undersecured as of the petition date. In other words, the §547(b)(5) burden had already been satisfied so it did not need to be discussed. The trustee in this case never showed that TCFC was undersecured at any point during the 90-day period and the bankruptcy court determined that TCFC was fully secured as of the petition date. The trustee did not satisfy his burden. See Richard F. Duncan, Preferential Transfers, the Floating Lien, and Section 547(c)(5) of the Bankruptcy Reform Act of 1978, 36 Ark. L. Rev. 1, 20 (1987) ("[I]t is not necessary to reach the question of application of section 547(c)(5) until after the trustee has met his burden of proving all of the necessary elements of a preference under section 547(b)."); James J. White & Daniel Israel, Preference Conundrums, 98 Com. L.J. 1, 4 (1993) ("It is important to remember, however, that 547(c)(5) applies only to a creditor who is undersecured ninety days before bankruptcy. The creditor who is fully secured cannot be attacked under 547(b). There is no initial deficiency and later transactions cannot improve the creditor's position.").

B.   *The burden of tracing the funds used to make the preferential payments is on the trustee*

The trustee contends that its use of the "add-back" method is correct because TCFC has not shown that the source of the allegedly preferential payments was sales of TCFC's collateral. In Castletons, it was undisputed that all of the preference period payments came from sales of assets subject to the creditor's floating lien. See In re Castletons, 990 F.2d at 555. In this case, however, the payments came from a commingled account that contained monies from the sales of other goods not subject to TCFC's lien. When Smith's made a sale, the proceeds were deposited into commingled bank accounts. Smith's bank swept the accounts daily, leaving them with zero balances overnight. Thus, the challenged payments were not made directly from the proceeds of the sales of TCFC's collateral. On the other hand, there is no evidence indicating that Smith's did not sell off enough of TCFC's collateral to account for all of the challenged payments. . . .

[W]e believe that it is part of the trustee's §547(b)(5) burden to trace the funds used to make the payments to sales of merchandise not subject to TCFC's liens. See In re Robinson Bros. Drilling, Inc., 6 F.3d 701, 703 (10th Cir. 1993) ("Under 11 U.S.C. §547(g), a trustee seeking to avoid an allegedly preferential transfer under §547(b) 'has the burden of proving by a preponderance of the evidence every essential, controverted element resulting in the preference.'") (quoting 4 Collier on Bankruptcy ¶547.21[5] at 547-93 (15th ed. 1993)); cf. In re Prescott, 805 F.2d 719, 726-27 (7th Cir. 1986) (placing burden on trustee to establish value of collateral and to show that value of collateral was less than the amount of indebtedness at time of transfer). One might argue that the creditor will be in a better position than the trustee to prove whether or not the alleged preferential payments came from the proceeds of the sale of its own collateral. On the other hand, in bankruptcy, it is the trustee who accedes to the debtor's books and records and has easier access and a better ability to divine the financial activities of the debtor in its last months of operation. Regardless of which side is better equipped to decipher the debtor's final financial actions, we hold that the language of the statute places the burden of demonstrating the source of such preferential payments squarely on the trustee.[3] See In re Lease-A-Fleet, 151 B.R. at

---

3. Our decision furthers the paramount policy behind §547: equality of distribution among creditors of the debtor. See In re Schwinn Bicycle Co., 200 B.R. 980, 993 (Bankr. N.D. Ill. 1996). If a floating lien creditor genuinely did not profit from a preference period transfer, then the creditor should not be forced to disgorge those payments. We agree with the dissent that §547 also tries to dissuade creditors

348 ("It is therefore an unfortunate fact of life that a preference plaintiff must effectively prove a negative (that the defendant is not a totally secured creditor), even though the secured creditor is the party with most access to proof of the validity of its own security interests.").

Commingled funds or not, §547(b)(5) places the burden on the trustee to show that the payments at issue came from a source other than sales of TCFC's collateral. Here there is no suggestion that any sales of products funded by TCFC were not subject to TCFC's priority lien. Instead, both parties stipulated that TCFC held a valid security interest in Smith's property. It is true that the route the payment took to TCFC was indirect, but we are not prepared to release the trustee from his burden under §547(b)(5) simply because the payments did not, demonstrably, come directly from sale of TCFC's collateral. See In re Compton Corp., 831 F.2d 586, 591 (5th Cir. 1987) ("The federal courts have long recognized that '[t]o constitute a preference, it is not necessary that the transfer be made directly to the creditor.'") (quoting National Bank of Newport v. National Herkimer County Bank, 225 U.S. 178, 184, 32 S. Ct. 633, 56 L. Ed. 1042 (1912)). It is up to the trustee to show that the payments did not come from TCFC's collateral before he can use the add-back method to satisfy his §547(b)(5) burden. . . .

CONCLUSION

We affirm the decision of the bankruptcy court in all respects. [The forceful dissent of Judge Graber is omitted.]

IV. FRAUDULENT TRANSFERS

Under §548 or §544(b) of the Bankruptcy Code, the trustee can avoid any "transfer" (including the creation of an Article 9 security interest) that is a *fraudulent transfer*. The law as to what is or is not a

---

from rushing to extract payments from the debtor shortly before bankruptcy. We do not think that our decision controverts this policy or that this is a case involving a race to the debtor's assets. The trustee offered no evidence that TCFC was less than 100 percent secured at the time of any of the 36 payments. For the payments it made to TCFC, the debtor received additional financing to keep its business afloat. Rather than encouraging a race to dismember the debtor, our decision to place the burden on the trustee to show that TCFC did not receive more by virtue of the payments than it would under a hypothetical liquidation encourages TCFC and other creditors to continue extending credit under floating liens.

fraudulent transfer has been developing for centuries, but is generally summarized in the Uniform Fraudulent Transfer Act (UFTA), which most states have adopted. There, an existing or later creditor (and the bankruptcy trustee per §544(b)) may avoid two types of fraudulent transfers: those where the transferee from an insolvent debtor does not give "reasonably equivalent value in exchange," and those where the transferor and the transferee have the *actual intent* to defraud the debtor's creditors.

PROBLEM 359

When Arnold Austin retired as an international diplomat, he was famous but much in debt. He decided to make money by writing his memoirs, which were certainly best-seller material. He gave a security interest in the right to receive royalty payments from his publisher to his wife as collateral for "the many debts I owe her," and she filed a financing statement in the proper place five months before Arnold filed his bankruptcy petition. Can the trustee avoid this security interest? (At common law one of the *badges of fraud*—situations in which fraud is presumed—was a voluntary transfer made by the debtor to a family member. United States v. West, 299 F. Supp. 661 (D. Del. 1969).) See G. Gilmore §45.3.1; King v. Ionization Intl., Inc., 825 F.2d 1180, 5 U.C.C. Rep. Serv. 2d 228 (7th Cir. 1987).

V. NON-CONSENSUAL LIENS AND THE TRUSTEE

Section 547(b) of the Bankruptcy Code condemns as preferential all judicial liens acquired by a creditor within the 90 days preceding the bankruptcy filing if taken while the bankrupt was insolvent.

As for statutory liens (the garage mechanic, etc.), they are effective under §545 against the trustee if (a) they would be good against a BFP and (b) they do not arise only on insolvency. The reason for this last rule—statutory liens that arise only on insolvency are void against the trustee—is this: originally the Bankruptcy Code permitted the separate states to specify which general creditors would get priority payments when the bankrupt's estate was distributed. When that power was taken away from the states, the states battled back by rewriting their priority statutes as statutory lien statutes—providing, for example, that unpaid employees would have an automatic lien on the employer's assets if the employer became insolvent but not otherwise. Since Congress didn't want the states to be able to dictate priorities in a federal insolvency proceeding, §545 and its predecessor were redrafted to avoid this type of statutory lien.

Chapter 24

PROCEEDS

I. THE MEANING OF PROCEEDS

Proceeds is defined in §9-102(a)(64) [*cash proceeds*, a subcategory of proceeds is defined in §9-102(a)(9)], and the priority rules for proceeds are contained in §9-315. Read those sections.

PROBLEM 360

When Rosetta Stone bought a new car from Champollion Motors, Inc., she traded in her five-year-old car, made a $200 down payment by giving the dealer her check, and signed a promissory note for the balance payable to the dealership. Rameses National Bank had a perfected security interest in Champollion Motors' inventory.

(a) Does that security interest continue in the car once it is delivered to Ms. Stone? See §9-320(a).

(b) Under §9-315(a) the bank's security interest will continue in *proceeds,* as defined in subsection (1). What are the proceeds of the car sale?

(c) Is the attachment of the creditor's security interest in the proceeds automatic, or must they be claimed in the original security agreement? See §9-203(f).

Farmers Cooperative Elevator Co. v. Union State Bank

Iowa Supreme Court, 1987
409 N.W.2d 178, 4 U.C.C. Rep. Serv. 2d 1

LARSON, J. Rodger Cockrum operated a farm and hog confinement operation in Madison County, Iowa. For several years financing for a substantial portion of the operation came from [Union] State Bank of Winterset (Union State). In February 1981, Union State loaned Cockrum a large sum of money and took a security agreement covering

> all equipment and fixtures, including but not limited to sheds and storage facilities, used or acquired for use in farming operations, whether now or hereafter existing or acquired; all farm products including but not limited to, *livestock, and supplies used or produced in farming operations whether now or hereafter existing or acquired.* . . .

(Emphasis added.)

In December 1983 and January 1984, Cockrum entered into several purchase money security agreements with Farmers Cooperative Elevator Company (CO-OP) for livestock feed. See Iowa Code §554.9312 (1983). For each transaction, CO-OP filed a financing statement with the Secretary of State, which stated:

> This is a purchase money security interest which covers Collateral described as all feed sold to Debtors by Secured Party and all of Debtors' feeder hogs now owned or hereafter acquired including . . . additions, replacements, and substitutions of such livestock, including all issues presently or hereafter conceived and born, the products thereof, and the proceeds of any of the described Collateral.

Cockrum defaulted on his obligations to both Union State and the CO-OP. CO-OP commenced an action against Cockrum seeking possession of collateral. (International Barter Corporation was also joined as a defendant, but its petition under chapter 11 of the Bankruptcy Act stayed further proceedings against it, and it is not involved in the present action.)

Union State filed a statement of indebtedness and requested that its security interests be established as a first security lien on Cockrum's hog inventory and any sale proceeds therefrom. CO-OP responded by filing an amendment to its petition, joining Union State as a defendant and alleging that its right to the hogs is superior to Union State's.

On CO-OP's motion to adjudicate law points, the district court ruled that Union State's security interest in the hogs was prior and superior to the CO-OP's. CO-OP has appealed from that decision.

We first address CO-OP's argument that its interest in the livestock and proceeds therefrom is superior to Union State's under section 554.9312(4) [now §9-324(a) — Ed.]. That section provides:

> A purchase money security interest in collateral other than inventory has priority over a conflicting security interest in the same collateral or its proceeds if the purchase money security interest is perfected at the time the debtor receives possession of the collateral or within twenty days thereafter.

"Purchase money security interests" are defined in section 554.9107 [now §9-103 — Ed.]:

> A security interest is a "purchase money security interest" to the extent that it is
> a. taken or retained by the seller of the collateral to secure all or part of its price; or
> b. taken by a person who by making advances or incurring an obligation gives value to enable the debtor to acquire rights in or the use of collateral if such value is in fact so used.

Union State concedes that CO-OP held a purchase money security interest in the feed. The question, however, is whether such a priority interest continues in livestock which consume the feed.

In essence, one who takes a purchase money security interest under section 554.9107(a) is the equivalent of the old conventional vendor—a seller who has, in effect, made a loan by selling goods on credit. See J. White & R. Summers, Uniform Commercial Code §25-5, at 1043 (2d ed. 1980). Put more simply, a purchase money security interest "is a secured loan for the price of new collateral." Henderson, Coordination of the Uniform Commercial Code with Other State and Federal Law in the Farm Financing Context, 14 Idaho L. Rev. 363, 375 (1978). In this case, CO-OP took the purchase money security interests

to secure the price of the feed, not the hogs. Consequently, by definition, CO-OP does not have a purchase money security interest in the hogs.

CO-OP, nevertheless, argues that their priority interest in the feed
continues to be superior in the hogs pursuant to section 554.9203(3)
because the hogs are "proceeds" of the feed. That section provides,
"[u]nless otherwise agreed a security agreement gives the secured
party the rights to proceeds provided by section 554.9306." Subsection
1 of section 554.9306 defines proceeds to include "whatever is received
upon the sale, exchange, collection or other disposition of collateral or
proceeds."

CO-OP contends that the "other disposition of collateral" language in section 554.9306 [now §9-315(a)—Ed.] includes ingestion
and the biological processes involved when livestock consume feed,
and as a result, fattened livestock are proceeds of the feed they consume. Such an argument was rejected in a case on all four hooves, so to
speak. In First National Bank of Brush v. Bostron, 564 P.2d 964, 966
(Colo. App. 1977), the court emphasized that "[the livestock producer]
received nothing when he disposed of the collateral by feeding it to
the . . . cattle . . . the collateral was consumed, and there are no traceable proceeds to which the security interest may be said to have
attached."

We agree with the result reached by the Colorado court. Ingestion
and biological transformation of feed is not a type of "other disposition" within the contemplation of section 554.9306. For UCC purposes,
the hogs are not proceeds of the feed.

CO-OP also argues that it should prevail over Union State pursuant to section 554.9315(1) [now §9-336—Ed.], which provides in
part:

> If a security interest in goods was perfected and subsequently the
> goods or a part thereof have become part of a product or mass, the
> security interest continues in the product or mass if
>   a. the goods are so manufactured, processed, assembled or
> commingled that their identity is lost in the product or mass. . . .

CO-OP contends that its superior interest in the feed continued in the
hogs because the feed became commingled with the hogs.

Section 9-315 of the Uniform Commercial Code is probably the
least litigated and discussed section of article 9. See Hawkland Uniform
Commercial Code Series §9-315:01, at 256 (1986) (hereinafter Hawkland). The only reported case examining this question is *Bostron.*
There, the court concluded

that cattle are neither a "product" nor a "mass" as these terms are used in the statute. The reference in subsection (a) to "manufactured, processed, assembled, or commingled" precludes any other interpretation. The feed which the cattle ate did not undergo any of these transformations, that is, it was not manufactured, processed, assembled or commingled with the cattle. . . . Once eaten the feed not only loses its identity, but in essence it ceases to exist and thus does not become part of the mass in the sense that the Code uses the phrase.

Bostron, 564 P.2d at 966.

Examining the *Bostron* decision and the question presented by the present case, one Uniform Commercial Code commentator has said:

Other than section 9-315, no Code provision clearly suggests a contrary result, and section 9-315 does not seem to apply since the goods have not been manufactured, processed or commingled. Rather, their identity has been lost through ingestion, a process apparently not contemplated by section 9-315.

Hawkland at 262.

When construing a statute, we search for an interpretation that is sensible, workable, practical and logical. Emmetsburg Ready Mix Co. v. Norris, 362 N.W.2d 498, 499 (Iowa 1985). CO-OP's argument, although creative, stretches the language of section 554.9315 beyond our interpretation guideposts.

Because of our disposition on the merits, we need not address Union State's procedural issues. We have considered all arguments raised and find no error.

Affirmed.

While Article 9 does not usually apply to security interests taken in either insurance policies as collateral (the common law or other statutes regulate these transactions), insurance payments that qualify as *proceeds* are regulated by the Code; §9-109(d)(8). For example, if the collateral is a car that is destroyed in a traffic mishap and the car owner receives compensation from an insurance company, the insurance money is *proceeds,* and any security interest in the car attaches to these monies.

Similarly, if the car owner sells the car and deposits the buyer's money in a bank account, the account now is *proceeds,* and the car money can be traced into the bank account and tapped by the unpaid secured creditor. Read §§9-315(a)(2) and 9-315(b)(2).

PROBLEM 361

Farmers' Friend Credit Association loaned Farmer Bean money secured by his crops. In 2011 the federal government paid Farmer Bean not to grow any crop that year. Is the government payment the "proceeds" of the crop? See In re Weyland, 63 Bankr. 854, 2 U.C.C. Rep. Serv. 2d 624 (Bankr. E.D. Wis. 1986); Annot., 79 A.L.R.4th 903.

II.   *PRIORITIES IN PROCEEDS*

PROBLEM 362

The Aquarius Auto Audio Shop (AAAS) sold and installed stereo systems in cars. Its inventory was financed by the Canis Major Bank and Trust Co., which had a perfected security interest in present and after-acquired inventory. When Aquarius sold the systems, it sometimes was paid cash, sometimes extended credit without signed contracts, and sometimes made credit customers sign contracts promising payment and granting AAAS a security interest in the systems. When Aquarius needed further financing, it took a later loan from the Cassiopeia Finance Company, granting the lender a security interest in its accounts receivable and its chattel paper. Cassiopeia knew all about the prior loan and inventory security interest of the Canis Major Bank at the time it filed its financing statement in the proper place. Aquarius defaulted on both loans, and both secured parties claimed the accounts and chattel paper (only Canis Major claimed the inventory). Canis Major's theory was that the accounts and chattel paper were *proceeds* of the inventory. The chattel paper was in Cassiopeia's possession; it had not yet collected any of the accounts receivable. Who should prevail? See §§9-315, 9-330(a), 9-322(a) and (b); White & Summers §24-17. What result where the accounts receivable financer filed first?

PROBLEM 363

Shadrach Heating and Air Conditioning, Inc., borrowed $15,000 from the Meshach Merchants Financing Association (MMFA) in order to purchase a new furnace for its own home office. When one of its important clients needed an identical furnace in a hurry, Shadrach Heating sold it its own new furnace, which it installed in the client's place of business. The $17,000 check it received in payment was put into Shadrach's checking account (balance prior to this deposit: $81) with the Abednego State Bank. Thereafter, Shadrach made one further deposit of $5,000, followed a week later by a withdrawal of $5,040.

(a) Are proceeds from the furnace sale still in the bank accounts? See Universal C.I.T. Credit Corp. v. Farmers Bank, 358 F. Supp. 317, 13 U.C.C. Rep. Serv. 109 (E.D. Mo. 1973) (the general rule is that "in tracing commingled funds it is presumed that any payments made were from other than funds in which another had a legally recognized interest," called the *lowest intermediate balance* rule). Section 9-315(b) permits tracing of *identifiable* proceeds; see also Official Comment 3 to this section. Note §4-210(b).

(b) If Shadrach Heating defaults on its loan repayment to MMFA and also on an unsecured promissory note currently held by the Abednego State Bank, can the bank exercise its common law right of setoff and pay itself out of the checking account, or is its setoff right junior to MMFA's security interest in the proceeds? See §9-340.

HCC Credit Corp. v. Springs Valley Bank & Trust Co.

Supreme Court of Indiana, 1999
712 N.E.2d 952, 38 U.C.C. Rep. Serv. 2d 1066

SULLIVAN, J. Lindsey Tractor Sales, Inc., sold 14 tractors to a customer and used the $199,122 proceeds to pay off the debt it owed Springs Valley Bank & Trust. Yet HCC Credit Corporation had financed Lindsey's purchase of the tractors and held a valid and perfected security interest in both the tractors and the proceeds from their sale. Because we hold that the payment to the bank was not in the ordinary course of the operation of Lindsey's business, HCC is entitled to recover the $199,122.

BACKGROUND

Lindsey Tractor Sales, Inc., purchased wholesale farm equipment from Hesston Corporation for resale in Lindsey's French Lick farm machinery sales and service business. At the times relevant to this case, HCC Credit Corporation provided financing for the purchases.

Written contracts governed the relationship between Hesston and HCC and Lindsey, including a security agreement. In the security agreement, Lindsey granted HCC a security interest in all the equipment it purchased from Hesston and in the proceeds from the sale of the equipment. Lindsey also agreed to pay HCC immediately for equipment sold from the proceeds of the sale. However, at no time did Hesston or HCC require Lindsey to deposit or segregate proceeds from the sale of Hesston products in a separate account.

The parties agreed and the trial court found that the security agreement was binding and enforceable against Lindsey, that Lindsey understood the purpose and effect of the security agreement (including the requirement of paying for equipment immediately when sold), and that HCC had a valid and perfected security interest in the equipment and proceeds from the sale thereof.

In 1991, the Indiana State Department of Transportation agreed to purchase from Lindsey 14 Hesston tractors. Lindsey acquired the tractors from Hesston on credit provided by, and subject to the security agreement in favor of, HCC. Lindsey received payment from the State on August 15, 1991, and deposited the proceeds of $199,122 in the company's checking account at Springs Valley Bank & Trust. At the time of the deposit, Lindsey had $22,870 in other monies on deposit in the account. On the next day, August 16, 1991, Lindsey wrote a check on this account payable to the bank for $212,104.75.

Lindsey's payment to the bank of the proceeds from the sale of the tractors was applied to pay debts owed by Lindsey to the bank. These debts were evidenced by four promissory notes dated January 23, 1987, November 19, 1990, February 7, 1991, and February 13, 1991. All four represented previously refinanced debts and three of them were not yet due when they were paid on August 16. The bank and Lindsey did not discuss paying off the four notes with Lindsey prior to their payment, nor did the bank seize the account to pay the notes. More specifically, Lindsey did not tell anyone associated with the bank that $199,122 of the $212,104.75 used to pay off the notes was from the sale of Hesston products. On the other hand, during the previous eight years Lindsey had borrowed funds or refinanced debts in excess of 100 times with the bank. The average debt balance outstanding during that period was between $100,000 and $200,000. After the notes were paid with the proceeds from the sale of the tractors, Lindsey owed the bank between $2,000 and $15,000.

Lindsey filed a bankruptcy liquidation proceeding in December of 1991, and dissolved shortly thereafter.

In the trial court, HCC sought to recover the $199,122 in proceeds from the sale of Hesston tractors that the bank received from Lindsey. Each party moved for summary judgment, agreeing that there were no genuine issues of material fact. The trial court granted summary judgment in favor of the bank and the Court of Appeals affirmed. HCC Credit Corp. v. Springs Valley Bank & Trust, 669 N.E.2d 1001 (Ind. Ct. App. 1996).

DISCUSSION

I

Under both the terms of the security agreement between the parties and the provisions of Article 9 of the Uniform Commercial Code as adopted by our legislature, HCC had a valid and perfected security interest in the $199,122 proceeds from the sale of the tractors. See Ind. Code §26-1-9-306(2) [now §9-315(a)—Ed.] ("a security interest continues . . . in any identifiable proceeds including collections received by the debtor"). If this were the end of the matter, there is no question but that HCC would be entitled to the money: UCC Article 9 gives the "secured party, upon a debtor's default priority over 'anyone, anywhere, anyhow' except as otherwise provided by the remaining [UCC] priority rules." Citizens Nat'l Bank of Whitley County v. Mid-States Dev. Co., 177 Ind. App. 548, 557, 380 N.E.2d 1243, 1248 (1978) (citing Ind. Code §26-1-9-201; other citations omitted).

But in promulgating the 1972 version of Article 9 of the Uniform Commercial Code, the National Conference of Commissioners on Uniform State Laws (NCCUSL) appended the following "official comment":

> Where cash proceeds are covered into the debtor's checking account and paid out in the operation of the debtor's business, recipients of the funds of course take free of any claim which the secured party may have in them as proceeds. *What has been said relates to payments and transfers in the ordinary course.* The law of fraudulent conveyances would no doubt in appropriate cases support recovery of proceeds by a secured party from the transferee out of ordinary course or otherwise in collusion with the debtor to defraud the secured party.

UCC §9-306 cmt. 2(c) (1972), 3 U.L.A. 441 (1981) (emphasis supplied). We will refer to this official comment in this opinion as "Comment 2(c)."

Although our legislature has never adopted the NCCUSL comments as authoritative, there seems to be general agreement that, at least to some extent, Comment 2(c) is an exception to the Indiana UCC's general priority rules. The bank argues that in this case, the proceeds were paid out of Lindsey's checking account in the operation of Lindsey's business and that the payment was made in the ordinary course without any collusion with the debtor. As such, the bank contends, Comment 2(c) operates to provide that the bank received the $199,122 free of any claim which HCC had in it as proceeds.[1] The trial court and Court of Appeals adopted this rationale. HCC now seeks transfer, arguing that its perfected security interest entitles it to the proceeds.

II

At a certain level of abstraction, this case requires us to assess the relative rights of a secured creditor to the proceeds of its collateral and of a third party to whom the debtor transfers those proceeds. Sound commercial policy considerations can be marshaled in support of both the rights of the secured party and the rights of the transferee.

A

Commercial policy considerations supporting the rights of a secured party are well set forth well by Judge Garrard in *Citizens National Bank.* In that case, the debtor sold collateral in which a party held a valid and perfected security interest. When the debtor deposited the proceeds in the debtor's bank account, the bank exercised a contractual right of set-off. In weighing the bank's right to set-off against the secured party's interest in the proceeds, the court found that a secured party should be able to rely on its compliance with the UCC's requirements for perfection and its search of the public recording system as against the unrecorded interest of the setting-off bank. 177 Ind. App. at 559, 380 N.E.2d at 1249. "Were this otherwise," Judge Garrard wrote, "a secured party with an interest in proceeds could not rely on recording." Id. Instead, he reasoned, the secured party would be required to take additional steps to insure full protection such as requiring special accounts or inquiring into loan transactions which are not a matter of public record. 177 Ind. App. at 559, 380 N.E.2d at 1250. "Putting such a duty on a secured party, as well as permitting a bank to prevail if that duty is not met, undercuts significant values of

---

1. As discussed under Background, supra, Lindsey deposited the proceeds from the tractors' sale into the business's checking account and then used those proceeds, along with other funds in the account, to pay the bank. The commingling of the proceeds with other funds does not cut off HCC's claim. It is well settled that in appropriate circumstances, "a secured party may trace 'identifiable proceeds' through a commingled bank account and into the hands of a recipient who lacks the right to keep them." Harley-Davidson Motor Co., Inc. v. Bank of New England-Old Colony, N.A., 897 F.2d 611, 620 (1st Cir. 1990) (collecting cases).

certainty, efficiency and reliance which are at the heart of the [UCC's] emphasis on public filing." Id.

The court also noted that while it might be a safe practice for a secured party to require that proceeds be payable to it before future advances to the debtor are made, "it is purposefully not required by the [UCC] for the maintenance of a proceeds security interest since it tends to curtail commercial practice and business operation." Id. In holding for the secured party, Judge Garrard concluded that if UCC Article 9 "is to be a comprehensive system for the perfection of security interests in personal property we see no reason for requiring special standards, with their increased costs, that must be met if a secured party is to prevail over a bank's right of set-off. The [UCC's] priority rules are sufficient." Id.

In *Citizens National Bank*, the conflicting interests were between the creditor's perfected security interest and the bank's right to set-off. In the case before us, the conflicting interests are between HCC's perfected security interest and the bank's asserted right as ordinary course transferee.[2] As such, the result in *Citizens National Bank* does not dictate the result here. But *Citizens National Bank* helps us understand the policy interests that favor enforcing HCC's perfected security interest—that requiring secured parties to take steps beyond those specified in Article 9 to protect their interests "undercuts significant values of certainty, efficiency" and "tends to curtail commercial practice and business operation."

B

Just as Judge Garrard gives sound policy reasons in *Citizens National Bank* for enforcing perfected security interests, there are sound policy reasons for allowing third party transferees to retain proceeds of another's collateral. When he was a judge of the United States Court of Appeals for the First Circuit, Justice Breyer had occasion to address this subject: "If . . . courts too readily impose liability upon those who receive funds from the debtor's ordinary bank account—if, for example, they define 'ordinary course' of business too narrowly—then ordinary suppliers, sellers of gas, electricity, tables, chairs, etc., might find themselves called upon to return ordinary payments . . . to a debtor's secured creditor, say a financier of inventory."

---

2. It is clear that the bank did not seize Lindsey's account for purposes of paying the four notes. Indeed, the trial court found that Lindsey did not consult with the bank before paying the notes and that the bank did not know that the funds it received were the proceeds of the sale of Hesston tractors or that HCC had any claim thereto.

Harley-Davidson Motor Co., Inc. v. Bank of New England-Old Colony, N.A., 897 F.2d 611, 622 (1st Cir. 1990) (internal citation omitted).

Judge Breyer was also able to "imagine good commercial reasons for not imposing, even upon sophisticated suppliers or secondary lenders, who are aware that inventory financiers often take senior secured interests in 'all inventory plus proceeds,' the complicated burden of contacting these financiers to secure permission to take payment from a dealer's ordinary commingled bank account. These considerations," he continued, "indicate that 'ordinary course' has a fairly broad meaning; and that a court should restrict the use of tracing rules to conduct that, in the commercial context, is rather clearly improper." Id.[3]

Harley-Davidson makes a strong statement of the policy interests supporting the bank's claim to the $199,122. But it is interesting to note that despite Judge Breyer's conception of the commercial utility of a "fairly broad meaning" for "ordinary course," his court was unwilling to find that the transferee bank in the *Harley-Davidson* case was entitled to summary judgment.

III

Judge Garrard's opinion in *Citizens National Bank* and Judge Breyer's in *Harley-Davidson* each illustrates the way the UCC streamlines legal impediments to commerce: reducing the burden on perfected secured parties in the former and reducing the burden on ordinary course payees in the latter. But the drafters of the UCC recognized that these two efforts could come into conflict as they do in this case. Comment 2(c) is meant to resolve that conflict.

Comment 2(c) is not a statute and is not written in the form of a statute; it does not set forth a tightly-worded rule, followed by equally tightly-worded elements necessary to establish its application. Rather, it is a narrative collection of three sentences from which we conclude

---

3. We note that in their most recent revision of Article 9, the American Law Institute and National Conference of Commissioners on Uniform State Laws have proposed that this liberal approach be codified. A new section would be added to Article 9 providing that "transferee of funds from a deposit account takes the funds free of a security interest in the deposit account unless the transferee acts in collusion with the debtor in violating the rights of the secured party." UCC §9-329 [now §9-332(b)—Ed.] (1998). "Broad protection for transferees helps to ensure that security interests in deposit accounts do not impair the free flow of funds. It also minimizes the likelihood that a secured party will enjoy a claim to whatever the transferee purchases with the funds. Rules concerning recovery of payments traditionally have placed a high value on finality. The opportunity to upset a completed transaction, or even to place a completed transaction in jeopardy by bringing suit against the transferee of funds, should be severely limited." Revision of UCC Article 9, §9-329, cmt. 3 (Reporters' Interim Draft Aug. 7, 1997).

that a recipient of a payment made "in the ordinary course" by a debtor takes that payment free and clear of any claim that a secured party may have in the payment as proceeds. The Comment also tells us that the payment (1) will be in the ordinary course if it was made "in the operation of the debtor's business" but (2) will not be in the ordinary course if there was "collusion with the debtor to defraud the secured party." We do not take these two factors to be the equivalent of statutory elements but rather descriptive of two parameters for determining "ordinary course." That is, whether a payment was made in the ordinary course will be a function of (1) the extent to which the payment was made in the routine operation of the debtor's business and (2) the extent to which the recipient was aware that it was acting to the prejudice of the secured party.[4]

As to the routine operation of business parameter, payment of sales tax collections or F.I.C.A. withholdings would obviously be at the most routine end and a one-shot payment of subordinated debt not yet due would be at the least. At various points between these extremes would fall payments ordered by how routine they were to both debtor and transferee—measured by such factors as their size, their frequency, whether the debtor received merchandise or services in return, whether the payment was on an obligation overdue, due or not yet due, etc. The cases have explored such payments as those for monthly marketing expenses, retainers to legal counsel by companies in financial difficulty, offsets against pre-existing debts, and periodic term loan payments in this or related bankruptcy contexts.

As to the awareness of prejudice parameter, it is hard to imagine the recipient of the monthly utility or rent payment having any knowledge that it was being paid with proceeds. At the other end of the spectrum is actual fraud in which debtor and recipient have colluded against the secured party.[5] Between these poles will fall

---

4. We explicitly reject the notion that Comment 2(c)'s "payments and transfers in the ordinary course" are the equivalent of UCC §1-201(9)'s "buyer in the ordinary course of business." Without giving extensive treatment to this point, we observe that §1-201(9)'s definition arises in the context of "buying" which is not always applicable in Comment 2(c) disputes (including this one). See ITT Commercial Fin. Corp. v. Bank of the West, 166 F.3d 295, 306 (5th Cir. 1999); Merchants Nat'l Bank & Trust Co. v. United States, 202 Ct. Cl. 343 n.3 (1973). We also note that §1-201(9) contains a knowledge requirement on the part of the buyer which differs from that which we find required by Comment 2(c). . . .

5. Compare Commerce Bank, N.A. v. Tifton Aluminum Co., Inc., 217 B.R. 798, 803 (W.D. Mo. 1997) (transferee knew of the secured party's interest in the proceeds and that the secured party had informed the debtor that it was not authorized to use any of the proceeds); NCNB Texas Nat'l Bank v. Standard Iron & Steel Co., Inc., 1990 WL 37929 (D. Kan. Mar. 16, 1990) (transferee privy to intimate knowledge of debtor's

payments where the recipient knows that a security interest exists but does not know that the payment is being made in violation of that interest; payments where the recipient had sufficient notice to put a reasonable recipient, exercising prudent business practices, on notice that something was awry; and payments where the recipient has information causing it to suspect strongly that a payment violates a secured party's interest, yet takes deliberate steps to avoid discovering more.

The nature of the relationship between the debtor and the transferee can give rise to a presumption of the transferee's awareness of prejudice, especially where the transferee itself is a lender. Such a secondary lender whose debt is subordinated to the secured party's or who has explicitly excluded the debtor's obligations to the secured lender in computing the debtor's borrowing base will generally be presumed to have actual knowledge of prejudice to the secured party. This occurs because the secondary lender has extended credit to the debtor with the express understanding that the secured party stands in a superior position to be repaid, at least in certain circumstances.

We reaffirm that a security interest continues in any identifiable proceeds of collateral including collections received by the debtor. Ind. Code §§26-1-9-201 & 306(2). We also reaffirm that Comment 2(c) is the law of Indiana: a recipient of a payment made "in the ordinary course" by a debtor takes that payment free and clear of any claim that a secured party may have in the payment as proceeds. And we hold that whether a transfer of proceeds is "in the ordinary course" requires an assessment of both (1) the extent to which the payment was made in the routine operation of the debtor's business and (2) the extent to which the recipient was aware that it was acting to the prejudice of the secured party. Because we agree that "imposing liability too readily on payees . . . could impede the free flow of goods and services essential to business," *J.I. Case*, 991 F.2d at 1277, we further hold that the transfer will be free of any claim that a secured party may have in it as proceeds unless the payment would constitute a windfall to the recipient. A windfall occurs in this context when the recipient has no reasonable expectation of being paid ahead of a secured creditor because of the extent to which the payment was made outside the routine operation of the debtor's business, because of the extent to which the recipient was aware that it was acting to the prejudice of the secured party, or because of both of these factors in combination.

---

financial situation); Universal C.I.T. Credit Corp. v. Farmers Bank of Portageville, 358 F. Supp. 317, 324 (E.D. Mo. 1973) (debtor told the transferee bank that the secured party had revoked its floor plan financing arrangement and that debtor wanted the bank to be "safe" on its loan).

While the determination of "ordinary course" is a question of law, sometimes an evaluation of the extent to which the payment was routine or the extent of the recipient's knowledge will require factual analysis. In such a situation, summary judgment would be inappropriate.

IV

Before applying these principles to the case before us, it is important to discuss J.I. Case Credit Corp. v. First National Bank of Madison County, 991 F.2d 1272 (7th Cir. 1993), a decision of the United States Court of Appeals for the Seventh Circuit applying Indiana law to a substantially identical problem. (*J.I. Case* served as the principal authority for the Court of Appeals in this case.)

As in the case before us, the debtor in *J.I. Case* deposited proceeds from the sale of secured agricultural equipment in his business checking account where it was commingled with funds from other sources. The debtor then used the commingled funds to pay creditors other than the secured creditor, including his bank lender. After careful analysis of whether these payments were "payments and transfers in ordinary course" within the meaning of Comment 2(c), the court concluded:

> [U]nder Comment 2(c), a payment is within the ordinary course if it was made in the operation of the debtor's business and if the payee did not know and was not reckless about whether the payment violated a third party's security interest.

991 F.2d at 1279. The court held that the payments were made in the ordinary course of business and the secured party was not entitled to recover them because both (1) the bank did not know that the debtor's payments violated the secured party's security interest (although the bank did know about the secured party's security interest) and (2) the bank did not receive payments from the debtor in reckless disregard of the fact that those payments violated the secured party's security interest. Id.; accord, ITT Commercial Fin. Corp. v. Bank of the West, 166 F.3d 295, 307 (5th Cir. 1999).

Without expressing any view as to the outcome of *J.I. Case*, it is clear that the Seventh Circuit's approach focussed exclusively on the awareness of prejudice parameter. . . . [W]e generally agree with this analysis. But the court did not independently examine the extent to which the debtor's payment to the bank was made in the routine operation of the debtor's business. For this reason, we decline to follow *J.I. Case*.

V

We hold that Lindsey's payment of $199,122 to the bank here was not a payment in the ordinary course of the operation of Lindsey's business. There is no disagreement as to the following facts. See Record at 19-20; 374; 418. The bank was aware that HCC had a valid and perfected security interest in Lindsey's tractor inventory. The bank took this into account in making its decision to extend credit to Lindsey and did not take a security interest in any of the collateral covered by HCC's security agreement. During the eight years prior to the payment at issue here, Lindsey had borrowed funds or refinanced debt in excess of 100 times with the bank and the average debt balance owed was between $100,000 and $200,000. Two of the notes Lindsey paid off represented a refinancing of approximately $225,000 in continuing debt carried by the bank. After the notes were paid off, Lindsey was in the unprecedented position of owing the bank only between $2,000 and $15,000. The bank's senior loan officer agreed with HCC's counsel that the $199,122 payment was "extraordinary" and constituted the largest ever made on any debt Lindsey owed the bank. The officer also said, "Anytime a significant loan balance is paid off you have to look at it as something that would not be a normal trade transaction, like paying interest or something like that."

The payment to the bank constituted the proceeds of collateral in which HCC had a valid and perfected security interest. The payment was used to liquidate a substantial secured debt which, for the most part, was not due. It was an extremely large payment, the likes of which Lindsey had never made before. And although the bank was not advised that the source of the payment it received constituted the proceeds of HCC's collateral, the bank knew of HCC's perfected security interest. As such, it had extended credit to Lindsey with the express understanding that HCC stood in a superior position to be repaid, at least in certain circumstances. We conclude that the payment was not in the ordinary course of Lindsey's business. For the bank to prevail would result in a windfall—a windfall because the bank had no reasonable expectation that Lindsey could or would liquidate its debt due the bank in advance of paying HCC for the tractors financed—at the expense of HCC which had taken all measures required by the UCC to protect its interest. As a result, the exception to the Indiana UCC's priority rules provided by Comment 2(c) does not apply and HCC, not the bank, is entitled to the $199,122.

CONCLUSION

Having previously granted transfer, thereby vacating the decision of the Court of Appeals, we now reverse the judgment of the trial court and remand this matter to the trial court with directions that summary judgment be entered for HCC and for any further proceedings that may be required.

NOTE

In a footnote the court states that the revised Article 9 has a section more explicitly protecting the transferee in the ordinary course in this situation. Read §9-332(b) and its Official Comments and decide if the case would have come out differently had that section then been in effect.

PROBLEM 364

Octopus National Bank loaned $200,000 to Big Department Store and took a security interest in its inventory "now owned or after-aquired," which it perfected by filing a financing statement on July 5. Antitrust National Bank loaned $100,000 to Total Store, Inc., and took a security interest in its inventory "now owned or after-aquired," which it perfected by filing a financing statement on September 25. Without the consent of either creditor, the two retailers merged the following year, when the inventories of both were worth $300,000. The new entity was named Total Department Store. Which bank has priority in this situation? See §§9-102(a)(56), 9-203(d) and (e), 9-508 (and its helpful Official Comments), 9-325, 9-326, and the latter's Official Comments; White & Summers §24-11; Jean Wegman Burns, New Article Nine of the UCC: The Good, The Bad, and The Ugly, 2002 Ill. L. Rev. 29, 70-75.

Read §9-315(d) carefully, and work your way through the following Problem.

PROBLEM 365

On August 2, when the filed financing statement in favor of the Last National Bank covered "all business machines," the debtor engaged in the transactions listed below. Decide for each transaction if the bank should take action before August 22 or if the financing statement is sufficient as filed:

(a) The debtor traded a computer for another computer.

(b) The debtor traded another computer for a painting to be hung in the office.

(c) The debtor traded a duplicating machine for a used car (and state law requires a lien interest in a vehicle to be noted on the certificate of title as the sole means of perfection).

(d) The debtor sold a calculator to a friend for cash and that same day used the cash to buy a painting.

(e) The debtor sold an adding machine for $500 and put the cash in a bank account at a different bank; on August 2 that bank exercised its right of setoff against the account. See §9-340.

(f) The debtor sold a coffee maker for $200 and gave the money to a Salvation Army volunteer that same day; see §9-332(a).

PROBLEM 366

Balboa Bank & Trust Company floor-planned the inventory of Erickson Motors and perfected its security interest in the inventory (and proceeds) by filing in the proper place. See §9-311(d). Erickson Motors sold a car to John Smith, who paid $1000 down and signed a contract obligating him to pay $25,000 more. The car dealership assigned this contract to the Cartier Finance Company, which took possession of the contract and notified Smith he was to make future payments to Cartier. Smith made no payments at all because the car had serious mechanical difficulties, and eventually the parties cancelled the transaction and the car was returned to Erickson Motors on September 11. On September 12 a representative of Cartier Finance Company came to the dealership and took possession of the car, claiming it was *proceeds* from the contract of purchase, which Cartier still had. Balboa Bank objected and claimed a superior interest in the car, asserting its priority in the inventory of the dealership. Who prevails here? See §9-330(c) and its Official Comments 9 and 10.

For a complete review of priority problems, some involving proceeds and some not, read Official Comments 4 through 9 of §9-322. If you can understand them all, you are on top of the subject matter of this course.

Chapter 25
DEFAULT

I. PRE-DEFAULT DUTIES OF THE SECURED PARTY

PROBLEM 367

Andy Doria was the owner of 100 shares of Titanic Telephone, which he pledged to the Morro Castle National Bank as collateral for a $10,000 loan. At the time of the pledge, the stock was selling for $100 a share. The security agreement was oral, and the bank filed no financing statement.

(a) If the stock began to fall in value and if on November 4, when it was selling at $80 a share, Andy called the bank and told the bank to sell, is the bank responsible if it does not and the stock bottoms out at $1.50 a share? Read §9-207; see, e.g., Federal Deposit Ins. Corp. v. Air

Atl., Inc., 389 Mass. 950, 452 N.E.2d 1143, 36 U.C.C. Rep. Serv. 1744 (1983).

(b) Would it help the bank's position if the pledge agreement contained a clause saying that the bank was not responsible for its own negligence in dealing with the stock? Read §1-102(3); see Brodheim v. Chase Manhattan Bank, N.A., 75 Misc. 2d 285, 347 N.Y.S.2d 394, 13 U.C.C. Rep. Serv. 139 (Sup. Ct. 1973); G. Gilmore, ch. 42.

(c) Andy's dealings with the bank became more complicated, and eventually the bank held, as pledgee, Andy's stocks in five different companies. One of these, Lusitania Foundry, offered a stock split option that had to be exercised by December 31, so Andy wrote the Morro Castle National Bank and, explaining that his records had become confused, asked the bank how many shares of Lusitania Foundry it held. The bank replied that it possessed 50 shares (this was a typographical error; it actually held 150). Andy tendered 50 shares of equivalent stock to the bank in exchange for a return of 50 shares of Lusitania Foundry, on which he then exercised the stock option, which proved very profitable. On January 3, Andy learned he owned 100 more shares that the bank held; it was too late to take the stock option on these shares. Does Andy have a cause of action against the bank under §9-207? Under §9-210? What damages can he recover? See §9-625(b) and (f).

PROBLEM 368

Mazie Minkus borrowed $2,000 from the Mount Brown State Bank and, as collateral, pledged to the bank her stamp collection (valued at $2,000). She used the money for a South American vacation. While she was away, the bank, which was located in an unstable geological area, was destroyed in an earthquake. The stamp collection went with it. Fortunately, the bank was fully insured by a policy with the Gibbons Insurance Company, which, inter alia, paid the bank $2,000 for the loss of the stamp collection. Gibbons then notified Mazie that she should pay the $2,000 debt to the insurance company, which was using the doctrine of subrogation to step into the shoes of the bank. Need she pay? See §9-207(b)(2); G. Gilmore §42.7.

II.   DEFAULT

State Bank of Piper City v. A-Way, Inc.

Illinois Supreme Court, 1987
115 Ill. 2d 401, 504 N.E.2d 737, 3 U.C.C. Rep. Serv. 2d 379

WARD, J. The plaintiff, State Bank of Piper City, filed a complaint in the circuit court of Iroquois County against the defendant, A-Way, Inc., to enforce its security interest in grain and the proceeds from sales of grain held by the defendant on account for a debtor of the plaintiff. The circuit court granted the defendant's motion to dismiss the complaint and denied the plaintiff's motion to vacate the order of dismissal. On the plaintiff's appeal, the appellate court reversed and remanded (135 Ill. App. 3d 1010), and we granted the defendant's petition for leave to appeal (103 Ill. 2d R. 315). . . .

In February 1982, the plaintiff was awarded a judgment in the amount of $131,083.91 against William C. Brenner upon his default on promissory notes that had been secured, under article 9 of the Uniform Commercial Code (UCC) (Ill. Rev. Stat. 1979, ch. 26, par. 9-101 et seq.), by a security interest in grain owned by Brenner which was stored in the defendant's warehouse. In a supplementary proceeding to enforce its judgment (Ill. Rev. Stat. 1981, ch. 110, par. 73), the plaintiff served the defendant with a citation to discover assets that it held on Brenner's behalf. The defendant responded by an affidavit acknowledging the accuracy of an attached ledger sheet with information regarding Brenner's account. The ledger sheet listed, inter alia, the number of bushels of grain the defendant held for him, 5,141.20, and the costs of drying and storing the grain. The plaintiff then moved for a citation order requiring the defendant to pay the plaintiff $5,141.20, confusing the number of bushels with their value, "as partial satisfaction for the judgment entered" in its suit against Brenner. The court held a hearing at which the defendant failed to appear, and allowed the plaintiff's motion. Acting upon the order, the defendant sold the grain, obtaining $11,310.64; of that amount, the defendant remitted $5,141.20 to the plaintiff and applied the balance to outstanding charges on Brenner's accounts.

Approximately eight months later, realizing its mistake, the plaintiff brought this action under article 9 of the UCC (Ill. Rev. Stat. 1979, ch. 26, par. 9-101 et seq.), to enforce its security interest in the proceeds of the grain sale over and above $5,141.20. The court dismissed the plaintiff's complaint on the grounds that the doctrines of merger and res judicata barred the suit. As stated, the appellate court reversed the dismissal.

The defendant first contends that the trial court properly dismissed the plaintiff's complaint under the doctrine of merger and that any rights the plaintiff had under the promissory notes of Brenner merged into the judgment, extinguishing any interest it had in the grain. "The general rule is, that by a judgment at law or a decree in chancery, the contract or instrument upon which the proceeding is based becomes entirely merged in the judgment. By the judgment of the court it loses all of its vitality and ceases to bind the parties to its execution. Its force and effect are then expended, and all remaining legal liability is transferred to the judgment or decree. Once becoming merged in the judgment, no further action at law or suit in equity can be maintained. . . ." (Doerr v. Schmitt (1941), 375 Ill. 470, 472, quoting Wayman v. Cochrane (1864), 35 Ill. 152, 154; Rock Island Bank & Trust Co. v. Stauduhar (1978), 59 Ill. App. 3d 892, 900.) Second, under principles of res judicata, it says, citing Hughey v. Industrial Com. (1979), 76 Ill. 2d 577, 582-583, that the plaintiff is barred from bringing the present action because the issue now raised could have been litigated in the citation proceeding.

The defendant's contentions have not been directly addressed by this court. We judge that, under the language of article 9 of the UCC (Ill. Rev. Stat. 1979, ch. 26, section 9-501(1)(5)) and from constructions in other jurisdictions, these contentions are without merit.

Section 9-501(1) [now §9-601—Ed.] of the UCC serves to broaden the options available to a secured creditor upon a debtor's default. . . . Section 9-501(1) of the UCC states:

> When a debtor is in default under a security agreement, a secured party has the rights and remedies provided in this Part [concerning default]. . . . He may reduce his claim to judgment, foreclose or otherwise enforce the security interest by any available judicial procedure. . . .The rights and remedies referred to in this subsection are cumulative.

(Ill. Rev. Stat. 1979, ch. 26, par. 9-501(1).)

When a secured creditor has chosen to reduce his claim to judgment "the lien of any levy which may be made upon his collateral by virtue of any execution based upon the judgment shall relate back to the date of the perfection of the security interest in such collateral" (Ill. Rev. Stat. 1979, ch. 26, par. 9-501(5)) and serve as a continuation of the secured creditor's original perfected security interest (Ill. Ann. Stat., ch. 26, par. 9-501(5), Uniform Commercial Code Comment, at 322 (Smith-Hurd 1974)). Thus, a secured creditor's effort to collect its debt through the judicial process will not "operate to destroy his security interest vis-à-vis the debtor or to impair its priority [interest] over third parties" (2 G. Gilmore, Security Interests in Personal Property sec. 43.7, at 1209-1210 (1965); [citations omitted]).

The doctrine of merger does not, contrary to the defendant's argument, preclude a secured creditor from enforcing its security interest in the property given as collateral.

In Ruidoso State Bank v. Garcia (1978), 92 N.M. 288, 587 P.2d 435, cited above, a secured creditor earlier had brought suit to enforce its security interest in two vehicles which it had previously levied upon in satisfaction of a judgment against its debtors upon their default on promissory notes. The vehicles, however, had been released upon a trial court's finding that they were exempt property. Subsequently the secured creditor brought the suit involved. The debtors argued, inter alia, that by foreclosing on the notes the secured creditor caused the security agreements executed by the debtors to merge in the judgment, precluding their subsequent enforcement. The court rejected this contention, holding:

> Merger does not apply here for the reason that the Bank [, the secured creditor,] had two separate causes of action. It could sue and reduce the debt to judgment. In that case the debt would be merged into the judgment. However, the debt would be carried forward so that the Bank's rights under the security agreement would not be destroyed. The security agreements, under the statutory prohibition [i.e., under article 9 of the UCC], would not be merged into the judgment.

Ruidoso State Bank v. Garcia (1978), 92 N.M. 288, 290, 587 P.2d 435, 437. . . .

Here even though the notes merged in the judgment precluding further action on the notes (Doerr v. Schmitt (1941), 375 Ill. 470, 472; Rock Island Bank & Trust Co. v. Stauduhar (1978), 59 Ill. App. 3d 892, 900), that merger did not preclude the plaintiff from bringing this action to enforce its security interest in the grain. That security interest was provided for in security agreements separate from and independent of the notes. The security agreements provided that upon the debtor's default the secured creditor "shall have all of the rights and remedies of a secured party under the Illinois Uniform Commercial Code," remedies which are, as previously stated, "cumulative." Furthermore, the "lien of any levy," which was made upon the grain pursuant to the plaintiff's judgment against Brenner, related back to the time of perfection of the security interest. (Ill. Ann. Stat. ch. 26, par. 9-501(5), Uniform Commercial Code Comment, at 322 (Smith-Hurd 1974).) Thus, the merger of the note in the plaintiff's judgment against Brenner and the plaintiff's citation to discover assets proceeding did not affect the plaintiff's security interest in the remaining grain-sale proceeds.

The defendant next contends that the plaintiff is barred under res judicata from bringing the present action against A-Way, Inc.:

> The doctrine of res judicata provides that "a final judgment rendered by a court of competent jurisdiction on the merits is conclusive as to the rights of the parties and their privies, and, as to them, constitutes an absolute bar to a subsequent action involving the *same* claim, demand or cause of action." (Emphasis added.) [Citation.] When res judicata is established "as a bar against the prosecution of a second action between the same parties upon the same claim or demand . . . it is conclusive not only as to every matter which was offered to sustain or defeat the claim or demand, but as to any other matter which might have been offered for that purpose. . . ." Housing Authority for La Salle County v. YMCA (1984), 101 Ill. 2d 246, 251-252.

Because of the provision under article 9 of the UCC for multiple and cumulative remedies upon the debtor's default, res judicata will not bar a secured creditor from exhausting his remedies under the UCC. . . .

Although the decisions cited involved successive actions against a debtor in default, there is no reason not to apply the same principles to situations, as here, involving third parties. Not to do so would defeat the purpose of article 9 in providing a secured creditor with multiple remedies upon a debtor's default.

That the order entered in the citation proceeding against the defendant was a final order (Illinois Brewing & Malting Co. v. Ilmberger (1910), 155 Ill. App. 417, 418) does not, under res judicata, preclude the plaintiff from bringing the present action. The order was entered in execution of the plaintiff's judgment against Brenner. Here, the plaintiff is acting in its capacity as a secured creditor attempting to enforce its article 9 security interest in the surplus proceeds from the sale of the grain, proceeds which it mistakenly omitted in the citation proceeding. The action of the plaintiff in the citation proceeding does not bar the plaintiff from proceeding here.

The defendant argues too that if the plaintiff is permitted to proceed with this action it will suffer undue hardship because it has applied the proceeds remaining from the sale to its other accounts of Brenner. The argument appears to border on effrontery. The defendant in the argument admitted that it knew the amount of the plaintiff's judgment against Brenner; that it was aware that the plaintiff had made a mistake in requesting that it pay the plaintiff 5,141.20 dollars instead of bushels; and that it did not disclose to the plaintiff the amount it received from sale of the grain. These may have been considerations in the defendant's not appearing at the citation proceeding. If we were to conclude that fraud had been present, which under our analysis we need not do, res judicata, of course, would not be applicable. Hughey v. Industrial Com. (1979), 76 Ill. 2d 577, 583; McNely v. Board of Education (1956), 9 Ill. 2d 143, 151-152.

For the reasons given, we hold that the trial court erred in dismissing the complaint. The judgment of the appellate court reversing and remanding the cause is affirmed.

Judgment affirmed.

The secured party's Part 6 Article 9 rights come into being whenever there has been a *default* by the debtor. The Code, however, does not define *default*, and the only judicially recognized form of default is failure to pay the debt on time; see Cofield v. Randolph County Comn., 90 F.3d 468, 30 U.C.C. Rep. Serv. 2d 374 (11th Cir. 1996). Since the Code is silent on the meaning of the term, the security agreement must fill in the blanks. It is the lawyer's job to draft the security agreement so as to cover the possible exigencies with appropriate clauses triggering default and the ability to foreclose. One way to do this is by a specific definition of the term *default* so that it includes not only failure to pay on time but also failure to perform any of the terms of the agreement. *Default* may also be defined to cover certain specific problems: death of the debtor, an assignment for the benefit of creditors, institution of any insolvency proceeding, impairment of the collateral, etc.

If through inadvertence, mistake, or deliberate bad faith the creditor repossesses when there is no right to do so, the creditor is guilty of conversion (and breach of contract) and will have to pay all damages caused thereby. In re Martin Specialty Vehicles, Inc., 87 Bankr. 752, 6 U.C.C. Rep. Serv. 2d 337 (Bankr. D. Mass. 1988).

Some security agreements provide simply that default is the failure to observe the conditions and promises of the security agreement and then include an acceleration clause similar to this one:

The parties agree that if at any time the secured party deems itself insecure because in good faith it believes the prospect of payment or performance is impaired, it shall have the right to declare a default and accelerate payment of all unpaid sums or performance or, at its option, may require the debtor to furnish additional collateral.

Read §1-208 carefully.

PROBLEM 369

When Mr. and Mrs. Bankruptcy bought a mobile home from Nervous Motors, Inc., they signed a purchase money security agreement in favor of the seller that contained an acceleration clause identical to the one above. Which of the following events, in your opinion, is sufficient to trigger the proper use of the clause?

(a) A very bad financial quarter for Nervous Motors, Inc.?

(b) A serious drop in the state of the economy?

(c) Knowledge that the Bankruptcys have been talking to a lawyer (could the seller here make use of §2-609)?

(d) A report (which simple investigation would show to be false) that the Bankruptcys have failed to pay their grocery bills for the last two months?

(e) An anonymous phone call that states the Bankruptcys are getting ready to move the mobile home to Mexico?

(f) The confiscation of the mobile home and the arrest of the Bankruptcys for possessing marijuana? See Blaine v. General Motors Acceptance Corp., 82 Misc. 2d 653, 370 N.Y.S.2d 323, 17 U.C.C. Rep. Serv. 641 (Sup. Ct. 1975). See §1-208 and its Official Comment; G. Gilmore §43.4; Annot., What Constitutes "Good Faith" Under UCC §1-208, 61 A.L.R.3d 244. The courts disagree on the *good faith* standard: compare Black v. Peoples Bank & Trust Co., 437 So. 2d 26, 37 U.C.C. Rep. Serv. 641 (Miss. 1983) (objective-reasonable person test) with Van Horn v. Van De Wol, Inc., 6 Wash. App. 959, 497 P.2d 252, 10 U.C.C. Rep. Serv. 1143 (1972) (purely subjective test). An exhaustive discussion of the meaning of §1-208 is contained in the well-written opinion in Watseka First Natl. Bank v. Ruda, 135 Ill. 2d 140, 552 N.E.2d 783, 10 U.C.C. Rep. Serv. 2d 1073 (1990). In First Natl. Bank in Libby v. Twombly, 689 P.2d 1226, 39 U.C.C. Rep. Serv. 1192 (Mont. 1984), the court awarded punitive damages for a bad faith acceleration.

(g) Would §1-208 be relevant at all if Mr. and Mrs. Bankruptcy had signed a demand promissory note (one that permits the creditor to call the loan any time the creditor wishes)? See the Official Comment to §1-208 and Solar Motors, Inc. v. First Natl. Bank of Chadron, 4 Neb. App. 1, 537 N.W.2d 527, 28 U.C.C. Rep. Serv. 2d 63 (1995).

The courts stretch to protect the debtor whenever the secured party's "insecurity" is unwarranted. See Lane v. John Deere, 767 S.W.2d 138, 8 U.C.C. Rep. Serv. 2d 609 (Tenn. 1989). For particularly outrageous conduct on the part of the creditor, punitive damages are favored. See Annot., Punitive Damages for Wrongful Seizure of Chattel by One Claiming Security Interest, 35 A.L.R.3d 1016.

Klingbiel v. Commercial Credit Corp.

United States Court of Appeals, Tenth Circuit, 1971
439 F.2d 1303, 8 U.C.C. Rep. Serv. 1099

BROWN, J. When Vern Klingbiel (Purchaser), went outside his home in St. Louis, Missouri, on the morning of June 22, 1966, he found his brand new (1966) Ford Galaxie 500 gone. Later he was to learn that in the dark of night and with skillful stealth the car—despite its being fully locked—had been taken away, not by some modern auto rustler, but by an anonymous representative of the Automobile Recovery Bureau acting for Commercial, the installment finance company, which was described with remarkable accuracy as a "professional firm." Little did he know that with this sudden, unexplained disappearance of an automobile, which—with all its chrome and large mortgage—was still his, so much had been unleashed. First, of course, was his anguish at his loss. More significant for us, time, tide, litigation, trial, victory and appeal was to instruct him in the intricacies of the fine print of the purchase mortgage contract he signed and, perhaps to his awe, the Uniform Commercial Code.

A Kansas jury, under the Judge's careful instructions, which we find to be unexceptionable, did not think much of this treatment and by its verdict awarded some small actual damages plus punitive damages in a sum almost twice the purchase price of the car.

Fleeing from this judgment as a matter of principle, if not principal, Commercial quite naturally and properly seeks a haven in the terms of the contract[1] and, as an anchor to windward, the acceleration

---

1. For convenience of reference the bracketed numbers are inserted (e.g., [i], [a], [b], [c], etc.);

This Mortgage may be assigned by Seller [Dealer], and when assigned, all rights of Seller shall vest in its assignee [Commercial] and this Mortgage shall be free from any claims or defenses whatsoever which Purchaser may have against Seller . . . [i] If Purchaser [a] defaults on any obligation or breaches any agreement or warranty

and good faith provisions of the Kansas Uniform Commercial Code. We find the attack unavailing and affirm.

WHAT HAPPENED

The case was tried largely on stipulated facts. On May 26, 1966, Vern Klingbiel, a resident of St. Louis, Missouri, entered into an installment contract with Dealer for the purchase of a new Ford Galaxie automobile. This installment contract showed a time sales price of $4,907.56. Purchaser made a down payment of $400.00, tendering to Dealer a personal check in the amount of $300.00 and a second check in the amount of $100.00, the latter being signed in his wife's name. This left a time balance of $4,507.56, to be paid in 36 equal, successive monthly installments of $125.21, the payments to commence on June 26, 1966, under the mortgage contract containing the acceleration and enforcement provisions (see Note [1] supra). Commercial shortly became the assignee, on a dealer recourse basis, for the consideration of $3,400.00.

Subsequently, but before Purchaser's first monthly installment became due, Commercial felt itself insecure, and it directed the Automobile Recovery Bureau of St. Louis, Missouri to repossess the automobile. On June 22, 1966—four days before Purchaser's first monthly installment was due and at a time when he was not in default —the repossessing professionals, without notice, demand, communication, or correspondence with Purchaser, removed his locked automobile from the front of his house in the dead of night, [and] delivered it to Commercial[2] along with Purchaser's personal property. . . .

---

under this Mortgage, or [b] if Seller should feel itself or Vehicle insecure, [c] the unpaid portion of the Time Balance and any expense (including taxes) shall without notice, at the option of Seller, become due forthwith. [ii] Purchaser agrees in any such case [a] to pay said amount to Seller, upon demand, or [b] at the election of Seller, to deliver Vehicle to Seller. [iii] This Mortgage may be foreclosed [a] in any manner provided by law, or [b] Seller may, without notice or demand for performance or legal process, except such as may be required by Law, lawfully enter any premises where Vehicle may be found, and take possession of it. [iv] Seller may retain all payments made by Purchaser as compensation for the use of the Vehicle while in Purchaser's possession. [v] Any personal property in Vehicle at the time of repossession which has not become a part thereof may be held temporarily by Seller for Purchaser, without liability thereof. . . . All rights and remedies hereunder are cumulative and not alternative.

2. Purchaser did not have the slightest idea that his car had been repossessed. He notified the police that it was missing, in the belief that it had been stolen, and it was the police who finally uncovered what had actually transpired.

OUT OF THE VERBAL WILDERNESS

The skillful Trial Judge having been aware that this contract . . . was not written for those who run to read discerned its true meaning by recognizing its true sequential structure. Unlike Commercial which assumes that the right to accelerate without notice or demand is synonymous with the right to repossess without notice or demand, the Judge carefully distinguished between the two. Acceleration, he charged, was permissible without notice or demand. But upon acceleration Commercial then had to make demand or give notice to Purchaser so that the admitted failure of notice/demand . . . made Commercial's repossession an unlawful conversion.

The Court's instruction tracked the terms of the contract correctly. Though under clause [i][b] (note [2], supra) "Time Balance" might from acceleration become due at any time without notice, if Commercial felt itself insecure, the very next provision in the contract provides "[ii] Purchaser agrees in any such case [a] to pay said amount to Seller, *upon demand*, or, [b] at the election of Seller, to deliver vehicle to Seller." (Emphasis added.) Clause [ii][a][b] with its alternative stated in the disjunctive does not speak in terms of rights which Commercial has. Rather it speaks in terms of *actions* which Purchaser must take depending on the choice opted by Commercial. It could require Purchaser to pay off in full or it could require redelivery. But before Purchaser was bound to do either Commercial had first to indicate which course was required. The two words, "upon demand," are not only conspicuous, they are unavoidable.

Not yet overborne, Commercial would further have us construe the contract so as to declare that no notice was necessary prior to repossession by falling back on clause [iii][b] which provides: "[iii] This mortgage may be foreclosed [a] . . . or [b] Seller may, without notice or demand for performance or legal process, . . . lawfully enter any premises where Vehicle may be found, and take possession of it."

Even the austere stipulation vividly portrays Commercial's conduct and presages its predicament: On June 22, 1966, Automobile Recovery Bureau, St. Louis, Missouri, at the telephone direction and request of Commercial Credit Corporation, without notice, demand, communication or correspondence with plaintiff, some time during the night, took the locked 1966 Ford Galaxie automobile off the street in front of plaintiff's home, and delivered the car to Commercial Credit Corporation at St. Louis, Missouri. Commercial Credit Corporation had no communication, either written or oral, with plaintiff prior to taking the automobile. Commercial Credit Corporation requested, ordered, authorized and directed the repossession of the 1966 Ford Galaxie 500 automobile from Vern Klingbiel because it felt itself, or vehicle, insecure.

This is equally unavailing. At the outset, this clause follows—does not precede—but follows clause [ii] which, [a][b] as we have held, calls for notice/demand before Purchaser is required to act upon a declared acceleration. Equally important, in the sequential structure of the contract this refers only to a *foreclosure*. This means that there must be a default on the part of the Purchaser. This can take the form of Purchaser's failure to perform as in [i][a] or an acceleration under [i][b]. Certainly in the case of predefault acceleration, as a result of the manner in which this contract is constructed, clause [ii][b] in effect calls for notice/demand to precipitate a default. The failure or refusal of Purchaser after such notice/demand would of course, be a [i][a] default, thus setting in train the foreclosure provisions of [iii][a] or [b], including *at that stage* even the most stealthy repossession by night riders. But this privilege is not available by skipping from [i][b] to [iii][b] over the head of [ii][a][b]. . . .

We think there was evidence, if believed by the jury, to warrant the inference of more than simple inadvertence or a technical conversion. There was first the circumstance of the stealthy retaking without notice of any kind, although notice clearly was called for as we have held. At that time Purchaser was not in default. Further, Purchaser's own personal property was taken along with the automobile. This was never returned to him, nor did he receive recompense for it. In fact, Commercial never even contacted Purchaser to inform him of the repossession. He had to find out through his own effort and investigation. There are many other factors unnecessary to catalogue which sustain the punitive damage finding.

This leaves only the objection to the Court's instruction on actual damages. Clearly there was sufficient evidence to cover the three elements submitted by the Court for the loss of value of the automobile, Purchaser's personal property, and the loss of the vehicle for an intervening period.

The objection is pointed at the term "actual value" rather than market value of the car. Assuming, but not deciding that it was error, such error was harmless. The "actual" damages awarded totalled $770.00. Of this sum $120.00 was for the loss of Purchaser's personal property, which Commercial fully concedes is correct. Purchaser's testimonial estimate of the loss from the loss of use of the car, which clearly is a permissible element of damages, was approximately $500.00. Thus, this leaves only $150.00 for the loss of value of the automobile itself. This modest recovery does not demonstrate any harm.

Affirmed.

PRACTICAL NOTE

On default, the debtor's attorney should read the security agreement carefully to see if expressly or impliedly it gives the debtor a right
to notice before repossession. Conversely, the secured party's attorney
should make sure the security agreement avoids statements like "upon
demand," which may give rise to such an implication.

Where a bank pursued its foreclosure remedy under the guise of a
state attachment procedure that was clearly unconstitutional, the plaintiffs in Guzman v. Western State Bank of Devil's Lake, 540 F.2d 948, 21
U.C.C. Rep. Serv. 332 (8th Cir. 1976), took the unusual step of suing
under the Civil Rights Act, 42 U.S.C. §1983, and recovered nearly
$10,000 in actual damages and $30,000 in punitive damages. The court
expressly found the bank guilty of bad faith.

PROBLEM 370

Natty Birdwhistle bought a car with money borrowed from
Repossession Finance Company (which perfected its interest in the
car). The security agreement provided that "time was of the essence"
and that the acceptance by the finance company of late payments was
not a waiver of its right to repossess. Natty always paid 10 to 15 days
late. One month Repossession Finance had had enough, and it sent a
man out who took the car (using a duplicate set of keys) from the
parking lot of the factory where Natty worked. Has a default occurred?
See §2-208; Moe v. John Deere Co., 516 N.W.2d 332, 25 U.C.C. Rep.
Serv. 2d 997 (S.D. 1994); G. Gilmore §44.1, at 1214: "[C]ourts pay
little attention to clauses which appear to say that meaningful acts are
meaningless and that the secured party can blow hot or cold as he
chooses." If Repossession's conduct has waived the right to repossess if
Natty is late, what can it do to reinstate the "time is of the essence"
clause? See §2-209(5).

NOTE: CREDIT INSURANCE AND DEFAULT

If the debtor has died or become ill or disabled, so that the credit
insurance taken out at the time the original contract was signed should
pay the debt, there is authority for the proposition that the secured

creditor must look first to the credit insurance before repossessing. Owens v. Walt Johnson Lincoln Mercury, Inc., 281 Or. 287, 574 P.2d 642 (1978).

III. REPOSSESSION AND RESALE

Section 9-609 authorizes the secured party to skip going through judicial processes and to repossess the collateral on the debtor's default if this can be done without a "breach of the peace." For the meaning of that elusive term, see White & Summers §25-6; Census Fed. Credit Union v. Wann, 403 N.E.2d 348, 28 U.C.C. Rep. Serv. 1207 (Ind. App. 1980); Comment, Breach of Peace and Section 9-503 of the Uniform Commercial Code—A Modern Definition for an Ancient Restriction, 82 Dick. L. Rev. 351 (1978); Annot., What Conduct by Repossessing Chattel Mortgagee or Conditional Vendor Entails Tort Liability, 99 A.L.R.2d 358. Grant Gilmore:

> In the financing of business debtors repossession causes little trouble or dispute. In the underworld of consumer finance, however, repossession is a knock-down, drag-out battle waged on both sides with cunning guile and a complete disregard for the rules of fair play. A certain amount of trickery seems to be accepted: it is all right for the finance company to invite the defaulting buyer to drive over to its office for a friendly conference on refinancing the loan and to repossess the car as soon as he arrives. It is fairly safe for the finance company to pick up the car on the street wherever it may be parked, although there is always a danger that the buyer will later claim that he had been keeping a valuable stock of diamonds in the glove compartment. But the finance company will do well to think twice before allowing its man to break into an empty house, even though a well-drafted clause in the security agreement gives it the right to do exactly that. And if the housewife, who is invariably pregnant and subject to miscarriages, sits on the sofa, stove, washing machine or television set and refuses to move, the finance company man will make a serious mistake if he dumps the lady or carries her screaming into the front yard. Juries love to award punitive damages for that sort of thing and the verdict will often be allowed to stand.

G. Gilmore §44.1, at 1212-1213.

Williamson v. Fowler Toyota, Inc.

Oklahoma Supreme Court, 1998
1998 Okla. 14, 956 P.2d 858, 36 U.C.C. Rep. Serv. 2d 951

ALMA WILSON, J. The issue is whether a creditor is liable for the trespass and the resulting damages caused by an independent contractor employed by the creditor to repossess secured collateral pursuant to 12A O.S. 1991, §9-503. We hold that the statute creates a nondelegable duty on the creditor to refrain from breaching the peace when repossessing secured collateral, and therefore the creditor is liable for any breach of the peace by the independent contractor. We also hold that the independent contractor's wanton and reckless disregard of the property rights of another may be imputed to the employer and exemplary damages awarded pursuant to 23 O.S. 1991, §9.

FACTS

The basic facts in this matter are uncontested. Fowler Toyota, Inc., (Fowler) sold a 1982 Chevrolet Chevette to Robert Gilmore on January 20, 1993, for $3,042.50. Gilmore paid $300.00 down, and agreed to twenty-one bi-weekly payments of $125.00, and one final payment of $117.50 to be paid on December 26, 1993. Gilmore also gave Fowler a security interest in the Chevette. Gilmore became ill and subsequently died from his illness. Sometime during his illness, Gilmore donated the car to Camp Hudgens but stopped making payments on the Chevette. The caretaker of Camp Hudgens took the car to Williamson, located north of McAlester, Oklahoma, to examine it and assure the car was safe to sell. Williamson had no knowledge of any lien on the Chevette, nor did he know that Fowler had declared Gilmore to be in default and had hired Clint McGregor to repossess the Chevette.

Williamson testified that the Chevette was in his possession about thirty days. On October 10, 1993, he came to work and observed that his gate was open and that the lock and chain he customarily attaches and which he had locked the night before were both missing. He checked the premises to determine what, if anything, had been taken, and discovered that the Chevette was gone. He called the police, who came to investigate. Within a couple of hours, the police told Williamson that the car had been repossessed by Fowler Toyota of Norman, Oklahoma.

Clint McGregor repossesses automobiles for Fowler Toyota and other automobile dealers. He was hired to repossess the Chevette, but was not told its location. He discovered that the car was at Williamson

Auto from one of Gilmore's relatives. McGregor testified that he learned where the Chevette was located after dark, and then drove to McAlester. He found Williamson Auto, and testified that he called the phone number listed on the building, but received no answer. He found the gate to Williamson Auto locked with a chain which he cut with bolt cutters. McGregor testified that he regularly carried bolt cutters and still carried them at the time of the trial. McGregor then entered the lot, pushed the Chevette out and towed it to Norman. He testified that before he left McAlester, he contacted the police to inform them that he had repossessed the Chevette.

When he turned the Chevette over to Fowler for his fee, he told them what he had done to repossess the vehicle. Neither he nor Fowler attempted to contact Williamson Auto. Fowler told McGregor not to trespass to repossess automobiles in the future. Fowler eventually sold the Chevette. Fowler still uses McGregor to repossess vehicles.

Williamson estimated his losses at $15.00 for the lock and chain, and $30.00 (one hour) of billable time. He sued Fowler and was awarded $45.00 in actual damages, and $15,000.00 in punitive damages. The Court of Civil Appeals reversed, and we have previously granted certiorari.

Employer's Liability for Tortious Acts of Independent Contractor

Fowler asserts that it is not liable for the actions of McGregor, because he was an independent contractor. Fowler maintains it had no prior knowledge that McGregor intended to break into Williamson Auto to retrieve the Chevette, and that when Fowler was told of his actions, the company expressed its disapproval and informed him that he was not to repeat the activity. In support of its argument that it is not liable for McGregor's actions, Fowler cites Hudgens v. Cook Industries, Inc., 1973 OK 145, ¶11, 521 P.2d 813, for the general rule that an employer is not liable for the torts of an independent contractor. But more fully stated, Hudgens provides:

> The rule in Oklahoma is that a person who performs work through an independent contractor is not liable for damages to third persons caused by the negligence of the contractor except where the work is inherently dangerous or unlawful or where the employer owes a contractual or defined legal duty to the injured party in the performance of the work. [Citations omitted.]

Hudgens, 1973 OK 145, ¶11, 521 P.2d 813. *Hudgens* was a negligence case. The rule stated in *Hudgens* includes an exception for work that is inherently dangerous or unlawful or where the employer owes a contractual or defined legal duty to the injured party in the performance of the work.

Fowler argues that it does not fall within the exceptions to the general rule that an employer is not liable for the torts of an independent contractor. Fowler cites 12A O.S. 1991, §9-503 [now §9-609—Ed.] in support of its reasoning that since creditors are expressly granted the right by statute to repossess collateral, the work of repossessing an automobile cannot be held to be inherently dangerous. But in fact, other jurisdictions have held precisely the opposite.

One such case is Hester v. Bandy, 627 So. 2d 833 (Miss. 1993). In this case involving the repossession of a 1982 Ford van, the Supreme Court of Mississippi held that "when one employs another to perform a task in which a serious danger to person or property, a crime, or some tort can reasonably be anticipated in its performance, it is no defense to say the act causing the harm was committed by an independent contractor." *Hester,* 627 So. 2d at 843. In reaching its conclusion, the *Hester* court construed its §9-503 from the Uniform Commercial Code. *Hester,* 627 So. 2d at 836, citing Miss. Code Ann. §75-9-503 (Supp. 1992). The court observed that under the statute the secured party had a right to take possession of the vehicle without any judicial process if it could be done without breach of the peace. *Hester,* 627 So. 2d at 840.

The facts of *Hester* reveal that after moving a car to get to the van, the repossessor, an independent contractor, took the van out of the debtor's driveway at 3:00 in the morning. When the debtor went outside to see what was happening, he saw two men attaching a "quick snatch harness" from a truck to the van, and he began yelling at them. In pursuing them as they left, he fell into a ditch and was injured.

Considering whether or not the independent contractor had committed a tort, the Mississippi court held that the tactic chosen by the repossessor guaranteed generating fright or anger, or both, if discovered in progress by the Hesters, and was therefore fraught with the peril of provoking a breach of the peace of the most serious kind. The court continued that when the debtor attempted to physically resist the repossession, this terminated the right of the repossessor to continue, because in doing so he caused a breach of the peace, and he committed a tort. *Hester,* 627 So. 2d at 841.

After concluding that the repossessor had committed a tort, the Mississippi court determined whether the secured party was liable for the tort of the independent contractor. Mississippi's rule is the same as

Oklahoma's, that one is not liable for the torts of an independent contractor unless the work or service is illegal, dangerous or harmful. *Hester*, 627 So. 2d at 841. But the Mississippi court quoted Bonaparte v. Wiseman, 89 Md. 12, 42 A. 918 (1899), that one who is about to cause something to be done that will probably be injurious to third persons is liable based upon the principle that he cannot set in motion causes that are dangerous to the person or property of others without taking all reasonable precautions to anticipate, obviate, and prevent their probable consequences. *Hester*, 627 So. 2d at 842. The question as to whether injury might reasonably have been anticipated as a probable consequence was a question of fact for the jury. *Hester*, 627 So. 2d at 842. The Mississippi court, using the same Uniform Commercial Code statute as Oklahoma's, and the same common law rule as Oklahoma's concerning liability for independent contractors, reached the opposite conclusion as that espoused by Fowler.

In Clark v. Associates Commercial Corp., 877 F. Supp. 1439 (D. Kan. 1994), a case citing and quoting from *Hester*, the United States District Court discussed the current state of the law in the various jurisdictions throughout the United States concerning vicarious liability of secured creditors in using independent contractors to repossess motor vehicles. The United States District Court in Kansas found it must apply Tennessee law, since that is where the repossession took place. The Tennessee law required the secured party to repossess peaceably and found the duty to be nondelegable. Therefore a secured party in Tennessee is vicariously liable for wrongful acts of a repossessor even if the repossessor is an independent contractor. *Clark*, 877 F. Supp. at 1443, citing McCall v. Owens, 820 S.W.2d 748, 751-752 (Tenn. Ct. App. 1991). The United States District Court observed that a number of courts had held that the duty to repossess peaceably under UCC §9-503 was nondelegable. The court continued that other courts have simply held that a secured creditor can be held liable for the torts of its repossessor even though the repossessor was acting as an independent contractor.

Oklahoma's Uniform Commercial Code provides for self-help repossession by a secured party provided the repossession is accomplished without breach of the peace. In construing the same section in Alabama's Uniform Commercial Code, the Supreme Court of Alabama considered what constituted breach of the peace. The court, after citing the Restatement (Second) of Torts §183 (1965), comment h, observed that under the Restatement principle, the use of force, such as breaking or removing a padlock, does not comport with concepts of reasonableness and peaceableness, and was therefore a violation of the prohibition in the Uniform Commercial Code.[3] Madden v. Deere Credit Services, Inc., 598 So. 2d 860, 865 (Ala. 1992). The court concluded that when collateral is located inside fences or is otherwise enclosed, the secured creditor's privilege is considerably abridged. *Madden*, 598 So. 2d at 866, citing Rogers v. Allis-Chalmers Credit Corp., 679 F.2d 138 (8th Cir. 1982). The court continued that the creditor's privilege is most severely restricted when repossession can be accomplished only by the actual breaking or destruction of barriers designed to exclude intruders, and gave as an example cutting a chain used to lock a fence that enclosed the debtor's property. *Madden*, 598 So. 2d at 866, citing Laurel Coal Co. v. Walter E. Heller & Co., 539 F. Supp. 1006 (W.D. Pa. 1982), and Bloomquist v. First National Bank of Elk River, 378 N.W.2d 81 (Minn. App. 1985). The court concluded that the potential for breaches of the public peace and tranquility as a result of unauthorized intrusions on property escalates in direct proportion to the presence of fences, gates, signs, and other indicia of nonassent to entry. *Madden*, 598 So. 2d at 867.

McGregor cut a chain locking the gate to Williamson Auto and entered without the permission of the owner. Trespass involves an actual physical invasion of the real estate of another without the permission of the person lawfully entitled to possession. Fairlawn Cemetery Ass'n v. First Presbyterian Church, 1972 OK 66, ¶14, 496 P.2d 1185. Stated another way, a trespasser is one who enters upon the property of another without any right, lawful authority, or express or implied invitation, permission, or license, not in the performance of any duty to the owner or person in charge or on any business of such person, but merely for his own purposes, pleasure, or convenience, or out of curiosity. Texas-Louisiana Power Co. v. Webster, 127 Tex. 126, 134, 91 S.W.2d 302, 306 (1936), Holder v. Mellon Mortgage Co., 954 S.W.2d 786, 796 (Tex. Ct. App. 1997). The trial court in the case at bar gave the jury instructions on both trespass and breach of the peace, and the jury found for the plaintiff.

The right of self help that belongs to the creditor is not transferable to another and the creditor's duty to exercise this right in a

---

3. The Restatement comment provides: "h. Use of force. The privilege stated in this Section is one of entry in a peaceable and reasonable manner to remove the thing from the land. It does not justify the use of any force to enter, to remove the thing, or to prevent interference by the possessor. Since the conditional seller or other actor has parted freely and voluntarily with his original possession, he is not privileged to recover it by force, and must resort to his remedy at law. Compare §101 and Comments. The actor will therefore be liable if he breaks and enters the land, as by removing a padlock."

peaceable manner is not delegable. We are persuaded to agree with the jurisdictions that have construed the Uniform Commercial Code, and the common law rule, as stated in *Hudgens*, to hold that in the repossession of secured collateral, the secured party has a nondelegable duty to repossess the secured collateral without breach of the peace. Fowler is therefore liable for McGregor's trespass and breach of the peace.

RATIFICATION OF ACTS OF REPOSSESSING AGENTS

The trial court instructed the jury that if Fowler accepted the repossessed automobile with knowledge that McGregor cut the chain and removed the lock in order to gain access to Williamson Auto, that the jury could find that Fowler had ratified the acts of McGregor, and were liable as though Fowler had committed the acts or gave McGregor specific authority to do so. This instruction was apparently based on Henry v. Carpenter, 1961 OK 253, 366 P.2d 928, which holds: "Where a master with full knowledge of the wrongful acts of his servant, accepts the benefits derived from the servant's conduct by retaining an article which he took from another, master thereby ratifies the acts of the servant, and becomes liable as though authority had been given." *Henry*, 366 P.2d at 930. Fowler argues that *Henry* does not apply because the case involved an employer-employee relationship, and Williamson argues that *Henry* does apply because the same rationale supporting the holding in that case applies to employer-independent contractor relationships. Although we do not find error in the trial court's instruction, this Court is holding as a matter of law that a secured creditor is under obligation to preserve the peace whether an employee or an independent contractor is repossessing the collateral on behalf of the creditor. The duty to preserve the peace is nondelegable.

PUNITIVE DAMAGES

Fowler argues that the trial court erred in instructing the jury on punitive damages, and by further authorizing the jury to award damages in excess of the actual damages suffered. The punitive damages statute found in title 23, §9, was amended in 1995. Prior to 1995, §9 provided:

> A. In any action for the breach of an obligation not arising from contract, where the defendant has been guilty of conduct evincing a wanton or reckless disregard for the rights of another, oppression,

fraud or malice, actual or presumed, the jury, in addition to the actual damages, may give damages for the sake of example, and by way of punishing the defendant, in an amount not exceeding the amount of actual damages awarded. Provided, however, if at the conclusion of the evidence and prior to the submission of the case to the jury, the court shall find, on the record and out of the presence of the jury, that there is clear and convincing evidence that the defendant is guilty of conduct evincing a wanton or reckless disregard for the rights of another, oppression, fraud or malice, actual or presumed, then the jury may give damages for the sake of example, and by way of punishing the defendant, and the percentage limitation on such damages set forth in this section shall not apply.

B. The provisions of this section shall be strictly construed.

The trial court found, on the record and out of the presence of the jury by clear and convincing evidence that the conduct of McGregor evinced a wanton and reckless disregard for the rights of another, and was oppressive. The court then removed the percentage limitation on punitive damages, and after instruction from the court, the jury returned a verdict for punitive damages in the amount of $15,000.00. The pre-1995 version of §9 reflected what had long been the law, that punitive damages are allowable when there is evidence of reckless and wanton disregard of another's rights. Mitchell v. Ford Motor Credit, 1984 OK 18, ¶8, 688 P.2d 42. In *Mitchell,* the jury awarded punitive damages in the amount of $60,000.00 after an award for actual damages of $843.74. *Mitchell,* 1984 OK at ¶3, 688 P.2d 42. The court found that the award was far from excessive when considered in light of the facts adduced and the creditor's disclosed net worth. *Mitchell,* 1984 OK at ¶10, 688 P.2d 42. In cutting the lock off a gate of an auto-mechanic's shop belonging to Williamson, who had no relationship to the security agreement between Fowler and the debtor, Gilmore, McGregor certainly showed complete disregard for the rights of Williamson in securing his place of business. As we have held, Fowler's duty not to breach the peace when repossessing vehicles is nondelegable, and so Fowler is vicariously liable even for punitive damages for McGregor's actions. This properly places the responsibility on the secured creditor to make sure the party it hires acts within the law in repossessing collateral. Because some evidence was presented that Fowler's worth was in excess of $3,000,000.00, and Williamson asked the jury to award $30,000.00 in punitive damages, an award of $15,000.00 is certainly not excessive.[4] . . .

4. "When a defendant's conduct is such as to amount to fraud, oppression or malice, or the act is wilfully and wantonly done with criminal indifference to the plain-

Certiorari previously granted; Opinion of the Court of Civil Appeals is vacated; Judgment of the trial court is affirmed.

PROBLEM 371

Don Jose was in charge of repossession for Carmen Motors. One Monday morning the dealership told him that cars owned by four debtors (Escamillo, Micaela, Zuniga, and Morales) were to be picked up because the buyers had missed payments. Look at §9-609, and answer this question: is Carmen Motors required to give the debtors *notice* that they are in default before repossessing? Don Jose visited each of the debtors with the following results:

(a) Don Jose found Escamillo's car parked in his driveway at 2:00 A.M.; he broke a car window, hot-wired the car, and drove it away. Has a breach of the peace occurred? See Giles v. First Virginia Credit Services, Inc., 560 S.E.2d 557, 46 U.C.C. Rep. Serv.2d 913 (N.C. App. 2002). What if Escamillo heard the window break, rushed out, and began yelling? May Don Jose continue the repossession, or must he quit? If he goes away, may he try again later that night? See Wade v. Ford Motor Credit Co., 8 Kan. App. 2d 737, 668 P.2d 183, 36 U.C.C. Rep. Serv. 1433 (1983); cf. Griffith v. Valley of the Sun Recovery & Adjustment Bureau, 613 P.2d 1283, 29 U.C.C. Rep. Serv. 711 (Ariz. App. 1980) (repossessor liable in negligence for act of debtor's neighbor who used a shotgun to shoot a bystander during repossession melee).

(b) Don Jose showed up at Micaela's house accompanied by his brother (an off-duty sheriff who was wearing his sheriff's uniform). Don Jose told Micaela that he was repossessing the car, and she said nothing. Has a breach of the peace occurred? See Stone Mach. Co. v. Kessler, 1 Wash. App. 750, 463 P.2d 651, 7 U.C.C. Rep. Serv. 135 (1970) (*constructive force* also constitutes a breach of the peace); accord, First & Farmers Bank v. Henderson, 763 S.W.2d 137, 7 U.C.C. Rep. Serv. 2d 1305 (Ky. App. 1988) ($75,000 punitive damages).

(c) Don Jose broke into Zuniga's garage through the use of the services of a locksmith. The garage lock and door were undamaged. A clause in the contract provided that the secured party had the right to enter the debtor's premises to remove the property. Does the repossession comply with §9-609? See §9-602(6); Davenport v. Chrysler Credit

---

tiff's rights, exemplary damages are allowable. And, in such an action these damages are peculiarly within the province of the jury, whose verdict will not be interfered with lightly upon the claim of excessiveness." Oller v. Hicks, 1967 OK 240, ¶13, 441 P.2d 356 (1967).

Corp., 818 S.W.2d 23, 15 U.C.C. Rep. Serv. 2d 324 (Tenn. App. 1991); White & Summers §25-7.

(d) Don Jose phoned Morales and said that the car was being recalled because of an unsafe engine mount. Morales brought the car in that morning. When the time came to pick up the car, Don Jose simply smiled, said "April Fool; it's been repossessed!" and refused to return it. Is the repossession valid? Compare Cox v. Galigher Motors Sales Co., 213 S.E.2d 475, 16 U.C.C. Rep. Serv. 1390 (W. Va. 1975), with Ford Motor Credit Co. v. Byrd, 351 So. 2d 557, 22 U.C.C. Rep. Serv. 1294 (Ala. 1974), commented on in 40 Ohio St. L.J. 501 (1979).

Hilliman v. Cobado

New York Supreme Court, 1986
499 N.Y.S.2d 610, 1 U.C.C. Rep. Serv. 2d 327

HOREY, J. By an order to show cause the plaintiff has brought on a motion for injunctive relief. In particular the plaintiffs seek an order of this court that the defendant return 26 cattle which the defendant seized and removed from the plaintiffs' farm premises. While not specifically denominated as a motion brought under the provisions of CPLR 6301 it is clear that the motion in issue falls within the parameters of that section.

The factual background giving rise to the motion is this: the defendant sold the plaintiff a herd of cattle. Sale was initially to be effected under an instrument denominated a "collateral security mortgage" dated February 1, 1984. Under the terms of this instrument the sale was secured by a mortgage on the farm realty of the plaintiff purchaser. However, before delivery of the cattle, the defendant demanded additional security interest in the cattle to be sold.

As a consequence of this demand a second instrument entitled "chattel mortgage" dated February 8, 1984 was executed by plaintiffs. Under the terms of this instrument the defendant was given a chattel mortgage interest in "68 cows and 1 bull."

Both instruments had the same provisions for payment of the indebtedness (sale price) which was $48,200. Payment was to be made by plaintiff by even monthly payments of $1,000. Interest was provided at 11% per annum.

After the delivery of the cattle to the plaintiff, the plaintiff under a claim of right culled a number of the cattle delivered. The defendant took exception to this practice. As a result of negotiations a third instrument was executed. This was also denominated a "chattel mortgage." It is dated June 20, 1985. Under the terms of this instrument the collateral is recited to be "37 replacement cows." The balance due was fixed at $39,552.77. Provision for payment of this reduced amount continued as previously provided, viz., $1,000 per month with the balance drawing interest at 11% per annum. The court regards it as significant that the plaintiff has never been in default on the required contract payments. . . .

After the second chattel mortgage no specific default was alleged by the defendant. Inferentially it appears that he continued to be disturbed by the plaintiff's practice of culling poorer cattle from the herd. Suddenly without any prior warning, the defendant Cobado and two deputy sheriffs arrived at the premises of the plaintiff, Szata. Mr. Szata, a cripple, proceeding with the aid of a cane and his wife went out of their home to meet Cobado and the deputies. It was then that the deputies advised Mr. and Mrs. Szata that Cobado "was here to repossess the collateral under the terms of the security agreement."

Mr. Szata immediately replied that he was not in default and that Cobado was to leave the premises immediately and could not have the cattle.

Mr. Szata attempted to engage Cobado in conversation to no avail. Cobado simply turned and ran to the barn saying "to hell with this we're taking the cows."

Cobado entered the barn and started releasing the cattle from their stanchions.

A brief conversation ensued between Deputy Buchardt and Mr. and Mrs. Szata. Deputy Buchardt told them that Cobado had a violent temper and a reputation for violence. The Deputy also told Mr. Szata that if he (Szata) got out of line he would be arrested.

After an unfruitful attempt to call their attorney, Mr. and Mrs. Szata went to the barn and again told Cobado to stop. Cobado simply laughed at them and continued to release the cattle and drive them around in the barn.

At this time while Cobado was beating the released cattle and trying to herd them through a small opening in the barn door a Fay Hilliman, the mother-in-law of Mr. Szata and the mother of Mrs. Szata arrived at the barn. She joined the Szatas in ordering Cobado to desist. Cobado ignored them and continued to push the cattle through the barn opening.

Before the cattle were loaded onto the trucks assembled Lt. Ernie Travis of the Cattaraugus County Sheriff's Department appeared on the scene. He advised Cobado that if he, Cobado, left with the cattle he would be arrested. Cobado ignored the warning and when he left with the cattle he was arrested for possession of stolen property. Later Mr. Szata was charged with fraudulent sale of mortgaged property. As of the argument of the motion at bar no disposition had been made of either criminal charge. . . .

The second instrument executed, viz., the first chattel mortgage dated February 8, 1984, securing "68 cows and 1 bull" contained the following provisions for seizure, to wit:

> In conjunction with, addition to or substitution for those rights, secured party, at his discretion, may (1) *enter debtor's premises peaceably* by secured party's own means or with legal process and take possession of the collateral, or render it unusable or dispose of the collateral on the debtor's premises and the debtor agrees not to resist or interfere. . . .

(p.2 chattel mortgage dated February 8, 1984.) Italics added.

The third instrument, executed, viz., the second chattel mortgage dated June 20, 1985 contains an identical provision for seizure as that in the chattel mortgage of February 8, 1984, set forth above.

The quoted provisions from the two chattel mortgages follow an immediate prior contract provision also referable to default and repossession which provided that upon default "the *secured party will have all the rights*, remedies and privileges *with respect to repossession*, retention and sale of the collateral and disposition of the proceeds *as are accorded to a* secured party by *the applicable section of the UCC* respecting 'default' in effect as of the date of the security agreement."

This court finds nothing in conflict between the clause in each chattel mortgage providing the secured party with the right to enter "debtor's premises peaceably" and the immediate prior provision in those chattel mortgages stating that the secured party has those rights as to repossession which are accorded under the UCC This is for the reason as we have seen that the repossession rights granted under the UCC may only be exercised "without breach of the peace" §9-504 UCC quoted supra.

Since the motion turns to consideration of "breach of the peace" we look to decisional law for definition of that term.

In People v. Most, 171 N.Y. 423 (Ct. of Appeals 1902, Opn. by Vann, J.), our highest court stated that a breach of the peace was well known at common law. The court then defined it as follows:

> It is a disturbance of public order by an act of violence, or by any act likely to produce violence, or which by causing consternation and alarm, disturbs the peace and quiet of the community.

171 N.Y. 423 at 429.

The right to self help by way of repossession is an assignment of the exclusive power of the sovereignty of a state. This is true because it represents a delegation of the exclusively governmental function of resolving disputes. See generally Sharrock v. Dell Buick, 45 N.Y.2d 152 at 162 and Fuentes v. Shevin, 407 U.S. 67 at 93. The delegation of the right of repossession to a secured party is not a carte blanche one. Rather it is specifically limited and exercisable only without a breach of the peace. Its exercise should be strictly confined to those situations, rare as they may be, when the repossession can be accomplished peaceably. Physical confrontation or the threat thereof is not necessary to effect a breach of the peace.

Certain it is that in ignoring the order of the purchasers to desist and remove himself from the premises; in ignoring the admonition of Lt. Travis of the Sheriff's Department to desist; in demonstrating his contempt for all restraint by his statement "to hell with this we're taking the cows"; by proceeding to release the cows, beating and herding them to the trucks, without heed of the warning that his continuance would result in his arrest, the defendant Cobado not only engaged in conduct which was likely to produce violence and consternation but did in fact produce violence, consternation and disorder.

This court finds as a matter of fact and law that the retaking of the plaintiff's cattle was a "breach of the peace."

Accordingly the decision of the court is that the defendant Cobado forthwith at his cost and expense redeliver the cattle repossessed by him to the plaintiff inclusive of any calves born to those cattle during his possession thereof.

PROBLEM 372

Octopus National Bank (ONB) financed Mary Melody's purchase of a new car, in which it perfected its security interest. The loan agreement provided that on default the bank had all the rights listed in Part 6 of Article 9 of the UCC and that the parties agreed that the bank would not be liable for conversion or otherwise if there were other items in the car at the time it was repossessed. Mary missed a payment, and ONB's agent took the car in the dead of night from its parking place in front of her home. She protested the next day, claiming that her golf clubs were in the trunk. ONB looked there but couldn't find the clubs. When she sued, ONB defended on the basis of the security agreement's exculpatory clause. Is it valid? See Ford Motor Credit Co. v. Cole, 503 S.W.2d 853, 14 U.C.C. Rep. Serv. 259 (Tex. Civ. App. 1973).

If ONB finds the clubs and returns them promptly on her demand, is the bank still guilty of conversion? See Thompson v. Ford Motor Credit Co., 324 F. Supp. 108, 9 U.C.C. Rep. Serv. 128 (D.S.C. 1971).

It is important to remember that if the debtor files a petition in bankruptcy, §362 of the Bankruptcy Code creates an automatic stay of any creditor collection activity. This automatic stay forbids not only repossession but also even more prosaic attempts to collect the debt, such as dunning letters. The automatic stay does not depend on formal court notice that the bankruptcy petition has been filed; it is in effect from the moment of the filing. Creditor action taken without knowledge of the filing must be undone on learning that the debtor's bankruptcy has already occurred. But any true information that reaches the creditor from whatever source that the bankruptcy has been filed invokes the protection of the automatic stay. Deliberate creditor conduct thereafter violating the stay would not only be in contempt of court, but could also lead to the invocation of §362(h): "An individual injured by any willful violation of a stay provided by this section shall recover actual damages, including costs and attorneys' fees, and, in appropriate circumstances, may recover punitive damages." Let the lender beware.

PROBLEM 373

Wonder Spa gave Antitrust National Bank (ANB) a security interest in its accounts receivable and chattel paper in return for a loan. When Wonder Spa missed two payments in a row, ANB notified the spa's customers that future payments should be made directly to the bank. Does the bank have this right? Read §9-607 and its Official Comment 2; see §9-406(c). If the spa stops opening its doors, need its former customers keep paying ANB? (The spa contracts did not mention the possibility that the contracts would be assigned.) See §9-404(a); G. Gilmore, ch. 41. The ability of customers to raise defenses against the finance company is bound up in the law of negotiable instruments— see Unico v. Owen, 50 N.J. 101, 232 A.2d 405, 4 U.C.C. Rep. Serv. 542 (1967), the leading case—and special consumer protection statutes, e.g., Uniform Consumer Credit Code §3.404, and regulations such as the FTC's Holder in Due Course rule, 16 C.F.R. §433 (1975); Annot., 39 A.L.R.3d 518. Section 9-403 carefully preserves any other rule of law that protects consumers from waiving their rights to assert their defenses against assignees of their obligations.

After repossession, the secured party may in some circumstances (§§9-620 to 9-622, explored below) simply keep the collateral and give up further remedy (this is called *strict foreclosure*). More typically the repossessing creditor will resell the collateral and, if the resale does not pay the debt in full, then sue the debtor for any *deficiency* (or, if the resale more than pays the debt, return the *surplus* to the debtor[5]).

Section 9-610 and the sections that follow it regulate the resale. Note that in most cases §9-611(c) dictates that the secured party must give the debtor *notice* of the time and place of the sale. The reason for this notice is twofold: on getting it, the debtor may elect to use the §9-623 right of redemption (about which more later), or the debtor can attend the sale or send potential buyers who will enter real bids and, by actively competing in the bidding, bring a fair price for the collateral. The notice requirement is much litigated: what must it say, who must it go to, and what happens if it is not given? These issues are raised by the Problems below, which also consider another §9-610 matter, the §9-610(b) mandate that "every aspect of a disposition of collateral, including the method, manner, time, place, and other terms must be commercially reasonable." As to the meaning of *commercially reasonable*, see G. Gilmore §44.5.

PROBLEM 374

After Nightflyer Loan Company had repossessed Lynn Brown's car, it decided to advertise it for bids in a local newspaper. Is this a private or a public sale? See Official Comment 7 to §9-610. How much in advance of the resale must she be given notice? See §§9-611, 612. What should the notice say? See §9-614 (for the notice to be given to non-consumer debtors, see §9-613). After the resale, Nightflyer simply sent her a statement saying that the amount she now owed was $3,200. She is unsure how Nightflyer came up with this figure, and comes to you, her attorney/cousin, for advice. What are her rights here? See §§9-616, 9-625(c) and (e). The price obtained at the resale seems suspiciously low to her. How relevant is that? See §9-627(a). She suspects that the reason the sale brought so little is that the only bidder was Nightflyer Loan Company itself. Can they do that? See §§9-610(e), 9-615(f), and 9-626(a)(5); White & Summers §25-10(d). If she succeeds

---

5. You can imagine how often this happens. "Like neutrinos, surpluses are believed to exist but are never observed," White & Summers §25-13, at 919.

in reducing the amount she owes, can she also get actual damages for the harm they have caused her? See §9-625(d); White & Summers §25-13(e).

PROBLEM 375

Mr. and Mrs. Miller decided to open a restaurant, for which purpose they needed $80,000. They went to Apocalypse National Bank, which agreed to loan them the money if they (1) got a surety, (2) signed an agreement giving the bank a security interest in the restaurant's equipment and inventory, and (3) pledged to the bank additional collateral having a value of $20,000 or more. The Millers got Mrs. Miller's father (Mr. Stuhldreher) to sign as surety; they signed the security agreement; and they borrowed $20,000 worth of stock from Mr. Miller's cousin, Mr. Layden. The stock was registered in Layden's name at the time it was pledged to the bank, but the bank had it re-registered in the bank's name so that it could be sold easily in the event of default. The bank did, however, file its finanacing statement in the appropriate office. Subsequently, the Millers borrowed another $5000 from Northbend Credit Union, which also took a security interest in the restaurant's equipment, and filed a financing statement. The restaurant then became involved in an unfortunate food poisoning incident, and business fell off dramatically. The Millers (who were in the midst of a divorce) missed two payments on the loan. The bank sent its collection agent, Mr. Crowley, out to the restaurant, and he repossessed the assets he found there. Mr. Crowley sent a written notice to Mr. Miller (who he knew was now living in a hotel), telling him that the stock would be sold on the open market (no specific date given) and that the restaurant equipment would be sold at public auction on December 1 at the offices of the Crowley Collection Agency. Crowley phoned Mr. Stuhldreher (the surety) and told him the same thing. He sent a written notice to Mr. Layden (the stock owner), but the letter came back marked "Moved—No Forwarding Address." If asked, either Mr. or Mrs. Miller would have supplied Crowley with Layden's new address. Crowley sold the stock for $10,000 on the open market (that was its current selling price) and auctioned off the restaurant equipment on December 1 for $500 (only one bid was received— Crowley himself was the bidder; he later resold the equipment to other restaurants for $10,000). Crowley turned over the proceeds from the two sales ($10,500 total) to Apocalypse National Bank, which then brought suit against the Millers and Mr. Stuhldreher for the deficiency. Answer these questions:

(a) Is a surety entitled to a notice under §9-611? That is, is he a *debtor*? Read §§9-102(a)(28)(A), 9-102(a)(71), 9-611(c). Was Mr. Layden a *debtor* too? See Official Comment 2a to §9-102. Does the *oral* notice to Mr. Stuhldreher satisfy §9-611(b)? See §§1-201(38), 9-102(a)(7), and 9-611's Official Comment 5.

(b) Were any parties entitled to notice of the *stock* sale? See §9-611(d). How about the sale of the equipment? See §9-611(c). If no notice was sent to Northbend Credit Union before the equipment was sold, did Mr. Crowley, himself take free of its security interest when he bought the equipment at the foreclosure sale? See §617. Did the buyer from Crowley? See §2-403(1).

(c) Is the notice sent to Mr. Miller sufficient as to Mrs. Miller? See Tauber v. Johnson, 8 Ill. App. 3d 180, 291 N.E.2d 180, 11 U.C.C. Rep. Serv. 1106 (1972).

(d) Does §9-611 require the creditor to whom a notice is returned by the post office to take further steps to notify the debtor? See Official Comment 6.

(e) If the restaurant equipment is also named as collateral in a junior filed financing statement, must the bank notify that secured party of the resale? See §9-611(c) and (e).

(f) Who has the burden of proof as to the commercial reasonableness of the sales? See §9-626(a)(2).

(g) If Crowley had given the equipment sale no publicity, has a *public* sale occurred, and, if so, was it *commercially reasonable*? See §9-610, Official Comment 7.

(h) When a secured party repossesses goods and sells them at a foreclosure sale, will this give rise to the Article 2 sales warranties being made to the purchaser at the sale? See §§2-312, 9-610(d) and (e), and the latter's Official Comment 11.

PROBLEM 376

The Bunyan State Bank held a perfected security interest in the logging equipment of the Blue Ox Timber Company. When Blue Ox defaulted on its loan repayment, Bunyan repossessed the equipment. The sale was held the next day in the middle of a snowstorm. The equipment sold for very little (there was only one bidder, and he complained that it was hard to know the condition of the equipment because it was so dirty, being covered with mud from the backwoods). Bunyan sued Blue Ox for the amount still due. Answer these questions:

(a) Was the notice period too short? See §9-612.

(b) Is the secured party required to wash the collateral prior to sale? See §9-610(a); Weiss v. Northwest Acceptance Corp., 274 Or. 343, 546 P.2d 1065, 19 U.C.C. Rep. Serv. 348 (1976); Timothy R. Zinnecker, The Default Provisions of Revised Article 9 of the Uniform Commercial Code: Part I, 54 Bus. Law. 1113, 1149-1151 (1999).

(c) Did it violate §9-610(b) to conduct the sale in the snowstorm? Liberty Natl. Bank & Trust Co. v. Acme Tool Div. of the Rucker Co., 540 F.2d 1375, 19 U.C.C. Rep. Serv. 1288 (10th Cir. 1976).

PROBLEM 377

When you explained to your client, Repossession Finance Company, all the rights that debtors have when the creditor seizes the collateral and resells it, the president of the company asked you to draft a clause in the security agreement waiving these rights. How should you do this? See §9-602 and its Official Comment. Can guarantors (as opposed to the primary debtor) waive these rights? See §9-602, Official Comment 4.

PROBLEM 378

Facade Motors granted a security interest in its inventory to Octopus National Bank (ONB), which duly perfected by filing a financing statement in the proper place. Subsequently Facade Motors granted an identical security interest to Nightflyer Finance Company to get short-term credit. When Facade failed to repay the second debt, Nightflyer repossessed the inventory and sold it. Must it somehow account to ONB for the proceeds of the resale? See §§9-608, 9-615, and Official Comment 5 to §9-610.

Penalties for Noncompliance. Amazingly, under the prior version of Article 9, it was unclear what the penalty was for a secured party who did not follow the required rules when disposing of the collateral, and the states reached differing results, some resolving the matter for non-uniform statutes. Some courts held that failure to comply resulted in a forfeiture of the creditor's right to collect a *deficiency* (the difference between the amount owed and the amount realized at the foreclosure sale)—this was called the *absolute bar* rule. Others allowed a deficiency but made the creditor overcome a *rebuttable presumption* that had the rules been followed there would have been no deficiency and allowed the creditor to pursue the debtor for the amount still due only if the creditor could overcome this presumption by adequate proof.

PROBLEM 379

Facade Motors repossessed the car that Portia Moot used in her law practice but failed to send her any notice of the foreclosure sale, which brought only half the amount she still owed on the car. May it still sue her for the deficiency? See §9-626(a) and its Official Comments. What are Portia's rights? See §9-625. If Portia had purchased the car for her *personal* use, what is the rule? See §9-626(b). Why would the drafters have done this?

IV.   REDEMPTION AND STRICT FORECLOSURE

Centuries of property law have established the right of the defaulting debtor to recover the collateral by curing the default. The courts of equity first enforced this right of *redemption,* and it has become a common maxim that the courts will not permit anything to "clog the equity of redemption." See G. Gilmore §43.2; Indianapolis Morris Plan Corp. v. Karlen, 28 N.Y.2d 30, 268 N.E.2d 632, 319 N.Y.S.2d 831, 8 U.C.C. Rep. Serv. 939 (1971).

PROBLEM 380

When Paul Morphy borrowed $2,000 from the Lasker State Bank in order to finance a trip to Iceland, the bank made him sign an agreement giving the bank a security interest in Paul's private yacht. He agreed to repay the loan at the rate of $200 a month. He took the trip and on his return made the first payment on time. He failed to make the second payment on the due date, and the next day the bank repossessed the yacht. Paul raced to the bank with the late payment. He had $200 in cash, which he tendered. The bank refused to take the money. The bank's loan officer, a Mr. Anderssen, pointed to an acceleration clause in the security agreement that made the entire amount due if a payment was missed. Anderssen demanded the total unpaid balance. Need Paul pay off everything? See §9-623 along with its Official Comment 2. A leading pre-Code case on this problem (which contains a very quotable discussion of the issue) is Street v. Commercial Credit Corp., 35 Ariz. 479, 281 P. 46 (1929); cf. Rogers v. Associates Commercial Corp., 632 P.2d 1002, 32 U.C.C. Rep. Serv. 635 (Ariz. App. 1981). For Code cases, see Urdang v. Muse, 114 N.J. Super. 372, 276 A.2d 397, 8 U.C.C. Rep. Serv. 1220 (1971); Robinson v. Jefferson Credit Corp., 4 U.C.C. Rep. Serv. 15 (N.Y. Sup. Ct. 1967); Krahmer, Creditors, Consumers and Article 9 of the UCC, 5 U. Tol. L. Rev. 1, 6-10 (1973). There is pre-revision authority for the proposition that misdescription of the redemption rights bars any action for the deficiency. First Natl. Bank v. DiDomenico, 302 Md. 290, 487 A.2d 646, 40 U.C.C. Rep. Serv. 7 (1985).

Strict foreclosure occurs when the creditor repossesses the collateral and simply keeps it in satisfaction of the debt. No deficiency is sought. The debtor (or other creditors having junior security interests) may not be pleased with strict foreclosure in all situations. Read §§9-620 to 9-622.

PROBLEM 381

Art Auctions, Inc. (AAI), sold Dudley Collector a $5,000 painting by Smock Pallet, a famous artist. Dudley paid $1,000 down and agreed to pay over $1,000 a month thereafter. The finance charge was $151.20; the annual percentage rate was 18 percent. The contract contained a clause saying that in the event of default, AAI could repossess the painting and keep it without reselling it or, at its option, could resell it and sue for the deficiency. Dudley made three more payments and then missed the last one, being temporarily short of funds. AAI, without notice, sent one of its agents to Dudley's home. Dudley's teenage son let the agent in, and he simply removed the painting from the wall and walked out, saying, "Thank you." Dudley immediately tendered $1,000 to AAI and demanded the painting. AAI refused (the painting is now worth $7,000). Four months later Dudley filed suit. What is the basis of his cause of action, and to what relief is he entitled? See §§9-620(e) and (f), 9-625(b) and (c). If Dudley had made only one payment and then defaulted, causing AAI to repossess, could AAI have sent him a proposal that it would keep the painting and forgive *half* the remaining debt only? See §9-620(g).

PROBLEM 382

When Repossession Finance Company declared a default and repossessed all the office equipment of attorney Portia Moot, as allowed by the security agreement, the company then did nothing with the collateral except let it sit in a storage room for 17 months. Finally it conducted a resale with appropriate notices and then sued Portia for the deficiency. She defended by arguing that actions speak louder than words and that, in effect, by doing nothing for such a long period, the finance company had constructively elected strict foreclosure and had forfeited any right to a deficiency. Is this correct? See Official Comment 5 to §9-620.

Reeves v. Foutz & Tanner, Inc.

New Mexico Supreme Court, 1980
94 N.M. 760, 617 P.2d 149, 29 U.C.C. Rep. Serv. 1450

SOSA, C.J. These suits were brought as separate actions but were consolidated by the Court of Appeals because the issues were essentially the same. The trial court held for plaintiffs, the Court of Appeals reversed, and we reverse the Court of Appeals.

Plaintiffs Reeves and Begay are uneducated Navajo Indians whose ability to understand English and commercial matters [is] limited. Each of them pawned jewelry with the defendant whereby they received a money loan in return for a promise to repay the loan in thirty days with interest. The Indian jewelry left with defendant as collateral was worth several times the amount borrowed. The plaintiffs defaulted and defendant sent each of them a notice of intent to retain the collateral, though Reeves claimed she never received notice. The retention was not objected to by either plaintiff. Defendant then sold the jewelry in the regular course of its business.

The question we are presented with is whether a secured party who sends a notice of intent to retain collateral, in conformance with §9-505 of the Uniform Commercial Code [now §9-620—Ed.], may sell the collateral in its regular course of business without complying with §9-504 [now §9-610—Ed.]? We decide that the secured party in this case could not sell the collateral without complying with §9-504.

The Uniform Commercial Code provides a secured party in possession with two courses of action upon the default of the debtor. Section 9-504 provides generally that the secured party may sell the collateral, but if the security interest secures an indebtedness, he must account to the debtor for any surplus (and the debtor must account for any deficiency). Section 9-505(2) provides the secured party with the alternative of retaining the collateral in satisfaction of the obligation. Under this section, the secured party must give written notice to the debtor that he intends to keep the collateral in satisfaction of the debt. The debtor is then given thirty days to object to the proposed retention and require the sale of the property according to §9-504.

In the present case we will assume that defendant gave proper notice to both Reeves and Begay of its intention to retain the collateral and that neither objected within thirty days. The trial court found that the defendant, in accordance with its normal business practice, then moved the jewelry into its sale inventory where it was sold to Joe Tanner, president of defendant corporation, or to Joe Tanner, Inc., a corporation owned by Joe Tanner and engaged in the sale of Indian jewelry. There was no accounting to plaintiffs of any surplus. The trial court also found that the defendant did not act in good faith in disposing of the jewelry, taking into consideration the relative bargaining power of the parties.

The defendant argues that the trial court should be reversed because it applied §9-504. It essentially argues that once it complied with §9-505(2) and sent the notice of intent to retain, it could do as it pleased with the property once the thirty days had elapsed without objection. The debtor-creditor relationship terminates, they claim, and the creditor becomes owner of the collateral.

The plaintiffs argue that the trial court was correct in applying §9-504 to require that any surplus from the sale of collateral be returned to the debtor. They urge that the intention of the secured party should control and where he intended to sell the collateral and did sell the collateral in the normal course of business, he must comply with §9-504 which governs sales of such collateral.

Neither party to this action has cited a case which has dealt directly with the issue here, but amicus has referred us to a Federal Trade Commission case on the subject where it was stated:

> In the Draftsmen's Statement of Reasons for 1972 Changes in Official Text, the Draftsmen summarized the purpose of §9-505 as follows:
>
> > Under subsection (2) [9-505(2)] of this section the secured party may in lieu of sale give notice to the debtor and certain other persons that he proposes to retain the collateral in lieu of sale.
>
> The foregoing language strongly suggests that waiver of surplus and deficiency rights under §9-505 is appropriate only when prompt

resale of repossessed collateral in the ordinary course of business is not contemplated by the creditor. . . . That being so, use of §9-505 by an automobile dealer, particularly one not disposed to pursue deficiency judgments, would appear calculated solely to extinguish surplus rights of consumers, which we do not believe was the intended purpose of §9-505.

In the Matter of Ford Motor Company, Ford Motor Credit Company, and Francis Ford Inc., 93 F.T.C. Rep. —, 3 C.C.H. Trade Reg. Rep. 21756, 21767 (FTC Docket No. 9073, Sept. 21, 1979). The Commission went on to say that a creditor of this type is not foreclosed from using §9-505(2) so long as he intends to retain the collateral for his own use for the immediately foreseeable future, rather than to resell the collateral in the ordinary course of business. We agree with the approach used by the Federal Trade Commission.

The Court of Appeals reasoned that once the creditor elected to retain the collateral, and followed the mechanics of §9-505, the property became his to keep or to sell. We do not find fault with this reasoning, but it misses the point. Defendant can do as he pleases with the property, but where he intends to sell the property in the regular course of his business, which is in substance selling the property as contemplated by §9-504, he must account for a surplus in conformity with §9-504.

The defendant also argues that plaintiffs could have objected to the retention, thus forcing a sale in compliance with §9-504. But because there was never any actual intent to retain under §9-505(2), the failure of plaintiffs to timely object does not foreclose their claim. Moreover, the fact that plaintiffs could have objected means nothing in this context; their objection would only have served to cause a sale of the goods, which sale was already intended by defendant.

The defendant also argues that the trial court erred in finding that it acted in bad faith. We need not reach this question because bad faith was not material to the trial court's conclusions of law and judgment, which we find to be proper.

The defendant next claims error in the fact that the trial court allowed interest on the judgment from November 1, 1974. The date is the approximate day on which the loss took place and is apparently not controverted. The amount due the plaintiffs was a sum certain once the jewelry was sold, as calculated according to the provisions of §9-504. It was not error for the court to allow prejudgment interest or to allow interest as a portion of the damages. Sundt v. Tobin Quarries, 50 N.M. 254, 265, 175 P.2d 684, 690-691 (1946).

The judgment of the trial court is affirmed.

QUESTION

Is this case right? Does the court mean that any time the creditor elects to use §9-620, that creditor is forbidden the right to resell the collateral? After this decision, and assuming the court would reach the same result under the revision of Article 9, can it be said that §9-620 is a dead letter in New Mexico?